Acta Conventus Neo-Latini Albasitensis

Acta Conventus Neo-Latini

General Editor

Florian Schaffenrath (*Ludwig Boltzmann Institut für neulateinische Studien*)

Editorial Board

Donatella Coppini (*University of Florence*)
Jean-François Cottier (*University of Paris—Sorbonne*)
Claudia Schindler (*University of Hamburg*)
Carolina Ponce Hernández (*University of Mexico*)
Farkas Gábor Kiss (*University of Budapest*)
John C. Leeds (*Florida Atlantic University*)
Joaquín Pascual Barea (*University of Cádiz*)
Sonja Schreiner (*University of Vienna*)

VOLUME 17

The titles published in this series are listed at *brill.com/acta*

Acta Conventus Neo-Latini Albasitensis

Proceedings of the Seventeenth International Congress of Neo-Latin Studies (Albacete 2018)

General Editors

Florian Schaffenrath
María Teresa Santamaría Hernández

Editors

Jean-François Cottier, Carla Maria Monti,
Marianne Pade, Stefan Tilg, Juan J. Valverde Abril

BRILL

LEIDEN | BOSTON

Cover illustration: Map of the city of Albacete from 1767. Regional government of Castilla-La Mancha, Museo Provincial de Albacete

Library of Congress Cataloging-in-Publication Data

Names: International Congress of Neo-Latin Studies (17th : 2018 :
    Albacete, Spain) | Schaffenrath, Florian, editor. | Santamaría Hernández,
    Ma. Teresa (María Teresa), editor. | Cottier, Jean-François, editor.
Title: Acta conventus neo-latini albasitensis : proceedings of the
    seventeenth International Congress of Neo-Latin Studies (Albacete 2018)
    / general editors, Florian Schaffenrath, María Teresa
    Santamaría Hernández ; editors, Jean-François Cottier [and 4 others].

Other titles: Acta conventus neo-latini ; v. 17.
Description: Leiden ; Boston : Brill, 2020. | Series: Acta conventus
    neo-latini, 2212–6007 ; vol. 17 | Includes index. | English, French, German,
    Spanish and Italian.
Identifiers: LCCN 2020008661 (print) | LCCN 2020008662 (ebook) |
    ISBN 9789004427099 (hardback) | ISBN 9789004427105 (ebook)
Subjects: LCSH: Latin philology, Medieval and modern—Congresses. |
    Latin literature, Medieval and modern—History and criticism—Congresses.
Classification: LCC PA8002 .I57 2018 (print) | LCC PA8002 (ebook) |
    DDC 470.9—dc23
LC record available at https://lccn.loc.gov/2020008661
LC ebook record available at https://lccn.loc.gov/2020008662

Typeface for the Latin, Greek, and Cyrillic scripts: "Brill". See and download: brill.com/brill-typeface.

ISSN 2212-6007
ISBN 978-90-04-42709-9 (hardback)
ISBN 978-90-04-42710-5 (e-book)

Copyright 2020 by Koninklijke Brill NV, Leiden, The Netherlands.
Koninklijke Brill NV incorporates the imprints Brill, Brill Hes & De Graaf, Brill Nijhoff, Brill Rodopi,
Brill Sense, Hotei Publishing, mentis Verlag, Verlag Ferdinand Schöningh and Wilhelm Fink Verlag.
All rights reserved. No part of this publication may be reproduced, translated, stored in a retrieval system,
or transmitted in any form or by any means, electronic, mechanical, photocopying, recording or otherwise,
without prior written permission from the publisher.
Authorization to photocopy items for internal or personal use is granted by Koninklijke Brill NV provided
that the appropriate fees are paid directly to The Copyright Clearance Center, 222 Rosewood Drive,
Suite 910, Danvers, MA 01923, USA. Fees are subject to change.

This book is printed on acid-free paper and produced in a sustainable manner.

Contents

XVIIth International Congress of Neo-Latin Studies XI
Programme XIII
Presidential Address XXX
 Ingrid A. R. De Smet
List of Illustrations XXXIV

Plenary Papers

1 Le *De Alea* (1561) de Pascasius, ou l'invention des addictions et de la thérapie analytique 3
 Jean-François Cottier

2 Petrarca e la natura 24
 Carla Maria Monti

3 "Conquering Greece": On the Correct Way to Translate in Fifteenth-Century Humanist Translation Theory 45
 Marianne Pade

4 Autor/Erzähler und Fiktion im neulateinischen Roman: Ein Beitrag zu einer historischen Narratologie 68
 Stefan Tilg

5 Apuntes sobre la transmisión textual de la versión latina de la *Política* de Leonardo Bruni 91
 Juan J. Valverde Abril

Communications

6 La *Compendiosa Historia Hispanica* (1470) como fuente en el primer Renacimiento castellano 117
 Guillermo Alvar Nuño

7 L'humaniste suisse Heinrich Glaréan (1488–1563), *vir bonus dicendi et docendi peritus* 130
 David Amherdt

8	La relevancia de los paratextos de las primeras ediciones de Marciano Capela para la crítica textual 143 *Manuel Ayuso*
9	Fonctions et effets des titres-résumés dans les miscellanées philologiques de la Renaissance 156 *Valéry Berlincourt*
10	From *puer* to *iuuenis*: Peder Hegelund's Self-Reflecting Portrayal of Danish Christian III in the *Epicedion de Inclyto et Serenissimo Rege Christiano III* 167 *Anders Kirk Borggaard*
11	Shaping a Poem: Some Remarks on Paul of Krosno and His Horatianism 178 *Elwira Buszewicz*
12	Le scritture esposte e il latino in Italia fra XIV e XV secolo 189 *Nadia Cannata*
13	Commenter Quinte-Curce au XVIᵉ siècle : Premières observations 202 *Lucie Claire*
14	Bernardo Michelozzi e Francesco Pucci, amici di penna 213 *Claudia Corfiati*
15	The Bird-Catcher's Wiles: Pietro Angeli da Barga's *De Aucupio* 223 *Ingrid A. R. De Smet*
16	La tradición latina renacentista del *De simplicium medicamentorum facultatibus* de Galeno 236 *Marina Díaz Marcos*
17	Aspects of Nature and People in Early Travel Literature (Fifteenth to Sixteenth Centuries) 248 *Roumpini Dimopoulou*
18	Bonaventura Vulcanius in Spain: Some Poems 259 *Ignacio J. García Pinilla*

19   La versión latina del tratado aristotélico *De sensu* (*Parva naturalia*) de Sepúlveda   273
       Paraskevi Gatsioufa

20   The Practicing Poet: Petrarch, Dedalus, and the Dynamics of Poetic Creativity in the *Bucolicum carmen*   284
       Donald Gilman

21   The *Epigrammata Antiquae Urbis* (1521) and the Muses: a Little-Known Chapter in Sixteenth-Century Latin Poetry   294
       Gerard González Germain

22   La figure du tyran dans les *Adages* d'Érasme   312
       Lika Gordeziani

23   From Caesar to the Rantzaus: Allegory, Fiction and Reality in Heinrich Rantzau's *De obitu nobilissimae matronae Annae Rantzoviae Domini Ioannis Rantzovij coniugis Ecloga*   323
       Trine Arlund Hass

24   Epigramme et épopée : quelques exemples tirés de l'épigramme lyonnaise des années 1530–40   335
       Sylvie Laigneau-Fontaine

25   Ovidio neo-latino tra Cinque e Seicento: un percorso italo-europeo   347
       Marco Leone

26   *Nunc erit beatior* ... L'homme et la nature dans la troisième épode de Maciej Kazimierz Sarbiewski   354
       Maria Łukaszewicz-Chantry

27   L'art de conférer chez Érasme   367
       Eric MacPhail

28   Mankind's Public and Private Roles in *Collectanea Moralis Philosophiae* (1571)   376
       Ana I. C. Martins

VIII

29 Prefazioni e dediche nelle edizioni degli storici greci tra politica e divulgazione 389
Maria Stefania Montecalvo

30 Dutch Late Humanism and Its Aftermath: the Reception of Hugo Grotius' Biblical Scholarship 401
Henk Nellen

31 The Merging of Linguistic Idioms in the Commentary Genre: the Case of Alejo Vanegas of Toledo (1542) 413
Daniel Nodes

32 La *quaestio An terra moveatur an quiescat* di Giovanni Regiomontano 428
Pietro Daniel Omodeo e Alberto Bardi

33 Los cuatro epigramas latinos de Alonso García en alabanza del *Libro de la melancholia* (Sevilla, 1585) de su discípulo Andrés Velásquez 439
Joaquín Pascual-Barea

34 Amato Lusitano: El relato patográfico del morbo gálico 450
María Jesús Pérez Ibáñez

35 Nuevos retos para el estudio de la poesía jesuítica latina del siglo XVIII 462
Carlos Ángel Rizos Jiménez

36 Fonti scientifiche in contesti scolastici: La metafora medica nei commenti a Persio del Secondo Quattrocento 472
Federica Rossetti

37 Continuidad y variación en el tratamiento de la rabia: de Gratio (s. I) a Aurifaber (s. XVI) 483
María de Lourdes Santiago Martínez

38 Magnetism's Transformation from Natural Phenomenon to Literary Metaphor 496
Raija Sarasti-Wilenius

CONTENTS

39 Natural and Artificial Objects in Conrad Gessner's Book on
"Fossils" 506
Petra Schierl

40 Educazione e politica nelle lettere di Costanza da Varano 518
Margherita Sciancalepore

41 Städtelob und Zeitkritik: Die Frankfurt-Episode im *Iter Argentoratense*
(1544) des Humanisten Georg Fabricius 525
Robert Seidel

42 Seven Types of Intertextuality, and the Emic/Etic Distinction 537
Minna Skafte Jensen

43 A Dowry Recovered after Three Decades: Diego Gracián's Spanish
Editions of Ioannes Dantiscus' *Hymns* Revisited 550
Anna Skolimowska

44 Neo-Latin and Russian in Mikhail V. Lomonosov's *Panegyric for Elizaveta
Petrovna* (1749) 562
Anna Smirnova

45 De interpretibus Iacobi Vanierii e Societate Jesu sacerdotis inter poetas
Hungaros 576
László Szörényi

46 The Weaver of Light: Divine Origin of Nature and Natural Science in
Carlo Noceti's *Iris* 586
Irina Tautschnig

47 Notas sobre la correspondencia manuscrita de Christoph Sand 598
Pablo Toribio

48 *Cum Apolline Christus*: Personal Mottos of Humanists from the Czech
Lands 610
Marta Vaculínová

49 Lettere alla corte aragonese: L'epistolario di Antonio Galateo, i re di
Napoli e l'Accademia 618
Sebastiano Valerio

50 The Latin and the Swedish Versions of J. Widekindi's *Historia Belli Sveco-Moscovitici Decennalis*: the Nature of the Differences 627
Arsenii Vetushko-Kalevich

51 Il bestiario "non inutile e giocondo" dell'umanista Pier Candido Decembrio 640
Éva Vígh

52 Der Humanist in der Krise: Zur Rolle der Poesie im Leben des Rigaer Humanisten David Hilchen 651
Kristi Viiding

53 *Nepenthes* – Trank der Helena: Die umstrittene Identität eines ‚homerischen' *pharmakon* in gelehrten Debatten des 17. Jahrhunderts 663
Benjamin Wallura

54 Martinus Szent-Ivany's Notion of *scientia*: Some Preliminary Notes on the Semantics of Neo-Latin Science 675
Svorad Zavarský

Index 689

International Association for Neo-Latin Studies

Seventeenth International Congress
Albacete, 29 July–3 August 2018

Humanity and Nature: Arts and Sciences in Neo-Latin Literature
Homines et Natura: Artes et Scientiae in Litteris Neo-Latinis Traditae

Executive Committee

President: Ingrid A. R. De Smet
First Vice-President: Marc Laureys
Second Vice-President: María Teresa Santamaría Hernández
Secretary: Raija Sarasti-Wilenius
Treasurer: Enikő Békés
Past President: Craig Kallendorf
Chair of Publications: Astrid Steiner-Weber
Chair of Digital Resources: Johann Ramminger

Organizing Committee

Chair: María Teresa Santamaría Hernández
Coordinator: Joaquín Pascual Barea
Member: Ignacio Javier García Pinilla
Member: Marina Díaz Marcos
Secretary: Rocío Martínez Prieto

Advisory Board

Donatella Coppini
Jean-François Cottier
Elisabeth Klecker
Jolanta Malinowska
Carolina Ponce Hernández
José Manuel Rodríguez Peregrina
Claudia Schindler
Marjorie Curry Woods

Sponsors & Partners

Universidad de Castilla-La Mancha:
Rectorado
Vicerrectorado de Investigación y Política Científica
Facultad de Humanidades de Albacete
Grupo de I+D *Interpretes Medicinae*
Departamento de Filología Hispánica y Clásica
Escuela de Traductores de Toledo
Ludwig Boltzmann Institut für Neulateinische Studien
Diputación Provincial de Albacete
Instituto de Estudios Albacetenses
Ayuntamiento de Albacete
Ayuntamiento de Alcaraz
Ayuntamiento de Chinchilla

Programme

MONDAY, 30 JULY 2018

09.00–10.00 Opening Ceremony

10.00–11.00 Plenary lecture I

JUAN J. VALVERDE ABRIL: Apuntes sobre la transmisión textual de la versión latina de la *Política* de Leonardo Bruni

11.30–13.00 Paper Sessions

Session I: Scientia Latina I: Neo-Latin as a Means of Promoting and Disseminating Early Modern Science (chair: Dominik Berrens)

Martin Korenjak: *O animum gravem, mundi capacem!* Heroes of the Scientific Revolution
Johanna Luggin: Explaining the Brain to Eighteenth-Century Readers: Claude Griffet's Didactic Poem *Cerebrum* (1727)
Irina Tautschnig: The Weaver of Light: Divine Origin of Nature and Natural Science in Carlo Noceti's *Iris*

Session II: Los paratextos de las ediciones de clásicos latinos en el Renacimiento y su relevancia para la crítica textual (chair: Antonio Moreno Hernández)

Manuel Ayuso García: La relevancia de los paratextos de las primeras ediciones de Marciano Capela para la crítica textual
Rosa Díaz Burillo: Aportaciones críticas de las epístolas dedicatorias transmitidas en las primeras ediciones impresas de la *Farsalia* de Lucano (1469–1512)
Antonio Moreno Hernández: Valor crítico de los paratextos de las primeras ediciones humanísticas de los *Commentarii* de César

PROGRAMME

Session III: Transnational Encounters in the Dutch Republic of Letters (chair: James A. Parente Jr.)

Henk Nellen: Dutch Late Humanism and its Aftermath: The Reception of Hugo Grotius' Biblical Scholarship

Jan Bloemendal: Cultural Dynamics: Neo-Latin Dramas between Nationality and Transnationality

James A. Parente Jr.: The Anthology as Site of Transnational Literary Exchange in the Low Countries

Session IV: Eloquence I (chair: Miguel Ángel González Manjarrés)

David Amherdt: L'Humaniste suisse Heinrich Glareanus, *vir bonus dicendi et docendi peritus*

Ferran Grau Codina: *Aliud est Grammatice, aliud Latine loqui:* La pureza de la lengua latina según Fadrique Furio Ceriol

John C. Leeds: Anti-Ciceronian Prose and Reformation Ideology: The Mandatory Archaism of Richard Sampson

Session V: Erasmus (chair: Ignacio Javier García Pinilla)

Lika Gordeziani: La Figure du tyran dans les *Adages* d'Érasme

Eric MacPhail: L'Art de conférer chez Érasme

Ronald Truman: Erasmus and Spain at the End of the Sixteenth Century: Two Examples

15.00–16.30 Paper Sessions

Session I: *De laude interpretationis*: Laurence Humphrey's Theory of Vernacular and Religious Translation (chair: Marianne Pade)

Outi Merisalo: The Divine Task of the Translator according to Laurence Humphrey

Annet den Haan: Laurence Humphrey and Biblical Translation

Session II: Neo-Latin Poets as Social Actors: Evidence from Central Europe (chair: Enikő Békés)

Lucie Storchová: Everyday Communication Practice in Central European Humanism: Georg Handsch and his Excerpt Journals from a Microhistorical Perspective

Marta Vaculinová: *Christus, natura, Apollo*: Symbola and Insignia of Humanists from the Lands of the Crown of Bohemia

Farkas Gábor Kiss: Immortalizing the Occasional: The *Poemata* of Johannes Sambucus

Session III: Las *Curationum medicinalium centuriae septem* de Amato Lusitano (chair: Ana Isabel Martín Ferreira)

Miguel Ángel González Manjarrés and Victoria Recio Muñoz: Las ediciones de la primera *Centuria* de Amato Lusitano. Difusión, valoración y *stemma*

María Jesús Pérez Ibáñez and José Ignacio Blanco Pérez: El relato patográfico de la sífilis en Amato Lusitano

Ana Isabel Martín Ferreira and Cristina De la Rosa Cubo: Amato en la obra del cirujano ¿portugués? Juan Fragoso

Session IV: Neo-Latin Translations (chair: Ferran Grau)

José Manuel Cañas Reíllo: World, Man and Nature in the Latin Translation of the *Translatio Chaldaica* in the Polyglot Bible of Alcalá

Mercedes Ortega Castro: La versión latina de la *Política* de Pierre de la Ramée

Kevin Zilverberg: The Interlinear Latin Translation of Greek *Daniel* in the Complutensian Polyglot Bible

Session V: Religion (chair: John C. Leeds)

Wolfgang Kofler: *Peccator deicida*, *Pastor bonus* und *Pius Samaritanus*: drei Brixner Meditationsspiele von Joseph Resch

Floris Verhaart: The Uses of Latin in Enlightenment Debates on Religious Tolerance and Politics: The Case of Petrus Burmannus Secundus (1713–78)

Ľubomíra Wilšinská: Being a Good Monk: An Example of a Neo-Latin Literary Work Written by R. P. Joannicius Basilovits OSBM (1742–1821)

17.00–18.30 Paper Sessions

Session I: Writing Culture in Latin: Ethnographic Fictions of Early Colonial Spanish America (chair: Bobby Xinyue)

Petra Šoštarić: Vinko Paletin's *De iure et iustitia belli*
Erika Valdivieso: Lies and Fictions of Colonial Peru: *Exsul Immeritus Blas Valera*

Session II: Passing Knowledge through Neo-Latin: Latin and Greek Sources and Terminology in Swedish and German University Disputations (chair: Martin Korenjak)

Meelis Friedenthal: The Terminology of Immaterial Substances in Swedish Universities during the First Half of the Seventeenth Century
Kaarina Rein: Language in the Medical Works of the Seventeenth-Century University of Tartu
Janika Päll: From Greek and Latin to Neo-Latin and Humanist Greek or *vice versa*: Borrowing and Adapting in University Disputations

Session III: Medicine I (chair: María Jesús Pérez Ibáñez)

Enikő Békés: Physician or Quack? Two Examples of Paduan Astrological Medicine: From Pietro d'Abano to Galeotto Marzio
Fabio Della Schiava: When the Historian is Like a Physician: a Reconsideration of Medicine in the Middle Quattrocento
María Teresa Santamaría Hernández: Humanist Medical Latin as an Instrument of Scientific Renewal: its Role in the Progress of European Medicine

Session IV: Nature I (chair: Victoria Recio Muñoz)

Astrid M. H. Nilsson: The Fascination of Nature: Marginalia in a Renaissance Marco Polo Manuscript
Raija Sarasti-Wilenius: Magnetism Transferred from Nature to a Trope
Caroline Stark: The Mirror of Nature in Lorenzo Bonincontri and Gioviano Pontano

Session V: Petrarch (chair: Íñigo Ruiz Arzalluz)

Donald Gilman: Petrarch, Daedalus, and the Dynamics of Poetic Creativity
István Dávid Lázár: Petrarca et Vallis Clausa
Vibeke Roggen: Sophonisba's Descent to the Underworld in Petrarch's *Africa*

PROGRAMME

Tuesday, 31 July 2018

09.00–10.30 Paper Sessions

Session I: Poetical Exegesis and Scientific Knowledge: Technical Sources in Renaissance Commentaries on Classics (chair: Angela Fritsen)

Felicia Toscano: *Quo pacto nos humanitatis professores eam tenebimus quam ne unquam delibavimus?* Nature and Science in Fifteenth-Century Commentaries on Ovid's *Fasti*

Daniela Caso: Pomponio Leto's Commentary on Columella's *De re rustica* x (*De cultu hortorum*): the Sources

Federica Rossetti: Scientific Sources in School Contexts: Commentaries on Persius in the Fifteenth Century

Session II: (Humanist) Greek in its Neo-Latin context. Examples from the Swedish Empire (chair: Peter Sjökvist)

Tua Korhonen: Applying for Bursary in Classical Languages: Two examples from the University of Turku, Finland

Erkki Sironen: Laudes linguae Graecae in orationibus academicis Latine et Graece conscriptis Imperii Svecici saeculi XVII

Johanna Akujärvi: Neo-Latin Texts and Greek Paratexts. On the Potential Importance of Liminary Texts for Interpretation

Session III: The Art of Transforming Horace in 16th-Century Poland and Italy (chair: Grażyna Urban-Godziek)

Elwira Buszewicz: Paul of Krosno and the Horatian Ode in Renaissance Poland

Francesco Cabras: Elegies and Poetry on Nature: Receiving Horace in Jan Kochanowski's *Elegiarum libri quattuor*

Giacomo Comiati: *Despiciens hominum tumultus*: Living a Good Life through Horatian Imitation in Marcantonio Flaminio's Alcaic Odes

Session IV: Hunting (chair: Outi Merisalo)

Ałła Brzozowska: *Carmen de bisonte* by Nicolaus Hussovianus. A Didactic Poem on Hunting or a Political Speech?

Ingrid De Smet: The Bird-Catcher's Wiles: Pietro Angeli da Barga's *De Aucupio*

María de Lourdes Santiago: Semejanzas o diferencias en algunas prescripciones médicas brindadas en el *Cynegeticon* de Gratio y en el Κυνοσοφίον

11.00–12.00 Plenary lecture II

STEFAN TILG: Autor/Erzähler und fiktionales Erzählen im neulateinischen Roman: Ein Beitrag zu einer historischen Narratologie

12.00–13.30 Paper Sessions

Session I: Neo-Latin and Education I (chair: Claudia Schindler)

Simon Wirthensohn: Komisches in lateinischen Schulkomödien
Isabella Walser-Bürgler: Whose Love of Which Statement? Inaugural Orations at Early Modern German Universities

Session II: Territoriale Instabilität und kulturelle Kontinuität am Beispiel der Kulturlandschaft Flandern in der Frühen Neuzeit (chair: Marc Laureys)

Roswitha Simons: Das Flandernlob in den Schriften von Antonius Sanderus
Marc Laureys: Real and Imagined Communities in Justus Rycquius's *Parcae*
Alexander Winkler: Italiennostalgie, ultramontane Netzwerke und Regionalidentität im Werk des Simon Ogerius

Session III: Drama (chair: Jan Bloemendal)

Neven Jovanović: De corpore dramatum Latinorum in Croatia actorum restituendo
Florian Schaffenrath: The Metamorphosis of King Nebuchadnezzar in Neo-Latin Drama between the Seventeenth and Eighteenth Centuries
Stefan Zathammer: Joseph Reschs *Sanctus Ingenuinus—Liebe deß Vatterlands:* Ein Heiligendrama über einen Heiligen, der gar keiner ist?

Session IV: Travels (chair: Jeannine De Landtsheer)

Roumpini Dimopoulou: Aspects of Nature and Population in Early Travel Literature (Fifteenth-Sixteenth Century)
Robert Seidel: Städtelob und Zeitkritik: Das *Iter Argentoratense* (1544) des Georg Fabricius
Diana Sorić and Teuta Serreqi Jurić: Antun Vrančić's *Iter Buda Hadrianopolim*: Historical and Literary Context

PROGRAMME

Session V: Spanish Themes (chair: Teresa Jiménez Calvente)

Ignacio Javier García Pinilla: Poemas latinos de Bonaventura Vulcanius sobre tema 'hispánico': Ecos de Burgos, Alcalá y Toledo
Guillermo Alvar Nuño: La *Compendiosa historia Hispanica* (1470), ¿fuente para los humanistas de la siguiente generación?
Joaquín Pascual Barea: Los cuatro epigramas latinos de Alfonso García alabando el *Libro de la melancholia* (Sevilla, 1585) de Andrés Velázquez

15.30–17.00 Paper Sessions

Session I: Neo-Latin and Education II (chair: Isabella Walser-Bürgler)

Valerio Sanzotta: Cristoforo Landino professore allo Studio fiorentino: le *recollectae* al corso sull'*Eneide* del 1462–63
Laura Refe: Il maestro fa scuola: Poliziano, allievi e collaboratori tra lavoro personale e Studio fiorentino (1480–94)

Session II: Genussmittel – Heilmittel – Projektionsobjekt: Frühneuzeitliche Diskurse und Debatten zu Luxusgütern in der neulateinischen Literatur und Fachschriftstellerei (chair: Alexander Winkler)

Ronny Kaiser: *Quis adeo vecors et barbarus fuerit ...?* Das Bier zwischen Natur, Kultur und medizinischer Wirksamkeit bei Johann Placotomus (1550) und Thaddaeus Hagecius (1585)
Benjamin Hübbe: Das homerische *pharmakon nepenthes* (Od. 4, 219–32). Die umstrittene Identität eines Mittels gegen Kummer und Sorgen in frühneuzeitlichen Debatten des 17. Jhs.
Claudia Schindler: Der Kakao: Ein europäisches Getränk? Luxus, Rausch und Wirksamkeit in Tommaso Strozzis *De cocolatis opificio* (1689)

Session III: Letters and Networks (chair: Jean-Louis Charlet)

Carolin Ritter: Ovids heimliche Rache an Augustus: Der Brief *Iulia Augusto* aus Mark Alexander Boyds *Epistulae Heroides* (1592)
Mª Ángeles Robles: R. Bentley y P. Burmann: misivas y ediciones en torno a la epístola de Laodamía
Gilbert Tournoy: On the Tracks of New *alba amicorum* from the Netherlands

Session IV: Panegyric (chair: María de Lourdes Santiago)

Teresa Jiménez Calvente: Los Reyes Católicos y su misión providencial: la semblanza panegírica de los monarcas en el *De rebus Hispaniae memorabilibus* de Lucio Marineo Sículo

Ágnes Máté: Literary Image of Renaissance Queenship: The Marriage of Isabella Jagiellon (1519–59)

Anna Smirnova: Neo-Latin and Russian in M. V. Lomonosov's *Panegyric for Elizaveta Petrovna* (1749)

Session V: Humanists I (chair: José Manuel Cañas Reíllo)

Ojārs Lāms: *De incertitudine rerum humanarum*: Intersection of Humanist Ideas and Historical Topicalities of Livonia in Creative Work of Georg Ciegler

František Šimon: Gregor Macer Szepsius, Dichter und Naturwissenschaftler

Pablo Toribio: Christoph Sand (1644–80): The Career of a Heterodox Scholar

17.30–19.00 Paper Sessions

Session I: The Edge of Fiction: Literary Self-fashioning and the Use of Real-Life Models (chair: Marc Laureys)

Trine Arlund Hass: What's in a Name? Fluctuations between Reality and Fiction in Bucolic Names

Anders Kirk Borggaard: Fashioning the Self through the Fashioning of Others: Funerary Literature as a Stage for the Aspiring Humanist

Lærke Maria Andersen Funder: Establishing a Brand: Defining Theoretical Positions in Academic Writing: The Case of Ole Worm

Session II: Philosophy I (chair: Pablo Toribio)

Gianmario Cattaneo: What Did the Ancients Think about Plato? Three Unpublished Texts about the Plato-Aristotle Controversy

Paraskevi Gatsioufa: Las versiones latinas renacentistas del tratado aristotélico *De sensu et sensato*

Ana Isabel Martins: Humanity's Public and Private Roles in *Collectanea Moralis Philosophiae* (1571)

PROGRAMME

Session III: Jesuits (chair: Tua Korhonen)

José Carlos Miralles Maldonado: Simone Poggi's Neo-Latin Fables: a Jesuit in the Footsteps of Phaedrus
Carlos Ángel Rizos Jiménez: Evolución de la poesía jesuítica latina del siglo XVIII
Aline Smeesters: An Exploration in the Tradition of Jesuit Neo-Latin Poetics (Seventeenth Century)

Session IV: Letters (chair: Caroline Stark)

Jean-Louis Charlet: Les *Épîtres* de Jean Second: étude métrique
Marcela Slavíková: Discussing a Critical Edition of Johann Amos Comenius's Correspondence: Genres, Styles, and Languages
Florence Bistagne: Giovanni Pontano au mirroir de sa correspondance familière

WEDNESDAY, 1 AUGUST 2018

09.00–10.30 Paper Sessions

Session I: Lettere a principi e amici: funzioni dell'epistola nel Quattrocento (chair: Claudia Corfiati)

Margherita Sciancalepore: Educazione e politica nelle lettere di Costanza da Varano
Claudia Corfiati: *Vix scripseram superiorem epistolam*: Bernardo e Francesco
Sebastiano Valerio: Lettere alla corte aragonese. L'epistolario di Antonio Galateo, i re di Napoli e l'Accademia

Session II: Scientia Latina II: Heroes of the Scientific Revolution: Neo-Latin Scientific Culture and the Universities (chair: Dominik Berrens)

David McOmish: Teaching Science: Didactic Poetry and the Commentary Tradition in the Universities
William M. Barton: Science in the University Dissertation: 'Grey Literature' and the Reception of Scientific Knowledge in the Early Modern German University. A Case Study
Alberto Bardi: Disputing Science at Early-Modern Universities: The Case of Cartesian Scholasticism

Session III: Pedagogical Contexts for Latin Drama in Early Modern England (chair: Elizabeth Sandis)

Ágnes Juhász-Ormsby: Teaching Classical Drama in the Tudor Classroom: School Commentaries and Bilingual Editions of Terence in Sixteenth-Century England

Elizabeth Sandis: Testing the Boundaries of Propriety on the University Stage: Grammar, Gender, and Cross-Dressing at Oxford and Cambridge

Tommi Alho and Aleksi Mäkilähde: Neo-Latin Gunpowder Plot Plays at the King's School, Canterbury: Contextualizing the Tradition

Session IV: Antiquarianism (chair: Colette Nativel)

Joan Carbonell Manils: Difusión e impacto de los *Epigrammata Antiquae Urbis* (Romae 1521) en el segundo tercio del siglo XVI

Gerard González Germain: The *Epigrammata Antiquae Urbis* (1521) and the Muses: A Little-Known Chapter in Sixteenth-Century Latin Poetry

Elisabeth Schwab: Letters on Ancient Things: Antiquarian News bei Francesco Petrarca, Poggio Bracciolini, and Bartolomeo Fonzio

Session V: History and Poetry (chair: Johann Ramminger)

Anne Bouscharain: Une Ambassade espagnole à Rome: Deux silves du Mantouan en l'honneur d'Íñigo López de Mendoza (1486)

Béatrice Charlet-Mesdjian: Poésie et Politique, de la *concordia* au *divortium*: Étude de trois poèmes d'Ercole Strozzi (Ferrare, 1473?–1508)

Íñigo Ruiz Arzalluz: El término *epitome* en el título de algunas obras latinas del primer Humanismo

11.00–12.00 Plenary lecture III

CARLA MARIA MONTI: Petrarca e la natura

12.00–13.30 Paper Sessions

Session I: Funzioni dell'epistola umanistica nell'età moderna: nei dintorni dei classici (chair: Claudia Corfiati)

Maria Stefania Montecalvo: Prefazioni e dediche nelle edizioni degli storici greci tra politica e divulgazione

PROGRAMME

Marco Leone: Ovidio neo-latino fra Cinque e Seicento

Francesco Saverio Minervini: L'epistolario fittizio, epistolario reale: lo scambio Bettinelli-Foscolo

Session 11: Eurotales: A proposal for the Latin Quarter in a Museum of the Voices of Europe (chair: Margaret Sönmez)

Margaret Sönmez: Roman Epigraphy and its Medieval and Early Modern Doubles: Public Script and Latin i

Nadia Cannata: Roman Epigraphy and its Medieval and Early Modern Doubles: Public Script and Latin ii

Peter Kruschwitz: The 'Voice' of Monuments: Monumental Latin and Communication Across Space, Time, and Medium

Session iii: Nature ii (chair: Raija Sarasti-Wilenius)

Petra Schierl: Conrad Gessner on Fossils and Pencils

Sonja Schreiner: *De vita plantarum in genere* (1844) oder: Die botanische Dissertation des "Retters der Mütter" Ignác Fülöp Semmelweis (1818–65)

Éva Vígh: Il bestiario "non inutile e giocondo" dell'umanista Pier Candido Decembrio

Session iv: Drama and History (chair: Neven Jovanović)

Elia Borza: Henri ii Estienne et ses commentaires à Sophocle: un travail « philosophocléen »

Magdaléna Jacková: Prologues, Choruses and Epilogues in Three Tobias Plays from the Czech Lands

Jozef Kordoš: *An et ubinam Draco existat?* The Dragons of Hungary in Joannes Baptist Grossinger's *Universa historia physica regni Hungariae* (1793–97)

Session v: Philosophy ii (chair: María Leticia López Serratos)

Alejandro Cantarero de Salazar: Una defensa de la juventud en el Quinientos hispánico: *De iuventute* (1556) de Sebastián Fox Morcillo

Lars Nyberg and Johanna Svensson: The World according to a Seventeenth-Century Swedish Polymath: Georg Stiernhielm's Philosophical Works

Peter Sjökvist: Truth, Etymology and Simple Word Pun in Thorild's *Maximum seu archimetria* (1799)

Thursday, 2 August 2018

09.00–10.30 Paper Sessions

Session I: L'Épigramme néo-latine aux confins des autres genres (chair: David Amherdt)

Virginie Leroux: Les *ekphraseis* de Grudius: épigrammes et *eicones*
Sylvie Laigneau-Fontaine: Épigrammes et épopée dans les *Nugae* de Nicolas Bourbon

Session II: Prose (chair: Jean-François Cottier)

Judith Deitch: The Making of Genius: *Ingenium* in Constantijn Huygens's Prose Autobiography (1629–31)
Jean-Nicolas Mailloux: La Formation oratoire de la noblesse d'épée pendant les Guerres de religion. Un cas d'espèce: l'*Oratio quam habuit Lutetiae Parisiorum* d'Odet Goyon de Matignon Thorigny
Ide François: The Death of a Child: Francesco Filelfo's *Consolation to Marcello* in Context

Session III: Spain and Latin America (chair: José Carlos Miralles Maldonado)

Michał Czerenkiewicz: Neo-Latin *Hispanica* and their Reception in Seventeenth-Century Cracovian Print Culture (Schedels' Printing Office)
Jeannine De Landtsheer: Justus Lipsius and the New World
Anna Skolimowska: Monument for Father-in-Law or Revenge of Injured Son-in-Law? Spanish Edition of Ioannes Dantiscus's *Hymns* by Diego Gracián Revisited

Session IV: Humanists II (chair: Rosa Marina Sáez)

Juan Ramón Ballesteros Sánchez: El sueño del humanista: Isaac Casaubon y la edición de Artemidoro (1603) de Nicolás Rigault
Angela Fritsen: The Humanist Bartolomeo Merula: Scholar at Whose Service?
María Asunción Sánchez Manzano: Mambrun, Le Moyne, Le Brun: Ancient and New Epic

15.00–16.30 Paper Sessions

Session I: Reinterpreting the Trivium: On the Teaching of Rhetoric and Logic in the Southern Netherlands during the 16th and 17th Centuries (chair: Jan Papy)

Christophe Geudens: Rhetoric Strikes Back: On the Reception of *De Inventione dialectica* in the Southern Low Countries (c. 1515–60)

Xander Feys: The Teaching of Rhetoric in 16th-Century Louvain: The Case of Cornelius Valerius (1512–78)

Steven Coesemans: Didactical and Philosophical Evolutions in Seventeenth Century Louvain Logic Teaching

Session II: Basinio da Parma (chair: Florian Schaffenrath)

Christoph Pieper: Isotta tra gli uomini: il secondo libro del *Liber Isottaeus* di Basinio da Parma

Christian Peters: Panegyric Chancer or Agent of Epic Renewal? Basinio da Parma and his Humanist Predecessors

Session III: Intertextuality (chair: María Asunción Sánchez Manzano)

José Ignacio Andújar Cantón: Reminiscencias neolatinas en *El rapto de las Sabinas* de Francisco García Pavón

Minna Skafte Jensen: Seven Types of Intertextuality

Arsenii Vetushko-Kalevich: The Latin and Swedish Version of J. Widekindi's *Historia Belli Sveco-Moscovitici*: Sources, Purposes, Readers

Session IV: Hungary (chair: Kristi Viiding)

Katarína Karabová: *Scriptores rerum Hungaricarum docti*: Selected Views of the Hungarian Historiography from the End of the Eighteenth Century

László Szörényi: Iacobus Vanierus (Jacques Vanière, 1664–1739) poeta Gallus et poesis Latina Hungaricaque in Hungaria

Martin Zborovjan: Samuel Spilenberger, Doctor, Pharmacist and Humanist (1572–1654): His occasional poems

17.00–18.00 Plenary lecture IV

JEAN-FRANÇOIS COTTIER: Le *De Alea* (1561) de Pascasius : l'invention des addictions et de la thérapie analytique

FRIDAY, 3 AUGUST 2018

09.00–10.30 Paper Sessions

Session I: Commenter les historiens latins au XVIᵉ et au XVIIᵉ siècles (chair: Valéry Berlincourt)

Lucie Claire: Sur quelques commentaires à Quinte-Curce du XVIᵉ siècle
Kevin Bovier: Commenter Tacite en milieu académique: le cours de Francesco Robortello à Padoue (1566)
Marijke Crab: Commenting on Suetonius in the Seventeenth Century

Session II: Neo-Latin Language Studies: Fields & Methodologies I (chair: Daniel Nodes)

Šime Demo: Neo-Latin as a Linguistic Phenomenon: Some Conceptual and Methodological Challenges
Johann Ramminger: Classical Latin Prose and the Humanists: The Search for the Exemplary Author
Lydia Janssen: *Latini sermonis usus apud eos sit continuus*: Latin and the Pedagogical Ideals of the Viglius College (1569–1797) in Louvain

Session III: Science and Antiquarianism (chair: Minna Skafte Jensen)

Gábor Almási: Astrology in the Cross-Fire: The Context of the *De Cometis dissertationes novae* (Basel: Perna, 1580)
Colette Nativel: Naissance de l'Archéologie: les débats autour du vêtement des Anciens
Svorad Zavarský: Martinus Szent-Ivany's Notion of *scientia*

10.30–11.30 Ask a Mentor

Informal session addressed to postgraduates and early career researchers about applying for jobs, funding, getting published, etc. (chair: Ingrid De Smet)

11.00–12.00 Poster Presentations

Alejandro Cantarero de Salazar: Dialogyca BDDH: hacia un corpus completo del diálogo hispano-latino en el Renacimiento español
Martin Korenjak: *Scientia Latina*: Early Modern Scientific Literature and Latin
José Carlos Miralles Maldonado: Charles Lebeau, autor del *Quijote*
María Teresa Santamaría Hernández: *Galenus Latinus*: La recuperación del corpus galénico latino del Humanismo médico renacentista
Svorad Zavarský with Katarína Karabová, Ľubomíra Wilšinská and others: *Nexus Slavorum Latini*: Intersections of Neo-Latin and Slavonic Studies

12.00–13.30 Paper Sessions

Session I: Neo-Latin Menippean Satire Three Ways: The Theory, Themes, and Practice of a Popular Early Modern Genre (chair: Ingrid De Smet)

Paolo Gattavari: Art, Architecture and Philosophy in Leon Battista Alberti's *Momus*: A Difficult Dialogue
Olivia Montepaone: *Turpe enim est centonibus loqui*: Menippean Satire in I. Casaubon's *De satyrica Graecorum poesi et Romanorum satira*
Jennifer K. Nelson: Biting the Hand that Feeds You: Writing Satire in Barberini Rome

Session II: Neo-Latin Language Studies: Fields & Methodologies II (chair: Paul White)

Daniel Nodes: The Merging of Linguistic Idioms in the Commentary Genre: The Case of Alejo Vanegas of Toledo (1542)
Alena Bočková: Balbín's *Diva Montis Sancti* (1665) and its Vernacular Versions as a Type of Early Modern Translations
Valéry Berlincourt: Les Enjeux multiformes des paratextes dans les "miscellanées philologiques" de la Renaissance

Session III: Women (chair: Florian Schaffenrath)

Rosa Mª Marina Sáez: Paradigmas femeninos en el *De institutione feminae christianae* de Luis Vives

Annamária Molnár: Donne tra fonti e invenzione. Boccaccio e le figure femminili del *De mulieribus claris*

Jan Papy: What Makes a Woman Beautiful? Ernestus Vaenius's *Tractatus physiologicus de pulchritudine* (Brussels, 1662)

Session IV: Poetry III (chair: Dirk Sacré)

Maria Chantry: *Nunc erit beatior* ...: L'homme et la nature dans la IIIᵉ Épode de Maciej Kazimierz Sarbiewski

Grażyna Urban-Godziek: Sixteenth-century Horatianism in Poland: The Models of Jan Kochanowski's Lyrical Cycles in Latin and Polish

Kristi Viiding, Der Humanist in der Krise. Zur Rolle der Literatur und Poesie im Leben des Rigaer Humanisten David Hilchen

15.30–17.00 Paper Sessions

Session I: The Certamen Hoeufftianum (1844/45–1978) and the Rediscovery of its Archives (chair: Trine Arlund Hass)

Xavier van Binnebeke: Digging up the Forgotten Classics of Modernity

Nicholas De Sutter: Tragedies at Sea: The *Titanic* and the *Lusitania* in the *Certamen Hoeufftianum*

Dirk Sacré: Modern Times. William H.D. Rouse (1863–1950) as a Competitor in the *Certamen Hoeufftianum*

Session II: Medicine II (chair: Juan Jesús Valverde Abril)

María José Brañes: *Morbum canere*: Juan Ignacio Molina y sus elegías neolatinas acerca de la viruela

Marina Díaz Marcos: La tradición latina renacentista del *De simplicium medicamentorum facultatibus* de Galeno

Rocío Martínez Prieto: La transmisión de la medicina árabe en el Renacimiento: traducciones y ediciones latinas

PROGRAMME

Session III: Poetry IV (chair: Stefan Tilg)

Martins Laizans: *Ars gratia scientiae*: The Case of Basilius Plinius Livonus
Paul White: Jean Passerat's *De nihilo* and its Legacy

Session IV: Politics (chair: Svorad Zavarský)

Kateřina Bobková-Valentová: Il teatro per i sovrani. Le rappresentazioni teatrali delle scuole gesuitiche preparate per le visite dei regnanti
María Leticia López Serratos: El pensamiento humanístico-político en la preceptiva dialéctica de Rodolfo Agrícola
Lav Šubarić: The War of Prophets in Vienna in 1791: *Eleutherii Pannonii Mirabilia Fata*

Session V: Grammar and Lexicography (chair: Farkas Gábor Kiss)

Marcela Andoková and Ivan Lábaj: Teaching Tense and Aspect in the Slovak and Czech Grammar Textbooks of the Sixteenth-Eighteenth Centuries: The Tradition of Priscian and Donatus Revisited
Ľudmila Buzássyová: The Concept of *Artes grammaticae* in the Grammatography from the Territory of Present-day Slovakia of the 17th–18th Centuries
Ralf Van Rooy: A Greek Word in a Neo-Latin Guise: The Curious Case of διάλεκτος–*dialectus*

17.30–18.30 Plenary lecture V

MARIANNE PADE: 'Conquering Greece': On the Correct Way to Translate in 15th-Century Humanist Translation Theory

18.30–19.00 Closing Ceremony

Presidential Address

Ingrid A. R. De Smet

Ilustrísimo Señor Decano Cebrián Abellán
Estimado Profesor García Pinilla,
Doctissimi collegae et socii Societatis Internationalis Studiis Neolatinis Provehendis,
Dear friends and guests of the University of Castilla-La Mancha and of the city of Albacete,

Como Presidente actual de la Sociedad Internacional de Estudios Neolatinos, me siento honrada de expresar nuestra satisfacción por estar aquí en el campus de Albacete de la Universidad de Castilla-La Mancha, para el decimoséptimo Congreso Internacional de nuestra Sociedad. Más de doscientos delegados están reunidos hoy aquí para abordar los aspectos más recientes de la investigación en su campo. Han venido de todas partes de Europa, desde Finlandia hasta el sur de Italia, desde Portugal hasta Letonia y Eslovaquia; varios colegas han cruzado el Atlántico, viniendo de los Estados Unidos y México. Esta reunión de nivel mundial no hubiera sido posible sin el arduo trabajo y la hospitalidad ofrecida por el comité organizador local, dirigido por la Profesora María Teresa Santamaría Hernández. Efectivamente, la Facultad de Humanidades del Campus de Albacete nos ha abierto siempre sus puertas, y ya tuvimos un ejemplo de la gran hospitalidad española en la magnífica recepción de ayer. El Comité Ejecutivo de la IANLS valora especialmente el apoyo proporcionado por la Profesora Santamaría Hernández y su equipo (Profesor Joaquín Pascual-Barea, Ignacio-Javier García-Pinilla, Rocío Martínez Prieto, Marina Díaz Marcos y otros) al igual que el apoyo por parte del Rectorado, el Vicerrectorado de Investigación y Política Científica, la Facultad de Humanidades, el Grupo de Investigación *Interpretes Medicinae*, y el Departamento de Filología Hispánica y Clásica de la Universidad de Castilla La Mancha. También queremos destacar el apoyo de otras instituciones españolas e internacionales: la Escuela de Traductores de Toledo, el Instituto de Estudios Albacetenses, y el Ludwig Boltzmann Institut für Neulateinische Studien. Agradecemos igualmente el importante apoyo de las autoridades regionales y locales: la Diputación Provincial de Albacete, y los Ayuntamientos de Albacete, Alcaraz y Chinchilla. La investigación académica no se lleva a cabo en una torre de marfil: aquí, con vosotros, nos encontramos en una universidad joven, que proporciona un ambiente dinámico, estimulante, y muy abierto para nuestros investigadores.

PRESIDENTIAL ADDRESS   XXXI

En effet, depuis le tout début, notre Association a été caractérisée d'un tel esprit d'échange, de collaboration et d'innovation: au sein de l'IANLS, en dehors des compartiments imposés par les anciennes structures universitaires, un étudiant de philologie classique pouvait – et peut toujours – très bien parler à un professeur de philosophie, un hispaniste à un historien de la Réforme, un francisant ou un angliciste à un poète latin de chair et os. De nos jours, on préconise le dialogue interdisciplinaire; je vous assure que ce sont les néo-latinistes qui l'ont inventée ! Plaisanterie mise à part, nos congrès de Louvain, Amsterdam, Tours, Bologne, St Andrews, Wolfenbüttel, Toronto, Copenhague, Bari, Ávila, Cambridge, Bonn, Budapest, Uppsala, Münster et Vienne, et maintenant celui d'Albacete témoignent de cette solidarité sans frontières, qui s'exprime aussi dans les diverses langues utilisées par nos conférenciers, y compris le latin, et qui fait écho à la république des lettres d'antan, où le latin était encore la langue courante. Le cadre international de la « culture néolatine » et le bi- ou multilinguisme qui l'accompagnent (car le néo-latin est toujours une langue seconde) sont alors des thèmes brûlants de nos enquêtes. Cet espace néo-latin, par ailleurs, va bien au-delà de l'Europe, alors que nos collègues étudient le latin au Nouveau monde, au Japon ou en Chine. À l'heure des replis, un peu partout dans le monde, sur les identités nationales, régionales, et religieuses, à l'heure d'une hausse dans les mesures protectionnistes, il vaut la peine de souligner la longue tradition des citoyens du monde – l'internationalisation avant la lettre – dont nous sommes les héritiers et les représentants.

In questo penso anche alla famosa *peregrinatio academica.* In effetto, nel periodo che studiamo come neolatinisti, cioè nel Rinascimento del Quattro- e Cinquecento, ma anche dopo, giovani studiosi e professori viaggiavano da un paese all'altro per raggiungere diverse università, lì dove le idee umanistiche si erano stabilite. Quindi è per giusti motivi che il programmo più conosciuto di mobilità studentesca, il programma *Erasmus+* finanziato della Unione Europea, prenda il suo nome dal celebre autore neolatino, Desiderio Erasmo. Nonostante le sui origini modeste, le sue peregrinazioni lo portavano dai Paesi Bassi in Francia, in Svizzera, in Italia e in Inghilterra, ciò senza dire nulla della suo enorme rete di corrispondenza. La mobilità crea la via alla comprensione e alla comunicazione.

The study of Neo-Latin offers many opportunities for a deep understanding of the roots of Western European culture and of questions and issues that still vex us today. I do not suggest that we will find ready answers and solutions to current problems in the texts of ere, merely that they equip us with a capacity for nuance and that they offer a long-term perspective on problems whose complexity and longevity many may well underestimate.

When I read extracts from Erasmus with my students, for example, they are struck by his evocation of the horrors of war and the benefits of peace. Similarly, let us not forget how Erasmus and his contemporaries, such as Guillaume Budé or Juan Luis Vives, shared a firm belief in the value of study. A good, rounded education, in the eyes of many Neo-Latin writers, and a timely return to one's books (the *otium cum dignitate* so desired by Cicero) are indispensable for good statesmanship. Those for whom the *muti magistri* hold no appeal should at least surround oneself with knowledgeable advisers. This is not an irrelevant principle in these days where politicians put education at the heart of their campaigns and policies, but are ready to dismiss expert views when these do not align with their vision. We call for integrity and objectivity at every level, clamour for free speech or an end to corruption. Our Neo-Latin writers did the same, only they spoke of *probitas, veritas, parrhesia* (let's throw in a bit of Greek, just as they did) or a *vita ab omni ambitu aliena.* (*Omnia mutantur, nihil interit!*)

The *studia humanitatis* were seen as foundational in the Neo-Latin world. However, humanities are not considered the opposite of science, at least not until the Enlightenment. On the contrary, it is the rediscovery and critical reconsideration of Ancient texts, often through the medium of Latin, that gave rise to some of the most significant scientific and medical advances: think of a Vesalius or Gabriel Harvey. The University of Albacete is very fortunate indeed to be home on a research cluster on the history of medicine, where Latin features firmly at its core, witness the edition of Pedro Jaime Esteve's Latin verse paraphrase (1552) of Nicander's *Theriaca* which Teresa Santamaría Hernández has produced for us as a memento of this conference. Was Latin not instrumental too in the development of Renaissance architecture, as illustrated by Leon Battista Alberti's *De re aedificatoria* and the *Wirkung* of Vitruvius? The contribution of Neo-Latin to fields that are traditionally associated with the vernacular has seen a sharp rise in scholarly interest: besides medicine and science, the *artes technicae*, including military tactics, and the relation between humans and animals have come under scrutiny. Eco-criticism has entered the realm of Neo-Latin. The broad theme of our congress, proposed by Teresa, is thus right on trend: *Homines et natura*, or *Humanity and nature: arts and sciences in Neo-Latin literature* – and so are the complimentary conference bags made out of environmentally friendly material!

However, as is customary at our congresses, we will also hear many papers on other topics. We should not forget to study Latin in relation to law or theology, nor should we neglect the aesthetics and philological aspects of Neo-Latin productions such as rhetoric and style, prosody and linguistics. Research priorities set by governments, universities, and funding bodies, the potential for public engagement and impact are nudging developments in our field – often with fine results in the shape of exhibitions, digital databases and reconstructions, podcasts and interviews. But we must be mindful of the risks. Of a return to nationalistic inward-looking attitudes, for example. Must Swedish Neo-Latinists only study Neo-Latin texts produced or found in Sweden, even if Sweden boasts internationally recognized experts on the Italian Renaissance? It is just a hypothetical scenario, and I have no issue with the Swedish government, but that would be absurd. And if not we, then who will argue for the value of less fashionable activities or skills such as palaeography, text editing, or the sheer humdrum of learning and teaching Latin grammar, in a world that demands quick results? Luckily we have among us, here at Albacete, not only a great number of dyed-through-the-wool enthusiasts, but also several up-and-coming researchers, some of whom are joining us for the first time: we bid you welcome!

Traurigerweise muss ich Sie noch an die Kolleginnen und Kollegen, Freundinnen und Freunde unserer internationalen Gesellschaft erinnern, die seit dem letzten Kongress verstorben sind: Line IJsewijn-Jacobs (verstorben 2016); Mariano Madrid Castro (1960–2017); Alain Michel (1919–2017), Präsident unserer Internationalen Gesellschaft für Neulateinische Studien von 1982 bis 1985; Karl August Neuhausen (1939–2017), ein treues Mitglied; Paola Tomé (verstorben 2017) und Eckhard Kessler (1938–2018). Wir wollen einen Augenblick lang in Stille unserer dahingegangene Freunde und Kollegen gedenken. *Requiescant in pace.*

[…] I wish you all a very fruitful Neo-Latin congress: *Faustus felixque sit Decimus Septimus Conventus Neo-Latinus! Dixi.*

University of Warwick

Illustrations

1.1 Généalogie de Juste Turq 6

1.2 Pascasii Justi, Eclouiensis, Philosophiae et Medicinae Doctoris, *Alea, sive de curandi pecuniam ludendi cupiditate*, Libri II. J. Operinus, Bâle, 1561 (Bayerische Staatsbibliothek, VD 16, J 923, p. 2) 10

21.1 Hamilton (ON), McMaster University, D 1160, front pastedown (The William Ready Division of Archives and Research Collections, McMaster University Library) 304

21.2 London, The Warburg Institute, CKN 336.M19, f. [aa8r] (The Warburg Institute and Library) 306

21.3 Trento, Biblioteca Comunale, t-G 2 c 157, f. [aa8v] (Biblioteca Comunale di Trento) 308

21.4 Gdansk, Biblioteka Gdańska PAN, Ce 7706 4°, verso of the front flyleaf (Pomeranian Digital Library, no. 4537) 310

Plenary Papers

CHAPTER 1

Le *De Alea* (1561) de Pascasius, ou l'invention des addictions et de la thérapie analytique

Jean-François Cottier

Abstract

Expliquer la redécouverte et la profonde originalité d'un texte médical (*De Alea*) publié en latin par le médecin-philosophe flamand Pascasius Juste Turcq en 1561 pour dénoncer le jeu addictif et proposer une thérapie cognitive : tel est l'objet de l'article ici proposé. Après avoir, dans une première partie, établi un état de la question et retracé le parcours personnel de l'auteur, la seconde partie analyse le contexte médical et philosophique du traité. On peut en effet considérer que le *De Alea* constitue un nouvel acte de naissance de la maladie addictive. Cette naissance ne coïncide évidemment pas avec celles des drogues ; elle implique plutôt une vision médicale du problème, avec une recherche de ses causes, et de remèdes appropriés, qui ne soient pas simplement – comme ce fut durant des siècles le cas pour tous les intempérants – le recours au jugement religieux et moral, puis à la punition.

Keywords

Justus Pascasius – *De alea* (1561) – Neo-Latin medical treatise – addiction – game

Le traité *De Alea sive de curanda ludendi in pecuniam cupiditate libri duo* (1561)[1] a été étudié pour la première fois dans un petit article en néerlandais de la revue *Brabantia* en 1952,[2] puis il a fait l'objet d'une analyse approfondie par Toon

---

1   Éditions anciennes du texte : Justus Pascasius, *Alea sive de curanda ludendi in pecuniam cupiditate libri II* (Bâle, 1561) ; Justus Pascasius, *Alea sive de curanda in pecuniam ludendi cupiditate libri duo*, éd. Johann von Münster (Neustadt, 1617) ; Justus Pascasius, *De Alea libri duo*, éd. Marcus Zuerius Boxhorn (Amsterdam, 1642).

2   Léon Elau, « Pascasius Justus Turcq. Een zestiende-eeuws speelziek jonker en medicus uit Eeklo, lijfarts an de markies van Bergen-op Zoom, » *Brabantia* 1 (1952), 194–208. Mention est faite de notre ouvrage par Ludwig Alvensleben dans son *Encyclopädie der Spiele* (Leipzig, 1853), 11–2.

© KONINKLIJKE BRILL NV, LEIDEN, 2020 | DOI:10.1163/9789004427105_002

Van Houdt en 2008.[3] En 2014, nous avons publié avec Marc Valeur et Louise Nadeau un livre à son sujet, étude fondée sur une première traduction intégrale du texte.[4] En décembre de la même année Susan-Türkis Kronegger-Roth a publié un ouvrage tiré de sa thèse doctorale soutenue à Salzbourg en 2000 et qui donnait une édition du texte latin avec une traduction allemande accompagnée d'un appareil de notes.[5] Cette redécouverte de Pascasius a peu à peu porté ses fruits, et désormais son *De Alea* est connu des spécialistes de l'histoire des jeux[6] et des addictions.[7] On saisit mieux également l'intérêt et l'originalité de ce petit traité longtemps ignoré : Pascasius est le premier à ne plus considérer le jeu comme une faute morale mais comme une maladie analysable de manière clinique, il est le premier aussi à proposer une méthode de traitement psycho-analytique, et ce bien avant Freud !

Pascasius : médecin, philosophe et joueur

De la vie de Pascasius, nous ne savons que ce que nous apprennent une courte biographie rédigée par le linguiste Marcus Zuer Van Boxhorn, à qui revient l'initiative de l'édition de 1642, quelques détails dans la lettre de dédicace de l'édition *princeps*, la préface au lecteur et des bribes d'informations disséminées dans le corps du traité, qui se présente comme la version écrite d'une conférence donnée à Bologne :[8]

---

3 Toon Van Houdt, « Healing Words. Ancient Rhetoric and Medicine in Pascasius Justus' Treatise *Alea sive de curanda ludendi in pecuniam cupiditate* (1561), » *Res publica litterarum. Documentos de trabajo del grupo de investigacion 'Nomos'* 18 (2008), 2–16 (ci-après Van Houdt).

4 *Pascasius, Du jeu de hasard, ou De la manière de soigner le désir de jouer pour de l'argent* (1561), éd. Jean-François Cottier, Louise Nadeau et Marc Valleur (Montréal, 2014).

5 *Pascasii Iusti Ecloviensis Philosophiae at Medicinae Doctoris alea sive de curanda ludendi in pecuniam cupiditate libri II (Basilae, MDLXI). Die zwei Bücher des Pâquier Joostens aus Eekloo, Doktors der Philosophie und der Medizin, über das Glücksspiel oder die Heilung der Spielleidenschaft,* éd. Susan Kronegger-Roth (Kiel, 2015).

6 Voir en particulier Andreas Hermann Fischer, *Spielen und Philosophieren zwischen Spätmittelalter und Früher Neuzeit* (Göttingen, 2016), 253–97 (étude analytique du traité et bonne mise en perspective historique), et « Problem of Excessive Play : Renaissance Strategies of Ludic Governmentality, » dans *Playthings in Early Modernity. Party Games, Word games, Mind Games,* éd. Alison Levy (Kalamazoo, 2017), 205–17.

7 Jean-François Cottier, « Les anciens pouvaient-ils être ‹ addicts › ? Réflexion contemporaine pour une histoire des addictions : à propos du *De Alea* (1561) de Pascasius, » *Les usages de drogues comme traitement de soi,* éd. Laure Westphal et Thierry Lamote (Paris, 2018), 20–31.

8 « Quare nihil etiam ut a me desiderari possit (nam et gratum hoc adolescentibus et multo etiam magis utile omnibus, quos effrenata vexat alea, fore judicavi), volui, quae unica ac

C'est pourquoi, pour autant que je puisse émettre un désir, je n'ai rien voulu d'autre (car j'ai jugé que ce serait agréable aux jeunes gens, et bien plus utile encore à tous ceux que le goût effréné du jeu tourmente) que développer dans deux livres ce que j'avais écrit dans un premier temps et dans l'intention que j'ai dite sous forme d'une simple et unique conférence, puis exposer certaines règles de soins et de remèdes : ceux qui les suivront en lieu et place d'un moyen d'aggraver leur maladie, ce que font les remèdes dont ils sont présentement armés, pourront se soigner à bon prix, se détourner de toute passion du jeu et se débarrasser d'un grave tourment.

Il revient au lecteur curieux de reconstituer le puzzle, auquel il manque toutefois quelques pièces maîtresses.

Son nom

L'auteur se présente sur la page de titre comme *Pascasius Justus Ecloviensis* respectant ainsi la tradition du temps, qui consiste à faire suivre son nom latinisé par celui de sa ville natale. Ce nom en trois parties se donne un air latin, avec son *praenomen*, son *nomen* et son *cognomen*. Notre Pascasius était assez facétieux, comme il ressort de certains passages de son ouvrage – on le devine par exemple derrière ce « Belge rouquin, un peu flambeur »[9] qu'il décrit dans un passage et il y aurait fort à parier que cette similitude était intentionnelle et qu'il s'est plu à se forger ainsi une *gens Justa*.[10]

Reprenons les trois termes un par un. *Ecloviensis* ne pose aucun problème. Il nous indique que notre personnage est né à Eeklo en Flandre orientale.

---

simplici oratione a me prius, quo dixi animo, conscripta fuerant, duos in libellos diducere atque posteriore veluti curationis et remediorum quasdam formulas exponere ; quas qui pro ingravescentis aegritudinis modo sequantur, praesentibus remediis instructi et levi mederi et omni sese ludendi cupiditate evolvere ac gravi expedire cura possint », Pascasius, *De alea*, Préface au lecteur, éd. 1561, p. 23. Voir Van Houdt (voir ci-dessus, n. 3), 8 : « Nor does his style smack of scholastic aridity. As the author points out in the preface to the reader, his treatise originated from a public oration held in Bologna. In reworking his speech, Pascasius made sure to adopt a smooth and quiet style best suited for an exposé that was more aimed at instruction than emotional stimulation. », et Fischer, *Spielen* (voir ci-dessus, n. 6), 257-60.

9   « quod nuper Bononiae rubicundulus quidam Belga fecit », Pascasius, *De alea* 1,5, éd. 1561, p. 55.

10 Nous verrons un peu plus bas que le prénom *Juste* était de tradition familiale.

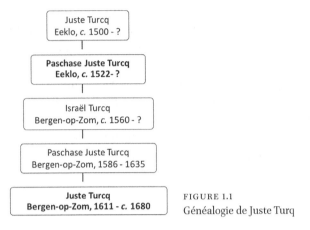

FIGURE 1.1
Généalogie de Juste Turq

Pascasius, Paschase en français, est un prénom, rare il est vrai, mais qui s'honore tout de même de deux saints,[11] *Justus* correspond au français Juste (et non au patronyme *Joostens*), alors que la lettre de dédicace de la troisième édition, celle de 1642, nous apprend que le patronyme de Pascasius est Turcq. Cette lettre dédie en effet le livre à un Juste Turcq, dont il est dit qu'il était l'arrière-petit-fils de l'auteur du traité. Juste est donc un second prénom, qui appartient à la tradition de cette famille, comme celui de Paschase. Notre auteur s'appelle donc Paschase Juste Turcq, il est natif d'Eeklo.

Sa vie

Sa date de naissance ne figure pas dans la notice biographique, laquelle se contente de nous dire qu'il « fut dans la fleur de l'âge vers 1540 ».[12] Par ailleurs, Pascasius dit lui-même dans sa lettre de dédicace datée du 14 septembre 1560 à Pavie, qu'il est loin de sa patrie « depuis dix-huit ans » et qu'il est entré « encore jeune homme » comme secrétaire *a litteris et studiis* au service de Mgr Poggio,[13] légat pontifical en Espagne, poste occupé pendant huit ans. Si l'on retranche de 1560, date de la lettre de dédicace, les dix-huit années passées à l'étranger on obtient l'année 1542 comme date de son arrivée en Espagne. En recoupant les deux indications « encore jeune homme » (en 1542, donc) et « fleur de l'âge vers 1540 », on voit que les deux dates concordent. Et si la fleur de l'âge est aux

---

11   Paschase de Vienne (mort vers 310), et surtout le théologien Paschase Radbert, auteur du premier grand traité sur l'eucharistie et la transsubstantiation des espèces (c. 790–865).
12   *Vita autoris*, rédigée et insérée par le linguiste flamand Marcus Zuer Van Boxhorn dans l'édition de 1641, f. **v.
13   Cardinal Giovanni Poggio (1493–1556).

alentours de la vingtaine, ce qui peut être l'âge d'un « jeune homme » aux yeux d'un quarantenaire, on peut tenir que Pascasius a dû naître vers 1522.

Que peut nous apprendre par ailleurs la carrière de Giovanni Poggio, auprès de qui Pascasius a passé huit ans ? Ce prélat a séjourné en Espagne, comme nonce (juillet 1529–mars 1541), puis comme légat (mars 1541–décembre 1551), enfin comme légat *a latere* (décembre 1551–mars 1553). Or dans la lettre de dédicace, Pascasius nous dit que Poggio était légat quand il était à son service, ce qui correspond à la période 1541–51. Comme d'après nos précédentes déductions, il serait resté à son service de 1542 ou 1543 à 1550 ou 1551, tout coïncide avec le second séjour en Espagne du cardinal Poggio.

Séjour en Espagne

Secrétaire du légat pontifical, Pascasius a donc dû vivre essentiellement à Tolède, lieu de séjour de la Cour.[14] Mais il donne dans son traité l'impression de connaître assez bien l'Espagne : sans doute ses fonctions l'amenaient-elles à la parcourir. Mais l'Espagne dont il nous parle est surtout celle du Jeu. Ce n'est pas dans les salons distingués de la bonne société qu'il a appris le mot *tahur*, terme verlan correspondant à *hurta* « voleur », qui sert à désigner le joueur chevronné et retors. Il a fréquenté les tripots et c'est certainement en Espagne qu'il a été pris par le démon du « jeu naufrageur : *praeceps alea* ».[15] C'est également en Espagne qu'il rencontre Jacques de Claerhout auquel il envoie, par l'entremise de son dédicataire, un exemplaire de son traité.

Séjour en Italie

Il arrive ensuite en Italie, en traversant donc la France, 1550–52, où il fréquente les universités de Rome, Bologne, Padoue et Pavie, qui sont en effet, à cette époque, « très illustres » comme le dit la *lettre-préface*. Pour un séjour de dix ans, cela fait une moyenne de deux ans et demi par université, sans que nous puissions affirmer lesquelles il a fréquentées le plus longuement.

---

14 La Cour d'Espagne est à Tolède jusqu'en juin 1561, date à laquelle Philippe II la transporte à Madrid, qui bénéficiait d'une politique d'urbanisme depuis 1492. Le palais de l'Escurial, commandé par Philippe II en 1557, ne sera jamais résidence royale permanente sous son règne.

15 « Cum in omni omnium hominum vita duo sint praecipua mala, saevus nimirum amor et praeceps alea », Pascasius, *De alea*, Préface au lecteur, éd. 1561, p. 17.

La suscription du traité le désigne comme « Docteur en Philosophie et en Médecine »,[16] titres acquis en Italie. Et il est plus que probable qu'il fut l'élève de Jérôme Cardan, de vingt ans son aîné, qui enseigna la médecine dans les trois dernières de ces universités et qui fut directeur à deux reprises de la faculté de médecine de Pavie (1544–51 et 1559–61). Ce grand médecin contribua en particulier à remettre en cause l'approche aristotélicienne et galénique de la médecine,[17] participant, ce faisant, aux grands progrès médicaux du XVIe siècle. C'est au reste sans doute cet ordre chronologique qu'il faut retenir : Pascasius a pu profiter d'un voyage à Rome de Mgr Poggio pour gagner cette ville et fréquenter en premier son université, au moment où celui-ci quittait sa fonction de légat pour celle de légat *a latere*. Nous pouvons donc fixer au courant de l'année 1551 l'arrivée de Pascasius en Italie.

Par ailleurs, à en croire sa propre biographie, *De vita propria*,[18] Cardan a lui-même été, comme Pascasius, un joueur compulsif.[19] Il n'y aurait donc rien de surprenant à ce qu'il eût assisté à la conférence donnée à Bologne par Pascasius, même s'il n'y était pas professeur à l'époque. On peut aller jusqu'à émettre l'hypothèse que ce soit lui qui ait incité Pascasius à s'intéresser aux aspects médicaux entraînés par un goût excessif du jeu.[20]

Pascasius semble au moment de son ouvrage un joueur repenti, ou du moins en rémission ; aurait-il d'ailleurs été crédible dans son exposé, s'il avait été connu comme joueur ? Ces choses-là se savent toujours, surtout dans le milieu académique.[21] Quel rôle a pu jouer Cardan dans l'organisation de la conférence, dans les idées qu'il y a développées ? Quels rapports, autres que professeur-élève, les deux hommes ont-ils entretenus ? Questions malheureusement sans réponse.

À Bologne, il noue des liens avec les frères Philippe et Jean de Marnix, ses cadets d'une vingtaine d'années. Ils appartiennent à une puissante famille d'origine savoyarde et Philippe fera une brillante carrière politique et littéraire comme ardent défenseur du calvinisme en Flandres. Avec l'un, il entretient une véritable amitié et il a soigné l'autre, gravement malade. Il fréquente

---

16   Voir Érasme, « Quod optimus medicus idem sit et philosophus » (Galien), *Colloques*, ASD I :1, 664–669.

17   Owsei Temkin, *Galenism. Rise and Decline of a Medical Philosophy* (Ithaca-Londres, 1973), et Nancy G. Siraisi, *The Clock and the Mirror. Girolamo Cardano and Renaissance Medicine*, (Princeton, 1997).

18   *De vita propria* (1575–76), première édition : 1643 ; traduction : *Gerolamo Cardano. Ma vie*, trad. Jean Dayre (Paris, 1936) ; édition révisée par Étienne Wolff (Paris, 1992). Sur Cardan, voir *La pensée scientifique de Cardan*, éd. Jean-Yves Boriaud (Paris, 2012).

19   Mais jusqu'en 1542, selon ses dires, date à laquelle Pascasius arrive en Espagne.

20   Voir Van Houdt (voir ci-dessus, n. 3), 7.

21   Fischer, *Spielen* (voir ci-dessus, n. 6), 253–5.

d'autres jeunes gens de la bonne société de son pays : Jacques de Claerhout (dont il avait fait la connaissance en Espagne) et Charles de Souastre, neveu par alliance du dédicataire du traité.

Retour en Flandres

On sait qu'il quitta l'Italie à peu près au moment de la publication de son traité sur le jeu, car c'est sûrement sur le chemin du retour, qu'il fait halte à Bâle pour confier le manuscrit de son traité à un éditeur. Il n'est pas sans importance qu'il ait choisi le Bâlois Jean Oporin qui avait édité en 1543 le grand traité d'anatomie de son contemporain André Vésale, traité dans lequel il corrigeait les erreurs les plus flagrantes de Galien.

Si l'on en croit la biographie de Marcus Boxhorn, il devint le médecin personnel de Jean IV de Glimes (1528–67), marquis de Berg-op-Zoom,[22] où il s'établit et qui vit naître ses enfants et après eux ses petits-enfants et arrière-petits-enfants. Selon certaines sources, il a été premier magistrat de cette ville, mais c'est douteux, car la biographie donnée par Marcus Boxhorn n'aurait pas manqué de le mentionner ; il s'agit certainement d'une confusion avec ses descendants, dont son arrière-petit-fils Juste, qui est donné, dans la lettre dédicatoire de l'édition de 1642, du même Marcus Boxhorn, comme bourgmestre (*consul*) de Berg-op-Zoom.

C'est par ailleurs peu après son retour, en 1566, qu'éclate la Guerre de Quatre-vingts-ans, qui devait aboutir dans un premier temps, en 1581, sous la conduite de Guillaume de Nassau, Prince d'Orange, à la création des Provinces-Unies indépendantes, qui regroupaient les provinces les plus septentrionales des Pays-Bas. Le duc d'Alençon[23] fut appelé, au nom des Provinces-Unies, par Guillaume d'Orange pour devenir prince « protecteur de la liberté des Pays-Bas » (1579) et devint duc de Brabant en 1582. Il choisit Pascasius comme médecin. C'est précisément cette année-là, en mars, que Pascasius fut appelé au chevet de Guillaume d'Orange, gravement blessé par une arquebuse à Anvers ;[24] il parvint à stopper l'hémorragie de la gorge et sa réputation n'a pu qu'en être grande. Suite à une grave maladresse politique, le duc d'Alençon fut

---

22 Sur ce personnage, voir Van Houdt (voir ci-dessus, n. 3), 6. Berg-op-Zoom, Brabant septentrional.
23 François de France (1574–84).
24 Le 18 mars 1582, Jean Jaureguy (1562–82) attentat à la vie de Guillaume d'Orange, qui succomba finalement à un autre attentat le 10 juillet1584, sous les coups de feu de Balthazar Gérard. Voir aussi Fischer, *Spielen* (voir ci-dessus, n. 6), 259–60.

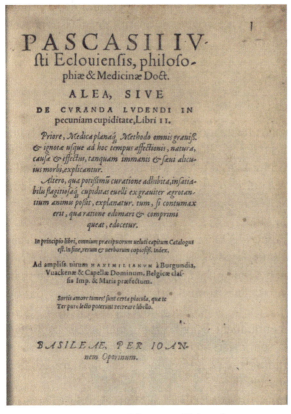

FIGURE 1.2 Pascasii Justi, Eclouiensis, Philosophiae et Medicinae Doctoris, *Alea, sive de curandi pecuniam ludendi cupiditate*, Libri II. J. Operinus, Bâle, 1561 (Bayerische Staatsbibliothek, VD 16, J 923, p. 2)

contraint, en 1583, de quitter les Flandres pour rentrer en France où il mourut un an plus tard : Pascasius avait alors une soixantaine d'années.

Sur les circonstances de sa mort, nous ne savons absolument rien de certain. La notice biographique se contente de nous dire que « le jeu a totalement causé sa perte ».[25] S'agit-il d'une manière pudique de parler d'un suicide ? Ce n'est qu'une conjecture et il faut renoncer à savoir ce qu'il est devenu après 1591, date à laquelle on perd sa trace. Après tout, il aurait eu à cette date environ soixante-dix ans, âge vénérable pour l'époque, et la « perte » dont parle la notice biographique pourrait être « seulement » sociale et professionnelle.

---

25   « Aleam vero admodum deperiit », éd. 1642, f. ** v.

Le *De Alea* : jouer n'est pas pécher

Le traité intitulé *Le Jeu* est à replacer pour sa part dans le changement qui s'opère dans les usages médicaux vers le milieu du XVIe siècle, période où l'on voit fleurir toute une série de monographies médicales qui transformèrent peu à peu le rapport des médecins avec les textes grecs de référence et leurs commentaires scolastiques. La lecture se fait critique et l'anatomie connaît des progrès remarquables. L'apport le plus caractéristique de ces monographies est qu'elles permettent de combiner la doctrine médicale traditionnelle avec les observations cliniques des praticiens.[26] C'est le principe suivi par notre médecin, qui fonde son analyse à la fois sur son expérience personnelle et sur sa lecture critique d'Aristote et de Galien qu'il complète de celle de Virgile, de Sénèque et des autres auteurs classiques. Ces progrès ne bouleversent toutefois pas les principes fondamentaux de la médecine, tels qu'ils se sont élaborés dans l'Antiquité, d'Hippocrate à Galien et qui perdureront jusqu'au XIXe siècle.

Pour mieux comprendre l'apport de Pascasius, on peut commencer par lire la page de titre de l'édition *princeps* de 1561 qui annonce un traité en deux livres, précédé d'une table des matières assez détaillée :[27]

> Dans le premier, on analyse de manière complète, selon une méthode claire et médicale, la nature, les causes et les effets d'une affection fort grave et inconnue jusqu'à ce jour, vue comme une maladie aussi terrible que cruelle.
>
> Dans le second, on expose le meilleur traitement possible à appliquer pour pouvoir ôter le désir insatiable et honteux de l'esprit des malades le plus gravement atteints ; et en cas de résistance, on y enseigne de quelle manière la dompter et la contenir.
>
> Au début du livre, se trouve un catalogue des principaux chapitres, et à la fin un index des sujets et des mots les plus importants.

Dès l'introduction notre auteur insiste par ailleurs d'une part sur sa qualité de médecin, et sur le caractère technique de son livre, destiné avant tout aux praticiens, qu'il appelle à poursuivre ses travaux. Mais surtout, il affirme être le premier à explorer ce sujet :[28]

---

26   Voir Van Houdt (voir ci-dessus, n. 3), 8 ; Nancy G. Siraisi, *Medieval and Early Renaissance Medicine. An Introduction to Knowledge and Practice*, (Chicago, 2009), 187–93.

27   Page de titre.

28   « Neque enim quisquam, ne veterum quidem, usque adhuc inventus est, qui quod sciam, animi affectionis hujus impetus et motus, quos habet gravissimos, quales sint aut unde veniant, ulla oratione aut stylo nobis proposuerit, nemo qua se ratione erigere afflicti

Or, autant que je le sache, il ne s'est trouvé personne jusqu'aujourd'hui, même chez les Anciens, qui nous ait exposé dans un traité ou une œuvre littéraire les élans et les bouleversements de cette affection de l'esprit, et elle en comporte de très graves, leurs caractéristiques et leur origine ; personne n'a expliqué par quel moyen ceux qui en sont gravement affligés peuvent se relever, par quelle stratégie leur esprit malade peut se rétablir. Bien plus, il n'y a pas un seul auteur qui nous ait donné à voir le spectacle du joueur dans une comédie !

Il aurait pu par ailleurs privilégier une forme littéraire plus poétique, mais son but, médical, est de décrire, de donner une étiologie, et de proposer un traitement à l'addiction au jeu, dont il souligne le caractère funeste et pour l'individu et pour la société. Sa table des matières – qu'il ne suit d'ailleurs pas tout à fait – pourrait être celle d'un de nos traités contemporains sur le jeu compulsif. Il se propose par exemple dans le premier livre de traiter de la description du jeu excessif, et notamment :

– de la définition du jeu de hasard ;
– de l'origine, chez l'homme, du désir compulsif et aveugle de jouer ;
– des effets du jeu et de leurs conséquences ;
– de la rechute : « pourquoi, le plus souvent, ceux qui s'écartent du jeu de hasard, parce qu'ils y ont subi une lourde perte [...] changent rapidement, voire très rapidement, du tout au tout, et finissent par courir avec un désir plus grand vers le même fléau [...] » ;
– de ce que l'on nomme aujourd'hui des erreurs cognitives : « Pourquoi la plupart des joueurs, avant de se mettre à jouer, pensent-ils pouvoir accommoder par quelque calcul les caprices de la Fortune, et à ce point diriger les mises et les enchères et la disposition du jeu, comme par leur propre volonté [...] ».[29]

Le livre 2 doit, lui, s'attacher à la recherche des causes, et à la proposition de remèdes : les causes relèvent à la fois du corps et de l'esprit. Il s'agit de ce que les Grecs nommaient une « *pathè* » c'est-à-dire « une maladie de l'esprit ». Mais cette maladie de l'esprit correspond aussi à un trouble corporel : l'excès de chaleur du sang, qui devient comparable à celui des buveurs de vin. Quant au traitement, et c'est ce qui rend aussi ce traité passionnant et important, il réside d'après Pascasius dans l'usage de la parole, seule capable d'agir sur cet

---

graviter aut quo consilio recreare et reficere aegrotum animum possint, explicavit, immo ne in comœdia quidem unus aliquis spectandum nobis aleatorem dedit », Pascasius, *De alea*, éd. 1561, p. 17–8.

29   *Problemata*, éd. 1561, 10 et *passim*.

Le joueur et son addiction

Malgré le titre *De Alea* donné au traité, Pascasius ne traite pas vraiment du jeu : pas de description des différents usages des dés et des cartes, ni d'exemples de règles ou d'usages. Tout cela est manifestement connu et abordé par d'autres, en particulier par son maître Cardan.[30] Notre auteur traite lui de la manière de guérir le joueur de sa passion pour le jeu, ce qui suppose d'aborder la question de ses motivations et des raisons pour lesquelles ils s'enferrent dans la dépendance. À le lire, la passion pour le jeu ne réside pas dans l'activité du jeu elle-même, mais dans la personne du joueur. C'est là une réflexion essentielle : pour Pascasius, qu'il s'agisse de montrer son habileté, de prendre des risques en se confrontant au hasard, ou simplement de se distraire et de passer le temps, le jeu fait partie des activités licites et non condamnables en soi. Pour lui, le problème n'est donc pas situé dans l'objet de l'addiction, mais dans la personnalité du joueur qui y est, pour diverses raisons, vulnérable :[31]

> Le goût du jeu est donc une passion effrénée de jouer de l'argent, passion qu'enflamme un espoir de gain virulent et crédule, autrement dit une maladie grave affectant durablement l'esprit, laquelle, en se fondant sur la vision erronée d'un avenir issu de la maîtrise du hasard, est déclenchée par un désir passionné de jouer aussi effréné qu'exaltée Il en découle en premier lieu qu'il n'est pas du tout question ici de ceux qui n'ont pas du jeu une pratique immodérée, à savoir ceux qui s'adonnent dans le seul but d'exercer leur esprit aux jeux où prévalent la réflexion et la stratégie ;

---

30   *Liber de ludo aleae*, (c. 1564, éd. 1663) : Girolamo Cardano, *Liber de ludo aleae*, éd. Massimo Tamborini (Milan, 2006). Voir aussi Øystein Ore, *Cardano, the Gambling Scholar* (Princeton, 1953) ; David Bellhouse, « Decoding Cardano 's Liber de Ludo Aleae, » *Historia Mathematica* 32 (2005), 180–202, et Thierry Derpaulis, « Cardan et Joostens : portraits croisés de joueurs au XVIe siècle (Le jeu excessif à a Renaissance) » *Ludica* 15/16 (2009–10), 135–42.

31   « Est igitur alea effrenata quaedam ludendi in pecuniam cupiditas animosa credulaque spe lucri flagrans vel est gravis quaedam et diu manens animi affectio, quae vitiosa futuri ex ducta sorte boni opinione constans effrenata quadam et exultante cupiditate ad ludendum concitatur. Ex quo primum illud patet minime de illis hic agi, qui immoderate alea non abutuntur, hoc est, qui vel iis ludis, in quibus ratio et consilium valet, ingenii exercitatione tantum incumbunt vel qui, ut labores leniant, animos recreent atque ocium consumant, quovis ludi genere ludo contendunt », Pascasius, *De alea* 1,2, éd. 156,1, p. 30.

ni de ceux qui jouent pour se distraire l'esprit, se reposer de leur travail ou meubler leur temps libre, quel que soit le type de jeu où ils s'affrontent.

Pourquoi joue-t-on ?

L'appât du gain semble être la motivation première du jeu, et, de nos jours encore, nombre de théories explicatives se fondent sur la rationalité économique pour tenter de comprendre la conduite des joueurs. Pourtant, notre auteur insiste beaucoup sur le fait que le moteur du jeu n'est pas l'avarice, et il l'affirme non sans précautions, puisqu'à ce sujet il contredit une sentence d'Aristote. Pour lui, le joueur est tout le contraire d'un avare :[32]

> Les joueurs cependant ne sont pas dans la quête sans retenue de l'argent pour lui-même, ni le moins du monde par cupidité, mais pour quelqu'une des possibilités de l'utiliser et d'en jouir ; ils le recherchent dans la volupté et leur passion est de se le procurer par le hasard des dés : nous les voyons accumuler les dépenses pour tout ce qui touche au plaisir, suivre leurs désirs, s'accorder de beaux habits, se consacrer à leur corps, faire bonne chère et pour le reste vivre à grands renforts de dépenses et surtout dépenser largement pour ce qui touche au jeu et à ses gains et pour ce qui sert le mieux les plaisirs ; absolument rien de tout cela ne relève du nom hideux de cupidité, mais ressortira plutôt à une absence de retenue dans la passion et le désir – sauf à préférer imaginer une cupidité d'un nouveau genre, passionnée et superbe !

L' « espoir crédule » du gain annonce ce que Bergler[33] appellera en 1957 « l'optimisme » du joueur pathologique qui est centrale dans la spirale du jeu excessif. Plus étonnants encore sont les passages de notre traité qui évoquent l'impression que peut avoir le joueur de contrôler le hasard, ainsi que ses superstitions. Les descriptions cliniques de Pascasius semblent annoncer les recherches les

---

32 « Cum tamen non propter se minimeque avare, sed qua diversa ratione utantur et frui possint, luxuriose illam expetant et comparare jacta sorte aleatores studeant (iis enim rebus, quae sunt libidinis, sumptus suggerere, cupiditatibus obsequi, vestitu indulgere, corporibus deservire, obsonare et profusis sumptibus caetera vivere, immo etiam de sorte et lucro prolixe largiri assistentibus maximeque voluptatum ministris videmus), ne pars quidem ista avariciae nomine sordido, sed potius luxuriosae cupiditatis libidinisque genere continebitur ; nisi si quis forte novum quoddam et animosum ac superbum avariciae genus confingere malit », Pascasius, *De alea*, Préface au lecteur, éd. 1561, p. 19.

33 Edmund Bergler, *The Psychology of Gambling* (New York, 1957), 198.

plus actuelles sur l'illusion de contrôle et l'ensemble des cognitions erronées ou croyances irrationnelles des joueurs.[34] En effet, à plusieurs reprises, Pascasius note qu'il est absurde de s'en remettre au sort, démontrant qu'il ne s'inscrit pas dans une tradition selon laquelle jouer serait « tenter Dieu », interroger des oracles, attendre une réponse de puissances supérieures. Son hasard est déjà le nôtre, alors que les travaux de Pascal, qui posera les fondements du calcul des probabilités, ne viendront que près d'un siècle plus tard. Cette vision du hasard lui permet de dénoncer ce qu'aujourd'hui on nommerait les « illusions de contrôle » ou les « cognitions erronées » des joueurs.

Non seulement il existe un manque de rationalité économique, mais il faut bien admettre une dimension « dostoïevskienne », de « jeu pour le jeu ». Les joueurs pathologiques de Pascasius semblent avoir l'intuition de ce qu'aujourd'hui on nomme les lois du hasard en les reconnaissant comme exactes. En même temps, ils ont un rapport subjectif au hasard qui transcende la rationalité empirique et ils se situent dans un autre univers, celui de leurs croyances illusoires sur le hasard et les jeux de hasard et d'argent. Et c'est cette déraison qui leur tient lieu de loi.

Une maladie de l'esprit

Galien reste pour Pascasius la référence incontestable en médecine. C'est en conformité avec les conceptions galéniques qu'il explique la passion du jeu comme échauffement, dégagement de vapeurs, corruption des humeurs. Le joueur pathologique est « chaud », et nous sommes évidemment tentés de faire un parallèle avec les discours actuels de psychologie cognitive qui distinguent le joueur « à froid » et le joueur « à chaud », en situation de jeu. Ce rapprochement est sans doute moins superficiel qu'il n'y paraît. Lorsque nous faisons des expériences sur la conduite des joueurs, il faut, pour mettre en évidence l'excitation du jeu, que ces expériences aient lieu en situation réelle, que le joueur mise son propre argent, prenne des risques. Nous pouvons alors objectiver l'excitation et les émotions à travers l'augmentation du rythme cardiaque, de la conduction cutanée, autant de signes d'excitation : nous

---

34 C'est dans un article de Ellen Langer, en 1975, que le terme semble avoir été introduit, en référence au comportement des joueurs dans six situations de jeu différentes. Robert Ladouceur a repris ce concept de manière fort heureuse dans le traitement cognitivo-comportemental des joueurs à partir de 1986. Edmund Langer, « The illusion of control, » *Journal of Personnality and Social Psychology* 32 (1975), 311–28.

admettons facilement que le jeu entraîne des modifications corporelles, qu'il y a parallélisme psycho-physiologique.

Le monde de Pascasius n'est pas le nôtre, et le corps n'y est pas encore séparé de l'âme. La bile et la mélancolie sont convoquées par Pascasius au titre de l'étiologie. Celle-ci relève assez simplement de l'échauffement du sang et des vapeurs qui montent au cerveau. Le jeu est alors comparé à la passion amoureuse et à la colère – « ira furor brevis est »[35] – lors de laquelle le sang bout à gros bouillons. L'ivresse, l'effet du vin, est aussi un réchauffement : au début, les conséquences en sont positives, surtout si la constitution de l'individu est froide, qu'il s'agit d'un timide, d'un craintif, de ce qu'on appellerait aujourd'hui un introverti. Mais, au-delà d'une certaine dose, l'excès de chaleur et de vapeurs conduit à la perte de la raison. Il semble donc que Pascasius comprend le jeu pathologique comme un cas particulier de ce que nous appelons aujourd'hui les « addictions », et qu'il met en avant une sorte de dénominateur commun à ces comportements :[36]

C'est ainsi qu'Aristote assure que cet *optimisme* se trouve en nous par l'effet d'une trop grande chaleur naturelle, qui, comme le vin, enflamme les hommes, les excite et transporte leur esprit. Entre autres passages, il a laissé dans sa *Rhétorique* cette phrase où il parle de la nature et des habitudes des jeunes gens : « Et les jeunes gens sont d'un optimisme confiant ; ils s'échauffent naturellement, comme les gens pris de vin ».[37] C'est certes une glose, mais bien digne d'Aristote, où on lit : *L'optimisme provient d'une chaleur naturelle abondante, comme celle que procure le vin.* Or si le vin, comme le dit Horace, *permet aux espérances d'être réalités,*[38]

---

35   « La colère est une courte folie », Horace, *Ep.* 1,2,62.

36   "Itaque εὐελπιστίαν hanc a naturae caliditate largiore insitam in nobis esse, quae uti vinum homines excitat, erigit et exultare animis facit, Aristoteles author est. Qui cum multis locis, tum Rhetoricorum libris de juvenum natura et moribus loquens sic scriptum reliquit : καὶ, ἔφη, εὐέλπιδες, ὥσπερ γὰρ οἱ οἰνομένοι, οὕτω διάθερμοί εἰσιν οἱ νέοι ὑπὸ τῆς φύσεως, hoc est : Juvenes bona et confidenti sunt spe ; natura enim incalescunt, non aliter atque vino poti.Apposita sane atque Aristotele digna sententia : A naturae abundante calore spem bonam tanquam a vino proficisci scribit. Neque vero vinum alia causa, ut Horatius inquit,'Spes jubet esse ratas',quam quia cum afflatu et motus aliqua vehementia calidiores homines facit.Neque solum calor εὐελπιστίαν ut vinum generat, verum etiam, si copiosus magis existat, perinde atque vinum et desipere homines facit.", Pascasius, *De alea* 1,5, éd. 1561, p. 43.

37   Aristote, *Rhét.* 1389a 2–4. La citation est tronquée : « Ils sont enclins à l'espérance ; cela vient de ce que la nature donne de la chaleur à la jeunesse, comme aux gens abreuvés de vin. »

38   Horace, *Ép.* 1,5,17.

c'est uniquement parce qu'en même temps qu'un souffle et une certaine violence des élans, il apporte à l'homme une chaleur plus intense. Et, comme le vin, la chaleur n'entraîne pas seulement l'optimisme, mais aussi, si elle se révèle plus abondante, elle fait délirer les hommes, exactement comme le vin.

La passion amoureuse, nous dit-il, est connue et décrite depuis longtemps, et ses conséquences dramatiques ont été l'objet de textes littéraires comme de traités médicaux. Notons qu'il s'agit bien là d'un thème majeur et vieux comme le monde. Notre culture, dans laquelle dominent la science et la raison, valorise pourtant grandement la passion amoureuse, Tristan et Iseut, Roméo et Juliette étant devenus des prototypes de l'amour vrai et souhaitable. Il en va autrement dans le monde de notre auteur, qui nous paraît presque cynique à propos de l'amour : alors que le plus souvent il ne s'agit que d'une pulsion sexuelle, la passion confère à l'objet désiré une importance délirante. La formulation de Pascasius s'inscrit dans une tradition de « l'amour-médecin », voulant que l'acte sexuel puisse être le remède à la passion morbide.[39] Il faut donc montrer que le jeu peut également être l'objet d'un investissement aussi morbide, que derrière l'idée du gain se trouve une espérance aussi folle. Pascasius donne quelques exemples saisissants de cette démesure de l'amour du jeu : parmi d'autres « on en a vu jouer leurs dents ou leurs sourcils, et j'ai même vu un Vénitien jouer sa propre femme »[40] ou celui de ce joueur qui fait coucher sur son testament sa volonté qu'après sa mort, ses os soient transformés en dés, et sa peau en revêtement d'une table de jeu.

La passion déborde la raison et la volonté, et bien des formules de notre texte sont aujourd'hui reprises, à l'identique, pour décrire l'impuissance de « l'*addict* » devant son « produit de choix ». Ce divorce entre la volonté et le désir est fort bien décrit comme la difficulté à se déprendre de l'objet de la passion :[41]

---

39   *Amour, sexualité et médecine aux XVᵉ et XVIᵉ siècles*, éd. Olga Anna Duhl (Dijon, 2009).

40   « Sed nec defuere, qui dentibus et superciliis lusisse visi sunt ; sicut et ipse Venetum, qui in uxorem suam luserat, vidi » Pascasius, *De alea* 1,2, éd. 1561, p. 38.

41   « Atque ut in corporis doloribus accidit, quorum qui maximus est, aliorum sensum omnem occultat, ita etiam in animi affectibus idem fieri constat. Omnem enim aliam cogitationem et sensum vehemens cura deponit. Sed non usque adeo mirum est, si qui tranquillo tempore imperare sibi non possunt, iidem damni tempestate ventisque oppressi ultima tentant. Illud potius admiratione dignum est multos adeo inveniri, qui cum affectus magnitudinem et vim saepe senserint eumque multis modis exitiosum esse et re saepe sint experti, et palam confiteantur, ideoque quidvis potius facere quam ludere adhuc velle dicant et conentur sedulo, tamen quasi vi coacti sint, ita ne cupientes quidem abstinere possunt. Unde clara et pervulgata, sed fracta et abjecti animi voce cum Medea

Et de même qu'en cas de douleur physique, la plus importante éclipse la sensation de toutes les autres, on voit bien qu'il en va de même dans les maladies de l'esprit : un tourment violent écarte toute autre pensée ou sensation. Et il n'y a pas lieu de s'étonner que ceux qui n'arrivent pas à se contrôler par temps calme, en viennent aux dernières extrémités quand ils sont en proie à la tempête et aux vents. Il faudrait plutôt s'étonner qu'il s'en trouvât même beaucoup qui après avoir maintes fois ressenti la grandeur et la force de leur affection et de mille façons combien elle leur était funeste, après en avoir fait maintes fois l'expérience concrète, qu'il s'en trouvât beaucoup, donc, pour le reconnaître même ouvertement, au point d'aller même jusqu'à affirmer vouloir n'importe quoi plutôt que jouer et de tendre tout leur zèle et leurs efforts vers ce but, et pour cependant, comme poussés par une force, ne pas pouvoir s'empêcher ne serait-ce que d'en avoir envie. D'où la parole illustre et très célèbre, mais brisée et issue d'un esprit abattu, de Médée qui s'écrie devant tous : *Je vois le bien et je l'approuve /Mais je fais le mal* [...][42]

Le traitement par la parole

Suis Dieu[43]
Qui que tu sois, si l'amour pernicieux du jeu te tient captif
Et qu'il te brûle pour ton malheur, lis-moi, tu seras libre !
Ne réplique pas : tout en invoquant les divinités, tu romps tes serments
Et tu continues, misérable, à jouer, te jouant de toi et des dieux.
Le verbe triomphe de tout[44] : c'est un dieu, il gouverne les cœurs !
Suis-le ! Il vainc les dieux, il vainc les esprits !

---

omnes exclamant :*Video meliora proboque, deteriora sequor* », Pascasius, *De alea* 1,2, éd. 1561, p. 35–6.

42 Cf. Ovide, *Mét.* 7,20–1.

43 Ἕπου Θεῷ : Il s'agit soit d'une maxime delphique (Voir Cicéron, *fin.* 3,73), soit de l'un des oracles des Sept Sages de la Grèce (Voir Érasme, *Adages* 1138) : les deux hypothèses ne sont pas incompatibles. Selon Plutarque, le sens en serait « Obéis à ta raison », le commandement de la raison étant un oracle envoyé par un dieu. – On ne trouve ce petit poème que dans l'édition bâloise de 1561. Il est par ailleurs intéressant de noter que le dernier mot du traité reprend la même maxime. Sur cette pratique lettrée dans les milieux humanistes, voir p. ex. *The Neo-Latin Epigram : A Learned and Witty Genre*, éd. Susanna de Beer, Karl Enenkel et David Rijser (Leuven, 2009).

44 πᾶν γὰρ ἐξαιρεῖ λόγος : Euripide, *Phén.* 516. Il faut entendre le mot « verbe » au double sens du mot grec « logos » : « parole » et « pensée », d'où « parole raisonnée ».

LE *DE ALEA* (1561) DE PASCASIUS, OU L'INVENTION DES ADDICTIONS

Mais ce qui fait vraiment la grande originalité du traité de Pascasius c'est son affirmation que le jeu excessif relève d'une maladie physique puisqu'il s'agit de chaleur du sang, de mélancolie, de vapeurs, d'humeurs corrompues et que le traitement qu'il propose à l'exclusion de toute autre médication, relève de ce qu'on appellerait aujourd'hui une psychothérapie. Le remède souverain est, en effet, pour notre médecin la parole :[45]

> Nous l'avons dit, la principale cause du jeu, *l'optimisme*, est produite chez les gens obéissant à leur penchant naturel par un excès de chaleur comparable à celle que provoque le vin chez les gens pris de boisson. Et ainsi, *le contraire soignant son contraire* et puisqu'il faut supprimer la cause pour supprimer l'effet, il apparaît clairement que c'est le refroidissement qui seule peut et doit être le remède privilégié pour guérir ce mal. Or il en est bien ainsi et, nous l'affirmons expressément, que on peut apporter aux gens ce refroidissement principalement par la parole – *parole dompteuse d'âme* comme l'a bien dit le bon poète[46] – ou bien par le jugement et la réflexion intellectuels.

Pascasius donne de nombreux exemples de paroles qui ont pu agir sur le corps, en mettant fin à un état passionnel, en « refroidissant » le corps. Cet effet est, avant tout, obtenu grâce à l'appel à la raison, à la réflexion, à l'intelligence : il s'agit de mettre fin à l'illusion du gain, à la croyance que l'on peut disposer du hasard.

Les racines des psychothérapies

L'appel à la raison est donc le principal remède au jeu excessif, si l'on admet, comme le fait une grande part de la littérature scientifique actuelle, que l'un des traitements du jeu pathologique doit reposer sur la « restructuration

---

45 « Diximus a calore nimio, qualis vino potorum hominum calor est, εὐελπιστίαν, aleae praecipuam causam, in hominibus, qui naturae propensioni obediunt generari. Itaque si contraria contrariorum sunt remedia remotaque causa removeri effectus debet, certe refrigerationem esse, quae sola vel potissimum huic malo remedio esse possit et debeat, non obscure videtur. Atqui sic est et nos refrigerationem hanc vel maxime oratione, quae recte a bono poeta dicta est flexanima, sive cogitationis aestimatione et motu induci in hominibus posse diserte asserimus », Pascasius, *De alea* 2,1, éd. 1561, p. 90.

46 Pacuvius, *Tragédies* 177 : « O flexanima atque omnium regina rerum oratio ! » (« Ô parole, dompteuse d'âme et reine de toutes choses ! »), cité par Cicéron, *De l'Orateur* 2,187.

cognitive », ou sur la correction des croyances infondées et des erreurs logiques des joueurs. Pour guérir, le joueur doit gagner en savoir et en sagesse, et pour prévenir les rechutes, il doit s'y appliquer dans l'ensemble des domaines de son existence, se répéter des formules à visée « préventive », se tenir à l'écart de ce qui pourrait le faire « flamber » à nouveau.

Dans son texte, Pascasius semble se rapprocher étonnamment des idées des cognitivistes qui se sont intéressés au traitement de l'information à partir du milieu des années 1960. On peut même se livrer au périlleux exercice d'utiliser un vocabulaire contemporain pour décrire le modèle explicatif de Pascasius. On dirait donc aujourd'hui que Pascasius attribue aux cognitions (attributions, croyances et attentes) les comportements des joueurs pathologiques et qu'en conséquence, il s'intéresse à ce que les joueurs pathologiques pensent. Pour lui, le jeu pathologique résulte de distorsions cognitives – notamment l'illusion de contrôle du hasard ou l'insensibilité face aux préjudices infligés aux proches. Ces erreurs entrainent le joueur dans un cercle vicieux où, même s'il perd, les distorsions cognitives et les croyances erronées sont maintenues. Le joueur doit rester vigilant toute sa vie pour remplacer ses idées fausses par des cognitions plus réalistes et plus adaptatives. Cela dit, les mots de Pascasius sont ceux de son temps, et toute reconceptualisation constitue une conduite de risque à laquelle il peut être difficile de résister devant un texte qui semble rejoindre tant de nos préoccupations actuelles.

Les origines de nos psychothérapies ?

Aux arguments logiques et intellectuels conduisant à la thérapie par la parole, Pascasius se doit d'ajouter une dimension plus clairement morale : non seulement le joueur doit se convaincre que l'idée du gain est une illusion, mais il doit aussi savoir que la réalité même du gain est de l'ordre de la faute morale, puisqu'il s'agirait de prendre l'argent des autres sans le mériter. Pascasius tient pourtant, manifestement, à ne pas pour autant se transformer en prêtre : de même que le hasard n'a rien à voir avec une quelconque volonté divine, il est inutile d'en appeler à Dieu, et à ses représentants. La loi que l'on viole en s'accaparant le bien d'autrui est une loi naturelle, nécessaire à l'harmonie de la communauté. Le thérapeute peut cependant faire appel aux écrits saints, et recourir à l'évocation de grandes figures emblématiques, dont le Christ est un exemple. Par ce moyen, il trouve un autre chemin que celui de la raison pure pour influencer le corps trop chaud du patient. C'est par l'émotion, par les fortes impressions, que l'on opère ici, en dehors d'un cheminement logique.

Se trouvent donc esquissées dans ce traité, à propos du traitement d'une addiction, ce qui pourrait être une racine historique des psychothérapies, avec la mise en avant du traitement par la parole. Nous avons en effet suggéré que ce traité pouvait être le premier ouvrage consacré à la thérapie cognitive, sans toutefois mentionner l'alliance thérapeutique. De fait, cette racine historique est en quelque sorte à deux branches. La première, que nous avons évoquée précédemment, consiste à faire appel à la raison, à l'intelligence. Il s'agit de convaincre le patient de ses erreurs, de lui donner les moyens intellectuels de résister aux tentations et de lui faire des suggestions quant à un style de vie qui le protégera des rechutes. En devenant pratique régulière ou mode de vie, elle tend à se rapprocher des buts de la philosophie grecque, recherche du bien non seulement pour le pur plaisir intellectuel mais aussi comme guide pour une vie meilleure. La raison devient le conducteur du char ailé de l'âme, tiré par les chevaux de la passion charnelle et de la fougue juvénile, énergies en soi positives, mais qu'il faut savoir diriger et contrôler. L'autre volet de ces psychothérapies relève plus de la morale, et le médecin se substitue ici plus clairement au prêtre. En impressionnant son patient par ses citations grandioses, en mettant en avant la connaissance d'une loi « naturelle », il agit sur les émotions et les sentiments, peut-être en jouant, de façon transférentielle en quelque sorte, le rôle du prêtre ou celui des parents. Dans ces deux modes d'action de la parole thérapeutique, il n'est question ni de contrainte, ni de coercition, ni de discipline imposée, ni de pénitence.

Pascasius se situe d'emblée comme médecin. Il affirme en introduction qu'il veut « rechercher comment soulager et soigner cette très grave affection et comment en adoucir la douleur ».[47] Il suggère aussi que le joueur doit être aidé s'il veut se débarrasser de ses croyances infondées et de ses erreurs logiques. Ce travail de collaboration, dont il ne précise jamais l'exacte nature, devrait porter fruit. S'il ne fait pas explicitement état d'alliance thérapeutique au sens actuel du terme, il dit clairement qu'il veut donner de l'espoir aux joueurs pathologiques et à ceux qui travaillent avec eux. Or, donner de l'espoir est un des fondements de l'alliance thérapeutique, le dénominateur commun à toutes les approches cliniques efficaces d'aujourd'hui. Il s'agit d'une inférence, mais comment ne pas postuler que la qualité de la relation avait aussi son importance dans l'issue du traitement à la Renaissance ? Pascasius était joueur, et sa conception de la dépendance et de l'addiction est inséparable de son expérience personnelle comme joueur qui se jugeait pathologique. Il faut faire

---

47 « [...] ad gravissimi affectus solatia remediaque et doloris levamenta inquirenda excitarem », Pascasius, *De alea,* Préface, éd. 1561, p. 20.

l'hypothèse que ses descriptions de l'expérience subjective du joueur et du traitement prennent racine dans le travail d'introspection qu'il préconise et qu'il a dû faire lui-même.

Conclusion

Pascasius nomme, dans une langue du XVIᵉ siècle, le sentiment intime de perte de liberté dont sont victimes les joueurs pathologiques. Notre auteur se réfère à son maître Galien et il pose qu'il y a une *envie* chez le joueur, et que cette envie présente une composante organique inscrite dans le tempérament du sujet. Bien que le joueur se sente possédé par une force plus grande que lui-même cette force n'est ni satanique ni insurmontable. Le sujet peut changer, s'améliorer : il existe des moyens qui sont à sa portée pour redevenir raisonnable. Il faut que le joueur confronte ses pensées erronées, modifie son style de vie. Il doit aussi savoir qu'il reste vulnérable à des rechutes.

Il est plus silencieux sur le processus de changement, sur l'aspect émotionnel essentiel qui redonne de l'espoir, qui engage le sujet dans un processus de changement. Nous savons que c'est souvent un attachement, une relation avec une autre personne – un proche ou un thérapeute – qui constitue ce catalyseur. Pour plusieurs joueurs, la décision d'aller chercher de l'aide ainsi que l'alliance thérapeutique, le transfert qui s'établit alors avec le clinicien agissent en synergie avec l'intention de s'améliorer. Cela dit, Pascasius évoque les dimensions morale et spirituelle qui accompagnent la rupture avec les jeux de hasard et d'argent. Il est moralement inacceptable de dépouiller ses concitoyens, et cela doit constituer une motivation au changement. Cette conception de la trajectoire addictive est proche de la nôtre à la fois dans sa conceptualisation et dans ses applications cliniques.

Pascasius, enfin nous a appris que la Renaissance n'a pas seulement mis au monde un humanisme créateur. Ce XVIᵉ siècle a aussi mis de l'avant les idées qui sont encore nôtres en ce qui a trait aux addictions, inscrivant dès 1561 les addictions dans l'histoire de la médecine. Cet auteur a aussi proposé une thérapie de restructuration cognitive pour diminuer l'illusion de contrôle des joueurs, un des creusets du travail clinique actuel avec nombre de joueurs pathologiques. Son œuvre se lit comme on regarde les portraits d'hommes du Titien, son contemporain : les habits sont du XVIᵉ, mais le regard est actuel malgré les siècles qui nous séparent. On voudrait entreprendre une conversation, poursuivre une discussion, poser des questions comme si le temps qui a passé depuis cinq siècles et demi n'avait pas d'importance, tant certains propos sont actuels.

> Que faut-il pour qu'un coup de dés réussisse ?
> Rien, sinon que la chance lasse,
> S'installe obscurément sur l'os de l'as
> Et mette en l'air les tétines du double six.[48]

Université de Paris/EA 4410 Cérilac

---

48   Jean Cocteau, *Allégories*, « L'Incendie » (Paris, 1941), 64.

CHAPTER 2

Petrarca e la natura

Carla Maria Monti

Abstract

Petrarch went to natural surroundings often and loved them, so that his work and the picture of himself which he intended to transmit to posterity has been deeply influenced by this feeling. He describes himself reading, writing, praying not inside his room, but in the open, lying down on the grass or leaning against a tree, like the poet Vergil in the opening page of the Ambrosian Vergil. For this reason, the sketch of Vaucluse, drawn by Boccaccio in the margins of the Pliny MS Paris Lat. 6802, is not to be interpreted as a naturalistic landscape, but as a symbolic representation of the poet himself. The actual climb to Mont Ventoux, filtered through classical and patristic echoes, becomes the story of an ascetic experience in *Fam.* 4,1. Finally, the poet who tries to grow laurel in his gardens, use it as the very symbol of his poetry.

Keywords

Francesco Petrarca – *Epistolae familiares* – Neo-Latin landscape description – Vaucluse – Mont Ventoux

La predilezione per il paesaggio campestre, di Valchiusa in particolare, l'amore per il giardinaggio, la descrizione di ascensioni alpine sono alcuni degli aspetti che caratterizzano il rapporto di Petrarca con la natura. Non c'è alcun dubbio che Petrarca abbia realmente frequentato e molto amato gli ambienti naturali, ponendosi in controtendenza, almeno per quanto riguarda la montagna, rispetto agli uomini del suo tempo e piuttosto in consonanza con atteggiamenti propri dell'uomo moderno: egli ha nutrito un piacere vero nello stare in campagna, coltivare il giardino, salire le montagne, e nello stesso tempo ha arricchito questa esperienza di molteplici significati e risonanze nel momento in cui l'ha trasposta nella finzione letteraria. Il paesaggio naturale ha ceduto proprie caratteristiche alla costruzione letteraria del poeta, facendo da sfondo e illuminando la sua autorappresentazione, ma nello stesso tempo la sua

© KONINKLIJKE BRILL NV, LEIDEN, 2020 | DOI:10.1163/9789004427105_003

PETRARCA E LA NATURA

presenza in questi luoghi ha trasformato e nobilitato la percezione che di essa
ne ebbero i visitatori.

Ritratto di poeta nel paesaggio

In uno dei suoi numerosi ritratti di Petrarca, quello affidato alla voce *Sorgia*
del *De montibus* 3,114, Giovanni Boccaccio presenta l'amico nel suo ambiente
naturale, il paesaggio di Valchiusa, che non è sfondo neutro ma parte integrante della definizione poetica e morale del personaggio, di cui evidenzia alcuni
tratti profondi:[1]

> SORGIA a surgendo dictus in Narbonensi provincia, loco qui dicitur Vallis
> Clausa, fons nobilissimus est. [...] Celebris quidem et antiquorum preco-
> nio et aquarum copia et piscium atque herbarum fertilitate est, sed longe
> celebrior in posterum factus novi hospitis carmine et incolatu. Apud
> hunc quidem nostro evo solitudinis avidus, eo quod a frequentia homi-
> num omnino semotus videretur locus, vir inclitus Franciscus Petrarca
> poeta clarissimus, concivis atque preceptor meus, secessit nova Babilone
> postposita et parvo sibi comparato domicilio et agello, agricultoris sui
> contentus obsequio, abdicatis lasciviis omnibus cum honestate atque
> sanctitate mirabili ibidem iuventutis florem omnem fere consumpsit.
> Etsi solitudinis amenitate plurimum teneretur, non tamen detestabili aut
> vacuo ocio tempus trivit, quin imo sacris et assiduis vacans studiis inter
> scopulos montium umbrasque nemorum, teste sonoro fonte, *Affricam* li-
> brum egregium heroico carmine gesta primi Scipionis Affricani cantans
> arte mira composuit, sic et *Buccolicum carmen* conspicuum, sic *Metricas
> epistolas* plures, sic et prosaice *Invectivas in medicum* et epistolas multas
> et laudabiles ad amicos: ac insuper ad Philippum Cavalicensem episco-
> pum *De vita solitaria* librum tam exquisito atque sublimi stilo ut divino
> potius quam humano editus videatur ingenio. Quam ob rem quasi obso-
> leto veteri aquarum miraculo, post eius discessum etatis fervore superato
> tanquam sacrarium quoddam et quodam numine plenum eius hospi-
> tium visitant incole, ostendentes locum miraculi ignaris et peregrinis.

---

1   Giovanni Boccaccio, *De montibus, silvis, fontibus, lacubus, fluminibus, stagnis seu paludibus
et de diversis nominibus maris*, a cura di Manlio Pastore Stocchi, in *Tutte le opere di Giovanni
Boccaccio*, vol. 8, a cura di Vittore Branca (Milano 1998), 1892–93.

> Nec dubium quin adhuc filii, nepotes et qui nascentur ab illis ampliori cum honore tanti vatis admiratione vestigia venerentur.

Il poeta è fissato nell'atto di comporre le sue grandi opere non nel chiuso della cameretta, secondo la consueta immagine del poeta nello studiolo consegnataci da tante miniature incipitarie, ma *en plein air* nella solitaria bellezza della fonte della Sorga, "lungi al romor degli uomini",[2] tra le rocce, i boschi ombrosi e la fonte sonora: "hominum omnino semotus [...] sacris et assiduis vacans studiis inter scopulos montium umbrasque nemorum teste sonoro fonte". Il paesaggio è parte integrante del ritratto di Petrarca poeta.

Del resto è Petrarca stesso che si presenta in questo modo in molti luoghi della sua opera.[3] Sentiamo quanto dice in *Fam.* 6,3,68–70, a Giovanni Colonna attribuita al 1338:[4]

> Risalendo il fiume Sorga si raggiunge la fonte, che non è seconda a nessuna altra e dà origine a quel limpidissimo fiume, sopra di essa vi è un'altissima rupe, oltre la quale non è possibile andare. Giunto lì troverai finalmente Francesco, seduto in terra ("in terram depositus") [...] lo vedrai da mane a sera vagar da solo tra i prati, i monti, le fonti, le selve, i campi ("solivagum herbivagum montivagum fontivagum silvicolam ruricolam"); fuggire le orme degli uomini, cercare luoghi appartati, amare

---

2 Giosuè Carducci, *Odi barbare*, "Ruit hora", vv. 1–2: "O desiata verde solitudine lungi al rumor de gli uomini!"

3 Le edizione utilizzate per le opere di Francesco Petrarca sono le seguenti: Laura Refe, *I fragmenta dell'epistola 'Ad posteritatem' di Francesco Petrarca* (Messina 2014); Francesco Petrarca, *L'Africa*, edizione critica per cura di Nicola Festa (Firenze 1926); Pétrarque, *L'Afrique. Affrica. Livres I–V, Livres VI–IX*, édition, traduction et notes de Pierre Laurens (Paris 2006 e 2018); Domenico De Venuto, *Il Bucolicum Carmen di F. Petrarca. Edizione diplomatica dell'autografo Vat. lat. 3358* (Pisa 1990) e Pétrarque, *Bucolicum carmen*, texte latine, traduction et commentaire par Marcel François et Paul Bachmann, avec la collaboration de François Roudaut, prèface de Jean Meyers (Paris 2001); Francesco Petrarca, *Canzoniere. Rerum vulgarium fragmenta*, a cura di Rosanna Bettarini (Torino 2005); Francesco Petrarca, *De gestis Cesaris*, a cura di Giuliana Crevatin (Pisa 2003); Pétrarque, *Les remèdes aux deux fortunes. De remediis utriusque fortune*, texte établi et traduit par Cristophe Carraud (Grenoble 2002); Francesco Petrarca, *De vita solitaria. Buch I*, ed. Karl A. E. Enenkel (Leiden 1990) e l'opera completa a cura di Guido Martellotti, in F. Petrarca, *Prose* (Milano – Napoli 1955), 285–591; Francesco Petrarca, *Epistulae metricae. Briefe in Versen*, herausgegeben, übersetzt und erläutert von Otto und Eva Schönberger (Würzburg 2004); *Le Familiari*, a cura di Vittorio Rossi, I–IV (Firenze 1933–43); Francesco Petrarca, *Res seniles. Libri I–IV, Libri V–VIII, Libri IX–XII, Libri XIII–XVII*, a cura di Silvia Rizzo con la collaborazione di Monica Berté (Firenze 2006, 2009, 2014, 2017).

4 Qui e in seguito mi servo con adattamenti della traduzione di Enrico Bianchi, in Francesco Petrarca, *Opere. Canzoniere – Trionfi. Familiarium Rerum Libri*, con testo a fronte (Firenze 1992).

i luoghi ombrosi, godere degli antri muscosi e dei prati verdeggianti [...] libero di giorno e di notte, lieto della compagnia delle Muse, del canto degli uccelli, del mormorio delle ninfe, con pochi servi e in compagnia di molti libri; e ora stare in casa, ora passeggiare, ora fermarsi, ora posare il capo e le membra stanche sull'erba tenera ("tenero in gramine lassatum caput et fessa membra proicere").

L'alta tessitura retorica del testo, denunciata dall'utilizzo insistito di *composita epitheta*, anche di neoformazione, sottolinea i tratti caratterizzanti del poeta *solitarius* in interazione con il paesaggio valchiusano. Da notare l'immagine finale del Petrarca seduto, anzi sdraiato sull'erba, che nella sua forte pregnanza visiva costituisce quasi un marchio di queste descrizioni.

In *Fam.* 15,3,10–15, indirizzata a Zanobi da Strada nel 1353 scrive:

Questa è la mia vita, mi alzo nel mezzo della notte, di primo mattino [il riferimento è all'ora liturgica del Mattutino] esco di casa, e nei campi come in casa, *studio, medito, leggo, scrivo*. Ogni giorno vado in giro per aridi monti, rugiadose valli e antri, passeggio spesso sull'una e l'altra riva della Sorga da solo, preso nei miei pensieri e *preteritorum memor ventura delibero*, sotto lo sguardo di Dio. [...] Sono alle sorgenti della Sorga, questo luogo è la mia Roma e la mia Atene, la mia patria. Qui ci sono i miei amici, legati a me per consuetudine famigliare e che hanno vissuto con me, ma anche quelli che son passati sulla terra prima di me or son molti secoli, che io conosco solo per il tramite delle loro opere e ammiro per le loro imprese, per l'indole e i costumi, la vita, la lingua, l'ingegno, qui venuti in questa stretta valle da ogni luogo e da ogni età, e io spesso mi intrattengo con loro e più dolcemente con essi parlo che con quelli che credono di essere vivi. [...] Così libero e sicuro vado vagando e tra tali compagni sono solo.

Per studiare meditare leggere e scrivere Petrarca non si rifugia nel porto del suo studiolo (cfr. *Rvf* 234,1 "O cameretta già che fosti un porto") ma esce di casa, alla ricerca di luoghi naturali belli e solitari. Lo accompagnano gli antichi, nella memoria o in forma di libri, e lì memore del passato, compone le opere nuove che giungeranno ai posteri.

La compagnia degli amici antichi è addirittura messa in scena in *Fam.* 12,8,1–4, indirizzata nel 1352 all'amico Lapo da Castiglionchio. Petrarca racconta di aver trascorso una villeggiatura nel suo Elicona transalpino insieme a Cicerone, che era rimasto impressionato dal luogo, che vedeva per la prima volta. "Mi parve dunque che Cicerone ne rimanesse colpito e si trattenesse con me volentieri e vi passammo insieme dieci giorni tranquilli e sereni", lontano dalla folla della città ma in compagnia di innumerevoli uomini illustri ed egregi, legati a vario titolo a Cicerone e viventi nelle sue opere. Fuor di metafora Petrarca aveva portato con sé a Valchiusa un codice con le opere di Cicerone, probabilmente quello con le quattro orazioni *Pro Milone, Pro Plancio, Pro Sulla* e *De imperio Cn. Pompei*, che gli aveva prestato lo stesso Lapo nel 1350 e che gli restituirà solo nel 1355, come racconta *Fam.* 18,12: "Cicero tuus quadriennio et amplius mecum fuit." Ma potrebbe essersi trattato anche del codice con un'ampia raccolta ciceroniana Troyes, Bibliothèque Municipale, 552.[5] Cicerone confessa che "nunquam se magis in Arpinate suo, ut verbo eius utar, gelidis circumseptum fluminibus fuisse quam ad fontem Sorgie mecum fuit". La somiglianza stabilita tra la gelida fonte della Sorga e i gelidi fiumi di Arpino (*Tusc.* 5,26,74 "gelidis fluminibus circumfusum") senza dubbio sottilmente insinua un parallelismo tra Petrarca e Cicerone.

Ma non è solo Valchiusa a suscitare questa consonanza profonda tra il poeta e i luoghi campestri, lo sono anche le altre sue residenze, per quanto Valchiusa ne rimanga l'archetipo. Nella *Fam.* 17,5 Petrarca dichiara di aver concepito la lettera all'amico Guido Sette, che ha proprio come tema la *ruralis vite laus* (21 ottobre 1353), dalla campagna di S. Colombano nel milanese, poco prima del calar del sole, seduto su una zolla erbosa, sotto l'ombra di un grande castagno. Ne aveva deposto il testo nella memoria e poi l'aveva scritto al suo ritorno in casa (*Fam.* 17,5,15):

> Te igitur cogitans et rus illud, dum tibi ista dictarem memorie credidi – neque enim scribendi instrumenta aderant –; illa autem, ubi domum est reditum, depositum bona fide restituit. Scripsi igitur hec ad vesperam in thalamo non philosophico poetico ve sed regio, que meditatus eram non multo ante solis occasum, solus ibi, *herboso cespiti insistens sub ingentis umbra castanee.*

Queste parole confermano che egli ebbe l'abitudine di leggere, scrivere o concepire le sue opere all'aperto seduto sull'erba all'ombra di un albero. Nella lettera da S. Colombano ritorna a tessere le lodi di Valchiusa, dove Guido Sette si era recato in assenza di Petrarca, quale luogo perfetto della sua *solitudo* e della sua attività poetica: "Nusquam iudice me preclara ingenii opera magnificentius excuduntur: loquor expertus" (*Fam.* 17,5,4–5). Tratteggia ancora una volta gli elementi essenziali della bellezza naturale che lo caratterizza: le acque

---

5 È censito in Michele Feo, "La biblioteca," in *Petrarca nel tempo. Tradizione lettori e immagini delle opere*, a cura di Michele Feo (Pontedera 2003), 488 e immagine a 493.

PETRARCA E LA NATURA

limpide, i pesci argentei (Petrarca fu pescatore), i prati e i rari buoi al pascolo, il salubre venticello leggero (*aura*) che soffia tra gli alberi, gli uccelli che cantano sui rami, il mormorio del ruscello. Ma la menzione specifica dell'usignolo e della tortora è mediata attraverso la singolare citazione di versi propri, tra l'altro non attestati altrove. La descrizione della natura si realizza non solo attraverso la voce dei poeti classici ma anche tramite la sua stessa poesia.

Anche in un'opera in versi, l'*Epyst.* 1,4,14–24, a Dionigi da Borgo San Sepolcro, ci sono altrimenti espresse le stesse immagini del paesaggio di Valchiusa: le acque della Sorga mormoranti, il monte roccioso, i boschi ombrosi, il clima mite, i prati verdeggianti, i pioppi, i fiori e le erbe, gli animali selvatici e un'ampia varietà di uccelli, in particolare ritorna la menzione della tortora e dell'usignolo. Notevole in questo testo il mirabile intreccio tra descrizione naturalistica ed elementi mitologici e poetici.

In un'altra epistola metrica, la 2,16 a Barbato da Sulmona, Petrarca tratteggia la campagna di Selvapiana in termini del tutto consonanti con la descrizione valchiusana: colli, boschi, faggi, erbe, acqua, uccelli, fonte. Da notare che anche in questo caso, come nella *Fam.* 17,5, troviamo il poeta accomodato su un letto non fatto da mano d'uomo ma opera meravigliosa della natura, che è amica dei suoi poeti (vv. 36–39):

> Floreus in medio torus est, quem cespite nullo
> Erexit manus artificis, sed amica poetis
> Ipsa suis natura locum meditata creavit.

La sentenza "natura amica poetis suis" definisce in modo folgorante l'interrelazione profonda esistente tra natura e poesia nella concezione petrarchesca.

In *Africa* 9,216–19 Ennio chiede al suo *dux* Omero chi sia il giovane seduto in una chiusa valle, circondato da teneri lauri, il capo cinto da verde corona, intento in profonda meditazione:

> Hic ego – nam longe clausa sub valle sedentem
> Aspexi iuvenem –: 'Dux o carissime, quisnam est,
> Quem video teneras inter consistere lauros
> Et viridante comas meditantem incingere ramo?

Si tratta evidentemente di Petrarca, che è detto giovane non in senso anagrafico ma in quanto poeta nuovo rispetto ai due antichi.

Questa immagine ha avuto anche una sua precoce realizzazione pittorica, sebbene il personaggio rappresentato non sia Petrarca ma Virgilio. Mi riferisco alla miniatura a piena pagina posta da Simone Martini attorno al 1338 davanti al monumentale Virgilio fatto costruire dal padre di Petrarca, il cui programma iconografico fu immaginato dal Francesco stesso. In essa, come è noto, si vedono tre personaggi – un pastore, un contadino e un condottiero – posti a rappresentare le tre opere virgiliane in ordine retoricamente ascendente, *Bucoliche Georgiche Eneide*, cui segue Servio, che tira una tenda e indica Virgilio. Il sommo poeta è seduto su un prato fiorito e appoggia la schiena ad un albero, ha in mano il calamo e sulle ginocchia reca il libro che sta scrivendo, il capo è coronato di verde fronda, probabilmente d'alloro, il volto ispirato è rivolto verso l'alto.[6] Con i suoi intensi elementi naturalistici questa miniatura è, a mio parere, la più antica realizzazione dell'idea petrarchesca di come vada ritratto il poeta, sia esso Virgilio o Petrarca. La sovrapponibilità tra i due ritratti è facilmente riconoscibile.

Il *De vita solitaria* aggiunge ulteriori particolari al ritratto del poeta nel paesaggio campestre. *En plein air* non si svolgono solo la lettura, la scrittura, lo studio, ma anche la preghiera, le *laudes Dei*: "Iste [il *solitarius*] ubi primum *floreum sedile* salubremque nactus collem *constitit*, iubare iam solis exorto, in diuturnas *Dei laudes* pio letus ore prorumpens" (*De vita solitaria*, 1,2). La preghiera mattutina delle Lodi è recitata non in cappella, nella cella o nella stanza ma sul già noto sedile di fiori posto su un'altura salubre, dove anche la voce dell'orante può unirsi al mormorio del ruscello e al dolce canto degli uccelli. Le lodi di Dio, gli studi liberali, la composizione di opere nuove e la memoria di quelle antiche sono le attività che occupano il tempo del *solitarius*: "inter laudes Dei et liberalia studia et novarum inventionem rerum ac veterum memoriam" (1,2). Petrarca ha sperimentato che il suo ingegno in nessun luogo è più fecondo che nei boschi e sui monti: "ego nusquam felicius quam in silvis ac montibus ingenium experiar, nusquam michi paratius et magnifici sensus occurrant [...] et equa conceptibus verba respondeant" (1,7). Come ribadisce in

---

6   Riproduzione della miniatura in *Petrarca nel tempo* (vedi sopra, n. 5), 473 e Francesco Petrarca, *Le postille del Virgilio Ambrosiano*, a cura di Marco Baglio, Antonietta Nebuloni Testa e Marco Petoletti, presentazione di Giuseppe Velli (Roma – Padova 2006), dove è collocata nel contro-frontespizio. Su di essa indico solo la bibliografia più recente: Maria Monica Donato, "*Veteres* e *novi, externi* e *nostri*. Gli artisti di Petrarca: per una rilettura," in *Medioevo: immagine e racconto. Atti del Convegno internazionale di studi* (*Parma, 27–30 settembre 2000*), a cura di Arturo Carlo Quintavalle (Milano – Parma 2003), 433–55, a 446–49; Gaudenz Freuler, "Simone Martini," in *Dizionario biografico dei miniatori italiani*, a cura di Milvia Bollati, pref. di Miklós Boskovits (Milano 2004), 943–45. Eve Duperray, *L'or des mots. Une lecture de Pétrarque et du mythe littéraire de Vaucluse des origines à l'orée du XXᵉ siècle. Histoire du pétrarquisme en France* (Paris 1997), 34–35, vede nella figura di Virgilio cinto d'alloro una anticipazione dell'immagine del *laureatus*.

PETRARCA E LA NATURA

Fam. 8,3,12: a Valchiusa, nel posto che è diventato sfondo alla sua attività creativa, più che in qualsiasi altro ambiente ha sentito l'impulso della creazione letteraria: "Nullus locus aut plus otii prebuit aut stimulos acriores."

Certo non è il luogo a fare i poeti ma la capacità di superare il livello del linguaggio comune degli uomini, anche se Petrarca ha notato che per lui ciò si verifica con maggiore facilità e prontezza negli spazi aperti: "ego nusquam felicius quam in silvis ac montibus ingenium experiar, nusquam michi paratius et magnifici sensus occurrant" (*De vita solitaria* 1,7). Così gli è capitato spesso di guardare a una propria poesia composta sui monti come fosse il capretto più grasso e più scelto dell'intero gregge e, consapevole dell'origine della sua naturale bellezza, di rivolgersi ad essa con le parole: "Gramen alpinum sapis, ex alto venis", hai sapore d'erba alpina, vieni dall'alto (*De vita solitaria* 1,7). Non solo dall'alto dei monti, ma da quello del linguaggio sovraumano della poesia.

Nella *Senile* 10,2, a Guido Sette, testo autobiografico complementare alla *Ad Posteritatem*, Petrarca ritorna a parlare del proprio regime di vita a Valchiusa. Egli passeggia tranquillo e solitario tra i boschi di giorno e di notte nella quiete campestre della valle, che risuona del chiaro mormorio del torrente, del muggito dei buoi e del canto degli uccelli che intonano i loro concerti tra le fronde degli alberi. Il luogo è così poco esposto ai pericoli del mondo che può vagare per campi e montagne senza paura di essere assalito da fantasmi, animali o persone: "Unde autem ea tanta fiducia si queritur, nempe umbras larvasque non metuo, *lupus* nunquam in ea valle visus erat, hominum pavor nullus" [74] e ancora "ubi in montibus noctu *solus ac securus erraverim*" [85]. Questa sicurezza gli viene dall'essere poeta. Dietro queste parole credo vada colta l'eco dei versi dell'*Ode* 1,22 di Orazio, in cui il poeta "Integer vitae scelerisque purus" nell'atto di far poesia non ha paura di nulla, può addirittura affrontare inerme il lupo della selva sabina (vv. 9–12):

> Namque me silva lupus in Sabina,
> dum meam canto Lalagen et ultra
> terminum curis vagor expeditis,
>   fugit inermem.

Questa immagine oraziana fu molto amata da Petrarca che la richiama anche in *Rvf* 176, 1–4:

> Per mezz'i boschi inhospiti et selvaggi,
> onde vanno a gran rischio uomini et arme,
> vo securo io, ché non po' spaventarme
> altri che 'l sol ch'à d'amor vivo i raggi

come è già stato da tempo notato.[7] Inoltre questa immagine si risente in *Fam.* 15,3,15: "Sic *liber ac securus vagor* et talibus comitibus *solus* sum", oltre che nella *Familiare* a lui indirizzata 24,10,114–15: "dum cantas Lalagen nudus et asperum / et *solus* tacita fronte fugas *lupum*". La memoria dei poeti si mischia con la suggestione dei luoghi.

Nella *Senile* 10,2 scudo ai pericoli della notte non è solo l'essere poeta ma Cristo stesso, il cui presidio è invocato nella preghiera notturna: "Quotiens autem reris me *nox* atra solum procul in campis invenerit? Quotiens per estatem media nocte surrexerim et *nocturnis Cristo laudibus persolutis* unus ego" [72]. Con riferimento alle parole dell'inno di Compieta *Te lucis ante terminum* (vv. 2–6):

> rerum Creator poscimus,
> ut pro tua clementia
> sis praesul et custodia.
> Procul recedant somnia,
> et noctium phantasmata

richiamate nell'espressione "nempe umbras larvasque non metuo" [74].[8]

Il famoso disegno di Valchiusa presente sui margini del Plinio Par. lat. 6802, f. 143v, ora assegnato alla mano di Boccaccio, è sigillato dalla definizione, questa sì di mano di Petrarca, "transalpina solitudo mea iucundissima".[9] Esso contiene

---

7   Francesco Maggini, "Un'ode di Orazio nella poesia del Petrarca," *Studi petrarcheschi* 3 (1950), 7–12.

8   Un fitto *pastiche* da passi della Compieta del sabato è presente nella descrizione delle ore del *solitarius* in *De vita solitaria* 1,2,24 (come è stato ben messo in luce nel commento di Enenkel, vedi sopra, n. 3, a 72): "Iste vel apricum fontem, vel herbosam ripam, vel equoreum litus adit, gaudens diem illum sine dedecore transivisse, et lucis ante terminum adversus secuture noctis pericula dolosque et insidias, ac rabiem leonino more rugientis adversarii, vigilem sobrietatem atque orationis et fidei clipeum, *adversus somnia pollutionemque et nocturna fantasmata*, excubare sibi solitam clementiam sui creatoris implorat; atque in manus eius commendato spiritu et angelis suis ad habituli proprii custodiam invocatis, se se in suam domum recipit, ut nichil iniusti questus, sic nil male cupidinis, multum vero decore laudis referens multumque quotidie in melius mutati animi."

9   Riproduzione in *Petrarca nel tempo* (vedi sopra, n. 5), 487. Nello stesso volume ("Le cipolle di Certaldo e il disegno di Valchiusa," 499–512) Michele Feo ripercorre la storia dell'attribuzione del disegno, e porta elementi a sostegno della paternità petrarchesca. L'ipotesi che l'autore sia Boccaccio, avanzata per primo da François Avril, ha trovato recentemente ampio sostegno dal confronto con i disegni presenti nel suo Marziale (Marco Petoletti, "Il Marziale autografo di Giovanni Boccaccio," *Italia medioevale e umanistica* 46 [2005], 35–55, a 41 n. 20; ma si veda anche Maurizio Fiorilla, *Marginalia figurati nei codici di Petrarca*, Firenze 2005) ed è ora prevalente tra gli studiosi, da ultimo Francisco Rico, "Boccaccio e Petrarca: *De vallibus clausis*,

PETRARCA E LA NATURA

alcuni elementi naturalistici: la roccia, la grotta da cui sgorga la fonte, le erbe palustri, l'airone cinerino con in bocca un pesce; altri invece sono stati ritenuti del tutto arbitrari: la strada che si arrampica sulla roccia e la chiesetta in cima ad essa. Il poeta è assente, diversamente da quanto avviene nella voce *Sorgia* del *De montibus*, anch'essa di mano di Boccaccio, seppur in veste di scrittore. Boccaccio, che non aveva visto il luogo, non credo abbia lavorato di pura fantasia ma, in accordo e su indicazione dell'amico, ha realizzato non un semplice bozzetto naturalistico ma un'immagine ricca di suggestioni simboliche, forse addirittura cifrate, come è stato ampiamente notato. Francisco Rico per esempio ha indicato che l'airone, ritenuto nei bestiari volatile prudentissimo, sarebbe un puntuale ritratto di Petrarca, che si alimentava di frequente di frutta e pesciolini (come dice in *Fam.* 13,8,9). Quanto al monte sarebbe il paradigma supremo di tutti i saperi e di tutte le virtù incarnate da Petrarca, oltre che "il simbolo, onnipresente nelle lettere medievali, di un'ascensione 'in monte Domini'".[10] Addirittura Rossend Arqués ha sostenuto che il disegno sia la rappresentazione grafica del nome: la forma dell'airone sarebbe la *f* di *Franciscus*, mentre il monte di pietra indicherebbe il cognome *Petrarca*, arca di pietra. I tratti essenziali di Valchiusa espressi nel disegno sarebbero dunque l'anagramma del Petrarca stesso, anzi ne rappresenterebbero l'essenza più profonda.[11] Certo Boccaccio aveva ben presente *Epyst.* 1,4 a Dionigi da Borgo San Sepolcro, come dichiara in *De vita et moribus* 10,[12] che offre una descrizione del luogo, in cui spicca la menzione del monte scosceso:

---

       montibus, silvis et fluminibus," in *Gli antichi e i moderni. Studi in onore di Roberto Cardini*, a curia di Lucia Bertolini e Donatella Coppini (Firenze 2010), 1169–82, ristampato da 1169 a 1176 nel capitolo IV "La Valchiusa di Boccaccio," in *Ritratti allo specchio* (Roma – Padova 2012), 73–83 con riproduzione e in più qualche tavola di confronto con i disegni del Marziale. È interessante notare che Feo, "Le cipolle di Certaldo" (vedi sopra), 509, ipotizza che concezione iconografica e realizzazione del disegno possano essere ascritte a due persone diverse: "è di conseguenza certo che l'idea del disegno sia del Petrarca e che sia stata realizzata da lui stesso o da persona amica sotto i suoi occhi."

10   Francisco Rico, "Boccaccio e Petrarca" (vedi sopra, n. 9), 1174; Idem, *Ritratti allo specchio* (vedi sopra, n. 9), 80.

11   Rossend Arqués, *"Per umbram fons ruit*. Petrarca in Elicona. Paesaggio e Umanesimo," *Quaderns d'Italià* 11 (2006), 245–72.

12   Ed. a cura di Renata Fabbri, in *Tutte le opere di Giovanni Boccaccio*, 5/1 (1992), 900–02: "dum adhuc iuveniles anni fervescerent, humana vitans consortia cepit solitudine delectari, petiitque inter *montes arduos* umbrisque arborum perpetuis occupatos, vallem quandam quam incole nec immerito 'Vallem Clausam' nominant ab antiquo, que non hominum artificio sed nature magisterio multis est delectabilibus exornata, quod ipsemet heroyco carmine caliopeo modulamine mensurato fratri Dyonisio de Burgo theologie magistro describit pulcerrime politeque."

Si nichil aut gelidi facies nitidissima *fontis*
Aut *nemorum* convexa cavis archana latebris
Ac placidis bene nota feris Driadumque cathervis
Et Faunis accepta domus, nichil ista poetis
Oportuna sacris sub apricis *rupibus* antra   5
Permulcent animum; nec clementissimus *aer*
Allicit ac *montis preruptus* in ethera vertex
Liberiore situ liquidas extentus ad auras;
Collibus aut Bromius frondens, aut silva Minerve
Gratior aut Veneri; nec utranque tegentia ripam   10
Herculeis *umbrosa* comis distinctaque subter
Floribus innumeris et dulce virentibus *herbis*
Prata trahunt oculos; aut hic qui separat arva
Atque soporifero *Clausam* qui murmure *Vallem*
Implet inexhausto descendens alveus *amne*.[13]   15

Ma l'elemento della chiesetta in cima alla roccia, che è stato recentemente interpretato come una libera invenzione del Boccaccio per alludere alla profonda religiosità petrarchesca, già da Nolhac era stato ricollegato alla cappella dedicata a S. Vittore, ancora esistente in cima al colle nel sec. XVII.[14] In *De vita solitaria* 2,14 Petrarca rivela di aver da tempo il desiderio di innalzare nel suo giardino, che sta sopra la fonte e sotto le rocce, un altare (probabilmente una cappella) dedicato a Maria: "Quas ego iampridem, Cristum testor, siqua voto facultas affulserit, illic in ortulo meo, qui fontibus imminet ac rupibus subiacet, erigere meditor, non Nimphis, ut Seneca sentiebat, neque ullis fontium fluminumque numinibus, sed Marie." A mio avviso la presenza nel disegno della chiesetta testimonia questo voto petrarchesco. Bisognerà riconoscere che come nel caso della miniatura del Virgilio Ambrosiano anche in questo Petrarca abbia avuto un ruolo nell'elaborazione del progetto iconografico in stretta collaborazione con Boccaccio. Petrarca *finxit*, Boccaccio *pinxit*.[15]

L'idea che il nome di Petrarca possa essere espresso attraverso l'immagine del paesaggio campestre valchiusano, trova riscontro nell'appellativo bucolico che Petrarca scelse per sé: *Silvanus* (*Bucolicum carmen* 10) o *Silvius* (*Bucolicum*

---

13   Su Petrarca e il paesaggio: Karlheinz Stierle, "Paesaggi poetici del Petrarca," in *Il paesaggio. Dalla percezione alla descrizione*, a cura di Renzo Zorzi (Venezia 1999), 121–37; Carlo Tosco, *Petrarca: paesaggi, città, architetture* (Macerata 2011), 103–29.

14   Pierre de Nolhac, *Pétrarque et l'humanisme* (Paris 1907[2]), vol. 2, 270.

15   Carla Maria Monti, "Petrarca finxit. La miniatura del Virgilio Ambrosiano e il disegno di Valchiusa nel Plinio Parigino," *Aevum* 93 (2019), 481–94.

PETRARCA E LA NATURA

carmen 1 e 2), l'abitatore delle selve. Del resto nel *Bucolicum carmen* gli elementi stilizzati del paesaggio valchiusano, fonti, selve, monti, colli, campi e uccelli canori, sono intensamente presenti. Singolare invece che il nome compaia anche fuori da questo contesto, per siglare alcune postille, segno del profondo significato che esso riveste. Intensissima la presenza di questo *nickname* nelle postille a Quintiliano (Par. lat. 7720), ne ricordo una: "Silvane, audi; te enim tangit,"[16] ma c'è anche nel Par. lat. 4846 con la *Topographia Hibernica* di Giraud de Barri: "Vade illuc Silvane, quid stas?" (f. 22v). Nel Par lat. 2103, che trasmette varie opere agostiniane, a f. 112r vi è addirittura una postilla in cui, alludendo probabilmente alla figlia, la chiama *Silvanella*, cioè piccola figlia di *Silvanus*.[17] In *Fam.* 10,4,20 ricorda il motivo per cui molti lo chiamano con questo nome: "propter insitum ab ineunte etate urbis odium amoremque silvarum, propter quem multi ex nostris in omni sermone sepius me Silvanum quam Franciscum vocant." Certo non sarà sfuggito a Petrarca che Silvano, nome del dio della natura incolta, ricorre tre volte nell'opera dell'amato Orazio.[18]

Se da un lato gli elementi del paesaggio naturale sono costitutivi del ritratto che il Petrarca offre di sé, dall'altro è la sua presenza in un luogo a trasformare la percezione che di essa ne ha il visitatore. Per quanto esso possa essere memorabile per qualità intrinseche, sarà tramandato alla memoria dei posteri perché è stato nobilitato dalla residenza del poeta. Questo vale anche per la Sorga: essa era assai celebre già nei tempi antichi e negli *auctores* per il miracolo della sua fonte carsica, ma, dopo che nei sui pressi vi ha vissuto Petrarca, il luogo viene additato alla venerazione di ignari e pellegrini solo perché ha ospitato il poeta, come scrive Boccaccio in *De montibus* 3,114. Del resto già Petrarca aveva detto in *Fam.* 8,3,9 che Valchiusa sarebbe stata conosciuta per il suo nome non meno che per la sua fonte, per quanto mirabile: "Quodsi apud te [...] sine iactantia gloriari licet, pace montium ac fontium silvarumque, quid usque nunc loco illi, non dicam clarius, sed certe notius incolatu meo accidit?"

Boccaccio va anche oltre: non solo la presenza viva del poeta ma anche quella delle sue ceneri possono trasformare un luogo in meta di pellegrinaggio.

---

16   de Nolhac, *Pétrarque et l'humanisme* (vedi sopra, n. 14), vol. 1, 92–93; Maria Accame Lanzillotta, "Le postille *del Petrarca a Quintiliano. Cod. Par. lat. 7720*," *Quaderni petrarcheschi* 5 (1988), 87.

17   Elisabeth Pellegrin, "Nouveux manuscrits annotés par Pétrarque à la Bibliothèque nationale de Paris," *Scriptorium* 5 (1951), 265–78, ma cito dalla ristampa nel volume *Bibliothèques retrouvées* (Paris 1988), 107–20, a 108. Si aggiunga il "Nota Silvane" a margine di *Enarrationes in Psalmos* 139,14 (Paris, Bibliothèque nationale de France, lat. 1989, f. 152va), su cui Giuseppe Billanovich, "Petrarca, Boccaccio e le *Enarrationes in Psalmos* di S. Agostino," (1960), ora in *Petrarca e il primo Umanesimo*, (Padova 1996), 68–96, a 82.

18   Francesco Trisoglio, *Silvano*, in *Enciclopedia oraziana*, vol. 2 (Roma 1997), 487.

Scrivendo a Francescuolo da Brossano dopo la morte di Petrarca (*Epistola* 24) egli afferma che i pellegrini si recheranno ad Arquà venendo da Oriente e da Occidente tratti solo dalla fama del sacro nome:[19]

> Venient et forsan aliquando niger Yndus aut ferox Hispanus vel Sauromata, sacri nominis admiratione tracti, et tam egregii hominis tumulum spectantes pia cum reverentia conditas salutabunt reliquias, suum infortunium execrantes quod vivum non viderint quem defunctum visitasset.

La fama antica del miracolo della fonte della Sorga sarà superata da quella del soggiorno di Petrarca; l'oscuro *vicus* di Arquà diverrà famoso in tutto il mondo perché custode anche solo delle sue spoglie.

Petrarca giardiniere

Sui fogli rimasti bianchi del ms. Vat. lat. 2193, che contiene tra l'altro significativamente Palladio *De agricultura*, dal 1348 al 1369 Petrarca ha vergato alcuni appunti di orticoltura, in cui spiccano quelli dedicati ai tentativi di piantare allori nei propri giardini.[20] Essi acquistano spessore se messi a fianco della sua produzione poetica, in particolare del sonetto *Rvf* 228, dove ai versi 1–4 si parla del lauro piantato in mezzo al cuore e si continua (vv. 5–8) con una versione metaforica del Petrarca giardiniere, menzionando la zappatura "vomer di pena" (vomere di dolore); la ventilazione "con sospir' del fianco" (ventilato dai sospiri emessi dal cuore); l'innaffiatura "piover giù dagli occhi". Gli esperimenti con le piante d'alloro nei vari giardini di Petrarca non hanno avuto molto successo, mentre l'alloro incorruttibile del campo letterario si è rivelato assai più resistente: "nell'*hortus conclusus* delle *Rime sparse* sono fioriti gli allori della sua corona poetica."[21]

Petrarca si è dedicato anche alla coltivazione di altre piante: viti, issopo e rosmarino, alberi da frutto (meli e peschi), salvia, ruta, erba del prato, spinaci,

---

19　Giovanni Boccaccio, *Epistole*, a cura di Ginetta Auzzas, in *Tutte le opere di Giovanni Boccaccio*, a cura di Vittore Branca, vol. 5/1 (Milano 1992), 728.

20　Pierre de Nolhac, "Pétrarque jardinier," in *Pétrarque et l'humanisme* (vedi sopra, n. 14) vol. 1, 259–68; Nicholas Mann, "Dall'orto al paesaggio: Petrarca tra filologia e natura," in *Petrarca e i suoi luoghi. Spazi reali e paesaggi poetici alle origini del moderno senso della natura*, a cura di Domenico Luciani e Monique Mosser (Treviso 2009), 57–70.

21　Nicholas Mann, "Il Petrarca giardiniere (a proposito del sonetto CCXXVIII)," in *Lectura Petrarce* 12 (1992), 235–56.

PETRARCA E LA NATURA

bietole, finocchi e prezzemolo. I suoi esperimenti orticoli non sono rimasti confinati all'ambito di una pura attività pratica, ma sono stati consegnati alla memoria dei posteri attraverso la scrittura, depositata in codici di autori illustri.

In *Fam.* 13,12,5 e 7 l'uso della metafora agricola ricorre anche a proposito della sua grande opera incompiuta. L'*Africa* è stata con fatica *exarata*, 'arata' o 'scritta' secondo il doppio significato che può assumere il verbo latino, ma non è stata rifinita: non gli è stata data l'ultima sarchiatura ("supremo sarculo") per tirare via sassi e erbacce, non è stata ancora tolta la terra in eccesso con il rastrello ("nondum glebas inutiles rastris attrivi"), non sono stati posti i graticci per pareggiare il terreno sconnesso ("nondum superductis cratibus scabrioris agelli cumulos coequavi"), né sono stati tagliati con la falce i pampini sovrabbondanti e la siepe irsuta ("nondum frondator luxuriantes pampinos et hirsutam sepem falce compescui"). Del resto il termine *cultus* indica nel contempo la coltivazione e la cultura, e *cultor* il coltivatore e il cultore.[22] Lo sperimentalismo del giardiniere – negli appunti dichiara *placet experiri* – che prova arditi innesti o trapianti fuori dalle regole della disciplina fa certamente il paio con lo sperimentalismo poetico.

Nell'opera di Petrarca la menzione di frutti e piante, pur facendo riferimento ad eventi reali, spesso contiene una seconda chiave di lettura, che allude alla produzione letteraria. Per esempio nella *Fam.* 7,15 Petrarca, rispondendo alla richiesta di erbe e piante da parte di Luchino Visconti, dice di aver dato incarico al giardiniere di predisporne l'invio, ma anche di averla interpretata in senso metaforico: come poeta egli non potrà che offrire poesia ("dum ortulanus herbis et arboribus, ego verbis et carminibus incumbam"). Si noti la somiglianza fonica dei termini usati per indicare i prodotti dell'uno e dell'altro. La lettera si conclude con l'invio di un breve carme, la *Epyst.* 3,6, destinato ad accompagnare i virgulti di alberi: versi e piante vengono offerti insieme.[23]

Nella già citata *Fam.* 17,5 Petrarca invita l'amico Guido Sette a servirsi allo stesso modo dei libri del poeta e del suo orto: "*utere libellis nostris*, qui crebro nimis absentem dominum lugent mutatumque custodem; *utere ortulo*, qui

---

22 "Colo – lis, lui colere cultum quinque habet significationes: colo civitatem idest habito; colo terram idest aro; colo formam idest orno; colo deum idest veneror; colo parentes idest diligo. Quas quinque significationes ostendunt illi versus trutanici (Eberh. 17, 63–64): 'agros, rus, formam, superos colit atque parentes: / hos orat, hoc habitat, ornat, honorat, amat'" (Uguccione da Pisa, *Derivationes*, edizione critica princeps a cura di Enzo Cecchini et alii, Firenze 2004, C 220,1).

23 Carla Maria Monti, "Gli esordi del pensiero politico signorile di Petrarca: i testi per Luchino Visconti," *Studi medievali e umanistici* 15 (2017), 43–80, a 57.

similem, quem quidem ego viderim, toto orbe non habet" (8). Il parallelismo è subito dopo replicato a proposito delle piante e della sua casa:

> *Utere arbustis* e quibus *antiqua* suis manibus Bachus et Minerva plantarunt, *nova* vero meis ipse manibus non tantum nepotibus umbram factura sed nobis; *utere parva domo et agresti lectulo*, qui ubi te gremio exceperit, mei presentiam non requiret." (10)

Come un perfetto ortolano fornisce anche indicazioni sui tempi della semina, indirizzando l'amico a piantare qualcosa di nuovo: "serite ibi, oro, novum aliquid" [10]. Sospetto che gli *arbusta antiqua* e *nova* alludano a uno sperimentalismo anche di tipo letterario.

La montagna

Il Mont Ventoux è una montagna alta 1912 metri nel dipartimento Vaucluse a nord-est d'Avignone. Ancora oggi costituisce una delle più belle escursioni di tutta la Provenza e dalla sua cima la vista spazia da Marsiglia alle Alpi, alle Cevenne, addirittura ai Pirenei, si tratta di uno dei più vasti panorami d'Europa. La salita al Ventoux era fatica molto rude ancora nel XIX secolo, come testimonia il naturalista e splendido narratore Jean-Henri Fabre.[24] Come ebbe a dire Giosue Carducci quella di Petrarca fu "la prima, modesta ed esaltante allo stesso tempo, prova di alpinismo turistico-escursionistico di cui si abbia notizia. [...]". Non solo, la sua descrizione nella *Fam.* 4,1 "è il primo brano letterario che tratti compiutamente e analiticamente un argomento strettamente connesso con la montagna", cioè è la "prima pagina alpinistico-letteraria della storia".[25]

Fondamentale resta la lettura fattane da Giuseppe Billanovich: "Il poeta di 'Solo e pensoso i più deserti campi' e 'Di pensier in pensier, di monte in monte' esercitò continuamente occhi e piedi nelle passeggiate solitarie. Ma se il Petrarca ebbe occhi per vedere, ebbe occhi ancora migliori per leggere." E ancora: "Anche il gusto delle ascensioni, ignoto ai suoi contemporanei, egli lo imparò, prima che camminando, leggendo, naturalmente leggendo i classici:

---

24 Jean Henri Fabre, *Souvenirs entomologiques*, vol. 1 (Paris 1920), 209–23.

25 Da Vittorio Pacati, "Ventoux, montagna simbolo," *Lo scarpone. La rivista del Club Alpino italiano*, 7 (luglio 2005), 18–19. Giosue Carducci, *Opere. X. Studi, saggi e discorsi* (Bologna 1898), 149–60.

soprattutto i testi classici di storia e di geografia",[26] cioè Livio, Pomponio Mela e Vibio Sequestre, da lui fortemente valorizzati.[27]

È la stessa *Fam.* 4,1 a mettere in luce che il gusto delle ascensioni era ignoto ai contemporanei di Petrarca, quando riporta il parere del vecchio pastore incontrato per via (7–8). Egli dichiara che sul monte non era mai salito nessuno, se non lui stesso molti anni prima spinto da giovanile ardore ("iuvenilis ardoris impetu supremum in verticem ascendisse"), quello stesso ardore che muoveva il novello alpinista, "sola videndi imaginem loci altitudinem cupiditate ductus" (1), ma l'aveva fatto con grave rischio per la sua persona, grande fatica e nessun guadagno. È già molto che non evochi il sacro terrore che nell'antichità classica e cristiana avvolgeva le montagne. Petrarca si presenta dunque come il primo a salire sui monti per desiderio di sfida, di conquista, di altezza, ma anche per desiderio di conoscenza, o almeno è il primo che in questi termini ce lo racconti. La *Familiare* è un vero archetipo del *récit d'escalade*.

Petrarca parte dall'esperienza, dalla visione diretta: ha sempre avuto davanti agli occhi il monte Ventoux e a un certo punto ha deciso di fare una buona volta ciò che ogni giorno faceva ("Cepit impetus tandem aliquando facere quod quotidie faciebam"), cioè salire su quel monte (2). La frase è sibillina e pone sullo stesso piano, usando lo stesso verbo, il fare e il desiderare, il compiere la salita e sognarla attraverso l'immaginazione. La molla è la *videndi cupiditas* ma il modello è offerto da un *exemplum* classico, quello di Filippo v di Macedonia, salito sul monte Emo per vedere il campo di battaglia, come raccontano, pur con alcune differenze, che Petrarca non manca di sottolineare, Livio (40,21,2) e Pomponio Mela (2,17). Mancano invece gli esempi biblici che ci aspetteremmo: non c'è alcun Mosè sul Sinai o Elia sull'Horeb. Anche se il campo di battaglia che Petrarca guarderà dall'alto sarà quello interiore. Del resto la movenza sintattica "Di pensier in pensier, di monte in monte" di *Rvf* 129,1 è presente qui nella forma ormai scopertamente ascetica "de virtute in virtutem preclaris gradibus ambulandum est" (13).

---

26 Giuseppe Billanovich, "Petrarca e il Ventoso," *Italia medioevale e umanistica* 9 (1966), 389–401, ristampato in Idem, *Petrarca e il primo Umanesimo* (Padova 1996), 168–84, a 169. Non rendo conto qui dell'enorme bibliografia successiva su questa lettera, ricordo solo: Roberto Mercuri, "Genesi della tradizione letteraria italiana in Dante, Petrarca e Boccaccio," in *Letteratura italiana. Storia e geografia*, 7/1 (Torino 1987), 344–49 (per gli echi danteschi); Georges Güntert, "Petrarca e il Ventoso: dalla « cupiditas videndi » al desiderio « scribendi ». L'epistola familiare IV, 1 come autoritratto letterario-morale," in *Petrarca e i suoi lettori*, a cura di Vittorio Caratozzolo e Georges Güntert (Ravenna 2000), 143–56; Giulia Radin, "Fonti patristiche per il Ventoso: nuove proposte di lettura," *Lettere italiane* 56/3 (2004), 337–67.

27 Giuseppe Billanovich, "Dall'antica Ravenna alle biblioteche umanistiche," *Aevum* 30 (1956), 319–53.

Da notare l'alternanza dei verbi *ascendere* e *conscendere* usati ad indicare la salita: Petrarca dichiara di essere salito, *ascendi*, per desiderio di vedere (1); Filippo V di Macedonia "Hemum montem thesalicum *conscendit*" (2); Francesco e Gherardo prima "hodie tandem cum singulis famulis montem *ascendimus*" (6), poi "soli duntaxat *ascensui* accingimur alacresque *conscendimus*" (8); il pastore dice "supremum in verticem *ascendisse*" (7). Ma la salita adombra una progressione spirituale: "ad ipsius te beate vite culmen oportet *ascendere*" (14). Come dirà Francesco una volta giunto in cima, anche l'animo è chiamato a salire insieme al corpo: "nunc exemplo corporis animum ad *altiora subveherem*" (26). L'ascensione si è trasformata in una ascesi e la visione delle meraviglie della creazione, illuminata dalle *Confessiones* di Agostino, gli ha aperto gli occhi del cuore invitandolo ad indagare le profondità del mondo interiore (27). Del resto questa è un'esperienza normale per gli alpinisti, che spesso approfittano del raccoglimento della montagna per fare un bilancio della propria vita. I piani reale, letterario e spirituale sono tenuti continuamente compresenti nel testo.

La salita è compiuta insieme al fratello Gherardo, che anche in questo caso, come in molti altri, è l'*alter ego* del poeta, il suo doppio, e ne incarna le aspirazioni interiori positive. Gherardo saliva in cima per la via più breve (*compendiaria via*), cioè *ad altiora tendebat*, Francesco allungava la strada tornando anche indietro e prendendo la via più lunga (*longior via*), cioè *ad ima vergebat*, con il significato morale che queste espressioni comportano (9). Uno solo è il protagonista, abitato da tensioni interiori opposte, che qui vengono personificate da Francesco e Gherardo.

Se la decisione di salire è propiziata dalla lettura dei classici il raggiungimento della cima è illuminato dalla citazione diretta di Agostino:

> Deum testor ipsumque qui aderat, quod ubi primum defixi oculos, scriptum erat: "Et eunt homines admirari alta montium et ingentes fluctus maris et latissimos lapsus fluminum et occeani ambitum et giros siderum, et relinquunt se ipsos." (27)

La citazione agostiniana insiste sul fatto che la sete bruciante di conoscenza dei luoghi naturali, la "sola videndi insignem loci altitudinem cupiditas" (1), va trasformata in pari desiderio di conoscere se stessi. In *De remediis* 1,58,4 *De viridariis* osserverà che non è nella bellezza dei luoghi né in alcun altra cosa ma nell'animo che risiede la felicità: "Repeto igitur: non in locis neque ullis preter animum in rebus habitat omnis vestra felicitas." Come ebbe a dire Giuseppe Billanovich: "Tito Livio e Pomponio Mela persuasero Petrarca a immaginare la grande ascensione, s. Agostino [...] gli insegnò a trasformare l'ascensione in una conversione."[28] Non a caso la rubrica della lettera, secondo il titolo secco *De curis propriis*, non annuncia il resoconto di una escursione ma intende narrare una vicenda solenne della sua anima. Anche se io ritengo, diversamente da Billanovich, che l'escursione sia effettivamente avvenuta.

Ma la montagna su cui Petrarca è salito più volte è stata senz'altro il Monginevro, che praticò fin dalla giovinezza per passare dall'Italia alla Francia e viceversa, poiché cercò di evitare per quanto gli fu possibile il viaggio per mare. Della salita al Monginevro e del panorama che da lì si ammira ha parlato in luoghi notissimi della sua produzione, primo fra tutti in *Epyst.* 3,24, la famosa "Cara Deo tellus", in cui viene magnificata la visione dell'Italia che si apre salendo il Monginevro dalla Francia (vv. 13–18):

> Te letus ab alto
> Italiam video frondentis colle Gebenne.
> Nubila post tergum remanent; ferit ora serenus
> Spiritus et blandis assurgens motibus aer
> Excipit. Agnosco patriam gaudensque saluto:
> Salve, pulcra parens, terrarum gloria, salve.

Nei testi dedicati a questa salita si risente sottilmente che egli si sta paragonando a Cesare, che aveva composto vari suoi libri durante il medesimo itinerario alpino, e perfino un poema intitolato *Iter*, come riferisce Svetonio nella vita a lui dedicata, *Iul.* 56,5 (cfr. *Res mem.* 1,12, 7 e *De gestis Cesaris* 26,11 e 13). L'espressione svetoniana "in Alpium transitu" viene fatta propria da Petrarca quando racconta questa salita, si veda *Fam.* 11,9 scritta *Gebenne montis e vertice*: "In transitu Alpium tibi hec scribo." Il *transitus Alpium* dunque è una frequente esperienza di vita ma anche una citazione.

Un altro testo dedicato alla salita al Monginevro dall'Italia verso la Francia è il carme extravagante e poco noto *Linquimus Italiam*, che offre una splendida descrizione della tormenta in montagna.[29]

> *In ipsis Alpium radicibus a parte Ytalie.*
> Linquimus Italiam, paulatim terra tumescit
>   et pedemontana valle tenemus iter.

---

28 Billanovich, "Petrarca e il Ventoso" (vedi sopra, n. 25), 173.

29 Francesco Petrarca, *Improvvisi. Un'antica raccolta di epigrammi*, a cura di Monica Berté (Roma 2014) 57–65, che pubblica criticamente il testo con le rubriche che nei manoscritti lo accompagnano.

In ascensu Alpium.
Surgimus assidue, rigidam iam scandimus Alpem
    asperiorque graves semita lassat equos.
Iupiter horrisono descendens turbine sevit
    et terras oculis eripuere nives.
In ipso transitu Alpium et descensu.
Iam glaciale solum convexaque summa Gebenne
    transgredimur, iam nos concomitantur aque.
Saxosus gelidusque viam Durentia monstrat
    et Rodani ripas arvaque nota petens.
Ventus ab adverso violento murmure perflat
    precipitansque nivem turbidus ora ferit.
Itala post tergum remanet pucherrima tellus,
    quam vetat etherei cernere montis apex;
Ante procul colles et gallica rura patescunt.
    Gentibus hic fuerat terminus, est et erit.

Il carme è dunque articolato in tre tempi: inizio dell'iter ascensionale in val di Susa alle pendici delle Alpi (vv. 1–2); inizio della scalata su sentieri rocciosi sempre più aspri, dove fa gradualmente la sua comparsa la tempesta di neve (vv. 3–6); acme della scalata sulla vetta ghiacciata del Monginevro e passaggio del valico alpino, sotto il vortice del vento e il turbinio della neve, e inizio della discesa sul versante francese (vv. 7–16). Tre verbi odeporici e alpinistici ne connotano i tre movimenti: *Linquimus* (v. 1), *Surgimus* (v. 3), *transgredimur* (v. 8). Sono le stesse battute che scandiscono il meditatissimo testo dell'ascensione al Ventoso, che parte "in radicibus montis" (*Fam.* 4,1,6) e descrive le fasi della scalata con lessico tecnico della stessa tipologia: "montem ascendimus" (6); "ascensui accingimur alacresque conscendimus" (8); "fatigatio subsequitur [...] in rupe subsistimus. Inde iterum digressi provehimur, sed lentius: et presertim ego montanum iter gressu iam modestiore carpebam [...] ad altiora tendebat" (9); "Collis est omnium supremus [...] Illius in vertice planities parva est; illic demum fessi conquievimus" (16); "Tunc vero montem satis vidisse contentus [...] ad ima pervenimus" (29). Nel carme *Linquimus* i tratti realistici prevalgono sugli echi classici.[30]

---

30   Gabriella Albanese-Paolo Pontari, "*Lyra minima*. Petrarca e le Alpi," in *Esercizi di lettura per Marco Santagata*, a cura di Annalisa Andreoni, Claudio Giunta e Mirko Tavoni (Bologna 2017), 121–56, a 127–28.

Modelli

Petrarca presenta se stesso sempre in relazione ai grandi modelli costituiti dagli autori del passato, suoi amici ancor più consonanti degli amici viventi. Questo accade anche nel caso del suo rapporto con la natura, come abbiamo già visto in qualche caso. L'esemplificazione più abbondante di ciò si trova nel *De vita solitaria*, in particolare nel secondo libro, in cui vi è una ampia rassegna di autori rappresentati *sub specie Petrarce*. Anche Cicerone diviene *solitarius* o per lo meno si afferma con nettezza che egli poté scrivere le sue grandi opere quando fu costretto a lasciare la città e a rifugiarsi in campagna. Dunque la schiera dei modelli petrarcheschi è amplissima. Farò solo due esempi, uno classico, Orazio, e uno medievale, Bernardo.

Nella lunga *Fam.* 6,3 a Giovanni Colonna Petrarca esprime il piacere che proverebbe nel visitarlo a Tivoli, che anticamente fu residenza del suo amato Orazio. La descrizione che segue, relativa al soggiorno petrarchesco sulle rive della Sorga, suggerisce una sorta di identificazione con l'Orazio *ruris amator* che fra le acque e le frescure del Tivoli compone i propri carmi: "circa nemus uvidique / Tiburis ripas operosa parvus / carmina fingo" (*Carm.* 4,2,30–32). In *De vita solitaria* 2,12 ricorda che per Orazio la campagna è il luogo ideale per scrivere versi, e addirittura in *Epist.* 2,2,77 ha stabilito quasi una regola: tutti gli scrittori amano i boschi e fuggono le città ("Scriptorum chorus omnis amat nemus et fugit urbes"), regola che Petrarca dice di aver seguito, imitandone la formulazione in un verso di una sua epistola metrica, che riporta: "Quem secutus ego in epystola quadam eandemque restringens ad poetas, dixi: 'Silva placet Musis, urbs est inimica poetis'" (*Epyst.* 2,3,43).

In *De vita solitaria* 2,7 Petrarca racconta, sulla base della *Vita Bernardi* (*PL* 185:240), che il santo soleva dire che tutta la sua erudizione si era formata nei boschi e nei campi, non con le discipline degli uomini ma con la meditazione e la preghiera: non aveva avuto alcun maestro oltre alle querce e ai faggi. Non è un caso che abeti e faggi siano anche i compagni della solitudine petrarchesca (cfr. *Rvf* 10,6 e 176,8). Petrarca vorrebbe che la propria sapienza fosse la stessa di Bernardo, acquisita meditando e pregando in campagna e nei boschi: il suo regime di vita, o almeno quello che ci racconta, pare modellato su Bernardo. Tra l'altro Bernardo aveva un fratello di nome Gerardo, che dopo essersi dedicato alla vita militare aveva abbracciato la vita monastica. Il parallelismo con la vicenda di Gherardo Petrarca non può sfuggire.

Chiudo segnalando che i luoghi naturali prediletti da Petrarca e da lui utilizzati per la propria costruzione autobiografica e poetica coincidono non credo casualmente con quelli cantati nella Bibbia, che unisce all'affresco potente della natura creata da Dio quello della natura a servizio dell'uomo.

Vi è la bellezza naturale selvaggia e quella dei luoghi coltivati: monti e colline, ghiaccio e neve, nubi e pioggia, vento e tempesta, fiumi e fonti, boschi, alberi e erbe, mare, mostri marini e pesci, animali selvatici e domestici, uccelli, cedri del Libano, alberi da frutta e coltivazioni dell'uomo, frumento e vite, erba e fiori. I testi biblici più rappresentativi sono i *Salmi* e il *Cantico dei tre fanciulli* (*Dn* 3,64–81), la cui conoscenza fu profondamente interiorizzata da Petrarca attraverso la recita quotidiana del Breviario.[31] Ricordo solo l'incipit del salmo 120: "Levavi oculos meos in montes unde veniet auxilium meum", che sembra risuonare all'inizio della *Fam.* 4,1: "mons autem hic late undique conspectus, fere semper in oculis est."

In Petrarca opera e vita sono il prodotto di una doppia mimesi: un'opera fortemente autobiografica, una vita modellata sull'opera, e vita e opera modellate sugli esempi dell'antichità. Questo vale anche per il rapporto con gli ambienti naturali: la rappresentazione della vicenda biografica è trasfigurata nel gioco di specchi della letteratura.

Università Cattolica del S. Cuore – Milano

---

31   Giulio Goletti, "Il Breviario del Petrarca," in *Petrarca nel tempo* (vedi sopra, n. 5), 513–15.

CHAPTER 3

"Conquering Greece": On the Correct Way to Translate in Fifteenth-Century Humanist Translation Theory

Marianne Pade

Abstract

In his award-winning monograph on *The Lost Italian Renaissance* (2004), Christopher S. Celenza argued that the Latin writings of Italian Renaissance intellectuals have been largely ignored since the Renaissance was first 'discovered', precisely because they were written in Latin. This holds true also for humanist translation theory: though we possess a large corpus of humanist Latin texts on translation, it is rarely touched upon by modern translation specialists.

In this article I shall focus on fifteenth-century discussions of translation and show how Renaissance translators often addressed questions that loom large in contemporary translation studies. The humanists discussed what we today would call domesticating versus foreignizing translation, rewriting, intertextuality, the stylistic analogue—amongst other things. My paper also shows that there were different phases in humanist translation, and that the wildly experimenting tendencies of the first half of the century eventually gave way to a more traditional approach.

Keywords

Francesco Petrarca – Coluccio Salutati – Manuel Chrysolaras – Neo-Latin translation studies – domesticating translation

For readers in any way familiar with fifteenth century humanist translation theory, the subtitle of this article will immediately bring to mind Leonardo Bruni's fundamental treatise *De interpretatione recta*—which in James Hankins' excellent translation became *On the Correct Way to Translate*.[1]

---

1 Gordon Griffiths, James Hankins and David Thompson, *The Humanism of Leonardo Bruni*, (Binghamton, NY, 1987), 217–29.

46   PADE

The very title of Bruni's treatise, *De interpretatione recta*, has probably been one of the reasons why modern translation studies have tended to ignore humanist translation theory: Since what the humanists wrote about translation is often prescriptive rather than descriptive, it would *a priori* not have any theoretical value. In her popular textbook called *La teoria della traduzione nella storia*, Siri Neergaard talks about Bruni's treatise as belonging to the 'pre-scientific' phase of reflection on translation. According to her, translators from Cicero and St Jerome and until after Bruni were not professional translators in 'our' sense of the word—whatever that is—they were poets, writers and philosophers;[2] it was only from the middle of the last century that one could talk about theoretical studies of translation. What was before was normative.[3] When Neergaard discards the scientific and theoretical value of humanist reflection on translation, it may also have to do with the format in which it was expressed. Much of it is found in peri- and epitexts, such as prefaces and letters and dedications that bear little resemblance to what we today recognize as scholarly literature, and their writers regularly argue with images or through intertextual allusions, using a mode of discourse that is very dissimilar to that of modern scholarship.[4]

Moreover, from the nineteenth century scholarly interest in the humanists' translations tended to focus on their value as sources for some lost variant in the Greek original.[5] Due to the prevailing humanist translation method, they were often highly unsuited for that, and the translations have therefore been much criticized for being imprecise and overly rhetorical.

But perhaps the most important reason why humanist translation theory is so often completely overlooked by modern translation scholars is

---

2 "questi autori non erano traduttori professionali nel senso in cui noi oggi intendiamo questa attività: erano poeti, letterati e filosofi," *La teoria della traduzione nella storia. Testi di Cicerone, San Gerolamo, Bruni, Lutero, Goethe, von Humboldt, Schleiermacher, Ortega y Gasset, Croce, Benjamin*, ed. Siri Nergaard (Milano 1993, third edition 2007), 10.

3 Ibid., 10–2.

4 *Issues in Translation* (see above, n. *), III.

5 For examples of this regarding Lorenzo Valla's 1453 translation of Thucydides, see Friedrich E. Poppo, *Thucydidis De bello Peloponnesiaco* (Leipzig, 1821–38), pars 2, vol. 1, 72; Eugen Julius Golish, *De Thucydidis interpretatione a Laurentio Valla latine facta disquisitionis specimen* (Öls, 1842); Egidius Josephus Leonard Ludwig Eugen Cordewener, *De Thucydidis Vaticani codicis quod ad libros septimum et octavum attinet praestantia cum Vallae Historiae Belli Peloponnesiaci interpretatione collata* (Amsterdam, 1897); *Thucydides Historiae*, vol. 1, ed. Giovan Battista Alberti (Roma, 1972), cxix–cxxxii; and Filippo Ferlauto, *Il testo di Tucidide e la traduzione latina di Lorenzo Valla* (Palermo, 1979).

ON THE CORRECT WAY TO TRANSLATE IN HUMANIST TRANSLATION THEORY   47

the regrettable fact that the basic texts are written in Latin. James Hankins once called the Latin literature of Early Modern Europe a "lost continent" or, if not lost, then definitely a largely overlooked part of the intellectual heritage of Europe.[6] In 2004, in the award-winning monograph *The Lost Italian Renaissance*, Christopher S. Celenza argued that a major part of the intellectual and cultural activity of the Italian Renaissance has been largely ignored since the Renaissance was first 'discovered': namely the vast body of works— literary, philosophical, poetic, and religious—written in Latin. This literature was initially overlooked by scholars of the Renaissance, because they were not written in the vernacular Italian which alone was seen as the supreme expression of the culture of the peninsula. This lack of attention, which continued well into the twentieth century, has led interpreters to misread key aspects of the Renaissance. For one thing, this literature establishes the intellectual traditions from which such well-known vernacular writers as Machiavelli and Castiglione emerge[7]—or in the case of translation theory the French Etienne Dolet. Of course, humanist translation theory has attracted the attention of a number of eminent Neo-Latin scholars, but if one looks at most modern literature on the history of translation studies, one of the fastest developing fields of the humanities, humanist translation is sadly overlooked:

George Steiner's *After Babel* has been hailed as one of the classic twentieth-century works on translation, and Steiner himself revised it twice after it was first published in 1975. He does touch upon ancient, medieval and early modern translation, but everything about the theory, practice and history of translation from Cicero and Horace up to around 1800 is treated in only a couple of pages.[8] First published in 1980, Susan Bassnett's *Translation Studies* is still regarded as essential reading for anyone interested in the field. At the beginning of the volume she offers a history of translation theory, beginning with the ancient Romans and encompassing key twentieth-century structuralist work. Here she states that one of the first writers to formulate a theory of translation was the French humanist Etienne Dolet—in the mid-sixteenth century.[9] But as we shall hear, Italian humanists discussed translation theory more

---

6   James Hankins, "A Lost Continent of Literature," in *The Lost Continent: Neo-Latin Literature and the Birth of European Vernacular Literature*, ed. J. Hankins (Cambridge, MA, 2001), 21–7.

7   Christopher Celenza, *The Lost Italian Renaissance* (Baltimore – London, 2004).

8   George Steiner, *After Babel. Aspects of language and translation* (Oxford, 1975; second edition 1992, third edition 1998), 248–9.

9   Susan Bassnett, *Translation Studies* (London – New York, 1980, fourth edition 2014), 53.

than a hundred years before Dolet, whose treatise mentioned by Bassnett is in fact not much more than an abbreviated translation of Bruni's.[10] In the following, I shall therefore argue that (a) there was a continuous discourse on translation from the early Renaissance and onwards, only not where and in the forms modern scholarship would recognize it, and not in a language most modern scholars can read; (b) humanist discourse on translation addressed—*avant la lettre*—a number of issues that have loomed large in Translation Studies in this and in the last century; and (c) the history of humanist Translation Studies is closely bound to the history of humanism itself. Recent interpretations of the humanist movement, as Patrick Baker's *Renaissance Humanism in a Mirror* (Cambridge, 2015), have stressed its linguistic nature, and as I hope to show, humanist translation was very much part of this linguistic project.

Petrarch

Petrarch may with some justification be called the father not only of humanism, but also of humanist translation, although he never managed to learn any Greek to speak of.[11] In spite of that he was instrumental in changing the course of Greek studies in the West: He was among the first to express a vivid interest in Greek rhetoric, poetry and biographical writings, genres that had been completely ignored by medieval translators, and together with Boccaccio he commissioned a Latin translation of the Homeric poems, the first Latin translations of any part of Homer since Antiquity. He also began to criticise medieval translation practice, thus anticipating central elements of fifteenth-century metadiscourse on translation.

Petrarch looked at the Greek world through the lens of classical Latin writers. He wanted to become acquainted with the orators and the philosophical writers upon whom Cicero had drawn, and with Homer who had inspired Virgil. His admiration, however, was never more than moderate, and he always maintained the superiority of Latin culture (Petrarca, *Fam.* 6,1,11–2).[12]

---

10 See my "Neo-Latin and Vernacular Translation Theory in the Fifteenth and Sixteenth Centuries: 'The tasks of the translator' according to Leonardo Bruni and Étienne Dolet," in *Neo-Latin and the Vernaculars. Bilingual Interactions in the Early Modern Period*, ed. Florian Schaffenrath and Alexander Winkler (Leiden – Boston, 2018), 96–112, there 106–10.

11 The paragraph is based on my discussion in *The Reception of Plutarch's* Lives *in Fifteenth-Century Italy*, 2 vols. (Copenhagen, 2007), vol. 1, 67–72.

12 When possible, I refer to Neo-Latin texts with the sigla used by Johann Ramminger in *Neulateinische Wortliste* (www.neulatein.de), where also the standard editions used in this article are listed.

> Quid de ingeniis loquar? imitatio unum insigne par siderum lingue latine, Ciceronem et Virgilium, dedit, effecitque ne iam amplius Grecis ulla in parte eloquentie cederemus; dum hic Homerum sequitur, ille Demosthenem, alter ducem suum attigit, alter a tergo liquit,

> Why do I speak of natural ability? Imitation created that one eminent pair, the stars of the Latin tongue, Cicero and Virgil, and thus brought about that we no more yield to the Greeks in any part of eloquence. While Virgil follows Homer and Cicero Demosthenes, the first of them equalled his guide, whereas the second left his behind.[13]

We may be almost certain that Petrarch never read a word of Demosthenes and that he had no direct knowledge of Homer at the time he wrote this letter. As would be the case with many of his fifteenth-century followers, he saw familiarity with Greek literature as something that would deepen his understanding of the Latin *auctores*.[14] We know how deeply he admired Virgil and the extent to which he imitated him e.g. in his *Eclogues* and the *Africa*,[15] so it is no surprise that that he showed a keen interest in Homer from his earliest years, collecting whatever information he came upon about the ancient poet. Later he and Giovanni Boccaccio would persuade Leonzio Pilato, a Greek speaking native of Calabria, to produce a complete Latin translation of the Homeric poems, the first ever. The result, however, was disappointing. Upon seeing a sample of Leonzio's translation, Petrarch wrote to Boccaccio, quoting Jerome (*chron. epist.* p. 4, l. 8) who had said that any translator who did not believe it necessary to change the word order for the sake of language, should try to render Homer into Latin word-for-word, or just in prose. He would find the word order ridiculous and that most eloquent of poets hardly able to speak.[16]

---

13   Unless otherwise stated, translations are my own.

14   James Hankins, "Chrysoloras and the Greek Studies of Leonardo Bruni," in *Manuele Crisolora e il ritorno del greco in occidente. Atti del Convegno Internazionale (Napoli, 26–29 giugno 1997)*, ed. Riccardo Maisano and Antonio Rollo (Napoli, 2002), 175–97, there 195.

15   Margit Berghoff-Bührer, *Das* Bucolicum carmen *des Petrarca. Ein Beitrag zur Wirkungsgeschichte von Vergils Eclogen* (Bern – Berlin etc., 1991); *Le postille del Virgilio Ambrosiano*, ed. Marco Baglio, Antonietta Nebuloni Testa and Marco Petoletti, 2 vols. (Roma – Padova, 2006).

16   *Epystole Extravagantes* 46 (var. 25), § 2, ed. Alessandro Pancheri in F. Petrarca, *Lettere disperse: varie e miscellanee* (Milano, 1994).

Leonzio, unfortunately, had done exactly what Jerome warned against, translating Homer into Latin word for word; what in the autograph manuscripts looks like a first draft, an interlinear translation where the Latin equivalent is written above the Greek words, is in fact the finished product. Petrarch's reaction to it is actually more surprising than Leonzio's translation method, as it had been normal practice in medieval translation to render the original word for word, and nobody seems to have minded. Admittedly, the majority of these translations were of scientific or philosophical texts in which the result was less absurd than when the word-for-word method was applied to literary or poetical texts, such as the Homeric epics.[17] Still, as we shall see later, medieval translations of e.g. Aristotle were fiercely criticised by humanist translators—though the practice was never totally abandoned.

Coluccio Salutati

Clumsy as they were, the new translations of Homer enjoyed an immediate success and were avidly sought after, for instance in the group around Florence's humanist chancellor Coluccio Salutati (1331–1406). A fervent admirer of Petrarch, Coluccio also appropriated the former's revolutionary views on translation method, or rather on the importance of a satisfactory Latin style, also in a translation. We have an example of that in a letter to the young Antonio Loschi, who had apparently resolved to embellish Leonzio's Latin *Iliad*—although he had no Greek. Coluccio evidently did not see that as a problem, for he eagerly encouraged the undertaking: Loschi should reproduce the style of Homer, of which, in some mysterious way, they both had clear notions. Concentrating on the content, Loschi should rewrite Leonzio's Latin in such an ornate and splendid style that not only the story and the phrases, but

---

17   On Leonzio's translations, see Agostino Pertusi, *Leonzio Pilato fra Petrarca e Boccaccio. Le sue versioni omeriche negli autografi di Venezia e la cultura greca del primo Umanesimo* (Venezia – Roma, 1964, rist. Firenze, 1980); Marianne Pade, "Un nuovo testimone dell' *Iliade* di Leonzio Pilato; il Diez. B. Sant. 4 della Staatsbibliothek, Stiftung Preussischer Kulturbesitz, di Berlino," in *Posthomerica 3*, ed. Franco Montanari and Stefano Pittaluga (Genova, 2001), 87–102 and eadem, "The *Fortuna* of Leontius Pilatus' Homer. With an edition of Pier Candido Decembrio's *Why Homer's Greek verses are rendered in Latin prose*," in *Classica et Beneventana. Essays Presented to Virginia Brown on the Occasion of her 65th Birthday*, ed. Frank T. Coulson and Anna A. Grotans (Turnhout, 2008), 149–72.

ON THE CORRECT WAY TO TRANSLATE IN HUMANIST TRANSLATION THEORY   51

also his very words would ring Homeric—such as they understood it: "verbis Homericum illud, quod omnes cogitamus, exhibeas atque sones."[18]

Coluccio had himself done something similar to Simon Atumanus' Latin translation of Plutarch's *De cohibenda ira*, completed in Avignon in 1373. Like Leonzio's Homer, Simon's version followed the Greek text *ad verbum*, and just like Petrarch, Coluccio was appalled when he read it: the Latin of the translation was too obscure to attract the reader, and it was impossible even to guess the sense intended by Plutarch. Coluccio was grateful to Simon for having translated the treatise, but it grieved him that the little which one could know of Plutarch's writings was unpleasant to read and hardly understandable. He therefore decided to rework Simon's version into better Latin. Grasping the sense, he had not troubled himself about the order of words or of the elements of Plutarch's narrative, and to enliven the prose he had sometimes inserted questions or exclamations where there were none in the original. The result, he believed, was Latin instead of half Greek (Salvtati, *ep.* 8,23, a. 1390).[19]

> [...] quem tractatum [scil. Simon's translation] avide discurrens, mecum indignari cepi tantam esse illius translationis obscuritatem tamque horrido stilo compositam, quod nulla prorsus alliceret suavitate lectorem, nec facile pateret quid nobis tantus philosophus tradidisset [...] habeo tamen illi optimo viro gratias, qui nobis qualitercunque Plutarchum dedit [...] fuit enim [...] ut ex hoc libello percipere possumus, eruditissimus philosophorum. moleste ferens igitur nos vel hoc modicum sic habere Plutarchi, quod nec libenter legere nec facile possit percipi quid sentiret, cogitavi mecum opusculum illud de sue translationis obscuritate planiore dicendi genere in lucem intelligentie revocare [...] amplectendo sententiam, noverint me de verborum aut rerum ordine non curasse. nec mirentur etiam, si forsan invenerint aliqua per interrogationem scripta, que sint in prima translatione solum posita narrative. ornatus enim gratia, manente sententia, licitum est continue narrationis quendam tepore accendere et per exclamationes aut interrogationum stimulos excitare. denique pro semigreca translatione remitto tibi latinum tractatum, clarum, ut arbitror.

To the modern reader, Coluccio's procedure may seem surprising, but, as Réka Forai has recently pointed out, that kind of rewriting of existing texts was

---

18   Salvtati, *ep.* 7,23 (1393) to Antonio Loschi.
19   On Coluccio's advice to Loschi and his own rewriting of the *De cohibenda ira*, see Pade, *The Reception* (see above, n. 11), vol. 1, 74–6 and 97–8.

actually a normal pre-modern practice. Intralingual rewriting had been advocated already by Quintilian, in Book 10 of his *Institutio Oratoria*, as a useful stylistic exercise and practiced ever since. When circumstances changed, for instance by the emergence of new stylistic standards, new versions of existing texts might be produced to accommodate these.[20]

Manuel Chrysoloras and the Greek *proprietas*[21]

Petrarch's and Coluccio's reactions to Leonzio's Homer both show a focus on the Latin style of the translation, in the case of Coluccio to the extent that he encouraged a very free rewriting of it, without recourse to the original. This preoccupation with style in the target language, here Latin, will be a recurrent theme in much fifteenth-century humanist translation theory, and it was discussed also by the first successful teacher of Greek in the West, Manuel Chrysoloras (ca. 1350–1415). He was a high-ranking Byzantine diplomat who had been invited by Coluccio to come to Florence to teach Greek. No doubt as an act of cultural diplomacy he accepted, hoping to remind the Italians of the close community of religion and culture that once existed between Greeks and Romans and thereby gaining allies for his country in its fight against the Ottoman Turcs.

Our main source for Chrysoloras' views on translation is a letter of a pupil of his, Cencio de'Rustici. Cencio recalls how Manuel thought that literal, word-for-word translation was worthless and a very free translation apt to interpret rather than translate the original. He recommended a middle course: "Sed ad sententiam transferre opus esse aiebat hoc pacto ut ii qui huiusmodi rebus operam darent, legem sibi ipsis indicerent, ut nullo modo proprietas greca immutaretur" (Instead one should render meaning, he said. Those who took pains with matters of this sort should make it a rule for themselves not to alter the Greek *proprietas* in any way).[22]

---

20   Réka Forrai, "Translation as Rewriting: A Modern Theory for a Premodern Practice," in *Issues in Translation Then and Now: Renaissance theories and translation studies today*, ed. Annet den Haan, Brenda Hosington, Marianne Pade and Anna Wegener, *Renaessanceforum* 14 (2018), 25–50.

21   The following is based on my discussion in "Chrysoloras on Translation: a note on the meaning of *proprietas graeca*," in *God latin. Festskrift til Peter Zeeberg i anledning af hans 60-årsdag den 21. april 2017. Studies in Honour of Peter Zeeberg on the Occasion of his Sixtieth Birthday 21 April 2017*, ed. Birgitte Bøggild Johannsen, Karin Kryger and Karen Skovgaard-Petersen, *Renaessanceforum* 12 (2017), 53–60.

22   Ludwig Bertalot, "Cincius Romanus und seine Briefe," *Quellen und Forschungen aus italienischen Archiven und Bibliotheken* 21 (1929–39), 209–55, now idem, *Studien zum italienischen und deutschen Humanismus*, ed. Paul Oskar Kristeller (Roma, 1975), vol. 2, 133.

ON THE CORRECT WAY TO TRANSLATE IN HUMANIST TRANSLATION THEORY   53

The word that interests me here is the one I have not translated, namely *proprietas*: the translator should do his outmost, "ut nullo modo proprietas greca immutaretur". *Proprietas* is used once more in the same passage, when Cencio relates Manuel's warnings against the overly free translation: "nam si quispiam, quo luculentius apertiusque suis hominibus loquatur, aliquid grece proprietatis immutarit, eum non interpretis sed exponentis officio uti" (For if anyone was to alter the Greek *proprietas* somehow, with the object of speaking better and more clearly to his own people, he would act the part of a commentator rather than that of a translator).[23]

Though we are reminded of the classical *loci* on translation, especially (Ps)Cicero's *On the best kind of orator* (14), Horace's *Art of Poetry* (vv. 133–34), and the passage in Jerome's letter to Pammachius (*ep.* 57) where he quotes them, the word *proprietas*, which Cencio uses it twice in five lines, is not in any of the three classical texts just mentioned. According to the *Thesaurus linguae Latinae*, the word *proprietas* has a wide range of meanings, but in grammatical and rhetorical contexts it is often used to signify the relationship between signified and signifier, about the way words used correctly may express the special characteristic of the thing it denotes. Some of the examples quoted regard translation or differences between Greek and Latin, and in several instances *proprietas* is used about a quality of the original, not just the actual phrasing, but also the concept it denotes.[24] For instance, in the preface to his translation of Eusebius' *Chronicle*, Jerome uses *proprietas* about something that is difficult or almost impossible to render in translation (*chron. epist.* 2,6):

> Significatum est aliquid unius uerbi proprietate: non habeo meum quo id efferam, et dum quaero implere sententiam, longo ambitu uix breuis uiae spatia consummo.

> A meaning may be conveyed by the *proprietas* of a single word, but in my vocabulary I have no comparable word; and when I try to accommodate the full sense, I take a long detour around a short course.[25]

Seen in this light, Chrysoloras'/ Cencio's use of *proprietas* begins to make sense. It denotes the Greek innate quality or the special Greek characteristic of the

---

23   Ibid.
24   "de ratione, quae intercedit inter verba et res iis significatas: usu communi spectat ad verba proprie posita, quae res suas significant secundum naturam, notionem primariam," Marijke Ottink, "Proprietas," *Thesaurus linguae Latinae* 10,2,14 (Lipsiae, 2004), col. 2085–92, there § Βιαα, c. 2086.
25   Translation from Rita Copeland, *Rhetoric, Hermeneutics and Translation in the Middle Ages* (Cambridge, 1991), 47.

original, both with regard to phrasing and content, and even if it is almost impossible to render in Latin, the translator must none the less strive to maintain it. As Ernesto Berti, one of the most eminent students of humanist translation, phrased it: "Chrysoloras asks the translator not to superimpose himself, or his Latinity, on the Greek original."[26] Thus, while Chrysoloras wanted to avoid the aesthetically displeasing in a translation, he would not at all costs have the translator aim at "the absence of any linguistic or stylistic peculiarities [...] [thus] giving the appearance that [the translation] reflects the foreign writer's personality or intention [...]—the appearance, in other words, that the translation is not in fact a translation, but the 'original'," as Lawrence Venuti phrased it in his influential *The Translator's Invisibility*.[27] And Venuti goes on, this "illusion [...] is an effect of a fluent translation strategy, of the translator's effort to insure easy readability by adhering to current usage, maintaining continuous syntax, fixing a precise meaning".[28] The result of fluency as a translation strategy is what in modern translation studies is called domestication, that is a translation where the reader is confronted with the foreignness of the original as little as possible. That was definitely not what Chrysoloras wanted, on the contrary, he wanted the West to acknowledge the East. With his call to translators not to change the *proprietas graeca*, Chrysoloras is advocating what we today would call foreignizing translation. Or as Schleiermacher famously said in an 1813 lecture on the different "methods" of translation, "there are only two. Either the translator leaves the author in peace as much as possible and moves the reader towards him; or he leaves the reader in peace, as much as possible, and moves the author towards him."[29] Justly proud of his country's cultural heritage and wanting Western readers to experience it, Chrysoloras would move *them* towards the Greek author.

Though Chrysoloras in other respects influenced his Italian students profoundly, it seems that he did not convince all of them of the need to preserve *proprietas graeca* in translation, nor does the word *proprietas* become a stable part of the lexicon of humanist translation studies. The reason for this,

---

26 Ernesto Berti, "Traduzioni oratorie fedeli," *Medioevo e Rinascimento* 2 (1988), 245–66, there 254–5. For Chrysoloras' teaching, see also Concetta Bianca, "Traduzioni interlineari dal greco nel circolo del Salutati: Jacopo Angeli, Niccolò Niccoli, Leonardo Bruni?," in *Manuele Crisolora e il ritorno del greco in occidente. Atti del Convegno Internazionale (Napoli, 26–29 giugno 1997)*, ed. Riccardo Maisano and Antonio Rollo (Napoli, 2002), 133–50.

27 Lawrence Venuti, *The Translator's Invisibility. A History of Translation* (London – New York, 1995, second edition 2008), 1.

28 Ibid.

29 Quoted from Andrè Lefevere, *Translating Literature: The German Tradition from Luther to Rosenzweig* (Assen, 1977), 74.

On the Correct Way to Translate in Humanist Translation Theory — 55

I believe, is that subsequent translation theoreticians, with Leonardo Bruni leading the way, were far more focused on the target language or culture, as both Petrarch and Salutati had been. They wanted to import the original into that culture, that is to produce totally domesticating translations. They actually developed a new vocabulary and refined imagery to describe their goal.

Leonardo Bruni and Others on Greek Studies

A protegè of Salutati's and one of Chrysoloras' most successful students, Leonardo Bruni (1370–1444) wrote both about translation and about the role of Greek studies. As an old man, in the *History of his Own Time*, he looked back at his youth, stressing the connection between the blossoming of letters he had experienced then, and the return of Greek studies to Italy (Bruni, *rer. gest. comm.* p. 429):

> Litterae quoque per huius belli intercapedines mirabile quantum per Italiam increvere, accedente tunc primum cognitione litterarum graeca-rum, quae septingentis iam annis apud nostros homines desierant esse in usu.

> When there was a pause in this war, the study of letters, too, flourished wonderfully, because then for the first time people became acquainted with Greek literature, which had ceased to be familiar to us as long as seven hundred years ago.

Bruni was far from being alone in associating Italy's cultural reawaken-ing with the return of Greek studies. In a letter to his son Battista, Guarino Veronese (1374–1460) praised the achievements of his revered teacher, Manuel Chrysoloras, describing the latter's sojourn in Italy as inaugurating a new era. *Humanitas* (good education) would recover its old vigour which, since it had survived until then, seemed to portend a new 'Roman Age': So, Chrysoloras, a teacher of Greek, brought about a Roman renaissance. Guarino appropriately quotes Cicero's *De oratore* (1.14), where we hear that Roman eloquence began to flower after the Latins had studied Greek rhetoric, literature, and philoso-phy. Now in Guarino's time the Latin language, which through long neglect had become stained and impure, was cleaned and illuminated by Chrysoloras' remedies.[30]

---

30   Guarino, *ep.* 862 (1452).

56 PADE

This thought was expressed even more directly by Francesco Filelfo (1398–1481), another pupil of Chrysoloras', in 1428, i.e. before the fall of Constantinople:[31]

> Non enim graecas literas tantopere omnes discere studemus quo iis apud Athenienses Byzantiosue utamur, sed ut illarum subsidia et ductu Latinam literaturam et eloquentiam melius teneamus et lautius.

> The reason we all study Greek is not so much to use it with the Athenians or the Byzantines. Rather, with the support and guidance of Greek letters we wish to get to know and master Latin letters and Latin eloquence better and more elegantly.

What to me is remarkable in these quotations, is not so much the interest in Greek studies, for that we find also in the Middle Ages. It is the belief that only with the return of Greek to the West could the classical culture Rome once possessed be revived from its very core, a culture that had been allowed to decay and become barbarous for centuries. At the very centre of this project, the revival of the classical culture of Rome, was the study of grammar, meaning both the lexical and the syntactic analysis of the two classical languages. The project originated with Petrarch, as we have seen, and its central idea is common in fifteenth-century humanist writings. Translators played a crucial role in the project. Their work was not just instrumental in making the Greek texts accessible, it was in itself a highly acclaimed rhetorical and linguistic exercise.[32] As Lucia Gualdo Rosa has argued in a seminal article, the centrality of this project was uncontested during the first half of the fifteenth century, and it only began to be questioned in the 1470s when Latin lost ground to Italian in some domains. This development is echoed also in the humanists' discourse on translation.[33]

---

31 Filelfo, "Praefatio in Aristotelis Rhetoricam ad Alexandrum," in *G. Trapezuntii rhetoricorum libri V* (Venetiis, 1523), ff. 136r–136v.

32 On the prestige of translators, see my "Greek into Humanist Latin: Foreignizing vs. domesticating translation in the Italian Quattrocento," *Issues in Translation* (see above, n. *), 1–23, there 1–3.

33 Lucia Gualdo Rosa, "Le traduzioni dal greco nella prima metà del '400. Alle radici del classicismo europeo," in *Hommages à Henry Bardon*, ed. Marcel Renard and Pierre Laurens (Bruxelles, 1985), 177–93. Now in eadem, *La* paideia *degli umanisti. Un'antologia di scritti* (Roma, 2017), II [21–37].

Leonardo Bruni: Exploring Strategies of Domesticating Translation[34]

When it comes to Bruni's writings on translation, the influence of Chrysoloras is clear, but Bruni remains faithful to the Petrarchan idea: The project is always the revival or development of Latin culture. While he seems to adhere to a middle course in translation that Chrysoloras recommended and Sabbadini famously called "faithful rhetorical translation",[35] Bruni's discourse on translation tends to prioritise the target culture, that is fifteenth-century Latin humanist culture. This is clear already in his famous 1404 letter to Niccolò Niccoli that came to function as a preface to his translation of Plato's *Phaedo*. Where Chrysoloras wanted the translator to maintain the *proprietas graeca*, Bruni has another agenda: carefully describing Plato's stylistic qualities, that is *how* he is in Greek, he states that his aim is to import this into the Latin world, because "hoc enim ipse Plato praesens me facere jubet, qui cum elegantissimi oris apud Graecos sit, non vult certe apud Latinos ineptus videri."[36] There would remain no "linguistic or stylistic peculiarities"—as Venuti puts it—to remind the reader that Bruni's translation was in fact not the original.

Some years later, in the 1417 preface to his Latin translation of Aristotle's *Nicomachaean Ethics*, Bruni uses a similar imagery to explain why a new translation of the text was needed:[37]

> si quis illi nunc sensus est rerum nostrarum, iampridem credendum est <eum> huic absurditati et inconcinnitati traductionis infensum et tantam barbariem indignatum hos suos libros esse negare, cum talis apud Latinos videri cupiat, qualem apud Graecos sese ipse exhibuit.

---

34   I have discussed Bruni's writings on translation as a plea for domesticating strategies in "Greek into Humanist Latin" (see above, n. 31). Some of the examples discussed here also figure in that same article.

35   Remigio Sabbadini, *Il metodo degli umanisti* (Firenze, 1922), 23–7.

36   "Plato himself asks me to do that, for a man who wore a most elegant aspect among the Greeks, surely does not want to appear crude and clumsy among the Latins", Bruni, *ep.* 1,1 (1,8 M.). For a discussion of Bruni's letter in the context of humanist translation theory, see my "Translating Thucydides: The Metadiscourse of Italian Humanist Translators," in *The Metadiscourse of Italian Humanism*, ed. Annet den Haan, *Renaessanceforum* 11 (2016), 1–22, there 3–8.

37   Bruni, *praef. Aristoteles eth. Nicom.* p. 158. *Eum* is added by Hans Baron, *Leonardo Bruni Aretino. Humanistisch-Philosophische Schriften; mit einer Chronologie seiner Werke und Briefe* (Leipzig – Berlin, 1928), 77.

if *Aristotle* has now any idea about what goes on here, one must assume that he has been long enraged by the harshness and awkwardness of the translation [*i.e. the medieval one*] and that, offended by such barbarism, he denies that the books are his. For he wants to appear among the Latins, as he showed himself to the Greeks.

If we recall Schleiermacher's words about the two "methods" of translation (see above, n. 28), one where "the translator leaves the author in peace as much as possible and moves the reader towards him", and the other where "he leaves the reader in peace, as much as possible, and moves the author towards him," Bruni clearly chose the second, the one we now call domesticating translation.

In all likelihood, it was in the letter to Niccoli, in the same passage as the one quoted above, that Bruni first effected an extremely influential semantic expansion with regard to the verb *traducere*. He began to use it for 'to translate', a meaning it never had in ancient Latin. At first, as we see, the metaphor is still clearly felt:[38]

ego autem Platoni adhereo quem ego ipse mihi effinxi et quidem latine scientem, ut iudicare possit, testemque eum adhibeo *traductionis* sue, atque ita *traduco* ut illi maxime placere intelligo.

I stay with Plato—I have imagined him knowing Latin, so that he can form his own judgement, and I use him as authoritative witness of his *move* [*into Latin*]; and I *lead him over* [*into Latin, i.e.* translate] as I understand pleases him best.

Domesticating Translation in Other Words

The metaphor inherent in using *traducere* for 'to translate' may in itself be said to announce the stance of many humanists towards translation: the foreign text should be imported into their world, it should be domesticated, and the author lead to the reader. We also find this attitude expressed in other metaphors used by translators: Guarino Veronese said that Chrysoloras led Greek letters, that

---

38   For this important semantic development, see Johann Ramminger, "Language Change in Humanist Latin: The Case of *traducere* (to translate)," *Analecta Romana Instituti Danici* 40–1 (2015–16), 35–62. I have used Ramminger's translation of the passage, ibid., p. 38.

had long been exiled from Latium, back to the Latins;[39] Francesco Barbaro led Cato back from exile, in his translation of Plutarch's life, and he gives Aristides, the Greek half of the pair, both Roman citizenship and Latin literacy[40]—to name only a few examples of what we might call the journey-to-Italy and citizenship metaphors.

In the famous preface to his 1452 translation of Thucydides, the letter of dedication to Pope Nicholas V, Lorenzo Valla (1407–57) went in a different direction, one that parallels his thoughts in the *Elegantie* about the Latin language, the *sermo romanus*, as the true *Imperium* and *dominatus* of Rome, and far more lasting than the political Empire.[41] In the letter to Nicholas, Valla compares himself, and the other translators employed by the Pope, to commanders send out by a Roman emperor "ut omnem, quoad possemus, Greciam tue ditioni subiiceremus, id est ut grecos tibi libros in latinum traduceremus".[42] If the Latin language is the true and lasting Empire of Rome, then to enrich that language by translating (worthwhile) books into it is to expand the Empire. But it is also, according to Valla, to bring foreign texts under Latin rule, i.e. to domesticate them. Nicholas, who commissioned a large number of Latin translations from the Greek, apparently shared this view on translation, for upon receiving another translation commissioned by him, Niccolò Perotti's Latin translation of Polybius, he wrote: "Tanta enim facilitate et eloquentia transfers ut historia ipsa nunquam graeca sed prorsus latina semper fuisse uideatur."[43]

Chrysoloras' plea for the translator to preserve the *proprietas graeca* was evidently ignored, if the ideal had become that not a trace of a work's original ethnic flavour should survive the translation process. Not surprisingly, this did not meet with approval in all quarters. As Paul Botley has shown, Michael Apostolis, an impoverished Greek teacher, complained that the Italians tried gradually to obliterate the Greek language and practically made the Greeks

---

39   "[Chrysoloras,] qui profugas dudum ex Latio litteras grecas ex innata liberalitate reducens ad nostrates" Guarino, *praef. Plutarch vitae* 18,1, c. 1412.

40   "intra paucos dies Aristidem [...] non ciuitate sed quod amplius est Latinis litteris donare, et Catonem illum grauissimum longo ut aiunt postliminio ad nostros homines reducere mihi licuerit" Barbaro, *praef. Plutarch vitae* 9,1, a. 1416.

41   Mariangela Regoliosi, *Nel cantiere del Valla. Elaborazione e montaggio delle "Elegantie"* (Roma, 1993), 64–71.

42   "To bring as much as possible of Greece under your rule, that is to translate Greek books into Latin for you." Quoted from the dedication copy of Valla's translation, MS Vat. lat. 1801, f. 1r. See also Pade, *Translating Thucydides* (see above, n. 35), 3.

43   "You translate with such ease and eloquence that this work of history seems never to have been Greek, but Latin through and through." Nicholas V, letter to Perotti, 29.8.1452, quoted from MS Vat. lat. 1808, f. 1v.

60   PADE

into Romans.[44] In a different context, Lawrence Venuti would call this "ethno-centric violence".[45]

How to Create the Illusion

Where Pope Nicholas said that Perotti's Latin Polybius "seems never to have been Greek" (see above, n. 42) and Apostolis accused Italian translators of turning the Greeks into Romans, modern translation scholars would talk about transparency, that is when "the absence of any linguistic or stylistic peculiarities makes it seem transparent, giving the appearance [...] that the translation is not in fact a translation, but the 'original'."[46] Using of course different words, humanist translators often discussed how to create the illusion of transparency.

One method might be called interlingual rewriting (as opposed to intralingual, see above and n. 19), undertaken to adapt the text to the taste of a new readership: In the preface to his translation of Xenophon's *Cyropaedia* from the mid-forties, Poggio Bracciolini declares himself to be an adherent of fluent, strongly domesticating translation: He had not rendered single words, he says, nor even every little sentence or conversation, because he knew that although it was not inelegantly said in Greek, it would not agree with the taste of learned men in Latin. He had followed the story, leaving out what detracted from the flow or could only with difficulty be aptly expressed in Latin:[47]

> Non autem verba singula, non sententiolas omnes, non collocutiones, quae quidem frequentius inseruntur, expressi, quippe qui sciam multa graece haud infacunde dici quae apud nos non absque fastidio legi a doctis possent; sed historiam sum secutus, ea quandoque omittens quae neque veritati rerum detraherent et concinne dici latine vix posse viderentur.

Shortly afterwords, in the preface to his translation of Diodorus Siculus (I–V), he again described how he sacrificed fidelity for the sake of Latinity: Adhering to the laws of the target language, *noster dicendi mos*, he had rendered factual

---

44   Paul Botley, *Latin Translation in the Renaissance: The Theory and Practice of Leonardo Bruni, Giannozzo Manetti and Desiderius Erasmus* (Cambridge, 2004), 168.

45   Venuti, *The Translator's Invisibility* (see above, n. 26), 1.

46   Ibid.

47   Poggio Bracciolini, *Opera Omnia,* ed. Riccardo Fubini (Torino, 1969), vol. 4, 676. For this quote, see also Maria Pasqualina Pillolla, "Infidus interpres," in *Tradurre dal greco in età umanistica. Metodi e strumenti*, ed. Mariarosa Cortesi (Firenze, 2007), 45–61, there 46.

ON THE CORRECT WAY TO TRANSLATE IN HUMANIST TRANSLATION THEORY   61

content, but omitted the circumlocutions or digressions, *ambages*, so common in Greek.[48]

In the preface to his 1449 translation of Demosthenes' masterpiece, *On the Crown* (in Latin *Pro Ctesiphonte*), Lorenzo Valla described how he had gone about adapting the Greek oration to a Latin humanist context. It also amounts to a rewriting of the original (Valla, *Demosthenes Ctes.* 195):

> Est enim relinquendus frequenter character ipse graecus, excogitandus novus, pariendae figurae, numeris omnino serviendum.

> One has to free oneself from the very style of the Greek. It must be thought anew, with new figures of speech, and one must altogether accommodate prosody.

Another method humanist translators often describe is what Venuti would call the 'stylistic analogue', that is when the translator can identify an analogy between the source text and some works in the target language, and attempts to exploit that in his/her translation.[49] This is a strategy that may be seen as radically domesticating, and if we examine the way it was used in humanist translation, I believe it was:

It is almost a topos in humanist writings on translation to identify classical Latin authors who imitated a classical Greek writer, or, in other words, to identify Latin writers whose style was 'stylistic analogous' to specific Greek ones. Lorenzo Valla did that in the preface to his Latin Thucydides when he mentioned that Sallust was known to have been an imitator of the Greek historian. Moreover, in the translation itself, Valla in fact regularly translates Thucydides' Greek into Sallustian phrases, clearly wanting readers to recognize and admire the intertextuality between his translation and its hypotext, since he sometimes remarked upon the procedure in the margin of his manuscript.[50]

Dissenting Voices: In Favour of Foreignization

In *On the Correct Way to Translate*, Leonardo Bruni explicitly warns the translator against leaving anything in Greek, that is to transliterate Greek terms

---

48   Poggio, *Opera* (see above, n. 46), vol. 4, 682.
49   Antonia Pozzi, *Breath: Poems and Letters*, trans. Lawrence Venuti (Middletown, CT, 2002).
50   For other examples of this, see Pade, "Translating Thucydides" (see above, n. 35), 8–12.

instead of finding Latin equivalents.[51] This had been normal practice in Medieval translation for instance with regard to the political lexicon, but in his retranslation of Aristotle's *Nicomachean Ethics* (1417), Bruni had effectively done away with much of the accepted terminology of the scholastics for Greek political institutions. The fierce polemic that followed the publication of his *Ethics* translation was especially concerned with this aspect of his practice.[52] However, it was not only Bruni's scholastic adversaries for whom Latinity was less important than unequivocal terminology, foreign or not. Also writers that we today count as humanists could argue that foreignization was an option.

Guarino Veronese was one of them. While still studying with Chrysoloras in Constantinople, he translated Isocrates' *To Demonicus* (1405), a very popular political treatise. Quoting Quintilian who had acknowledged the procedure amongst the ancients, Guarino admitted in his preface that he was prepared to retain Greek words in his translations if Latin equivalents were not available— for instance *monarchia* or *democratia*. He also playfully excuses the Greek flavour of his translation by asking how an old man, already gray, i.e. Isocrates, who had only recently learned the foreign language, could be expected to[53]

> pronounce accurately the very gracefulness of our language and the flow of our speech? It is hardly possible that his speech will not, every now and then, keep some of its native flavour. I actually mixed some of his Greek words into the narrative. We are not used to them, but if they are not too many they bestow an attractive variety. So why do people look askance at me if I, for my individual share, should succeed in enriching our paternal language [Hor. ars 57] by bringing something from elsewhere? Especially

---

51   "ut [...] non mendicet illud aut mutuo sumat aut in Graeco relinquat ob ignorantiam Latini sermonis," Bruni, *interpr.* p. 85. Bruni wrote the treatise between 1424 and 1426.

52   For this see James Hankins, "Notes on Leonardo Bruni's Translation of the Nicomachean Ethics and its Reception in the Fifteenth Century," in *Les traducteurs au travail: Leurs manuscrits et leurs méthodes. Actes du Colloque* [...] (*Erice, 30 septembre–6 octobre 1999*), ed. Jacqueline Hamesse (Tournhout, 2001), 427–47; expanded version in idem, "The Ethics Controversy," in *Humanism and Platonism in the Italian Renaissance*, ed. James Hankins (Roma, 2003), vol. 1, 193–239; and my "Popular Government Revisited: New Texts on Greek Political History and Their Influence in Fifteenth-Century Italy," *Neulateinisches Jahrbuch* 19 (2017), 313–38.

53   "[...] ipsum linguae nostrae nitorem integrumque orationis cursum diligenter enuntiet? Vix enim esse poterit ut aliqua ex parte proprium patriae non sapiat eloquium; immoque eiusdem nobis insueta graeca nonnunquam inter narrandum verba miscui, quae uti nimia non sunt, sic gratioris aliquid varietatis aspergunt. Praeterea cur, si 'pro parte virili' 'patrium ditare sermonem' et aliunde aliqua simul ferre si possim 'invidear?' praesertim cum id ex ipso Quintiliano in oratoriae artis institutione licere compererim, qui 'et concessis quoque graecis, inquit, utimur verbis, ubi nostra desint' [*inst.* 1,5,8]" Guarino, *ep.* 2.

when I found out from Quintilian himself, in *The Orator's Education*, that "we admittedly use Greek words where no Latin terms are available [*inst.* 1,5,8]."

Like Bruni, Guarino was a student of Chrysoloras' and perhaps an even greater admirer of his teacher, and when he talks about Isocrates's language "keeping some of its native flavour" it is difficult not to think of Chrysoloras insisting that translations preserve the *proprietas graeca*. Though Guarino would occasionally experiment with extremely domesticating translation strategies, for a political text like *To Demonicus* he accepted the use of transliterated technical vocabulary, although the effect would be foreignizing. He not only accepted it, he felt that he enriched the Latin language. Moreover, it could be argued that in fact he did enrich it. Guarino actually coined a number of very successful loanwords from the Greek that he first used in translations. One of them is still with us in I believe most European languages, namely *myriad* meaning 10.000 or 'an indefinitely great number'. Guarino first used it in 1412 and considerately announced the novelty in the margin of the manuscript.[54]

The Gradual Return of Literal Translation

Francesco Filelfo was another student of Chrysoloras' who apparently had difficulties with the radical domestication advocated by Bruni. He does not comment upon the praxis of transliteration, but protests against the prevailing dogma, that translations ought to be *ad sensum*. Shortly after Bruni had published *On the Correct Way to Translate*, Filelfo wrote, apropos of the translation of a philosophical text: "Correct translation is a big and difficult thing. For when it comes to philosophy one often has to translate word by word."[55]

As we know, St Jerome distinguished between translation of Scripture that should be *ad verbum*, because the very word order was part of the sacred text, and translations of all other kinds of texts where a free translation, *ad sensum*, was preferable. With Filelfo we now see that another text type, namely philosophy, could be exempt from the exacting demands of the *ad sensum* rendering, and, as his allusion to Bruni implies, from the stylistic demands of domesticizing translation.

---

54   See Pade, *The Reception* (see above n. 11), vol. 1, 255–6.

55   "Magna res igitur ac difficilis est interpretatio recta [= Bruni]: est enim in arte verbum saepius e verbo exprimendum," Filelfo, *Praefatio* (see above n. 30), f. 136r.

We find a more detailed system of distinctions between genres in the writings of Pier Candido Decembrio (1399–1477). The son of Uberto, Pier Candido had revised his father's and Chrysoloras's translation of Plato's *Republic*, apparently to turn it into more up-to-date Latin, and he had a long rivalry with Leonardo Bruni. Pier Candido's views on translation were summed up by his friend Antonio da Rho in the 1443 *Dialogus in Lactantium*. According to da Rho, Pier Candido argued that different translation techniques were appropriate for different kinds of texts: sacred texts should be rendered in a strictly literal way; paraphrase was permissible for rhetorical or poetical texts where the translator should aim to preserve the literary effect of the original. In between was the kind of translation appropriate for historical and philosophical texts, which should be neither too literal nor so loose that the exact contents of these texts were not rendered.[56]

Another scholar who for some purposes shied away from the freer *ad sensum* versions was George of Trapezunt (1395–1484). In his polemic with Theodore Gaza, he wanted to defend Aristotle against the whims of humanist translators and actually had the courage to say that he preferred the medieval *ad verbum* translations to the new 'platonizising' ones.[57] We find the point of view again in the preface to his translation of Demosthenes' *On the Crown* (1444–46) where he proposed a differentiated system of translation methods that in every case would allow the method to be adapted to the genre of the work being translated:[58]

> Non enim unus modus in traducendo est, sed pro rerum subiectarum varietate varius atque diversus. Qui ardua, sensu intellectuque difficilia, et plerumque vel apud ipsos auctores suos ambigua in aliam linguam vertit, is verba magis exprimat quam sensum ne, cum eum sensum sequatur quem ipse capiat, alios negligat forte meliores ac altiores. [...] Hanc traducendi rationem divine scripture Aristotelisque voluminibus convenire nemo nisi omnino imperitus dubitabit. Qui historicum aliquem vertit, is de verbis nihil laboret, sed cum rem totam percepit, latius strictiusve, dum historico genere dicendi utatur, eam more suo in Latinum vertat licebit. Qui autem oratoris alicuius Greci orationem Latinam facere

---

56 James Hankins, *Plato in the Italian Renaissance*, 2 vols. (Leiden – New York, 1990), vol. 1, 120–1 n. 28; and idem, "Translation Practice in the Renaissance: the Case of Leonardo Bruni," *Études classiques IV. Actes du colloque* Méthodologie de la traduction: de l'Antiquité à la Renaissance, ed. Charles Marie Ternes (Luxembourg 1994), 154–75, there 158.

57 Gualdo Rosa, "Le traduzioni dal greco" (see above, n. 32), 189.

58 Latin text in John Monfasani, *Collectanea Trapezuntiana* (Binghamton, 1984), 94; English translation from Hankins, *Plato* (see above, n. 55), vol. 1, 187.

cupit, is ignorare non debet non verba, non sensum illius solum sibi sequendum, sed multo magis orationis genus et dicendi varietatem Latine, quantum facere potest, esse exprimendam.

There is no one way to translate; rather, the method should be varied in accordance with the subject matter. Things that are sublime and difficult to understand or to sense—things which are quite often ambiguous for the very authors themselves—[such things] the translator should express literally rather than according to the sense, lest, in following the sense as he understands it, he should happen to neglect other deeper and better senses. [...] Only the utterly ignorant will doubt that this method of translating is suitable for the Holy Scriptures and the works of Aristotle. In translating an historian, [on the other hand], the translator will not concern himself with the words, but, having once understood the entire subject, he will be permitted to translate it after his fashion, more loosely or more strictly, so long as he observes the diction proper to the genre of history. The translator who wants a Greek orator to speak Latin, however, must not merely avoid misunderstanding the words, he must not only follow his author's sense, but more importantly he must reproduce in Latin, as far he can, the type of speech and the variety of [his author's] diction.

We notice that George on the one hand includes philosophy, at least Aristotle, in the kind of texts that should be translated literally; on the other, for the genres where he advocates a freer *ad sensum* translation, he acknowledges the need to attempt to render the style of the original and observe genre conventions.

Some years later, Gianozzo Manetti composed his *Apologeticus* (1454–56). As with Bruni's *On the Correct Way to Translate*, it was written as a defense of one of his own translations, the new Latin version of the Psalms. In Book Five, where in general he is very close to Bruni's precepts, Manetti maintains that though translation *ad sententiam* is fine with other genres, as rhetoric, historiography and poetry, one had to proceed more carefully with philosophy and Scripture ("graviorem quandam ac severiorem traductionem exigere et postulare videntur").[59] We again notice that it is not just with Scripture one should avoid free translation, Manetti advocates a closer translation also for philosophy.

From around the middle of the fifteenth century, more and more voices, also from scholars we tend to see as humanists, are in favour of literal, word-for-word

---

59   Manetti, *apol.* 5,46.

66   PADE

translation. One of them was that of the Greek cardinal Bessarion. In his 1453 commentary on the Gospel of St John, he wrote (Bessarion, *in Illud* p. 626):

> Oportet enim qui aliquid ex una in aliam transfert linguam, et linguam ipsam nosse quam transfert, et ejus non modo sententiae veritatem, sed etiam verba de verbis exprimere, idque praesertim in sacris litteris.

> If someone translates from one language into another, he must master the language of the original, and not just render the meaning of what is said in it, but also translate word for word. This is especially important in translations of Scripture.

As Petrarch had done almost a hundred years previously—and many humanists after him—, Bessarion quotes St Jerome's letter to Pammachius, but his purpose is the opposite of Petrarch's: he want to advocate close, literal translation, and not just for Scripture.

Conclusions

In her article on "Le traduzioni dal greco" that I mentioned earlier, Lucia Gualdo Rosa argued that there was a profound change, or a crisis, in the humanist movement in the second half of the fifteenth century, and especially from the 1470s and onwards. The optimism of the first part of the century gave way to internal strife, of political, religious, and also rhetorical and literary character. In this crisis the *volgare* became more important—the *volgare* that humanists had looked on with contempt in the first half of the century. Translations into the *volgare* again became more *en vogue*, and the new translators were critical of the strong linguistic orientation of their colleagues of the early Quattrocento.[60]

In other words, in the first 70 years of the fifteenth century, in what I am tempted to call the 'heroic' age of humanism, Latin was not only the most common and the most prestigious literary and scientific language. It was during this period that we find almost uncontested the dream of reviving the linguistic universe of Ancient Rome, yes, even the dream of reaching a linguistic level that could vie with that of the ancients. *Aemulatio* is a core concept, both in translation and in original writings. It was also, as I hope to have shown, during that period that Neo-Latin, humanist translation was at its wildest.

---

60   Gualdo Rosa, "Le traduzioni dal greco" (see above, n. 32), 189.

Heeding Petrarch and ignoring Chrysoloras' pleas for preserving the *proprietas graeca*, leading humanists like Leonardo Bruni and Lorenzo Valla developed and described radically domesticating translation strategies, for instance what modern translation scholars have dubbed the stylistic analogue. Of course the picture was never uniform, and there were always dissenting voices, like that of Guarino, who felt that foreignizing translations, that would for instance introduce Greek loanwords, were not only permissible, they were actually enriching the Latin humanist culture. Moreover, by the second half of the century, humanists like Pier Candido Decembrio and Gianozzo Manetti questioned the prevailing dogma of *ad sensum* translation for every kind of text but Scripture, and Bessarion implicitly allowed word-for-word translation as the general method. However, hand in hand with the cultural optimism that characterized Italian humanism during the first five or six decades of the fifteenth century, we saw an almost boundless belief in the possibilities of the Latin language and of translation into Latin. This resulted in a theorization of the translation process that anticipates many of the themes discussed in modern translation studies—a fact that I hope will eventually be acknowledged in histories of the humanities.

Acknowledgments

I wish to express my gratitude to the executive committee of IANLS for inviting me to give a plenary paper at the 2018 Congress of the Association in Albacete; I am very conscious of the honour and all the more grateful, because IANLS is an association that has been important to me in many ways during most of my scholarly life. I also wish to thank two eminent members of IANLS who both in various ways inspired my talk. The first is Lucia Gualdo Rosa who over the years published a series of fundamental articles on fifteenth-century humanist translation and with her encyclopedic knowledge was instrumental in establishing the chronology for humanist translation theory, I shall propose in this talk. The second is Brenda Hosington, whom I first met through the IANLS, and—more importantly—with whom I started to bring humanist translation theory into dialogue with modern translation studies. See the introduction to the volume *Issues in Translation Then and Now: Renaissance Theories and Translation Studies Today*, ed. Annet den Haan, Brenda Hosington, Marianne Pade and Anna Wegener, *Renaessanceforum* 14 (2018), III–V.

Danish Academy in Rome/ Aarhus University

CHAPTER 4

Autor/Erzähler und Fiktion im neulateinischen Roman: Ein Beitrag zu einer historischen Narratologie

Stefan Tilg

Abstract

Drawing on the emerging field of 'historical narratology' and on Frank Zipfel's analysis of concept(s) of literary 'fiction', this contribution focuses on the categories of 'fiction' and 'narrative voice' in the Neo-Latin novel. Its major example is John Barclay's *Argenis* (1621), but a number of other novels also receives consideration. In terms of fictionality, the overwhelming majority of these novels can be described as hybrid: a story that tends towards historical facticity is narrated with unabashedly fictional techniques to an audience that usually expects facts and immediate historical relevance. This hybrid set-up, which is seen as an exception in modern theory, constitutes the default case of the Neo-Latin novel. It is interpreted here as bound up with the presence of the author behind the narrative voice: with very few exceptions (such as Holberg's *Iter subterraneum* of 1741), the speaker of a Neo-Latin novel is the 'author' rather than the 'narrator' of modern narrative theory. This can be put in the larger contexts of the general pragmatic view of literature in early modern literature; the author-centric tradition of classical literature; and the assumed roles of Neo-Latin novelists as 'teachers' (satirists, moralists, educators, philosophers etc.) that mostly correspond to their real social roles e.g. as diplomats or preachers.

Keywords

John Barclay – historical narratology – Neo-Latin novel – fictionality – author and narrator

1 Historische Narratologie

Während die klassische strukturalistische Narratologie entweder ganz ahistorisch oder auf die Moderne fokussiert war, verstärkt sich seit etwa

© KONINKLIJKE BRILL NV, LEIDEN, 2020 | DOI:10.1163/9789004427105_005

zwanzig Jahren der Trend zu einer historischen Erzählforschung, die auch antike, mittelalterliche und frühneuzeitliche Texte als Gegenstand narratologischer Analyse in den Blick nimmt. Die Anglisten Ansgar Nünning und Monika Fludernik haben in den Jahren 2000 und 2003 manifestartige Beiträge dazu veröffentlicht.[1] Sie fordern eine diachrone Erweiterung des Analysecorpus der modernen Narratologie, weil wir durch die Untersuchung geschichtlicher Neufunktionalisierungen von Erzählformen Neues über diese Erzählformen selbst, aber auch über das kulturelle Milieu lernen können, in dem sie sich manifestieren. Nünning skizziert in diesem Sinn z.B. das Projekt einer Geschichte des unzuverlässigen Erzählers. Grundlegende narratologische Kategorien wie „Unzuverlässigkeit" oder „Erzähler" bleiben in diesen Ansätzen universal gedacht, werden aber in einen je spezifischen historisch-kulturellen Kontext eingebettet, in dem sie auf je eigene Weise eingesetzt werden und wirken. Eine etwas andere Spielart historischer Narratologie, in der moderne narratologische Kategorien fundamentaler hinterfragt wurden, hat sich v.a. von der germanistischen Mediävistik aus verbreitet.[2] So argumentiert z.B. Gert Hübner in einem 2010 erschienenen Band zur Historischen Narratologie aus mediävistischer Perspektive,[3] dass die scheinbare interne Fokalisierung, also das Hineinschauen in das Innenleben einer Figur, in mittelhochdeutschen Erzähltexten gerade *nicht* mit den Begrifflichkeiten der modernen Narratologie als Perspektivierung oder Fokalisierung zu interpretieren, sondern historisch korrekter aus der zeitgenössischen Rhetorik abzuleiten sei. Dort fallen diese Phänomene unter den Begriff der *evidentia*, der Anschaulichkeit, mit der ein Sprecher die Glaubwürdigkeit seiner Erzählung durch das Sich-Hineinversetzen in eine Figur verstärken will. In diesem Verständnis von historischer Narratologie werden moderne narratologische Kategorien in vormodernen Texten also nicht nur anders kontextualisiert und funktionalisiert, sondern *sind* ihrem Wesen nach eigentlich schon andere als die in den vormodernen Texten geltenden. Der eine Ansatz einer historischen Narratologie betont also mehr die Kontinuität, der andere mehr die Differenz. Beide Ansätze gehen aber von den modernen Kategorien aus. In

---

1 Ansgar Nünning, "Towards a Cultural and Historical Narratology: A Survey of Diachronic Approaches, Concepts, and Research Projects," in *Anglistentag 1999 Mainz: Proceedings*, hg. Bernhard Reitz und Sigrid Rieuwert (Trier, 2000), 345–73; Monika Fludernik, "The Diachronization of Narratology," *Narrative* 11.3 (2003), 331–48.

2 Eine interdisziplinäre Übersicht über dieses Forschungsfeld bietet jetzt der Band *Handbuch Historische Narratologie*, hg. Eva von Contzen und Stefan Tilg (Stuttgart, 2019).

3 Gert Hübner, "*evidentia*: Erzählformen und ihre Funktionen," in *Historische Narratologie, mediävistische Perspektiven*, hg. Harald Haferland und Matthias Meyer (Berlin, 2010), 119–47.

beiden Ansätzen haben sie heuristischen Wert, und sei es nur, um wesentliche Differenzen überhaupt erst einmal erkennen und benennen zu können.

2 Historische Narratologie und neulateinischer Roman

Im vorliegenden Beitrag versuche ich, einen historisch-narratologischen Zugang einmal für die neulateinische Literatur auszuprobieren, wobei ich wohl auch eher Differenzen als Kontinuitäten betonen werde. Da der Roman das Untersuchungsobjekt *par excellence* der modernen Narratologie ist, schien es mir naheliegend, mich meinerseits auf den neulateinischen Roman zu konzentrieren. Auch mit dieser Einschränkung auf ein Genre wären die Möglichkeiten historisch-narratologischer Ansätze natürlich vielfältig, weshalb ich mit den Begriffen der ‚Fiktion' und der Trennung von ‚Autor' und ‚Erzähler' weiter auf zwei fundamentale Kategorien des modernen romanhaften Erzählens fokussiert habe. Die weithin anerkannte Minimaldefinition eines Romans, wie wir sie z.B. im *Reallexikon der deutschen Literaturwissenschaft* lesen können,[4] lautet ja, dass ein Roman eine lange, selbständig veröffentlichte, *fiktionale* Erzählung in Prosa sei. Fiktionalität gehört demnach zum elementaren Wesensmerkmal eines Romans, und folgt man der modernen Narratologie, erfordert jede fiktionale Erzählung auch einen Erzähler, der nicht mit dem Autor identisch ist (dazu später noch mehr). Ich werde mich in meinem Beitrag also dem neulateinischen Roman unter den Gesichtspunkten seiner *Fiktion* und seiner *Erzählstimme* zuwenden. Ich werde dabei von modernen Begriffen ausgehen in der Absicht, gerade dadurch charakteristische Eigenheiten des neulateinischen Romans in seiner epochalen und kulturellen Gebundenheit besser sichtbar zu machen. Im besten Fall wäre das dann auch eine Art Werbung oder ein Manifest für die Berücksichtigung historisch-narratologischer Ansätze in der neulateinischen Philologie.

Abgesehen davon, dass ich dieses Unterfangen hier nur sehr schemenhaft ausführen kann, möchte ich ausdrücklich aber noch zwei Vorbehalte äußern. Erstens: Obwohl ich als Neulateiner über den neulateinischen Roman spreche, ist vieles von dem, was hier verhandelt wird, sicher auch im volkssprachlichen Roman zu finden. Der neulateinische Roman war ein Kind seiner Zeit und Teil einer größeren literarischen Kultur.[5] Trotzdem werde ich am Ende dieses

---

4 Hartmut Steinecke, "Roman," in *Reallexikon der deutschen Literaturwissenschaft*, hg. Klaus Weimar, Bd. 3 (Berlin, 2003), 317–22, hier 317.
5 Dazu u.a. *Der neulateinische Roman als Medium seiner Zeit – The Neo-Latin Novel in Its Time*, hg. Stefan Tilg und Isabella Walser (Tübingen, 2013).

AUTOR/ERZÄHLER UND FIKTION IM NEULATEINISCHEN ROMAN 71

Beitrags ein paar spezifisch lateinische Rahmenbedingungen benennen, die vielleicht nahelegen, dass manche der von mir beschriebenen Eigenheiten auf den lateinischen Roman der Frühen Neuzeit in noch stärkerem Ausmaß als auf den volkssprachlichen zutreffen. Zweitens: Der neulateinische Roman ist in keiner Hinsicht eine monolithische Gattung und lässt sich auch in punkto Fiktion und Erzählstimme nicht auf *einen* gemeinsamen Nenner bringen. Es gibt aber Kernbereiche und signifikante Tendenzen, die ich herausarbeiten will. Mein Ausgangspunkt ist dabei der mit Abstand erfolgreichste und einflussreichste neulateinische Roman, John Barclays *Argenis*, sowie die Technik des Schlüsselromans, die er anwendet. Zumindest unter den von mir gewählten Gesichtspunkten – Fiktion und Erzählstimme – lässt sich ausgehend von diesem Zentrum meiner Analyse vieles auch auf andere neulateinische Romane übertragen bzw. können die anderen Beispiele leicht in Relation zu diesem Zentrum positioniert werden. Ich werde deshalb nur die *Argenis* ausführlicher, ausgewählte andere Romane vergleichsweise kurz behandeln.

3   ,Fiktion': Fiktivität, Fiktionalität und Fiktionsvertrag

Bevor ich mich Barclay zuwende, muss ich allerdings noch den für mich zentralen Begriff der Fiktion näher definieren, der erfahrungsgemäß recht beliebig und in verschiedenen Sprach- und Wissenschaftskulturen äußerst divergent verwendet wird. Ich stütze mich dabei auf Frank Zipfels mittlerweile zu einem international vielbeachteten Referenzwerk gewordene 2001 erschienene Monographie zum literaturwissenschaftlichen Fiktionsbegriff.[6] Die Stärke von Zipfels Buch ist besonders seine Trennung verschiedener Ebenen der Fiktion, was sehr zur analytischen Klarheit beigetragen hat. Ich fasse Zipfels Trennung von Fiktionsebenen hier deshalb etwas ausführlicher zusammen, weil ich noch öfter darauf zurückkommen werde und nur so deutlich sichtbar wird, an welchen Stellen Fiktion im neulateinischen Roman sich womöglich von moderner Fiktion abhebt. Zipfel unterscheidet insgesamt fünf Ebenen der literarischen Fiktion, von denen die erste und zweite text- bzw. erzählimmanent sind und der klassischen narratologischen Unterscheidung von *fabula* und *syuzhet, histoire* und *discours* oder *story* und *discourse* entsprechen. Hier werden also die erzählte Welt und die sprachlich realisierte Erzählung unterschieden. Die dritte bis fünfte Ebene sind text- bzw. erzähl*extern*. Ich fasse sie hier der Einfachheit halber zu einer einzigen Ebene zusammen.

---

6   Frank Zipfel, *Fiktion, Fiktivität, Fiktionalität: Analysen zur Fiktion in der Literatur und zum Fiktionsbegriff in der Literaturwissenschaft* (Berlin, 2001).

Die erste Ebene der Fiktion ist die (erfundene) erzählte Geschichte, die sich im Wesentlichen aus Figuren und ihren Handlungen in einem bestimmten Setting zusammensetzt. Fiktion auf dieser Ebene heißt im deutschen Fachdiskurs ‚Fiktivität'; erfundene Figuren und Sachverhalte sind also ‚fiktiv', nicht ‚fiktional'. Reale, nicht-erfundene Geschichten wären dagegen ‚faktisch'. Im modernen Roman wird die Erfundenheit der Geschichte als Normalfall betrachtet. In James Joyces *Ulysses* z.B. irrt die Hauptfigur Leopold Bloom am 16. Juni 1904 durch Dublin. Es gab faktisch aber keinen Leopold Bloom, der am 16. Juni 1904 durch Dublin irrte, ergo ist die Geschichte fiktiv.

Die zweite Ebene der Fiktion ist die sprachliche, textliche, diskursive Erzählung mit ihren narrativen Erzähltechniken. Fiktion auf dieser Ebene heißt im deutschen Fachdiskurs ‚Fiktionalität'. ‚Fiktional' sind also Erzählungen qua Erzählungen; die erfundenen Geschichten, Personen und Dinge, von denen sie erzählen, werden dagegen ‚fiktiv' genannt. Der Gegenbegriff zu ‚fiktionalen' Erzählungen wären ‚faktuale' Erzählungen. Die fundamentale Grundverfasstheit fiktionaler Erzählungen ist, dass sie von einem seinerseits erfundenen Erzähler erzählt werden, der viele Dinge weiß und behauptet, die der historische Autor als solcher so nicht wissen und behaupten könnte. Faktuales Erzählen dagegen kommt ohne den vom Autor getrennten Erzähler aus. Hier verantwortet der Sprecher selbst, was er sagt. Abgesehen von der grundlegenden Autor/ Erzähler-Unterscheidung ist die Paradetechnik fiktionalen Erzählens in der 3. Person die interne Fokalisierung, also das – realistischerweise nicht erklärbare und deshalb wieder auf Erfundenheit beruhende – Hineinschauen des Erzählers in das Innere seiner Figuren (im *Ulysses* z.B. haben wir dieses Hineinschauen bis zum Exzess des Bewusstseinsstroms). Bei einem Ich-Erzähler würde dem ein unrealistisches, übermenschliches Erinnerungsvermögen entsprechen, wenn also ein Ich-Erzähler so detailreich erzählt, dass das offensichtlich nichts mit einer normalen faktualen Erzählung zu tun hat.

Die weiteren Ebenen drei bis fünf sind die Ebenen des Textproduzenten, des Textrezipienten und der institutionell-gesellschaftlichen Kommunikationssituation. Nimmt man diese Ebenen zusammen, geht es hier letztlich um die kulturellen Rahmenbedingungen, um die Frage, ob in einem bestimmten Milieu Autor und Publikum stillschweigend aufgrund von konventionellen Fiktionssignalen und Rezeptionshaltungen so etwas wie einen ‚Fiktionsvertrag' schließen können; ob in einem gegebenen Literaturbetrieb – um mit Coleridges geflügeltem Wort zu sprechen – so etwas wie eine „willing suspension of disbelief" möglich ist; ob also Produzenten und Rezipienten einer literarischen Fiktion sich auf sie einlassen und sie schätzen, obwohl sie eigentlich ja wissen, dass die in der Fiktion getätigten Behauptungen keine direkte Referenz in der Wirklichkeit haben.

AUTOR/ERZÄHLER UND FIKTION IM NEULATEINISCHEN ROMAN 73

4   Barclays *Argenis* (1621) und ihr Fiktionskonzept

Ausgehend von Barclays 1621 erschienener *Argenis* werde ich nun im Folgenden zeigen, wie und auf welchen Ebenen sich die Fiktion des neulateinischen Romans von typisch moderner Fiktion dadurch unterscheidet, dass sie stärker auf Elementen des Faktischen und auf einer faktualen Erzählsituation aufbaut, in der die Erzählstimme die des Autors und nicht die eines von ihm getrennten Erzählers ist.

Das Setting der *Argenis* ist ein imaginäres, vorrömisches Sizilien, wobei sich Teile der Handlung auch in der weiteren Welt des Mittelmeers und Europas abspielen. Schon der Anfang des Romans macht mit seinem Einstieg *in medias res*, seiner Fokalisierung auf die Wahrnehmung eines Individuums und seinem Spannungsaufbau klar, dass wir es hier mit einem fiktionalen Text zu tun haben. Ich zitiere ein Stück weit das lateinische Original (1,1,1–2) mit der jüngsten deutschen Übersetzung von Gustav Waltz 1891,[7] die heute natürlich auch schon ziemlich antiquiert wirkt:

> Nondum Orbis adoraverat Romam, nondum Oceanus decesserat Tibri, cum ad oram Siciliae, qua fluvius Gelas maria subit, ingentis speciei iuvenem peregrina navis exposuit. […] Ille insuetus navigii malis procubuerat in arenam quaerebatque circumactum pelagi erroribus caput sopore componere, cum acutissimus clamor, primum quiescentis mentem implacida imagine confundens, mox propius advolutus somni otium horrore submovit. Silva erat in conspectu, raris quidem sed in ingens spatium effusis arboribus, subter quas tumuli, fruticum dumorumque caligine, velut ad insidias surrexerant. Hinc repente in campum erumpit femina optimi vultus, sed quae corruperat oculos fletu […] Incitatus verberibus equus non sufficiebat in cursum effusae […] At illa ubi potuit exaudiri: „O quicumque es, si virtutem, inquit, amas, ah succurre Siciliae, quam in fortissimo viro praedones nefarii oppugnant! Nec diu me orare patitur instans malum, nec leviter deprecari pro Poliarcho possum, quem non hinc procul grassatorum ferox turba circumsedit improviso facinore. Ego inter tumultum effugiens, te primum opportune, nec plus forsitan in illius salutem quam in gloriam tuam, vidi.“

---

7   Text: *John Barclay: Argenis,* hg. Mark Riley und Dorothy Pritchard Huber (Assen, 2004); Übersetzung: *Argenis: Politischer Roman vom Anfang des XVII. Jahrhunderts,* hg. Gustav Waltz (München, 1891).

Noch war Rom nicht das Staunen der Welt, noch der Ozean nicht ein Sklave des Tiber, da stieg bei der Mündung des Flusses Gelas ein ungemein schöner Jüngling aus fremdem Schiff ans sizilische Land. [...]. Der Meerfahrt ungewohnt, streckte sich der Fremdling alsbald in den Sand, um dem umhergeworfenen Haupt einige Ruhe zu gönnen. Aber der Erholung sollte nur wenig sein. Ein durchdringendes Geschrei füllte den Geist des kaum Eingeschlafenen mit unruhigen Traumbildern, es kam näher und näher und scheuchte den Frieden des Schlummers mit Schrecken davon. Dem Ufer nah stand ein dünner, doch weitausgedehnter Wald, und unter ihm zogen sich Hügel hin, deren dichtes Strauch- und Dorngestrüpp für Wegelagerer wie gemacht schien. Aus diesem sprengte ein Weib von der glücklichsten Gesichtsbildung, doch die Augen durch Weinen entstellt [...]. Fort und fort hieb sie auf ihr Pferd los, und immer noch lief es ihr zu langsam: so sehr war sie auf Eile bedacht. [...] Kaum in seine Hörweite gelangt, stieß die Reiterin die Worte aus: „Wer immer Du bist, edler Fremdling, komme, wenn Du die Tugend liebst, Sizilien zu Hilfe, das Lotterbuben im tapfersten aller Männer bekämpfen. Die dringende Gefahr verbietet mir viele Worte, und doch sollt' ich Dich aufs äußerste anflehen für Poliarchus, den unweit von hier eine wilde Räuberschar meuchlings überfallen hat. Ich floh während des Tumults, und nun seh' ich Dich so gelegen daherkommen – dem Bedrängten zum Heil, und Dir selber zum Ruhme!"

So beginnen fünf Bücher voller Rückblenden, unerwarteter Wendungen, Kämpfe, Liebeshändel, Reden, Gefühle und Gedanken der Protagonisten. Versucht man, die nicht-linear und in zahlreichen Strängen erzählte Handlung zu linearisieren und zu vereinfachen, kommt man ungefähr auf folgende Geschichte: Das Königreich Sizilien unter König Meleander ist von Religionskonflikten zerrissen und von einer Revolution von Adeligen unter Führung eines Lycogenes bedroht. Meleander wird aber überraschend von einem aus Afrika ankommenden Ritter (unserem anonymen Ankömmling des Incipits, der später als Archombrotus identifiziert wird) und einer Flotte des Königs von Sardinien, Radirobanes, gerettet. Nach der Niederschlagung der Revolte kommt es zu einem Konflikt der Protagonisten um die Königstochter Argenis, die *damsel in distress* der Anfangsszene. Sie wird umworben von a) Poliarchus, dem König von Gallien, der inkognito auf Sizilien weilt und bereits vor dem Einsetzen der Handlung ihr Herz gewonnen hat. Poliarchus ist der „tapferste aller Männer" der Anfangsszene, der überfallen wurde und für den sich Argenis beim gerade angekommenen Archombrotus einsetzt; b) Archombrotus selbst, dem Ritter aus Afrika, der sich aus Liebe zu Argenis

AUTOR/ERZÄHLER UND FIKTION IM NEULATEINISCHEN ROMAN 75

mit seinem Freund Poliarchus entzweit; und c) Radirobanes, dem König von Sardinien, der König Meleander nur deshalb zu Hilfe kommt, weil er es auf seine Tochter Argenis abgesehen hat und sie entführen will. Radirobanes wird aber vertrieben, und bevor sich die ehemaligen Freunde Poliarchus und Archombrotus wegen Argenis die Köpfe einschlagen können, entpuppt sich Archombrotus als Argenis' Halbbruder. Poliarchus darf endlich seine Argenis heiraten, Archombrotus erhält Poliarchus' Schwester zur Ehe.

Vorderhand ist das eine Liebes- und Abenteuergeschichte, hintergründig aber auch eine politische Allegorie. Darauf deutet schon die Widmung an den französischen König Ludwig XIII. (1601–43). Hier erläutert Barclay den Charakter seines Romans als eine Art Fürstenspiegel und weist Ludwig, den echten *Galliae rex*, besonders auf seine Ähnlichkeit mit der Hauptfigur, dem König von Gallien, Poliarchus, hin:[8]

> Videbis virtutum vitiorumque certamina, nullibi quam vestris in aulis atrociora [...] Tuas saepe virtutes reperies; tua in aliis heroibus simplicius facta miraberis. Popularem denique tuum, tot fatis, tot hostibus exercitum Poliarchum, ipsa virtutis et dignitatis similitudine habebis cariorem.

> Du wirst darin den Kampf der Tugenden und der Laster sehen, der nirgends mit größerer Erbitterung geführt wird, als eben an euren Höfen [...] Du wirst oft deine eigenen Tugenden finden; deine Taten wirst du an fremden Helden unbefangener bewundern. Deinen von so vielen Wechselfällen des Schicksals und so viel Feinden heimgesuchten Landsmann Poliarchus wirst du wegen seiner Ähnlichkeit zu dir in Tugend und Würde nur um so lieber gewinnen.

Weitere Analogien zwischen Realgeschichte und erzählter Geschichte sind leicht zu finden. Das von Religionskriegen und Revolutionsbestrebungen zerrüttete Sizilien steht für die jüngere Geschichte Frankreichs während der Hugenottenkriege (1562–98) und des Aufstiegs der Bourbonen unter Heinrich IV. (1553–1610), Ludwigs Vater. Sardinien unter seinem anmaßenden und ehrgeizigen König Radirobanes ist als Spanien unter Philipp II. (1527–1598) zu erkennen. Archombrotus' Heimatland Mauretanien wird von einer Königin beherrscht, die das Parlament fragen muss, bevor sie Steuern einhebt, und die die angreifende Flotte Sardiniens zerstört: Dahinter kann nur das England der parlamentarischen Monarchie unter Elizabeth I. (1533–1603) stehen, das die spanische Armada 1588 zerstört hat. Barclay selbst hat

---

8 Riley/Pritchard-Huber, *Argenis* (s.o., Anm. 7), 94, Z. 8–13.

sein Verfahren historisch-politischer Allegorese in Kapitel 2,14 der *Argenis* reflektiert: Hier lässt er den am Hof Meleanders tätigen gelehrten Schriftsteller Nicopompus, der unschwer als ein Alter Ego Barclays zu identifizieren ist, einem Priester und einem Dichter gegenüber den Plan für ein neuartiges Werk entwickeln. Der unmittelbare Kontext des Gesprächs ist eine Diskussion über die Gefährlichkeit von Kritik und Belehrung an Fürstenhöfen. Nicopompus setzt in dieser prekären Situation auf indirekte Kritik (2,14,4–5):

> Ita ego non subito et aspero questu, veluti reos, citabo ad tribunal illos qui rempublicam turbant – par odio non essem! – sed inscios circumducam per suavissimas ambages, ut etiam eos delectet sub alienis nominibus accusari. [...] Grandem fabulam historiae instar ornabo. In ea miros exitus circumvolvam [...] Dum legent, dum tamquam alienis irascentur aut favebunt, occurrent sibi ipsis agnoscentque obiecto speculo speciem ac meritum suae famae. Forte pudebit eas partes diutius agere in scena huius vitae, quas sibi cognoscent ex merito contigisse in fabula. Et ne traductos se querantur, neminis imago simpliciter exstabit. Dissimulandis illis multa inveniam, quae notatis convenire non poterunt. Mihi enim non sub religione historiae scribenti libertas haec erit [...] Praeterea et imaginaria passim nomina excitabo, tantum ad sustinendas vitiorum virtutumque personas, ut tam erret qui omnia, quam qui nihil, in illa scriptione exiget ad rerum gestarum veritatem.

So will ich die Staatsumwälzer nicht mit plötzlichen und schroffen Beschuldigungen wie Verbrecher vor den Richterstuhl schleppen. Ich wäre deren Hass nicht gewachsen! Vielmehr will ich sie, ohne dass sie dessen gewahr werden, durch anmutigen Umschweif so führen, dass sie noch ein Vergnügen bei der Anklage empfinden sollen [...] Eine große, der Geschichte ähnliche Fabel will ich erzählen und wunderbare Begebenheiten hineinflechten. [...] Während meine Leute lesen, während sie gleichsam Fremden grollen oder geneigt sind, begegnen sie sich selber und erkennen im vorgehaltenen Spiegel sich und ihren Wert. Vielleicht schämen sie sich, auf dem Schauplatz des Lebens eine Rolle weiter zu spielen, die sie in dieser Erzählung als die ihrige anerkennen müssen. Aber sie sollen sich nicht über Verhöhnung ihrer Person beklagen können; keiner soll ganz so, wie er ist, dargestellt werden. Um sie unkenntlich zu machen, leih' ich ihnen Züge, die mit ihrem wirklichen Bilde unvereinbar sind, und meine Feder, die nichts von den Gewissensskrupeln des Historikers weiß, kann sich eine solche Freiheit wohl erlauben. [...] Überdies will ich die Laster und Tugenden, zur lebendigeren Anschaulichkeit ihres Wesens, allenthalben an erfundene Namen knüpfen: so dass einer, der in dieser Schrift alles für bare Münze nimmt, sich ebensowohl irrt, als einer, der nichts darin für wahr hält.

Barclay ordnet seine Erzählung also zwischen einer faktischen *historia* und einer fiktiven *fabula* ein.[9] Er weist seine Leser ausdrücklich an, Entsprechungen zu Personen und Vorgängen der historisch-politischen Wirklichkeit zu suchen, es damit aber auch nicht zu übertreiben. Diese ausdrücklich beabsichtigte Spannung zwischen Faktizität und Fiktivität der erzählten Geschichte wurde von Barclays Lesern begeistert aufgenommen, tendenziell aber auch in Richtung Faktizität aufgelöst. Das bevorzugte Mittel dafür waren die *claves*, die ‚Schlüssel‘, die seit der in Leiden 1627 erschienenen Elzevier-Ausgabe den Drucken der *Argenis* beigegeben wurden. Seit damals sprechen wir übrigens von ‚Schlüsselromanen‘ – wir verdanken Barclay bzw. seinen postumen Herausgebern dieses Konzept und diesen Begriff. Formal konnten die *claves* die historisch-politische Allegorie entweder diskursiv in einem fortlaufenden Text erklären oder tabellarisch die fiktiven Namen den (mutmaßlich) faktischen gegenüberstellen. Die erwähnte Ausgabe Leiden 1627 enthielt beide Formen zugleich, häufiger anzutreffen ist in der Folge die tabellarische Form, wohl schlicht deshalb, weil sie die wesentlichen Informationen auf einen Blick enthält. Nicht verschwiegen sei hier, dass auch die *claves* und die weitere paratextuelle Tradition der *Argenis*-Ausgaben nicht immer von einer klaren Entsprechung von fiktiven und faktischen Namen ausgingen. Im tabellarischen Schlüssel von 1627 werden z.B. *certa* und *media* unterschieden, also sichere und mittel-sichere Identifikationen; und in der Edition Leiden 1630 erschien gar ein *Discursus* [...] *de nominibus Argenidaeis*, der heftig gegen die mittlerweile eingerissene Praxis der vereinfachenden politisch-historischen Identifikationen polemisierte. Solche Warnungen blieben aber die Ausnahme. Die übliche Lektürepraxis war, Barclays Fiktion auf die historische Realität zurückzuführen. Barclay selbst war daran nicht ganz unschuldig, auch wenn er auf einer unaufgelösten und letztlich nicht aufzulösenden Spannung zwischen *historia* und *fabula* insistierte.

---

9   Die Begriffe *historia* und *fabula* wurden spätestens seit dem 1. Jahrhundert v. Chr. in der rhetorischen Theorie der *narratio* gebraucht, um Erzählungen nach ihrem Realitätsbezug und ihrer Wahrscheinlichkeit zu kategorisieren (*Rhetorica ad Herennium* 1,8,11–1,9,14; Cicero, *De inventione* 1,19,27). Eine *historia* ist demnach wahr und (*eo ipso*) wahrscheinlich, eine *fabula* unwahr und unwahrscheinlich. Das in der antiken Rhetorik dazwischen angesiedelte *argumentum*, das unwahr, aber wahrscheinlich ist, geriet in der mittelalterlichen und neuzeitlichen Rezeption oft in den Hintergrund.

5 Barclays Fiktionskonzept in modernen fiktionstheoretischen Kategorien

Wenn man nun das Fiktionskonzept der *Argenis* mit den eingangs vorgestellten Kategorien Zipfels abgleicht, ergibt sich Folgendes:

1) Fiktivität der erzählten Geschichte: In gewisser Weise ist Barclays Geschichte gleichermaßen erfunden wie nicht-erfunden. Natürlich gab es nie einen Poliarchus oder einen Radirobanes, andererseits verweisen die erfundenen Figuren und Handlungen mehr oder weniger deutlich auf Figuren und Handlungen der historischen Realität. Die klassische narratologische *story-discourse* Unterscheidung, die von einer fiktiven *story* ausgeht, greift hier jedenfalls zu kurz. Man könnte vielleicht sagen, die *story*-Ebene wird im Schlüsselroman ihrerseits noch einmal in einen fiktiven Vordergrund und einen faktischen Hintergrund aufgespalten. Man kann sich aber auch fragen, inwiefern Barclay im Kontext seines dezidiert politischen Programms überhaupt primär eine fiktive Geschichte erzählen will – dazu später noch mehr, wenn ich die Autor/Erzähler-Unterscheidung behandle.

2) Fiktionalität der Erzählung: Wie mein Textbeispiel vom Anfang der *Argenis* gezeigt hat, sind typisch fiktionale Erzähltechniken wie die interne Fokalisierung realisiert. Die Erzählstimme gibt uns direkten Einblick in die Gedanken- und Gefühlswelt der Protagonisten. Gerade in vormoderner Literatur gibt es so etwas natürlich auch in der Geschichtsschreibung – man denke nur an die zahlreichen Reden der Akteure in historiographischen Werken seit Herodot. Trotzdem wird niemand die *Argenis* mit Historiographie verwechselt haben. Die fiktionalen Erzählmittel sind dafür schlicht zu massiv eingesetzt. Ob wir auch einen vom Autor getrennten Erzähler als fundamentale fiktionale Erzähltechnik annehmen sollten bzw. warum wir das nicht tun sollten, möchte ich an dieser Stelle noch offen lassen.

3) Fiktionsvertrag: Es gab in der Frühen Neuzeit punktuell immer wieder die Idee eines Fiktionsvertrags zwischen Autor und Leser, auf dessen Grundlage die Zweifel an der Realität des Erzählten willentlich ausgesetzt werden konnten. Ein prominentes frühes Beispiel wäre Philip Sidney, der in seinem ca. 1579 geschriebenen und 1595 veröffentlichten Traktat *The Defence of Poesy* den didaktischen Wert unterhaltsamer Fiktion explizit gegen die an historische Realität gebundene Geschichtsschreibung und die allzu trockene Philosophie abhob. Dass dies aber die ganze Frühe Neuzeit hindurch eine eher apologetische Position war, legt schon das Wort *Defence* in Sidneys Titel nahe. Insbesondere das ausgedehnte Erzählen in Prosa tat sich schwer, sich von der Historiographie und ihrem faktischen Anspruch zu verabschieden. Das zeigt

sich nicht zuletzt auch in einem Locus classicus der barocken Romanpoetik in Deutschland, Sigmund von Birkens Vorrede zum Roman *Aramena* (1669) seines Gönners, Herzog Anton Ulrich von Braunschweig.[10] Hier unterscheidet Birken drei Arten von „Geschichtsschriften": 1) die „Annalen" – gemeint ist die eigentliche Historiographie; 2) die „Gedichtgeschicht", in der historische Hauptumstände durch erfundenen Nebenumstände erweitert sind – gemeint sind hier Epen im Stil von Homers *Ilias*; und schließlich 3) das „Geschichtgedicht", das entweder reale Geschichte „unter erdichteten Namen" und teils erfundenen Umständen oder „ganz-erdichtete Historien" umfasst, die aber trotzdem noch wie Historien bzw. Geschichtsschriften aussehen sollten. Als Beispiel für die dritte Kategorie wird u.a. die *Argenis* genannt. Barclay konnte also nicht wie selbstverständlich auf einen Fiktionsvertrag bauen. Er selbst lädt zu einer historisierenden Lektüre ein, und sein Publikum hat diese historisierende Lektüre durch das Schlüsselwesen weiter ausgebaut.

Zusammenfassend kann man in der *Argenis* eine hybride Mischung von Fiktionselementen erkennen. Eine zur Faktizität neigende Geschichte wird mit fiktionalen Mitteln einem Publikum erzählt, das an freie Fiktion nicht so recht gewöhnt war und sich eine geschichtliche Dimension erwartete.

6 Ähnliche Fiktionskonzepte in anderen neulateinischen Romanen

Das ist nun ein Rezept, wie es für viele neulateinische Romane so oder so ähnlich gilt. Zunächst einmal natürlich für alle Schlüsselromane, und das sind – in der Nachfolge Barclays – etwa die Hälfte aller neulateinischen Romane. Nicht immer muss dabei ein expliziter Schlüssel beigegeben oder auffindbar sein. Zur 1687 erstmals veröffentlichten *Austriana regina Arabiae* des bayerischen Juristen Anton Wilhelm Ertl z.B. gab es keinen Schlüssel. Trotzdem zeigt sich der Schlüsselcharakter des Werks klar genug in der Vorrede des Autor, in der er „die Wahrheit unter schönem Schein" abbilden ("sub specioso commento adumbrata veritas") und die triumphierende Unschuld ("triumphans innocentia") Habsburgs „in fremde Begriffe verpackt" ("peregrinis involuta vocabulis") darstellen will. Auch viele in der 1. Person erzählte satirische Romane sind Schlüsselromane. Traditionsbildend ist hier wieder Barclay, diesmal mit dem 1605–07 in zwei Teilen erschienenen *Euphormionis Lusinini Satyricon*, zu dem erstmals in der Ausgabe Straßburg 1623, also noch vier Jahre vor der *Argenis*, eine *clavis* erschien. Ausgehend von der zentralen Entschlüsselung der

---

10   Vgl. z.B. Rosmarie Zeller, „*Fabula* und *Historia* im Kontext der Gattungspoetik," *Simpliciana* 20 (1998), 49–62, hier 52–3.

Hauptfigur Euphormio als Barclay selbst, wurde der ganze Roman als Satire des Autors auf seine Zeit auf Grundlage seiner eigenen Biographie verstanden.

Eine gewisse Faktizität der Geschichte wird aber auch in allen Romanen gesucht, die zwar keine klar erkennbaren Schlüsselromane sind, aber sich doch (wie die *Argenis*) als Fürstenspiegel gerieren. Ein Beispiel wäre die *Methodus doctrinae civilis, seu Abissini regis historia* (1628) des am bayerischen Hof tätigen jesuitischen Staatstheoretikers Adam Contzen. Contzen erzählt in seiner *historia* das Leben des zeitgenössischen äthiopischen Kaisers Sissinios (1572–1632) und die Einrichtung seines Staats als Vergleichsgröße zu Kurfürst Maximilian I. (1573–1651) und dem frühabsolutistischen Bayern.[11] Der fiktive Abissinus ist relativ weit vom historischen Sissinios entfernt, weil Contzen laut seiner Vorrede nicht *quae facta sunt, sed facienda, vitandaque* beschreiben will. Darüber hinaus ist Abissinus nicht ein direktes Vorbild für Maximilian, da der Protagonist des Romans auch negative Züge hat, vor denen Contzen warnen möchte. Trotzdem ist der konstante Abgleich von fiktiven und faktischen Personen, Institutionen und Handlungen ein Grundprinzip des Romans.

Dieser konstante Abgleich zwischen fiktiver und faktischer Geschichte ist auch für alle utopischen Romane typisch, die das Modell fiktionaler Erzählung mit dem Modell der *Utopia* von Thomas More kreuzten (wobei die *Utopia* selbst ein Dialog in platonischer Tradition und keine Erzählung im engeren Sinn ist). Ein Beispiel hierfür wäre die christliche Utopie von Samuel Gotts *Nova Solyma* (1648), in der zwei Studenten aus Cambridge Jerusalem besuchen, und zu ihrem Erstaunen dort erkennen, dass die Juden zum Christentum konvertiert sind und einen idealen christlichen Staat errichtet haben. In solchen utopischen Entwürfen ist der Leser zwar nicht zu einer faktischen, aber doch zu einer kontrafaktischen Lektüre eingeladen, in der die erzählte Geschichte immer noch ständig auf die gerade anders geartete historische Realität verweist. Anders als bei freier Fiktivität, bleibt utopische Kontrafaktik ohne den konstanten Abgleich mit den historischen Fakten unverständlich.

Schließlich gibt es neben Schlüsselromanen, Fürstenspiegeln und Utopien auch eine Reihe von neulateinischen Romanen, die unter Einsatz fiktionaler Erzählmittel *true stories* aus der Geschichte als Exempel menschlicher Tugenden und Schwächen oder auch der Conditio humana ganz allgemein erzählen. Der Jesuit Johannes Bissel literarisiert in seinen *Argonautica Americana* (1647) z.B. die wahre Geschichte eines spanischen Abenteurers, der vor der

---

11   Vgl. z.B. Dieter Breuer, "Adam Contzens Staatsroman: Zur Funktion der Poesie im absolutistischen Staat," in *Literatur und Gesellschaft im deutschen Barock: Aufsätze*, hg. Conrad Wiedemann (Heidelberg, 1979), 77–126 (zu den historischen Quellen bes. 92–3).

Küste Mittelamerikas gestrandet ist, sich in existenzbedrohenden inneren und äußeren Nöten durch den Dschungel kämpft und schließlich in Lima sein Seelenheil in der Societas Jesu findet. Zieht man alle faktischen und kontrafaktischen Geschichten vom Corpus der neulateinischen Romane ab, bleibt nur noch wenig übrig. Leon Battista Albertis mit Figuren der klassisch-antiken Mythologie durchgespielter Anti-Fürstenspiegel *Momus* (ca. 1444–50) ist so frei, dass er sich weder mit einem bestimmten Fürsten noch mit bestimmten historischen Fakten leicht in Verbindung bringen lässt. Die Fürstenspiegelfunktion wird hier mehr über das moralisch-allegorische Potenzial der mythologischen Figuren realisiert. Ludwig Praschs *Psyche Cretica* (1685) ist ihrerseits eine moralische Allegorie, hier auf die menschliche Seele, ihren göttlichen Bräutigam Amor und ihre teuflischen Widersacher. Beide Autoren bzw. Werke sind in vieler Hinsicht außergewöhnlich – Alberti ist immer außergewöhnlich, weil er Alberti ist; Prasch hat seinen Roman als Reformroman und als experimentelle Illustration der von seiner Frau, Susanne Prasch, in ihren *Réflexions sur les Romans* (1684) niedergelegten Forderungen nach einem christlich-allegorischen Roman verfasst. Keiner der beiden Autoren geht in seiner fiktiven Welt so weit, alles neu zu erfinden: Alberti schließt sich an die klassische Mythologie an, Prasch an Apuleius' Märchen von Amor und Psyche. Gibt man diesen Vorlagen einmal denselben Status wie die ebenfalls vorgängige und nicht-erfundene geschichtliche Realität, dann scheint mir der einzige neulateinische Autor, der eine komplett fiktive Geschichte erzählt, Ludvig Holberg mit seinem *Nicolai Klimii Iter Subterraneum* (1741) zu sein. Auch dieser Roman, in dem merkwürdige Gesellschaften und Charaktere im Inneren der Erde beschrieben werden, ist natürlich eine Zeitsatire – sie ist aber so frei und allgemein, dass klare Parallelen zu einzelnen Individuen und historischen Vorgängen gar nicht oder allenfalls sehr punktuell feststellbar sind. Ich komme auf diesen Roman als besonders außergewöhnlichen und aussagekräftigen Fall zurück.

7 Fiktions-Kreuzungen und die sie bestimmende Regel

Ich habe eine bestimmte Art von Fiktions-Hybridität festgestellt, die in den neulateinischen Romanen häufig vorkommt: historisierende Geschichte, fiktionale Erzählung, in einem Milieu, in dem freie Fiktion zumindest in Prosa nicht so üblich wie heute war. Diese Hybridität wird von modernen Fiktionstheorien kaum berücksichtigt. Dafür ist wieder Zipfel aufschlussreich, der zwar auch Fiktions-Hybridität kennt, aber so, dass der neulateinische Regelfall bei ihm die Ausnahme bildet. Zipfel geht von der Grundannahme aus, dass faktische

Geschichten faktual erzählt werden und fiktive Geschichten fiktional. Man vergleiche zu den verschiedenen Kreuzungen dieser Ebenen folgende Tabelle:[12]

Erzählen / erzählte Geschichte	faktisch	fiktiv
faktual	Faktualer Erzähltext	Fingierte Faktualität > Fiktionaler Erzähltext
fiktional	Grenzfälle	Fiktionaler Erzähltext

Ganz unproblematisch sind nach Zipfels Grundannahmen die Fälle des faktisch-faktualen und des fiktiv-fiktionalen Erzählens. Faktisch und faktual sind z.B. Alltagserzählungen im Stil von „Gestern habe ich dies und jenes getan" – der Inhalt solcher Erzählungen ist, jedenfalls dem Anspruch nach, faktisch; es werden keine fiktionalen Erzählmittel wie interne Fokalisierungen gebraucht. Die fiktionale Erzählung einer fiktiven Geschichte wäre der Fall eines typischen modernen Romans wie des *Ulysses*. Unproblematisch ist für Zipfel aber auch das fiktiv-faktuale Erzählen, in dem eine erfundene Geschichte realistisch, ohne typisch fiktionale Diskurselemente erzählt wird. Ein Beispiel wäre Max Frischs *Homo Faber*, in dem Walter Faber seine Geschichte so dokumentarisch erzählt, dass sie auch in einem Tagebuch stehen könnte. Wenn wir nicht wüssten, dass er und seine Geschichte fiktiv sind, würden wir es seiner Erzählung auch nicht ansehen. Allerdings sehen wir, dass der Name des Autors auf dem Buch Max Frisch und der Name des Ich-Erzählers Walter Faber ist. Kein Paratext vermittelt uns, dass Max Frisch und Walter Faber dieselbe Person sind, und wir kennen die Konvention unseres Literaturbetriebs, dass in so einem Fall der Autor eine Erzählerfigur erfindet. Das faktuale Erzählen einer fiktiven Geschichte ist nach Zipfel also nur eine Scheinfaktualität, ein fingiertes faktuales Erzählen, weil eine Minimalbedingung fiktionalen Erzählens, nämlich die erfundene Erzählerfigur, auch in diesem Fall erfüllt ist. Auf der erfundenen Erzählerfigur beruht die ‚fingierte Faktualität', die solche Erzählungen letztlich wieder zu einem fiktionalen Erzähltext macht. Problematisch ist für Zipfel allerdings der Fall des faktisch-fiktionalen Erzählens, weil hier die Regel, dass faktische Geschichten faktual und fiktive Geschichten fiktional erzählt werden, unrettbar gebrochen wird. Von Zipfel genannte Beispiele sind Formen des

---

12 Nach Zipfel, *Fiktion* (s.o., Anm. 6), 168. Die institutionell-gesellschaftliche Ebene der Fiktion ist hier ausgeblendet.

historischen Romans, in dem alle Figuren – und nicht nur Rahmenfiguren – der Geschichte entnommen sind; fiktionale (Auto-)Biographien realer Personen (etwa Marguerite Yourcenars *Erinnerungen des Hadrian,* 1951) oder ‚nonfiction novels' (dt. ‚Tatsachenromane') wie der Klassiker *Kaltblütig* (1965) von Truman Capote, in dem der Autor einen realen Mordfall faktisch minutiös recherchiert und mit allen Mitteln fiktionaler Erzählkunst romanhaft dargestellt hat. Zipfel interpretiert diese Fälle als bewusste Grenzüberschreitungen, die mit ihren paradoxen Effekten die eigentliche Regel bestätigen (wonach eben faktische Geschichten faktual und fiktive Geschichten fiktional erzählt werden). Die ‚Regel' aber – und das weiß Zipfel grundsätzlich auch, ohne es historisch durchzudeklinieren – ist letztlich vom jeweiligen historisch-kulturellen Milieu abhängig, d.h. von der institutionell-gesellschaftlichen Ebene, den Konventionen des Literaturbetriebs. Für die Moderne stimmt Zipfels Schema deshalb genauso, wie es für den lateinischen Roman der Frühen Neuzeit nicht stimmt. Hier ist die fiktionale Erzählung faktischer oder zumindest zur Faktizität neigender Geschichten die Regel, nicht die Ausnahme.

8 Auktoriale Erzählstimme und Fiktionskonzept im neulateinischen Roman – das Beispiel Barclays

Nun könnte man die institutionell-gesellschaftliche Ebene, die das in der Frühen Neuzeit so möglich macht, in vieler Hinsicht analysieren. Ich möchte hier mit dem Verhältnis von Autor und Erzähler einem narratologisch zentralen Schnittpunkt zwischen historisch-kultureller Realität und Textwelt weiter nachgehen. Meine These ist: Im neulateinischen Roman erwartete man sich grundsätzlich nicht, dass ein Autor nur auf dem Buchdeckel steht und dann ein erfundener Erzähler übernimmt; man erwartete sich vielmehr, dass der Autor auch derjenige ist, der erzählt. Dadurch liegt dem fiktionalen Erzählen des neulateinischen Romans eine eigentlich faktuale Erzählsituation zugrunde, die dann auch mit der Präferenz für faktische, historisierende Geschichten korreliert.

Ich bleibe zunächst beim Beispiel der *Argenis*. Der Autor Barclay verschwindet hier nicht nach dem Titelblatt, sondern definiert die Erzählstimme des Romans in mehreren Paratexten. In seiner Widmung an Ludwig XIII. erläutert Barclay sein, Barclays, literarisches Programm. Dass die folgende Erzählung seine, Barclays, ist, wird durch den Genitiv des Besitzes unmittelbar vor dem Textbeginn nochmals klar: *Ioannis Barclaii Argenis.* Sollte es der Leser im Lauf der Lektüre doch einmal vergessen, dass Barclay spricht, wird er in jeder Kopfzeile jeder Doppelseite daran erinnert: *Io. Barclaii Argenis.*[13] Seit der zweiten Auflage Paris 1622 war es üblich, ein Porträt des Autors voranzustellen, damit man sich besser vorstellen konnte, wer hier sprach.[14] In diversen Ausgaben war auch eine Vita des Autors enthalten; und natürlich entschlüsselten die *claves* die Figur Nicopompus, die die Schlüsseltechnik der *Argenis* in der erzählten Welt entfaltet, als Barclay selbst.

Tatsächlich kannte man diesen Autor auch als jemand, dem man eine verhüllte Geschichte über die europäische Zeitgeschichte abnahm. Barclay war ein europäischer Spitzendiplomat seiner Zeit, der an verschiedenen Fürstenhöfen wirkte und wusste, wie es dort zuging. Berühmt ist die zuerst in der Barclay-Vita der *Argenis*-Ausgabe von 1659 überlieferte Anekdote, dass Kardinal Richelieu täglich in der *Argenis* gelesen habe, um über das Staatswesen zu lernen, und dass sie damit zum Aufstieg Frankreichs zur europäischen Supermacht im 17. Jahrhundert beigetragen habe.[15] Ohne den faktischen Anspruch des Erzähltexts und ohne die Autorität von Barclay selbst als hinter ihm stehender Erzählstimme wäre es kaum möglich, sich so eine Anekdote überhaupt auszudenken.

Nun kann man sagen, dass eine Identifikation von Autor und Erzähler bei einem Roman in der 3. Person relativ einfach ist. Schwieriger scheint sie im Fall einer Ich-Erzählung zu sein, wenn der Ich-Erzähler einen anderen Namen als der Autor hat. Ein Beispiel dafür ist Barclays *Satyricon*, in dem der erzählende Protagonist ein gewisser Euphormio aus dem Phantasieland Lusinia ist. Ich habe aber schon erwähnt, dass Euphormio von Barclays Lesern als Barclay selbst entschlüsselt wurde. Das konnte handschriftlich geschehen wie auf manchen Titelblättern der anonym erschienenen Erstausgabe von 1605, auf denen *Euphormionis* mit *Io. Barclaii* glossiert wurde.[16] In späteren Ausgaben wie der ersten mit *clavis* versehenen von 1623 lesen wir schon auf dem Titelblatt: *Euphormionis Lusinini sive Ioannis Barclaii Satyricon.* Figur und Autor werden also explizit identifiziert (was sich natürlich auch in der *clavis* widerspiegelt: "Euphormio: Ioannes Barclaius, Auctor Satyrici"). Barclay selbst provozierte diese Identifikation mit einer ganzen Reihe von Signalen, etwa mit zahlreichen autobiographische Reminiszenzen wie Euphormios problematischer Erziehung durch die Jesuiten, die auch Barclays eigene war; oder mit der metaleptisch wirkenden Widmung der Figur Euphormios an Barclays realen

---

13   Nicht in der modernen Edition von Riley/Pritchard-Huber, *Argenis* (s.o., Anm. 7).

14   Vgl. Riley/Pritchard-Huber, *Argenis* (s.o., Anm. 7), 2.

15   Seite 4 der unpaginierten Vita.

16   Siehe z.B. das Exemplar der Stadtbibliothek Lyon, SJ x 433/28 Bibliothèque jésuite des Fontaines.

AUTOR/ERZÄHLER UND FIKTION IM NEULATEINISCHEN ROMAN 85

Gönner dieser Zeit, König Jakob I. von England ("Augustissimo Regi Iacobo Primo [...] Euphormio S. D."). Euphormio war also letztlich keine autonome Figur, auch nicht der erzählten Welt, sondern ein Deckname bzw. Pseudonym des satirischen Autors, der mit viel fiktionalen und einigen fiktiven Mitteln vor allem Faktisches erzählen wollte.

9   Ähnliche Autorenkonzepte in anderen neulateinischen Romanen und der Prüfstein von Holbergs *Iter subterraneum* (1741)

Auch in anderen neulateinischen Romanen ist der Autor als Erzählstimme oft gut hörbar. In Ertls *Austriana regina Arabiae* z.B. erscheint der Autor mit seiner Berufsbezeichnung (*iurisconsultus*) auf dem Titelblatt, wohl auch deshalb, damit wir ihm die Expertise zutrauen, mit der er seine als Liebesgeschichte verbrämte Geschichte über die zeitgenössische Politik erzählt. Wie Barclay entwickelt er sein literarisches Programm in einer Widmung an einen Fürsten. Am Ende des Erzähltexts tritt er als Erzähler hervor mit dem Schlusssatz: "Ego applaudente orbe universo id unum prolixe voveo, ut Austriana Esset In Orbe Ultima!" (Ich stimme in den Beifall des gesamten Erdkreises ein und wünsche nur dieses eine von Herzen: Alles Erdreich sei Austriana untertan!). Adam Contzen steht in seiner *Abissini regis historia* ebenfalls mit seiner Berufsbezeichnung (*SS. Theol. Doctor*) auf dem Titelblatt und schaltet der Erzählung eine programmatische Widmung vor. Zudem ist der Übergang von auktorialer Programmatik und eigentlicher Erzählung hier insofern fließend, als das mit *historiae usus* überschriebene Kapitel 1 der Erzählung den offen auktorialen Diskurs der Widmung mit Überlegungen zum Nutzen der (fiktionalisierten) *historia* als Vermittlerin politischer Lehren weiterführt. Die Erzählstimme wird auf diese Weise explizit als jene des Autors eingeführt. Johannes Bissel, der Verfasser der *Argonautica Americana*, ist zwar ganz offensichtlich ein anderer als der Ich-Erzähler seiner Geschichte, der historische spanische Abenteurer Pedro de Victoria. Doch wie Bissel in seinem Vorwort erläutert, will er auch nur der Herausgeber und Verbesserer von Pedros Geschichte sein, die dieser selbst 1610 veröffentlichte und die Bissel in einer deutschen Übersetzung von 1622 vorlag. Die Erzählstimme ist demnach nach wie vor jene Pedros, auch wenn Bissel dessen vergleichsweise simplen Bericht mit den Mitteln fiktionaler Erzählkunst literarisiert und erweitert. Nicht immer sind die Verhältnisse so klar signalisiert: Gotts utopische *Nova Solyma* z.B. ist anonym erschienen und enthält als einzigen Paratext ein sog. *Autocriticon*, in dem auf die Defizite des jugendlichen Werks und auf das Zögern des Autors bei der Veröffentlichung hingewiesen wird. Der Autor als Erzähler ist dem

Werk aber durch einen poetologischen Exkurs eingeschrieben, in dem die beiden Cambridger Studenten, die die Institutionen des neuen Jerusalems kennenlernen, eine Lehrstunde beim Schulmeister Alphaeus erhalten.[17] Dieser zeigt ihnen sechs Schreibgriffel, die für verschiedene Genres stehen. Der sechste und letzte Schreibgriffel ist eine Mischung aus allen anderen: Er steht für den Roman. Jüngst, so Alphaeus, habe ein Schriftsteller einen nützlichen christlichen Roman geschrieben, wobei auch die anonyme Publikation diesem christlichen Programm entsprochen habe – unschwer lässt sich hinter diesem Schriftsteller der anonyme Autor der *Nova Solyma*, Samuel Gott, erkennen. So oder so ähnlich lassen sich für fast alle neulateinischen Romane mehr oder weniger deutliche Hinweise auf eine Identifikation von Autor und Erzähler finden. Der einzige Roman, bei dem mir das nicht gelungen ist, ist – wieder – Holbergs *Nicolai Klimii iter subterraneum*, das sich, 1741 entstanden, damit vielleicht auch schon als besonders ,modern' erweist. Das anonym erschienene *Iter subterraneum* enthält keine mit dem Autor in Verbindung zu bringenden Paratexte. Das erste Kapitel, in dem der Protagonist durch einen Erdspalt in der Nähe von Bergen in eine unterirdische Welt fällt, ist überschrieben mit *Autoris descensus ad inferos*. Es wird aber explizit gesagt, dass dieser *descensus* im Jahr 1664 stattfand – Holberg wurde erst 1684 geboren. Der *autor* der erzählten Welt ist also offenbar eine autonome Figur und kein bloßer Deckname für den realen Autor. Dazu passt auch, dass der Ich-Erzähler hier eine überaus dubiose Figur ist, die sich z.B. in maßloser Herrschsucht zum Tyrannen in der unterirdischen Welt aufschwingt.

Zur schärferen Kontrastierung der Besonderheit des Holberg'schen Ich-Erzählers ist ein Vergleich mit einem anderen Ich-Erzähler hilfreich, dessen Lebenszeit ebenfalls vor diejenige des Autors fällt. In Giovanni Vittorio Rossis satirisch-dystopischem Roman *Eudemia*, der erstmals 1637 erschien, erzählt ein gewisser Flavius Vopiscus Niger wie er nach einer misslungenen Verschwörung gegen Kaiser Tiberius aus Rom flüchten musste, zur fernen Insel Eudemia gelangte und dort eine Kolonie von früher schon ausgewanderten Römern kennenlernte. Die Beschreibung der oft lasterhaften und korrupten Sitten und Gebräuche dieser ausgewanderten Römer ist dann der eigentliche Inhalt des Romans, der in vieler Hinsicht ein Schlüsselroman ist. Die antiken Römer Eudemias sind ein Spiegelbild der barberinischen Römer aus Rossis eigener Zeit. Es kursierten auch regelrechte *claves* zur *Eudemia* (obwohl den Editionen

---

17   Zu dieser zentralen, einen Großteil von Buch 3 (und damit die Mitte des insgesamt 6 Bücher umfassenden Romans einnehmenen) Szene bes. Jennifer Morrish, "Virtue and Genre in Samuel Gott's *Nova Solyma*," *Humanistica Lovaniensia* 52 (2003), 237–317, hier 258–71.

AUTOR/ERZÄHLER UND FIKTION IM NEULATEINISCHEN ROMAN

selbst kein Schlüssel beigegeben war).[18] Der Name des Ich-Erzählers, Flavius Vopiscus, ist identisch mit dem Namen des letzten der antiken Scriptores Historiae Augustae, des einzigen, der von sich selbst etwas erzählt. Im Vorwort zu seiner *Vita Aureliani* schildert der Scriptor Flavius Vopiscus, wie ihn beim römischen Hilaria-Fest, bei dem alles unterhaltsam zugehen und gesagt werden sollte ("Hilaribus, quibus omnia festa et fieri debere scimus et dici"), der römische Stadtpräfekt zum Verfassen einer Geschichte des Kaisers Aurelian aufforderte. Diese Geschichte könne gern auch fiktive Elemente enthalten, da sich ja auch bisher noch kein einziger Historiker vollständig an die Wahrheit gehalten hat. Das passt wunderbar als literarisches Programm für unseren Autor Rossi, der eine scherzhafte Satire auf die Mächtigen seiner Zeit schreiben wollte, die wie Barclays *Argenis* zwischen *historia* und *fabula* oszillierte. Der romanhafte Ich-Erzähler Flavius Vopiscus ist also über den Scriptor Flavius Vopiscus leicht als Autorenfigur zu entschlüsseln (obwohl das meines Wissens bisher noch niemand so getan hat).

Zahlreiche weitere Indizien legen diese Identifikation nahe: Rossi war ein prominentes Mitglied der römischen Gelehrtengesellschaft *Accademia degli Umoristi*, von der auch weitere Mitglieder im Roman satirisch porträtiert werden. Dieser Gesellschaft ging es, wie der Name ,Umoristi' schon andeutet, um den Witz in der Literatur, wozu wieder der witzige Auftrag an den Scriptor Flavius Vopiscus beim römischen Hilarienfest passt. Außerdem stellt sich Rossi in seinem programmatischen Vorwort ausdrücklich in die satirische Tradition Barclays. Wie in Barclays *Argenis* ist sein Autorenname auch auf jeder Kopfzeile jeder Doppelseite zu lesen. Spätere Ausgaben stellten ein Autorenbild und Gedichte auf die Eloquenz des Autors voran. Rossis Fall ist also trotz oberflächlicher Gemeinsamkeiten ganz anders zu beurteilen als der Holbergs, wo wir keine einschlägigen Paratexte, keinen auf den Autor verweisenden Namen des Ich-Erzählers oder andere Hinweise auf den Autor haben.

Wenn ich mit meinen Analysen recht habe, ist Holbergs Roman der einzige neulateinische Roman, der den Autor vom Erzähler trennt. Gleichzeitig ist er, wie schon früher gesagt, der einzige, der seine Geschichte komplett frei erfindet. Das *Iter subterraneum* bestätigt damit *ex negativo* meine These, dass die tendenzielle Faktizität der erzählten Geschichten narratologisch mit der Erzählstimme des Autors korreliert, ja logisch wohl auf dieser beruht, weil der reale Autor eine reale Erzählsituation herstellt, die eine reale oder stark an die Realität angelehnte Geschichte zur Folge hat.

---

18   Ingrid De Smet, *Menippean Satire and the Republic of Letters 1581–1655* (Genf 1996), 76, Anm. 71; Jennifer Nelson verdanke ich den Hinweis auf eine bei De Smet nicht erwähnte handschriftliche *clavis*: Cambridge, Mass., Houghton Library, MS Lat 306.1.

10 Moderne und neulateinische Narratologien

Die für neulateinische Romane typische Hybridität von Fiktionselementen kann ich am Ende nun folgendermaßen präzisieren und kontextualisieren: Auf der Ebene der erzählten Geschichte gibt es eine starke Tendenz zur (v.a. historisch gedachten) Faktizität. Auf der Ebene der Erzählung ist offene Fiktionalität typisch. Wir haben immer charakteristisch fiktionale Erzählmittel wie das Hineinschauen in das Innere der Figuren bei einer Erzählung in der 3. Person oder das unrealistisch wohlgeformte und detailreiche Erinnern bei einer Ich-Erzählung. Das, was Zipfel „fingierte Faktualität" nennt, also so zu erzählen, als ob der Roman ein faktuales Genre wie ein Tagebuch, ein authentischer Reisebericht oder eine echte Biographie sein könnte, interessierte die neulateinischen Romanciers offenbar nicht. Sie sahen das Nützliche an der Fiktion gerade in der unterhaltsamen fiktionalen Erzählweise, mit der faktische Inhalte eingängiger transportiert werden konnten. Anders als uns das die strukturalistische Narratologie und die moderne Fiktionstheorie nahelegen möchten, erzählten Sie dabei in der Regel mit ihrer eigenen Stimme als Autoren, selbst dann, wenn sie einen Ich-Erzähler als Alter Ego vorschoben. Die damit hergestellte faktuale Erzählsituation passte zur tendenziellen Faktizität ihrer Geschichten, mit denen sie mehr oder weniger direkt in den gesellschaftlichen Diskurs eingreifen wollten.

Eine wichtige institutionelle Rahmenbedingung dafür war ganz allgemein sicher das vergleichsweise pragmatische Literaturverständnis der Frühen Neuzeit, in dem Literatur mehr als direkter Beitrag zu gesellschaftlichen Debatten denn als autonomes Kunstwerk verstanden wurde. Für die starke Autorenzentriertheit speziell der lateinischen Romane kann man aber auch noch weitere Gründe finden: Die neulateinischen Romanciers arbeiteten in einem mit Bezug auf die antiken Klassiker, die kanonischen *auctores*, ohnehin schon traditionell stark autorenzentrierten literarischen System. Darüber hinaus verstanden sie sich, ausgehend von Autoren wie Lukian und Petron, der Menippeischen Satire, der neulateinischen Utopie und dem Christentum als Satiriker, Moralisten, Erzieher und Weltverbesserer, und für ihre im weitesten Sinn didaktischen Anliegen standen sie letztlich auch mit ihrer eigenen Person ein. Sie konnten das nicht zuletzt deshalb glaubwürdig tun, als die Rollen die sie im realen Leben spielten, mit ihrer Autorenrolle korrelierte: Staatsromane wurden von Diplomaten, Politikern und Staatstheoretikern geschrieben, religiöse Romane von Predigern und Ordensmännern. Mit den eminent lateinisch besetzten Feldern der Politik und Religion ist das Gros der neulateinischen Romane dann auch schon abgedeckt.

Jede Zeit hat ihre kulturellen Rahmenbedingungen, die das Erzählen, aber auch die Theorie des Erzählens in bestimmte Bahnen lenken. Auch die textimmanente Narratologie à la Genette war nur vor dem Hintergrund eines modernen Literaturbetriebs möglich, in dem der Autor sich aus dem Text und den Paratexten immer weiter zurückzog, bis nur noch sein Name auf dem Buchdeckel übrig blieb und so der Eindruck entstehen konnte, dass er mit der Erzählung selbst erzähllogisch nichts mehr zu tun hat. Diese Logik ist aber zutiefst zeitbedingt. Wenigen Autoren und Lesern neulateinischer Romane wäre es eingefallen, den Erzähltext als vom Autor getrenntes, hypostasiertes Gebilde anzusehen. Es wäre ihnen schon allein deshalb nicht eingefallen, weil der Autor in der faktischen Dimension der erzählten Geschichten und in zahlreichen Paratexten überall herumschlich und so seine eigene Erzählstimme hören ließ. Zipfel, der für seine Fiktionstheorie ein aus der Linguistik abgeleitetes Kommunikationsmodell von Sender-Nachricht-Empfänger auf Erzähltexte anwendet, kennt wohl den Autor als Sender, lehnt ihn aber als Sprechinstanz für fiktionale Texte ab, weil man aus der Perspektive des Autors nicht erklären könne, warum Behauptungssätze (die der linguistischen Definition gemäß nun einmal immer wahr oder falsch sind) in fiktionalen Texten Dinge behaupten, die es gar nicht gibt (die also weder wahr noch falsch sind). Aus der Perspektive eines textimmanenten Erzählers aber löse sich das Paradox auf, weil es aus der Perspektive des Erzählers die von ihm behaupteten Dinge sehr wohl gebe, eben in der erzählten Geschichte. Ich weiß nicht, ob dieser linguistisch-aussagenlogische Ansatz das Erzählen *irgendeiner* Zeit zufriedenstellend beschreibt. Unsere lateinischen Zeitgenossen der Frühen Neuzeit legten jedenfalls ein anderes Erzählmodell zugrunde, in dem dem Autor die Imaginationskraft zugestanden wurde, fiktive Elemente zu erfinden und sich in Figuren hineinzuversetzen, ohne sich deshalb gleich in aussagenlogische Widersprüche zu verstricken. Diese Rolle der spielerischen Phantasie kommt z.B. bei Barclay dadurch zum Ausdruck, dass er seinen Euphormio aus dem Land „Lusinia" kommen lässt, was üblicherweise von *lusus*, „Spiel", abgeleitet wird. Johann Valentin Andreae erklärt am Beginn seiner christlichen Utopie *Christanopolis* (1619) seine Reise in die gleichnamige utopische Stadt damit, dass er noch einmal „die Fahrt auf das Akademische Meer hinaus" ("visum est, academicum mare, quantumvis persaepe infestum mihi, iterum tentare") wagen wollte, das „Schiff der Phantasie" bestieg ("conscensa phantasiae nave") und so inmitten der „tausend Gefahren, die die Wissbegierde nach sich zieht" ("mille curiositatis periculis"), vor Christanopolis strandete. Johannes Bissel entdeckt laut seinem Vorwort zu den *Argonautica Americana* seine Neigung zum amerikanischen Setting dadurch, dass in seiner Phantasie die Tiroler

Alpen, in denen er gerade auf Kur weilte, zu den südamerikanischen Anden wurden, was in seinem Kopf eine ganze Reihe von mentalen amerikanischen *imagines* nach sich zog. Allgemein lehrte die antike Rhetorik, die damals nach wie vor das Grundgerüst literarischer Bildung war, wie durch *enargeia* bzw. *evidentia* Anschaulichkeit hergestellt wird, indem der Redner seine Phantasie betätigt und sich Umstände und Personen ausmalt.

Eine historische Narratologie, die über die hier vorgestellte Skizze zum neulateinischen Roman hinausgeht, hätte all das zu berücksichtigen und mit der modernen Perspektive zu verrechnen. Sie könnte damit aufzeigen, was in vormodernen Kontexten anders ist, aber unter Umständen auch wieder so manche Anregung in die moderne Theoriebildung zurückspiegeln. Der Autor ist ja dort auch schon längst zurückgekommen, wie z.B. der *Rückkehr des Autors* betitelte Sammelband von 1999 plakativ beweist.[19] Und unter den vielen Möglichkeiten, ihn zurückzubringen, ist die über die mentale Dimension des Erzählens (der sich jüngst die kognitive Narratologie annimmt) und die einer Rhetorik fiktionaler Erzähltexte nach frühneuzeitlichem Vorbild vielleicht nicht die schlechteste.

Albert-Ludwigs-Universität Freiburg

---

19   *Rückkehr des Autors: Zur Erneuerung eines umstrittenen Begriffs*, hg. Fotis Jannidis, Gerhard Lauer, Martín Martínez und Simone Winko (Tübingen, 1999).

CHAPTER 5

Apuntes sobre la transmisión textual de la versión latina de la *Política* de Leonardo Bruni

Juan J. Valverde Abril

Abstract

La valoración desde el punto de vista de la crítica textual de los testimonios que transmiten la traducción latina de la *Política* de Leonardo Bruni es todavía una tarea pendiente de la filología latina humanística. Tras el estudio del comportamiento de diecisiete testimonios (diez manuscritos y siete ediciones impresas) de dicha obra mediante la comparación de unos pasajes significativos, es posible establecer un primer grupo de manuscritos, bastante homogéneo tanto en lo que respecta al estado del texto que transmiten como a sus características físicas, creados para el estudio académico (entre ellos están F^3, M^2, M^a, M^c; y también M^1, aunque éste presenta especificidades propias); y un segundo grupo, formado por ejemplares de lujo, cuyo texto transmitido resulta más heterogéneo (P, F^4, V^1 y V^2). Un papel crucial en la transmisión parece jugar el manuscrito F^1 (Florencia, BML, MS Plut. 89 sup. 54), pues en él se observan lecturas dobles que definen esos dos grupos descritos. En cuanto a las ediciones impresas, estas presentan igualmente un estado del texto muy variado; no obstante, puede seguirse una línea de transmisión que parte de la edición de Valencia por Lambert Palmart en 1473 (v) y pasa por la "revolucionaria" recensión de Jacques Lefèvre d'Étaples, impresa en París por Henri Estienne en 1506 (p^{fs}), hasta llegar a las ediciones basilienses de Johann Oporin en 1538 y 1542 (o^1 y o^2 respectivamente).

Keywords

Aristotle – *Politics* – Leonardo Bruni – Neo-Latin translations – Textual criticism

Según el relato tradicional se considera que fue el Duque de Gloucester, ya no sólo por querer asimilarse a los nobles imbuidos del nuevo espíritu humanístico en el patronazgo de los hombres de letras, sino también para hacerse con un texto que sirviera para la instrucción política de su pupilo, Enrique VI de

© KONINKLIJKE BRILL NV, LEIDEN, 2020 | DOI:10.1163/9789004427105_006

Inglaterra,[1] quien encomendó a Bruni que tradujera la *Política* de Aristóteles. Se ha conservado, en efecto, una misiva en la que Bruni acepta ese encargo del Duque, y que se puede fechar en marzo de 1434, aunque algunos adelantan esa fecha hasta 1433.[2] En cualquier caso, precisamente el año de 1434, Palla Strozzi fue desterrado a Padua, donde permaneció hasta el final de sus días, llevando consigo, es de suponer, su copia manuscrita de la *Política*. El hecho de que en la descripción del legado de Palla Strozzi no figure el manuscrito de la *Política* no es prueba para demostrar que no lo llevara consigo.[3] Por consiguiente, si es cierta la noticia de Vespasiano da Bisticci y se acepta este relato tradicional para la composición de esta obra, Bruni debió quedarse sin su modelo griego a poco de empezar su trabajo.

Sin embargo, no hay que olvidar que ya en el *De interpretatione recta* (una obra que se suele fechar en una horquilla de tiempo que va de 1420 a 1426, aunque las voces más autorizadas circunscriben su composición a los tres años finales de dicho periodo, 1424–26),[4] aparecen traducidos al latín algunos párrafos de la *Política*, que luego fueron retomados tal cual en la versión bruniana de esta obra.[5] De ello puede deducirse que Bruni trabajaba en la traducción de este tratado aristotélico desde mediados de los años veinte. Recuérdese además que el Aretino concluyó su traducción de la *Ética* entre 1418 y 1420, y de los *Económicos* en 1420; por ello es lógico pensar que, tras la conclusión de estos trabajos, Bruni emprendiera la traducción de la tercera obra de filosofía

---

1   Alfonso Sammut, *Unfredo duca di Gloucester e gli umanisti italiani* (Padova, 1980), 147; Susanne Saygin, *Humphrey, Duke of Gloucester (1390–1447) and the Italian Humanists* (Leiden, 2001), 57–68.

2   Bruni, *Epist.* 6,14, en Francesco Paolo Luiso, *Studi su l'epistolario di Leonardo Bruni*, ed. Lucia Gualdo Rosa (Roma, 1980), en 122–3; Lucia Gualdo Rosa, "Una nuova lettera del Bruni sulla traduzione della *Política* di Aristotele," *Rinascimento* 23 (1983), 113–24, en 117.

3   Michele Curnis, "La rinascita della *Política* in greco: codici, copisti, committenti nel XV secolo," en *La armonía del conflicto. Los fundamentos aristotélicos de la política. Actas del Congreso Internacional sobre la Política de Aristóteles*, ed. Francisco L. Lisi Bereterbide (Sankt Augustin-Madrid, 2012), 17–42, en 24 y ss.

4   Sobre este opúsculo bruniano puede verse en español Antonio Guzmán Guerra, "Leonardo Bruni Aretino, *De interpretatione recta*," en *Textos clásicos de teoría de la traducción*, ed. Miguel Ángel Vega (Madrid, 1994), 94–104; Maurilio Pérez González, "Leonardo Bruni y su tratado *De interpretatione recta*," *Cuadernos de Filología Clásica. Estudios Latinos* 8 (1995), 193–233; y Fernando Romo Feito, *De interpretatione recta de Leonardo Bruni: un episodio en la historia de la traducción y la hermenéutica* (Vigo, 2012).

5   Las referencias ya aparecían en la edición de Hans Baron, *Leonardo Bruni Aretino, Humanistisch-philosophische Schriften* (Leipzig, 1928; reimpresión en Wiesbaden, 1969), pero también en la nueva edición de Paolo Viti, *Opere letterarie e politiche di Leonardo Bruni* (Torino, 1996), 145–94, que precisamente reproduce los párrafos omitidos por Baron: así, los pasajes de Aristot., *Pol.* 7,1,3, y 7,5,7, se encuentran en *De interpretatione recta* 1,15; y Aristot., *Pol.* 4,10,6–7, un poco más adelante, en *De interpretatione recta* 2,2.

LA TRANSMISIÓN TEXTUAL DE LA VERSIÓN LATINA DE LA *POLÍTICA*   93

moral aristotélica. Por tanto, cuando el Duque de Gloucester escribió a Bruni instándolo a hacer una nueva traducción de la *Política*, ya debía estar sobre aviso (quizá por mediación de Gerardo Landiano) de que hacía tiempo que el Aretino había comenzado ese trabajo.[6]

En cualquier caso, la gestación del mismo no fue fácil, debido a las obligaciones profesionales de Bruni como canciller de Florencia, y se prolongó por varios años. Hacia comienzos de 1436 ya debía existir un esbozo de la traducción completa. La obra no quedó concluida, sin embargo, hasta los primeros meses de 1437, porque es precisamente en marzo de ese mismo año cuando Bruni gestionó la dedicación de su traducción al pontífice Eugenio IV.[7] Pero parece ser que Bruni se cuidó de que no circulara públicamente, hasta que el Duque de Gloucester recibiera la copia prometida, quizá ya en 1438, pues esta es la fecha de composición que presentan algunos manuscritos y la fecha a partir de la cual Bruni remitió copias de su traducción, primero a los Señores de Siena, en noviembre de 1438, y poco después a Alfonso de Aragón.

A partir de esa fecha la traducción bruniana de la *Política* se difundió por toda Europa, como demuestra el volumen impresionante de manuscritos que la conservan y que han llegado hasta nosotros, así como el número de ediciones impresas.[8]

Pues bien, a pesar del enorme interés habido en los últimos tiempos sobre las traducciones greco-latinas realizadas en época humanística, y en especial sobre las hechas por Bruni, no existe una aproximación crítica a todo ese material bibliográfico, más allá de la propia catalogación de Hankins, siendo esa labor un paso previo inexcusable para la realización de una edición crítica de la versión latina de la *Política* realizada por Bruni. En este trabajo se coteja el texto transmitido por algunos de esos testimonios textuales, tanto manuscritos como impresos, seleccionados al azar y considerando su accesibilidad, en unos pasajes concretos,[9] al objeto de delinear unas líneas básicas en la transmisión textual de esta traducción bruniana.

---

6   James Hankins, "The Dates of Leonardo Bruni's later Works," *Studi medievali e umanistici* 5–6 (2007–2008), 11–50.

7   Gualdo Rosa, "Una nuova lettera" (véase arriba, n. 2), 118–9.

8   En concreto, se han contabilizado un total de doscientos seis manuscritos y cincuenta y una ediciones de esta traducción bruniana. Véase James Hankins, *Repertorium Brunianum: A critical Guide to the Writings of Leonardo Bruni, vol. I, Handlist of Manuscripts* (Roma, 1997); y también del mismo autor, "Translations practice in the Renaissance: The Case of Leonardo Bruni," en *Méthodologie de la traduction: de l'antiquité à la Renaissance. Théorie et praxis*, ed. Charles Marie Ternes y Monique Mund-Dopchie (Luxembourg, 1994), 154–75.

9   Para la división en capítulos y parágrafos de la *Política* sigo la edición de J. Aubonnet, *Aristote: Politique, I: Livres I–II* (Paris, 1960). En concreto los pasajes cotejados son: 1,2,5 (52b9–16); 1,2,10 (53a6–10); 1,3,1–2 (53b1–12); 1,6,5 (55a21–28); 1,6,9 (55b4–9); 1,8,4–5 (56a19–29); 1,9,15

Así pues, los manuscritos empleados (todos ellos databales en el siglo XV) han sido los siguientes:

F^1 = Florencia, Biblioteca Medicea Laurenziana, MS Plut. 89 sup. 54.
F^3 = Florencia, BML, MS Plut. 90 sup. 86.
F^4 = Florencia, BML, MS Plut. 79,26.
M^1 = Madrid, Bibioteca Nacional de España, MS 6927.
M^2 = Madrid, BNE, MS 7321.
M^a = Madrid, Biblioteca de la Real Academia de la Historia, MS 9/5693.
M^c = Madrid, Biblioteca Histórica de la Universidad Complutense, MS 114.
P = París, Bibliothèque nationale de France, MS lat. 6310.
V^1 = Valencia, Biblioteca Universitaria, MS 293.
V^2 = Valencia, BUV, MS 388.

Y las ediciones impresas:

a = Strasbourg: Johann Mentelin, 1469.
v = Valentiae: Lambert Palmart, 1473.
b = Barcinone: Nicolaus Spindeler, *ca.* 1481.
r = Romae: per magistrum Eucharium Silber, 1492.
p^{fs} = Apud Parisios: ex officina Henrici Stephani, 1506.
o^1 = Basileae: [Io. Oporinus], 1538.
o^2 = Basileae: [Io. Oporinus], 1542.

Tanto por el estado del texto que transmiten como por las características físicas que los configuran, puede establecerse una primera familia textual formada por el manuscrito de Florencia, BML, MS Plut. 90 sup. 86 (F^3), y los tres matritenses, BNE, MS 7321 (M^2), BRAH, MS 9/5693 (M^a), y BHUC, MS 114 (M^c). En efecto, estos cuatro manuscritos presentan una serie de características comunes muy evidentes (arcaizantes las unas, junto a otras más innovadoras), como son el hecho de estar escritos todos ellos en letra gótica, pero no en dos columnas, sino a línea tirada; presentar letras capitales miniadas, adornadas con líneas, en rojo y violáceo, y el texto dividido por calderones, en su mayoría, con tinta de otro color; y, por último, presentar un abigarrado conjunto de glosas, comentarios y anotaciones en los márgenes y también entre las líneas

---

(57b35–40); 1,11,9 (59a9–18); 2,1,2 (60b36–61a1); 2,2,2 (61a15–20); 2,5,6–7 (63a27–37); 2,5,19 (64a17–22); 2,6,7 (65a17–25); 2,6,15–16 (65b22–34); 2,6,20 (66a14–19); 2,8,1 (67b22–30); 2,8,6 (68a6–11); 2,8,25 (69a24–28); 2,9,8–11 (69b27–70a8); 2,9,25 (70b37–71a3); 2,10,2–4 (71b24–41); 2,11,4–5 (72b38–73a9); 2,11,12 (73b2–7).

LA TRANSMISIÓN TEXTUAL DE LA VERSIÓN LATINA DE LA *POLÍTICA*   95

del texto principal.[10] La orla decorativa que aparece en el fol. 6r del manuscrito complutense es una impostación posterior a imitación del estilo florentino, puesto que el tipo ilustrativo de este manuscrito es el mismo que el del resto que configura este grupo, como se observa en los folios interiores del mismo.

En lo que respecta a las relaciones textuales de estos manuscritos, es evidente que configuran una rama específica dentro de la tradición textual, pues son frecuentes las lecturas propias que comparten entre ellos. Dejando a un lado las variantes fonéticas o gráficas y las omisiones que pueden presentarse de forma independiente, comparten estos manuscritos fenónemos textuales como son las alteraciones en el orden de palabras, las sustituciones léxicas, los cambios entre las formas del paradigma flexivo. Ejemplos de estas lecturas propias en los pasajes cotejados son los siguientes:

> 1,2,5 duabus igitur] igitur duabus $F^3M^2M^aM^c$ || 1,6,5 simul] simpliciter $F^3M^2M^aM^cr$ || 1,8,4 atqui] atque $F^3M^2M^aM^c$ || 1,11,9 uigente] urgente $F^3M^2M^aM^c$ || 2,2,2 suscipit] suscepit $F^3M^2M^a$: succipit M^c || 2,2,2 atqui] atque $F^3M^2M^aM^c$ || 2,2,2 domum²] domus $F^3M^2M^aM^c$, *etiam* F^1 *scripserat* domus, *sed corr.* domum *in margine* || 2,5,19 gymnasia] gimnasia F^3 : ginnasia M^av : gignasia M^2M^c || 2,6,7 oportet] opportet $F^3M^2M^aM^c$ || 2,6,16 ut¹] *om.* $F^3M^2M^aM^c$ || 2,6,20 tertio²] tercio $F^3M^2M^aM^cavb$ || 2,8,1 farcto] facto $F^3M^2M^aM^c$ || 2,8,6 quippiam] quipiam F^3 : quidpiam $M^2M^aM^c$ || 2,10,3 fere Graeci omnes] Graeci fere omnes $F^3M^2M^aM^c$.

Pero dentro de este grupo de cuatro manuscritos la relación que se establece entre el manuscrito de Florencia, BML, MS Plut. 90 sup. 86 (F^3), y el de Madrid, BRAH, MS 9/5693 (M^a), parece más estrecha que con el resto de la familia, pues comparten en exclusiva lecturas propias, como es la introducción en el texto de un escolio (1,11,9), la existencia de omisiones resueltas de la misma forma (2,6,16), o la presencia de lecturas comunes frente a toda la tradición manuscrita estudiada.

> 1,8,5 cuique] unicuique F^3M^a || 1,11,9 pauxillum] pusillum alias pauxillum F^3M^a || 2,1,2 sit] est F^3M^a || 2,2,2 magis domus] domus magis *scripserant* F^3 *et* M^a, *sed corr.* F^3 *in litura et scribendo inter lineas* magis domus, M^a *fort. alia manu punctis subscriptis* magis *traiecit ante* domus || 2,5,19 sunt] sint

---

10   En relación al aparato de notas y comentarios del manuscrito de Madrid, BRAH, MS 9/4693, puede verse Juan J. Valverde Abril, "Glosas a la *Política* de Aristóteles en la versión latina de Leonardo Bruni Aretino (ms. Madrid, RAH, 9/5693): Proemio y Libro I," *Boletín de la Real Academia de la Historia* 206 (2009), 287–337.

F³Mª || 2,6,7 sunt] *Mª uidetur correxisse* : sint *F³* || 2,6,7 autem] *om. F³Mª* || 2,6,7 ciuiliter uiuere] uiuere ciuiliter *F³Mª* || 2,6,16 non recte. Forsan enim Lacedaemoniorum rem publicam] *om. F³Mª, sed suppl. F³ in margine, Mª inter lineas* || 2,6,20 potentiae] potencie *F³Mªa* || 2,9,10 initio] inicio *F³Mªav* || 2,11,12 auctor] actor *F³Mª* || 2,11,12 legis] logis *F³Mª, sed Mª uidetur correxisse.*

Y siendo esto así, cada uno de estos dos manuscritos presenta a su vez lecturas propias; lo que indica que cada uno tiene su propia idiosincrasia y que aun procediendo de una fuente común no son copia el uno del otro.

Como característica propia del manuscrito florentino, BML, MS Plut. 90 sup. 86 (*F³*), hay que señalar que en él no aparece completo el texto del prefacio a la traducción, frente a los tres manuscritos matritenses, que sí lo presentan. Por lo demás, la idiosincrasia del copista se observa no sólo en las peculiares grafías que emplea para algunos términos, que no se observan en otros testimonios de la tradición textual estudiados, sino también en el hecho de que parece no entender bien las abreviaturas empleadas por su modelo, o incluso en la sustitución de unos términos por otros aparentemente sin un motivo claro. Las lecturas propias y exclusivas son las siguientes:

1,2,5 Hesiodus] Exiodus *F³* || 1,2,5 quotidiana] quothidiana *F³* || 1,2,5 est[1]] *om. F³* || 1,2,5 quotidianae] quothidianae *F³* || 1,3,1 cum] quum *F³* || 1,6,9 alium esse] et alium esse *F³* || 1,8,5 cum] quum *F³* || 1,9,15 uariatur] uariantur *fort. F³* || 1,9,15 acquisitionis] acquisicionis *F³a* || 1,9,15 acquisitio] acquisicio *F³a* || 1,11,9 cum] quum *F³* || 2,2,2 unam enim] enim unam *scripserat F³, sed* enim *in litura, iterauit post* unam || 2,2,2 censemus] censsemus *F³* || 2,2,2 perimit] perimitit *scripserat F³, sed uidetur litteras* ti *in litura deleuisse* || 2,5,7 praeterea] propterea *F³* || 2,6,7 impossibiles] imposibiles *F³* || 2,6,7 ipsam] p ipsam *F³* || 2,6,15 cum] quum *F³* || 2,6,16 constitutio] constitucio *F³a* || 2,6,16 gubernatio] gubernacio *F³a* || 2,6,16 si] sui *F³* || 2,8,1 inuenit] adinuenit *F³* || 2,8,1 capillorum] capilorum *F³V²* || 2,8,1 ornatu] hornatu *F³* || 2,8,6 quippiam] quipiam *F³* || 2,8,6 afficerentur] aficerentur *F³* || 2,8,6 bellando] *inter lineas F³* || 2,8,25 considerationem] consideracionem *F³a* || 2,9,8 primus] primo *F³* || 2,9,8 omnes] *om. F³* || 2,9,10 hostes] ostes *F³* || 2,9,11 assuefacti] asuefacti *F³a* || 2,9,11 at] aut *F³* || 2,9,25 decernendi] discernendi *F³v* || 2,9,25 diffidat] difidat *F³* || 2,10,2 cum] quum *F³* || 2,10,2 cognationem] cognacionem *F³a* || 2,10,4 institutio] institucio *F³a* || 2,11,12 assuescere] asuescere *F³a* || 2,11,12 assumere] asumere *F³* || 2,11,12 prospexisset] prospexiset *F³*.

LA TRANSMISIÓN TEXTUAL DE LA VERSIÓN LATINA DE LA *POLÍTICA*

Por su parte, y en lo que respecta a las lecturas específicas del manuscrito de Madrid, BRAH, MS 9/5693 (M^a), la mayoría de sus lecturas propias son variantes ortográficas (como el empleo de la hache en el anafórico, u otras formas exóticas); presenta también algunas omisiones, como se observa en los siguientes ejemplos:

1,2,5 his] hiis M^aa || 1,2,5 domus est] est domus M^a || 1,2,10 et] *om.* M^a || 1,2,10 apes] apex M^a || 1,3,1 his] hiis M^aa || 1,8,5 distinxit] distincxit M^a || 1,11,9 cumque] cũique M^a || 1,11,9 pecuniarum] peccuniarum M^a || 2,5,6 proficient] proficientur M^a || 2,5,6 his] hiis M^aa || 2,5,6 gubernantur] gubernant M^a, *sed corr. alia manu* || 2,5,19 communia] omnia M^a || 2,5,19 omnia] communia M^a || 2,6,15 aedificiorum] hedifficiorum M^a || 2,6,16 his] hiis M^aab || 2,6,20 solis] solum *fort.* M^a || 2,6,20 primis] primisque M^a || 2,6,20 et] *om.* V^lM^a || 2,8,25 his] hiis M^aa || 2,9,10 in mulieres] *om.* M^a || 2,9,11 assuefacti] assuefactam M^a || 2,9,25 ut[2]] *om.* M^a || 2,10,3 Rhodum] Thodum *scripserat* M^a, *sed corr.* || 2,11,4 quam] *traiecit* M^a *ante* eligunt || 2,11,5 quaedam[2]] *om.* M^a, *sed suppl. supra lineam.*

Los otros dos manuscritos matritenses, BNE, MS 7321 (M^2), y BHUC, MS 114 (M^c), parecen guardar a su vez entre ellos una estrecha relación. Lo primero que llama la atención es el parecido extremo de la letra de ambos códices, aunque se dejan ver ciertas diferencias sutiles en la forma de determinadas letras. En atención a ello podría pensarse que ambos manuscritos proceden del mismo copista. Además estos dos manuscritos comparten variantes propias frente al resto de la tradición textual:

1,11,9 pauxillum] pusillum M^2 : *om.* M^c, *inter lineas* pusilum *scripsit* || 2,5,19 gymnasia] gignasia M^2M^c || 2,6,7 sua regione] regione sua M^2M^c || 2,6,16 optimam rem publicam] rem publicam optimam M^2M^c || 2,10,2 Lyctii] Lucii M^2M^c || 2,10,3 perioeci] parieti M^2 : perieti M^c.

Sin embargo, el comportamiento del copista es muy diferente para estos dos manuscritos en lo que respecta a la reproducción del texto. Ello se observa en las lecturas propias de cada uno de estos dos testimonios. Como ejemplos de estas lecturas propias de M^2 hay que citar los siguientes:

1,2,5 appellat] appellant M^2 || 1,3,1 quibus ex partibus] ex quibus partibus M^2 || 1,3,1 constat] constituitur M^2 || 1,3,1 quaeque] quam *fort.* M^2 || 1,3,1 existant] existunt M^2a || 1,6,5 eos] *om.* M^2 || 1,8,5 modo] *om.* M^2 || 1,8,5 idem] iddem M^2 || 1,8,5 illarum[1]] illorum M^2 || 1,8,5 illarum[2]] illorum M^2 || 1,9,15 acquisitionis] adquisitionis M^2 || 1,9,15 acquisitio] adquisitio M^2 || 2,1,2 quidem[1] est] *iterauit M^2 inter folios* || 2,2,2 suppositionem] suspictionem M^2 || 2,2,2 tamen non] non tamen M^2 || 2,6,15 utique] *iterauit M^2 inter folios* || 2,6,20 cuncti] cunti M^2 || 2,9,8 illisque] *post* illisque M^2 mulieribus administrabantur *add., sed deleuit in lit.* || 2,9,11 Lycurgus] hiturgus M^2 || 2,9,25 sufficienter] suficienter M^2 || 2,10,2 diuersatum] diuerssatum M^2 || 2,10,2 autem] *om.* M^2 || 2,10,4 aggressus] agressus M^2V^1.

A su vez, las lecturas propias de M^c son muy frecuentes y peculiares. Destacan las gráficas, como el empleo de la geminada /ll/ o /dd/, en palabras donde no corresponden, la confusión b/v, motivada sin duda por el modo de representar ambas letras en la escritura gótica. Otras veces, el escriba parece no entender la palabra que está copiando, o la entiende mal. Por lo demás, tiene una severa tendencia a la lectura automatizada. En otras ocasiones añade palabras de su cuenta. En el caso de los sustantivos griegos, suele ofrecer lecturas irracionales:

1,2,5 Hesiodus] Esiodus M^c || 1,2,5 aratorem] aiutorem M^c || 1,2,5 quotidiana] cothidiana M^c || 1,2,5 homocapos] homocapados M^c || 1,2,5 utilitatis] utillitatis M^c || 1,2,5 quotidianae] cotidianae M^c || 1,2,10 belli] uelli M^c || 1,3,2 de dominica, de coniugali, de paterna] de coniugali, de dominica, de paternali M^c || 1,6,5 quidam] quiddam M^c || 1,6,5 posuere] possuere M^c || 1,6,5 atque] ac M^c || 1,6,5 atque] ac M^c || 1,6,9 manifestum] magni festum M^c || 1,6,9 et quod] quod M^c || 1,6,9 determinatum] terminatum M^c || 1,6,9 quod] quo M^c || 1,11,9 Mileto] Milleto M^c || 1,11,9 arrasque] arasque M^c || 1,11,9 ditari] dictari M^c || 1,11,9 illis] *post* sed *traiecit* M^c || 2,2,2 domum[1]] domus M^c || 2,5,6 diuisae] diuisse M^c || 2,5,6 incusationes] incussationes M^c || 2,5,6 etiam nunc] nunc etiam M^c || 2,5,19 quam ob] ob quam M^c || 2,5,19 permittentes] permitentes M^c || 2,5,19 possessionem] possessiones M^cV^1 || 2,6,7 utilia] utillia M^c || 2,6,15 aedificiorum] edifficiorum M^c || 2,6,15 prosit] prossit M^c || 2,6,16 hanc] hanc esse M^c || 2,6,16 forsan[1]] forsam M^c || 2,6,16 sin] sim M^c || 2,6,16 forsan[2]] forssan M^c || 2,6,16 Lacedaemoniorum] Lacedeniomorum M^c || 2,6,16 probabit] prouabit M^c || 2,6,20 assumptio] assuptio M^c || 2,6,20 assumuntur] assunnitur M^c || 2,6,20 omnes] omnis M^c || 2,8,1 Milesius] Millesius M^cv || 2,8,1 quidem] quiddem M^c || 2,8,1 aestate] state M^c || 2,8,6 utile] utillem M^c || 2,8,6 occubuissent] obcubuissent M^c || 2,8,6 alendos] allendos M^c || 2,8,6 prouisum] prouissum M^c || 2,8,25 omittamus] obmittamus M^c || 2,9,8 quoniam] qui M^c || 2,9,8 uenerea] benerea M^c || 2,9,9 refert] reffert M^c || 2,9,9 bellum] uellum M^c || 2,9,10 contigisse] contingisse M^c || 2,9,11 domo] a domo M^cb || 2,9,11 abessent] abesset

M^c || 2,9,11 Argiuis] organis M^c || 2,9,11 bellum] uellum M^c || 2,9,11 irrefragantes] infragamtes M^c || 2,9,11 conatus] cognatus M^c || 2,9,25 decernendi] dicernendi $M^c p^{fs} o^1$ || 2,9,25 diffidat] deffidat M^c || 2,10,2 Charilli] Charsii M^c || 2,10,2 coloni] colloni M^c || 2,10,3 coloniam] colloniam M^c || 2,10,4 Siciliam] Ciciliam M^c || 2,10,4 conuenientiam] conueientiam M^c || 2,10,4 Cretica] Crethica M^c || 2,10,4 Laconica] Lacedemonica M^c || 2,11,4 neque] nec M^c || 2,11,5 rei publicae] re publica M^c || 2,11,12 quidem] quiddem M^c || 2,11,12 sumptus] suptus M^c || 2,11,12 opulentiam] opullentiam M^c || 2,11,12 praestantium] prestantum M^c.

Además, aunque no son muchas, estos dos manuscritos presentan lecturas comunes con M^a, discriminando a F^3:

2,10,2 tutelam] tutellam $M^1 M^2 M^a M^c$ || 2,10,3 Peloponneso] Poloponenso F^3 : Peloponenso $M^2 M^a M^c V^1 b$ || 2,11,4 reprehensorum] reprehensionum $M^2 M^a M^c$ || 2,11,12 oportet eos] eos opportet $M^2 M^a M^c$.

Por su parte, el manuscrito de Madrid, BNE, MS 6927 (M^1), escrito en letra gótica bastarda, de origen español, presenta también, como los anteriores un nutrido corpus de notaciones marginales. Incluye no sólo la *Política*, sino también las otras dos obras de filosofía moral del Estagirita, así como otras obras y opúsculos de Bruni. Coincide con los cuatro manuscritos anteriores en muchas lecturas, aunque a ese consenso también se sumen en ocasiones otros testimonios:

1,2,10 esse animal] animal esse $F^3 F^4 M^1 M^2 M^a M^c V^1 V^2 avbrp^{fs} o^1 o^2$ || 1,11,9 hieme] hyeme $M^1 M^2 M^a M^c vbrp^{fs} o^1 o^2$ || 2,5,7 uicissim] uicisim $F^3 M^1 M^2 M^a M^c$ || 2,6,16 potentium] potentum $F^3 F^4 M^1 M^2 M^a M^c V^1 vb$ || 2,6,16 media] mediam $F^3 M^1 M^2 M^a M^c ar$ *et etiam* F^1 *scripserat* mediã, *sed signum nasale est in litura* || 2,8,1 hieme] hyeme $F^3 F^4 M^1 M^2 M^a M^c vbrp^{fs} o^1 o^2$ || 2,9,11 militiam] miliciam $F^3 M^1 M^2 M^a M^c av$ || 2,11,5 referendi[2]] refferendi $F^3 M^1 M^2 M^a M^c$ || 2,11,12 opulentiam] opulenciam $F^3 M^1 M^a a$: opullentiam M^c.

A veces esa coincidencia es sólo con alguno de los cuatro ya vistos, pero no con todos:

1,2,5 Charondas] Karondas $M^1 M^c$ || 1,2,5 quidem] quidam M^1 *et fort.* M^c || 1,2,10 nihil] nichil $F^1 M^1 M^2 M^a M^c ap^{fs}$ || 1,11,9 pretio] precio $F^3 M^1 M^2 M^a V^1 avbrp^{fs} o^1$ || 1,11,9 uellent] uelent $F^3 M^1$ || 2,6,7 sint] sunt *b et*

M^1M^2 *in compendio* || 2,6,16 his] iis $M^1V^2p^{fs}o^1o^2$: hiis M^aab || 2,6,16 optimatium] optimatum $F^3M^1M^2M^cV^2$: optimatuum M^a || 2,8,6 reperissent] repperissent $F^4M^1M^aP$ || 2,8,25 differentia] differencia M^1M^aa || 2,9,9 insolentia] insolencia M^1M^aav || 2,9,10 indulgentia] indulgencia $F^3M^1M^aa$ || 2,9,25 forsan] forsam $M^1M^aM^c$ || 2,10,2 tutelam] tutellam $M^1M^2M^aM^c$ || 2,10,2 Lyctii] Licii $F^3M^1V^2v$ *et* M^a, *sed uidetur scripsisse* Litcii, t *in rasura* : Lucii M^2M^c || 2,10,2 obtinentia] obtinencia $F^3M^1M^aa$ || 2,10,4 conuenientiam] conuenienciam $F^3M^1M^aa$: conueientiam M^c || 2,11,4 pretii] precii $M^1M^2M^aM^cV^1avbrp^{fs}o^1$ || 2,11,5 potentiam] potenciam F^3M^1a || 2,11,5 referendi[2]] refferendi $F^3M^1M^2M^aM^c$ || 2,11,12 opulentiam] opulenciam $F^3M^1M^aa$.

Pero lo peculiar de este manuscrito es que presenta numerosas lecturas particulares. Entre ellas hay que citar, por supuesto, las peculiaridades gráficas, aunque no sean tan numerosas como en otros testimonios; pero este manuscrito destaca sobre todo por la libertad con la que el copista obra con respecto al texto: no sólo sustituye unos términos por otros (1,3,1; 1,11,9; 2,8,25; 2,10,4; etc.), quizá porque no entienda la abreviatura que encuentra en su modelo, y otras veces sin motivo aparente; sino que incluso cambia la redacción de la frase cuando detecta una variante que no da sentido al texto y acomoda el léxico y la sintaxis de la frase a ella (2,6,15).

1,3,1 perficitur] conficitur M^1 || 1,8,4 sunt] *om.* M^1 || 1,8,4 illo] ab illo M^1 || 1,11,9 obiiceretur] subijceretur M^1 || 1,11,9 subito] postea M^1 || 2,1,2 necessarium] neccesarium M^1 || 2,1,2 enimuero nulla esse communia impossibile constat esse cum ciuitas sit communio quaedam[2]] *om.* M^1V^2 || 2,1,2 ac] et M^1v || 2,1,2 ciues[2] autem socii unius ciuitatis[2]] *om.* M^1 || 2,2,2 suppositionem] supponitionem M^1 || 2,5,6 ut est] et est ut M^1 || 2,5,19 quale] quod M^1 || 2,6,7 ciuitatem] *om.* M^1 || 2,6,15 substantiam] substanciam M^1 || 2,6,15 ne] in M^1 || 2,6,15 diuisio] diuisione M^1 || 2,6,15 non] num M^1 || 2,6,20 uerum non omnes necesse erat ex tertio] *om.* M^1, *sed suppl. alia manu in margine* || 2,8,1 Piraeum] Pyreum M^1 : Pireum *omnes reliqui testes exceptis* ro^2 || 2,8,1 in cetera] incerta *scripserat* M^1, *sed corr.* || 2,8,6 occubuissent] ocubuissent M^1 || 2,8,25 aliorum est] est aliorum M^1 || 2,8,25 temporum] operum M^1 || 2,9,8 huiuscemodi] huiusmodi $M^1vbp^{fs}o^1o^2$ || 2,9,8 administrabantur] ministrabantur M^1 || 2,9,25 dicet] licet M^1 || 2,9,25 sic etiam] ita M^1 || 2,9,25 et[2]] *om.* M^1 || 2,10,3 circum] circa F^4M^1b || 2,10,3 Peloponneso] Peloponensi M^1 || 2,10,3 Rhodum] Rhodium M^1 || 2,10,4 defunctus] deffunctus M^1 || 2,10,4 institutio] consuetudo M^1 || 2,11,4 aut[1]] et M^1o^2 || 2,11,5 concordent[1]] concordant M^1 || 2,11,12 ac] at M^1 || 2,11,12 prospexisset] prospexit M^1.

La transmisión textual de la versión latina de la *Política*

Los cinco códices hasta ahora descritos forman parte del grupo de manuscritos privados empleados para la lectura universitaria. Pero existen también otros que por sus características gráficas pueden calificarse como ejemplares de lujo. Para hablar de ellos, hay que comenzar, no obstante, tratando el manuscrito de Florencia, BML, MS Plut. 89 sup. 54 (*F¹*).

Este manuscrito florentino parece ser un ejemplar para uso privado. Está escrito en letra humanística y en su colofón aparece fechado en 1438, aunque es incierto si esta es efectivamente la fecha de copia o la que se encontraba ya en su modelo. Desde el punto de vista textual es un manuscrito muy interesante, porque, de un lado, presenta un texto muy cuidado y depurado de grafías consideradas hoy como exóticas; pero, de otro, está configurado de tal forma, con la inclusión de determinadas correcciones y lecturas dobles, que muy bien puede ser el punto de inflexión a partir del cual se bifurca la tradición textual: de un lado quedarían los manuscritos empleados en contextos universitarios, como los vistos con anterioridad, y de otro los ejemplares de lujo. Para determinar el valor exacto de este testimonio y de sus correcciones es de importancia capital poder determinar cuál es la procedencia de dichas correcciones y lecturas dobles.

Entre las lecturas propias que presenta cabe citar las siguientes:

> 1,8,4 hoc] uel hoc *F¹, sed* uel *punctis subscriptis notauit* || 1,9,15 augere] agere *F¹, corr.* augere *supra lineam ipsa manu* || 2,1,2 autem] *om. F¹, sed in margine suppl.* || 2,1,2 impossibile] impossibile est *F¹, sed* est *del. in litura* || 2,2,2 unum] hominem *scripserat F¹, sed corr.* unum *in margine* || 2,2,2 domum²] domus *scripserat F¹, sed corr.* domum *in margine* || 2,5,6 aliqua²] alia *scripserat F¹, sed corr. in margine* aliqua || 2,6,15 domos] domus *scripserat F¹, sed notauit litteram* u *puncto subscripto et supra scripsit* o || 2,6,16 media] mediã *scriperat F¹, sed signum nasale est in litura* || 2,6,16 constituit] constitutiot *scripserat F¹, sed cancellauit tertiam* t *et secundam* o *punctis subscriptis* || 2,8,6 autem] quoque *scripserat F¹, sed corr. in margine* || 2,8,25 enim] *om. F¹, sed suppl. in margine* || 2,9,25 nam] sed *scripserat F¹, sed corr. in margine* || 2,10,2 qui] ii qui *scripserat F¹, sed cancellauit* ii, *ut solet, punctis subscriptis* || 2,10,2 quomodo] quando *scripserat F¹, sed corr. in margine* || 2,10,2 ac] et *scripserat F¹, sed cancellauit puncto subscripto et corr. inter lineas* || 2,11,4 magis¹] *iteratum del. F¹ in litura.*

Muy cercano a este códice desde el punto de vista genealógico es el manuscrito de París, BNF, MS lat. 6310. Se trata de un ejemplar de lujo, membranáceo, que perteneció al Cardenal de Borbón.

Sigue en lo fundamental el texto que presenta *F¹*, y parece interpretar acertadamente sus correcciones. Pero no es seguro que sea su modelo directo.

La existencia de lecturas propias, aunque pocas, apunta a que ambos manuscritos proceden de una fuente común. Las lecturas propias de P en los pasajes cotejados son las siguientes:

> 1,2,5 his] iis P || 1,11,9 oleae] olei M^aPo^2 || 2,2,2 censemus] *om. P* || 2,8,6 est] etiam P || 2,9,9 nociuae] nocuit P || 2,9,11 multas enim continet utilitatis partes] *om. P* || 2,11,4 ipsi] ipsa *P.*

El resto de manuscritos considerados en este trabajo son todos ejemplares de lujo, similares a este manuscrito parisino. Por ello cabría esperar que, en lo que respecta al texto que presentan, se inscribieran en esta línea de transmisión representada por el manuscrito florentino F^1 y el parisino (P). Sin embargo, son muchas las lecturas comunes que comparten con los manuscritos académicos antes vistos.

Entre estos manuscritos de lujo está otro manuscrito de Florencia, BML, MS Plut. 79,26 (F^4), en vitela, con letras capitales decoradas al comienzo de cada libro, y con orla en la portada. En lo que respecta al texto, comparte con los manuscritos académicos las siguientes lecturas, aunque a ese consenso se puedan sumar también otros testimonios:

> 1,2,10 esse animal] animal esse $F^3F^4M^1M^2M^aM^cV^1V^2avbrp^{fs}o^1o^2$ || 1,8,5 earum] eorum $F^3F^4M^2M^aM^cV^1V^2abr$ || 2,2,2 unum] hominem $F^3F^4M^2M^aM^cV^1V^2b$ || 2,5,19 sustinentibus] substinentibus $F^1F^4M^aM^cV^1$ || 2,5,19 sustinebunt] substinebunt $F^4M^aM^cV^1$ || 2,6,16 potentium] potentum $F^3F^4M^1M^2M^aM^cV^1vb$ || 2,8,1 Hippodamus] Hyppodamus M^1r : Hypodamus $F^4M^aM^c$: Hipodamus M^2V^2 : <Hip>podamus vb || 2,8,1 hieme] hyeme $F^3F^4M^1M^2M^aM^cvbrp^{fs}o^1o^2$ || 2,8,6 reperissent] repperissent $F^4M^1M^aP$ || 2,10,2 qui] ii qui $F^3F^4M^2V^2bp^{fs}o^1o^2$ *et scripserat etiam* F^1, *sed cancellauit* ii *punctis subscriptis* : hi qui M^cvr : hii qui M^aV^1a || 2,10,3 circum] circa F^4M^1b || 2,11,4 iam] *om.* $F^3F^4M^2M^aM^c$ || 2,11,5 attinet] actinet F^3F^4.

Pues bien, a pesar de ser un ejemplar de lujo, la escasa pericia del copista, al menos en lo que respecta a la reproducción del contenido del texto, queda demostrada con las lecturas propias que el códice presenta. Entre estas lecturas propias hay que citar las frecuentes omisiones, motivadas por salto de igual a igual; y también, la utilización casi sistemática de la grafía -y- para la representación del fomena /i/ en los términos de origen griego. Pero lo más notorio son los cambios léxicos a los que somete el texto, bien porque no entienda lo que hay escrito en el modelo, o porque haga de él una interpretación particular.

1,2,5 duabus] duobus F^4 || 1,2,5 homosipios] homosypios $F^4p^{fs}o^2$ || 1,2,5 Epimenides] Epymenides *corr.* F^4 || 1,2,5 non] uero F^4 || 1,6,5 continget] contingit F^4a || 1,8,4 diuersas] diuersis F^4 || 1,11,9 pauxillum] pausillum F^4 || 1,11,9 fecisse] fecisset F^4 || 1,11,9 Mileto] Myleto F^4 || 1,11,9 in Chio] in Chyo F^4 || 1,11,9 nemine] uenires F^4 || 2,5,6 unoquoque] nunc quoque F^4 || 2,6,7 uicina] uicima *seu* uicinia F^4 || 2,6,16 igitur ut communissimam omnium hanc constituit] *om.* F^4 || 2,6,20 censu postea totidem ex secundo postea ex tertio uerum] *om.* F^4 || 2,8,1 sumptuoso] specioso F^4 || 2,8,1 farcto] fracto F^4V^1a || 2,8,6 prius fuerit] prius fuerit prius F^4 || 2,8,6 est] et F^4 || 2,9,9 quid] quod F^4 || 2,10,2 cognationem] cognitionem F^4 || 2,10,3 enim[3]] *om.* F^4 || 2,10,3 modicum] medicum F^4 || 2,10,4 Peloponneso] Peloponense F^4 || 2,10,4 Camerinam] Camerina F^4 || 2,11,5 quaedam[2]] quaedam uero F^4 || 2,11,12 magistratum] magistratus *scripserat F^4, sed puncto subscripto* s *cancellauit et* u *per signum nasale notauit* || 2,11,12 prospexisset] perspexisset F^4.

Por su parte, el manuscrito de Valencia, BUV, MS 293 (V^1), escrito en vitela, con letra humanística redonda de origen italiano, presenta letras capitales doradas y miniadas. En la orla de la portada aparece el escudo del rey de Aragón sostenido por ángeles. Perteneció a la Biblioteca Palatina de Nápoles. El Duque de Calabria, Fernando de Aragón, lo hizo traer a España tras la muerte de su madre en 1533. En lo que respecta a su texto, se muestra cercano al anterior manuscrito florentino, y asimismo concuerda con los manuscritos académicos:

1,2,10 esse animal] animal esse $F^3F^4M^1M^2M^aM^cV^1V^2avbrp^{fs}o^1o^2$ || 1,8,4 earum] eorum $F^3F^4M^2M^aM^cV^1V^2abr$ || 1,11,9 pretio] precio $F^3M^1M^2M^aV^1avbrp^{fs}o^1$ || 2,2,2 unum] hominem $F^3F^4M^2M^aM^cV^1V^2b$ || 2,6,16 potentium] potentum $F^3F^4M^1M^2M^aM^cV^1vb$ || 2,6,20 tertio[1]] tercio $M^2M^aM^cV^1avb$ || 2,8,1 farcto] fracto F^4V^1a || 2,8,1 aggressus] agressus $F^3V^1p^{fs}$ || 2,10,3 Peloponneso] Peloponenso $M^2M^aM^cV^1b$ || 2,10,4 aggressus] agressus M^2V^1 || 2,11,4 pretii] precii $M^1M^2M^aM^cV^1avbrp^{fs}o^1$.

También presenta lecturas propias que muestran las faltas en las que suele incurrir cuando copia el texto:

1,2,5 Charondas] Carondas V^1 || 1,2,5 homosipios] homosypios $F^4p^{fs}o^2$ || 1,2,5 quotidianae] quottidianae V^1a || 1,3,1 minutissimis] minutissimis rebus V^1 || 1,3,1 unumquodque] unumquod V^1 || 1,6,5 prouenit] prouenerit V^1 || 1,6,9 determinatum est] determinatum V^1 || 1,6,9 alium parere] *om.* V^1

|| 1,8,4 diuersitates] diuersitas $V^{1}v$ || 1,9,1 uariatur] uariat V^{1} || 1,11,9 quasi] quam *fort.* $V^{1}v$ || 2,1,2 quidem[1]] quippe V^{1} || 2,1,2 constat esse] esse constat V^{1} || 2,1,2 est] *om.* V^{1} || 2,2,2 eo procedente] eo procedere *scripserat* V^{1}, *sed eadem manu corr.* || 2,2,2 ut] et V^{1} || 2,5,19 sunt] *om.* V^{1} || 2,5,18 quid] quid plus V^{1} || 2,6,15 ne] de V^{1} || 2,6,20 et] *om.* $V^{1}M^{a}$ || 2,8,1 esse uolens] uolens esse V^{1} || 2,8,6 lege] longe V^{1} || 2,8,25 omittamus] omictamus V^{1} || 2,9,11 repugnabant] repugnant V^{1} || 2,10,2 Charilli] Carilli $V^{1}avbro^{2}$ || 2,11,4 eligunt] eliguntur V^{1} || 2,11,5 ipsorum] eorum V^{1} || 2,11,12 rationabile] racionabile V^{1} || 2,11,12 in] *om.* $V^{1}v$.

Por último, el otro manuscrito valenciano aquí considerado, BUV, MS 388 (V^{2}), es un manuscrito copiado por Giovanni Rinaldo Mennio, en letra humanística redonda. En el fol. 6r se encuentra la portada, con orla de oro y colores con emblemas, trofeos y ángeles que sostienen el escudo de los soberanos de Nápoles. Se discute si perteneció a Juan II, rey de Aragón, quien lo adquirió en 1470, o al homónimo arzobispo de Zaragoza, Juan de Aragón. En cualquier caso, como el códice anterior, fue traído a España por el Duque de Calabria.

Pese a su belleza no es este un manuscrito que destaque por su calidad textual. Ya las noticias de los catálogos informan de las numerosas omisiones en las que incurre el copista; pero es que además cambia las formas del paradigma flexivo, se come determinadas sílabas e introduce formas que no tienen ningún sentido. Entre las lecturas propias que presenta se pueden citar las siguientes:

1,6,5 retinentes] renitentes V^{2} || 1,6,5 nam lex iustum quid est seruitutem quae ex bello prouenit iustam posuere et simul non aiunt] *om.* V^{2} || 1,8,4 vitae] uites V^{2} || 1,8,4 faciunt] faciant V^{2} || 1,9,15 uidetur] uidentur V^{2} || 1,11,9 infructuosum] fructuosum V^{2} || 2,2,2 ciuitas] ciuitatis V^{2} || 2,5,19 permittentes] permittens V^{2} || 2,6,7 et[1]] *om.* V^{2} || 2,6,16 his] iis $M^{1}V^{2}p^{fs}o^{1}o^{2}$ || 2,6,16 sin] sint V^{2} || 2,8,6 qui] quae V^{2} || 2,8,6 quippiam] cuippiam V^{2} || 2,9,10 inferentes] inferentibus V^{2} || 2,10,3 perioeci] pexicii V^{2} || 2,10,3 fere Graeci omnes] frege Graeci omnes V^{2} || 2,10,3 Rhodum] Rodum $V^{2}v$ || 2,11,4 optimatum] optimam V^{2}.

Cuando coincide con otros manuscritos, suele hacerlo con el de Florencia, BML, MS Plut. 79,26 (F^{4}) y el otro valenciano, BUV, MS 293 (V^{1}), aunque en ocasiones esas lecturas son también compartidas en parte o en su totalidad por los manuscritos académicos. Pero los pasajes en que ello sucede no son muy numerosos:

LA TRANSMISIÓN TEXTUAL DE LA VERSIÓN LATINA DE LA *POLÍTICA* 105

1,2,5 esse animal] animal esse $F^3F^4M^1M^2M^aM^cV^1V^2avbrp^{fs}o^1o^2$ ‖ 1,8,5 earum] eorum $F^3F^4M^2M^aM^cV^1V^2abr$ ‖ 2,1,2 enimuero nulla esse communia impossibile constat esse, cum ciuitas sit communio quaedam²] *om. M^1V^2* ‖ 2,2,2 unum] hominem $F^3F^4M^2M^aM^cV^1V^2b$ ‖ 2,6,16 his] iis $M^1V^2p^{fs}o^1o^2$ ‖ 2,6,16 optimatium] optimatum $F^3M^1M^2M^cV^2$ ‖ 2,8,1 capillorum] capilorum F^3V^2 ‖ 2,10,2 qui] ii qui $F^3F^4M^2V^2bp^{fs}o^1o^2$ *et scripserat etiam F^1, sed cancellauit* ii *punctis subscriptis* ‖ 2,10,3 Peloponneso] Peloponesso PV^2a.

En lo que respecta a las ediciones, es considerada como edición príncipe de esta versión latina de la *Política* la publicada en Estrasburgo en una fecha quizá anterior a 1469 por el impresor Johann Mentelin (*a*).[11]

Esta edición emplea de forma sistemática la representación fonética latina, tal como se encontraba en muchos manuscritos. Así, las lecturas propias que presenta son en su mayoría variantes gráficas de los términos, motivadas por la fonética de los mismos. En consecuencia, es regular la notación palatalizada del grupo -*ti*- más vocal. Por lo demás, duda en la notación de determinados términos, y tiene serios problemas en la reproducción correcta de los nombres griegos:

1,3,1 sint] *om. a* ‖ 1,3,1 perquirenda] perquerenda *a* ‖ 1,6,5 quidam] quidem *a* ‖ 1,6,9 rationem] racionem *a* ‖ 1,8,5 comedunt] commedunt *a* ‖ 1,9,15 amplificatio] amplificacio *a* ‖ 1,11,9 emptionem] empcionem *a* ‖ 1,11,9 in Chio] nichio *a* ‖ 2,1,2 considerationis] consideracionis *a* ‖ 2,2,2 tanquam] tamquam *a* ‖ 2,2,2 unum] hominem unam *a* ‖ 2,2,2 etiam] eciam *a* ‖ 2,5,6 incusationes] incusaciones *a* ‖ 2,5,6 etiam nunc] eciam nunc *a* ‖ 2,6,7 suppositiones] supposiciones *a* ‖ 2,6,7 etiam] eciam *a* ‖ 2,6,15 aliquid] aliquit *a* ‖ 2,6,15 etiam] eciam *a* ‖ 2,6,16 potentium] potencium *a* ‖ 2,6,16 optimatium] optimacium *a* ‖ 2,8,1 abscidit] abscindit *a* ‖ 2,8,1 capillorum] cappillorum *a* ‖ 2,8,1 sumptuoso] sumptuosu *a* ‖ 2,8,1 etiam] eciam *a* ‖ 2,9,9 enim²] non *a* ‖ 2,9,9 etiam] eciam *a* ‖ 2,9,25 aliquis] alias *a* ‖ 2,9,25 sic etiam] sic eciam *a* ‖ 2,9,25 mentis] ciuitatis *ao²* ‖ 2,10,2 Lyctii] Liti *a* ‖ 2,10,3 Asia] Alia *a* ‖ 2,11,5 senatu] sanatu *a* ‖ 2,11,12 sumptus] sumtus *a*.

---

11   El ejemplar empleado para este estudio es el conservado en la Bayerische Staatsbibliothek, con signatura 2, Inc.s.a. 96b, accesible en formato digital a través de la web: [sine titulo: *Aristotelis Ethica ad Nicomachum – Politica – Oeconomica*, Leonardo Bruni interprete] (Strasbourg, Johann Mentelin, 1469).

Cuando presenta lecturas compartidas con otros testimonios su comportamiento es variado. Pero si nos atenemos a los errores que reproduce presentes en otros testimonios, esta edición se encuentra cercana a los manuscritos V^1 y F^4:

1,2,5 his] iis P : hiis M^aa || 1,2,5 quotidianae] quothidianae F^3 : quottidianae V^1a : cotidianae M^c || 1,2,10 nihil] nichil $F^1M^1M^2M^aM^cap^{fs}$ || 1,3,1 existant] existunt M^2a || 1,3,1 his] hiis M^aa || 1,6,5 continget] contingit F^4a || 1,8,4 atqui] atque $F^3M^2M^aM^c$: at qui av || 1,8,5 earum] eorum $F^3F^4M^2M^aM^cV^1V^2ar$ || 1,9,15 acquisitionis] acquisicionis F^3a || 1,9,15 acquisitio] acquisicio F^3a || 1,11,9 obiiceretur] obiceretur $F^1M^2M^aM^cav$ || 1,11,9 pretio] precio $F^3M^1M^2M^aV^1avrp^{fs}o^1$ || 2,2,2 suppositionem] supposicionem F^3a || 2,5,6 immo] ymo $M^2M^aM^ca$ || 2,5,6 unoquoque] uno quoque V^1av || 2,5,6 his] hiis M^aa || 2,6,7 in ferenda] inferenda av || 2,6,16 constitutio] constitucio F^3a || 2,6,16 gubernatio] gubernacio F^3a || 2,6,16 media] mediam $F^3M^1M^2M^aM^car$ *et etiam* F^1 *scripserat* mediã, *sed signum nasale est in litura* || 2,6,16 his] hiis M^aa || 2,6,20 potentiae] potencie F^3M^aa || 2,6,20 assumptio] assumpcio F^3a || 2,6,20 tertio^1] tercio $M^2M^aM^cV^1av$ || 2,6,20 tertio^2] tercio $F^3M^2M^aM^cav$ || 2,8,1 farcto] fracto F^4V^1a || 2,8,6 his] hiis M^aM^ca || 2,8,25 his] hiis M^aa || 2,8,25 differentia] differencia M^1M^aa || 2,8,25 considerationem] consideracionem F^3a || 2,9,9 insolentia] insolencia M^1M^aav || 2,9,10 initio] inicio F^3M^aav || 2,9,10 indulgentia] indulgencia $F^3M^1M^aa$ || 2,9,11 militiam] miliciam $F^3M^1M^2M^aM^cav$ || 2,9,11 assuefacti] asuefacti F^3a || 2,10,2 Charilli] Carilli V^1avro^2 || 2,10,2 cognationem] cognacionem F^3a || 2,10,2 qui] hii qui M^aV^1a || 2,10,2 obtinentia] obtinencia $F^3M^1M^aa$ || 2,10,3 perioeci] perieci $F^1F^3F^4M^1M^aPV^1a$ || 2,10,3 Peloponneso] Peloponesso PV^2a || 2,10,4 conuenientiam] conuenienciam $F^3M^1M^aa$ || 2,10,4 institutio] institucio F^3a || 2,11,4 pretii] precii $M^1M^2M^aM^cV^1avrp^{fs}o^1$ || 2,11,5 intentionem] intencionem F^3M^aa || 2,11,5 potentiam] potenciam F^3M^1a || 2,11,12 assuescere] asuescere F^3a || 2,11,12 largitionem] largicionem F^3M^ca || 2,11,12 opulentiam] opulenciam $F^3M^1M^aa$ || 2,11,12 praestantium] prestancium $F^3M^1M^aa$.

Otra edición incunable es la que apareció en Valencia hacia el año de 1473 en las prensas de Lambert Palmart (v).[12] Por la presencia en esta edición de ciertas lecturas particulares se podría considerar que es de poca calidad: muchas veces sus variantes no dan sentido a la frase, y el cajista interpreta mal

---

12   El ejemplar consultado es el conservado en la BNE, accesible a través de la web: *Ethica, Oeconomica, Politica* (Valentiae, Lambert Palmart, *ca.* 1473).

LA TRANSMISIÓN TEXTUAL DE LA VERSIÓN LATINA DE LA *POLÍTICA*

las abreviaturas que encuentra en su modelo, se come sílabas, no entiende los nombres griegos, copia palabras sin sentido, cambia los términos por otros del paradigma flexivo, e incurre en alguna que otra omisión.

> 1,2,5 homocapos] homo capos v || 1,2,5 utilitatis] utilitas v || 1,2,10 et quam] quam v || 1,3,1 de] et de v || 1,3,1 de dominica] dominica v || 1,6,5 prouenit] peruenit v || 1,11,9 in Chio] inthio v || 2,1,2 quidem^2] enim v || 2,2,2 etiam] *om. v* || 2,5,19 cetera] circa v || 2,6,7 et^1] etiam et v || 2,6,16 optimatium] optimam v || 2,6,20 assumptio] assumtio v || 2,6,20 solis] talis v || 2,8,1 quoque] *traiecit v ante* in cetera || 2,8,1 farcto] forsito v || 2,8,6 quasi] q v || 2,9,10 indulgentia] indulgenciam v || 2,9,11 ipsos] ipsas v || 2,9,11 continet] continent v || 2,9,25 corporis] corpus v || 2,10,2 susceperant] susceperunt v || 2,10,2 eam coloniam] camcolonam v || 2,10,3 perioeci] pergeci v || 2,10,3 illis legibus] *om. v* || 2,10,3 sita] cito v || 2,10,3 hinc] huic v || 2,10,3 Peloponneso] Penopnenso v || 2,10,4 Siciliam] Siculam v || 2,10,4 aggressus] egressus v || 2,10,4 Camerinam] Comirrinam v || 2,11,12 adispiscuntur] adipiscimur v || 2,11,12 sumptus] subtus v || 2,11,12 praestantium] praestantiam v.

Pero el de esta edición resulta ser un testimonio importante, porque en él van a aparecer lecturas que la tradición de las ediciones posteriores consagra como buenas. Así, las lecturas compartidas con otros testimonios son las siguientes:

> 1,2,10 esse animal] animal esse $F^3F^4M^1M^2M^aM^cV^1V^2avrp^{fs}o^1o^2$ || 1,2,10 sit constituta] constituta sit $vp^{fs}o^1$ || 1,3,1 oportet] oporteat $vp^{fs}o^1$ || 1,8,4 atqui] at qui av || 1,8,4 diuersitates] diuersitas V^1v || 1,9,15 at] ac $vp^{fs}o^1o^2$ || 1,9,15 itaque] quare $p^{fs}o^1o^2$: atque v || 1,11,9 obiiceretur] obiceretur $F^1M^2M^aM^cav$ || 1,11,9 quasi] quam *fort.* V^1v || 1,11,9 hieme] hyeme $M^1M^2M^aM^cvrp^{fs}o^1o^2$ || 1,11,9 pretio] precio $F^3M^1M^2M^aV^1avrp^{fs}o^1$ || 2,1,2 quidem^1 est] est quidem $vp^{fs}o^1$ || 2,1,2 ac] et M^1v || 2,1,2 quidem^2] enim v : *om.* $p^{fs}o^1$: quaedam o^2 || 2,2,2 atqui] at qui vr : atque $F^3M^2M^aM^c$ || 2,2,2 posset quispiam] quispiam posset $vp^{fs}o^1o^2$ || 2,5,6 diuisae] diuersae $vp^{fs}o^1$ || 2,5,6 immo] imo vo^1 || 2,5,6 unoquoque] uno quoque V^1av || 2,5,7 sua] *om.* $M^cvp^{fs}o^1$ || 2,5,7 quisque] unusquisque $vp^{fs}o^1$ || 2,5,19 different] differrent $M^2M^aM^cvr$ || 2,5,19 gymnasia] ginnasia M^av || 2,6,7 in ferenda] inferenda av || 2,6,15 quintuplum] quincuplum *fere omnes testes exceptis av* || 2,6,16 forsan^1] forsitan $vp^{fs}o^1$ || 2,6,20 potentiae] potentia vro^2 || 2,6,20 tertio^1] tercio $M^2M^aM^cV^1av$ || 2,6,20 tertio^2] tercio $F^3M^2M^aM^cav$ || 2,8,1 Milesius] Millesius M^cv || 2,8,1 hieme] hyeme $F^3F^4M^1M^2M^aM^cvrp^{fs}o^1o^2$ || 2,8,25 quocumque] a quocunque $vrp^{fs}o^1o^2$ || 2,9,8 huiuscemodi] huiusmodi $M^1vp^{fs}o^1o^2$ || 2,9,9 at enim]

et enim *v* : etenim $p^{fs}o^1o^2$ || 2,9,9 insolentia] insolencia M^1M^aav || 2,9,10 initio] inicio F^3M^aav || 2,9,11 militiam] miliciam $F^3M^1M^2M^aM^cav$ || 2,9,11 Messeniis] Messanis F^4v || 2,9,25 decernendi] discernendi F^3v : dicernendi $M^cp^{fs}o^1$ || 2,9,25 et[1]] *om.* $vp^{fs}o^1$ || 2,10,2 Lyctii] Licii $F^3M^1V^2v$ *et* M^a, *sed uidetur scripsisse* Litcii, t *in rasura* || 2,10,2 qui] ii qui $F^3F^4M^2V^2p^{fs}o^1o^2$ *et scripserat etiam* F^1, *sed cancellauit* ii *punctis subscriptis* : hi qui M^cvr : hii qui M^aV^1a || 2,10,3 hinc] hic p^{fs} : huic *v* || 2,10,3 Rhodum] Rodum V^2v || 2,11,4 pretii] precii $M^1M^2M^aM^cV^1avrp^{fs}o^1$ || 2,11,12 praestantium] praestantiam *v* : praestantiae $p^{fs}o^1$.

Dejando a un lado las coincidencias de tipo ortográfico con otros testimonios, aquí interesan sobre todo las coincidencias con la edición de 1506 realizada por Jacques Lefèvre d'Étaples (p^{fs}). Es poco probable que el humanista francés dispusiera de un ejemplar de dicha edición. Quiere ello decir que las coincidencias con esta edición se deben a un testimonio anterior, no considerado aquí, pero que parece representar una línea de transmisión textual distinta, y quizá más depurada, que las vistas hasta ahora.

La siguiente edición cronológicamente hablando, considerada en este estudio es la publicada en Barcelona, por Nicolás Spindeler, datada en 1481 (*b*).[13] Presenta lecturas propias muy llamativas, que inducen a calificar esta edición como poco valiosa:

1,2,5 homosipios] homosopios *b* || 1,2,5 Cretensis] Chethensis *b* || 1,6,5 retinentes] retinens *b* || 1,6,5 bello] lege *b* || 1,6,9 quod] quam *b* || 1,11,9 superlucratum] perlucratum *b* || 1,11,9 hoc] *om. b* || 2,5,6 in ciuitatibus] ciuitatibus *b* || 2,5,19 different] differunt *b* || 2,5,19 Cretenses] Chretenses *b* || 2,6,15 cuique] unicuique *b* || 2,6,20 quarto] ex quarto *b* || 2,8,1 et[1]] *om. b* || 2,8,6 prius fuerit] fuerit prius *b* || 2,8,25 quocumque] quotcumque *b* || 2,9,10 Argiuis] archiuis *b* || 2,9,25 quod[1]] quid *b* || 2,10,3 perioeci] periechi *b* || 2,10,3 fere Graeci omnes] fere omnes Graeci *b* || 2,10,4 insularum] insulas *b* || 2,11,4 aut[1]] ac *b* || 2,11,4 sint] sunt *b* || 2,11,12 gerere] genere *b*.

Las lecturas divergentes que comparte con otros testimonios son las siguientes:

1,2,10 esse animal] animal esse $F^3F^4M^1M^2M^aM^cV^1V^2avbrp^{fs}o^1o^2$ || 1,8,5 earum] eorum $F^3F^4M^2M^aM^cV^1V^2abr$ || 1,11,9 hieme] hyeme $M^1M^2M^aM^cvbrp^{fs}o^1o^2$ || 1,11,9 pretio] precio $F^3M^1M^2M^aV^1avbrp^{fs}o^1$ ||

---

13   Se ha consultado el ejemplar de la BNE disponible en internet: *Politica* (Barcinone, Nicolaus Spindeler, ca. 1481).

2,2,2 unum] hominem $F^3F^4M^2M^aM^cV^1V^2b$ || 2,5,6 his] iis $bp^{fs}o^1o^2$ || 2,5,19 sint] sunt b et M^1M^2 in compendio || 2,6,16 potentium] potentum $F^3F^4M^1M^2M^aM^cV^1vb$ || 2,6,16 his] hiis M^aab || 2,6,20 tertio[1]] tercio $M^2M^aM^cV^1avb$ || 2,6,20 tertio[2]] tercio $F^3M^2M^aM^cavb$ || 2,8,1 hieme] hyeme $F^3F^4M^1M^2M^aM^cvbrp^{fs}o^1o^2$ || 2,9,8 huiuscemodi] huiusmodi $M^1vbp^{fs}o^1o^2$ || 2,9,10 domo] a domo M^cb || 2,10,2 Charilli] Carilli V^1avbro^2 : Charili M^a : Charsii M^c || 2,10,2 Lyctii] Lictii F^4b || 2,10,2 qui] ii qui $F^3F^4M^2V^2bp^{fs}o^1o^2$ et scripserat etiam F^1, sed cancellauit ii punctis subscriptis || 2,10,3 circum] circa F^4M^1b || 2,10,3 Peloponneso] Peloponenso $M^2M^aM^cV^1b$ || 2,11,4 pretii] precii $M^1M^2M^aM^cV^1avbrp^{fs}o^1$.

Un hito importante en la transmisión del texto de la *Política* traducido por Bruni es la edición de Roma de 1492, publicada por Eucario Silber (*r*).[14] En efecto, esta edición presenta una novedad con respecto a las restantes; y es que junto a la traducción de Bruni, en los márgenes de cada página aparece el comentario de Tomás de Aquino a la *Política*, que, como es sabido, está realizado sobre la traducción de esta obra aristotélica realizada por Guillermo de Moerbeke. Ello tiene no pocas consecuencias para el establecimiento del texto de la traducción bruniana en esta edición, porque la yuxtaposición de ambos textos puede favorecer que algunas lecturas de la antigua traducción pasen a la de Bruni. Las lecturas propias que presenta esta edición son las siguientes:

1,2,5 Charondas] Charundas ro^2 || 1,2,5 homosipios] homosyphioes r || 1,2,5 homocapos] homocapnos ro^2 || 1,6,9 quare et] quare r || 1,11,9 coegisset] eoegisset r || 2,8,1 Pireum] Piraeum ro^2 || 2,9,9 idem] ita r || 2,10,2 Lyctii] Lytii r || 2,10,3 perioeci] parechi r || 2,10,4 ac] ac et ro^2.

Las lecturas compartidas por esta edición con otros testimonios en los pasajes cotejados son las siguientes:

1,2,10 esse animal] animal esse $F^3F^4M^1M^2M^aM^cV^1V^2avbrp^{fs}o^1o^2$ || 1,6,5 simul] simpliciter $F^3M^2M^aM^cr$ || 1,8,5 earum] eorum $F^3F^4M^2M^aM^cV^1V^2abr$ || 1,11,9 hieme] hyeme $M^1M^2M^aM^cvbrp^{fs}o^1o^2$ || 1,11,9 pretio] precio $F^3M^1M^2M^aV^1avbrp^{fs}o^1$ || 2,2,2 atqui] at qui vr || 2,2,2 unum] hominem

---

14   El ejemplar consultado es el conservado igualmente en la Bayerische Staatsbibliothek, con signatura 2 Inc.c.a. 2682a, accesible en internet: [sine titulo: Aristotelis Politica Leonardo Aretino interprete cum commentariis diui Thomae] *Augustinus Piccolhomineus Magistro Ludouico Ordinis Predicatorum Procuratori* [...] *SPD* (Romae, per magistrum Eucharium Silber, 1492).

unum $rp^{fs}o^1o^2$ || 2,5,19 different] differrent $M^2M^aM^cvr$ || 2,6,16 media] mediam $F^3M^1M^2M^aM^car$ et etiam F^1 scripserat mediã, *sed signum nasale est in litura* || 2,6,20 potentiae] potentia vro^2 || 2,8,1 Hippodamus] Hyppodamus M^1r || 2,8,1 hieme] hyeme $F^3F^4M^1M^2M^aM^cvbrp^{fs}o^1o^2$ || 2,8,1 quocumque] a quocunque $vrp^{fs}o^1o^2$ || 2,9,11 Messeniis] Meseniis ro^2 || 2,9,11 Lycurgus] Ligurgus M^1avr || 2,10,2 Charilli] Carilli V^1avbro^2 || 2,10,2 qui] hi qui M^cvr || 2,11,4 pretii] precii $M^1M^2M^aM^cV^1avbrp^{fs}o^1$

Pero la edición que supone un cambio radical en el texto latino de Bruni es la realizada por Jaques Lefèvre d'Étaples y publicada en París en 1506 (p^{fs}).[15]

Como es sabido, pocos años antes se había publicado la edición aldina de las obras de Aristóteles en griego. Lefèvre d'Étaples somete la versión de Bruni a una comparación minuciosa con el texto griego aldino y cambia en la traducción bruniana todos aquellos pasajes en los que esta discrepa de dicho texto griego. Otros cambios se deben a un simple deseo de mejorar estilísticamente el texto de Bruni. Las lecturas propias que presenta en los pasajes cotejados son muy numerosas y dan una idea del cambio profundo a que fue sometido el texto:

1,2,10 simul] simul natura $p^{fs}o^1o^2$ || 1,2,10 cupidus] cupidus [est *add.* o^1] ueluti qui nullo retinetur iugo, ut neque uolatilia $p^{fs}o^1o^2$ || 1,2,10 gregarium] gregarium animal $p^{fs}o^1o^2$ || 1,3,1 de his utique tribus] de tribus utique his partibus $p^{fs}o^1$ || 1,3,1 unumquodque] unaquaeque $p^{fs}o^1$ || 1,3,2 coniugali] nam et ipsa proprio nomine non nominatur *add.* $p^{fs}o^1o^2$ *post* coniugali || 1,3,2 disciplina] re familiari $p^{fs}o^1$: sint autem hae tres quas diximus *add.* $p^{fs}o^1o^2$ *post* disciplina || 1,6,5 retinentes] usurpantes $p^{fs}o^1o^2$ || 1,6,5 aiunt] arbitrantur $p^{fs}o^1o^2$ || 1,6,5 alicuius iusti] aliquod iustum $p^{fs}o^1o^2$ || 1,6,5 et] atque p^{fs} : atqui o^1 || 1,6,5 non aiunt] non iustam esse aiunt $p^{fs}o^1o^2$ || 1,6,5 alioquin] alioqui $p^{fs}o^1$ || 1,6,5 continget] contiget p^{fs} || 1,6,9 non] quod $p^{fs}o^1o^2$ || 1,6,9 quibus] quibus ob idipsum $p^{fs}o^1$: quibus quod ob idipsum o^2 || 1,8,4 nam] quapropter $p^{fs}o^1o^2$ || 1,8,4 itaque] quare $p^{fs}o^1o^2$ || 1,8,4 faciunt] fecerunt $p^{fs}o^1o^2$ || 1,8,5 uictus] uictus atque delectum $p^{fs}o^1o^2$ || 1,8,5 earum] ipsarum $p^{fs}o^1o^2$ || 1,9,15 eiusdem] eiusdem rei $p^{fs}o^1o^2$ || 1,9,15 existens] cum sit $p^{fs}o^1o^2$ || 1,9,15 eiusdem] ipsius $p^{fs}o^1o^2$ || 1,9,15 est usus] usus $p^{fs}o^1o^2$ || 1,9,15 huius uero] illius uero $p^{fs}o^1o^2$ || 1,9,15 itaque] quare $p^{fs}o^1o^2$: atque v || 1,9,15 pecuniam] nummorum substantiam $p^{fs}o^1$

---

15   *Contenta. Politicorum libri octo. Commentarij. Economicorum duo. Commentarij. Hecatonomiarum septem. Economiarum publ. unus. Explicationes Leonardi in oeconomica duo* (Paris, 1506). El texto de Lefèvre d'Étaples fue reimpreso en 1511, 1515 y 1521.

|| 1,11,9 cui cum] cum enim $p^{fs}o^1$ || 1,11,9 obiiceretur] obiiceretur illi $p^{fs}o^1$ || 1,11,9 studium] studium propter inopiam $p^{fs}o^1o^2$ || 1,11,9 hieme] hyeme $M^1M^2M^aM^cvbrp^{fs}o^1o^2$ || 1,11,9 pretio] precio $F^3M^1M^2M^aV^1avbrp^{fs}o^1$ || 1,11,9 esse] est $p^{fs}o^1$ || 2,1,2 considerationis] confoederationis (confederationis p^{fs}) $p^{fs}o^1$ || 2,1,2 ciues[1]] ciues omnes $p^{fs}o^1$ || 2,1,2 quaedam[1]] quaedam et quaedam non $p^{fs}o^1$ || 2,1,2 paritas] aequalitas $p^{fs}o^1$ || 2,2,2 paritas] aequalitas $p^{fs}o^1$ || 2,2,2 eo procedente] ea si procedat $p^{fs}o^1o^2$ || 2,2,2 ut] atque $p^{fs}o^1$ || 2,2,2 faciendum] faciundum $p^{fs}o^1$ || 2,5,6 diuisae] diuersae $vp^{fs}o^1$ || 2,5,6 incusationes] incusationes adinuicem $p^{fs}o^1$ || 2,5,6 per] ob $p^{fs}o^1$ || 2,5,6 erunt] erunt ad usum $p^{fs}o^1o^2$ || 2,5,6 his] iis $bp^{fs}o^1o^2$ || 2,5,6 aliqua[2]] et aliqua $p^{fs}o^1$ || 2,5,7 forent uniuscuiusque] ut ita dicam propriis $p^{fs}o^1$ || 2,5,7 et uehiculis] si forte in uiis in agris et regionem quis indiguerit $p^{fs}o^1$ || 2,5,19 sustinentibus] erit iis qui sustinent $p^{fs}o^1$: accedet sustinentibus o^2 || 2,5,19 praetexunt] machinentur $p^{fs}o^1$ || 2,5,19 qui] illi enim $p^{fs}o^1$ || 2,5,19 gymnasia] *post* illis *traiecerunt* $p^{fs}o^1$ || 2,6,7 sunt] *om.* $p^{fs}o^1$ || 2,6,7 pro arbitrio] ad optionem $p^{fs}o^1$ || 2,6,15 attribuit] *post* attribuit *add.* $p^{fs}o^1$ separatim diuidens || 2,6,16 uult] apparet $p^{fs}o^1$: apparet *in margine add.* o^2 || 2,6,16 plebis gubernatio] popularis status $p^{fs}o^1$ || 2,6,16 potentium] potentia $p^{fs}o^1$ || 2,6,16 omnium] omnium aliarum ciuitatum $p^{fs}o^1$ || 2,6,16 optimam] optimam post primam $p^{fs}o^1$ || 2,6,20 senatus assumptio] consiliariorum delectio $p^{fs}o^1$ || 2,6,20 assumuntur] assunnitur M^c : deliguntur $p^{fs}o^1$ || 2,6,20 omnes] omnibus $p^{fs}o^1$ || 2,6,20 erat] erat iis qui $p^{fs}o^1$ || 2,6,20 quartorum] et quartis $p^{fs}o^1$ || 2,8,1 autem] autem Euryphontis $p^{fs}o^1o^2$ || 2,8,1 diuisionem] diuisiones $p^{fs}o^1$ || 2,8,1 abscidit] incidit $p^{fs}o^1$ || 2,8,1 superfluus] uitae esse superflue $p^{fs}o^1$ || 2,8,1 uili] frugali $p^{fs}o^1$ || 2,8,1 farcto] calido $p^{fs}o^1$ || 2,8,6 his] iis $p^{fs}o^1o^2$ || 2,8,6 non] nondum $p^{fs}o^1$ || 2,8,6 prius fuerit] apud alios fuisset $p^{fs}o^1$ || 2,8,6 lex] lex nunc $p^{fs}o^1$ || 2,8,6 aliis] in aliis $p^{fs}o^1o^2$ || 2,8,25 uel] an $p^{fs}o^1o^2$ || 2,8,25 aut] an a $p^{fs}o^1$ || 2,9,8 quoniam] nam $p^{fs}o^1$ || 2,9,8 sunt] uidentur $p^{fs}o^1$ || 2,9,8 ad uenerea illisque obnoxii] ad eam quae masculorum aut ad eam quae mulierum conuersationem $p^{fs}o^1$ || 2,9,8 itaque] quapropter $p^{fs}o^1$ || 2,9,9 insolentia] audacia $p^{fs}o^1$ || 2,9,11 cum per] nam propter $p^{fs}o^1$ || 2,9,11 multum] multum temporis $p^{fs}o^1$ || 2,9,11 abessent] abfuerant $p^{fs}o^1$ || 2,9,11 Argiuis] aduersus Argiuos $p^{fs}o^1$ || 2,9,11 primo] *om.* $p^{fs}o^1$ || 2,9,11 mox] deinde $p^{fs}o^1$ || 2,9,11 Arcadibus] aduersus Arcadas $p^{fs}o^1$ || 2,9,11 Messeniis] Mesenios $p^{fs}o^1$ || 2,9,11 irrefragantes] exercentes $p^{fs}o^1o^2$ || 2,9,11 assuefacti] assuefactos $p^{fs}o^1o^2$ || 2,9,11 utilitatis] uirtutis $p^{fs}o^1o^2$ || 2,9,11 abstinuisse] abstinuisse tandem $p^{fs}o^1$ || 2,9,25 quod[1]] si $p^{fs}o^1$ || 2,9,25 boni] aequi et boni $p^{fs}o^1$ || 2,9,25 enimuero] attamen $p^{fs}o^1$ || 2,10,2 plurimum] tunc plurimum temporis $p^{fs}o^1$ || 2,10,2 tunc] quae tunc $p^{fs}o^1$ || 2,10,2 obtinentia] obtinuerant $p^{fs}o^1$ || 2,10,3

perioeci] accolae $p^{fs}o^1$ || 2,10,3 esse] *om.* $p^{fs}o^1$ || 2,10,3 hinc] hic p^{fs} : huic v || 2,10,3 illinc] illic $p^{fs}o^2$ || 2,10,3 circa] a loco qui circa $p^{fs}o^1$: loco qui circa o^2|| 2,10,4 enim[4]] autem $p^{fs}o^1o^2$ || 2,11,4 imperatorem] reges $p^{fs}o^1$ || 2,11,4 neque ex uili aut praecellenti] neque id temere, sed si quid praestantius est eorum qui eliguntur quam quod affinitas afferat aut aetas $p^{fs}o^1$ || 2,11,5 reprehensorum] eorum quae reprehendi solent $p^{fs}o^1$ || 2,11,5 imperatores] reges $p^{fs}o^1$ || 2,11,5 populus ipsorum dominus] dominus ipsorum populus $p^{fs}o^1$ || 2,11,12 est[1]] est uendendo $p^{fs}o^1$ || 2,11,12 assumere] ad magistratum assumere $p^{fs}o^1$: assumere ad magistratum o^2 || 2,11,12 probabiliusque] satius quoque $p^{fs}o^1$ || 2,11,12 fuit] fuisset $p^{fs}o^1o^2$ || 2,11,12 uirorum] bonorum uirorum $p^{fs}o^1$ || 2,11,12 abiecisset] prouidisset $p^{fs}o^1$.

Cuando coincide con otros testimonios en sus lecturas lo hace fundamentalmente con la edición de Valencia de 1473.

1,2,5 homosipios] homosypios $F^4p^{fs}o^2$: ὁμοσιπύους, id est, eadem arca utentes o^1 || 1,2,10 esse animal] animal esse $F^3F^4M^1M^2M^aM^cV^1V^2avbrp^{fs}o^1o^2$ || 1,2,10 nihil] nichil $F^1M^1M^2M^aM^cap^{fs}$ || 1,3,1 sit constituta] constituta sit $vp^{fs}o^1$ || 1,3,1 oportet] oporteat $vp^{fs}o^1$ || 1,9,15 at] ac $vp^{fs}o^1o^2$ || 1,9,15 itaque] quare $p^{fs}o^1o^2$: atque v || 1,11,9 hieme] hyeme $M^1M^2M^aM^cvbrp^{fs}o^1o^2$ || 1,11,9 pretio] precio $F^3M^1M^2M^aV^1avbrp^{fs}o^1$ || 2,1,2 quidem[1] est] est quidem $vp^{fs}o^1$ || 2,1,2 quidem[2]] enim v : *om.* $p^{fs}o^1$: quaedam o^2 || 2,2,2 posset quispiam] quispiam posset $vp^{fs}o^1o^2$ || 2,5,6 diuisae] diuisse M^c : diuersae $vp^{fs}o^1$ || 2,5,6 his] iis $bp^{fs}o^1o^2$ || 2,5,7 sua] *om.* $M^cvp^{fs}o^1$ || 2,5,7 quisque] unusquisque $vp^{fs}o^1$ || 2,6,16 his] iis $M^1V^2p^{fs}o^1o^2$ || 2,6,16 forsan[1]] forsitan $vp^{fs}o^1$ || 2,8,1 hieme] hyeme $F^3F^4M^1M^2M^aM^cvbrp^{fs}o^1o^2$ || 2,8,1 aggressus] agressus $F^3V^1p^{fs}$ || 2,8,25 quocumque] a quocunque $vrp^{fs}o^1o^2$: quotcumque b || 2,9,8 huiuscemodi] huiusmodi $M^1vbp^{fs}o^1o^2$ || 2,9,9 at enim] et enim v : etenim $p^{fs}o^1o^2$ || 2,9,25 decernendi] dicernendi $M^cp^{fs}o^1$ || 2,9,25 et[1]] *om.* $vp^{fs}o^1$|| 2,10,2 qui] ii qui $F^3F^4M^2V^2bp^{fs}o^1o^2$ *et scripserat etiam* F^1, *sed cancellauit* ii *punctis subscriptis* || 2,10,3 hinc] hic p^{fs} : huic v || 2,10,3 illinc] illic $p^{fs}o^2$ || 2,11,4 pretii] precii $M^1M^2M^aM^cV^1avbrp^{fs}o^1$ || 2,11,12 praestantium] praestantiam v : praestantiae $p^{fs}o^1$.

Otro hito importante en la transmisión de esta traducción bruniana es la edición que salió de las prensas de Johann Oporin en Basilea en 1538 (o^1).[16] Esta

---

16   *Aristotelis Stagiritae* [...] *Opera quae quidem extant omnia, latinitate vel iam olim vel nunc recens a viris doctissimis donata, & graecum ad exemplar diligentissime recognita. Acc. in singulos libros optimis ex autoribus argumenta, commentarii vice studiosis futura. Item Io.*

LA TRANSMISIÓN TEXTUAL DE LA VERSIÓN LATINA DE LA *POLÍTICA*　　　113

edición, que corrió a cargo de Luis Vives y Philipp Melanchthon, sigue fiel-
mente el texto editado por Lefèvre d'Étaples. Sólo se aparta de él en contadas
ocasiones, para corregir alguna errata o para incidir en algún detalle no considerado por el editor francés:

> 1,2,5 homosipios] homosypios $F^4p^{fs}o^2$: ὁμοσιπύους, id est, eadem arca
> utentes o^1 || 1,2,10 cupidus] cupidus [est *add.* o^1] ueluti qui nullo retinetur
> iugo, ut neque uolatilia $p^{fs}o^1o^2$ || 1,6,5 et] atque p^{fs} : atqui o^1 || 1,6,5 contin-
> get] contiget p^{fs} || 2,10,3 hinc] hic p^{fs} || 2,10,3 illinc] illic $p^{fs}o^2$.

En cambio, la edición salida también de las prensas de Oporin en 1543 (o^2),[17]
publicada tras la aparición de la segunda edición basiliense del texto griego, se
muestra mucho más comedida a la hora de reproducir los cambios de Lefèvre
d'Étaples. Antes bien, los rechaza en su gran mayoría, y restituye las lecturas de
la tradición textual no espuria. De todos los enumerados con anterioridad sólo
acepta los siguientes cambios:

> 1,2,10 simul] simul natura $p^{fs}o^1o^2$ || 1,2,10 cupidus] cupidus [est *add.* o^1]
> ueluti qui nullo retinetur iugo, ut neque uolatilia $p^{fs}o^1o^2$ || 1,2,10 grega-
> rium] gregarium animal $p^{fs}o^1o^2$ || 1,3,2 coniugali] nam et ipsa proprio
> nomine non nominatur *add.* $p^{fs}o^1o^2$ *post* coniugali || 1,3,2 disciplina] re
> familiari $p^{fs}o^1$: sint autem hae tres quas diximus *add.* $p^{fs}o^1o^2$ *post* discipli-
> na || 1,6,5 retinentes] usurpantes $p^{fs}o^1o^2$ || 1,6,5 aiunt] arbitrantur $p^{fs}o^1o^2$
> || 1,6,5 alicuius iusti] aliquod iustum $p^{fs}o^1o^2$ || 1,6,5 non aiunt] non iustam
> esse aiunt $p^{fs}o^1o^2$ || 1,6,9 non] quod $p^{fs}o^1o^2$ || 1,8,4 nam] quapropter $p^{fs}o^1o^2$
> || 1,8,4 itaque] quare $p^{fs}o^1o^2$ || 1,8,4 faciunt] fecerunt $p^{fs}o^1o^2$ || 1,8,5 uictus]
> uictus atque delectum $p^{fs}o^1o^2$ || 1,8,5 earum] ipsarum $p^{fs}o^1o^2$ || 1,9,15 eius-
> dem] eiusdem rei $p^{fs}o^1o^2$ || 1,9,15 existens] cum sit $p^{fs}o^1o^2$ || 1,9,15 eiusdem]
> ipsius $p^{fs}o^1o^2$ || 1,9,15 est usus] usus $p^{fs}o^1o^2$ || 1,9,15 huius uero] illius uero
> $p^{fs}o^1o^2$ || 1,9,15 itaque] quare $p^{fs}o^1o^2$: atque v || 1,11,9 studium] studium
> propter inopiam $p^{fs}o^1o^2$ || 1,11,9 hieme] hyeme $M^1M^2M^aM^cvbrp^{fs}o^1o^2$ ||
> 2,2,2 eo procedente] ea si procedat $p^{fs}o^1o^2$ || 2,5,6 erunt] erunt ad usum
> $p^{fs}o^1o^2$ || 2,5,6 his] iis $bp^{fs}o^1o^2$ || 2,8,1 autem] autem Euryphontis $p^{fs}o^1o^2$
> || 2,8,6 his] iis $p^{fs}o^1o^2$ || 2,8,6 aliis] in aliis $p^{fs}o^1o^2$ || 2,8,25 uel] an $p^{fs}o^1o^2$

---

    *Lodovico Vivis Valentini de libris Aristotelicis censura nunc recens & nata et ed. Ad haec de
vita Aristotelis, deque genere philosophiae, ac scriptis eiusdem commentatio doctissima, per
Philippum Melanchthonem* (Basileae, 1538).

17　*Aristotelis Stagiritae, philosophorum omnium facile principis, opera quae in hunc usque
diem extant omnia, latinitate partim antea, partim nunc primum à Viris doctissimis donata,
& Graecum ad exemplar diligenter recognita* (Basileae, 1542).

|| 2,9,11 irrefragantes] exercentes $p^{fs}o^1o^2$ || 2,9,11 assuefacti] assuefactos $p^{fs}o^1o^2$ || 2,9,11 utilitatis] uirtutis $p^{fs}o^1o^2$ || 2,10,3 illinc] illic $p^{fs}o^2$ || 2,10,4 enim[4]] autem $p^{fs}o^1o^2$ || 2,11,12 fuit] fuisset $p^{fs}o^1o^2$.

E introduce lecturas propias:

1,6,9 quibus] quibus ob idipsum $p^{fs}o^1$: quibus quod ob idipsum o^2 || 2,5,19 sustinentibus] erit iis qui sustinent $p^{fs}o^1$: accedet sustinentibus o^2 || 2,10,3 circa] a loco qui circa $p^{fs}o^1$: loco qui circa o^2 || 2,11,12 assumere] ad magistratum assumere $p^{fs}o^1$: assumere ad magistratum o^2.

Concluye aquí esta breve valoración crítico-textual de estos diecisiete testimonios textuales de la traducción bruniana de la *Política*. Aunque el número considerado es corto y no ha sido posible establecer un *stemma codicum*, ya se han establecido unas primeras líneas generales para el estudio de la transmisión textual de esta obra de Bruni, que podrán ser corroboradas en estudios futuros con el cotejo de otros testimonios.

Universidad de Granada

Communications

CHAPTER 6

La *Compendiosa Historia Hispanica* (1470) como fuente en el primer Renacimiento castellano

Guillermo Alvar Nuño

Abstract

La producción escrita de Rodrigo Sánchez de Arévalo (1404–70) ha sido considerada en un discreto segundo plano por los estudiosos de la Castilla del s. xv, y ello a pesar de que gozó de una pluma prolija. La *Compendiosa Historia Hispanica* (Roma, 1470) fue una crónica que hizo imprimir en Roma justo al final de su vida, pero, a pesar de la extensión de la obra y de que debió gozar de un prestigio grande en su época, no existe ningún trabajo que haya estudiado la influencia que ha podido tener en autores posteriores. La presente contribución tiene por objetivo señalar en qué medida fue conocida por otros eruditos castellanos y, a continuación, cómo ha resultado ser fuente directa para dos autores: Antonio de Nebrija y fray Gonzalo de Arredondo.

Keywords

Rodrigo Sánchez de Arévalo – *Compendiosa Historia Hispanica* (1470) – Neo-Latin historiography – Lorenzo Galíndez de Carvajal – Antonio de Nebrija

1 Introducción y objetivos del estudio

La producción escrita de Rodrigo Sánchez de Arévalo (1404–70) ha sido considerada en un discreto segundo plano por los estudiosos de la Castilla del s. xv, y ello a pesar de que gozó de una pluma prolija. Su faceta de historiador no ha corrido mejor suerte. Tate lo explicaba de la manera siguiente:[1]

> La razón por la que Sánchez de Arévalo nunca ha figurado de manera destacada en la historia cultural de Castilla es que, como otros clérigos

---

[1] Robert Brian Tate, *Ensayos sobre la historiografía peninsular del siglo XV* (Madrid, 1970), 74.

contemporáneos y compañeros suyos, Carvajal, Torquemada y Juan de Mella, pasó los años más activos de su vida en Italia al servicio del Vaticano.

A ello hay que añadir que, salvo dos obritas redactadas en castellano, el resto de su obra fue redactada en latín. La *Compendiosa Historia Hispanica* (Roma, 1470) fue una crónica que hizo imprimir en Roma justo al final de su vida. Se trata de la primera Historia de un país moderno que fue impresa, y pretendía dar a conocer los hechos de la Península Ibérica en los círculos intelectuales de la curia papal, en otras palabras, fue escrita para un público internacional. A pesar de la extensión de la obra, y de que debió gozar de un prestigio grande en su época – se conservan 13 copias manuscritas de la *editio princeps* así como dos reediciones –,[2] no existe ningún trabajo que haya estudiado la influencia que ha podido tener en autores posteriores. La presente contribución tiene por objetivo señalar en qué medida fue conocida por otros eruditos castellanos y, a continuación, cómo ha resultado ser fuente directa para dos autores: Antonio de Nebrija y fray Gonzalo de Arredondo.

2   Autores que conocieron la obra de Rodrigo Sánchez de Arévalo

Hay algunos datos que prueban que la *Compendiosa Historia Hispanica* de Rodrigo Sánchez de Arévalo fue conocida por los cronistas de época de los Reyes Católicos, especialmente por aquéllos que se educaron en Salamanca. Lorenzo Galíndez de Carvajal es un ejemplo claro de ello. Se licenció en Leyes por el Estudio de Salamanca y regentó la cátedra de Vísperas de Leyes en 1497 y la de Prima desde 1504 en dicha Universidad. Además, fue consejero de los Reyes Católicos, censor de cronistas de reinados anteriores y cronista regio él mismo. Realizó una mención escueta, pero elogiosa, de la *Compensiosa Historia Hispanica* de Sánchez de Arévalo en su *Crónica del Rey don Juan el Segundo*, que era una revisión de la crónica redactada por Fernán Pérez de Guzmán. En el prefacio a su obra, dedicado el rey Carlos I, Galíndez de Carvajal advertía de los peligros que corrían los monarcas al delegar en terceros el gobierno del Estado[3] y describía al buen monarca como aquél que cumplía con su Oficio Real. Y concluye el prefacio con la cita a la que aludo:[4]

---

2   Cf. Guillermo Alvar Nuño, *Estudio, edición crítica y traducción de la* Compendiosa Historia Hispanica *de Rodrigo Sánchez de Arévalo* (Madrid, 2017), 150.

3   Lorenzo Galíndez de Carvajal, *Crónica del Rey don Juan el Segundo*, BAE LXVIII, (Madrid, 1877), 274: "Y que nunca la confianza que tienen de sus ministros sea tan excesiva, que los descuide del todo para olvidar el cargo que tienen."

4   Galíndez de Carvajal, *Crónica* (véase arriba, n. 3), 275.

LA *COMPENDIOSA HISTORIA HISPANICA* (1470)

Y porque para esto se podrian traer grandes exemplos y muchas auctori-
dades, que aunque hiciesen caso, saldrian fuera de mi propósito, bastará
si esta materia les agradare y quisieren en ella mas alargarse, que vean á
Eneas Sivio Papa Pio, en su tratado: *De miseriis curialium*; y á nuestro Don
Rodrigo, Obispo de Palencia, en su *Crónica* deste Rey, y en su *Speculum
uitae humanae*, quando habla en esta materia.

Se sabe que Galíndez de Carvajal poseyó un manuscrito, el MS f.i.18 de la
Biblioteca del Real Monasterio de El Escorial, fechado en el s. XVI,[5] en el que
hoy se conservan dos obras, el *Cronica Hispaniae* de Lucas de Tuy y la *Historiae
Hispanicae libri IV* [sic] de Arévalo, es decir, su *Compendiosa Historia Hispanica*.
En el fol. 1v de dicho ejemplar se puede leer la siguiente nota al margen:

Hic incipit prologus et historia diaconi lucae tudensis extracta jubssu
petri ponce epi. placentini ex libro vetusto membranis conscripto, reper-
to in bibliotheca doctoris laurentii galindez de carvajal.

Según dicha nota, este ejemplar fue copiado de otro que perteneció a la biblioteca privada de Lorenzo Galíndez de Carvajal y, aunque el texto citado
hace referencia a la obra de Lucas de Tuy, tanto esta obra como la crónica de
Arévalo fueron copiadas por la misma mano.[6] En la hoja de guarda del manuscrito hay también una anotación de la mano del humanista Ambrosio de
Morales (1513–91). Cuando el rey Felipe II estaba adquiriendo obras para la
Biblioteca de El Escorial, envió a Morales a revisar qué obras poseía el obispo Pedro Ponce de León (1509–73), un gran coleccionista de libros que llegó
a reunir una gran biblioteca;[7] entre sus fondos se encontraba el mencionado
ejemplar de la *Compendiosa* conservado en El Escorial.[8]

Por otro lado, Galíndez de Carvajal escribió de su puño y letra una anotación
de un pasaje en el margen de otra de las copias de la *Compendiosa Historia
Hispanica*, conservada en el MS Colección Salazar cod. G-2, [ahora 9/451

---

5 Cf. Guillermo Antolín, *Catálogo de los códices latinos de la Real Biblioteca del Escorial*, vol. 2
   (Madrid, 1911), 144.
6 Se puede leer una descripción del manuscrito f.i.18 en Alvar Nuño, *Estudio* (véase arriba,
   n. 2), 167–8.
7 Cf. Méndez Hernán, "Notas para el estudio de la platería, y sus patronos, en la ciudad de
   Plasencia. El orive Lorenzo Mesurado," en *Estudios de Platería*, ed. Jesús Rivas Carmona e
   Ignacio José García Zapata (Murcia, 2006), 451–4.
8 Sobre este asunto, cf. Gregorio Andrés Martínez, "Carta de Pedro Ponde de León, obispo de
   Plasencia a Felipe II sobre las reliquias y librerías de su obispado y sus actividades literarias,"
   Revista de estudios extremeños 23.1 (1967), 5–21.

(9-3-4)].[9] El pasaje y la anotación en cuestión se encuentran en el fol. 282v. Para entender la anotación de Lorenzo Galíndez de Caraval, es necesario leer el pasaje de la *Compendiosa Historia Hispanica*; decía Sánchez de Arévalo lo siguiente (*Comp.* 4,36,89–98):[10]

> Post predicta Henricus Hispalim rediit duxitque uxorem dominam Iohannam, filiam Eduardi regis Portugalie, facto tamen primo diuortio apostolica auctoritate a domina Blanca, filia Iohannis regis Aragonum consanguinea sua, quam prius duxerat uxorem. Expleuit autem solemnia nuptialia dominus archiepiscopus Turonensis orator missus per dominum Carolum VI regem Francie ad eundem regem Henricum. Deinde Henricus ex eadem Iohanna regina genuit inclytam filiam Elisabeth, quam cuncti regni status in primogenitam iurarunt simul et receperunt.

De ahí que Galíndez de Carvajal realizara la siguiente corrección:

> Aditio.
> Fallitur uehementer auctor complacere cupiens pocius Henrrico quam ueritati. Nam hec non Elisabet, sed Iohanna Henrrici huius exposita uel inposita filia fuit, uulgo Beltraneja nuncupata, que fuit iurata adulatorie uel adulterine ut regi et regine complacerent iurantes neque misterio uacat Elisabet pro Iohanna hac nuncupatur adulterina filia Deo agente sublata nomine. Sic fuit priuata sucesione uel a legitima quam Iohannis regis filia Elisabet nominata sic Deo uiuente fuit prelata in regnorum sucesione et felicissime uidimus regnasse.
> Caruajal.

Parece difícil que Sánchez de Arévalo, capellán de Enrique IV y embajador suyo al más alto nivel, a quien, por cierto, dedicó su obra histórica, se confundiera de un modo tan palmario, pues se trataba de una cuestión de la máxima relevancia. Lo más plausible es pensar que Arévalo tuviera este pasaje redactado antes del Tratado de Guisando (1468), en el cual se nombró Princesa de

---

9 Parte de la información codicológica de este manuscrito ha sido consultada en Baltasar Cuartero Huerta y Antonio de Vargas-Zúñiga, *Índice de la colección de don Luis Salazar y Castro*, vol. 21 (Madrid, 1958), 13. Por otro lado, conviene mencionar que tanto el manuscrito escurialense (f.1.18) como el de la RAH (9/451), son copias de otro ejemplar que ya no existe o está desaparecido. El análisis de variantes textuales de ambos ejemplares se encuentra en Alvar Nuño, *Estudio* (véase arriba, n. 2), 181–3.

10 Todos los textos latinos de la *Compendiosa* han sido extraídos de Alvar Nuño, *Estudio* (véase arriba, n. 2).

LA *COMPENDIOSA HISTORIA HISPANICA* (1470)

Asturias y heredera del reino de Castilla a Isabel en detrimento de Juana la Beltraneja. Al redactar la *Compendiosa*, se habría presentado en un primer momento a Juana la Beltraneja como heredera jurada por los estados del reino, pero, tras la firma del tratado, Arévalo debió corregir de manera apresurada el pasaje, sustituyendo el nombre de Juana por el de Isabel.

Otro autor que conoció la obra de Rodrigo Sánchez de Arévalo fue Diego Rodríguez de Almela.[11] Ambos eran discípulos de un mismo maestro, Alfonso de Cartagena y, de hecho, Almela era además familiar de Cartagena. Ostentó los cargos de cronista y capellán de Isabel la Católica. De acuerdo con Tate y Torres Fontes,[12] Almela estuvo en Roma por asuntos de su capítulo catedralicio en 1464, y después por más tiempo entre 1466 y 1467, por lo que el contacto entre ambos debió ser duradero y fecundo. Allí conoció los escritos históricos de Arévalo, en concreto, una versión previa a la *Compendiosa* y que la tradición textual ha conocido como *Breuis historia Hispanie*.[13] A cambio, Almela le daría a conocer su *Valerio de las estorias escolásticas*, obra citada con frecuencia en la *Compendiosa Historia Hispanica*. En Roma, Almela "[pudo cumplir] anhelos propios, así como el reencuentro con su amigo Arévalo, mayor que él y más experimentado, que le facilitaría puerta abierta para conocer y convivir en el ambiente humanista de la corte pontificia".[14]

Un último autor de quien hay pruebas irrefutables de que conoció a Sánchez de Arévalo fue Elio Antonio de Nebrija. Éste, al escribir su tratadito pedagógico *De liberis educandis* (1509), tuvo como modelo buscado[15] el opúsculo *Breuis tractatus de arte, disciplina et modo alendi et erudiendi filios, pueros et iuuenes* de Sánchez de Arévalo, escrito hacia el año 1453.[16] Se ha apuntado la

---

11   Acerca de la influencia de Sánchez de Arévalo en Rodríguez de Almela, cf. Robert Brian Tate, "An Apology for Monarchy. A Study of an Unpublished 15th-Century Castilian Historical Pamphlet," *Romance Philology* 15 (1961), 111–23.

12   Brian Tate, "An Apology" (véase arriba, n. 7), 118; Brian Tate, *Ensayos* (véase arriba, n. 1), 115; Juan Torres Fontes, *Diego Rodríguez de Almela: Valerio de las Estorias Escolásticas e de España* (Murcia, 1994), XVIII–XX.

13   Cf. Alvar Nuño, *Estudio* (véase arriba, n. 2), 130–1.

14   Torres Fontes, *Diego* (véase arriba, n. 6), XIX–XX.

15   Acerca de la terminología de dependencia textual entre obras diferentes, como es el caso de 'modelo buscado', vid. Gérard Genette, *Palimpsestes. La littérature au second degré* (París, 1982); Antonio Alvar Ezquerra "Tipología de los procedimientos intertextuales en la poesía latina antigua," *IX Congreso Español de Estudios Clásicos: Madrid, 27 al 30 de septiembre de 1995*, vol. 5 (Madrid, 1998), 3–16.

16   Cf. José López de Toro, "El primer tratado de pedagogía en España (1453)," *Boletín de la Universidad de Granada* 5 (1933), 262–5, cuyos datos confirmaron Lorenzo Velázquez y Pedro Arias, "Rodrigo Sánchez de Arévalo. Manera de criar a los hijos," *Cuadernos de anuario filosófico* 9 (1999), 5–128, en 22–42, y Tomás González Rolán y Pilar Saquero Suárez-Somonte, "La primera huella de Plutarco latinizado en la Castilla de mediados

122   ALVAR NUÑO

posibilidad de que los dos escritores castellanos se hubieran podido conocer en Roma en 1463, siendo ya Arévalo alcaide de la fortaleza papal de Sant'Angelo y encontrándose Nebrija de camino a Bolonia.[17]

3 La *Compendiosa Historia Hispanica* como fuente directa

La *Compendiosa Historia Hispanica* gozó de un éxito relativo. Tuvo el honor de tener una *editio princeps* (Roma, 1470) en la imprenta de Ulrich Han, lo que hizo que fuera la primera crónica de un país moderno en ser impresa. Tuvo, además, una difusión manuscrita razonable, pues de ella se han conservado 13 manuscritos y una traducción al italiano; sin embargo, todos ellos datan del siglo XV o de principios del XVI.[18] Hubo que esperar a 1579 para ser reeditada (Andreas Wechsel, Frankfurt) y su última reimpresión tuvo lugar en 1603, en la colección *Hispania illustrata* de Andreas Schott. Hay dos razones que justifican que no gozara de un éxito mayor: por un lado, el latín de Arévalo, cuyo estilo era más escolástico que humanista y, por otro, la actitud ciertamente favorable que mostraba en su crónica hacia Enrique IV, monarca bajo el que había medrado profesionalemente.

Con todo, la obra dejó su impronta en algunos autores,[19] de los que se pretende destacar a dos en esta contribución. El primero, Nebrija, pues hasta ahora había pasado inadvertido que la *Compendiosa Historia Hispanica* de Arévalo sirvió de fuente directa en la redacción del prólogo castellano a las *Introduciones latinas contrapuesto el romance al latín* (*ca.* 1488), que fue tan ponderado por Rico como ejemplo de humanismo.[20] La versión bilingüe de las

---

      del siglo XV: el tratado pedagógico de Rodrigo Sánchez de Arévalo," *Revista de Estudios Latinos* 7 (2007), 131–52, en 137–8.

17   Cf. Velázquez y Arias, "Rodrigo" (véase arriba, n. 10), 23–4.

18   Cf. Alvar Nuño, *Estudio* (véase arriba, n. 2), 150.

19   Como es lógico, la *Compendiosa* influyó primero en el seno del círculo de discípulos de Alfonso de Cartagena. Es muy interesante el caso de Diego Rodríguez de Almela, pues existió una influencia mutua: de éste hacia aquél, cf. Antonio López Fonseca y José Manuel Ruiz Vila, *Rodrigo Sánchez de Arévalo. Deberes y funciones de generales, capitanes y gobernadores* (Madrid, 2011), 46–57, y Alvar Nuño, *Estudio* (véase arriba, n. 2), 128–31, pero también en sentido contrario, como señaló Tate, "An Apology" (véase arriba, n. 6), 118. Otro discípulo de Cartagena, Mosén Diego de Valera, también conoció la *Compendiosa*, según ha señalado Miguel Ángel Ladero Quesada "Fray Gonzalo de Arredondo, cronista de Enrique III, Juan II y Enrique IV de Castilla. Texto inédito," *Medievalismo* 16 (2006) 271–88, en 273: "Almela y Valera conocían ya la obra de Sánchez de Arévalo". Estas relaciones merecen ser estudiadas con mayor detenimiento.

20   Me parece indispensable recuperar algunas de las afirmaciones de Rico en torno al prólogo a las *Introduciones latinae, contrapuesto el romance al latín*; en concreto, Francisco Rico

LA *COMPENDIOSA HISTORIA HISPANICA* (1470)

Introductiones latinae se realizó por orden de la propia reina ("ipsius Reginae imperio") para que las monjas de Castilla pudieran conocer algo de lengua latina sin salir de sus monasterios y conventos.[21] No es difícil imaginar que Nebrija conociera la *Compendiosa* de Arévalo, ya que debió lograr cierta difusión en Castilla al poco de ser impresa;[22] por otro lado, se sabe que Nebrija firmó un contrato[23] como lector en la Universidad de Salamanca el 4 de julio de 1475, y el 22 de enero del año siguiente firma la Cátedra de Prima Gramática, que había obtenido por oposición. Lo más probable es que la biblioteca de la Universidad poseyera ya un ejemplar de la *Compendiosa* que pudo ser consultado Nebrija.

La presencia de la *Compendiosa* en las *Introductiones* no es literal; sin embargo, Nebrija siguió en términos generales la disposición de la información geográfica tal como la presentó Sánchez de Arévalo, así como parte del léxico que éste había empleado. Nebrija resumió en pocas palabras lo que en Arévalo abarcaba los capítulos uno (elogio del aire y ubicación de Hispania), dos (elogio a la feracidad de la tierra hispana), tres (elogio a las riquezas minerales y otras materias primas) y cuatro (elogio a las cualidades de las gentes de Hispania), que son una *Laus Hispaniae*, convertida en tópico literario,[24] pero muy fundamentada con la inclusión de autores clásicos, tanto latinos como griegos en traducción latina.[25] Nebrija, además, siguió el mismo orden

---

"Un prólogo al Renacimiento español. La dedicatoria de Nebrija a las *Introduciones latinas* (1488)," en *Seis lecciones sobre la España de los Siglos de Oro*, ed. Pedro Manuel Piñero Ramírez y Rogelio Reyes Cano (Sevilla – Burdeos, 1981), 59–94, en 66–7: "No es necesario comentar aquí con la detención conveniente, frase por frase, esas páginas admirables [sc. el prólogo de las *introduciones latinas, contrapuesto el romance al latín*]. Por ahora, pretendo sólo sacarlas un poco del olvido en que se arrastran, frente al desproporcionado cacareo en torno al preámbulo de la *Gramática castellana*," y en 68–9: "Nebrija se propone deslumbrarla con una visión más afín a la florentina de la 'lengua del imperio' que al intangible 'imperio de la lengua': el auge del castellano debe seguir al imperio de Castilla, cual ocurrió con asirios o egipcios, hebreos, griegos y romanos."

21 Cf. Rico, "Un prólogo" (véase arriba, n. 15), 62–4.

22 A día de hoy, se conservan 68 ejemplares de la *editio princpes*, de los que 15 se encuentran en bibliotecas españolas. Todas las copias manuscritas de la *Compendiosa* fueron realizadas a partir de la *editio princeps*. Sobre este asunto, cf. Alvar Nuño, *Estudio* (véase arriba, n. 2), 150–214.

23 Cf. Miguel Ángel Esparza y Vicente Calvo, *Introducciones latinas contrapuesto el romance al latín* (Münster, 1996), VII–VIII.

24 Acerca de la tradición de la *Laus Hispaniae* como tópico literario, vid. Antonio Alvar Ezquerra, "Spain," en *Europatria*, ed. Francisco Oliveira (Coímbra, 2013), 433–80.

25 Cf. Alvar Nuño, *Estudio* (véase arriba, n. 2), 81: "Esta primera parte es acaso la menos histórica *sensu stricto*, y también la más personal, pues contiene una fuerte carga ideológica. Una buena parte de ella está consagrada a anticipar los contenidos del grueso de la obra. Sánchez de Arévalo echó mano de una cantidad enorme de fuentes clásicas – geógrafos griegos y romanos – cuya función consistía, como se ha visto, en robustecer las ideas del

narrativo que el dispuesto por Arévalo, con una sola excepción: intercambió los capítulos dos y tres de la *Compendiosa*, de modo que presentó en su prólogo a las *Introduciones* primero el elogio a los metales y materias primas, y luego lo concerniente a la feracidad de Hispania. Para mostrar cómo usa Nebrija el texto arevaliano, valgan como ejemplos de romanceamiento y transformación la descripción de la abundancia de metales preciosos en Hispania:

> No quiero agora dezir como **toda esta preñada de minedos de oro, de plata, de hierro y de todos los otros metales** la inuencion delos quales no menos que todas lasotras buenas artes esta oy entre nos otros perdida.

Que se corresponde con el siguiente pasaje de la *Compendiosa* (*Comp.* 1,3,8–12):

> **Est itaque Hispanie terra mineris auri et argenti et aliorum metallorum ditissima**, si solerter inquiruntur. **Ferrariis quoque ultra ceteras orbis plagas abundat**, adeo ut etiam aquas generet, quibus ferrum acrius temperatur.

Y el elogio a las cualidades de los hispanos:

> Vengo alo ques proprio del ombre: ninguna otra nacion, como dize Trogo Pompeio, **es tan sufrida de hambre, calor, frio, trabaio**, tan constante & fiel en las alianças publicas & amistades priuadas – **como parece en los saguntinos & aquel sieruo que en vengança de su señor mato al principe & capitan delos carthagineses-, tan cobdiciosa dela honra & saber & osar morir por ella.**

Que están tomados de los siguientes pasajes de la *Compendiosa*:

> Demum ut uirtutes corporeas non omittamus, habent Hispani corpora, ut ueteribus placuit, ad **inediam et labores aptissima**, quarumuis corporis et animi fatigationum patientissima, duram obseruant et astrictam parsimoniam, uigilias, **solem et hiemem, famem quoque ac sitim pati, et queuis pericula pro patria sustinere et pro honore adire paratissimi sunt.** (Comp. 1,4,41–46)

---

autor ante un público humanista. Los primeros cuatro capítulos hablan de los diferentes aspectos geográficos de Hispania: salubridad de su aire, fertilidad y fecundidad de su tierra, abundancia mineral e industrial, y virtudes y devoción de los habitantes de la Península."

LA *COMPENDIOSA HISTORIA HISPANICA* (1470)   125

> Huic genti obedire dominis natura est, non quidem uiolentia, sed amore, et cui semel dedere fidem, prestitere simul et uitam. **Testis est, ut cetera taceamus, illa Saguntinorum non modo fortitudo sed expectata ad socios fides**, ut Liuius, deinde Valerius, referunt. (Comp. 1,4,116–120)

> Cuius rei celebratur etiam bello **Punico serui Hispani fides et patientia, qui ultus dominum inter tormenta risu exultauit serenaque letitia crudelitatem seuientium uicit.** (Comp. 1,4,134–136)

Otro autor que se sirvió ampliamente de la Historia de Arévalo fue fray Gonzalo de Arredondo, quien redactó en castellano la *Coronica brevemente sacada de los excelentisimos fechos del vienaventurado caballero de gloriosa memoria conde Fernan Gonçales.*[26] A pesar del título, se narran los sucesos históricos castellanos hasta el reinado de Enrique IV. Ladero Quesada fechó esta obra poco después de 1480,[27] es decir, diez años después de la publicación de la *Compendiosa Historia Hispanica.* Él ya se dio cuenta de la dependencia textual de Arredondo con Sánchez de Arévalo – la otra fuente principal de la *Coronica de Fernan Gonçales* fue la *Corónica de España* de Diego de Valera, impresa en Sevilla en 1482, quien a su vez conocía la obra de Arévalo–. Sánchez de Arévalo y Diego de Valera son, por tanto, los modelos buscados, que determinan la arquitectura compositiva de la *Coronica de Fernan Gonçales.* Los relatos históricos de los tres autores se insertan en la línea historiográfica del goticismo castellano,[28] que hundía sus raíces en el inicio mismo de la Reconquista[29] y que tuvo un primer punto culminante durante los reinados de Fernando III y Alfonso X y un segundo renacer a mediados del siglo XV gracias a la *Anacephaleosis* de

---

26 Se ha consultado el MS RAH 9/2047. Sobre los códices conservados de esta obra, vid. José Simón Díaz, *Bibliografía de la Literatura Hispánica*, vol. 6 (Madrid, 1973), 69–71.

27 Ladero Quesada, "Fray Gonzalo" (véase arriba, n. 13), 272–3.

28 Cf. José Manuel Nieto Soria, "La realeza," en *Orígenes de la monarquía hispánica: Propaganda y legitimación (ca. 1400–1520)*, ed. José Manuel Nieto Soria (Madrid, 1999), 25–103, en 42: "Es precisamente en la persona del prelado recién nombrado [Alfonso de Cartagena] donde encontramos el eslabón determinante en el que se engarzan los autores de obras históricas de mediados del siglo XV preocupados, cuando no obsesionados, por legitimar históricamente los intereses de la monarquía castellana, en conexión con un cierto concepto de hispanidad, como es el caso de Rodrigo Sánchez de Arévalo, junto a aquellos otros autores más tardíos que harán otro tanto, ya en plena coincidencia con el reinado de los Reyes Católicos, entre los que cabe destacar al canónigo de Murcia y capellán y cronista real Diego Rodríguez de Almela."

29 Cf. Gaëlle Le Morvan, "Reinos e imperio: la *Historia Legionensis* (llamada *Silensis*) y la reivindicación leonesa de la herencia visigótica," *e-Spania* 14, URL: http://e-spania.revues .org/2168 [visitado por última vez el 10-06-2019].

Alfonso de Cartagena.[30] La *Compendiosa Historia Hispanica* constituye un eslabón fundamental en esta cadena, pues su propio modelo buscado era la *Anacephaleosis*.

Fray Gonzalo de Arredondo, pues, romanzó *ad pedem litterae* extractos muy amplios de la *Compendiosa*: valgan como ejemplo dos pasajes que mencionó Ladero Quesada (2006) confrontando uno y otro texto. Así vertió Arredondo al castellano la descripción de don Álvaro de Luna realizada por Arévalo:

> Et ut paucis agamus, idem Aluarus prudens, sagax et astutus plurimum fuit, quia ut Redemptor ait: "Filii huius seculi prudentiores sunt filiis lucis." Fuit denique simulans ea uelle que nollet. His uero quos oderat affabilis et quasi beneuolus apparens, balbutiens sed facetus eloquio erat, repentinis responsionibus aut consiliis melior quam meditatis, ut alter Tiberius. Verum fuit in bellis strenuus insuper et animosus, nec defuerunt qui dicerent eum magis felicem quam strenuum aut fortem. Denique plurimas uirtutes participabat, si eas cum magis expediebat, non deseruisset aut recte uti uoluisset. Fauit ei fortuna longo tempore, et tamdiu cuncta ei prospere obuenerunt quamdiu regio honori et bono publico animum dedit. Demum uero eius consilio et animi magnitudine acta sunt. Demum uero cum status sui incrementa, ut aiunt, supra modum quereret et, ut paucis agam, cuncta suo arbitrio uellet, uirtutes pristinas sua dominandi cupidine obumbrauit. (*Comp.* 1,3,8–12)

> E porque muchos en silençio pongamos, fue este don Albaro muy prudente e sagaz e astuto ca segund nuestro redenptor dize los fijos de este siglo más prudentes son que los fijos de la luz, e simulaba aquellas cosas querer que no quería, ca era afable al paresçer e simulábase veníbolo a los que mal quería, e en las responsiones o consejos más prudente de presto que no en las pensadas vien, ansí como aquel Tiberio, e en las vatallas muy estrenuo, e sobre todo animoso. Mas no desfallesçieron quienes dixiesen que era más dichoso que no strenuo o fuerte en las vatallas e ansi por conseguiente participaba en muchas virtudes si de ellas según natura quisiera usar, enpero favoresçiole la fortuna muy luengo tiempo e tanto todas las cosas le venieron prósperas quanto tovo su ánimo e coraçón a la corona real e vien público, en el qual tiempo muchas cosas nobles por su consejo e mananimidad ansi en paz como en guerra fueron

---

30   Sobre la recuperación de una perspectiva historiográfica panhispánica, cf. Robert Brian Tate, "The Rewriting of Historical Past. *Hispania et Europa,*" en *L'histoire et les nouveaux publics dans l'Europe médiévale (XIII–XV siècles)*, ed. Jean Philippe Genet, (París, 1997), 241–57.

LA *COMPENDIOSA HISTORIA HISPANICA* (1470) 127

fechas. E finalmente como su estado por grand codiçia sobremanera quisiese alçar, sus virtudes primeras olbidó e por su causa muchas cosas malas ordió e fizo ansí con grandes como con pequeños en estos reygnos de España. (*Coronica Fernan Gonçales* cap. 23, fol. 364r)

Quizás el pasaje más interesante que romanceó Gonzalo de Arredondo fue el de la muerte de Álvaro de Luna, pues en él se refiere la última confesión del condestable antes de ser decapitado. Si es de creer la noticia que transmite Arredondo, el religioso que acompañó a Álvaro de Luna en su hora suprema fue, precisamente, Sánchez de Arévalo, único de los historiadores de su época que contó al detalle este episodio. Así dice, en primer lugar, el pasaje de Arévalo (*Comp.* 4,33,62–63):

> Nouimus nos uirum uita et sapientia integerrimum qui Aluarum in foro ad supplicium adductum consolabatur, inter cetera dicens ea lege humanam prosperitatem atque uitam ipsam quam illico dimissurus esset, suscepisset, ut aliquando ab eo auferri deberet. Quia, nostro Seneca teste, nihil fortuna eripit nisi quod dedit, immo, ut Iulius Celsus ait, quos fortuna beneficiis lustrat, ad duriorem casum reseruat.

Éste evitó mencionarse a sí mismo de manera expresa como el sacerdote que acompañaba a Álvaro de Luna en dicho pasaje, aunque la alusión explícita a haber conocido personalmente a quien consolaba al condestable, así como a la conversación que mantuvieron ambos, deja poco lugar a dudas. Por su parte, Gonzalo de Arredondo vertió el pasaje de la manera siguiente, dejando claro que fue quien asistió al noble castellano (*Coronica Fernan Gonçales* cap. 23, fol. 368r):

> E como el mismo don Álbaro de Luna, maestre de Santiago, estouiese puesto en un mui alto estrado en meytad de la plaça de Valladolid para le degollar, el muy reverendo don rodrigo Sánchez obispo de Palencia le aconsolando entre otras cosas dezía al maestre que le plugiese de grado y a Dios enconmendando su prosperidat e vida a Dios la ofresçer pues segund Séneca ninguna cosa la fortuna lleba sino lo que dio, y segund aquel Julio Çelso dize a aquellos que la fortuna faboresçe con benefiçios a muy dura cayda los guarda.

Por último, Ladero Quesada[31] se sorprendió de que Arredondo hiciera a Isabel la Católica hija de Enrique IV y Juana de Portugal con las siguientes palabras:

---

31   Ladero Quesada, "Fray Gonzalo …" (véase arriba, n. 13), 274.

"Algo más adelante, hace alusión al segundo matrimonio del monarca con Juana de Portugal aunque comete la equivocación inexplicable – salvo por error del copista – de hacer hija de esta unión … ¡a Isabel!" Como se ha mostrado al inicio de esta investigación,[32] el error es en realidad muy fácilmente explicable, y es que Gonzalo de Arredondo no estaba haciendo otra cosa que verter en lengua castellana a Sánchez de Arévalo, pero sin reflexionar sobre lo que escribía. Y, cosas de la vida, del mismo modo que Lorenzo Galíndez de Carvajal le enmendó la plana a Rodrigo Sánchez de Arévalo, un lector anónimo de finales del s. XVI enmendó nuevamente este grosero error,[33] cometido ahora por Arredondo (*Coronica Fernan Gonçales* cap. 24, fol. 369v):

> E finalmente segund su nobleza todas las cosas noblemente fechas vinose a Sevilla donde resçebió por mujer a la mui noble doña Juana fija de Eduardo rey de Portogal pero hecho primero el apartamiento por autoridat apostólica de doña Blanca, fija del rey don Juan de Aragón, su parienta, la qual toviera primero por mujer. E acabó estos solenes casamientos el muy reverendo señor arçobispo de Turonia enviado por enbaxador del muy noble don Carolo sexto de Françia el mesmo rey don Enrique. Y ovo este noble rey don Enrrique de su reigna doña Juana a doña ~~Ysabel~~ **Juana** a la qual todos los grandes del reygno la juraron y resçebieron por primojénita.

4   Conclusiones

A primera vista, la *Compendiosa Historia Hispanica* (1470) no tuvo un éxito rotundo y fue rápidamente relegada al olvido por los historiadores posteriores. Sin embargo, sí parece claro que fue una obra conocida, sobre todo entre los eruditos formados en la Universidad de Salamanca, tal y como demuestran las evidencias manuscritas, y también entre otros discípulos de Alfonso de Cartagena. Al analizar las relaciones textuales con obras posteriores con más detenimiento, se advierte una cierta influencia en diferentes ámbitos. Así, los datos geográficos que proporcionó en la descripción de la Península Ibérica fueron reutilizados por Rodríguez de Almela en su *Compendio historial* y por Antonio de Nebrija en sus *Introductiones latinae*. Por otro lado, la línea historiográfica del goticismo retomada por Alfonso de Cartagena y con la que

---

32   En el primer pasaje citado (*Comp.* 4, 36, 89–98).

33   Resalto en negrita la corrección del lector del s. XVI.

LA *COMPENDIOSA HISTORIA HISPANICA* (1470)   129

logró destacados éxitos diplomáticos y literarios,[34] cobra nuevas fuerzas gracias a la *Compendiosa Historia Hispanica* de Sánchez de Arévalo, pues logra relanzar el goticismo como sistema de propaganda política al servicio de los intereses políticos de la monarquía castellana. Esta manera de historiar gozó de un vigor renovado desde finales del s. xv y a lo largo del s. xvi, y convivió con los modelos historiográficos de estilo italianizante – valgan de ejemplo el *Paralipomenon* de Joan Margarit, las *Antiquitates Hispaniae gentis* de Alfonso de Palencia o el *De laudibus Hispaniae* de Lucio Marineo Sículo –;[35] por fin, la *Compendiosa* sirvió claramente de modelo directo a Gonzalo de Arredondo en la redacción de su *Coronica de Fernan Gonçales*, quien no dudó en verter al castellano pasajes enteros de ella.[36]

Universidad de Alcalá (UAH)
Instituto universitario de investigación en Estudios Medievales y Siglo de Oro
(IEMSO)

---

34   Los éxitos diplomáticos se debieron a los discursos *De preeminentia* (1436) y *Allegationes super conquesta Insularum Canariae contra Portugalenses* (1437); los literarios, a la *Anacephaleosis* (1456).

35   Cf. Teresa Jiménez Calvente, "Teoría historiográfica a comienzos del siglo XVI," en *Imágenes históricas de Felipe II*, ed. Alfredo Alvar Ezquerra (Madrid, 2000), 197–215; acerca de la imporancia política de las *Antiquitates Hispaniae*, vid. Helena de Carlos Villamarín, *Las antigüedades de Hispania* (Spoleto, 1996) y Pablo Fernández Albadalejo "*Materia de España* y *Edificio* de historiografía: algunas consideraciones sobre la década de 1540," en *En torno a las comunidades de Castilla. Actas del congreso internacional Poder, conflicto y revuelta en la España de Carlos I*, ed. Fernando Martínez Gil (Cuenca, 2002), 109–30, en 110–4.

36   El presente trabajo ha sido realizado dentro del marco del proyecto de investigación FFI2016-75143-P, Práctica literaria y mitología en el s. xv en Castilla. Comento a Eusebio y Breviloquio del Tostado: edición crítica del texto latino y castellano, perteneciente al Programa Estatal de Fomento de la Investigación Científica y Técnica de Excelencia, Subprograma Estatal de Generación del Conocimiento.

CHAPTER 7

L'humaniste suisse Heinrich Glaréan (1488–1563), *vir bonus dicendi et docendi peritus*

David Amherdt

Abstract

Cet article se penche sur la vision de l'éducation et de l'enseignement de celui qui fut le *praeceptor* de la Suisse catholique, le poète et savant suisse Heinrich Glareanus (1488–1563), à travers l'examen de ses poèmes, de ses manuels scolaires, des notes de cours prises par ses élèves, et enfin de sa correspondance et des témoignages de ses contemporains. Il se dégage de cette étude l'image d'un savant passionné par l'Antiquité et désireux de diffuser les principes de l'humanisme chrétien. Sans jamais perdre de vue la formation morale des jeunes gens, il met l'accent sur leur formation littéraire, et donc sur la lecture des anciens Grecs et Latins. Mais il ne laisse pas pour autant de côté la formation scientifique, secondaire, sans doute, mais importante, car elle permet de lire les auteurs avec plus de profit et est le véhicule d'une culture générale qui sera utile aux élèves dans leur vie quotidienne et professionnelle. Heinrich Glareanus, homme pétri d'humour, bon et bienveillant, habile communicateur et pédagogue hors pair, mérite assurément d'être qualifié de *vir bonus dicendi et docendi peritus*.

Keywords

Heinrich Glareanus – *Duo elegiarum libri* (1516) – *De geographia* (1527) – Neo-Latin education treatise – Swiss humanism

> Huc ego deductus, dum non mihi barba rigeret,
> Scilicet ut sanctas artes moresque pudicos
> Haurirem et nunquam moriturae nomina famae.[1]

∴

---

1 « C'est ici que je fus conduit, à l'époque où ma barbe n'était pas encore dure, / Afin de me pénétrer des saints arts et des mœurs / Pudiques et de la gloire d'une renommée impérissable. »

© KONINKLIJKE BRILL NV, LEIDEN, 2020 | DOI:10.1163/9789004427105_008

Tel est le regard, non dépourvu d'ironie, que jette sur son arrivée à Cologne, en 1507, celui qui deviendra le *praeceptor* de la Suisse catholique. Glaréan affirme s'être fixé trois buts au moment de faire son entrée à l'Université : la gloire d'une renommée impérissable, bien naturelle chez un jeune homme de dix-neuf ans pénétrant dans le temple du savoir, mais surtout l'éducation dans les belles lettres et dans les bonnes mœurs ; ce sont là les deux objectifs principaux de l'éducation humaniste, le deuxième étant par ailleurs considéré comme le plus important.[2]

Ces deux objectifs ont été, sa vie durant, ceux d'Heinrich Loriti (né dans le canton de Glaris, d'où son surnom de Glareanus), qui a consacré toute sa carrière à l'éducation des jeunes gens, à Bâle, Paris et Fribourg-en-Brisgau.[3] *Poeta laureatus*, professeur et humaniste, éditeur et commentateur de textes, auteur d'ouvrages scientifiques, notamment sur la musique, Glaréan incarne le maître idéal : sa pensée et son action sont entièrement tournées vers la formation qu'il dispensait aux étudiants de l'université et à ceux qui résidaient dans son internat.

Glaréan n'a pas laissé de réflexion théorique systématique sur sa vision de l'éducation et de l'enseignement. Celle-ci peut toutefois être déduite de ses œuvres en vers et en prose, des notes prises par ses élèves et des témoignages de ses contemporains. Notre but est d'examiner ces divers aspects afin de donner l'image la plus précise possible de Glaréan en tant qu'éducateur.

1 L'œuvre poétique : les *Elegiae* à ses élèves

Commençons par une œuvre de jeunesse, qui sert idéalement notre propos, puisque ce sont des poèmes adressés par Glaréan à ses élèves. Il s'agit des dix

---

Glaréan, *Carmen totam fere Glareani vitam complectens*, v. 31–3, dans *Das Epos vom Heldenkampfe bei Näfels und andere bisher ungedruckte Gedichte*, éd. Konrad Müller, Hans Keller (Glaris, 1949), 156. La composition de ce poème autobiographique remonte selon toute vraisemblance aux années 1535–38 ; voir *Das Epos vom Heldenkampfe*, 43–44, ainsi que Franz-Dieter Sauerborn, « '... atque suum familiarem nominarint'. Der Humanist Heinrich Glarean (1488–1563) und die Habsburger, » *Zeitschrift des Breisgau-Geschichtsvereins „Schau-ins-Land"* 120 (2001), 57–75, ici 59. En l'absence d'indication contraire, les traductions sont les nôtres.

2 Voir par exemple Érasme, *De utilitate colloquiorum*, dans *Colloquia*, éd. Léon-Ernest Halkin, Franz Bierlaire et René Hoven (Amsterdam, 1972), 741.

3 Pour un état de la question sur les études glaréaniennes, voir *Heinrich Glarean – ein Universitätslehrer in Freiburg im 16. Jahrhundert*, numéro spécial des *Freiburger Universitätsblätter* 53 (2014), 5–62 ; *Heinrich Glarean's Books. The Intellectual World of a Sixteenth-Century Humanist*, éd. Ian Fenlon et Inga Mai Groote (Cambridge, 2013) ; *Heinrich Glarean oder : Die Rettung der Musik aus dem Geist der Antike ?*, éd. Nicole Schwindt (Kassel, 2006).

pièces formant le deuxième livre des *Duo elegiarum libri* publiés à Bâle chez Froben en 1516.[4] Avec beaucoup d'affection, le maître y exhorte les jeunes gens à la vertu, en particulier à la chasteté, et les encourage à s'attacher au Christ et aux saints.[5]

Dans ces concentrés d'enseignement chrétien, l'exhortation à la piété baigne dans une atmosphère antique, puisque le jeune professeur multiplie les *exempla* de héros antiques ayant brillé par leur vertu. On trouve un beau spécimen de ce mariage entre christianisme et tradition antique dans l'élégie 2,4 : Glaréan, après avoir exhorté Daniel Ifflinger à s'attacher au Christ et à la Sainte Vierge, lui propose des exemples de vertus dans les personnes, légendaires ou historiques, de Coclès, Clélie, Decius, Fabius, Camille, Caton et Cicéron.[6]

Dans ces poèmes éminemment « pédagogiques », qui ne sont pas exempts d'un certain moralisme (d'ailleurs souvent présent chez Glaréan, et dont l'exacerbation peut être mise sur le compte de son jeune âge), on distingue trois visées. La première est évidemment la formation à la vertu en général, et à la piété en particulier.

L'insistance sur les héros romains suggère une deuxième visée : familiariser les étudiants avec des personnages exemplaires du passé, leur présenter des modèles exaltants dignes d'être imités. Ces figures remarquables sont des pièces clés dans l'édifice éducatif de Glaréan. On les retrouve notamment dans son long poème patriotique et éminemment pédagogique, la *Descriptio Helvetiae* (1519), où l'humaniste, en plus d'enseigner aux jeunes gens la géographie et l'histoire de la Suisse, a pour but de leur montrer la grandeur du passé

---

4   Voir David Amherdt, « Les élégies de Glareanus aux jeunes étudiants : des conseils pour la vie (éternelle), » dans *Munera Friburgensia. Festschrift zu Ehren von Margarethe Billerbeck*, éd. Arlette Neumann-Hartmann et Thomas Schmidt (Bern, 2015), 263–77.

5   De tels recueils de poèmes moraux, voire moralisateurs, sont plutôt rares à l'époque. On peut toutefois rapprocher les élégies de Glaréan, pour ce qui est de la manière aussi bien que du ton, d'un ouvrage beaucoup plus ample jouissant à l'époque d'une certaine renommée, les quatre livres des *Elegiae morales* de Johannes Murmellius, publiés en 1508 chez Quentel à Cologne.

6   *Eleg.* 2,4,13–15 et 23–28 : « Posce salutiferum syncaero pectore Christum ; / Virgo, decus coeli, sit tua cura velim. / Quicquid habes dedit ille tibi, corpusque animumque. / [...] Solam virtutem post funera scito perennem, / Haec te nobilitat perpetuumque facit. / Romanum spectes incurvo poplite Coclem ; / Virgo natans Tybrim Cloelia nota tibi, / Et Decii et Fabii, et clara virtute Camillus, / Moratusque alto cum Cicerone Cato. » (« Recherche d'un cœur sincère le Christ porteur de salut ; / J'aimerais aussi que la Vierge, gloire du ciel, soit ton souci. / Tout ce que tu possèdes, il te l'a donné, le corps comme l'âme. / [...] Sache que seule la vertu reste pour toujours après la mort, / C'est elle qui t'ennoblit et te rend éternel. / Contemple à genoux le Romain Coclès ; / Elle t'est connue, la vierge Clélie qui traversa le Tibre à la nage, / Et les Decius et les Fabius, et Camille à l'éclatante vertu, / Et Caton, qui séjourne avec le grand Cicéron. »)

L'HUMANISTE SUISSE HEINRICH GLARÉAN (1488–1563)

de la Confédération et de les encourager à imiter les vertus des héros des temps anciens.[7] Il se plaît en outre à y chanter la puissance de la Suisse et ses grands hommes, comme Guillaume Tell, qu'il égale aux héros antiques, mettant ainsi en scène une sorte de *translatio imperii* de Rome vers l'Helvétie.

Cette *translatio imperii* va de pair avec une *translatio studii*. En faisant l'éloge, dans sa *Descriptio*, des héros de l'Helvétie, Glaréan veut aussi montrer que les Suisses sont capables d'écrire en latin aussi bien que leurs prédécesseurs qui chantaient les héros de Rome. Or, pour espérer que la Confédération porte fièrement le flambeau poétique, il est essentiel de donner aux jeunes gens une formation littéraire. C'est à cette tâche que Glaréan a consacré toute sa vie, et c'est aussi ce qu'il fait, modestement, dans les élégies, dont on découvre là la troisième visée : en même temps qu'il leur fait la morale, Glaréan éduque ses élèves dans les belles lettres, non en théorie, mais en prêchant d'exemple : il leur montre comment on fait de la poésie chrétienne sur le modèle antique, en imitant les Latins tant pour ce qui est du fond que de la forme.

L'ensemble de la production poétique de Glaréan, très variée (elle va du poème de circonstances au panégyrique, en passant par l'ode et l'autobiographie), est pétri de motifs antiques et participe à son effort pour former ses jeunes lecteurs dans les belles lettres. La présence des figures exemplaires de l'Antiquité y est, elle aussi, constante. Enfin, le souci pour la piété du lecteur traverse toute son œuvre poétique, qui comporte d'ailleurs un grand nombre de pièces sur des sujets religieux : poèmes en l'honneur du Christ et de saints divers (Thomas d'Aquin, Fridolin, etc.) ; poème sur l'origine des chartreux, etc.[8]

2   L'œuvre en prose. Les épitomés et les manuels

Une partie non négligeable de l'œuvre de Glaréan est directement consacrée à la formation scolaire ou universitaire de ses étudiants. Il a en particulier

---

7   Voir en particulier les v. 390–410 de l'*Helvetiae descriptio : panegyricum. Beschreibung der Schweiz : Lob der dreizehn Orte*, éd. Werner Näf (St.-Gall, 1948), 90 ; traduction partielle par David Amherdt dans *Guillaume Tell et la libération des Suisses*, éd. Jean-Daniel Morerod et Anton Näf (Lausanne, 2010), 84–5.

8   Sur l'œuvre poétique de Glaréan, et en particulier sur ses poèmes religieux, voir Barbara Mahlmann-Bauer, « Frömmigkeit zwischen Reformation und Gegenreformation im antiken Gewand. Das Beispiel der Gedichte Heinrich Glareans, » dans *Welche Antike ? Konkurrierende Rezeptionen des Altertums im Barock*, t. 2, éd. Ulrich Heinen (Wiesbaden, 2011), 667–721, qui dresse la liste des poèmes du manuscrit Clm 28325 de la Bayerische Staatsbibliothek de Munich, qui regroupe la quasi-totalité de l'œuvre poétique de Glaréan.

composé un grand nombre d'épitomés, issus de ses cours et destinés à enseigner une matière de manière claire et simple.

En 1516 déjà, alors qu'il enseigne à Bâle, Gléréan fait paraître son *Isagoge in musicen*, manuel d'introduction à la musique. La même année, il publie un *De ratione syllabarum brevis isagoge*, sur les règles de la quantité des syllabes et de la métrique latine, accompagné d'un *De figuris* sur les principales figures de rhétorique. Son effort pour faciliter l'apprentissage du latin apparaît aussi dans la publication, en 1526, de l'*Ars minor* de Donat muni d'explications de son cru[9] et accompagné, au fil des éditions, de résumés, également de sa plume, sur divers aspects de la grammaire (*De generibus nominum, De constructionis regulis et syntaxi*, etc.). En 1557, il publie, avec Johann Wonnegger, en latin et en allemand, une version abrégée du *Dodekachordon* (1547), son grand ouvrage sur la musique ; il ne s'agit pas là à proprement parler d'un manuel, mais plutôt d'un texte universitaire s'adressant à un lectorat d'étudiants des arts libéraux.[10]

Trois épitomés utilisés par Gléréan dans son enseignement retiendront particulièrement notre attention : le *De geographia*, le *De VI arithmeticae practicae speciebus* et le *De asse*. Les épîtres dédicatoires de ces manuels consacrés à des disciplines scientifiques du *quadrivium* sont particulièrement précieuses pour établir les priorités de Gléréan dans l'enseignement des jeunes gens.

La première édition du *De geographia* paraît à Bâle en 1527.[11] Il s'agit d'un manuel présentant les diverses notions de géographie accompagnées de nombreux schémas. Dans l'*epistola dedicatoria*, adressée au théologien polonais Johannes a Lasco, Gléréan fait d'emblée cette affirmation, essentielle pour notre propos : « sans elle [la géographie], toute lecture des anciens auteurs est obscure et le récit des hauts faits ennuyeux. »[12] Le but premier de la géographie est ainsi de faciliter la lecture des auteurs, cette dernière constituant la base de la formation.[13] Gléréan ajoute cependant que la géographie a également une

---

9   *Ael. Donati methodus, scholiis utilissimis illustrata* (Bâle, 1526).

10   *Musicae epitome sive compendium ex Glareani Dodecachordo* (Bâle, 1557) ; *Uß Glareani Musick ein ußzug* (Bâle, 1557). Sur ce texte, voir Inga-Mai Groote, « Studying music and arithmetic with Glarean : contextualizing the *Epitomes* and *Annotationes* among the sources for Glarean's teaching, » dans Groote, *Heinrich Glarean's Books* (voir ci-dessus, n. 3), 193–222, ici 201.

11   Sur le *De geographia*, voir Christine R. Johnson, « Between the Human and the Divine : Glarean's *De geographia* and the Span of Renaissance Geography », dans Groote, *Heinrich Glarean's Books* (voir ci-dessus, n. 3), 138–58.

12   *De geographia liber unus* (Bâle, 1527), fol. 1v : « absque hac caeca est omnis veterum authorum lectio, surda rerum gestarum narratio. »

13   Quelques années plus tard, dans l'épître dédicatoire du *De VI arithmeticae practicae speciebus epitome* (Fribourg-en-Brisgau, 1539), 4, Gléréan répète que c'est pour permettre une meilleure explication des auteurs qu'il enseignait ces éléments de géographie, qu'il décida

L'HUMANISTE SUISSE HEINRICH GLARÉAN (1488–1563)

utilité dans la vie publique aussi bien que privée :[14] le bon professeur n'oublie pas que ses étudiants seront bientôt confrontés à la vie professionnelle. La géographie est donc une science appliquée, qui vise à la fois à la compréhension des classiques et à l'utilité pratique.[15]

La première édition du *De VI arithmeticae practicae speciebus epitome* paraît en 1539 à Fribourg-en-Brisgau. Il s'agit, de même que le *De geographia*, d'un manuel issu de ses cours.[16] Un tiers de l'ouvrage est consacré à la grammaire des nombres (adjectifs cardinaux, ordinaux, distributifs ; adverbes multiplicatifs, etc.) ;[17] le reste traite du calcul, des suites de nombres et des proportions, Glaréan illustrant ces notions par des exemples tirés de la littérature. Or, l'épître dédicatoire confirme le rôle clé joué par la lecture des textes dans l'enseignement tel que le conçoit notre humaniste, qui commence par rapporter l'opinion d'Érasme selon laquelle « rien ne fait davantage de tort aux grands écrivains que ces fâcheux auteurs d'épitomés, tel L. Florus pour Tite-Live, Justin pour [Trogue] Pompée. »[18] Glaréan souligne ici l'importance essentielle de la lecture *intégrale* des textes latins et grecs originaux. Il poursuit en faisant remarquer que dans le domaine des sciences, en revanche, il n'y aucun inconvénient, au contraire, à faire des résumés. Il précise ensuite – c'est ce qui nous intéresse surtout ici – que son traité est au service des « matières supérieures »,

---

ensuite de publier : « Ad enarrandos eximios authores praelegere solebam Geographica quaedam, quae postea edidi » (« Lorsque je commentais les meilleurs auteurs, j'avais l'habitude d'expliquer des éléments de géographie, que j'ai ensuite édités. »)

14 *De geographia*, fol. 1v : « [...] in publicis consultationibus inque dirimendis controversiis quoties de ditionis finibus ambigunt principes, vel fideli consilio vel aequo iudicio iuvat civitatem. Nihilo secius interim et in privatis actionibus plurimum adferens et commoditatis et voluptatis » (« [...] dans les délibérations publiques et dans le règlement de différends – lorsque des princes discutent à propos des frontières de leur territoire –, elle est utile à la cité par son fidèle conseil ou son juste jugement. Au reste, il n'en va pas différemment dans les discussions privées, où elle est source de beaucoup de profit et de plaisir. »)

15 Voir Groote, « Studying music » (voir ci-dessus, n. 10), 199.

16 Voir l'épître dédicatoire du *De VI arithmeticae*, 3–5, adressée à l'un de ses anciens étudiants, Charles de Wehingen ; voir aussi Groote, « Studying music » (voir ci-dessus, n. 10), 199.

17 Voir ibid., 200.

18 *De VI arithmeticae*, 3 : « D. Erasmum illum Roterodamum [...] dicere saepe audivimus magnis authoribus nihil aeque nocere atque epitomarum illos importunos scriptores, quemadmodum Livio L. Florum, Trogo Iustinum. » Voir l'adage 2001, « *Herculei labores* », où Érasme rapporte l'opinion de ceux qui pensent que les abrégés sont responsables de l'oubli et de la perte des auteurs anciens ; il cite précisément l'exemple de Florus et de Tite-Live, et celui de Justin et de Trogue Pompée, *Adagiorum chilias tertia*, t. 1, éd. Felix Heinimann et Emanuel Kienzle (Amsterdam, 1981), 30. Glaréan reprendra ce reproche dans l'épître dédicatoire des *In Iustini historias* [...] *annotationes* (Bâle, 1562), 3–4.

c'est-à-dire, comme on le comprend à la fin de l'extrait proposé en note, la lecture des auteurs.[19] Il confirme cette priorité quelques lignes plus bas lorsqu'il affirme qu'en écrivant ce livre, il a voulu faciliter la compréhension des auteurs qu'il explique chez lui (« domi »), c'est-à-dire dans son internat.[20] La maîtrise de la langue apparaît ainsi comme essentielle dans son projet éducatif : sans elle, on ne peut comprendre les auteurs et, qui plus est, on ne s'exprime pas de manière adéquate. C'est ce que confirme la *Praefatiuncula*, où Glaréan affirme qu'il est honteux de parler n'importe comment dans une langue dont on ignore les mots et les règles.[21] Enfin, tout comme la géographie, l'arithmétique a une visée pratique. Glaréan explique ainsi qu'elle permet une meilleure compréhension de la géographie (calcul du diamètre de la terre, par exemple) et de la musique (calcul des intervalles, par exemple).[22] Il s'agit donc également d'une science appliquée.

Le but du *De asse* (1550),[23] comme l'indique l'épître dédicatoire au conseiller impérial Johann Georg Paungartner, est de mettre de l'ordre dans le chaos qui règne dans la description et la définition des poids et des mesures.[24] Ici aussi, l'objectif est de faciliter la lecture des Anciens ; Glaréan affirme en effet : « Il

---

19   *De VI arithmeticae*, 3 : « At multo aliud esse negocium in tradendis disciplinis. Ibi vero compendium saepe prodesse ac pluribus ansam dare ad maiora capessenda » (« Mais c'est une tout autre affaire lorsqu'il s'agit de transmettre les sciences. Dans ce domaine, effectivement, un résumé est souvent utile et fournit à bien des gens l'occasion de comprendre de très grandes choses ») ; et 5 : « Itaque cogitavi, qua in aliis uti soleo, de unica brevitate, et ut ea potissimum tractarem, quae ad maiora illa intelligenda ducerent ac inservirent, non quae absolutum in ea arte facerent ; neque enim id requirebant, quos tum praelegebam, authores » (« Voilà pourquoi mon unique but a été la brièveté, que j'utilise aussi dans les autres domaines, et j'ai voulu exposer de préférence les thèmes qui permettent de comprendre les matières supérieures et se mettent à leur service, non ceux qui représentent la perfection dans cet art – ce n'est d'ailleurs pas ce qu'exigeait la lecture des auteurs que j'expliquais alors. »)

20   Ibid., 6 : « Tibi autem hunc dedicare volui, ut quando alia in authoribus, tanta cura, tantula praesertim adhuc aetate perlegeris, et hic si non magnum facerem arithmeticum, degustationem tamen praeberem ad authores, quos domi meae praelego, intelligendos non prorsus contemnendam » (« Or j'ai voulu te le dédier. Il te sera utile lorsque tu liras d'autres auteurs (et ce sera avec bien des difficultés, surtout à ton âge encore tendre) : même si je ne fais pas ici de la grande arithmétique, je t'en propose du moins un avant-goût loin d'être tout à fait inutile à la compréhension des auteurs que j'explique chez moi. »)

21   Ibid., 7 : « Turpe siquidem est artem quavis profiteri lingua, cuius voces ac loquendi usum ignores. »

22   Ibid., 4–5.

23   Sur le *De asse*, voir Menso Folkerts, « Roman weights and measurements in Glarean's *Liber de asse et partibus eius*, » dans Groote, *Heinrich Glarean's Books* (voir ci-dessus, n. 3), 159–79.

24   *Liber de asse et partibus eius* (Bâle, 1550), fol. A2r–v.

n'est rien qui soit plus utile à l'explication des passages les plus obscurs des grands auteurs qu'un traité de ce genre. »[25]

Dans le reste de l'œuvre en prose, constitué surtout par les annotations sur des auteurs antiques, d'ailleurs elles-mêmes souvent issues de son enseignement,[26] le souci pour la formation des étudiants, qui ne sont généralement pas le premier public de ces textes, est moins directement apparent, même si les visées pédagogiques n'y sont jamais totalement absentes, qu'elles soient littéraires ou morales.[27]

3 Les notes de ses élèves

La méthode d'enseignement de Glaréan a été récemment mise en lumière par plusieurs études, en particulier celles d'Inga Mai Groote et de son équipe, qui a comparé les livres de la bibliothèque de Glaréan annotés par l'humaniste lui-même, avec les notes de ses étudiants dans leurs propres exemplaires. Il s'agit surtout de textes d'auteurs classiques (César, le *De officiis* de Cicéron, Horace, Tite-Live, Suétone) ou de la Renaissance (Valla), mais aussi de ses propres manuels d'arithmétique, de géographie et de musique, par exemple,[28] ainsi que de sa *Chronologia* (1540).[29] Ce sont d'une part des notes prises à partir des propos du professeur (notes personnelles ou notes dictées) lors de cours publics (à l'université) ou privés (dans son internat), d'autre part et surtout des copies ou transcriptions fidèles de gloses à partir d'un exemplaire préparé par Glaréan pour ses élèves.

L'étude de ces notes tend à montrer que Glaréan était un professeur passionnant, original et amusant,[30] doté d'un grand sens pédagogique, qui tendait

---

25   Ibid., fol. A3r : « Nihil enim est quod aeque ad magnorum scriptorum obscurissimos locos explicandos deserviat atque huiusmodi tractatio. »

26   C'est le cas, par exemple, de ses *Annotationes* sur le *De bello Gallico* de César (Fribourg-en-Brisgau, 1538) ; voir Jean-Claude Margolin, « Glaréan, commentateur du '*De bello Gallico*', » *Caesarodunum* 22 bis (1985), 183–212, ici 194.

27   Voir notamment Claudia Wiener, « Glarean's didactic, » dans Groote, *Heinrich Glarean's Books* (voir ci-dessus, n. 3), 223–47.

28   Pour une liste de ces cours, voir Groote, « Glarean als Universitätslehrer : *Musica zwischen Allgemeinbildung, Poetik und kultureller Identität*, » dans *Heinrich Glarean – ein Universitätslehrer* (voir ci-dessus, n. 3), 24.

29   Anthony T. Grafton et Urs B. Leu, *Henricus Glareanus's (1488–1563)* Chronologia *of the Ancient World. A Facsimile Edition of a Heavily Annotated Copy Held in Princeton University Library* (Leiden, 2014).

30   Groote, « Studying music » (voir ci-dessus, n. 10), 207–8.

à se concentrer sur les principes généraux et les idées centrales,[31] avec une certaine propension aux jugements moraux[32] et un souci constant de faire voir l'actualité de ces textes pour l'époque présente, en tirant des parallèles entre l'Antiquité et son temps.[33] Il profitait en outre de ses cours dans tous les domaines pour améliorer chez ses élèves la maîtrise du latin, l'étude des *eximii authores* restant la base de l'éducation ;[34] enfin, la piété revêtait une importance que l'on retrouve dans l'ensemble de son œuvre.[35]

4   La correspondance et les témoignages des contemporains

La correspondance de Glaréan nous présente un homme plein d'humour et de bienveillance, soucieux de la santé physique, intellectuelle et morale des jeunes Helvètes qu'il forme dans son internat. Alors que dans ses écrits Glaréan est généralement très exigeant au sujet des règles éthiques, sa correspondance révèle un maître qui, dans la pratique, est tout sauf un censeur rigide ; il fait au contraire preuve d'indulgence et de compréhension devant les frasques de ses étudiants, dont certains trouvaient auprès des jeunes filles, en particulier à Paris, un complément aux joies des études.[36]

La fibre pédagogique de Glaréan se révèle également dans l'organisation de l'internat qu'il dirigeait à Paris, où il pratiquait l'éducation par le jeu : afin de familiariser les étudiants au fonctionnement de la République romaine, et aussi sans doute pour les préparer à l'exercice de la politique, il avait organisé son école comme une sorte de République romaine, avec diverses charges attribuées aux élèves ; il terminait d'ailleurs parfois ses missives avec des formules telles que « Salutat te Senatus populusque Romanus Lutetiae ! »[37] Dans une

---

31   Inga Mai Groote et Bernhard Kölb, « Glarean the Professor and His Students' Books : Copied Lecture Notes, » *Bibliothèque d'humanisme et Renaissance* 73 (2011), 61–91, ici 63.

32   C'est le cas en particulier de ses notes sur Suétone ; voir ibid., 75.

33   Groote, « Studying music » (voir ci-dessus, n. 10), 203. Ainsi, les notes prises par ses étudiants révèlent que dans son explication de Suétone il comparait les comices de Rome avec la Landsgemeinde des cantons suisses ; voir Groote, « Glarean als Universitätslehrer » (voir ci-dessus, n. 28), 27 ; « Studying music » (voir ci-dessus, n. 10), 214.

34   Voir ci-dessus, n. 13, ainsi que Groote, « Studying music » (voir ci-dessus, n. 10), 221.

35   Ainsi, il considère que la maîtrise du système musical renforce le contenu du texte et meut à la piété : c'est la *docta pietas* ; voir Groote, « Glarean als Universitätslehrer » (voir ci-dessus, n. 28), 35.

36   Voir par exemple sa lettre de juillet 1520 à Oswald Myconius, éd. Albert Büchi, *Glareans Schüler in Paris (1517–1522) nebst 15 ungedruckten Briefen* (Stans, 1928), n° XIII, 414.

37   Ibid., n° VIII, 414 ; n° X, 418 ; n° XI, 419 ; n° XII, 423 ; n° XIII, 426.

L'HUMANISTE SUISSE HEINRICH GLARÉAN (1488–1563)

lettre à Oswald Myconius, on apprend ainsi que ses élèves ont reçu diverses charges en rapport avec l'organisation de l'internat : l'un est *censor*, un autre *praetor, quaestor publici aerarii, tribunus plebis* ou *triumvir*.[38]

Par le biais de sa correspondance et de son oeuvre en vers et en prose, Glaréan met habilement en scène sa propre image de professeur, et ses disciples feront de même à sa mort.[39] Ainsi, l'anthologie de poèmes publiée à Bâle, chez Froben, quelques mois après sa mort par Jodocus Castner, un ancien étudiant de Glaréan, souligne ses qualités d'enseignant dans les divers domaines du savoir.[40]

Si Glaréan eut à subir les critiques des autorités académiques le priant de mieux contrôler le comportement de ses pensionnaires ou de ne plus critiquer les luthériens dans ses cours,[41] si son caractère facétieux lui fit parfois subir les foudres de ses ennemis,[42] il semble bien que jamais ses qualités d'enseignant n'aient été mises en doute.

Parmi les témoignages de ses contemporains, nous retiendrons pour terminer celui d'Érasme, qui, en 1516 déjà, fait l'éloge de Glaréan, qui se trouve alors, tout comme lui, à Bâle. Il loue sa soif de savoir et ses qualités d'enseignant : « Ce qu'il sait, il l'enseigne volontiers et clairement. » Il fait aussi l'éloge de son caractère vif et joyeux, et précise qu'il a horreur des beuveries, des jeux de hasard, des propos indécents et des prostituées, au point qu'il refuse même qu'on fasse mention de ces choses, ce qui montre que Glaréan mettait

---

38   Ibid., n° IX, 415–416.

39   Voir Ian Fenlon et Inga Mai Groote, « Heinrich Glarean's World, » dans *Heinrich Glarean's Books* (voir ci-dessus, n. 3), 2–4.

40   Jodocus Castner, *De obitu* [...] *Henrichi Loriti Glareani* [...] *epicedion et epigrammata quaedam funebria* (Bâle, 1563), notamment 13.

41   Voir notamment Heinrich Schreiber, *Heinrich Loriti Glareanus. Seine Freunde und seine Zeit* (Fribourg-en-Brisgau, 1837), 36, 83 et 86 ; Otto Fridolin Fritzsche, *Glarean. Sein Leben und seine Schriften* (Frauenfeld, 1890), 26 et 56–8.

42   Franz-Dieter Sauerborn, « Glarean – das *enfant terrible* unter den Basler Humanisten ? Anmerkungen zu seiner Biographie und Persönlichkeit, » dans *Wort und Klang*, éd. Lothar Käser (Bonn, 1995), 301–27, montre bien que si Glaréan n'était peut-être pas toujours facile à vivre, il était loin d'être « l'enfant terrible » et incontrôlable que ses ennemis, protestants en particulier, ont essayé de faire de lui. Voir aussi Fenlon/Groote, « Heinrich Glarean's World » (voir ci-dessus, n. 39), 5. Sur son esprit facétieux et son humour, voir David Amherdt, « Rire et humour dans la correspondance d'Heinrich Glareanus, » *Actes du colloque « Le rire des épistoliers »* (*Brest, 8–9 juin 2017*), à paraître ; Paul Gerhard Schmidt, « Henricus Glareanus. Universalgelehrter mit Witz und Leidenschaft, » dans *Poeten und Professoren : eine Literaturgeschichte Freiburgs in Porträts*, éd. Achim Aurnhammer et Hans-Jochen Schiewer (Fribourg-en-Brisgau, 2009), 115–30.

lui-même en pratique les règles éthiques qu'il inculquait à ses élèves.[43] En fin de compte, cette rigueur intellectuelle et morale, à laquelle s'ajoute un grand enthousiasme, permet de décrire Glaréan, selon l'expression de Caton légèrement modifiée, comme un *vir bonus dicendi et docendi peritus* : un homme bon, savant, excellent professeur, qui, en rhéteur accompli, met en pratique ce qu'il enseigne, ce qui est la meilleure façon d'entraîner (*movere*) son auditoire vers le bien, de le convaincre, en plus, bien sûr, de l'instruire (*docere*) de manière agréable (*delectare*).

Conclusion

La vision du savoir défendue par Glaréan, à l'instar, par exemple, de celle d'Érasme, dont l'influence sur lui est évidente,[44] est une vision globale : il s'agit d'une éducation pour la vie, qui ne comprend pas seulement la formation littéraire et scientifique, mais aussi, et peut-être surtout, la formation morale, sans laquelle il est impossible de parler de véritable éducation.[45]

L'importance de la formation morale est perceptible aussi bien dans les écrits que dans l'exemple de la vie de Glaréan ; il sait qu'il n'y a pas d'enseignement efficace si le maître ne met pas lui-même en pratique ce qu'il professe : il

---

43 *Opus Epistolarum Des. Erasmi Roterodami*, éd. Percy Stafford Allen, t. 2 (Oxford, 1910), 208, lettre n° 394 du 7 mars 1516, à Urbain Rieger ; trad. dans *La correspondance d'Érasme*, éd. Marcel A. Nauwelaerts (Bruxelles, 1973), 302 : « Quod nescit, discit avide ; quod scit, docet libenter et candide. Moribus alacribus ac festivis ac prorsus omnium horarum homo. Addam extremum calculum, quem ego vel in primis estimandum arbitror : ingenium integritati natum. Abhorret a compotationibus istis temulentis, abhorret ab alea, a turpiloquio, a scortis, ita ut harum rerum ne mentionem quidem ferret possit » (« [...] Il est d'un caractère vif et joyeux, et c'est de plus l'homme de toutes les heures. J'ajouterai un dernier trait, que je trouve estimable entre tous : il est foncièrement honnête. Il a horreur des beuveries d'ivrognes, il a horreur des jeux de hasard, des propos indécents, des prostituées, à tel point qu'il ne peut même pas souffrir d'entendre parler de ces choses. ») Voir aussi ibid., 457 (lettre n° 529 du 14 février 1517, à Étienne Poncher).

44 Dans son œuvre, Glaréan se réfère fréquemment à Érasme, qu'il a fréquenté et avec qui il a correspondu, comme à son maître.

45 Le caractère global de l'éducation se retrouve chez Guillaume Budé, dont l'humanisme se veut « total, encyclopédique » et accorde une grande importance à la mystique chrétienne ; voir Marie-Madeleine de la Garanderie, que nous citons, « Guillaume Budé, philosophe de la culture, » *Bulletin de l'Association Guillaume Budé* 49 (1990), 371–81, ici 374. On notera d'ailleurs que Glaréan, lors de son séjour à Paris (1517–22), a fréquenté Budé ; voir notamment Schreiber, *Heinrich Loriti* (voir ci-dessus, n. 41), 41 et Fritzsche, *Glarean* (voir ci-dessus, n. 41), 21.

se doit d'être lui-même irréprochable. Et c'est bien ce que Glaréan semble avoir été, aussi bien dans ses écrits que dans ses actes.

La lecture des textes des écrivains grecs et latins fournit l'essentiel de ce qui est nécessaire à la bonne formation des jeunes gens. Les sciences quant à elles ont, dans ce contexte, un rôle secondaire : elles permettent de lire les auteurs avec davantage de profit, et aussi de mieux s'exprimer ; elles donnent également-ment aux élèves ce qu'on pourrait appeler une culture générale, qui sera mise à profit lors de la lecture des textes, mais aussi dans la vie pratique.

Cet enseignement basé sur les textes vise avant tout à former des esprits clairs capables de faire face aux défis de leur profession future. C'est une forma-tion éminemment utile, non utile au sens où on l'entend souvent de nos jours, où la notion d'utile est directement liée au profit et à une certaine efficacité pratique et où la véritable formation de l'esprit, qui passe nécessairement par la littérature, est souvent négligée au profit du tout, tout de suite.

L'éducation prônée par Glaréan est une éducation globale, avons-nous dit ; elle ne l'est pas seulement dans le sens qu'elle tient compte aussi bien de l'âme que de l'intellect des jeunes gens, mais aussi dans le sens qu'elle ne néglige aucun aspect de la formation ; il est à cet égard très intéressant de constater que Glaréan, savant universel, a su lui-même transmettre toutes ces facettes du savoir.

Son œuvre et les témoignages directs ou indirects sur sa manière de faire cours donnent de lui l'image d'un homme dont l'enseignement était original, attirant, centré sur l'essentiel et d'une grande clarté, cette exigence de clarté dans l'exposition du savoir révélant d'ailleurs un esprit éminemment didac-tique ou pédagogique. La citation suivante, tirée de ses annotations sur Denys d'Halicarnasse, fournit à tout professeur une leçon fondamentale : « [...] ut do-ceamus ingenue absque fuco ! »[46] Tout Glaréan est dans cette phrase !

---

46   *In Dionysii Halicarnasei* [...] *Antiquitatum Romanarum librum primum* [...] *annotationes*, Bâle, 1532, fol. Z1r : « At in annotationibus saepe maior utilitas ad lectorem redit minusque fastidii est, praesertim si a digressionibus caveatur, idque unum spectemus ut doceamus ingenue absque fuco, nec pudeat dicere : hoc ignoro, hoc dubito, hoc nescio » (« Or les annotations sont toujours plus utiles et moins ardues pour le lecteur, surtout si on se garde de faire des digressions ; et c'est à cela seul que nous devons veiller : enseigner sim-plement et sans fard, et ne pas avoir honte de dire : cela, je l'ignore ; de cela, je ne suis pas sûr ; cela, je ne le sais pas. ») Dans la phrase précédente Glaréan affirmait, faisant une dis-tinction éclairante entre commentaires et annotations : « In commentariis tamen longe maior licentia expatiandi et ingenii ostentatio esse solet » (« Dans les commentaires, ce-pendant, on a d'ordinaire une plus grande latitude pour aller dans les détails et pour faire ostentation de son intelligence ») – à vrai dire, rien de plus étranger à Glaréan que le désir de faire ostentation de son génie !

Enfin, les témoignages de ses contemporains, sa correspondance, l'ensemble de ses écrits, bref, tout porte à croire que ce professeur passionné de religion et d'Antiquité, désireux de diffuser les principes de l'humanisme auprès des jeunes gens, était un homme bon et bienveillant, un habile communicateur et un pédagogue hors pair, un *vir bonus dicendi et docendi peritus*. Glaréan était bien le *praeceptor Helvetiae catholicae*, un savant universel et un maître universel, un humanisme au sens propre du terme, c'est-à-dire qui mettait l'homme au centre, et auquel, ajouterions-nous volontiers, rien de ce qui est humain n'était étranger.

Université de Fribourg (Suisse)

CHAPTER 8

La relevancia de los paratextos de las primeras ediciones de Marciano Capela para la crítica textual

Manuel Ayuso

Abstract

Desde la *editio princeps*, impresa en Vicenza en 1499, hasta la primera edición completa del s. XVI, publicada en 1532 en Basilea, diversos tipos de paratextos acompañan al texto editado del *De nuptiis Philologiae et Mercurii* con diversa tipología y con muy variadas finalidades. Los impresores y editores de estos primeros impresos, como Bodianus, Dubravius o H. Petrus, intervienen en la configuración del texto mediante los paratextos con actuaciones que van más allá de la corrección de erratas o la simple enmienda. En algunos casos las ediciones ofrecen a través de sus paratextos variantes textuales y conjeturas, pero también datos de posibles modelos textuales, de preferencias del editor por una u otra forma, del modo en que el texto ha sido corregido, etc. Estudiar estos hechos mejora nuestro conocimiento del texto transmitido en el Humanismo, pero también es un instrumento útil para la crítica textual actual del texto de Capela.

Keywords

Martianus Capella – early modern editions of *De nuptiis Philologiae et Mercurii* – Hugo Grotius – Bonaventura Vulcanius – Franciscus Vitalis Bodianus

1 Introducción*

La edición de Grotius de Leiden 1599, la última del XVI, fue durante los siglos cruciales del desarrollo de la filología la *vulgata* de Marciano Capela y los

---

* Este artículo se ha realizado dentro de los proyectos FFI2015-67335-P y PGC2018-094609-B-100 (Estudio filológico de los textos clásicos latinos transmitidos en impresos incunables y post-incunables conservados en España), cofinanciados por el Ministerio de Ciencia, Innovación y Universidades y el Fondo Europeo de Desarrollo Regional (FEDER).

© KONINKLIJKE BRILL NV, LEIDEN, 2020 | DOI:10.1163/9789004427105_009

estudiosos de este texto de los siglos XVII, XVIII y principio del XIX emplearon la edición de Groot como texto base.

El peso de este trabajo lo demuestran los ejemplares de la edición de Leiden conservados anotados por Salmasius, Vossius,[1] o Bentley,[2] por citar algunos ilustres nombres. La siguiente edición completa de la obra de Kopp, que ve la luz en Fráncfort en 1836, es, en suma, la repetición de la de Grotius con comentarios y añadidos de algunos manuscritos y de los estudiosos anteriores. En las ediciones publicadas tras los hallazgos de Lachmann, la cantidad de variantes, correcciones y conjeturas del sabio holandés incorporadas al texto es muy significativa.

Con estos datos queda justificado el interés del estudio de esta edición, que bebe de las anteriores, que en el caso de Marciano Capela son escasas, al contrario de lo que sucede con los manuscritos que transmiten la obra, pues mientras que las ediciones anteriores completas son solo 6–13 contando los impresos parciales –, los manuscritos son casi un cuarto de millar.[3]

2   Las Primeras ediciones

Las ediciones de la obra completa de Capela vieron la luz en 1499 (Vicenza), 1500 (Modena) – copia de la anterior –, 1532 (Basel), 1539 (Lyon) – copia de la anterior repetida en 1592 (Lyon) –, 1577 (Basel) y 1599 (Leiden). He aplicado el principio de la *eliminatio editionum descriptarum* descartando las ediciones de 1500, 1539 y 1592.

Por otro lado, he estudiado en un trabajo reciente[4] las relaciones de dependencia entre las ediciones incunables y postincunables, tratando también los datos transmitidos en los paratextos. Entre las conclusiones más relevantes de este trabajo está la de descartar que el ms. BPL36[5] fuera uno de los modelos de la *editio princeps*, aunque así se dice en varias ediciones críticas desde Dick

---

1   Cf. Astrid C. Balsem, "Collecting the Ultimate Scholar's Library: The *Bibliotheca Vossiana*," en *Isaac Vossius (1618–1689) Between Science and Scholarship*, ed. Eric Jorink y Dirk Van Miert (Leiden, 2012), 299.

2   William H. Stahl, *Martianus Capella and the Seven liberal arts*, vol. 1, (New York, 1971), 11.

3   Cf. Claudio Leonardi, "I codici di Marziano Capela," *Aevum* 33 (1959) 433–89 y Claudio Leonardi, "I codici di Marziano Capela," *Aevum* 34 (1960) 1–99.

4   Manuel Ayuso, "La forma textual de las ediciones incunables de Marciano Capela: modelos, relaciones e influencia en la tradición impresa del inicio del s. XVI," *Calamus renascens* 15 (2014), 17–56.

5   Leiden, Universiteitsbibliotheek, MS. BPL 36.

LOS PARATEXTOS DE LAS PRIMERAS EDICIONES DE CAPELA　　　145

1925 hasta la última de Navarro 2016.[6] También se establece la filiación de los otros impresos con respecto a la *editio princeps*, su modelo. Las relaciones se sintetizan en Ayuso, "La forma" (véase n. 3), 39. En otros trabajos he estudiado este grupo de ediciones y sus paratextos.[7]

3　　Las ediciones más significativas en crítica: La *editio princeps*

En la *editio princeps* la información más significativa para la crítica textual transmitida en los paratextos se contiene en el prefacio, en el cual Bodianus informa de haber realizado una intensa labor de enmienda de más de 2000 correcciones con la ayuda de Domenicus Portensis, y de la disposición de varios modelos. En segundo lugar, las *castigationes* finales proporcionan un reducido número de variantes textuales. De estos datos de los paratextos se demuestra el uso de más de un modelo, probablemente tres.

El segundo impreso de más peso para la crítica de este periodo es la edición con comentario de los libros I y II de Dubravius, Viena 1516, pues hace algunas conjeturas y contribuciones al texto verdaderamente notables para la época. Los paratextos que transmiten esta información son el comentario intercalado del texto y los *errata* finales.

Veamos ahora los tres impresos restantes del s. XVI, las ediciones de Petrus (Basilea 1532), Vulcanius (Basilea 1577) y Grotius (Leiden 1599). Los ejemplos que voy a proponer son preferentemente de los dos primeros libros donde se presenta la fábula del matrimonio de Filología y Mercurio.

Pues bien, en uno de los paratextos de la edición de Grotius, carta al lector anterior a sus *notae* (fols. †1r–2v), se reconoce que el modelo fundamental del impreso ha sido la edición de Vulcanius, su maestro (Basilea 1577), pero también las ediciones de Petrus (Basilea 1532) y de Bodianus (Vicenza 1499) (fol. †1v):

> Nos ei sucessimus, usi ante omnia ipsius Vulcanij editione [...] Textu nostro secuti fuimus, Veicetino praeterea codice quem [...] ab Ios. Scaligero

---

6　A. Dick, (Leipzig, 1925); J. Willis, (Stuttgart, 1983), J.-Y. Guillaumin (Paris, 2003); F. Navarro, (Madrid, 2016).

7　Antonio Moreno y Manuel Ayuso, "La evolución de la concepción editorial de los primeros impresos incunables y postincunables de la obra de Marciano Capela (1499–1599)," *Dialogues d'Histoire Ancienne*. 39,1 (2013) 121–74. Antonio Moreno y Manuel Ayuso, "Los paratextos de las ediciones humanísticas de obras latinas de la Antigüedad; El tratamiento de la portada, el Prefacio y el colofón en las ediciones de Marciano Capela (ss. XV y XVI)," *Agora Estudos Clássicos em Debate* 17 (2015), 51–133.

accepimus, impresso ante annos centum, anno nempe a salute nostra MCCCCXCIX. Lugdunensi etiam libro anni MDXXXII. Basileano quoque anni MDXXXIX. Qui iterum mutata fronte prodiit anno MDXCII.[8]

4   La edición de Basilea 1532

Pasemos, pues, a la edición de 1532. En Moreno-Ayuso "La evolución" (véase arriba, n. 6), 149–50 damos cuenta de una *vita* de origen medieval, el primer paratexto relevante. Esta *vita Martiani* de origen medieval que suele estar incorporada a los manuscritos desde los testimonios más antiguos, sufrió múltiples ampliaciones y modificaciones. En todo caso, es un indicio para descubrir alguno de los posibles modelos de la edición.

El segundo elemento paratextual significativo para la crítica son las apostillas marginales, que precedidas por † ofrecen una variante a una parte del texto, llamada también con †. Las apostillas presentes en el texto son de dos clases: variantes textuales y títulos o indicaciones al texto, que no se preceden por †. Estos *marginalia* se distinguen además por ir en cursiva de menor cuerpo que el texto.

Las glosas presentadas no son muy abundantes y lo más llamativo es que se ciñen a los dos primeros libros y el inicio del III, donde solo hay títulos. Son en total 58 variantes, de las cuales 30 se localizan en el libro I y las restantes 28 en el II. Esto lleva a pensar que el modelo de las mismas pudiera ser un manuscrito que transmitiera solo esta parte de la obra, si bien esto puede deberse a otras razones, como un interés especial del editor por esta parte de la obra. Las *variae lectiones* ofrecidas son de cierta entidad y entre ellas hay omisiones, adiciones y transposiciones, lo cual significa muy probablemente que no se deben a razones paleográficas u ortográficas, sino más bien a que provienen de un modelo de otra rama de la transmisión. Por ejemplo, en fol. 28r (Mart. Cap. 2,151) presenta como variante "a novitate, novi novitate".[9] En fol. 35r frente a "a patrem deumque", señala "deum patremque" (Mart. Cap. 2,202), entre otras que podríamos indicar. Fuera de estas variantes, el texto editado coincide en lo esencial con el de la *editio princeps*.

Solo con el análisis de los paratextos, parece que el modelo, llamémoslo alternativo, ha de ser un manuscrito que contenga los dos primeros libros y una vita. En cualquier caso, está probado que Petrus contó con más de un modelo para su edición y que uno obviamente fue la *editio princeps*, su principal

---

8   Grotius invierte los nombres de Basilea y Lion sin duda por error.

9   En la edición de Lyon 1539 precede la indicación *alias* a esta variante.

LOS PARATEXTOS DE LAS PRIMERAS EDICIONES DE CAPELA

modelo, y, al menos, alguno de los manuscritos de Basilea, de los que se trata más adelante.

5 Basilea 1577

Continuando con el orden cronológico, el siguiente impreso es el de Basilea 1577 de Vulcanius. En el transcurso del siglo las humanidades han experimentado un gran avance que se refleja en buena medida en este trabajo.[10] Los paratextos de que consta son más, más amplios y con informaciones más substanciales. Los paratextos útiles para la crítica de textos son los siguientes: 1) la carta dedicatoria, 2) las glosas marginales, 3) las *annotationes* finales y 4) los *errata*.

La carta dedicatoria a Groesbeek informa de algunas de las fuentes de las que se ha servido el flamenco para elaborar su trabajo (fol.):(3r):[11]

> In Martiano Capella eundem ordinem sum secutus, quem, cum non minus quam Isidorus corruptus esset, ad vetustissimorum codicum fidem quos mihi partim typis excusos, partim manu exaratos Clarissimus vir & iuvandae rei literariae studiosissimus Basilius Amerbachius I. C. suppeditavit, emendavi: & scholiis partim veteribus, partim meis illustravi.

En esta declaración el editor informa del uso de modelos impresos, que muy probablemente son las ediciones anteriores de Basilea 1532 y la *princeps*, así como algunos manuscritos calificados como antiquísimos. Estos modelos le fueron proporcionados por B. Amerbach, nieto de J. Amerbach.

Antes de referirme a los demás paratextos, puedo adelantar que el texto de Vulcanius sigue en lo esencial a las ediciones anteriores, aunque se aprecia ya una labor de enmienda mayor que la que llevó a cabo Petrus, su predecesor.

Con los datos proporcionados en esta dedicatoria por parte de Vulcanius he indagado los posibles modelos manuscritos de Vulcanius y creo haber encontrado algunos.

En Ayuso, "La forma" (véase arriba, n. 3) 3–12, dábamos cuenta del proyecto editorial que llevó a cabo J. Amerbach. Como resultado se elaboró un manuscrito conservado primero en el gabinete Amerbach de Basilea y posteriormente

---

10   Sobre la figura de B. Vulcanius, cf. *Bonaventura Vulcanius : Works and Networks, Brugge 1588–Leiden 1614*, ed. Hélène Cazes (Leiden, 2010).

11   ):(es la extraña manera de denominar este cuaderno en la edición de Vulcanius.

148 AYUSO

en la Biblioteca Universitaria de la ciudad suiza (BU FV40).[12] Todos los indicios apuntaban a que debió de ser empleado como modelo en las dos ediciones basilenses de 1532 y 1577 mencionados en su epístola por Vulcanius. Este hallazgo queda confirmado por el análisis de los datos, si bien presenta importantes matices en el uso que hicieron ambas ediciones del mismo, de los que trato más abajo.

Según el catálogo de la BU de Basilea, ms. FV40 contiene el *De nuptiis* (fols. 1v–174v) y una parte inicial del comentario de Remigio de Auxerre en los márgenes (fols. 1v–12v) hasta Mart. Cap. 1,32, y otras glosas. Incluye explicaciones de Leontorius de los términos griegos – añadidos como hojas suplementarias –, comentarios en el margen de J. Amerbach y el título de pertenencia de B. Amerbach (fol. 1r),[13] además de diagramas (fols. 175v–178v). Dick, aunque lo consultó, consideró que reproducía casi todas las faltas de los modelos peores y no lo colacionó. Las ediciones posteriores lo han ignorado por completo.

Otro dato importante es que también creo haber detectado otro posible modelo de estos editores, me refiero al ms. FV17, también de la Biblioteca de la Universidad de Basilea.[14] Este códice, según los datos del catálogo, del s. XI, contiene los dos primeros libros de Marciano Capela, junto con el comentario de Remigio de Auxerre con la *vita*, que incluye también la parte inicial del libro III (fols. 36v–38r). Además, un texto menor de Gerberto de Aurillac. Junto a estos dos textos el ms. transmite glosas interlineales y marginales de varias épocas y manos. El ms. está dispuesto en dos columnas de las cuales la interior (a), en un cuerpo de texto mayor, transmite el *De nuptiis* y la exterior (b) el *Commentum Remigii*. También incluye una *vita* alternativa. Este segundo ms. de Basilea ha sido colacionado en las ediciones de Dick, Chevalier y Navarro.

6   La *vita* de Basilea 1577 y los mss. de Basilea

Volvamos, pues, a la *vita* de la edición de 1532 (fol. 2ar–v), ligada a la tradición del comentario de Remigio. Esta *vita* coincide en gran parte de manera muy fiel, con diferencias poco significativas, con la del ms. FV17. Este manuscrito

---

12   Basel, Universitätsbibliothek, MS. FV40. Se puede acceder a lña descripción completa: http://www.ub.unibas.ch/digi/a100/kataloge/mscr/mscr_f/BAU_5_000117210_cat.pdf.

13   Sobre la relación de B. Amerbach con Vulcanius, cf. Hugues Daussy, "L'insertion de Bonaventure Vulcanius dans le réseau international protestant," en Cazes, *Bonaventura Vulcanius* (véase arriba, n. 10), 167–84.

14   Basel, Universitätsbibliothek, MS. FV17. Se puede acceder a la descripción completa en: https://www.ub.unibas.ch/digi/a100/kataloge/mscr/mscr_f/BAU_5_000084973_cat.pdf.

LOS PARATEXTOS DE LAS PRIMERAS EDICIONES DE CAPELA

contiene dos *vitae* diferentes en los fols. 1v y 38br–v, que son refundidas en el impreso de la siguiente manera: 1) Las primeras 22 líneas se toman del texto íntegro transmitido en fol. 38br.[15] 2) Tras un espacio en blanco, las siguientes líneas y hasta la línea 11 de la página siguiente (fol. 39av), concuerdan con el comienzo de la otra *vita* de este ms., más extensa, y transmitida al comienzo del mismo (fol. 1v).[16] No obstante, también se transmite la segunda parte de esta *vita* en el ms. FV40, fol. 1v, aunque con ciertas variantes separativas del ms. FV17 y de la edición de Petrus; y 3) Siguen 25 palabras más ("Introducitur hoc loco [...] naturalium conceptionum") a modo de cierre de la vita que hemos identificado en el fol. 1v, lin. 21–22 del ms. FV40.

Así pues, la *vita* parece una composición hecha por Petrus a partir de los dos modelos manuscritos de que dispone. Este modo de proceder, que comprobamos en la elaboración de la *vita*, parece el mismo que le guía para la *constitutio* del texto y las notas marginales.

En efecto, el uso del ms. FV17, no se limitó a la *vita*, ya que hemos podido identificar variantes, algunas de las cuales se pueden ver más adelante, que no se testimonian ni en los impresos anteriores, ni en el ms. FV40. No obstante, Petrus sigue este manuscrito para enmendar el texto de Bodianus en ciertos pasajes solo, pues algunas de las variantes separativas de este ms. no son incorporadas al texto ni a los *marginalia*.

7   Las variantes marginales en Basilea 1532 y 1577

Las variantes marginales de Petrus se transmiten en muchos casos en los mss. de Basilea: 4 están en FV17 y 27 en FV40. Las restantes 27 no se toman de ninguno de ambos modelos. Muchas de estas variantes de FV40 no se recogen en ninguno de los aparatos críticos, excepto en el de Navarro, el cual incorpora las variantes de FV40 como procedentes de Petrus.

Las variantes sin correspondencia en ninguno de ambos manuscritos son generalmente correcciones triviales, por ejemplo, "minio" por "nimio", o de origen paleográfico u ortográfico, como "videbatur" por "videbantur", aunque no se puede descartar que Petrus dispusiera de algún modelo más. En todo caso,

---

15   Se trata de la vita transmitida en llamado comentario anónimo, cf. Sinéad O'Sullivan, *Glossae aeui Carolini in libros I–II Martiani Capellae De nuptiis Philologiae et Mercurii* (Turnhout 2010), 3–4, en la cual faltan estas últimas líneas, lo cual probaría en efecto que Petrus usó el manuscrito FV17.

16   La vida de Remigio de Auxerre.

del examen de estos datos transmitidos en los paratextos quedan identificados estos dos modelos de Basilea.

Pasemos ahora a examinar los paratextos de la siguiente edición de Vulcanius. Transcurridos 45 años el flamenco edita la obra de Marciano junto con Isidoro y un compendio de gramática.

En este intervalo de tiempo que media entre ambas ediciones la técnica editorial y filológica había realizado notables progresos, como se comprueba en los paratextos de este impreso. Entre los datos usados que nos parecen más reveladores, además del prefacio, del que ya he tratado, quiero destacar los *marginalia*, que son precedidos alternativamente por las indicaciones "al." o "forte" distinguiendo así algunas veces las variantes *ope codicum* – la mayor parte – de las conjeturas *ope ingenii*. Con este procedimiento se incluyen más de un centenar de *variae lectiones* en un precedente embrionario de una edición crítica, que amplía el de Petrus. Se aprecia también el avance en la técnica editorial de Vulcanius en el hecho de que a veces propone dos variantes (e.g. col. 111), y con lo cual se demuestra también el uso de al menos tres modelos.

En contraste con Petrus, Vulcanius ofrece variantes marginales en todos los libros, aunque la presencia de estas variantes es mucho más amplia en los dos primeros libros. Pues bien, de nuevo una parte muy importante de estas está presente en alguno de los dos manuscritos basilenses. El ms. FV17 parece ser la principal fuente de lecturas alternativas en los dos primeros libros a juzgar por el número de variantes presentes en el mismo, pues de las 89 variantes presentadas por Vulcanius para los dos primeros libros este ms. contiene 33. Le sigue de cerca el ms. FV40, que presenta 32 variantes. En varios casos la variante está en ambos mss.

Las variantes que ofrece Vulcanius en los márgenes son de dos clases: lecturas que ya reproduce Petrus, y nuevas variantes que Petrus no recogía en sus *marginalia*. Además, Vulcanius incorpora al texto editado una buena parte de las variantes de Petrus.

Veamos algunas de las variantes, el texto editado y su presencia en alguno de los mss.:

renitentis : renidentis	FV17, FV40 (col. 14): (Mart. Cap. 1,76)
om. : canoris	FV17 (col. 20): (Mart. Cap. 2,117)
materie : temperie	FV17 (col. 6): (Mart. Cap. 1,16)
alligat : illigat	FV40 (col. 9): (Mart. Cap. 1,32)
Conse : Cosse	FV40 (col. 11): (Mart. Cap. 1,54)

Un buen número de lecturas de ambos manuscritos se incorporan al texto editado, distanciándose así de la edición de Petrus y, por ende, de la *editio princeps*. Esto demuestra que Vulcanius emplea las lecturas de sus manuscritos de forma no mecánica, examinando cada caso. No obstante, el texto editado de Vulcanius sigue siendo fiel en muchos pasajes controvertidos al texto de Bodianus.

Solo con estos paratextos la edición de Vulcanius da un gran paso adelante, pero además incorpora por primera vez en las ediciones completas de Marciano Capela un comentario de unas 800 líneas, que titula *annotationes*. La mayor parte de entradas son breves aclaraciones a términos obscuros, antigüedades, términos griegos y algunas cuestiones métricas. No obstante, también nos proporciona algunas informaciones útiles para la crítica.

En primer lugar, se lee tras la llamada a *Emenso* (col. 226) que se ha tomado una lectura de un *codex* de Venecia. Sin embargo en los *errata* (col. 242) se corrige por *Vicentiae*. Este dato es de suma importancia, pues demuestra que Vulcanius no solo empleó la edición anterior de Petrus, sino también la de Bodianus de 1499 de manera directa.

El segundo pasaje (col. 233) presenta una variante, que por alguna razón desconocida no incorporó al margen. La variante ofrecida es "boematum" de la cual afirma que la tiene un manuscrito antiguo: "Quidam V.[etus] C.[odex] habet boematum" (Mart. Cap. 2,114) y añade que proviene del griego Βοηµάτων. Pues bien, esta variante está en FV40. Esto corrobora que Vulcanius usó este manuscrito.

En otra de las entradas (col. 230; Mart. Cap. 1,46) presenta la variante "Mars" a "Lars" apostillando "Vetus codex habet." En esta ocasión es FV17 el que transmite tal variante. Con esto se demuestra que Vulcanius emplea ambos manuscritos para corregir su texto, pero también que no hace distinciones entre ambos a la hora de referirse a sus variantes.

En la siguiente entrada del comentario útil para la crítica textual Vulcanius presenta la variante "obliquabat" (col. 230; Mart. Cap. 1,67), pero esta vez la anuncia con "alia exemplaria habent." La distinta forma de presentarlo obedece a una razón clara: es más de uno el modelo que transmite esta forma; en efecto, tanto el ms. FV40, como la anotación al margen de Petrus contienen la forma citada.

Tras las *annotationes* en el último paratexto de esta edición, los *errata*, se añaden algunas variantes que no estaban y se corrigen algunas otras. La mayor parte de estos comentarios fueron introducidos como variantes al margen por Grotius.

Así pues, con el análisis de los paratextos de este impreso hemos demostrado el uso de 4 modelos al menos y comprobado el progreso en la técnica editorial de este impreso, que fue el texto de partida para la siguiente edición.

8   Leiden 1599

En efecto, la edición de Grotius vió la luz 22 años después, aunque sabemos que Grotius, niño prodigio, empezó a trabajar en ella 4 años antes a la edad de 12 años. En este impreso los paratextos son de suma importancia para la crítica de textos.

La edición cuenta con un prefacio en forma de carta dedicatoria al futuro Enrique IV de Francia, poco relevante para el texto. Sin embargo, después del *De nuptiis* y antes del comentario Grotius añade una carta dirigida al lector anónimo en la que ofrece la información más amplia hasta el momento de la técnica filológica, del uso e identificación de modelos y de los criterios de selección de variantes.[17]

Gracias a estas informaciones podemos establecer el uso de 4 códices aún presentes en la Biblioteca de la Universidad de Leiden. Asimismo, informa de la selección de un *codex* como *optimus*, el ms. BPL 36, y del uso de la edición de Vulcanius como texto base y de las otras ediciones anteriores. Proporciona sucintamente cierta información codicológica, en particular dice que su ms. contiene la suscripción al final del libro I y otros detalles.

También descarta el uso de las ediciones de Lyon aplicando prematuramente la regla de la *eliminatio descriptorum exemplarium*. Sobre el establecimiento del texto, Grotius confirma que las variantes que considera más seguras se han incorporado al texto, en cambio, las que necesitan una explicación se han incluido en las notas finales o *februa*.

Todas estas informaciones dan una idea del enorme progreso que han experimentado los *studia humanitatis* y la técnica editorial de la edición de textos clásicos. Esta tarea no podría haber sido asumida sin el concurso de grandes humanistas, a la mayoría de los cuales nombra expresamente, empezando por Vulcanius, Scaliger, los hermanos Lindenbrog, su padre Janus Grotius y Meursius. También dispuso de la ya entonces muy considerable biblioteca de la universidad de Leiden, muchas de cuyas obras cita expresamente.[18]

El segundo elemento paratextual que voy a tratar, los *marginalia*, sigue la estela marcada por su maestro y predecesor Vulcanius. Este elemento se enriquece enormemente con respecto a las variantes que transmite Vulcanius,

---

17   Sobre la labor de Grotius como filólogo, cf. Herm-Jan van Dam, "Hugo de Groot: Filoloog en dichter in Leiden," en *De Hollandse jaren van Hugo de Groot (1583–1621)*, ed. Henk J. M. Nellen y Johannes Trapman (Hilversum 1996), 67–86.

18   Sobre la relación con los sabios más prominentes de Leiden puede consultarse una amplísima bibliografía. Ofrecemos algunos ejemplos: Dirk van Miert, "Scaliger, Vulcanius, Hoeschelius and Early Byzantine History," en Cazes, *Bonaventura Vulcanius* (véase arriba, n. 10), 363–88.

LOS PARATEXTOS DE LAS PRIMERAS EDICIONES DE CAPELA 153

pues en el caso de los dos primeros libros casi duplican las variantes pasando de 89 a 167, y incorporando en algunas de las notas marginales dos variantes.

Las variantes de Vulcanius están recogidas casi en su totalidad, en algunos casos incorporadas al texto, pero además, Grotius repitió las variantes que Vulcanius había ofrecido en sus anotaciones, demostrando un uso muy cuidadoso de la edición anterior.

Puesto que Grotius cuenta con un grupo de modelos muy amplio,[19] es lógico que buena parte de esta lecturas alternativas provengan de algunos de los manuscritos a los que se refiere en el prefacio. Esto se constata en muchas de ellas:

una cum coniuge : una coniuge   Vossianus Latinus F. 48 (fol. 2) (Mart. Cap. 1,3)

pertrahebat: pertrahebant   BPL 87, BPL 88, Vossianus Latinus F. 48 (fol. 8) : (Mart. Cap. 1,15)

Llama la atención también que alguna de las variantes, que Vulcanius no ofrece en sus márgenes, estén también presentes en el ms. FV40 de Basilea y no en los otros modelos. Este hecho me plantea la hipótesis de que Vulcanius se hubiera llevado a Leiden notas con las variantes de FV17 y FV40, cosa que me parece lo más verosímil. Veamos algunos ejemplos:

crocino : coccino   FV40 (fol. 36) : (Mart. Cap. 2,140)

conscensionis : consessionis   FV40 (fol. 37) : (Mart. Cap. 2,143)

En general, Grotius mantiene las variantes anotadas por Vulcanius, también imprime algunas de las variantes de Petrus que Vulcanius había omitido. Solo he localizado una variante que Vulcanius ofrece (col. 20), coniciens : coniiciens (Mart. Cap. 2,118), ausente del impreso de Grotius.

La mayor parte de variantes nuevas provienen de los modelos de Leiden, como era previsible. No obstante, la intervención sobre el texto no se limita a ofrecer estas variantes al margen, sino que incorpora también directamente al texto variantes de sus modelos, pues según él mismo declara ha corregido el texto de Vulcanius en más de 300 lugares.

Diversos indicios de la *selectio* y *constitutio textus*, quedan a la vista en el estudio del siguiente paratexto, sus notas. Sus notas o *Februa* son en realidad el comentario más extenso publicado hasta la fecha que se alarga más de 70 pp. Las informaciones expuestas son de diversa índole y también siguen en esto el

---

19   Los manuscritos son estos: Leiden, Universiteitsbibliotheek, BPL 87, BPL 88, Vossianus Latinus F. 48.

154 AYUSO

camino de las de Vulcanius explicando a menudo términos obscuros, antigüedades, arcaísmos, cuestiones métricas, y otras, además de cuestiones relacionadas con la crítica de textos.

En su Carta al lector Grotius anuncia que sus notas son lo más reducidas
posibles y que escasamente ha introducido excursos, que las cosas que requieren más explicaciones, necesitarían más espacio. También explica en carta al
lector las abreviaturas empleadas: "MS manuscriptus, L. lege, F. forte; M. malo,
melius", pero la información que se extrae es deficiente para la crítica, pues
normalmente no identifica el manuscrito concreto del que extrae la variante.

Entre los muchos comentarios útiles para la crítica, Grotius reconoce a
veces el uso de las conjeturas para corregir *loci insani* con el término habitual, *conieci*, cuando es él mismo el autor, o citando al autor de la misma, e.g.
Scaliger.

En ciertos casos esclarece el uso de un modelo determinado con fórmulas
como "ex codice Veicetino" para referirse a la *editio princeps* o "in manuscripto
meo" indicando que la variante está en Ms. BPL 36. Sin embargo, la mayor parte
de las variantes se exponen sin identificar el modelo.

También emplea el término *glossema* o *glossa* para referirse a anotaciones
al margen de los modelos que no forman parte del texto propiamente dicho,
pero que en las ediciones y manuscritos a veces se incorporaron al mismo. No
obstante, también usa este término para referirse a comentarios de otros textos, como el de Isidoro, que cita a menudo, sin duda tomados de la edición de
Vulcanius de 1577.

En algunos de los comentarios se muestra su pericia en la crítica. Por ejemplo en fol. B3r propone la corrección de un verso: "conspicis astra virgo" en
lugar de "astra virgo conspicis", para la cual añade esta explicación: "peccat his
versus [...] transpositis vocibus." En otros casos corrige adiciones y omisiones.

Tras un análisis de las variantes propuestas en los *Februa* se observa que
provienen a menudo de distintas lecturas de los mss. de Leiden, pero también
de discrepancias entre estos y la edición de Vulcanius o los mss. de Basilea.
Veamos algunos ejemplos:

desparata : disparata disperata   FV40   BPL88 / BPL36, BPL87 (fol. A5v;
                                     Mart. Cap. 1,11)
at nobis praescire : at praescire deis BPL36 / BPL88 (fol. A6r; Mart. Cap. 1,21)
Concubiae : connubia   FV17 / BPL88 (fol. A6v; Mart. Cap. 1,37)

Así pues, en los *Februa* se observa que la procedencia de la mayor parte de
las variantes es de los mismos modelos que en las notas marginales: los mss.
de Leiden y los de Basilea. El criterio para introducirlas en este o en aquel

LOS PARATEXTOS DE LAS PRIMERAS EDICIONES DE CAPELA

paratexto, lo explica el propio Grotius: se reservan los *Februa* para los lugares que requieren más explicación.

En resumen, el conjunto de los paratextos de Grotius proporciona una información muy valiosa, que en muchos casos apoya y corrobora la información del análisis del texto, pero también ofrece claves que no están en otros sitios, de modo que su análisis se hace muy conveniente para conocer mejor el texto, en este caso, de Marciano Capela. Se constata con todo ello el uso y la identificación de los modelos que hemos mencionado.

Los modelos de la edición de Grotius se consideran poco significativos en los últimos trabajos de crítica textual, pues pertenecen a una recensión carolingia muy interpolada, aunque fue la *vulgata* del s. IX y X. Sin embargo, el texto de Grotius sigue gozando de un gran prestigio en los estudios de Capela.

9　Conclusiones

La tradición impresa del texto de Marciano Capela ha marcado y mediatizado en buena medida la interpretación que se ha hecho del texto y las ediciones críticas actuales, de una manera que considero ha sido particularmente intensa. Conocer esta parte de la tradición es, por tanto, de especial importancia. Para conocer esta parte de la tradición, creo que el estudio de los paratextos es vital, pues permite llegar a conclusiones que solo con el estudio del texto no son accesibles.

Creo que he podido demostrar en este y en otros trabajos muchos de los modelos de estas ediciones, en particular de los mss. de Basilea, pero falta un trabajo muy importante: determinar los modelos o, al menos, la rama de la tradición manuscrita de la que se sirvió Bodianus para elaborar su *editio princeps*.

　　Universidad Nacional de Educación a Distancia

CHAPTER 9

Fonctions et effets des titres-résumés dans les miscellanées philologiques de la Renaissance

Valéry Berlincourt

Abstract

Les recueils de remarques critiques et exégétiques sur les textes antiques se multiplient depuis la fin du XVe siècle dans le sillage de Calderini, Beroaldo et Poliziano, comme en témoignera plus tard l'énorme compilation de Gruter (*Lampas, sive Fax artium liberalium, hoc est Thesaurus criticus*, Francfort/Main, 1602–12/1634). Le discours érudit de ces *observationes, annotationes, miscellanea, variae lectiones*, qui a notamment pour modèle les *Nuits Attiques* d'Aulu-Gelle, privilégie la variété et la liberté. Ces 'commentaires collectifs' se prêtent à être utilisés comme ouvrages de référence grâce au développement des index. Le présent article porte sur un autre type de paratexte fréquent dans de tels recueils : les titres-résumés placés en tête de chaque section. Il aborde les fonctions et effets de ces titres-résumés en relation avec les modes d'utilisation potentiels des recueils de 'miscellanées philologiques', mais aussi et surtout avec la prédilection pour la variété et la liberté qui caractérise leur discours.

Keywords

Janus Gruter – *Lampas* (1602–12) – Neo-Latin commentaries – philological miscellanea – paratexts

1 Introduction

Chez les humanistes de la Renaissance, l'activité d'exégèse des textes antiques se pratique sous la forme du commentaire continu ou sélectif consacré à un texte singulier, mais aussi sous celle du recueil de remarques portant sur une

© KONINKLIJKE BRILL NV, LEIDEN, 2020 | DOI:10.1163/9789004427105_010

LES TITRES-RÉSUMÉS DANS LES MISCELLANÉES PHILOLOGIQUES   157

pluralité de textes,[1] initiée par Domizio Calderini,[2] Filippo Beroaldo[3] et Angelo Poliziano.[4] Les ouvrages en question, qui se réclament de modèles antiques tels que les *Nuits Attiques* d'Aulu-Gelle et l'*Histoire variée* d'Elien, portent des titres fondés sur des termes comme *observationes* ou *annotationes* mais aussi sur des expressions qui évoquent la diversité comme *miscellanea* et *variae lectiones* ;[5] on peut leur donner le nom général de 'commentaires collectifs' mais aussi de 'miscellanées philologiques'.[6]

Les recueils de miscellanées philologiques abordent des auteurs et des sujets fort variés, en un foisonnement qui reflète l'idéal humaniste d'un savoir universel. Ils accordent d'ordinaire une place prépondérante à l'explication et à la critique textuelle, souvent en relation avec la discussion de questions d'histoire culturelle, mais incluent parfois d'autres matières (notamment des anecdotes). Ils constituent un genre érudit aux contours fluctuants mais perçu

---

1 Sur cette forme de commentaire, voir notamment Raphaële Mouren, « La *varietas* des philologues au XVIe siècle : entre *varia lectio* et *variae lectiones,* » dans *La varietas à la Renaissance*, éd. Dominique de Courcelles (Paris, 2001), 5–31 ; Jean-Marc Mandosio, « La miscellanée : histoire d'un genre, » dans *Ouvrages miscellanées et théories de la connaissance à la Renaissance*, éd. Dominique de Courcelles (Paris, 2003), 7–36 ; Ann Blair, « The Collective Commentary as Reference Genre, » dans *Der Komentar in der Frühen Neuzeit*, éd. Ralph Häfner, Markus Völkel (Tübingen, 2006), 115–31 ; Klara Vanek, *Ars corrigendi in der frühen Neuzeit : Studien zur Geschichte der Textkritik* (Berlin, 2007), 137–53 ; Harm-Jan van Dam, « Adversaria, Annotationes, Miscellanea, » dans *Brill's Encyclopaedia of the Neo-Latin World*, éd. Philip Ford, Jan Bloemendal et Charles Fantazzi (Leiden – Boston, 2014), 921–3 ; et l'excellente étude de cas de Maïté Roux, *Les Variae lectiones de Marc-Antoine Muret : l'esprit d'un homme, l'esprit d'un siècle* (mémoire de Master Lyon / ENS-SIB, 2011). Je remercie Jeanine de Landtsheer de m'avoir communiqué un texte inédit sur les *Variae lectiones* de Juste Lipse.

2 « Ex tertio libro Obseruationum Domitii », in [*P. Papinius Statius : Silvae*], Rome, 1475 ; cf. Maurizio Campanelli, *Polemiche e filologia ai primordi della stampa : le 'Observationes' di Domizio Calderini* (Roma, 2001).

3 [*Annotationes centum*], Bologne, 1488 ; cf. *Filippo Beroaldo the Elder : Annotationes centum*, éd. Lucia A. Ciapponi (Binghamton NY, 1995).

4 *Miscellaneorum centuria prima,* Florence, 1489. *Angelo Poliziano : Miscellaneorum centuria secunda*, éd. Vittore Branca et Manlio Pastore Stocchi (Firenze, 1972).

5 Sur les titres, voir notamment Mandosio, « Miscellanée » (voir ci-dessus, n. 1), Vanek, *Ars corrigendi* (voir ci-dessus, n. 1), 137–41 et Roux, *Variae lectiones* (voir ci-dessus, n.1), 33–9.

6 'Commentaire collectif' : e.g. Blair, « Collective Commentary » (voir ci-dessus, n. 1). 'Miscellanées philologiques' : e.g. Dirk van Miert, « Hadrianus Junius' *Animadversa* and His Methods of Scholarship, » dans *The Kaleidoscopic Scholarship of Hadrianus Junius (1511–1575) : Northern Humanism at the Dawn of the Dutch Golden Age*, éd. Dirk van Miert (Leiden – Boston, 2011), 96–135.

comme un ensemble, ce que démontre le fait qu'ils sont réunis dans des compilations[7] et pris en compte conjointement dans des ouvrages de référence.[8]

Le discours que construisent les miscellanées privilégie la discontinuité et la fragmentation, passant d'une matière à l'autre en toute liberté. En particulier dans les paratextes introductifs, ces propriétés discursives sont légitimées par l'autorité des précédents antiques et vantées comme une stratégie destinée à charmer et divertir le lecteur, à maintenir son intérêt en éveil, et à l'aider ainsi à assimiler les connaissances présentées. Sur le plan structurel, les recueils concernés sont divisés en sections,[9] désignées la plupart du temps comme des chapitres.[10] Ces unités, une centaine chez Beroaldo et Poliziano, souvent entre quinze et trente par livre chez Piero Vettori (25, puis 38 livres)[11] ou Marc-Antoine Muret (8, puis 15 livres, auxquels s'ajoutent 4 livres posthumes),[12] n'occupent couramment qu'une à trois pages environ mais peuvent être bien plus étendues. Une caractéristique de la division en sections, qui a pour principal modèle Aulu-Gelle, est que celles-ci sont, pour l'essentiel, indépendantes les unes des autres.[13] La segmentation des miscellanées ne sert donc nullement à mettre en évidence un arrangement logique, comme le fait par exemple celle des traités antiquaires;[14] liée au mode de production de ce discours que l'auteur élabore progressivement au gré de son inspiration, elle en souligne plutôt l'éclectisme.

---

7   Ces compilations apparaissent dès la fin du xve siècle; la plus vaste est de loin la *Lampas* (ou *Fax artium liberalium,* ou encore *Thesaurus criticus*) de Jan Gruter (Francfort/Main, 1602–1612 et supplément 1634).

8   C'est le cas de répertoires bibliographiques comme les *Pandectae* de Conrad Gessner (Zurich, 1548), discutés dans Mandosio, « Miscellanée » (voir ci-dessus, n. 1), mais aussi du volume de Benedetto Biancuzzi (Blancucius) qui indexe de nombreux recueils d'« observationes, miscellanea et variae lectiones » (Rome, 1597).

9   Sur les sections, voir notamment Roux, *Variae lectiones* (voir ci-dessus, n. 1), 31–5, 43–6 et 53–54.

10   Il arrive que les sections reçoivent d'autres dénominations (*schediasmata, dialogismi,* etc.), mais aussi, on le verra ci-dessous, qu'elles ne soient pas explicitement désignées comme telles.

11   *Variarum lectionum libri XXV,* Florence, 1553; *Variarum lectionum XIII novi libri*, Florence, 1568; *Variarum lectionum libri XXXVIII* [...], Florence, 1582.

12   *Variarum lectionum libri VIII,* Venise, 1559; *Variarum lectionum libri XV,* Anvers, 1580; *Variarum lectionum libri IV et Observationum iuris liber singularis*, Augsbourg, 1600.

13   Il ne s'agit là que d'une tendance générale. Des liens manifestes existent par exemple entre certains chapitres consécutifs des *Animadversa* de Junius, comme le relève van Miert, « Hadrianus Junius' *Animadversa* » (voir ci-dessus, n. 6), 100–2.

14   Sur le rôle de la segmentation dans les ouvrages antiquaires, voir e.g. Karl Enenkel, « *Ars antiquitatis*: Erkenntnissteuerung und Wissensverwaltung in Werken zur römischen Kulturgeschichte (ca. 1500–1750) », dans *Cognition and the Book: Typologies of Formal Organisation of Knowledge in the Printed Book of the Early Modern Period*, éd. Karl Enenkel et Wolfgang Neuber (Leiden, 2005), 51–123, ici 91–112.

2   Les titres-résumés de sections

Les paratextes des miscellanées philologiques comprennent, outre les éléments introductifs comme les épîtres dédicatoires et les préfaces, des indications relatives au contenu de ces recueils.[15] On y trouve parfois des *marginalia* (manchettes), surtout utilisés pour fournir les références des citations et mettre en évidence des explications, corrections ou discussions thématiques, et beaucoup plus souvent des index, qui recensent principalement les auteurs ainsi que les sujets et/ou les mots abordés et permettent aux miscellanées de servir d'ouvrages de référence.[16] Deux autres types de paratextes sont indissociables de la segmentation du discours : titres-résumés placés en tête de chaque section pour annoncer son contenu, et table des matières consistant en une liste des sections et incluant très souvent, elle aussi, des titres-résumés.[17] Ces deux derniers types de paratextes constituent, tout comme la division en sections, une propriété formelle récurrente de ce genre érudit.[18] Plus encore que pour les tables des matières, présentes dans plus de la moitié des recueils, ceci est vrai pour les titres-résumés placés en tête des sections, qui figurent dans la grande majorité d'entre eux (et dont il est démontrable au moins dans certains cas qu'ils ont bien été rédigés par les auteurs).[19] En voici quelques exemples tirés des *Miscellanea* de Poliziano :

---

15   Sur les paratextes de contenu, voir notamment Roux, *Variae lectiones* (voir ci-dessus, n. 1), 34–5, 43, 52, 54–5.

16   Sur cet aspect des miscellanées, voir Blair, « Collective Commentary » (voir ci-dessus, n. 1) ; pour une perspective plus générale, Ann Blair, *Too Much to Know : Managing Scholarly Information Before the Modern Age* (New Haven, 2010), 117–72. On ajoutera ici deux faits particulièrement significatifs, à savoir que Gruter (voir ci-dessus, n. 7) indexe les divers ouvrages qu'il inclut dans sa compilation, et surtout que Biancuzzi (voir ci-dessus, n. 8) publie un volume exclusivement consacré à l'indexation de nombreux recueils de miscellanées.

17   Roux, *Variae lectiones* (voir ci-dessus, n. 1) parle de 'titres/sommaires'.

18   Certains recueils de miscellanées ne contiennent toutefois aucun des deux, comme Caspar Schoppe, *Suspectarum lectionum libri quinque* [...] (Nuremberg, 1597).

19   Dans le cas de Poliziano ces paratextes existent déjà dans la version autographe : Branca et Pastore Stocchi, *Angelo Poliziano* (voir ci-dessus, n. 4), 39 ; cf. Ciapponi, *Filippo Beroaldo* (voir ci-dessus, n. 3), 20–4 sur les enjeux de leur apparition chez Poliziano, par comparaison avec Beroaldo chez qui ils étaient absents. Dans le cas de Robortello ils sont indirectement revendiqués par l'auteur dans sa préface, comme on le verra ci-dessous. Dans celui de Muret ils sont aussi l'œuvre de l'auteur, même si pour la partie posthume, publiée sur la base de brouillons épars, ils sont des ajouts de l'éditeur André Schott ; sur ce point, voir Lucie Claire, « Sur la publication posthume des commentaires de Marc-Antoine Muret (Augsbourg et Ingolstadt, 1600–1604), » dans *Apta compositio : formes du texte latin au Moyen Age et à la Renaissance*, éd. Christiane Deloince-Louette, Martine Furno et Valérie Méot-Bourquin (Genève, 2017), 413–32, ici 422.

Caput xvii.

Correctus in tragoedia Senecae locus : atque ex graeca remotiore fabula declaratus super nemiaeo leone. (f. d5^v)

Caput xviii.

Quid sit apud Iuuenalem fraterculus gigantis : quidque apud alios Terrae filius : ibidemque de Mani uocabulo. (f. d6^r)

Caput xviiii.

Super aspiratione citata quaepiam : simul enarratum Catulli nobile epigramma. (f. e1^r)

Caput xxviii.

Panici terrores qui uocentur : eoque locupletissimi citati testes. (f. f1^v)

Les liens qui unissent les titres-résumés placés en tête des sections et les titres-résumés inclus dans une table des matières sont particulièrement visibles dans le fait que, lorsqu'ils coexistent dans un même ouvrage, leurs énoncés sont d'ordinaire identiques.[20] Ces deux types de paratextes ont, dans une large mesure, un modèle antique dans les *lemmata* des *Nuits Attiques* d'Aulu-Gelle, et les endroits qu'ils occupent – en tête de chaque section et souvent aussi dans une table générale – correspondent à ce que l'on trouve, comme aboutissement d'un processus complexe de transmission, dans les premières éditions imprimées de cette œuvre.[21]

Dans les pages qui suivent, on examinera les fonctions que les titres-résumés remplissent ainsi que les effets qu'ils produisent.

---

20 Parmi les rares exceptions, citons Pierre Pithou, *Adversariorum subsecivorum libri II* (Paris, 1565).

21 Sur la transmission manuscrite des *Nuits Attiques*, voir Leofranc Holford-Strevens, *Aulus Gellius : an Antonine Scholar and his Achievement* (Oxford, 1988, éd. rév. 2003), 30 et 333–7 : dans une phase ancienne, les *lemmata*, qui étaient originellement réunis dans une table des matières générale à la fin de la préface, ont été répartis au début des différents livres sous la forme de tables des matières partielles, e.g. Cité du Vatican, Biblioteca Apostolica Vaticana, MS Reg. lat. 597 = O (s. IX^1, livres 9–20) et MS Vat. lat. 3452 = V (s. XII^2, livres 1–7), puis dans une phase ultérieure chaque *lemma* a été inséré en tête de son chapitre respectif (e.g. Florence, Biblioteca Medicea Laurenziana, MS plut. 79.29 (a. 1446), où ces éléments paratextuels coexistent avec des tables des matières partielles figurant au début des différents livres). Les premières éditions ont des *lemmata* en tête de chaque chapitre, associés à une table des matières générale : Rome, 1469 = *editio princeps*, ISTC ig00118000 (où la table est en fin d'ouvrage) ; Rome, 1472, ISTC ig00119000 (où la table est en fin d'ouvrage) ; Venise, 1472, ISTC ig00120000 (où la table est en début d'ouvrage).

3   Marquage des sections

Dans la situation usuelle, l'opération consistant à diviser le discours en sections est expressément marquée par des désignations telles que 'caput primum / secundum / tertium' etc., comme dans les exemples de Poliziano cités ci-dessus. A l'égard de cette opération, les titres-résumés qui précèdent chaque section sont dès lors redondants, même si leur impact visuel peut contribuer à mettre en évidence la division du discours, notamment quand il est accru par la mise en œuvre de procédés typographiques multiples.[22]

Il arrive cependant que les titres-résumés revêtent une fonction essentielle dans la segmentation du discours. Dans le recueil publié en 1543 par Francesco Robortello,[23] les sections ne sont pas désignées explicitement par des termes comme 'caput primum' etc. :

LOCVS HORATII IN
Poetice declaratus.   (f. 19r)

LOCVS PROPERTII
emendatus.   (f. 43r)

De la sorte, les titres-résumés, du reste particulièrement brefs (un point sur lequel on reviendra), s'avèrent être dans le corps de cet ouvrage – et même dans l'ouvrage entier car aucune table des matières n'y est présente – le seul élément qui révèle l'existence des sections. Le fait que, dans sa préface, Robortello dit avoir divisé son recueil en 'chapitres' confirme que, à ses yeux, insérer des titres-résumés dans son texte équivaut à le découper en unités de cette nature.

La démarche de Robortello consistant à assigner exclusivement aux titres-résumés la fonction de marquer les sections constitue une exception : on ne la retrouve ailleurs que dans de très rares cas.[24]

---

22   Voir e.g. Roux, *Variae lectiones* (voir ci-dessus, n. 1), 51 à propos des *Variae lectiones* de Muret.

23   *Variorum locorum annotationes tam in Graecis, quam Latinis authoribus* (Venise, 1543). Dans la seconde édition augmentée du même recueil de Robortello, qui figure dans *De historica facultate disputatio* [...] (Florence, 1548) sous le titre « In varia loca, quae tam in Graecis scriptoribus quam in Latinis passim leguntur, annotationum libri duo », puis dans son recueil postérieur intitulé « Variorum locorum in antiquis scriptoribus, tum Graecis, tum Latinis annotationes », inclus dans *De convenientia supputationis Livianae ann. cum marmoribus Rom. quae in Capitolio sunt, eiusdem De arte, sive ratione corrigendi veteres authores disputatio, eiusdem Emendationum libri duo* (Padoue, 1557), les chapitres sont en revanche explicitement désignés comme tels.

24   Notamment Giovanni Battista Pio, « Annotationes <priores> » (« Annotamenta » dans la table des matières), inclus dans une compilation contenant aussi les miscellanées de

4 Indication du contenu des sections

Outre le rôle, d'ordinaire accessoire, qu'ils jouent par rapport au marquage des sections, les titres-résumés – placés en tête des sections ou réunis en une table – ont pour fonction intrinsèque de signaler pour chaque section quelles matières et en particulier quels auteurs et thèmes y seront commentés. D'un ouvrage à l'autre, cette fonction s'exerce selon des modalités diverses (qui entraînent à leur tour, comme on le constatera plus loin, des différences en ce qui concerne des fonctions – et effets – plus spécifiques).

Le contenu informatif des titres-résumés est très variable. Dans les miscellanées de Robortello, il s'avère très maigre, puisqu'il se limite presque toujours, comme dans les exemples cités ci-dessus, à la mention de l'auteur ou du texte discuté ainsi qu'à celle de l'opération effectuée (correction, explication).[25] Dans de nombreux recueils il ne porte pas seulement sur les auteurs et les textes, mais inclut aussi des précisions sur les questions traitées, une situation qui s'observe déjà chez Poliziano, puis entre autres chez Vettori :

> *Locus emendatus in Liciniana, ubi Cicero uitam suam tuetur contra uoces*
> *maleuolorum, eum ut nimis deditum studiis literarum, insectantium.*
> Cap. XI. (éd. 1553, p. 21 [livre 2])

Du reste, l'accent peut résolument être mis sur les thèmes, comme dans le dernier des exemples de Poliziano cités plus haut, ou chez Hadrianus Junius, qui recourt très volontiers à cette pratique :[26]

> *Cur Cupressus feralis arbor fuerit ab*
> *antiquis habita, rationes.* Cap. XX. (p. 53 [livre 1])

Il arrive que les indications de contenu soient assez substantielles, comme dans les *Electa* de Juste Lipse :[27]

Calderini, Beroaldo et Poliziano : Filippo Beroaldo, *Annotationes centum, eiusdem Contra Servium grammaticum notationes* [...] (Brescia, 1496) et Petrus Nannius, Συμμίκτων *sive Miscellaneorum decas una* (Lyon, 1548). Dans le recueil postérieur de Pio, *Annotamenta* (Bologne, 1505), les chapitres sont explicitement désignés comme tels.

25 Il en va de même dans les *Antiquae lectiones* de Lipse et souvent aussi dans ses *Variae lectiones* (voir ci-dessous, n. 30). Concernant Robortello, les titres-résumés de son ouvrage postérieur de 1557 (voir ci-dessus, n. 23) se limitent le plus souvent à la mention, non pas de l'auteur antique dont il explique ou corrige le texte, mais de l'érudit dont il s'attelle à démontrer l'erreur.

26 *Animadversorum libri sex* [...], Bâle, 1556.

27 *Electorum liber I, in quo, praeter censuras, varii prisci ritus* (Anvers, 1580) ; *Electorum liber primus, in quo, praeter censuras, varii prisci ritus* et *Electorum liber secundus, in quo mixtim*

CAP. I.

Refutata uulgi opinione de scriptore Controuersiarum. Non esse Annaeum Senecam philosophum. ostensum id ab aetate, a uita, a stylo. Esse illius patrem. id quoque clare ostensum. Senecarum stemma. Locus unus correctus.   (éd. 1580, p. 17 [livre 1])

De surcroît, le degré de détail des informations fournies varie lui-même grandement. Certains titres-résumés offrent un reflet précis du contenu des sections : tandis que dans les *Electa* de Lipse leur ampleur donne une fidèle image de la consistance des chapitres, dans les *Variae lectiones* de Muret leur brièveté correspond à la simplicité de composition de chaque unité. En revanche, dans d'autres cas les titres-résumés ne représentent que très partiellement le contenu des sections : ceux de Janus Palmerius sont fort maigres par rapport à la notable longueur des chapitres qui constituent son ouvrage.[28]

5   Aide à la consultation

Par leur rôle d'indicateurs de contenu, les titres-résumés peuvent orienter l'activité du lecteur, et notamment soutenir une forme de consultation consistant à parcourir les matières du recueil dans la perspective de sa structure, c'est-à-dire telles qu'elles sont réparties section par section.

Leur appui potentiel à une telle utilisation dépend de leur consistance et de leur degré de détail, qui, on l'a vu, varient considérablement, mais aussi de l'endroit où ils sont placés : les ouvrages incluant des titres-résumés groupés en une table, comme ceux de Poliziano ou de Vettori ou les *Electa* de Lipse, qui donnent accès conjointement aux contenus de toutes les sections, se prêtent bien mieux à un survol que ceux qui comprennent seulement des titres-résumés en tête de chaque section. Or cette dernière situation, qui s'observe par exemple chez Robortello et Junius ou encore dans les *Suspiciones* de Jan Gruter,[29] est presque aussi fréquente que la première. Ceci suggère que les titres-résumés n'ont pas forcément pour principale justification de servir la consultation.

Du reste, l'aide que les titres-résumés sont capables d'apporter à un survol reste limitée même quand ils sont informatifs et réunis en une table générale. Précisément parce qu'ils exposent les contenus de l'ouvrage sous l'angle de sa division en sections, ils sont bien moins efficaces à cet égard que les index, qui

---

     ritus et censurae (Anvers, 1585).

28   *Spicilegiorum commentarius primus* [...] (Francfort/Main, 1580).

29   *Suspicionum libri IX* [...] (Wittenberg, 1591).

permettent une consultation ciblée. Si les titres-résumés peuvent fournir un appui effectif à une forme de consultation, c'est surtout – pour ainsi dire par défaut – dans les recueils qui ne contiennent pas d'index, comme par exemple les *Variae lectiones* et les *Antiquae lectiones* de Lipse[30] ou encore les *Variae lectiones* de Dirk Canter.[31] Or il s'avère qu'ils coexistent fréquemment avec des index, ce qui tend à confirmer que leur présence – ou du moins leur persistance à une période où les index sont devenus courants – ne s'explique pas prioritairement par le soutien qu'ils offriraient à cette modalité d'utilisation.

6 Mise en évidence de la nature du discours érudit

Outre l'aide, limitée, qu'elles fournissent à la consultation, les indications de contenu procurées par les titres-résumés sont susceptibles de mettre en évidence certaines propriétés du discours érudit des miscellanées.

Si on les considère de manière globale, les titres-résumés d'un ouvrage peuvent attirer l'attention sur le fait que celui-ci est centré sur les textes, comme c'est le cas des *Variae lectiones* et des *Antiquae lectiones* de Lipse, ou qu'il privilégie au contraire l'histoire culturelle, comme c'est le cas de ses *Electa*. Cet effet, lui aussi, s'exerce surtout quand les titres-résumés sont réunis en une table des matières : pour en revenir aux exemples cités en début d'article, la concentration sur la correction et l'explication des textes est plus manifeste dans le recueil de Poliziano, qui dispose d'une telle table, que dans celui de Robortello, où les titres-résumés figurent uniquement en tête de chaque section.

Par ailleurs, les titres-résumés d'un ouvrage considérés dans leur globalité, et plus encore dans leur séquence, peuvent agir comme des marqueurs de son éclectisme, en montrant qu'il traite des sujets très divers et que ses sections successives passent librement de l'un à l'autre. Quand les titres-résumés sont seulement placés au début des sections, comme chez Junius, l'effet en question n'est perceptible que si l'on feuillette ou lit le recueil. Il est en revanche d'emblée évident quand ils sont réunis en une table comme déjà chez Poliziano, puis par exemple chez Muret :

> CORRECTVS & explicatus locus e primo libro Aristotelis de arte dicendi. Cap. I.
> De Psyllis, & ophiogenesin. Allatus locus Varronis, cuius testimonio usus erat Plinius. Cap. II.

---

30   *Variarum lectionum libri IIII* (Anvers, 1569). *Antiquarum lectionum commentarius* [...] (Anvers, 1575).

31   *Variarum lectionum libri duo* (Anvers, 1574).

LES TITRES-RÉSUMÉS DANS LES MISCELLANÉES PHILOLOGIQUES

Sententiam illam, Patria est, ubicunque bene est, acute a Lysia reprehensam.   Cap. III.

De ui uerbi alloquor. Horatii in odis explicatus locus.   Cap. IIII.

De Callisthene & Philisto. locus Ciceronis emendatus, & declaratus. Capitales interdum a ueteribus ingeniosos dictos esse.   Cap. V.

(éd. 1559, Ff2ᵛ [livre 2])

Cet effet de mise en évidence de la nature du discours érudit est essentiellement indépendant de la forme des titres-résumés, courts et simples comme ceux de Muret et surtout de Robortello, ou longs et complexes comme ceux des *Electa* de Lipse. Un effet additionnel se produit cependant quand ces différentes formes se combinent au sein d'un même ouvrage. Une telle configuration révèle que la variété discursive de l'ouvrage concerné résulte aussi d'une alternance entre des discussions focalisées sur une matière spécifique et des discussions sophistiquées (impliquant le cas échéant plusieurs matières). On la rencontre notamment dans les *Adversaria* d'Adrien Turnèbe :[32]

Vir uirum legit.   Cap. 7.

(éd. 1573, p. 11 [livre 25])

Curione non egere, Per curionem dici iubere.   Cap. 8.

(éd. 1573, p. 12 [livre 25])

Statio, Lampridius emendatur, Iuuentutis princeps, Frumentarii, Laticlauii honos, Rudiarii, Delinimenta, Bellonae ministri, Gigantes anguipedes cur, Secutores, Dirae, Porta Libitinensis, Penula.   Cap. 17.

(éd. 1573, p. 20 [livre 25])

Capitolinus emendatur & explicatur, Tolerantia, Praesul, Vates, Magister, Ampiruare, Redantruare, Seuiri, Ius relationis secundae, tertiae, quartae & quintae, Signum dare, Dies utiles, & non utiles, Bucolici milites, Bucolia, Semiermes, Diocnitae, Iudex, Donatiuum.   Cap. 18.

(éd. 1573, p. 22 [livre 25])

Par ailleurs, des titres-résumés longs et complexes sont capables de mettre en évidence certains aspects du discours érudit quand on les prend en compte non seulement dans leur succession, mais aussi de façon intrinsèque (et donc indifféremment selon qu'ils sont placés en tête des sections ou réunis en une table des matières). Cet effet intrinsèque des titres-résumés longs et complexes tient au fait que la pluralité d'énoncés qu'ils contiennent indique comment

---

32   *Adversariorum tomus primus duodecim libros continens,* Paris, 1564 ; *Adversariorum tomus secundus duodecim libros continens,* Paris, 1565 ; *Adversariorum tomus tertius, libros sex continens,* Paris, 1573.

166   BERLINCOURT

s'enchaînent les divers éléments d'une section. Il peut consister à souligner, le cas échéant, que son agencement interne obéit lui-même aux principes de variété et de liberté qui prévalent plus généralement dans la composition du recueil, mais aussi à faire apparaître qu'il repose au contraire sur une forte cohérence thématique, comme dans cet exemple tiré des *Electa* de Lipse.

CAP. VIII.

De Frumentatione, accurata conlectanea. Eius origo prima. Indicatum in Liuii loco mendum. Appiani in Gracchi lege apparens error. Sallustii insignis emendatio. Menstruum seruorum. Clodii Annonaria lex. Recensus populi, & in ea uoce Suetonius correctus. Dionis error in tempore Recensus Augusti. Persius explicatus & Plinius. Ambigua Capitolini lectio. Caelius in Epistolis ad Cicer. correctus bis. De origine Praefecti & Curatorum annonae. Minutia Frumentaria. Appuleius emendatus. Panis gradilis, & alia compluria.   (éd. 1580, p. 55 [livre 1])

Ce titre-résumé très développé signale sans équivoque que la section concernée, dont il détaille la structure, constitue une sorte de petite dissertation consacrée à une question spécifique. Il traduit ainsi très clairement la propension des *Electa* à mettre l'accent sur des sujets antiquaires, annoncée en page de titre (livre 1 "in quo, praeter censuras, varii prisci ritus"; livre 2 "in quo mixtim ritus et censurae").

7   Conclusion

Ces quelques observations sur les titres-résumés de sections des miscellanées philologiques ont notamment montré qu'une part de leurs fonctions et effets sont différents, ou s'exercent de façon différente, selon l'endroit que ces paratextes occupent. Remarquons ici, pour conclure, que les ouvrages, nombreux, dont les titres-résumés placés en tête de chaque section (disposition en soi la plus fréquente) ne s'accompagnent pas de titres-résumés groupés dans une table encouragent – voire imposent s'ils ne contiennent pas d'index – des formes d'utilisation qui, chacune à sa manière, sont intimement liées à la variété caractéristique du discours des miscellanées : une lecture linéaire soumise à l'agencement éclectique créé par l'auteur, ou un feuilletage permettant au lecteur de s'arrêter au gré de ses propres envies sur telle ou telle section qui retient son attention.

Université de Genève

CHAPTER 10

From *puer* to *iuuenis*: Peder Hegelund's Self-Reflecting Portrayal of Danish Christian III in the *Epicedion de Inclyto et Serenissimo Rege Christiano III*

Anders Kirk Borggaard

Abstract

In Renaissance Europe, the death of a king could spell disaster for the existing power structure but at the same time prove to be a grand opportunity for the aspiring individual. To contemporary humanists, the tradition of composing Neo-Latin funerary literature immortalising and eulogising the deceased effectively turned the occasion into an opportunity for them to show off their skills in prose and poetry by fashioning literary monuments that preserved the memory and virtues of the deceased while simultaneously serving as convenient vehicles for the self-fashioning of their ambitious authors. In this paper, I demonstrate how the literary fashioning of others could thus be a way of fashioning oneself by turning the eulogy of the *laudandus* into a means of self-fashioning for the *laudator*. This will be done through an examination of how Peder Hegelund (1542–1614), a Danish schoolboy and aspiring humanist only 17 years old, used the recently deceased King Christian III of Denmark-Norway as a mirror of his own aspirations in his *Epicedion de Inclyto et Serenissimo Rege Christiano III* (1560). Focusing my attention on an episode portraying the youthful years of the future king, I argue that Hegelund created an image of the young king-to-be which paralleled that of a sixteenth century schoolboy, thereby enabling him to present himself through the figure of young Christian as a bright young man with a promising future.

Keywords

Peder Hegelund – *Epicedion de Inclyto et Serenissimo Rege Christiano III* (1560) – Neo-Latin funerary literature – King Christian III of Denmark-Norway – literary self-fashioning

© KONINKLIJKE BRILL NV, LEIDEN, 2020 | DOI:10.1163/9789004427105_011

In[1] 1559, Peder Hegelund (1542–1614), a 17-year-old schoolboy from Ribe, put pen to paper and began composing an *epicedion* celebrating King Christian III of Denmark-Norway (1503–59), who had passed away on New Year's Day that same year. But rather than keeping to the customary content and structure of an *epicedion*, Hegelund turned his work into a detailed poetic biography of the king, recounting his entire life from cradle to grave while praising his many and pious *res gestae*.[2] Simultaneously, Hegelund found a clever way of adding himself to the narrative, as I will demonstrate in this paper, through a little known episode from the early years of the king. Having spent his youth in the duchies of Schleswig-Holstein, Christian was crowned king in 1537 after his victory in the Count's Feud, the civil war-like interregnum that followed the death of his father, Frederik I (1474–1533). A fervent Lutheran since his youth, Christian's first action as king was to swiftly carry out the Reformation within the entire realm, and he furthermore transformed the educational system after the Melanchthonian model in order to educate a new humanist elite for the preservation of the reborn Gospel, as well as the benefit of the entire kingdom. Christian's reign therefore witnessed an academic and humanist flourishing hitherto unequalled in the Danish realms, and the favourable conditions enjoyed in this scholarly environment produced a great social mobility that especially benefitted the new class of humanists. The death of their Danish Maecenas could therefore spell disaster for the still nascent humanist community, but simultaneously the humanist tradition of composing works lamenting the deceased and praising their deeds and virtues presented the humanists with the possibility of influencing or positioning themselves within the new situation *rege mortuo*. In effect, to the inventive humanist, death became a great (literary) opportunity.[3]

---

1   This paper was written during my PhD fellowship funded by the Carlsberg Foundation and Aarhus University.

2   For a brief overview of the genre, see Ingeborg Gräßer, *Die Epicedien-Dichtung des Helius Eobanus Hessus* (Frankfurt am Main, 1994), 13–8.

3   On death as a literary opportunity, see Birgitte Bøggild Johannsen, "Ars moriendi more regio: Royal Death in Sixteenth Century Denmark," *Journal of Early Modern Christianity* 1 (2014), 51–90; Gräßer, *Epicedien-Dichtung* (see above, n. 2), 13–8; Gary Ianziti, "Pier Candido Decembrio and the Suetonian Path to Princely Biography," in *Portraying the Prince in the Renaissance. The Humanist Depiction of Rulers in Historiographical and Biographical Texts*, ed. Patrick Baker et al. (Berlin, 2016), 237–70. For the genre as a political and ideological tool, see e.g. John S. McManamon, *Funeral Oratory and the Cultural Ideals of Italian Humanism* (Chapel Hill, 1989); Sharon T. Strocchia, *Death and Ritual in Renaissance Florence* (Baltimore, 1992). In a Northern European context, scholarly attention has focused on this kind of literature in the vernacular as a means of religious propaganda in the confessional struggles of the sixteenth century. See e.g. the volume *Preparing for Death, Remembering the Dead*, ed. Tarald Rasmussen and Jon Øygarden Flaeten (Göttingen, 2015), and especially the contributions by

Many grasped this opportunity, and one of these was the young Hegelund in Ribe.[4] His *Epicedion de Inclyto et Serenissimo Rege Christiano III, Rege Daniae & Noruegiae, &c.*[5] was published in Basel in 1560 as part of a greater volume on the death of Christian III composed by Hans Thomesen (1532–73), Hegelund's headmaster at the grammar school in Ribe.[6] Until now, the work of Hegelund has been neglected by scholars and simply dismissed as lacking in every kind of originality.[7] While it is true that Hegelund was not alone in opting for a biographical approach to his royal panegyric—indeed three other humanists produced very similar biographical accounts in both poetry and prose, one of them being schoolmaster Thomesen[8]—Hegelund nevertheless managed to provide his work with both originality and a unique personal dimension that sets his work apart from the other contemporary biographies. Within his ambitious 1192 verses of elegiac couplets, Hegelund pays special attention to an episode that took place during the early years of Christian's life. As a young man, Christian was sent to the court of his maternal uncle, Elector Joachim I of Brandenburg, and when the elector was summoned to the Diet of Worms in 1521, young Christian followed him to the famous Diet where Luther would defend his writings and eventually be condemned as a heretic. While the Diet undeniably was an important experience for the future reformer-king, Hegelund chooses to portray it more as a transitional test of character in the life of a young man on his road from boyhood to adulthood and future greatness.

This paper will therefore examine this short but key narrative (vv. 149–278), in which I will argue that Hegelund fashions the narrative of young Christian in a way that effectively transforms the image of the *laudandus*, Christian, into a mirror for the personal ambition of the *laudator*, Hegelund. Using narratology as an approach to the *Epicedion* can help illustrate how Hegelund uses the biographical raw material left behind by Christian as a means for his own self-fashioning. In his plenary paper, "Autor/Erzähler und Fiktion im neulateinischen Roman: Ein Beitrag zu einer historischen Narratologie," Stefan Tilg

---

Claudia Resch (153–72), Sivert Angel (173–98), Arne Bugge Amundsen (223–40), and Eivor Andersen Oftestad (281–312).

4 A complete overview of the literary production is still lacking. I have so far been able to identify more than 20 pieces of prose and poetry composed 1559–61, one in 1563.

5 Hereafter referred to as *Epicedion*. Unless otherwise stated, all page/verse numbers refer to this.

6 Hans Thomesen, *Oratio De illustriss. principe ac domino, D. Christiano Tertio, Rege Daniae, & Noruegiae, &c. [...] Adiectum est et epicedion, scriptum à Petro Hegelio Ripensi* (Basileae, 1560; LN 1582 8°).

7 Bjørn Kornerup, *Ribe Katedralskoles Historie: Studier over 800 Aars dansk Skolehistorie*, vol. 1 (København, 1947), 306: "Uden al Originalitet".

8 The three are Hans Thomesen, Johannes Sascerides, and Hieronymus Osius, see below.

demonstrated how a fictitious *fabula* could incorporate elements of history, *historia*, into the narrative *syuzhet* of the Neo-Latin novel.[9] A similar albeit reversed technique is found in the *Epicedion* of Hegelund. As Christian died, his life became a common *archive* of dormant, biographical information—the *historia* to the *syuzhet*—which could be re-activated by an inventive humanist into a *functional memory*—the *syuzhet* to the *historia*.[10] At the same time, the king being dead meant that his memory was now *fair game*, and the selection of *historia* could consequently be framed in a way suited to the aims of authors like Hegelund through elements more closely related to the realm of *fabula* than to biographical *historia*.[11]

I will therefore approach the *Epicedion* in three steps. First, I will outline how the aforementioned narrative is framed as a transitional event, both within the greater narrative of the *Epicedion* proper and within the life of Christian as man of great deeds. Next, I examine how Hegelund fashions the character of the young Christian into a parallel of himself by playing on the close relationship between author and narrator using both the literary narrative itself and his own *Lectori Salutem*. Finally, I will discuss the parallelism created by Hegelund in comparison to the other contemporary depictions of the same events, as well as its influence on the remainder of the *Epicedion* and the message it tries to convey.[12]

The Diet of Worms as a Transitional Event

The *Epicedion* opens with a lengthy *exordium* (vv. 1–106) after which the biographical *narratio* progresses chronologically from a brief description of Christian's lineage (vv. 107–34) and primary education at home in the hands

---

9   See Stefan Tilg, "Autor/Erzähler und Fiktion im neulateinischen Roman: Ein Beitrag zu einer historischen Narratologie," this volume 68–90.

10 Here using terms from *Cultural Memory Studies* formulated by Aleida Assmann, see e.g. Aleida Assmann, "Canon and Archive," in *Cultural Memory Studies: An International and Interdisciplinary Handbook*, ed. Astrid Erll and Ansgar Nünning (Berlin, 2008), 97–107; Aleida Assmann, *Cultural Memory and Western Civilization: Functions, Media, Archives* (New York, 2011; first German edition 1999), 119–34. A similar idea is found in the theoretical framework of the SFB 644, *Transformationen der Antike*; see Hartmut Böhme, "Einladung zur Transformation," in *Transformation. Ein Konzept zur Erforschung kulturellen Wandels*, ed. Hartmut Böhme et al. (München, 2011), 7–37.

11 Cf. Patrick Baker on Giannozzo Manetti's very idealized and almost hagiographical depiction of the recently deceased Niccolo Niccoli; Patrick Baker, *Italian Renaissance Humanism in the Mirror* (Cambridge, 2015), 130.

12 See n. 8.

of Wolfgang von Utenhof (vv. 135–48) to the events in Germany, the episode examined in this paper (vv. 149–278). Next follows a narrative on Christian's manly deeds (vv. 279–698), and finally Hegelund depicts his pious departure from this world (vv. 699–1114). The events in Germany thereby bridge the educational years of Christian and his first deeds as a grown man, and Hegelund emphasises the narrative importance of this passage by spending 130 verses of the 1000 verse long *narratio* on this single episode—more or less the same as spent on the entire Count's Feud that resulted in Christian's coronation in 1537.

Leaving behind the home schooling of Wolfgang von Utenhof where Christian learnt the "Phoebeas artes", our passage opens as young Christian is sent to Germany and the electoral court of Joachim I of Brandenburg to be further educated and cultivated as a prince by his uncle (vv. 149–76). This educational stay culminates when Christian follows Joachim to the Diet of Worms (vv. 177–278), and in the following, the by now learned and Lutheran Christian travels home, where "Eripuitque patrem tenebris, noctique profundae, / Per Stygios fumos, Pontificumque dolos,"[13] before embarking on a career as a military commander and proto-reformer. The Diet therefore constitutes the final chapter in the education of young Christian, and Hegelund shows special care for this episode by furnishing it with a detailed, lingering description otherwise only used for the Count's Feud (vv. 425–92) and Christian's deathbed and burial (vv. 707–988; 1073–1114). However, where we might expect the Diet, which is explicitly introduced as having to do with the *causa Lutheri*,[14] to be yet another educational experience in which the future Lutheran king comes into contact with Luther or Lutheran ideas, the rebel monk vanishes completely, in turn leaving the stage open to the young Christian who instead becomes the one answering the all-important question of "quae doctrina placeret".[15] The episode at Worms is thereby transformed into an occasion for the young man at the end of his education and thus on the brink of adulthood to prove his talents as a final test of character before venturing on to more serious tasks such as war and reformation. This reading is supported by Hegelund's own concluding remarks as he leaves behind the events in Worms framing them as *praeludia* for the greatness he is about to describe: "Haec magnis non magna tuis praeludia gestis [...] His tandem missis, maiora ad caepta feramur [...]."[16]

---

13   Vv. 293–4 (p. 78).
14   "Qui tum Vuormaciae dubias discernere causas / Deberent, etiam docte Luthere tuam." vv. 179–80 (p. 74).
15   "Prodidit is coràm sibi quae doctrina placeret, / Hanc ueluti furtim quam prius addidicit." vv. 193–4 (p. 74).
16   Vv. 275–9 (p. 78).

As a result, the Diet becomes a threshold both within the greater narrative and in Christian's life as a man of great deeds. This function is ultimately made possible by the education that Christian receives and, more importantly, by the physical and mental development that he experiences in the period leading up to the Diet. For although he had been educated by von Utenhof and his uncle, neither of them had taught him the Lutheran values necessary to declare "quae doctrina placeret" and thus to fulfil the role assigned to him by Hegelund. Instead, Christian is portrayed as having acquired this knowledge "furtim", and so his early attraction to Lutheranism becomes a testament to the genius and potential residing within the young man at this transitional point in time.[17] Christian's personal development is therefore central to his role at the Diet, and Hegelund is diligent in describing how Christian evolves into the young man full of potential.

Hegelund begins by stressing that Christian arrives in Germany as a boy not even 15 years old.[18] Throughout the period from his arrival to the convocation of the Diet, he is continuously described as "puer", which is the same epithet as used while Wolfgang von Utenhof was educating Christian at home. There, he was a "puer" with "pectora puerilia" and an "aetas mollis et apta regi",[19] but during his time with Joachim, he evolves from "nec adhuc iuuenis" to "penè puer" and finally to "praeclare puer".[20] He does, however, remain firmly within the category of *puer*. This changes very suddenly just before the Diet of Worms is convened: "Iam tibi cor fuerat iuuenili in corpore canum, / Iam pueri ingenium turba senilis amat."[21] From this point on, Christian is referred to as "iuuenis" instead of the former "puer",[22] but Hegelund goes a long way to point out how the nature of the young Christian is one of duality, or rather transition. As expressed in the close and chiastic relationships between both "cor canum— iuuenili corpore" and "cor canum—pueri ingenium", Christian currently takes

---

17   See above n. 15.

18   "Hinc ned adhuc iuuenis, cum uix tria lustra teneret, / Inuisit terram Marchio clare tuam:" vv. 149–50 (p. 73).

19   "Ergò tibi puero fuit haec pia cura parentis, / Custodes uitae iunxerat atque duces." vv. 135–6 (p. 72); "Formabas aptis puerilia pectora uerbis, / Dum fuit huic aetas mollis et apta regi." vv. 141–2 (p. 72).

20   "Hinc nec adhuc iuuenis, cum uix tria lustra teneret, / Inuisit terram Marchio clare tuam:" vv. 149–50 (p. 73); "Ad te penè puer teneris perrexit ab annis, / Deliciaeque patris, deliciaeque tuae." vv. 155–6 (p. 73); "Ò praeclare puer, simul his uersatus in oris, / Clarior es uerbi luce nitente Dei." vv. 167–8 (p. 73).

21   Vv. 171–2 (p. 74).

22   "Et tua signa sequens iuuenis comparuit heros, / Tunc annis instans post tria lustra tribus." vv. 185–6 (p. 74); "At iuuenis Princeps, nil turgida uerba moratus, / Mirator solum, non uenerator erat." vv. 233–4 (p. 76). Notice how he also becomes "heros" and "princeps".

part in all three stages of life, and Hegelund further underlines the transitional nature of this point in time by reversing the chronological order of the adjectives in "iuuenili corpore" and "pueri ingenium". Transitioning from boy to man, Hegelund seems to say, Christian's youthfulness entailed a certain boyish crudeness despite the intelligence residing within his "cor canum". This is almost reminiscent of the commonplace apology of a young writer excusing his inexperienced lack of style, and we ought to keep this in mind considering the 17-year-old author of the *Epicedion*. As young Christian shortly after makes his way to Worms, Hegelund again informs us of his age: the young man with the aged heart is now 17 years old.[23]

An *Exemplum* for the Aspiring Schoolboy

While this attention to detail may be seen as biographical precision, it is simultaneously a key element in Hegelund's auto-reflexive depiction of Christian, as he uses it to effectively create a setting that would have been well known in the life of a sixteenth century schoolboy like himself. In the *Ordinatio Ecclesiastica* of 1537, Christian's own educational reform, this point in time was recognised as a time of transition, in this case from grammar school to the university:[24]

> Praeterea debent ludimagistri indolem discipulorum suorum diligenter obseruare [...] Quos vero ingenio valere deprehenderint / ad decimum sextum usque aetatis annum in ludo detineant. Ab eo autem anno accuratissime dispiciant qui ea quae caeperunt suis studiis / foeliciter aliis communicaturi sint / et qui id non incommode facturi videntur domino offerantur / et priuatis vel publicis stipendiis / ad publica studia ablegentur.

As this shows, in the scholarly environment of the time, Christian's age would have been closely associated with transition and the need for a test of character—a situation familiar to the author of this very text, the schoolboy Hegelund. He is to be examined before he can matriculate at the university, and by framing Christian as a Danish schoolboy, Hegelund opens up the possibility of mirroring himself in the young Christian at Worms.

---

23   Vv. 185–6 (p. 74) (see above n. 22).
24   *Ordinatio Ecclesiastica Regnorum Daniae et Norwegiae et Ducatuum / Sleswicensis / Holtsatiae etcet.* (Hafnie, 1537; LN 196 8°), fol. xxxviiir–v.

The parallel relationship between the two young men becomes more pronounced when we take into account how Hegelund presents himself to his reader in the prefatory *Lectori Salutem*. Although short and generic—the king is worthy of praise, but Hegelund's slender muse is not worthy of the task—it ends in a three-part sequence in which Hegelund describes the circumstances for the composition of his work.[25] Here, he informs his reader that he is only a simple "alumnus", whom his headmaster, Hans Thomesen, has ordered to compose a work that far exceeds the abilities of his muse.[26] Secondly, he confesses that it was due to his youthful audacity that he nevertheless dared to treat the lofty subject, and Hegelund suggestively uses "iuueniliter" in connection with his state of mind at the time of composition, the corresponding "iuuenis" being the word used to describe Christian prior to and in Worms. Finally, he expresses the hope that his work will be well received even though it might be quite rough around the edges. Stylistic shortcomings, he believes, should be pardoned when dealing with grand themes. Here, it is the thought that counts.

While these are all prefatory tropes appropriate for a young writer 'excusing' his lack of style, we found a similar apologetic tone in the description of the wise but unpolished Christian, as pointed out above.[27] Furthermore, both passages share the same three-part structure, and I therefore propose that we approach the preface as a kind of *Lesersteuerung*, albeit not as one that instructs us in the proper reading of the description of Christian, but rather as one that reappears as an echo within this passage and thereby reminds us of Hegelund, the other young man currently facing a somewhat similar situation.

If we now compare the sequence from the *Lectori Salutem* to the description of Christian, we do indeed find striking similarities. We initially learn that Christian was sent to the court of his uncle to be educated, and we may accordingly perceive Christian as an *alumnus* of the electoral court. Here, uncle Joachim has the explicit role of educator, and just as Thomesen commanded young Hegelund to compose his *Epicedion*, it is similarly Joachim who bids the "iuuenis" to accompany him to Worms.[28] Secondly, Hegelund is diligent in noting that while Christian's young age and inexperience naturally should

---

25   "Scribere qui iussit, quique impulit, edidit idem: / Cuius ego è multis unus alumnus eram. / Et sumus haec, fateor, nimium iuueniliter ausi: / Candide tu Lector consule cuncta boni. | Et rude si lectu dignabere (si modò) carmen, / Des ueniam: in magnis si uoluisse sat est." Hegelund, *Lectori*, p. 66, vv. 9–14.

26   Thomesen explains in the preface to his *Oratio* that he gave the deceased king as the theme for the poems which the students had to compose *more ueteri* for the celebration of St. Thomas' day 1559; Thomesen, *Oratio* (see above, n. 6), 7. See also Kornerup, *Ribe Katedralskoles Historie* (see above, n. 7), 264.

27   See e.g. Tore Janson, *Latin Prose Prefaces: Studies in Literary Conventions* (Stockholm, 1964), 132.

28   Vv. 149–88 (pp. 73–74).

have kept him from participating directly in the affairs of the Diet, his age simultaneously required him to use the opportunity to present "Indolis excelsae signa probanda", the phrase "signa probanda" suggestively hinting at the idea of Christian being a schoolboy about to be examined.[29] However, arriving at the third and final part of the sequence, we encounter a telling difference between the content of the *Epicedion* and the *Lectori Salutem*. While Hegelund hopes for a positive response to his work, Christian has already finished his transitional test of character, and more importantly, he did so with great success. This difference effectively turns young Christian into the embodiment of Hegelund's own personal and professional ambitions, and it is therefore of great importance to describe how Christian, his *exemplum*, passed his test in Worms despite the difficulties of youth.

At the Diet (vv. 177–278), Hegelund presents us with a congregation of noblemen, clergy, the Holy Roman Emperor, and young Christian with his uncle Joachim. A monk, "Epicuri de grege porcus" and symbol of the papist church, ascends a temporarily constructed podium from which he begins a thundering speech condemning the blasphemy of the time, "fanda et nefanda". His behaviour is best described as histrionic, and during his laughable performance, the monk falls on his knees in pretended prayer. This is too much for the pious Christian, and he therefore decides to speak his mind. When he notices that the rope girdling the monk has fallen through a crack in the podium, he creeps closer, stealthily reaches under the platform, and ties several tight knots on the end of the rope. Trapped on all four and by now infuriated, the monk cries out to the Emperor, demanding the punishment of whoever was responsible for the blasphemous prank.

In the ensuing confusion, Christian calmly raises his head and admits his guilt: "En autor facti, dixit, quem quaeritis adsum, / Haud insons aliquis nunc mea facta luat."[30] Surprisingly, this is met not with criticism but with a positive response from everyone except the monks, and the noblemen even find great pleasure in the lively character of the young man. What can at best be described as crude and juvenile behaviour—indeed, Hegelund twice addresses his actions as "iocus"[31]—evidently becomes a way for Christian to successfully demonstrate his talents and his genius, and he effectively declares "quae doctrina placeret" through the prank he plays on the monk. Hegelund thereby

---

29 "Et licet hunc aetas rebus prohibebat agendis, / Quae grauibus causis non satis apta fuit: / Quod tamen huic licuit, quodque hunc fecisse decebat, / Indolis excelsae signa probanda dedit." vv. 189–92 (p. 74).

30 Vv. 267–8 (p. 77); cf. Verg., *Aen.* 1,595.

31 "Aspicit obseruans gestus, et uultibus haeret: / Ille furens bilem commouet atque iocos." vv. 235–6 (p. 76); "Ex illo princeps es Christi nomine dignus, / Attulit iste tuus seria multa iocus." vv. 273–274 (p. 77).

illustrates that great things can be found in youthful crudeness, and the actions of Christian together with the response of the noblemen almost seem to mirror the gnome with which Hegelund ends the *Lectori Salutem*: "Des ueniam: in magnis si uoluisse sat est."[32]

The *laudandus* as a mirror of the *laudator* and the ambitions of a young author

Christian's successful test in Worms had made it obvious to all that the young man possessed great potential, and Hegelund accordingly moves on to spend the remaining verses recounting the deeds of the adult Christian. He sings of wars, reformation, and great piety in life as well as death, and since these are all subjects fit for men and kings, Christian the schoolboy is now a thing of the past. Instead, he is elevated to a regal *exemplum* for his son and successor, Frederik II (1534–88), to whom the entire volume is dedicated.[33] However, by combining the biographical raw material from the early years of Christian's life with elements brought in from the world of the Danish grammar school, Hegelund creates a unique narrative in which the king also becomes an example for the simple schoolboy, who sees in the politically and religiously important Diet a familiar transitional test of genius.

How this addition from outside the biographical *historia* governs the narrative becomes clear when comparing it to the three descriptions of the same event in other contemporary biographies. In an *epicedium* by Johannes Sascerides, a work steeped in Lutheran piety, the narrative on Germany and Worms is treated with extreme brevity and portrayed as a purely religious event in which Christian receives the light of the true Gospel and becomes a pious Lutheran.[34] Something similar is the case in the *Oratio* of schoolmaster Thomesen and the *Res Gestae* of Hieronymus Osius, German humanist and *poeta laureatus* of Christian III.[35] While both Thomesen and Osius address the incident at Worms as an omen of Christian's future, they do so solely in relation to his work as a reformer. In the words of Thomesen,[36]

---

32 See n. 25.

33 This exemplarity is also emphasised in the preface of Thomesen, see n. 26.

34 Johannes Sascerides, *Epicedium in obitum Serenissimi Potentissimiq: principis Christiani Tertij Daniae. &c. Regis* (Hafniae, 1559; LN 1440 4°), fols. A4v–Br.

35 Thomesen, *Oratio* (see above, n. 6); Hieronymus Osius, *Res Gestae inclyti ac serenissimi Domini D. Christiani III Regis Daniae &c. descriptae carmine heroico* (Vitebergae, 1563; VD16 O 1320).

36 Thomesen, *Oratio* (see above, n. 6), 17–8. Cf. Osius, *Res gestae* (see above, n. 35), fols. A5v–A6r.

uidetur CHRISTIANVS hoc facto, quasi laeto omine, certum prae-
buisse indicium, de secuta per eum in his regionibus Euangelij propa-
gatione, reiectis monachis, sacrificulis, atque id genus alijs hypocritis
quamplurimis.

This is remarkably different from the *iocus iuuenilis* portrayed by Hegelund.
Rather than framing the episode only as a religious omen of a life dedicated
to the propagation of the true Gospel, Hegelund uses his narrative to present
Christian's unrefined yet wise and auspicious rejection of Catholicism as the
"signa probanda" and "non magna praeludia" given by a young man in a situation of transitional examination. This ultimately connects to what is, in my
opinion, the most significant difference between Hegelund and his three sen-
iors: none of the others addresses the point that Christian, due to his young
age, had no business interfering with the Diet. Only Hegelund emphasises the
awkward circumstance that Christian's inexperience ought to have silenced
him while his age placed him in a transitional setting that forced him to speak
up anyway.

To Hegelund, this was a key detail, as he felt himself to be in a similar situation when composing his praise for a king too great for his pen. To him, the
Epicedion was effectively his Worms. As we saw in the *Ordinatio Ecclesiastica*,
gifted schoolboys "domino offerantur / et priuatis vel publicis stipendiis / ad
publica studia ablegentur,"[37] and in his preface to the new king, Frederik II,
schoolmaster Thomesen does exactly this.[38] Hegelund in turn responds by
demonstrating his talents, and through the *exemplum* of young Christian,
skilfully fashioned into a parallel of himself, he reminds us that great things
can come from humble—or youthful—beginnings. Christian's successful test
of character at Worms foreshadowed the reception Hegelund hoped his work
would receive, and if we follow the parallel with Christian to its logical end,
Hegelund almost seems to suggest that given the right support—the "publicis stipendiis" promised by Frederik's father Christian—he will have similar
potential, albeit in a scholarly context. Who could have known that after further studies at the university, Hegelund would in fact become one of the most
important schoolmasters and bishops of the Danish Renaissance? He did nevertheless warn us, in the spirit of his *exemplum*, that this work was only *non
magnum praeludium* for his future greatness.

Aarhus University

---

37   See above n. 24.
38   Thomesen, *Oratio* (see above, n. 6), 8.

CHAPTER 11

Shaping a Poem: Some Remarks on Paul of Krosno and His Horatianism

Elwira Buszewicz

Abstract

Paul of Krosno (ca. 1474–1517) was a Polish humanist, poet and teacher of the sixteenth-century Krakow University milieu. Scholars have so far presented him either as an enthusiastic propagator of humanist ideas, or as an erudite, 'bookish', and moderately talented poet. Some scholars also maintained that his poetry was too focused on religious topics and (consequently) unable to reflect the variety of subjects that other contemporary Renaissance poets dealt with in their works. This paper aims to go against this latter opinion, by discussing Paul of Krosno's poetic process and some of the existing forms of classical Latin literature's reception in his lyrical production. Indeed, Paul of Krosno extensively imitated Horace's works, by following not only the metrical patterns of Horace's *Carmina*, but also rendering his 'spirit'—the 'nature' of the Horatian odes—in his poetry. The author focuses on many of Paul of Krosno's poems and hymns written according to the Horatian forms, in order to study the multi-faceted and wide-ranging forms of his Horatian reception (displayed both in the themes he focused on, and in the features he displayed in his works, such as poetical structures, metres, and rhetorical forms).

Keywords

Paul of Krosno – Neo-Latin lyric poetry – reception of Horace – Polish humanism

The Poet and His Milieu

Paul of Krosno[1] was a humanist poet and teacher in the sixteenth-century milieu of Kraków University. He was born about 1470 in Krosno, a sub-Carpathian

---

1 The only monograph on the poet is by Albert Gorzkowski, *Paweł z Krosna. Humanistyczne peregrynacje krakowskiego profesora* (Kraków, 2000).

© KONINKLIJKE BRILL NV, LEIDEN, 2020 | DOI:10.1163/9789004427105_012

SHAPING A POEM: REMARKS ON PAUL OF KROSNO AND HIS HORATIANISM   179

royal borough founded by Casimir the Great, King of Poland, and fortified by Ladislaus Jagiello in the early fifteenth century. It rapidly became a centre for the manufacture of clothing and prospered commercially; already during the fifteenth century Krosno was called "parva Cracovia", probably because of its parish schools. The next century was the golden age in its history.

Paul was the only son of a townsman, the mayor (*proconsul*) of his native town, John Procler. In 1491, he matriculated as a student at Kraków University as "Paulus Johannis de Crosna."[2] At this time humanist ideas were beginning to resonate in the minds of many of the social climbers among those university scholars who rejected the scholastic teaching of the time—though often it is not easy to draw a dividing line between 'scholasticism' and 'humanism'.

We do not know how long Paul stayed in Kraków, but we encounter him in 1499 (without a bachelor's degree) at the University of Greifswald in Pomerania. He matriculated there on August 3, the same day as Johannes Dantiscus (1485–1548).[3] At Greifswald he had the opportunity to meet Peter of Ravenna, who taught Roman and canon law there at the time.[4] After obtaining the bachelor's degree, Paul returned to Kraków in 1500 and started lecturing as an *extraneus*. He graduated with a master's degree in 1506. There were several intervals in his academic career in Kraków: he fled the city during epidemics of the plague, in the winter of 1508, and to Hungary in the summer of the same year. Thanks to his student Sebastién Magyi, he was introduced to Gábor Perényi, one of the most powerful Hungarian nobles of the period, who became his generous patron.[5] He visited Várad (now Oradea in Romania) and Nagyszőlős (now Vynohradiv in Ukraine). The following year he went to Vienna to publish his poems. In the spring of 1511 we encounter him back in Kraków. Now a *collega minor*, he recommenced his lectures, commenting on Virgil, Claudian, Ovid's *Heroides*, and Lucan. Sometimes he was absent and colleagues replaced him for classes on Virgil, Persius or Seneca. In 1516 Paul delivered his last lecture "in poesi". There are no further records of him, except for a handwritten note about his death, on a page of an edition of his poems, that he died of a cerebral stroke in 1517 in the small town of Sącz: "In Sandecz apoplexia obit anno 1517

---

2   *Metrica seu Album Studiosorum Universitatis Cracoviensis, pars prima, inde ab anno 1400 usque ad annum 1508*, BJ MS 258, III (manuscript in the Jagiellonian Library), fol. 377ᵛ.

3   On Dantiscus see Cristina Neagu, "East-Central Europe," in *The Oxford Handbook of Neo-Latin*, ed. Sarah Knight and Stefan Tilg (Oxford 2015), 517; Harold B. Segel, *Renaissance Culture in Poland: The Rise of Humanism, 1470–1543* (Ithaca, 1989), 161–90; Piotr Urbański, "Joannes Dantiscus and Italian Neo-Latin Poetry," in *Acta Conventus Neo-Latini Cantabrigiensis*, ed. Jean-Louis Charlet (Tempe, 2003), 555–63.

4   Gorzkowski, *Paweł z Krosna* (see above, n. 1), 84–6.

5   Segel, *Renaissance Culture* (see above, n. 3), 110.

(millesimo quingentesimo decimo septimo) in Novembr[i] fugiens pestem Crac[oviam] infest[antem]."[6]

The Poems and Their Reception

Some of Paul's poems were published in print, others survived in manuscript. The only major Renaissance edition of his poems appeared in Vienna in 1509.[7] Some texts were also published separately[8] or added as commendatory verses for other authors' books.[9]

---

6 Gorzkowski, *Paweł z Krosna* (see above, n. 1), 94–6.

7 The book was entitled *Pauli Crosnensis Rutheni artium liberalium magistri Poetaeque quam suavissimi Panegyrici ad divum Ladislaum, Pannoniae regem victoriosissimum et sanctum Stanislaum, praesulem ac martyrem Poloniae gloriosissimum et pleraque alia connexa carmina non sine magna suavitate condita.* The volume contains a foreword addressed to Gábor Perényi and a collection of poems in diverse metres: 1) *Ad libellum ut in Pannoniam se conferat* (Phalaecian), 2) *Panegyricus in laudem d. Ladislai* (elegiac couplet), 3) *Panegyricus in laudem d. Stanislai* (elegiac couplet), 4) *Elegiacon ad S. Barbaram,* 5) *Imnus extemporaneus ad D. Mariam* (lesser Sapphic), 6) *Saphicon endecasillabum ad S. Catharinam,* 7) *Saphicon in Virginalem Conceptionem,* 8) *In Natalem Christianum* (elegiac couplet), 8) *Ode ad G. Perenaeum pro novo anno* (Alcaic), 9) *Ad Janum Deum bifrontem* (lesser Sapphic), 10) *Epigrammata in insignia Gabrielis de Peren[yi]* (elegiac couplet) 11) *Ode ad Apollinem* (Fourth Asclepiadian), 12) *Ad Thaliam* (lesser Sapphic), 13) *Ad G. Perenyi salutatorium* (elegiac couplet), 14) *Eucharisticon ad eundem* (lesser Sapphic), 15) *Elegiacon ad ... Stephanum Bathoriensem Castellanum Budensem,* 16) *Propempticon ad Sebastianum Maghium* (elegiac couplet), 17) *Ad eundem* (elegiac couplet), 18) *Invitatorium ad eundem* (elegiac couplet), 19) *Ad Stan[islaum] Turzo praepositum Varadiniensem* (Fourth Archilochian), 20) *In cenam eiusdem* (lesser Sapphic), 21) *In laudem Joannis Winterburger, impressoris solertissimi* (elegiac couplet), 22) *In invidum* (elegiac couplet).

8 Paulus Crosnensis, *Epithalamion, hoc est Carmen Connubiale in nuptias illustrissimi ac invictissimi principis et domini: domini Sigismundi Regis Poloniae nobilissimaeque ac pudicissimae Barbarae filiae inclyti et Magnifici domini Stephani Palatini Pannoniae. Cepussique Comitis perpetui a Magistro Paulo Crosnensi Rutheno concinnatum* (Kraków, 1512); idem, *Saphicon de inferorum vastatione et triumpho Christi* (Kraków, 1513; reprinted in 1514); idem, *Carmina de felicissimo reditu ex Vienna Austriaca Illustrissimi* [...] *Sigismundi Regis Poloniae* (Kraków, 1515); idem, *Panegyricus ad divum Stanislaum Praesulem sanctissimum et martyrem victoriosissimum, ac Patronum Regni Poloniae beneficientissimum* (Kraków, 1522).

9 Cf. Ioannes Stobnicensis, *Introductio in Ptholomei Cosmographiam cum longitudinibus et latitudinibus regionum et civitatum celebriorum* (Kraków, 1512). Paul wrote two commendatory epigrams to the book: 1. *Magister Paulus Crosnensis Lectori studioso,* 2. *Distichon:* "Adspice quam parvo, lector studiose, libello / Clausa sit immensi machina magna soli" ("Just look, o diligent reader, what a little book encloses the mighty machine of the boundless earth"). The translations, if not otherwise indicated, are mine.

SHAPING A POEM: REMARKS ON PAUL OF KROSNO AND HIS HORATIANISM   181

Modern scholars have not been very interested in this poet. The first collected edition,[10] compiled by Bronisław Kruczkiewicz, appeared in the 1880s. Some years later Michał Jezienicki discovered and described a Breslau manuscript containing many previously unknown poems and some of Paul's prose works.[11] But it was not until 1962 that a corrected and enlarged verse collection was published thanks to the efforts of Maria Cytowska.[12]

Philologists' opinions on Paul's poetic activity have varied. Some have called him a "church poet" whose medievalism filtered through his superficial humanist culture,[13] which was considered *imitatio servilis*. Others, especially Cytowska, see him as an enthusiastic protagonist of humanist ideas, the first native Polish poet who managed to create his 'school' at the university.[14] In Harold B. Segel's opinion, he was metrically correct and erudite, but rather "bookish" and not very talented; his poetry was allegedly too religious and did not reflect the variety of subjects typical of the best Renaissance poets.[15] The monographer Gorzkowski locates Paul's work within a wider and deeper context of Renaissance culture, arguing against some of the stereotypical views and accentuating his merits as a true humanist and teacher.

Indeed, Paul of Krosno was the first native Polish scholar and poet whose work displayed a considerable variety of metres. This was emphasized by the renowned Belgian scholar Claude Backvis, who wrote of Paul with evident fascination:[16]

> Si un éloge de la Vierge se contente de distiques élégiaques, le gros de son oeuvre nous vient affublé de strophes saphiques, asclépiades B ou alcaïques, de rhythmes logaédiques hendécasyllabes [...] ou phaleciens. Une

---

10   Paulus Crosnensis et Ioannes Vislicensis, *Carmina*, ed. Bronislaw Kruczkiewicz (Kraków, 1887).

11   Michał Jezienicki, "O rękopisie Biblioteki królewskiej i uniwersyteckiej we Wrocławiu z r. 1515 [...] tudzież o pismach w nim zawartych", *Archiwum do Dziejów Literatury i Oświaty w Polsce* 9 (1897), 268–9.

12   Paulus Crosnensis, *Carmina*, ed. Maria Cytowska (Warsaw, 1962). Further cited as *Carmina* 1962.

13   Tadeusz Sinko, "Historia poezji łacińskiej humanistycznej w Polsce," in *Dzieje literatury pięknej w Polsce*, part 1 (Warsaw, 1918), 130.

14   Maria Cytowska, "Twórczość Pawła z Krosna na tle ówczesnej literatury humanistycznej," *Meander* 16 (1961), 502. Also Ignacy Lewandowski poses Paul of Krosno between the most important Polish/Latin poets of Renaissance, presenting some of his poems in a bilingual anthology entitled *Antologia poezji łacińskiej w Polsce. Renesans* (Poznań 1996), there 65–81.

15   Segel, *Renaissance Culture in Poland* (see above, n. 3), 113–5.

16   Claude Backvis, "La poésie latine en Pologne pendant la première phase de l'Humanisme," *Neohelicon* 3 (1975), 31–2.

épitre adressée à Stanislas Thurzo se présente même en un mètre particulièrement recherché, combinaison d'archiloquien majeur et de senaire iambique catalectique. Est-ce l'effet d'un pur hasard?

Metrical Choices and Poetic Inspirations

We may observe Paul's predilection for the lesser Sapphic stanza. He wrote many poems in this metre, among which we find the *Saphicon de inferorum vastatione et triumpho Christi*, on the triumphant descent of Christ into hell before his resurrection, which seems a rather 'untypical' heroic epyllion from the point of view of choice of metre.[17] Prudentius treated the subject in his *Cathemerinon* (9,70–81), but in a completely different metre.[18] Paul's poem contains 66 Sapphic stanzas, that is, 264 lines. As regards the metre, Crosnensis may have drawn inspiration from Giovanni Pontano's *Orpheus*, since Pontano's poetry circulated in Hungary in manuscript form. Instead of choosing a mythological catabasis, Paul narrates a religious one, like others which appeared in the period (mainly in hexameters), for example Erasmus's *Carmen heroicum*, Hessus' *Victoria Christi ab inferis*, or Macarius Mutius' *De triumpho Christi*.[19] The printed version of Paulus's poem has an invocation to Apollo, which was absent in the manuscript version. The whole work is syncretic—joining not only mythical and Christian, but also epic and hymnic elements.

Let us take a brief look at the stanzas in which we observe a contest between Pluto-Lucifer and Christ. Pluto wants the infernal doors to remain closed, guarding Hell against Christ's entrance:[20]

> Ocius, fidi famuli, labantes
> Cardinum postes reparate, et antra
> Claudite abstrusa, et ruitura duro
> Ostia saxo.

---

17   There is also a medieval epic poem in this metre, Saxo Grammaticus's *Lay of Ingellus*: see Karsten Friis-Jensen, "The *Lay of Ingellus* and its Classical Models," in *Saxo Grammaticus. A Medieval Author Between Norse and Latin Culture*, ed. Karsten Friis-Jensen (Copenhagen, 1981), 67–71.

18   This is the *Hymnus omnis horae*, which begins as follows: "Da, puer, plectrum, choreis ut canam fidelibus / dulce carmen et melodum, gesta Christi insignia, / hunc Camena nostra solum pangat, hunc laudet lyra". Translation in *The Poems of Prudentius*, trans. Sister M. Clement Eagan (Washington, 1962), 59: "Boy bring my quill of ivory, that I may to sounding lyre / Sing in sweet and tuneful trochees Christ and His immortal deeds. / Him alone my Muse shall honor, Him alone my lyre shall praise."

19   Cf. Gorzkowski, *Paweł z Krosna* (see above, n. 1), 243.

20   *Carmina* 1962, 177.

Hurry up, faithful servants! Repair the tottering door and close off the hidden caverns, and block the gate, which could otherwise collapse, with a hard rock.

However, the devils are obedient not to him, but to the Lord, who invokes the psalmic or hymnic formula *Tollite portas*:[21]

Non minus princeps revocandus instat
Verba sublata memorata fundens
Voce : "Caelesti, fera monstra, Regi
  Tollite portas."

However, the Prince, who was to be dismissed, presses on, raising his voice and uttering memorable words: "Open up the doors, you wild monsters, to the King of Heaven!"

The poem was supplemented with another, *Hymnus in diem Paschalem,* rooted both in Horatian imagery and in the early Christian tradition, including Patristic literature, the hymns of Prudentius, and especially Venantius Fortunatus's *Ad Felicem episcopum de Pascha.*[22]

Let us now examine some of the Horatian elements in Paul's hymn. We encounter here the *mutat terra vices* theme (from Horace, *carm.* 4,7). The Horatian poem is Archilochian, but Paul again chooses the Sapphic stanza, not following the metre, but the imagery and sometimes words and phrases. Horace describes a scene of transformation from winter to spring, underlining that "the snows have dispersed, already grass is returning to the meadows and leaves to the trees; the earth goes through its changes, and the rivers decrease their flow between the banks."[23] The Polish poet amplifies and sacralises this landscape, adding more light, dignity and colour:[24]

Ecce quae turpi iacuit colore,
Terra, nunc fructus recreat virentes,
Sponte producens foliis honorem,
  Gramina campis.

---

21 *Carmina* 1962, 177.
22 Gorzkowski, *Paweł z Krosna* (see above, n. 1), 251; Elwira Buszewicz, "Obraz Chrystusa Zmartwychwstałego w polskiej poezji nowołacińskiej," in *Via pulchritudinis. Wątki biblijne w literaturze i kulturze polskiej*, ed. Albert Gorzkowski et al. (Kraków, 2010), 268–71.
23 Prose translation by Gregson Davis, *Polyhymnia. The Rhetoric of Horatian Lyric Discourse* (Berkeley, 1991), 155.
24 *Carmina* 1962, 182.

Silva crinitis redimita ramis
Perditum rursus revocat decorem
Et gelu nuper glaciali abacta
    Tecta resumit.
Prata mirando renitent nitore,
Floribus passim graphice refecta
Et velut picti variata lucent
    Sidera caeli.

And now the earth, which lay with a dismal complexion, is regenerating its green crops, spontaneously bestowing charm on the leaves, and grass on the fields. The forest, crowned with long-leafed branches, recovers once again its lost beauty and its covering, which was lately driven off by the icy chill. The meadows, picturesquely ornate on all sides with flowers, are resplendent with an amazing brightness, shining like diverse stars on a decorated sky.

Paul's poem may even be regarded as a polemic with the ancient poet, from whom he quotes the expression "gramina campis". In Horace's *carm.* 4,7, an enthusiastic praise of spring ends with a warning: "Thou wast not born for aye," for "we are dust and dreams".[25] Horace focuses mainly on the moment at the end of a mortal life, when surprisingly the cyclical progression of the four seasons must be seen as non-cyclical, linear. Thus, every human being is like an autumn leaf falling before a "lifeless winter,"[26] a long winter of death. In Paul's stanzas the joyful metamorphosis of Nature brings more delight, because spring is seen as a figure of the Resurrection and as such is more important than a pagan spring—it assures us of immortal life. Here the transformation of the earth seems to be only a part of a total Paschal metamorphosis of the Universe, which regains its cosmic harmony: all four elements are reconciled in peace and all the lights in the sky present a triumphant spectacle.[27]

The Sapphic stanza was used also in some of Crosnensis's brief lyrical invocations to the gods—or rather, as he explains, to the only, though polyonymous, God, who is the source of power and inspires every human enterprise. These are intended as examples for students to read before writing their own texts. Entitled *To Jove*, *To Apollo*, *To Bacchus*, *To Mercury*, *To Pallas*, and *To the Muses*,

---

25   Horace, *carm.* 4,7,7, "Immortalia ne speres", and 4,7,16, "pulvis et umbra sumus", in A. E. Housman's translation, in *The Poems of A. E. Housman*, ed. Archie Burnett (Oxford, 1997), 118.

26   Gregson Davis, *Polyhymnia* (see above, n. 23), 156.

27   Cf. Elwira Buszewicz, "Obraz Chrystusa" (see above, n. 22), 269.

SHAPING A POEM: REMARKS ON PAUL OF KROSNO AND HIS HORATIANISM   185

these invocations do not allow us to think that the teacher wanted his students to pray to pagan divinities. It is a typical humanist *metonomasia*, representing the pagan deities as allegories of the Christian God, the Saints, or "as symbolic entities, [which] demonstrated how to portray poetically that divine energy that manifested itself visually on earth."[28] But we also find some longer invocations and hymnic odes in Horatian metres addressed to the Saints and pagan gods, in Alcaic stanzas (*Invocatio ad divam Virginem, Alia invocatio in diem natalem divae Virginis, Ad gloriosam Virginem super choros angelorum assumptam invocatio, Ad Divum Sebastianum martyrem militemque gloriosissimum carmen*) or in Sapphics (*Alia invocatio ad divam Virginem Mariam, Alia [...] ad sanctam Annam, Ad omnes sanctos invocatio alia, Hymnus extemporaneus ad divam Virginem Mariam, Saphicon hendecasyllabum ad sanctam Catharinam, Saphicon in virginalem Conceptionem*, but also *Ad Ianum, Ad Thaliam*) and also in Fourth Asclepiadian (*Ode [...] ad Apollinem*).[29]

Horatian Clichés and Moods

The didactic intent is even more explicit in some poems expressing humanist principles, written in Sapphics or Alcaics, which may have been versified résumés of or introductions to various lectures delivered at the university. They include poems like *Carmen laudes artis poeticae [...] demonstrans, Exhortatio ad virtutem, Carmen Horatii poetae vitam [...] perstringens* as an example of a verse biography, and *In laudem Valerii Maximi, In laudem Terentianae lectionis*. On the one hand, we observe in them the Horatian immortality-of-poetry topos, including the praise of poets; on the other, they lack a Horatian density, offering a series of clichés, typical of what we may call academic poetry. "Academic poets" structured their thoughts and imagination by reading not only the ancient poets, but also Renaissance commonplace books.[30] Thus, some of Paul's ideas may seem rather watered down or even banal, especially to a modern reader, who, of course, may find commonplaces in Horace too, but, aware of that, still appreciates the Roman poet's sophisticated and playful conceits.

---

28   Stella Revard, *Pindar and the Renaissance Hymn-Ode, 1450–1700* (Tempe, 2001), 145.

29   Horace wrote his hymns to pagan deities in Sapphic (*carm.* 1,10) or Alcaic stanzas (*carm.* 1,35; 2,19); this might have influenced Paul's metrical choices.

30   As Ann Moss convincingly shows, naming them "a memory store of quotations, which could be activated to verbalize present experience in the langue of familiar moral paradigms and with reference to a cultural history shared by writer and reader": Ann Moss, *Printed Commonplace-Books and the Structuring of Renaissance Thought* (Oxford, 1996), VI.

Paul's odes of this kind are devoid of Horace's intimacy, of a persona talking in private to a friend, but also—through the text—to every reader. Paul's lyrical "you" is generally any audience interested in the subject, the *studiosa iuventus, quicumque, quisque.* We can say the same about two commendatory odes added to Paul's editions of Seneca's tragedies: *Lectori studioso* to *Thyestes*[31] and *Ad lectorem* to *Troas.*[32] The former looks like a kind of lay sermon on the supremacy of the goods of the soul over the goods of Fortune and the goods of the body, while the latter, describing Fortuna's terrible power, is not only a didactic but also a reflective ode, spiced with melancholy, anticipating certain poetic moods which would later be characteristic of the Jesuit lyre:[33]

> Quae caeca, comis, blanda, potens, rapax,
> Incerta, fallax, instabilis, vaga,
>   Iniusta, saeva, trux, maligna,
>   Lubrica mobiliorque ventis [...]
> Quae cuncta technis, fraude, dolo gerit,
> Et mille gentes artibus implicat,
>   Muscas ut irretire arachne
>   Officiosa solet tenellas.

> Who [Fortuna] as blind, kind, powerful, grasping, uncertain, false, unstable, vague, unjust, cruel, wild, malicious, mobile and faster than the winds [...], who controls everything, using crafty plans, fraud, and stratagems, and entangles thousands with her artful tricks, like a diligent spider that ensnares the tiny flies.

If we compare Paul's Fortuna with the powerful goddess in Horace's *carm.* 1,35, she does not seem a divine power that may be worshipped or invoked in a prayer like "Preserve Caesar." Instead she assumes a rather demonic dimension, deceives people, makes them as blind as she is. Crosnensis addresses his melancholic warning to "whoever wants to know about all the goddess' deception," gathers numerous conventional epithets and comparisons and composes them in the metre of the Alcaic stanza.

However, there is a poem *Ad Stanislaum Thurzonem*, in which we observe a direct address and familiarity in pure Horatian style, and moreover in a sophisticated Horatian metre. This poem may even be called a Horatian cento,

---

31   *Lucius Annaeus Seneca, Tragoedia secunda Thyestes*, ed. Paulus Crosnensis (Vienna, 1513).

32   *Lucius Annaeus Seneca, Tragoedia sexta, quae Troas inscribitur, ex Avantii annotationibus castigatissime impressa*, ed. Paulus Crosnensis (Vienna, 1513).

33   *Carmina* 1962, 171.

showing *similia* with *carm.* 1,4; 1,7; 1,9; 4,7, and *Ep.* 13. Hence it is Horatian in mood and in imagery, related to the *carpe diem* theme. With its sparkling winter imagery, it resembles Janus Pannonius' farewell poem to Várad.[34]

Paul is a true Horatian in his description of the winter landscape of Várad. He expresses his fear of old age. His poem has a studied metre and prosody, and is full of alliteration:[35]

> Poplitibus properat turpis cito nam senecta curvis
> > Graduque letum nos premit citato.
> Nunc placido laeti, nunc tempore victitemus, ecce
> > Pallens adest languoribus senecta [...]
> Ergo hilares pariter cantabimus igneos amores
> > Iuxta focum flagrantibus caminis.
> Grandia sumamus quoque pocula more Sarmatarum
> > Et musta scyphis aureis bibamus.
> Quis scit, an exspectet lux crastina propero meatu,
> > Seu pensa ducant longius sorores?

For ugly old age is fast approaching on crooked limbs, and death is pressing upon us with hasty step. Now, now let us seize the good time with joy. Here is Old Age, pale with her diseases, already by our side. [...] So we shall merrily sing the flames of love, near the fire burning in the fireplaces. Let us also take up great cups, like Sarmatians, and drink new wine from golden goblets. Who knows whether tomorrow's fast-approaching dawn still awaits us or the Sisters [= the three Fates] draw out our threads further?

Paul's next ode, in Sapphic stanzas, apparently to the same addressee, is also related to the *carpe diem* and *nunc est bibendum* themes. Confronted with the reality behind the two texts, their lyrical situation is enigmatic. The tone is too familiar and patronizing for what we might expect in a patron—client relationship (especially in comparison with the poems addressed to Gabor Perényi). Even the identity of the addressee is a riddle. The dedication reads:

---

34 The similarity was noticed by Ilona Kristóf, "Eruditio ac lepor. Humanizmus vo Varadíne pred Moháčom", in *Historia nostra. Sociálno historické štúdie zo spoločnej slovensko-maďarskej minulosti*, ed. Zoltán Borbély and Annamária Kónyová (Prešov, 2015), 7. For a Hungarian version of the article, see "Humanizmus a Mohács előtti Váradon", in *Arcana tabularii: Tanulmányok Solymosi László tiszteletére*, ed. Attila Bárány, Gábor Dreska and Kornél Szovák (Budapest-Debrecen, 2014), 705–23. However, Pannonius's poem is not so Horatian and is written in the Phalaecian metre.

35 *Carmina* 1962, 148.

Ad dominum Stanislaum Thurzo praepositum Varadiniensem. Polish scholars identify the addressee as "Stanislaus Thurzo, the future bishop of Olomouc".[36] However, the event is dated November 1, 1508, when Stanislaus Thurzo was no longer a "future bishop of Olomouc," since he had been appointed to the see already in 1497. Moreover, we know that another representative of the Thurzo family, namely Sigismund, was Bishop of Várad from 1505. How could the poet not have known that? Probably the lyrical situation was imaginary rather than real. However, as Cytowska asserts, Stanislaus Thurzo held the prepositure of Várad from 1488.[37] It is possible that for an unknown reason his earlier dignity was seen as more important at the Várad court. The familiar tone may be explained if we recall that Stanislaus Thurzo was Paul's peer, and a former student of Kraków. The poems addressed to him tend to be rewarded with patronage from the Thurzo family, but they are imbued with a predominantly Horatian spirit and not similar to those written to him as Bishop of Olomouc by Ursinus Velius or Georgius Logus.[38]

To conclude, I would like to emphasize that in imitating Horace, Paul of Krosno tried not only to follow the metrical patterns but also to render some of the moods and the 'nature' of Horatian odes. As a Horatian, however, he was definitely not another Horace; we could even say that he was not an excellent poet. His project of a collection of the *Carmina*, a *silva*, similar to Pontano's *Parthenopeus*,[39] was not continued by his pupils and followers, most of whom preferred elegiac compositions, which he had cultivated as well. Perhaps Paul's Horatian richness was a blind alley in the history of the Neo-Latin ode in Poland, perhaps it was to some extent wasted, or at least reduced to some scholarly exercises. But labelling him as bookish and less talented may be unfair: as a humanist teacher in Renaissance Kraków writing poems of his own, he may well have launched an epiphany, showing his students the possibilities of expressing their own truth *modo Horatiano* and gaining a humanist culture—that is, a new identity.

Jagiellonian University, Kraków

---

36   Cf. Gorzkowski, *Paweł z Krosna* (see above, n. 1), 109–10.

37   *Carmina* 1962, 147.

38   Cf. Jana Kolářová, "Latin Poems Dedicated to Stanislaus Thurzo, Bishop of Olomouc," in *Augustinus Moravus Olomucensis. Proceedings of the International Symposium to mark the 500th Anniversary of the Death of Augustinus Moravus Olomucensis (1467–1513), 13th November 2013, National Széchényi Library, Budapest,* ed. Péter Ekler and Farkas Gábor Kiss (Budapest, 2015), 139–47.

39   Cf. Matteo Scoranzo, *Poetry and Identity in Quattrocento Naples* (London, 2016), 20.

CHAPTER 12

Le scritture esposte e il latino in Italia fra XIV e XV secolo

Nadia Cannata

Abstract

Sitting between Classical, Renaissance and Neoclassic forms and style, medieval and Early Modern epigraphy constitutes in the common perception a kind of deviation from established norms, whereby Roman epigraphic style and Latin were bent and adjusted to suit a production which was addressed to a public for which Latin was the only 'writable' language and yet which could not effectively either write or understand it properly. Consequently, the elaboration of a commonly shared canon for its production was probably impossible, and indeed was never attempted—either in relation to the script(s) to be used or indeed to the language(s) employed. Public script bears a particularly stringent relationship with the community for which it is produced, and it therefore yields important information about its linguistic culture. The paper will present new research on inscriptions produced in Italy in which Latin and modern vernaculars coexist and intertwine in a new symbiosis in which neither seems entirely independent of the other. The materials are drawn from a new database of vernacular inscriptions produced in Italy and reveal a hitherto uncharted picture of linguistic culture and of the role the Latin model had played in relation to modern languages before the Renaissance canon became predominant.

Keywords

Neo-Latin inscriptions – Neo-Latin epigraphy – vernacular epigraphy – Romance linguistics – language history

Le scritture che ogni società lascia su muri e monumenti, che si leggono a corredo di dipinti o nelle titolazioni di libri e documenti, o anche graffite in segno di approvazione o protesta – inequivocabile segnale di una partecipazione diretta del pubblico di varia estrazione alla vita delle città e ai simboli del potere – è un potente specchio sia della cultura grafica e linguistica di

© KONINKLIJKE BRILL NV, LEIDEN, 2020 | DOI:10.1163/9789004427105_013

ogni comunità, sia, soprattutto, del suo rapporto con la memoria e con i mezzi utilizzati per la sua condivisione. L'epigrafia monumentale e le scritture esposte tardo-medievali e primo-rinascimentali furono modellate, naturalmente, sui modelli classici e costituiscono una particolare forma di imitazione dell'antico e di rivisitazione della tradizione latina.

Il latino ha costituito in Europa fino alle soglie dell'età moderna l'unico modello di scrittura disponibile – sia in termini di organizzazione dello scritto inteso per l'esposizione, sia come lingua di comunicazione. Tuttavia il latino ha coesistito con i volgari moderni lungo almeno sette secoli, dal IX al XV e ad essi si è intrecciato in una nuova simbiosi e interdipendenza. Lo studio di questa nuova simbiosi è l'oggetto di questa presentazione, che discuterà della relazione fra i due sistemi linguistici nelle scritture esposte della prima età moderna (XIV–XV) fornendo una serie di esempi utili a cogliere il ruolo culturale che il latino ha ricoperto nelle comunità riguardate, come ponte e garanzia di memoria.

Un censimento sistematico dell'intero patrimonio di iscrizioni in volgare prodotte in Italia fino al XV secolo, intrapreso di recente, ha rivelato un numero molto alto di testimonianze, oltre cinquecento, delle quali vorrei discutere in questa sede due aspetti: la presenza del latino come modello grafico e linguistico, e il rapporto che il volgare stabilisce con la lingua madre per la condivisione pubblica della memoria.[1] Gli spazi di esposizione della scrittura sono infatti generalmente gestiti dalle comunità alle quali lo scritto si rivolge – sia che si tratti di spazi cittadini, di luoghi della liturgia, di oggetti di uso comune o privato. In ogni caso, la funzione che il latino occupa in questi documenti rappresenta

---

1   Gli studi fondativi sull'argomento si devono ad Armando Petrucci. Si veda, in particolare, il suo studio pionieristico *La scrittura. Ideologia e rappresentazione* (Torino, 1986). Fra i contributi principali in materia si vedano inoltre almeno Dario Covi, *The Inscriptions in Fifteenth Century Florentine Painting* (New York – London, 1986); Francesco Sabatini, Sergio Raffaelli e Paolo D'Achille, *Il volgare nelle chiese di Roma*, (Roma, 1987); *Visibile parlare: le scritture esposte nei volgari italiani dal Medioevo al Rinascimento*, ed. Claudio Ciociola (Napoli, 1997); Albert Dietl, *Die Sprache der Signatur. Die mittelalterlichen Künstlerinschriften Italiens*, (München – Berlin, 2008); Paolo D'Achille, *Parole: al muro e in scena. L'italiano esposto e rappresentato* (Firenze, 2012); Ronnie Ferguson, *Saggi di lingua e cultura veneta*, (Padova, 2013); Francesca Geymonat, "Scritture esposte," in *Storia dell'Italiano scritto*, ed. Giuseppe Antonelli, Matteo Motolese e Lorenzo Tomasin, (Roma, 2014), vol. 3, 57–100. Per il censimento delle iscrizioni in volgare d'Italia si vedano: Luna Cacchioli e Alessandra Tiburzi, "Lingua e forme dell'epigrafia in volgare," in *Studj Romanzi* 10 (2014), 311–52; Luna Cacchioli, Nadia Cannata e Alessandra Tiburzi, "Italian Medieval Epigraphy in the Vernacular (IX–XV c). A New Database," in *Off the Beaten Track. Epigraphy at the Border*, ed. Antonio E. Felle e Andrea Ruocco, (Oxford, 2016), 91–129; Nadia Cannata, "Scrivere per tutti. Il volgare esposto in Italia (secc. IX–XV)," *Critica del Testo* 21 (2018), 33–76; Il database è disponibile sul sito www.edvcorpus.com/wp; i volumi con il catalogo descrittivo completo sono in preparazione.

LE SCRITTURE ESPOSTE E IL LATINO IN ITALIA FRA XIV E XV SECOLO 191

un dato per la ricostruzione della storia culturale d'Italia assai eloquente e che merita di essere indagato.[2]

Di seguito una tavola sinottica con la datazione dei reperti censiti:

TAVOLA 1   Numero totale di iscrizioni censite in Italia (suddivise per secoli)

Iscrizioni anteriori all'anno 1000	3
Iscrizioni databili al XI secolo	4
Iscrizioni databili al XII secolo	14
Iscrizioni databili al XIII secolo	22
Iscrizioni databili entro il XIII secolo	43 (7,3%)
Iscrizioni databili al XIV secolo	204 (35%)
Iscrizioni databili al XV secolo	292 (50,1%)
Totale	582

I documenti che qui interessano, datati ai secoli XIV (204) e XV (292) furono prodotti in schiacciante maggioranza fra Veneto e Toscana; e cumulativamente essi rappresentano il 69% delle testimonianze; se poi alla Toscana aggiungiamo anche l'Italia centrale o mediana, nella quale si colloca il 50,2% dell'intera produzione, la concentrazione di testimonianze nell'area centrale della penisola sale addirittura all'85%.

Analogo quadro emerge per il secolo seguente: la concentrazione percentuale di iscrizioni prodotte in Italia centrale e mediana arriva addirittura al 66,4%; le testimonianze venete (e, soprattutto, veneziane) scendono notevolmente – si passa da 70 a 35 – e costituiscono appena l'11,9%. Interessante anche il numero di testimonianze localizzate in Emilia Romagna, mentre restano poco documentati il resto dell'Italia settentrionale (13 in tutto, il 4,5%) e l'Italia meridionale e le isole (24 pezzi, 8,2%).

Quanto alle funzioni dello scritto esposto, come era forse presumibile nel corso del XIV secolo, circa la metà delle iscrizioni censite sono avvisi di natura pubblica, dunque testi legati alla vita politica e cittadina; mentre la percentuale scende in misura significativa alle soglie del moderno, e con essa anche la percentuale di iscrizioni funerarie, mentre salgono repentinamente le didascalie – si tratta soprattutto di didascalie esplicative che accompagnano e contestualizzano le vicende sacre narrate nei dipinti, e le firme di artista.

---

2 Petrucci, *Visibile parlare* (vedi sopra, n. 1), 45.

TAVOLA 2   Iscrizioni databili al XIV secolo

Regione	Numero iscrizioni	Avviso pubblico	Didascalia	Iscrizione funeraria	Graffito
Toscana	70	28	21	21	
Veneto	70	45	19	3	3
Emilia Romagna	16	7	6	3	
Roma	10	1		9	
Umbria	7	2	5		
Marche	6	4	2		
Lazio	6	2	4		
Abruzzo	4			4	
Sicilia	4	1	2	1	
Sardegna	3	1		2	
Friuli	2	1	1		
Campania	2		2		
Puglia	2	1	1		
Lombardia	1		1		
Liguria	1	1			
TOTALI	204 (100%)	94 (45,8%)	64 (31,5%)	43 (21,2)	3 (1,5)

TAVOLA 3   Iscrizioni databili al XV secolo

Regione	Numero iscrizioni	Avviso pubblico	Didascalia	Iscrizione funeraria	Graffito scritture su oggetti
Toscana	71	29	21	21	
Umbria	46	5	35		5
Marche	40	13	27		
Veneto	35	18	14	3	
Emilia Romagna	26	10	9	7	
Lazio	20	3	17		
Roma	11		2	9	
Campania	7	2	5		
Sicilia	7	3	4		

TAVOLA 3   Iscrizioni databili al XV secolo (*cont.*)

Regione	Numero iscrizioni	Avviso pubblico	Didascalia	Iscrizione funeraria	Graffito scritture su oggetti
Abruzzo	6	1	1	4	
Puglia	6		4	2	
Piemonte	5		5		
Sardegna	3		3	1	
Friuli	2		2		
Lombardia	2		2		
Liguria	2	1	1		
Trentino	2		2		
Basilicata	1		1		
TOTALI	292 (100%)	85 (29,1%)	155 (53,1%)	47 (16,1)	5 (1,7%)

Il latino e la scrittura

Ogni processo di scritturazione di una lingua comporta, mi pare, un duplice atto di traduzione: poiché non tutte le lingue che si parlano si scrivono, anzi, il numero delle lingue 'scrivibili' è significativamente inferiore al numero delle lingue che si parlano, anzitutto occorre che chi si appresta a comporre un testo destinato alla scrittura lo 'traduca' nella lingua della scrittura accolta e condivisa dalla comunità entro la quale scrive.

Qualunque documento prodotto in area romanza fino al XV secolo è normalmente classificato come 'latino' o 'volgare', dove con 'volgare' si intende il sistema delle lingue naturali, distinguendole dal latino. La classificazione, introdotta da Dante, è basata su una distinzione di natura ontologica fra le lingue: le volgari (o naturali, o materne) e le due grammatiche, latino e greco, opera umana e non divina. Si tratta di due universi linguistici complementari per Dante, che servono per descrivere un universo linguistico caratterizzato, diremmo oggi, dalla diglossia.

È evidente dunque che non è possibile immaginare una storia di una qualunque lingua romanza che sia indipendente dal latino, perché il latino è parte integrante dell'universo linguistico romanzo, avendo rappresentato il modello grazie al quale le nuove lingue acquisirono una forma scritta, e pertanto, una tradizione e la stabilità necessarie per potere essere univocamente individuate e finalmente nominate come esistenti.[3] Se è vero che la cultura linguistica dell'Italia basso medievale è intessuta di latino, va da sé che qualunque testo prodotto in quell'epoca e regione, in qualsivoglia lingua sia scritto, è parte di una cultura linguistica complessa che è strutturalmente bilingue. Una conferma indiretta di questo dato si trova nella documentazione offerta dalle scritture esposte.

Osservando le iscrizioni di Toscana e Veneto si nota subito che almeno due terzi delle iscrizioni trecentesche di entrambe le regioni contengono porzioni di testo in latino, per esempio nelle formule di datazione, o nelle didascalie che accompagnano la firma di un artista, posta magari in calce ad un testo tutto in volgare, come negli affreschi del Buon Governo a Siena: "Ambrosius Laurentii de Senis hic pinxit;" o nell'iscrizione sulla vera da pozzo in Campo dell'Angelo Raffaele a Venezia: "Marco Arian fiio che fo de ser Antuono Arian me fecit." Ancora nel Quattrocento circa la metà delle iscrizioni di entrambe le regioni presentano una porzione di testo in latino, che siano datazioni, espressioni formulari, citazioni evangeliche o bibliche, dichiarazioni di committenze, firme di artisti o altro.

Dunque innanzi tutto può essere utile domandarsi per ciascuno dei documenti oggetto del nostro studio quale sia la loro relazione con il latino. I casi in cui le firme o le indicazioni di committenza sono in latino sono numerosissimi; e frequenti anche i casi in cui l'iscrizione volgare risuona di echi di liturgie che i fedeli conoscevano come latine. In un contesto in cui, come si diceva, la presenza di entrambe le lingue è immanente, mi sembra tuttavia che si possano distinguere due categorie generali:

1) iscrizioni nelle quali le due lingue si fondono al punto da risultare quasi indistinguibili;

2) iscrizioni nelle quali sembrerebbe agevole separare i due sistemi, e nelle quali il latino è generalmente utilizzato nelle parti formulari e il volgare nelle parti per così dire 'libere'.

Esaminiamo qualche esempio, non anteriore al XIV secolo. Si veda il graffito datato 1305 con il quale il pittore che affrescò la chiesa di San Zeno a Cerea firma la sua opera: "E[g]o sum Ioh(an)es c'à fato questa scritura in dies [...] fate piture corando MCCCV scripis Ioh(an)e;" o l'iscrizione nella chiesa di santa Fosca a Roncadelle di Ormelle (1348): "+ MCCCXLVIII a dì XX de luli Bortolameus da Ronchadele, filion chondam Piligrini de Stabluco, fecit sagrarum questa glexia de Santa Fosca" o infine l'altra iscrizione modenese di un secolo posteriore: "+ 1440 ho(c) op(us) fe' fare Coradus olim notarius Campigaiani de suo mez." Si

---

3 Nadia Cannata, "Lontano da dove? Tradizioni culturali e coscienza linguistica in Europa," *Critica del testo* 19 (2016), 63–91.

LE SCRITTURE ESPOSTE E IL LATINO IN ITALIA FRA XIV E XV SECOLO

tratta di tre esempi nei quali il latino formulare si sovrappone e confonde con il volgare con il quale appare d'altra parte perfettamente fuso. L'oscillazione finisce in uno dei casi citati per creare forme linguistiche inesistenti (ma perfettamente interpretabili sul piano grafico) che risultano dal tentativo di scrivere e ridurre entro un preteso canone del latino espressioni quotidiane. Così interpreto "sagrarum", nel significato di 'consacrato', da un supposto "sacratum" soggetto ad assimilazioni consonantiche e sonorizzazioni comuni, e scritto con un interessante latinismo grafico '–um' per 'o' a formare una parola enigmatica e, in quella forma, evidentemente non pronunciata.

Comunissimo naturalmente è anche il caso in (2), testimoniato, ad esempio, nella famosa lastra di Francesco Roncaglia (1396) che affronta ai due lati dello stemma familiare il testo latino ("Hoc sepulcrum fecit fieri Franciscus filius (con)d(am) s(er) Iacob(i) De Ronhaleis civius Mutin(e) de cinq(uan) ti(n)a Sante Agathe p(ro) se (et) suis her<e>dib(us) M(illesim)o CC[C L] XXXXVI") al monito in volgare ("Eio fue quelo ch(e) tu è e tu serà quelo ch(e) e' sum mi, la morte s'aspeta ogni dì, p(re)ga Dio p(er) mi ch(e) eio lo p(re)garò p(er) ti").

Alcuni dei casi più notevoli di convivenza o fusione fra le due lingue si verificano in iscrizioni poste a corredo di immagini che costituiscono un tema iconografico di valenza liturgica o devozionale. È il caso, ad esempio, dei *Giudizi Universali* dipinti a cavallo fra XIV e XV e in pieno XV secolo sulle pareti della collegiata di Santa Maria Assunta a San Gimignano da Taddeo di Bartolo, o da pittori meno noti a Castignano, nelle Marche, ad Amatrice, Pofi, Fianello e Montebuono nel Lazio, a Sant'Agata dei Goti, a Ventaroli in Campania e in Puglia, a Soleto;[4] tutti vari nelle raffigurazioni, ma sostanzialmente identici nello schema della rappresentazione: le immagini potenti, spaventose e colorate dei peccatori sono corredate da didascalie identificative, in volgare, che ne identificano attività e mestieri, e sono spesso accompagnate dalla citazione evangelica da Matteo ("Venite benedicti, Percipite regnum") e dal "Surgite mortui venite ad iuditium".[5] L'iconografia e la forma delle didascalie, la loro impostazione grafica ricorrente – descrizioni lapidarie rappresentate entro un cartiglio accanto alla figura, stravolta e grottesca, del peccatore – nonché il latino che le accompagna, formano uno stile che si ripete in tutta la penisola,

---

4 Michel Berger, "S. Stefano di Soleto e i suoi affreschi," in *Paesi e figure del vecchio Salento*, ed. Aldo De Bernart (Galatina, 1980), 81–128 e 113–4; Daniela Ferriani, "I Giudizi Universali di Castignano e di Loreto Aprutino: iconografie a confronto," in *Atti del Convegno di Studi Immagini della memoria storica* (Montalto Marche, 2000), 13–43 e 403; Chiara Frugoni, *Lavorare all'inferno. Gli affreschi di Sant'Agata de' Goti* (Roma, 2004).

5 *Matth.* 25,34 e Ps. Hieronymus, *Regula Monacharum*, cap. 30, *De consideratione extremi dei iudicii*: "Semper tuba illa terribilis vestris perstrepet auribus: Surgite, mortui, venite ad iudicium." (*PL* 30,403–38: 430).

inequivocabilmente unitario, benché i dipinti siano dedicati a fedeli che vivevano in comunità fra loro lontane, e non solo linguisticamente. Essi sfruttano un linguaggio evidentemente condiviso e comunemente inteso, e diffuso in modo omogeneo. Così a Castignano in provincia di Ascoli Piceno il giudizio universale raffigura il "[... t]avernaro, L'omo che fa vergogna alla molge"; e a Montebuono in provincia di Rieti "biastimaturi" e "lusuriusi"; a Sermoneta sono effigiati "spriuri" ('spergiuri') e "manigolti"; a Pofi ancora l'"usuraro", il "sodomita" e ancora il "tavernaro", a Soleto è raffigurato fra i dannati il "βουτζερη", "buccerius" a Sant'Agata dei Goti e "voziero" a Ventaroli. Meno diffusa, ma comunque significativa la presenza di una iconografia unica per il cosiddetto *Cristo della domenica* (Firenze, Basilica di San Miniato al Monte, Castel Sant'Angelo sul Neera, e nel Santuario di Santa Maria delle Grazie detto della Cona Passatora presso Amatrice), nei quali la figura del Cristo accompagnata dagli attrezzi di lavoro si accompagna con una didascalia in volgare che ricorda la proibizione del lavoro nel giorno di festa.

Ancora più interessante il caso costituto dell'orazione latina (ma, come vedremo riprodotta con vari gradi di volgarizzazione) "O domine Iesu Christe, adoro te in cruce pendentem," antichissima preghiera settentrionale di epoca forse carolingia composta per la cerimonia dell'*Adoratio crucis* del venerdì santo, che compare in almeno quattro diverse iscrizioni poste a corredo dell'immagine del *Christus patiens*. Secondo una leggenda che ebbe grande fortuna alla fine del Trecento e nel secolo successivo, a Gregorio Magno che diceva messa in Santa Croce in Gerusalemme sarebbe apparsa l'immagine del Cristo con i segni della Passione. Il papa avrebbe così creato un'indulgenza per chi avesse recitato l'orazione davanti all'immagine.[6]

I quattro dipinti con questo tema che contengono iscrizioni in volgare sono ancora una volta tutti quattrocenteschi e distribuiti al Nord, al Centro e nel Meridione estremo:

(1) la cosiddetta *Lauda di Vanzone* (Vercelli) del 1404;

(2) il *Cristus Patiens* – tempera su legno di fattura umbra datata all'ultimo quarto del xv secolo – oggi a Colonia presso il Wallarf-Richartz Museum;

(3) la *Pietà* di Giovanni di Averara, del 1486, conservata nella chiesetta dei disciplini a Clusone (Bergamo);

(4) il grande affresco rappresentante la Pietà e Messa di san Gregorio, dotato di didascalie in latino e in siciliano databile intorno al 1495 della Collegiata di Sant'Andrea a Piazza Armerina (Enna).

---

6 Claudio Ciociola, "Visibile parlare: agenda," *Rivista di letteratura italiana* 7 (1989), 9–77.

In (1) leggiamo (trascrivo in corsivo le parti in latino):[7]

> *Sancto gregorio papa missa celebrante: apparuit ei dominis noster Iesus Christo sub effigie pietatis: et compassione motus concessit cuilibet* [...] *penitenti confesso et contrito devote dicenti* [...] *infra scriptas* [...] *q(ui) nquepater n(oste)r totidem Ave Maria* [...] *flexis* [...] *tali imagine pietatis quatuordecim ind*[...] *annor(um) alii postea summi po(n)tifices addide-ru(n)t indulge(n)tia* [...] *trasce(n)ndit XXIJ milia annor pro qualibet vice dicenti:*
> O Signore mio Jesu Christo te adoro in croce pendente
> e corona de spine in testa portante, te prego
> che la tua croce me libera dalo angelo percutiente.
> Pater noster e Ave Maria.
> O Signore mio Jesu Christo te adoro in croce impiagato
> de felle et aceto abeverato, te prego che le tue piaghe
> siano remedio a l'anima mia.
> O Signore mio Jesu Christo te adoro in croce morto
> in la sepoltura metudo, de spetie condito.
> Te prego che la tua morte sia mia vita.
> Pater noster e Ave Maria. [...]

In (2) l'iscrizione inverte l'ordine dei due testi, premettendo la laude al raccon-to dell'episodio di san Gregorio e al conteggio delle indulgenze, che è volga-rizzato. Nella laude il testo ha due stanze in meno, ma per il resto mostra una stretta relazione con la versione piemontese.

> O Signore Jesu Christo, io te adoro incroce pendente, e la corona despine incapo portante; io te prego che la tua croce me libere da l'angelo perco-tente. O Signore Jesu Christo, io te adoro incroce piagato, de fele et aceto abeverato, et sì te priego che le tuoe piaghe sieno remedio del'anima mia. O signore Jesu Christo io te adoro nel sepolcro posto, nel lençuolo col'on-guento ingulupato, et sì te priego che latua ii morte sia remedia de l'ani-ma mia.
> Sancto Gregorio essendo papa et dicendo lamessa gl'aparve il no-stro signore Jesu Christo in forma de piatade, onde vedendolo sancto Gregorio fo mosso a piatade et devotione et sì fece queste oratione a sua reverentia; et sia concesso ad onne persona confessa et contrita che

---

7   Erminio Ragozza, "Laudari in affreschi del sec. XV e la tradizione di preghiere valsesiane," *Novarien* 7 (1975–76), 68–74.

le dirà inançe ala piatade cum cinque pater nostri et cinque Ave Maria averà quator[d]ece milia anni de vera indulgentia; et molti altri pape ànno agionto intanto che suma in tucto Vintasette milia anni et trentasei dì de vera indulgentia.

L'affresco di Giovanni di Averara (3) fornisce una versione ridotta del testo latino con la parte che riguarda il conteggio delle indulgenze volgarizzata:[8]

> *Rinus fi[lium?] hoc opus .+. fieri / die 4* novembris *1486*
> *O domine ChristuIesu a patre adoro te in cruce pendente coronam spineam in capite portantem deprecor te ut tua crux luit me ab angelo percutiente. Deus domine [yhesu xriste] adoro te in cruce vulneratum fele et aceto potatum deprecor te ut tua vulnera sint re medium anime mee. Deus [yhesu xriste] adoro te in sepulcro positum aromatibus conditum deprecor te ut tua morssit vita mea amen.* Chi [...]ne cum cinqui Pater Noster e cinqui Ave Marie averano xx milia ani de indulgentia concessa per molti sumi pontifici · Iohannes de Averaria pinxit

Circa un decennio più tardi, e a più di un migliaio di chilometri di distanza, a Piazza Armerina (Enna) fu dipinto uno straordinario affresco (4), che sviluppa su un'intera parete il tema iconografico.[9] L'opera si sviluppa su due registri: nel primo si trova Cristo, al centro, in piedi nel sepolcro, con la croce alle sue spalle, le verghe, lo staffile, le croci dei ladroni, le donne in pietà e alcuni degli episodi e strumenti legati alla Passione (il bacio, il rinnegamento di Pietro, le pie donne, le parole dei due ladroni e del centurione). Piccoli cartigli dipinti a fianco delle immagini ospitano citazioni evangeliche (di cui indico si seguito la fonte), naturalmente in latino, e didascalie in siciliano, che trascrivo per intero di seguito. Nel registro inferiore è raffigurata la Messa di San Gregorio, e in due cartigli laterali il dettaglio delle indulgenze dovute per la devozione all'immagine, in latino e in un volgare siciliano intessuto di latino. Infine, i primi tre versi dell'orazione, in latino.

> [a sin della croce]
> *uestem meam / [...] <mi>serunt sortem* (Gv 19,24)
> *   concilium fecerunt principes sacerdotes/ et similiter uniuersi populi contra [...]*

---

8   Andrea Frugoni, *Incontri nel Medioevo*, (Bologna, 1979), 217–49.

9   Tancredi Bella, *S. Andrea a Piazza Armerina, priorato dell'Ordine del Santo Sepolcro: vicende costruttive, cicli pittorici e spazio liturgico* (Caltanissetta, 2012).

[sul braccio sinistro della croce]

Pater dimitte illis quia nesiunt quid faciunt (Lc 23,34) / *dico tibi hodie eris mecum in paradiso* (Lc 23,43)

Memento mei domine cum ueneris/ in regnum tuum (Lc 23,42)

Lu iudiu ch(e) spu/ ta a xpu

Li buxuli di lunguen/ tu dila madalena

mulier ecce filius/ tuus

Longin(us) uidit et testa/ uit

[al centro]

INRI

[a destra della croce]

La cena

Dedit eis signum

Petrus negauit cu(m)/ ancilla

petrus ancilla

[a sin Giuda che bacia il Cristo]

IUDAS

[sul braccio destro della croce]

Eli eli lamacza abatani [...]ntio: in manus tuas D(omi)ne/ com(m)endo spiritum meum consumactum est

Si tu es xps salus fac tecum nos

Sona beni

Ecce mater tua

Iosep haramatia

Centurio dixit uere fili(us)/ Dei er<at> iste (Mt. 27,54)

[nel registro inferiore, a commento della scena della Messa di San Gregorio]

[1 all'interno del cartiglio di sinistra]

Summanu tuti li prisenti indulgentij conchesi et confirmati ala dicta figura di la pietati di nostru Signuri Jesu Xristu per sanctu Grigoli papa di Ruma et altri papa et episcopi XX. M. annorum et trichentu 42 iorni di piradunanza per volta che si dichi la orationi *genibus flexis genibus flexis videlicet Pater Noster Ave Maria* per la passioni di Xristu

Papa Nicola confirma li predicti indulgentij et asupplixi chi s ...22... annorum di indulgentij [...] *Papa Pius romanus omnia supradicta confirmavit et adidit [...] anorum et 20 dies de indulgentia. Et deinde pro sequentibus orationibus genibus flexis ab memoriam passionis Domini, videlicet 15 Pater Noster et Ave maria concessit indulgentiam omnium peccatorum suorum.*

[2 all'interno del cartiglio di destra]

> [...] *indulgentie*
> [...] *ad septem*
> *primo ad delictorum expiacionem. Tercio ad penitentie supplectionem.*
> *Quarto ad pene purgatorij diminucionem. Quinto ad penitentis pene debite*
> *exterminacionem. Sexto ad* [...]*ionis graciam petrat*[...]*m. Septimo ad ma-*
> *ioris gracie augmentationem*
> *Domine Jesu Xriste adoro te in cruce pendente co*[...] *spinea in capite*
> *portante <de> precor te ut tua crux liberet e ab angelo <percuten>te.*

Come si vede anche nelle parti volgarizzate la distanza fra latino e volgari è minima, al punto che vi sono brani per i quali sarebbe assai difficile determinare
quale dei due codici sia quello effettivamente in uso. Leggiamo in (2): "sia *concesso* ad onne persona confessa et contrita che le dirà inànçe ala piatade [...]
quator[d]ece milia anni de vera indulgentia; et molti altri pape ànno *agionto*
intanto che *suma* in tucto Vintasette milia anni e trentasei dì [...]" che com-
pendia il "concessit et confirmavit" e traduce l'"addidit" in (1) e (3); mentre in
(4) troviamo "Summanu tuti li p[risen]ti indulgentij conchesi et [co]nfirmati"
con l'interessante mantenimento di 'sommare' per il latino "addere" e, naturalmente il volgare 'conchesi' e 'confirmati' per il latino "concessit et confirmavit". Perciò non sarà sorprendente il fatto che, a pochi chilometri da Piazza
Armerina, nell'Abbazia di San Salvatore a Caltanissetta, si trova un affresco
pressoché identico a questo, anche se di proporzioni più ridotte, raffigurante
il Cristo della Passione e la Messa di San Gregorio. Il dipinto è evidentemente
coevo, l'iconografia identica, il corredo testuale indubbiamente discende da
una fonte comune, ma i testi sono esclusivamente in latino. La frase del centurione "vere filius dei erat" (Mt 27,54) ricompare identica nel cartiglio posto
sotto la sua figurina anche a Piazza Armerina; inoltre, anche il cartiglio sotto-
stante porta un testo quasi identico:

> *Nota quae indulgencie valent ad septem: primo ad delictorum ingnorancie*
> *et expiationem; secundo ad venialium peccaturum detercionem; tercio ad*
> *penitencie* [...] *supplectionem; quarto ad pene purgatorii diminucionem;*
> *quinto ad penitencie pene debite exterminacionem; sexto ad velociorem*
> [...] *impetracionem; septimo ad maioris gracie augmentacione.*

Mentre il testo negli affreschi di medesimo soggetto in Umbria, Piemonte e
Lombardia – pur mantenendo un colorito locale – conserva chiara la eco del
volgare letterario ormai diffuso in pieno Quattrocento in Italia e oltre, colpi-
sce che le due testimonianze siciliane, pur in tutto analoghe nell'iconografia
e nell'impostazione generale, possano in qualche misura quasi ignorarne la

presenza e risolvere la questione della scritturazione del volgare negli unici due poli di riferimento che in esse possiamo identificare: il latino liturgico e il volgare siciliano, presenti persino in una data così tarda, in modo si direbbe interscambiabile. È evidente che gli affreschi di Caltanissetta e Piazza Armerina sono testimonianze inseparabili fra loro, per l'identità del soggetto e dell'iconografia che lo rappresenta, per la evidente relazione che li lega e perché sono espressione di un tessuto culturale organicamente bilingue, che in entrambi ancora esclude dal proprio orizzonte la lingua letteraria invece già largamente praticata e nota altrove, ma che in effetti in nessuna delle iscrizioni siciliane è stata utilizzata.

Tuttavia e ciononostante, le due Messe di San Gregorio sono strettamente connesse anche ai dipinti lombardi, piemontesi e umbri e certamente anche ad altri che il tempo avrà inghiottito, benché questi utilizzino le medesime fonti per un corredo testuale formato attraverso la relazione non fra due, ma fra tre poli: il latino della liturgia, la lingua locale dell'uso e il volgare letterario d'Italia.

Ogni lingua ne contiene altre: i volgari romanzi respirano il latino classico, il latino liturgico, le nuove lingue letterarie e le lingue d'uso, come anche le *scripte* rustiche, e, naturalmente la lingua delle immagini; e ancora i colori delle emozioni, la paura del Giudizio e l'angoscia della Passione. Ogni iscrizione romanza prodotta entro il Quattrocento abbraccia e nasconde tutte queste voci e mostra come il latino in alcune zone d'Europa, fra le quali certamente l'Italia, ancora in epoca rinascimentale vive in fondo due vite: l'una, figlia di una continuità culturale ininterrotta, in cui non si intravvede ancora frattura fra il latino e le lingue moderne e l'altra, invece, che noi identifichiamo più direttamente con la modernità, nella quale il latino è oggetto di imitazione e veicolo per la restaurazione di una civiltà perduta.

La moderna storiografia ha, io credo, il compito di conciliare queste due realtà entrambe vive, almeno fino al Cinquecento.

Università di Roma "La Sapienza"

CHAPTER 13

Commenter Quinte-Curce au XVIᵉ siècle : Premières observations

Lucie Claire

Abstract

Bien que Quinte-Curce soit l'un des historiens latins préférés des lecteurs de la Renaissance, les commentateurs s'intéressent peu à ses *Histoires d'Alexandre*, et tard. Érasme (Strasbourg, 1518) et Ulrich von Hutten (Strasbourg, 1528) sont les premiers à y consacrer quelques notes. Heinrich Glarean (Bâle, 1556), François Modius (Cologne, 1579) et Valens Acidalius (Francfort-sur-le Main, 1594), qui leur succèdent dans cette entreprise, donnent plus d'envergure au geste exégétique. À partir de l'étude de ce corpus, il s'agira de confronter les pratiques, de mesurer les évolutions et de dégager les lignes de force des commentaires à Quinte-Curce au cours du XVIᵉ siècle, afin d'évaluer quelle est leur singularité dans la tradition du commentaire humaniste sur les historiens latins.

Keywords

Heinrich Glarean – Franciscus Modius – Valens Acidalius – Neo-Latin commentaries – Reception of Curtius Rufus

Quinte-Curce est l'un des historiens latins préférés des lecteurs de la Renaissance, comme en témoigne le grand nombre de ses éditions, tant latines que vernaculaires.[1] Les commentateurs, eux, s'intéressent peu à son œuvre. Il existe un important décalage chronologique entre le mouvement de publication des éditions du texte et celui de ses commentaires : presque une cinquantaine d'années sépare la *princeps*, publiée vers 1471 par l'imprimeur

---

1 Sur la réception de Quinte-Curce à la Renaissance, qui excède le cadre de cet article, voir Lucie Claire, « Les éditions latines des *Historiae* de Quinte-Curce, de la *princeps* à Johannes Freinsheim, » dans *Postérités européennes de Quinte-Curce : de l'humanisme aux Lumières (XIVᵉ–XVIIIᵉ siècle)*, éd. Catherine Gaullier-Bougassas (Turnhout, 2018), 99–126.

© KONINKLIJKE BRILL NV, LEIDEN, 2020 | DOI:10.1163/9789004427105_014

COMMENTER QUINTE-CURCE AU XVIE SIÈCLE : PREMIÈRES OBSERVATIONS   203

vénitien Wendelin de Spire, et le premier commentaire de 1518. En outre, pour la période 1471–1597, face à une cinquantaine d'éditions latines,[2] on recense seulement cinq commentaires, tous cantonnés à l'aire germanique, et dont la présente contribution entend offrir une vue synthétique.

Érasme et Ulrich von Hutten sont les premiers à consacrer quelques notes aux *Historiae* de Quinte-Curce : le premier fait paraître ses *Annotationes* à Strasbourg en 1518 en même temps qu'une édition du texte,[3] quand les *Flores* du second, consacrés à Salluste et à Quinte-Curce, sont publiés de manière posthume, à Strasbourg encore.[4] Les deux travaux, fort intéressants, ne donnent pas encore au geste exégétique toute son envergure, puisqu'ils se focalisent sur l'*usus scribendi* de Quinte-Curce en proposant de brèves reformulations de certaines tournures ou expressions, qui peuvent être lapidaires et résister à l'appellation même de commentaire. Succèdent à Érasme et à Hutten dans cette entreprise Heinrich Glarean (*Annotationes*, Bâle, 1556),[5] François Modius (*Notae*, Cologne, 1579)[6] et Valens Acidalius (*Animaduersiones*, Francfort-sur-le-Main, 1594).[7] Ils explorent d'autres démarches dans leurs travaux, tantôt traditionnelles, comme l'approche philologique, qui vise à retrouver la vérité du texte latin, tantôt plus originales, induites par la spécificité du texte de Quinte-Curce. C'est la diversité même de ces cinq commentateurs qui me conduit à adopter ici une démarche chronologique plutôt que thématique : si les points de convergence existent, ils sont trop peu nombreux pour justifier cette dernière. Un second élément vient conforter le choix de l'analyse chronologique : les cinq commentaires dessinent une véritable chaîne exégétique. Les trois derniers en particulier doivent se comprendre comme une réponse au commentaire précédent, avec une dimension polémique très marquée : Acidalius construit ses *Animaduersiones* contre les *Notae* de Modius, elles-mêmes écrites en réaction aux *Annotationes* de Glarean.

---

2   Lucie Claire, « Bibliographie des éditions latines des *Historiae* de Quinte-Curce, de la *princeps* à Johannes Freinsheim, » dans Gaullier-Bougassas, *Postérités européennes* (voir ci-dessus, n. 1), 127–47.

3   *Quintus Curtius De rebus gestis Alexandri Magni regis Macedonum. Cum Annotationibus Des. Erasmi Roterodami* (Strasbourg, 1518).

4   *C. Salustii et Q. Curtii Flores*, éd. Ulrich von Hutten (Strasbourg, 1528).

5   *Q. Curtii De gestis Alexandri Magni Macedonum regis libri XII.* [...] *Hen. Glareani Annotationes* [...] (Bâle, 1556).

6   *Q. Curtii Rufi Historiarum Magni Alexandri Macedonis libri octo, noue editi et recogniti a Francisco Modio Brugensi* [...] *Seorsum excusae eiusdem Modii in eundem Curtium Notae* (Cologne, 1579).

7   Valens Acidalius, *In Q. Curtium Animaduersiones. Quibus superstites scriptoris eius omnes libri post accuratam Fr. Modii censuram plurimis etiam locis, aliique nonnulli quibusdam obiter, emendantur, illustrantur* (Francfort-sur-le-Main, 1594).

Les *Annotationes* d'Érasme

Les *Annotationes* d'Érasme forment non seulement le premier commentaire à Quinte-Curce, mais aussi le plus bref : elles occupent en tout et pour tout quatre pages et demie d'un in-folio. Elles figurent deux fois dans l'édition des *Historiae* préparée par Érasme : d'abord récapitulées sous forme de liste alphabétique entre l'épître dédicatoire et le texte de Quinte-Curce, elles se trouvent ensuite dans les marges du volume, en regard du passage concerné. Les presque cent trente *Annotationes* visent un objectif exclusif, à l'exception de quatre notes dans lesquelles Érasme propose de corriger le texte de Quinte-Curce :[8] la transposition, dans un latin classique, de certains termes ou expressions utilisés par l'historien. La majorité des *Annotationes* est avancée de manière sèche par l'humaniste.[9] Si, par exemple, on regarde les lemmes répertoriés sous la lettre I,[10] on se rend compte qu'Érasme donne un synonyme du terme employé par Quinte-Curce dans une langue plus classique pour les trois premières entrées de la lettre, bien qu'il s'agisse d'usages qui peuvent se rencontrer aussi chez Cicéron : « iactatio » est mis pour « iactantia » ou « ostentatio », « iam » pour « praeterea » ou « ignoratio » pour « ignorata res ». Parfois le commentateur intervient et se transforme en juge de la bonne latinité de Quinte-Curce : la tournure « imperare sociis naues »[11] est ainsi considérée comme une innovation de Quinte-Curce, mais qui respecte l'*elegantia* (« noue sed eleganter »). Quand un usage s'écarte trop de la norme cicéronienne, Érasme donne une occurrence proche qu'il a relevée chez l'Arpinate : l'expression sans doute un peu audacieuse « inhibere remis nauim »,[12] qui suscite encore une note dans les éditions modernes, est comprise par l'humaniste comme signifiant « reniti remis ut sistant »[13] et trouve son meilleur défenseur en Cicéron lui-même qui, dans une lettre à Atticus à laquelle renvoie Érasme,[14] explique le sens que peut revêtir « inhibere » dans le vocabulaire technique de la marine : le verbe désigne une manœuvre particulière des rames qui, pour Cicéron, n'équivaut pas à une suspension des rames. On peut observer le même procédé à propos

---

8   Quatre et non trois : je rectifie Claire, « Les éditions » (voir ci-dessus, n. 1), 110.

9   Il faut signaler qu'en 1518 également, Érasme publie à Bâle une édition de Suétone accompagnée d'*Annotata* d'un type assez proche. À leur sujet, voir Marijke Crab, « Henricus Petri's Editions of Suetonius : Printing and Commenting the *Lives of the Twelve Caesars* in Sixteenth-Century Basle, » *Viator* 48.1 (2017), 297–314, ici 306–8.

10   Érasme, *Annotationes* (voir ci-dessus, n. 3), fol. 3r.

11   Quinte-Curce, 3,1,20.

12   Ibid., 4,4,9.

13   Henri Bardon comprend, lui, cette expression comme signifiant « faire reculer l'embarcation ». Voir *Quinte-Curce, Histoires*, éd. Henri Bardon, tom. 1 (Paris, 1961), 61.

14   Cicéron, *Att.* 13,21,3.

de l'expression « insidere iugum »[15] (pour « occupare iugum ») : Érasme la rapproche, peut-être de manière abusive, de la tournure virgilienne « insistere limen ».[16]

Ce qu'il faut retenir de la démarche d'Érasme, c'est son désir d'établir Quinte-Curce comme un modèle de bonne latinité et d'élégance. Si cette volonté se devine lors de la lecture du commentaire, elle est formulée sans ambiguïté dans l'épître dédicatoire de l'édition. Érasme y qualifie Quinte-Curce de « candidus et tersus », après avoir invoqué l'autorité de Cicéron dès les premiers mots :[17]

> Si M. Tullius omnium suffragiis uberrimus et inexhaustus facundiae fons fatetur eloquentiae uenam facillime inarescere, ni quotidiana legendi dicendique exercitatione sufficias, Herneste princeps, non tantum imaginibus inclyte, quid mihi credis accidisse, cui cum uix tenuis quidam orationis riuulus contigerit, iam anni complures in eo studiorum genere consumpti sunt, quod adeo ad expoliendam orationem non facit, ut quamlibet etiam benigne fluentem copiam possit extinguere, ac dictioni quantumuis nitenti situm ac rubiginem obducere ? Quid enim inutilius ad tuendam rhetorices politiem, quam tumultuaria lectione sursum ac deorsum per omnes authores eosque interim inconditos raptari ?

L'imitation suppose, en plus de l'entraînement recommandé par Cicéron, du discernement : tous les auteurs ne doivent pas être aveuglément imités. La lecture qui ne sait pas cibler les meilleurs se révèle stérile. Érasme suggère ici que l'œuvre de Quinte-Curce appartient à la catégorie des textes qui permettent à l'éloquence de se perfectionner. Dix ans plus tard, un jugement similaire est formulé dans le *Ciceronianus* : Buléphore recommande à Nosopon la lecture de Quinte-Curce, en raison des discours qui s'y trouvent. Le maniaque de l'imitation de Cicéron rejette cependant l'historien, au motif que ses tournures diffèrent trop souvent de celles de l'Arpinate.[18]

Les *Flores* d'Ulrich von Hutten

Alors qu'Érasme place son travail sous le patronage de Cicéron, Hutten s'en remet à l'autorité de Quintilien, au motif que le rhéteur préconise la lecture

---

15   Quinte-Curce, 3,9,10.
16   Virgile, *En.* 6,562.
17   Érasme, *Annotationes* (voir ci-dessus, n. 3), fol. 1v.
18   Érasme, *Dialogus cui titulus Ciceronianus siue De optimo genere dicendi* (Bâle, 1528), 348.

des historiens à l'apprenti orateur.[19] L'épître dédicatoire, bien qu'elle n'ait pas été composée par Hutten, indique quel est l'objectif des *Flores*, au titre déjà éloquent : proposer un répertoire d'exemples à imiter relevant de la meilleure latinité, tant chez Salluste que chez Quinte-Curce. Hutten s'inscrit ainsi dans la tradition inaugurée par Érasme, qu'il a connu personnellement par ailleurs,[20] et intègre presque toutes les *Annotationes* de son prédécesseur à ses *Flores*. Sa démarche possède néanmoins une dimension anthologique plus prononcée et couvre une part bien plus importante du texte de Quinte-Curce : les *Flores* occupent environ cent trente pages d'un in-octavo. Leur volume s'explique en partie par le fait qu'Hutten cite toujours intégralement le texte de Quinte-Curce à l'appui de son *flos*.

Les *Flores* sont disposés par Hutten livre à livre, selon l'ordre dans lequel ils apparaissent dans les *Historiae* de Quinte-Curce. Il en résulte un ensemble d'un maniement malaisé en l'absence d'une présentation alphabétique, à la différence des *Annotationes* d'Érasme. Les *Flores* se caractérisent cependant par une variété plus grande que ces dernières et soulignent toutes les richesses de la langue déployée par Quinte-Curce. À ce titre, il me semble légitime de les faire figurer dans le corpus de cette étude bien qu'ils ne constituent pas *stricto sensu* un commentaire, au sens de texte rédigé qui offre un examen critique à des fins d'élucidation.

Si Hutten choisit parfois, comme Érasme, d'offrir une transcription classique du terme curtien à l'aide de la préposition « pro », il donne surtout des exemples d'usage. Son analyse de la langue des *Historiae* se révèle ambitieuse. Je laisse de côté les quelques remarques où Hutten se contente, au moyen de l'impératif « attende », d'attirer l'attention du lecteur sur une proposition, sans donner aucune précision sur ce qui mérite l'intérêt. Dans l'ensemble, ses *Flores* scrutent les moindres détails du style des *Historiae*. Hutten se montre sensible, par exemple, à l'usage des cas : il signale une occurrence de « lachrymare » avec le datif ou de « consuli » avec l'accusatif.[21] Il note aussi que certains verbes peuvent être employés de manière absolue, comme « laxare ».[22] Les *Flores* mettent en outre en relief toute une série d'associations de mots sélectionnées en vertu de leur élégance : des combinaisons d'une épithète et d'un

---

19   Quintilien, 10,1,31–34.

20   Hutten rencontre Érasme en 1514. Si dans un premier temps, les relations entre les deux humanistes sont marquées du sceau de l'amitié, elles se détériorent rapidement : voir l'exposé très complet de Monique Samuel-Scheyder, « Ulrich von Hutten et Érasme, » dans *Ulrich von Hutten, Expostulatio*, éd. Alexandre Vanautgaerden (Turnhout, 2012), 11–133.

21   Hutten, *Flores* (voir ci-dessus, n. 4), fol. F11v (à propos de 3,12,6) et fol. I8v (à propos de 6,10,28, qu'on lit différemment aujourd'hui).

22   Ibid., fol. G4r (à propos de 4,3,6).

substantif particulièrement heureuses (« scelestum consilium »),[23] des effets de *variatio* agréables (« dimicare de/pro », « bellum/proelium » ou « metuere/formidare »)[24] ou des antithèses expressives (« nouus/fatigatus »)[25] sont ainsi mentionnés. Enfin, Hutten signale quelques procédés d'écriture : un « credo » employé avec ironie ou une phrase dont la chaîne d'accord passe d'un singulier collectif au pluriel retiennent son attention.[26]

Si les *Flores* entendent d'abord fournir un répertoire d'exemples à qui se pique d'éloquence latine, ils livrent également une étude riche de la langue et du style de Quinte-Curce. Il est difficile de ne pas les rapprocher d'un travail quasiment contemporain, produit dans le même milieu de l'humanisme alsacien par une connaissance d'Hutten :[27] en 1533, Beatus Rhenanus fait paraître le *Thesaurus constructionum locutionumque et uocum Tacito solennium*, qui présente plusieurs points de convergence avec les *Flores*. Même si Beatus ne se plie pas à l'ordre alphabétique dans son *Thesaurus*, les entrées sont structurées de manière moins éclatée : une rubrique du *Thesaurus* donne tous les exemples d'emploi qui se trouvent chez Tacite, quand Hutten use d'un système de renvoi au moyen de l'adverbe « supra », peu lisible, ou signale une expression à chacune de ses occurrences chez Quinte-Curce, comme la tournure « cordi esse », qui revient au moins à six reprises dans les *Flores*.

Les *Annotationes* d'Heinrich Glarean

Les deux cent deux *Annotationes* de Glarean forment un ensemble foisonnant et passionnant. Le Suisse, qu'on sait friand des historiens grecs et latins,[28] explore dans son commentaire de multiples pistes, souvent originales et inattendues. Il fait preuve, lui aussi, d'un intérêt pour la question de la (bonne) latinité de Quinte-Curce et signale le recours à certaines figures (amphibologie,

---

23   Ibid., fol. F5v (à propos de 3,7,13).

24   Ibid., fol. G4r (à propos de 4,3,19), fol. H3r (à propos de 4,14,15) et fol. H4r (à propos de 4,16,17).

25   Ibid., fol. F7v (à propos de 3,11,6).

26   Ibid., fol. F4r (à propos de 3,2,16) et fol. F6r (à propos de 3,8,23).

27   Sur les relations qui unissent les deux humanistes, voir Monique Samuel-Scheyder, « Le séjour d'Ulrich von Hutten à Sélestat en novembre 1522, » dans *Beatus Rhenanus (1485–1547) et une réforme de l'Église : engagement et changement*, éd. James Hirstein (Turnhout, 2018), 397–433.

28   Voir Marijke Crab, « Glareanus's Commentaries on the Ancient Historians : The Case of Valerius Maximus (1553), » *Neulateinisches Jahrbuch* 16 (2014), 7–27, ainsi que son chapitre consacré à Glarean dans *Exemplary Reading : Printed Renaissance Commentaries on Valerius Maximus (1470–1600)* (Münster, 2015), 173–206.

hystéron-protéron, zeugma, hypophore, syllepse),[29] ainsi que les passages où l'usage curtien rencontre celui de Cicéron, de Quintilien ou encore de Tite-Live, garants de l'*elegantia*, voire s'en écarte parfois.[30] Il lui arrive cependant, bien plus souvent, de souligner le manque de clarté de l'historien. La proposition « locus est oppido obscurus » se trouve à plusieurs reprises au début de telle ou telle *annotatio*.[31]

Au-delà des questions de clarté et d'élégance, d'autres lignes de force traversent le travail de Glarean. Le lecteur ne peut qu'être frappé de l'intérêt marqué de l'humaniste pour les questions historiques et géographiques. *A priori*, la chose ne paraît guère étonnante lorsqu'on commente un texte d'historien. Mais Glarean diffère des autres commentateurs d'historiens latins : il s'intéresse relativement peu à l'histoire dans ses dimensions stylistique et antiquaire. Les *realia* ne le stimulent guère et, à l'exclusion d'une remarque sur les mystères de Samothrace ou d'une autre sur le sésame,[32] l'exotisme de Quinte-Curce ne retient pas son intérêt. Glarean se prend plutôt de passion pour les questions liées à la chronologie, ce qui ne surprend pas de la part de l'auteur d'une table chronologique de Tite-Live.[33] Il va jusqu'à proposer une réorganisation d'ensemble des *Historiae* : à la partition traditionnelle en dix livres, il oppose une structure annalistique en douze livres, chaque livre retraçant *grosso modo* une année du règne d'Alexandre.[34] Un exposé propédeutique est consacré à cette question dans son édition et des considérations sur l'agencement de l'œuvre reviennent au seuil de chaque livre concerné par la réorganisation envisagée. Glarean aime encore confronter la version des faits transmise par Quinte-Curce à celle donnée par d'autres historiens d'Alexandre, comme le montre l'exemple de l'*annotatio* 165, où sont successivement confrontés Diodore, Strabon et Arrien. Glarean souligne de plus que les sources divergent non seulement sur le lieu et le moment exact de l'action, mais aussi sur le nombre de gardes d'Alexandre. L'intérêt pour les chiffres est du reste constant chez lui.

La véritable singularité du commentaire se situe encore ailleurs cependant. Elle réside dans le goût de Glarean pour la géographie, auteur du reste d'un manuel consacré à cette discipline.[35] Ce goût s'incarne dans une attention

---

29 Glarean, *Annotationes* (voir ci-dessus, n. 5), n° 10, 17, 31, 103 et 171.

30 Ibid., n° 60 et 109 (Cicéron), 166 (Quintilien) et 108 (Tite-Live).

31 Ibid., n° 40, 98, 115 ou 138.

32 Ibid., n° 136 et 116.

33 *T. Liuii Patauini Latinae Historiae Principis quicquid hactenus fuit aeditum* [...]. *Addita est Chronologia Henrici Glareani*, éd. Heinrich Glarean (Bâle, 1531).

34 La réorganisation consiste à scinder en deux livres les actuels livre 4 (livres 4 et 5 chez Glarean) et livre 10 (livres 11 et 12 chez Glarean).

35 Heinrich Glarean, *De geographia liber unus* (Bâle, 1527).

à l'ethnographie, ainsi qu'à la configuration des lieux des batailles.[36] La géographie permet en outre au commentaire de remplir sa traditionnelle fonction d'élucidation : Glarean fournit à son lecteur plusieurs exposés sur des lieux mentionnés par Quinte-Curce, afin d'évaluer la fiabilité du savoir légué par l'historien. Ainsi, Glarean juge ses informations sur l'Inde avec sévérité.[37] Surtout, la géographie est promue au rang de savoir auxiliaire de la philologie. Glarean assigne en effet à son travail une ambition philologique : il veut rénover le texte de Quinte-Curce, corrompu par la faute des « librarii » : leur incurie est critiquée à maintes reprises – lieu commun de la littérature exégétique. Si Glarean ne recourt guère aux témoins manuscrits pour émender, suivant l'usage dominant de son temps, il ne cesse de mobiliser ses connaissances géographiques pour corriger les *Historiae*. Le philologue doit être à ses yeux « peritus geographiae », expression que l'on rencontre en plusieurs occasions.[38] La géographie lui permet en particulier de corriger les nombreux noms de peuples orientaux, souvent mal orthographiés par les copistes.

Enfin, dernière originalité de l'entreprise de Glarean : le désir d'actualisation du texte de Quinte-Curce. L'humaniste n'hésite pas à proposer quelques parallèles aussi originaux que pertinents entre la réalité représentée par Quinte-Curce et son monde à lui. Je me contenterai de brefs exemples. À deux reprises, Glarean compare l'expression latine d'un nombre à une tournure équivalente en langue vernaculaire, tantôt en français, tantôt en allemand.[39] Il glisse aussi parfois vers le miroir du prince et tire profit d'une action d'Alexandre pour présenter de brèves réflexions sur l'exercice du pouvoir, comme dans l'*annotatio* 14. La dernière phrase, formulée au présent de vérité générale, propose une petite maxime à partir de l'attitude d'Alexandre qui, dans ce passage,[40] se divertit dans la ville de Soles qu'il vient de prendre : « Neque enim proxima semper incedunt exercituum duces, maxime dum piscantur. » Dans l'*annotatio* 180, Glarean souligne, à propos de la cruauté d'Alexandre à l'égard du satrape Orsinès,[41] qu'il n'existe aucun modèle de cruauté supérieur aux empereurs romains Tibère, Caligula et Néron.

---

36   Par exemple Glarean, *Annotationes* (voir ci-dessus, n. 5), n° 19, 20 et 54.
37   Ibid., n° 145.
38   Ibid., n° 41, 63 ou encore 119.
39   Ibid., n° 6 et 171.
40   Quinte-Curce, 3,7,2.
41   Ibid., 10,1,22–38.

Les *Notae* de François Modius

Les *Notae* de Modius accompagnent une édition de Quinte-Curce qui a fait date dans l'histoire du texte en raison de sa très grande qualité.[42] Il est donc cohérent que la préoccupation majeure de Modius dans ses *Notae* soit d'ordre philologique. À l'exclusion de quelques remarques sur l'*elegantia* ou la *venustas* de Quinte-Curce, les *Notae* offrent une copieuse liste de corrections argumentées et ont pour objectif de restaurer le texte des *Historiae*. Modius dispose de nombreux outils pour mener son entreprise à bien. Tout d'abord, il recourt de manière systématique aux manuscrits. Dans la préface de ses *Notae*, il indique avoir utilisé un manuscrit provenant de Toulouse, d'autres venant de la cathédrale de Cologne, ainsi qu'un manuscrit originaire de l'abbaye de Siegburg ; il signale même s'être mis en quête d'autres témoins dans les bibliothèques des environs, en vain.[43] L'évocation des « membranae » et des « codices scripti » revient avec régularité et donne même une couleur particulière au style de Modius : les manuscrits sont souvent personnifiés par l'humaniste, pour qui ils « iubent », « laudant », « accusant » ou « delirant ».[44] Modius recourt à ces témoins avec discernement. Il est conscient que les plus anciens doivent être privilégiés,[45] tout en possédant assez de connaissances paléographiques pour les utiliser à bon escient : par exemple, jusqu'à Modius, les éditions donnent « pugnare mouerat » en 8,14,6. L'humaniste propose de corriger en « pugna se mouerat », en fondant sa correction sur la proximité des lettres R et S dans l'écriture lombarde – ou bénéventine.[46]

Comme ses contemporains, Modius accorde une certaine importance aux éditions imprimées, mais sans jamais les préférer aux manuscrits. Il possède plusieurs d'entre elles sur sa table de travail : des éditions lyonnaises sont souvent citées, ainsi qu'une édition anversoise,[47] l'édition de Johann Gymnich (Cologne, 1538) et l'édition de Simon de Colines (Paris, 1533 et 1543, qui reprend l'édition d'Érasme en réalité), qu'il juge la meilleure d'entre toutes.[48] Modius complète son information par la fréquentation des commentaires de ses prédécesseurs : Érasme, Hutten et Glarean sont mentionnés. En outre,

---

42   Claire, « Les éditions » (voir ci-dessus, n. 1), 111–4.

43   Modius, *Notae* (voir ci-dessus, n. 6), 2–3. Ces différents manuscrits n'ont pu être identifiés : voir Simon Dosson, *Étude sur Quinte Curce, sa vie et son œuvre* (Paris, 1886), 355–6, ainsi que Quinte-Curce, *Historiae*, éd. Carlo M. Lucarini (Berlin, 2009), XLII–III.

44   Par exemple Modius, *Notae* (voir ci-dessus, n. 6), 25, 62, 99, 113 ou 119.

45   Ibid., 18.

46   Ibid., 156.

47   Plusieurs éditions sont imprimées à Anvers au XVIᵉ siècle, voir Claire, « Bibliographie » (voir ci-dessus, n. 2), entrées n° 15, 25, 28, 39 et 43.

48   Modius, *Notae* (voir ci-dessus, n. 6), 167.

COMMENTER QUINTE-CURCE AU XVIᴱ SIÈCLE : PREMIÈRES OBSERVATIONS   211

son excellente maîtrise de la littérature latine en général et de la littérature consacrée à Alexandre (Diodore de Sicile, Plutarque, Arrien, Justin) lui permet de comparer l'usage curtien à d'autres tournures et de corriger *ope ingenii* si nécessaire. Enfin, Modius étaye en plusieurs passages sa correction par l'autorité de son ami Janus Mellerus Palmerius. Toutes ces compétences variées, employées à propos, valent à de nombreuses *Notae* de Modius de porter juste et de continuer à être retenues par les éditeurs actuels.

Il reste à souligner la dimension polémique très prononcée des *Notae*. Les « librarii » sont la cible des critiques du philologue, comme souvent. Modius incrimine également les « operae typographici ».[49] Les mots peuvent être durs : Modius qualifie les corrupteurs du texte de Quinte-Curce de sycophantes, de petits maîtres ou encore d'aveugles.[50] L'objet de toute sa véhémence se nomme cependant Glarean, dont la pratique de commentateur semble visée dans l'épître dédicatoire des *Notae*, de manière anonyme mais limpide, à travers cette *recusatio* :[51]

> Non ingrederer quoque anxiam disputationem de nominibus propriis hominum, urbium, populorum, fluminum, locorum : denique numero copiarum et si qua sunt similia. Ac ne illa quidem notarem, quae ad historiam pertinent.

Il est difficile de proposer un refus plus fort de la conception exégétique de Glarean. Ce dernier n'est du reste jamais épargné au fil du commentaire de Modius, où les attaques *ad personam* sont fréquentes, dans un style agressif qui singe parfois les *Annotationes* de Glarean, comme lorsque Modius reprend l'expression chère à son prédécesseur « locus est oppido obscurus ».[52]

Les *Animaduersiones* de Valens Acidalius

Le désir de polémiquer avec son prédécesseur caractérise aussi les *Animaduersiones* d'Acidalius, qui inscrit sur la page de titre le nom de Modius. Les *Animaduersiones* épousent, comme le travail de Modius, une perspective philologique et constituent un ensemble imposant : elles couvrent près de trois cents pages d'un in-octavo. La qualité des *Animaduersiones* est cependant inversement proportionnelle au volume de l'ouvrage et à la virulence des

---

49   Ibid., 82, 89, 96, 100, 101 et 159.
50   Ibid., 93 et 98.
51   Ibid., 4.
52   Ibid., 111.

critiques adressées aux *Notae* de Modius. Le propos s'avère en général inepte, creux et infondé. Les arguments en faveur des corrections textuelles rejetées ou suggérées sont inexistants, au mieux faibles. On peut repérer le schéma suivant pour nombre d'*Animaduersiones* : la note s'ouvre par une attaque contre Modius (dont la leçon peut être néanmoins retenue), puis elle propose une correction de la leçon de Modius, qui est rarement construite sur des arguments scientifiquement recevables. Un court exemple illustrera mon propos : en 4,12,7, Valens Acidalius conteste la correction de Modius, « immixtos », donnée par les manuscrits, et avance une autre correction, « immixtas », à partir de la leçon des imprimés, « mixtas ».[53] Son seul argument, présenté sous la forme d'une question rhétorique, est la disposition des mots : à ses yeux, mieux vaut que « mixtas » ou « immixtas » porte sur « copias », plutôt que « immixtos » porte sur « pedites ». L'exemple choisi ici est de taille raisonnable : parfois, la logorrhée s'étend sur de nombreuses pages et rend la lecture indigeste.

Pour conclure, si le nombre de commentaires à Quinte-Curce recensés au XVIe siècle peut paraître pauvre au regard de la popularité de l'historien, la variété et la singularité des démarches viennent compenser cette faiblesse. Quand leurs contemporains qui s'intéressent à Salluste ou à Tacite se concentrent sur les *realia*, la philologie ou l'*elegantia*, les cinq commentateurs des *Historiae* se désintéressent de l'information historique de Quinte-Curce et entreprennent la rénovation du texte au moment où la tradition exégétique est installée. L'originalité des pratiques pourrait s'expliquer par les différents publics visés. Même si les paratextes sont avares de renseignements à ce sujet, il semble probable qu'Érasme et Hutten s'intéressent à Quinte-Curce dans une perspective pédagogique et que Modius écrive à l'attention de lecteurs érudits, quand le jeune Acidalius cherche à se constituer un réseau de protecteurs à Wroclaw.[54] Le lectorat de Glarean paraît plus délicat à cerner. Quoi qu'il en soit, en explorant des chemins inattendus, les cinq travaux donnent à Quinte-Curce une place originale dans la tradition du commentaire humaniste sur les historiens latins.

Université de Picardie Jules Verne
UR UPJV 4284 TrAme

---

53   Acidalius, *Animaduersiones* (voir ci-dessus, n. 7), fol. 41r.

54   Après l'épître dédicatoire du volume, chaque livre des *Animaduersiones* est précédé d'une épître dédicatoire singulière. Les neuf lettres sont adressées à des personnalités de Wroclaw, où Acidalius se rend après son séjour en Italie (1590–93). Voir Beate Hintzen, « Acidalius, Valens, » dans *Der neue Pauly. Supplemente 6. Geschichte der Altertumswissenschaften : Biographisches Lexikon*, éd. Peter Kuhlmann et Helmuth Schneider (Stuttgart, 2012), 2–3.

CHAPTER 14

Bernardo Michelozzi e Francesco Pucci, amici di penna

Claudia Corfiati

Abstract

Da tempo è nota la corrispondenza che Francesco Pucci, allievo del Poliziano, tenne per lungo tempo con il suo compagno di studi e amico Bernardo Michelozzi, fratello del più noto diplomatico fiorentino Niccolò. Il Pucci si era trasferito a Napoli presso lo *studium* e, dopo un primo periodo di difficoltà, aveva trovato buona accoglienza sia presso gli Aragonesi, che gli affidarono la gestione della Biblioteca, sia presso i *sodales* della Accademia Pontaniana, di cui sicuramente fece parte. Recentemente sono state scoperte alcune nuove lettere, frammenti inediti di un dialogo molto interessante che i due umanisti praticavano in latino e in greco classico con una certa disinvoltura e non senza un gusto per il *ludus* e per la battuta scherzosa, caratteristica questa che spesso ha reso difficile la comprensione dei precisi contesti cui si riferiscono. Le nuove acquisizioni, inserendosi fortunatamente negli intervalli lasciati vuoti dalla tradizione fino a questo momento, permettono di affrontare una interpretazione più sicura dell'insieme dei testi: in questo contributo se ne offre un primo inedito saggio.

Keywords

Francesco Pucci – Bernardo Michelozzi – Neo-Latin epistolography – Accademia Pontaniana – humanism in Naples

Nel 1963 Mario Martelli segnalava la presenza di cinque lettere inedite di Francesco Pucci a Bernardo Michelozzi nel fondo Ginori Conti della Biblioteca Nazionale di Firenze, alla cui recensione e catalogazione stava lavorando.[1] L'interesse da parte sua nei confronti di queste lettere nasceva dalla presenza

---

1 Mario Martelli, "Lettere inedite di Francesco Pucci, 'librero major' nella Biblioteca aragonese," *La Bibliofilia* 65 (1963), 225–37.

© KONINKLIJKE BRILL NV, LEIDEN, 2020 | DOI:10.1163/9789004427105_015

in esse di evidenti allusioni ad Angelo Poliziano, maestro del Pucci,[2] allusioni tuttavia che non riuscivano a trovare una loro univoca interpretazione, dal momento che i due corrispondenti, compagni di scuola e amici strettissimi, utilizzavano nella loro scrittura una forte reticenza, dovuta forse alla non opportunità di far girare per l'Italia i loro giudizi su personaggi in vista e vicini a Lorenzo, ma anche – come credo – al fatto che la loro familiarità rendeva superflue dichiarazioni esplicite. In poche parole, i due alludono, scherzano, giocano, divertendosi, come avrò modo di mostrare, ma a noi lettori moderni risultano ben poco comprensibili, perché di quel contesto ci manca moltissimo, non solo in termini di date o dati, ma di sentimenti, esperienze, parole.[3] Una delle ragioni per cui queste lettere sono rimaste, dopo lo studio di Martelli, inedite, è forse proprio da rintracciare nella precarietà di qualsiasi forma di interpretazione, nella parzialità delle informazioni (perché si conosceva solo il testo di Pucci e non quello del Michelozzi), nella occasionalità fin troppo evidente di questi documenti.

Quando nel 2016 ho avuto la fortuna di rintracciare nel fondo degli Autografi Patetta della Biblioteca Apostolica Vaticana (nella parte non ancora catalogata e recensita) un gruppo di lettere di Bernardo al suo amico Francesco,[4] ho provato l'illusione, piacevole ma effimera, che la perfetta complementarietà dei testi potesse finalmente aiutare a far luce sul significato complessivo della corrispondenza. Certo, credo che alla fine del mio studio, che ora è solo agli esordi, e che è finalizzato alla edizione del carteggio nel suo complesso, al di là di ogni ragionevole dubbio, qualcosa in più rispetto a quello che aveva congetturato con grande finezza Martelli, si dovrà pur comprendere. Ad oggi tuttavia molte sono le incertezze, le lacune, gli interrogativi su questa vicenda.

Partiamo da alcune considerazioni metodologiche. In merito agli epistolari degli umanisti sono state scritte pagine importanti, anche perché – ma non è il caso, forse, dei nostri – lo scrivere lettera era considerato dagli intellettuali cresciuti alla scuola di Petrarca un genere letterario a tutti gli effetti. Di Pucci però – a meno che non si voglia credere ad una nota molto stringata

---

2 Su Francesco Pucci si veda Mario Santoro, *Uno scolaro del Poliziano a Napoli: Francesco Pucci* (Napoli, 1948); Tammaro De Marinis, *La biblioteca napoletana dei re d'Aragona* (Milano, 1952), vol. 1, 186–7 e 254–7; Claudia Corfiati, "Un corrispondente fiorentino da Napoli: Francesco Pucci," in *Angelo Poliziano e dintorni. Percorsi di ricerca*, ed. Claudia Corfiati e Mauro de Nichilo (Bari, 2011), 65–102; Franco Pignatti, "Pucci, Francesco," in *Dizionario Biografico degli Italiani* 85 (Roma, 2016), 555–9.

3 Per Bernardo Michelozzi rimando a Claudia Corfiati, "*In aulam pontificiam me contuli*: Bernardo Michelozzi e Giovanni de' Medici," in *Leone X. Finanza, mecenatismo, cultura*, Atti del Convegno Internazionale, Roma, 2–4 novembre 2015, ed. Flavia Cantatore et al. (Roma, 2016), 277–93.

4 Vedi Claudia Corfiati, "'Nuove' carte Michelozzi," *Studi medievali e umanistici* 13 (2015), 273–8.

BERNARDO MICHELOZZI E FRANCESCO PUCCI, AMICI DI PENNA 215

di Eberhard Gothein, nella quale segnalava la presenza di *Lettere* del Pucci nella collezione Arditi,[5] informazione che stimola nella fantasia del filologo l'idea che il professore avesse raccolto la sua corrispondenza –, di Pucci, dicevo, non abbiamo una raccolta organica, ma solo quanto riviene dall'archivio Michelozzi, immaginato, più che da Bernardo, dal fratello cancelliere Niccolò, e conservato bene nei secoli grazie all'eredità di alcune famiglie fiorentine, fino alla sua improvvida dispersione agli inizi del Novecento. A casa Michelozzi d'altronde non si realizzò una raccolta di lettere ordinata, una trascrizione o un regesto, sicché abbiamo le missive di Francesco, in bella copia e originali, con il segno della ceralacca e l'indirizzo sul verso; quelle di Bernardo invece sono bozze, realizzate velocemente in una scrittura sciatta e approssimativa, senza data, firma e nemmeno congedo o intestazione (che evidentemente scriveva solo nella copia da spedire). In alcuni casi è ancora in dubbio che si tratti di epistole spedite all'amico Pucci o ad altri, data la mancanza di qualsiasi riferimento al destinatario. Quello che è sicuro è che si tratta di un frammento piccolissimo di una corrispondenza ricca e frequente, soprattutto nei primi anni del trasferimento di Francesco a Napoli. In questa occasione offro un solo esempio, che serva anche ad illustrare l'importanza delle nuove acquisizioni dal fondo Patetta.

Quando il Pucci lasciò Firenze, è assai probabile che abbia fatto una tappa a Roma e poi subito dopo si sia spostato a Napoli. Questa parte della sua vita è del tutto oscura in verità, ma le ricerche sono ancora in corso.

Una delle prime esperienze napoletane che sente il bisogno di raccontare all'amico è una lunga gita a Pozzuoli, un *topos* – diremmo noi – letterario, nonché una meta turistica obbligata. Purtroppo la lettera in cui raccontava questa sua gita non ci è arrivata, ma egli ne fa esplicito riferimento in una successiva, la prima a noi giunta contenente una data chiara. È il 7 marzo del 1484, e Francesco si preoccupa di correggere un dato antiquario che aveva riportato in un'epistola a Bernardo, che non è immediatamente precedente a questa, dal momento che usa l'avverbio "olim" per indicare il tempo della sua scrittura. In verità quello che vuole raccontare a Bernardo è il fatto che di questa sua 'scoperta' ha dato ampio sfoggio "in publico Gymnasio magno auditorum consessu".[6]

---

5 Nel raccontare infatti di aver visto il *De funere Ferdinandi* di Tristano Caracciolo nella biblioteca del bibliofilo salentino, aggiungeva un cenno al Pucci: "Sammlung Arditi, dort auch Pucci's Briefe," in Eberhard Gothein, *Die Culturentwicklung Süd-Italiens in Einzel-Darstellung* (Breslau, 1886), 546.

6 Si era fidato di quello che i dotti 'locali' gli avevano riferito, ovvero che la grotta di Cocceio, il tunnel di tufo che collega Napoli, o dovremmo dire Cuma, al lago Averno, non era opera del ricco Lucullo, ma – come si trovava scritto in Strabone – di Cocceio appunto, che aveva

Gli Autografi Patetta ci hanno restituito oggi la risposta di Bernardo, o meglio la bozza della sua risposta, che dovette scrivere a stretto giro di posta, come vedremo. Per prima cosa lo ringrazia per avergli riferito dell'errore sulla grotta di Cocceio, e soprattutto della sua vittoria: interpreta infatti in senso quasi politico il fatto che il Pucci a lezione abbia potuto vincere l'ostinata opinione dei suoi colleghi napoletani, portando un punto di vantaggio alla patria Firenze. Lo mette in guardia tuttavia dal cullarsi troppo di tali successi: il nemico infatti (l'avversario o il concorrente in cattedra) è sempre sull'allerta e potrebbe attaccarlo da un momento all'altro. È difficile – secondo il Michelozzi – sradicare credenze diffuse da tanto tempo anche se ci si appoggia ad autori antichi, anche con lo strumento cioè della testimonianza storica e della filologia: da questo punto di vista Pucci avrebbe dovuto forse – così gli suggerisce l'acuto amico – consultare e poter citare il testo di Strabone in greco e non nella traduzione latina a sua disposizione. Non rimprovera apertamente Francesco di questo, anche perché trovare uno Strabone greco a Napoli all'epoca era impossibile:[7] a Firenze – così racconta – c'erano solo due codici del geografo greco, ma si trovavano nelle mani di qualcuno che non li lasciava nemmeno toccare. Bernardo quindi si offre di fare la ricerca del passo in lingua originale, ma sa già che gli sarà oltremodo difficile.[8]

Giustifica subito dopo il fatto di non aver scritto all'amico riferendogli di un viaggio fatto al seguito di Gentile Becchi in Francia, per portare il saluto al nuovo sovrano Carlo VIII.[9] Questa missione fu organizzata per il novembre

---

lavorato sotto Agrippa. L'aspetto filologico di questa ricostruzione del Pucci cui ho già accennato altrove sarà approfondito in sede di edizione del testo, cfr. Corfiati, "Un corrispondente fiorentino" (vedi sopra, n. 2).

7   Si veda Aubrey Diller e Paul Oskar Kristeller, "Strabo," in *Catalogus translationum et commentariorum. Medieval and Renaissance Latin Translations and Commentaries*, vol. 2 (Washington, 1971), 225–33. Già dal 1469 circolava a stampa la traduzione di Guarino Veronese dei libri I–X, insieme a quella di Gregorio Tifernate per i libri XI–XVII, curata da Giovanni Andrea Bussi. Nella biblioteca aragonese poi vi era più di una copia del testo, ma solo in traduzione: basti ricordare il prezioso codice Paris, Bibliothèque Nationale de France, MS Latin 4798 o ancora Città del Vaticano, Biblioteca Apostolica Vaticana, MS Ott. Lat. 1447. Per Firenze si veda Aubrey Diller, *The textual tradition of Strabo's Geography* (Amsterdam, 1975), 147–8, dove si accenna ad una supervisione di Demetrio Calcondila nell'allestimento di un codice greco di Strabone per i Medici (l'attuale Paris, Bibliothèque Nationale de France, MS Grec. 1394).

8   Sicuramente, se noi oggi andiamo a leggere i passi latini (tratti dal testo di Guarino) citati da Pucci, comprendiamo quanto raffinata fosse la cultura di Bernardo, capace di domandarsi se non ci fosse qualche problema di traduzione in quelle parole, che risultano infatti difficilmente comprensibili, in parte per colpa della scelta del Pucci.

9   Cfr. André Rochon, *La Jeunesse de Laurent de Médicis (1449–1478)* (Paris, 1963), 31–5; Cecil Grayson, "Becchi Gentile," in *Dizionario Biografico degli Italiani*, vol. 7 (Roma, 1970), 491–3 e Vittore Branca, *Poliziano e l'umanesimo della parola* (Torino, 1983), 38.

BERNARDO MICHELOZZI E FRANCESCO PUCCI, AMICI DI PENNA 217

del 1483 e prevedeva delle tappe ben precise, a Milano, nel Monferrato, presso il Duca di Savoia. Michelozzi testimonia all'amico il suo desiderio di scrivere un testo in prosa, una *historia*, per raccontare quella esperienza, e gli promette di spedirglielo al più presto. Solletica poi la sua curiosità riferendogli, in greco, che un tal 'famoso concittadino nostro', il primo giorno della quaresima ha iniziato a commentare i libri del Pentateuco in Orsanmichele. Nel testo della bozza si legge così:[10]

> πολίτης ἐκεῖνος ὁ ἡμέτερος vetus testamentum primo τεσσαρακοστῆς die, in dive Mariae, quem ortum Sancti Michaelis nuncupamus, enarrare incepit: omnia novit graeculus exuriens.

Da questa sua nota scopriamo che è appena iniziata la quaresima e che siamo in un periodo di tempo di poco successivo al ritorno del Michelozzi dalla missione in Francia: nel 1484 il mercoledì delle ceneri cadeva il 6 marzo, quindi il giorno prima che Pucci gli spedisse la lettera. Il tempo intercorso tra la spedizione e la ricezione deve essere stato abbastanza breve, qualche giorno, e Michelozzi gli risponde subito.[11] Ma chi è questo concittadino del Pucci, lettore del Pentateuco? Bernardo fornisce pochi indizi al riguardo: si dichiara incerto sulle sue competenze in materia (il che potrebbe far pensare che non si tratti di un teologo) e rimanda a un qualcosa che il Pucci gli aveva scritto proprio riguardo a questo personaggio e che lui riferisce in greco.[12] Le ultime tre righe dell'epistola di Bernardo contengono ancora un ulteriore indizio: il personaggio cui allude ha una cultura e degli interessi ecclettici, ora studia il latino infatti, ora il greco, ora l'ebraico, ora il caldaico.[13]

---

10   Città del Vaticano, Biblioteca Apostolica Vaticana, Fondo Autografi Patetta 1245, cart. 5, n. 7, fol. 2r (segnatura provvisoria). L'ultimo emistichio è citazione da Iuv., *Sat.* 3,77–8.

11   Se mantenessimo la proposta di Martelli che datava la lettera del Pucci al 1485, pensando all'uso fiorentino di far iniziare l'anno il 25 marzo, ci troveremmo in difficoltà dal momento che in quell'anno la Pasqua occorreva il 3 di aprile e dunque le ceneri il 20 febbraio, data un po' troppo lontana dalla lettera di Pucci e quindi dalla risposta dell'amico, per giustificare l'accenno da parte di Bernardo a queste 'lezioni'.

12   "Velim illum ἐν τῷ βήματι aspiceres perlegentem, in aures credo insusurrares, quid ad me superioribus litteris scripsisti, αὐτότατός ἐστι, τὸ γὰρ χάος παλαιὸν εἰς ἡμᾶς φέρει, δυνάμει μέντοι, ἀλλ᾽οὐ πράξει," Città del Vaticano, Biblioteca Apostolica Vaticana, Fondo Autografi Patetta 1245, cart. 5, n. 7, fol. 2r (segnatura provvisoria). Al momento non abbiamo traccia di una lettera di Francesco con una frase in latino o in greco di questo tono, per cui non riusciamo a comprendere se non una critica metodologica.

13   È notevole come lo studio delle cinque lingue diventerà fondamentale nel programma di riforma di Savonarola: cfr. Angelo Michele Piemontese, "Lo studio delle cinque lingue presso Savonarola e Pico," in *Europa e Islam tra i secoli XIV e XVI*, ed. Michele Bernardini, Clara Borrelli, Anna Cerbo e Encarnación Sánchez García (Napoli, 2002), vol. 1, 179–202.

Questo commento pubblico al Pentateuco, cui allude il Michelozzi, non sembra rimandare ad un vero e proprio corso sulle sacre scritture, come quello che il giovane Girolamo Savonarola aveva iniziato a tenere presso il convento di San Marco dal 1482.[14] E non si può trattare nemmeno di un quaresimale: in quei mesi, oltre al frate domenicano, che predicava in San Lorenzo,[15] vi era anche l'agostiniano Mariano da Genazzano presso il monastero delle Murate[16] e sicuramente altri, ma le parole di Bernardo non sembrano far riferimento ad una omelia, quanto piuttosto ad un lavoro sul testo della traduzione latina geronimiana della Bibbia.[17] Tra l'altro stava per arrivare in città, se non era già presente, Giovanni Pico della Mirandola,[18] i cui interessi per la cultura ebraica e cabalistica, che prendono forma proprio in questi mesi, sono ben noti, e nella cui biblioteca ricchissima di testi greci, latini, ebraici e caldaici non mancherà

All'ecclettismo di questo personaggio, anche se in modo ironico, alluderebbe anche la citazione da Iuvenale di cui *supra*.

14   Cfr. Roberto Ridolfi, *Vita di Girolamo Savonarola* (Firenze, 1974), 20–31, che a sua volta rimanda a Giuseppe Schnitzer, *Savonarola*, trad. Ernesto Rutili (Milano, 1931), 82–3.

15   Girolamo Cinozzi, che fu tra i primi uditori e biografi del frate domenicano, racconta che i suoi primi esperimenti di approccio al popolo fiorentino non erano stati molto apprezzati, soprattutto durante la quaresima del 1484: *Scelta di predice e scritti di Fra Girolamo Savonarola, con nuovi documenti intorno alla sua vita*, ed. Pasquale Villari e Eugenio Casanova (Firenze, 1898), 11. Girolamo aveva iniziato a predicare presso il monastero benedettino delle Murate e in Orsanmichele, durante la quaresima del 1483: vedi Alessandro Gherardi, *Nuovi documenti e studi intorno a Girolamo Savonarola* (Firenze, 1887²), 39–40. Per la quaresima del 1484 risulta che avesse predicato a San Lorenzo, cfr. Schnitzer, *Savonarola* (vedi sopra, n. 14), 87–9. Copiosa è la documentazione sui 'quaresimali' del frate: cfr. Armando F. Verde, "Girolamo Savonarola: il quaresimale di S. Gimignano (1486). *Rationes flagellorum* e *Rationes fidei*," *Memorie Domenicane* 20 (1989), 167–253 e soprattutto Giulio Cattin, *Il primo Savonarola. Poesie e prediche autografe dal codice Borromeo* (Firenze, 1973). Si veda inoltre Zelina Zafarana, "Per la storia religiosa di Firenze nel Quattrocento. Una raccolta privata di prediche," *Studi medievali*, ser. III, 9.2 (1968), 1017–113.

16   Daniela Gionta, "Pomicelli, Mariano (Mariano da Genazzano)," in *Dizionario Biografico degli Italiani*, vol. 84 (Roma, 2015), 671–7.

17   Forse potrebbe trattarsi di una lezione integrativa; difficile pensare a un ciclo di *sermones* legati a qualche congregazione religiosa (e spesso tenuti da laici): vi accenna Isidoro del Lungo, *Florentia. Uomini e cose del Quattrocento* (Firenze, 1897), 191–203. Sulla confraternita si veda Saverio La Sorsa, *La compagnia d'Or San Michele, ovvero una pagina della beneficenza in Toscana nel secolo XIV* (Trani, 1902). Sui *Sermones* del Poliziano, editi in Giancarlo Tanturli, "I *Sermoni* di Angelo Poliziano," *Archivum mentis* 6 (2017), 223–48, si veda Giovannangiola Tarugi, "Scritti religiosi di Angelo Poliziano," in *Il pensiero italiano del Rinascimento e il tempo nostro. Atti del V Convegno internazionale del Centro di Studi Umanistici (Montepulciano, 8–13 agosto 1968)*, ed. Giovannangiola Tarugi (Firenze, 1970), 43–108.

18   Così Arnaldo Della Torre, *Storia dell'Accademia platonica in Firenze* (Firenze, 1902), 747–60.

BERNARDO MICHELOZZI E FRANCESCO PUCCI, AMICI DI PENNA   219

di lì a qualche anno anche una traduzione latina del *Commento al Pentateuco* di Menechem da Recanati, realizzata su sua commissione da Flavio Mitridate.[19] Sono dunque interessi, questi testimoniati dal misterioso personaggio, condivisi con il circolo di intellettuali più vicini alla cultura medicea, condivisi con lo stesso Ficino, che in quei mesi aveva appena completato la seconda redazione del suo *De christiana religione*, e i cui contatti con la tradizione ebraica sono oggi meglio noti e studiati.[20]

La nostra curiosità su chi sia il lettore di Orsanmichele cresce ancora di più se colleghiamo – come necessità vuole – a questa lettera di Bernardo la risposta del Pucci. Si tratta questa volta di una delle epistole segnalate da Martelli, che naturalmente ora possiamo rileggere con occhi diversi e soprattutto formulando nuove domande. Francesco infatti esordisce dicendo che ha aspettato che passasse la Quaresima per scrivere al suo amico: dopo aver assaggiato la carne di capretto infatti, terminato ogni rigore religioso, può tornare alle cose piacevoli. Per prima cosa gli racconta di una sua nuova battaglia filologica a proposito di un passo di Plinio, vinta naturalmente sfoggiando la sua conoscenza dei testi classici; quindi passa a commentare la seconda parte della lettera dell'amico dove si parla di quel 'concittadino', appunto. Gli dice infatti:[21]

Alteram epistulae tuae partem intelligere non potui: nulla enim coniectura assequi valeo quisnam sit ille πολίτης ἐκεῖνος ὁ ὑμέτερος; si scripsisses

---

19   Su questo personaggio si veda *Flavio Mitridate mediatore fra culture nel contesto dell'ebraismo siciliano del XV secolo. Atti del convegno internazionale di studi, Caltabelotta, 30 giugno–1 luglio 2008*, ed. Mauro Perani e Giacomo Corazzol (Palermo, 2012); in particolare per i rapporti con Giovanni Pico della Mirandola, che da lui imparò il caldaico, si veda Giovanni Dell'Acqua e Ladislao Münster, "I rapporti di Giovanni Pico della Mirandola con alcuni filosofi ebrei," in *L'opera e il pensiero di Giovanni Pico della Mirandola nella storia dell'Umanesimo, Convegno internazionale (Mirandola, 15–18 settembre 1963)* (Firenze, 1965), 149–68 e François Secret, "Nouvelles precisions su Flavius Mithridates maitre de Pic de la Mirandole et traducteur de Commentaires de Kabbale," in *L'opera e il pensiero* (vedi sopra), 169–87. Nella biblioteca del Conte della Mirandola vi era più di una copia del Pentateuco: cfr. Pearl Kibre, *The Library of Pico della Mirandola* (New York, 1936), 37–48.

20   Cfr. Guido Bartolucci, "Il *De christiana religione di Marsilio Ficino* e le 'prime traduzioni' di Flavio Mitridate," *Rinascimento* 44 (2006), 345–55 e quindi Marsilio Ficino, *De Christiana religione*, ed. Guido Bartolucci (Pisa, 2019), in part. per il rapporto con la cultura ebraica, 34–52.

21   Firenze, Biblioteca Nazionale Centrale, Fondo Ginori Conti, 29a. "La seconda parte della tua lettera non l'ho potuta capire: con nessuna ipotesi sono capace di comprendere chi mai sia quel vostro concittadino, se avessi scritto 'nostro' avrei pensato ad Angelo. Forse fu errore di penna. Se è così, mi viene in mente quel detto *quid sus Minervam?* Perché indugio con tante parole? Io ancora a stento trattengo il riso. Mi sembra di vedere Aristarco annotare le Scritture. O povero Girolamo, che alla fine ha ricevuto oggi in sorte un tanto rigido censore!"

ἡμέτερος intellexissem περὶ Ἀγγέλου: calamus fortasse aberravit ἐν τῷ γράμματι. Quod si est, succurrit illud τὶ χοῖρος πρὸς Ἀθηνᾶν? Quid multis moror? Ego adhuc vix risum compesco. Videre videor Aristarchum ὀβελίζοντα γράμματα τὰ ἱερά. O infelicem Hieronimum, qui nunc tandem tam rigidum censorem sortitus est!

Dunque Bernardo non aveva più scritto in bella ἡμέτερος come leggiamo noi oggi nella brutta copia, ma ὑμέτερος, non sappiamo quanto consapevolmente.[22]

Neanche Pucci è riuscito a comprendere chi mai si fosse messo a leggere la Bibbia a Orsanmichele, sicché congettura – previa proposta *emendatio* dell'evidente, per lui, *lapsus calami* – che si tratti di Angelo Poliziano: Bernardo avrebbe dovuto scrivere 'nostro' concittadino e non vostro, però.[23] Se così fosse, aggiunge Pucci utilizzando un detto di Cicerone, che traduce in greco, "che ha a che fare il maiale con Minerva?" Ovvero – e in questo concorda con Bernardo, a quanto pare – "chi glielo fa fare a mettersi a fare il grammatico sulle sacre scritture?" È da intendere così sia il riferimento ad Aristarco, grammatico per eccellenza, sia a Girolamo, che a questo punto non può essere Girolamo da Panzano, secondo l'ipotesi allora sensatissima di Martelli, ma San Girolamo, l'autore della vulgata, che il *grammaticus* onnisciente, il Poliziano, andrebbe a pungere sul vivo della sua versione, censurandone gli errori.

Michelozzi gli risponde. Sono passati un po' di giorni: con la lettera del Pucci siamo oramai oltre il 18 aprile, quindi è probabile che questa ultima di Bernardo si dati tra la fine del mese di aprile e i primi giorni di maggio del 1484.

Per prima cosa si dichiara divertito dal fatto che il Pucci ha praticato l'astinenza dalle carni per il periodo prescritto dalla quaresima e gli risponde con un epigramma;[24] quindi torna a lodare le imprese accademiche dell'amico e

---

22 I rapporti tra Poliziano e Michelozzi non dovettero essere sempre cordiali: da questo carteggio privato vien fuori un atteggiamento ironico da parte di Bernardo, che forse esprime qui in maniera più autentica che altrove il senso di disagio che una parte dei 'fiorentini' sicuramente provava nei confronti di chi giovane provinciale aveva conquistato in breve tempo la stima e la fiducia del signore. Per altri dettagli rimando ai due precedenti lavori citati nelle note 2 e 3.

23 L'ostinazione, l'entusiasmo, il successo, l'audacia di questo *lector* sembrano rimandare a tipici tratti del suo carattere, così come ci viene ritratto altrove; cfr. Branca, *Poliziano* (vedi sopra, n. 9) e la famosa lettera del luglio del 1486 di Girolamo da Panzano a Bernardo Michelozzi (ivi edita, 74–75), che recita: "Politianus tuus nunc maxime, ut inquit ille, sua se iactat in aula ac totus est in illa sua silvula explicanda. Qua in re aiunt non esse illi opus interprete: mirum est quam omnes suos sensus exprimat, atque etiam reconditos. Saepius sibi ipsi plaudit atque blanditur multisque in locis sibi placuisse ingenue fatetur" (75).

24 Si tratta di un componimento formato da esametri latini alternati con pentametri greci. Il contenuto è leggero e divertente, per non dire dissacrante (così poi commenterà l'amico),

BERNARDO MICHELOZZI E FRANCESCO PUCCI, AMICI DI PENNA 221

a consigliargli prudenza, nonostante testimoni la necessità che tutti i giovani Fiorentini emigrati, non solo Francesco (ma anche lui, se gliene sarà data occasione, farà lo stesso), si sforzino di mostrare la grandezza della loro patria, mettendo a frutto la loro cultura e la loro educazione.

Nel commentare in greco poi la parte che riguarda il personaggio misterioso che leggeva il Pentateuco, così si esprime:[25]

> Quam partem epistolae meae nullis vaquis te potuisse coniecturis assequi in promptu, ut mihi quidem videtur, est, nec putes calamum aberrasse οὐ γὰρ ἡμέτερον ἀλλ᾽ὑμέτερον ἠβουλόμην ἐν τῷ σε τε καὶ τοὺς αὐτοῦ φίλους ἄλλους δεῖξαι. οὐκ ἐμοὶ γὰρ οὐδαμῶς ὁ σὸς πολίτης καὶ τῶν τοιούτων, οἵ αὐτοῦ ἔρανται, περὶ τοῦτον τελευταῖον ὄν λέγεις ἠσθόμην, cui qua fortuna τὸ πεντατεῦχος τὸ μωσαικός enodanti succederet (de me sileo) aliorum sit iudicium. Sunt tamen, nec hi quidam pauci nec indocti, qui dicant "in sua ille harena versetur, ad suos redeat poetas", quod ille persentiscens sepius ἐν τῇ ἐξαίδρᾳ, (saepius) de his dum obloquitur eorumque impudentiam accusat, crimen – mihi crede – gravat. Affui ego.

A me sembra che l'ipotesi di Pucci sia confermata da Bernardo, che dichiara di aver scritto consapevolmente ὑμέτερον (vostro) per non confondersi nella schiera dei *suoi* ammiratori, nella quale c'è anche Francesco. E quando nelle righe successive aggiunge che nella folla dei suoi uditori vi erano persone, non

---

    secondo un modulo praticato in epoca tardo antica da Ausonio: la quaresima infatti viene presentata come il momento in cui ci si mantiene con gran difficoltà in bilico tra la propria volontà, che coraggiosamente ci tiene saldi fino alla fine, e la sorte (che lui chiama in causa con l'immagine dei dadi) che da un momento all'altro ci può far cadere in tentazione. E sul filo di quest'ultima immagine, nella seconda parte del carme ammonisce l'amico a stare attento a che – finita l'astinenza – non si faccia sedurre dall'antica dolcezza di Partenope, ma anzi come Ulisse si turi le orecchie e resista, vincendo la città e Amore. Anche in questo caso Francesco ha difficoltà a capire e nella risposta sarà divertito e perplesso sugli scherzi dell'amico.

25   Città del Vaticano, Biblioteca Apostolica Vaticana, Fondo Autografi Patetta 1245, cart. 5, n. 7, fol. 1r (segnatura provvisoria): "Quella parte della mia lettera che dici di non essere riuscito a comprendere con nessuna congettura, è ben chiara, come sembra a me e non credere che abbia sbagliato a scrivere. *Non infatti nostro ma vostro volevo dire, indicando te e gli altri suoi amici. Non ha niente a che fare con me infatti in nessun modo il tuo concittadino: ho sentito parlare di quello di cui parli da ultimo, da quei tali che ne sono innamorati.* Con quale esito poi abbia commentato il Pentateuco di Mosè, sia giudizio altrui. Vi sono alcuni, tuttavia, e questi né pochi né ignoranti, che direbbero 'che se ne stia nella sua sabbia, che torni ai suoi poeti.' E questo lui lo ha intuito bene e spesso dalla cattedra, e mentre interloquisce con loro, stigmatizza la loro sfacciataggine, credimi, aumenta la gravità del delitto. Io c'ero".

certo ignoranti, che lo ammonivano a tornarsene dai suoi poeti e a lasciar stare i testi sacri, ci fa capire che non si tratta di un teologo. Su questo episodio i due non torneranno più (abbiamo la risposta di Pucci a questa lettera): si erano intesi, loro.

Al momento non è altrimenti documentabile quanto si ricava da queste pagine e che potrebbe costituire un episodio stravagante della biografia del Poliziano, ma non è escluso che ulteriori ricerche possano corroborare e chiarire ulteriormente la questione. L'interesse per i testi sacri, anche se saltuario e di natura per lo più linguistica e filologica, è testimoniato soprattutto per anni successivi, legato alla sua amicizia con Giovanni Pico e al progredire dei suoi studi linguistici al di fuori dei confini della letteratura classica:[26] restano suggestive tuttavia le parole con cui Angelo apre, non sappiamo quando, una lettera indirizzata ad un aspirante poeta, Johannes Gottius, del quale aveva letto – nonostante gli impegni – i *carmina*: "Cum per hos quadragesimae proximos dies enarrandis populo sacris litteris essem occupatus [...]."[27]

Università degli studi di Bari

---

26   Cfr. Lucia Cesarini Martinelli, "Poliziano e i Padri della Chiesa," in *Umanesimo e Padri della Chiesa, Manoscritti e incunaboli di testi patristici da Francesco Petrarca al primo Cinquecento*, ed. Sebastiano Gentile (1997), 93–100; eadem, "La versione del Poliziano di un opuscolo di s. Atanasio," *Rinascimento* 8 (1968), 311–21; Francesco Bausi, "Bibbia e umanesimo," in *La Bibbia nella letteratura italiana. V. Dal Medioevo al Rinascimento*, ed. Grazia Melli e Marialuigia Sipione (Brescia, 2013), 363–98; Maria Pia Sacchi, "Oltre la filologia: Poliziano e il sacro," ibid., 471–87 e Claudio Bevegni, "Presenze dei Padri della Chiesa greci nelle opere di Angelo Poliziano," in *Significato e funzione della cattedrale, del giubileo e della ripresa della patristica dal Medioevo al Rinascimento. Atti del XXIII Convegno Internazionale (Chianciano Terme-Pienza 18–21 luglio 2011)*, ed. Luisa Rotondi Secchi Tarugi (Firenze, 2013), 295–309. Si veda inoltre Salvatore Camporeale, "L'esegesi umanistica del Valla e il simposio teologico di Lorenzo il Magnifico a Palazzo Medici. L'intervento di Poliziano," in *Poliziano e il suo tempo. Atti del VI Convegno internazionale (Chianciano-Montepulciano 18–21 luglio 1994)*, ed. Luisa Rotondi Secchi Tarugi (Firenze, 1996), 283–95, in cui si recuperano le testimonianze in merito ad una disputa tra grammatica e teologia nel giugno del 1489.

27   Angeli Politiani *Omnia opera* (Venetiis, 1498), f. fiiv; questa lettera è citata come documento e testimonianza della religiosità del Poliziano per la prima vota in Gerardi Ioannis Vossii *De veterorum poetarum temporibus libri duo* (Amstelaedami, 1643), 80; si veda la discussione riportata in Friderici Ottonis Menckenii *Historia vitae et in literas meritorum Angeli Politiani* (Lipsiae, 1736), 429–48.

CHAPTER 15

The Bird-Catcher's Wiles: Pietro Angeli da Barga's *De Aucupio*

Ingrid A. R. De Smet

Abstract

Pietro Angeli da Barga's *De aucupio* or *Ixeuticon* was first published in Florence in 1566 with a dedication to Francesco de' Medici. The unfinished didactic poem on fowling, or the trapping of birds with nets, snares, or glue sticks, corroborated the Tuscan humanist's reputation as a Latin poet, in the wake of his more voluminous and grandiloquent, the *Cynegetica* ("On Hunting", first published at Lyon in 1561) but well before his famous epic masterpiece, the *Syrias*. This paper reassesses the enduring appeal of Angeli's *De aucupio* and its artistic merit. After considering its place in the georgic and cynegetic traditions of the Renaissance and Early Modern period, our study focuses on Angeli's treatment of the moral and material aspects of bird-trapping, an art by which humans notoriously outwit nature.

Keywords

Pietro Angeli da Barga (Petrus Angelius Bargaeus) – *De aucupio* or *Ixeuticon* (1566) – Neo-Latin didactic poetry – history of hunting – fowling and trapping

"Elegante, vero, vivo, tutto odoroso di campagna e di selva": such is the praise which the nineteenth-century poet and scholar Giovanni Pascoli famously bestowed on Pietro Angeli da Barga's *De aucupio* or *Ixeuticon*.*,[1] The work was first published in Florence in 1566 with a dedication to Francesco de' Medici and a short, liminary poem by Mario Colonna, as well as an elegiac *parergon* on the defeat of the Gothic general Radagasio below Fiesole, dedicated to Cosimo

---

* I owe thanks to Prof. Florian Schaffenrath and Dr Gloria Moorman for their assistance with accessing the manuscript material cited in this paper.

1 Giovanni Pascoli, *Il Bargeo*, ed. Marinella Tartari Chersoni (Bologna, 1994), 43.

© KONINKLIJKE BRILL NV, LEIDEN, 2020 | DOI:10.1163/9789004427105_016

de' Medici.[2] This didactic poem on fowling, or the trapping of birds with nets, snares, or glue sticks, corroborated the Tuscan humanist's reputation as a Latin poet, in the wake of his more voluminous and grandiloquent *Cynegetica* ("On Hunting", first published at Lyon in 1561) but well before his famous epic masterpiece, the *Syrias* (Paris, 1582–584).[3] The *De aucupio* was reprinted with Angeli's *Poemata omnia*, first in Florence in 1568, and again in Rome in 1585.[4] From the eighteenth century onwards, it has also been translated several times into Italian, by Giovanni Pietro Bergantini (1735), Girolamo Pongelli (1780), and Giuseppe Chimienti (1931).[5] This paper reassesses the basis for the enduring appeal of Angeli's *De aucupio*: what was its place in the georgic and cynegetic traditions of the Renaissance and Early Modern period? Above all, what exactly can a Latin work such as this tell us about the moral and material aspects of bird-trapping, an art by which humans notoriously outwit nature?

An Unfinished Masterpiece?

First, a word must be said about the scope of the poem itself. The dedicatory epistle of 1566, which disappeared from subsequent editions (except Bergantini's), contains the oft-repeated assertion that the text, consisting of a single Book, was still incomplete, but that the poet had three further Books on the stocks:[6]

---

2 Pietro Angeli, *De aucupio liber primus ad Franciscum Medicem Florent[inorum] & Senens[ium] principem. Eiusdem Elegia de Radagasi et Getarum cæde ad urbem Florentiam. Ad Cosmum Medicem Florent[inorum] et Senens[ium] Ducem* (Florence, 1566). On the *Elegia* and its context, see Henk Th. van Veen, "Art and Propaganda in Late Renaissance and Baroque Florence: The Defeat of Radagasius, King of the Goths," *Journal of the Warburg and Courtauld Institutes* 47 (1984), 106–18.

3 Alexander Winkler, "Pietro Angeli da Barga's Syrias (1582–91) and Contemporary Debates over Epic Poetry," in *Neo-Latin and the Vernaculars: Bilingual Interactions in the Early Modern Period*, ed. Florian Schaffenrath and Alexander Winkler (Leiden, 2018), 212–31.

4 Pietro Angeli da Barga, *Poemata omnia ab ipso diligentiss[ime] recognita & plurimis varij generis carminibus et indice capitum singulorum lib[rorum] copios[i]s[sime] aucta [...] Item Marii Columnae quaedam carmina* (Florence, 1568), 185–214; idem, *Poemata omnia* (Rome, 1585), part 1, 176–202.

5 "L'Uccellatura a vischio di Pietro Angelio Bargeo," in *Il falconiere di Jacopo Augusto Tuano [...] Coll'Uccellatura a vischio di Pietro Angelio Bargeo [...] poemetto pur latino, similmente tradotto, e commentato. Ozii, e ameni studii di G. P. Bergantini* (Venice, 1735), separate title-page and pagination; *L'uccellagione de Pietro Angelio Bargeo volgarizzata*, trans. Girolamo Pongelli (Naples, [1780]); *Aucupium o l'uccellagione di Pietro Angeli di Barga*, trans. Giuseppe Chimienti (Trieste, 1931).

6 Angeli, *De aucupio* (see above, n. 2), fol. 3r.

Etsi hominis esse videatur minime gravis ea in lucem edere, FRANCISCE MEDICES Princeps potentissime, quae nondum absoluta sunt: ego tamen nihil veritus huiusmodi de me opinionem hunc primum librum de AVCVPIO divulgari, et in manus hominum pervenire facillime sum passus. Quod cum a me quatuor scripti sint, unus hic imprudenti exciderit, et a multis descriptus cum fuerit, lacer propemodum ac plurimis in locis pessime affectus circumferatur.

Although, most mighty Prince Francesco de' Medici, it may seem typical of a man who is not in the least bit serious to publish an unfinished work, I was not at all afraid that I would earn that kind of reputation and happily allowed this First Book of my work "On the Art of Fowling" to be disseminated and to be placed in the hands of the public. Indeed, whilst I had composed four Books, I carelessly allowed this one to slip away: copied by many, it circulates in an imperfect state, badly afflicted in many places.

Whilst we know that Angeli started composing his poem in October 1562, and finished the first book in 1564,[7] thus leaving some time for a manuscript to circulate, his statement to Francesco de' Medici must be treated with caution. In many respects, the so-called First Book appears to be a self-contained and well-rounded unit, that closes on an evocation of pastoral bliss. Secondly, there is no trace of the three further Books which Angeli implies he had already drafted. On the contrary, his eighteenth-century biographer Salvini records an anecdote, according to which Angeli wittily explained there had been no point in finishing the work, since his previous didactic endeavour, the *Cynegetica*, had brought him no profit, only criticism:[8]

Iis additus est postea liber de Aucupio unus, cum tamen, ut totum illud argumentum complecteretur, quatuor libros scribere constituisset; itaque rogatus aliquando, cur inchoatum opus reliquisset, respondit, se quoniam in venando nihil cepisset, et in ejus Venationis apparatu a canibus propemodum absumtus esset, ne, quae sui reliquiae supererant, ab Accipitribus, et Vulturiis exederentur, aucupii fortunam experiri noluisse.

To his [poem on hunting] he later added a single book on the art of fowling, whereas he had in fact planned to write four books, to cover

---

7   Guido Manacorda, "Petrus Angelius Bargaeus (Piero Angeli da Barga)," *Annali della R. Scuola Normale Superiore di Pisa: Filosofia e Filologia* 18 (1905), 1, 3–71, 73, 75–105, 107–31, there 17.

8   Salvino Salvini, *Fasti consolari dell'Accademia Fiorentina* (Florence, 1717), 289–316, there 309.

the entire subject. So when he was once asked why he had abandoned the work he had started, he replied that, since he had caught nothing by hunting and had almost been devoured by the hounds in the full flush of that hunt, he had no desire to experience the fate of a fowling expedition, lest whatever was left of him be scavenged by birds of prey and vultures.

The printed text of the extant single Book varies somewhat in the three contemporary printed issues, whilst the Biblioteca Laurenziana preserves a miscellaneous manuscript which includes an autograph text of the *De aucupio*'s first Book, with ample revisions, often on the opposite page, left blank for that very purpose.[9] The sequence and extent of the variants in this manuscript and its successive editions deserve to be plotted in a critical edition, which is lacking so far and lies beyond the scope of the present study. In what follows, then, I shall concentrate on the *editio princeps* of 1566, i.e., the version in which Angeli formally released his text into the public domain, unless otherwise stated.

The *De Aucupio* in the Didactic-Georgic and Cynegetic Traditions

Angeli's reputation as a Neo-Latin didactic poet is well-established. In an important article on Latin georgic poetry of the Italian Renaissance, published in 1999, Yasmin Haskell associated Angeli's "recreational didactic" with the "manly" hunting poems of Natale Conti (the *De venatione libri IIII*, published in Venice in 1551) and Angeli's own *Cynegeticon libri VI*, already mentioned;[10] for all these texts, Haskell rightly identifies Vergil's *Georgics* as a principal model, but she sees the *De aucupio* as "something of a generic hybrid, [...] sharing ground with poems of the sericultural / horticultural variety" (150), such as Girolamo Vida's *Bombycon libri II* (on silkworms) or Giuseppe Milio's later *De hortorum cultura*, both of which were dedicated to women. Haskell's suggestion that Angeli's *De aucupio* "admit[s] of at least one female reader" (ibid.), viz. the girl Chloris addressed in the final section of the Book, however, is problematic: I shall return to this conundrum at the end. Meanwhile, let us note that the *De aucupio* exhibits the common hallmarks of the didactic genre, combining a pedagogic lexis and technical contents with aetiological myths, and periphrases to indicate times and seasons, or to identify certain kinds of birds by referring to their patron deity. Angeli's Classical sources,

---

9   Florence, Biblioteca Laurenziana, MS Acquisti e Doni 437 ("Memorie. Mss. autografi di Pietro Angeli detto il Bargeo"), 169–234.

10   Yasmin Haskell, "Work or Play? Latin 'Recreational' Georgic Poetry of the Italian Renaissance," *Humanistica Lovaniensia* 48 (1999), 132–59.

moreover, go well beyond Vergil, with *iuncturae* borrowed from Horace, Ovid (the *Metamorphoses* especially), Lucan, Lucretius, Propertius and so on.

At the same time, Angeli's work is also a well-known exponent of the rich vein of hunting, hawking and fowling treatises produced in late Medieval and Renaissance Italy, and it rightly features in Giuliano Innamorati's 1965 landmark anthology of Italian texts on falconry, fowling and other types of hunting.[11] Among Angeli's most significant predecessors are Pietro de Crescenzi's *Ruralia commoda* (a Medieval text, which continued to circulate widely in the sixteenth century), Belisario Acquaviva's *De aucupio*, printed in 1519, but also Jacopo di Porcia's tract *De venationibus et aucupationibus*, the original manuscript of which was thought to have been lost but is in fact preserved at Innsbruck.[12] These are all in prose. Angeli's *De aucupio* further anticipates Italian vernacular treatises such as *Il Canto degl'augelli* by Antonio Valli da Todi: published in Rome in 1601 with engravings made from drawings by Antonio Tempesta, Valli's treatise describes in both words and images the various kinds of traps and techniques for catching various species of songbirds. Studying these texts helps us understand and evaluate the 'trade secrets' that Angelio's text contains.

Last but not least, Angeli's *De aucupio* coincides with the dawn of ornithology as a modern science, which found expression in both Latin and the vernacular: eleven years after William Turner's *De historia avium* appeared in Cologne in 1544, Pierre Belon published his *Histoire de la nature des oiseaux* in Paris, in 1555; it drew on Belon's own observations during his travels and on specialist illustrations of birds made by artists in England, Italy, Flanders and France. In that same year, 1555, Conrad Gesner's *De avibus* was printed in Zürich. Bird-catchers were also an important source of information for this emerging science: Gesner, for example, refers to his consultation of contemporary fowlers and falconers on several occasions.[13] Ulisse Aldrovandi's encyclopaedic *Ornithologiae libri III*, on the other hand, was first published between 1599 and 1603; Aldrovandi's systematic treatment of different species of birds routinely includes discussions of how birds might be used by humans

---

11   Mario Carrari, "Saggio bibliografico delle opere italiane sulla caccia dal secolo XV agli anni nostril," *Aevum* 13 (1939), 193–221; *Arte della caccia. Testi di falconeria, uccellagione e alter cacce*, ed. Giuliano Innamorati (Milan, 1965), vol. 2, 111–91 (reproducing Bergantini's translation, as in n. 5 above).

12   Andrea Benedetti, "Il Trattato della caccia, uccellagione e pesca del conte Jacopo di Porcia," *Il Noncello* 19 (1962), 47–81 (reproducing the text on the basis of a 1917 transcript). Innsbruck, Universitäts- und Landesbibliothek Tirol, Cod. 286, fols 41rb–49r ("De venationibus et aucupationibus per Iacobum Comitem purliliarum").

13   Conrad Gesner, *De avibus* (Zürich, 1555), 8, 12, 54, 109, 274, 698, 724 and 729.

as food, kept for delectation, or indeed be themselves used in the hunt. Just as Gesner occasionally drew on literary sources, so Angeli's poetry—not just the *De aucupio*, but also the *Syrias*—features among the many texts quoted and consulted by Aldrovandi.[14] It is among these early ornithologists that an interest and awareness arose of Ancient poems on bird-catching: Gesner had access to Eutecnius Sophistes's paraphrase in prose of the *Ixeuticon* ascribed to Oppian of Corycos (not yet distinguished from Oppian of Apamea) and knew of the recently discovered fragments of a poem *De aucupio*, then attributed to Nemesianus.[15] Angeli's *De aucupio* sports the more learned, alternative title *Ixeuticon* from 1585 onwards;[16] this suggests that he only became aware of these 'new' texts after 1568. It is not clear either to what extent Angeli's poem draws on his own observations or experience: his extensive travels—notably in the Eastern Mediterranean, but also through Italy and to France—supposedly fed into the hunting techniques described in the *Cynegetica*, but that notion, stemming from an *a posteriori* claim by the poet, has been disputed.[17] Nevertheless, Manacorda, writing in 1905, believed—perhaps rather indulgently—that Angeli spent enough time in his native mountain region to have taken instruction from the locals on fowling, before making the subject his own and bringing it alive in his poetry.[18] But let us now turn to Angeli's poem itself and the art that it proclaims to teach.

Angeli's Survey of Bird-Catching Techniques: Humans vs. Nature

Have you ever tried to catch a butterfly with your bare hands, let alone a bird, other than perhaps a duckling or a chicken with clipped wings, on a farm when you were little? Mere speed and dexterity are rarely enough. Since time immemorial fowlers have notoriously developed various tools and techniques to capture their prey, achieving a high level of complexity by the sixteenth and seventeenth centuries.[19] The fowlers' tricks and tools thus inspired a range

---

14   Ulisse Aldrovandi, *Ornithologiae, hoc est, De avibus historiae libri XII* (Bologna, 1599–1603), vol. 1, 741; vol. 2, 367 and 396; vol. 3, 41.

15   Ingrid A. R. De Smet, *La Fauconnerie à la Renaissance. Le "Hieracosophion" (1582–84) de Jacques Auguste de Thou* (Geneva, 2013), 165–6. On Angeli's debt to Oppian of Apamea's and Nemesianus's texts on venery, see Edilio Marelli, "Bargaeus," *Aevum* 32 (1958), 537–48, there 540–2.

16   Pietro Angeli, *Poemata omnia, diligenter ab ipso recognita* (Rome, 1585), 177.

17   Manacorda, "Petrus Angelius Bargaeus" (see above, n. 7), 9. For Marelli, however, "fuit ipse venator inter venatores" (see above, n. 15, 540).

18   Manacorda, "Petrus Angelius Bargaeus" (see above, n. 7), 35.

19   For a long-term view, see Anne Eastham, "Papageno down the Ages: A Study in Fowling Methods, with Particular Reference to the Palaeolithic of Western Europe," in *Homenaje a*

THE BIRD-CATCHER'S WILES: PIETRO ANGELI DA BARGA'S *DE AUCUPIO* 229

of metaphors and emblems portraying deceitful practices. This cunning is highlighted from the very beginning of Angeli's poem: "Hinc quibus *insidiis* auceps instructus et armis / *Decipiat* volucres [...]" ("What tricks and tools a bird catcher must know to deceive the birds [...]").[20] The word "fraus" occurs a dozen times in the poem, and just once, outside fowling practices proper, as "sine fraude"; there are likewise eight occurrences of "insidiae" or "insidiosus", as of "dolus" or "dolosus". The question is, however, whether in this particular context the fowler's deceit is to be understood as truly negative and morally reprehensible (as in Haskell's reading of the poem) or as a rightful stratagem and proof of human ingenuity; the vernacular expression "caccia con insidie" certainly seems to have been neutral. The Renaissance admittedly construed fowling as a less noble sport than hawking, in which one bird species (a raptor) combats another, at the beck and call of its master. But in many regions of Renaissance Italy, aristocrats and princes (including princes of the Church) readily enjoyed bird-catching as a pastime too—and an edifying one at that. Given Angeli's noble dedicatee, the reference to the fowler's tools as weaponry ("arma") presents the *auceps* as a fighter preparing himself for combat. Indeed, where the poem describes methods that require the input of more than one person, it is implied that this well-armed fowler dispatch his friends to the more ancillary tasks such as beating. In one case, the companion is referred to as a "faithful Achates, who has come with you to share the sweet labour of the hunt" ("fidus Achates, [...] praedae socius gratique laboris", [19]) thus by implication casting the fowler as a second Aeneas, or noble, epic hero, facing a canny foe.

What, then, do the bird-catcher's wiles and instruments entail? After the customary introduction, Angeli highlights the diversity of (wild) birds: different techniques, therefore, are required according to the species and the season. A first section thus concerns the trapping of ducks and similar water fowl. All gins must be carefully concealed as the birds will fly off at the slightest misgiving: "there must be no traces of your tacit deceit," says the poet, "no planed poles or stakes, [...]" ("absint tacitae vestigia fraudis / Absint et culti ferro palique sudesque [...]", 11). In other words, all signs of human activity or intervention must be concealed, or the birds will disappear, "leaving the young fowler lurking in his small, straw hut, to point his hands and eyes skyward and make all sorts of vows just to Neptune" ("Et iuvenem parvi latitantem in stramine culmi, / Tendentemque manus, oculosque ad sidera, et uni / Plurima Neptuno facientem vota relinquent", ibid.).

    Jesús Altuna. Trabajos sobre paleontología, arqueozoología, antropología, arte, arqueología y patrimonio arqueológico (San Sebastian, 2005–06), vol. 1, 369–97.

20   Angeli, *De aucupio* (see above, n. 2), 5 (my emphasis).

The technique of catching water birds by means of ropes coated in glue, which are then set afloat in a pond, leads to a consideration of the best kinds of birdlime, which can be made from the resin of various types of tree, mixed with substances such as liquid honey and olive oil. Other methods include mixing poisonous seeds among the bait that is scattered about, or tranquillizing the wild birds by adding wine or dregs to water holes and springs: sozzled birds make for easy prey!

Swans and cranes are caught with nets rigged across a river by means of tall masts and pulleys, set up on either bank; beaters then move noisily along the stream to drive the birds towards the expansive nets, at dusk. In winter, partridges and geese may be caught in frost-covered fields, at dawn and with carefully hidden clap-nets and an assistant (the aforementioned "fidus Achates") who pretends to labour the land, carefully driving the grazing flock of birds towards the ambush. The poet further discusses funnel traps for partridges, who even lead their own chicks into them in search of food. He explains how to shape these nets, some of them curved like a scorpion's tail. Other devices include the use of a bright light to mesmerize birds by night (so they can easily be netted by an associate) or decoy calls imitating the partridges' familiar sound ("crepitacula [...] avium notos imitantia cantus", 23), not to mention fine snares made out of horsehair. Dogs are used in the hunt for quail and partridge. An ingenious method for catching crane involves a hollow gourd smeared in bird lime with a buzzing insect inside, to entice the crane to put its beak into the neck of the treacherous fruit. Next come jackdaws and other flocking birds, before the poet turns to the use of little owls to attract prey, with a female proving more effective than the male. The horned owl is deployed in hunting corvids (magpies, crows or similar). Finally, the poet turns his attention to the hunt for smaller birds, such as fieldfare, best captured in wooded areas in October.

In Angeli's poem, humans heavily rely on artefacts. Prominent are the various types of nets—some of them taller than a person and wider than his outstretched arms: they are furled on the ground, and sprung by pulling a rope, hoisted on rigs, or draped between trees. The fowler therefore does not hesitate to intervene in the landscape, which he will alter and adapt to suit his requirements. Thus Angeli describes in some detail how to construct a duck decoy (i.e., a large-scale trap) by cordoning off an area around a pond with wattle fences, and digging a squat funnel-shaped canal away from the main water, again suitably fenced off. The water birds are then driven into this narrowing escape route—except that the gully offers no escape, merely permits carnage. The passage is reminiscent of a fowling technique used on Ischia in 1527 at the court of Alfonso d'Avalos, which according to Paolo Giovio allowed

THE BIRD-CATCHER'S WILES: PIETRO ANGELI DA BARGA'S *DE AUCUPIO*   231

the massacre of more than 300 birds.[21] Other forms of managing the environment included purposely planted coppices called "ragnaie" named after the fine nets ('mist nets' or "ragne") that could be hung there to catch small birds.[22] Writing in Latin, Angeli explicitly alludes to the Tuscan word "ragna", suggesting it was Arachne, 'Spiderwoman' herself, who taught mankind to weave the eponymous nets.[23] Humans thus do not just dominate nature, they can also imitate it and learn from it.

We have seen that Angeli's fowlers make use of other animals in their craft. The dogs (pointers) will come as no surprise to modern readers, nor will the deployment of live call-birds and decoys, such as domestic ducks and geese, whose function it is to convey to their wild counterparts that the area is safe. Such decoys could also be artificial, i.e. painted images set out near the nets. More curious, by modern standards, is that tethered owls, or indeed the buzzing beetle locked inside the gourd, are used to play on the natural aggression or curiosity of the prey: ravens, magpies and crows will mob a tethered owl, as the presence of this nocturnal animal clearly poses a threat to the diurnal birds. When the latter tire from their attack, the expectation is that they should perch on a nearby tree that is rigged with glue sticks or spikes, causing the birds to fall onto the ground. Similarly, lengths of limed string are attached to flocking birds, which are then released into an airborne flock, so that their fellow birds would get caught, setting the tangled clusters to tumble down. Whilst a bird-catcher might "disguise himself with fronds and twigs" ("sese occulit auceps / Frondibus et ramis", 30) or lurk in a well-camouflaged hut with a tunnel-like entrance, large farm animals, such as a donkey, ox, or even a horse offer the fowler moving cover for the surreptitious approach of his prey—a technique known in Italian as "accavalamento".

In Angeli's poem, the animal world is thus completely subjugated to the fowler's purpose: to lure thrushes, for example, the fowler will bring call-birds kept in covered cages; by whistling himself, he then gets the caged birds "to emit their gentle song from their chest, to twitter at the right time, and to vary

---

21 Paolo Giovio, *Notable Men and Women of Our Time*, ed. Kenneth Gouwens (Cambridge, MA, 2013), 536–51 (*Appendix*), there 548–51.

22 On the management of these groves, see the tract *Del modo di piantare e custodire una ragnaia e di uccellare a ragna*, attributed to the Florentine Giovanni Antonio Popoleschi (1551–1617), in Innamorati, *Arte* (see above, n. 11), vol. 2, 327–41, and Hervé Brunon, "La Chasse et l'organisation du paysage dans la Toscane des Médicis," in *Chasses princières dans l'Europe de la Renaissance*, ed. Claude d'Anthenaise and Monique Chatenet (Arles, 2007), 219–49, there 230–4.

23 Angeli, *De aucupio* (see above, n. 2), 29. For this *topos* see Plutarch, *Mor.*, 12,66 (*De sollertia animalium*); Polydore Vergil, *On Discovery*, ed. Brian P. Copenhaver (Cambridge, Mass. – London, 2002), 394 (3,6,2).

their tune" ("Invitat lenes effundere pectore voces, / Et tempestivum garrire, ac flectere cantum", 30). However, so Angeli advises, "if among those birds, you happen to have a thrush that likes to be loud and shrill, do not hesitate to silence it by smashing its brain: that vile traitor warns the others to fly far away and to set their course towards safer shores."[24]

Barga likewise describes a practice for catching crows, similar to a technique of the *caccia alla cornacchia* still detailed in a nineteenth-century account of bird-catching in the Veneto.[25] According to Angeli, a live crow is "exhibited on its back" ("cornicem [...] supinam / Exponunt", 26)—that is, probably with its wings stretched out, so 'crucified' to a flat piece of wood—in the middle of a ploughed field: at the bird's shrieks, others fly in to investigate. But one of those may be then caught in the call-bird's talons, offering itself as yet another easy picking for the fowler. Angeli uses highly emotive language in this passage, imparting human-like emotions to the birds, yet he has no qualms in transitioning to the next section by stating that "such scenes are a pleasure for our eyes and a delight for the soul" ("haec cum sint oculis gratissima nostris / Oblectentque animum", ibid.). Rare indeed are the sixteenth-century authors who consider the suffering of animals as anything but serving human interests.

Angeli does give some thought to the reasons why humans hunt birds. He variously casts fowling as a punishment for the birds' ruining of freshly sprouting crops or for an ancient, mythical fault (22, 28). Another, very practical motivation is the availability of a non-commercial food source in a society that relies for a great deal on self-sufficiency ("unde avibus laeti vescamur inemptis", 22). The Vergilian echo aside (*Georg.* 4,133 "dapibus [...] inemptis"), the notion of nobles procuring their own food during their rural retreats became something of a *topos*. Paradoxically, the birds that are caught with cunning contribute to an honest meal ("epulas inter sine fraude paratas", 32). Strong social implications underlie these statements: as Jacopo di Porcia remarked, probably at the beginning of the sixteenth century, whilst fowling (*aucupatio*) keeps nobles out of mischief, peasants delight in it in the hope of making money ("de inimica voluptati nobilium aucupatione [...], qua spe lucri plurimum delectantur rustici"[26]). Angeli echoes this common belief, albeit in broader terms, at the end of his poem, where the civilizing—and indeed ennobling—benefits of the countryside are listed to lure Chloris away from the city:[27]

---

24   "Quas inter tibi siquis erit, qui stridere acutum / Turdus amet, hunc tu cerebro compescere fracto / Ne dubita. Monet iste alios discedere longe / Proditor, et tutas cursum contendere ad oras [...]", Angeli, *De aucupio* (see above, n. 2), 30.

25   "Cenno sopra la caccia nella Provincia di Venezia," in *Venezia e le sue lagune*, ed. Giovanni Correr (Venice, 1847), vol. 2.1, 245–59, there 247.

26   Innsbruck, Universitäts- und Landesbibliothek Tirol, Cod. 286 (see above, n. 12), fol. 47r.

27   Angeli, *De aucupio* (see above, n. 2), 32.

THE BIRD-CATCHER'S WILES: PIETRO ANGELI DA BARGA'S *DE AUCUPIO*

Hic tibi cum vili nusquam commercia vulgo
[...] erunt: hic puriter aevum
Degere, tranquillamque per otia ducere vitam,
Otia perpetuam semper comitantia pacem.

Here there will be no trading whatsoever with the lowly populace [...], but here you may spend your time honestly and lead a quiet life of leisure— the leisure that steadily accompanies eternal peace.

Fowling, it is implied, similarly enhances the personal qualities of the fowler: the young man ("iuvenis") must be impervious to damp and cold conditions; as a "callidus [...] auceps" ("shrewd fowler", cf. Ovid, *Met.* 11,73), he must learn to plan, to be patient and disciplined, and to persevere. The reward for his effort, then, is the joy and excitement one experiences at the moment of capturing and killing the prey, symbolized in a blooding rite: "jubilant and gleeful, he smears his face and both his hands with blood as he slaughters the wretched prey" ("[...] laetus ovansque / Ora manusque ambas miserarum in caede cruentat").[28]

An Odd Conclusion

Fowling, just like poetry, emerges as a source of honour and glory. The artistic flair of Angeli's poem is debatable, however, and consonant with Lilio Gregorio Giraldi's laconic statement about early versions of the *Cynegeticon* and some of Angeli's eclogues ("De eo speranda sunt in dies meliora") or Alberto Asor-Rosa's tempered judgment of Angeli's qualities as a commentator and translator of Ancient texts.[29] Readers have questioned the incongruous double negation in the poet's early, customary claim that he will be covering new ground. The meaning is clear; the morpho-syntax, however, is not:[30]

---

28   Ibid., 10. Cp. Haskell, "Work or Play" (as above, n. 10), there 152, for a discussion of this passage but without acknowledgment of its ritualistic aspect. As 'blooding' (daubing the cheeks and forehead of a hunter with the prey's blood, especially to celebrate a first kill) is mostly associated with venery, Angeli may well offer us a unique testimony.

29   *Lilio Gregorio Giraldi, Modern Poets*, ed. John Grant (Cambridge, Mass. – London, 2011), 198. Alberto Asor-Rosa, "Angèli, Pietro," in *Dizionario Biografico degli Italiani*, vol. 3 (Rome, 1961), 201–4, there 202.

30   Angeli, *De aucupio* (see above, n. 2), 6 (my emphasis). For the debate, see for instance Bergantini's commentary (as in n. 5), there 14–5. Angeli's expression may have been influenced by the double negation used in the vernacular: e.g. *non vi entrò nessun poeta* [...].

234   DE SMET

> *Non* ego nunc primum, qua vatum incedere *nullus*
> Est ausus, *nulla* usquam extant vestigia, *nulli*
> Ingressus aditusque patent; immo omnia clausa,
> Omnia sunt obstructa, et sentibus obsita densis, [...]

> Now I first [venture] where no poet has dared to tread: there are no tracks
> to follow; no entrance or vestibule beckons: indeed, all is closed, blocked,
> and covered in thick brambles [...]

There is at least one other instance where a double negation causes confusion, not to mention other passages where the wording is downright clumsy or obscure.

The long closing passage at the end of the Book, inviting Chloris to come and enjoy the delights of the countryside is also problematic. Haskell interprets this invitation as the poet's own.[31] However, it is cast as a direct speech, which Angeli's poetic persona (the narrator as the purveyor of knowledge) imagines the young apprentice-fowler ("iuvenem") will utter, when he claims some well-deserved rest and recreation in his lady's company after the effort of bringing in a bountiful catch thanks to his craft. Might this love-starved, young fowler not be more likely identified with Angeli's still fairly young dedicatee Francesco de' Medici, who had married Joanna of Austria on 18 December 1565? Let us note that Angeli's *Epithalamium in nuptias Francisci Medicis Florentinor[um] & Senens[ium] principis, et Ioannae Austriacae reginae* [...] (Florence, 1566) appeared in the same year as the *editio princeps* of the *De aucupio*. However, the fowler then suggests that Chloris might well like to hear him sing of hunting and the techniques for each animal employed, even though Chloris is described as "surdam" ("deaf", 31) earlier on: the expression is no doubt not to be taken literally! The identity of the "iuvenis" has imperceptibly shifted to Angeli himself.

After this not-so-subtle allusion to Angeli's earlier *Cynegetica*, the poet ends with a nod to Chloris's family and an assurance of his love. Researchers such as Virginia Cox have certainly made us much more aware of Italian Renaissance women as readers and authors of vernacular and indeed some Latin verse,[32] whilst Angeli is said to have been enamoured of Fiammetta Soderini, a poetess in her own right, in his youth.[33] Yet the pastoral name Chloris is perhaps too ge-

---

31   Haskell, "Work or Play" (see above, n. 10), 151.

32   Virginia Cox, *Lyric Poetry by Women of the Italian Renaissance* (Baltimore, MD, 2013).

33   Manacorda, "Petrus Angelius Bargaeus" (see above n. 7), there 8. Angeli's *Poesie Toscane* make several meaningful allusions to a beloved named *Fiamma* (e.g. inc. "Non è Fiamma

THE BIRD-CATCHER'S WILES: PIETRO ANGELI DA BARGA'S *DE AUCUPIO*   235

neric to imply a real person and a genuine, female reader, as Haskell surmised. Indeed, the table of contents of the *De aucupio* in the 1585 edition refers to this capstone passage as "an allegorical digression in which the poet commends his efforts to Francesco de' Medici Archduke of Florence and Siena" ("Digressio, qua ἀλληγορικῶς commendat labores suos Francisco Medici Florentinorum et Senensium Principi").[34] This by all accounts contorted ending to the poem has all the hallmarks of a hastily concocted conclusion, composed perhaps in order to rush the poem to print when its successive Books were not yet ready but when new opportunities for patronage arose.[35]

●●●

In conclusion, whilst Angeli da Barga's poem *On Fowling* is steeped in the rich tradition of Ancient and Neo-Latin didactic-georgic poetry, it also offers us remarkable contemporary insights into Renaissance practices of bird-catching. Angelio portrays fowling as a meaningful pastime, suitable for nobles such as his dedicatee Francesco de' Medici. I have contested the sinister interpretation that has been given to the bird catchers' wiles ("insidiae, dolus, fraus"), suggesting instead that their deception of their prey as well as the various mechanical contraptions described in the poem (nets, lime sticks, decoys etc.) should be seen, from a sixteenth-century perspective, as a triumph of human ingenuity. The artistic accomplishment of the poem arguably leaves to be desired: the concluding passage to the poem, with its slipping points of view, especially constitutes an unsatisfactory finale but must be read in the context of Angeli paying homage to Francesco de' Medici. Such shortcomings, however, did not stop Angeli's *De aucupio* from being listed in the hallowed ranks of cynegetic poetry, extolling that very arena in which humans pit themselves against nature.

University of Warwick

---

mortal la Fiamma ond'arsi / Et ardo [...]"); the *Poesie* were published in Florence in 1589 with the *Poesie Toscane* of his friend Mario Colonna, a more explicit poetic admirer of Soderini's, and with Angeli's translation of Sophocles's *Oedipus Tyrannus*.

34   Angeli, *Poemata Omnia* (see above, n. 14), Index, Capita rerum, quae tractantur in libro Ixeuticorum, seu de aucupio, no page number.

35   Note that there are ample corrections to the end of the Book in the Florentine MS Doni e Acquisti 437 (see above, n. 9), 230–3.

CHAPTER 16

La tradición latina renacentista del *De simplicium medicamentorum facultatibus* de Galeno

Marina Díaz Marcos

Abstract

Antes de 1480 solo un par de textos médicos tenían nuevas traducciones humanistas. En el caso del tratado sobre los simples de Galeno (*De simplicium medicamentorum facultatibus*), sin edición crítica ni traducción en lengua moderna, hay unas veintidós ediciones en latín entre 1490 (la de Bonardo) y 1625 (la última *Giuntina*). La primera contiene una traducción medieval latina procedente del árabe y del griego. No obstante, las ediciones latinas posteriores, que contienen la traducción propiamente humanista realizada desde el griego por Theodoricus Gerardus Gaudanus, intentan modernizar el texto. El objetivo principal de este estudio será trazar la historia del *De simpl. med. fac.* durante el Renacimiento para mostrar sus diferentes versiones. La presencia o no de prefacios también puede ser relevante porque en ocasiones contienen información sobre nuestro tratado. El resultado final mostrará que, en general, se concedió más importancia al hecho de reorganizar el material para hacer accesible la obra que a editarla o corregirla. Es importante, pues, este análisis si tenemos en cuenta que en Occidente, durante el Renacimiento, esta obra de Galeno fue conocida principalmente a través de la versión latina, a pesar de su redescubrimiento en el siglo XVI en su lengua original, el griego.

Keywords

Theodoricus Gerardus Gaudanus – Neo-Latin translations – Reception of Galen – *De simplicium medicamentorum facultatibus*

© KONINKLIJKE BRILL NV, LEIDEN, 2020 | DOI:10.1163/9789004427105_017

1　Introducción[1]

Hasta la segunda mitad del siglo XV no se publican las primeras traducciones latinas de corte humanista[2] de textos griegos médicos, las cuales, una vez editadas, sustituyeron a los manuscritos, que constituían la base de consulta habitual de las fuentes por parte de los autores.

Los primeros traductores humanistas, que trabajaron solo con manuscritos, se centraron principalmente en Galeno, cuyas obras fueron vertidas al latín varias veces más o menos al mismo tiempo. Un ejemplo es Niccolò Leoniceno (1428–1524),[3] quien publicó los primeros trabajos genuinos en griego de Galeno (aunque la primera edición griega, la de 1525, se la debemos a Aldo Manuzio), tradujo once de ellos del griego al latín y recopiló una cantidad considerable de manuscritos. El mérito de los editores humanistas radica, pues, en el redescubrimiento de diversos tratados importantes desconocidos anteriormente en Occidente y en la depuración del canon galénico.

Una traducción latina de gran importancia realizada en este período por Theodoricus Gerardus Gaudanus,[4] sin edición crítica ni traducción en lengua moderna, es la del *De simplicium medicamentorum facultatibus* (o "tratado de los *Simples*") de Galeno. En este artículo vamos a llevar a cabo la comparación de dicha traducción en las distintas ediciones renacentistas, cuyo resultado final nos mostrará que el texto de Gaudanus no ha sido apenas modificado ni suplantado por una nueva traducción humanista, pero sí comentado y corregido por los editores.

Conviene subrayar también el valor de los paratextos (prefacios y anotaciones impresas y manuscritas) presentes en dichas ediciones, ya que en algunos

---

1　Este trabajo se inscribe dentro de las líneas de investigación del proyecto *Galenus Latinus: Recuperación del Patrimonio de la Medicina Europea II* (FFI2016-77240-P) del grupo I+D *Interpretes Medicinae* (INTERMED), que lidera la Red de Excelencia Opera Medica: Recuperación del Patrimonio Textual Grecolatino de la Medicina Europea II (RED2018-102781-T).

2　Es decir, traducciones realizadas directamente del griego al latín sin el eslabón intermedio del árabe.

3　Richard J. Durling, "A Chronological Census of Renaissance Editions and Translations of Galen," *Journal of the Warburg and Courtauld Institutes* 24 (1961), 230–305, en 236; y Stefania Fortuna, "The Prefaces to the First Humanist Medical Translations," *Traditio: Studies in Ancient and Medieval History, Thought and Religion* 62 (2007), 317–35, en 320.

4　Irene Calà, "Theodoricus Gerardus Gaudanus traduttore di Galeno," *Medicina nei secoli* 25.3 (2013), 1105–16, en 1106.

casos pueden contener información de interés sobre el origen, fuentes, traductores, etc. de nuestra obra.[5]

2 El tratado de los *Simples*: cuestiones previas

La tradición latina del *De simplicium medicamentorum facultatibus* presenta un interés manifiesto ya desde antiguo para la historia del desarrollo de una ciencia de los remedios simples y compuestos. Es un tratado de farmacología compuesto por once libros, los cuales se han transmitido de manera bipartita desde los primeros testimonios en griego, llegando a generar una tradición propia: por un lado, los libros I–V o parte teórica (propiedades del cuerpo y medicamentos simples) y, por otro, los libros VI–XI o parte práctica (cualidades de remedios simples particulares).[6]

En su tradición manuscrita existen testimonios griegos bastante antiguos, a diferencia de otras obras, pero también traducciones en siríaco, árabe y latín, ya sea por vía directa o indirecta.[7] Por ello, no es de extrañar la coexistencia de arabismos, vulgarismos y helenismos, a menudo deformados, en las versiones latinas medievales. Esta situación, repetida también en otras obras, provocó a finales del siglo XV la reacción de algunos estudiosos que, rechazando las traducciones arabo-latinas, se afanaron en depurar los textos antiguos consultando las versiones griegas de las obras y recuperando el latín de época clásica.

Los *Simples* han sido mal comprendidos y mal conocidos hasta la publicación de sus primeras ediciones renacentistas:

– La griega de Aldo Manuzio, la *Aldina* (1525), para la que se utilizaron manuscritos griegos que, posteriormente, sirvieron para corregir el texto latino.[8]

---

5 Solo prestaremos atención a los prefacios de las ediciones cuando aporten información sobre la traducción humanista de los *Simples*, puesto que ya han sido estudiados en Stefania Fortuna, "The Latin Editions of Galen's *Opera omnia* (1490–1625) and their prefaces," *Early Science and Medicine* 17 (2012), 391–412, en 399–407; y Fortuna, "The prefaces" (véase arriba, n. 3), 317–35.

6 Caroline Petit, "La tradition manuscrite du traité des Simples de Galien. *Editio princeps* et traduction annotée des chapitres 1 à 3 du livre I," en *Histoire de la tradition et édition des médecins grecs – Storia della tradizione e edizione dei medici greci*, eds. Véronique Boudon-Millot, Jacques Jouanna, Antonio Garzya y Amneris Roselli (Nápoles, 2010), 143–65.

7 Ivan Garofalo, "Un sondaggio sul *De simplicium medicamentorum facultate di Galeno*," en *Studi arabo-islamici in onore di Roberto Rubinacci nel suo settantesimo compleanno*, ed. Clelia Sarnelli Cerqua (Nápoles, 1985), vol. 1, 317–25.

8 La segunda edición, la *Basileensis*, es de 1538.

DE SIMPLICIUM MEDICAMENTORUM FACULTATIBUS DE GALENO

- La latina de Theodoricus Gerardus Gaudanus,[9] que aseguró la difusión del tratado en el Renacimiento y que fue publicada de manera póstuma en 1530 por Johannes Sturm[10] (1507–89). Gaudanus, un médico y humanista, nació en Gouda (Holanda) a finales del siglo XV en el seno de una familia acomodada. Lo poco que sabemos de él es que comenzó sus estudios de medicina en la Universidad de Lovaina en mayo de 1510 y, gracias a la epístola dedicatoria que acompaña las otras dos traducciones que realizó (el *De curandi ratione per sanguinis missionem* y el *De hirundinibus*, ambas publicadas en 1529), que contrajo una enfermedad en 1528 que causó su muerte un año después. Su traducción de los *Simples* se reimprimió hasta el siglo XIX, cuando encontramos la edición de Kühn, que recoge todas las obras de Galeno en 20 volúmenes.

No obstante, existía ya una edición de 1490[11] que contenía la versión medieval de nuestro tratado: los libros I–V, a los que se unía el VI, traducidos por Gerardo de Cremona (s. XII) del árabe al latín, y los libros VII–XI,[12] vertidos también al latín en el siglo XIV, pero desde el griego, por Niccolò de Reggio. Esta edición constituía el único testimonio por el que se conocía el tratado a comienzos del siglo XVI hasta la publicación de la obra de Gaudanus.

3   El *De simplicium medicamentorum facultatibus* de Galeno en las ediciones renacentistas

Los *Simples*, traducidos solo dos veces al latín, fueron editados veintidós veces entre 1490 y 1625 en las *Opera omnia* de Galeno:[13] siete en su versión arabo-latina o medieval hasta 1528 y dieciséis en la grecolatina o humanista entre 1541 y 1625.[14] Esta segunda traducción fue reimpresa veintisiete veces,

---

9   Calà, "Theodoricus" (véase arriba, n. 4), 1105–7.
10   Charles Schmidt, *La vie et les travaux de Jean Sturm* (Strasburg, 1855), 8–17.
11   Caroline Petit, "La tradition latine du traité des Simples de Galien: étude préliminaire," *Medicina nei Secoli* 25.3 (2013), 1063–90, en 1072–3.
12   Niccolò también tradujo el libro VI, pero a partir del griego. Sin embargo, la traducción árabo-latina de Gerardo es la que se ha transmitido en las ediciones medievales.
13   Fortuna, "The Latin editions" (véase arriba, n. 5), 394.
14   Para las ediciones de los *Simples*: Durling, "A Chronological" (véase arriba, n. 3), 250–79; Stefania Fortuna, "Galeno latino, 1490–1533," *Medicina nei secoli* 17.2 (2005), 469–506; Stefania Fortuna, *Galeno. Catalogo delle traduzione Latine* (2008) http://www.galenolatino .com/index.php?id=16&clean=1, consultado el 5 de septiembre de 2019; Fortuna, "The Latin Editions" (véase arriba, n. 5), 394–5, 399, 407; Stefania Fortuna, "René Chartier e le edizioni latine di Galeno," en *René Chartier (1572–1654). Éditeur et traducteur d'Hippocrate et Galien. Actes du colloque international de Paris (7 et 8 octobre 2010)*, ed. Véronique

según Clara Domingues,[15] entre 1530 y 1596. Para su consulta, nos hemos servido de catálogos y bases de datos como los siguientes: BIU Santé, Gallica BnF, Göttinger Digitalisierungszentrum, Google Books, Bayerische StaatsBibliothek, e-rara, etc.

3.1 Primer grupo: la traducción medieval

Dentro de este grupo de ediciones que contienen la traducción medieval latina del tratado, nos detendremos, esencialmente, en la de 1490, ya que nuestro objetivo principal son las humanistas:

– 1490, 27 de agosto, Venecia: Filippo Pinzi, ed. Diomedes Bonardo. 2 vols. *in folio.*

Esta edición, bajo el nombre de *Opera*, contiene 78 traducciones latinas de tratados de Galeno exclusivamente medievales[16] (65 en el primer volumen y 13 en el segundo[17]), ya que Bonardo tenía la intención de presentarlo "ex fonte [...], ex eius riuulo minime."[18] El texto se dispone en dos columnas, su decoración es escasa y no contiene portada, pero sí un breve prefacio llevado a cabo por Bonardo. En él, el editor explica las circunstancias de su trabajo: la dificultad para buscar en las bibliotecas italianas manuscritos con las obras de Galeno y la edición de las mismas, pues habían sido corrompidas por la ignorancia de los copistas.

Los *Simples*, se localizan en el volumen 2 y presentan la agrupación de los libros que corresponde a los distintos traductores medievales:

– Libros I–VI (22v–63v): *De simplicibus.* Tr. Gerardo de Cremona. Contienen en los márgenes variantes encontradas en otros manuscritos.
– Libros VII–XI (64r–85v): *De simplici medicina.* Tr. Niccolò de Reggio. Esta parte ha sido enriquecida posteriormente con glosas a los diferentes simples.

Tras esta edición, se sucedieron otras a modo de corrección o simplemente reimpresión en las que se fue haciendo evidente el paso de las traducciones medievales a las humanistas. La traducción de Bonardo se transmite hasta la edición de 1528 de Rivirius e incorpora a partir de la de Suriano anotaciones marginales que se reimprimen en las seis siguientes ediciones. Es conveniente

---

Boudon-Millot, Guy Cobolet, Jacques Jouanna (Paris, 2012), 303–24; Vivian Nutton, *John Caius and the manuscripts of Galen* (Cambridge, 1987), 21–2.

15 Petit, "La tradition latine" (véase arriba, n. 11), 1079.
16 Fortuna, "Galeno latino" (véase arriba, n. 14), 472–3.
17 Los dos volúmenes corresponden a la división árabe del conocimiento médico en teoría y práctica.
18 Fortuna, "The prefaces" (véase arriba, n. 3), 323.

DE SIMPLICIUM MEDICAMENTORUM FACULTATIBUS DE GALENO 241

mencionarlas,[19] aunque no sean significativas para nuestro estudio, porque constituían la única vía para conocer el tratado antes de la publicación de la traducción de Gaudanus:

– 1502, Venecia: Bernardino Benagli, ed. Girolamo Suriano. 2 vols. *in folio*.
– 1513–14, Venecia: Bernardino Benagli, ed. Scipione Ferrari. 2 vols. *in folio*.
– 1515–16, 12 de junio, Pavía: Giacomo Pocatela, ed. Pietro Antonio Rustico. 3 vols. *in folio*.
– 1522, 5 de enero, Venecia: Lucantonio Giunta, ed. Scipione Ferrari. 3 vols. *in folio*.
– 1528–33, 5 de enero-marzo, Venecia: Lucantonio Giunta (vols. 1–6) con la colaboración de Aurelio Pinzi (vols. 3–4), eds. Scipione Ferrari (vols. 1–2) y Marziano Rota (vols. 3–4). 4 vols. *in folio* + 2 vols. supl. *in folio* (1531, 23 de julio; 1533, agosto).
– 1528, Lyon: en calcografía Gabiana; ed. Joannes Nebriensis Rivirius. 3 vols. *in quarto*.[20]

3.2 Segundo grupo: la traducción humanista en las ediciones renacentistas

La traducción latina de Theodoricus Gerardus Gaudanus realizada directamente a partir del griego fue publicada por primera vez en 1530 y, más tarde, en las grandes ediciones de obras galénicas posteriores al año 1541, aunque con ciertas correcciones y variaciones.

– 1530, 1 de septiembre, Paris: Johannes Sturm, ed. Simon de Colines. 1 vol. *in folio*.

Esta traducción fue terminada por Gaudanus el 5 de abril de 1529, como indica él mismo en la página 265 de su obra (ahora no se enumera por folios), pero fue publicada de manera póstuma el 1 de septiembre de 1530 por Johannes Sturm.[21] Gaudanus hace desaparecer la división de los libros en dos partes, titulando así su obra: *Claudii Galeni Pergameni De simplicium medicamentorum facultatibus libri undecim, Theodorico Gerardo Gaudano interprete.*[22]

El tratado ocupa 265 páginas precedidas de otras 10 más, sin numerar, que incluyen un *Index alphabeticus* con todos los simples de la obra, una carta manuscrita y un prefacio o carta-dedicatoria de Sturm a Jean de Hangest (1501–77),

---

19   Para más información sobre estas ediciones y sus prólogos, editores, impresores, etc. cfr. Fortuna, "Galeno latino" (véase arriba, n. 14), 472–86; para el listado de obras de cada edición, ibid., 486–99.

20   Ibid., 483. Esta edición, según Fortuna, no fue señalada por Durling en su elenco de ediciones.

21   Ya indicado en la p. 239 (cf. *supra*).

22   Este título será ampliado a lo largo de las diferentes ediciones.

en el que elogia las traducción de Gaudanus frente a las *Barbarorum copiae*, que habían deformado el texto.

En cuanto a sus características formales, el texto se dispone en una columna con las líneas numeradas de 5 en 5 y presenta una decoración más elaborada que las ediciones medievales. Por un lado, en la parte teórica, Gaudanus divide cada libro en capítulos (libro I: 38; II, III y V: 27; IV: 22) y ofrece una breve descripción sobre el contenido de los mismos. Por otro lado, los libros de la parte práctica comienzan con una introducción (la más extensa de dos páginas y media en el libro VI), seguida de la descripción (sin arabismos) de cada simple, en la que primero se ofrece el nombre latino y debajo información detallada sobre el mismo: propiedades, efectos, procedencia (en ocasiones), enfermedad contra la que se puede utilizar, etc.

Las anotaciones, generalmente manuscritas, suelen ser palabras latinas que se incorporan al texto o aclaraciones o explicaciones del mismo con equivalentes en griego. Se encuentran tanto en los márgenes interiores y exteriores como sobre la línea del texto y son fruto del trabajo de revisión y corrección posterior, gracias a la consulta de manuscritos, las dos ediciones griegas o la *translatio uetus*. Un ejemplo es el que encontramos sobre el título ya impreso del primer libro, en la página 1, donde aparece el nombre de la obra escrito a mano, tanto en griego como en latín: Περὶ κράσεων τῶν ἁπλῶν φαρμάκων / *De simplicium medicamentorum facultatibus*. Otro es "humida [...] ac mollia" (libro 1, p. 5, línea 19) en cuyo margen aparece ὑγρὰ καὶ πλαδαρά (vid. fol. 2, línea 26 de la *Aldina*) seguido de "humida et tremula legit uetus interpres". En la segunda parte, cada simple va acompañado de sinónimos latinos también escritos a mano: "Aegyrus" (p. 131, línea 24), por ejemplo, también con el nombre de "Alba uulgo". En esta entrada, además, se incorpora una de las únicas correcciones impresas que encontramos en esta edición, ya anunciada aquella por Pablo de Egina y referida a la palabra "tertio" (p. 131, línea 25): "*Arbitror legendum, primo. nam sic etiam habet Paulus Aeg."

Diez son las ediciones humanistas que transmiten la traducción de Gaudanus junto con el resto de obras de Galeno, dispuesta en una columna y con subdivisiones en el texto:

– 1541–45, Venecia: Dominico Farri, eds. Agostino Ricchi y Vittore Trincavelli. 8 *sectiones* (10 vols.), *in octauo*.

Es una de las ediciones más importantes de Galeno, cuyas obras son agrupadas aquí en ocho *sectiones* temáticas: biología, anatomía, fisiología, higiene y dietética, semiótica, patología, terapia y farmacología. Los *Simples* son la última obra de la *sectio secunda* (vol. 3) y su texto se dispone ahora en líneas numeradas de 10 en 10.

DE SIMPLICIUM MEDICAMENTORUM FACULTATIBUS DE GALENO

Esta edición incluye anotaciones "luculentissimae" en los márgenes basadas en manuscritos griegos (aún desconocidos) y las ediciones griegas, hecho que ya anuncia Ricchi en la portada de la *sectio secunda* o en el índice de obras de esta, en el que podemos leer: "[...] a nobis ex multorum ueterum Gręcorum exemplarium collatione [...] restituti". Estas notas sirven para explicar una parte del texto: p. 781, líneas 6–7: "Cohibet porro impetus in uenerem [...]." Margen: "Contra uenere." o para ofrecer una variante al texto latino (p. 777, línea 12): "lumbricos interimat." Margen: "lumbricos interimit."

Esta edición presenta los simples con el término latino, mientras que el resto de ediciones de este segundo grupo optan por el nombre griego. Por ejemplo, "abrotonum" frente a "abrotonon". También es la única que incluye un índice de simples al inicio del volumen.

Ricchi dedica además un prefacio al simple "aphonitrum", en el que explica que se han tenido que utilizar testimonios griegos ("habet capitis illius initium in gręcis codicibus impressis, atque in plerisque manuscriptis") para corregirlo y diferenciarlo de "aphrolitrum", es decir, "aphrolitrum ab †aphonitro differt" (libro 9, p. 937–8, línea 30).

– Cuatro ediciones *Giuntinas*,[23] en las que el profesor de medicina Giovanni Battista Montano propuso un nuevo modo de organizar las obras de Galeno, más amplio que el de la edición de Ricchi y Trincavelli. Esta clasificación, que fue seguida en las posteriores ediciones humanistas, consiste en 7 *classes* (biología, anatomía y fisiología, higiene y dietética, patología, semiótica, farmacología, cirugía y terapia), a las que se añaden otras 3 más (trabajos introductorios, trabajos *extra ordinem* y trabajos espurios).

Las *Giuntinas* recogen el mayor número de obras de Galeno jamás publicadas, especialmente traducciones humanistas, y presentan el texto en folios numerados (no páginas) y subdividido en capítulos y secciones alfabéticas que van de la A a la D y de la E a la H.

Agostino Gadaldini (y Montano en la *Giuntina* de 1541–42) fue el encargado de revisar nuestro tratado basándose en las ediciones griegas, manuscritos griegos antiguos y la traducción latina medieval.[24] La obra encabeza la *quinta classis*, dedicada a los tratados de farmacología, a lo largo de las cuatro *Giuntinas*.

---

23   Fortuna, "The Latin editions" (véase arriba, n. 5), 400–4.
24   Petit, "La tradition latine" (véase arriba, n. 11), 1079.

- 1541–42, Venecia: Giunta, eds. Agostino Gadaldini y Giovanni Battista Montano. 10 vols. (10 *classes*), *in folio*.

Esta edición contiene en su mayoría obras humanistas. Reimpresa ocho veces hasta 1625, fue planeada por Giunta, pero, al morir en 1538, se detiene el proyecto. Más tarde, sus hijos, Tommaso y Giovanni Maria, llevan a cabo la empresa. La difícil preparación de la edición de obras de Galeno es descrita por Gadaldini[25] solo en el prefacio de esta edición.

Incluye correcciones y variantes impresas en los márgenes realizadas a partir de algunos manuscritos (en parte desconocidos) y las ediciones griegas, pero serán las de la *Giuntina* de 1550 las que se incorporen al texto en las posteriores ediciones.

- 1550, Venecia: Giunta, ed. Agostino Gadaldini. 10 vols. (10 *classes*), *in folio*.

A partir de esta *Giuntina* se persigue un trabajo filológico. Las anotaciones marginales, ya impresas, marcan el equivalente de una palabra *in graeco*, variantes latinas (*al.*) o correcciones realizadas a partir de *antiqui codices graeci*.

- 1556, Venecia: Giunta, ed. Agostino Gadaldini. 10 vols. (10 *classes*), *in folio*.

Esta edición es importante porque modifica el texto con las correcciones latinas de la de 1550, que se incluyen en las sucesivas *Giuntinas*. Por ejemplo, en el fol. 6r, en el título del capítulo 21, se ha incorporado la palabra "utriusque" que aparecía en el margen en la edición anterior. En cuanto a las anotaciones, aunque son escasas, se mantienen en ocasiones aquellas referidas a variantes latinas (también en la edición de 1565), como, "al. Asclepiadeus" (fol. 8, línea 6), o a códices griegos, como la última del fol. 5r: "†Antiqui codices graeci legunt ἐν πολλῷ παρεσπαρμένον id est in multa quantitate dispersum, et ita legit et antiqua translatio", referida a "multo tempore praeparatum".

- 1565, Venecia: Giunta, ed. Agostino Gadaldini. 12 vols. (10 *classes*), *in folio*.

Esta edición incluye dos nuevos volúmenes que contienen una presentación de la obra y un índice. Aquí, los *Simples* aparecen en el sexto, pero todavía en la *quinta classis*.

Gadaldini toma el texto de la edición de 1556 ya corregido, como indica Tomasso Giunta en el prefacio, y añade algunas de esas variantes marginales procedentes de códices griegos. La novedad de esta edición radica en las referencias que se hacen a otras obras, también en los márgenes. Por ejemplo, en el fol. 40r, en la entrada de *abrotonon*, hay una mención a los *Aforismos*.

- Tres ediciones impresas por Froben y Episcopius, en las que los *Simples* son la primera obra del tercer volumen, *tomus quintus* (*quinta classis*), dedicado

---

25   Ivan Garofalo, "Agostino Gadaldini (1515–1575) et le Galien latin," en *Lire les médecins grecs*, ed. Véronique Boudon-Millot y Guy Cobolet (París, 2004), 317–21.

DE SIMPLICIUM MEDICAMENTORUM FACULTATIBUS DE GALENO 245

a los medicamentos simples y compuestos. El texto en las dos primeras ediciones se dispone en dos columnas numeradas (ahora no por folio o por página), con secciones de la A a la D y con párrafos con numeración romana; en la tercera, reproduce la *Giuntina* de 1556, tanto en contenido como en división interna.

– 1542, marzo, Basilea: Hieronymus Froben y Nikolaus Episcopius, ed. Hieronymus Gemusaeus. 4 vols. (8 *tomos*, 10 *classes*), *in folio*.

Esta edición y la siguiente son reimpresiones de la *Giuntina* de 1541–42. Tras el largo prefacio de Gemusaeus, ya incluido en esa *Giuntina*, como apunta una nota manuscrita, hay una carta dirigida al lector sobre la nueva división de la obra en *tomos* (aunque se siguen manteniendo las *classes* dentro de estos).

Las anotaciones manuscritas que explican, al principio de cada libro de los *Simples*, el argumento, son copiadas posteriormente de la tercera edición de este grupo, la de 1561–62. Se sabe que son bastante posteriores a la fecha de publicación por una referencia a la *Giuntina* de 1586 que figura en la portada general.

– 1549, Basilea: Hieronymus Froben y Nikolaus Episcopius, ed. Janus Cornarius. 4 vols. (8 *tomos*, 10 *classes*), *in folio*.

Esta edición es igual que la anterior, pero incluye 18 nuevas traducciones llevadas a cabo por Cornarius, pero no de los *Simples*. El editor del tratado no incluye las anotaciones marginales, pero sí añade en la primera parte un resumen de todos los capítulos que conforman cada libro, a modo de índice. En la segunda, divide más claramente los simples en epígrafes.

– 1561–62, Basilea: Hieronymus Froben y Nikolaus Episcopius, ed. Conradus Gesnerus. 4 vols. (10 *classes*), *in folio*.

Gesnerus reproduce el texto de la *Giuntina* de 1556 para los *Simples*, aunque no con todas las anotaciones marginales que ofrecen el equivalente en los testimonios griegos, y añade una importante bibliografía sobre Galeno. También, en el título de nuestro tratado, menciona a Gadaldini como primer editor de la traducción de Gaudanus.

– 1549–51, Lyon: Jean Frellon, ed. Conradus Gesnerus. 4 vols. (6 *tomos*), *in folio*.

Esta edición es básicamente una reimpresión de las *Giuntinas* de 1541–42 y 1550 y no incluye ninguna novedad.

3.3 *Tercer grupo: la traducción humanista en las ediciones renacentistas (tardías)*

A partir de 1560, la medicina de Galeno entra en declive y disminuye el número de publicaciones de su obra:

– 1562–63, Venecia: Vincenzo Valgrisi, ed. Giovanni Battista Rasario. 9 vols. (9 *classes*), *in folio*.

246   DÍAZ MARCOS

Rasario[26] trabaja, revisa y modifica estilísticamente casi 60 obras de Galeno (no de los *Simples*) y propone un nuevo orden basado en el *De partibus artis medicae*, obra de Galeno que solo es conocida a través de la traducción medieval latina realizada por Niccolò de Reggio. Se trata de seis *classes* (biología, anatomía y fisiología; semiótica; patología; dietética; farmacología; terapia) más un índice, comentarios a Hipócrates y trabajos espurios. A pesar de los cambios, los *Simples* siguen apareciendo en la *quinta classis* e incluyen los comentarios de la edición de Gesnerus, pero en los márgenes internos.

Las siguientes ediciones, que reproducen la *Giuntina* de 1565 con algunos cambios en el orden de las obras, se imprimieron durante 50 años en que el estudio de Galeno se había debilitado. En ellas, se persiguió un trabajo filológico basado ahora solamente en las ediciones griegas. En las tres últimas *Giuntinas*, Paolini se queja de que, aunque ha querido comparar todos los textos griegos y latinos, no obstante, los impresores no le han dado el tiempo suficiente para dicha tarea.

Solo las mencionaremos por no ser consideradas casi renacentistas:

- 1576–77, Venecia: Giunta, ed. Girolamo Mercuriale. 11 vols. (11 *classes*), *in folio*.
- 1586, Venecia: Giunta, ed. Giovanni Costeo. 11 vols. (11 *classes*), *in folio*.
- 1596–97, Venecia: Giunta, ed. Fabio Paolini. 11 vols. (11 *classes*), *in folio*.
- 1609, Venecia: Giunta, ed. Fabio Paolini. 11 vols. (11 *classes*), *in folio*.
- 1625, Venecia: Giunta, ed. Fabio Paolini. 11 vols. (11 *classes*), *in folio*.

4 Consideraciones finales

El trabajo de los humanistas tuvo un impacto particularmente sensible en el dominio de la farmacología, donde había mucho que hacer para establecer un vocabulario claro y coherente. Los encargados de asimilar esta medicina y su terminología tenían ante sí graves problemas de selección de fuentes y una serie de principios establecidos de tipo lingüístico o literario entre los que se tenían que mover, en muchos casos sin tener toda la información y libertad necesarias para la constitución de una lengua técnica médica a la que de un modo más o menos consciente aspiraban.

Las obras de Galeno fueron traducidas varias veces durante el Renacimiento por este motivo, a excepción de los *Simples*, que se transmitieron en la versión latina de Gaudanus hasta el siglo XIX. Desde las primeras ediciones

---

26   Christina Savino, "Giovanni Battista Rasario and the 1562–1563 edition of Galen: Research, exchanges and forgeries," *Early Science and Medicine* 42 (2012), 413–45, en 414.

DE SIMPLICIUM MEDICAMENTORUM FACULTATIBUS DE GALENO

humanistas, esta obra va a editarse unas veintidós veces con ayuda de códices griegos antiguos, las ediciones griegas, etc., aunque sin demasiados cambios, ya que las pocas variantes que se introducen están relacionadas con los nombres de los simples. Mientras que en la edición de Ricchi y Trincavelli son presentados con el término latino (por ejemplo, "abrotonum"), en el resto se utiliza el griego ("abrotonon"). No obstante, en ocasiones Ricchi añade ambos términos. Por ejemplo, "Bolbos emeticos. Bulbus uomitorius".

Parece que los editores del Renacimiento dieron más prioridad al hecho de hacer accesible la obra[27] mediante la organización del material del que disponían que a editarla. Así, en las nuevas agrupaciones temáticas de los tratados galénicos basadas en *classes*, *tomos* o *sectiones* los *Simples* encabezan aquella parte dedicada a obras farmacológicas (no en la edición de Ricchi y Trincavelli, en la que ocupan el último lugar). En general, se tiende a mejorar la disposición del texto en capítulos, secciones y líneas numeradas con cifras o letras. También la labor de revisión y corrección hizo que los márgenes se enriquecieran con notas, variantes de manuscritos y resúmenes de los capítulos o secciones. Sin embargo, las únicas ediciones que incorporan estas mejoras al texto son las de Basilea de 1549 y 1561–62 y la *Giuntina* de 1556.

En cuanto a los prefacios, solo la edición de Ricchi y Trincavelli dedica una parte a nuestra obra mediante la inserción de un índice de simples y una entrada especial en la que se tratan cuestiones sobre el "aphonitrum".

En definitiva, estas ediciones de la traducción humanista de los *Simples* y sus constantes revisiones e intentos de mejora constituyen un componente importante de la historia de la farmacología porque proporcionan nueva información sobre la historia de la terminología farmacológica y botánica.

Escuela de Traductores de Toledo – Universidad de Castilla-La Mancha

---

27   Clara Domingues, "L'aménagement du continent galénique à la Renaissance: les éditions grecques et latines des oeuvres complètes de Galien et leur organisation des traités," en *Lire les médecins grecs à la Renaissance*, ed. Véronique Boudon-Millot y Guy Cobolet (París, 2004), 163–79.

CHAPTER 17

Aspects of Nature and People in Early Travel Literature (Fifteenth to Sixteenth Centuries)

Roumpini Dimopoulou

Abstract

Western Europeans (fifteenth–sixteenth century) travelled to Southeastern Greece and the Mediterranean by land or sea for various purposes, such us commerce, pilgrimage to the Holy Land or diplomatic missions. Erudite Italian humanists interested in antiquity toured the Greek islands and partly explored continental Greece. They recorded their journeys in the early travelogues. Travellers with a certain theoretical baggage recount the historical past, drawing upon Greek and Latin literature, as well as their personal experiences from their travels. The present paper focuses on the perception of nature and people, as presented in three different types of literary genres: an isolario, a diary and a narrative poem. Cristoforo Buondelmonti in his isolario *Liber insularum archipelagi* (1420), Ciriaco d' Ancona in his *Diaries* from his early and later travels (1400–45), and Hugo Favolius in his epic poem *Hodoeporici Byzantini libri III* (1563) enrich their reminiscences of the classical past with representations of Greek nature and comments upon the people they encounter. This article aims to explore the varied approaches of the writers and the aspects of Greek nature and the local people, which are enhanced in their travel accounts.

Keywords

Cristoforo Buondelmonti – Ciriaco d' Ancona – Hugo Favolius – Neo-Latin travel literature – Greek landscape

From the fifteenth century, but mainly the sixteenth, there is a proliferation of travelogues relating to Greece. Lettered authors, animated by memories of Ancient Hellas, have already painted a preconceived picture of Greece, which many times not even an actual visit to this land was able to overturn. Memory, remembrance and experience, real or false, shape the writing.

© KONINKLIJKE BRILL NV, LEIDEN, 2020 | DOI:10.1163/9789004427105_018

ASPECTS OF NATURE AND PEOPLE IN EARLY TRAVEL LITERATURE   249

This paper focuses on views about Greek nature and people, as these are imprinted in the works of three travellers who ventured to Greece in the fifteenth and sixteenth centuries. Agents of Italian Humanism, all three, from different starting points and with different motives, they have bequeathed us three different genres of travel texts in Latin: an isolario, a diary and an epic poem.

The cleric Cristoforo Buondelmonti, scion of an aristocratic family of Florence, was born around 1385.[1] By 1414 he was living in Rhodes, polishing his Greek, travelling and searching for manuscripts. Experiences of his peregrinations in the Aegean islands, Constantinople and Crete are recorded in his two works in Latin, *Descriptio Insule Crete* (1417) and *Liber Insularum Archipelagi* (*c.* 1420).[2] The latter, dedicated to Cardinal Giordano Orsini, is an exemplary isolario with 79 coloured maps and corresponding descriptions of islands and archipelagos, which became a model for subsequent isolaria. The work survives in a lot of manuscripts (about 70), the autograph by the author has not been identified and there is no critical edition of the text either. A host of manuscripts are dated to the fifteenth century and continued until the seventeenth century, while before its publication it was translated into Italian, English and French.[3]

---

1   The terse biographical information relates to his humanist education and his brief ecclesiastical career in his birthplace. See Robert Weiss, "Buondelmonti Cristoforo," *Dizionario Biografico degli Italiani* 15 (1972), 198–200. Cf. Benedetta Bessi, "The Ionian Islands in the Liber Insularum of Cristoforo Buondelmonti," in *The Ionian Islands: Aspects of their History and Culture*, ed. Anthony Hirst and Patrick Sammon (Newcastle upon Tyne, 2014), 225–8; Giuseppe Ragone, "Il Liber insularum Archipelagi di Cristoforo dei Buondelmonti: Filologia del testo, filologia dell' imagine," in *Humanisme et culture géographique à l'époque du Concile de Constance. Autour de Guillaume Fillastre. Actes du Colloque de l' Université de Reims, 18–19 November 1999*, ed. Didier Marcotte, (Turnout, 2002), 184–7; Claudia Barsanti, "Constantinopoli e l'Egeo nei primi decenni de XV secolo: La testimonianza di Cristoforo Buondelmonti," *Rivista dell' Istituto Nazionale d' Archeologia e Storia dell' Arte* 56 (2001), 83–254; Hilary Louise Turner, "Christopher Buondelmonti: Adventurer, explorer and cartographer," in *Géographie du monde au Moyen Âge et à la Renaissance*, ed. Monique Pelletier (Paris, 1989), 207–9.

2   See Cristoforo Buondelmonti, *Descriptio Insule Crete et liber insularum, Cap XI: Creta*, ed. Marie-Anne van Spitael, (Heraklion, 1981). Francesca Luzzati Laganà, "La funzione politica della memoria di Bisanzio nella Descriptio Cretae (1417–1422) di Cristoforo Buondelmonti," *Bulletino dell' Istituto Italiano per il Medio Evo e Archivio Muratoriano* 94 (1988), 395–420. Cf. Cristoforo Buondelmonti, *Perigrafi tis nisou Kritis: Enas gyros tis Kritis sta 1415*, ed. Martha Aposkite (Heraklion, 1996).

3   See Ragone, "Il Liber insularum Archipelagi" (see above, n. 1). Cf. Augusto Campana, "Da Codici di Buondelmonti," in *Silloge Bizantina in onore di Silvio Giuseppe Mercati* (Rome, 1957), 32–52. Essentially, it was a best seller of the Renaissance. The first printed edition of the Latin text, with commentary, edited by G. L. von Sinner, is dated to 1824: *Christoph. Bondelmontii*

Also active in the fifteenth century was Ciriaco d' Ancona (1391–1452), who is considered a founder of Classical Archaeology.[4] Born in Ancona, into a noble family of merchants, he was initiated into the allure of travel when he was only nine years old.[5] He combined his professional involvement in trade with overseas voyages, sailing throughout the Eastern Mediterranean. Gradually, his mercantile travels were transformed into journeys of discovery. He toured Egypt, Asia Minor, Italy and Greece.[6] His interests ranged from studying buildings, purchasing rare codices and precious objects, drawing monuments and statues, which resulted in the creation of a voluminous diary and an archive of sketches and records. His copying of thousands of inscriptions, many of which are now lost and are preserved only in his daybook jottings, is considered his most important contribution to scholarship.[7]

Among travellers in the sixteenth century is the Flemish physician Hugo Favolio (1523–85), who was born at Middlebourg in Zeeland into a bourgeois

---

Florentini Librum Insularum Archipelagi e codicibus Parisinis regiis nunc primum totum edidit, praefatione et annotatione instruxit (Leipzig, 1824); while Émile Legrand gives a French translation and a translation into Greek of an unknown author from a sixteenth-century manuscript: *Description des îles de l'Archipel, par Christophe Buondelmonti. Version grecque par un anonyme, publiée d'après le manuscrit du Sèrail* (Paris, 1897). Recent publications present facsimiles of individual manuscripts of the maps and Buondelmonti's Latin text transcribed and translated: MS 1475 fMa of the James Ford Bell Library, University of Minnesota, in Cristoforo Buondelmonti, *Description of the Aegean & other Islands*, ed. Evelyn Edson (New York, 2018) [with supplemental material by Henricus Martellus Germanus], and MS G13, from Düsseldorf, in *Cristoforo Buondelmonti, Liber insularum archipelagi. Universitäts-und Landesbibliothek Düsseldorf Ms. G 13*, ed. Irmgard Siebert and Max Plassmann (Wiesbaden, 2005); Cf. *Cristoforo Buondelmonti, Liber insularum archipelagi*, ed. Karl Bayer (Wiesbaden, 2007).

4 See *Cyriac of Ancona: Life and Early Travels,* ed. Charles Mitchell, Edward W. Bodnar and Clive Foss (Cambridge, MA, 2015), 1–171; *Cyriac of Ancona: Later Travels,* ed. Edward W. Bodnar and Clive Foss (Cambridge, MA, 2003), ix–xviii; *Francesco Scalamonti, Vita viri clarissimi et famosissimi Kyriaci Anconitani,* ed. Charles Mitchell and Edward W. Bodnar (Philadelphia, PA, 1996); Jean Colin, *Cyriaque d'Ancône: Le voyageur, le marchand, l'humaniste* (Paris, [1981]). Cf. also Michail Chatzidakis, *Ciriaco d'Ancona und die Wiederentdeckung Griechenlands im 15. Jahrhundert* (Mainz, 2017); Giorgio Mangani, *Il vescovo e l'antiquario: Giuda Ciriaco, Ciriaco Pizzecolli e le origini dell'identità adriatica anconitana* (Ancona, 2016); Richard Stoneman, *Land of the Lost Gods. The Search for Classical Greece* (New York, 2010), 22–36 and Marina Belozerskaya, *To Wake the Dead. A Renaissance Merchant and the Birth of Archaeology* (New York, 2009).

5 Scalamonti, *Vita viri clarissimi* (see above, n. 4), 13, 102; Colin, *Cyriaque d'Ancône* (see above, n. 4), 13–4; Edward William Bodnar, *Cyriacus of Ancona and Athens,* (Brussels, 1960), 18.

6 Bodnar/Foss, *Cyriac of Ancona* (see above, n. 4), x–xi.

7 Ibid., ix–x; *Cyriacus of Ancona's Journeys in the Propontis and the Northern Aegean, 1444–1445,* ed. Edward W. Bodnar and Charles Mitchell (Philadelphia, PA, 1976), 1.

ASPECTS OF NATURE AND PEOPLE IN EARLY TRAVEL LITERATURE

family of Pisan origin.[8] Educated at the University of Louvain and in the famed Medical School of Padua, Favolio accompanied the diplomatic mission of King Charles V to Constantinople. His impressions of the journey are recounted in the three books of *Hodoeporicon Byzantinum libri III,* a travel text written in Latin verse, in dactylic hexameters, numbering over 5 000 lines. The editio princeps, of which 12 copies are attested, was published in Louvain in 1563, almost eighteen years after Favolios's return from Constantinople. The first book narrates the voyage through the Adriatic from Venice to Ragusa and then the journey through the Balkans as far as Constantinople. The second book is devoted to Constantinople and the delegation's negotiations with Suleiman I. The work is concluded with the third book, narrating the sea voyage homeward from Constantinople to Venice.

The three travellers did not follow the same routes, most of the places they visited do not coincide, while their views about the same place differ. In Buondelmonti's testimonies for the Cyclades, Ciriaco d'Ancona's for the Peloponnese and Crete, and Favolio's for the islands in the Ionian Sea, an attempt is made to reconstitute aspects of Greek nature and to sketch the local populations in the "geographical space of Greece", both mainland and island.

The Greek landscape is distinguished by mountainous massifs,[9] rich vegetation and the watery element. The rocky Cyclades,[10] essentially scattered peaks of mountains sunk in the Aegean Sea, end, according to Buondelmonti,[11] in steep coasts with a few wandering animals:[12] goats roam the rugged terrain of

---

8   For further biographical information on Favolio see Roumpini Dimopoulou, *Hugo Favolius, Hodoeporici Byzantini Liber III (1563)* (PhD Thesis in Greek, University of Athens, 2006), 23–8, and André Deisser, *Sur la Route de Constantinople. Le premier livre de l'Hodoeporicum Byzantinum (1563) par Hugo Favolius, édition critique, traduction, commentaire* (PhD Thesis, University of Liège, 1992), 23–7. Cf. Marc Laureys, "Classical Tradition and Contemporary Experience in Hugo Favolius's Hodoeporicon Byzantinum (1563)," in *Artes Apodemicae and Early Modern Travel Culture, 1550–1700*, ed. Karl A. E. Enenkel and Jan de Jong (Leiden, 2019), 293–311.

9   For study of the aesthetics of mountains and literary references to them see William M. Barton, *Mountain Aesthetics in Early Modern Latin Literature* (London, 2017).

10   For the historical examination of the natural environment, the inhabitants and the settlement development of the Cyclades see, *Cyclades. Istoria tou topiou kai topikes istories. Apo to Fysiko perivallon sto istoriko topio*, ed. Lina G. Mendoni and Nikos Margaris (Athens, 1998).

11   All of the following quotations from the *Liber Insularum Archipelagi* are taken from Sinner's 1824 edition (see above, n. 3); all page references in parentheses are to that edition.

12   Further bibliography on Buondelmonti's descriptions of individual Cycladic islands can be found in Roumpini Dimopoulou, "Buondelmonti's Delos: Restoring the Present with Reminiscences of the Past Embellished by Borrowings," *Mediterranean Chronicle* 6 (2016),

Seriphos, "per abrupta viarum aeghae innumerabiles vagari cernuntur" (83), Herakleia and Keros, "in quibus multa aegrarum societas repetitur quae vagatur ubique" (98), as well as of Mykonos, "quae arida tota cum aegis multis comprobatur" (90), while on Sikinos, little donkeys move about with difficulty, "in qua aselli, forte per insulam relicti, usque nunc errantes per asperas ripas, magno [...] labore" (79). The barren crags of Antiparos offer refuge to flocks of birds, mainly eagles and hawks, whose nests cover them and are launching pads for them to hunt their prey,[13]

> ab aquilisque falconibus non est derelicta. Quisve poterit quot foleae per scopulum parantur in anno, [...] tanta est congeries aviumque folearum et praesertim aquilarum, quae dum in loco praedam conducit, [...] sola praedam non manducat (95).

The austere rocky massifs of the Cyclades reveal the unique geological wealth of the islands. In Santorini, Buondelmonti recalls the eruption of the volcano that caused the submergence of part of the island and gave Therasia its crescent shape, "propter vulcani combustionem medietas in profundum maris est submersa, cuius particulam ad modum lunae exustam videmus, et Therasia hodie nuncupatur" (78). Paros's pristine white marble from afar looks like snow, "et gignit adeo marmor candidissimum, ut a longe videntes nivem esse dicant" (94). A very hard dense black stone known as emery is quarried on Naxos, "petra nigerrima et durissima dicta Smeriglo" (96), where a vein of gold is left untouched for want of a specialist artisan to mine it, "Vena auri in aliquibus invenitur partibus, quam domini ob defectum artificis intactam demittunt" (97).[14]

Ciriaco d'Ancona[15] in the Peloponnese[16] gazes at the snow-capped peaks of imposing Taygetos, "niveos montis vertices" (328) from its eastern foothills, "ad orientales Taygeti montis radices" (328), and refers to its new name, Agios Ilias, given by the locals, "montem vero non usquam claro suo nomine Taygeton,

---

97–118; Georgios Tolias, "Gyro apo enan sticho tou Virgiliou: I Syros sta nisologia," in *Chartes kai Istories: Ellinikes topographies tis Anagennisis*, ed. Giorgos Tolias (Thessaloniki, 2008), 15–40.

13   The detailed narration is enriched with memories from Pliny, *hist. nat.* 10,4.

14   On the same island there is also a salina, "Ibique prope salinarum panditur locus" (97).

15   Quotations from Ciriaco's Latin text are taken from the 2003 edition by Bodnar and Foss (see above, n. 4); all page references in parentheses are to that edition.

16   For travellers' testimonies about the Peloponnese see Anna Lambropoulou and Aggeliki Panopoulou, "H Fraggokratia kai to despotato tou Moreos," in *Oi Metamorfoseis tis Peloponnisou (4os–15os ai.)* (Athens, 2000), 59–82.

quin Hagion Heliam late ab incolis vocitatum audimus" (328), from the chapel built at the top, "sacrum Heliae prophitae sacellum accolae ostentarunt" (328), according to Christian habits.

On Crete, captivated by the high mountains and the lush vegetation, "montanas illas nobiles ciparisseas videremus" (184), he clambers up the rocky slopes of the White Mountains, "scrupeos arduosque per colles ad ipsos Leucos montes ascendimus" (184) and he admires the countless cypress trees and the tall fragrant conifers that seemingly threaten the sky with their green foliage, "plerasque vidimus altas coniferas redolentes coelumque comis minantes perpetuoque virentes, insigne decus nemorum cypressus" (186).

The absence of mountains is characteristic of Favolio's[17] memories of the Ionian Sea. Sporadic references to the cliffs and the high acropolises of the islands, "alta Cythera" (295: 1335), "altae saxa Ithacae" (295: 1622–23), "subimus Phaeacum aerias [...] arces" (307: 1674–75), lead to the *Aeneid*,[18] and are not actual original impressions from the voyage.

Apart from the mountains the variety of vegetation also confirms the polymorphism of the Greek landscape. The forests on the mountains of Crete, alternate with the low vegetation cover of Cyclades. According to Buondelmonti, fruit trees thrive on the islands' waterless soil, on Siphnos "omnium virescit pomorum" (83), and on Naxos "abundantia [...] frugumque" (96), "per vallem fructiferam usque viridarium" (97–8), as well as fertile vineyards, "fertilitate vinearum" (96).[19] On Kythnos they make their own wine from the vines and also produce meat and silk, "in vino vero blado, sericoque carnibus bene habetur" (85).

In the Peloponnese, Ciriaco d'Ancona identifies the ruins of the ancient city of Messene, scattered in the fields amidst verdant countryside, with tranquil gardens and leafy trees, "per agros et virentia rura amoenosque et frondosis arboribus" (306). In Laconian Mani, he comes across villages with cultivated fields, vineyards and olive groves in abundance, "villas inspeximus cultis agris vinetisque et oliveis arboribus uberes" (312). From his rambles on the coasts of the Mani Peninsula he conveys the picture of the deep-green valley densely planted with vines, the many trees and the pleasant meadows, "pulchram et densis hinc inde vineis arboribusque et amoenis pratis virentem et placidissimam vallem hilari animo conspexissem" (322).

---

17   Quotations from Favolios's Latin text of Book 3 of the *Hodoeporici Byzantini* are taken from Dimopoulou, *Hugo Favolius* (see above, n. 8); local references in parentheses include both the page numbers and the individual verses.

18   Virgil, *Aen.* 1,680 "alta Cythera", *Aen.* 3,291 "Aerias Phaeacum abscondimus arces".

19   Cf. Plinius, *nat. hist.* 4,25 "Naxus [...] Dionysiada a vinearum fertilitate, alii Siciliam minorem".

Favolio's very few mentions of the flora of the Ionian Islands are linked with gazing at them from a distance and resonate the remembrances of his classical readings, as in the case of Zacynthos with his green low vegetation, "virentibus herbis" (303: 1582), introduced as "Zacynthos nemorosa" (303: 1581), another verbal loan from Vergil.[20] The Greek landscape emerges from the water, which becomes also the 'vehicle' of the voyage. In the arid Cyclades of Buondelmonti the watery element defines the outline of the island groups, frames the maps and is limited textually to isolated references. On Kythnos a stream with head-waters high up the mountain flows across the island into the sea, "In monte vero [...] turris erigitur, a qua rivulus aquarum rigat usque salum domesticus" (84), whereas on Naxos there is a small river, "parvo flumine" (98). For Kea the unique property of water temporarily to dull the senses of those who test them is recorded, "fons invenitur, cuius aquae potu faciunt homines hebetes sensu, et, postquam ad digestionem venerint, mens ad pristinam reducitur sanitatem" (86). On Tenos the abundance of water is linked etymologically with the historical name Hydrousa, which Aristotle attributed to the island, "Aristoteles propter aquarum abundantiam Hydrusam hanc nominat, quod latine aquatica sonat" (88). On Delos the Inopos spring at the foot of Mount Cintius is believed to be linked to the river Nile because of the movement of its waters,[21] "fons est qui crescit et, decresit ei tempore et hora Nili fluminis" (92).

Ciriaco d'Ancona relates that on Crete, in the foothills of Mount Dikte the mountainous landscape is enriched by the waters of the spring of Artemis Diktaia, "ad mirificum Dictaeae Dianae fontem venimus" (198), which rise from the mountain's summit and flow noisily through a jagged rock hewn by their pressure, "alto a vertice scisso suapte ruina saxo a summo montis cacumine excataruentem et angustae scissurae anfractibus sonoro ruente latice," (198) forming a small lake, a natural water basin ruffled by many waves, "profundo repleto lacu naturali rotunditate urna" (198). The unique colourful rainbow encircling the basin enhances the perfection of the creation, "polycromateum sub nubibus in solem mille vibrantem coloribus arcum Iunoniam Iridem" (200).

In Favolio's epic descriptions the watery element predominates.[22] The sea is transformed by changes in the direction of the winds and travellers sailing the routes of Odysseus participate in the adventure and revel in unique images. On Zakynthos, a balmy breeze favours the ship's departure, "Iamque ratem ventus,

---

20 Virgil, *Aen.* 3,271 "Zacynthos nemorosa".

21 Cf. Dimopoulou, "Buondelmonti's Delos" (see above, n. 14), 110.

22 He composes the relevant excerpts with citations from corresponding passages from Vergil's *Aeneid*, which he processes and enriches with linguistic loans from Silius Italicus, Ovid, and others.

et gratior aura vocabat / Aetheris, hinc rursus declive capescimus aequor" (304: 1601–02), and sailing swifter than the javelin and the arrow, the vessel vies with the winds, "Evolat uncta ratis, mox inde per aequoris undas / Ocyor et iaculo, et ventos aequante sagitta" (304: 1606–07). Close to the cliffs of Ithaca, the captain's skilful manoeuvre turns the vessel to the open sea and he cuts through the waves, navigating safely (305: 1622–25):

> Ipsa suis nota indigenis, cum protinus altae
> Saxa Ithacae, externis nimis importuna carinis
> Evitans navarcha ratem detorquet in altum,
> Quaque magis tutum, medias intersecat undas.

The light ship passes by Actium and, propelled by the impetuous fluctuation of the wind, ploughs foamy furrows through the rippling sea (306: 1648–51):

> Hic dudum celeri substrata per aequora cursu,
> Ventorumque levis rapido aestu concita puppis
> Evolat, infinditque salum, rostroque bisulcas
> Undique agens spumas crispantia marmora radit.

In the midst of the open sea, wet winds rage and the ship with its billowing sails cuts through the frothy waves, "In mare vela vocant, [...] / Ut tamen acta ratis vasti sub aperta profundi est, / Ilicet exorti nimbosis flatibus udi / Tendunt vela Noti, fugimus spumantibus undis" (306: 1656–60).

Apart from the sea voyage, mythological memories from Ovid's *Meta-morphoses* guide Favolios's lyrical verses about the rivers that flow into the Ionian Sea: the Alpheios, "Alpheus, nunc Rophea" (Rouphias), the dark waters of which mix with the sea and, as the poets say, unite with the Sicilian waters of Arethousa in a single flow (303: 1575–80):[23]

> Qua procus Alphaeus refluis immergitur undis,
> Et freta caeruleis miscet Neptunia lymphis.
> [...]
> Occultas egisse vias subter mare, et arcte
> Sicelis hunc Aretusa tuis miscerier undis
> Assuetum, et tecum stagnari gurgite in uno

---

23   Cf. Ovid, *Met.* 5.572–641.

and the Naupaktian Acheloos[24]—"Achelous," whose sandy waters overflow, accumulating mud, and ooze in the stagnant *Echinades* (305: 1625–29),[25]

> Qua Naupactaeus lymphis Achelous inundans
> Semper arenosis coenum, limumque recentem
> Aggerit, et resides stagnantis Echinadas auget
> Alluvione soli, celebratas carmine quondam.

On the bleak outlying islands, the disadvantaged inhabitants keep alive their own beliefs, which nurture and are nurtured by the fear of death. According to Buondelmonti the threat of raids by Turks and pirates leads to the decline and desolation of most islands. On Ios, every evening after sunset the islanders climb up, with great effort, to the well-fortified castle, "postquam ad occasum perventum erit, in munitissimum magno labore ascendum castellum" (99). Before daybreak, they send the old ladies out to explore and, as soon as the all-clear signal is given, the gates are opened for everyone; thus they spend their life in a state of fear, "mane autem facto, vetulas ad speculandum per insulam, ante auroram mittunt, et dato ab eis signo, portae panduntur in totum, et sic vitam transeunt cum tremore" (99). The incredible barbarity of the Ottomans is imprinted in the text about the islet of Kalogeros, where Turks who lose their vessel at sea find refuge on the rocks. Three days later, they are rescued by a passing Christian ship, they recover and, on returning home, they sell their saviours into slavery (88):

> cumque semel Turcorum ratis ibi mergeretur, ad salutem in scopulis hominum eventum est. Tertia vero die Christianorum puppis coram affuit eis. Quae, misericordia mota super omnes, illos semivivos evasit in altum. Qui, post cibum convalescentes, in Christianos irruere, et navigantes in patriam, Christianos, tantae evasionis causas, ad continuam posuere servitutem.

The author is moved by the lonely life of the womenfolk of the Cyclades. There is special mention of the women of Siphnos, the island's main inhabitants, who, due to the lack of men, live a chaste life, "habitant denique hic pauci et miserabiles, quorum numerus pars maxima sunt mulieres, quae, per defectum virorum, usque ad senium vitam vi castam deducunt" (83). On Naxos, a great number of women spend a life of deprivation and solitude until ripe old

---

24 This is a linguistic debt to Ovid, *Ov. F.* 2.43.

25 Cf. Ovid, *Met.* 8.577–889.

ASPECTS OF NATURE AND PEOPLE IN EARLY TRAVEL LITERATURE 257

age, without marital bonds, keeping their virginity all their life, not because of obsession with its value but because men are absent, "numerum magnum reperi mulierum quae, copula virorum carentes, usque ad decrepitam aetatem in virginitate resident, non zelo constantiae meritae, sed ex defectu hominum, finem complent virginalem" (97).

Buondelmonti's information on the local people is complemented by intermittent references to their dietary habits: on Seriphos they prefer sun-dried meat, "carnes quarum assatae a sole diu in cibum a colonis sumuntur" (83), whereas on Syros they eat barley bread, carob pods and kid (goat), "ordeaceo pane cum carrubis et aegharum carnibus vescuntur" (93).

Ciriaco's journal entries on the local people focus mainly on the survival of ancient customs and echo his antiquarian interests. In a particularly detailed narrative he describes the everyday life of the Laconians dwelling on the shores of the Tainaros Peninsula, who, he maintains, keep ancient habits alive, "hisdem locis homines [...] antiquum servare ritum cognovimus" (322). The inhabitants build their houses in the fields with polygonal masonry according to the ancient technique, "suas per ruras casas magnis polygonisque et antiqua arte compositis lapidibus aedunt" (322). With their bare hands they dig out cisterns in line and they protect them with high rocks, "cisternas quoque manu longo tramite effodientes ingentibus et septipedum saxis protegunt" (322). They speak like the ancient Greeks, "Ita et loquendi antiquum quodammodo servare morem cognovimus" (322), and, even though Christians, when referring to the dead, they say that they have gone to Hades, "mortuos nanque suos quosvecunque suae relligionis homines ἐς τὸν Ἄδην, scilicet ad inferos, migrasse dicunt" (322). They eat crushed nuts with olive oil, barley bread, "dapes enim eorum fractae quoque fabae oleoque conditae multo" (322, 324), and although they drink water every day, "potum vero aqua est" (324), they drink wine only at festivals, "raro vel nisi pro solemnibus laetis vinum gustant et panegyricis festis" (324).

Ciriaco d'Ancona also records the organization of an annual athletic contest, observing the ancient ceremonial, "quo quot annis indigena proxima quoque iuventus antiquo de more" (322), in a specific place surrounded by stones, with the prizes presented by the local lord, "locum lapidibus ingenitis terminatum ostentarunt [...] positis a principe premiis, agonem exercent quem ἀνδρόδρομον πεντασστάδιον quoque vocant" (322). Young men dressed only in a linen tunic run barefoot over a distance of five stadia, competing for a monetary prize, "v scilicet stadiorum spatio virorum cursu contendunt, exutis quidem pedibus, et interiori linea tantum tunica induti" (322).

Among Favolio's few and random remarks on the people of the Ionian Islands characteristic is the case of Cephalonia, with the sad picture it presents

after the removal of the Christian inhabitants and its settlement by dangerous heathen Turks. He speaks of derelict reed huts with rickety roofs of wicker
from the marshes (304–5: 1609–18):

> speculamur ab alta
> Arva Cephalenum, populis exhausta professis
> Relligione pia Christum, novus incola quae nunc
> Occupat, heu, nostris longe infestissimus hostis.
> [...]
> Nuper ubi amplivagis vallatae moenibus urbes
> Surgebant aliquot nunc, [...]
> reliqua aggestis inculta mapalia culmis,
> Raraque tecta vides malesarta palustribus ulvis.

Through examining three different geographical regions of Greece in three
different travel texts we come to the conclusion that Buondelmonti's isolario
imprints the picture of the Cyclades with the barren rocks and sparse vegetation, and with limited references to the watery element. In the diary entries of
Ciriaco d'Ancona, the traveller from Ancona focuses on the high mountainous
massifs, the forests and the low vegetation cover of the plains, with olive trees
and vineyards. Alternating seascapes dominate Favolio's verses recounting his
voyage in the Ionian, while all three travellers focus on the wretched populations and denounce the brutalities of the Ottoman Turks.

The views of nature and of people in Greece vary according to the textual
genre, the duration of the travels and the reason for them, as well as the interests of each author. They result from the experience of the journey, while
resonances of their humanist leanings function complementarily. Greek nature changes but is present. Its beauty and splendour delights the travellers
and does not fall short of their expectations. The Greeks, impoverished and
unhappy suffer under the Ottoman yoke. These unique testimonies capture
the real and not the imaginary picture of Greece in the fifteenth and sixteenth
centuries, and are important sources for the study of this obscure period.

National and Kapodistrian University of Athens
Department of Italian Language and Literature

CHAPTER 18

Bonaventura Vulcanius in Spain: Some Poems

Ignacio J. García Pinilla

Abstract

Algunos poemas de ocasión de Bonaventura Vulcanius (1538–1614) corresponden a sus años de permanencia en España (1559–71). Casi todos ellos se conservan, a veces con variantes, en dos manuscritos de la colección Vulcaniana de Leiden. En este paper se identifican once piezas de este grupo y se aportan las claves que permiten interpretarlos; en efecto, se refieren a lugares diversos (Burgos, Alcalá de Henares, Toledo), se distribuyen en todo el arco temporal de esos doce años y aluden a diferentes personas o a sucesos de repercusión pública, cuya identificación aporta información sobre la situación y actividad de Vulcanio en ese período. Cuando es preciso, se establece cuál es la versión definitiva de algunos de estos poemas, ya que conservamos diferentes versiones de varios de ellos, con variantes de autor.

Keywords

Bonaventura Vulcanius – collection Vulcaniana – Neo-Latin occasional poetry – Spanish humanism

1   His Early Years in Spain

The aim of this paper is to offer new perspectives on the activities of Bonaventura Vulcanius (Bruges 1538–Leiden 1614) during his years in Spain, from 1559 to 1570, using as source material eleven short poems dating from that period and written by him.[1] After an initial period of study in Leuven and

---

1   An updated bibliography on Vulcanius can be found in Eduardo del Pino González, "La versión latina de Bonaventura Vulcanius de las 'Coplas a la muerte de su padre' del español Jorge Manrique," *Bibliothèque d'Humanisme et Renaissance* 79 (2017), 395–417; see also *Bonaventura Vulcanius, Works and Networks, Bruges 1538–Leiden 1614*, ed. Hélène Cazes (Leiden – Boston, 2010). Some bibliographic details of his stay in Spain are clarified in Gilbert Tournoy, "La correspondance de Bonaventura Vulcanius: quelques notes de lecture," *Humanistica Lovaniensia* 60 (2011) 315–25, esp. 316–8.

© KONINKLIJKE BRILL NV, LEIDEN, 2020 | DOI:10.1163/9789004427105_019

Cologne (1555–59), Vulcanius settled in Spain for almost eleven years. After his return to the north, he held different positions in Cologne (1573), Geneva (1575), and Basel; in 1577 he became secretary to Marnix de Sainte-Aldegonde in Antwerp and, from 1581, worked as professor of Greek and Latin in Leiden. He was renowned as an editor and translator of the classics, as well as for tutoring students like Daniel Heinsius and Hugo Grotius.

Vulcanius' years in Spain have received little scholarly attention. He served cardinal Francisco de Mendoza y Bobadilla, bishop of Burgos, from 1559 until the bishop's death in 1566,[2] working as his librarian and copyist; he was also given the task of making Latin translations of Greek texts—at least of St Cyril's unpublished works.[3] This outstanding cardinal's library was inherited by his brother, Fernando de Mendoza, archdeacon of Toledo, and Vulcanius consequently moved to that city.[4] When Fernando de Mendoza died in 1570, Vulcanius accepted an invitation to return to the Low Countries and enter the Duke of Medinaceli's service, although in the end he did not take up that post.

2 Collection of Poems

Most of Vulcanius' poetic compositions were gathered into various manuscripts, principally those held in Leiden, Universiteit Bibliotheek MS Vul. 97 and Vul. 103 (hereafter, Vul. 97 and Vul. 103). Alfons Devitte and Harm-Jan van Dam have published studies on them.[5] The latter, for example, highlights the fact that many poems are found in both manuscripts, or even in both parts of Vul. 103, frequently with authorial variants; he also observes variants

---

2 There is not any detailed biography of this noble humanist cleric. There is a synthesis and bibliography in Inmaculada Pérez Martín, "El helenismo en la España moderna: libros y manuscritos griegos de Francisco de Mendoza y Bovadilla," *Minerva* 24 (2011), 59–96, with interesting clues as to Vulcanius.

3 See Gilbert Tournoy, "A Life-long Dream: Bonaventura Vulcanius and his Edition of St Cyril of Alexandria (I)," *Calamus Renascens* 12 (2011), 185–255.

4 On the changing fortunes of the library during Vulcanius' time as librarian, see Gregorio de Andrés, "Historia de un fondo griego de la Biblioteca Nacional de Madrid. Colecciones: cardenal Mendoza y García de Loaisa," *Revista de Archivos, Bibliotecas y Museos* 77 (1974), 5–65, esp. 10–6.

5 Alfons Dewitte, "Bonaventura Vulcanius Brugensis: Hoogleraambt, Correspondenten, edita," *Sacris erudiri* 26 (1983), 312–63; Harm-Jan van Dam, "'The Honour of Letters': Bonaventura Vulcanius, Scholar and Poet", in Cazes, *Bonaventura Vulcanius* (see above, n. 1), 47–68.

BONAVENTURA VULCANIUS IN SPAIN: SOME POEMS 261

when comparing some of the printed poems to the handwritten versions. Furthermore, van Dam points out the epigrammatic tone, characterised by brevity and wit, of the poems written during Vulcanius' sojourn in Spain.

3 Poems Dating the Spanish Period. Versions

There are twelve poems of Vulcanius datable to his Spanish period. He wrote other compositions related to Spain, or even in Spanish, but these were composed years later, frequently against Spanish barbarians, and so we do not include them here. All the poems from the Spanish period are in elegiac couplet form, except two, which use the Sapphic stanza. The order of the poems' presentation here does not coincide with any manuscript order, even though Vul. 103 II follows an order that may have been created by Vulcanius himself, possibly in relation to some proposed publication. Instead, I have opted for a chronological order, given the considerable uncertainty involved in dating such short pieces, and because I prefer to give priority to what the poems can contribute to Vulcanius' biography. Ten of the poems from the Spanish period are included in Vul. 103 II, seven in Vul. 97, one in Vul. 103 I, and two in other manuscripts.

Of the twelve poems, I have chosen not to study the epigram *In Sotum et Guadalupam*,[6] even though, judging by the names, in all probability it refers to the Spanish years. However, it furnishes no specific information for our purpose; it merely mocks a married couple: her for being adulterous and him for being a sodomite.

3.1

Carmen Bonauenturae Vulcanii,
ad Philippum Hispaniarum Regem,
ex Belgica reducem, confecto iam bello

Splendidior radiis emergit ab aequore Phoebus,
Pura magis solito cornua Luna gerit,
Ornataeque comas Horae vacuo aethere ludunt
Et tenero vernans gramine terra viret.

---

6 This poem is found in Vul. 97, fol. 14r.

Oblitique irarum homines conuiuia curant,   5
    Aspiciunt aequis terram oculis superi
Gratantur regem Hesperiae pacemque reductam
    Phoebus, Luna, Horae, Terra, Homines, Superi.

copies: Vul. 103 II fol. 91r (M); Vul. 97 fol. 16r (L); British Library MS Sloane Add. 2764, fol. 45r (B)
Tit.: In reditum Philippi II Hisp. Regis ex Belgio in Hispaniam confecto bello cum Gallia L ; Ad Philippum II. HISP. REGEM pace cum Galliarum rege confecta in Hispaniam e Belgio reducem M
6 aequis ML : laetis B   7 Hesperiae BM *p. corr.* L : Hesperiaeque L   *in fine add.* Toleti Anno Domini M. D. LX. M

Supported by the royal historian Juan Páez de Castro,[7] who was then living in Brussels, Vulcanius was able to enter the service of the cardinal bishop of Burgos, don Francisco de Mendoza y Bobadilla. This prelate was a nobleman with humanist interests whose library included a notable collection of Greek and Latin manuscripts.[8] Páez had been Mendoza's librarian in Rome, and it was probably his praise for Vulcanius' abilities that convinced the cardinal to employ him. In order to fulfil his duties, Vulcanius had to travel from the Low Countries to Burgos. He made the journey to Spain in 1559, possibly in Philip II's entourage as it made its way back to the Peninsula. What is likely the oldest poem written by Vulcanius in Spain relates to this journey and extols the Peace of Cateau-Cambresis, as can be seen in the title lines. If this is so, Vulcanius must have arrived in Toledo with the court in November 1559. Yet the copy in Vul. 103 II is dated at Toledo in 1560. This reference does not imply that the poem was written at this later date, however. More likely, Vulcanius used the excitement of the welcome ceremonies as an opportunity to add his contribution. Its tone is identical to that of other poetry composed for the occasion, in which extolling the Peace is a constant theme.[9] It is possible that it dates from the beginning of 1560, before the royal wedding in Guadalajara

---

7   On him, see especially Arantxa Domingo Malvadi, *Bibliofilia humanista en tiempos de Felipe II: la biblioteca de Juan Páez de Castro* (Salamanca, 2011).

8   In relation to this library, see Charles Graux, *Los orígenes del fondo griego del Escorial*, trans. Gregorio de Andrés (Madrid, 1982), 104–12 and especially Inmaculada Pérez Martín, "El helenismo" (see above, n. 2).

9   *El recebimiento, que la universidad de Alcalá de Henares hizo a los Reyes* [...] (Alcalá de Henares, 1560); *Álvar Gómez de Castro, Recebimiento que la imperial ciudad de Toledo hizo a la magestad de la reina nuestra señora Isabel* [...], ed. Concepción Fernández Travieso (A Coruña, 2007).

BONAVENTURA VULCANIUS IN SPAIN: SOME POEMS   263

(29 January). This indicates that Vulcanius did not immediately go to Burgos after arriving in Spain, but remained for some time with the royal court. This seems reasonable since cardinal Mendoza was then accompanying the Queen from the French border to Guadalajara.

3.2

In Ambrosium Morales Eunuchum, cui Arcuum triumphalium extruendorum cura data erat Compluti, cuius versus aliquot in impluuio Collegii Complutensis (loco ex lotio foetido) erant positi, in quibus antepenultimam in *spectacula* corribiebat, primam in *solum*, pro *terra*, produxerat.

> Complutense solum, magno spectacula regi
>   Dum facis, hac vesci se iubet ambrosia.
> (*erat enim locus foetidus ex lotio*)
>   *Ambrosius respondet:*
> Parce poeta precor, nam qui mala carmina feci,
>   semiuir ut, sic et semipoeta fui.

mss.: Vul. 103 11 fol. 93v (M); Vul. 97 fol. 16v (L)
Tit.: Ambrosium **M** : quendam Ambrosium **L** Eunuchum **M** : Spadonem **L** extruendorum **M** : construendorum **L** cuius—aliquot **M** : in aduentu regis et reginae Elizabethae, et **L** Complutensis **M** : Complutensi **L** loco—positi **M** : versus aliquot statuerat **L**
2 *sub* ambrosia *add.* erat enim locus foetidus ex lotio **L**

This short epigrammatic dialogue refers to the humanist from Cordoba, Ambrosio de Morales,[10] to whom Vulcanius attributes one of the epigraphs that embellished Elizabeth of Valois' reception in Alcala, which took place on 3 February 1560. This epigram reveals the identity of the hitherto-unknown author of the unmetrical epigraph. Juan Francisco Alcina had attributed it tentatively to Álvar Gómez de Castro, while Isabel Alastrué was more inclined to think it was indeed Ambrosio de Morales.[11] Vulcanius was very well informed, and so was able to make poetic sport of Morales' castrated condition. Regarding the date of poem: Vulcanius need not have written it immediately after the verses were presented at the Valois reception; a little later, in the spring of 1560,

---

10 Jenaro Costas Rodríguez, "Morales, Ambrosio de," in *Diccionario de Humanistas Españoles*, ed. Juan Francisco Domínguez (Madrid, 2012), 572–600.

11 Juan Francisco Alcina Rovira, *Repertorio de la poesía latina del Renacimiento en España* (Salamanca, 1995), 109; Isabel Alastrué Campo, *Alcalá de Henares y sus fiestas públicas (1503–1675)* (Madrid, 1990), 95.

a book was published containing all the poems and scenes of the event, and he could have read it there.[12] It is plausible to suppose that Vulcanius composed his epigram in Toledo, an environment where undoubtedly he had more time as well as readers who could enjoy his mockery. We do not know how long he stayed in Toledo with the cardinal before moving to Burgos.

3.3

Ad Illustriss. ac Rmum. D. D. Cardinalem de Mendoza Episcopum Burgen. αὐτοσχεδίως

> Magna mihi peragranda via est, amplissime Praesul,
>   Graeciaque est iussu magna adeunda tuo.
> Nil mihi tam gratum ac tua iussa capessere, quamque
>   Currere in amplexus, docte Cyrille, tuos.
> Sed quis per tantos solisque viaeque labores,   5
>   Sit nisi homo, possit, ferreus, ire pedes?
> Sis igitur facilis mihi non iniusta petenti et
>   Fac Flandro superem taedia vectus equo:
> Auspiciis sic ibo tuis citiusque redibo
>   Quaeque redux referam praemia pluris erunt.   10

mss.: Vul. 103 II fol 92v (**M**); Vul. 97 fol. 16r (**L**); Vul. 103 I no fol. (**N**)
Tit.: Ad Cardinalem Mendozam, cuius iussu Cyrillum e Graeco in Latinum vertebat. Petens equum **L** : Ad Cardinalem Mendozam, cuius auspiciis Cyrilli ἀνέκδοτα vertebat **M**
1 longa **N** : magna **LM** | peragranda **LM** : peragenda **N**   7 Sis igitur **N** : Ergo veni **LM** | petenti et **N** : precanti et **M** : precanti **L**   9 auspiciis sic ibo tuis **N** *p. corr.* **L** : sic ibo ad tua iussa citus **M** *mrg. aliter* **L** : sic alacer ibo citius **L** | citiusque **L** : citiorque **M** : laetusque **N**   10 referam praemia **LM** : reddam munera **N**

The poem consists of an amusing request for a horse made by Vulcanius to cardinal Mendoza. Therefore, the poem must precede the latter's death on 28 November 1566. It confirms that Vulcanius' work on St Cyril required him to travel; this allows one to surmise that not all the manuscripts of this Church Father acquired by cardinal Mendoza belong to his Italian period.[13] The poem

---

12   The unmetrical epigraph criticised by Vulcanius is in *El recebimiento* (see above, n. 9), fol. Br.

13   According to Pérez Martín, "El helenismo" (see above n. 2), 90, n. 117, the manuscript used by Vulcanius to translate St Cyril's *De adoratione in spiritu* has not survived.

BONAVENTURA VULCANIUS IN SPAIN: SOME POEMS 265

may indicate a journey from Arcos (Burgos) to Toledo in search of a new copy to complete the Cyril collection.

3.4

Ad Burgenses ἀναρχίας
ἐκκλησιαστικῆς studiosos

Graecia dum Paridis caecos ultura furores
  Ingenti peteret Pergama vasta manu,
Tenta fuit dudum fatis iraque deorum
  Pestifera Graecos depopulante lue.
At vero ignari quae tantos ferre tumultus   5
  Posset, et iratos culpa tenere deos,
Calchantem responsa petunt, qui protinus illis
  Tristibus ex adytis talia dicta refert.
Chrysidis exposcit violati Phoebus honorem
  Nec nisi pacato est vate paranda salus.   10
Credidit extemplo male relligiosa vetustas
  Pacatoque fuit reddita vate salus.
Sit mihi fas etiam clero populoque labanti
  Grassantis causas explicuisse mali.
Quis non has poenas contemti praesulis ergo   15
  Aque Deo mitti vindice flagra videt?
Incipite, heu, miseri pastorem agnoscere vestrum,
  Haec pietas vobis causa salutis erit.

copies: Vul. 97 fol. 19v (L); Vul. 103 II fol. 91r (M)
Tit.: In Burgensem clerum Anarchiae studiosum, grassante pestem **M**
4 Graecos **L** : populum **M** 5 at—ignari **L** : ignarique homines **M** 7 protinus illis **L** : fretus Achille **M** 8 tristibus—adytis **L** : intrepidus Graecis **M** 9 violati **L** : violatum **M** | Phoebus **M** : Phebus **L** 10 pacato **L** : placato **M** 11 extemplo male **L** : oraclo cito **M** 12 pacatoque **L** : placatoque **M** | reddita vate **L** : Chryside parta **M** 15 contemti **L** : contempti **M** 16 mitti **L** : immitti **M**

The situation presented in this poem is a plague at Burgos, which the author compares to the one which devastated the Greeks at Troy; in doing so, he attributes the cause of both to disobedience to the will of God. The poem reflects the terrible plague which ravaged the city of Burgos in 1565 and is estimated to

266   GARCÍA PINILLA

have killed 40% of the population.[14] The reference to the disobedience of the Burgos priests could be related to the cardinal's efforts to introduce the decrees of the Council of Trent and the canons' resistance to a canonical visit—which indeed could not be carried out until 1566.[15] On 18 July 1565 the cardinal signed a four-month concord with the canons, which provides the date *ante quem* for the poem.

> 3.5
> Quisquis es a claris ducens maioribus ortum
>   visque tuum a prima discere stirpe genus,
> his adytis responsa pete et contentus abibis
>   et faciet votis sat liber iste tuis.
> Nam quis auus proauusque et sanguinis ultimus auctor   5
>   Non melius vates Delphicus expediat.
>   B. Vulcanius Brugensis

copies: Biblioteca General de la Universidad de Zaragoza, MS 98; Biblioteca Nacional Argentina en Buenos Aires, MS FD 702, *explicit*; Arquivo Nacional da Torre do Tombo (Lisboa), Livraria, MS 632, *explicit*; Biblioteca del Real Monasterio del Escorial MS h-ii-21, fol. 377r; BNE, MS 11497, *explicit*; Barcelona, Biblioteca de Catalunya, MS 531 *explicit*.
ed.: *Anuario del Cuerpo facultativo de archiveros, bibliotecarios y anticuarios* 2 (1882), 207; Gutiérrez Cabezón, "Algunas poesías latinas de Páez de Castro," *La Ciudad de Dios* 94 (1913), 203.

This is the only one of the eleven selected poems which is not found in the Leiden manuscripts. These six lines are located at the end of some manuscript copies of *Libro delos linajes de España*, a Castilian translation from the Portuguese original of don Pedro Alfonso of Portugal, count of Barcelos. Both the translation and the preserved manuscripts are related to the circles of the cardinal of Burgos and the historian Juan Páez de Castro, so they precede the former's death.[16] It is not surprising that Vulcanius had access to these

---

14   See José Manuel López Gómez and Esther Pardiñas de Juana, "Un testimonio inédito sobre la epidemia de peste de 1565 en Burgos," *Boletín de la Institución Fernán Gónzález* 221 (2000), 227–50.

15   See Nicolás López Martínez, "El cardenal Mendoza y la Reforma tridentina en Burgos," *Hispania Sacra* 31 (1963), 61–137, there 83–8.

16   The cardinal obtained a copy of the work through Pedro Jerónimo de Aponte. This can be inferred from a note found in MS C-143 de la Real Academia de la Historia, fol. 1r: "Historia de los linages de España, que escribió el conde D. P., hijo de D. Dionís, Rey de Portugal. Sacada de dos originales de un tenor de mano de Ambrosio de Morales y

BONAVENTURA VULCANIUS IN SPAIN: SOME POEMS

documents as the cardinal's librarian. In addition, it is well known that one manuscript of this work (the one held in Lisbon, Arquivo Nacional da Torre do Tombo; Livraria, ms. 632) belonged to don Diego of Castilla, who was in fact dean of the cathedral of Toledo at the time that Vulcanius moved to the city and entered the service of the deceased cardinal's brother, Fernando de Mendoza. This poem is linked to another facet of Vulcanius' activity in the cardinal's service: that of copyist.

3.6
Ad D. Fontium medicum Toletanum aegrotans

> Dum Toletanam celebris per urbem
> Tecta magnatum medicus frequentas,
> An piget, Fonti, tenuis subire
>   Limen amici,
> Cui latens aegros populatur artus   5
> Aestus, et dulci male grata somno
> Vexat, indicitque famem sitimque
>   Improba tussis?
> Non tibi maius precium salutis
> Decolor persoluat Arabs vel Indus,   10
> Quam tuas saeclis celebrans futuris
>   Carmine laudes.
> Ergo ades, quaque es potis arte cura
> Oro per Musas, ita te vocantem
> Audiat Phoebus, faueatque votis   15
>   Dexter Apollo.

copies: Vul. 97 fol. 23v (L); Vul. 103 11 fol. 92r (M)
Tit.: Ad doctorem medicum De la fuente. aliter Fontius **L**
11 saeclis **L** : seclis **M**

Rodrigo de la Fuente, physician and professor at the University of Toledo, enjoyed extraordinary prestige, to the point of being painted by El Greco and mentioned by Cervantes.[17] Here Vulcanius describes him as a busy doctor

---

Jerónimo de Zurita, coronistas de Castilla y Aragón, que copiaron del traslado que, por orden de D. Francisco de Mendoça y Bobadilla, cardenal de Burgos, trajo Pedro Jéronimo de Aponte, receptor de Granada, que la sacó del original que está en Lisboa, en la recámara del rey de Portugal" (modernised spelling).

17 On him, see David Martín López, *Orígenes y evolución de la Universidad de Toledo (1485–1625)* (Toledo, 2014), 206–9.

visiting the wealthiest families' homes, and asks him to come to his sick-bed, where he lies weakened by illness. The mutual confidence depicted in the poem suggests that it was composed after 1566, when Vulcanius was settled in Toledo. It is also evidence of Vulcanius' substantial involvement in Toledo's academic and humanistic circles, of which Dr de la Fuente was a member.

3.7

De Vulcano et Vulcanio:
de incendio bibliothecae Car[lis] Fr. a Mendoza, Car[lis] Episcopi Burgensis

Ardens Vulcanus per pinea tecta furebat,
   Tecta quibus Latium et Graecia tota latet.
Diuitiae, Mendoza, tuae, quem Hispania luget
   Ereptum terris purpureique Patres.
Obstitit at Phoebi Vulcanius ictus amore   5
   Et vetuit flammae longius ire minas.
Vulcanus contra: "Quis mi Vulcanius obstat
   Ausus, et irato est obuius ire deo?"
Dixit et immittens piceum in praecordia fumum,
   "I modo et haec", inquit, "tu tibi σῶστρα refer."   10
Ast ego Tardipedi "Parua haec dispendia", dixi,
   "Pieridum saluae sint modo diuitiae."

copies: Vul. 97 fol. 19r (L); Vul. 103 II fol. 93r (M)
Tit.: In eiusdem bibliothecam ab incendio abs se seruatam, post Car[lis] obitum **M**
7 obstat **L** *p. corr.* **M** : inquit **M**

This poem refers to a fire that had threatened the cardinal's library (an incident not documented in other sources) sometime after his death. Hence the poem was written after 28 November 1566 and before Vulcanius' departure from Spain. It could have been composed in Arcos or, alternatively, after the library (along with Vulcanius) had moved to Toledo and into the keeping of archdeacon Fernando de Mendoza, brother of the deceased. The poem seems to have been written close to the cardinal's death; we also know from Vulcanius himself that one part of the library was for sale in Toledo in 1569.[18]

---

18   See Tournoy, "A Life-long Dream" (see above, n. 3), 190.

BONAVENTURA VULCANIUS IN SPAIN: SOME POEMS   269

3.8 and 3.9
    In SS. IVSTVM ET PASTOREM
      reduces Complutum

Complutum nobis patria et commune sepulchrum
    Pro Christi caesis relligione fuit.
Sed ne nos raperent vastantes omnia Mauri,
    Id metuens Oscam nos pia turba tulit.
Atque octingentos illic requieuimus annos   5
    Molliter, exilii sed graue pressit onus.
Donec pacata Hesperia Maurisque repulsis
    Barbarico tellus libera facta metu est.
Tum veteres dedit in sedes remeare Philippus,
    Pergrato nobis et patriae officio.   10
Tu reduces ergo tandem ede, patria, diuos
    Et regi grates, nos ut habemus, habe.

copies: Vul. 103 II fol. 91v

      De iisdem

Dum sacros IVSTO pueri senesque
Et tibi, PASTOR, celebramus hymnos
Longa post tandem patriae Henareae
    Secla reductis
Est meo merces studio tributus   5
Annulus fuluo fabrefactus auro,
Quem super pulchrae viridans Diones
    Ridet ocellus.
Hunc ego donec super est futurum
Quidquid est vitae digitis fouebo,   10
Rite Complutum geminosque Diuos
    Carmine dicens.

copies: Vul. 103 II fol. 91v
3 Henareae *p. corr.* : atque amicis *a. corr.* 11 Complutum ... Diuos *p. corr.* :
complutum ... diuos *a. corr.*

These two poems, as is evident from their headings, belong to the same context.
The first, in elegiac distiches, is put in the mouth of the child martyrs Justus
and Pastor, having been composed on the solemn occasion of the reception

of their relics in Alcala de Henares, on 7 March 1568.[19] Ambrosio de Morales published a work in which he described, among other things, the ceremonies which took place then.[20] From this work we know that the church of Alcala organised a literary contest with various categories, offering several prizes for each. Vulcanius' second poem of the two reveals that the first triumphed in one of the categories, for which the author was awarded a ring ("merces", v. 5). And in fact, according to Ambrosio de Morales, the first prize in lyric poetry was a gold ring set with an emerald.[21] Although both poems relate to the same occasion, there was a margin of time separating them in which the jury made its decision. One is led to wonder whether the ring which Vulcanius is wearing in the first known portrait of him, a 1596 engraving, is in fact that prize;[22] if it is, it would appear that the pride he expressed in 1568 was still alive a quarter of a century later.

3.10

ISABELLAE VALESIAE Hisp. reg. κενοτάφιον Toleti

Hospes qui tumuli molem miraris inanis
    Siste, et Reginae tristia fata lege.
Regibus orta sacris, et magno nupta Philippo
    Connubio fregi maxima bella meo.
Magnanimosque inter reges noua foedera sanxi,   5
    Quam vellem nullo dissoluënda die.
Excepit summo me tota Hispania plausu
    Atque hyemes fouit Mantua laeta nouem.
Vixi cara meis et dulci cara marito
    Cui duo donaui pignora grata tori. 10
Orbamque Hesperiam germano haerede beassem
    Ni Lucina suam saeua negasset opem.
Sic ego cum foetu sum ruda morte perempta
    Cum mihi lustra minus quinque peracta forent.

---

19   Lola González, "Los Santos mártires Justo y Pastor. Transmisión y praxis cultural en España en la segunda mitad del siglo XVI (1568)," *Criticón* 101 (2008), 55–67, there 55–8.

20   Ambrosio de Morales, *La vida, el martyrio, la inuencion, las grandezas y las translaciones de los gloriosos niños martyres san Iusto y Pastor: y el solemne triumpho con que fueron recebidas sus santas reliquias en Alcala de Henares* (Alcalá de Henares, 1568).

21   Ibid. 67v: "Ille igitur quem [...] maiori cum lepore et venustate decantasse censuerint iudices, anulo ex auro purissimo cum smaragdo orientalis Indiae donabitur".

22   It is reproduced in Kasper van Ommen, "The portraits of Bonaventura Vulcanius," in Cazes, *Bonaventura Vulcanius* (see above, n. 1), 103–19, there 115.

BONAVENTURA VULCANIUS IN SPAIN: SOME POEMS

I nunc et sceptris vel firmae fide iuuentae   15
    Quisquis es et Parcas parcere nosse puta.

Obiit Mantuae Carpetanorum Ann. M.D.LXVIII 4 Non. Oct.
Aetatis suae anno xxiii

B. V.

copies: Vul. 97 fol. 18v (L); Vul. 103 II fol. 92v (M)
Tit.: EPIPHAPHIUM ISABELLAE Valesiae Reginae Hisp. L | *a.* κενοτάφιον
del. tumulus **M**
8 hyemes **M** : hiemes L   13 perempta L : peremta **M**   16 nosse L : posse
M   19 B. V. *om.* **M**

The announcement of the death of the queen, Elizabeth of Valois, reached
Toledo on 8 October 1568, but the quarrel between the city authorities and the
cathedral chapter made it difficult to organise the funeral rites.[23] These were
delayed a month and a half, finally being celebrated in the cathedral between
21 and 23 November. According to some extant accounts, the catafalque raised
for the occasion exceeded anything previously known, "into whose composition and decoration the plastic arts, the fondness for symbolic-allegorical expression, and the fashion for the epigraphic poured their best inventiveness".[24]
This poem, which represents a conversation between the deceased queen and
a visitor astounded by the catafalque, must have formed part of that third
group of inventions. There is some evidence that Vulcanius maintained good
relations with Toledo's ecclesiastical circles, and that he was appreciated to
the point of being assigned the task of composing some verses for the solemn
funeral rites.

3.11

Toleti An. 1569 prid. Caterinae.
In Leonem Grammaticum Hispanum

Hebraico iactas, Leo, te callere magister
    Primaque te linguae nosse elementa negas.
Quid superest nisi te linguam cum lacte bibisse?
    Haec materna tibi et lingua paterna fuit.

---

23   Jerónimo López de Ayala, *Toledo en el siglo XVI después del vencimiento de las comuni-
      dades* (Madrid, 1901), 28–9 and 117.
24   Ibid., 29.

copies: Vul. 97 fol. 19r (L); Vul. 103 11 fol. 93v (M)
Tit.: In LEONEM quendam Hisp. **M**
1 Hebraico **M** : Hebraice L

This short epigram is the only one of these eleven compositions to which the author himself gave an exact date: the day before Saint Catherine's Day, 24 November 1569. St Catherine was the patron saint of the university of Toledo, from which we understand that the setting of the poem is a festive one. This composition contains a common anti-Semitic trope, attributing a *converso* lineage to the grammarian León in order to denigrate him. However, this in itself is not enough to attribute an anti-Semitic character to Vulcanius; a previous poem reveals his high esteem for Dr Rodrigo de la Fuente, a well-known *converso*. The information we have does not allow us to determine to whom the poem was addressed: neither friar Luis de León (who was a professor at that time) nor León de Castro (who was in fact a Hellenist) seem to be suitable candidates.

4   Conclusion

From editing and studying these eleven selected poems, we have gathered further information about Vulcanius' eleven-year sojourn in Spain. It appears that he travelled with Philip 11's court not only on the journey into Spain, but all the way to Toledo, where he established his first contacts with humanist circles. His appointment by the cardinal of Burgos to work on St Cyril involved him in a number of journeys. As the cardinal's secretary, he witnessed the tensions between his master and the cathedral chapter, during which time there was a terrible plague in Burgos. He served not only as librarian and secretary of the episcopal residence in Arcos de la Llana, near Burgos, but he occasionally worked as a copyist (in Greek, Latin or Spanish) for the cardinal and the historian Juan Páez de Castro, with whom he enjoyed a close relationship until Castro's death in 1571. After the cardinal's demise, Vulcanius prevented a major fire in his library, which would have caused tremendous losses for classical studies. He won a poetry contest organised in Alcala de Henares in 1568. Finally, because of his prestige as a poet, his verses, composed perhaps on commission, were included on Elizabeth of Valois' catafalque in the cathedral of Toledo.[25]

University of Castilla-La Mancha (Toledo, Spain)

---

25   I am indebted to Jonathan L. Nelson for the English version of this paper.

CHAPTER 19

La versión latina del tratado aristotélico *De sensu* (*Parva naturalia*) de Sepúlveda

Paraskevi Gatsioufa

Abstract

La traducción latina de los *Parva Naturalia* realizada por Juan Ginés de Sepúlveda conoció dos ediciones, la primera en Bolonia en 1522, y la segunda, una década más tarde, en París. En otras versiones latinas humanísticas de dicha obra aristotélica no se incluye el tratado *De sensu*; pero para Sepúlveda formaba parte integrante de la colección aristotélica. Para realizar su traducción, de poco le sirvieron las versiones medievales ya existentes. Su pretensión al emprender esta nueva traducción fue, en efecto, la de superar esas antiguas versiones, tanto desde el punto de vista de la expresión linguística, como desde el punto de vista del estado del texto a partir del cual se hace la traducción. En este sentido, el estudio detallado y la comparación del texto latino con los originales griegos permiten determinar los fundamentos griegos de los que Sepúlveda se valió para hacer su traducción del opúsculo *De sensu*. Evidentemente la edición Aldina es el primer texto griego de referencia sobre el que Sepúlveda realizó su versión, pero la redacción de ciertos pasajes en la traducción del humanista cordobés permite poner en relación esta traducción con la segunda familia de códices griegos que transmiten la obra, y sobre todo con el manuscrito Vat. gr. 253 y su descendencia.

Keywords

Reception of Aristotle – *De sensu* – Juan Ginés de Sepúlveda – Neo-Latin translations – Textual transmission

Las versiones latinas de las obras de Aristóteles son un capítulo de suma importancia dentro de la literatura latina humanística y también en relación con la historia de la transmisión del texto griego aristotélico. Entre las traducciones realizadas por Juan Ginés de Sepúlveda hay que situar la versión del opúsculo *De sensu* (Περὶ αἰσθήσεως καὶ αἰσθητῶν), una obra esencial dentro del corpus de los *Parva Naturalia*. En las páginas que siguen me centraré

© KONINKLIJKE BRILL NV, LEIDEN, 2020 | DOI:10.1163/9789004427105_020

en el estudio de sus características y en el de su relación genealógica con los manuscritos griegos que transmiten la obra. La identificación del modelo griego sobre el que Sepúlveda realizó su traducción es una tarea de extraordinaria dificultad, no solo porque en la versión latina es difícil reconocer el término original griego que subyace a ella, sobre todo si la traducción no sigue el procedimiento del *verbum de verbo*, sino también y sobre todo porque es probable que use más de un modelo para su traducción. Además, ni que decir tiene que dicho trabajo requiere la existencia previa de un *stemma codicum* para la obra en cuestión. En mi opinión, un *stemma* es completo cuando se integran en él los comentarios, en este caso bizantinos, realizados por los comentaristas de Aristóteles, y también las traducciones medievales y renacentistas. Solo entonces es posible percibir de forma clara y precisa la historia de la transmisión manuscrita de una obra, la historia de su tradición.

Sobre las traducciones medievales del *De sensu* he publicado un trabajo en el que se comprueba que la *vetus translatio* depende de los códices griegos que en el *stemma* por mí establecido pertenecen a la primera familia.[1] En ella se sitúan entre otros manuscritos más jóvenes, el *vetustissimus* Par. gr. 1853 y el Vat. gr. 261. Esa traducción es muy fiel al texto griego, está hecha palabra por palabra, y tuvo como modelo un manuscrito cercano al Par. suppl. gr. 314. Sobre la *translatio nova* de Moerbeke en breve tendré resultados.

Sepúlveda aristotélico

Sobre la formación filosófica de Sepúlveda y su actividad traductora en Italia es sabido que en la Universidad de Alcalá de Henares tuvo sus primeros contactos con la filosofía. En dicha universidad cursó durante tres años las materias correspondientes al estudio de filosofía (Súmulas, Lógica y Física), de la mano de Sancho Carranza de Miranda, un notable teólogo y filósofo de su tiempo. Tras su estancia en Alcalá, Sepúlveda pasó a Bolonia, donde ocupó la plaza de becario que había quedado vacante en el Colegio de San Clemente, recomendado por el Cardenal Cisneros. En la ciudad italiana Sepúlveda se entregó al estudio de la filosofía bajo el magisterio de Pietro Pomponazzi, seguidor de Aristóteles, que le imbuye su pasión por la obra del Estagirita, pero por la obra original griega, no la vertida al latín en la Edad Media. Sepúlveda logró altas cotas en su conocimiento del latín y del griego, y también de la filosofía aristotélica, como

---

1 Paraskevi Gatsioufa, "Observaciones críticas sobre las traducciones latinas de *Parva naturalia*," en *Miscellanea Latina*, ed. María Teresa Muñoz García de Iturrospe y Leticia Carrasco Reija (Madrid, 2015), 77–84.

demuestra el hecho de que desde pronta edad su nombre sonó como especialista en Aristóteles entre los círculos humanísticos italianos.[2]

En total pasó ocho años en Bolonia, hasta 1523. Para esa fecha ya habían salido de las prensas varias traducciones suyas, como *Parva naturalia* y *De ortu et interitu* (*De generatione et corruptione*); además preparaba la traducción de otras tres obras: *Meteorologica, De mundo ad Alexandrum* y el *Comentario a la Metafísica* de Alejandro de Afrodisíade.

Su primera traducción aristotélica en ver la luz fue, por tanto, la versión latina del grupo de opúsculos que se reúnen bajo la denominación de *Parva Naturalia*, aunque Sepúlveda incluyó en esa traducción otros tratados que no pertenecen a los tratados bio-psicológicos del Estagirita bajo ese mismo nombre. No fue posible a los editores de la Real Academia de la Historia, que hicieron una edición de los *opera omnia* de Sepúlveda a finales del siglo XVIII, localizar un ejemplar de dicha traducción. Fue el Conde de Aranda, embajador de Carlos III en Francia, quien descubrió un ejemplar en la Biblioteca Real de París y envió a los editores académicos una descripción detallada del mismo. Su edición príncipe data de 1522, y conoció una segunda edición en París, una década más tarde.[3]

En los primeros folios del volumen (2–4) aparece una carta dedicatoria a Julio de Medici, en la que entre otros aspectos expone los presupuestos teóricos y revela el método que ha seguido al elaborar su traducción. En esa carta Sepúlveda presenta una breve historia de las traducciones latinas de Aristóteles; así, divide en tres fases ese proceso histórico: la primera, anterior a Juan Argirópulo, se caracteriza por seguir el método de traducción denominado *verbum de verbo*, de donde se deducen los numerosos errores que se hallan en esas traducciones; la segunda etapa significó un notable avance gracias a la figura de Argirópulo; y, por último, la tercera, representada por él mismo, tiene como objetivo seguir la labor inacabada del sabio bizantino. Sepúlveda resume los criterios que siguió en el siguiente párrafo:

---

2 Elena Rodríguez Peregrina, "Juan Ginés de Sepúlveda y sus traducciones comentadas de los filósofos griegos," *Revista de Filología Latina* 4 (1984), 235–46.

3 Como el objetivo del trabajo es identificar el modelo griego en que se basó Sepúlveda para su traducción de este tratado, interesa más la primera edición (Bolonia, 1522), pues en ella se encontrarán las lecturas más auténticas: *Libri Aristotelis quos vulgo latini parvos naturales appellant e graeco in latinum sermonem conversi Ioanne Genesio de Sepulveda Cordubensi interprete; Impressum fuit hoc opus per me Hieronymum de Benedictis Bononiae, Anno domini M.DXXII. Die vero XV maii.* En la segunda edición es muy probable que se hayan introducido nuevas lecturas.

Ego vero quantum in me fuit dedi operam, ut latinitas aures tuas quam minime offenderet. Et in vertendis hoc tenui temperamentum, ut non verbum verbo redderem, moleste sedula et iam olim a doctis viris explosa fidelitate, nec rursus ut paraphrastis more dilatarem nimis compressa, et justo difusiora resecarem, sed Aristotelis vestigiis insistens, quae unum simplicemque sensum habere visa sunt, haec verborum non admodum sollicitus latine et ornate quam maxime possem enunciarem, lubrica vero et ancipitia loca quae in diversos sensus trahi possent ita verti, ut latina oratio eandem multiplicitatem integram ingeniis reservaret. Haec quidem certe volui, an praestiterim aliorum sit judicium. Illud certe testari possum, multum me in hoc opere laboris exhausisse, quippe ad communes interpretum difficultates illa mihi non parva accessit, quod salebrosa via nec ea brevis sine duce peragenda fuit, qui priorum interpretum labore idcirco iuvari non potui [...]. Qua ratione ductus dificillima quaedam loca quae nulla fideli interpretatione satis poterant expediri appositis scholiis explicare tentavi, quibus adiuta interpretatio diligentem et ingeniosum lectorem commentariorum necessitate magna ex parte, ut spero, levabit.

Yo, en la medida de mis posibilidades, he puesto todo mi empeño en que mi estilo latino perturbara lo menos posible tus oídos; y a la hora de traducir he seguido un procedimiento moderado, no trasladar palabra por palabra, en aras de una fidelidad excesivamente celosa y reprobada ya por los eruditos, pero tampoco alargar según la costumbre de los parafraseadores lo que es demasiado sucinto ni abreviar lo razonadamente difuso, sino, siguiendo las huellas de Aristóteles, enunciar correctamente en latín y de la forma más bella que pudiera aquello que parece tener un sentido unívoco, sin preocuparme en exceso por las palabras; en cambio los pasajes difíciles y ambiguos, que pueden ser interpretados en diversos sentidos, los he traducido de tal modo que el texto latino reproduzca para los eruditos de forma íntegra esa misma multiplicidad de sentido. Este ha sido ciertamente mi propósito, si lo he conseguido otros deberán juzgarlo. Yo sin duda puedo dar fe de que he dedicado mucho esfuerzo a este trabajo, puesto que a las dificultades comunes de los traductores se ha unido en mi caso otra no pequeña, la de tener que recorrer sin guía un camino escabroso y no precisamente corto, dado que no he podido ayudarme del trabajo de anteriores traductores [...]. Llevado por este motivo he intentado aclarar, añadiendo unos escolios, aquellos pasajes dificilísimos para los que no había una traducción fiel que pudiera transmitirlos de manera suficientemente clara. La traducción apoyada sobre ellos librará al lector diligente y reflexivo en gran medida, según espero, de tener que consultar los comentarios.

Su prioridad primera es que su expresión lingüística respete la pureza impuesta por la norma latina. Por lo demás, no sigue el uso de traducir palabra por palabra, de donde se deduce que su traducción es más bien *ad sententiam*, pero sin llegar a caer en el defecto de amplificar lo que es conciso o de simplificar lo que es difuso. Su intención es siempre la de mantenerse fiel a Aristóteles y traducir por una expresión unívoca lo que es unívoco en latín, o por una expresión multívoca lo que puede resultar ambiguo en el texto aristotélico. De poca ayuda le han servido en su labor de traductor las versiones anteriores de esa misma obra, haciendo referencia, sin duda, a las traducciones medievales. En aquellos pasajes en que el pasaje es difícil de interpretar, unas notas al margen intentarán aclarar el sentido del texto. Por su parte, los folios 5 y 6 contienen otra epístola dedicatoria, dirigida a Alberto Pio, otro de sus protectores.

En la versión de Sepúlveda los opúsculos que integran la colección de *Parva naturalia* son *De incessu animalium*, *De sensu et sensibilibus*, *De memoria et meminisse* (*reminiscentia*), *De somno et vigilia*, *De insomniis*, *De divinatione per somnum*, *De motu animalium*, *De longitudine et brevitate vitae*, *De iuventa et senecta* (*juventute et senectute*), *vita et morte ac de spiratione*, *De spiratione* (*respiratione*).

Es importante señalar que de estas obras *De incessu animalium* y *De motu animalium* no pertenecen propiamente al corpus de *Parva Naturalia*. Pero tampoco sorprende que aquí aparezcan junto a los tratados de *Parva Naturalia*, porque en muchos de los testimonios griegos se transmiten junto a ellos. Y no es sorprendente que la traducción de Sepúlveda de *De generatione et corruptione* se publique al mismo tiempo, ni que luego sigan los *Meteorologica* y el *Commentario* de Alejandro de Afrodísíade a la *Metafísica* de Aristóteles. Exactamente así se transmiten en buena parte de los códices griegos.

En relación a la declaración de principios que Sepúlveda hace de su método de traductor, de la lectura de su traducción resulta evidente que, a pesar de lo que él mismo dice, sí hace ampliaciones, y lo más importante, cambia la sintaxis del original griego, uniendo frases cortas en un periodo más largo, e invirtiendo el orden de sus miembros, en la creencia de que así transmite mejor el sentido. En mi opinión, su traducción es 'libre' en la mayoría de los casos. Es cierto que no tiene nada en común al menos con la *vetus translatio*. En definitiva, se trata de una traducción que alcanza gran calidad, aunque en algún que otro pasaje resulte poco fiel al original. Por lo demás, no veo que la traducción de Sepúlveda incorpore en su primera edición elementos de ningún comentario bizantino, como insinúa Alejandro Coroleu para la segunda edición.[4] Al contrario de la costumbre de los comentaristas, Sepúlveda se mantiene fiel al texto aristotélico.

De sensu en la traducción de Sepúlveda

Sepúlveda leyó con toda seguridad el texto de Aristóteles a partir de la edición de Aldo Manuzio publicada en Venecia entre 1495 y 1498.[5] Pero, para realizar su traducción, también empleó al menos un manuscrito, como se verá a continuación.

Para identificar el modelo sobre el que se hace una traducción o una copia hay que basarse en los errores, las transposiciones, las omisiones, las adiciones, el cambio de vocabulario, el uso de glosas, etc. Pero, en el caso particular de las traducciones latinas (que no suelen ser absolutamente literales), las transposiciones no tienen valor en la mayoría de los casos para identificar el modelo, y con mucha frecuencia tampoco las adiciones.

Según mis colaciones, la traducción de Sepúlveda tiene estrecha relación con el texto griego de la edición aldina y con una subfamilia de la segunda familia (*familia* β) del *stemma codicum* por mí elaborado, identificada con la sigla ι, y constituida por los manuscritos Ambr. gr. H 50 sup. (x), Par. gr. 2034, Marc. gr. Z. 214 (Hᵃ), y Vat. gr. 253 (L). Apógrafos de L son los manuscritos Bon. gr. 2302, Bodl. Auct. T. 3. 21, Ricc. 81, Bodl. Can. gr. 107.

En la siguiente tabla se relaciona la traducción latina con el texto griego de los manuscritos mencionados y de la aldina:[6]

---

4   Alejandro Coroleu, "La contribución de Juan Ginés de Sepúlveda a la edición de los textos de Aristóteles y de Alejandro de Afrodisias," *Humanistica Lovaniensia* 43 (1994), 231–45, en 234. En su opinión, Sepúlveda hace uso con frecuencia en sus traducciones del extenso corpus de comentaristas, griegos y latinos, sobre todo para los *Parva naturalia* y para su segunda edición revisada. Dice Coroleu que para *De memoria* y *De insomniis* Sepúlveda usó la paráfrasis de Temistio en traducción latina, y no en el texto griego; por lo que respecta a *De sensu*, lanza la hipótesis de que podría haber consultado el comentario de Alejandro de Afrodisíade editado en la imprenta aldina en 1527. Pero eso solo puede ser válido, como él mismo advierte, para la edición corregida de 1532, no para la edición príncipe de 1522.

5   *Aristotelis Opera omnia* (Venetiis, 1495–98), vol. 3, fol. 247r–259v.

6   El asterisco señala aquellos pasajes en los que hay desviaciones, es decir, en los que no coincide la traducción latina con la subfamilia ι (o incluso con la segunda familia), o con la edición aldina, o con ambas. Con *cett.* se entiende la lectura 'correcta' y más extendida, la de la vulgata. Por supuesto, existen muchas variantes transmitidas por varios testimonios que no se consideran aquí.

LA VERSIÓN LATINA DEL TRATADO ARISTOTÉLICO *DE SENSU* DE SEPÚLVEDA 279

436a1	postquam ... dissertum iam est : ἐπεὶ ... διώρισται πρότερον Aldina *familia* β : ἐπεὶ ... διώρισται *cett.*
436a14	quattuor omnino sunt coniugationes : τέσσαρες οὖσαι συζυγίαι τὸν ἀριθμὸν μόναι Aldina ι : τέσσαρες οὖσαι συζυγίαι τὸν ἀριθμόν *cett.*
436a17	contingant : συμβαίνουσι Aldina ι : συμβαίνει *cett.*
436b2	cuncta vero quae dicta sunt : ante τὰ λεχθέντα *add.* πάντα Aldina ι
436b9	reddita causa cui haec affectio animalibus accidat : καὶ διὰ τί συμβαίνει τοῖς ζώοις τοῦτο τὸ πάθος Aldina ι : τί ἐστι καὶ διὰ τί συμβαίνει τοῖς ζώοις τοῦτο τὸ πάθος *cett.*
436b10	diximus : εἴρηται Aldina ι : εἴρηται πρότερον *cett.*
436b12	propia vero : ἰδίᾳ δέ *familia* β : ἰδίᾳ δ' ἤδη *cett.*
436b14	in libro de anima : ἐν τῷ περὶ ψυχῆς Aldina ι : ἐν τοῖς περὶ ψυχῆς *cett.*
*436b17	nutriendi : γευστικοῦ μορίου Aldina ι : θρεπτικοῦ μορίου *cett.*
437a9	morum, statum, numerum : κίνησιν, στάσιν, ἀριθμόν Aldina ι : κίνησιν, ἀριθμόν *cett.*
437a24	respiendens ignis apparet : φαίνεται πῦρ ἐκλάμπον Aldina ι : φαίνεται πῦρ ἐκλάμπειν *cett.*
437a26	nam tunc quoque in tenebris fit : γίνεται γὰρ καὶ τότε ἐν σκότει Aldina *familia* β : γίνεται γὰρ καὶ τότε σκότος *cett.*
437a32	non tamen ut lumen faciant : οὐ μέντοι φῶς γε ποιεῖν Aldina *familia* β : οὐ μέντοι φῶς γε ποιεῖ *cett.*
437b8–9	duo simul et unum esse : ἅμα δύο καὶ ἓν εἶναι Aldina ι : ἅμα ἓν καὶ δύο εἶναι *cett.*
437b16	in humido : ἐν ὑγρῷ Aldina ι : ὑγρῷ *cett.*
437b21	maxime : μάλιστα Aldina ι : μᾶλλον *cett.*
*438a1	diffunditur : ἐχείατο (L Hᵃ) *vel* ἐχεύατο *familia* β : λοχάζετο Aldina *familia* α *recte*
*438a15	solidior : εὐυπυποληπτότερον Aldina *familia* β : εὐπιλητότερον *cett.*
438a19	oculus impendio lucet splendetque : τῇ λαμπρότητι ὑπερβάλλον ἐστὶ καὶ τῇ στιλπνότητι Aldina ι : τῇ ψυχρότητι ὑπερβάλλον καὶ τῇ λαμπρότητι *cett.*
438b16	quod si in his contingit : ὥστε εἴπερ ἐπὶ τούτων συμβαίνει Aldina *familia* β : ὥστ' εἴπερ τούτων τι συμβαίνει *cett.*
438b21	actu : ἐνεργείᾳ *om.* L : *non om.* Aldina Ricc. Can.
438b23	quare necesse est sensus hoc fit quod prius erat potentia : ὥσθ' ὑπάρχειν ἀναγκαῖον αὐτὴν ὃ δυνάμει πρότερον Aldina ι : ὥσθ' ὑπάρχειν ἀνάγκη αὐτὴν (*vel* αὕτη) δυνάμει πρότερον *cett.*

439a16	in volumine de anima : ἐν τῷ περὶ ψυχῆς Aldina ι : ἐν τοῖς περὶ ψυχῆς cett.
439a23	communis : καινή L : κοινή Aldina Auct. Ricc. Can.
*439a28	extremum esse constat : εἴη παντὶ δῆλον Aldina ι : εἴη ἄν τι δῆλον cett.
439b8	corporibus inest : ἐνυπάρχει τοῖς σώμασιν Aldina ι : ὑπάρχει ἐν τοῖς σώμασιν cett.
440a17	omnium rerum : ἁπάντων Aldina ι : πάντως cett.
440a19–20	quam tactu atque defluxibus : ἢ ἁφῇ καὶ ταῖς ἀπορροίαις Aldina familia β : ἁφῇ καὶ μὴ ταῖς ἀπορροίαις cett.
440a28	distantia : διαστήματος Aldina ι : ἀποστήματος cett.
440b3	in libro de mistione : ἐν τῷ περὶ μίξεως Aldina ι : ἐν τοῖς περὶ μίξεως cett.
440b12	hoc maxime fieri : τοῦτο μάλιστα γίγνεσθαι Aldina ι : τοῦτο γίγνεσθαι cett.
*440b13–14	quo intelligitur necessarium esse : ἀλλὰ τὶς ἀνάγκη ... δῆλον Aldina ι : ἀλλ᾽ ὅτι ἀνάγκη ... δῆλον cett.
440b23	ac de mistis quidem alias est a nobis disputatum : καὶ περὶ μὲν τῶν μιγνυμένων καὶ ἐν ἄλλοις διώρισται Aldina ι : καὶ περὶ τῶν μιγνυμένων cett.
*441a1	odoratum : τὴν αἴσθησιν ταύτην Aldina ι : τὴν ὄσφρησιν cett.
441a14–15	et arescentes tempore ex dulcibus fieri austeros : καὶ ἐξικμαζομένους διὰ τὸν χρόνον αὐστηροὺς ἐκ γλυκέων Aldina Auct. Ricc. Can. : καὶ ἐξικμαζομένους δὲ καὶ κειμένους (vel κινουμένους) διὰ τὸν χρόνον αὐστηροὺς ἐκ γλυκέων cett.
441a30	qui fructibus insunt : ἐν τῷ περικαρπίῳ ι : ἐν τοῖς περικαρπίοις Aldina Bon. Auct. cett.
441b4	idcirco : διό Aldina familia β : καί cett.
441b5	post χυμόν add. eadem est ratio humorum, qui per alia commeant : post χυμόν add. καὶ τὰ διὰ τῶν ἄλλων (vel ἁλῶν) ὁμοίως Aldina familia β
441b6	(fontium diversitas) numerosa : πολλαί om. ι : non om. Aldina Ricc. Can.
441b14	quatenus ipsis inest repugnantia : ὑπάρχει ἐν αὐτοῖς ἐναντιότης Aldina ι : ὑπάρχει ἐναντιότης ἐν ἑκάστῳ cett.
442a3	ad librum de generatione : ἐν τῷ περὶ γενέσεως Aldina ι : ἐν τοῖς περὶ γενέσεως cett.
442a18–19	acer austerus : ὁ δὲ δριμὺς καὶ αὐστηρός Aldina ι : ὁ δὲ αὐστηρὸς καὶ δριμύς cett.
442a21	utrorumque : ἀμφοτέρως Aldina Ricc. Can. : ἀμφοτέρων cett. : om. ι

LA VERSIÓN LATINA DEL TRATADO ARISTOTÉLICO *DE SENSU* DE SEPÚLVEDA 281

442b6	acutum obtussumque : τὸ ὀξὺ ἢ τὸ ἀμβλύ ι : τὸ ὀξὺ καὶ τὸ ἀμβλύ Aldina Ricc. Can. *cett.*
442b17	et ceterarum figuratum : *ante* σχημάτων *add.* ἄλλων Aldina *familia* β
442b19	dulce pugnat cum amaro : τὸ γλυκὺ τῷ πικρῷ Aldina ι : τῷ γλυκεῖ τὸ πικρόν *cett.*
442b23–24	sed de sapore et gustabili : καὶ περὶ μὲν τοῦ χυμοῦ καὶ γευστοῦ Aldina ι : καὶ περὶ μὲν τοῦ γευστοῦ καὶ χυμοῦ *cett.*
*442b29	sapidum humidum : τὸ ἔγχυμον ὑγρόν : *om.* Aldina L Hᵃ
443a1	influere et inundare : πλυτικὸν καὶ ῥυπτικόν Aldina ι : πλυντικὸν ἢ ῥυπτικόν *cett.*
443a4	odorati : ὀσφραινόμενοι Aldina ι : ὀσφραινόμενα *cett.*
443a8	a sapido profisci : ἀπ' ἐγχύμου ἐστί Aldina *familia* β : ἅπαν χυμοῦ ἐστί *cett.*
*443a10	aer : ἀήρ *om.* Aldina *familia* β
443a26	utrumque : καὶ ἄμφω Aldina ι : ὡς ἄμφω *cett.*
443b6	iam vero si effectus ... similis est in humoribus atque in aere : ἔτι δὲ εἰ ὁμοίως ἐν τοῖς ὑγροῖς ποιεῖ καὶ ἐν τῷ ἀέρι Aldina ι : ὅτι δ' ὁμοίως ἐν τοῖς ὑγροῖς ποιεῖ καὶ ἐν τῷ ἀέρι *cett.*
443b7–8	quin odores proportine saporibus respondeant : ὅτι δεῖ ἀνάλογον εἶναι τὰς ὀσμὰς τοῖς χυμοῖς Aldina *familia* β : ἔτι δεῖ ἀνάλογον εἶναι τὰς ὀσμὰς τοῖς χυμοῖς *cett.*
443b21	nam cum sint affectio altricis potentiae : διὰ γὰρ τὸ τοῦ θρεπτικοῦ εἶναι πάθος Aldina Bon. Ricc. Can. : διὰ γὰρ τὸ τοῦ θρεπτικοῦ εἶναι πάθησιν ι : διὰ γὰρ τὸ τοῦ θρεπτικοῦ πάθη εἶναι (*vel* εἶναι πάθη) *cett.*
443b23	ne odores : οὐδ' αἱ ὀσμαί Aldina *familia* β : οὐδ' ὅσοις μή *cett.*

El manuscrito Ambr. H 50 sup. se data entre finales del siglo XII y principios del XIII.[7] Por su parte, el Par. gr. 2034 se data en el siglo XIII.[8] La traducción de Sepúlveda presenta más afinidad con el códice Marc. gr. Z. 214; se data a finales

---

7 Véase su descripción en Aemidius Martini y Dominicus Bassi, *Catalogus codicum graecorum bibliothecae Ambrosianae* (Milano, 1906), vol. 1, 525–6. Es de procedencia constantinopolitana; una datación en los últimos años del siglo XII parece más probable. Cf. Giancarlo Prato, "I manoscritti greci dei secoli XIII e XIV: Note paleografiche," en *Paleografia e codicologia greca. Atti del* II *colloquio internazionale (Berlino-Wolfenbüttel, 17–21 ottobre 1983)*, ed. Dieter Harlfinger et al. (Alessandria, 1991), vol. 1, 131–49.

8 Henri Omont, *Inventaire sommaire des manuscrits grecs de la Bibliothèque National. Seconde partie, Ancien fonds grecs: Droit – Histoire – Sciences* (Paris, 1888), 182. Entre sus poseedores se encuentran Juan Láscaris y Niccolò Ridolfi.

del siglo XIII y a comienzos del siglo XIV.[9] Pero la relación más estrecha se establece con el Vat. gr. 253 (L), manuscrito que se data en el siglo XIV y procede del círculo de Máximo Planudes en Constantinopla.[10] También he comprobado que establece una relación todavía más estrecha con los cuatro apógrafos de L, manuscritos que proceden de este a través de escalas intermedias, configurando dos grupos de dos manuscritos cada uno: del primero forman parte el Bon. gr. 2302 y el Oxon. Bodl. Auct. T. 3. 21; del segundo el Ricc. 81 y el Oxon. Bodl. Can. 107. Esa fuente perdida común, derivada de L, y de la que proceden esos dos grupos, o un manuscrito cercano a ella, también perdido, es con toda probabilidad el modelo de Sepúlveda.

El códice Bon. gr. 2302 fue copiado por el copista e impresor Zacarías Kallierges en Padua a finales del siglo XV o comienzos del siglo XVI, pero más probablemente en esta segunda fecha.[11] Por su parte el Bodl. Auct. T. 3. 21 fue copiado por dos colaboradores de Kallierges, Jorge Alexandrou y Demetrio Moschos, en la misma época y en la misma provincia del Véneto.[12] De ahí se deduce que una copia del Vat. gr. 253 debió haberse producido en Roma, y a partir de ella se sacó un apógrafo que llegó al Véneto y que sirvió como modelo para estos dos códices. Otro apógrafo de esa copia sirvió como modelo para los códices Ricc. 81 y Oxon. Bodl. Can. 107. El primero de estos se compone de dos partes: la primera fue copiada por Harmonio Ateneo en Roma en la segunda mitad del siglo XV, mientras que su segunda parte, de copista anónimo, data de los siglos XVI–XVII.[13] El último códice, el Bodl. Can. 107, es para el tratado *De sensu* un ejemplar del impreso del año 1542, mientras que el resto de tratados en él contenidos proceden de la mano de Vitantonius Gremesius.[14]

---

9   Véase su descripción en Elpidio Mioni, *Aristotelis codices graeci qui in bibliothecis Venetiis adservantur* (Padova, 1958), 130; y sobre su datación definitiva Marwan Rashed, *Die Überlieferungsgeschichte der aristotelischen Schrift De generatione et corruptione* (Wiesbaden, 2001), 245–50. Es un manuscrito en pergamino de procedencia constantinopolitana. El año de 1432 se encontraba en Italia, en la posesión de Pietro Vitali, Abad de Grottaferrata; de él pasó a Besarión. Después de la muerte de este en 1472, el manuscrito pasó a Venecia; y durante la Academia Aristotélica de Trento se encontraba en esa ciudad en los años 1545–46, como préstamo de la Biblioteca Marciana.

10 Véase su descripción en Iohannes Mercati y Pius Franchi de Cavalieri, *Codices Vaticani Graeci* (Roma, 1923), vol. 1, 330–1.

11 Véase su descripción en Paul Moraux *et al.*, *Aristoteles Graecus. Die griechischen Manuskripte des Aristoteles* (Berlin – New York, 1976) 63–4.

12 Una descripción del mismo puede verse en Henry O. Coxe, *Greek Manuscripts, Bodleian Library* (Oxford, 1969, reprinted with corrections from the edition of 1853), 7–88.

13 Moraux, *Aristoteles Graecus* (véase arriba, n. 11), 362–3.

14 Su descripción se halla en Coxe, *Greek Manuscripts* (véase arriba, n. 12), 98.

Conclusión

Aunque la traducción de Sepúlveda guarda estrecha relación de un lado con la subfamilia ι, y dentro de ella aun más estrecha con L y con sus apógrafos, y de otro con la edición aldina, sin embargo, en algunas ocasiones no comparte los errores ni de la aldina, ni de la subfamilia ι, ni de ambas fuentes, o incluso tampoco de la segunda familia, en su conjunto. Todo ello hace pensar que Sepúlveda usó también otro modelo del que provienen las correcciones y desviaciones del texto, aunque es tarea difícil, si no imposible, identificarlo, dado que las lecturas correctas puede haberlas tomado de un manuscrito de cualquier otra familia.

En mi opinión, Sepúlveda incorpora las correcciones, tomándolas no de un manuscrito perteneciente, por ejemplo, a la primera familia, sino de ese manuscrito perdido, descendiente de L y del que dependen sus cuatro apógrafos. Se trata, en efecto, de una fuente perdida, en la que también se producen correcciones de toda la segunda familia, de la subfamilia ι y de L. De no ser así, entrarían en la traducción de Sepúlveda errores procedentes de esa otra familia, así como rasgos característicos de ella. De hecho, en las copias de L se puede observar que muchos pasajes están libres de errores propios de la segunda familia y de la subfamilia ι, y de su modelo L. Por todo ello, estoy convencida que esa es la fuente que empleó Sepúlveda, la fuente común de los cuatro apógrafos de L. No es de extrañar que entre estos se encuentre un manuscrito bononiense; hay que recordar que Sepúlveda se encontraba en Bolonia, cuando realizó su traducción, y allí debió conocer esta rama de la tradición manuscrita.

Universidad de Salamanca

CHAPTER 20

The Practicing Poet: Petrarch, Dedalus, and the Dynamics of Poetic Creativity in the *Bucolicum carmen*

Donald Gilman

Abstract

Through the mythological figure of Dedalus, Petrarch delineates a process of poetic imitation. In complementing theorizations in his *Collatio laureationis* and letters, he presents in *Bucolicum carmen* IV the picture of a practicing poet who conveys divine insight through intelligible poetic form. As inventor-architect and, according to medieval mythographers, as a craftsman endowed with wisdom, Dedalus employs an *ingenium* or divinely instilled natural talent that he applies, through study and labor, to artistic creativity. Dedalus is neither an inspired poet-*vates* who unconsciously transmits divine message nor a versifier who slavishly replicates conventional thought in poetic form. Rather, Petrarch sees Dedalus in terms of Horatian poetics that combines the uses of divinely endowed natural talent and acquired technique. Theory, though, is not always consistent with practice, for the aspiring poets in the third and tenth eclogues struggle to attain perfection. The reach often exceeds the grasp.

Keywords

Francesco Petrarca – *Bucolicum carmen* – Neo-Latin pastoral poetry – reception of Horace – medieval mythography

As a practicing poet, Petrarch recorded the struggles and strains of poetic creativity. Throughout his writings he details a process that requires natural talent and technical skill. In his *Collatio laureationis* (or *Coronation Oration*) and in his letters, he sees the practicing poet sharing qualities of the inspired poet-seer who conveys divine insight but, because of human limitations, draws

© KONINKLIJKE BRILL NV, LEIDEN, 2020 | DOI:10.1163/9789004427105_021

upon acquired techniques.[1] Petrarch does not propose a systematic treatise on poetic creativity. Rather, analyses of scattered statements lead to an emerging picture of a poet seeking to express cosmic and human truth through eloquent expression. As visionary and craftsman, the mythological architect-inventor Dedalus parallels his concept of the practicing poet. The figure of Dedalus does not at first appear to be a key to an understanding of Petrarch's poetics. However, as Leonard Grant has noted, Petrarch employs a "riddling" in his *Bucolicum carmen*, and "allusions are everything."[2] Thus, an examination of Petrarch's representation of Dedalus, within the contexts of medieval mythography and his theoretical statements, may assist us in refining his thoughts on the dynamics of poetic creativity.

Completed in Milan in 1357, with revisions lasting another ten years,[3] the twelve poems that comprise Petrarch's *Bucolicum carmen* extol the simple pleasures of pastoral life.[4] Like Virgil, Petrarch creates in pastoral poetry an

---

1   For studies on Petrarch's poetic theory, see Aldo Bernardo, *Petrarch, Scipio, and the "Africa"* (Baltimore, 1962), chaps. 9 and 10; Pietro Paulo Gerosa, *Umanesimo cristiano del Petrarca* (Turin, 1966), chaps. 1 and 15; Charles Trinkaus, *In Our Image and Likeness: Humanity and Dignity in Italian Humanist Thought*, 2 vols. (Chicago, 1970), chap. 1; idem, *The Poet as Philosopher: Petrarch and the Formation of Renaissance Consciousness* (New Haven, 1979), chap. 4; Ronald Witt, "Coluccio Salutati and the Conception of the *Poeta Theologus*," *Renaissance Quarterly* 30 (1977), 538–63; Jennifer Petrie, *The Augustan Poets, the Italian Tradition, and the "Canzoniere"* (Dublin, 1983), chap. 2; Marjorie O'Rourke Boyle, *Petrarch's Genius: Pentimento and Prophecy* (Berkeley – Los Angeles, 1991); Dennis Looney, "The Beginnings of Humanistic Oratory: *Coronation Oration*," in *Petrarch: A Critical Guide to his Complete Works*, ed. Victoria Kirkham and Armando Maggi (Chicago, 2009), 131–40; Mario Pomilio, *Petrarca e l'idea di poesia* (Rome 2016).

2   W. Leonard Grant, *Neo-Latin Literature and the Pastoral* (Chapel Hill, 1965), 87. Petrarch comments on ambiguity in his *Liber sine nomine*, ed. Giovanni Cassio (Florence, 2015), Praef. 3 and 7, and provides exegetical readings of the first eclogue in *Familiares* 10,4, *Le Familiari*, ed. Vittorio Rossi, 4 vols. (Florence, 1933–42), vol. 2, 301–3 and of the second and fifth eclogues respectively in *Varia* 49 and 42, *Lettere di F. Petrarca*, ed. Giuseppe Fracassetti, 5 vols. (Florence, 1892), vol. 5, 416–7 and 402–3.

3   For the dating of the eclogues, see Nicholas Mann, "'O deus, qualis epistola!': A New Petrarch Letter," *Italia medioevale e umanistica* 17 (1974), 207–43, and "The Making of Petrarch's *Bucolicum carmen*: A Contribution to the History of the Text," *Italia medioevale e umanistica* 20 (1977), 127–82; and Enrico Fenzi, "Sull'ordine di tempi e vicende nel *Bucolicum carmen* di Petrarca," *Per leggere* 15 (2015), 8–24.

4   For critical commentary on Petrarchan pastoral, see Enrico Carrara, *La poesia pastorale* (Milan, 1909), 87–111; Carlo Calcaterra, *Nella selva del Petrarca* (Bologna, 1942); Konrad Krautter, *Die Renaissance der Bukolik in der lateinischen Literatur des XIV. Jahrhunderts: von Dante bis Petrarca* (Munich, 1983), chaps. 3–5; Guido Martellotti, "Dalla tenzone al carmen bucolico: Giovanni del Virgilio, Dante, Petrarca," in *Dante e Boccaccio e altri scrittori*

ideal of leisure that goes beyond time and space. The pain of earthly realities, though, punctures this picture. In describing in individual poems strife, death, amorous tribulations, and political intrigues, he presents a dissonance between the permanent, idyllic landscape of nature and the temporal experience of human hardship. Poetic creativity forms part of this tension and displacement.

Dedalus appears in the fourth eclogue where two shepherds discuss the benefits of poetic genius.[5] Gallus, in seeking insight into this mystery, recognizes his poetic deficiencies and seeks from Tirrenus answers to his success in creating inspired verse. Gallus notes that poetry is a craft requiring technical skills, and that the lyre is the instrument. Tirrenus elaborates on its qualities. Both Gallus and Tirrenus identify Dedalus as its inventor, but Tirrenus sees the instrument as a means to convey a transcendent harmony. Like other interlocutors in pastoral poetry, both shepherds disclose the sorrows of earthly existence. However, in viewing Tirrenus's misery, Dedalus selects him as recipient of the lyre to assuage his suffering. The music produced by Tirrenus is therapeutic, transporting him from earthly ache to spiritual consolation. Tirrenus refuses Gallus's pleas to exchange his goats for the lyre; Gallus, resigning himself to his inadequacies, acknowledges Tirrenus as favored by the gods. Through the figures of these shepherds, then, Petrarch subtly delineates two sorts of poets: the versifier-craftsman and the divinely endowed poet. According to Gallus, the cords of the lyre and the arrangement of numerical proportions result in music. However, the lyre goes beyond a tool to exercise learned skills; it is the means to express a vision of solace and harmony. As creator of the lyre, Dedalus becomes exemplar and benefactor.

Although Dedalus appears as a builder and joiner in Greek epic poetry,[6] Petrarch probably draws upon four narratives told by Ovid and Virgil to portray his semi-divine qualities: (1) the creation of a labyrinth that retains the Minotaur;[7] (2) the fabrication of wax wings that enables Dedalus and his son

---

dal'Umanesimo a "Romanticismo," ed. Guido Martellotti (Florence, 1983), 71–8; Giuseppe Mazzotta, *The Worlds of Petrarch* (Durham, N.C., 1993), 153–9; Stefano Carrai, "Pastoral as Personal Mythology in History (*Bucolicum carmen*)," in *Petrarch: A Critical Guide to Complete Works* (see above, n. 1), 165–77.

5 For studies of this poem, see Calcaterra, *Nella selva* (see above, n. 4), 119–44; Nicholas Mann, "In margine alla quarta ecloga: piccoli problemi di esegesi petrarchesca," *Studi petrarcheschi* 4 (1987), 17–32, and Enrico Fenzi, "'Dedalus' (*Bucolicum carmen* IV)," *Letteratura italiana antica* 7 (2006), 1–24.

6 Sarah P. Morris, *Daidalos and the Origins of Greek Art* (Princeton, 1992), chap. 1. Piero Boitani, *Winged Words: Flight in Poetry and History* (Chicago, 2007), chaps. 1, 2, and 6, studies the changing perceptions of Dedalus.

7 Ovid, *Met.* 8,156–70. All references to ancient Greek and Roman texts correspond to the most recent editions of the Loeb Classical Library.

PETRARCH, DEDALUS, AND THE DYNAMICS OF POETIC CREATIVITY 287

Icarus to escape Crete but ends in Icarus's death;[8] (3) the design of a temple to Apollo in Cumae;[9] and (4) his role as teacher of his nephew Perdix who, upon inventing the saw, incited Dedalus's jealousy and resulted in Perdix's death.[10] Pliny, in his *Historia naturalis* (7,198), summarizes Dedalus's discovery and uses of carpentry that include the saw, axe, and drill. Dedalus, though, was not simply a craftsman. Plato, in his *Meno* (97D), remarks that Dedalus transforms static figures into animate objects; and, according to Pausanias (*Description of Greece* 2,4,5), he was a divinely inspired artist.[11]

Medieval mythographers comment on these anecdotes, and Dedalus emerges as a sort of demi-god. As a father, he grieves the death of his son; as a rival, he envies Perdix. But his art seems sparked by the divine. Hyginus, Servius, and Isidore of Seville recount stories of the labyrinth, Dedalus's escape, and Icarus's and Perdix's death;[12] and Hyginus notes that Athena endowed him with the art of craftsmanship.[13] Martianus Capella, moreover, refers to the artistry of Dedalus's carpentry. In his description of geometry in *De nuptiis Philologiae et Mercurii*, he describes a woman who crafts figures on an abacus that, in their beauty and intricacy, identify her as "the offspring of Dedalus of Labyrinth fame."[14] Bernard Silvestris elaborates on Martianus's description. In his commentary on Virgil's *Aeneid* (6,14–31), he recounts Dedalus's construction of Apollo's temple decorated with sculpture depicting stories and histories, and he points out Dedalus's engineering skills to design wings to escape Minos's oppression. Study and labor explain, in part, Dedalus's achievements, but he also attributes to him reason and intellect that lead to insight and wisdom.[15] Pierre Besuire, in his *Metamorphosis ovidiana moraliter*, sees Dedalus as an artificer but stresses his sagacity.[16] Allegorically, the labyrinth that imprisons Dedalus symbolizes sin, and Dedalus's intelligence and craft to design wax wings afford

---

8   Ovid, *Met.* 8,183–235; *Trist.* 3,4,21–2 and 3,8,5–16; *Ars am.* 2,19–98.

9   Virgil, *Aen.* 6,14–41.

10 Ovid, *Met.* 8,236–59.

11 Morris, *Daidalos* (see above, n. 6), 223, 247–8.

12 Hyginus, *Fabularum liber* (Basel, 1531; reprint New York, 1976), *Fabulae*, 39–40; Servius, *Commentaire sur "l'Énéide" de Virgile, Livre 6*, ed. Emmanuelle Jeunot-Mancy (Paris, 2012), 9–15; Isidore of Seville, *Etymologiae*, ed. W. M. Lindsay (Oxford, 1911), 15,36.

13 Hyginus, *Fabulae* (see above, n. 12), 39.

14 Martianus Capella, *De nuptiis Philologiae et Mercurii*, ed. A. Dick and J. Préaux (Stuttgart, 1978), 289 "labyrinthus Daedalus eam credendus sit geniusse".

15 Bernard Silvestris, *The Commentary on the First Six Books of the "Aeneid" of Vergil Commonly Attributed to Bernardus Silvestris*, ed. Julian W. Jones and Elizabeth F. Jones (Lincoln, Neb., 1977), 36–7.

16 Pierre Besuire, *Metamorphosis ovidiana moraliter* (Basel, 1543; reprint New York, 1979), fols. 53v–4r and 63r–v.

his escape and become the means to contemplate God. Dedalus, moreover, conveys apt advice to his son Icarus to resist flying too close to the sun and risking the melting of the wings. Presumption, though, overtakes Icarus, and the wings dissolve, resulting in his plunge into the sea and drowning. In exercising virtue, Dedalus maintains a middle course between the sun and sea and, according to Bersuire, is blessed with "artistic skill and knowledge," and endowed with "wisdom and subtlety."[17] In 1394 Francesco Piendibeni, in following Benvenuto da Imola's commentary, identifies Dedalus as "Yhesus Cristus."[18] However, unlike Christ, Dedalus errs, facilitating Pasiphaë's incest with the bull, and yielding to envy that ends in Perdix's death.[19]

Dedalus's gift of the lyre that incites Tirrenus to compose verse indicates the conjoining of the human and heavenly. Materially, it is an artfully crafted instrument whose ivory frame and cords enable the poet-musician to create lyrics both through the use of the bow and pick and through the harmonious arrangement of musical notes. As its inventor and benefactor, Dedalus is its "supreme craftsman."[20] Poetic creation, however, goes beyond artifice, raising spirits, banishing sorrow, and freeing man from unrelenting hardship. In linking the practice of *musica humana* with the harmony of *musica mundana*, Petrarch reinforces the notion of the poet as craftsman and visionary. As the earthly cords of the lyre reflect the cosmic movements of the stars, the poet transmits in intelligible form his glimpse into the beauty of universal harmony.

Through the figure of Dedalus and the image of the lyre, Petrarch portrays the practicing poet as an intermediary who perceives into the working of cosmic harmony, but who must also acquire learned techniques to convey these insights. The practicing poet is therefore both visionary and craftsman. In fact, Petrarch attributes to Dedalus an *ingenium* or natural talent that, according

---

17   "arte et scientia", "sapientia et subtilitate", Ibid., fol. 54r.

18   *Il "Bucolicum carmen" e i suoi commenti inediti*, ed. Antonio Avena (Bologna, 1906), 265; see also Fausto Ghisalberti, "L'Ovidius Moralizatus di Pierre Bersuire," *Studj Romanzi* 23 (1933), 129–30, and *Petrarch's "Bucolicum Carmen,"* trans. and annotated Thomas G. Bergin (New Haven, 1974), 224–5.

19   Earlier commentators did see Dedalus as a god, Ibid., Avena, 202, but also as a "subtilissimus vir et ingeniosus," Ibid., 201. According to Calcaterra, *Nella selva* (see above, n. 4), 120–1, modern critics, such as Rossetti, Carrara, and Mazzoni, see Dedalus as both god and man but do not identify him as Christ. See Ibid., Bergin, for varying interpretations of Dedalus.

20   *Il Bucolicum Carmen di F. Petrarca*, ed. Domenico De Venuto (Pisa, 1990), 4,6 "artificum stupor". English translation corresponds to Ibid., *Petrarch's "Bucolicum Carmen,"* trans. Bergin, 49.

to Horace, produces "a god of human nature."[21] As Mario Pomilio has demonstrated, *ingenium* provokes divine insight but is hardly a frenzy; and, through his analyses of Cicero's *Pro Archia* and *Tusculan Disputations*, he defines its dynamics as an interrelation of inspiration and talent.[22] Thus, according to Isidore of Seville, Varro sees *ingenium* as a working of the *vis mentis* activated by an impulse or *spiritus*.[23] Like divine inspiration, *ingenium* is, as Bernard Silvestris describes it, an infused force or *daimon* within man. This natural disposition becomes part of the rational soul essential in discovering an appropriate object of imitation, and in discriminating fact from fantasy.[24] In his *Coronation Oration*, delivered earlier in 1341, Petrarch does not differentiate inspiration from talent. His use of the words "rapere" and "afflare" suggests the force of an uncontrolled enthusiasm, but the source of poetry, he states, evolves from a human talent granted to him by God who, according to Persius, is "master of the arts and bestower of genius."[25] *Ingenium*, then, shares characteristics with inspiration; but, unlike the unlettered bard, the practicing poet employs his talent to perceive cosmic realities and to acquire techniques essential in writing a verse that sets forth truths "physical, moral, and historical."[26]

As Roman critics had theorized, nature and art are complementary forces that define the dynamics of poetic creativity or oratorical discourse.[27] Similarly, Petrarch remarks in his *Seniles* 12,2 that the poet seeks the truth of things and

---

21   Horace, *Ep.* 2,2,188 "naturae deus humanae". See also Horace, *Sat.* 1,4,43–4. For a detailed description of *ingenium*, see Jane Chance Nitzsche, *The Genius Figure in Antiquity and the Middle Ages* (New York, 1975). See also George M. A. Grube, *The Greek and Roman Critics* (London, 1965), 244, 323–32, and Charles O. Brink, *Horace on Poetry* (Cambridge, 1971), 323–35, 422–3.

22   Pomilio, *Petrarca* (see above, n. 1), 163–87.

23   Isidore of Seville, *Etymologiae* (see above, n. 12), 8,7,3; Pomilio, *Petrarca* (see above, n. 1), 192–3.

24   Nitzsche, *The Genius Figure* (see above, n. 21), chap. 3, examines Bernard Silvestris's description of Genius, the bestower of *ingenium*, as an agent infusing man with a divine but human talent consistent with theories proposed by Servius, Guillaume de Conches, and Remigius of Auxerre.

25   Persius, *Satires*, prologue 10 "magister artis ingeniique largitor", quoted by Petrarch, *Collatio laureationis*, in *Scritti inediti di Francesco Petrarca*, ed. Attilio Hortis (Trieste, 1894), 319. English translations are taken from Ernest Hatch Wilkins, *Studies in the Life and Works of Petrarch* (Cambridge, Mass., 1955), 306. Later, Bruni makes a similar statement in his *Vita di Dante* (1496), in *Leonardo Bruni Aretino: Humanistich-Philosophische Schriften*, ed. Hans Baron (Leipzig, 1928), 59–61.

26   Hortis, *Scritti* (see above, n. 25), 320 "nunc fisica nunc moralia nunc hystorias"; trans. Wilkins, *Studies* (see above, n. 25), 306.

27   Horace, *Ars poetica*, 408–11; Cicero, *Pro Archia* 15, and *De Oratore* 113–59; Quintilian, *Institutio oratoria* 2,19. See Brink, *Horace on Poetry* (see above n. 21), 382, 394–400.

then conveys it in through fiction.[28] "Poetry," as he notes in *Familares* 10,4, "is not contrary to theology,"[29] and truth proceeds from God. Thanks to his use of natural talent, he finds the object of his imitation in earthly phenomena, human experience, theological teaching, and literary texts. In *Seniles* 7,1 Petrarch affirms the poet as an agent of God. But he is also a *doctus imitator*, who consciously determines the moral validity of his subject matter and then converts his insight into an expression that, as he observes in *Seniles* 2,3, engenders and perfects art.

Two centuries later, the French poet-humanist Pierre de Ronsard delineates three sorts of poets: (1) the poet-prophet who, infused by divine insight, unconsciously transmits his vision in verse; (2) the "poète humain" who, through use of native talent, draws upon visionary and human experience and learned techniques; (3) the versifier who relies solely upon rhetorical resources.[30] Petrarch suggests these distinctions. However, instead of analyzing the theoretical traditions and premises of these types of creativity, he describes the challenges, triumphs, and disappointments of the human poet who, like Dedalus and Tirrenus, perceives the divine and then molds it to artistic form.

In the first eclogue Petrarch presents two shepherds: Silvius who seeks release from stress, and Monicus who has discovered tranquility in contemplation.[31] Silvius recognizes the therapy of music and, motivated to apply study and labor to the making of song, seeks an inspiration that he has lost. Indolence afflicts him. Monicus suggests that poetic creativity springs from one source that emits two rivers. Silvius corrects this statement, identifying one river produced from two sources: a sacred stream that cleansed Apollo and a torrent turning fields to ashes. These references require explanation; and, in a letter (*Familiares* 10,4) to his brother Gherardo, a Carthusian monk, Petrarch offers an allegorical interpretation. Two springs, the "Jor" and "Dan," form the Jordan, descending to the ashen fields of the Sodomites and denoting the river where

---

28   References to the *Seniles* correspond to *Res seniles*, ed. Silvia Rizzo and Monica Berté, 4 vols. (Florence, 2010–18).

29   "dicam theologiam poeticam esse de Deo," *Le Familiari*, (see above, n. 2), vol. 2, 301; English translations are taken from *Letters on Familiar Matters*, trans. Aldo S. Bernardo, vol. 1 (Albany, 1975), vols. 2–3 (Baltimore, 1982, 1985), vol. 2, 69. See also Cicero, *Pro Archia* 8,18, and Petrarch, "Invective contra medicum," *Invective*, ed. Francesco Bausci (Florence, 2005), 27.

30   Donald Gilman, "Ronsard's Concept of the 'Poète humain,'" *Bibliothèque d'Humanisme et Renaissance* 45 (1982), 89–95.

31   For analyses of this poem, see E. Fenzi, "Verso il *Secretum*: *Bucolicum carmen* I, *Parthenias*," *Petrarchesca* 1 (2013), 13–53, and Elisabetta Tarantino, "Bucolicum Carmen I (Parthenias)," in *Filologia e storia letteraria: Studi per Roberto Tissoni*, ed. Carlo Caruso and William Spaggiari (Rome, 2008), 47–56.

John baptizes Christ. The earthly and heavenly commingle; and Silvius sees the image of the conflicting aspects of the Jordan as the subject of his epic: Scipio Africanus who, as general, knows the tragedies of human existence, but who, as hero and "celestial youth,"[32] restores political order. Silvius, then, is hardly an unthinking amanuensis; and, through his *ingenium* and craft, he seeks to create verses reconciling human experience and heavenly reality worthy of Orpheus.[33]

Silvius's journey to the creation of verse metaphorically parallels Dedalus's flight between earth and heaven and is, according to Monicus, difficult and hazardous. Through the image of the laurel, Petrarch elaborates on these challenges. In the third eclogue he depicts the misery of Stupeus's unrequited love for Daphne.[34] Music affords consolation; and, like Dedalus and Silvius, Stupeus undertakes a journey, spurning wealth, and seeking contentment. Inflamed by love, and enduring hardship, he spies a laurel and, heeding the advice of Calliope, produces a harmony that moves Daphne. Both *ingenium* and labor testify to Stupeus's success, but motivation is needed. Like Gallus and Silvius, Stupeus endures a restlessness that poetry relieves. In *Familiares* 9,5, Petrarch describes the therapy of writing to alleviate grief and, in *Familiares* 3,1, sees poetry as a means to find spiritual satisfaction. In his *Coronation Oration* he elaborates on the creative source of poetry, identifying it as a love that, overtaking the poet, results in praise of the Republic, personal glory, and the teaching of virtue. Study and labor are equally important. Petrarch's explication of lines from Virgil's *Georgics* (3,291–2) suggests the difficulties of creation: "But a sweet longing urges me upward over the lonely slopes of Parnassus."[35] The motivation of "dulcis amor" must be complemented by the toil of study; and, after determining the object of imitation, the poet must employ learned techniques to compose delightful fiction. Like Dedalus who steers a course between earth and sky, the practicing poet navigates a *via media* that combines the ideal of the inspired poet-prophet and the slavish replications of the versifier.

Through the image of the laurel, then, Petrarch subtly describes its magical qualities to produce verse and to ease the pain of earthly existence. In describing its properties in the *Coronation Oration*, he recognizes that, through its fragrance, it conjoins the earthly and heavenly. The implications of this metaphor

---

32 "iuvenis sidereus," *Le Familiari* (see above, n. 2), vol. 2, 309; trans. Bernardo, (see above, n. 29), vol. 2, 75.

33 Petrarch, *Bucolicum carmen* (see above, n. 20), 1, 123.

34 For an analysis of this poem, see Michele Feo, "Per l'esegesi della III ecloga del Petrarca," *Italia medioevale e umanistica* 10 (1967), 385–401.

35 Hortis, *Scritti* (see above, n. 25), 311 "Sed me Parnasi deserta per ardua dulcis raptat amor"; trans. Wilkins, *Studies* (see above, n. 25), 300.

extend to worldly glory and divine insight. Like the source of the two rivers in the first eclogue, the poet touched by the laurel reconciles earthly accomplishments and priestly functions. In providing shade, the laurel affords a leisure or *otium* after the exertions of strife or study that facilitate human activity. But as a sacred tree associated with Apollo, god of poetry and prophecy, it enables the practicing poet to visualize truth in dreams. Theory, though, clashes with practice. As we have seen, Petrarch differentiates between the inspired poet-*vates* who unconsciously transmits divine truth and the practicing poet who expresses his glimpse of cosmic order through learned techniques. Study and labor are required, and the poet must identify and transform his object of imitation by employing rhetorical tropes and techniques. Truth remains constant, but poetic expression varies, producing a veil of fiction, and inducing delight. In receiving the laurel crown from Robert of Anjou, Petrarch acknowledges his accomplishments as a practicing poet who, thanks to his *ingenium* and mastery of versification, creates a vision surpassing insipid verse. But the dialectic that links enduring truth and poetic fiction is tenuous. Unlike the ancient poet-*vates*, Petrarch doubts his capacity to perceive and transmit immortal truth.

This fracture between aspiration and attainment expands Petrarch's thoughts on the dynamics of poetic creativity. In the tenth eclogue he returns to the description of the laurel, but the rewards afforded to Petrarch the poet-laureate are contrasted with the lack of fulfillment described by the shepherd Silvanus. Like Petrarch, Silvanus had discovered the magical qualities of the laurel. Experiencing the poverty caused by untilled lands, Silvanus detects the aroma of a laurel, forsakes worldly concerns, and finds relief in the plant. Arduous cultivation, however, requires the acquisition of techniques and labor that he identifies as a long journey. A lengthy catalogue of poets and philosophers relates the nurturing of the laurel to poetic creativity. But, if Silvanus is pursuing a path similar to Dedalus's escape, Silvius's rocky road, or Stupeus's arduous search, cultivation or the acquisition of techniques must be complemented by the supernatural qualities of the laurel. In this eclogue Silvanus grieves the loss of the laurel that has been uprooted and planted in heaven. In recalling Petrarch's doubts of securing immortal truth in the *Coronation Oration*, Silvanus's recognition of human limitations defines the trials of the practicing poet who experiences the challenges of translating *intelligibilia* into *sensibilia*.

The figure of Dedalus, then, enables Petrarch to present an insight into the dynamics and difficulties of poetic creativity. Combining divinely endowed genius with technical expertise, study, and labor, Dedalus as inventor and craftsman creates tools conceptually perceived and materially realized. According to medieval mythographers, Dedalus applies his talent to architecture and engineering that demonstrate his insight and wisdom. But Petrarch, in attributing to him the invention of the lyre, also associates him with poetic creativity. In following Dedalus's example and benefiting from his gift, Tirrenus and earlier Silvius glimpse into the nature of creativity. In many respects Petrarch's theorizations recall Horace's poetics; for, like Horace's picture of the aspiring poet, Petrarch's practicing poet employs the complementary resources of natural talent and learned techniques.[36] At the conclusion of his *Ars poetica*, Horace attacks mad, uneducated poets.[37] Similarly, Petrarch does not depict the poet as an agent unconsciously conveying divine insight. On the other hand, the poet is not merely a versifier: Horace sees wisdom as the source and font of good writing,[38] and Petrarch's Gallus pleads for the capacity to escape earthly realities through the music of Dedalus's lyre. Natural talent or *ingenium* reflects therefore the innate capacities of the practicing poet to find an object of imitation to be shaped to artistic form. In brief, according to Charles Trinkaus, Petrarch molds a *theologia poetica* to the demands of *theologia rhetorica*.[39] In the *Coronation Oration* Petrarch comments on the interaction of nature and art in a poetic process that requires motivation, study, and labor. The laurel crown rewards a trek over "the lonely slopes of Parnassus" that parallels the long and strenuous journeys of the shepherds Silvius and Stupeus. Disappointment lurks behind this struggle. Dedalus, in spite of his attainments, experiences grief. Like the shepherds in Petrarch's eclogues who seek escape from earthly and attainment of spiritual tranquility, Silvanus, in the tenth eclogue, perceives, in the metaphorical meaning of the laurel, both the transitory emptiness of trite verse and the lasting permanence of inspired poetry. The reach, though, often exceeds the grasp; for, in ascending the difficult slopes of Mt. Parnassus, the practicing poet knows the dynamics and strains of a process that demands the use of divinely endowed talent and acquired technical skill.

Ball State University

---

36 In a perceptive analysis, Karsten Friis-Jensen, "Petrarch and the Medieval Horace," in *The Medieval Horace*, ed. Karin Margareta Fredborg, Minna Skafte Jensen, Marianne Pade, and Johann Ramminger (Rome, 2015), 173–88, especially 183–7, sees Tirrenus as a mask for Petrarch's Horatian poetics. See also Walther Ludwig, "Horazrezeption in der Renaissance oder die Renaissance des Horaz," *Entretiens sur l'Antiquite classique* 39 (1993), 305–79, especially 312–25; and Michele Feo, "Petrarca, Francesco," in *Enciclopedia oraziana* (Rome, 1998), vol. 3, 405–25.

37 Horace, *Ars poetica*, 453–76.

38 Ibid., 309.

39 Trinkaus, *In Our Image and Likeness* (see above, n. 1), chap. 15; idem, *The Poet as Philosopher* (see above, n. 1), chap. 4.

CHAPTER 21

The *Epigrammata Antiquae Urbis* (1521) and the Muses: a Little-Known Chapter in Sixteenth-Century Latin Poetry

Gerard González Germain

Abstract

In 1521, the editor Giacomo Mazzocchi published in Rome the anonymous *Epigrammata Antiquae Urbis*, the first printed collection of ancient inscriptions found in the city of Rome. An analysis of the annotations in the surviving copies of the book shows that, besides the antiquarian, the *Epigrammata* had a different, more 'literate' type of reader, who focused—solely or primarily—on metrical inscriptions; who added Neo-Latin poems by renowned authors, and who appended compositions otherwise unknown, which were probably their own. Four such poems are edited and briefly studied here.

Keywords

Giacomo Mazzocchi – *Epigrammata Antiquae Urbis* (1521) – Neo-Latin epigrams – marginalia – antiquarianism

1 Introduction[1]

It has long been asserted that the publication of the *Epigrammata antiquae Urbis* (ed. Giacomo Mazzocchi, Rome 1521) marked a milestone in antiquarian studies, due to the crucial developments in the fields of philology, topography and printing that were necessary to tackle such a challenging task. Similarly, previous research has underscored the key role that the *Epigrammata* played

---

1 The research leading to these results has received funding from the Spanish Government (FFI2016-77723-P). Inscriptions are identified by the number of the *Carmina Latina Epigraphica* (hereafter cited as *CLE*), ed. Franz Buecheler, Ernst Lommatzsch (Leipzig, 1895–1927), and the *Corpus Inscriptionum Latinarum* (hereafter cited as *CIL*), ed. Theodor Mommsen et al. (Berlin, 1863–), 18 vols.

© KONINKLIJKE BRILL NV, LEIDEN, 2020 | DOI:10.1163/9789004427105_022

THE *EPIGRAMMATA ANTIQUAE URBIS* (1521) AND THE MUSES 295

as the basis of most epigraphic inquiries into the city of Rome for at least the following fifty years,[2] although it is only now that the actual extent and depth of this influence is beginning to emerge.

One aspect of the *Epigrammata*'s reception which has not yet been considered is its relationship with Neo-Latin poetry. In the early Cinquecento, collecting inscriptions had displaced manuscript hunting as the most productive means of recovering ancient Latin texts. The *Epigrammata* was a repository of sixty ancient epigrams—plus ten other forgeries—, most of which were printed here for the very first time. The vast majority were funerary poems, written mostly in elegiac couplets, although hexameters and a few iambic and trochaic metres were found as well.

In this paper, I intend to prove that, besides the antiquarian, the *Epigrammata* had a different, more 'literate' type of reader, who for the most part appears to have disregarded the inscriptions' historical, archaeological or linguistic significance and to have focused—solely or primarily—on metrical inscriptions and poetic expressions, both as ancient epigrammatic literature and as a source of inspiration for Neo-Latin poetry. Evidence of this particular type of readership comes from the annotations left by several sixteenth-century readers in the surviving copies of the book. More specifically, my analysis will take into consideration three complementary cases: readers who annotated—exclusively or predominantly—the verse inscriptions; readers who added Neo-Latin poems by renowned authors; and readers who appended compositions otherwise unknown, which were probably their own.

2 Locating and Reading the Ancient Poems

A few readers left sporadic annotations almost exclusively in the book's verse inscriptions. Interestingly enough, in most of these cases the annotations date from the sixteenth century, whereas later annotators show a larger array of antiquarian interests. One such early sporadic reader was Paolo Spineda, doctor of civil law from Treviso, who marked several poems with manicules and squiggles.[3] A copy in Madrid presents several metrical texts highlighted,

---

2 See Richard Cooper, "Epigraphical Research in Rome in the Mid-Sixteenth-Century: The Papers of Antonio Agustín and Jean Matal," in *Antonio Agustín between Renaissance and Counter-Reform*, ed. Michael H. Crawford (London, 1993), 95–111; Concetta Bianca, "Giacomo Mazzocchi e gli *Epigrammata antiquae urbis*," in *Studi di antiquaria et epigrafia per Ada Rita Gunella*, ed. Concetta Bianca et al. (Roma, 2009), 107–16.

3 Princeton University Library, Oversize 10214.62q, fols. 3v (*CLE* 899), 32r (*CLE* 964), 46v (*CLE* 1339), 56r (*CLE* 1107), 59v (*CLE* 201), 85v (*CLE* 1375), 130v (*CLE* 1028 and *CIL* VI 24*), 145r (*CLE*

one of them identified with the word "carmina".[4] Another copy at the Folger Shakespeare Library includes, besides a few expressions from the inscriptions copied in the margins, a profuse annotation comparing the word "Anchialo" on one funerary poem to Martial's "Anchialum" (*epig.* 11,94,8).[5]

At least three humanists, well versed in antiquity, distinguished the verse inscriptions from those which were non-metrical. This was the case of the Portuguese antiquarian André de Resende (c. 1500–73): having found a copy in the King's library, he passed it on to his pupil Francisco de Holanda (who afterwards drew extensively on it), not before marking every single metrical inscription he could find with the imperative form "adverte versus" or with the single word "versus".[6] Similarly, a profuse annotator of a copy kept in Valencia, who focused chiefly on aspects of Roman history and religion, also distinguished most of the verses in the book, oftentimes with a manicule or a simple strike, but also with the words "versus" and "carmina".[7] Finally, what may be the most interesting evidence of a specific study of the *Epigrammata*'s poems, comes not from a surviving copy but from an epigraphic miscellany known as the *Codex Memmianus*,[8] which contains the epigraphic papers of Jean Maludan (dating from the 1550s), assembled and expanded by his pupil Henri de Mesmes (1532–96), a bibliophile and an excerpter of classical and modern authors.[9] The manuscript contains, almost certainly in de Mesmes's own hand, three pages of quick excerpts under the heading *Ep(igramma)ta*

   1106), 150v (*CIL* VI add. 3*), 158v (*CLE* 802), 164r (*CLE* 995), 173v (*CLE* 1051) and 180r (*CIL* VI 2k*). The ex-libris "D(omini) Pauli de Spinet(is) Tarvis(ini) l(egum) doct(oris)" is found on the end paper. According to the exhibition *Incunaboli. Antichi libri a stampa dal mercato antiquario alla Biblioteca dell'Archiginnasio* (cur. Anna Manfron, Bologna, 2010; retrieved from http://badigit.comune.bologna.it/mostre/incunaboli/index.html), Paolo Spineda received his doctorate in 1492 at the university of Padua.

4 Madrid, Real Academia de la Historia, 14/2052, fols. 7r–v (*CLE* 249), 39v (*CLE* 1249), 46v (*CLE* 1339), etc.; the annotation "carmina" is found in fol. 180r (*CIL* VI 2k*).

5 Folger Shakespeare Library, 209-001f, fol. 101r (*CLE* 973). I would like to thank Prof. William Stenhouse for drawing my attention to this copy.

6 Lisbon, Biblioteca Nacional de Portugal, RES. 1000A¹. See Sylvie Deswarte-Rosa, "*Sous la dictée de la Sibylle*. Épigraphie et Poésie. Un exemplaire des *Epigrammata Antiquae Urbis* annoté par André de Resende et Francisco de Holanda," in *Peregrinationes ad inscriptiones colligendas. Estudios sobre epigrafía de tradición manuscrita*, ed. Gerard González Germain (Bellaterra, 2016), 73–134, there 92–5.

7 València, Universitat, Biblioteca Històrica, BH Z-13/103, fols. 35v, 59v, 70r (vertical strikes); 3v, 30r, 32r 46v (manicules); 22r, 28v, 85v ("versus"), and 97r, 101r, 130v, 133r, 145r ("carmina").

8 See *CIL* IX, p. XXXV; *CIL* XIII, p. 260 no. XXXVII; Nathan Badoud, "La table claudienne de Lyon au XVIe siècle," *Cahiers du Centre Gustave Glotz* 13 (2002), 169–95, there 188.

9 See Gerald Sandy, "Two Renaissance Readers of Apuleius: Filippo Beroaldo and Henri de Mesmes," in *Authors, Authority, and Interpreters in the Ancient Novel: Essays in Honor of Gareth L. Schmeling*, ed. Shannon N. Byrne et al. (Groningen, 2006), 239–73, there 251–71.

THE *EPIGRAMMATA ANTIQUAE URBIS* (1521) AND THE MUSES

versibus scripta, which is an actual index of the poems in the book, providing the page, position of the text within the page and *incipit*.[10]

3   Adding Neo-Latin Poems

Other humanists decided to accompany the book with a single poem, usually after the colophon or in the flyleaves at the beginning or end of the book. This is further evidence of the book's appeal to the literate reader, and it sheds light on the book's reception by these humanists.

A copy now in Cologne is such a specimen.[11] An Italian humanist included new antiquarian material at the end of the book, and on the frontispiece he copied Ovid's celebrated *Tempus edax rerum* passage,[12] which became a leit-motiv of Renaissance antiquarianism—most famously, in Herman Posthumus' *Landscape with Roman Ruins* (1536).

Three Italian copies, otherwise clean of annotations, each present a Latin poem by a renowned poet of the first half of the Cinquecento at the end of the book. Gian Francesco Gamurrini (1835–1923) donated a copy to the Arezzo library that bore the ex-libris "Laelii Benuccii" on the frontispiece,[13] and included Ariosto's own *Epitaphium Ludovici Areosti* written between the end fly-leaf (vv. 1–4) and a separate slip of paper preserved with the book (vv. 5–15). Gamurrini thought the poem was an autograph of Ariosto, whose copy of the *Epigrammata* would have then passed through his wife Alessandra Benucci to a distant member of the family; but in 1963 Mutini rejected the idea that the copy of the poem had been written by Ariosto, and dated it instead after the *editio princeps* of the text in 1553.[14]

---

10   Paris, Bibliothèque nationale de France, MS lat. 5825 I, fols. 59r–60v.

11   Köln, Universitäts- und Stadtbibliothek, WAX27.

12   Ov., *met.* 15,234–6 "Ovidius. Tempus edax rerum tuque invidiosa vetusta / omnia destru-itis viciata dentibus (a)evi / paulatim nigra consumitis omnia morte." The original poem has "lenta" instead of "nigra"; while the annotator may have quoted from memory, the same mistake is found in Giovanni Tortelli's *Orthographia* (on the entry "Deus"), and in Ambrogio Calepino's *Dictionarium* (on the entry "Saturnus", which depends on Tortelli); both works were reprinted repeatedly throughout the sixteenth century.

13   Probably Lelio Benucci from Siena, son of Lattanzio Benucci (1521–98); see Maria Antonietta Garullo, "Notizie sulla vita e sull'opera di Lattanzio Benucci « giureconsulto sanese »," *Scaffale aperto* 5 (2014), 9–48, there 17–8.

14   Arezzo, Biblioteca Città di Arezzo, GAM P 67. See Claudio Mutini, "Nota sull'« Epitaphium Ludovici Areosti »," *Bibliothèque d'Humanisme et Renaissance* 25 (1963), 198–206. Since then, both the flyleaf and the slip of paper have been removed from the book and their present location is unknown.

A clean copy that belonged to the epigrapher Giovanni Labus (1775–1853) has, on the end pastedown, an epigram copied by a sixteenth-century Italian hand with no indication of authorship or title.[15] This poem was published in the 1576 corpus prepared by Giovan Matteo Toscano,[16] where it was attributed to the Modenese poet Francesco Maria Molza (1489–1544),[17] and entitled *In venustam quandam puellam*. It tells of a beautiful woman who has given up her previous libidinous life for a chaste one.[18]

Finally, a copy in Cortona (Arezzo) presents, on the verse of the last printed page, a poem with the heading *R(everendissi)mi car(dina)lis Ravennat(is)*.[19] The composition does indeed belong to the cardinal and archbishop of Ravenna Benedetto Accolti the Younger (1497–1549),[20] and was published in 1562 under the title *Lycoris*: it is a pastoral composition in which Lycoris laments the absence of Daphnis.[21] It is noteworthy that the readings of the ninth verse differ between the printed edition and the handwritten version;[22] an eventual study of Accolti's poetry may help determine whether these are meaningless mistakes or they attest to a manuscript tradition of the poem.

4   Composing New Poems

Undoubtedly, the most interesting evidence of the *Epigrammata*'s poetic influence comes from several otherwise unknown poems copied by the owners of the book. While we cannot be certain that these were their own creations, the fact that they are not attested elsewhere makes it plausible that they were written in the owners' inner circle. At the moment, we know of four such poems. We will examine each case individually.

---

15   Roma, Istituti Culturali di Roma, Biblioteca Memoria, ST1. L2.Sc1.P8.

16   Iohannes Matthaeus Toscanus, *Carmina illustrium poetarum Italorum* (Lutetiae, 1576), fol. 54v.

17   See Franco Pignatti, "Molza, Francesco Maria," *Dizionario biografico degli italiani* (hereafter cited as *DBI*) (Roma, 2011), vol. 75, 451–61. The handwriting is certainly not Molza's, for which see idem, "Francesco Maria Molza," in *Autografi dei letterati italiani. Il Cinquecento*, vol. 2 (Roma, 2013), 257–70.

18   *Francesco Maria Molza, Elegiae et alia*, ed. Massimo Scorsone and Rossana Sodano (Torino, 1999), 192 no. XXXI (among the "Componimenti attribuiti al Molza in edizioni cinquecentine").

19   Cortona, Biblioteca del Comune e dell'Accademia Etrusca, Cinq. 392.

20   See Eugenio Massa, "Accolti, Benedetto, il Giovane," in *DBI*, vol. 1 (Roma, 1960), 101–2.

21   [Francesco Berni], *Carmina quinque Hetruscorum poetarum nunc primum in lucem edita* (Florentiae, 1562), 131.

22   "Exurgent latis gemmantia gramina campis" instead of "exurgent pictis gemmantia gramina fundis".

THE *EPIGRAMMATA ANTIQUAE URBIS* (1521) AND THE MUSES 299

A copy in Hamilton, Ontario, which bears an ex-libris from one Giovanbattista Colucci da Pescia,[23] contains a poem on the front pastedown, by a hand which is not Colucci's, and which reappears once within the book.[24] The poem bears the title *De obitu Caesaris Sacci 1523 m(ense) Aug(usto)*, and was very probably composed and recorded shortly after the publication of the *Epigrammata*. Cesare Sacchi, born in Lodi, was a poet and orator and a client of the condottiero Gian Giacomo Trivulzio, who frequented the Roman literary circle of Johannes Corycius.[25] His death on August 5th, 1523, is recorded in an obituary of Italian humanists written around 1525,[26] and Pierio Valeriano mentions his sudden death while he was having dinner with Cardinal Scaramuccia Trivulzio.[27]

The poem [fig. 1; appendix no. 1] consists of 16 phalaecian hendecasyllables. It begins by addressing the deceased, who needs not to lament his arrival at sunless Hades (vv. 1–3): he is in fact being mourned by Rome, the Muses, Minerva, Apollo, and his fellow poets (vv. 4–11). In the conclusion, the author states that Sacchi lived while he could, and foresees that Death will not dissipate his memory, since he will be known to the lands of East and West, together with the Roman authors (vv. 12–16).

The poem was clearly written by one of Sacchi's Roman *aonii sodales* to whom v. 10 alludes. He demonstrates a good command of the meter and, although the subject and structure of the poem are certainly not original, some verses (especially the mourning of Phoebus and the poets) are quite felicitous. Likewise, the borrowings from Vergil—for the description of Hades (v. 3)—and

---

23   He may be the Giovanbattista Colucci who appears prominently in the deliberations of the Comune di Pescia during the years 1526–32: see Massimo Braccini, *Le deliberazioni del Comune di Pescia (1526–1532). Regesti* (Roma, 2000), *ad indicem*.

24   On the margin of *CIL* VI 18817 (fol. 67r), a funerary inscription put by a wife to his late husband, the annotator has written: "ex summo amore coniugum".

25   See Giovanni Agnelli, "Cesare Sacco e sua famiglia," *Archivio storico per la città e comuni del circondario di Lodi* 7 (1888), 129–44. He contributed two poems to the *Coryciana* collection (no. 17 and 29), and was mentioned in Francesco Arsilli's *De poetis urbanis* (261–4): see Jozef IJsewijn, *Coryciana* (Roma, 1997), *ad indicem*.

26   Mauro de Nichilo, *I viri illustres del cod. Vat. lat. 3920* (Roma, 1997), 80–1: "Caesar Sacchus, Laudensis, homo multae lectionis litterarum Latinarum et multae memoriae, mortuus est Romae nonis Augusti MDXXIII."

27   Pierio Valeriano, *De litteratorum infelicitate*, 2,48: "Caesaris autem Sacci repentina mors uni illi forsan commoda, nobis vero, qui iucundissima eius lepiditate fraudati sumus, visa est acerbissima. Laudensis is fuit, Iacobi Triultii familiaritate clarus eiusque factionis adsectator acerrimus, vir alioqui Graece Latineque doctissimus, versu prosaque oratione non inelegans, mathematicarum optime sciens. Dum autem apud Scaramuzam cardinalem Triultium a cena fabulatur, subitaria paralysi suffocatus interiit e vestigio". See Julia H. Gaisser, *Pierio Valeriano on the Ill Fortune of Learned Men* (Ann Arbor, 1999), 210–1 and 323.

Horace—for the poet's victory over death (vv. 12–13)—are certainly fitting,[28] as is Sacchi's comparison to the Roman poets, which is established through two metaliterary references: Ovid's assertion of Gallus's immortality, and Horace's mention of two ancient and two contemporary authors.[29]

The copy kept at the Warburg Library in London bears only two marginal annotations, both noting the presence of verses in the book.[30] This same Italian hand, probably from the first half of the Cinquecento, added an epigram [fig. 2; appendix no. 2] in elegiac verse directly after the colophon. The poem tells of a husband and wife who have lived without any disagreement until the moment of planning their funeral (vv. 1–4): each one wants to die first wishing the other a long life following that loss (vv. 5–8). The poem ends with a celebration of such a harmonious marriage (vv. 9–10).

This is probably the poem that most closely resembles Roman verse inscriptions, where it is common to find the deceased talking in first person, the praise of conjugal love or clauses such as "viximus", "sine lite" (v. 1) or "dulcissima coniunx" (v. 7).[31] But most of these clauses are found as well in elegiac poetry, both ancient and Neo-Latin. In this regard, the only certain borrowing I have detected is the final hemistich "contigit ante mori", which derives from an epigram of Martial that tells of the affection of two brothers, each of whom wanted the other to survive him—from where the motif of this epigram clearly derives.[32]

A copy in Trento, with annotations within the book by a sixteenth-century Italian hand, contains, in the verse of the last printed page, a particularly interesting testimony of Renaissance French poetry [fig. 3; appendix no. 3].[33] It consists of an elegiac epitaph in the form of a dialogue between a traveler and the deceased,[34] followed by a poetic rendering into French. The Latin text

---

28 Verg., *Aen.* 6,534: "tristis sine sole domos"; Hor., *carm.* 3,30,6–7: "multaque pars mei / vitabit Libitinam".

29 Ov., *am.* 1,15,29–30: "Gallus et Hesperiis et Gallus notus Eois / et sua cum Gallo nota Lycoris erit"; Hor., *ars* 53–5: "quid autem / Caecilio Plautoque dabit Romanus ademptum / Vergilio Varioque?"

30 London, Warburg Institute, CKN 336.M19, fol. 130r ("notandum est hoc distichon"; referred to *CIL* VI p. 251* *add.* 3*) and 130v ("nota hoc epigramma"; referred to *CIL* VI 24*).

31 "Viximus" (as the first word of the verse): *CLE* 754, 995, 1237, 1305, 1431, 1550b, 2080, 2106. "Dulcissima coniunx" (as the end of a hexameter): *CLE* 773, 794, 986, 1429. "Sine lite": *CLE* 134, 477, 561, 1112, 1571.

32 Mart., *epigr.* 9,51. Apart from the aforementioned clause (v. 2), it also has "Elysios nemorisque" (v. 5) which may have influenced the "Elysium [...] nemus" of v. 6. In Mart., *epigr.* 1,36, which deals with the same subject, the brothers get into a dispute ("nobilis [...] pietatis rixa", v. 3) over who should die first.

33 Trento, Biblioteca Comunale, t-G 2 c 157.

34 These dialogues are not unknown in ancient funerary epigraphy (see e.g. *CLE* 995, found in fol. 92r of the *Epigrammata*), but they became a literary type since Pontano's *Tumuli* (1,5, 12, 23, 41, 44, 48).

THE *EPIGRAMMATA ANTIQUAE URBIS* (1521) AND THE MUSES 301

bears the subscription "1543 Mallarius faciebat", whereas the French is signed as "Abraham le Machays Gallice donabat";[35] both texts are written by the same French humanist hand, clearly at the same time.

The deceased ("praeses Gentileus" in Latin, "president Gentil" in French) is a well-known historical figure. René Gentil, a native of Tortona, in the Duchy of Milan, was made councilor of the Parliament of Paris in 1522, and then president of the *Chambre des Enquêtes* in 1528. In 1542 he was accused of official misconduct, and hanged at the gibbet of Montfaucon on September 25, 1543.[36]

The rise and fall of such a prominent figure served as inspiration for several poems. Théodore de Bèze dedicated one of his *Epitaphs* to him, published in his *Iuvenilia* (1548);[37] a French funerary poem was already printed in 1544;[38] and the Protestant Rasse des Noeux included, in a poetic collection assembled in the 1560s, two further Latin poems and another one in French.[39]

The poem in the copy of the *Epigrammata* is not found elsewhere, and in fact has remarkable differences with the other known poems of Gentil's execution. These attacked or mocked Gentil rather harshly, whereas ours inquires for his wrongdoings, and then he is given the opportunity to speak for himself: resembling a stoic philosopher, he declares that his fate had been sealed from his birth, and that he had been fortunate enough to escape it in Italy.

It is tempting to identify the author with Nicolas Maillard (Nicolaus Mallarius), doctor of theology at the Sorbonne from 1522, correspondent of Erasmus in 1531, dean of the Faculty of Theology in 1558 and leader of a delegation of Paris theologians to the Council of Trent in 1562.[40] His poetic activity is attested in the printed works of others, where he published several poems

---

35   On the possible identity of Mallarius, see below; nothing is known, on the other hand, about the translator.

36   See Édouard Maugis, *Histoire du Parlement de Paris de l'avènement des rois Valois à la mort d'Henri IV* (Paris, 1913–1916) vol. 1, 169, 179, 356–58; vol. 3, 152, 165; Mario Ascheri, *Un maestro del 'Mos Italicus': Gianfrancesco Sannazari della Ripa* (Milano, 1970), 24–6.

37   *Inc.* "fracto gutture stare quem revinctum"; see Kirk M. Summers, *A View from the Palatine: The* Iuvenilia *of Théodore de Bèze* (Tempe, 2001), 130–1 no. 16, and 163.

38   *Inc.* "Entre longbards iadis prins ma naissance"; see Clément Marot, *L'enfer* [...]. *Plus ballades & rondeaulx dependents de l'argument* ([Lyon], 1544), fol. 39v.

39   Paris, Bibliothèque nationale de France, MS Français 22560, 2nd part, fols. 35r (*inc.* "Scalarum e gradibus Gemoniarum") and 50v–51r (*inc.* "Insubres ortum, cultum Romuleia tellus"; "Lors que Gentil au gibet on menoit"). The French poem recurs in other sixteenth-century collections: ibid., MS Dupuy 736, fol. 218v; MS Dupuy 843, fol. 125r.

40   See James K. Farge, *Biographical Register of Paris Doctors of Theology 1500–1536* (Toronto, 1980), 296–301 no. 323; idem, "Nicolas Maillard," in *Contemporaries of Erasmus* (Toronto, 1986), vol. 2, 369–70.

between 1516 and 1544, all but one in elegiac verse, and with an apparent taste for classical mythology.[41]

The last poem [fig. 4; appendix no. 4] is found in the copy that formed part of the library of Giovanni Bernardino Bonifacio (1517–97),[42] which he donated to the city of Gdansk in 1591, thus becoming the core of today's Gdansk Library of the Polish Academy of Sciences.[43] Two hands appear in the volume: one marked some names, passages and poems that he found interesting, and compiled an index of some of them at the end; the other wrote a poem on the verso of the flyleaf prior to the frontispiece. Since both hands seem to belong to Italian humanists and do not match Bonifacio's,[44] they most probably antedate his departure from Italy in 1557.

The epigram, in elegiac verse, bears the heading *Roma loquitur* and is 12 verses long. The city of Rome begins by deploring that, having once been the center of the world and covered with marble, long ago she lay prostrate and defenseless against barbaric ruin (vv. 1–4). However, to finally honor the dead, she has recently come in this new semblance ("in effigiem hanc"), so that the remembrance of Rome's golden past will serve as a model for the addressee and their children, who will strive to cast out this foulness (vv. 5–10). In the conclusion, Rome proclaims that the virtue of the ancient Romans is already shining on the forehead of a young man (vv. 11–12).

The new "semblance" of Rome that shows its pristine glory should refer to the book itself: thus, the poem would have been made especially for the *Epigrammata*, which in turn explains its prominent location, mirroring the frontispiece. Since the allusion to the addressee's both noble linages (v. 9 "amborum [...] clari de stirpe parentum") and to a young man (plausibly the addresse's son) appear too specific to be merely rhetorical, we may venture that the inscribed copy was a gift to the addressee, who possibly shared the dedicator's interest in the recovery of Rome's ancient glory, in which the epigraphic collection participated.

---

41   An epigram in Bernardinus Rincius, *Sylva* (Paris, 1518), is full of classical references (e.g. to the *Charites*): see Stephen Bamforth, Jean Dupèbe, "The *Silva* of Bernardino Rincio (1518)," *Renaissance Studies* 8:3 (1944), 256–315, there 312–3. Another one in Jérôme de Hangest's *Moralia* (Paris, 1521) mentions *Apollo*.

42   Mandfred Welti, *Die Bibliothek Giovanni Bernardino Bonifacio, Marchese d'Oria 1517–1597. Der Grundstock der Polnischen Akademie der Wissenschaften* (Bern, 1985), 95 and 301 no. 400. On Bonifacio, see Domenico Caccamo, "Bonifacio, Giovanni Bernardino," *DBI* (Roma, 1970), vol. 12, 197–201.

43   Gdańsk, Biblioteka Gdańska PAN, Ce 7706 4°.

44   I have compared the annotations with two autograph letters kept in Basel, Universitätsbibliothek, Frey-Gryn Mscr II 2, fols. 7r–8r.

5 Conclusion

Evidence of the *Epigrammata*'s reception as an anthology of ancient epigrammatic poetry can be found both in the marginalia to the verse inscriptions of the book and in the literary pieces added in several copies. There can be no doubt that these are related to the reading of the inscriptions, especially those in verse. Indeed, they share the same genre, the epigram, ranging from six to sixteen verses, and their preferred meter is in both cases the elegiac verse.

The subject of the handwritten epigrams is not always connected with the book—Molza's and Accolti's poems are the clearest examples. More often, however, the content of the epigrams does respond to the work they were written into, most of the compositions being contemporary verse epitaphs: Ariosto's, Cesare Sacchi's, René Gentil's, and the unnamed couple's. While these poems drew inspiration from ancient funerary epigrams such as those found in the book, they belonged to a consolidated, independent literary genre in the Renaissance. Finally, one poem falls into the category of antiquarian poetry: the epigram where Rome itself recounts its past glory and successive misfortune. This is also the only case where the text is specifically connected to the book; the rest of the poems were probably not intended as paratexts (they are placed preceding or following the book and lack any direct borrowing from or allusion to the inscriptions), but rather as suitable additions to the *Epigrammata*'s content.

To conclude, the exclusive interest in the metrical inscriptions and the addition of literary epigrams can be attributed to an audience quite distinct from that of the antiquarians, since most of the evidence analyzed here is found in copies with no other signs of interest in the inscriptions. As we have seen, most of these annotations can be dated to the first decades after the publication of the book, in stark contrast with the antiquarians, who continued to annotate their copies throughout the Cinquecento, and sometimes still in the seventeenth or eighteenth century. It is possible that the non-antiquarian reader found, in the second half of the century, other epigrammatic collections that suited their taste better.[45] Finally, one wonders whether Mazzocchi was appealing to this particular type of reader, to broaden the book's audience—and therefore its saleability—, when he chose the title *Epigrammata*, and not *epitaphia*, *vetustates*, *antiquitates* or *inscriptiones*, which had been the terms used in printed epigraphic collections until then.[46]

---

45   E.g. Gulielmus Bercherus, *Epitaphia et inscriptiones lugubres* (London, 1566); Tobias Fendt, *Monumenta sepulcrorum cum epigraphis* (Breslau, 1574); Laurentius Schrader, *Monumentorum Italiae quae hoc nostro saeculo et a Christianis posita sunt libri quatuor* (Helmstedt, 1592); Nathan Chytraeus, *Variorum in Europa itinerum deliciae* (Herborn, 1594).

46   Nicolaus Marschalk, *Epitaphia quaedam mire vetustatis* (Erfurt, 1502); Conrad Peutinger, *Romanae vetustatis fragmenta* (Augsburg, 1505); idem, *Inscriptiones vetustae Romanae*

Appendix. Unpublished Poems in the Copies of the *Epigrammata antiquae Urbis*

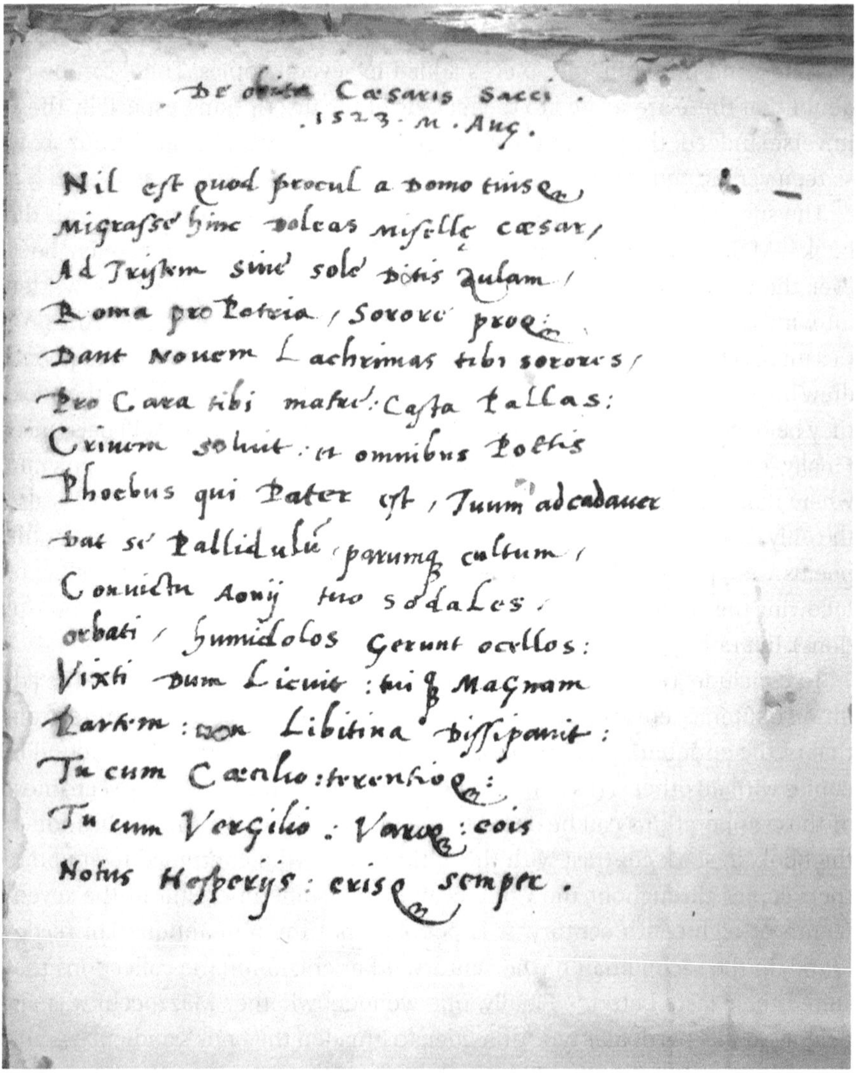

FIGURE 21.1   Hamilton (ON), McMaster University, D 1160, front pastedown
THE WILLIAM READY DIVISION OF ARCHIVES AND RESEARCH
COLLECTIONS, MCMASTER UNIVERSITY LIBRARY

---

et earum fragmenta (Mainz, 1520); Johannes Huttich, *Collectanea antiquitatum in urbe atque agro Moguntino repertarum* (Mainz, 1520).

THE *EPIGRAMMATA ANTIQUAE URBIS* (1521) AND THE MUSES

1. Hamilton (ON), McMaster University, D 1160 (front pastedown):

De obitu Caesaris Sacci, 1523 m(ense) Aug(usto)
Nil est quod procul a domo tuisque
migrasse hinc doleas, miselle Caesar,
ad tristem sine sole Ditis aulam.
Roma pro patria, sorore proque
dant novem lachrimas tibi sorores;   5
pro cara tibi matre, casta Pallas
crinem solvit, et omnibus poetis
Phoebus qui pater est tuum ad cadaver
dat se pallidulum parumque cultum,
convictu Aonii tuo sodales   10
orbati humidolos gerunt ocellos.
Vixti dum licuit, tuique magnam
partem non Libitina dissipavit.
Tu cum Caecilio Terentioque,
tu cum Vergilio Varoque Eois   15
notus Hesperiis erisque semper.

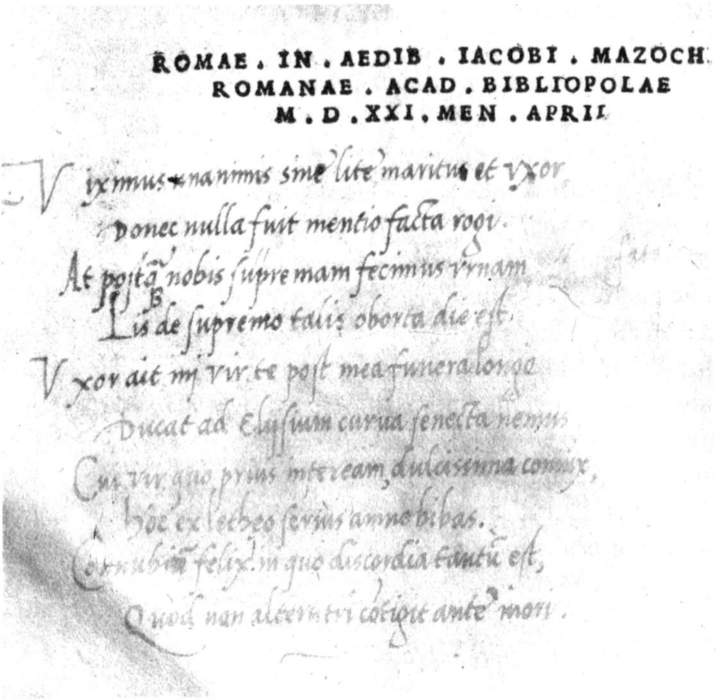

FIGURE 21.2   London, The Warburg Institute, CKN 336.M19, f. [aa8r]
THE WARBURG INSTITUTE AND LIBRARY

THE *EPIGRAMMATA ANTIQUAE URBIS* (1521) AND THE MUSES

2. London, The Warburg Institute, CKN 336.M19 (after the colophon):

Viximus unanimes[47] sine lite maritus et uxor
    Donec nulla fuit mentio facta rogi.
At postquam nobis fatalem[48] fecimus urnam
    lis de supremo talis oborta die est.
Uxor ait: "mi vir, te post mea funera longe   5
    ducat ad Elysium curva senecta nemus".
Cui vir, "quo prius inteream, dulcissima coniunx,
    hoc ex lethaeo serius amne bibas".
Connubium felix! in quo discordia tantum est
    quod non alterutri contigit ante mori.   10

---

47   *corr. ego* : unanimis *MS.*
48   fatalem *corr. i.m. MS* : supremam *MS.*

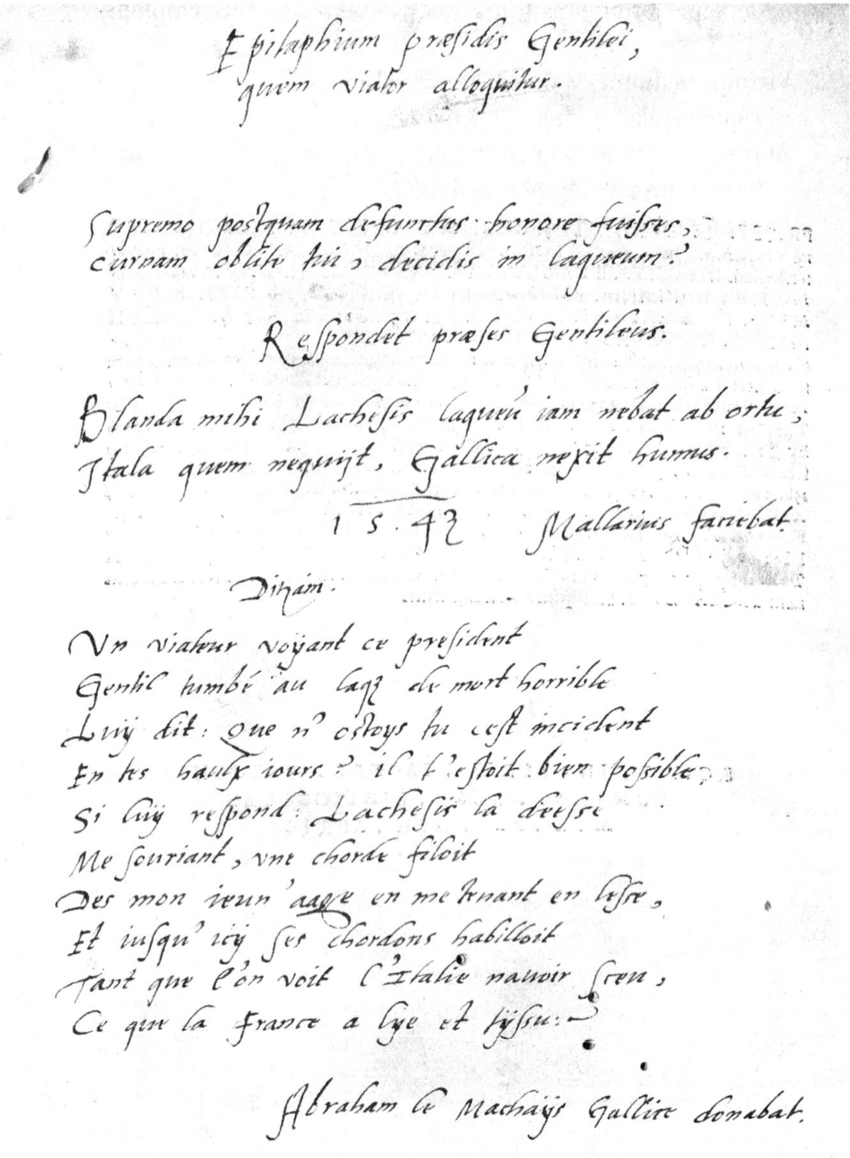

Epitaphium præsidis Gentilei,
quem viator alloquitur.

Supremo postquam defunctus honore fuisses,
curnam oblite tui, decidis in laqueum?

Respondet præses Gentileus.

Blanda mihi Lachesis laqueum iam nebat ab ortu,
Itala quem nequijt, Gallica nexit humus.

1 5 42   Mallarius faciebat

Dizain.

Vn viateur voyant ce president
Gentil tumbé au lacq de mort horrible
Luij dit: que n' estoys tu cest incident
En tes haultz iours? il t'estoit bien possible.
Si luij respond Lachesis la deesse
Me souriant, vne chorde filoit
Des mon ieun' aage en me tenant en lisse,
Et iusqu' icij ses chordons habilloit
Tant que l'on voit l'Italie nauoir freu,
Ce que la France a lye et tijssu:

Abraham le Machaijs Gallice donabat.

FIGURE 21.3   Trento, Biblioteca Comunale, t-G 2 c 157, f. [aa8v]
BIBLIOTECA COMUNALE DI TRENTO

THE *EPIGRAMMATA ANTIQUAE URBIS* (1521) AND THE MUSES

3. Trento, Biblioteca Comunale, t-G 2 c 157 (verso of last printed page):

Epitaphium praesidis Gentilei, quem viator alloquitur
Supremo postquam defunctus honore fuisses,
   cur nam, oblite tui, decidis in laqueum?
Respondet praeses Gentileus:
Blanda mihi Lachesis laqueum iam nebat ab ortu,
   Itala quem nequiit, Gallica nexit humus.
                    1543 Mallarius faciebat.

Dizain:
Un viateur voyant ce president
Gentil tumbé au laque de mort horrible
luy dit: "que n'ostoys tu cest incident
en tes haulx jours? Il t'estoit bien possible."
Si luy respond: "Lachesis la deesse   5
me souriant, une chorde filoit
des mon jeun'aage, en me tenant en lesse,
et jusqu'icy ses chordons habilloit
tant que l'on voit l'Italie n'avoir sceu
ce que la France a lye et tyssu."   10
            Abraham le Machays Gallice donabat.

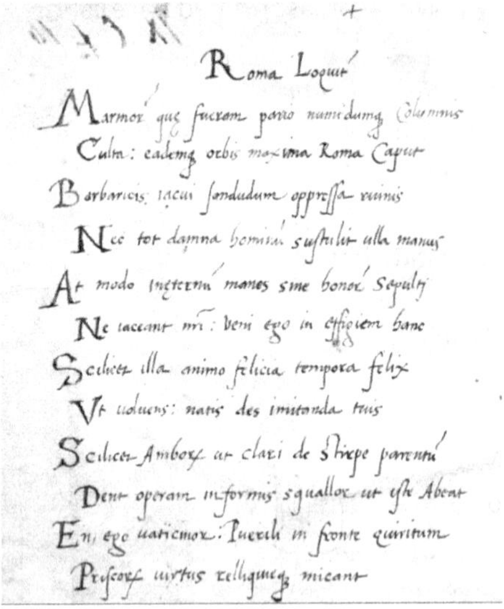

FIGURE 21.4 Gdansk, Biblioteka Gdańska PAN, Ce 7706 4°, verso of the front flyleaf

POMERANIAN DIGITAL LIBRARY, NO. 4537

THE *EPIGRAMMATA ANTIQUAE URBIS* (1521) AND THE MUSES

4. Gdansk, Biblioteka Gdańska PAN, Ce 7706 4° (verso of the front flyleaf):

Roma loquitur:
Marmore quae fueram Pario Numidumque columnis
    culta, eademque orbis maxima Roma caput,
barbaricis iacui iandudum oppressa ruinis
    nec tota damna hominum sustulit ulla manus.
At modo in aeternum manes sine honore sepulti   5
    ne iaceant nostri, veni ego in effigiem hanc
scilicet illa animo felicia tempora felix
    ut volvens natis des imitanda tuis
scilicet amborum ut clari de stirpe parentum
    dent operam informis squallor ut iste abeat.   10
En, ego vaticinor: puerili in fronte Quiritum
    priscorum virtus relliquiaeque micant.

Universitat Autònoma de Barcelona (UAB)

CHAPTER 22

La figure du tyran dans les *Adages* d'Érasme

Lika Gordeziani

Abstract

Comme nous le savons, les *Adages* subissent un changement important dans la version parue en 1515. Érasme apparaît désormais dans cet ouvrage non seulement comme un érudit, mais aussi comme un penseur. En effet, il profite souvent de l'occasion que lui offre une expression antique pour s'exprimer sur les sujets qui lui tiennent à cœur. Un de ces sujets est l'abus du pouvoir. Des remarques et des réflexions sur le mauvais monarque, ou le tyran, sont assez récurrentes dans l'ensemble du recueil. Dans la mesure où les *Adages*, appartiennent à la lignée d'ouvrages didactiques d'Érasme et s'adressent à l'élite, aux nobles qui côtoient la cour, il nous a paru intéressant de voir ce qui est dit dans ce recueil de la figure du tyran et de son pouvoir. Dans cet article, nous proposons une étude en trois temps : nous nous attachons d'abord au portrait moral et physique du tyran et au mode de fonctionnement de son pouvoir, puis aux circonstances contribuant à la tyrannie, et, enfin, aux moyens par lesquels on peut s'y opposer. Nous nous appuyons principalement sur les commentaires-essais dont sont munis les adages *Aut regem aut fatuum nasci oportere* et *Scarabaeus aquilam quaerit*, puisqu'ils sont consacrés à la question du gouvernement, mais aussi sur d'autres commentaires, plus ou moins célèbres, qui contiennent des remarques importantes à cet égard.

Keywords

Desiderius Erasmus – *Adagia* – Neo-Latin political literature – tyrant – early modern political discourse

Comme nous le savons, dans la version parue en 1515, les *Adages*[1] subissent un changement important. Érasme apparaît désormais dans cet ouvrage non

---

1 Nos éditions de référence sont celles de l'ASD (2.1–8) et de Jean-Christophe Saladin (Paris, 2011). Pour les traductions françaises des adages et de leurs commentaires nous nous appuyons toujours sur celles de l'édition de Jean-Christophe Saladin.

seulement comme un érudit, mais aussi comme un penseur.[2] En effet, il profite souvent de l'occasion que lui offre une expression antique pour s'exprimer sur les sujets qui lui tiennent à cœur,[3] ce qui fait apparaître dans le recueil des commentaires-essais[4] tels que ceux des adages *Aut regem aut fatuum nasci oportere* (« Il faut naître roi ou fou » n°201), *Spartam nactus es, hanc orna* (« Le sort t'a remis Sparte : fais-la resplendir » n°1401), *Sileni Alcibiadis* (« Les silènes d'Alcibiade » n° 2201), *Scarabeus aquilam quaerit* (« Un scarabée qui pourchasse un aigle » n°2601), *Dulce bellum inexpertis* (« La guerre paraît douce à ceux qui n'en ont pas l'expérience » n° 3001).[5] Un des sujets mis en valeur dans cette nouvelle version des *Adages* est le mauvais usage du pouvoir,[6] ce qui s'explique sans doute par le fait qu'au moment où elle est préparée (1509–14), l'humaniste voit avec grande inquiétude le monde chrétien entraîné dans une guerre permanente par la soif insatiable de conquêtes et les incessantes revendications de quelques princes.[7]

Il faut dire que des remarques et des réflexions sur le mauvais monarque, ou le tyran, sont assez récurrentes dans l'ensemble du recueil, et que nous n'en trouvons pas seulement dans les cinq essais mentionnés ci-dessus. Dans la mesure où les *Adages*, appartiennent à la lignée d'ouvrages didactiques d'Érasme et, même s'ils ne sont pas dédiés à un roi, s'adressent néanmoins à l'élite, aux nobles qui côtoient la cour,[8] il nous a paru intéressant de voir ce qui est dit dans ce recueil de la figure du tyran et de son pouvoir. Dans cet article, nous proposons une étude en trois temps, en nous attachant d'abord au portrait moral et physique du tyran et au mode de fonctionnement de son pouvoir, puis aux circonstances contribuant à la tyrannie, et, enfin, aux moyens par lesquels on peut s'y opposer. Pour cela nous nous appuyons principalement sur les commentaires des adages *Aut regem aut fatuum nasci oportere* et *Scarabaeus aquilam quaerit*, consacrés à la question du gouvernement, mais aussi sur d'autres commentaires plus ou moins célèbres, qui contiennent des remarques importantes concernant cette question.

---

2 Margaret Mann Phillips, *The 'Adages' of Erasmus. A Study with Translations* (Cambridge, 1964), 35.

3 Ibid., 84.

4 Jacques Chomarat, *Grammaire et rhétorique chez Érasme* (Paris, 1981), 768.

5 Notons toutefois que les adages *Dulce bellum inexpertis, Sileni Alcibiadis* et *Scarabeus aquilam quaerit* figurent déjà dans l'édition aldine (1508) en tant qu'adages n° 1404, 1706 et 1913, mais ils n'occupent pas une place particulière et leurs commentaires sont beaucoup plus courts.

6 Phillips, *The 'Adages' of Erasmus* (voir ci-dessus, n. 2), 36.

7 Pierre Mesnard, *L'essor de la philosophie politique au XVIème siècle* (Paris, 1969), 90.

8 Le baron William Mountjoy, le dédicataire du recueil, est d'ailleurs proche du jeune roi Henri VIII d'Angleterre.

Tout d'abord, une mise au point terminologique s'impose. Rappelons que le sens dans lequel Érasme emploie le plus souvent le terme *tyrannus* diffère de la signification initiale du mot grec dont il est l'équivalent, dans la mesure où il se rapporte à la qualité du souverain et non à son statut. Si le τύραννος grec désigne « celui qui usurpe le pouvoir absolu dans un État libre »,[9] le *tyrannus* érasmien est tout souverain qui gouverne mal, quelle que soit la manière dont il a obtenu son pouvoir. Comme le note Pierre Mesnard dans son ouvrage *L'essor de la philosophie politique au XVIème siècle*, la conception juridique du tyran est remplacée par une conception morale.[10] Toutefois, il faut dire que, si au nombre des tyrans de l'époque archaïque figurent Pittacos de Mytilène et Pisistrate d'Athènes, connus pour leur modération et leur bienveillance, la tyrannie, en tant que forme de gouvernement, est critiquée par les philosophes à partir de l'époque classique à cause du fait qu'elle confère au monarque un pouvoir arbitraire et illimité.[11] C'est en s'appuyant sur la classification d'Aristote,[12] selon laquelle la tyrannie est une aberration de la royauté (Παρέκβασις δὲ βασιλείας μὲν τυραννίς),[13] qu'Érasme oppose le tyran au roi.[14] Néanmoins, le terme *rex* ne désigne pas toujours un bon souverain. À plusieurs reprises, Érasme rappelle sa valeur péjorative, en se référant à la réalité romaine. Quand il essaie d'expliquer l'association des rois aux fous, il rappelle aux lecteurs que cet adage était né chez les Romains, pour qui le mot *rex* était aussi odieux que les mots *barbarus* et *tyrannicus*, s'opposant à la liberté publique à laquelle ils tenaient avant tout.[15] Il rappelle la connotation négative du mot *rex* également quand il s'en prend à la vanité des souverains de son époque, disant que ce titre que les grands personnages romains évitaient, le considérant comme démesuré et craignant d'attirer de l'hostilité, certains maintenant s'en satisfont à peine y ajoutant toute une liste d'éclatantes épithètes illusoires.[16] Quand il parle d'un bon souverain, Érasme semble privilégier le terme *princeps*. Certes, ce terme se rapporte au statut, dénué en soi de connotations éthiques, de la personne

---

9 *Le Grand Bailly, Dictionnaire grec-français d'Anatole Bailly*, éd. E. Egger, revue par L. Séchan et P. Chantraine (Paris, 2000), 1977. Toutefois, Mario Turchetti note que l'usurpation n'est pas un caractère distinctif de la tyrannie ancienne, puisque certains tyrans avaient eu accès au pouvoir de manière légitime. Voir Mario Turchetti, *Tyrannie et tyrannicide de l'Antiquité à nos jours* (Paris, 2013), 35.

10 Mesnard, *L'essor de la philosophie* (voir ci-dessus, n. 7), 120.

11 Turchetti, *Tyrannie et tyrannicide* (voir ci-dessus, n. 9), 34–7.

12 Comme le rappelle Pierre Mesnard, les emprunts à Aristote à propos du tyran sont nombreux chez Érasme, voir Mesnard, *L'essor de la philosophie* (voir ci-dessus, n. 7), 128.

13 Aristot., *Eth. Nic.*, 8,10,1160a. Cf. *Pol.*, 5,1310b.

14 *Scarabeus aquilam quaerit* (n° 2601, *ASD* 2.6 : 400).

15 *Aut regem aut fatuum nasci oportere* (n° 201, *ASD* 2.1 : 314).

16 *Scarabeus aquilam quaerit* (n° 2601, *ASD* 2.6 : 401).

LA FIGURE DU TYRAN DANS LES *ADAGES* D'ÉRASME   315

la plus importante de l'État, du chef. À plusieurs reprises, il désigne même les
monarques critiqués. Pourtant, dans le commentaire de l'adage *Aut regem aut
fatuum nasci oportere*, Érasme insiste sur le fait que c'est un nom que l'on devrait mériter par un bon gouvernement.

1   Le tyran et son pouvoir

Voyons d'abord comment est représentée la figure du tyran, et ce qui est dit
exactement de sa manière de gouverner. Si le τύραννος grec était parfois un bon
souverain, le *tyrannus* érasmien, quant à lui, est un monarque tout à fait odieux
et nuisible. Il est le Mal en personne, et il conduit son peuple à la ruine. Plus
précisément, en tenant compte de ce que disent les commentaires d'adages,
on peut décrire le tyran comme un être cruel, insatiable, insensé, capricieux,
à la fois redoutable et craintif, dangereux pour tous et haï de tous. Sa présence
à la tête de l'Etat est un véritable fléau pour son peuple. Nous voudrions ici
attirer l'attention sur quelques points qui nous semblent particulièrement
importants.

– Le tyran est un souverain insensé, qui n'a pas la sagesse requise chez un
   monarque.

Après s'être interrogé sur la légitimité de l'opposition établie dans l'adage *Aut
regem aut fatuum nasci oportere*, et avoir constaté qu'en réalité la plupart des
rois ont été insensés, Érasme insiste sur l'importance de la sagesse[17] et dit
qu'un chef d'État, s'il est sot, l'est pour le grand malheur du monde entier, en
revanche, s'il est sage, il l'est pour le grand bien de tous. Puis, il souligne que
le seul critère valable dans l'appréciation d'un chef d'État est la sagesse, et reprend la thèse de Platon, selon laquelle les États ne peuvent être heureux que
si l'on confie le gouvernement aux philosophes, ou si ceux auxquels il est échu
de gouverner s'attachent à la philosophie.[18] Il s'ensuit de là qu'un bon souverain est un souverain sage, et qu'en revanche celui qui n'a pas cette vertu est un
mauvais souverain. Or, pour parler de ce dernier l'humaniste emploie le mot

---

17   Comme le rappelle Mario Turchetti, la sagesse requise chez un chef d'État est à la fois bon
       sens, intelligence, érudition, raison, prudence, clairvoyance et elle correspond à la science
       politique. Voir la *Formation du prince chrétien*, trad. Mario Turchetti (Paris, 2015), 80–1.

18   Plat., *Resp.*, 5,473cd. Cette idée, à laquelle Érasme adhère complètement, est reprise dans
       le commentaire de l'adage *Scarabeus aquilam quaerit* (n° 2601, *ASD* 2.6 : 400) et l'*Institutio
       principis* (*ASD* 4.1 : 144–5). Comme le note Fiorella De Michelis Pintacuda, il s'agit avant
       tout de la *Philosophia Christi*. Voir Fiorella De Michelis Pintacuda, « L'*Instiutio principis
       christiani* di Erasmo da Rotterdam, » *Mélanges de l'École française de Rome. Moyen Âge,
       Temps modernes*, 99 (1987), 261–73, ici 268.

tyrannus. En associant le mal à la déraison, Érasme est probablement influencé par Platon.[19]

– Le tyran est un monstre dangereux caché sous le masque des apparences.

L'idée que le tyran est un être dangereux est récurrente dans les *Adages*. L'expression *Porro a Jove atque a fulmine* (« Loin de Zeus et de ses foudres » n° 296) sert à rappeler qu'il vaudrait mieux se tenir à l'écart des puissants, en particulier des tyrans, qui peuvent perdre un homme d'un seul signe de tête si bon leur semble.[20] Ceux qui côtoient la cour ne sont pas les seuls à être en péril. Comme le rappelle le commentaire de l'adage *Aut regem aut fatuum nasci oportere*, le tyran est, par sa sottise, funeste à la terre entière (« orbis totius malo stultus est »).[21] Pour accentuer l'aspect dangereux du tyran, Érasme présente celui-ci comme une créature effrayante. Il le compare aux animaux de proie comme l'aigle,[22] le loup[23] et lion.[24] Comme le signale Pierre Mesnard,[25] Érasme suit la tradition biblique où les loups et les lions désignent les princes tyranniques.[26] Si le tyran est rapproché des animaux redoutables, il est lui-même décrit comme une sorte de monstre. Comme dit l'adage n°102, les tyrans ont plusieurs oreilles et yeux (« Multae regum aures atque oculi »).[27] Certes, le mot employé est *rex*, mais dans le commentaire Érasme prend soin de préciser qu'il s'agit d'un roi tyrannique qu'il qualifie de « portentum ».[28] En outre, après avoir expliqué que l'adage désigne de manière allégorique la multitude d'espions que les tyrans ont à leur service, l'humaniste ajoute que les tyrans non seulement ont plusieurs yeux qui voient partout et plusieurs oreilles, longues comme celles des ânes,[29] mais aussi autant de mains, de pieds, ventres.[30] Un tel portrait monstrueux apparaît également quand Érasme dit que les aigles humains ont de très nombreuses oreilles, autant d'yeux, de serres, de becs, et de ventres.[31] Si l'humaniste insiste sur l'aspect repoussant du tyran, c'est sans doute parce qu'en réalité, la tyrannie n'est pas toujours facile

---

19   Plat., *Protag.*, 345c.

20   *Porro a Jove atquea fulmine* (n° 296, ASD 2.1 : 401–2).

21   *Aut regem aut fatuum nasci oportere* (n° 201, ASD 2.1 : 306).

22   *Scarabeus aquilam quaerit* (n° 2601, ASD 2.6 : 401–2).

23   *Scarabeus aquilam quaerit* (n° 2601, ASD 2. 6 : 408–10).

24   *Leonis catulum ne alas* (« Ne nourris pas le petit du lion » n° 1277, ASD 2.3 : 292).

25   Mesnard, *L'essor de la philosophie* (voir ci-dessus, n. 7), 120–1.

26   Zeph 3.3 ; Ez 22.27.

27   *Multae regum aures atque oculi* (n° 102, ASD 2.1 : 216).

28   Ibid.

29   Ibid. Cf. l'adage *Midas auriculas asini* (« Les oreilles d'âne de Midas » n° 267, ASD 2.1 : 376–8).

30   *Multae regum aures atque oculi* (n° 102, ASD 2.1 : 216).

31   *Scarabeus aquilam quaerit* (n° 2601, ASD 2.6 : 405).

à percevoir. En effet, le commentaire du célèbre adage *Sileni Alcibiadis* avertit le lecteur qu'il ne doit pas se laisser tromper par les signes extérieurs de la majesté, car ce souverain aux titres imposants et à l'allure divine risque d'être un silène inversé :[32] si l'on regardait à l'intérieur, on verrait un tyran qui est pour son peuple une véritable Ἰλιάδα κακῶν (« une *Iliade* de malheurs »), comme dit le proverbe grec.[33]

– Si le tyran ruine son peuple, c'est parce que sa manière de gouverner est malsaine.

Premièrement, le tyran gouverne non pour le peuple, mais pour lui-même. Cette idée empruntée à Aristote[34] est particulièrement développée dans le commentaire de l'adage *Scarabeus aquilam quaerit,* où l'humaniste déplore le fait qu'alors que le roi devrait entièrement se consacrer au bien-être de son peuple, la plupart des souverains méritent l'injure ignominieuse qu'Achille lance à Agamemnon : δημοβόρος βασιλεύς[35] (« roi dévoreur-de-son-peuple »). En effet, ils n'ont qu'un seul but, faire en sorte que tout ce qu'ils font leur serve à détourner les richesses collectives dans leur cassette personnelle, véritable tonneau percé et « aquilarum in morem innoxiarum avium visceribus se suosque saginent pullos » (« s'engraisser, eux et leur progéniture, à la manière des aigles, avec les viscères d'inoffensifs oiseaux »).[36] L'adage Ἐγχέλεις θηρᾶσθαι (« chasser des anguilles »), répertorié en latin sous la forme *Anguillas captare* (« Capturer des anguilles » n° 2579), permet de rappeler que pour piller plus librement le peuple, les souverains tyranniques n'hésitent pas à provoquer des guerres et des séditions, tournant à leur propre avantage le malheur qu'ils provoquent ainsi dans l'État.[37]

Deuxièmement, le tyran abuse de son pouvoir absolu. Plusieurs commentaires mettent l'accent sur le fait que le tyran est un être capricieux et que ses caprices coûtent cher à ses sujets.[38] Plusieurs commentaires insistent

---

32   *Les Silènes d'Alcibiade*, éd. Jean-Claude Margolin (Paris, 1998), XLV–XLVI. Sur la méfiance d'Érasme à l'égard de l'apparente magnificence voir aussi James D. Tracy, *The Politics of Erasmus. A Pacifist Intellectual and His Political Milieu* (Toronto, 1978), 36.

33   *Sileni Alcibiadis* (n° 2201, ASD 2.5 : 168). Pour l'expression Ἰλιάδα κακῶν voir l'adage *Ilias malorum* (n° 226, ASD 2.1 : 338).

34   Aristot., *Eth. Nic.*, 8,10,1160b. Cf. *Pol.* 5,1310b–1311a.

35   Hom., *Il.* 1,231.

36   *Scarabeus aquilam quaerit* (n° 2601, ASD 2.6 : 400–2).

37   *Anguillas captare* (n° 2579, ASD 2.5 : 381–2).

38   Voir par exemple ceux des adages *Aut regem aut fatuum nasci oportere* (n° 201, ASD 2.1 : 310), *Porro a Jove atque a fulmine* (n° 296, ASD 2.1 : 401–2), *Festina lente* (n° 1001, ASD 2.3 : 20), *Anguillas captare* (n° 2579, ASD 2.5 : 381–2).

sur l'aspect arbitraire d'un gouvernement tyrannique.[39] Dans celui de l'adage *Festina lente* (« Hâte-toi lentement » n°1001), Érasme redoute la mise en place d'une tyrannie barbare, semblable à celle qui existe chez les Turcs où tout serait soumis aux lubies d'un seul homme.[40]

Troisièmement, le pouvoir du tyran s'appuie sur la sottise et sur la peur. Il est à noter que bien que tout-puissant, le tyran est craintif. Il a peur que l'on ne s'empare de son pouvoir. Il peut redouter des êtres beaucoup plus faibles que lui, mais plus ingénieux. Cette idée est exprimée dans le commentaire de l'adage *Scarabeus aquilam quaerit* à travers l'image de l'hostilité de l'aigle envers le petit oiseau trochile (le roitelet), qui tout en étant faible et fuyard, est doté d'habileté et d'ingéniosité grâce à quoi il réussit à vaincre l'aigle.[41] La terreur d'être détrôné fait aussi que le tyran déclare la guerre à tous ceux qui ont une opinion différente de celles de la multitude. Transposée dans le monde des oiseaux, cette inimitié est représentée par celle de l'aigle et du cybindis, une sorte d'épervier nocturne qui voit clair la nuit.[42] Selon Pierre Mesnard, cet oiseau symboliserait le penseur politique.[43] Le pouvoir du tyran se nourrit donc de la sottise du peuple. Le tyran est également hostile envers ceux qui ont le courage de s'exprimer librement, et comme l'aigle au cygne, il s'en prend à la race des poètes. En effet, les poètes, même au risque de leur vie, n'hésitent pas à attaquer les autorités dans leurs écrits.[44] Si le tyran a peur de la liberté d'opinion, c'est que sa toute-puissance se fonde sur la terreur qu'il inspire et qui provoque l'asservissement de ses sujets. Il accepte d'être haï de tout le monde, pourvu qu'on le craigne.[45] Ce principe est illustré par l'adage *Oderint, dum metuant* (« Qu'ils me haïssent, pourvu qu'ils me craignent » n° 1862).[46]

2   Le chemin vers la tyrannie

Érasme ne se contente pas de brosser un portrait monstrueux du tyran et de souligner l'aspect malsain de la tyrannie, il s'interroge également sur la voie qui mène à un tel régime.

---

39   *Scarabeus aquilam quaerit* (n° 2601, ASD 2.6 : 400), *Haec potior* (« La minorité l'emporte » n° 528, ASD 2.2 : 54–6) et *Non probantis* (« De qui refuse de donner son approbation » n° 2701, ASD 2.6 : 484).

40   *Festina lente* (n° 1001, ASD 2.3 : 20).

41   *Scarabeus aquilam quaerit* (n° 2601, ASD 2.6 : 408).

42   Ibid.

43   Mesnard, *L'essor de la philosophie* (voir ci-dessus, n. 7), 126.

44   *Scarabeus aquilam quaerit* (n° 2601, ASD 2.6 : 408).

45   *Scarabeus aquilam quaerit* (n° 2601, ASD 2.6 : 409).

46   *Oderint, dum metuant* (n° 1862, ASD 2.4 : 252).

LA FIGURE DU TYRAN DANS LES *ADAGES* D'ÉRASME

Dans le commentaire de l'adage *Aut regem aut fatuum nasci oportere,* il se demande si le peuple n'est pas lui-même responsable des malheurs qui l'accablent, dans la mesure où il ne confie pas le pouvoir à celui qui le mérite par son expérience, mais il admet que le pouvoir échoie à quelqu'un uniquement parce qu'il est né dans une famille noble. Alors que celui qui veut devenir aurige doit d'abord en apprendre la technique, s'y exercer, s'y préparer, on estime que la naissance suffit pour devenir chef d'un État, quoique cette dernière fonction soit la plus difficile. Alors que l'on tient compte des compétences d'un pilote de navire, responsable de quelques passagers et d'une maigre marchandise, on considère suffisant que le chef d'État soit né comme tel, lui qui est responsable de tant de vies. Érasme met donc en cause ici la transmission héréditaire du pouvoir royal, la jugeant périlleuse puisqu'elle met le pouvoir entre les mains de celui dont on ne sait encore s'il va être un bon souverain. C'est non sans amertume qu'il reconnaît que ce mode de transmission de pouvoir est trop ancré dans les mœurs pour être changé et que l'on est donc obligé d'accepter que l'on naisse chef d'État, et que[47]

> cuicunque sors faverit, sive probus sit ille sive improbus, sive stultus sive sapiens, sive sanus sive motae mentis, modo figuram habeat hominis, ei summa rerum credenda est. Hujus arbitrio mundus bellis et caedibus miscebitur, sacra ac prophana omnia perturbabuntur

> quel que soit l'homme que la Fortune a favorisé, qu'il soit honnête ou malhonnête, stupide ou sage, sain d'esprit ou dérangé, pourvu qu'il ait figure humaine, il faut lui confier la plus haute charge. Selon son bon vouloir, le monde sera ruiné par des guerres et des massacres, tout ce qui relève du sacré et du profane sera profondément bouleversé.

À cela s'ajoute le fait que le futur souverain est corrompu par la mauvaise éducation qu'il reçoit. Plus loin, dans le même commentaire,[48] Érasme déplore le fait que les futurs souverains, ceux qu'il faudrait élever de la meilleure manière possible, sont élevés de la manière la plus corrompue et la plus négligée. L'enfant qui est destiné à gouverner le monde est confié à des femmelettes complètement insensées qui, non seulement ne lui apprennent rien qui soit digne d'un souverain, mais le détournent de sa fonction, si le précepteur lui donne un sage conseil ou si l'enfant est naturellement enclin à la bienveillance. Ce qu'elles font, c'est de lui enseigner à agir en tyran. On lui montre qu'il lui est permis de faire tout ce qui lui plaît, il entend dire que toutes les propriétés de

---

47   *Aut regem aut fatuum nasci oportere* (n° 201, *ASD* 2.1 : 310).
48   *Aut regem aut fatuum nasci oportere* (n° 201, *ASD* 2.1 : 312–4).

tous ses sujets appartiennent au prince, que le prince est au-dessus des lois. Enfin, « depuis son enfance, il n'apprend à jouer rien d'autre qu'à la tyrannie » (« dum adhuc puer est, nihil aliud discit ludere quam tyrannidem »).[49]

Ainsi corrompu, le futur souverain est aussi entouré de flatteurs. Aux mauvaises nourrices s'ajoutent le précepteur, les ministres, les représentants de l'Église.[50] Enfin, personne n'ose contredire. Tous se montrent obséquieux, se souciant non de la patrie mais de sa propre fortune.[51] Se comportant ainsi, l'entourage abêtit le monarque. Érasme le dit explicitement, profitant de l'occasion que lui offre l'explication de l'adage grec Σοφοὶ τύραννοι τῇ σοφῶν συνουσίᾳ, en latin *Sapientes tyranni sapientum congressu* (« Les rois deviennent sages au contact des sages » n° 2497) qu'il modifie à la fin du commentaire. En effet, il souhaite que cet adage plaise aux souverains de son époque, dont on dirait plutôt Μωροὶ τύραννοι τῶν κολάκων συνουσίᾳ (« Le commerce des flatteurs rend les princes fous »).[52]

Enfin, non seulement ceux qui côtoient le monarque sont responsables de son abêtissement, et donc de sa future tyrannie, mais le peuple l'est aussi. Nous avons noté plus haut qu'il commet l'erreur d'admettre la transmission héréditaire du pouvoir, créant le risque qu'une tyrannie se mette en place. À cette imprudence, si l'on peut dire, s'ajoute le fait qu'il ne juge pas le chef d'État selon les bons critères. Dans le commentaire de l'adage *Aut regem aut fatuum nasci oportere*, Érasme se plaint de ce que la populace stupide admire tout chez son souverain, sauf ce qu'elle devrait exiger de lui. Elle apprécie la noble naissance, la jeunesse, la beauté, la hauteur, la force, la richesse, l'éloquence, le talent dans le chant et la danse, la capacité de boire, l'habileté aux jeux, au lieu de considérer la qualité vraiment digne d'un souverain, c'est-à-dire la sagesse.[53]

3   Remèdes à la tyrannie

Malgré le fait qu'Érasme présente le tyran comme l'incarnation du mal, nulle part il n'invite au tyrannicide,[54] et il est contre la révolution ; il est d'avis qu'au lieu de lutter contre la tyrannie, il faudrait la prévenir.

---

49   *Aut regem aut fatuum nasci oportere* (n° 201, ASD 2.1 : 312).
50   Ibid.
51   Ibid. Cf. *Scarabeus aquilam quaerit* (n° 2601, ASD 2.6 : 402 et 404).
52   *Sapientes tyranni sapientum congressu* (n° 2497, ASD 2.5 : 343–4).
53   *Aut regem aut fatuum nasci oportere* (n° 201, ASD 2.1 : 306).
54   Daniel Ménager, « Tyrannie, » dans *Éloge de la folie, Adages, Colloques, réflexions sur l'art, l'éducation, la religion, la guerre, la philosophie, correspondance*, éd. Claude Blum, André Godin et Jean-Claude Margolin (Paris, 1992), CCXXXIII.

LA FIGURE DU TYRAN DANS LES *ADAGES* D'ÉRASME   321

En effet, la tyrannie est un mal dont on ne peut se libérer sans grand dommage. Il vaudrait donc mieux éviter un tel régime, plutôt que de le combattre une fois qu'il est établi. Cet avertissement apparaît notamment dans les commentaires des adages *Multitudo imperatorum cariam perdidit* (« La foule des généraux a ruiné la Carie » n° 1607), *Ut fici oculis incumbunt* (« Comme des kystes qui grossissent dans les yeux » n° 1765) et *Leonis catulum ne alas* (« Ne nourris pas le petit du lion » n° 1277). L'adage *Leonis catulum ne alas* nous conseille de ne pas soutenir un pouvoir qui pourrait l'emporter sur les lois, puisqu'une fois mis en place, on ne pourra plus le combattre sans porter dommage à l'État. Érasme dit de manière explicite qu'un tyran ne doit pas être admis, mais que s'il l'est, on doit le supporter (« Tyrannus aut ferendus est, aut non recipiendus »).[55] Dans le commentaire de l'adage *Ut fici oculis incumbunt*, les tyrans sont comparés à des kystes qu'il est urgent d'enlever des yeux, mais dont l'ablation est extrêmement douloureuse.[56] Quant à l'adage *Multitudo imperatorum cariam perdidit*, il nous avertit que si la tyrannie est le pire des maux, la polyarchie, qui équivaut à l'anarchie, est encore pire. Cet adage, dont le sens est proche des paroles qu'Ulysse prononce dans l'*Iliade*[57] lorsqu'il veut arrêter le tumulte des soldats achéens, trahit la peur d'une révolution.[58]

On pourrait éviter la tyrannie en donnant une bonne éducation à celui qui devra plus tard gouverner l'État. Étant donné que le système de la monarchie héréditaire ne peut pas être ébranlé (« esto, receptius est quam convelli possit »),[59] il faut prendre soin de choisir un bon précepteur pour l'héritier du trône, afin que celui-ci reçoive une bonne éducation et comprenne ce que c'est qu'un véritable *princeps*,[60] il faut que le futur souverain, détenteur du pouvoir absolu, soit entouré de sages, comme le rappelle l'adage *Sapientes tyranni sapientum congressu*. Il faut que l'on cesse d'apprécier chez le souverain des qualités qui ont peu d'importance dans l'administration d'un État et que l'on exige celle qui est cruciale : la sagesse. Un autre moyen d'éviter la tyrannie serait de faire en sorte que le pouvoir ne soit pas concentré entre les mains d'une seule personne. Érasme le suggère dans le commentaire de l'adage *Festina lente*,[61] où il dit que pour le bien de l'État il faut qu'il y ait un équilibre de pouvoirs, mais

---

55   *Leonis catulum ne alas* (n° 1277, ASD 2.3 : 294).

56   *Ut fici oculis incumbunt* (n° 1765, ASD 2.4 : 190).

57   Hom., *Il.* 2,204.

58   *Multitudo imperatorum cariam perdidit* (n° 1607, ASD 2.4 : 92).

59   *Aut regem aut fatuum nasci oportere* (n° 201, ASD 2.1 : 310).

60   Ibid. Pour plus de détails sur les principes que le précepteur doit inculquer au futur souverain voir Lika Gordeziani, « The *Adagia* as an *Institutio Principis*, » *Erasmus Studies* 38 (2018), 219–34.

61   *Festina lente* (n° 1001, ASD 2.3 : 20).

aussi dans celui de l'adage *Servatori tertius* (« Une troisième pour le Sauveur » n° 1701), où il parle des mesures que l'on prenait à Sparte pour tempérer la gestion des affaires publiques et éviter ainsi de sombrer dans une tyrannie.[62]

En guise de conclusion, on pourrait dire que le tyran est le résultat que l'on obtient en acceptant que le pouvoir absolu soit transmis de manière héréditaire au lieu de le confier à celui qui le mérite par ses compétences, en corrompant par une mauvaise éducation et des flatteries la personne destinée à gouverner, et en la jugeant selon de mauvais critères. Plus que le tyran, c'est son entourage et le peuple qui sont incriminés. Tout en brossant un portrait monstrueux du tyran, l'humaniste met l'accent sur le fait que ses sujets font tout pour favoriser l'établissement d'un tel régime politique. En insistant sur la responsabilité du peuple, Érasme annonce le Contrat Social,[63] mais en adoptant un point de vue pessimiste : on ne fait rien pour éviter la mise en place d'une tyrannie et on doit endurer ensuite un gouvernement despotique. D'autre part, plusieurs commentaires trahissent l'attitude négative envers le pouvoir absolu. Si Érasme accepte la monarchie,[64] la concentration du pouvoir entre les mains d'une seule personne l'inquiète, et il laisse entendre que, tenant compte de la réalité, il est adepte d'un gouvernement où le pouvoir est tempéré et équilibré. Enfin, nous pourrions penser qu'en accentuant les points faibles du tyran (sa sottise, ses craintes), Érasme semble vouloir ébranler le mythe de la toute-puissance du tyran.

Université Paris Diderot-Paris 7

---

62   *Servatori tertius* (n° 1701, ASD 2.4 : 151–2).

63   Cf. Lester K. Born, « Notes on the Political Theories of Erasmus, » *The Journal of Modern History* 2.2 (Jun. 1930), 226–36, ici 227 ; Eberhard von Koerber, *Die Staatstheorie des Erasmus von Rotterdam* (Berlin, 1967), 33 et 47.

64   Cf. Von Koerber, *Staatstheorie* (voir ci-dessus, n. 63), 44 : « Die reine Monarchie war sein Ideal. »

CHAPTER 23

From Caesar to the Rantzaus: Allegory, Fiction and Reality in Heinrich Rantzau's *De obitu nobilissimae matronae Annae Rantzoviae Domini Ioannis Rantzovij coniugis Ecloga*

Trine Arlund Hass

Abstract

This paper is the first treatment of the eclogue *De obitu nobilissimae matronae Annae Rantzoviae Domini Ioannis Rantzovij coniugis Ecloga* presumably written by Heinrich Rantzau and published in Leipzig and Schleswig in 1582 as part of *Epitaphia aliquot in obitum Annae Walstorpiae*. The paper focuses on the use of the name Daphnis, which is intimately connected to the bucolic genre and through its use in Classical poems evokes certain associations and expectations, and the non-bucolic proper name of the deceased, Anna, which is used too. She is called by her proper name once while most frequently referred to as "Daphnidis uxor". It is discussed how allegory is employed in the construction of a narrative and how the text balances reality and fiction in its construction of an appealing picture of the Rantzau family starting with Heinrich Rantzau's mother, Anna Walstorp. It is examined how the authoritative reading of Vergil's eclogue 5, the primary model for funerary eclogues involving a Daphnis, influences the decoding of allegory in Rantzau's poem. The examinations employ and discusses Tilg's considerations of fiction (based on Frank Zipfel's categories) contained in this book.

Keywords

Heinrich Rantzau – *De obitu nobilissimae matronae Annae Rantzoviae Domini Ioannis Rantzovij coniugis Ecloga* (1582) – Neo-Latin pastoral poetry – allegory – fictionality

This paper[1] examines the intermingling of fiction and reality through the use of allegory by studying the use of a non-bucolic name as well as a well-known

---

1 The paper was written during my postdoctoral scholarship at the Danish Academy in Rome and Aarhus University, funded by the Carlsberg Foundation.

© KONINKLIJKE BRILL NV, LEIDEN, 2020 | DOI:10.1163/9789004427105_024

bucolic name in *De obitu nobilissimae matronae Annae Rantzoviae Domini Ioannis Rantzovij coniugis Ecloga* (referred to below as *De obitu*), which was published in Leipzig and Schleswig in 1582 as part of the work *Epitaphia aliquot in obitum Annae Walstorpiae.*[2]

The main focus in the following is the way in which Heinrich Rantzau[3] constructs an appealing picture of his family, starting with his mother. To this purpose, the concepts regarding allegory and its function introduced by Teskey will be applied. In the entry "Allegory" in *The New Princeton Encyclopedia of Poetry and Poetics* he writes:[4]

> An allegory arouses *hermeneutic anxiety* and supplies instructions for *interpretative play*. By engaging in such play, the reader builds a coherent structure of meaning that is then imagined to have been hidden in advance and to have been merely discovered by the reader. Hermeneutic anxiety and interpretative play are allegory's primary aesthetic effects. They are complemented by a sense of penetrating through the text toward a singularity—Dante would call it a *punto*—that is at the heart of the mystery of the world. Only there may one rest from interpretation. We may refer to this last as *the narcosis of repose in the truth*. Thus, the three phases of response to an allegory are *hermeneutic anxiety, interpretative play*, and *narcosis of repose in the truth*.

Accordingly this treatment is particularly concerned with the creation and relief of *hermeneutic anxiety* in Heinrich Rantzau's designations of the deceased, and how Rantzau presents the premises of an interpretative play in his construction of a fictive, allegoric narrative about his mother. It is furthermore considered how a well-known Classical model seems to be instrumental in directing the reader to the interpretation of the allegory and thus to the reality of his own world (Dante's *punto* or Teskey's *truth*), or rather, the version of it that Rantzau conveys.

The use of allegory as a communicative devise transgressed genres in this period—we find it in all sorts of texts as well as in visual media. Readers and

---

2 LN 570 4°; VD16 R 242 (entire publication) and VD16 R 239 (the eclogue). The entire work has no. 217 (Schleswig) and no. 218 (Leipzig) in Peter Zeeberg, *Heinrich Rantzau. A Bibliography* (Copenhagen, 2004).

3 Unless otherwise stated, "Rantzau" refers to Heinrich Rantzau in this text.

4 Gordon Teskey, "Allegory," in *The New Princeton Encyclopedia of Poetry and Poetics*, ed. Roland Greene et al. (Princeton, 2012, fourth edition), 37–40, there 37 (Teskey's emphasis).

audiences in general must be considered skilled in and ready for decoding allegories whether it be in a novel, an emblem or, as in this case, a poem. With respect to the relationship between reality and fiction, allegoric literature such as Rantzau's poem resembles the so-called *Fiktions-Hybridität* that Tilg has identified in Neo-Latin novels in his plenary paper.[5] Looking at the definitions of fiction by Zipfel discussed by Tilg, Rantzau's poem can be defined to some extent by using the term *Fiktivität*; as this text is made up by invented figures and their actions (here this is conversation) in a particular place; but as in the case of Tilg's example, although the *discourse* is clearly fiction, this is not an invented *story*.[6] Bucolic poetry is not a narrative genre per se; but as something like a plot structure can be defined in Rantzau's text it makes sense to talk about narratological concepts in relation to this text. The *story* in this eclogue is one that fits Tilg's suggested redefinition of Zipfel's classifications: "[...] die story-Ebene wird im Schlüsselroman ihrerseits noch einmal in einen fiktiven Vordergrund und einen faktischen Hintergrund aufgespalten."[7] In *De obitu*, reality has been mingled with and then presented in an allegorical fictional text.

After analyzing the poem's different ways of designating the deceased, their implication for the allegorical nature and interpretation of the text is discussed, as well as the effect of the fictionalization of the historical reality through the use of allegory with inclusion of Tilg's point of view on this.

Heinrich Rantzau, His Family and His Work

As the title reveals, the occasion of the poem is the death of Johann Rantzau's wife, Anna Walstorp. She was born in 1510 at Steinberg, the child of Gert Walstorp and Katharina Rantzau; and she died at Breitenburg Castle, which was built by her husband, in the valley of the Stör in Holstein on 29 December 1582. She was married (c. 1523) to Johann Rantzau (1492–1568), Knight of the Golden Spur, general, governor of the duchies of Schleswig and Holstein and member of the Danish privy council. After his death, most of his honorary positions were transferred to their oldest son, Heinrich Rantzau.

Although it was not generally regarded as a favourable sign for noblemen, Heinrich Rantzau authored and orchestrated publications. He had professionals

---

5   Stefan Tilg, "Autor/Erzähler und Fiktion im neulateinischen Roman: Ein Beitrag zu einer historischen Narratologie," this volume section 7 = pp. 81–83. Tilg discusses Frank Zipfel, *Fiktion, Fiktivität, Fiktionalität: Analysen zur Fiktion in der Literatur und zum Fiktionsbegriff in der Literaturwissenschaft* (Berlin, 2001).

6   Zipfel, *Fiktion, Fiktivität, Fiktionalität* (see above, n. 5).

7   Tilg, "Autor/Erzähler und Fiktion" (see above, n. 5), section 5, = pp. 78–79.

revise his own writings and hired writers on commission and procured a great number of copies of the works, distributing them personally in his own circles and asking his agents to make sure they were put in the hands of influential people all over Europe. Zeeberg, who has examined Rantzau's bibliography, regards the broad scope of this distribution as the reason why several works were printed simultaneously in several locations, as is the case with the work on which this paper focuses.[8] Rantzau was very anxious to stage his family through literature, such as funerary literature produced on the occasion of the death of family members—parents, siblings and children. The epicedia were issued on the relevant occasions but also collected in editions that Rantzau had distributed as he did with other *Rantzoviana*.[9]

De obitu is part of a publication containing six laments of Walstorp, of which the first four are attributed directly to Heinrich Rantzau by the statement of his name or initials in connection with the title; the fifth is attributed to Henning Conradinus, poet, teacher and co-author of several *Rantzoviana*. The eclogue, text number six, is not unequivocally attributed to an author here, but in a later edition, *Henrici Ranzouii epitaphia De obitum patris, matris, fratris, et sororis, nec non filiorum suorum: adiectum est praeterea opusculum de somniis eorumque eventibus* (Lepizig, 1584),[10] Heinrich Rantzau's initials are placed after the title of the eclogue. This paper is not concerned with the question of attribution, referring simply to Rantzau as the author of the eclogue as he is clearly the sender of the publication.

In the eclogue, the link between the *literal* world[11]—the fictional, bucolic world of the text—and the *figural*[12]—the historical context of the author— is ensured by the paratext and the poem's embeddedness among other texts written on the same occasion. This is the last of the six laments and the penultimate text in the work. For that reason, the eclogue's statement of theme and occasion in the title is iterative and at this point, although varied, almost formulaic.

---

8   The passage on Heinrich Rantzau's use and production of literature draws on Zeeberg, *Heinrich Rantzau* (see above, n. 2), 9–63. Other important works on Heinrich Rantzau are Dieter Lohmeier, "Heinrich Rantzau und die Anfänge der neulateinischen Literatur in Schleswig-Holstein," in: *Humanismus im Norden. Frühneuzeitliche Rezeption antiker Kultur und Literatur an Nord- und Ostsee*, ed. Thomas Haye (Amsterdam, 2000), 1–61, and Wiebke Steinmetz, *Heinrich Rantzau (1526–1598)* (Frankfurt am Main, 1991).

9   Cf. Zeeberg, *Heinrich Rantzau* (see above, n. 2), 39–40.

10   VD16 R 243, Zeeberg, *Heinrich Rantzau* (see above, n. 2) no. 219.

11   Teskey, "Allegory" (see above, n. 4), 37.

12   Ibid.

Daphnis in Different Realities

The title of the eclogue clearly explains that this is a poem about the passing of Anna Walstorp. It highlights her social status ("nobilissimæ matronae [...] Ioannis Rantzovij coniugis"), thus making it clear that Walstorp should be regarded as the main character of the poem as well as indicating that her privileged status has much to do with her marriage to Johann Rantzau. Heinrich Rantzau also presents her as Johann Rantzau's wife ("coniunx") and "matrona" in the general title and in the title of the eclogue, again referring to her marital status. In the titles of the first and third lament, however, she is referred to as his mother.

In the eclogue proper, Anna Walstorp is referred to as "Daphnidis uxor", with two exceptions. This survey presents all the occasions on which she is mentioned, using various designations.

> Designations for Anna Walstorp:
> Haud ignota fuit tibi *nostri Daphnidis uxor* [...] (v. 29)
> Sic quoque uirtutum *nostri pia Daphnidis uxor* ... (v. 41)
> [...] Floribus ornatur: sic *nostri Daphnidis uxor* (v. 45)
> [...] Hic sumus edocti, *quia nostri Daphnidis uxor* (v. 58)
> Nam uobis, nostri periit *quia Daphnidis uxor* [...] (v. 63)
> Clamantes, *genetrix* cur sic nos alma relinquis (v. 67)
> *Anna* mane, uel nos tecum quas ibis in oras [...] (v. 68)
> [...] Ergo quod occubuit *nostri pia Daphnidis uxor* [...] (v. 80)
> Si spectes corpus *nostri pia Daphnidis uxor* [...] (v. 96)
> [...] Haud minus e gremio *nostri pia Daphnidis uxor* [...] (v. 107)
> Haud frustra nuper *quia nostri Daphnidis uxor* [...] (v. 132)
> [...] Quod terras liquit *nostri pia Daphnidis uxor* [...] (v. 142)
> [...] Ecce stat ante meum *nostri pia Daphnidis uxor* [...] (v. 151)
> (*Daphnidis uxorem* monstrans) *quia* sedula cultrix [...] (v. 169)
> uiuit enim *nostri* uiuit *pia Daphnidis uxor* [...] (v. 180)

Walstorp is referred to as "Daphnidis uxor" 13 times, 12 of which occur at the end of a line. This designation very often occurs together with "nostri" (11 times) and "pia" (7 times), and sometimes with "quia" (4 times). Of these words, "quia" is less significant in terms of content but does contribute to the creation of a formulaic way of mentioning the deceased. The expression "Daphnidis uxor" is not quite a refrain, as it does not occur at regular intervals, but it does have a similar effect: it is iterated throughout the poem, thereby reminding readers constantly of the honorary identity marker presented in the title, her husband.

He, however, has been adapted to the bucolic, allegorical universe as he is fictionalised with the prototypical bucolic name Daphnis.

In classical bucolic poetry, Daphnis is the name of a mastersinger. He is mourned as a deceased mythical singer who invented the pastoral in Theocritus' first idyll and in Vergil, *Eclogue* 5. In Vergil's poem, the death of Daphnis is mourned first, but then his ascension to heaven is celebrated in the eclogue's second part. The name is rather frequently used for deceased celebrated in Neo-Latin funerary eclogues, which are most often based on Vergil's poem.[13] As the following shows, there are several formal similarities between Vergil's and Rantzau's text, for which reason it seems relevant also to consider the name as a referent or intertext.

Rantzau's poem roughly follows the general structure of Vergil's, as these surveys of the two poems show:

Vergil, *Eclogue* 5
1–19: Mopsus and Menalcas meet, discuss themes for song
20–44: Mopsus' song: The bucolic universe stands still to mourn Daphnis
45–55: Praise of Mopsus, introduction of following song
56–80: Menalcas' song: Daphnis has risen to Olympus, the bucolic universe is joyful
81–90: The singers exchange gifts

Rantzau, *De obitu*:
1–28: Menalcas and Mopsus meet. Purpose: relieve sorrow with conversation
29–36: They sing of the deceased's qualities
37–70: Menalcas: the world mourns the deceased*
71–129: Mopsus: consolation arguing that only the body dies while the soul lives forever*
130–140 Eulalius joins the two, is in a better mood
141–176: Eulalius: has seen Christ and angels fetch the deceased

---

13   For a general exemplary survey of Neo-Latin epicedia see Leonard W. Grant, *Neo-Latin Literature and the Pastoral* (Chapel Hill, 1965), 290–330; four of his examples refer to the deceased as Daphnis. For a newer, general introduction to Neo-Latin pastoral, see David Marsh, "Pastoral," in *Brill's Encyclopaedia of the Neo-Latin World*, ed. Philip Ford, Jan Bloemendal and Charles Fantazzi (Leiden, 2014), 425–36 and Estelle Haan, "Pastoral," in *A Guide to Neo-Latin Literature* ed. Victoria Moul (Cambridge 2017), 163–79. For a treatment of the pastoral epicedium, see Ellen Zetzel Lambert, *Placing Sorrow. A Study of the Pastoral Elegy Convention from Theocritus to Milton* (Chapel Hill, 1976).

177–182: Sadness is gone; life can go on with duties etc., Daphnis' wife looks over the world from heaven.
(*strictly speaking not monologues, but the mentioned interlocutor promotes the stated idea with encouragement from the other interlocutor.)

Rantzau's text features interlocutors named after Vergil's: Mopsus and Menalcas; and it, too, begins with a lament. It also ends with a celebration of the protagonist's ascension to heaven, describing how she is brought to paradise. There are variations on a macro- and micro-level in Rantzau's poem. For instance, the consolatory ascension is not worded by Menalcas as in Vergil's poem. Rantzau's Menalcas is lamenting while Mopsus offers consolation, but even the consolation is different. It has a theological nature, arguing that only the body dies while the soul will live on. Anna's ascension to heaven is described by a third interlocutor, Eulalius, who is an addition to the Vergilian structure. Eulalius reports that he has seen the ascension in a dream, and his unfolding of an eyewitness report is presented as an embedded narrative. This offers the internal and external audiences of the text the experience of the miraculous happening in real time. In one sense, Eulalius' narrative iterates Mopsus' theological argument; it offers practical proof of it and thus real comfort that allows life to go on.

As already stated, the designation "Daphnidis uxor" is a bucolic, allegorised, fictional version of the designation of Walstorp found in the eclogue's title and on the title page. Reusing the name of Vergil's deceased shepherd effectively integrates Walstorp in the bucolic universe and furthermore makes it possible to include the protagonist of the classical model repeatedly, although it is not Daphnis' death that is mourned. Using this term causes hermeneutic anxiety and invites interpretative play because it masks reality and although it is fairly easy to conjecture that Daphnis represents Johann Rantzau it does require the reader to pause in order to make the identification. However, in Rantzau's text, the connection to the historical reality (Daphnis = Johann Rantzau) does not take us all the way to *il punto* or the *truth*. That requires consideration of the contemporary understanding of Rantzau's model.

At this time, the readings of the late antique commentaries, and Servius in particular, were almost as famous as Vergil's eclogues themselves.[14] The commentary often accompanied Vergil's text and formed the foundation of Vergilian exegesis for centuries, not least during the Renaissance. Consequently, studying Servius is an effective way of obtaining insight into (part of) the horizon

---

14   See David Scott Wilson-Okamura, *Virgil in the Renaissance* (Cambridge – New York, 2010), 252–66 for a survey of printed commentaries on Vergil.

of expectations of Renaissance readers and writers concerned with Vergil and bucolic poetry. About Daphnis, Servius writes:[15]

> [M]ulti dicunt, simpliciter hoc loco defleri Daphnim quendam pastorem [...] alii dicunt significari per allegoriam C. Iulium Caesarem, qui in senatu a Cassio et Bruto viginti tribus vulneribus interemptus est: unde et 'crudeli funere' volunt dictum [v. 20]. sed si de Gaio Caesare dictum est, multi per matrem Venerem accipiunt, per leones et tigres populos quos subegit, per thiasos sacra quae pontifex instituit, per formosum pecus populum Romanum. alii volunt Quintilium Varum significari, cognatum Vergilii [...]

Reading Daphnis as Julius Caesar became the most successful interpretation in the exegetic tradition.[16] One could say that the figured meaning of Vergil's text, as attested by Servius and others, adds a new layer to the figured meaning of Rantzau's text. To a reader who knows Vergil through the commentary tradition and thus is used to thinking of Daphnis as representing Julius Caesar, the evocation of Johann Rantzau as Daphnis in a context resembling that of Vergil's Daphnis suggests that he, when presented as Daphnis, should also be likened to Daphnis' figured meaning, Julius Caesar.[17] Johann Rantzau was famous for his accomplishments as a general and politician, and thus fits Caesar's general characteristics better than if he is simply identified with the mastersinger of the bucolic world.

In the interpretative play, the borders between reality and fiction thus disappear. The literal and figured meanings of Vergil's Daphnis have become intertwined, and the historical reality of antiquity serves just as well as mythological or fictional material when it comes to constructing the *discourse* of Rantzau's poem. Rantzau in a way introduces a new protagonist when comparing to the model, both the literal and figured narrative, but he does so by

---

15 Servius on Vergil, *Ecl.* 5,20.

16 For a survey of the scholarly tradition on Daphnis' identification, see e.g. Edward Coleiro, *An Introduction to Vergil's Bucolics with a Critical Edition of the Text* (Amsterdam, 1979), 147–9.

17 The name Daphnis is commonly used as a masque for princes in bucolic poetry. Danish Erasmus Laetus and Hans Lauridsen Amerinus use Daphnis as masque for King Christian III and King Frederik II respectively; Grant, *Neo-Latin Literature* (see above, n. 17), 324 and 330 mentions that François Petremot of Paris presents Charles IX as Daphnis, Davide Hume of Godscroft presents King James as Daphnis and that John Barklay of Pont à Mousson presents the murdered Henri IV as Daphnis. See also Lambert, *Placing Sorrow* (see above, n. 13), 85 on Neo-Latin pastoral and the influence of Vergil, *Eclogue* 5.

FROM CAESAR TO THE RANTZAUS: ALLEGORY, FICTION AND REALITY 331

expanding the existing universe as he identifies her through her relationship to Daphnis, the original protagonist. In the following, the construction of this new character as an expansion is studied further, as well as how the model and its traditional interpretative context serves as a guide in the interpretive play.

Anna genetrix

In vv. 67 and 68 two deviations from the normal way of designating Walstorp occur: she is referred to as "genetrix" and simply with her first name, "Anna". As we said above, Rantzau rather than simply inventing a new character, makes further creative use of his classical model in the inclusion of his mother in the bucolic, elegiac world. Looking at the two instances where Walstorp is not presented as *uxor*, it becomes clear that he, although far from quoting Vergil, nevertheless establishes some parallels to the Vergilian text:

> Rantzau, *De obitu* 65–70 (**nymphs,** *mother, vocative*)
> [...] O quotiens votis nil proficientibus illam
> Storaides **nymphæ** reuocarunt, talia frustrà
> Clamantes, *genetrix* cur sic nos alma relinquis?
> *Anna* mane, vel nos tecum, quas ibis in oras,
> Transfer et hinc vultu te nunquam subtrahe nostro:
> Sed precibus cunctis stat inexorabile fatum.
> Vergil, *Ecl.* 5,20–25 (**nymphs,** *mother, vocative*)
> Exstinctum **Nymphae** crudeli funere Daphnim
> flebant (vos coryli testes et flumina **Nymphis**),
> cum complexa sui corpus miserabile nati
> atque deos atque astra vocat crudelia *mater*.
> non ulli pastos illis egere diebus
> frigida, *Daphni*, boves ad flumina; nulla neque amnem [...]

As the various highlighting in the quotations shows, both passages present mourning nymphs (Vergil has "nymphae" and "Nymphis", while Rantzau has "Storaides nymphae", thus connecting his nymphs to the local river Stör); in both texts the deceased is addressed directly (Vergil has "Daphni", Rantzau has "genetrix" and "Anna"); and in both texts denominations of feminine ancestry are found (Vergil has "mater", Rantzau has "genetrix").

Rantzau transforms Vergil's "mater", who mourns alongside the nymphs, into the object of mourning. The change of words from "mater" to "genetrix" strengthens the connection to the figural world of Vergil's poem, since Servius explained that if Daphnis is Caesar, then the mother in the poem must be understood as Venus, the divine ancestress of the *gens Julia* through whom Caesar and Augustus legitimised their power ("multi per matrem Venerem accipiunt"). Rantzau thus introduces the function in which Walstorp is immediately relevant to him, but more than that he directs attention towards genealogy, and thus to a mother role that goes beyond the immediate relationship between her and her child.

In the following line (v. 68), Walstorp is addressed as Anna. This disrupts the carefully established allegorical fiction, as the use of the actual name of the deceased naturally does not trigger hermeneutic anxiety: figured and literal meaning coincide. The apostrophe using her proper name is spoken by Menalcas, but he is presenting the laments of the nymphs of the Stör. This means that there is a reciprocal movement: the narrator becomes one level remote when the level of meaning is made more easily accessible; this somewhat compensates for the collapse of the distance between literal and figured worlds although this distance is of a different sort. Naming the deceased in a reversed way confirms the fictional contract of the Neo-Latin writers and readers that Tilg describes, based on which he says that "die Zweifel an der Realität des Erzählten willentlich ausgesetzt werden konnten."[18] It reminds us that *De obitu* is about reality—apart from the title and context, this is our key to unlocking the fictional, allegorical code. If there was any doubt about how the allegorical world relates to the real world, it has now been resolved.

Referring to Walstorp as "Anna" may also be a way for Heinrich Rantzau to let his mother stand out from the parallel established in the line before. Although she is honoured as the Julians honoured Venus, she is represented in her own right.

Concluding Remarks: Effects of Allegory and Fiction

As seen above, it is suggested that the funerary eulogy of Anna Walstorp presents the Rantzau family, to some extent, as parallel to the Julian dynasty in Rome. This parallel is established most notably, in a quantitative sense, through the designation of Walstorp as "Daphnidis uxor". As contemporary readers would associate the name Daphnis with Vergil's Daphnis, who is traditionally understood as masking Julius Caesar, this is the main vehicle of the parallel. It both governs the allegorical reading of the poem and projects an image of Heinrich Rantzau's parents as a unit. It is stylistically convenient because it

---

18   Tilg, "Autor/Erzähler und Fiktion" (see above, n. 5), section 5, p. 9.

enables Heinrich Rantzau to use the name of Vergil's deceased, although it would not work for his own protagonist.

The use of Walstorp's first name and the term "genetrix" promotes her role in the Rantzau narrative from being an anonymous wife and mother to gaining a proper identity and being associated with the divine ancestress of the Julians. Breaking the otherwise consistently applied allegory by referring to Walstorp as Anna allows her to formally assume the role of a key that unlocks the connection between reality and fiction. It also contributes to the originality of Rantzau's text, as this name, unlike Daphnis, is independent of the model. The name Anna points us in the direction of reality, the immediate decoding of the allegorical message (= this is a poem about the death of Anna Walstorp). The name Daphnis, on the other hand, leads us to the next level of understanding—the reason why this topic is presented in the form of an eclogue (= Anna's husband is comparable to one of the greatest generals of Rome who was mourned by Vergil in a similar poem, so this family can be understood as a contemporary parallel to the Julians). Together, the two names lead the reader to *il punto*. The apostrophe with *genetrix* in v. 67 also brings into focus Walstorp's role in the genealogy of the Rantzaus and specifically in relation to Heinrich Rantzau. His role must not be forgotten, as he is if not the author then still the sender of this text. The alignment of his parents with prestigious classical models, just as well as the presentation of especially his mother as able to rival the glory and piety of the models is evidently attractive. Heinrich Rantzau does not appear in the poem, as far as can be extracted, but if the world of references constructed by him means that a reader would associate him, as son and sender of the lament, with the next hero of the Julian line after Caesar, he would surely not mind. However, there are no direct indications of this in the text proper, just the general, unexpressed idea that the glory of ancestors shines onto their descendants.

On the point of possibilities and purposes, this last section returns to the discussion of fiction. In his final discussion, and by contrast with Zipfel, Tilg stated that the Neo-Latin novelists "[...] sahen das Nützliche an der Fiktion gerade in der unterhaltsamen fiktionalen Erzählweise, mit der faktische Inhalte eingängiger transportiert werden konnten."[19] However, when the facts are wrapped in a fictional or allegorical veil, more diligence is required by the reader in decoding the text. Rantzau's allegories are not particularly cryptic; but the allegorical mode nonetheless requires reading along a vertical axis, penetration through

---

19   Tilg, "Autor/Erzähler und Fiktion" (see above, n. 5), section 10, 88–90.

the layers of intertexts and meanings.[20] This means that the horizontal reading aiming at the plot and the end is paused repeatedly as the reader is considering matters like who is represented by this and that name, where he has seen this and that phrase before and what parts familiar or unfamiliar elements are playing in the new context.[21] If readers do not stop to consider questions like these they would only access the literal world of the text and thus be unable to extract the *truth* from it. In a world where allegory is a way of communication in so many media that would have been unsatisfactory and inspired further pausing or perhaps even returning to previous passages or entirely re-reading. I am not far from Tilg in his understanding of the usefulness of fiction to the Neo-Latin writers, as long as "eingängiger" is not necessarily taken to mean that perception is immediately easier. What is gained is rather a deeper, more lasting understanding—the imprinting of a memory—caused by the diligent reading process and the reader's experience of piercing through the layers of meaning and recognising what it is all actually about.

The Danish Academy in Rome & Aarhus University

---

20 Cf. Julia Kristeva, "Word, Dialogue and Novel," in *The Kristeva Reader*, ed. Toril Moi (New York, 1986), 35–59.
21 Cf. Peter Brooks, *Reading for the Plot* (Cambridge, 1992).

CHAPTER 24

Epigramme et épopée : quelques exemples tirés de l'épigramme lyonnaise des années 1530–40

Sylvie Laigneau-Fontaine

Abstract

A Lyon, s'est formé dans les années 1530 un groupe particulièrement homogène de quatre poètes néo-latins, membres du sodalitium Lugdunense : Bourbon, Dolet, Ducher et Visagier. Ce sont tous des poètes épigrammatistes et ils ont une pratique de ce genre littéraire tout-à-fait cohérente. L'une des caractéristiques de leur poésie est le goût du jeu avec les genres littéraires. Selon les analyses du théoricien Robortello, l'épigramme serait une « particule » des autres genres : la poésie du sodalitium Lugdunense peut apparaître comme une bonne mise en oeuvre de ces analyses. Les épigrammes de ces poètes empruntent en effet à divers genres et en particulier, alors que l'épigramme se situe tout en bas de l'échelle des genres, à l'épopée. La communication cherchera à cerner ces mécanismes et à déterminer les motifs de ces jeux avec le code épique, lesquels peuvent à l'évidence être d'ordre encomiastique, mais sont aussi parfois la marque d'un humour au second degré et d'une distance vis-à-vis de soi-même des plus amusantes.

Keywords

Nicolas Bourbon – Etienne Dolet – Gilbert Ducher – Jean Visagier – Neo-Latin epigram

Le groupe que l'histoire a retenu sous le nom de *sodalitium Lugdunense* est constitué d'intellectuels lyonnais qui, autour des années 1530–40, se retrouvaient en particulier dans l'atelier de l'imprimeur Gryphe. Parmi eux, des antiquaires, des médecins, quelques mécènes et beaucoup d'écrivains, pour certains en langue française (Maurice Scève) et pour quatre d'entre eux, tous auteurs d'épigrammes, en latin : il s'agit de Nicolas Bourbon, Etienne Dolet,

© KONINKLIJKE BRILL NV, LEIDEN, 2020 | DOI:10.1163/9789004427105_025

Gilbert Ducher et Jean Visagier,[1] qui semblent avoir constitué en quelque sorte l'âme du *sodalitium*.[2] Tous ont de l'épigramme une conception identique, conforme à ce qui apparaît déjà chez Catulle ou Martial : le premier, dans la pièce liminaire de ses *Carmina*, qualifiait son œuvre de *libellum* et de *nugae* ; le second, dans une scène bien célèbre (12,94), feignait d'avoir d'abord tenté tous les autres genres avant de se résoudre à descendre, par degrés, jusqu'à l'épigramme, soit le genre le plus modeste. À la Renaissance, l'humaniste suisse Vadian est le premier à s'intéresser à ce genre littéraire et le caractérise essentiellement par sa *breuitas* ;[3] ses successeurs, tous postérieurs à nos poètes, poursuivent dans la même voie : Simon de Vallambert affirme ainsi que l'épigramme doit être formulée *breuiter*[4] et Robortello voit dans l'épigramme une « particule » (« particulam ») des autres genres.[5] Pour l'instant, c'est essentiellement ce diminutif du terme *pars* qui m'intéresse.

L'épigramme est donc le genre humble par excellence, et nos auteurs soulignent cette caractéristique : un des *topoi* antiques qu'ils exploitent le plus souvent est le motif de la *recusatio*, emprunté aux élégiaques latins. C'est le cas de Bourbon dans la pièce 1,7 de ses *Nugarum libri octo*, dans laquelle, après avoir explicitement refusé les sujets didactiques, épiques ou tragiques, il affirme (v. 9–10) :

> Haec (inquam) qui nosse uoles tam grandia, abito :
> Ista tibi est alio fonte leuanda sitis.

---

1 Nicolas Bourbon, *Epigrammata* (Lyon, 1530) ; *Nugae* (Paris, Vascosan ; Bâle, Cratander, 1533) ; *Nugarum libri octo* (Lyon, 1538 et Bâle, 1540) ; édition moderne des *Nugae* de Cratander S. Laigneau-Fontaine (Genève, 2008). Etienne Dolet, *Carmina* (Lyon, 1538) ; édition moderne C. Langlois-Pézeret (Genève, 2009). Gilbert Ducher, *Epigrammatôn libri duo* (Lyon, 1538) ; édition moderne S. Laigneau-Fontaine et C. Langlois-Pézeret (Paris, 2015). Jean Visagier, *Epigrammatum libri duo* (Lyon, 1536) ; *Epigrammatum libri quattuor, eiusdem Xenia* (Lyon, 1537) ; *Hendecasyllaborum libri quattuor* (Paris, 1538) ; *Inscriptionum libri duo* (Paris, 1538). Les traductions ici proposées sont empruntées aux éditions citées ou sont personnelles. Sauf exception mentionnée, les citations de Bourbon sont tirées des *Nugarum libri octo* de 1538.

2 Pour des précisions sur le *sodalitium*, Ducher, *Epigrammatôn libri* (voir ci-dessus, n. 1), 33–82.

3 Joachim Vadianus, *De poetica et carminis ratione*, éd. Peter Schäfer (München, 1973–1977), tom. 1, 84.

4 Simon de Vallambert, *Epigrammaton somnia* [...] (Lyon, 1541), cité par Marie-Madeleine Fontaine, « Quelques traits du cicéronianisme lyonnais : Claude Guillaud, Florent Wilson, Barthélémy Aneau et Simon Vallembert, » dans *Scritture dell'impegno dal Rinascimento all'età barocca*, éd. Enea Balmas (Turin, 1998), 69.

5 Francesco Robortello, *Paraphrasis in librum Horatii qui uulgo De Arte poetica ad Pisones inscribitur* [...] (Florence, 1548) ; éd. dans Bernrd Weinberg, *Trattati di poetica e retorica del Cinquecento* (Bari, 1974), 509.

Si tu veux (dis-je) savoir de si grandes choses, passe ton chemin :
  C'est à une autre source que ta soif doit s'étancher.

Les sujets « grandia » sont donc fermement refusés à l'ouverture du recueil. La même idée se trouve chez Ducher, exprimée avec encore plus de modestie, sous la forme du récit d'une tentative avortée qui rappelle la première pièce des *Amours* d'Ovide ; le poète, qui a tenté de s'élever au genre de l'éloge en chantant les hauts faits du chevalier de Malte Georges de Vauzelles,[6] voit soudain apparaître devant lui une Calliope sarcastique qui lui fait comprendre que ce poids est supérieur à ses forces.[7] Cela explique que tous nos poètes qualifient leurs œuvres de « poèmes légers », de « bagatelles » (« nugae, apinae »), de « riens » (« flocci ») ou d'« œuvrettes », fruits de la faiblesse d'une inspiration basse.[8]

Néanmoins, il ne s'agit que d'une pure posture et ces auteurs ont au contraire une grande confiance en leur talent et en l'importance de leur œuvre. Loin des bagatelles, leurs recueils traitent parfois de sujets sérieux, dans lesquels ils s'engagent avec toute la puissance de leurs convictions : l'exemple le plus frappant est sans aucun doute la pièce 489 des *Nugae* de 1533 de Bourbon, intitulée « Ode à la gloire de Dieu très grand très bon », longue pièce de vingt-et-une strophes saphiques, qui chante la certitude des humanistes de voir triompher, avec les *literae politiores*, une civilisation meilleure, plus humaine.[9] On pourrait trouver, chez les autres, d'autres pièces aussi militantes, qui prouvent que les poètes du *sodalitium* n'en restent pas toujours à des sujets futiles. D'ailleurs, la définition de l'épigramme donnée par Robortello, « particule des autres genres », indique bien qu'elle peut emprunter ses sujets à tous les genres. Aussi ces auteurs n'hésitent-ils pas, parfois, à faire dériver leurs épigrammes vers l'épopée, si éloignés que soient ces deux genres sur l'échelle traditionnelle des genres littéraires.

Ils font tout d'abord passer un souffle épique dans les pièces dans lesquelles ils évoquent de glorieux personnages, auxquels ils rendent ainsi hommage. Bourbon, choisi par Jacques Galiot de Genouillac pour être le précepteur de

---

6 Sur la famille Vauzelles, voir Elsa Kammerer, *Jean de Vauzelles et le creuzet lyonnais (1520–1550)* (Genève, 2013).

7 Ducher, 2,64,6 : « Esse meis impar uiribus illud onus. »

8 « Leuis » : Ducher, 1,1,4 ; Bourbon, 3,55,5 ; Visagier, *Epigr.*, 1,183,12. « Nugae » : Bourbon, 1,133,31 ; 1,147,1 ; Dolet, 3,1,13–14 ; Visagier, *Epigr.*, 1,210,5 ; « Apinae » : Ducher, 1,197,8. « Floccus » : Visagier, *Epigr.*, 1,183,13. Diminutifs : Ducher, 2,233,10 ; Bourbon, 1,3,5 […].

9 Jugée dangereuse pour le poète qu'elle a contribué à envoyer en prison pour idées trop ouvertement évangéliques, la pièce fut supprimée des éditions de 1538 et 1540. Sur la biographie de Bourbon, voir l'introduction à mon édition citée des *Nugae* (voir ci-dessus, n. 1).

ses fils, ne pouvait pas honorer son employeur et protecteur en demeurant dans le genre humble. C'est donc en usant de *topoi* épiques qu'il évoque ce proche de François Ier, Grand Maître de l'artillerie, Grand Ecuyer de France (Bourbon, 1,56,3–12) :[10]

> Iure tibi, Galeote, data est heroica palma,
>> Pacis et armorum laus tibi prima fuit.
> Quid memorem insignem uirtutem et fortia facta
>> Quorum tota memor Gallia semper erit ?
> Nunc etiam uiridis superest et cruda senectus,
>> Visque animi crescens ingeniique uigor. [...]
> Hectora set si non digne cantauit Homerus
>> Nec potuit, moueo cur ego maius opus ?

> C'est à juste titre, Galiot, que te fut accordée la palme héroïque,
>> Et que ta gloire, en paix comme en guerre, a été au firmament.
> A quoi bon rappeler ton insigne vertu et tes courageux exploits,
>> Dont toute la France se souviendra toujours ?
> Maintenant encore, tu gardes une verte et solide vieillesse,
>> Ta force d'âme et la vigueur de ton esprit ne font que croître. [...]
> Mais si Homère a été incapable de chanter Hector dignement,
>> Que vais-je entreprendre une œuvre plus vaste encore ?

L' « heroica palma » fait ici référence à l'Ordre de saint Michel, conféré à Galiot en 1526[11] et assimile ce dernier aux grands héros antiques ; le procédé de la prétérition permet à Bourbon de faire allusion à ses exploits résumés par la formule « fortia facta » empruntée à Virgile (*Aen.*, 1,642), tout comme le vers 5, réécriture du vers 6,304 de l'*Enéide* (« Iam senior, sed cruda deo uiridisque senectus »). Enfin, le dernier distique, qui reprend le vers programmatique de Virgile au début du chant 7,[12] assimile Galiot à la fois à Enée et à Hector par la conditionnelle ; la louange des exploits de Galiot chez Bourbon est l'équivalent, chez Virgile, de l'évocation des combats d'Enée ; c'est évidemment

---

10   Sur ce personnage, voir par exemple Philippe Contamine, « Un seigneur de la Renaissance : Jacques de Genouillac, dit Galiot, maître de l'artillerie et Grand Ecuyer de France (1465–1546), » *Actes du groupe de recherches et d'études historiques de la Charente saintongeoise* 16 (1995), 277–94.

11   Cet ordre avait été créé en 1469 par Louis XI, à la fois pour répliquer à la création de l'Ordre de la Toison d'Or par Philippe le Bon et pour récompenser ses chevaliers les plus fidèles.

12   *Aen.*, 7,44–45 : « [...] Maior rerum mihi nascitur ordo, / maius opus moueo. »

aussi une manière, pour le poète lui-même, de s'assimiler à ses prestigieux prédécesseurs.

Bien souvent, pour évoquer les hauts personnages qu'ils entendent honorer, nos poètes abandonnent le distique, le mètre préféré de l'épigramme, au profit de l'hexamètre lui-même. C'est par exemple le cas de la pièce 1,16, que Dolet consacre à Henri de Lautrec et Claude-Guy de Laval,[13] qualifiés de « foudres de guerre » (« belli fulmina ») sur le modèle de Virgile, *En.*, 6,842, ou encore de l'épigramme 1,169 de Ducher, adressée « au seigneur Jean Stuart, illustrissime duc d'Albany »,[14] dans laquelle il s'emploie à grandir la figure de ce régent du royaume d'Ecosse, anti-Anglais et passé au service de François Ier (v. 1–6) :

> Belligeri fuerint Diomedes, Teucer, Achilles
> Quosque sibi celebres olim peperisse coronas,
> Hostibus edomitis, prodit cariosa uetustas.
> Tu contra Martem, nedum illos, uincis, et unus
> Pugnando Aeneae similis, stratagemate Ulyssi,
> Obsidione urbes penetras, certamine castra.

> Si belliqueux qu'aient été Diomède, Teucer, Achille
> Et tous ceux qu'on célèbre pour avoir gagné des couronnes,
> Une fois leurs ennemis domptés, les années les ont fait pourrir et oublier.
> Toi au contraire, tu vaincs Mars (et à plus forte raison ces héros) ; seul,
> En combattant, pareil à Énée et avec les ruses de guerre d'Ulysse,
> Tu pénètres dans les villes par le siège et dans les camps par le combat.

Publiée deux ans après le décès d'Albany, cette pièce fait de lui un héros plus grand que ceux de l'*Iliade* – destinés à l'oubli –, plus grand même que le dieu de la guerre : Ducher se garde évidemment de mentionner qu'en 1525, mandaté par François Ier pour marcher contre les forces impériales, Albany avait dû renoncer, ses hommes ayant fait défection aux Français pendant la bataille.

Même sans chanter un homme en particulier, les épigrammes qui font allusion aux guerres ou aux combats sont aussi de celles dans lesquelles la dérive vers l'épopée est la plus prégnante. Lorsqu'en 1536, François Ier se lance

---

13 Sur Henri de Foix, voir par exemple Verdun-Louis Saulnier, « Recherches sur Nicolas Bourbon l'Ancien, » *Bibliothèque d'Humanisme et Renaissance* 16 (1954), 172–91, ici 176.

14 Sur Albany, voir par exemple Arlette Jouanna et al., *La France de la Renaissance. Histoire et dictionnaire* (Paris, 2001), 1090–91.

340 LAIGNEAU-FONTAINE

de nouveau dans les guerres d'Italie et revendique le Milanais, Dolet adresse une pièce d'encouragement *Ad copias Gallicas in Italiam influentes* (Dolet, 1,57,1–6) :[15]

> Fata uocant, petite Italiam, Galli ; id iubet retextus,
>   id ordo fatorum iubet retextus.
> Italiam Galli petite ! Ira furorque sortis in uos
>   resedit : ad arma securi redite !
> Ecce Deus, Deus ecce Deus Mars Barbaris amicus
>   Nimium antea pedem parat referre !

> C'est l'appel du destin, attaquez l'Italie, Français : c'est le cours
> du Destin, inversant sa trame, qui l'ordonne.
> Attaquez l'Italie ! La colère et la fureur du Sort contre vous
> ont cessé : reprenez sans crainte les armes !
> Le voici le dieu, oui, le voici le dieu, le dieu Mars qui, trop proche ami
> des Barbares naguère, s'apprête aujourd'hui à reculer !

Quoique Dolet use non de l'hexamètre mais, conformément à son goût d'une métrique rare et précieuse, du « quatrième archiloquien », c'est bien une tonalité épique qui se dégage de cette pièce, sensible non seulement dans la présence du dieu Mars, mais aussi par l'intertexte tiré de l'*Enéide* : l'expression « fatorum ordo » figure en 5,707 et, surtout, au chant 6, c'est par le même syntagme « deus ecce deus » que la Sibylle annonce que le dieu prend possession d'elle-même, avant d'indiquer à Enée qu'il pourra détacher de l'arbre le rameau d'or nécessaire pour entrer aux Enfers « si les destins l'appellent » (« si te fata uocant », à la même place à l'ouverture du vers[16]). Substituant ici sa voix à celle de la prêtresse d'Apollon, Dolet, loin de l'humilité épigrammatique, se fait *uates* pour encourager les troupes françaises au combat.

C'est un autre moment des guerres d'Italie que Bourbon a chanté, ou plutôt déploré : la défaite par laquelle se solda, en 1528, l'invasion du royaume de Naples par Lautrec. Pour évoquer le typhus qui frappa l'armée française, le poète invoque la responsabilité de Mars, jaloux de l'ardeur des Français (Bourbon, 2,172,11–14) :

---

15   Ce titre est peut-être un clin d'œil ironique à Cicéron, *prov. cons.*, 32 : « Ipse ille Marius [...] influentis in Italiam Gallorum maximas copias repressit » : ce que les Gaulois n'ont pas réussi à faire, les Français y parviendront.

16   *Aen.*, 6,46 et 147.

QUELQUES EXEMPLES TIRES DE L'EPIGRAMME LYONNAISE (1530–40)   341

> Conserere ergo manus campo declinat aperto,
>   Aggrediturque alia Mars superare uia.
> O fati inuidiam ! Grassans per Gallica castra
>   Ille deus pestis uirus ubique ferit !

> Mars refuse donc d'en venir aux mains dans la plaine découverte,
>   Et entreprend de vaincre par un autre moyen :
> O destin plein de haine ! Le voilà qui traverse le camp français,
>   Ce dieu, et qui, partout, le frappe du poison de la peste.

Ce dieu frappant l'armée française rappelle bien entendu Apollon qui, au début de l'*Iliade*, envoie la peste sur l'armée grecque : il fallait hausser le ton pour transformer cette « hideuse catastrophe », pour reprendre le mot de Francis Hackett,[17] en un combat injuste entre un dieu malveillant et de courageux humains, et expliquer ainsi d'une manière satisfaisante pour l'orgueil français la défaite, due en réalité en grande partie à l'incurie du maréchal Odet de Lautrec.

En dehors des pièces qui évoquent spécifiquement des guerriers ou des combats, l'extragénéricité épique peut aussi être employée pour obtenir un effet de solennité. Bourbon, en 1,122 des *Nugarum libri octo,* adresse à François de Thou, le secrétaire d'Henri de Lautrec, une pièce de trente hexamètres d'un assez beau souffle, intitulée *Deploratio temporis* : elle évoque les catastrophes qui s'abattent sur le royaume de France, incendies, déluges, foudre, épidémies, famines, mais aussi et surtout guerres (v. 23–26) :

> Bella set in primis, bella, ô dii, qualia bella
> Quae fore uel quiuis pastor uel durus arator
> Praesciat, in promptu caussa est discordia regum
> Atque humana sui semper mens nescia fati.

> Mais, pire que tout, les guerres, les guerres, ô dieux, des guerres telles
> Que n'importe quel berger, n'importe quel laboureur dur à la tâche
> Les sent survenir, et dont la cause, évidente, est la discorde entre les rois,
> Et l'esprit humain toujours ignorant de sa propre destinée.

Le lyrisme du ton, la répétition emphatique de « bella », l'apostrophe aux dieux traduisent l'émotion de Bourbon et éloignent la pièce du registre des « bagatelles ».

---

17   Francis Hackett, *François Ier* (Paris, 1937), 415.

C'est un usage assez comparable du registre épique que l'on peut relever dans certaines pièces de Ducher et de Visagier: néanmoins, il ne s'agit plus pour le poète de faire partager au lecteur sa terreur devant une situation dramatique, mais de lui faire sentir son indignation devant l'attitude de certains personnages. En 4,18, Jean Visagier évoque la figure d'Antonio de Leiva, le *capitán general* des troupes de Charles Quint, à qui l'empereur dut en particulier sa victoire à Pavie ; Visagier laisse entendre les paroles de Leiva qui veut causer la ruine de la France puis commente : « O scelus, o immane nefas, ignobile crimen ! » (v. 19). Cette expression, présente au chant 6 de l'*Enéide* dans la description des grands criminels des Enfers,[18] est destinée à assimiler Leiva à l'un de ces criminels. Dans le même ordre d'idées, c'est à un ennemi des Belles Lettres que s'en prend Ducher en 2,9. Le poète, après avoir indiqué les méfaits d'un nommé Claude Mondor, qui « conspir[e] contre les savants de toute [s]a force »,[19] formule le vœu suivant : « Dii tibi pro meritis ea iusta praemia reddant » (v. 9 : « les dieux, pour tes mérites, te rendent, dans leur justice, les récompenses que voici »). Ce vers est une réécriture des vers de l'*Enéide* dans lesquels Priam s'adresse à Pyrrhus, qui vient d'assassiner son fils Politès et qui s'apprête à le mettre indignement à mort.[20] La haine sincère que Ducher ressent à l'égard de Mondor, ici assimilé à l'immonde Néoptolème, lui fait hausser le ton et justifie cet intertexte épique : c'est une véritable guerre que les humanistes livrent aux ennemis des Belles Lettres.

Chez Bourbon – et chez lui seul – peut être relevé un autre usage de l'extragénéricité épique, un usage parodique. C'est le cas dans la pièce 3,148, intitulée *De se ipso et Rubella puella*, qui narre en vingt-sept distiques élégiaques la première rencontre entre le poète et son égérie. Elle s'ouvre sur une atmosphère bucolico-élégiaque : Bourbon, qui endosse ici la *persona* de l'*ego* élégiaque, se promène à l'aurore dans un riant paysage de frondaisons et de roseraies, sous le souffle du zéphyr et au milieu des chants des oiseaux, lorsque soudain, en une épiphanie amoureuse, lui apparaît « une jeune fille, solitaire et magnifique, / qui [lui] sembl[e] une déesse et non une mortelle » ;[21] le coup de foudre est réciproque et, bientôt, les amants échangent mille baisers, lorsque surgit soudain la nourrice de la jeune fille, qui était à sa recherche et se jette sur elle (v. 43–50) :

---

18 *Aen.*, 6,624 « Vsi omnes immane nefas ausoque potiti. »

19 Ducher, 2,9,7 « Conspirans etiam in doctos, molimine toto. »

20 *Aen.*, 2,535–7 « [...] pro talibus ausis / di, si qua est caelo pietas quae talia curet, / persoluant grates dignas et praemia reddant. »

21 Bourbon, 3,148,7–8 « Sola mihi occurrit soli pulcherrima uirgo / non mihi mortalis, sed dea uisa fuit. »

QUELQUES EXEMPLES TIRES DE L'EPIGRAMME LYONNAISE (1530–40)

Inuolat in pulchros crines et uerberat ora,
  Ora quibus potuit Iuppiter ipse capi !
Adcurro, illa stetit contra mortemque minatur,
Lumina scintillant, esse putes Furiam.
Atque ubi tentaui succurrere fidus amator,
  Stringunt sacrilegae guttura nostra manus.
Et ni chara cito accessisset amica Rubella,
  Nunc ego cum Stygiis manibus umbra forem.

La voilà qui se jette sur ses beaux cheveux et qui frappe son visage,
  Ce visage qui aurait pu séduire Jupiter lui-même !
J'accours, elle me fait face et me menace de mort,
  Avec ses yeux luisants, elle a tout d'une Furie.
Et quand, en amant fidèle, j'ai essayé de secourir mon amie,
  Ses mains sacrilèges se serrent autour de ma gorge.
Si ma tendre amie, si Rubella n'était pas arrivée bien vite,
  A présent je ne serais plus qu'une ombre avec les mânes, sur le Styx

De bucolique et élégiaque qu'elle était, la scène est devenue épique : se trouvent en effet en présence un monstre terrifiant aux yeux luisants,[22] véritable Furie sortie des Enfers, une jeune fille en détresse et un héros en proie à un danger mortel ; leur groupe est mis en scène dans un récit auquel présents de narration et construction paratactique apportent une grande force d'évidence, tandis que le v. 45 possède une *iunctura* proprement épique.[23] Mais, dans le même temps, l'épopée est déconstruite par la parodie : le héros se révèle en fin de compte incapable d'agir et n'est sauvé que par sa belle, le monstre n'est qu'une vieille femme, l'expression « oculi scintillant » ne se trouve pas dans une épopée, mais dans une comédie de Plaute[24] et la clausule « umbra forem » figure dans l'élégie 3,7 des *Amours*, l'élégie du fiasco, dans laquelle Nason se plaint d'une défaillance passagère auprès de sa belle : il y a intertextualité plus glorieuse ...

Le même emploi parodique se trouvait déjà dans la pièce 2,164. Bourbon raconte à son frère, dans cette pièce de cinquante-deux hexamètres, une mésaventure qui lui est arrivée : alors qu'il chevauchait près de Vienne, en Isère, sous une assez forte tempête, son cheval l'a brusquement désarçonné, il est

---

22 Cf. Ovide, *Mét.*, 3,33 : « igne micant oculi » (le dragon qui attaque les compagnons de Cadmus).

23 Cf. Stace, *Théb.*, 11,295 : « In te ardens frater ferrum mortemque minatur. »

24 Plaute, *Men.*, 745.

tombé dans le Rhône et n'a dû son salut qu'à un passant qui l'a aidé à sortir du fleuve. Dès le début, la description de la tempête en fait une sorte d'apocalypse (v. 4–11) :

> Dum furit horrificis agitatus flatibus aër
> et sternit segetes, uellit radicitus ornos,
> sublimeisque aedes et summas deiicit arces,
> et glomerat densas immani turbine nubes
> aequoraque et fluuios uexat saeuoque boatu
> mortaleis omneis et murmure territat orbem,
> dilacerat naues, inuoluit et obruit undis,
> solus eram [...]

> L'air grondait, agité de souffles déchaînés ;
> Il couchait les moissons, déracinait les ornes,
> Renversait les plus hauts édifices, les citadelles les plus élevées,
> Rassemblait en un tourbillon monstrueux d'épais nuages,
> Bouleversait plaines et fleuves et, de son cruel mugissement
> Et de son grondement, terrifiait tous les mortels sur la terre,
> Disloquant les navires, les ensevelissant et les engloutissant sous les eaux.
> J'étais seul. [...]

L'adjectif « horrificus », qui appartient exclusivement à la langue épique,[25] donne le « la » : le ton sera celui de la grandeur et de l'horreur ; dans la suite, les expressions ou *iuncturae* épiques abondent ;[26] le Rhône lui-même se transforme en une mer en furie, sous les flots de laquelle des flottes entières disparaissent, et le vers 10 se termine sur une clausule lucrétienne.[27] Après cette longue protase, sous la forme d'une proposition temporelle étendue sur sept vers, la brièveté abrupte de l'apodose (« solus eram ») est clairement destinée à poser le poète en héros solitaire – pré-romantique ! – face à la violence des éléments.

Il serait trop long d'évoquer la suite du texte, qui est à l'avenant : le Rhône, « plus barbare que Scylla, que la Syrte et la monstrueuse Charybde », le poète

---

25   Lucrèce, 2,609 ; Virgile, *Aen.*, 3,225 ; Lucain, 2,372 ; Silius Italicus, 2,501 ; Valerius Flaccus, 2,97 et 518.

26   « Sternere segetes » est une variation sur « sternere agros » (Virgile, *Aen.*, 2,306) ; « immensi turbine » est présent chez Virgile (*Aen.*, 6,594) et Silius Italicus (12,538) ; le « murmur » de la tempête rappelle celle du chant 4 de l'*Enéide* (4,160).

27   Lucrèce, 5,413 : « [...] obruit undis » (certains éditeurs modernes lisent aujourd'hui « obruit urbes »).

QUELQUES EXEMPLES TIRES DE L'EPIGRAMME LYONNAISE (1530–40)   345

qui, tel le sage épicurien du début de chant 2 de Lucrèce, « regard[e] du haut d'un rocher, les bateaux faire naufrage »[28] Néanmoins, l'allusion à cette figure est sans doute ici destinée à encourager le lecteur à une lecture au second degré, dans la mesure où notre sage ne va pas tarder à se retrouver cul par-dessus tête et plongé dans les eaux mêmes qu'il contemplait avec sérénité. Tout à coup, en effet, raconte-t-il, « d'un chemin étroit, voici que bondit devant moi une chèvre » :[29] l'arrivée, dans ce paysage de fin du monde, d'un animal aussi prosaïque (qui va faire cabrer le cheval), surprend et fait sourire : dans l'épopée bourbonienne, c'est une chèvre qui tient lieu d'ennemi ! Dès lors, il convient de relire les tout premiers vers de la pièce (v. 1–3) :

> Si uacat atque placet casum cognoscere nostrum
> Quem referam paucis, audi, charissime frater,
> Quanquam animus meminisse stupet concussus et horret.

> Si tu as du temps, et l'envie d'apprendre le malheur qui m'est arrivé
> (je te le raconterai en peu de mots), écoute, mon bien cher frère,
> quoique mon âme, à ce souvenir, se fige sous le choc et s'horrifie.

On aura reconnu là, bien sûr, les mots par lesquels Enée annonce qu'il va accéder au souhait de Didon et raconter la dernière nuit de Troie, malgré la douleur que cela lui procure (*Aen.*, 2,10–13) :

> Sed si tantus amor casus cognoscere nostros
> et breuiter Troiae supremum audire laborem,
> quamquam animus meminisse horret luctuque refugit,
> incipiam.

> Mais si tu as une telle envie de connaître nos malheurs,
> et d'entendre brièvement raconter le dernier jour de Troie,
> quoique mon âme, à ce souvenir, s'horrifie et s'enfuie de chagrin,
> je commencerai.

Le poète joue des différents modes d'imitation et de transformation des vers virgiliens et inverse la situation d'énonciation : Enée est contraint par Didon à faire son récit, Bourbon impose le sien à son frère « si [celui-ci] a le temps ».

---

28   Bourbon, 2,164,15 : « Barbarior Scylla, Syrti uastaque Charybdi » ; 17 : « E summaque rates pereunteis rupe uidebam. »

29   Ibid., 16 « Eque uia angusta, subito ecce mihi obuia capra ! »

L'intertexte épique, ici, est au service du jeu : Bourbon se plaît à grossir sa mésaventure aux dimensions de la grande catastrophe antique pour amuser son lecteur, à condition du moins que celui-ci reconnaisse la citation, bien entendu non explicitement mentionnée comme telle.

Ainsi, les modalités de l'extragénéricité épique dans l'épigramme lyonnaise des années 1530–40 sont multiples. L'imitation de l'épopée est d'abord destinée à magnifier (ou déplorer) de grands événements et de grands hommes, à « hausser la voix » pour produire des vers dignes des grands sujets. Elle est aussi employée lorsque les poètes veulent évoquer des idées qui leur tiennent à cœur et qui ne sauraient être exprimées sans une certaine forme de solennité. C'est que tous les membres du *sodalitum Lugdunense*, malgré leurs protestations de modestie, malgré le choix du genre littéraire qui est le leur, sont intimement persuadés du pouvoir immense qui est celui de leur poésie, lorsqu'ils abandonnent l'humble *labor* du *poeta* pour se laisser emporter par le *furor* du *uates*. Cette certitude a pu pousser Lucien Febvre, dans son ouvrage assassin pour les « Apollons de collège », à parler de l'« énorme, stupéfiante et candide vanité » de ces poètes.[30] Pourtant, des pièces comme celles de Bourbon que j'ai analysées pour finir montrent bien que ces derniers font preuve d'un humour et d'un second degré interdisant de prendre leurs forfanteries au pied de la lettre : ce qui se lit derrière ces affirmations qui semblent, certes, manquer de modestie, c'est la volonté d'explorer toutes les formes et toutes les modalités de la littérature et d'adopter les *personae* de tout auteur ; c'est, finalement, avant tout l'expression d'un amour intense des Belles-Lettres, dont Bourbon fut un des premiers à chanter la « Renaissance » et pour lesquelles il affirme être prêt à tout endurer.[31]

Université de Bourgogne Franche-Comté

---

30   Lucien Febvre, *Le problème de l'incroyance au XVIᵉ siècle. La religion de Rabelais* (Paris, 1974 [1942]), 20–1.

31   Bourbon, 8,15,1–4 : « Qui tam multa tuli usque adhuc et ecce / qui tam multa fero, et feram libenter, / renascentium amore litterarum / non lassesco. »

CHAPTER 25

Ovidio neo-latino tra Cinque e Seicento: un percorso italo-europeo

Marco Leone

Abstract

Il modello dell'ovidiana epistola eroica si caratterizza per una fortunata e ampia diffusione in tutta Europa tra Cinque e Seicento, anche con una serie di varianti inedite e originali. Fra queste, c'è la variante neo-latina, con due raccolte del poeta britannico Marc Alexander Boyd, le *Epistulae Quindecim* (1590) e gli *Epistulae et hymni* (1592), o con l'opera, più tarda, del gesuita Jakob Balde (*Urania victrix*, 1663). In particolare, nel caso delle due raccolte di Boyd, la *variatio* consiste, rispettivamente, nella costituzione di un gruppo di lettere responsive a quelle ovidiane e in un ampliamento dei temi e dei personaggi già presenti nel modello archetipico (una strada, quest'ultima, battuta da numerosi epigoni cinque-seicenteschi del genere). Nel caso dell'*Urania victrix* di Balde si assiste, invece, a una radicale trasformazione del paradigma originario, che assume la forma di *certamen* o di agone retorico. L'intervento si propone di approfondire temi, caratteristiche e strutture dell'epistola eroica in neo-latino fra XVI e XVII secolo, con specifico riferimento agli esempi di Boyd e di Balde.

Keywords

Marc Alexander Boyd – *Epistulae Quindecim* (1590) – Jakob Balde – *Urania victrix* (1663) – Neo-Latin heroides

Si sa già molto dell'elegia medievale e umanistico-rinascimentale, di cui l'epistola eroica rappresenta una sottospecie, e anche su quella di età barocca la strada è oramai aperta in virtù di approfondimenti dedicati.[1] Quest'ultima

---

1   Per una storia del genere elegiaco, fra Medioevo e Barocco, cfr. Vania De Maldè, "Appunti per la storia dell'elegia volgare in Italia tra Umanesimo e Barocco," *Studi Secenteschi* 36 (1996), 109–34; Silvia Longhi, "Il genere dell'elegia volgare," in eadem, *Le memorie antiche. Modelli classici da Petrarca a Tassoni* (Verona, 2011), 49–68. Per una storia europea del sotto-genere

si caratterizzò per una espansione oltre i confini nazionali, soprattutto in Francia, anche grazie alla mediazione di Marino, e in Inghilterra; e per mutazioni strutturali, dovute alla liquidità del genere, che venne a contaminarsi con l'epistola in versi di argomento amoroso. La sovrapposizione fra elegia, eroide ed epistola amorosa fu favorita dal fatto che l'elegia era rimasta fuori dalle codificazioni rinascimentali, forse come conseguenza della scarsa considerazione già ricevuta in epoca medievale: non si dimentichi che per Dante essa era l'ultima nella gerarchia degli stili e anche l'uso innovatore che ne fece Boccaccio (per soggetto e per temi) nella *Elegia di madonna Fiammetta* non acquisì, tuttavia, funzione modellizzante nelle epoche successive. Non stupisce allora, sulla base di queste premesse, che la forma dell'eroide abbia subito un profondo processo di cambiamento, tra la fine del Cinquecento e il primo trentennio del Seicento, cioè proprio in una fase di cruciale alterazione dei paradigmi letterari tradizionali: un cambiamento che in Italia si verificò paradossalmente sull'onda di una iniziativa letteraria solo progettata e mai realizzata, le epistole eroiche che il Marino annunziò nella *Lettera* premessa alla terza parte della *Lira*.[2] Anche se si tratta solo di un progetto, il suo autore lo dettaglia molto bene, aprendo l'eroide ovidiana non più solo al mito, ma anche alla storia e all'epica di Ariosto e di Tasso. Come spesso gli capitava, Marino non inventava di sana pianta, perché aveva alle sue spalle già qualche precedente tardo-cinquecentesco italiano e anche straniero, come si vedrà. Ma la sua consapevolezza, al riguardo, era ben maggiore rispetto agli altri riformatori del genere delle eroidi: il suo ambizioso tentativo era infatti quello di fondare una moderna epistola eroica, alimentandola della dialettica con gli antichi e includendovi opzioni inedite sino a quel momento. I suoi epigoni non si limitarono a involargli l'idea, ma apportarono ulteriori varianti sperimentali, non tutte contemplate dalla *Lettera*, dando luogo a una variegata fenomenologia. Il caso

---

dell'epistola eroica e, dunque, anche in riferimento alla sua fase barocca, cfr. il fondamentale studio di Heirich Dörrie, *Der heroische Brief. Bestandsaufnahme, Geschichte, Kritik einer humanistisch-barocken Literaturgattung* (Berlin, 1968). Ma vd. ora anche Lorenzo Geri, *L'epistola eroica nell'Europa barocca* (1590–1717) (www.enbach.eu/it/content/lepistola-eroica-nelleuropa-barocca-1590-1717#text40, consultato il 17 settembre 2019). In relazione allo specifico contesto italiano, cfr. Lorenzo Geri, "L'epistola eroica in volgare: stratigrafie di un genere seicentesco. Da Giovan Battista Marino ad Antonio Bruni," in *Miscellanea seicentesca*, ed. Roberto Gigliucci (Roma, 2012), 79–156, a cui si rimanda per un più completo regesto bibliografico, e Moreno Savoretti, *Il carteggio di Parnaso. Il modello ovidiano e le epistole eroiche nel Seicento* (Avellino, 2012).

2 Emilio Russo, "Le promesse del Marino. A proposito di una redazione ignota della lettera Claretti," in idem, *Studi su Tasso e Marino* (Roma – Padova, 2005), 101–88; Emilio Russo, *Marino* (Roma, 2008), 145–8; Lorenzo Geri, "La Lettera di Rodomonte a Doralice," *L'Ellisse. Studi storici di letteratura italiana* 6 (2011), 177–87.

OVIDIO NEO-LATINO TRA CINQUE E SEICENTO   349

più eclatante è quello delle *Epistole eroiche* di Antonio Bruni, la più autentica e fedele traduzione del progetto mariniano, che addirittura coniugano elegia ed idillio e che torcono l'eroide in chiave patetico-affettiva oppure storico-tragica, dandone talora una veste moralizzata e didascalica, fra omaggio e sfida emulativa nei confronti del caposcuola.[3]

Come si può notare, il paradigma di Ovidio sostanzialmente evaporò o, al più, rimase sullo sfondo, dinanzi a risultati così caratterizzati dal gusto variantistico e dalla tensione sperimentale. Né sorte molto diversa capiterà all'eroide latina, più legata all'archetipo ovidiano per ovvie ragioni linguistiche, ma soggetta comunque a notevoli processi di aggiornamento. Si potrebbe infatti credere che la sua veste classicistica possa aver rappresentato sulle prime una specie di argine a innovazioni troppo estreme, ma in realtà non fu così: le eroidi in latino e quelle nei volgari nazionali seguirono invece, sostanzialmente, lo stesso percorso di una accentuata e intensa revisione del modello tradizionale.

Al contrario dell'eroide in italiano e di quella nelle diverse lingue europee, l'eroide in latino costituisce tuttavia, ancora in larga parte, un territorio incognito, sul quale insistono indagini in corso, spesso da parte dei medesimi attori delle esplorazioni sulla lettera eroica in volgare,[4] anche se l'egemonia è tenuta, in tale ambito di ricerca, soprattutto dai classicisti stranieri.[5] Alcuni dati risaltano comunque con evidenza da subito a proposito di questa forma letteraria: per esempio, il fatto che essa abbia attecchito soprattutto fuori d'Italia, per l'azione di latinisti esteri. Ciò accadde forse perché in Italia la ricerca spasmodica di una *varietas* argomentativa aveva probabilmente contribuito a contraffare irrimediabilmente l'originale ovidiano, rendendo impraticabile la sua riproposta originale nella lingua antica; o forse perché il largo successo dell'eroide in italiano, con la sua annessa casistica di metamorfosi e di rifacimenti, aveva esaurito ormai ogni spazio di affermazione per quella in latino; oppure, ancora, perché erano nel frattempo mutati gli spazi di riferimento: mentre l'eroide in italiano aveva avuto nell'accademia il suo incunabolo privilegiato, anche come mezzo di comunicazione letteraria tra sodali, l'epistola eroica in latino prosperò invece nella rete internazionale dei collegi gesuitici, perché era divenuta frattanto tema di svolgimento retorico.

Se in Italia la grande fioritura della produzione volgare aveva inibito insomma, in qualche modo quella latina, altrove le cose andarono diversamente.

---

3 Gino Rizzo, "Introduzione," in *Antonio Bruni, Epistole eroiche*, ed. Gino Rizzo (Galatina, 1993), 9–63; Geri, "L'epistola eroica in volgare" (vedi sopra, n. 1), ad indicem.

4 Geri, *L'epistola eroica nell'Europa barocca* (vedi sopra, n. 1).

5 Susanna de Beer, "Elegiac Poetry," in *Brill's Encyclopaedia of the Neo-Latin World*, ed. Phliph Ford, Jan Bloemendal and Charles Fantazzi (Leiden – Boston, 2014), 387–98.

Per esempio, lo scozzese Alexander Boyd (1562–1601), che aveva anche soggiornato nella penisola italica, dove aveva avuto modo di apprezzare i poeti italiani in latino del suo tempo, pubblicò nel 1590 le *Epistulae quindecim*, in risposta a quelle ovidiane.[6] Anticipando una variante che sarà replicata più tardi anche dagli autori di eroidi in italiano (quella cioè delle lettere responsive), le *Epistulae quindecim* risentono, proprio sotto questo aspetto, delle *Contre Épistres d'Ovide* di Michel d'Amboise (1541), che aveva per l'appunto introdotto per primo l'invenzione del carteggio fra le eroine sedotte e gli uomini oggetto del loro amore, in un'epoca in cui Ovidio era utilizzato in Francia soprattutto come modello lirico (si pensi solo a Ronsard[7]) e non elegiaco. Boyd ebbe forse modo di conoscere l'opera di d'Amboise durante la sua permanenza in Francia, dove studiò legge a Parigi, Orléans e Bourges. Un'opera in francese influenzerà, dunque, a distanza di qualche decennio, con il suo originale congegno narrativo, un'altra in latino, che era stata allestita in Inghilterra da un autore scozzese educatosi però, durante la sua giovinezza, al culto della poesia latina del Rinascimento italiano. Non potrebbe esserci prova più significativa delle complesse intersezioni geografiche e linguistiche che riguardarono il genere dell'eroide cinque-seicentesca in Europa.

In realtà neanche la seconda silloge di Boyd, le *Epistulae Heroides et Hymni* (1592),[8] si rifà al paradigma classico in maniera del tutto ortodossa e regolare e anche in questo caso ci troviamo di fronte a una peculiare prospettiva transnazionale e translinguistica. Nella dedica a James Stuart VI, re di Scozia e futuro re d'Inghilterra col nome di Giacomo I, il poeta richiama la sua ammirazione per quell'aureo filone di poesia italiana in latino (da Bembo a Fracastoro) che egli aveva conosciuto da vicino e che ora cercava di esportare nel Nord Europa, non senza, però, significative innovazioni, che riguardarono anche la trattazione della materia erotica secondo peculiari venature libertine.[9] La raccolta di Boyde raggruppa infatti componimenti ispirati, sì, alle *Heroides*, ma con una selezione di personaggi totalmente nuova rispetto all'archetipo ovidiano. Spiccano invece l'inserimento di figure della storia romana o del mito non trattati da Ovidio, come l'episodio relativo alla storia d'amore fra Venere e Adone,

---

6   Geri, *L'epistola eroica nell'Europa barocca* (vedi sopra, n. 1), ad indicem.

7   André Baïche, "Le réalisme de Ronsard. Deux imitations, dans les Hymnes, d'Ovide et d'Apollonios et Virgile," in *Ovide en France dans la Renaissance*, ed. Henri Lamarque e André Baïche (Toulouse, 1981), 41–58.

8   *Ovidius redivivus. Die* Epistulae Heroides *des Mark Alexander Boyd. Edition, Übersetzung und Kommentar der Briefe Atalanta Meleagro (1), Eurydice Orpheo (6), Philomela Tereo (9), Venus Adoni (15)*, ed. Carolin Ritter (Hildesheim – Zürich – New York, 2010).

9   Edward Paleit, "Sexual and Political Liberty and Neo-Latin Poetics: The *Heroides* of Marc Alexander Boyde," *Renaissance Studies* 22 (2008), 351–67.

OVIDIO NEO-LATINO TRA CINQUE E SEICENTO

di significativa fortuna rinascimentale già prima della consacrazione poetica che ne farà Marino, o quello riguardante Sofonisba e Massinissa.[10]

Neppure l'eroide latina, dunque, conservò veramente i caratteri del modello fondativo, a parte l'uso del distico, anzi per certi versi precorse, già alla fine del Cinquecento, le evoluzioni barocche che riguarderanno quella praticata nei diversi volgari europei. La seconda raccolta di Boyd risalta, inoltre, per la sua cifra bilinguistica, poiché propone, accanto ai testi latini, anche il volgarizzamento in francese delle prime due epistole eroiche. Boyd sviluppa, insomma, il genere di matrice ovidiana su uno scacchiere intricato, basato sul confronto fra lingua antica e idioma moderno e sul rapporto con altre tradizioni letterarie (britannica e italiana). La sezione di *Hymni* si affianca, poi, alla sezione delle *Heroides* come un esperimento poetico sganciato dal paradigma di Ovidio, perché si concentra su una diversa forma letteraria, quella dell'inno dedicato a diverse specie floreali e ad alcuni simboli marziali ("hasta," "ensis," "cassis"). Se questi ultimi si spiegano con il profilo del dedicatario della raccolta, che era un re guerriero, i primi richiamano la tipologia dell'inno cristiano per l'allegorizzazione delle tipologie botaniche, corrispondenti a differenti virtù (peraltro ciascuno degli inni è rivolto a un sodale del poeta, con una sostanziale ripresa mimetizzata, dunque, della dialogicità epistolare). Ancor più significativo è, però, il fatto che la raccolta del 1592 si chiuda con una sezione di brevi epistole latine (*literularum curia*) indirizzate a diversi destinatari, perché Boyd testimonia così una particolare attitudine allo stile epistolare nel suo complesso, con le sue diverse configurazioni retoriche, non solo alla sua derivazione dell'epistola eroica in versi. E ciò risulta tanto più notevole, se si pensa che accadde in un tempo sincrono alla genesi e alla formazione dei primi libri di lettere:[11] sicché non appare per nulla casuale, nelle *Epistulae Heroides et Hymni*, questo gioco di specchi fra le differenti varianti del genere epistolare, tra prosa e poesia, che attesta, anche nel fronte classicistico, una calcolata azione di rimaneggiamento sperimentale su di esso.

Se le raccolte di Boyd, pur recependo le innovazioni delle eroidi in volgare e gli apporti da letterature estere, sembrano mantenere comunque, tutto sommato, un legame con l'originale, non si verifica lo stesso nel caso della più tarda *Urania victrix* (1663), opera senile del gesuita Jacob Balde (1604–68),

---

10   I personaggi delle *Epistulae* di Boyd sono i seguenti: Atalanta e Meleagro, Callioneira e Diomede, Silvia e Marte, Antigone ed Emone, Lamia e Demetrio, Euridice ed Orfeo, Clizia e Febo, Lavinia e Turno, Sofonisba e Massinissa, Paolina e Mundo, Piramo e Tisbe, Giulia e Augusto, Ottavia e Antonio, Venere e Adone.

11   Cfr., fra gli altri, *Le carte messaggiere. Retorica e modelli di comunicazione epistolare. Per un indice dei libri di lettere del Cinquecento*, ed. Amedeo Quondam (Roma, 1981); Lodovica Braida, *Libri di lettere. Le raccolte epistolari del Cinquecento tra inquietudini religiose e "buon volgare"* (Roma – Bari, 2009).

un ingegno versatile che si applicò a diversi generi letterari (comprese satira e parodia), affiancando all'*imitatio* dei classici la tendenza, tipica della coeva cultura gesuitica, a un loro ammodernamento, a tratti anche spregiudicato e anti-conformistico.[12] E in effetti, l'*Urania victrix* rappresenta davvero una trasfigurazione totale del modello ovidiano, ben più radicale delle rivisitazioni che offriva il coevo panorama delle lingue nazionali.[13] La ragione di ciò andrà ricercata nel fatto che, mentre Boyd era ancora legato, per origini e per formazione, alla corrente del tardo-umanesimo francese, in lui corroborato anche dal diretto contatto con la poesia italiana in latino del primo Cinquecento, Balde è invece espressione della cultura gesuitica della seconda metà del XVII secolo, in cui il genere dell'eroide latina era stato oramai ridotto, come già detto, al rango di esercitazione retorica nei collegi, dopo opportuno travestimento didascalico ed edificante; e aveva assunto una specifica curvatura sacra e parenetica, soprattutto in Germania e nei Paesi Bassi (paesi nei quali, peraltro, l'insegnamento ignaziano si era diffuso con particolare efficacia). Nell'articolata mappa geo-culturale del genere, l'incompiuta *Urania victrix* (delle tre parti previste di elegie fu composta solo la prima) rappresenta tuttavia un *unicum* assoluto, non incasellabile veramente in nessuna delle tipologie secentesche di eroide, e non pare avere alcun rapporto neppure con il precedente umanistico dell'*Urania* di Giovanni Pontano, il poemetto mitologico pure trapunto da numerose reminiscenze ovidiane.[14] Dedicata al pontefice Alessandro VII, che per questo insignì Balde di una medaglia d'oro, e, dunque, idealmente concepita per un contesto caratterizzato da pulsioni eticizzanti ed educative, l'*Urania* riprende dall'eroide sacra proprio il didascalismo, ma in una chiave molto più sofisticata sul piano dell'*inventio* (e, in effetti, il suo autore fu apprezzato docente di retorica in diversi collegi gesuitici di Germania). La sua struttura, che si rifrange in un vortice di superfetazioni interne, si sviluppa, infatti, sulla base del confronto epistolare, in forma di *altercatio*, fra *Urania*, cioè l'anima,[15] e i cinque sensi (con il relativo apparato di seduzioni e di blandizie). I sensi scrivono all'anima prima direttamente e poi per il tramite di interlocutori (due o tre per senso) che hanno a che fare in qualche modo con ciascuna delle

---

12   *La Lyre Jésuite. Anthologie de poèmes latins (1620–1730)*, ed. Andrée Thill (Genève, 1999), 101–46.

13   Vd. la moderna edizione antologica in francese, *Urania Victrix*, ed. Andrée Thill (Mulhouse, 1989). Esiste anche una edizione in tedesco, con ricca introduzione: *Urania Victrix: Die Siegreiche Urania. Liber I–II. Erstes und zweites Buch*, ed. Lutz Claren, Wilhelm Kühlmann, Wolfgang Schibel e Robert Seidel (Tübingen, 2003).

14   Francesco Tateo, "Ovidio nell'*Urania* di Pontano," in *Aetates ovidianae. Lettori di Ovidio dall'Antichità al Rinascimento*, ed. Italo Gallo e Luciano Nicastri (Napoli, 1995), 279–92.

15   L'anima viene a identificarsi con la Musa dell'astronomia, in quanto, come è spiegato nell'*Isagoge* con un complesso ragionamento teologico, si tratta di entità direttamente promanata dal cielo, dunque da Dio, e composta per questo di materia celeste.

OVIDIO NEO-LATINO TRA CINQUE E SEICENTO 353

funzioni sensoriali (per esempio, per l'udito a scrivere sono musicisti e poeti[16]),
e l'anima corrisponde a ogni interlocutore, infarcendo le proprie risposte con
una congerie di citazioni scritturali e patristiche che rendono l'epistole in versi
quasi il travestimento di un trattato teologico. La scelta della forma dialogica
ed epistolare, in luogo di quella trattatistica, è giustificata peraltro in alcune
pagine dell'*Isagoge*, sotto la rubrica *De stylo epistolari*.[17] In questa bizzarra e
singolarissima costruzione responsiva Ovidio e il modello dell'epistola eroica
fungono, in realtà, solo da fondale. Benché il poeta di Sulmona sia citato nella
Isagoge, cioè nell'introduzione all'opera (termine che lascia trasparire tutta l'e-
splicita pedagogia della raccolta), la sua presenza appare infatti del tutto sco-
lorita e disincarnata, perché nell'*Urania* lo scambio epistolare in distici si muta
sostanzialmente in un *certamen* tra spirito e corpo, dalle esplicite finalità gno-
miche e catechetiche, e questa gara si risolve ovviamente, come suggerisce lo
stesso titolo, nella vittoria finale di Urania. La retoricizzazione del paradigma
ovidiano appare dunque ben evidente dal suo camuffamento in agone, che è
una dimensione tipica della pedagogia gesuitica e che, in questo caso, deforma
alla radice l'*exemplum* elegiaco, adattandolo ai protocolli della *Ratio studiorum*
e strumentalizzandolo alla stregua di un semplice palinsesto.

Anche il versante dell'eroide in latino di età barocca, dunque, conobbe spe-
rimentalismi spavaldi, pur con esiti e processi molto diversi da quelli esperiti
nelle lingue moderne, e non fu semplicemente un'area di resistenza classicistica. In Italia l'epistola eroica in lingua italiana assorbì l'intera varietà di questa
forma letteraria, nel segno di un drastico aggiornamento stimolato dall'intui-
zione mariniana, che ebbe agganci anche con il panorama della produzione
extra-nazionale. Fuori d'Italia, per il campo latino, il percorso di innovazione
ebbe cause e sbocchi di altro segno, legati in massima parte all'ambiente gesuitico, ma ugualmente incidenti sulla fisionomia del genere; condusse addirittura in qualche caso, come si è visto, a riscritture estreme, con un impiego
estremamente duttile e flessibile dell'ipotesto ovidiano (in linea, del resto,
con la sorte di tanti altri classici metamorfizzati dai letterati appartenenti
all'Ordine di Sant'Ignazio[18]).

Università del Salento

---

16   L'intero schema dell'opera è il seguente: per il senso della vista, scrivono ad Urania pittori
e matematici; per l'udito, musicisti e poeti; per l'olfatto, unguentari e fabbricanti di farma-
ci; per il gusto, cacciatori, cuochi e maggiordomi; per il tatto, osti, servi di corte e soldati
vanagloriosi.

17   Iacobus Balde, *Urania victrix* (Monaco di Baviera, 1663), 26–9.

18   László Szörényi, "Il genere gesuitico 'Metamorphosis' e la poesia di Bernando Pannagl,"
in idem, *Arcades ambo. Relazioni letterarie italo-ungheresi e cultura neo-latina* (Soveria
Mannelli, 1999), 207–18.

CHAPTER 26

Nunc erit beatior ... L'homme et la nature dans la troisième épode de Maciej Kazimierz Sarbiewski

Maria Łukaszewicz-Chantry

Abstract

Dans son épode *Laus otii religiosi. Palinodia ad secundam libri Epodon Odam Q. Horatii Flacci*, Maciej Kazimierz Sarbiewski engage un dialogue littéraire avec son maître romain. Cette épode réunit deux visions différentes de la nature. Les environs de Niemenczyn sont décrits comme un *locus amoenus* à la manière d'Horace. Sarbiewski souligne toutefois que cette beauté de la nature est un reflet de la Beauté absolue, que toutes les créatures y sont réunies dans un même amour de Dieu. Le jésuite polonais exprime cette vérité par des images poétiques qui sont un écho de l'œuvre de son confrère italien Mario Bettini. Les deux conceptions de la nature proviennent donc de ces deux sources d'inspiration : d'Horace et de Bettini. En adoptant le regard de ce dernier (caractéristique de la spiritualité ignatienne de son époque), Sarbiewski engage une polémique avec le poète de Venouse. Au « beatus ille » – le personnage d'Horace –, il oppose un nouveau héros : « beatior ille », et propose une autre approche du bonheur. Pour le jésuite, la vie *inter naturae fines* n'est pas en soi suffisante. Pour trouver le bonheur, il faut découvrir que la nature est théophanie.

Keywords

Maciej Kazimierz Sarbiewski – *Laus otii religiosi* – Neo-Latin lyric poetry – reception of Horace – Mario Bettini

La troisième épode de Maciej Kazimierz Sarbiewski – surnommé l'Horace chrétien – est intitulée *Laus otii religiosi. Palinodia ad secundam libri Epodon Odam Q. Horatii Flacci : 'beatus ille qui procul negotiis'*. Le titre même signale qu'il s'agit d'une palinodie, c'est-à-dire d'un dialogue polémique avec un texte

---

© KONINKLIJKE BRILL NV, LEIDEN, 2020 | DOI:10.1163/9789004427105_027

original d'Horace.[1] Sarbiewski indique aussi dans le sous-titre les circonstances dans lesquelles son épode a été composée : c'était pendant ses vacances à Niemenczyn, dans la jolie villa des jésuites de Wilno (« Cum amoenam collegii Societatis Iesu Vilnensis Nemecinae villam per sextiles ferias inviseret »).[2] Cette information a son importance, car elle oriente l'interprétation du texte.[3]

Comme on le sait, la deuxième épode d'Horace commence par une formule de macarisme :[4]

> Beatus ille qui procul negotiis,
>   ut prisca gens mortalium,
> paterna rura bobus exercet suis
>   solutus omni faenore
> neque excitatur classico miles truci
>   neque horret iratum mare
> forumque vitat et superba civium
>   potentiorum limina.

Son personnage, le « beatus ille », trouve le bonheur loin des tentations et des dangers de la ville, en cultivant sa terre familiale et en vivant en accord avec la nature. Pour Horace, la vie simple à la campagne est donc comme un retour à l'âge d'or, aux premiers temps heureux où l'humanité savait se contenter de ce que la terre lui donnait, où chacun savait vivre de peu de chose. À l'opposé de ces temps de justice anciens, viennent les guerres et les voyages maritimes qui naissent de la cupidité, mère de tous les maux. À ces deux éléments, guerres et voyages, souvent évoqués en littérature comme signes de la perte irréversible de l'âge d'or, Horace ajoute encore l'usure, manifestation évidente de la cupidité. C'est donc après avoir rappelé ces obstacles au bonheur que le poète latin commence sa description de la vie simple et paisible *inter naturae fines*. Pourtant, tout son éloge de la vie à la campagne, y compris la mise en garde

---

1 À propos de la palinodie comme stratégie littéraire employée dans cette épode, voir Maria Łukaszewicz-Chantry, « Une parodie et une palinodie d'Horace, par M. K. Sarbiewski, » *Eos* 80 (1992), 313–28, ici 319–24.

2 Probablement en 1631. Voir John Sparrow, « Sarbiewski's 'Silviludia' and their Italian Source, » *Oxford Slavonic Papers* 8 (1958), 1–48, ici 32.

3 J'ai publié précédemment en polonais un essai d'interprétation de cette épode, voir Maria Łukaszewicz-Chantry, « Gdy jezuici odpoczywają, czyli jeszcze o trzeciej epodzie Macieja Kazimierza Sarbiewskiego, » dans *Iesuitae in Polonia. Poloni Iesuitae. Piśmiennictwo łacińskie czasów nowożytnych*, éd. Jarosław Nowaszczuk (Szczecin, 2017), 7–20. Je propose ici une version de cette étude modifiée et étendue au nouveau contexte de la comparaison avec l'œuvre de Bettini.

4 Horace, *Ep.* 2,1–8.

contre l'usure, est placé dans la bouche de l'usurier Alfius qui, après s'être exprimé de la sorte, se hâte de rentrer en ville pour y reprendre ses activités habituelles (*Ep.* 2,67–70) :

> haec ubi locutus faenerator Alfius,
>   iam iam futurus rusticus,
> omnem redegit Idibus pecuniam,
>   quaerit Kalendis ponere.

Ainsi, l'ironie contenue dans la fin du poème remet en question tout l'éloge de l'*otium rusticum* que l'on vient d'entendre. Alfius reste un usurier, les charmes de la vie simple et paisible dans un environnement bucolique et la contemplation d'un bonheur familial n'ont rien changé en lui.

Cette œuvre d'Horace était très populaire en Pologne aux XVIᵉ et XVIIᵉ siècles : elle a été paraphrasée plus de trente fois par des auteurs polonais.[5] Mais l'éloge de la vie à la campagne a été traité par ceux-ci sur un ton sérieux, pour présenter un idéal de vie rurale, en effaçant le personnage de l'usurier et en perdant ainsi toute l'ironie amère que contenait l'hypotexte. Cette importante modification tient à la différence de situation sociale à Rome et en Pologne. À Rome, l'usure était certes connotée négativement, mais c'était une occupation très répandue.[6] Il était tout à fait vraisemblable qu'un usurier romain s'achète une villa de campagne pour y mener une existence tranquille. Dans la Pologne des XVIᵉ et XVIIᵉ siècles en revanche, l'usure était exclusivement une activité de citadin, et plus particulièrement de Juifs. Il était inconcevable que la noblesse terrienne s'y adonne. Aussi la poésie chantant le bonheur de la vie campagnarde présentait-elle en réalité un idéal de vie rurale inaccessible à toute personne extérieure à la noblesse.[7] Il était impossible à un usurier de devenir hobereau.

Maciej Kazimierz Sarbiewski propose cependant une paraphrase différente de cette épode. Il conserve le personnage d'Alfius, mais c'est pour polémiquer

---

5 Voir par exemple : Adam Karpiński, « Parafraza jako aemulatio (na przykładzie staropolskich przeróbek epody Horacego ‹ Beatus ille qui procul negotiis ›), » dans *Retoryka a literatura*, éd. Barbara Otwinowska (Wrocław, 1984), 107–19 ; Maciej Eder, « Sobotóry Alfiusza. O Epodzie 2 Horacego i jej staropolskich parafrazach, » *Meander* 51 (1996), 287–96.

6 Sénèque, philosophe qui dans ses traités ne cache pas son mépris pour l'argent, aurait semble-t-il prêté lui-même de l'argent à intérêt à des villes entières : voir Dion Cassius, *Historia Romana* 61,10,3.

7 Eder, « Sobowtóry Alfiusza » (voir ci-dessus, n. 5), 294–5.

avec Horace.[8] La polémique s'annonce d'ailleurs dès le premier vers : « At ille, Flacce, nunc erit beatior », où le héros d'Horace, « beatus ille », se voit opposer un autre héros plus heureux, « beatior ille ».

Le deuxième personnage de l'épode – l'usurier Alfius – n'apparaît comme chez Horace que vers la fin du poème, laquelle contient aussi une pointe surprenante.[9] Sarbiewski prétend que si l'usurier Alfius voyait « cela » (« haec »), le paysan déçu qui est en lui ne voudrait certainement plus rentrer en ville pour y reprendre son métier habituel (99–102) :[10]

> Haec si videret faenerator Alphius,
>   Olim futurus rusticus,
> Quam collocaret Idibus pecuniam,
>   Nollet Kalendis ponere.

La question qui se pose est de savoir ce qu'Alfius a bien pu voir. Qu'est-ce qui a bien pu l'amener à abandonner l'usure et à changer de vie, chose qu'il ne fait pas dans le poème d'Horace, après avoir contemplé le *locus amoenus* ? L'épode de Sarbiewski nous apprend qu'Alfius a vu … des jésuites en vacances dans la région de Wilno. La conclusion d'Alfius est en effet précédée d'une longue description de leur repos tranquille à Niemenczyn, qui occupe toute la deuxième partie de l'épode. Pour rendre compte des charmes de l'existence dans cette campagne paisible, Sarbiewski suit les traces d'Horace, tout en se livrant bien sûr à certaines substitutions. La beauté de la nature est aussi apaisante à Niemenczyn que dans la campagne italienne, mais celle-ci est désormais lituanienne : on y retrouve la forêt et les verts pâturages, un lac et une rivière aux eaux claires, l'ombre des chênes et des peupliers, le chant des oiseaux.

Comme dans le *locus amoenus* d'Horace, la vie dans la campagne de Wilno est simple et heureuse, même si les repas ne sont bien sûr plus pris en famille, comme chez le poète latin, mais dans une communauté religieuse où règne une atmosphère fraternelle (93–8) :

---

8   Dans un sens, il polémique aussi avec les paraphrases polonaises d'Horace qui chantent l'idéal de la vie champêtre. Voir Piotr Urbański, *Theologia fabulosa. Commentationes Sarbievianae* (Szczecin, 2000), 141–2.

9   Rappelons que Sarbiewski a lui-même donné une célèbre définition de la pointe, qu'il appelle « concors discordia » dans son traité *De acuto et arguto sive Seneca et Martialis*, voir Maciej Kazimierz Sarbiewski, *Praecepta poetica. Wykłady poetyki*, éd. Stanisław Skimina (Wrocław, 1958), 10.

10   Texte de l'édition : *Maciej Kazimierz Sarbiewski, Lyrica quibus accesserunt Iter Romanum et Lechiados fragmentum*, éd. Mirosław Korolko (Warszawa, 1980), 451–5.

> At nec tacemus pone considentium
>> Dulcis manus sodalium ;
> Nec inficeta sermo differtur mora,
>> Sed innocentibus iocis,
> Multoque tinctus, sed verecundo sale
>> Innoxium trahit diem.

Toutefois, pour être introduit dans cette excellente compagnie de jésuites et jouir de leur *otium religiosum*, il est nécessaire de suivre un certain itinéraire spirituel. Celui-ci est présenté dans la première partie de l'épode. Le héros qui apparaît dès le premier vers est appelé à être heureux, mais pour atteindre le bonheur, il doit franchir plusieurs étapes. La première consiste à quitter les champs de son père : « paterna liquit rura » (3), ce qui est en contradiction avec les conseils que donnait Horace : « paterna rura bobus exercet suis » (3).

Quitter le champ, c'est abandonner les soucis auxquels l'agriculteur doit sans cesse faire face. Mais le sous-titre nous permet aussi d'interpréter ce départ dans un sens évangélique, où il s'agit alors de quitter sa maison et ses proches, de se détacher des biens matériels pour suivre le Christ.

Vient ensuite l'image de la réflexion dans la solitude (de la retraite au sens religieux du terme). Le héros de l'épode, le « beatior ille », se retire du monde pour réfléchir sur son existence (9–14) :

> Ergo aut profanis hactenus negotiis
>> Amissa plorat sidera
> Aut in reducta sede dispersum gregem
>> Errantis animi colligit,
> Postquam beatae lucra conscientiae
>> Quadrante liberavit suo.

Alors que chez Horace, le « beatus ille » regardait les troupeaux errants aux pâturages :[11]

> aut in reducta valle mugientium
>> prospectat errantis greges.

---

11   Hor., *Ep.* 2,11–2 ; Paraphrasant le Psaume 1 dans le style de l'épode d'Horace, Paulin de Nola emploie l'image des troupeaux errants comme métaphore des pécheurs qui vivent dans l'erreur (*Poema* 7,1–7).

L'HOMME ET LA NATURE DANS LA TROISIÈME ÉPODE DE SARBIEWSKI　　359

Sarbiewski montre son personnage en train de « rassembler » ses pensées erratiques :[12]

> Aut in reducta sede dispersum gregem
> 　Errantis animi colligit,
> Postquam beatae lucra conscientiae
> 　Quadrante libravit suo.

C'est une représentation poétique de l'examen de conscience, pratique très importante dans la spiritualité ignatienne.[13] Éviter le mal, examiner sa propre existence à la lumière de la loi divine, se repentir et chercher continuellement à s'améliorer sont des conditions pour vivre heureux. Mais ce n'est pas tout.

Pendant sa méditation nocturne, le « beatior ille » observe le ciel étoilé.[14] Le regard tourné vers les étoiles, l'homme vivant sur terre – cette « vallée de larmes » – aspire au bonheur futur du paradis. Les ténèbres de la nuit qui baignent la nature contribuent à l'état d'esprit du personnage : il se sent éloigné de Dieu et aspire à le retrouver. L'aube qui vient après la nuit symbolise le réveil spirituel. Lorsque le soleil vient éclairer le monde, il éclaire aussi le regard que l'homme porte sur la réalité qui l'entoure. Celui-ci commence à percevoir Dieu autour de lui, à découvrir des traces divines dans la nature qu'Il a créée (33–6) :

> Assueta caelo lumina in terras vocat,
> 　Lateque prospectum iacit,
> Camposque lustrat, et relucentem sua
> 　Miratur in scaena Deum.

Il prend conscience de la beauté surnaturelle dont toute la réalité est imprégnée. À ce propos, une autre œuvre de Sarbiewski, *Dii gentium*, peut être évoquée ici. C'est une encyclopédie de la mythologie antique. Dans le chapitre consacré à Amor,[15] Sarbiewski explique de manière très plastique comment la beauté divine invisible devient visible dans les créatures : tout comme un rayon de soleil invisible devient visible en traversant les nuages et prend alors

---

12　Sarb., *Ep.* 3,11–4.

13　Urbański, *Theologia fabulosa* (voir ci-dessus, n. 8), 93.

14　Les étoiles étaient perçues comme des trous dans la voûte céleste par lesquels filtrait une lumière surnaturelle. Voir Maria Łukaszewicz-Chantry, *Trzy nieba. Przestrzeń sakralna w liryce Macieja Kazimierza Sarbiewskiego* (Wrocław, 2002), 79–82.

15　Voir Maria Łukaszewicz-Chantry, « L'Amor aethereus chez Sarbiewski, » *Uranie* 8 (1998), 153–60.

diverses couleurs pour donner l'arc-en-ciel, la beauté divine devient visible en imprégnant le monde matériel.[16]

Inspiré de la philosophie platonicienne, Sarbiewski définit l'amour comme une aspiration au beau.[17] Dans l'épode, ce désir du beau absolu, toutes les créatures l'éprouvent, même les fleurs qui essaient de s'élever jusqu'aux étoiles (37–46) :[18]

> En, omnis, inquit, herba non morantibus
>> In astra luctatur comis ;
> Semota caelo lacrimantur, et piis
>> Liquuntur arva fletibus ;
> Ligustra canis, et rosae rubentibus
>> Repunt in auras bracchiis ;
> Astrisque panda nescio quid pallido
>> Loquuntur ore lilia,
> Et sero blandis ingemunt suspiriis,
>> Et mane rorant lacrimis.

En voyant toute la nature unie dans son amour et son désir de Dieu, l'homme aussi veut communier avec l'ensemble de la création et découvrir dans le monde les traces de son Créateur (47–52) :

> Egone solus, solus in terris piger
>> Tenace figor pondere ?
> Sic et propinquas allocutus arbores,
>> Et multa coram fontibus
> Rivisque fatus, quaerit auctorem Deum
>> Formosa per vestigia.

Un fait essentiel est ainsi révélé : la nature tout entière est une théophanie. Cette idée s'inscrit dans une tradition qui remonte à l'Ancien Testament, selon laquelle il est possible de connaître le Créateur à travers la réalité qu'il a créée.

---

16 Cf. *Maciej Kazimierz Sarbiewski, Dii gentium. Bogowie pogan*, éd. Krystyna Stawecka (Wrocław, 1972), 158.

17 Voir Piotr Urbański, « Wątki platońskie w twórczości Macieja K. Sarbiewskiego, » dans *Barok polski wobec Europy. Kierunki dialogu*, éd. Alina Nowicka-Jeżowa (Warszawa, 2003), 513–26.

18 Cf. Maren-Sofie Röstvig, *The Happy Man. Studies in the Metamorphoses of a Classical Ideal : 1600–1700* (Oslo, 1962), vol. 1, 77–8.

Comme nous pouvons en effet le lire dans le *Livre de la Sagesse* : « la grandeur et la beauté des créatures font, par analogie, contempler leur Auteur. » (Sg 13,5).

Il faut cependant souligner que Sarbiewski rend compte de cette vérité à travers des images poétiques empruntées à l'œuvre d'un autre jésuite, Mario Bettini. Il y a lieu de rappeler ici que l'une des œuvres de Sarbiewski, *Silviludia*, doit presque tout – et c'est peu dire – à cet auteur. Comme l'a découvert John Sparrow il y a soixante ans, le texte du jésuite polonais est en effet une *pia fraus* d'un drame pastoral de Mario Bettini intitulé *Ludovicus, Tragicum Sylviludium*.[19] Sparrow s'est également demandé s'il était possible de trouver d'éventuelles autres traces d'inspiration de Bettini dans les œuvres de Sarbiewski, et il a observé une similitude entre un passage de l'épode qui nous intéresse ici et certains vers de *Ludovicus* :[20]

> Sarbiewski :
> En, omnis, inquit, herba non morantibus
>   In astra luctatur comis ;
> Semota caelo lacrimantur, et piis
>   Liquuntur arva fletibus ;
> Ligustra canis, et rosae rubentibus
>   Repunt in auras bracchiis ;
> Astrisque panda nescio quid pallido
>   Loquuntur ore lilia,
> Et sero blandis ingemunt suspiriis,
>   Et mane rorant lacrimis.
> Egone solus, solus in terris piger
>   Tenace figor pondere ? (37–48)

> Bettini :
> En flosculi riparum
> Herbigenae volucres,
> Prae numinis amore,
> Fucatas foliorum

---

19 La pièce de théâtre *Ludovicus* a été présentée pour la première fois à Parme en 1612 (en latin) et à Bologne en 1614 (en italien), puis imprimée à Parme en 1622 et à Paris en 1624. Les *Silviludia* de Sarbiewski comptent 440 vers dont pas moins de 420 sont empruntés à Bettini (la pièce originale de Bettini se compose de 1400 vers). Voir Sparrow, "Sarbiewski's 'Silviludia'" (voir ci-dessus, n. 2), 16–20. Cf. Denise Aricò, *Scienza, teatro e spiritualità barocca. Il gesuita Mario Bettini* (Bologna, 1996), 157–90.

20 Sparrow, "Sarbiewski's 'Silviludia'" (voir ci-dessus, n. 2), 32–3.

Ad coelum alas explicant.
Odoris flant suspiriis
Fletuque madent roscido. [...]
En Ederae virentibus
Ad astra reptant brachiis, [...]
An solus ego (heu misero !)
Tot inter faces algeo ?
An solus ego ad terras
Devexo feror pondere ?

Act. 2, Sc. 4, 35–41, 46–47, 50–53[21]

La ressemblance entre ces deux visions de la nature qui aspire à l'Absolu est effectivement frappante. Sparrow, toutefois, considérait que les similitudes se limitaient à ce seul passage. Je ne pense pas que ce soit le cas. Voici deux autres passages de l'épode qui trouvent des correspondances dans le drame de Bettini :

Sarbiewski :
Camposque lustrat, et relucentem sua
    Miratur in scaena Deum
[...]
Sic et propinquas allocutus arbores,
    Et multa coram fontibus
Rivisque fatus, quaerit auctorem Deum
    Formosa per vestigia. (35–36, 47–50)

Bettini :
Floriparentes herbae,
Pratorum astra flores,
Vallesque nemorosae,
Gemmaeque florum rosae [...]
Impressi fida Numinis vestigia.
Sagacem deamantis
Cursumque vimque mentis
Beantis ad beata

---

21   Texte de la version établie par Sparrow à partir de l'édition : *Marii Bettini Ludovicus tragicum Sylvitudium* (Parma, 1622 ; Paris, 1624), voir Sparrow, "Sarbiewski's 'Silviludia'" (voir ci-dessus, n. 2), 35–48.

L'HOMME ET LA NATURE DANS LA TROISIÈME ÉPODE DE SARBIEWSKI

Vos ora praedae ducitis.
Tacita diae simulacra formae,
Quae ludibunda pinxit
Pennati dextra Amoris ;
Vos quidem, vos qua licet aemulamini
Authoris ora vestri.

Act. 2, Sc. 4, 1–4, 9–18

Dans ces vers également, les deux auteurs présentent une vision semblable de la nature qui porte les traces du Créateur. La même idée et une image semblable apparaissent d'ailleurs aussi dans une épigramme de Sarbiewski (*Divini Amores* 37) :[22]

Qualis est dilectus tuus ? (Cant. 5,9)
« Qualis erat tuus ille, tuus pulcherrimus ille ? »
    dicebat nuper barbara turba mihi.
Arripio dextra pennam laevaque tabellam
    et noto, Christe, tuo quidquid in orbe noto.
Pingo rosas, aurum, gemmas, viridaria, silvas,
    Arva, lacus, celeri sidera pingo manu.
Et tabulam monstrans : « Noster pulcherrimus », inquam,
    « qualis erat, vultis discere ? Talis erat. »

Il nous semble retrouver ici des échos de l'œuvre de Bettini. Mais il ne faut pas limiter la ressemblance au seul niveau des *similia* littéraires ou de l'intérêt partagé des deux auteurs pour le néoplatonisme. N'oublions pas qu'ils appartiennent tous deux à une même famille spirituelle, celle de la spiritualité ignatienne, dont l'un des traits majeurs est de rechercher Dieu en toute chose. Pour saint Ignace et ses disciples, le Mystère de l'Incarnation a eu des conséquences fondamentales. L'Incarnation s'est en effet soldée par un séjour permanent de Dieu dans le monde, et par conséquent, par la sanctification de ce dernier.[23] La réalité matérielle est ainsi devenue un lieu où il est possible de rencontrer Dieu.

---

22   Texte de l'édition : *Maciej Kazimierz Sarbiewski, Epigrammatum liber (Księga epigramatów)*, éd. Magdalena Piskała et Dorota Sutkowska (Warszawa, 2003), 52. À propos des épigrammes religieuses de Sarbiewski, voir Maria Łukaszewicz-Chantry, « Metafizyczne epigramaty Macieja Kazimierza Sarbiewskiego, » *Studia Classica et Neolatina* 8 (2006), 184–92.

23   Sarbiewski a également parlé du Mystère de l'Incarnation. Voir Maria Łukaszewicz-Chantry, « The Mystery of Incarnation in the Works of Maciej Kazimierz Sarbiewski, »

Dans un autre passage encore, le rapprochement entre les deux œuvres n'est plus aussi marqué – les ressemblances lexicales ne sont plus aussi évidentes – mais l'idée est analogue et transmise au moyen d'images semblables :

Sarbiewski :
Idem, propinqua nocte, stellatas vigil
   Cum vesper accendit faces,
Ut gaudet immortale mirari iubar,
   Terraque maiores globos
Et per cadentes intueri lacrimas
   Rimosa lucis atria,
Quae, Christe, tecum, Virgo, quae tecum colat
   Perennis heres saeculi !
Volvuntur aureis interim stellae rotis,
   Pigrumque linquunt exsulem,
Per ora cuius uberes eunt aquae,
   Somnos quod avertat graves. (15–26)

Bettini :
En erit (O beata !)
En erit illa dies,
Cum tui lumen oris
Mi dabitur tueri ?
En erit ut aetherea
Correpta face pectora
In cineres labascant ;
Tum rogo de vitali
Ad te mens ales advolet,
In teque niduletur ?
      Act. 2, Sc. 4, 25–34

Les deux poètes sont proches dans leur description du désir de contempler la lumière divine et de l'aspiration au ciel, objectif ultime, « retour au bercail » de l'homme dans sa véritable patrie. Le sentiment amer de la brièveté du séjour de l'homme en ce monde, mais aussi de la vie terrestre perçue comme un exil prolongé, est caractéristique du climat spirituel de cette époque et apparaît

---

dans *Pietas Humanistica. Neo-Latin Religious Poetry in Poland in European Context*, éd. Piotr Urbański (Frankfurt a. M., 2006), 129–40.

L'HOMME ET LA NATURE DANS LA TROISIÈME ÉPODE DE SARBIEWSKI

souvent dans la poésie religieuse, surtout chez les jésuites.[24] Sarbiewski a donc pu tirer son inspiration de nombreuses sources. Mais comme nous savons avec certitude qu'il connaissait Bettini – puisque Sparrow l'a « pris en flagrant délit » –, il nous est loisible de penser qu'ici aussi, le poète polonais s'est appuyé sur cet auteur italien.

Le motif de la recherche de traces du Créateur dans tout l'univers matériel termine la première partie de l'épode. Sarbiewski passe ensuite directement à la description des vacances dans la campagne de Wilno. Le « beatior ille », comme on peut le supposer, doit être là, à jouir des beautés de la nature en compagnie des jésuites. On peut supposer que son séjour à Niemenczyn est pour lui une occasion de contempler le Créateur dans la nature, même si le poème ne dit plus rien à ce propos. Le changement qui intervient dans la description de la nature est surprenant : il établit un contraste marqué entre les deux parties de l'épode. Là où la première partie mettait au premier plan les lys et les roses tournés vers le ciel, dans leur soif de l'Absolu, la deuxième partie met en scène des légumes (choux, fèves) et des fruits (fraises des bois bien mûres) destinés aux plaisirs de la bouche. Nous avons donc affaire à une construction assez risquée où les deux parties d'un même texte présentent deux approches diamétralement opposées de la nature qui – j'espère l'avoir démontré – proviennent de deux sources d'inspiration différentes. Horace, évoqué dans le titre, a servi de modèle à la deuxième partie de l'épode, tandis que les descriptions naturelles de la première partie sont inspirées de Bettini.

Le drame de Bettini permet d'ailleurs peut-être aussi de trouver une certaine explication à cette association inhabituelle. Dans une partie du deuxième acte intitulée *Cantiuncula*, en effet, le refrain suivant se répète (Act 2, Sc. 1, 5–6, 17–18, 29–30) :

O vita nullis vitiata curis
Rura colentum !

Ce chant fait l'éloge de la vie tranquille à la campagne, par opposition à la vie mouvementée des puissants. Il a pour toile de fond un *locus amoenus* qui rappelle le décor où évoluait le héros d'Horace, le « beatus ille ». Il est donc vraisemblable que la *Cantiuncula* ait rappelé à Sarbiewski l'existence d'une épode

---

24   Ces sentiments apparaissent dans d'autres œuvres de Sarbiewski, par exemple dans sa fameuse ode *Urit me patriae decor* (*Lyr.* 1,19). Voir Łukaszewicz-Chantry, *Trzy nieba* (voir ci-dessus, n. 14), 101–4 et Elwira Buszewicz, *Sarmacki Horacy i jego liryka. Imitacja-gatunek-styl. Rzecz o poezji Macieja Kazimierza Sarbiewskiego* (Kraków, 2006), 291–9.

d'Horace qu'il connaissait bien, l'ait amené à aborder ce poème par le prisme de Bettini, et dans cette optique, lui ait donné l'idée de se livrer à un jeu intertextuel avec son maître latin.

Pour conclure, nous pouvons dire que dans sa polémique avec Horace, Sarbiewski propose une conception différente du bonheur. Pour le jésuite, la vie *inter naturae fines* ne suffit pas en soi pour être heureux. Le bonheur se manifeste seulement à celui qui a découvert que la nature est une théophanie. L'*otium rusticum* est donc insuffisant : un *otium religiosum* est également nécessaire, comme l'annonce le titre de l'épode. Et dans cette polémique avec Horace, il convient de souligner que Sarbiewski n'était pas seul : il s'est appuyé sur son confrère italien Mario Bettini.

Université de Wrocław

CHAPTER 27

L'art de conférer chez Érasme

Eric MacPhail

Abstract

Érasme a choisi de sous-titrer son traité sur le libre arbitre, dirigé contre Martin Luther, διατριβή *sive collatio*. En conclusion, il nous laisse le jugement libre : « Contuli, penes alios esto iudicium. » Luther s'est souvenu de cet usage quand il a fermé son *De servo arbitrio* par la phrase bien autrement agressive, « Non contuli sed asserui et assero. » L'emploi du verbe "confero" chez Érasme et son refus chez Luther peuvent jeter une lumière importante sur leur différend. En même temps, cet usage nous rappelle une tendance profonde de l'oeuvre d'Érasme, son scepticisme. Je propose d'examiner, chez Érasme, le rapport entre scepticisme et *collatio* en faisant appel à l'essai *De l'art de conferer* de Montaigne, pour mieux situer le débat Érasme-Luther dans l'évolution de la pensée renaissante.

Keywords

Desiderius Erasme – Martin Luther – *De libero arbitrio* – *conferre* – scepticism

La controverse entre Érasme et Luther à propos du libre arbitre a suscité beaucoup d'intérêt parmi les historiens de la théologie, ce qui n'a pas toujours favorisé la réputation d'Érasme, jugé moins bien versé dans la théologie scholastique que son adversaire et moins apte à raisonner comme les *magistri nostri*.[1] C'est pour cela que je voudrais situer cette controverse dans un contexte plutôt littéraire, un contexte fourni par la littérature comparée, en tenant compte du rôle

---

1 Voir le témoignage d'Urbanus Rhegius cité par Erika Rummel, *The Confessionalization of Humanism in Reformation Germany* (Oxford, 2000), 54–61, ici 59. Pour une lecture du *De libero arbitrio* plutôt appréciative de la formation théologique d'Érasme, voir Ernst-Wilhelm Kohls, « La position théologique d'Érasme et la tradition dans le *De libero Arbitrio*, » dans *Colloquium Erasmianum* (Mons, 1968), 69–88. Plus caractéristique du mépris habituel à l'égard des compétences théologiques d'Érasme est E. Gordon Rupp, qui trouve qu'Érasme, en tant que théologien, « is always edifying and profitable, but hardly ever profound. » Voir *Luther and Erasmus : Free Will and Salvation* (Londres, 1969), 9.

© KONINKLIJKE BRILL NV, LEIDEN, 2020 | DOI:10.1163/9789004427105_028

joué par le verbe *confero* et le substantif *collatio* dans leur querelle. Érasme a choisi d'appeler son ouvrage *De libero arbitrio diatribe sive collatio*, et pour sa traduction, la première traduction française, Pierre Mesnard a proposé le titre *Essai sur le libre arbitre*.[2] Est-ce un choix innocent ? J'espère que non, parce que pour éclairer le projet d'Érasme, je propose d'interpréter son ouvrage à la lumière des *Essais* de Montaigne et surtout de l'essai *De l'art de conférer* (3,8). L'emploi que fait Montaigne du verbe *conférer* peut effectivement orienter notre lecture d'Érasme et peut servir surtout à souligner un aspect de son livre qui a tendance à inquiéter la critique érasmienne et à offenser les oreilles pieuses, à savoir son scepticisme. Dans le prologue de son traité sur le libre arbitre, Érasme lui-même se rapproche des sceptiques, mais Luther a retourné contre lui ce rapprochement avec une telle violence et une telle mauvaise foi, que depuis lors les Érasmiens, à quelques exceptions près, ne veulent plus entendre parler de scepticisme, pour mieux protéger l'orthodoxie de leur auteur. Mais cette sensibilité fait tort à ce que je veux comprendre comme le véritable objectif d'Érasme, qui est de décourager la persécution religieuse en décourageant les débats sur le dogme. Comme l'humaniste s'en plaint à Jean de Carondelet, dans l'épître-préface des *Œuvres* de Saint Hilaire de Poitiers, dès que la philosophie s'est emparée de la *doctrina Christi*, on a fait croître démesurément le nombre d'articles et on est passé aussitôt aux menaces et terreurs pour obliger les gens à croire ce qu'ils ne croient pas : « ut credant quod non credunt. »[3] C'est précisément pour résister à cette tendance qu'Érasme fait le sceptique dans le *De libero arbitrio*. Pour mieux apprécier la portée de ce scepticisme, je propose de lier ensemble Érasme et Montaigne, de les conférer dans la même histoire de la tolérance religieuse.

Pour esquisser rapidement le contexte de cette controverse, on peut évoquer quelques détails de la rupture entre Luther et l'Église au début des années 1520. Le 15 juin 1520, le pape Léon X promulgua sa bulle *Exsurge domine* qui condamnait les erreurs de Luther en quarante et un articles. A la fin de la même année, cette bulle provoqua la réponse de Luther intitulée *Assertio omnium articulorum* où Luther tient à réaffirmer tous ces articles, y compris l'article 36 qui parle du libre arbitre, lequel ne serait, d'après Luther, qu'une fiction et un mot vide de sens, parce que tout se passe selon une nécessité absolue. En fait, Luther prétend devoir révoquer l'article condamné, « liberum arbitrium post peccatum res est de solo titulo », pour le remplacer par une négation plus complète de la liberté humaine, « liberum arbitrium est figmentum in rebus

---

2 Érasme, *Essai sur le libre arbitre*, tr. Pierre Mesnard (Alger, 1945).

3 Épître 1334, ligne 379, see *Opus epistolarum Desiderii Erasmi Roterodami*, ed. Percy S. Allen, vol. 5 (Oxford, 1924), 181.

seu titulus sine re ».[4] C'est la phrase qu'Érasme allait qualifier de « durissima sententia ».[5] D'ailleurs, pour Luther, cet article représente l'essence de sa théologie, et il est donc d'autant plus lamentable que ses adversaires soient tous si stupides et aveugles à son propos.[6] Or c'est à cet article que répond Érasme dans son *Essai sur le libre arbitre*, qu'il publia enfin en septembre 1524, cédant ainsi à la pression de ses puissants protecteurs et mécènes, y compris le pape, alors Clément VII.

Dans son livre *De servo arbitrio*, où il prétend écraser le *De libero arbitrio*, Luther fait surtout attention à ce que l'on peut appeler le prologue ou la préface du livre d'Érasme, et il a raison d'y faire attention plus qu'au reste du texte. C'est ici au début, qu'Érasme propose de discuter d'une façon modérée avec Luther à propos du libre arbitre, en confrontant les textes et les arguments pour que la vérité devienne plus évidente, la vérité dont la recherche fait honneur aux studieux (*LB* 9 :1215C) :

> Proinde ne quis hanc pugnam interpretetur, qualis solet esse inter commissos gladiatores, cum unico illius dogmate conflictabor, non in aliud, nisi ut, si fieri queat, hac collisione Scripturarum et argumentorum fiat evidentior veritas, cuius indagatio semper fuit honestissima studiosis.

On peut remarquer ici l'emploi du substantif « collisio », qui correspond à l'emploi de « collatio » que fera plus loin Érasme. Il préfère discuter « sine conviciis » ou sans injures, et lui-même est si loin d'aimer l'assertion ou le dogmatisme, qu'il suivrait volontiers les traces des sceptiques chaque fois que cela lui est permis par l'Église et les Écritures (*LB* 9 :1215D) :

> Et adeo non delector assertionibus, ut facile in Scepticorum sententiam pedibus discessurus sim, ubicunque per divinarum Scripturarum inviolabilem auctoritatem et Ecclesiae decreta liceat.

Tout au moins, il préfère l'esprit sceptique à l'opiniâtreté de ceux qui, comme Luther bien entendu, ne supportent pas les avis contraires aux leurs (*LB* 9 :1215D).

---

4   *D. Martin Luthers Werke : Kritische Gesamtausgabe*, vol. 7 (Weimar, 1897), 146 (= *WA* 7 :146).

5   *Desiderii Erasmi Roterodami opera omnia*, ed. Jean Le Clerc, vol. 9 (Leiden, 1706), 1224D (= *LB* 9 :1224D).

6   *WA* 7 :148 « in hoc articulo, qui omnium optimus et rerum nostrarum summa est, dolendum ac flendum est, miseros sic insanire. »

> Atque hoc ingenium mihi malo, quam quo video quosdam esse praedi-
> tos, ut impotenter addicti sententiae nihil ferant, quod ab ea discrepet :
> sed quicquid legunt in Scripturis, detorquent ad assertionem opinionis,
> cui se semel manciparunt.

Jusqu'ici et tout le long de ce prologue, on peut avoir l'impression qu'Érasme ne s'intéresse pas trop au fond du problème, « car », comme dira Montaigne dans son essai *De l'art de conferer*, « nous sommes sur la maniere, non sur la matiere du dire. »[7] Érasme s'intéresse surtout à la manière dont on s'exprime et dont on conduit le débat, plutôt qu'à sa résolution.

Il convient de s'attarder un peu sur la phrase « ut facile in Scepticorum sententiam pedibus discessurus sim », dont la plupart des lecteurs, exception faite de Luther bien entendu, ont cherché à minimiser la signification. Érasme sceptique ? Luther dit oui, sceptique et irréligieux. En fait, qui supprime les assertions, supprime le Christianisme : « Tolle assertiones, et Christianismum tulisti » (*WA* 18 :603). S'abstenir de faire des assertions, c'est refuser la religion : « hoc esset nihil aliud, quam semel totam religionem ac pietatem negasse, aut asseruisse, nihil esse religionem, aut pietatem aut ullum dogma » (*WA* 18 :604). Depuis la publication du *De servo arbitrio* en 1525, on s'est montré extrêmement prudent sur la question du scepticisme chez Érasme. L'exception la mieux connue est celle de Richard Popkin, qui commence son histoire du scepti-cisme par Érasme, mais la critique érasmienne semble avoir fait très peu de cas de la thèse de Popkin malgré son importance pour l'histoire des idées.[8] Erika Rummel, au moins, a bien voulu parler du « scepticisme chrétien » d'Érasme, et elle a insisté sur le contexte épistémologique du débat sur le libre arbitre.[9] Mais sa notion du scepticisme semble exclure la suspension du jugement et favorise, au lieu de l'irrésolution, le consensus. En 2009 Irena Backus, dans un volume consacré au mémoire de Popkin, a rejeté catégoriquement toute asso-ciation d'Érasme avec le scepticisme.[10] Pour elle, le *De libero arbitrio* n'est rien moins que sceptique et nulle part Érasme ne suspend son jugement sur le libre

---

7   *Michel de Montaigne, Les Essais*, éd. Pierre Villey (Paris, 1978), 928. Désormais cité dans le texte par livre, chapitre et page (3,8,928).

8   Richard Popkin, *The History of Scepticism from Erasmus to Descartes* (New York, 1968), 1–16.

9   Rummel, *Confessionalization* (voir ci-dessus, n. 1), 54–61.

10 Irena Backus, « The Issue of Reformation Scepticism Revisited : What Erasmus and Sebastian Castellio Did or Did Not Know, » dans *Renaissance Scepticisms*, éd. Gianni Paganini et José Maia Neto (Dordrecht, 2009), 63–89.

L'ART DE CONFÉRER CHEZ ÉRASME

arbitre.[11] Manfred Hoffmann est largement d'accord avec cette interprétation, comme il l'a exprimé très clairement dans un article de 2004.[12] Pour ma part, je préfère comprendre le scepticisme d'Érasme en fonction de son attitude envers la persécution des hérétiques. Si on laisse ouverte la question du libre arbitre, sans prononcer un arrêt d'orthodoxie, on peut différer la persécution de ceux qui ne se conforment pas à cet arrêt. C'est dans cet esprit qu'Érasme rappelle à son adversaire que même si, lui, Luther a raison, même s'il dit vrai, il y a des vérités inopportunes qu'il ne faut pas publier partout.[13] Pareillement, il suggère qu'il y a des erreurs doctrinales qu'il vaut mieux tolérer que supprimer, « qui minore malo tolerantur quam tolluntur » (*LB* 9 :1217D). Ce jeu de mots entre « tolerare » et « tollere » est connu de tout lecteur des *Paraphrases* d'Érasme, car c'est en paraphrasant l'évangile selon Matthieu 13,40, à propos de la parabole du bon grain et de l'ivraie, qu'il dit : « Interim igitur mali bonis admixti ferendi sunt, quando minore pernicie tolerantur quam tollerentur » (*LB* 7 :80F). Cette phrase passe pour être le *locus classicus* de la tolérance chez Érasme.[14] S'il fait écho maintenant, dans le *De libero arbitrio*, aux paroles qu'il prêtait dans sa paraphrase à l'évangéliste, c'est qu'il est enclin à situer le débat sur le libre arbitre dans le même contexte de la punition ou de l'impunité des hérétiques.

Érasme semble résumer l'esprit de sa *Diatribe* quand il nous assure qu'il n'entend pas faire le juge en débattant, et qu'il est aussi prompt à apprendre qu'à enseigner : « disputatorem agam, non judicem : inquisitorem, non dogmatisten, paratus a quocunque discere » (*LB* 9 :1216B). C'est ce passage que je voudrais mettre en parallèle avec une phrase de l'essai *De l'art de conferer* qui est un des passages les plus célèbres et les plus admirés des *Essais*, où Montaigne explique pourquoi, dans la conférence, « la victoire du sujet » (3,8,925) lui est à peu près indifférente (3,8,928) :

> L'agitation et la chasse est proprement de nostre gibier : nous ne sommes
> pas excusables de la conduire mal et impertinemment ; de faillir à la

---

11   Ibid., 67 « In fact, if we examine Erasmus' argument in his treatise, it turns out to be anything but sceptical » ; 68 « What might appear sceptical about Erasmus' view is his weighing up of several opinions before giving his preference to the one that is most valid. [...] However, at no point does Erasmus suspend judgement. »

12   Manfred Hoffmann, « Reformation Ways of Speaking : Erasmus' Rhetorical Theology in *De libero arbitrio*, » *Erasmus of Rotterdam Society Yearbook* 24 (2004), 1–22.

13   « Licet verum dicere, verum non expedit apud quoslibet, nec quovis tempore, nec quovis modo » (*LB* 9 :1217E).

14   Voir Johannes Trapman, « Erasmus and Heresy, » *Bibliothèque d'Humanisme et Renaissance* 75 (2013), 7–24.

prise, c'est autre chose. Car nous sommes nais à quester la verité ; il appartient de la posseder à une plus grande puissance [...] Le monde n'est qu'une escole d'inquisition.

La vision du monde comme une école d'inquisition convient parfaitement à celui qui dit, « inquisitorem non dogmatisten ago ». L'idée de bien conduire la chasse, même si on doit faillir à la prise, fait une entière justice à la position d'Érasme, qui n'entend pas régler une fois pour toutes une question théologique mais propose plutôt à son interlocuteur de conduire ensemble une *indagatio veritatis* qui peut très bien s'avérer interminable.[15] Bref, cette louange de la chasse qui se prolonge sans résolution exprime bien l'érasmisme latent de Montaigne.

Vers la fin de son prologue, Érasme fait appel à l'esprit évangélique dont parlent si souvent Luther et ses partisans, espérant qu'ils le traiteront, lui Érasme la vieille outre, comme le Christ traita Nicodème et les apôtres Gamaliel (*LB* 9 :1220E) :

> Saltem eo loco nos habeant, quo Christus habuit Nicodemum, Apostoli Gamalielem. Illum licet crassum, sed discendi avidum, non repulit Dominus : hunc suspendentem sententiam, donec exitus rei doceret, quo spiritu gereretur, Discipuli non sunt adspernati.

La figure de Gamaliel, le juge qui suspend son jugement dans les Actes des Apôtres 5,34–9, sera un des *topoi* favoris des avocats de la tolérance religieuse tout le long du siècle, et Calvin lui-même, dans sa *Déclaration pour maintenir la vraie foi*, écrite pour justifier le supplice de Michel Servet, reconnaît l'importance accordée par ses adversaires à ce juge qui « demeure en suspens. »[16] Pour Sébastien Castellion, dédiant sa traduction latine de la Bible au roi Édouard VI d'Angleterre, Gamaliel donne l'exemple d'une irrésolution salutaire qui fait face au dogmatisme immodéré de leur époque.[17] L'auteur anonyme de l'*Apologie de Michel Servet*, attribué à l'hérétique italien Matteo Gribaldi, fait également l'éloge du sage juriste, « sapiens ille legisperitus, » qui a su résister au jugement

---

15   Voir Rummel, *Confessionalization* (ci-dessus, n. 1), 56 : « Erasmus, then, did not attempt to settle the theological question of free will but to give a methodological demonstration. » Mais si cela est vrai, le scepticisme d'Érasme est bien plus audacieux qu'elle ne voudrait l'admettre.

16   *Jean Calvin, Oeuvres*, ed. Francis Higman et Bernard Roussel (Paris, 2009), 916.

17   Castellion, « Préface à la *Biblia* (1551), » dans *Sébastien Castellion : des Écritures à l'écriture*, ed. Marie-Christine Gomez-Géraud (Paris, 2013) 433–41, ici 438. Référence reprise dans le *Traité des Hérétiques*, ed. Olivet (Genève, 1914), 137.

L'ART DE CONFÉRER CHEZ ÉRASME

précipité des autres.[18] Au milieu des controverses acharnées de la Réforme, Gamaliel représente les bienfaits du scepticisme.

Quand Érasme arrive au terme de son prologue, qui représente pour lui la moitié de son livre, « Absolvi dimidium huius libri » (1220E), bien qu'il soit toujours au début, il exprime l'espoir de faire ressortir la vérité « ex collatione Scripturarum » (1220F) ou de la confrontation des Écritures, en citant un échantillon des passages de la Bible qui parlent pour et d'autres qui parlent contre le libre arbitre. C'est cette *collatio* qui va occuper le gros du traité et que la plupart des lecteurs ont voulu comprendre comme un effort, de la part d'Érasme, pour créer un consensus, ou bien pour conserver le consensus autour du libre arbitre, en évitant les extrêmes. La *via media* plaît beaucoup à Érasme, comme on le voit bien dans ses *Annotations* au Nouveau Testament, dans l'édition de 1527, où il commente l'épître de Saint Paul aux Ephésiens 1,6 : « Nusquam apostolus hic non extollit gratiam extenuans operum humanorum fiduciam ; nunc sunt qui peccent in utranque partem. Medio tutissima via est. »[19] Dans la controverse entre la grâce et les bonnes œuvres, Érasme voit des péchés ou des hyperboles de part et d'autre (mais surtout du côté luthérien) et donc Manfred Hoffmann a raison de comprendre *collatio* comme « comparison leading to agreement. »[20] Érasme a mérité son renom comme l'apôtre de la concorde. Et pourtant, si je suis plus sensible à la portée sceptique qu'à la portée conciliatrice de la *collatio*, c'est parce que le consensus peut très bien être intolérant là où l'irrésolution favorise la tolérance.

En tout cas, à la fin de son exposé, Érasme déclare, en recourant au mot clé, « Hactenus ex divinis libris loca contulimus » (1241D), et il faut dire que les traducteurs ne sont pas tous à la hauteur de cette phrase. Mesnard dit assez inexplicablement, « Nous nous sommes bornés jusqu'ici à confirmer les passages de l'Ecriture » qui parlent pour et contre le libre arbitre,[21] tandis que Peter Macardle préfère « Up to this point we have collected Scriptural passages »[22] et Lesowsky « Bis jetzt haben wir Stellen aus der Heiligen Schrift zusammengetragen. »[23] Plus proche du *sensus germanus* est la nouvelle traduction de Georges Lagarrigue : « nous n'avons fait jusqu'ici que comparer les passages

---

18 *Apologia pro M. Serveto* dans *Ioannis Calvini opera quae supersunt omnia*, éd. Johann Wilhelm Baum, Eduard Cunitz et Eduard Reuss, vol. 15 (Brunswick, 1876), 55 (= *CO* 15 :55).

19 *Opera omnia Desiderii Erasmi Roterodami*, vol. 6, tome 9 (Leiden, 2009), 166 (= *ASD* VI-9 :166).

20 Hoffmann, « Reformation Ways of Speaking » (voir ci-dessus, n. 12), 17.

21 Érasme, *Essai* (voir ci-dessus, n. 2), 157.

22 *Collected Works of Erasmus*, vol. 76, *A Discussion of Free Will*, tr. Peter Macardle (Toronto, 1999), 74 (= *CWE* 76 :74).

23 *Erasmus, De libero arbitrio*, éd. Winfried Lesowsky (Darmstadt, 1969), 157.

des Livres saints. »[24] A mon sens, c'est Luther qui a le mieux compris la force de « contulimus » quand il reproche à Érasme d'avoir mis en scène une dispute *in utramque partem*. On lit dans le *De servo arbitrio* cette phrase adressée à Érasme, phrase qui commente le sous-titre *Diatribe sive collatio* (*WA* 18 :660) :

> Deinde sententia suspensa, in utranque partem disputas, Quid pro, quid contra dici possit, praeterea nihil agis toto isto libello, quem ob eandem causam Diatriben potius quam Apophasin vel aliud appellare voluisti, quod omnia collaturus, nihil affirmaturus scriberes.

Érasme refuse de prendre parti ou de trancher la question en dispute, favorisant ainsi une suspension de jugement. On sent à quel degré Luther s'indigne de cette technique franchement sceptique.

On connaît la dernière phrase du *De libero arbitrio* où l'auteur renonce à trancher la question : « CONTULI, penes alios esto judicium » (1248D). Ce qui peut nous frapper c'est l'emploi de *confero* au singulier, sans objet direct ou complément aucun. Que veut dire « j'ai conféré » ? Comment conférer tout seul ? Le « contuli » semble attendre un « contulimus » ou « contulerimus » ou même un « tecum contuli ».[25] De son côté Luther répondra par la phrase non moins célèbre, « NON CONTULI, SED ASSERUI ET ASSERO » (*WA* 18 :787). Mais Luther se trompe avec son « non contuli ». Il a effectivement disputé avec Érasme ; il a fait le *collator* malgré lui. C'est-à-dire que les deux écrivains se sont contredits et sont arrivés à une impasse pour mieux tenir la question en suspens. Ils ont disputé *in utramque partem* sans pouvoir résoudre leur différend : ils ont chassé sans rien prendre. Ce qui explique en partie pourquoi l'intervention d'Érasme dans ce débat n'a finalement satisfait personne.

Pour conclure je voudrais emprunter un morceau de sagesse à la critique montaignienne, notamment à l'article de Stéphan Geonget sur l'essai *De l'art de conférer*. Geonget explique le sens du mot « conférer » en le situant dans un contexte juridique qui n'est pas étranger au magistrat Montaigne : « Conférer, c'est d'abord rapprocher des articles, des points litigieux (dans le monde du droit mais aussi de la politique) et tomber d'accord sur une interprétation commune. »[26] Paradoxalement, cette recherche d'un accord ne réussit, d'habitude,

---

24 Luther, *Du serf arbitre* suivi de Désiré Érasme, *Diatribe : Du libre arbitre*, tr. Georges Lagarrigue (Paris, 2001), 541.

25 Voir l'article de Eric Pesty, « *Conférer* à la fin du XVIe siècle, » *Bulletin de la Société des amis de Montaigne* 7e série, 17–18 (2000), 109–20 qui analyse l'usage de *confero* chez les anciens et chez les néo-latins pour mieux éclairer l'emploi de *conférer* chez Montaigne.

26 Stéphan Geonget, « Les enjeux juridiques du terme de 'conférence' (III, 8), » *Bulletin de la Société internationale des amis de Montaigne* 65 (2017), 49–64, ici 56.

qu'à faire ressortir le désaccord : « Somme toute, ce que produit la conférence c'est moins un accord progressif que l'exhibition de plus en plus manifeste de ce qu'elle cherche à résoudre, c'est-à-dire des divergences. »[27] Dans le cas de l'essai, « L'art de conférer c'est précisément l'art de ne pas parvenir à la conférence, c'est-à-dire à cette unité et à cette résolution finale. »[28] Différer ainsi toute résolution finale n'est pas un échec mais un art, un art favorable à la tolérance. Et donc, « L'art de conférer » est bien le titre qui convient le mieux à l'ouvrage d'Érasme.

Indiana University

---

27   Ibid., 58.
28   Ibid., 62.

CHAPTER 28

Mankind's Public and Private Roles in *Collectanea Moralis Philosophiae* (1571)

Ana I. C. Martins

Abstract

The *Collectanea Moralis Philosophiae* (1571) organizes the Graeco-Latin patterns into *loci communes*, combining the pagan heritage and the Christian matrix. This encyclopaedic work is divided into three parts, one of which includes sentences from Seneca's works, the second, a compilation of opuscules from Plutarch's moral treatises, and the third, a collection of the noblest apophthegmata from the most important and influential philosophers. Conscious that human beings are just as prone to vice as to virtue, both for good and for evil, the purpose of Fray Louis of Grenade (1504–88) is to emphasize the conquest of *vita beata*, whose corollary is *ratio perfecta* and *felicitas*. The Dominican presents anthropological concerns, promoting ethical and moral ideals for the political man, in his public sphere and also in his personal and private sphere through a very modern awareness of the unresolved duality of our human nature. Among all these mankind's stereotypes, we will focus on two in particular: *discipulus et magister* or *doctor et auditor* (public sphere) and *pater et filius* (private sphere) so as to explore the symbolic power of these representations, explaining why they belong to our *consecutio* typology.

Keywords

Fray Louis of Grenade – *Collectanea Moralis Philosophiae* (1571) – Neo-Latin philosophical treatise – moral philosophy – dialectics

[...] Propone de este modo Fray Luis de Granada una especie de programa de adoctrinamiento moral cristiano, al estilo de los humanistas centroeuropeos, basado en la lectura piadosa de los tres principales

géneros literarios en los que la Antigüedad pagana fundaba la divulga-
ción filosófica.[1]

••

The Venerable Fray Louis of Granada (1504–88) was a Dominican, a master of
oratory and eloquence, an articulate preacher, sincere politician, a scathing
theologian, an acknowledged humanist of the Renaissance, and above all, an
intellectual engaged in his time and space. His honourable reputation spread
beyond the borders of his native Spain, and having accepted the invitation of
Portuguese Cardinal Dom Henrique (1512–80), the archbishop of Évora, the
Spanish Dominican chose Portugal as his second home, where he lived for
more than 30 years (1556–88) until his death. He also held significant social
and political sway at court, where he was royal confessor of D. Catarina. He
achieved social prestige, ecclesiastic respectability and was admired not only
for his solid knowledge and clear-sightedness—particularly regarding his work
on the interplay of shadow and light in spirituality—but also for his skills and
talent with words. His literary and spiritual works cover a broad spectrum of
themes, from the theological principals of Christianity to pagan philosophy.
Granada's eclectic and prolific publications could be framed in five typologies:
dialogues, sermons, prayers, letters, and biographies. He translated several
books from Latin to Spanish, and he also preached and wrote in Spanish, in
Portuguese and in Latin. Marcel Bataillon underlines that[2]

> a Luís de Granada estaba reservado fundir de manera más decisiva la he-
> rencia de interioridad del erasmismo con muchas otras tradiciones anti-
> guas o recientes [...] Ninguno fue más hábil para soldar, en una sola, joyas
> de proveniencia muy diversa.

His Latin trilogy—*Collectanea Moralis Philosophiae*, *Silva Locorum* and
Rhetorica Ecclesiastica—follows a catechetical-doctrinal program in order to
construct an itinerary of morality, looking for a universal sense of mankind in

---

1 Juan J. Valverde Abril, "Fray Luis de Granada, la Collectanea Y Erasmo," in *Acta Conventus Neo-Latini Upsaliensis: Proceedings of the Fourteenth International Congress of Neo-Latin Studies (Uppsala 2009)*, ed. Astrid Steiner-Weber (Leiden, 2012) 1178–87, there 1178.

2 Marcel Bataillon, *Erasmo y España, Estudios sobre la historia espiritual del siglo XVI*, (Buenos Aires, 1966), 594.

all his dimensions. Therefore, in this present study, our main goal is to identify and analyse all these public and private roles of mankind in the *Collectanea Moralis Philosophiae* (1571), recognizing their articulation and complementarity, proving how perennial and relevant are these representations of society. On the success of oratory and eloquence, Fray Louis defends the importance of *copia argumentorum et sententiarum* giving detailed instructions and citing several sentences from pagan authors who endorsed *auctoritas* and *grauitas*. In this theoretical treatment of emotion, and so as to serve the triple function of *docere, delectare, mouere*, the Dominican quotes Quintilian, refers to Aristotle, and treats *amplificatio* as one of the major aspects of rhetoric. The *amplificatio* effect is rooted in similes, allegories, metaphors, and parallelisms, which invite the reader to deepen reflection and argumentation, offering different perspectives for his hermeneutic training. In most cases, the natural world provides the examples, which favours the paganist idea of interconnection between all elements, even the most insignificant animals.

This encyclopaedic handbook gathers mostly Protestant authors, figures from classical antiquity and even voices and *corpora* by his contemporaries, analysing the Graeco-Latin standards of rhetoric, combining the pagan and the Christian legacies. The *Collectanea Moralis Philosophiae* is divided into three tomes:[3] the first includes selected sentences from the works of Seneca,[4] the second a compilation of opuscules from all the moral treatises of Plutarch,[5] and the third combines *series locorum* by ancient and modern authors, ranging from Cicero to Erasmus but also including Seneca and Plutarch.[6] Granada

---

3 Louis of Granada, *Collectanea Moralis Philosophiae in tres tomus distributa* [...] (Parisiis, 1582). This edition is the source of our study.

4 From *Epistulae ad Lucilium, Naturales Quaestiones, De Ira, De Prouidentia, De Beneficiis, Suasoria, De Tranquillitas animi, Consolatio ad Polibium, De remediis fortuitorum, De clementia, De constantia sapientis, De otio, De paupertate*.

5 From *Moralia: De exilio, De doctrina principum, De liberis educandis, De fortuna et uirtute Alexandri, De uirtute morum, De tuenda bona ualetudine, De officio auditoris, De disputatione philosophorum, De officio auditoris, De profectu morum, De docenda uirtute, De uitiosa uerecundia, De utilitate capienda ab inimicis, de utilitate capienda ex inimico, De discrimine adulatoris et amici, De cohibenda iracundia, De amicitia in multos difusa, In oratione consolatoria, De odio et inuidia, De audiendis poetis, De claris mulieribus, De curiositate, De uirtute et uitio, De cupiditate diuitiarum*.

6 Greek authors: Plutarchus, Claudius Aelianus, Aphthonius, Aristotle, Diogenes Laertius, Eusebius Cesarea, Favorinus, Herodianus, Herodotus, Philo of Alexandria, Philostratus, Antonius Melissa, Nicephorus Callistus, Stobaeus; Latin authors: Apuleius, Cassiodorus, Cicero, Flavius Eutropius, Aulus Gellius, Macrobius, Plinius, Priscianus, Quintilian, Scriptores Historiae Augustae (Flavius Vopiscus, Aelius Lampridius, Julius Julio Capitolinus), Seneca, Suetonius, Valerius Maximus; modern authors: Rodolphus Agricola, Adriaan van Baarland, Filippo Beroaldo, Brusonio Contursino, Cuspian, Baptista Inácio, Erasmus, Francisco

presents a collection of the noblest *apophthegmata* from the most important and paradigmatic figures and philosophers over the ages, organised in *loci communes*, in order to make all these humanistic subjects more easily accessible to any dedicated reader. Contrary to many works of this genre, his *dispositio* denies an alphabetical order, because the Dominican believed that the epistemological and philosophical affinity is much more important than the designation of concepts. In terms of internal structure, all volumes are further divided into subcategories (so called *classes*). The first volume presents the first *classis* containing sections on many different types of individuals and their social/public and individual/private roles ("prima classis, in qua ponuntur tituli ad diuersa genera statuum et personarum spectantes"[7]), the second *classis* contains *themata* concerning virtues and vices ("secunda classis locorum communium in qua de uirtutibus et uitiis agitur"[8]), the third *classis* includes several righteous themes, perhaps the noblest ones from the Friar's perspective ("tertia classis locorum communium quae uaria continet loca"[9]). The second and third volumes only have two *classes*: "prima classis in qua ponuntur tituli diuersa genera statuum et personarum spectantes" (vol. 2)[10] resp. "prima classis quae a Deo Opt. Max incipiens, duersorum sttuum personas complectitur" (vol. 3);[11] "secunda classis quae communia uirtutum et uitiorum loca [...]" (vol. 2)[12] resp. "secunda classis in qua uirtutum et uitiorum loci collocantur" (vol. 3).[13]

The *Collectanea* reveal more classical and pagan influences which explains its idiosyncrasy and our particular interest in it, given the inclusion of authors such as: Seneca, Cicero, Plutarch, Diogenes Laertius, Apuleius, Plato, Aristotle, and also medieval and contemporary authors, including the Portuguese Jerónimo Osório, Priscianus Caesariensis, Piccolomini (Pope Pius II) and Erasmus. Louis of Granada quotes the Germans Jakob Spiegel and Johannes

---

Senensis, Baptista Fulgosio, Guido Bituriensis, Jeronimo Osorio, Antonio Beccadeli, Panormita, Aeneas Silvio Picolomini, Pontano, Jakob Spiegel. We should underline that our Dominican follows a common methodology in sixteenth century and to compile the third tomus he was inspired by *Apophthegmata* of Lycosthenes. Regarding this aspect see Juan J. Valverde Abril, "Los Apophthegmata de Conradus Lycosthenes o las vicissitudes de la sabiduría humanística," in *Nardus et myrto plexae coronae. Symmikta Philologica ad Amicos in Iubilaeo obsequendos*, ed. Juan J. Valverde Abril and Gatsioufa Paraskevi (Granada, 2018), 419–69.

7   Louis of Granada, *Collectanea* (see above, n. 3), vol. 1, 1r.
8   Ibid., vol. 1, 22v.
9   Ibid., vol. 1, 113v.
10 Ibid., vol. 2, 140r.
11 Ibid., vol. 3, 222r.
12 Ibid., vol. 2, 161r.
13 Ibid., vol. 2, 241r.

Cuspian, as well as the Dutch, Adriaan van Baarland, who are *auctores damnati* in the inquisitorial index. We should not underestimate this information, as it reveals the Dominican's wide-ranging, unprejudiced and eclectic interest and culture.

During the Renaissance, the Christian *docta religio* abolished the boundaries between the sacred and the profane and, consequently, the church adopted and adapted the Platonic virtues—*iustitia, prudentia, fortitudo,* and *temperantia*—having added *fides, spes* and *amor* in a dialectic building.[14] This axiological architecture was carefully represented and articulated by Friar Louis of Granada in this *Collectanea Moralis Philosophiae*:[15] "Praestabis parentibus pietatem, cognatis dilectionem. Praestabis amicis fidem, omnibus aequitatem. Pacem cum omnibus habebis, bellum cum uitiis."[16]

Each volume is physically independent, but they play a complementary role exhibiting a coherent reading in their internal logic. Stoicism reverberates when Granada incorporates Seneca's ideals in the first volume: Philosophy is the only way to fulfil the virtue, and virtue is the only way to conquer freedom, happiness, and wisdom; the contempt for wealth is a progressive exercise; a frugal and prudent *modus vivendi* strengthens and improves *ethos*. Stoics were concerned with providing insight for the development of a practice of life, defending an active political engagement, always interconnected with a virtuous conduct and an inner harmony:[17]

> Non is solus Reipublicae prodest, qui candidatos extrahit, et tuetur reos, et de pace belloque censet sed qui iuuentutem exhortatur, qui in tanta bonorum praeceptorum inopia uirtute instruit, qui animos ad pecuniam luxuriamque cursu ruentes prensat, atque retrahit, in priuato publicum negotium agit.

---

14   Moralising literature and the apophthegmatic genre aligned other genres such as iconography and heraldry, when they represent the virtuous ethos of the *princeps* (*speculum principis*). On this aspect, see the triumph car of Albrecht Dürer, dedicated to Emperor Maximilian I.

15   See about *Iustitia* and *Iniustitia* Louis of Granada, *Collectanea* (see above, n. 3), vol. 1–3, 52r, 175r, 253r; about *Prudentia* and *Imprudentia* ibid., vol. 1–3, 50v, 174v, 251v; about *fortitudo* ibid., vol. 1 and 3, 72r and 261r; about *temperantia* ibid., vol. 1 and 3, 88v and 193v; about *fides* ibid., vol. 1, 31r; about *spes* and *desperatio* ibid., vol. 1, 31v, about *amor* (*amor in communi, amor mundi rerumque lebentium et earum contemptus, amor inimicorum, amor proximi contraque odium, amor sui*) ibid., vol. 1–3, 32r–36v, 164r, 244r and 276r.

16   Ibid., vol. 1, 52r.

17   Ibid., vol. 1, 15r.

MANKIND'S ROLES IN *COLLECTANEA MORALIS PHILOSOPHIAE*   381

In the second volume, Plutarch is included, based mostly on his *Moralia*, in representation of Platonism: the proximity between the transcendent and the human being, also through the practice of philosophy, justice, civic humanism and these virtues previously mentioned. In *topos proficientium status*, Granada says:[18]

> Videas equidem non paucos, qui cupidi admodum feruntur ad philosophiae studia: uerum mox ubi ad alia diuerterint negotia, effluit affectus prior, nulloque dolore torquentur philosophiae desiderio.

The Platonism established an isomorphic structure of the city and soul, conciliating public and private dimensions. Concerning this path of overcoming and learning, if we scrutinize the *Collectanea*'s index, we recognize a possible representation of three hierarchical principles. The paradigm and the perfect model of conduct are represented by *themata* such as *Deus, Dei Prouidentia, Dei iustitia* etc.; the platonic demiurge, a craftsman as a mediation between God and his creation is represented by *themata* concerning man in all his dimensions and roles like *rex/princeps, pater/filius, magister/discipulus*. Finally, we can discuss *topoi* such as *veritas, philosophia, sapientia, vita, mors, tempus* representing the incorporeal matter and the highest activity of the human soul, a transcendent principle of cosmic order. The third volume exhibits a different nature, gathering several authors and consequently this idiosyncrasy consolidates the syncretism of this encyclopaedic handbook, neither compromising nor invalidating this coherence.

Designed to focus on vices and virtues, the *Collectanea* construct moral and philosophical dialectics, opposing several *topoi* as a representation of conflictual forces, such as light and shadow, vice and virtue, God and the fragility of human nature. The author follows a particular and meticulous philological method to organize and to arrange all his sources, rooted in rhetorical and dialectical criteria, as can be understood from his introductory letter, in which he confesses that it is much more important to respect the moral and philosophical nature of the subjects than their alphabetical order.

Taking F. Buisson's classification of *Collectanea* as our reference—dialectical and philosophical work[19]—a pioneering hermeneutical reading can be constructed, by grouping all *themata* into four types of dialectics in terms of their internal structure, freeing us from the corset of the three *tomi*. The first group involves contrasting binomials ("agôn"), subdivided into those that share the

---

18   Ibid., vol. 2, 149r.
19   Ferdinand Buisson, *Répertoire des ouvrages pédagogiques du XVI siècle*, (Paris, 1968), 333.

same etymological root,[20] and those that have different etymological roots;[21] the second group contains the binomials of *consecutio*;[22] the third group corresponds to the contiguous pairs that can also be divided into those that share the same etymological root[23] and those that have different etymological roots.[24] The fourth and final group contains axiological binomials such as "conscientia bona et mala", "amicitia uera et falsa", "gloria uera et falsa", "libertas uera et falsa", and "uirtus bona et mala". These dichotomies could be a possible key of moral coherence and philosophical cohesion in this pedagogical program that seeks to harmonize so many authors and several epistemic influences under the same pedagogical program.[25]

Friar Louis of Granada wished to deepen anthropological concerns by endorsing ethical and moral ideals for the public and civic man ("homo politicus ac eloquens: magistratus/iudex; discipulus/magister; princeps/rex"), but also for the private man ("homo priuatus: pater/filius; uir/uxor, dominus/seruus"), revealing a very modern awareness of an unresolved duality in human nature. The human being is just as prone to vice as to virtue, hesitating between good and evil, and the purpose of this axiological structure is the conquest of the *vita beata*, whose corollary is *ratio perfecta* and *felicitas*, if indeed there is any conciliation of serenity, freedom, truth, conscience, wisdom—the human being's main goal. The topicality of Granada's message is closely related to this operative principle: reshaping man as the measure of all things, rediscovering and understanding his dual condition and his internal dialectic between virtue and vice, truth and lies, light and shadow, within his polymorphic and contradictory nature. Moreover, the richness of this sententious and apophthegmatic genre lies in its methodological possibilities and versatility not only because

---

20 Contrasting binominals are: "nobiles/ignobiles; fama/infamia; prudentia/imprudentia; iustitia/iniustitia; gratitudo/ingratitudo; sobrietas/ebrietas; patientia/impatientia; temperantia/intemperantia; spes/desperatio; constantia/inconstantia; obedientia/inobedientia".

21 "magnanimitas/pusillanimitas; inertia/diligentia; timor/audacia; auaritia/prodigalitas; pulchritudo/deformitas; mansuetudo/ira; abstinentia/gula; uita/mors, luxus/abstinentia; uir/uxor; dominus/seruus; uirtus/uitium; labor/otium".

22 "pueritia/adolescentia; pater/filius; magister/discipulus; doctor/auditor; rex/princeps; iudex/magistratus; admonitio/castigatio".

23 "potentes/potentia; nobiles/nobilitas; prosperitas/prosperitatus; senectus/senex; sapiens/sapientia; nobiles/nobilitas; amicitia/amicus".

24 "pax/concordia; otium/inertia; gloria/honor; parsimonia/frugalitas; pudor/uerecundia; sacrificium/oblatio; castitas/coelibatus; exemplum/imitatio; aduersitas/tribulatio; temperantia/perseuerantia;labor/industria; frugalitas/parsimonia; superbia/ambitio; secretum/silentium; fides/credulitas".

25 This taxonomy is a result of my PhD research.

MANKIND'S ROLES IN *COLLECTANEA MORALIS PHILOSOPHIAE* 383

the collectors can gather from different sources and places but also because the reader can choose a particular author or a specific subject and study what different philosophers, orators and poets have said about it. Concerning the versatility of this classical heritage and all these *loci communes*, we should evoke Léon Halkin's words:[26]

> Quand on connut les écrits des anciens, et leur morale parfois déjà si belle on fut amené à croire que la morale n'était pas exclusivement catholique et théologique, mais universelle et humaine.

Among all these social stereotypes, we will focus on two in particular: "discipulus et magister" or "doctor et auditor" (public sphere) and "pater et filius" (private sphere), so as to explore the symbolic power of these representations, explaining why they belong to our *consecutio* typology. The *magister* and the *pater* should have the same altruism and generosity in regards to the transmission of the best teachings.[27] These *topoi* are arranged in the first part of each volume in a sequential order, following the concepts of *Deus* and *Providentia*, respecting the hierarchical structure.[28]

The humanist *paideia* emphasizes the ideal of education as second nature and, for this reason, this paradigm is a keystone in our reading:[29]

> Socrates dicebat, optime natis ingenuisque potissimum adhibendam rectam institutionem. Idem enim in his usu uenire, quod in equis: in quibus, qui feroces sunt, ac generosae indolis, si statim a primis annis recte instituantur, egregii et ad omnem usum accommodi euadunt, sin minus, efferati, intractabiles, et ad nihil utiles sunt.

The pedagogical path demands strong dedication and perseverance, because when people became adults it is much more difficult to correct the vices that grew with them. One should also avoid fear, fragility, despair and distrust during this learning process:[30]

> Maiora uitia metuenda sunt, pauor, difficultas et desperatio et suspiciones. Educatio maximam diligentiam plurimumque profuturam desiderat.

---

26 Léon Halkin, *Erasme et l'humanisme chrétien* (Paris, 1969), 347.

27 Louis of Granada, *Collectanea* (see above, n. 3), vol. 1, 13v–15v, vol. 2, 146r–148r, vol. 3, 228r–229r.

28 Louis of Granada, *Collectanea*, vol. 1r–4r.

29 Ibid., vol. 3, 228r.

30 Ibid., vol. 1, 13r and vol. 2, 146v.

Facile est enim teneros adhuc animos componere. Difficulter rescindun-
tur uitia, quae nobiscum creuerunt. [...] Nouella aetas ad fingendum facilis et tenera est et ipsorum animis (dum molles adhuc extant) disciplinae
melius distillantur. Difficilius autem quae dura sunt, molliuntur.

An education on the path of freedom, respecting individual nature and desires, is the key point, under the conviction that the spirit is magnified with
freedom and languishes with servility: "Crescit licentia spiritus, seruitute
comminuitur."[31]

The *magister* should instil self-confidence in his *discipulus* as well as keep
the watchful eye and prudent attitude like a father, so as to regulate his inso-
lence, pride and haughtiness. They should also discover together that winning
does not mean harming. Thus, the role and the attitude of a father and a master are complementary and adjuvant, showing very few differences, such as in
terms of earning a salary, for example:[32]

Idem Lycurgus obiicientibus quod eloquentiae praeceptoribus daret
mercedem si quis inquit profiteatur se filios meos Mihi redditurum melio-
res, non mille drachmas sed omnium facultatum dimidium effunderem.

The teaching process has a mirror effect in the relation between father and
son, whether in obedience (if education is successful)[33]

Aelianus adolescens Eretriam post longam peregrinationem reuersus, rogatus a patre, quid disciplinae tanto temporis interstitio assecutus esset?
se breui ostensurum esse pollicetur. Verberibus igitur paulo post caesus
propter delictum admissum, patri nequaquam inobediens fuit et ait hoc
edoctum ut parenti castigandi obediret eiusque indignationes atque poenas aequo animo ferret.

or in disobedience, (if the transmission of values and knowledge fails):[34]

Diogenes cum puerum conspiceret indecore se gerentem paedagogum
illius baculo percussit dicens cur sic instituis? Indicans primae aetatis

---

31   Ibid., vol. 1, 13r.
32   Ibid., vol. 3, 228v.
33   Ibid., vol. 3, 228v.
34   Ibid., vol. 3, 229r.

MANKIND'S ROLES IN *COLLECTANEA MORALIS PHILOSOPHIAE*   385

formatoribus potissimum imputandum esse, si adolescens euadant male morati aut secus.

Benevolence and indulgence lead to assertiveness because they are characteristic of an education that is weak and lacking in discipline:[35]

> Nihil enim magis fecit iracundos, quam educatio mollis et blanda; [...] Quemadmodum medici amara quaedam uenena dulcibus immiscentes succis, comitem utilitatis amoenitatem inuenerunt ita et patres increpationum rigorem mansuetudine temperent est necesse.

The *dominus* should have the same benevolent attitude with his *seruus,* whose respect and loyalty are intertwined with intelligence and humility. Both the *seruus* and the *magister* serve each other in a symmetric and chiastic manner.

Vicious actions are easily imitated even if they are not as frequent as the virtuous attitudes:[36]

> Nutricum et paedagogorum retulere mox in adolescentia mores. Apud Platonem educatus puer, cum ad parentes relatus, uociferantem uideret patrem: "nunquam inquit hoc apud Platonem uidi." Non dubito quin citius patrem, quam Platonem imitatus sit.

Plato is a notable pedagogical reference throughout the discussion of these and others concepts:[37]

> Aptissime, igitur, diuinus ille Plato nutrices admonuisse uidetur, ut ne friuolas ac turpes fabellas pueris mandent, ne illorum animos ex initio stultitia et corruptis imbuant moribus [...] Si non fiunt mortales disciplina meliores, periisse impendia dixeris, quae fiunt in paedagogos a lacte ipso primum pueros in disciplinam accipientes. Nam ut nutrices manibus effigiant corpus ita illi mores componendo primum uirtutis uestigium collocant. Vnde Spartanus ille rogatus quid commodi afferret praeceptorum opera. Honesta inquit illi faciunt ut pueris etiam sint iucunda. Haud ab re antiquus ille Crates dicere solebat cui si licuisset ubi in altissimam urbis partem conscendisset se uociferaturum aiebat quorsum ruitis homines, qui omne in comparandis pecuniis uestrum

---

35   Ibid., vol 1, 13v and vol. 2, 148r.
36   Ibid., vol. 1, 13v.
37   Ibid., vol. 2, 146v.

studium facitis filiorum uero quibus eas relinquatis nullam sane curam suscipitis? Quibus addendum esse censeo, quod hi patres haud aliter faciunt quam qui magnam calceorum sedulitatem habent cum interim pedem ipsum parui pendant. Multi uero sunt parentes in quibus adeo numorum amor pariter et filiorum odium saepe numero increuit, ut ne maiora impendant salaria nullius existimationis homines natis suis deligant uilissimorum preciorum disciplinam ipsam insectantes. Ob quam rem Aristippus haud insul se quin urbano plurimum sermone quendam mentis inopem patrem carpsit. Quopiam enim ex eo percontante quantam instruendi gratia filii mercedem postularet mille drachmas dixit. Ille uero Hercule ait per magnum postulatum. Seruum enim comparare mille drachmis possum. Duos inquit habebis seruos et filium et quem mercaberis. Quid autem his admirandis accidat patribus post quam filios male nutrierint maleque instruxerint dicere aggrediar.

The construction of authority is not developed by imposition or by force. Granada explains that a king and a dictator are differentiated by a particular virtue: *clementia.* Following the same presupposition, the master suggests but does not command:[38]

Qui ut aliquam rem adeas, hortantur quidem, sed nihil ipsi suggerere, nullamue rationem quonam pacto id fieri oporteat afferre uidentur, sane non illis absimiles sunt qui lucernae ut ardeat lychnum emungunt et manu contrectant ceterum olei nihil omnino infundunt.

The humanistic preference for the genre of *speculum principis,* in which all the precepts that a prince should respect are presented, is based on the conviction that their behaviour should inspire the citizens and a father should reveal the same exemplary attitude:[39]

Ante omnia opus est, ut patres non solum nihil peccando uerum etiam honesta singula peragendo, manifestum sese filiis exemplar exibeant ut ita eorum uitam, quasi quoddam speculum, intuentes, ab operum simul et sermonum turpitudine se penitus euertant.

---

38   Ibid., vol. 2, 148r.
39   Ibid., vol. 2, 147r.

MANKIND'S ROLES IN *COLLECTANEA MORALIS PHILOSOPHIAE* 387

Action and discourse should be coherent and in agreement, strengthening each other:[40]

> Omnis doctor in uitae ratione peccans, turpior est, ob hoc quod in officio, cuius magister esse uult, labitur; Si agricolam arbor ad fructum producta delectat si pastor ex fetu gregis sui capit uoluptatem, si alumnum suum nemo aliter intuetur, quam ut adolescentiam illius suam iudicet quid euenire credis his, qui ingenia educauerunt, et quae tenera formauerunt, adulta subito uident? Assero te mihi meum opus es [...] In hoc gaudeo aliquid discere, ut doceam nec me ulla res delectabit, licet eximia sit et salutares, quam mihi sciturus sum. Si cum hac exceptione detur sapientia, ut illam inclusam teneam nec enunciem reiniciam. Nullius boni sine socio iucunda possessio est. Tu me inquis uitare turbam iubes, secedere et conscientia esse contentum ubi illa praecepta uestra quae imperant in actu mori? Quod ego tibi uideor interim suadere, in hoc me recondidi et fores clausi, ut prodesse pluribus possem. Nullus mihi per otium dies exit, partem noctis studiis uendico non uaco somno sed sucumbo et oculos uigilia fatigatos cadentesque in opere detineo. Secessi, non tantum ab hominibus, sed etiam a rebus et primum a rebus meis. Posterorum negotium ago. Illis aliqua quae possint prodesse conscribo salutares admonitiones, uelut medicamentorum compositiones, literis mando esse illas efficaces in meis ulceribus expertus quae etiam si personata non sunt, serpere desierunt. Rectum iter quod sero cognoui et lassus errando, aliis monstro.

We cannot neglect to mention that the driving force behind this form of achievement is a true and strong motivation ("Magna pars est profectus, uelle proficere"[41]) and the following *topoi—incipientium status* and *proficientium status*—represent the result of this idea: we are always evolving. The *discipulus* will become a *magister*, and the *filius* will become a *pater*. It is as if this evolution were a kind of natural law. Therefore, everything boils down to learning how to live in order to make the best choices, to achieve *sapientia, felicitas* and *virtus*, renouncing ambitions for worldly wealth. However, there is always the need for a general master in his hyponymous representations: a pedagogue, a father, rationality or even God because virtue is hard to find by ourselves

---

40 Ibid., vol. 1, 13v–14r.
41 Ibid., vol. 1, 16r "Progress is largely in the desire to want to progress."

and requires a leader; vices, on the contrary, are learned without a master. Furthermore, there is always time for us to learn:[42]

> Molestum est semper uitam inchoare, aut si modo magis sensus potest exprimi, male uiuunt, qui semper uiuere incipiunt. Quidam uiuere tunc incipiunt, cum desinendum est. Si hoc iudicas mirum adiiciam quod magis admireris. Quidam ante uiuere desierunt, quam inciperent.

In conclusion, *Collectanea Moralis Philosophiae* is aligned with the idea of *enkyklios paideia*, the cycle and perfectibility of human growth, because individual and collective learning is continuous and osmotic between private and public dimensions; it is a Sisyphus-like journey during which we never conquer and fulfil the whole *sapientia*. The moment we die is the right one where we are ready to start living. In addition, public virtues and private vices are not a possible or admirable paradigm: only a good *discipulus* can be a good *magister*; only a good son can be a good father. For this reason, this encyclopaedic work represents a kaleidoscope, reshaping forms of reading, encouraging several combinations and interpretations under different points of views, but the corollary is always the same: education guides us to prudence and knowledge, and philosophy is our accomplice, confidante and counsellor, promoting and consolidating our virtues in the performance of our responsibilities. These multiple approaches are given by the fluidity of these *themata*, being convinced that the discussion about *magister* and *discipulus*, or *pater* and *filius* is not confined to the discussion of their 'dictionary entries', but rather is open to other concepts and reflections.

Finally, we should underline that several *corpora* are combined in a coherent and consistent *corpus*, in a challenging and endless reading. As Granada said: "Celebre illud Hesiodi petae paruula si tentes super adiecisse pusillis idque frequens peragas magnus cumulatur aceruus."[43] We never say too much because we never read enough: "Nunquam nimis dicitur, quod nunquam satis discitur."

> University Rennes2 – France
> Faculty of Arts at University of Coimbra – Portugal

---

42   Ibid., vol. 1, 16r.
43   Ibid., vol. 2, 149r.

CHAPTER 29

Prefazioni e dediche nelle edizioni degli storici greci tra politica e divulgazione

Maria Stefania Montecalvo

Abstract

La divulgazione degli autori di storia romana in lingua greca si accompagna, nelle edizioni cinquecentesche, spesso *editiones principes*, con la giustificazione della utilità politica derivata dalla loro conoscenza. I dedicatari sono di fatto principi, sovrani o personaggi rilevanti dell'epoca: la Roma imperiale è esemplare e la dottrina politica esposta da autori 'monarchici' è ritenuta appropriata allo *speculum principis*. Scopo del contributo è appunto quello di illustrare alcuni casi di dediche e materiali prefatori ove "in restituendis optimis authoribus et ab oblivione vindicandis" è presente anche la riflessione politica, mettendo in luce l'intreccio tra considerazioni attuali e impiego delle fonti classiche.

Keywords

Neo-Latin philology – reception of Roman historiography – reception of Greek historiography – Neo-Latin translations

La divulgazione degli autori di storia romana in lingua greca (Dionigi d'Alicarnasso, Cassio Dione e Appiano) si accompagna, nelle edizioni quattro-cinquecentesche, con la giustificazione della utilità anche politica derivata dalla loro conoscenza. I dedicatari sono principi, sovrani o personaggi rilevanti dell'epoca: la Roma imperiale è esemplare e la dottrina politica ivi esposta è ritenuta appropriata allo *speculum principis*. I casi presi in considerazione in questo contributo riflettono uno studio ancora *in fieri* sulla fortuna degli storici greci in età umanistica.[1] Si tratta di dediche e materiali prefatori

---

1 Un percorso di ricerca che ha preso le mosse dallo studio della riscoperta di Cassio Dione in Occidente e dunque dalla considerazione dell'attività di Celio Secondo Curione a Basilea come classicista e professore di retorica, di cui ho dato qualche anticipazione in: "Note sulla

---

© KONINKLIJKE BRILL NV, LEIDEN, 2020 | DOI:10.1163/9789004427105_030

ove "in restituendis optimis authoribus et ab oblivione vindicandis" (sono le parole di Guillaume du Blanc nella lettera dedicatoria al cardinale George d'Armagnac, promotore della traduzione di Xifilino) si palesa l'intreccio tra considerazioni attuali e impiego delle fonti classiche.

A monte va ricordato l'interesse per la ricostruzione della storia romana nel suo dipanarsi nei secoli, grazie alla rinnovata conoscenza dei testi dell'antichità classica, e secondo una 'nuova' prospettiva, quella degli storici dell'impero in lingua greca,[2] diffusi dapprima in traduzione (in latino o in volgare) e solo in seguito pubblicati in greco:[3] è il caso ad esempio di Dionigi d'Alicarnasso, Appiano e Cassio Dione, dati alle stampe in traduzione alla fine del Quattrocento ed editi in greco solo alla prima metà del Cinquecento.[4] È ben noto l'impegno di papa Niccolò V (1447–55) che commissionò traduzioni da Tucidide, Erodoto, Senofonte, Platone, Aristotele, Teofrasto, Tolomeo, Strabone e che affidò a Pier Candido Decembrio la traduzione dei libri 16–20 di Diodoro Siculo[5] e di Appiano,[6] a partire dall'arrivo di Decembrio a Roma, nel 1450. Nella prefazione dell'edizione di Appiano l'umanista lamentava la perdita di opere importanti, in particolare di Livio, Curzio Rufo, Trogo e Tacito. Ed esponeva una considerazione ancora attuale: "quamquam haec vetus apud nos historiae querela sit ut rerum gestarum scripta deflere potium vacet quam inspicere."[7]

---

lettura di Cassio Dione in Celio Secondo Curione," in *Storie di testi e tradizione classica per Luciano Canfora*, ed. Rosa Otranto, Pasquale Massimo Pinto (Roma, 2018), 141–53; "Celio Secondo Curione: The Re-Discovery of Classicism, Religious Reform, and Political Change," in *Giordano Bruno: Will, Power, and Being – Law, Philosophy, and Theology in the Early Modern Era*, ed. Massimiliano Traversino (in corso di stampa presso Garnier).

2 Per una ricostruzione generale si veda Leighton D. Reynolds, Nigel G. Wilson, *Copisti e filologi* (Padova, 2016⁴); Nigel G. Wilson, *From Byzantium to Italy* (London, 1992; 2017²).

3 Ad essi va sicuramente accostata la ben nota tradizione delle biografie plutarchee, circolanti in traduzione già dagli anni Trenta del XV secolo e per la cui fortuna – e il ruolo di Salutati – rinvio ai contributi di Marianne Pade, soprattutto i due volumi de *The Reception of Plutarch's Lives in Fifteenth-Century Italy* (Copenhagen, 2007).

4 L'*editio princeps* di Dionigi d'Alicarnasso: 1546; di Appiano: 1551; di Cassio Dione: 1548. Sulla stampa in greco: Robert Proctor, *The Printing of Greek in the 15th Century* (Oxford, 1900; 1966), Victor Scholderer, *Greek Printing Types 1465–1927* (London, 1927); id., "Printers and Readers in Italy in the Fifteenth Century," *PBA* 35 (1949), 25–47; Léandre Vranoussis, "Manuscrits, Livres, imprimeries et maisons d'éditions," *JÖB* 32.1 (1982), 393–480; Paul Canart, "Scribes grecs de la Renaissance," *Scriptorium* 17 (1963), 56–82; Jean-Christophe Saladin, *La bataille du grec à la Renaissance* (Paris, 2000).

5 I precedenti erano stati assegnati al Bracciolini e al Trapezunzio. Decembrio tradusse solo i cap. 1–49 del libro 16 per l'avvenuta morte del papa (25.3.1455).

6 Cf. Massimo Zaggia, "La traduzione latina da Appiano di Pier Candido Decembrio: per la storia della tradizione," *SM* 34 (1993), 193–243. Già Johann Schweighaeuser, *De impressis ac manuscriptis Historiarum Appiani Alexandrini codicibus commentatio historico-critica. Accedit novae editionis specimen* (Argentorati, 1781).

7 Cito dalla *praefatio* dedicata a Niccolò V ("P. Candidi in libro Appiani [...] ad Nicolaum quint(u)m [...] Prefatio incipit felicissime"), c. 1v [non numerata], rr. 5–7 dell'edizione veneta del

L'interesse verso Appiano era anche dovuto alla peculiare disposizione della materia: una storia di Roma ordinata geograficamente poteva risultare utile a colmare i vuoti della conoscenza e fornire una prospettiva diversa. Lo rilevava già l'anonimo autore di una prefazione presente, oltre che nel ms. Vaticanus graecus 141 e nei discendenti della famiglia *i*, nell'attuale Monacensis graecus 374, il codice "Augsburgensis" ricordato da Xylander nella prefazione del 1558, presentando i 'materiali' necessari per la ricostruzione del passato di Roma: Dionigi d'Alicarnasso per i tempi anteriori al principato e Appiano per le *singularum provinciarum res*.

1. Ad uno dei successori di Niccolò V, Paolo II, al secolo Pietro Barbo, di nobile famiglia veneziana, fu dedicata la prima traduzione latina di Dionigi d'Alicarnasso. L'autore, Lampugnino (o Lampo, Lapo, Lappo) Birago, già collega e amico di Decembrio, intende giustificare la lettura dell'opera di un greco di epoca pagana.[8] La traduzione, pubblicata a Treviso nel 1480, dopo la morte di Paolo II, avvenuta nel 1474, si basò su due manoscritti messi a disposizione di Birago,[9] allievo e amico di Francesco Filelfo e già autore di uno *Strategicon* dedicato a Niccolò V,[10] proprio da parte del papa.[11]

La *virtus* e la *magnitudo* del pontefice, le gravi e molteplici sue occupazioni richiedono, a detta di Birago, una necessaria distrazione; la guida della Chiesa e del suo popolo si coniuga con l'interesse per il passato ("extendens etiam cogitationes tuas usque ad proceres illos priscos: fundatores urbis: tantique imperii: honori eorum: ac famae cum delectatione inservias"[12]). In questo passato rientra anche la giustificazione dei pagani:[13]

1477, conservata alla Bibliothèque Nationale de France (Arsenal, 4-H-999): *Opera quae supersunt, latine a P. Candido Decembrio* (Venetiis, 1477).

8   Ci si potrebbe chiedere se tale giustificazione fosse dovuta alla soppressione dell'accademia romana (1468).

9   Cf. Massimo Miglio, "La versione di Lampugnino Birago delle Antichità di Dionigi d'Alicarnasso," *Annali della Scuola speciale per Archivisti e Bibliotecari* 8 (1968), 73–83; id., "Birago, Lampugnino," *DBI* 10 (Roma, 1968), 161–2; Valérie Fromentin, "La tradition directe des Antiquités Romaines (livre I) et la question de la traduction latine de Lapus Biragus," *MEFRA* 101 (1989), 37–62, in part. 47–8. La studiosa ricostruisce l'attività di Birago in "La tradition manuscrite des Antiquités Romaines," *REG* 106 (1993), 102–19, in part. 113–9.

10   Si veda ora Iulian Mihai Damian (ed.), *Lo Strategicon adversum Turcos di Lampugnino Birago* (Roma, 2017).

11   Sulla precedente traduzione manoscritta, dedicata a Niccolò V, e relativa ai libri 1–2 e all'inizio del terzo cf. Fromentin, "La tradition directe" (vedi sopra, n. 9), 56–62 e Fromentin, "La tradition manuscrite" (vedi sopra, n. 9), 113.

12   Questa e le seguenti citazioni sono tratte dalla dedicatoria *Clementissimo ac sanctissimo Paulo secundo domino nostro papae* dell'edizione *De Origine urbis Romae libri undecim*, ed. Lapo Birago (Tarvisii, 1480), c. 1r [non numerata] rr. 13–15.

13   Ibid., c. 1r [non numerata] rr. 18–20.

392 MONTECALVO

> Voluisti tu tamen eis externa quoque addere testimonia: nec quemquam moveat: quod hos viros religiosissimos dixerim: qui verae fidei ignari fuerint: non illorum istud vicio: sed temporum infelicitate accidit.

In ciò si iscrive la riscoperta dei primi dieci libri delle *Antichità romane* di Dionigi di Alicarnasso, affidate a Birago e rimarchevoli perché in esse si ritrova[14]

> diligentia sane multa: et ars oratoria: magnoque artificio elaboratae orationes: religionumque illius temporis explicatio accuratissima: documentaque et exempla plurima: quae esse possint civili viro militarique ac religioso utilia simul et iocunda.

Ma soprattutto perché narrano il passato di Roma, un passato di cui può risultare significativo non l'inizio ("primordia tenuiora illa forsan"[15]), ma l'epoca della gloriosa espansione della *respublica* e dell'affermazione dei suoi protagonisti, soprattutto se si avesse la ventura di ritrovare l'intera opera di Dionigi:[16]

> incidere possemus in res maiores gestas cum veteribus: et cum novis hostibus: Gallis: Samnitibus: Tarentinisque: et Pyrrho: et in duces quoque clarissimos: Camillos Decios Torquatos: Maximos: Curios: Fabricios: aliosque praeterea quorum nomina vel sola illustrare: quamvis narrationem possent.[17]

2. Accanto ad Appiano e Dionigi, ad Erodiano, tradotto da Poliziano e pubblicato nel 1493 (ISTC ih00085000),[18] va ricordata la riscoperta di un altro significativo rappresentante della storiografia romana in lingua greca, Cassio Dione Cocceiano, conosciuto e tradotto dapprima tramite Xifilino che aveva epitomato lo storico severiano nella seconda metà dell'XI secolo, per ordine di Michele VII Parapinace (1071–78). La prima menzione della presenza di Dione

---

14   Ibid., c. IV [non numerata] rr. 9–12.

15   Ibid., c. IR [non numerata] rr. 31–32.

16   Se la ricostruzione di Fromentin, "La tradition manuscrite" è corretta, questa frase corrisponde davvero alla speranza di Birago di ritrovare un Dionigi completo, poiché la prima traduzione latina si era fondata su di un manoscritto che conteneva solo i primi due libri e parte del terzo (fino al cap. 23) delle *Antichità*.

17   *De Origine urbis* (vedi sopra, n. 12), c. IV [non numerata] rr. 1–5.

18   *Herodiani Historiarum libri octo, Angelo Politiano interprete* (Roma, 1493). Si veda Daniela Gionta, "Pomponio Leto e l'Erodiano del Poliziano," in *Agnolo Poliziano, poeta, scrittore, filologo,* ed. Vincenzo Fera, Mario Martelli (Firenze, 1998), 425–58.

in Occidente risale invero alla lista dei manoscritti che Aurispa portò con sé dal primo viaggio in Oriente, nel 1416.[19]

Lo storico severiano, anche in epitome, poteva interessare per l'impostazione biografica che caratterizza la sua opera a partire dal principato di Augusto. E appunto le vite di Nerva, Traiano e Adriano, tratte da Xifilino, furono tradotte da Giorgio Merula[20] durante il suo soggiorno milanese[21] e presentate come esemplate sul testo di Dione. La prima edizione a stampa apparve a Milano nel 1503, ma circolava in contemporanea una traduzione di Bonifacio Bembo, dedicata al cardinale Francesco Todeschini Piccolomini e databile al 1493/94 (ISTC ic00243000);[22] mentre la traduzione curata da Giorgio Aurispa del dialogo che Dione inserisce nel libro 38, tra Cicerone in esilio e Filisco, composta nel 1425, fu pubblicata postuma.[23] I libri a noi giunti dell'opera dionea (36–60,

---

19   Cf. Adriano Franceschini, *Giovanni Aurispa e la sua biblioteca: notizie e documenti* (Padova, 1976), 53–169: al nr. 138 dell'inventario (p. 84) figura una "Hystoria Dionis in gramatica greca, in membranis".

20   Si veda Gianvito Resta, "La cultura umanistica a Milano alla fine del Quattrocento," in *Milano nell'età di Ludovico il Moro. Atti del Convegno internazionale* (Milano, 1983), 201–12. Su Merula traduttore di Xifilino e l'identificazione del manoscritto Matritensis 4714 come sua fonte cf. Teresa Martínez Manzano, "Entre Italia y España: el Dión Casio de Giorgio Merula," *Νέα Ῥώμη* 13 (2016), 363–81.

21   Le vite vanno datate anteriormente al 1494 (anno della morte di Merula), e probabilmente prima del 1489, quando Jacopo di Volterra afferma di averle in sua mano, cf. Martínez Manzano, "Entre Italia" (vedi sopra, n. 20), 380. Secondo Giovanni Battista Pio, *Annotamenta Ioannis Baptistae Pii bononiensis*, (Bononiae, 1505), cap. 21, Merula avrebbe tradotto dodici vite dei Cesari, traendole da Xifilino, cf. Vincenzo Fera, "Tra Poliziano e Beroaldo: l'ultimo scritto filologico di Giorgio Merula," *Studi Umanistici* 2 (1991), 15, n. 1; Alessandro Daneloni, "Merlani, Giorgio," *DBI* 73 (2009), 679–85. È databile al 1503 un'edizione che le contiene, insieme con la *Vesaevi montis conflagratio* (Cass. D. 62,21–3): *Index operum quae in hoc volumine continentur: Censorini de Die natali liber aureus* [...] *Nervae Trajanique et Adriani Caesaris vitae ex Dione in latinum versae, a Georgio Merula. Item Vesaevi montis conflagratio ex eodem, Merula interprete* [...] *Nicolao Peroto et Francisco Philelpho interpretibus. Omnia collegit Tristanus Calchus, Mediolanensis* (s. l.). Su Calco si veda Annalisa Belloni, "Tristano Calco e gli scritti inediti di Giorgio Merula," *IMU* 15 (1972), 283–328.

22   Cf. Maria Grazia Blasio, "L'editoria universitaria da Alessandro VI a Leone X: libri e questioni," in *Roma e lo Studium Urbis. Spazio urbano e cultura dal Quattro al Seicento* (Roma, 1992), 298–9.

23   La data tradizionalmente indicata per la pubblicazione (*Philisci Consolatoria ad Ciceronem dum in Macedonia exularet e Graeco Dionis Cassii*, Parisiis 1510) va anticipata, in quanto essa si trova già nel *De interpretandis Romanorum litteris* di Valerio Probo, ed. Johannes Bonardus, (Venetiis per Ioannem de Tridino, 1498). Su Aurispa cf. Remigio Sabbadini, *Biografia documentata di Giovanni Aurispa* (Noto, 1890); id., *Carteggio di Giovanni Aurispa* (Roma, 1931) id., "Briciole umanistiche (Dione Cassio nel secolo XV)," *SIFC* 6 (1898), 397–406. Rimasero manoscritte la traduzione di Battista Guarino (estate 1463) del discorso di Antonio ai funerali di Cesare (Cass. D. 44.36–49), su cui cf. Battista Guarini, *Opuscula*, ed.

taluni lacunosi) furono poi diffusi prima in italiano, grazie alla traduzione curata da Niccolò Leoniceno data alle stampe nel 1533, ma composta tra il 1472 e il 1488 (su cui si basò Claude Deroziers per la traduzione francese del 1542: *Dion, historien grec, des faictz et gestes insignes des Romains*), mentre l'*editio princeps* curata da Robert Estienne fu pubblicata nel 1548 a Parigi.[24]

3. La scelta delle vite di Nerva, Traiano e Adriano poteva non essere casuale e, nel caso di Merula, poteva legarsi alla propaganda politica milanese degli Sforza. In altro ambito, vale la pena di prendere in considerazione un'edizione data alle stampe a Basilea nel 1518[25] presso Froben e curata da Erasmo[26] che proponeva un *continuum* cronologico, da Cesare al VII secolo:[27] cominciava con le vite dei Cesari di Svetonio, seguivano le vite di Nerva, Traiano e Adriano tradotte da Merula e presentate come dionee;[28] poi gli autori della *Historia Augusta* scanditi singolarmente (Elio Spartiano, Giulio Capitolino, Elio Lampridio, Vulcacio Gallicano, Trebellio Pollione, Flavio Vopisco Siracusio) cui si aggiungevano Sesto Aurelio Vittore, Eutropio, Paolo Diacono, Ammiano Marcellino, il compendio di Pomponio Leto e Egnazio Veneto.[29]

      Luigi Piacente (Bari, 1995), 367–93 e quella di Lauro Quirini del discorso di Cesare prima dello scontro con Ariovisto, su cui cf. Arnaldo Segarizzi, "Lauro Quirini umanista veneziano del secolo XV," *Memorie della Reale Accademia delle Scienze di Torino* 54 (1904), 1–28.

24   Sui manoscritti impiegati per queste edizioni, oltre alla *praefatio* di Boissevain (Berolini, 1895), cf. Johannes Maisel, *Observationes in Cassium Dionem* (Berolini, 1888), e id., *Beiträge zur Würdigung der Handschriften des Cassius Dio* (Augsburg, 1894).

25   Su questa edizione cf. James Hirstein, "Erasme, l'Histoire Auguste et l'histoire," in *Actes du Colloque international Erasme (Tours, 1986)*, ed. Jacques Chomarat, André Godin, Jean-Claude Margolin (Genève, 1990), 71–95.

26   Su Erasmo editore: Pierre Petitmengin, "Comment étudier l'activité d'Erasme éditeur des textes antiques," in *Colloquia Erasmiana Turonensia* 1 (Paris, 1972), 217–22; Eileen Bloch, "Erasmus and the Froben Press: The Making of an Editor," *The Library Quarterly* 35 (1965), 109–20. Su Erasmo traduttore: Erika Rummer, *Erasmus as Translator of the Classics* (Toronto, 1985).

27   *Ex Recognitione Des. Erasmi Roterodami. C. Suetonius Tranquillus. Dion Cassius Nicaeus. Aelius Spartianus. Iulius Capitolinus. Aelius Lampridius. Vulcatius Gallicanus V. C. Trebellius Pollio. Flauius Vopiscus Syracusius Qvibvs Adivncti Svnt. Sex. Aurelius Victor. Eutropius. Paulus Diaconus. Ammianus Marcellinus. Pomponius Laetus Ro. Io. Bap. Egnatius Venetus* (Basileae, 1518).

28   Oltre che nell'edizione del 1503 qui alla n. 21, la traduzione figura anche in un'edizione veneta del 1519 insieme con gli scrittori dell'*Historia Augusta* e il *de Caesaribus* di Egnazio Veneto (Giovanni Battista Cipelli).

29   Sulle edizioni della *Historia Augusta* cf. Angela Bellezza, *Historia Augusta* (Genova, 1959); su Leto in quest'edizione: Francesca Niutta, "Il *Romanae historiae compendium* di Pomponio Leto," in *Principato ecclesiastico e riuso dei classici gli umanisti e Alessandro VI*, ed. Davide Canfora, Maria Chiabò, Mauro de Nichilo (Roma, 2002), 321–54.

PREFAZIONI E DEDICHE NELLE EDIZIONI DEGLI STORICI GRECI   395

La dedica di Erasmo era rivolta a Federico III e Giorgio di Sassonia ed era tanto più significativa in quanto successiva alla pubblicazione dell'*Institutio principis christiani* (presso Froben nel 1516), dedicata, come è noto, a Carlo V, e fortemente influenzata dalla lettura dell'*Ad Nicoclem* isocrateo. Come nell'*Institutio*, nella dedica a Federico e Giorgio, Erasmo individuava nella deriva tirannica i rischi che un principe avrebbe potuto correre. E quindi la selezione dei modelli del passato da proporre al sovrano faceva emergere gli *optimi principes*, ovvero la dinastia antonina, sancendo così una vulgata storiografica che sarebbe durata ben al di là di Gibbon.

Secondo Erasmo ai principi non è richiesta la precisa conoscenza dei fatti storici, tuttavia sarebbe compito degli amici colti suggerire le giuste letture al principe:[30]

> Cum quibus enim amicis libentius confabuletur cordatus et pius princeps, quam cum iis, qui et semper praesto sunt, et sapiunt plurimum, et nihil loquuntur ad gratiam?

Tra queste si distingue la lettura degli storici:[31]

> Verum nullis ex libris, mea sententia, plus utilitatis capi possit, quam ex eorum monumentis, qui res publice privatimque gestas, bona fide posteris prodiderunt, praesertim si quis regalis Philosophiae decretis imbutus huc accesserit.

L'accento è posto sul valore esemplare, soprattutto per l'individuazione dei modelli da seguire e di quelli da evitare:[32]

> ex bonae fidei Scriptoribus super alias innumeras, haec praecipua capitur utilitas, quod non alia res aeque, vel bonorum Regum animos ad res cum laude gerendas accendit, vel Tyrannorum cupiditates cohibet ac refrenat.

Erasmo identifica come tiranni Nerone, Caligola, Eliogabalo e Commodo: a suo giudizio, nessun sovrano avrebbe voluto riprodurne il comportamento una volta che ne fosse venuto a conoscenza. Nonostante la "tanta malorum

---

30 *Ex Recognitione Des. Erasmi Roterodami C. Suetonius Tranquillus* (vedi sopra, n. 27), lettera dedicatoria *Illustrissimis Saxoniae ducibus, Federico sacri imperii electori &c. eiusque patrueli Georgio, Erasmus Roterodamus S. D.*, c. α2, rr. 11–2.

31 Ibid., c. α2, rr. 13–5.

32 Ibid., c. α2, rr. 18–21. È quanto più volte ricorre nell'*Institutio*, ad es. 1,7; sui cattivi esempi del passato cf. 1,28–9.

Principum turba", anche tra gli "ethnici" Federico e Giorgio potranno trovare "dignas sancto Principe cogitationes", udire "voces absoluto Principe dignas" e confrontare "exempla, in quibus nihil desideres."[33] E inoltre modelli di amministrazione imperiale:[34]

> qui Christiano animo Reipublicae gererent imperium, non sibi, qui tam laboriosae administrationis non aliud spectarent praemium, quam ut de rebus humanis benemererentur, qui publicam utilitatem liberorum affectibus, imo suae suorumque incolumitati praeferrent.

È la conferma della predilezione per gli Antonini:[35]

> O nos felices, si Christiani Principes suae quisque ditioni praestarent animum, quem[36] Trajanus, quem Antonini duo, quem Aurelius Alexander, orbi terrarum praestiterunt.

A loro si contrappongono i tempi attuali e, per il passato, Cesare, Ottaviano (rispetto al quale cambierà opinione in una versione diversa della lettera), Lepido e Antonio. Nel caso di questi ultimi "potestas ea, quam postea diis aequavit hominum consensus, impietate, caedibus, parricidiis, incestis, tyrannide, condita consecrataque fuit".[37]

Erasmo ripropone, in conclusione, una visione provvidenziale, e cristiana, della storia e quanto alla politica auspica la concordia tra i principi europei ("si Christianos principes inter se junget concordia"[38]), ben educati nella cristianità ("si principes sancte Christianeque instituti, simul atque susceperint regnum, pariter et animum regno dignum suscipiant"[39]) e lontani dalla tirannide ("publicis commodis metiantur consilia omnia ab omni Tyrannidis specie velut a peste abhorreant"[40]), condizione nella quale non vi sarebbe bisogno di un *monarcha*.[41]

---

33 Ibid., c. α3, rr. 21–3.

34 Ibid., c. α3, rr. 23–7.

35 Ibid., c. α3, rr. 27–9.

36 In un'altra versione, prima di Traiano: "Octavius jam confirmatus, quem Titi duo." Così si legge in *Desiderii Erasmi Roterodami Opera omnia emendatiora et auctiora* (Lugduni Batavorum, 1703), vol. 3.1, ep. 318, col. 326.

37 *Ex Recognitione* (vedi sopra, n. 30), c. α3, rr. 38–40.

38 Ibid., c. α4, rr. 5–6.

39 Ibid., c. α4, rr. 12–3.

40 Ibid., c. α4, rr. 13–4.

41 "Non desiderabit orbis monarcham, si Christianos principes inter se junget concordia." Queste parole e il contesto immediatamente successivo sono citate da Lucien Febvre,

PREFAZIONI E DEDICHE NELLE EDIZIONI DEGLI STORICI GRECI

4. Appiano, Dione, Xifilino erano dunque ancora alla metà del Cinquecento autori 'nuovi'. Nella lettera dedicatoria al cardinale George d'Armagnac,[42] promotore della traduzione di Xifilino, Guillaume du Blanc ne celebrava, nel 1551, il recupero: "magnam operam posuisti in restituendis optimis authoribus et ab oblivione vindicandis."[43] Dione, in quanto console e pretore, affermava Le Blanc basandosi su Suidas e Xifilino,[44]

> noverat [...] causas bellorum, caeterarumque rerum, quae ab ipsis gerebantur: quippe magnam partem audiebat in senatu, et optimatibus, atque adeo ipsis imperatoribus ita familiaris erat, ut ei facile esset eorum consilia cognoscere.

Questa valorizzazione di Dione e della sua opera trova conferma nella *praefatio* della traduzione latina di Dione, di poco successiva (1558), di Wilhelm Xylander a Johann Heinrich Herwart, mecenate e importante membro della città di Augsburg, che aveva avviato Xylander allo studio dello storico severiano.[45] In essa il dotto tedesco, tanto entusiasta dell'autore e dell'impresa da comporre una elegia *In Dionem suum*, sottolineava l'importanza dell'opera di Dione per la comprensione del passato di Roma, anche per chiarire ("uel

---

    L'Europa. Storia di una civiltà. Corso tenuto al Collège de France 1944–1945 (Roma, 1995), 169, lezione 18 (dalla lettera 586 di Erasmo nell'edizione Allen-Allen-Garrod, Oxford 1910).

42   Nell'*Histoire des Cardinaux* (Paris, 1647), vol. 4, 87, Antoine Aubery ricordava l'impegno e il ruolo di Armagnac come protettore delle lettere e fautore delle traduzioni citando questa dedica. Armagnac fu arcivescovo di Tolosa dal 1562 al 1577, periodo durante il quale sostenne i gesuiti e si distinse come amministratore e mecenate (Nicolas Bachelier fu tra i suoi protetti).

43   *Dionis Nicaei, Rerum Romanarum a Pompeio Magno, ad Alexandrum Mameae filium Epitome, Ioanne Xiphilino autore, & Gulielmo Blanco Albiensi interprete* (Parisiis, 1551). La citazione è tratta dalla lettera dedicatoria *Guiliemus Blancus Georgio Armeniaco, Illustrissimo atque amplissimo Cardinali suo S.* (c. A.ii, rr. 14–5). Dalla dedica si intravede anche uno spaccato della scena culturale romana dell'epoca. Il nipote di Le (o du) Blanc, anch'egli Guillaume, fu autore di poesie sulle rovine di Roma e percorse anch'egli la carriera ecclesiastica, ricoprendo il vescovato di Grasse. Su di lui cf. la notizia biografica anteposta all'edizione di Hyacinthus, curata da G.-J.-F. Souquet de La Tour (Paris, 1846). Su d'Armagnac e du Blanc cf. Richard Cooper, *Roman Antiquities in Renaissance France, 1515–65* (Farnham, 2013), 52–9.

44   Ibid., c. A.ii v, rr. 16–9.

45   *Dionis Cassii Nicaei Romanae historiae libri XXV, nimirum a XXXVI ad LXI, quibus exponuntur res gestae a bello Cretico usque ad mortem Claudii Caesaris [...] Nunc primum summa fide diligentiaque de Graecis Latini facti, Guilielmo Xylandro [...] interprete. His accesserunt ejusdem annotationes [...] Additum est Joannis Xiphilini e Dione Compendium, Guil. Blanco [...] interprete ; quae versio ab eodem Xylandro diligenter est [...] castigata [...] Adhaec, rerum et verborum copiosissimus index* (Basileae, 1558).

obscura explicari, uel deprauata restitui") passi di autori latini (Cicerone, Sallustio, Cesare, l'epitome liviana, Floro, Velleio Patercolo, Tacito, Svetonio) e greci (Plutarco e Appiano).[46] Xylander raccomandava la lettura dello storico poiché temeva il ritorno della "barbaries", ritorno che avrebbe potuto essere debellato, a suo avviso, grazie all'impegno da una parte degli "homines eruditi" dall'altra di "viri nobiles, magni ac virtute praediti" che potessero sostenerli e che così ne sarebbero stati nobilitati.[47]

5. Nella *praefatio*, Xylander alludeva a parti di Dione già tradotte, tra l'altro alla traduzione latina che Celio Secondo Curione, l'umanista italiano allora a Basilea perseguitato *religionis causa* e punto di riferimento per gli umanisti riformati italiani, aveva dato della coppia di discorsi che Dione inseriva nel libro 52 della sua opera dando la parola ad Agrippa e a Mecenate per consigliare Ottaviano sulla migliore forma di governo. Agrippa aveva proposto la *respublica*, Mecenate la *monarchia*. Curione, che aveva dato alle stampe nel 1554 Appiano portando a termine il lavoro di Gelenio, aveva pubblicato la traduzione di questi discorsi nel 1553,[48] con una prefazione (*argumentum*) nella quale sottolineava come in essi si trovassero "pene omnia [...] quae ad optimum principem instituendum requiri posse uideantur" e sottolineandone il valore: "Quae si, qui uocantur Principes hodie, uellent attendere, atque exprimere, melius res humanae haberent."[49]

Questa prefazione deve esser messa in relazione con la dedica che Curione aveva apposto all'edizione delle *Filippiche* ciceroniane apparsa nel 1551 in onore di Edoardo VI di Inghilterra.[50] Si trattava di un'edizione che conteneva anch'essa materiali dionei tradotti, e cioè quattro discorsi che lo storico severiano introduceva nei libri 44–46 dell'opera dando la parola a Cicerone per l'amnistia dei Cesaricidi, ad Antonio per funerali di Cesare, a Cicerone e Fufio Caleno per un agone retorico che inscenava la difficile situazione dell'anno 43 a. C. e rappresentava la *summa* dell'anticiceronianismo antico appunto nella

---

46 La citazione è tratta dalla *Ad nobilem et praestantissimum virum Ioannem Henricum Herwartum, patricium Augustanum, Guilielmi Xylandri Augustani Praefatio in Dionem a se conversum*, c. α6r [non indicato], r. 32–α6v, r. 2.

47 Ibid., c. α2v, rr. 15–23.

48 *Caelii Secundi Curionis selectarum epistolarum libri duo. Eiusdem orationum (inter quas et Agrippae contra monarchiam, et Mecaenatis pro monarchia, adversariae orationes duae, lectu dignissimae, ex Dione Latinitate donatae) continentur, Liber unus*, (Basileae, 1553).

49 Ibid., p. 134.

50 *M. Tullii Ciceronis Philippicae orationes XIIII in M. Antonium a Caelio Secundo Curione [...] perpetuis explicationibus illustratae. His accessere orationes quatuor ad Philippicarum argumentum pertinentes ex Dione historico, eodem Caelio Secundo Curione interprete [...]* (Basileae, 1551). Cf. più in dettaglio Montecalvo, "Note sulla lettura di Cassio Dione" (vedi sopra, n. 1).

PREFAZIONI E DEDICHE NELLE EDIZIONI DEGLI STORICI GRECI   399

replica di Caleno. La dedica di Curione a Edoardo VI, giovane re d'Inghilterra cui andavano le simpatie dei perseguitati italiani a causa delle scelte religiose, conteneva una riflessione politica sulla giustificazione della monarchia[51] e l'ammonimento contro la tirannia, riprendendo espressioni dionee, oltre che ciceroniane e sallustiane.

Queste riflessioni di Curione lasciano intravedere come il legame tra riflessione politica, edizioni dei classici (anche in traduzione) e scelta dei materiali in quanto veicolari del pensiero politico stesso si manifestasse attraverso precise scelte editoriali.

L'edizione degli autori di storia romana curata da Erasmo nel 1518 coincideva forse non a caso con l'elezione del successore di Massimiliano al trono imperiale;[52] la prefazione della traduzione dei discorsi di Agrippa e Mecenate rifletteva forse la delusione degli umanisti riformati per l'ascesa al trono d'Inghilterra di Maria la Cattolica dopo la morte di Edoardo VI; la riflessione sul principato aveva da una parte un riscontro negli storici greci d'età imperiale dall'altra nelle attuali considerazioni del *Principe* di Machiavelli, che Curione e i suoi allievi erano interessati a diffondere in latino. Non è forse un caso che nel 1580 la traduzione curata da Curione di questa coppia di discorsi di Agrippa e Mecenate venisse compresa nell'edizione latina del *Principe*, insieme con le *Vindiciae contra Tyrannos* e il *De iure magistratuum* di Teodoro di Beza.[53]

Antichi e moderni potevano dialogare per la risoluzione dei problemi attuali: "Nec dubitet tamen" chiosava Gabriel Harvey nelle note manoscritte apposte

---

51   "Neque enim negari potest, difficilius esse multos invenire bonos et sapientes, quam paucos, et paucos quam unum", la citazione è tratta dalla lettera dedicatoria al sovrano inglese *Caelius Secundus Curio, Eduardo VI Britanniae atque Hyberniae Regi serenissimo S. D.*, c. *2v, r. 3–4. Riecheggia il giudizio che Dione formulava all'inizio del libro 44 commentando criticamente l'uccisione di Cesare e rassegnandosi anche ad un monarca non virtuoso (Cass. D. 44,2,1–3).

52   Nello stesso anno, il 3 settembre 1518, il papa Leone X aveva inviato a Federico III, tra i candidati per il trono del sacro romano impero nel 1518/19, una rosa d'oro di virtù.

53   Silvestro Tegli, allievo di Curione, aveva pubblicato la traduzione del *Principe* nel 1560 presso Perna; Curione avrebbe pubblicato nel 1566 la traduzione di Guicciardini. Autore della traduzione del 1580 fu Giovanni Niccolo' Stoppani, allievo e amico di Curione, collaboratore di Perna dal 1568. Cf. Walter Kaegi, "Machiavelli in Basel," *Basler Zeitschrift für Geschichte und Altertumskunde* 39 (1940), 5–52; "Machiavelli a Basilea," in *Meditazioni storiche*, ed. Delio Cantimori, (Roma, 1960), 155–215; Leandro Perini, *La vita e i tempi di Pietro Perna* (Roma, 2002), in part. 177, 184–7; Thomas Maissen, "Why Did the Swiss Miss the Machiavellian Moment? History, Myth, Imperial and Constitutional Law in the Early Modern Swiss Confederation," *Republics of letters* 2 (2010), 105–20; Gábor Almási, "Experientia and the Machiavellian Turn in Religio-Political and Scientific Thinking: Basel in 1580," *History of European Ideas* 42 (2016), 857–81.

ad un'edizione liviana curata dal medesimo Curione (nella ristampa del 1555) ora a Princeton,[54]

> ex ipsis politicorum principiorum fontibus, altiores adhuc haurire privatae industriae, publicaeq[ue] gubernationis regulas, quam vel ab istis sunt, vel ab aliis observatoribus animadversae.

E considerava Polibio, Dionigi di Alicarnasso e Cassio Dione "insignes, et praestantes Romani Historici", cui attingere "et publico, privatoque usui", nonché Machiavelli come il miglior commentatore di Livio.[55]

Nel dialogo tra storia antica e attualità i dotti umanisti potevano dunque trovare un sistema di corrispondenze, ove ancora l'antichità poteva fungere da guida ed indicare modelli e, con le parole di Harvey, *gubernationis regulae*.

Università degli Studi di Foggia, Dipartimento di Studi Umanistici

---

54 Consultabile al link: http://arks.princeton.edu/ark:/88435/n870zq89q

55 La nota manoscritta cui ci si riferisce è posta alla pagina 22, prima del testo di Livio. Sulle note di Harvey cf. Anthony Grafton, Lisa Jardine, "'Studied for action': How Gabriel Harvey Read His Livy," *Past and present* 129 (1990), 30–78.

CHAPTER 30

Dutch Late Humanism and Its Aftermath: the Reception of Hugo Grotius' Biblical Scholarship

Henk Nellen

Abstract

In 1618, during his detention at Loevestein Castle, the Dutch humanist Hugo Grotius (1583–1645) began to work on a project that would occupy him for the remainder of his life: a commentary on the New Testament, later completed with annotations on the Old Testament. Grotius embarked on this project because he was convinced to have found a remedy for the continual dogmatic strife that divided the Christian Churches. He directed his research to placing the books of the Bible in their original historical context. If he could show Christian believers how the divine message had worked at the moment of its first expansion, it would be easy to retrace its quintessence and transpose it to the seventeenth-century world. This paper deals with the reception of Grotius' biblical annotations in Holland and France. It elaborates two major themes, for which Grotius' research soon proved to be both innovative and influential: divine inspiration and prophecies. Grotius' views on these two topics will be discussed as far as they surface in the works of scholars like André Rivet, Jean Leclerc, Richard Simon and Pierre Bayle.

Keywords

Hugo Grotius – Neo-Latin commentaries – exegesis – inspiration – prophecy

In 1619, during his detention at Loevestein Castle, the famous Dutch humanist Hugo Grotius (1583–1645) began to work on a project that would occupy him for the remainder of his life: a detailed commentary on the New Testament,[1] completed with (less extensive) annotations on the Old Testament. Grotius

---

1 Cf. *Briefwisseling van Hugo Grotius*, ed. Philip C. Molhuysen et al. (The Hague, 1928–2001), vol. 10, 842 and 15, 597, letters from Grotius to Willem de Groot and Nicolaes van Reigersberch, 31 December 1639 and 23 July 1644, cited in Henk Nellen, *Hugo Grotius: A Lifelong Struggle*

© KONINKLIJKE BRILL NV, LEIDEN, 2020 | DOI:10.1163/9789004427105_031

embarked on this project because he was convinced that it would serve as a remedy for the continual dogmatic strife that divided the Christian churches. He deliberately directed his research to placing the books of the Bible in their original historical context. If he could show Christian believers how the divine message had worked at the moment of its first expansion, it would be easy to identify its quintessence and transpose it to the seventeenth-century world. This paper deals with the reception of Grotius' biblical annotations in Holland and France, although a similar story could also be told for England and Germany. I elaborate on two major themes, for which Grotius' research soon proved to be both innovative and influential: prophecies and divine inspiration.[2] Grotius' views on these two topics will be discussed as far as they surface in the works of scholars like André Rivet, Jean Leclerc, Richard Simon, and Pierre Bayle.

Matthew's Birth Narrative

In the history of biblical hermeneutics and exegesis the quotations from the Old Testament in the New function as key elements for establishing the truth of the Christian religion. These quotations inspired Christian exegetes to claim that Christ was the promised Messiah whose expiatory death would take away the sins of mankind and open the doors of heaven to every pious believer. I limit myself to one example that will return repeatedly hereafter, a prophecy in Isaiah 7:13–5, that was used in Matthew 1:22–3. Isaiah uttered his prophecy at a time when God's chosen people were going through a troublesome period:

> [13] And he said, hear ye now, O house of David; is it a small thing for you to weary men, but will ye weary my God also? [14] Therefore the Lord himself shall give you a sign; behold, a virgin shall conceive, and bear a son, and shall call his name Immanuel. [15] Butter and honey shall he eat, that he may know to refuse the evil, and choose the good.

First a few words on the historical context of this passage that brings us back to the eighth century before Christ. Ahaz, king of Judah, the southern Hebrew

---

for Peace in Church and State, 1583–1645 (Leiden, 2014), 297. I am grateful to two anonymous reviewers for their careful comments and suggestions.

2 See for the following also Jacques Le Brun, "La réception de la théologie de Grotius chez les catholiques de la seconde moitié du XVIIe siècle," in idem, *La jouissance et le trouble. Recherches sur la littérature chrétienne de l'âge classique* (Geneva, 2004), 217–46, esp. 229–34.

DUTCH LATE HUMANISM AND ITS AFTERMATH   403

kingdom, feared to be overrun by two allied kings, Pekah of the northern kingdom Israel and Rezin of Aram-Damascus. He hoped to maintain himself by asking Tiglath-Pileser III, king of the mighty Assyrians, for support, a strategy that Isaiah tried to prevent, because the prophet abhorred the Assyrian despotism and destructive military force. In order to convince the hesitating Ahaz to put his trust in God, Isaiah promised the king that a change for the better was imminent. The historical context in the Old Testament seems to have disappeared when we turn to the quotation of Isaiah 7:14 in the New Testament and examine how, in the first chapter of his Gospel, the evangelist Matthew made use of Isaiah's prophecy:

> [22] Now all this was done, that it might be fulfilled which was spoken of the Lord by the prophet, saying: [23] Behold, a virgin shall be with child, and shall bring forth a son, and they shall call his name Emmanuel, which being interpreted is, God with us.

The evangelist applied the passage to Mary, Joseph's wife, who received the annunciation of the birth of a son, Jesus Christ. From the earliest days of Christianity the passage in Isaiah was heavily discussed. While elucidating the historical setting of the Old Testament prophecies, many exegetes tried to fit such prophecies into the history of the Jewish people. Because they were intent on proving that Christ's incarnation was the fulfillment of the Old Testament, they had to strike a thoughtful balance between a historical explanation and a messianic one. Often they took recourse to a typological framework by assuming a double sense: Old Testament 'types' prefigured or adumbrated persons or events in the New Testament. This was a time-honored approach which had already been explored by the New Testament writers and, in their wake, by church fathers like Origen, Jerome, and Augustine.[3] Christian apologists, however, generally defended Isaiah's prophecy as a prediction of Christ's birth from a virgin, in a direct, literal sense. Jerome, for instance, applied the prophecy in a Christological sense to the Virgin Mary giving birth to an all-powerful deity, who, although destined to be born in a faraway future, was able, once being called upon, to rescue the House of David. While elaborating on the historical context of the passage, Jerome also referred to literal

---

3   Stuart George Hall, "Typologie," in *Theologische Realenzyklopädie*, vol. 34 (Berlin, 2002), 208–24. See also, for the early modern context, Donald R. Dickson, "The Complexities of Biblical Typology in the Seventeenth Century," *Renaissance and Reformation* 23 (1987), 253–72, and Richard A. Muller, *Post-Reformation Reformed Dogmatics*, vol. 2, *Holy Scripture: The Cognitive Foundation of Theology* (Grand Rapids, 2003²), 469–82.

explanations that identified Immanuel as the son of Ahaz or the son of Isaiah himself.[4] Understandably enough, before and after Jerome many Christian exegetes wanted to defend their creed against attacks by Jews and non-believers, and for that reason they laid great emphasis on the quotation from Isaiah in Matthew's birth narrative as a direct proof that the Messiah had come. In this approach the original historical context in the Old Testament history of the Jewish people, described above, did not really count for much; the fact that the divinely inspired evangelist Matthew had put the prophecy in a completely different historical setting was ignored. If an exegete dared to apply the passage to Old Testament times exclusively, he would deprive Christian polemicists of an essential, or even *the* essential proof-text that bolstered the identity of Christ as the long awaited Messiah.

Grotius on Prophecies

In the course of the sixteenth and seventeenth centuries a process of historicization took place. Against this background an old exegetical discussion gained new momentum, namely the idea that the Old Testament quotations should be seen as conveying a double sense. On the one hand, there was a literal or historical interpretation that sought to place the Old Testament persons and events in their original, contemporary context. Isaiah's prediction of the imminent birth of a child should firstly be explained against the background of the political situation in which Judah's king Ahaz, caught up in the maelstrom of international politics in the Eastern Mediterranean, tried to keep his head above the waves. Isaiah predicted that the threat of the allies would disappear before a child, Immanuel, son of Ahaz or Isaiah, had reached adulthood. In the second instance a more sublime, but also vague, abstruse and mysterious reading of the text was called for, such as Matthew himself adhered to: Immanuel was the prefiguration or type that foreshadowed Christ. In this sense, and only in this secondary, typological sense, the passage referred to Christ. The typological interpretation took into account that Christ and his apostles had constantly referred to the Old Testament, precisely in order to associate themselves with the widespread belief that the advent of the long awaited Messiah was imminent.

In the seventeenth century the approach described above found a staunch defender in Hugo Grotius, who strongly opted for a first, historical

---

4 Jerome, *Commentaria in Isaiam prophetam* (*PL* 24:101–14, especially 110) and Nicholas Hardy, *Criticism and Confession: The Bible in the Seventeenth Century Republic of Letters* (Oxford, 2017), 212.

DUTCH LATE HUMANISM AND ITS AFTERMATH

interpretation that was complemented or, so to speak, upgraded by a vaguer, typological one. Grotius explained himself in great detail in his seminal work, the *Annotationes in libros Evangeliorum*, an impressive folio that saw the light in Amsterdam in 1641. He did so in his commentary on Matthew 1:22,[5] where the evangelist introduced the quotation from Isaiah, referred to above. In 1644 Grotius saw his *Annotata* on the Old Testament through the press, and in many places he again stressed the first, historical interpretation of many Old Testament prophecies, after which he adduced a secondary, typological one to secure a Christological explanation.[6] Most importantly, Grotius included in his commentary on Matthew 1:22 a substantial digression on all those New Testament passages that were introduced by the words "that it might be fulfilled" and pointed out that Christ and his disciples did not rely on these quotations as valid proofs that Christ was the Messiah. He expressly stated that they preached their ideas in the conviction that the truth of the Christian belief had already been established by the miracles Christ performed, in particular by his resurrection.[7] Although Grotius regarded the passage in Isaiah as an inspired prophecy on Christ's coming, he reduced such Old Testament quotations in the New Testament to supplementary evidence. It was his firm conviction that Jews and non-believers would only embrace the typological explanation of Isaiah's prediction, after they had acknowledged the authenticity of the Christian faith on the basis of the accounts of Christ's miracles in the Bible. Whether or not Grotius developed his controversial exegesis on his own initiative, it is certain that Socinian exegetes adhered to this line of reasoning fervently. Their leader Faustus Socinus had defended it in his anonymously published *De auctoritate Sacrae Scripturae*, a book that Grotius certainly studied,[8] and in more detail, in the *Lectiones sacrae*.[9]

Grotius must have been driven by the idea that the Old Testament prophecies had been divulged to cater to the needs of a contemporary audience, an

---

5   Hugo Grotius, *Opera omnia theologica* (Amsterdam, 1679; reprint Stuttgart, 1972), henceforward cited as *OTh*, vol. 2, part 1, 11–4 (ad Matthaeum 1:22).

6   Abraham Kuenen, "Hugo de Groot als uitlegger van het Oude Verbond," *Verslagen en mededeelingen der Koninklijke Akademie van Wetenschappen, afd. Letterkunde*, second series, 12 (1883), 301–32. See also *OTh* 1, 278 B 34–36 (ad Esaiam 7:1): "Non repetemus hic quae ad intellectum huius capitis et sequentis satis copiose congessimus ad Matth. 1:22–23."

7   *OTh* 2, part 1, 11 A 44–54, 12 B 13–6 and 38–44. See also on the pivotal role of miracles in Grotius' defense of the Christian faith, *De veritate religionis christianae* (*OTh* 3, 33–6 and 51–2).

8   Jan Paul Heering, *Hugo Grotius as Apologist for the Christian Religion: A Study of his Work De veritate religionis christianae (1640)* (Leiden, 2004), 106–8, 116–37, 148.

9   Ludwig Diestel, *Geschichte des Alten Testamentes in der christlichen Kirche* (Jena, 1869; reprint Leipzig, 1981), 391–2 and 430–4, and Peter T. van Rooden, *Theology, Biblical Scholarship and Rabbinical Studies in the Seventeenth Century: Constantijn L'Empereur* (Leiden, 1989), 147.

insight that forced him to highlight the historical meaning and postulate a fulfillment within Jewish national history, either after a short lapse of time or in a more distant era. How could Isaiah predict the birth of Christ as a sign of imminent relief for the Jewish people if this birth was bound to happen more than seven hundred years later? Nonetheless, he met with serious resistance, for example from André Rivet and Pierre-Daniel Huet,[10] who maintained the literal meaning of the prophecies as expressed in the Old Testament. According to these learned theologians, Isaiah's words foretold and even directly referred to the coming of Christ. The prophet had spoken about a virgin and this should be taken literally, in the person of Mother Mary who gave birth to Christ without sexual intercourse. As an erudite scholar who was well-versed in Old Testament exegesis, Rivet accepted a double fulfillment for many passages, but in the case of Isaiah 7:14 he reproached Grotius for endorsing an explanation that not only smacked of Socinianism, but showed methodical inconsistencies as well. In no way at all could the wife of Isaiah, a woman who lost her virginity by sleeping with the prophet, stand as a type or prefiguration of the Virgin Mary.[11] By such an explanation Grotius paved the way for Jewish exegetes who were bent on robbing Christian apologists of a key text that had underpinned the claims to truth of their religion since the days of Christ. For that reason Rivet rejected Grotius' notes on the Old Testament as "annotata Judaico-Sociniana".[12] The fiercest of rivals, Grotius and Rivet crossed swords on another topic as well. While Rivet upheld the supernatural revelation of the biblical canon, Grotius limited divine interference to the Old Testament prophecies and Christ's sayings mainly. From the following it will become clear that Grotius' views of divine inspiration met with both acclaim and rejection later in the century.[13]

Leclerc on Divine Inspiration

We now make a leap in time and come to a publication dating from 1685, Jean Leclerc's *Sentimens de quelques theologiens de Hollande*. This anonymously published book was a response to the famous *Histoire critique du Vieux*

---

10   Pierre Daniel Huet, *Demonstratio evangelica* (Amsterdam, 1680²), vol. 1, 490–1, 530–2 and 551.

11   Hardy, *Criticism and Confession* (see above, n. 4), 212–8, offers an incisive analysis of the debate between Grotius and Rivet.

12   Nellen, *Hugo Grotius* (see above, n. 1), 641, note 218.

13   Ibid., 633–634. Cf. [Jean Leclerc], *Défense des Sentimens* (see below, n. 27), 222–3 and 229–33.

DUTCH LATE HUMANISM AND ITS AFTERMATH 407

Testament by Richard Simon. Jean Leclerc was a Swiss Huguenot who became the most ardent defender of the intellectual legacy of Hugo Grotius. He acclaimed the Dutchman as a champion of tolerance and reedited his popular apology *De veritate*.[14] In the *Sentimens* he dedicated the largest part of a chapter to Grotius' posthumous reputation, which he tried to purge from all stains of heterodoxy, Socinianism in particular.[15] Furthermore, he described Grotius' significance for the history of biblical scholarship by summarizing what was important in Grotius' *Annotata* on the Old Testament. He mentioned the explanation of obscure passages on the basis of the frequent use of pagan sources, the adequate explanation of biblical idiom, and the correct interpretation of prophecies. Here Leclerc had the double fulfillment in view. He explicitly referred the reader to Grotius' "admirable" annotation on Matthew 1:22.[16]

In the *Sentimens* Leclerc shed light on another aspect of Grotius' exegesis: his restriction of the Bible's divine inspiration. This he did in a very peculiar way. In chapters eleven and twelve of his book he included a lengthy "Mémoire", written by a certain "Monsieur N."[17] In this explosive manifesto[18] the normative ethical value of the Bible was underscored, but its divine inspiration virtually denied. To be sure, most prophecies on the coming of the Messiah resulted from divine inspiration, but that was the only point Monsieur N. was willing to concede. The historical parts of the Bible did not need such supernatural support. The same applied to the Gospels, because they evidently depended on testimonies by eyewitnesses or thorough historical research. The truthfulness of these texts was beyond any doubt, but to assume direct intervention by God during their genesis was unnecessary.[19]

None other than Hugo Grotius provided the anonymous author of the *Mémoire* with essential material for his argument. A few examples may suffice.

---

14 *De veritate religionis christianae* (Amsterdam, 1709) and following editions. See also Leclerc, *Bibliotheque choisie* 27–2 (Amsterdam, 1713), 388–423, for a justification of Grotius' ideas on the double sense of prophecies.

15 [Jean Leclerc], *Sentimens de quelques theologiens de Hollande sur l'Histoire critique du Vieux Testament* (Amsterdam, 1685), 374–402 (letter 17).

16 Ibid., 387–9.

17 Ibid., 119–286.

18 Stefano Brogi, "'Foi éclairée' et dissimulation chez Jean Le Clerc," *La Lettre clandestine* 13 (2004), 35–56, there 45. Even liberal protestants like Philippus van Limborch and John Locke distanced themselves from the *Mémoire*. Cf. *The Correspondence of John Locke*, ed. Esmond S. de Beer, vol. 2 (Oxford, 1976), 742–3, 748–51 and 755–7, letters by van Limborch and Locke, dated 1, 6 and 18 October 1685.

19 Maria Cristina Pitassi, *Entre croire et savoir: Le problème de la méthode critique chez Jean Le Clerc* (Leiden, 1987), 16–9. See also Jean Roth, "Le 'Traité de l'Inspiration' de Jean Leclerc," *Revue d'Histoire et de Philosophie religieuses* 36 (1956), 50–60.

First, Monsieur N. explicitly quoted a passage taken from Grotius' annotations on Matthew 1:22, where the Dutch exegete inferred from stylistic variations in the books of the prophets that God's inspiration had not been continuous.[20] Next, Monsieur N. showed his skeptical attitude to the maxim of a permanent, unvarying divine inspiration by drawing attention to Grotius' observation that the Bible offered two versions of the Ten Commandments, in *Exodus* and *Deuteronomy* respectively, displaying striking differences. How had these differences crept into the text? Did Divine Providence drop a few stitches when revealing such a crucial decree to mankind in two distinct forms? To the unbiased observer the differences might give reason for doubting the impeccability of divine inspiration. In order to strengthen his plea for a severely reduced divine inspiration, Monsieur N. showed how Grotius had ridiculed those Jewish exegetes who tried to explain the differences away by supposing a simultaneous and fully identical proclamation of the Ten Commandments that did justice to the differences of both versions. Grotius' commentary was laconic indeed: the Bible described so many miracles that it was useless to add another one.[21] After having exalted Grotius together with Erasmus as the two most important contributors to modern exegesis, Monsieur N. quoted from Grotius' *Appendix de antichristo*, a pamphlet that provided him with the audacious statement that the prophets and apostles did not have constant revelations, but often proceeded by guesswork, just like other human beings.[22]

The Identity of Monsieur N. Revealed

It took some time before the identity of Monsieur N. was disclosed. As becomes clear from Leclerc's correspondence, it was the author of the *Sentimens* himself who had written the attack on the Bible's divine inspiration. Fearing that he was about to be exposed to a torrent of sharp criticisms, he only admitted his authorship in his confidential correspondence with a close friend,

---

20   Leclerc, *Sentimens* (see above, n. 15), 224.

21   Ibid., 224–5, quoting from Grotius, *Explicatio Decalogi* (Amsterdam, 1640), 7–8, or *OTh* 1, 35 B 25–50, *Annotationes ad Vetus Testamentum*, ad Exodum 20:1: "Satis multa sunt in sacris historiis miracula, ut nova extra necessitatem nullique usui comminisci nihil sit opus". Cf. *The Oxford Dictionary of the Jewish Religion*, ed. Raphael J. Zwi Werblowsky and Geoffrey Wigoder (New York, 1997), 683–4.

22   Leclerc, *Sentimens* (see above, n. 15), 262–4, quoting from Grotius, *Appendix de antichristo* (Amsterdam, 1641), 5–6. Cf. *OTh* 3, 475 B 18–9.

DUTCH LATE HUMANISM AND ITS AFTERMATH 409

Jacques Lenfant.[23] To the outside world he maintained the persona of a "Monsieur N.", whose treatise he had allegedly included to exhort more capable scholars, for example Richard Simon, to write a definitive rebuttal. The *Mémoire* aroused vehement reactions indeed, in the first place from Pierre Bayle, who gave in to Leclerc's pressure not to debunk the *Sentimens* in his widely read periodical, the *Nouvelles de la Republique des Lettres*. Amongst other things, Bayle removed a phrase from his review of the book in which he accused Monsieur N. of speaking like a zealous Socinian and a deist.[24] But he voiced his disapproval in the private atmosphere, by writing a personal letter to Leclerc, in which he fiercely condemned the book. He singled out the *Mémoire* as an exceptionally dangerous piece that contaminated people's minds with countless doubts and seeds of atheism. He had come to know Leclerc as a Remonstrant, a representative of a lenient form of Calvinism. This leniency resulted from the Remonstrants' wish to secure Protestantism from collapsing after the Synod of Dordrecht had embraced a cruel form of predestination that degraded mankind to a plaything of destiny. In direct contradiction to the pious objective of safeguarding religion against the horrible consequences of a doctrine that deprived believers of any form of personal responsibility, the *Sentimens* showed that Leclerc had no qualms in undermining religion in another, even more harmful way, namely by promoting an attack on such an essential tenet as divine inspiration. It was no surprise for Bayle that the Dutch theologians denounced the book as worse than Spinoza, "pire que Spinoza".[25]

---

23   Pitassi, *Entre croire et savoir* (see above, n. 19), 114–5, note 99, referring to letters later published in Jean Le Clerc, *Epistolario*, ed. Mario Sina and Maria Grazia Sina (Florence, 1987–1997), vol. 1, 303 and 386, Leclerc to Jacques Lenfant, 10 March and 4 September 1685. See also ibid., 370 (letter of 26 July 1685) and 548–9 (biography of Jacques Lenfant).

24   [Pierre] B[ayle], *Nouvelles de la Republique des Lettres*, mois de juillet 1685 (Amsterdam, 1685), art. 7, 767–77, and *Correspondance de Pierre Bayle*, vol. 5 (août 1684–fin juillet 1685), ed. Elisabeth Labrousse et al. (Oxford, 2007), 435–9, Leclerc to Bayle, 19 June 1684 [=19 July 1685]. The printer of the *Nouvelles de la Republique des Lettres*, Henri Desbordes, had given Le Clerc access to the manuscript draft of Bayle's review.

25   Le Clerc, *Epistolario* (see above, n. 23), vol. 1, 349–51, Bayle to Leclerc, 18 July [1685]; *Correspondance de Pierre Bayle* (see above, n. 24), 5, 430–2. Cf. Maria Cristina Pitassi, "Bayle, the Bible, and the Remonstrant Tradition at the Time of the *Commentaire philosophique*," in *Scriptural Authority and Biblical Criticism in the Dutch Golden Age*, ed. Dirk van Miert et al. (Oxford, 2017), 257–69, there 259–61. Bayle's apodictic rejection of the *Sentimens*, in particular the Grotius-based "Mémoire sur l'inspiration," led to an irreparable breach between the two scholars. Even more outspokenly than Bayle, Leclerc, hereafter aired his resentment in his correspondence. See, for the general context of the quarrel, Elisabeth Labrousse, *Pierre Bayle* (The Hague, 1963–64), vol. 1, 258–65; 2, 328–31, and Hans Bots et al., *De "Bibliothèque universelle et historique" (1686–1693): Een periodiek als trefpunt van geletterd Europa* (Amsterdam, 1981), 6–30.

Leclerc's answer to this letter is remarkable for the dishonesty with which he tried to exonerate himself. As he confessed, he initially even doubted whether Bayle, rather than reading the *Sentimens*, had relied on an informant who combined ignorance with hostility towards Leclerc. The author of the *Mémoire* was somebody else, as Leclerc boldly explained, and his Remonstrant friends had nothing to do with the piece. They had not seen it before it came off the press and they did not agree with its contents. Nonetheless, it merited approval, and it certainly did not destroy religion, as Bayle had pointed out. Instead of attacking religion, the *Mémoire* comprised the quintessence of the Christian creed: it confirmed the truth of Christ's miracles and resurrection, assumed that the New Testament contained the whole of Christ's teaching without lacking anything essential, and declared that the apostles faithfully reported on this teaching, sacrificed their lives for it and saw their message confirmed by divine miracles. While Bayle rejected the idea of a partial inspiration of Scripture as if it shook the foundations of belief, others would judge differently. Erasmus, Grotius and many more great men had adhered to a view that was very similar to that of the *Mémoire*.[26]

In his *Défense*, directed at Simon's attack on the *Sentimens*,[27] Leclerc again strenuously exerted himself to exculpate his fictitious friend, Monsieur N. While admitting that the unknown author had aroused great indignation among orthodox believers, he argued that this should not be adduced as a motive for avoiding discussion on the doctrine of inspiration. In fact, the issue was so important that silence entailed great damage to religion. In order to defend his position Leclerc sketched a pessimistic view of his times, in which the greater part of the sciences had attained a degree of perfection not seen before, however without making people any wiser. On the contrary, licentiousness and impiety were gaining ground in a scandalous way. Although many readers were uneducated and lacked sufficient knowledge of philosophy and criticism, they eagerly devoured impious books in Latin, French, English, and Dutch, those by Spinoza in the first place. They became convinced that, by attacking literal inspiration, writers like Spinoza had undermined the authority of Scripture— as if the philosopher's arguments could not be refuted. Consequently, they lapsed into deism or atheism. Leclerc felt forced to admit that it was impossible to repress those libertine attacks on divine inspiration altogether. By

---

26   Leclerc, *Epistolario* (see above, n. 23), vol. 1, 351–4, Leclerc to Bayle, 19 June 1684 [=19 July 1685]; *Correspondance de Pierre Bayle* (see above, n. 24) 5, 435–7.

27   [Jean Leclerc], *Défense des Sentimens de quelques théologiens de Hollande* (Amsterdam, 1686), replying to [Richard Simon], *Réponse au livre intitulé Sentimens de quelques théologiens* (Rotterdam, 1686).

DUTCH LATE HUMANISM AND ITS AFTERMATH411

publishing Monsieur N.'s *Mémoire* he had tried to exhort others to put forward irrefutable arguments concluding that Scripture was inspired both in contents and wording. As long as nobody had presented such arguments, however, the only remaining option was to allow Monsieur N. to demonstrate that his view of inspiration did not detract in any way whatsoever from the authority of Scripture.[28] For this reason, he provided Monsieur N. with the opportunity to further illustrate his views[29] and refute the objections of his adversaries,[30] after which Leclerc himself defended his friend once more against accusations of deism.[31]

Many years later, Leclerc still held on to the fiction of an anonymous Monsieur N. He did so most expressly in a letter to Richard Kidder, Bishop of Bath and Wells, who had incriminated him as a deist and disciple of Thomas Hobbes, on the grounds that he had questioned Moses' authorship of the Pentateuch. "I have nowhere stated that I favor the insights of Monsieur N.", Leclerc remarked.[32] By now, the real identity of Monsieur N. must have been an open secret in the Republic of Letters.[33] Even so, Leclerc preferred to maintain the fiction of a Monsieur N., thus betraying how much importance he attached to keeping up appearances: towards the outside world the correspondence served him as a means to safeguard his reputation against incessant accusations of heterodoxy.[34]

From what has been said before, some conclusions might be drawn. In the first place, we are justified to state that theology and exegesis form an important part in Grotius' *Nachleben*, something we tend to forget when, in this

---

28   Leclerc, *Défense* (see above, n. 27), letter 9, 218–23.

29   Ibid., letter 9, 223–9 and 229–190 [=236], containing a second "Mémoire," in two parts, delivered by "Monsieur N." to refute the criticisms against his first treatise.

30   Ibid., letter 10, 238–71, answers by Monsieur N. to sixteen objections raised against his views.

31   Ibid., letter 11, 272–204 [=304].

32   Leclerc, *Epistolario* (see above, n. 23), vol. 2, 141, letter of 13 December 1694, in reply to a letter of 9 November 1694 (ibid., 134–5), in which Kidder referred to *Five Letters Concerning the Inspiration of Holy Scripture* (London, 1690), the English translation of those chapters in the *Sentimens* (letters 11–12) and the *Défense des Sentimens* (letters 9–11) that included Monsieur N.'s *Mémoire* and its appendices. Kidder informed his correspondent that the book did not benefit his reputation across the Channel.

33   Cf. Leclerc, *Epistolario* (see above, n. 23), vol. 1, 414–5, Jean-Robert Chouet to Leclerc, 19 December 1685: Chouet praised the *Sentimens*, but he also warned his correspondent to be on his guard for his critics, who were eagerly preparing themselves to refute the book, the more so because it was generally assumed that Leclerc himself was the author of the controversial *Mémoire*: "[…] on veut estre persuadé que vostre Mr. N. et vous estes le mesme homme".

34   See also [Jean Leclerc], *Parrhasiana* (Amsterdam, 1701²), vol. 1, 365–6 and 376.

secularized age, we focus on his contribution to juridical thought, in particular natural law and the law of nations. In the second place, it is important to note that even long after his death Grotius was acclaimed and attacked for his contribution to exegesis for two main reasons: his historicizing approach to biblical prophecies and his reduction of divine inspiration. Both characteristics fit in a general development towards a more scientific, religiously neutral and secularizing biblical scholarship that helped to pave the way for the enlightened thinkers at the turn of the century. Finally, after more than thirty years Grotius' writings still inspired a kindred spirit like Jean Leclerc to articulate views on divine inspiration that went against the grain of orthodox theology, to the extent that he did not venture to uphold them personally in the public space of the Republic of Letters. More time was needed before enlightened ideas on the explanation of the Bible would take firm root.

Huygens Institute for the History of the Netherlands, Amsterdam

CHAPTER 31

The Merging of Linguistic Idioms in the Commentary Genre: the Case of Alejo Vanegas of Toledo (1542)

Daniel Nodes

Abstract

Humanist writers who extolled Ciceronian Latin exercised a broader idiomatic range in their writing. The letters of Piccolomini offer a familiar example where classical diction merges with biblical and medieval idioms. Their expanded linguistic range reflects the interaction of court and cathedral in Piccolomini's diplomatic missions, in which he served as both an imperial ambassador and a churchman at the highest levels of theological controversy. Nearly a century later, Alejo Vanegas (1498–1562), Master of Grammar in Toledo, another avowed devotee of Ciceronian Latin, published a commentary on the *Samarites Comoedia* (1539) at the request of the Sacristan of Toledo Cathedral who saw the play's educational value and wanted its lessons disseminated in Latin for the schools. Through a meticulous, even encyclopedic, commentary, Vanegas explained the play's poetics and literary sources as a competent humanist scholar, but the schoolmaster also devoted himself to explaining its ethical and doctrinal import, presenting theological explanations in the terminology of scholasticism. Vanegas's Latin reflects the blend of linguistic traditions, owing much to Erasmus but also drawing on the Latin of patristic and medieval theology and even reaching into the Spanish vernacular at key moments. Vanegas delivered well on his commission. His commentary is rooted in the needs of students for whom grammatical explanations and literary paraphrases were essential, but whose education also required the language of the Bible, the medieval scholars, and their own Spanish milieu. Vanegas thus epitomizes Neo-Latin's expanded linguistic and cultural range.

Keywords

Enea Silvio Piccolomini – Neo-Latin epistolography – Alexius Vanegas – *Samarites Comoedia* (1539) – humanist Latin

© KONINKLIJKE BRILL NV, LEIDEN, 2020 | DOI:10.1163/9789004427105_032

414   NODES

Piccolomini's Ciceronian Ideal at the Nexus of Court and Church, 1450–51[1]

In 1451, Enea Silvio Piccolomini led an embassy to Bohemia in the diplomatic service of Emperor Frederick III. The object was to arrange a council to calm the Bohemian opposition to Frederick's guardianship of their young king Lladislas. But he was also there as a bishop to try to restore the rebellious Hussites to Catholic orthodoxy. After the visit Enea wrote to the Spanish cardinal Juan de Carvajal, who had presided over his consecration as bishop in 1447 and was concerned with Bohemia and the matter of the Hussites, and gave a detailed report of the mission. Enea opens with a description of his visit to the Bohemian city of Tabor, a Hussite stronghold outside Prague, with its battle-hardened population standing as a minority against the Holy Roman Empire. He described the Taborites as "rusticanum et incompositum vulgus" ("a boorish and disheveled") and to that "vulgus" he applied Vergil's description of Deiphobus in the underworld as an apt portrait: "populataque tempora, raptis auribus, et truncas inhonesto vulnere naris" ("temples disfigured, ears ripped off, and nostrils torn with hideous wounds").[2]

Enea also described the two inspirational symbols carved on the city's outer defenses. One was a portrait of the legendary Hussite general Jan Žižka. Žižka had been blinded in both eyes in combat, one eye at a time, but was reputed never to have lost a battle; but Enea rather dismissively refers to him as "homo senex et utroque lumine cassus" ("an old man and blind in both eyes"), and this time Enea quotes Matthew's Gospel rather than Vergil or another classical author:[3]

> Quem [sc. Žižka] Thaborite non solum monoculum sed cecum quoque secuti sunt ducem, neque absurde; nam tali populo, qui nihil divinitatis intelligit, nihil religionis tenet, nihil equi rectique videt, quis ducatum prebere debuit nisi cecus? Impletur est illud salvatoris in eis: "Si cecus ceco ducatum prebeat, ambo in foveam cadunt."

And this [Žižka], not only blind in one eye but even completely blind, did the Taborites follow as their leader, and that is reasonable; for who

---

1 The author thanks the peer reviewers who made helpful suggestions about this article.

2 "Bischof Eneas an den Kardinal Juan Carvajal; Wiener-Neustadt, 21 August 1451," in *Der Briefwechsel des Eneas Silvius*, ed. Rudolph Wolkan (Vienna, 1908–18), vol. 3, pt. 1, no. 12, 22–57, there 23 (quoting *Aen.* 6,496–7).

3 Ibid., 24.

ought to give orders to such a nation that understands nothing about theology, has no grasp of anything of religion, sees nothing of what is fair and right, except a blind man? Fulfilled in them is what our Savior said, "but if a blind man guides another blind man, both fall into the pit" (Matthew 15.14).

Enea's earlier description of the sordidness of the Taborites, likening them to a figure in the Underworld, contains both physical and spiritual overtones about their condition. Here the physical blindness of their leader reinforces the image of the spiritual blindness of the people through Enea's effective merging of quotations from classical and biblical sources.

The other symbol Enea saw on Tabor's walls was an angel holding the Communion cup, "quasi," Piccolomini adds, "communionem sub specie vini suaderet populo" ("as if he were urging Communion by wine upon the people").[4] As a bishop meeting with Hussite representatives, his mission was to insist that they conform to the Roman rite, which by the thirteenth century prescribed Communion for the faithful by the species of bread only, without receiving wine. His letter observes that in his interview he defended the "confectio" of the two species, bread and wine, by the clergy; but for the laity there was "manducatio" but not "bibitio", later terms that he uses interchangeably with the classical "esus" and "potus". He made it his aim, he recalls, to speak before the Hussite representatives about so great a sacrament in more lofty terms, and it was Thomas Aquinas who supplied the loftiness: "Ut altius de tanto sacramento loquamur, triplex est, ut noster Aquinas ait, sanctus et profundissimus doctor, huius excellentissimus rei significatio triaque tempora respicit."[5] Enea explained Thomas's tripartite theology of the Eucharist in terms of the formal distinctions of medieval scholasticism: Communion is called "sacrificium" with reference to the past, recalling the Lord's passion; it is called "communio" with reference to the present and pertains to ecclesiastical unity, and it is called "viaticum" with reference to the future because it foretells of the enjoyment of God that is awaited and because it shows the way to the heavenly fatherland; and in that sense it is also called "eucharistia". Now "communio" and "viaticum" apply to all the faithful, but "sacrificium" applies to the clergy alone.

That is Enea in action, as it were; but around that time he also wrote vigorously in praise of the ideal of Ciceronian Latin. In his praise of Leonardo

---

4 Ibid., 23.
5 Ibid., 47.

Bruni in *De viris illustribus* (1445–50) he describes the rise and fall of the Latin language:[6]

> Ab ipsis etenim lingue latine repertoribus ornatus dicendi et studia litterarum continuo creverunt usque ad tempora Ciceronis, ubi vere plenitudinem acceperunt nec amplius crescere potuerunt, cum jam essent in culmine. Manserunt igitur postea per plures annos ac usque ad Jeronimum atque Gregorium viguerunt, non tamen absque minutione, exin perierunt funditus; nec enim post illa tempora qui ornate scripserunt reperitur.

> From its very founders, the Latin language developed continually in the elegance of its expression and literary study up to the time of Cicero, when it achieved its true fullness and could not possibly have evolved further, since it was already at its apex. It remained there for many years down to the likes of Jerome and [Pope] Gregory [1], although not without some diminution, and thereafter it died out utterly. For after that period no elegant writer of the language was to be found.

Along with the praise of Leonardo went his own efforts to achieve a classicizing, Ciceronian style, which tendency is especially evident in his letters.[7] Ruldolph

---

6 *Enea Silvio Piccolomini, De viris illustribus*, ed. Adrianus van Heck (Vatican City, 1991), 34.2–20; trans. Patrick Baker, "*De viris illustribus* and the self-conception of Italian humanism in the 15th Century," in *Acta Conventus Neo-Latini Upsaliensis*, ed. Astrid Steiner-Weber (Leiden, 2012), 189–98, there 192–3. See also Claudia Märtl, "Vier übersehene Viten aus Eneas Silvius Piccolominis *De Viris illustribus*," *Deutsches Archiv für Erforschung des Mittelalters* 72 (2016), 177–88.

7 For studies of Piccolomini's rhetoric, especially in the context of clergymen who supported papal monarchy and Catholic orthodoxy, see Charles E. Trinkaus, *In Our Image and Likeness: Humanity and Divinity in Italian Humanist Thought*, 2 vols. (Chicago, 1970); John W. O'Malley, *Praise and Blame in Renaissance Rome: Rhetoric, Doctrine, and Reform in the Sacred Orators of the Papal Court, c. 1450–1521* (Durham, NC, 1979); John F. D'Amico, *Renaissance Humanism in Papal Rome: Humanists and Churchmen on the Eve of the Reformation* (Baltimore, 1983); Rolando Montecalvo, "The new Landesgeschichte: Aeneas Silvius on Austria and Bohemia in Pius II," in *El più expeditivo pontifice: Selected Studies on Aeneas Silvius Piccolomini (1405–1464)*, ed. Zweder von Martels and Arjo Vanderjagt (Leiden, 2003), 55–86. For a general listing of works on Piccolomini see Franz Josef Worstbrock, "Piccolomini, Aeneas Silvius," in *Die deutsche Literatur des Mittelalters: Verfasserlexikon*, ed. Kurt Ruh, Guldolf Keil et al., vol. 7, pt. 2 (Berlin, 1987), 634–69; *Aeneas Silvius Piccolomini: Europe (c. 1400–1458)*, ed. Robert Brown and Nancy Bisaha (Washington, D.C., 2013). On Piccolomini's legation to the Hussites in 1451 see *Oration 'Res Bohemicas' of Enea Silvio Piccolomini (1455, Rome)*, ed. Michael von Cotta-Schönberg (online, 2019) hal-01180832.

Wolkan, the editor, knew that Enea himself courted that style in the original composition, but also revised the letters for publication: "Wie Eneas schon bei der ersten Redaktion bestrebt war, seine Briefe stilistisch zu feilen, so tut er dies auch jetzt."[8] The revisions show efforts to express ideas more clearly but at times simply to use a more formal turn of phrase. Wolkan notes, for example, that Enea changed the medieval "dieta" (Reichstag), to "conventio", revised an object infinitive ("fecissem regem scribere") with a substantive *ut*-clause after a verb of bidding ("orassem regem ut scriberet"). Similarly, for a simple factitive verb ("faciet"), he substituted the more elegant phrase "provinciam assumet"; and he converted a simple subject-verb-object construction ("rex auxilium mittit") to a sentence expressing the same simple idea through the dative case construction ("rex auxilio est"). More recently, Martin Wagendorfer, pointing to the continued absence of serious study of Piccolomini's language and style, has presented additional examples of Piccolomini's quest for a formally classical but not excessive style, offering, as he put it, "a snapshot of the linguistic habits of the Sienese in the 1450s." Among the examples Wagendorfer gives of changes in Piccolomini's style are "papa" to "pontifex", "passagium" to "expeditio", "vasalli" to "subditi", "instructio" to "mandatum", "terrigenae" to "populares", "audientia" to "audiri" or "aures prebere", "dietim" to "indies", "castrum" to "oppidum" etc.[9] The letters contain many similar classicizing efforts, but despite them all, it has been observed that Enea's Latin was "elegant if somewhat uneven," "did not rise to the highest humanistic standards," "never reached the highest humanist-classical standards," and, more ambiguously put, "His Latinity was fluent rather than 'elegant'."[10]

In light of that assessment, readers may ask, "What held him back?" The richest models of Latin style were made available a century before his birth, his whole life was literary, and he composed and published in a wide range of genres. The answer to questions about his perceived deficiencies in imitating classical form is found partly in his own explanation of the goal he set for himself as a letter-writer, which was to imitate the ancient style while avoiding what he saw as its eccentricities; but practical necessity as well achieved more than

---

8   Wolkan, *Der Briefwechsel* (see above, n. 2), xix.

9   Martin Wagendorfer, "Sprache und Stil," in *Eneas Silvio Piccolomini, Historia Austrialis*, ed. Julia Knödler, Pt. 1, (Hannover, 2009), lxi–lxxviii.

10   Gary R. Grund, "Review of *Aeneas Silvius Piccolomini: Europe (c. 1400–1458)*," *Renaissance Quarterly* 67 (2014), 1298; Craig Kallendorf, "Aeneas Sylvius Piccolomini," *Oxford Bibliographies*: DOI: 10.1093/OBO/9780195399301-0065 (accessed 12 July 2019); William. H. Woodward, ed., "The Treatise of Aeneas Sylvius Piccolomini, Afterwards Pius II, *De liberorum educatione* (1450)," in idem, *Vittorino da Feltre and Other Humanist Educators* (Cambridge, 1897, 1912), 134–58 (reprint Toronto, 1996), there 135.

simply a substandard classicism. Over against his classicizing tendency and lament of the decline of Latin after Cicero, Piccolomini's Latin was also supplemented and expanded by medieval concepts, and at times was dependent on scholastic Medieval Latin, which is evident in his abundant collection of letters. The Latin idiom of his 1451 letter to Cardinal Carvajal suited his legation that supported the papacy's refusal to acknowledge concessions over communion in two species that had been granted in the Hussite Compacts at the Council of Basel (1433–36).[11] And in 1462 it was Piccolomini as Pope Pius II who declared those compacts null and void. His merging of classical forms within an ecclesiological and theological message must, therefore, also be seen as his deliberate choice. By contrast, Nicholas of Cusa, although prevented from joining Piccolomini in Bohemia during his own papal legation of 1451–52, also negotiated with the Hussites through long treatises, defending the papacy and the Catholic form of communion against their claims. But in his anti-Hussite writings Cusa refrained even from Piccolomini's form of classicism.[12]

Latin's Expanded Range in Vanegas's Commentary on the *Samarites Commedia*, 1539

That reflection on Piccolomini's avowed linguistic ideal and his actual writing offers a more familiar example of the merging of linguistic idioms, especially between those typically labeled classical and Christian Latin, or, more specifically, scholastic and humanist, by a famous Ciceronian advocate in the humanist period. The search for an exemplary author was more complicated than the humanists' declarations often suggest; many writers of the Renaissance and Neo-Latin centuries praised an essentially Ciceronian standard while expanding Latin's linguistic and stylistic range. In the sixteenth century Alejo Vanegas (frequently Venegas) of Camarena and Toledo, 1498(9)–1562, was a renowned master of Latin and an educator committed both to the Latin classical idiom and its enrichment by other linguistic forms. Alejo Vanegas del Busto of Toledo was a lexicographer, author of devotional works, a humanist, and a grammarian. He was a professor of Latin, but despite his mastery of the classical idiom and his dedication to Latin as a teacher, he composed his first three books in

---

11 For Piccolomini's role in the council see Johannes Helmrath, *Das Basler Konzil 1431–1449: Forschungsstand und Probleme*, (Cologne, 1987).

12 See *Nicholas of Cusa: Writings on Church and Reform* (Cambridge, Mass., 2008), 2–85; 356–429. On Cusa's aborted legation to Bohemia see Donald Sullivan, "Nicholas of Cusa as Reformer: The Papal Legation to the Germanies, 1451–1452," *Mediaeval Studies* 36 (1974), 382–428, there 392.

Castilian while teaching Latin grammar in the then new Universidad de Toledo.[13] His first publication was *El Tractado de ortografía* (1531), on orthography and accentuation of Latin, Greek, Hebrew, and Spanish. In this work Vanegas gives many rules of orthography for the vernacular language and even argues for Castilian Spanish as equal to Latin. Vanegas taught at Toledo from 1526 to 1544 under the *catedratico* Cedillo. Two other books written by Vanegas during that time are also in Spanish. Vanegas had a patron in Diego de Mendoza, Count of Melito, and on the Count's death Vanegas published *Agonia del transito de la muerte* (Toledo, 1537), which he dedicated to Mendoza's wife, Ana de la Cerda, Countess of Melito. Vanegas was a strong supporter of Erasmus, and scholars have seen this work as derived from Erasmus's *Praeparatio ad mortem* (1534). The *Agonía* went through many editions to the end of the seventeenth century. It has been called by Marcel Bataillon "le chef-d'oeuvre de la littérature ascétique espagnole à l'époque de Charles-Quint."[14] Vanegas's third treatise in Spanish is the *Primera parte de las diferencias de libros que ay en el universo* (Toledo, 1540), an allegorical work on the major orders or systems: the 'books' of God, of nature, and of moral and religious knowledge.

Vanegas lived in the early decades of the Spanish *época dorada*. But that appellation does not mean that the state of education was in good condition. Erasmus and Vives described the impoverished schools and their ill-trained and poorly compensated teachers. In this environment, Vanegas pursued a vocation to teach grammar and form the character of young scholars.[15] He was influenced by the educational reform that was sweeping Europe, being a contemporary of Juan Luis Vives (1492–1540), who both lived one generation after John Colet (1467–1519), Erasmus (1466–1536), and Antonio de Nebrija (1444–1522).

A vivid testimony to this educational mission appears in Vanegas's commentary on the school drama by the Flemish schoolmaster Petrus Papeus titled *Samarites commedia* (1539). The play, enacting the rescue of a prodigal son by Jesus Christ as portrayed by another gospel story, the Good Samaritan of Luke's Gospel, is voiced in the language of Plautus and Terence with a cast of rogues, parasites, and a young harlot, all familiar to the Roman comedies. In 1542 Vanegas was commissioned by a prelate of Toledo to republish the play along with a commentary, not in Spanish but in Latin, that would teach

---

13 On Vanegas's life see Ildefonso Adeva Martín, *El Maestro Alejo Venegas de Busto: su vida y sus obras* (Toledo, 1987).

14 Marcel Bataillon, *Érasme et l'Éspagne: recherches sur l'histoire spirituelle du XVIe siècle* (Paris, 1937; reprint Geneva, 1998), 606.

15 Adeva Martín, *Venegas* (see above, n. 13), 49–52.

420   NODES

schoolboys the correct meaning of the play's themes as well as a thorough ap-
preciation of the poetic and rhetorical features of its Latin dialogue.

Vanegas's reverence for Cicero is evident from the commentary's dedicatory
letter to his patron, where in the first sentence Vanegas cites a definition of
comedy attributed to Cicero as the only author whose definition satisfies everyone: "unus Cicero omnibus satisfaciet."[16] The commentator's entries continue
to resort to Cicero as the court of appeal for style and word choice. In the entry
on the word *sycophantia* 'cunning,' 'calumny,' for example, used repeatedly by
Plautus, Vanegas observes that "Cicero numquam usus est hoc nomine", but he
approves of the phrase "corvus albus", because "Cicero usus est hac metaph-
ora." And to approve of the use of the verb "valeat" with the meaning of 'away
with him!', 'be off!,' Vanegas notes that such usage is found in Cicero.[17] And
while Vanegas introduced many sources and analogues to words in the play
from Cicero by way of Erasmus' *Adagia*, Vanegas never mentions Erasmus in
the commentary, while Cicero is the most frequently quoted authority therein.

That reverence for Cicero notwithstanding, the very subject matter of the
Samarites and the commission undertaken to comment on the play's moral
and theological lessons as well as its literary qualities required Vanegas to incorporate the language of Christian Latin theology. Just as was the case with Enea
Piccolomini's mission, here Vanegas's mission, in the form of a co-mission, had
both secular and ecclesiastical aims. About his project, it has been said:[18]

> Los escolios a *Samarites* son un ejemplo granado de aquella corriente
> humanista cristiana, encabezada por Nebrija y Arias Barbosa, según la
> cual ya no era total la dependencia de los autores paganos para el apren-
> dizaje de las humanidades, porque los había cristianos que habían va-
> ciado la nueva visión del mundo en bellas y armónicas formas expresivas.

Vanegas explains the moral and theological significance of the play for students
by invoking the vast biblical exegetical tradition about salvation and divine
benevolence in detail. Often there is a basis in Cicero, which is supplemented
by terms and concepts developed in the Christian era. When, for example, the
Samaritan of the play acknowledges that sometimes God rejects a person for
serious sins "quemquam abdicat ob flagitia" (768–9), Vanegas adds scholastic

---

16   *Parables on a Roman Comic Stage: Samarites, Comoedia de Samaritano Evangelico* (1539) *by
      Petrus Papeus Together with the Commentary of Alexius Vanegas of Toledo* (1542), ed. Daniel
      Nodes (Leiden, 2017), 174.
17   Ibid., 204–12.
18   Adeva Martín, *Venegas* (see above, n. 13), 292.

THE MERGING OF LINGUISTIC IDIOMS IN THE COMMENTARY GENRE   421

theology's explanation of how such rejection by God does not negate God's will that all persons be saved. God's antecedent will that all be saved exists *simpliciter*, unconditionally, but his will "secundum praesentem iustitiam", according to the sinner's particular moral state at the time of his having turned away from repentance, may be to reject.[19] That distinction between God's just vengeance "secundum quid", which is *consequent*, and his benevolent will, which exists *simpliciter* and is *antecedent*, is a distinction made throughout the explanations of scholastic theologians, including Thomas Aquinas.[20]

To complete the essential lesson to be drawn from the play, Vanegas adds technical distinctions between two kinds of repentance: "attritio", incomplete contrition or contrition for unwholesome reasons, say, fear of punishment, and true "contritio", motivated not by fear but by genuine sorrow for having directed an offense against God through sin. The distinction is expressed using words not found in the play, nor in Cicero, nor in the present sense by any classical author.

In a related comment on God's condemnation of the unrepentant despite "wanting all men to be saved" (1 Tim 2,4), Vanegas quotes from Peter Lombard and John of Damascus in the Latin translation made by Jacques Lefèvre D'Étaples (Paris, 1507), to explain a theological distinction among various aspects of the one will of God. At the heart of the entire matter is the concept of the *voluntas beneplaciti* of God, as it is used throughout the books of the Bible. The compound verb "beneplaceo" and the noun "beneplacitum" formed from it come into Latin in the Christian period from the Greek εὐδοχία,[21] and

---

19   "Abdicat, inquam, secundum praesentem iustitiam. Propterea enim Iob verebatur omnia opera sua, quia sciebat Deum non parcere delinquenti. Iob 6. Delinquenti ergo quo ad praesentem iustitiam Deus non parcit, benigne tamen et misericorditer parcit illi, qui postquam deliquit, vera poenitentia ductus, Dei misericordiam implorat. Quamuis enim 'Deus ulciscatur nos secundum peccata nostra' (Iudith 7). 'Christus Iesus qui est ad dexteram Dei interpellat pro nobis,' ad Romanos 8." Nodes, *Parables* (see above, n. 16), 50–1.

20   "Deus antecedenter vult omnem hominem salvari; sed consequenter vult quosdam damnari, secundum exigentiam suae iustitiae. Neque tamen id quod antecedenter volumus, simpliciter volumus, sed secundum quid. Quia voluntas comparatur ad res, secundum quod in seipsis sunt, in seipsis autem sunt in particulari, unde simpliciter volumus aliquid, secundum quod volumus illud consideratis omnibus circumstantiis particularibus, quod est consequenter velle. Unde potest dici quod iudex iustus simpliciter vult homicidam suspendi, sed secundum quid vellet eum vivere, scilicet inquantum est homo. Unde magis potest dici velleitas, quam absoluta voluntas. Et sic patet quod quidquid Deus simpliciter vult, fit; licet illud quod antecedenter vult, non fiat." Thom. Aq., *Summa Theo.* Prima pars. Q. 19 a. 6 ad 1.

21   As Jerome explains, "verbum εὐδοχία, quod Latinus sermo interpretatus est placitum, apud Graecos compositum est ex duobus integris ἀπὸ τοῦ εὖ καὶ τοῦ δοκεῖν, a bene et a placito, quod nos possumus dicere beneplacitum, quia non statim omne, quod placuit et

in most later uses it continues to reflect the language of the Bible or precisely to articulate the complex efforts to maintain the permanence of the divine will together with its allowance for human freedom of choice. This paradox is facilitated by the theological division of the *voluntas beneplaciti* between the antecedent will of God, *voluntas antecedens*, and the consequent will, *consequens*, the former being contingent on man's acting in consort with it, the latter tempered by divine justice. Thus, to say that God wills all to be saved is seen not to conflict with the frequent warnings about divine punishment of the unrepentant. Vanegas's commentary thus continues the practice of incorporating scholastic theological concepts and diction into a classical, chiefly Ciceronian, base that is in evidence in Enea Piccolomini from a century earlier. Christian Latin, including the language of medieval scholasticism, continued to be a tributary flowing into Neo-Latin.

Applications from the Spanish Vernacular at Key Moments in the Commentary

The master of Toledo helped open another tributary, flowing from the vernacular, in this case his native Castilian. While writing the commentary on *Samarites* in Latin, Vanegas remained a proponent of the Spanish language as a valid literary medium. He introduced Spanish proverbs and phrases into his study of classical philology, treating ancient and modern expressions as partners toward helping readers understand the play. Both the dialogue of the play itself and Vanegas's commentary include proverbs in Greek and Latin from classical authors, but Vanegas independently added phrases and anecdotes from Spanish to explain either the meaning of classical expressions or to explain characters' motives or dispositions.

For example, the protagonist, named Aegio, leaves his father's house in Jerusalem, deceived by devil's agents into believing that he has a lover awaiting him in Jericho. Papeus the playwright cleverly cast Aegio first as a type of the Prodigal Son, who left home because he was dissatisfied and lusted for adventure. This *contaminatio* of two gospel parables helps develop the play's moral and theological significance. Vanegas explains that both the devils' agents who tempt Aegio and the brigands who eventually beat him as he travels on the road to Jericho did not cause, nor even could have caused Aegio's ruin. Aegio was already inclined toward spiritual death and was self-defeated

---

bene placere potest, sed ibi tantum εὐδοκία hoc est beneplacitum dicitur, ubi quod placuit, recte placitum comprobatur." *Commentarium in Epistolam ad Ephesios* 1,5 (*PL* 26:449).

THE MERGING OF LINGUISTIC IDIOMS IN THE COMMENTARY GENRE 423

because he had willingly placed himself in so vulnerable a position: leaving his father's house, ignoring his tutor, and letting down his moral guard. The phrases Vanegas brings to bear on this episode operate on the spiritual as well as physical level. To reinforce that important lesson, when the devil orders the brigands to stop beating Aegio on the road to Jericho and says "Bene habet" ("He's had enough", 720), Vanegas describes Aegio's situation by two proverbs. The first is classical: *Salmacida spolia*, referring to the adage, "Salmacida spolia sine sanguine sine sudore" ("Son of Salmacis, win spoils that cost nor sweat nor blood"). The saying is from Cicero who quoted from Ennius in *De officiis*.[22] It refers to the pool of the nymph Salmacis, which makes effeminate all those who drink from it. Vanegas applies the classical proverb that refers to the weakening of anyone who drank from the Salmacian pool, to explain that it would have been pointless to inflict further wounds on Aegio. But then Vanegas introduces a contemporary Spanish proverb from Toledo, "a Moro muerto, gran lanzada," meaning the assault with a big thrust on a Moorish soldier who is already dead. Had he wished to remain in the classical idiom Vanegas could easily have drawn many other suitable proverbs to express the assault on an already defeated enemy. The proverbs "Leoni mortuo lepores insultant, iugulare mortuos, mortuum flagellas (νεκρὸν μαστίζεις), a mortuo tributum exigere, a mortuo tributum auferre," and "mortuos rursus occidere," are all described in Erasmus's *Adagia* as having noble sources in classical authors.[23] Papeus employs 110 classical adages found in Erasmus's collection, and Vanegas adds another 69 in his commentary. But despite all those expressions in literary Latin and Greek in this case, Vanegas still chose to comment on Aegio's situation by a vivid contemporary *castellano* proverb.

Vanegas also used opportunities provided by the play's own reference to the Spanish language to elucidate the remarks with additional examples from Spanish. In act three, as Aegio was passing through a crowded marketplace with his pedagogue, the two devil's agents, Hedylogus and Gulo, each tried to attract a crowd to lure Aegio. As his name would suggest, Hedylogus is the more successful because he flatters the crowd and promises to use magic to deliver whatever people want. Gulo, jealous of his rival's greater success, curses him: "Ut ei dii malum duint; sic Iberas nugas atque portentosas nenias blaterat" ("May the gods curse this fellow; he's babbling hyperbolic Spanish nonsense and bombastic gibberish" 386–8).

Vanegas offers detailed comments on both "Iberas nugas" ("Spanish trifles"), and "nenias", including an explanation of "nenias" as "disparatas

---

22 From Ennius, quoted in Cic., *Off.* 1,18,61; cf. Ovid, *Met.* 4,285–7.
23 Erasmus, *Adagia*, 3682–4.7.82; 0154–1.2.54; 0365–1.4.65; 0812–1.9.12, 1069–2.1.69, 4094–5.1.94.

hyperbolicasque cantilenas, quales in funeribus audiri solent" ("random and hyperbolic dirges as are accustomed to be heard at funerals").[24] That definition resembles one that Cicero gave in *De legibus*:[25]

> Etiam cantus ad tibicinem prosequatur, cui nomen neniae, quo uocabulo etiam apud Graecos cantus lugubres nominantur. Est autem nenia funebris cantus.

> A song follows to the music of the flute. To this song the name *nenia* is given, a word which signifies a song of mourning in Greek also. Nenia, moreover, is a funeral dirge.

But Vanegas continues, "Nostro idiotismo dicitur 'endecha'" ("in our language it is called 'endecha' [lament]").

Vanegas is the grammarian who in 1537 first recorded the correct derivation of "endecha" from the Latin "indicia" or LL "indicta" > Indo. Eur. *inDEIC*, that is "cosas proclamadas, en este caso alabanzas fúnebres declamadas".[26] It is a most fitting comment on "nenia", which is literally a funeral dirge but which often means only gibberish or random babbling. The connection, as Vanegas explains, is that the excessive weeping and sorrow that frequently occurs over a dead loved one is ill-advised because it suggests despair about the well-being of the dead in the afterlife. He writes that such excess defies natural reason: "El lloro demasiado se funda mas en la opinion de los hombres, dedonde las *endechas* tuvieron origen, que en la razon natural."[27]

In the world of the play, however, there is more than linguistic right to have a character describe the chaotic hawking of the devil's agent by the word "nenia". His speech was proleptic; it is as if he is singing in advance a dirge for young Aegio, as the young protagonist continues toward death, first of will, and then

---

24 Nodes, *Parables* (see above, n. 17), 244.

25 Cicero, *De leg.* 2,62,4.

26 *Etimologias de Chile*: http://etimologias.dechile.net/?endecha.

27 Alejo Venegas, *Agonía del tránsito de la muerte con los avisos y consuelos que cerca della son provechosos* (Toledo, 1537), punto sexto, cap. 5. Vanegas also included "endecha" in a glossary appended to the third version of his *Agonia* (1543). His etymology stressed the derivation of the plural "endechas" from the Latin "indicia", displays: "*Endechas* quiere dezir 'muestras de amor,' derivase de *indicia*, en el plural." Vanegas offered another etymology and suggested that it was derived from the Latin, "inde iaces, '-chas' por *iaces*, 'como si la endechera hablasse con el difuncto, diziendole, 'dime, como ende iazes.'" Vanegas's first etymology of "endecha", however, from the Latin "indicia" or "indicta", became and remains the accepted etymology. The *Diccionario de la lengua española* published by the Real Academia Espanola derives "endecha" from Latin "indicta 'anunciada'", just as Vanegas did in 1537.

of deed. Vanegas's inclusion of a linguistic reflection on the Spanish "endecha" thus vividly reinforces that precise etymology of "nenia". The audience sees that it wasn't long before Aegio was referred to as being struck by the brigands while already doomed to death. That was also a place where Vanegas's introduction of words from Spanish advanced readers' understanding of the plot's meanings on two levels effectively merged in "nenia": the one aimed at entrapping and harming Aegio physically, the other sounding the spiritual demise that he had brought on himself.

As a final example, we present a line spoken by the pedagogue, Eubulus, in his peroration where he explains the symbolism of the play's characters and details. When Eubulus explains the symbolism of the two coins given by the Samaritan to the innkeeper as representing the two covenants or testaments, that of Moses and of the Gospel, Vanegas first explains the Latin used in the play ("legis Moseae et euangelae") on grammatical terms as comprising two shortened adjectives with "legis", that is, "Moseae" for "Mosaicae" and "euangelae" for "euangelicae". Then Vanegas explains the basic noun form "euangelium" as the good news itself ("bonum et laetum nuntium"). Vanegas could have finished a serviceable comment there, but he found another opportunity to introduce a related definition. The word as used in the play, referring to the Good News itself, he writes, should not be confused with the word "evangelia", meaning the expression of satisfaction and good feeling that comes from hearing a pleasant report. Vanegas points to Cicero's use of "evangelia" according to that latter sense twice in a letter to Atticus, in reference to news of the acquittal of Valerius Messala:[28]

> *Euangelia* vero in plurali pro 'mercede' et 'praemio' iucundi allati nuncii in epistola ad Atticum bis usurpauit Cicero. Secundum quam significationem idem erit 'euangelium,' quod vulgo dicimus 'albricias.' In prima vero acceptione significat (vt diximus) ipsum laetum et iucundum nuntium.

> Cicero in the *Letters to Atticus* twice used 'evangelia' in the plural for the reward or prize of a good message that had been brought. And according to this meaning, 'evangelium' will mean the same as we say in Spanish *albricias* (glad tidings). But in the first reception it means (as we have said) the happy and pleasing message itself.

To help readers understand the difference Vanegas added that the word in that second sense will mean that same as the when the Spanish say "albricias", as

---

28 Nodes, *Parables* (see above, n. 17), 348.

one might say "bravo!", or as a synonym for "regalo!" ("what a treat!"). Vanegas mistook Cicero's feminine singular Greek form "euangelia" as the plural of "euangelium", but his aim was to assure readers that in the play the reference is to the good news of the Gospel itself. It is also noteworthy that "albrícias" is derived not from Latin but from Arabic albúśra > ár. clás. bušrà. At key moments, Vanegas's study, teaching and grounding in classical Latin, thus reaches out beyond Latin. Here, "albrícias" completes the play's movement first from the ominous "endechas" of the devil's agent, then to the spiritually dead Aegio described as "Moro muerto", and finally to the good news of the Samaritan's life-restoring gifts. Vanegas's addition of Spanish words and proverbs at precise and vital moments in the unfolding of the theological plot thus operate not only on the linguistic level but contribute to the understanding of the play's fundamental message, and all in a modern context. Toward the end of his life, Vanegas published additional writings in Spanish and continued to defend even more directly Spanish as a valid literary language. The later publications, mainly in the form of prologues, *aprobaciones*, and *censuras* to the writings of others, are written in Spanish. As this study has intended to show, however, even in his most learned Latin commentary on a Latin play, Vanegas made efforts to relate the vernacular idiom to Latin.

There is irony in that Vanegas's integration both of medieval Latin and his desire to promote *castellano*, a 'modern' language, has analogues in Cicero and Erasmus. Cicero began his *De finibus* by reprehending those of his fellow Romans who expressed contempt for their own Latin language and, as he describes the seriousness of the matter, even refused to take a book seriously unless it was in Greek. If one were to judge by the professed standards of Renaissance humanism, Cicero's defense of Latin was so great a success that in 1529 Erasmus in the *Ciceronianus* felt the need to reprehend his colleagues who expressed contempt for any style other than that modeled on Cicero. For the most part, the Ciceronian Latin so desired by the humanists included a desire to imitate Cicero's period-sentence structure but mainly "came down to no more than limiting onself to the vocabulary of the extant works of Cicero," as H. C. Gotoff observed, noting also that "Erasmus was too good a Latinist to ignore the stylistic failure of the doctrinaire Ciceronians, too interested in communicating to restrict his style in so slavish and perfunctory a manner."[29] It is right to pay tribute to Erasmus for his humorous critique of so limiting a view of Latin through his character Nosopon (playing on πρόσωπον, 'character'), who "for seven whole years touched nothing but Ciceronian books," in

---

29   H. C. Gotoff, "Cicero vs. Ciceronianism in the Ciceronianus," *Illinois Classical Studies* 5 (1980), 163–73, there 163.

order that he might eliminate from his own vocabulary every un-Ciceronian phrase. Erasmus, on the other hand, defended the expansion, rather the enrichment, of Latin by transcending Ciceronian limits, principally to include the language of Christian writers and the Bible.

Thus, the relation of Vanegas's Neo-Latin to its environment continued to develop. Hardly remaining isolated, it moved backward and forward in linguistic time from its classical core. The panels on *Neo-Latin Methodologies* in the Albacete congress set out to explore the nature of Neo-Latin, asking the important questions: What was the linguistic standard for Neo-latin? How did Neo-Latin evolve? The papers have offered case studies of Latin writings whose vocabulary and composition flowed from various tributaries into the classical mainstream. The evidence points to a broad linguistic field in which Neo-Latin, despite having a distinct classical foundation, is shown to be heir to all the ages and the beneficiary of that richness.

Baylor University, Waco, Texas

CHAPTER 32

La *quaestio An terra moveatur an quiescat* di Giovanni Regiomontano

Pietro Daniel Omodeo e Alberto Bardi

Abstract

The mathematician Johannes Schöner (1477–1547) published a brief disputation, or *quaestio disputata*, on the motion of the Earth, entitled *An terra moveatur an quiescat*, as part of his *Opusculum Geographicum* in Nuremberg in 1533 and ascribed the text to the renowned astronomer Regiomontanus (Johannes Müller von Königsberg, 1436–76). Although it rejected terrestrial motion, this disputation is a precious document for the history of science, as it reveals the mental attitudes and scientific interests of a network of scholars who played a crucial role in the advancement of early-modern astronomy. The publication of Regiomontanus's disputation in the first period of the printing press is evidence of the emergence of debates on the motion of the Earth in the years in which Copernicus' ideas had just began to circulate. This disputation suggests that the topic of the Earth's motion was disputable, and thus the immobility of the Earth according to the dominant cosmology of the time was not understood in dogmatic terms. We here provide the first translation of this text alongside a commentary on its content, structure and historical context.

Keywords

Johannes Regiomontanus – Johannes Schöner – *Opusculum Geographicum* (1533) – Neo-Latin science – motion of the earth

L'*An terra moveatur an quiescat* è una curiosa trattazione rinascimentale del problema del moto terrestre,[1] attribuita all'illustre astronomo matematico

---

[1] Desideriamo ringraziare le istituzioni che hanno reso questo lavoro possibile: il contesto ERC *EarlyModernCosmology* finanziato dal programma di ricerca e innovazione Horizon 2020 dell'Unione Europea (GA n. 725883), la Polonsky Academy del Van Leer Institute di Gerusalemme e la Dibner Library of the History and Science and Technology, Washington DC.

© KONINKLIJKE BRILL NV, LEIDEN, 2020 | DOI:10.1163/9789004427105_033

LA *QUAESTIO AN TERRA MOVEATUR AN QUIESCAT* DI REGIOMONTANO   429

tedesco Giovanni Regiomontano (Johannes Müller da Königsberg, 1436–76) dai suoi successori.[2] Il matematico Giovanni Schöner (1477–1547) la pubblicò nel 1533 nella città di Norimberga, dove era attivo, quale secondo capitolo di un suo *Opusculum geographicum*.[3] Agli occhi di Schöner la discussione dell'immobilità della terra, assieme a quella della sua sfericità e a nozioni base di geografia astronomica, era propedeutica per una trattazione specifica delle regioni del globo terrestre, con le loro denominazioni e coordinate geografiche, a cui è dedicata la seconda parte dell'*Opusculum*. Sin dal 1514 le ipotesi geocinetiche ed eliocentriche di Niccolò Copernico avevano cominciato a diffondersi a partire dai circoli universitari di Cracovia, ma l'opera maggiore dell'astronomo, il *De revolutionibus orbium coelestium*, che avrebbe rivoluzionato la teoria planetaria, era ancora incompleta.[4] Sarebbe apparsa nella stessa Norimberga dieci anni dopo la stampa dell'*Opusculum* grazie a Giorgio Gioacchino Retico (1514–74), giovane professore di matematica di Wittenberg, il quale era andato a conoscere Copernico in Varmia proprio su suggerimento di Schöner e aveva in seguito procurato il manoscritto del *De revolutionibus* allo stampatore Giovanni Petreio (ca. 1496–1550). In segno di riconoscenza per averlo così bene indirizzato, Retico aveva dedicato a Schöner la *Narratio prima* (Danzica, 1540), prima presentazione della teoria copernicana alla repubblica delle lettere.[5] Questo è il contesto scientifico e la temperie culturale nei quali si colloca la stampa del frammento sul moto terrestre attribuito a Regiomontano.[6] Siccome la pubblicazione si colloca ad un crocevia di idee

---

2 Discutiamo più ampiamente i contesti culturali del testo oggetto di studio in un saggio di prossima pubblicazione: Alberto Bardi e Pietro Daniel Omodeo, "The Disputational Culture of Renaissance Astronomy: Johannes Regiomontanus's *An terra moveatur an quiescat*," in *Early Modern Disputations and Dissertations in an Interdisciplinary and European Context*, ed. Robert Seidel (Leiden: Brill, in press).

3 Il titolo esteso è *Ioannis Schoneri Carolostadii Opusculum Geographicum ex diversorum libris ac cartis summa cura et diligentia collectum, accommodatum ad recenter elaboratum ab eodem globum descriptionis terrenae* ([Nuremberg]: [Petreius], 1533).

4 Marian Biskup, *Regesta copernicana* (*Calendar of Copernicus' Papers*) (Wrocław, 1973), 63–4, n. 91. Sulla prima recezione di Copernico si veda Pietro Daniel Omodeo, *Copernicus in the Cultural Debates of the Renaissance. Reception, Legacy, Transformation* (Boston-Leiden, 2014), 11–65.

5 Cf. Jarosław Włodarczyk, "Introduction," in *Georg Joachim Rheticus, Narratio prima or First Account of the Books* On the Revolutions *by Nicolaus Copernicus*, ed. Jarosław Włodarczyk (Warsaw, 2015), 9–70, in particolare 13.

6 Qui faremo riferimento all'edizione facsimile Johannes Regiomontanus, *Opera collectanea*, ed. Felix Schmeidler (Osnabrück, 1972), 37–9, ma abbiamo consultato anche una copia a stampa dell'*Opusculum* originale del 1533, conservata alla Dibner Library of the History and Science and Techonogy, Washington DC. Cf. Bern Dibner, "The Burndy Library in Mitosis. (Contemporary Collectors, XLIX)," *The Book Collector* 26 (1977), 12; Robert Westman,

astronomiche e dibattiti cosmologici di fondamentale importanza per la storia della scienza moderna, una sua riconsiderazione è auspicabile. Ci proponiamo di ricapitolarne i contenuti e pubblicare qui la prima traduzione in una lingua moderna. Indipendentemente dalla correttezza o meno dell'attribuzione a Regiomontano, l'ascrizione stessa e il contesto di ricezione sono sufficienti a farne un documento dell'accendersi di discussioni sul moto terrestre in contesto astronomico negli anni che precedono la pubblicazione del *De revolutionibus* copernicano. Inutile aggiungere che il rilievo delle posizioni espresse in una controversia non vanno misurate nei termini anacronistici di un'adesione alla tesi del moto terrestre o di un rigetto della stessa. Dal nostro punto di vista è la possibilità di documentare un dibattito o di aggiungere elementi di valutazione che merita l'attenzione dello storico della cultura scientifica, indipendentemente dai suoi esiti storici.

Il testo in questione ha la veste prettamente scolastica di una *quaestio disputata*.[7] Più precisamente, Regiomontano lo presenta quale *quaestio de motu locali*. La disputa, incentrata su un problema specifico quale, nel nostro caso, il moto terrestre, era tipico genere universitario. Infatti, la discussione degli argomenti *pro* e *contra* determinate tesi era esercizio fondamentale dell'educazione medievale e rinascimentale.[8] Nonostante Regiomontano sia stato spesso interpretato quale dotto umanista del cosiddetto 'Rinascimento matematico', estraneo alle forme 'barbare' della scolastica, testi come l'*An terra moveatur* attestano piuttosto la continuità delle varie espressioni della cultura scientifica quattrocentesca.[9] L'attenzione del Regiomontano per le forme e i contenuti dell'insegnamento universitario è altresì attestata da una sua famosa orazione sulla dignità degli studi matematici, da lui pronunciata a Padova nel 1464 in occasione di un corso di astronomia sferica basato su Alfragano. Petreio l'avrebbe pubblicata nel 1537 col titolo di *Oratio introductoria in omnes scientias mathematicas*, ponendola a premessa di due classici dell'astronomia islamica, i *Rudimenta astronomica* di Alfragano nella traduzione di Giovanni da

---

    Copernicus and the Astrologers: Dibner Library Lecture, December 12, 2013 (Washington, 2016), 44–8.

7 Brian Lawn, *The Rise and Decline of the Scholastic 'Quaestio disputata' with Special Emphasis on Its Use in the Teaching of Medicine and Science* (Leiden, 1993).

8 Anche a Vienna, l'università a cui Regiomontano fu maggiormente legato. Si veda Michael H. Shank, "Scientific tradition in Fifteenth-Century Vienna," in *Tradition, Transmission, Transformation: Proceedings of Two Conferences on Pre-Modern Science Held at the University of Oklahoma*, ed. F. Jamil Ragep e Sally P. Ragep (Leiden, 1996), 117–20.

9 L'immagine di Regiomontano umanista matematico è stata magnificata da Paul Lawrence Rose, *The Italian Renaissance of Mathematics: Studies on Humanists and Mathematicians from Petrarch to Galileo* (Genève, 1975), 90–117.

Siviglia e il *De motu stellarum* di Albategno nella versione di Platone da Tivoli.[10] Schöner, responsabile della revisione ed edizione di tali opere, utilizzò come base testuale un codice di Regiomontano.[11]

Non è mancato chi mettesse in dubbio addirittura l'attribuzione della disputa a Regiomontano. L'autore della più significativa prosopografia dello scienziato, Ernst Zinner, la considerò spuria ritenendo che Schöner fosse caduto in errore oppure avesse voluto ammantare l'argomento del prestigio della maggiore autorità scientifica della generazione precedente.[12] Tali dubbi o sospetti paiono però eccessivi sotto vari punti di vista. Innanzitutto la confutazione del moto terrestre non era controversa negli anni Trenta del Cinquecento e dunque non richiedeva il patrocinio di una *auctoritas* moderna potendo già contare su quelle classiche, *in primis* Tolomeo e Aristotele. Inoltre Schöner godeva di una posizione privilegiata da cui asseverare l'opera e le idee di Regiomontano in quanto apparteneva ad una comunità scientifica che aveva beneficiato dell'insegnamento dei suoi allievi o collaboratori diretti, tra cui Bernard Walther (1430–1504). In considerazione del contesto culturale di Norimberga e della familiarità degli scienziati tedeschi con l'opera di Regiomontano, ci pare altamente implausibile che un'indebita attribuzione potesse passare per buona senza rimostranze. La nostra valutazione non vuole certo sostituire la filologia d'autore ma integrarla in prospettiva storico-culturale. Non essendo stato trovato un testo equivalente negli autografi di Regiomontano, resta un margine di dubbio se il testo stampato da Schöner sia una copia di una stesura ad opera della mano del nostro oppure il frutto di appunti presi da un socio o un allievo dell'astronomo. Nonostante questo margine di incertezza, noi faremo qui riferimento alla breve disputa sul moto terrestre come testo non spurio di Regiomontano non solo perché riteniamo l'attribuzione plausibile fino a prova contraria, ma anche perché siamo persuasi che il suo valore storico-culturale, contestuale ai dibattiti del Cinquecento, non sia inficiato da un'eventuale quanto improbabile errata attribuzione da parte di Schöner.

La biblioteca e le carte del Regiomontano erano preservate in larga parte a Norimberga, sede da lui prescelta negli anni Settanta del Quattrocento per un progetto editoriale volto a restituire testi fondamentali della tradizione scientifica antica e medievale. La lista dei titoli da lui previsti è nota

---

10   Una discussione dell'orazione e della sua recezione potrà essere trovata nel saggio di prossima pubblicazione Pietro Daniel Omodeo, "Johannes Regiomontanus and Erasmus Reinhold on the History of Astronomy: Two Concepts of Renaissance," in *Translations and Their Consequences, 8th–16th Centuries*, ed. Sonja Brentjes (Berlin, in stampa).

11   Codice *Nurembergensis Cent.* VI 21. Cf. Ernst Zinner, *Regiomontanus: His Life and Work* (Amsterdam, 1990), 216.

12   Zinner, *Regiomontanus* (vedi sopra, n. 11), 203.

grazie ad un documento a stampa ("Haec opera fient in oppido Nuremberga Germania ductu Ioannis de Monteregio").[13] Il progetto editoriale, interrotto dalla morte prematura dell'iniziatore, prevedeva la pubblicazione di classici quali Euclide, Archimede, Teodosio e Tolomeo oltre ad *auctores moderni* quali Witelo, Giordano Nemorario e le *Theoricae novae planetarum* del maestro di Regiomontano, Giorgio Peuerbach (1423–61). Nella stessa serie sarebbero dovuti apparire anche i suoi lavori matematici. Petreio avrebbe ripreso in parte tale progetto dando alle stampe, tra l'altro, la trigonometria di Regiomontano (*De triangulis*, 1533) e l'*Ottica* di Witelo (*Perspectiva*, 1535).

La disputa che ci interessa si apre con la tesi controversa *Quod moveatur* ("che la terra si muova"). Regiomontano chiarisce subito che il moto in questione è quello locale e non uno degli altri tipi di moto contemplati dalla filosofia aristotelica, cioè quelli di alterazione, generazione e corruzione. Condizione per poter sostenere che la terra ruoti attorno al proprio asse, mentre i cieli sono in quiete, è che tutti i fenomeni celesti rimangano identici a quelli osservati e spiegati dall'astronomia aristotelico-tolemaica: "Omnia salvari possunt, quae in astris apparent" è presupposto imprescindibile.[14] Regiomontano riporta che "l'autore della *Sfera*" rigetta su questa base la dottrina del moto terrestre, con probabile riferimento a Giovanni di Sacrobosco e al suo testo standard per l'insegnamento dell'astronomia sferica medievale.[15] Egli non pare distinguere qui moto diurno e annuo, nonostante Tolomeo fosse stato attento a separare la confutazione del moto di rotazione da quella relativa al dislocamento della terra dal centro cosmologico.[16] Nel primo libro dell'*Almagesto* egli aveva dovuto fare i conti con la teoria del 'Copernico dell'antichità', Aristarco di Samo. Regiomontano non si confronta invece con una teoria particolarmente raffinata del moto terrestre. Si limita a riportare che i suoi antichi sostenitori basavano su di un'analogia grossolana tra la terra e la carne allo spiedo

---

13   Michela Malpangotto, *Regiomontano e il rinnovamento del sapere matematico e astronomico nel Quattrocento* (Bari, 2008), 211–7.

14   È il presupposto metodologico al centro della famosa trattazione di Pierre Duhem, *Sōzein ta phainomena: essai sur la notion de théorie physique de Platon a Galilée* (Paris, 1908). Si veda anche Peter Barker e Bernard R. Goldstein, "Realism and Instrumentalism in Sixteenth Century Astronomy: A Reappraisal," *Perspectives on Science* 6.3 (1998), 232–58.

15   Si veda il classico Lynn Thorndike, *The Sphere of Sacrobosco and Its Commentators* (Chicago, 1949). Si veda anche Matteo Valleriani, "The Tracts of the Sphere: Knowledge Restructured over a Network," in *The Structures of Practical Knowledge*, ed. Matteo Valleriani (Cham, 2017), 421–74.

16   Cf. Pietro Daniel Omodeo e Irina Tupikova, "Cosmology and Epistemology: A Comparison between Aristotle's and Ptolemy's Approaches to Geocentrism," in *Spatial Thinking and External Representation: Towards a Historical Epistemology of Space*, ed. Matthias Schemmel (Berlin, 2016), 131–58.

LA *QUAESTIO AN TERRA MOVEATUR AN QUIESCAT* DI REGIOMONTANO   433

l'argomento secondo il quale, come il fuoco non è mosso dal bisogno dell'arrosto, così non è il sole, bensì la terra a doversi muovere spinta dal desiderio del calore dell'astro diurno.

Una volta introdotta la "nota quaestio" Regiomontano sviluppa la sua trattazione attorno a due tesi, o *conclusiones*, una relativa al moto della terra nella sua interezza e una relativa al moto delle sue parti.[17] La rotazione da occidente a oriente è rigettata in base ad un noto argomento tolemaico, tratto dal primo libro dell'*Almagesto*, secondo cui la rapidità del moto dovrebbe produrre un forte vento e lasciarsi indietro tutto ciò che si trovi in aria. Se la terra ruotasse, gli uccelli che desiderassero volare verso oriente incontrerebbero la tenace resistenza dell'aria agitata in direzione contraria. Nubi e volatili dovrebbero scorrere continuamente verso occidente. Inoltre, sostiene Regiomontano sulla base di un classico argomento contro il moto terrestre, il moto verticale risulterebbe impossibile. Se per esempio si gettasse un oggetto in alto, perpendicolarmente al terreno, non potrebbe ricadere nel punto di partenza a causa dello slittamento del suolo.

Il moto della terra quale totalità è dunque bandito. Lo stesso non può dirsi delle parti, le quali, come si afferma nella *conclusio secunda*, sono in continuo movimento. Regiomontano riprende la dottrina medievale dei 'piccoli moti della terra' descritta da Pierre Duhem nei suoi classici studi su Leonardo da Vinci.[18] Essa fa riferimento a processi geologici di ridistribuzione della massa terrestre dovuta all'essiccamento della sua superficie e fenomeni di erosione ad opera delle acque. La necessità continua di ristabilire il centro di gravità dell'elemento terrestre fa sì che le parti scorrano senza posa al fine di garantire l'immobilità del tutto. Due corollari fanno seguito a questa tesi. Il primo afferma che il centro della terra non è sempre occupato dalla stessa parte ma è attraversato da parti che si susseguono le une alle altre. Ne consegue, nel secondo corollario, che la materia viene continuamente trasportata dall'alto al basso e viceversa. Regiomontano passa quindi dal moto astronomico della terra, da lui rigettato con decisione, alla discussione, e accettazione, di una sorta di 'moto convettivo' interno all'elemento terrestre. Prova ne siano le montagne e le rocce, erose dalla pioggia e dalle intemperie o riarse e compattate dai raggi del sole. Le radici degli alberi che restano scoperte sarebbero ulteriore attestazione dello sgretolarsi dei terreni.

---

17   La *quaestio* è nota soprattutto grazie alle dispute di autori medievali come Buridano e Oresme, ampiamente discussi da Marshall Clagett, *The Science of Mechanics in the Middle Ages* (Madison, Wisconsin, 1959). Ma si veda anche Pierre Duhem, *Un précurseur français de Copernic: Nicole Oresme (1377)* (Paris, 1909).

18   Pierre Duhem, *Études sur Léonard de Vinci: ceux qu'il a lus et ceux qui l'ont lu* (Paris, 1984), vol. 2, 332–6, "Leonard de Vinci et les origines de la géologie".

La disputa si chiude, come prevede il genere, con un sommario delle conclusioni raggiunte, "sic patet [...]". Regiomontano ricapitola secondo quale accezione ("qualiter") la terra si debba dire immobile e secondo quale possa essere detta invece in movimento. Dal punto di vista astronomico essa è ferma. Non potrà quindi ruotare sui poli al posto della sfera celeste ("sicut Sphaera"). Dal punto di vista della teoria degli elementi si dovrà invece asserire che la terra, o meglio le sue parti, siano mosse dalla loro gravità così come gli altri elementi (acqua, aria e fuoco) il cui moto è più facilmente riscontrabile. Questi avrebbero più propensione ad essere agitati a causa della loro maggiore leggerezza.

Si nega infine, "a ragion veduta" ("ad rationem"), che il moto terrestre possa "salvare tutti i fenomeni" ("quod omnia possint salvari"). Regiomontano osserva che le congiunzioni e opposizioni dei pianeti, nonché i loro specifici moti, ne risulterebbero sovvertiti. L'obiezione è bizzarra perché la rotazione della terra al centro del cosmo non avrebbe alcuna conseguenza sulle cosiddette 'teorie dei pianeti'. Solo la rotazione attorno al sole poteva sollevare dubbi circa la possibilità di preservare la teoria planetaria sulla cui base possono essere calcolate e previste congiunzioni, opposizioni e moti dei pianeti. Tolomeo aveva considerato il sovvertimento di tali aspetti una conseguenza dell'eccentricità della terra, ossia della possibilità di un suo spostamento dal centro del cosmo. Sorge quindi la domanda: che la conclusione eccentrica della disputa di Regiomontano segnali un'incipiente riflessione sulla possibilità (ovvero impossibilità) di attribuire alla terra anche il moto annuo?

Regiomontano refuta il moto locale della terra anche nell'*Epytoma in Almagestum Ptolemaei* (postuma, 1496), che rappresenta il maggior contributo di Regiomontano all'astronomia matematica latina. La *conclusio quinta* del primo libro è intitolata *Quod terra localem motum non habeat declarare*. Essa si limita a considerazioni relative alla rotazione assiale:[19]

> Ex superioribus constat terrae non accidere motum rectum. Sic enim medium mundi relinquere cogeretur, quod ante hac prohibuimus. Oporteret denique terram velocissime moveri mole sua id agente, unde reliqua corpora minus gravia terre adiacentia in aere relinquerentur si omnia gravia ad unum niterentur terminum, quod nusquam apparet. Terra demum circularem non habet motum. Si enim circa axem mundi moveretur ab occidente ad orientem, omnia que in aere moverentur semper versus occidentem moveri viderentur. Non enim possent consequi motum terrae. Cuius contrarium in nubibus motis atque avibus sepenumero experimur.

---

19   Giovanni Regiomontano e Giorgio Peuerbach, *Epytoma in Almagestum Ptolomei* (Venetiis, 1496), fol. a6v.

LA *QUAESTIO AN TERRA MOVEATUR AN QUIESCAT* DI REGIOMONTANO   435

> Idem quoque accideret: si aerem una cum terra hoc pacto moveri putaveris. Terra postremo circa alium quempiam axem non movetur. Sic enim altitudo poli nobis in terra quiescentibus varia haberetur. Quod cum nemini appareat, terram hac lege moveri non posse constat.

La discussione del solo moto terrestre di rotazione assiale si colloca evidentemente in un clima filosofico e scientifico precopernicano. Vi è comunque un capitolo iniziale dell'*Epytoma*, la *conclusio tertia*, dedicato alla dimostrazione della centralità della terra ("Terram in medio mundi sitam esse"). Esso esclude sin dall'inizio la possibilità che la terra possa mai occupare una posizione eccentrica rispetto al centro cosmologico e quindi, *a fortiori*, che possa ruotare attorno ad un centro differente da quello occupato dalla terra stessa.[20]

La coda della disputa sul moto terrestre inserisce la discussione all'interno di una cornice astronomica più ampia. Dopo aver trattato della sfericità e dell'immobilità della terra, si legge, occorre passare all'asse del mondo, ai vari circoli della sfera celeste e alla loro proiezione sul globo terrestre. Che la disputa fosse dunque il tassello di un mosaico più vasto? Di un'introduzione generale all'astronomia sferica? Può darsi, ma è più probabile che la conclusione sia un'intromissione di Schöner volta a incastonare il prezioso testo del 'maestro' nel suo *Opusculum geographicum*. Il capitolo primo, precedente l'*An terra moveatur*, tratta infatti della forma sferica del globo terrestre mentre le tematiche anticipate nella conclusione della disputa, asse terrestre e circoli celesti, vengono affrontate nei capitoli seguenti, tre e quattro.

Anche se la disputa di Regiomontano impallidisce alla luce degli sviluppi teorici del Cinquecento e la profondità dell'argomentazione non pare sufficiente per far fronte all'armamentario che Copernico avrebbe approntato, nondimeno essa costituisce un non trascurabile documento della cultura scientifica di quegli anni. Occorrerà ricordare che la funzione della disputa medievale non era tanto quella di riaffermare verità incontrovertibili quanto quella di soppesarle e sottoporle ad un rinnovato vaglio. Come ha sottolineato la storica dell'università parigina Olga Weijers, "la risposta finale data da un maestro di filosofia […] alle questioni disputate non era necessariamente vista quale la soluzione definitiva del problema. Costoro [sc. maestri e dottori] fanno spesso mostra di una certa modestia e sono pronti a rivedere la loro opinione." Inoltre "gli argomenti addotti a favore della posizione contraria, quella da refutare, venivano rigettati, certo, ma non venivano disprezzati o considerati privi di valore. Al contrario, essi contribuivano alla discussione, rivelando i vari aspetti del

---

20   Ibid., fol. a5v–a6r.

problema e aiutavano a mostrare la non validità della risposta contraria."[21] Da questo punto di vista la disputa di Regiomontano contro il moto terrestre e la considerazione da parte dei suoi lettori rinascimentali non vanno interpretate nei termini di una chiusura dogmatica. Attestano piuttosto che il moto terrestre era tema 'disputabile' e fu anche di fatto 'disputato' nel tardo Quattrocento e nel primo Cinquecento, all'alba dell'astro nascente di Copernico.

Appedice: Traduzione

Disputa di Giovanni Regiomontano se la terra si muova o stia ferma.
Capitolo 11

Si può sostenere che la terra si muove perché tutti i fenomeni legati agli astri possono essere salvati attraverso il moto circolare della terra da Occidente a Oriente. Di conseguenza, se diciamo che la terra viene mossa e il cielo sta fermo, non vi è nulla di incongruo. Al contrario pensa l'autore della *Sphaera*.[22] Una nota questione [*nota quaestio*] verte sul moto locale e non sul moto di alterazione (ossia di generazione o di corruzione), precisamente se la terra abbia un moto locale [*localiter moveatur*]. Già alcuni tra gli antichi ritenevano che il cielo stesse fermo e la terra si muovesse in circolo sui suoi poli, compiendo in un giorno una rotazione [*revolutio*] da Occidente verso Oriente. Così ci si immaginava che la terra fosse come la carne arrostita nello spiedo e il sole come il fuoco che arrostisce. Sostenevano, infatti, che, come il fuoco può fare a meno dell'arrosto, al contrario, non è il sole ad aver bisogno della terra, ma piuttosto la terra del sole.

Prima tesi. La terra non ha un moto circolare da Occidente verso Oriente circa i suoi poli né un moto giornaliero sul proprio centro, come pensavano costoro.[23] Ciò è abbastanza evidente, perché sarebbe più difficile andare verso Occidente che verso Oriente, cosa che è contro l'esperienza. Ci si aspetterebbe che anche l'aria vicino alla terra si muovesse in modo tale da essere di ostacolo a chi cammina. Persino gli uccelli non potrebbero volare bene verso Oriente [*contra orientem*] a causa dell'aria che li incalzerebbe e solleverebbe le loro penne. Infatti [non] vediamo gli uccelli volare meglio contro vento [*contra*

---

21   Olga Weijers, *A Scholar's Paradise: Teaching and Debating in Medieval Paris* (Turnhout, 2015), 122 (traduzione propria).

22   Probabile riferimento all'opera dell'astronomo parigino del secolo XIII Giovanni Sacrobosco, oppure all'astronomo islamico del secolo IX Al-Farghani, noto in Occidente come *Alfraganus*.

23   Costoro, "isti" nell'originale, si riferisce ai sostenitori della tesi aristotelico-tolemaica dell'immobilità terrestre.

LA *QUAESTIO AN TERRA MOVEATUR AN QUIESCAT* DI REGIOMONTANO

ventum] che seguendo il vento [*cum vento*].[24] Allo stesso modo ciò che viene gettato verso l'alto non ritornerebbe al punto di partenza e, per la stessa ragione, vedremmo le costruzioni rompersi a causa di un impeto molto violento. Tuttavia è ancora più evidente che la terra non si muove [*non moveatur*] di moto giornaliero per il fatto che gli uccelli si vedono muoversi in aria verso Oriente [*versus orientem*], e similmente fanno le nubi, cosa che non accadrebbe mai se la terra si muovesse in modo tale da dover essere mossa più velocemente tanto da superare essa stessa con il suo movimento il movimento di tutti gli esseri dell'aria, e quindi si vedrebbero gli uccelli e tutte le nubi muoversi verso Occidente [*versus occidentem*].

Seconda tesi. È evidente che qualsiasi parte della terra si muove di continuo localmente. Infatti, come di continuo la parte arida della terra a causa dei raggi solari si scalda, si consuma, si leviga, così molte piccole parti della terra e anche dell'acqua vengono portate dalla parte arida attraverso i fiumi verso il mare aperto. Da ciò deriva che la parte della terra coperta dall'acqua, che arriva anche a condensarsi e solidificarsi per la freddezza dell'acqua, è più pesante. Perciò conviene che essa si diriga in su verso l'altra tanto a lungo finché il centro di tutto il peso [*gravitas*] coincida col centro del mondo [*medium mundi*]. Di conseguenza qualsiasi parte della terra è mossa da un continuo moto locale.

Corollario. Non sempre la stessa parte della terra rimane nel centro del mondo, ma un'altra e così via.[25]

Corollario. Si constata che, dopo una lunga successione di tempo, presupposta la perpetuità del mondo, la parte della terra che per un certo tempo fu al centro del mondo viene in superficie e viceversa. Da ciò si ha la distruzione dei grandi monti e delle rocce, perché le parti della terra meno tenaci vengo erose dalle piogge, mentre rimangono le parti della terra più tenaci che cuociono continuamente per i raggi del sole e ricevono la durezza maggiore. In questo stesso modo, se qualcuno non vuole credere all'erosione della terra, guardi le radici degli alberi antichi nei boschi, e le vedrà già che escono fuori dalla terra, mentre invece un tempo dovevano risiedere dentro la terra. Così è chiaro in quale accezione intendiamo che la terra è immobile, cioè che non si muove in

---

24   Il testo stampato sarebbe: "Nam [non] melius volare videmus aves contra ventum quam cum vento." Riteniamo vi sia un refuso e che, per dare senso alla frase, serva introdurre la particella negativa.

25   La ristampa anastatica offerta a pp. 37–9 dell'*Opera collectanea* di Regiomontano a cura di Felix Schmeidler (vedi sopra, n. 6), riporta un testo latino corrotto da una macchia di inchiostro: "[a]lia et successive". Abbiamo conferma della nostra integrazione testuale grazie all'ispezione di una copia dell'*Opusculum Geographicum* in una copia del 1533, probabilmente l'esemplare di Schöner medesimo, custodita alla Dibner Library for the History of Science and Technology, Washington DC.

circolo rispetto al proprio centro, in quanto centro della sfera celeste.[26] In più essa non è in continua alterazione locale a causa del proprio peso, come invece gli altri elementi, i quali sono più leggeri e sono soggetti facilmente all'agitazione e al moto. Si deve ragionevolmente negare che tutte le apparenze[27] si possono salvare.[28] Infatti attraverso di esso (moto terrestre) non possono essere conservate né le congiunzioni né le opposizioni dei pianeti e le differenze dei loro moti. Inoltre non possiamo salvare il fatto che vediamo gli uccelli e le nubi di tanto in tanto muoversi verso Oriente [*versus orientem*], mentre si dovrebbero muovere sempre verso Occidente [*versus occidentem*].

Abbiamo così ammesso la rotondità e l'immobilità della terra, che insiste sul centro del mondo, cioè il centro di ciascun elemento e delle sfere celesti, senza ulteriori distinzioni di circoli. Ora è tempo di parlare dei circoli della sfera celeste, che si raffigurano tanto nel globo della terra quanto nel cielo, a partire dalla definizione dell'asse del mondo.

ERC *EarlyModernCosmology* (Horizon 2020, GA: 725883), Università Ca' Foscari di Venezia
Polonsky Academy for Advanced Study in the Humanities and Social Sciences
Van Leer Jerusalem Institute

---

26 *Sphaera* significa l'insieme delle sfere celesti.
27 Moti di corpi celesti e fenomeni legati ad essi visibili ad occhio nudo.
28 Giustificare con leggi che abbiano portata generali, siano cioè valide per tutti i corpi celesti considerati in un sistema cosmologico di riferimento.

CHAPTER 33

Los cuatro epigramas latinos de Alonso García en alabanza del *Libro de la melancholia* (Sevilla, 1585) de su discípulo Andrés Velásquez

Joaquín Pascual-Barea

Abstract

Edición, traducción y comentario de los epigramas de Alonso García al primer tratado sobre la melancolía impreso en Europa: el primero resume el contenido, y los restantes alaban al autor, su discípulo el doctor Andrés Velázquez (ca. 1535–1615), médico de la ciudad de Arcos de la Frontera y luego del Duque de Medina Sidonia en Sanlúcar de Barrameda. Analizamos las posibles fuentes literarias de estos dísticos elegíacos, su métrica y estilo, motivos y tópicos literarios, figuras, referencias geográficas y a médicos y dioses antiguos, y sus defectos. Comentamos el contenido de este libro dedicado al Duque de Arcos y basado en Hipócrates, Galeno y otros autores de la medicina antigua, medieval y moderna a los que también discute; el libro también trata sobre el cerebro, el estudio de las ciencias, los tipos de risa, la imaginación y el ingenio, y refuta la teoría del doctor Huarte de San Juan de que los frenéticos podían hablar latín o filosofar sin haber estudiado.

Keywords

Alonso García – Andrés Velázquez – Neo-Latin epigram – melancholy – reception of ancient medicine

1 El *Libro de la melancolía**

Los cuatro epigramas en latín sobre los que trataré a continuación aparecieron en 1585 en la primera monografía impresa en Europa sobre la melancolía.

---

* El presente trabajo se ha realizado en el seno del Proyecto de Investigación "*Galenus Latinus*: Recuperación del Patrimonio Escrito de la Medicina Europea II" (FFI2016-77240-P) y de la Red de Excelencia "Opera Medica: Recuperación del Patrimonio Textual Grecolatino de la Medicina Europea" (FFI2016-81769-REDT) del Ministerio de Ciencia, Innovación y Universidades.

© KONINKLIJKE BRILL NV, LEIDEN, 2020 | DOI:10.1163/9789004427105_034

A pesar de la intención divulgativa propia de un libro escrito en castellano, estamos ante un tratado erudito, como revelan sus abundantes citas de obras generalmente en latín con las referencias anotadas al margen. El autor describe las distintas partes y funciones del cerebro, y explica la melancolía como una enfermedad del cuerpo siguiendo la teoría de Hipócrates a través sobre todo de distintas traducciones latinas de los escritos de Galeno[1] y de los médicos musulmanes Avicena, Averroes y Al-Razi, así como de los comentarios de autores modernos como Marsilio Ficino, Jason Pratensis, François Valleriole, Jean François Fernel, Girolamo Fracastoro, Giovanni Manardo, Pero Váez, Pero de Peramato y Francisco Vallés. Con todo, en diversos lugares no solo busca el apoyo de esas y de otras autoridades, sino que también las discute y refuta. A lo largo de todo el libro mantiene un debate con el doctor Huarte de San Juan, quien diez años antes había tratado acerca de la sede del alma en su *Examen de ingenios para las sciencias*, admitiendo entre otras cosas que los frenéticos podían hablar latín o filosofar sin haber estudiado. Velásquez refuta esta teoría basándose tanto en obras científicas como en la Biblia, y sostiene que tales hechos sobrenaturales serían obra del demonio. El libro ha sido comentado hasta nuestros días en diversos estudios sobre la Historia de la Medicina,[2] y también sobre la literatura de los Siglos de Oro por la atención que Velásquez dedica al poder de la imaginación y la relación entre el ingenio y el temperamento melancólico,[3] entre ellos tres monografías sobre la melancolía publicadas en el presente siglo.[4]

Como rezan la portada y el *explicit*, el libro salió de la imprenta de Hernando o Fernando Díaz, quien entre 1568 y 1588 tuvo uno de los más famosos y activos talleres de impresión de Sevilla, hasta 1581 en la calle de la Sierpe (hoy Sierpes) y luego junto a San Antón.[5] Fue impreso "a costa de Alonso de Mata, mercader

---

1 Entre otros autores antiguos, también cita a Platón, Aristóteles, Areteo, Aecio, Alejandro de Trales y Pablo de Egina.

2 Véase Antonio Contreras Mas, "Libro de la melancholia by Andrés Velazquez (1585). Part 1. The intellectual origins of the book," *History of Psychiatry* 14–53 (2003), I, 25–40; "Part 2. Its context and importance," ibid., II, 179–93. Ismael del Olmo, "El lugar del alma en el debate médico de Huarte de San Juan y Andrés Velázquez," en *Historia Moderna: Tendencias y Proyecciones* (Mar del Plata, 2013), 187–95.

3 Véase Teresa Soufas, "Digressions on/of the Melancholy Mind in Lazarillo de Tormes and the Libro de la Melancholia," *Ometeca* 2 (1990), 19–133.

4 Roger Bartra, *Cultura y melancolía: Las enfermedades del alma en la España del Siglo de Oro* (Barcelona, 2001), 19–150, 200–9 y 230–3. Felice Gambin, *Azabache: Il dibattito sulla malinconia nella Spagna dei Secoli d'Oro* (Pisa, 2005; trad. española por Pilar Sánchez Otín, Madrid, 2008), 178–204 y 226–30. Belén Atienza, *El loco en el espejo: Locura y melancolía en la España de Lope de Vega* (Amsterdam, 2009), 107 y 115–6.

5 Véase Francisco Escudero y Perosso, *Tipografía Hispalense: Anales bibliográficos de la ciudad de Sevilla desde el establecimiento de la imprenta hasta fines del siglo XVIII* (Madrid, 1894), 28–9.

LOS CUATRO EPIGRAMAS LATINOS DE ALONSO GARCÍA EN ALABANZA   441

de libros", cuya presencia en Sevilla está documentada entre 1566 y 1594, año en que redactó testamento. Vivía en la plaza de San Francisco, y estaba casado en segundas nupcias con María de Medina, con quien tenía dos hijas pequeñas. Desde 1578 aparece vinculado al comercio de libros como editor y distribuidor en Sevilla y para América, y costeó al menos siete ediciones de diversas obras.[6]

2   Andrés Velásquez

Andrés Velásquez debió de nacer hacia 1535–40 en Arcos de la Frontera (Cádiz). Estudió en Osuna, donde se graduó de bachiller en febrero de 1554, y el 7 de octubre de 1555 probó haber oído un curso de Medicina. En octubre de 1557 aparece el licenciado Velázquez como padrino de bautismo de una niña en Arcos, y en torno a esos años es probable que estudiara en Alcalá de Henares, donde coincidiría con Huarte de San Juan. Estuvo casado con Ana de Vargas Rubiales, y fue padre al menos de dos hijos y de dos hijas, que emparentó con algunas de las más importantes familias de Arcos. Aquí bautizó a su hijo Juan en 1568, y ejerció la Medicina hasta 1608, teniendo desde 1571 el encargo público de atender a las prostitutas con un salario del municipio. Entretanto compuso su tratado en 1585, y en 1587 se permitió regalar un órgano al convento de San Agustín, uno de los indicios con que contamos de su desahogada situación económica. Tras la muerte en 1607 de su protector el Duque de Arcos, Rodrigo Ponce de León, a quien había dedicado su libro, pasó en 1608 a Sanlúcar de Barrameda, donde hasta su muerte en la segunda mitad de 1615 fue médico del Duque de Medina Sidonia, Alonso Pérez de Guzmán, quien había sido en 1588 el comandante de la fallida Armada Invencible del rey Felipe II contra Inglaterra.[7]

3   Los epigramas de Alonso García

Del autor de estos epigramas solo sabemos lo que cabe deducir de sus versos acerca de su capacidad versificadora en latín, así como de uno de sus títulos en que llama a Velásquez "su queridísimo discípulo". No consta sin embargo que fuera doctor,[8] ni dónde o en qué disciplina fue maestro de Velásquez, aunque a

---

6 Véase María del Carmen Álvarez Márquez, *La impresión y el comercio de libros en la Sevilla del quinientos* (Sevilla, 2007), 92–4 y 180–9.

7 Véase Roger Bartra, *El siglo de oro de la melancolía: Textos españoles y novohispanos sobre las enfermedades del alma* (México, 1998), 19–22, 33, 59–61, 109, 162–3.

8 Lo llaman doctor Anastasio Chinchilla, *Anales históricos de la Medicina en general y biográfico-bibliográfico de la española en particular* (Valencia, 1845), vol. 2, 147, quien copia

juzgar por estos poemas es probable que le hubiera enseñado la lengua latina en Arcos.

Al tiempo que añadían nuevos errores, algunos de los editores modernos de estos epigramas han corregido muchas de las erratas de la *editio princeps*, si bien todos ellos han mantenido la lectura "edidiscit" en lugar de "edidicit" en el verso décimo del primer epigrama, "auri feris" en lugar de "auriferis" al comienzo del segundo, y "rudi" por "rude" al final del último. Aparte del texto del primer epigrama editado por Chinchilla en 1845, he tenido en cuenta estas cuatro ediciones de la obra:

- Andrés Velásquez, *Libro de la melancholia, en el qual se trata dela naturaleza desta enfermedad, assi llamada Melancholia, y de sus causas y simptomas. y si el rustico puede hablar Latin, o philosophar, estando phrenetico o maniaco, sin primero lo auer aprendido. Compuesto por el doctor Andres Velasquez Medico de la Ciudad de Arcos de la Frontera. Dirigido al excelentissimo señor Duque della e su señor* (Sevilla, 1585), 6r–7r. Presenta numerosas erratas debidas al descuido y desconocimiento del latín por parte del impresor o linotipista; otras formas que difieren de las de época clásica deben achacarse más bien al autor de los poemas.

- Andrés Velázquez, *Libro de la Melancholia. Libro de la Melancolía* (Madrid, 1996). Facsímil de la primera edición a partir del ejemplar de la Hispanic Society of America, con la transcripción del texto en un segundo volumen. Esta transcripción (pp. 20–22) resuelve las abreviaturas de nasal (aunque escribe "nanque") y de algunas enclíticas "-que"; sigue el uso de /v/ consonante y /u/ vocal salvo en "inuentis"; añade coma tras "docti"; escribe "fuis" en lugar de "suis" con *s longa*; "doçti" en vez de "docti" con /ct/ ligadas por arriba; centra los versos; separa el primer poema en tres partes iguales y omite el título del último epigrama.

- Edición de Germán Franco y revisión y traducción de los textos latinos de Francisco Barrenechea, en Roger Bartra, *El siglo de oro de la melancolía: Textos españoles y novohispanos sobre las enfermedades del alma* (México, 1998), 255–372. La edición anotada está precedida de un estudio introductorio de Barrenechea (229–53), e incluye la traducción de los cuatro epigramas en nota a pie de página (260–2). En la edición de los poemas actualizan la puntuación y – salvo "Phalernum" – la mayor parte de las grafías latinas (también "Garsiae" en "Garciae"); mantienen la mayúscula inicial de los

---

el primero de los epigramas añadiéndole seis erratas; Antonio Hernández Morejón, *Historia bibliográfica de la Medicina española* (Madrid, 1846; facs. New York – London, 1967), vol. 3, 332, quien cree que le enseñó Medicina en Arcos; Zacarías Benito González, "Estudios teórico-prácticos sobre las enfermedades mentales," *El siglo médico* 13 (1866), 164.

LOS CUATRO EPIGRAMAS LATINOS DE ALONSO GARCÍA EN ALABANZA   443

versos; no centran los títulos de los poemas, y corrigen oportunamente muchas de las erratas del original.[9]

– Andrés Velásquez, *Libro de la melancholia*, ed. Felice Gambin (Viareggio, 2001). Mantiene algunas erratas del original, como "Hexasthicon" en el título del segundo epigrama, y "Auri feris" y "phrigiam ve coluunt" en el primer y cuarto verso del tercer epigrama, además de la errata "graviter" en lugar de "gnaviter" que ya traía Chinchilla en el verso undécimo del primer epigrama.

He mantenido la distribución en líneas centradas de tamaño menguante de los títulos de los dos primeros epigramas, así como las grafías renacentistas "authorem" y "arenis" en vez de las clásicas "auctorem" y "harenis", y "Garsia" y "Velasquez" en lugar de la forma actual de los apellidos "García" y "Velázquez". Pero corrijo otras formas que tampoco eran raras en la época, como la grafía /i/ por /y/ de "phrigiā" por "Phrygiam" y de "Hypocrates" por "Hippocrates" junto a la simplificación de geminadas; la representación con la aspirada griega /ph/ en lugar de la consonante fricativa inicial de "Falernum"; el traslado del signo de aspiración en "Hexasthicon" por "Hexastichon", y la monoptongación del diptongo /ae/ en /e/ en "que" por "quae" en el verso 12 del primer epigrama. Empleo /v/ para la consonante y /u/ para la vocal, en lugar de /v/ en inicial de palabra y /u/ en interior. No distingo la /s/ longa de la /s/ normal. También he modificado la puntuación de algunos versos; he añadido un signo de exclamación detrás de "heu", y las comillas del penúltimo poema. He corregido la separación de palabras en "debili" por "de bili", "quae ve" por "quaeve", "phrigiā ve" por "Phrygiamve", "per docti" y "per docte" por "perdocti" y "perdocte", "Auri feris" por "Auriferis", "De sine" por "Desine", e "inaurē" por "in aurem". He resuelto las abreviaturas de las nasales /m/ y /n/ y de la enclítica "-que", y escribo "et" en lugar del signo &. He regularizado el uso de mayúscula ("Epigramma, Medici, pierides, helicone, hebrus, pactolus lydos, hermus, cares, phrigiā, phoebus, phalernum"), que figuraba en la inicial de todos los versos.

Los cuatro epigramas fueron traducidos en la referida edición anexa al tratado de Bartra. Sin embargo, en el primer poema está mal traducida la oración de relativo del primer pentámetro ("y que casualmente anhela conocer las cosas exactamente") y el último hexámetro ("esta obra espléndida lo explica diligentemente"). En el segundo epigrama, al no percibir que es preciso sobreentender una forma de imperativo plural como "venite" o "adeste", y sin tener en cuenta que es palabra pirriquia, traducen "cito" por 'invoco' como si fuera un

---

9 Así, "facnltates" por "facultates", "laedantua" por "laedantur", "ea que" por "ea quae", "per docti/e" por "perdocti/e", "Hexasthicon" por "Hexastichon", "Hypocrates debili quae ve" por "Hippocrates de bili quaeve", "phrigiā ve coluūt" por "Phrygiamve colunt", "inaurem" por "in aurem", "de sine" por "desine".

verbo, que al ser transitivo habría necesitado un objeto directo ("vos"), cuando se trata del adverbio 'cito' que encontramos habitualmente en la poesía latina. Tampoco está bien traducido el último verso ("para que digáis allá arriba que en nada hubiera podido ser superado"), que ciertamente es poco elegante y confuso en latín.[10] En el primer verso del tercer epigrama, al no corregir "auri feris" en "auriferis", resulta una traducción absurda con "arenis" como "con fieras arenas de oro". Tampoco es acertada en el último epigrama la traducción del primer pentámetro como "al autor ilustre por el renombre de este libro", ni la del último verso que omite "ubique" y no recoge la alusión al refrán del texto entre paréntesis al traducirlo "como todos saben". Por tanto, la traducción de los epigramas se nos antoja aún más necesaria que su edición.

Los cuatro epigramas se basan en una serie de tópicos y motivos habituales en los poemas laudatorios de libros: el primero, que debe leer la obra quien desee conocer los principales temas que trata, que son referidos en los cinco primeros dísticos; el segundo, que Velásquez ha explicado en español la doctrina de Hipócrates y de Galeno; el tercero, que con su lengua y estilo enriquece la lengua española sobre Medicina, y el último, que el libro se vende por sí solo sin necesidad de alabanza, a partir de un proverbio latino muy difundido en el siglo XVI con distintas formulaciones: "Vino vendibili suspensa hedera nihil opus est, Falerno frustra suspenditur hedera," que alude a que un buen producto no necesita publicidad para venderse.

Aunque todos los epigramas comparten un mismo tono laudatorio, no resultan monótonos debido a la variedad en el tratamiento literario, ya que están dirigidos el primero al lector interesado en el contenido del libro, el segundo a las Musas para que coronen al autor por su elegancia, el tercero al autor del libro por enriquecer la lengua española, y el cuarto a recoger supuestamente las palabras que el propio dios Apolo le dirige al poeta para que deje de alabar una obra que por su calidad no lo necesita.

Son escasas las expresiones clásicas, que el autor probablemente había conocido en muchos casos de forma indirecta. Así, en las *Geórgicas* de Virgilio encontramos la secuencia "corpora morbo" (*georg.* 4,252) en la misma sede métrica, y "auro turbidus Hermus" (*georg.* 3,137); pero la secuencia pudo haberla leído en algún texto sobre Medicina, y la expresión "Hermus turbidus auro" se encuentra tal cual en una glosa al verso virgiliano. Las secuencias que hallamos en Ovidio, como "verba Latina" (*trist.* 4,1,90) y "tempora fronde" (*fast.* 4,656) en la misma sede métrica, y "mihi nescio quis" (*epist.* 15,109), pueden encontrarse igualmente con una mayor coincidencia textual en poemas de otros

---

10   No es más acertada la traducción de este epigrama que hizo Francisco Romero Cubero para J. A. Delgado y Orellana, *Hidalguía*, 31 (1983), 401–20 (410).

autores más recientes. Lo mismo cabe decir del sintagma "auriferis harenis" y de la expresión "tollere ad astra" que ya aparecen en Silio (16,560 y 3,164), y de las expresiones "in aurem [...] dicere" de Horacio (*serm.* 1,9,9–10), y "devexit ad astra virum" de Partenio, presbítero de Constantinopla (*carm.* 1,11).

Mucho más numerosas son las concomitancias con otros poemas neolatinos, tanto anteriores como posteriores a 1585, sin que tampoco se trate normalmente de una imitación directa. Muchos de ellos son también epigramas laudatorios, lo que nos indica que su origen más probable se encuentra en ese tipo de literatura, en muchos casos compuesta para los preliminares de otros libros. Así, en el primer poema, las secuencias "noscere forte cupis" y "hoc opus evolvat" en la misma sede métrica se dirigen con frecuencia al lector de un libro; y en otro epigrama podemos encontrar "verba latina loqui" en la misma sede y dependiendo incluso de "didici". Del segundo epigrama, "lauri [...] ornetis tempora" figura en un epigrama de Giano Vitale; "sacro ex Helicone" y "nil potuisse magis" en la misma sede de sendos epigramas de los humanistas alemanes Conrad Celtis y Ulrich von Hutten; "clarus uterque suis" en la misma sede de varios epigramas laudatorios medievales y renacentistas. Del tercer epigrama, el comienzo presenta secuencias muy similares a las de otros epigramas medievales y renacentistas, como "aurifluis Pactolus ditat arenis" en un poema de Rodolfo Tortario, y con otros epítetos similares ("fulvis, auriferis") y referidas a otros ríos (Hermus, Tagus) en poemas de Janus Dousa y de otros autores renacentistas, además de Silio Itálico; el final "ingenioque tuo" figura igualmente en la misma sede en otros poemas laudatorios.

Alonso García se sirve de distintos recursos expresivos propios de la poesía latina, como la reiteración de "risus" y la interjección "heu" en el segundo dístico, la reiteración de "quae" en el tercer verso del segundo poema, las asonancias entre los dos hemistiquios presentes en casi la mitad de pentámetros, la invocación a las musas del segundo poema, el sobrepujamiento figurado sobre el que está construido el tercer poema, o la divertida prosopopeya y el proverbio del último. Por lo demás, confieren cierto carácter poético a los epigramas las alusiones a los dioses del panteón greco-romano relacionados con la poesía: Febo, las musas Piérides y el monte Helicón; las referencias a la legendaria riqueza de los ríos Hebro de Tracia, y Hermo y su tributario Pactolo en Asia Menor;[11] el empleo metonímico de "Falernum" por "vinum", los epítetos compuestos "auriferis" y el más raro "fluctifragis" que remonta a Lucrecio (1,305), y otros términos o sintagmas propios de la poesía como "lauri fronde, hedera, lepore" e incluso "laudibus".

---

11   Los tres ríos, junto a otros varios, son mencionados entre los lugares ricos en oro en un *Epitome* de la *Cornucopia* de Ravisio Textor (Lyon, 1593), 7–8.

Debido al carácter circunstancial de los epigramas, también abundan en ellos términos y expresiones poco poéticas que es fácil hallar sobre todo en tratados de Medicina, especialmente en el primero que describe el contenido del libro: "temperiem cerebri, inter humana membra, exacte noscere, exitiale malum, corpora morbo, facultates animi rectrices, phrenesis, docti medici, apta nimis," etc. Otras expresiones prosaicas que figuran en tratados medievales y renacentistas de carácter jurídico sobre todo son "rusticus an possit" y "si petat ipse". Son fórmulas propias del latín coloquial secuencias como "quae non edidicit, ambigerem quibus, efferrem laudibus", o "nomine conspicuum".

García conoce bien por tanto la lengua latina de su época, y es capaz de componer dignamente unos epigramas latinos para los preliminares de ese libro según la costumbre y el estilo de la literatura humanista. Se trata sin embargo de una poesía convencional y repleta de tópicos, con la que ni siquiera busca demostrar su familiaridad con los poetas clásicos de la Antigüedad como hacen los poetas humanistas más ambiciosos. Algunas expresiones resultan incluso poco elegantes, como el empleo de "illae" con un valor cercano al del artículo, el uso transitivo de "loqui" y la perífrasis comparativa "parata magis" en el primer epigrama; el último verso del segundo epigrama, donde en vez del pleonástico "magis" más bien habríamos esperado otra palabra yámbica y comenzando por vocal pero semánticamente equivalente a "addi" ("ser añadido"). Algunos versos suenan un tanto duros debido tanto a la sintaxis enrevesada y al léxico prosaico ya referidos, como a la torpe disposición de las palabras en algunos dísticos, y a ciertas secuencias cacofónicas como "hedera suspensa" en el último epigrama.[12]

Por lo que se refiere a la métrica, aunque el autor demuestra conocer los fundamentos de la versificación dactílica, no siempre construye sus versos con la elegancia y el ritmo propios de los mejores poetas neolatinos. En el hexámetro, las cinco secuencias de dáctilos y espondeos que más emplea son también las cinco más frecuentes en la *Eneida* de Virgilio, especialmente DDSS (4 versos) y DSDS, DSSS, SDSS y SSSS (2 versos), y solo esta última es más rara en Marcial y en los poetas elegíacos;[13] además trae en un verso las secuencias SSDS, DDSD y SDSD. Sin embargo, resultan poco elegantes los hexámetros segundo del segundo poema y primero del tercero al presentar un monosílabo largo seguido de palabra espondaica después de la cesura ("de bili" y "non tantum"), aunque el verso no quede cortado en dos partes iguales gracias a la estrecha relación

---

12   Sobre este concepto de homeotéleuton véase David R. Shackleton Bailey, *Homoeoteleuton in Latin Dactylic Verse* (Stuttgart, 1994), 1, 4–9 y 219–41.

13   Véase Jesús Luque Moreno, *El dístico elegíaco: Lecciones de métrica latina* (Madrid, 1994), 55.

semántica de ambos términos.[14] La cesura más frecuente es la pentemímeres, si bien en el primer hexámetro coincide con una elisión en una posición poco adecuada. Emplea además trihemímeres y heptemímeres en el primer verso del último epigrama; en el segundo hexámetro del primer y del cuarto epigrama únicamente figura la trihemímeres, y el segundo hexámetro del tercero es especialmente desafortunado al carecer de cesuras y presentar elisión en "seu Hermus".

En cuanto al pentámetro, las secuencias más frecuentes son SS (9) y DS (4), además de DD (1) y SD (1), mientras que Marcial relega la secuencia de dos espondeos a la última posición, y los elegíacos antiguos a la tercera. Además de los habituales finales bisilábicos, y de dos tetrasílabos que tampoco condenan los manuales de la época ("fluctifragis" y "conspicuum"), hallamos un trisílabo ("medici") que tampoco es excepcional en Marcial o en Ausonio.[15]

4 Texto y traducción de los cuatro epigramas

Alfonsi Garsiae epigramma,
omnia fere, quae in hoc
opere continentur,
complectens

Temperiem cerebri, humana inter membra tenentis
    culmen, qui exacte noscere forte cupit;
et risus, quae et risus causae, quid quoque bilis
    atra sit, heu multis exitiale malum!;
atque huic gignendo pariter quae corpora morbo   5
    apta nimis, multo sintque parata magis;
deinde facultates animi laedantur ut illae,
    rectrices docti quas vocitant medici;
rusticus an possit, rapuit quem insana phrenesis,
    quae non edidicit, verba Latina loqui,   10
hoc opus evolvat praeclarum gnaviter, illud
    namque ea quae cecini, si petat ipse, dabit.

---

14   Sobre cómo algunos poetas neolatinos evitan contravenir la Ley de Marx he tratado en "Algunas particularidades de prosodia y métrica latinas del Renacimiento," en *Estudios de Métrica Latina,* ed. Jesús Luque Moreno, Pedro Rafael Díaz y Díaz (Granada, 1998), vol. 2, 747–66 (en 759–62).

15   Ibid., 56 y 71–2. Pantaleón Bartelón, *De ratione quantitatis syllabariae liber* [...] (Lyon, 1578), 39v, advertía: "Heroicum clauditur pulchre vel dissyllaba uel trisyllaba dictione; durius autem tetrasyllaba aut pentasyllaba. Durissime vero monosyllaba, nisi enclitica sit."

Epigrama de Alonso García
que comprende casi todo
lo que contiene
esta obra

Quien desee conocer con exactitud el equilibrio del cerebro,
que ocupa la cumbre entre los miembros del hombre;
y qué es la risa, y cuáles las causas de la risa, también
la melancolía, ¡ay! mal funesto para muchos;
e igualmente qué cuerpos son muy propensos, y mucho
más dispuestos para producir esta enfermedad;
luego cómo se lesionan las facultades del alma
que los médicos cultos llaman rectoras;
si un paleto poseído por un loco frenesí puede
hablar en latín sin haberlo aprendido,
hojee con diligencia esta obra ilustre, pues ella
le dará lo que he contado, si él mismo lo busca.

Eiusdem Alfonsi Garsiae, in laudem
perdocti Andreae Velasquez,
discipuli sui amantissimi,
Hexastichon

Huc cito, Pierides, sacro ex Helicone, Velasquez
    ut lauri ornetis tempora fronde mei.
Nam quae atra Hippocrates de bili quaeve Galenus
    dixere, inventis clarus uterque suis,
Hispane explicuit tanto pariterque lepore,   5
    supra ut dicatis nil potuisse magis.

Hexástico del mismo Alonso García
en alabanza del doctísimo Andrés
Velásquez, su queridísimo
discípulo

Aquí rápido, Piérides, desde el sagrado Helicón, para que adornéis
con ramas de laurel las sienes de mi querido Velásquez.
Pues lo que dijeron sobre la melancolía Hipócrates
o Galeno, uno y otro ilustre por sus hallazgos,
lo ha explicado en español igualmente y con tanta elegancia,
que debéis decir que superarlo más no era posible.

LOS CUATRO EPIGRAMAS LATINOS DE ALONSO GARCÍA EN ALABANZA

Aliud eiusdem

Auriferis Hebrus non tantum ditat arenis
    quos cingit ripis undique fluctifragis,
nec Pactolus Lydos, seu Hermus turbidus auro
    despectos Cares, qui Phrygiamve colunt,
quantum tu medicos lingua, perdocte Velasquez,   5
    Hispanos ditas ingenioque tuo.

Otro del mismo

No enriquece tanto el Hebro con sus auríferas arenas
a quienes ciñe en sus riberas que rompen por doquier la corriente,
ni el Pactolo a los lidios, o el Hermo turbio por el oro
a los despreciables carios, o a quienes habitan Frigia,
cuanto tú, doctísimo Velásquez, enriqueces a los médicos
españoles con tu lengua y con tu ingenio.

Aliud eiusdem

Ambigerem quibus efferrem dum laudibus huius
    authorem libri nomine conspicuum,
nescio quis mihi (credo Phoebus) dixit in aurem:
    "Desine tu tantum tollere ad astra virum.
Indiget haud hedera suspensa namque Falernum   5
    vendibile (ut vulgo fertur ubique) rude."

Otro del mismo

Mientras dudaba con qué alabanzas ensalzaría
al autor de este libro, noble por su apellido,
no sé quién (creo que Febo) me dijo al oído:
"Deja tú de elevar a los astros a tan gran varón.
Pues el vino que se vende en bruto no necesita que le cuelgue
la hiedra, como se dice vulgarmente por doquier."

Universidad de Cádiz

CHAPTER 34

Amato Lusitano: El relato patográfico del morbo gálico

María Jesús Pérez Ibáñez

Abstract

En las *Centurias*, Amato Lusitano recoge su experiencia profesional. Una de las enfermedades que aparece retratada es la entonces conocida como morbo gálico. Estudiar cómo Amato Lusitano aborda esta enfermedad en las distintas *curationes*, a qué pacientes trata y con qué medicamentos y recomendaciones, permite adentrarse en su modo general de componer el relato patográfico. Además, dada la 'novedad' que en la medicina del siglo XVI supone la enfermedad, el comportamiento de Amato permite ver cómo se refleja en su obra la polémica contemporánea y su vinculación con las autoridades médicas o su preferencia por la *experientia* como fuente de autoridad.

Keywords

Amato Lusitano – *Curationum Medicinalium Centuriae* (1549–66) – Neo-Latin medical treatise – syphilis – *morbus Gallicus*

1 Amato Lusitano (1511–68)[1,2]

João Rodríges de Castelo Branco es el médico portugués de origen judío conocido por el pseudónimo de Amato Lusitano (Amatus Lusitanus). Formado

---

1 Trabajo realizado en el Proyecto de Investigación "Estudios de medicina práctica en el Renacimiento: Las *Centurias* de Amato Lusitano" (MINECO, Secretaría de Estado de Investigación, Desarrollo e Innovación FFI2017-82381-P) y en el marco del GIR *Speculum medicinae* (VA099G18).

2 Sobre la biografía puede verse: Maximiano Lemos, *Amato Lusitano, a sua vida e a sua obra* (Oporto 1907); Ricardo Jorge, *Amato Lusitano: comentos à sua vida, obra e época* (Lisboa 1908); Jose Lopes Dias, *Amato Lusitano, Doutor João Rodrigues de Castelo Branco; ensaio bio-bibliográfico* (Lisboa 1942); Harry Friedenwald, "Amatus Lusitanus," en *The Jews and Medicine* (Baltimore 1944), 332–381; Mirko Malavolti, *Medici marrani in Italia nel XVI e XVII secolo*

© KONINKLIJKE BRILL NV, LEIDEN, 2020 | DOI:10.1163/9789004427105_035

en la Universidad de Salamanca, desarrolla la mayor parte de su carrera profesional fuera de la Península Ibérica, Lisboa, Amberes, Ferrera, Ancona, Roma, Florencia, Venecia, Pesaro, Ragusa (Dubrovnik) y Salónica, donde fallece de la epidemia de peste que como médico estaba atendiendo. En su amplia experiencia como médico (*post ca.* 1530),[3] igual que muchos de sus contemporáneos, tuvo que tratar la enfermedad llamada entonces morbo gálico.[4] Asimismo registra, al modo de un trabajo de campo,[5] parte de su experiencia en las *Curationum medicinalium Centuriae septem*, obra cuya publicación por libros se dilata desde el inicio de la composición en 1549 a la publicación de la *Septima centuria* en 1566 (su colofón es de 1561).[6]

2 Las *Curationes* de morbo gálico

Esta enfermedad, contagiosa y con graves síntomas asociados a la transmisión sexual, generó abundante bibliografía y variadas disputas entre los médicos

---

(Roma 1968); Joshua O. Leibowitz, "L'activité scientifique d'Amatus Lusitanus," *Asclepio* 8 (1956), 289–90; Antonio M. Lopes Andrade, "As tribulações de Mestre João Rodrigues de Castelo Branco (Amato Lusitano) à chegada a Antuérpia, em 1534, em representação do mercader Henrique Pires, seu tio materno," *Medicina na Beira Interior da Pré-Historia ao século XXI. Cadernos de Cultura* 23 (2009), 7–14; "De Antuérpia a Ferrara: o caminho de Amato Lusitano e da sua família," Ibid., 25 (2011) 5–16; "Amato Lusitano em Ancona: a tragédia da família Pires", Ibid. 26 (2012), 20–7 o J. A. David Morais, *Amato Lusitano. Reinterpretação historiográfica da sua biografia* (Lisboa 2015). Teresa Santander Rodríguez, *Escolares médicos en Salamanca* (*siglo XVI*) (Salamanca 1984) aporta las fechas de su vinculación a Salamanca. No agotamos la amplia bibliografía al respecto, como se desprende de los estudios de João Rui Pita y Ana Leonor Pereira, "Escritos maiores e menores sobre Amato Lusitano," *Medicina na Beira Interior da Pré-Historia ao século XXI. Cadernos de Cultura* 17 (2003), 6–17, "História da história de Amato Lusitano", Ibid., 27 (2013), 63–72 y "Estudos contemporâneos sobre Amato Lusitano", en *Humanismo e ciência. Antiguidade e Renascimento*, ed. A. M. Lopes Andrade (Aveiro 2015), 513–41. Una amplia bibliografía sobre el autor puede verse en http://amatolusitano.uva.es/bibliografia/.

3 Si aceptamos que siendo estudiante trabajó guiado por sus profesores en la Universidad de Salamanca.

4 Jon Arrizabalaga, John Henderson y Roger French, *The Great Pox. The French Disease in Renaissance Europe* (New Haven 1997), en 1–3, 8 y 18 señalan los riesgos de la identificación inmediata con la sífilis venérea.

5 "diário de bordo" según Isilda Teixeira Rodrigues, "Amato Lusitano e as problemáticas sexuais. Algumas contribuições para uma perspectiva de análise das *Centúrias de Curas Medicinais*," *Revista Lusófona de Ciência das Religiões* 6.11 (2007), 317–33 en 319; "cuadernos de campo" para Ana A. Macedo Lima, "La melancolía en la primera y segunda *Centúrias de Curas Medicinais* de Amato Lusitano," *Cauriensia* 7 (2012), 89–99, en 90.

6 João José Alves Dias, *Amato Lusitano e a sua obra. Séculos XVI e XVII* (Lisboa 2011). La primera edición completa de las siete *Centurias* (Lión 1580) es posterior a la muerte del autor.

de formación universitaria sobre el origen, la novedad, la denominación o el tratamiento adecuado.[7]

Amato Lusitano no entra en el debate teórico y doctrinal sobre esta enfermedad. Acepta la novedad de la misma y la terminología común y critica a los empíricos la falta de personalización al aplicar remedios "indiscrete" (*Curatio* 2,70). En relación a este mal destaca en Amato la preocupación por la terapéutica, en tanto que estudia los remedios 'nuevos': raíz de China y guayaco (de los que acepta sustitutos) y mantiene y matiza el heredado tratamiento con mercurio. También enfatiza su práctica, su actuación ante el enfermo, de este modo genera doctrina como nueva *auctoritas*, lo que le permite no mencionar a otras, que conoce y maneja.[8]

Suele decirse que las *Curationes* de Amato, de variada extensión, combinan el registro de su actuación clínica (*curationes*) y la precisión del médico erudito (*scholia*),[9] pues con el adecuado aparato doctrinal y teórico comenta su clínica como comentaría un texto académico. Combinar teoría y práctica[10] hace de él una autoridad[11] y de su obra una fuente de consulta, facilitada por la inclusión de los títulos de las *Curationes* ("in qua agitur de") en índices.[12] Sin embargo, de las 47 *Curationes* relativas al morbo gálico que tomamos en cuenta, solo 17

---

7   Una prueba son los textos de hasta 59 autores recogidos por Aloysius Luisinus, *De morbo Gallico omnia quae extant apud omnes medicos cuiuscumque nationis* (Venecia, 1566–1567). Sobre la denominación cf. María J. Pérez Ibáñez, "Un problema médico y terminológico (sífilis en el siglo XVI)," *Voces* 6 (1995), 61–79; "*Galli vocant istum morbum morbum eius cuius est*. Otra designación para el 'mal francés'," *Asclepio* 60 (2008), 267–79. Han expuesto diversas cuestiones en torno a este mal Arrizabalaga, Henderson, French, *The Great Pox* (véase arriba, n. 4).

8   María J. Pérez Ibáñez, "Amato ante el morbo gálico," en *Amato y la medicina de su tiempo*, ed. Miguel Á. González Manjarrés (Valladolid 2019, en prensa).

9   Gianna Pomata, "Sharing Cases: The *Observationes* in Early Modern Medicine," *Early Science and Medicine* 15 (2010), 193–236, en 210.

10   Iolanda Ventura, "Theory and Practice in Amatus Lusitanus's *Curationum medicinalium Centuriae*: The Case of Fevers," *Korot* 20 (2009–2010), 139–79 en 144–5: "a problematic but intriguing balance between medical theory and practice".

11   María J. Pérez Ibáñez, *El humanismo médico del siglo XVI en la Universidad de Salamanca* (Valladolid, 1997) 103. Los comentarios carecen de la organización interna de los escritos académicos. Pomata, "Sharing Cases" (véase arriba, n. 9) define a Amato como autoridad y pionero de este género que valora la práctica como forma de conocimiento.

12   Ventura, "Theory and Practice" (véase arriba, n. 10), 147–8, lo describe como obra para consulta donde los escolios son tan importantes como las *Curationes*, pues la intención del autor es formar un *corpus* teórico, vademécum para futuros lectores. Pérez Ibáñez, "Amato ante el morbo gálico" (véase arriba, n. 8) muestra que no es plenamente aplicable al morbo gálico.

AMATO LUSITANO: EL RELATO PATOGRÁFICO DEL MORBO GÁLICO   453

presentan *scholia*.[13] En esta situación Amato enfatiza su práctica, destaca su *experientia*.[14]

En este trabajo tratamos de ver con qué elementos construye el relato clínico del morbo gálico, atendiendo a las partes fijas de sus historias clínicas, el título y la *curatio* propiamente dicha, pues ya nos hemos ocupado de la posición e interés de los escolios.[15]

2.1   *Los títulos de las* Curationes

Los títulos, heredados de la literatura 'consiliar', suponen una tendencia tipificadora y generalizadora, en contraste con la teórica individualidad del caso concreto.[16]

Los títulos de las historias que tomamos en consideración no informan sobre el paciente[17] y pocos mencionan la enfermedad: *morbi gallicani* (*cur.* 1,50), *de morbo gallico* (4,54; 4,15; 4,69; 5,22; 5,25; 5,49; 5,56; 6,43; 6,48); otros asocian síntomas o afecciones concretas con ese mal (*cur.* 3,4: *de ulceribus a morbo Gallico contractis* [...]; 1,26; 1,29; 4,4; 4,55; 5,60; 5,68; 5,72; 6,22; 6,85); y otros (v.g. *cur.* 5,14: *de miro quodam artificio ad recuperandam vocem* [...] *amissam propter ulcus palato innatum*; 6,60: *de quodam qui* [...] *multa et varia abhorrebat*) no permiten sospechar que el morbo gálico es un importante antecedente médico, como se desprende de la lectura de las *Curationes*. Amato parece más interesado en la afección presente y en la intervención sobre ella.

Siguiendo los títulos de estas *Curationes*, veríamos que pueden reducirse a dos grandes bloques: los que recogen el nombre de la enfermedad y sus distintas manifestaciones (23 en total, como los de las *Curationes* 1,50 o 3,4 presentados en el párrafo anterior) y aquellos que en una primera instancia no mencionan la enfermedad (24 casos, como el 5,14 o 6,60 arriba recogidos), pero que el autor juzga interesantes. Pronto estos títulos integraron unos índices que permiten una búsqueda no siempre fácil de orientar para aspectos teóricos que pudieran tener utilidad en la práctica clínica relacionada con el morbo gálico.

---

13   Sólo cuatro *Curationes* con *scholia* mencionan en el título el morbo gálico: 3,4; 4,55; 4,69 y 5,22, Pérez Ibáñez, "Amato ante el morbo gálico" (véase arriba, n. 8). Cuando Amato no menciona el morbo gálico, aunque síntomas o tratamientos parezcan sospechosos, no lo tomamos en cuenta.

14   Pérez Ibáñez, "Amato ante el morbo gálico" (véase arriba, n. 8).

15   Ibid.

16   Pedro Laín Entralgo, *La historia clínica* (Madrid 1950), 132–3.

17   Excepto 2,31: *De methodo et vera regula propinandi decoctum radicis cynarum pro Iuio Tertio Pontifice Maximo ad illustrissimum ac iuxta humanissimum dominum Vincentium de Nobilibus Anconae aequissimum praesidem,* una epístola en que detalla las virtudes y modos de uso de la raíz de la China.

2.2   *Las* Curationes

En las *Curationes* propiamente dichas, describe la historia clínica del paciente y su intervención profesional, incluye el diagnóstico – en cierto modo resumido en el título – e indicaciones terapéuticas, que pueden ser muy detalladas e incluir la composición de los medicamentos prescritos. Suele indicar también el resultado positivo de su intervención.

2.2.1   El paciente

Tiende a comenzar hablando del paciente, la mayoría varones de distintas edades. A veces son contagiados por una mujer (*cur.* 2,60: "quum apud mulierem Gallica scabie foedatam [...] moraretur"; 3,61 "cum venusta sed Gallica scabie foedata muliere coivit"; 5,49: "a muliere meretrice discedens"). Otras veces transmiten la enfermedad a esposas e hijos, contagios involuntarios en tanto que tiempo atrás cursaron la enfermedad (*cur.* 1,49 *De quibusdam Gallicana scabie infectis*, cuenta cómo un bebe, hijo de un enfermo que al cabo de los años contagia a su esposa, transmite la afección a su nodriza y ésta a otras personas; 1,50: "interpositis quindecim annis, huius uxor, mulier honesta et robusta, puellam peperit exanthematibus Gallicanis [...] infectam.")

Una parte son hombres indeterminados (1,49 "quidam", 1,85 "iuvenis natus annos vigintiquinque", 5,72 "qui", 1,54 "vir") o de los que, a lo sumo, conocemos la profesión o rango (1,4 "miles", 1,90 "Graecus proxeneta", 2,29 "Monaculus divi Dominici", 3,4 "Reverendissimi Cardinalis Farnesii famulus", 3,61 "Iuvenis aurifex", 4,69 "Reverendus divi Dominici", 5,14 "Graecus nobilis", 5,22 "lapicida iuvenis", 6,80 "marinus vir insularis").

De otros varones ofrece datos para la identificación, al menos para los potenciales lectores de la época, y recurre a varios procedimientos, a veces combinados:

1. nombre o filiación, si son niños o jóvenes (1,26 "Christophorus Almeida", 1,64 "Arubas vir", 1,74 "Filius Gasparis Pisaurensis", 1,94 "Simon iuvenis", 2,60 "Filius Vincentii coriarii, qui apud fanum Divi Nicolai habitat", 3,18 "Puer Altarasii", 4,14 "Simon praedictarum[18] frater", 4,56 "probus vir Damianus Illyrucus", 5,10 "Fabritius de Medicis, illustris familiae apud Florentinos", 5,25 "Livius a Bertinoro, iuvenis").

2. Explicita la profesión (5,3 "Ioannes Baptista propola", 5,49 "Alovisius Florentinus, iuvenis [...], mercator", 5,56 "Luca, Ligurus, [...] rei maritimae maximus explorator", 5,73 "Laurentius de Gentilibus, publicus notarius Pisaurensis", 6,43 "Thamar Turca mercator ex Pergamo", 6,85 "Aeneas

---

18   Varias mujeres identificadas en relación a Margarella Scallia (4,11), cuando el referente suele ser un varón.

AMATO LUSITANO: EL RELATO PATOGRÁFICO DEL MORBO GÁLICO   455

Neapolitanus musicus") o grupo social (6,22 "Marinus Gondulanus, nobilis iuvenis Ragusaeus", 6,25 "Sebastianus Bubalius ex Ragusaeis Patritiis", 6,48 "Ioannis Luca [...] Patritius Ragusaeus", 6,60 "Bernardus Bonius ex Ragusaeorum patritia familia", 6,72 "Iacobus Basilius, nobilis Ragusaeus"). Estos dos procedimientos de identificación solo serían útiles para el propio médico o para algún lector muy cercano en el tiempo y el espacio.

3.   Ofrece datos precisos, aunque esta es la opción minoritaria: (1,75 "Vincentius Virgilius monachus ordinis Sancti Augustini apud Anconitanus prior dignissimus et Polydori Virgilii Urbinatis, viri hac nostra aetate ut eius attestantur monumenta doctissimi, consanguineus", 2,95 "Ludovicus Bononiensis extra urbem Romae ad 50. miliaria commisarius", 3,25 "Ioannes Politianus, vir nobilis et praefectus arcis Anconitanae, Rebeliniae dictae", 3,65 "filius Salonis, qui propter Cibetae catos, quos [...] in Italiam traxerat, Catarii nomen ademptus est", 6,42 "Iacobus homo Gallus et Henrici Francorum Regis in orientali plaga procurator").

Sus diez pacientes femeninas apenas tienen cabida como esposas o hijas (1,72 "uxor comitis", 4,55 "uxor Naucleris navis Belioti", 4,68 "filia illius qui vinum vendit", 6,46 "uxorem [...] eius, sc. Ioannis Lucae [...] patritii Ragusaei)". A veces señala el lugar de residencia (2,70 "mulier Illyrica quae ad caput montis habitat", 4,4 "Mulier nobilis quae ad mare habitat", 5,60 "mulier quae ad portum agit") o de procedencia (4,15 "mulier quae ex Iadera civitate apud Dalmatas Anconam venit", 5,21 "mulier iuvenis Senensis", 5,68 "mulier quae ex Sancto Lupidio ad me delata est").

Aunque hay alguna identificación muy precisa para los lectores del siglo XXI – quizá todavía más para los coetáneos del autor –, en general los nombres y datos de los pacientes parecen una *variatio* de unas formas de pronombre indefinido, una *variatio* que evoca y ofrece una apariencia de personalización e individuación del paciente.

2.2.2   Detalles particulares

La poco precisa identificación del paciente se asocia – a nuestro juicio – a que no siempre describe sus características fisiológicas, como complexión y temperamento,[19] algo sorprendente en quien insiste en la importancia de atenerse a las características particulares (6,60, escolio completo):

Non abs re Galenus dixit saepe ultra temperaturas universales particulares hominum esse deprehendendas, ut libro Artis curativae ad Glauconem et alibi saepe ut **iis in Centuriis** quoque nos adnotavimus.

---

19   En 5,22 explica el temperamento de la unción mercurial.

456 PÉREZ IBÁÑEZ

Si en ocasiones describe características del paciente (1,4 "aetate virili, robustus, fortis, natura melancholicus", 1,54 "qui morbo Gallico laborabat et multis lichenibus [...] scatebat, [...] robustus, ad temperaturam calidam declinans", 4,55 "quinquagenaria, obesa, potens et virago")[20] y luego detalla el transcurso de la enfermedad y su intervención, en más ocasiones identifica el mal sin detalles particulares (1,72 "quadragenaria, iam olim morbo Gallico infecta, gravissimo dolore circa os ventriculi premebatur", 2,70 "Mulier Illyrica, [...] quum strumam a Gallica scabie originem ducentem [...] haberet", 5,25 "iuvenis viginti natus annos, cum iamdiu morbo Gallico laboraret") y pasa a exponer el procedimiento terapéutico y el decurso de la enfermedad.[21]

Vamos sumando rasgos, título generalizador, paciente no identificado ni caracterizado médicamente son tendencias dominantes en la redacción de estos casos clínicos de Amato.

2.2.3   La enfermedad

Para las mujeres que atiende esta enfermedad puede ser pura sospecha (4,68 "ulcuscula [...] an a morbo Gallico originem traherent in dubium vertebatur") o algo inminente (4,4 "capillorum defluxio, vera et indubitata via ad morbum Gallicum, laborare coepit, demum ut morbo Gallico affecta curata fuit"). Normalmente es una enfermedad del pasado cuyas consecuencias percibe en el presente (1,72 "iam olim morbo Gallico infecta, gravissimo dolore circa os ventriculi premebatur", 4,15 "alios humores ab ipso morbo Gallico contractos vigere esset certum", 4,55 "ulcera maligna a morbo Gallico contracta [...] patiebatur", 5,21 "morbo Gallico olim infecta fuerat", 5,60 "iamdiu morbo Gallico vexata est").

Si menciona la vía del contagio, suele ser el esposo (5,68 "morbo Gallico laborabat, nam eo maritus antea laboraverat", 6,48 "uxorem [...] pari labe correptam facile fuit iudicare, iuvenem [...] ea peste indignam").

En los varones, aunque pueden combinarse varios elementos, la enfermedad se identifica con el morbo gálico (1,26 "morbo Gallico correptus erat", 2,60 "quum apud mulierem Gallica scabie foedatam [...] moraretur, duobus bubonibus circa inguina correptus fuit", 4,14 "iuvenem hunc limites morbi Gallici intrasse", 4,56 "ulcus Gallicanus erat");[22] o la intervención de Amato obedece a una, llamémosla, secuela de esa afección (1,4 "atrocissimum morbum [...] quem a Gallica scabie originem traxisse [...] comperi", 3,61 "cum [...] Gallica

---

20   También lo hace en 1,74; 1,75; 1,94; 3,25; 3,65; 4,14; 4,68; 5,56; 5,73; 6,25; 6,48 y 6,60.

21   Amato interviene a veces sobre la dieta del paciente: 1,54; 1,85; 2,60; 3,4; 3,18; 3,61; 4,15; 4,44; 4,68; 5,3; 5,14; 5,22; 5,49; 5,60; 5,68; 6,22; 6,25; 6,43; 6,48; 6,85.

22   De forma similar en 4,69; 5,3; 5,22; 5,56; 5,72; 6,22 o 6,42.

AMATO LUSITANO: EL RELATO PATOGRÁFICO DEL MORBO GÁLICO 457

scabie foedata muliere coivit, unde in virga ulcera […]", 3,65 "ab afectione Gallicana eius morbi seminaria originem trahere suspicarer").[23] También aparece la enfermedad entre los antecedentes del paciente (1,49 "quidam morbo Gallico infectus fuit et […] sanus evaserit", 1,85 "morbo Gallico olim sed leviter infectus fuit, a quo curatus […] interpositis annis […]", 3,4 "quum ulceribus antiquis a morbo Gallico contractis scateret et […] incuratus maneret").[24]

Los pacientes masculinos son más numerosos y, cuando se menciona tal detalle, aparecen como transmisores de la enfermedad a sus esposas o como los receptores de la enfermedad que les llega de mujeres. También ellos padecen más manifestaciones y variedades del morbo gálico. En cambio las pacientes de Amato, muchas menos, son contagiadas por sus esposos y o bien padecieron la enfermedad o bien la van a sufrir en el futuro sin que se expliciten vías de contagio.

2.2.4   La observación

Amato es un buen observador, incluso delicado, que cuida de no ser indiscreto. En 3,25 le interesan las fiebres de su identificado paciente (dan título a la *curatio*), otros síntomas permiten sospechar la causa de sus males. Amato sin relacionar las fiebres con el morbo gálico sutilmente apunta que cuando esto ocurre "vigebat Gallicanae scabiei humor". Tiene clara la vía de transmisión de la enfermedad ("a muliere meretrice discedens in plures eius universum corpus foedantes papulas incidit") y como la historia clínica lleva por título *De morbo gallico* (5,49) no menciona la afección en la *curatio*.

Por sus observaciones sabe que el rostro delata la enfermedad. Le parece un signo tan cierto que la *cur.* 6,48 (*de marito et uxore morbo Gallico infectis*) no comienza, como es habitual, presentando al paciente, sino con lo que parece una máxima: "Facies ut totius corporis inscriptio est, ita latentes hominum morbos indicare solet, eorum praesertim qui morbo Gallico vexantur." También generaliza sobre la alopecia y titula la *cur.* 4,4 (*de alopecia hodie vero et indubitato morbi Gallici signo*) e igualmente añade observaciones sobre un poco moderado régimen de vida, *cur.* 6,25: *De surditate contracta ob malum vitae regimen,* en cuyo desarrollo explicita:

> Iam diu est, morbo Gallico afflictus fuit qui postea inmoderatis rei veneriae usibus deditus et aeri nocturno assiduo expositus, in capitis gravedines et ipsius vertiginies […] incidit.

---

23   Igualmente en 1,54; 1,74; 5,10; 5,14; 5,25; 6,43; 6,60 o 6,85.
24   O en 1,50; 1,94; 5,3 y 6,72.

458 PÉREZ IBÁÑEZ

La insistencia en la propia observación permite que en las *Curationes* que nos ocupan apenas haya referencias o menciones de autoridades médicas.[25] Con este procedimiento, lejos del debate doctrinal, destaca su actuación como un médico cuya *experientia* le confiere autoridad.

2.2.5 La indicación del resultado

A menudo cerrando las *Curationes*, Amato Lusitano incluye el resultado de su intervención médica. Es abrumadoramente positivo en el caso de las *Curationes* relacionadas con el morbo gálico. Pocos casos permanecen en la indefinición, como *cur.* 3,61: "Sed morbus [...] ad trigesimum usque diem lente processit ut Guaiaci decocto postea pro eo extirpando opus fuerit."

Para esta declaración positiva emplea diversas formulaciones. Las que parecen proceder del paciente incluyen un adverbio de modo (1,74 "bene habuit", 3,65 "taurice valuit", 4,15 "optime se valere dixit", 4,68 "optime valuit", 5,21 "optime habere dixit", 5,22; 6,48 y 6,60 "recte habuit", 5,25 "recte valeret").

Las que emanan del médico tras su trabajo pueden señalar la duración del tratamiento y en ellas aparecen el adjetivo "sanus" o el participio "sanatus" y el sustantivo "sanitas":

> A) 1,54 "sanus factus est", 3,25 "ex toto sanus evasit", 4,55 "intra quadraginta dies ex toto sana evasit", 5,60 "ex toto sanata est", 5,68 "intra hoc [...] tempus sanata est", 6,22 "intra [...] tempus sanatus est", 6,43 "intra viginti dies sanus [...] evasit", 6,72 "ex toto sanus".
>
> B) 1,4 "sanitati fuerat restitutus", 1,72 "sanitati fuit restituta", 1,85 "sanitati integrae fuit restitutus", 1,94 "intra decem dies sanitati fuit restitutus", 2,60 "proximis viginti diebus sanitati fuit resitutus", 3,4 "sanitati tamen integrae colophonem addidit buxi decoctum per viginti dies ebibitum", 4,4 "ad sanitatem integram redacta", 5,10 "intra sexaginta dies pristinae sanitati restituimus", 6,85 "intra viginti dies pristinam sanitatem adeptus sit".

En pocas *Curationes* su paciente muere, como los bebés (1,49 y 1,50) nacidos de madre sana y padre en el pasado enfermo. Resulta interesante comprobar cómo varios fallecimientos derivan bien de la intervención de otros profesionales (5,56 "cum adhuc sese non omnino sanum dicerat, alium accersivit

---

25   Señalamos las *Curationes* en las que menciona autoridades y cuáles son estas: 3,25 (Hipócrates), 3,65 (Hipócrates, Galeno, Avicena, Mesué, Pablo de Egina y Aecio de Amida), 4,4 (Galeno), 4,14 (Galeno y Dioscórides), 4,69 y 5,68 (Galeno), 5,10 (Dioscórides), 6,25 (Galeno y Pablo de Egina), 6,42 (Alejandro de Tralles), 6,72 (Galeno y él mismo). En 2,60 él mismo es la única autoridad mencionada.

medicum qui ex mercuriali unguento eum illinivit, et ita sinistre ut [...] diem suum obiit");[26] bien de la poca preocupación del paciente (5,3 "pancratice habuit [...] cum ad [...] intempestiva convivia [...] frequens esset [...] repente apoplexia enectus obiit"). Así parece probar que una amplia experiencia médica es la mejor vía para la curación.

3 Consideraciones finales y ejemplos

Los datos presentados sobre las historias clínicas relacionadas con el morbo gálico no parecen fruto de la casualidad. El propio Amato da a entender que su obra no es un 'cuaderno de campo', apuntes rápidos al hilo de su intervención, sino el producto de la reflexión. En la *cur.* 5,14 en que presenta su novedoso obturador del paladar afirma que el registro del caso lo hace después ("Ex hoc namque instrumento arti medicae gloria non vulgaris ascita est, quo et nunc, dum haec Ragusii commemoramur, simile opus confecimus [...].")

Según lo apuntado más arriba, los títulos, que acaban insertos en índices, tienen un carácter generalizador, no siempre recogen el nombre de la enfermedad, si bien pueden incluir la mención de variedades de la misma. El paciente, entre cuyos antecedentes clínicos puede figurar el morbo gálico, apenas está individualizado, su nombre, filiación o profesión son casi *variationes* de un indefinido, y de él se destacan pocos detalles particulares (temperamento, complexión,...), algo que contraviene el principio médico de la adecuación del tratamiento a tales características individuales. Utiliza expresiones formulares y generalizadoras de los síntomas más significativos y suele señalar el resultado positivo, salvo imponderables, de quienes se atienen a su tratamiento.

Todos estos elementos parecen destacar aspectos dotados de validez universal, como intento de Amato por presentar algo que podríamos llamar 'caso-tipo' que elimina o reduce al máximo la individualidad del paciente y detalla aspectos prácticos del tratamiento de una enfermedad asociada o no a diversos síntomas o causa subyacente de afecciones concretas, aspectos prácticos acompañados de detalles de observación diagnóstica y de la evolución y duración de la prescripción. De este modo, Amato pone el foco en su *experientia* que no tiene por qué necesitar el aval de las autoridades o lo pone a su altura.

Esta enseñanza sobre la forma de actuación no se ofrece, como suele decirse, en los *scholia*, identificados como sede del aparato doctrinal y teórico. En el caso del morbo gálico los *scholia* son poco frecuentes, apenas se ligan a

---

26 También *cur.* 6,25.

Curationes cuyo título contiene clara referencia al morbo gálico e inciden en aspectos terapéuticos y dejan de lado otros aspectos doctrinales de la enfermedad.[27] El posible *vademécum* que formarían las *Curationum medicinalium Centuriae* no busca una enseñanza teórica, sino práctica puesta de relieve en las *Curationes*, no en los *scholia*.

Sirvan de ejemplo la *cur.* 4,4, y la 5,60 ambas sin escolios.[28] La primera presenta un título generalizador y una muestra de la capacidad de observación del clínico que es Amato al identificar como signo del morbo gálico la caída de cabellos. Apenas hay datos específicos sobre el temperamento y condiciones de la paciente. La experiencia de Amato se refuerza por su contraposición a la doctrina de Galeno.[29] Lo que pudo ser un caso concreto se convierte en una curación paradigmática de una manifestación concreta del morbo gálico (*cur.* 4,4):

Curatio IV. in qua agitur de alopecia hodie vero et indubitato morbi Gallici signo.

Mulier nobilis, quae ad mare habitat, pulchra si qua altera, ingenti febre correpta est, quam per integrum diem passa fuit. Sequenti die rauca facta syrupum ex capillo Veneris et glycirrhiza ebibit; tertio febris desiit, sed paucis aliis interiectis diebus alopecia, hoc est capillorum defluvio, vera et indubitata ad morbum Gallicum via, laborare coepit. Demum ut morbo Gallico affecta curata fuit et ad sanitatem integram reducta.

Caeterum, tametsi Galenus libro 11 de simplicium medicamentorum facultatibus, capitulo de pinguedine et adipe dicat vere esse proditum ursinum adipem alopecias curare, quo tamen probatiora medicamenta

---

27   Pérez Ibáñez, "Amato ante el morbo gálico" (véase arriba, n. 8).

28   Mientras se elabora la edición transcribimos siguiendo un ejemplar de la edición *Amati Lusitani doctoris medici praestantissimi Curationum medicinalium centuriae septem* (Burdeos, 1620).

29   La presencia de Galeno en la formación del médico occidental es amplia, más desde el siglo XIII con la incorporación de nuevos textos galénicos al *curriculum* universitario: el llamado "nuevo Galeno": L. García Ballester, "Arnau de Vilanova (*c.* 1240–1311) y la reforma de los estudios médicos en Montpellier (1309): El Hipócrates latino y la introducción del nuevo Galeno," *Dynamis* 2 (1982), 97–158. En el siglo XVI Galeno sigue siendo una fuente principal para el saber médico y una autoridad prácticamente incuestionable. Con todo, el peso que adquieren la *observatio* y la *experientia* permite a los médicos, como en este caso, cuestionar las afirmaciones de esa autoridad tan conocida, leída y estudiada. Sobre la importancia y la presencia de Galeno pueden verse, entre otros, Owsei Temkin, *Galenism: Rise and Decline of a Medical Philosophy*, (Ithaca – London 1973); Anthony Wear, "Galen in the Renaissance," en *Galen: Problems and Prospects*, ed. Vivian Nutton (London, 1981) 229–62; Luis García Ballester, *Galen and Galenism* (Aldershot, 2002); Susan P. Mattern, *Galen and the Rhetoric of Healing* (Baltimore, 2008).

AMATO LUSITANO: EL RELATO PATOGRÁFICO DEL MORBO GÁLICO 461

ipse habebat, nos huic ursorum adipi multum pro hoc curando vitio et pilis gignendis tribuimus. Experti enim sumus inter praecipua huic rei facientia remedia adipem hunc primatum habere.

Igual de generalizador es el título de la *cur.* 5,60, sin apenas datos específicos e individualizadores del paciente y con su aguda observación sobre los signos que delatan la enfermedad ofrece un rápido diagnóstico y un, por así decir, resumen de su actuación: modifica la dieta y aplica uno de los medicamentos habituales en él para el morbo gálico, marcando el tiempo que dura la prescripción:

Curatio LX. in qua agitur de urinae acredine mordacitateve ob ulcera a morbo Gallico contracta.

Mulier, quae ad portum agit et iamdiu morbo Gallico vexata est, ut quoque eius facie percipitur, in urinae ingentem acredinem mordacitatemve incidit. Caeterum haec proposito optimo victus ordine et cassiae Aegyptiacae pulpamento bis atque ter deglutito ac ebibitis decoctis quae materiam morbi Gallici respiciunt, guaiaci decoctum ad quadraginta dies ebibit et ex toto sanata est.

Universidad de Valladolid

CHAPTER 35

Nuevos retos para el estudio de la poesía jesuítica latina del siglo XVIII

Carlos Ángel Rizos Jiménez

Abstract

La literatura que produjeron los jesuitas durante el siglo XVIII experimenta una importante evolución a lo largo de esta centuria porque se pasa de un latín anclado en el barroquismo a un nuevo latín que recupera sus modelos clásicos. Esto se aprecia especialmente en la poesía, y la causa de este cambio se encuentra en el modelo académico que impulsan, desde la Universidad de Cervera, José Finestres y su mano derecha, Bartolomé Pou, cuyo decreto académico de 1756 marca un antes y un después. Aunque aparentemente este cambio está muy focalizado en un área geográfica muy concreta, la movilidad de los padres de la Compañía de Jesús hace que se propague por toda la provincia jesuítica de Aragón (Cataluña, Aragón, Baleares y Comunidad Valenciana) y, en última instancia, a raíz de la expulsión de 1767, a Italia y, desde allí, a toda Europa y el resto del mundo. Veremos la evolución de esta poesía con muestras procedentes tanto de textos impresos como de obras que nos han llegado manuscritas.

Keywords

Neo-Latin poetry – Jesuits – 18th century – José Finestres – Bartolomé Pou

El cierre de las universidades catalanas a raíz de los decretos de nueva planta propugnados por Felipe V y la apertura de una única universidad en Cervera en 1717 se ha visto generalmente como una gran pérdida, pero el papel que llevó a cabo la Compañía de Jesús en la Universidad de Cervera desde el colegio jesuítico de esta ciudad dio lugar a una época de gran esplendor humanístico que ha sido profundamente analizado por especialistas de la talla de los jesuitas

© KONINKLIJKE BRILL NV, LEIDEN, 2020 | DOI:10.1163/9789004427105_036

NUEVOS RETOS PARA EL ESTUDIO DE LA POESÍA JESUÍTICA LATINA   463

Ignacio Casanovas[1] y Miguel Batllori[2] y más recientemente por autores como Niccolò Guasti,[3] Manfred Tietz[4] o José Antonio Clúa.[5]

Ya aquellos evidenciaron el carácter marcadamente barroco de la latinidad practicada por los jesuitas hasta la primera mitad del XVIII, donde encontramos la clásica poesía encomiástica que salía de los colegios jesuíticos, y que es a partir de la segunda mitad, bajo el liderazgo de José Finestres, que encontramos la búsqueda del buen gusto recuperando el modelaje de los clásicos. Aunque disponemos de una pléyade de autores jesuitas que constituyen el cenáculo de Cervera, fueron sobre todo dos las figuras que promovieron la recuperación del buen gusto por la latinidad clásica: el aragonés Blas Larraz, "piedra angular del neoclasicismo latinizante de Cervera"[6] y el mallorquín Bartolomé Pou, que "reformó los estudios en los colegios de la Compañía de Aragón" (dice Buenaventura Serra y Ferragut) "habiendo encargado la religión [la Compañía de Jesús] su reforma a los dos mallorquines el P. Bartolomé Pou y el P. Sebastián Nicolau" (dice el padre Luis de Vilafranca),[7] el segundo de los cuales "no tuvo nunca contacto inmediato con Cervera. Pero en Tarragona pasó los primeros años de su vida religiosa, y ya allí se puso en relación con los jesuitas que, despertando de un sueño de incultura que duró dos siglos, se ponían de un salto en las avanzadas de un movimiento de restauración que a mediados de siglo estaba ya plenamente logrado. Y cumplió, como Pou, un cometido de difusión: nombrado profesor del Colegio de Zaragoza, impuso allí nuevos cánones clásicos – 'de buen gusto' decían entonces – contra la descomposición barroquista, y cinco años seguidos – de 1757 a 1761 – pronunció en la capital aragonesa los discursos inaugurales, que en 1764 vieron la luz pública."[8] Pou

---

1   Ignacio Casanovas, *Josep Finestres: Estudis biogràfics* (Barcelona, 1932) y Ignacio Casanovas, *La cultura catalana en el siglo XVIII: Finestres y la Universidad de Cervera* (Barcelona, 1953).

2   Miguel Batllori, *La cultura hispano-italiana de los jesuitas expulsos: españoles-hispanoamericanos-filipinos (1767–1814)* (Madrid, 1966).

3   Niccolò Guasti, *L'esilio italiano dei gesuiti spagnoli: identità, controllo sociale e pratiche culturali (1767–1798)* (Roma, 2006).

4   *Los jesuitas españoles expulsos: su imagen y su contribución al saber sobre el mundo hispánico en la Europa del siglo XVIII*, ed. Manfred Tietz (Madrid, 2001), con casi una treintena de estudios.

5   José Antonio Clúa, "La difusió dels escriptors clàssics a la Universitat del segle XVIIIè: Josep Finestres," en *La tradició clàssica: actes de l'XIè Simposi de la Secció Catalana de la Sociedad Española de Estudios Clásicos*, ed. Mercè Puig Rodríguez-Escalona (Andorra, 1996), 263–70; idem, "Anotacions sobre l'humanisme classicista jesuític a la Catalunya del segle XVIII: la Universitat de Cervera," *Calamus Renascens* 2 (2001), 43–75.

6   Batllori, *Cultura* (véase arriba, n. 2), 313.

7   Citados ambos por Miguel Batllori, *Cartas del padre Pou al cardenal Despuig* (Mallorca, 1946), 36.

8   Batllori, *Cultura* (véase arriba, n. 2), 478.

fue el "brazo derecho de Finestres en la restauración humanística. Ninguno le supera en dotes literarias y él vence a todos en la actividad y eficacia de su acción [...] Fue el divulgador más vasto de la cultura cervariense."[9] Ofreció un marco teórico a esta reforma a través de su obra *Ludi rhetorici et poetici in Academia Cervariensi ipsius decreto acti ab adolescentibus linguae latinae graecaeque studiosis* (1756), cuyos dos puntos esenciales resumió Casanovas:[10]

> 1ª, qué autores latinos se han de poner en manos de los estudiantes; 2ª, qué valor tiene la gloria de improvisar. La primera cuestión dividió en dos tendencias a los latinistas: unos querían que la lengua se aprendiese en Cicerón o en los autores del siglo de oro; otros admitían de buen grado la colaboración de autores más secundarios. El P. Pou se inclina abiertamente hacia el segundo grupo, aunque confiesa que, con ello, se aparta de la tradición de los antiguos jesuitas [...] Y de los ejercicios improvisados, tan celebrados en los grandes certámenes de Barcelona y en otros lugares, ¿qué juzga el P. Pou? 'Si hemos de exigir temas perfectamente elaborados, ¿qué cosa más contraria a este ideal podemos buscar que lanzarlos a hablar atropellada y repentinamente? Esta gloria de una facundia extemporánea, que en nuestros tiempos, quieren algunos imponer en todas partes y como cosa vulgar, ¿no ha sido siempre algo muy raro, aun en los hombres más eruditos y ejercitados? Pero, sea de ello lo que fuere, nuestro afán no es ni escribir mucho ni escribir a chorro, sino tan solo este: escribir bien.'

A propósito de Blas Larraz, dice Batllori: "La tarea depuradora y neoclasicista que el P. Larraz emprendía en las aulas universitarias era secundada y como preparada en las escuelas de gramática y retórica – en su sentido clásico y renacentista – de todos los colegios que la Compañía tenía en Cataluña, pero principalmente en el de Cervera."[11] Precisamente él, que escribiría en buen latín la célebre crónica de la expulsión de los jesuitas de la Provincia de Aragón, destacó como poeta, lo que podemos comprobar, por ejemplo, en su *Poema épico latino y su traducción española, con que la Real Universidad de Cervera aplaudía el arribo de sus Magestades y Altezas el Rey Nuestro Señor Don Carlos Tercero de Borbón, la Reyna Nuestra Señora Doña Amalia de Saxonia, y los Señores Infantes e Infantas, sus augustíssimos hijos* (1759).

---

9   Casanovas, *Cultura* (véase arriba, n. 1), 98.
10   Ibid., 146–8.
11   Batllori, *Cartas* (véase arriba, n. 7), 41.

NUEVOS RETOS PARA EL ESTUDIO DE LA POESÍA JESUÍTICA LATINA   465

Bartolomé Pou, que era "mucho mejor prosista latino que poeta",[12] nos dejó el poema *Bassidos libri III* (Bolonia, 1794), en dísticos elegíacos, dedicado a la profesora de filosofía y física Laura María Caterina Bassi Veratti, de la Universidad de Bolonia, que había muerto en 1778.

El barcelonés Antonio Mollet publicó un *Epithalamium serenissimorum Principum Delphini Galliarum et Mariae Teresiae Hispaniarum Infantis* (Cervera, 1745) en hexámetros para conmemorar el enlace (celebrado el 23 de febrero de ese año) entre María Teresa Rafaela de Borbón (octava hija de Felipe V) y el delfín de Francia, Luis Fernando de Borbón, hijo de Luis XV.

El también barcelonés José Pons i Massana, profesor de los colegios barceloneses de Cordelles y Belén, cultivó la épica didáctica en *Ignis: poema didascalicum* (Barcelona, 1760), sobre el que afirmó el también jesuita Joan Vilar i Costa: "No he pas de deturar-me a fer l'examen literari d'aquest poema, ni, al meu parer, ho demana, car basta saber que és una d'aquelles migrades produccions literàries de la poesia insípida i infeconda del XVIIIè segle, que es presentava a les Acadèmies en forma de vanes declamacions o bé s'encarcarava de dissertacions filosòfiques sens enginy poètic, sens foc de sentiment, sense volada d'inspiració. Això no hi fa que'l desembràs el qual mostra en la versificació i certes maneres de dir, ens fan ententre que l'Autor tenia forta coneixença de la literatura clàssica de l'antigor, especialment llatina."[13] José Pons llegó a Cervera en 1762 como profesor de Filosofía, contexto en el que hay que situar otro poema que se le atribuye, *Philocentria* (Bolonia, 1774), sobre las teorías de Newton. Jaume Medina[14] reeditó el primer poema y analizó su contenido. En la misma línea, Miquel Sitjar[15] publicó un artículo sobre el *Signum magnum* (1761) de Francesc Capdevila, aunque en este caso el poema analizado no es de un jesuita sino de un alumno que estudiaba en el colegio de la Compañía de Jesús de Vich; es una composición para conmemorar la festividad de San Luis Gonzaga. En ese contexto de poesía de certamen cabe situar los poemas del leridano Miguel Doria (1737–1819) que han centrado la atención de mis estudios,[16] pero en este caso son textos inéditos: *Christus Natus: ecloga inter Fuscum et*

---

12   Ibid., 145.
13   Joan Vilar i Costa, "Ensaig Bio-bibliogràfic sobre el canonista barceloní Josep Pons i Massana," *Anuari de l'Institut d'Estudis Catalans* 6 (1923), 87–123, en 103.
14   Jaume Medina, "*Ignis*: un poema jesuític del segle XVIII," *Faventia* 18,1 (1996), 105–17.
15   Miquel Sitjar, "Aproximació a la poesia jesuítica de certamen: el *Signum magnum* (1761) del ribatà Francesc Capdevila i Ventós," *Annals de l'Institut d'Estudis Gironins* 31 (1990–91), 205–12.
16   Carlos Rizos, "Una égloga latina a lo divino del siglo XVIII," *Cuadernos de Filología Clásica: Estudios Latinos* 14 (1998), 245–52; "Un *epos* hagiográfico latino del siglo XVIII dedicado a San Luis Gonzaga," *Florentia Iliberritana* 21 (2010), 405–44; *La poesia jesuítica llatina a Lleida al segle XVIII: Miquel Dòria (edició, traducció i estudi de la seva obra)* (Barcelona,

Marcum (de tema navideño) y *Ad Divum Aloysium epos* (dedicado a San Luis Gonzaga). Es también el caso de los poemas manuscritos que he encontrado en el Archivo Municipal de Lérida (fondo de la Compañía de Jesús): ocho poemas breves del zaragozano Joaquín Carnicer (1743–1819), 41 composiciones del barcelonés Francisco Lloses (1728–82), además de seis documentos más que contienen poesía anónima de distinta índole.[17]

En el colegio de Vich destacó Onofre Pratdesaba, que publicó un *Certamen oratorio y poético en que harán alarde de su educación los alumnos que en la Compañía de Jesús cursan las escuelas de la* [...] *ciudad de Vique* (1747),[18] que también nos dejó un par de poemas publicados en el exilio: *Borsi Aretini primi Ferrariensis Ducis prosopopoeia* (Ferrara, 1785; sobre Borso, primer duque de Ferrara) y *Ferdinandum sive Hispaniam a Mauris liberatam cum Ferdinandus Borbonius Serenissimus Asturiarum Princeps Salutaretur* (Ferrara, 1791; sobre Fernando vi).

Si nos salimos del círculo de Cervera, encontraremos otros poetas que nos han dejado obras en latín, pero apenas han recibido atención por parte de los investigadores. Sin salir de la provincia de Aragón, tenemos autores como los valencianos Tomás Serrano ("componiendo una interminable serie de chispeantes epigramas a lo Marcial, que solo vieron la luz en 1788"[19]), Antonio Pinazo (autor de una *Ode tricolos tetrastrophos in laudem Xaverii Bettinelli demortui*, Mantua, 1808; sobre el escritor mantuano Saverio Bettinelli) o Manuel Lassala ("poeta de salón dieciochesco, no dejaba pasar oportunidad alguna para fingir en versos latinos o italianos una emoción poética que ni sentía [...] el nombramiento de un nuevo cardenal y otros temas de menor fuste todavía, eran ocasión suficiente para templar su lira y disparar uno tras otro *carmina*, elegías, epitalamios, odas y sonetos. Fuera de estas composiciones originales – llamémoslas así, para entendernos –, tradujo Lassala del árabe en versos latinos esopianos las fábulas del sabio persa Lokman".[20] Incluso el padre Juan Andrés, más conocido como historiador, ha sido considerado como el responsable del *Certamen oratorio poético que celebran los alumnos humanistas de la regia, cesárea y pontificia universidad de Gandía* (Valencia, 1765) "en que 14 muchachos expuestos al examen público acreditaron su mucha instrucción en la versión de los autores latinos del siglo de Augusto, en la retórica, poesía, ritos romanos, historia y geografía, y algunos también su inteligencia en las lenguas

---

2016; tesis doctoral en línea, publicada – en lo esencial – en papel bajo el título *L'obra poètica llatina del jesuïta Miquel Dòria [1737–1819]*, Universitat de Lleida, 2019).

17   Carlos Rizos, "La poesia jesuítica a l'Arxiu de la Paeria de Lleida," *Shikar* 2 (2015), 77–84.

18   Este título nos recuerda el de otro jesuita, el gerundense Francisco Javier Dorca (1736–1806), que nos dejó un *Certamen poético griego y latino* (1751).

19   Batllori, *Cultura* (véase arriba, n. 2), 499.

20   Ibid., 500.

NUEVOS RETOS PARA EL ESTUDIO DE LA POESÍA JESUÍTICA LATINA 467

griega y hebrea; admiró a todos el lucimiento de estos ejercicios, y mucho más sabiendo que algunos solo medio año que concurrían a su aula."[21]

La renovación cultural la protagonizaron los jesuitas del XVIII desde la Universidad de Cervera *urbi et orbi,* es decir, para la ciudad de Cervera y toda su zona de influencia (Cataluña en primer lugar y toda la provincia jesuítica de Aragón en segundo término) y para todo el mundo hispano-jesuítico (también de Hispanoamérica y Filipinas) que se concentró en Italia durante los años de la expulsión (1767–73) y extinción (1773–1814). Y el requisito de esta escuela renovadora fue "un profund sentit estètic, crític i filosòfic de tota la cultura".[22] Esta supremacía de la provincia de Aragón es destacada también por el padre Batllori:[23]

> En Italia, casi todas las provincias españolas ofrecerán, al lado de autores que hoy ya no tienen sino un valor puramente bibliográfico, algunos grandes nombres, definitivamente engarzados a la historia de la cultura española: Isla, Arévalo, Arteaga, Hervás. Pero solo la provincia de Aragón – hasta entonces la última de España, en el orden cultural – puede presentar en el destierro una cultura media de tanta extensión y de tan alta calidad como la formada por los aragoneses Millás, Garcés y Requeno, por los mallorquines Pou y Nicolau, por los valencianos Andrés, Eximeno, Serrano, Lassala, Colomes, Pinazo, Montengón y Conca, por los catalanes Juan Francisco, Baltasar y José Antonio Masdeu, Pla, Llampillas, Aymerich, Prats y Gustà, por no citar sino a los que recibieron el espaldarazo crítico de Menéndez Pelayo o han interesado luego fuera de España.

Es por ello que también la principal poesía saldrá de los jesuitas de la provincia de Aragón, pero también tenemos importantes muestras en el resto de España y asimismo en Hispanoamérica. Como poetas latinos quizá nos tendremos que limitar solo a un par de nombres. El primero es el extremeño Faustino Arévalo, que en el exilio italiano nos dejó su tratado *Hymnodia hispanica* (Roma, 1786; que incluye algunos himnos latinos de creación propia)[24] y un *Ad D. Gregorium Doran Hispanium* [...] *Epigramma* (Roma, 1796; dedicado a un arquitecto). Luego encontramos la figura del segoviano Esteban de Arteaga,

---

21 Ibid., 523.
22 Casanovas, *Cultura* (véase arriba, n. 1), 137. Sigue aquí el discurso de Mateo Aymerich sobre la Academia Crítico-Literaria, incluido en su libro *Prolusiones philosophicae, seu verae et germanae philosophiae effigies criticis aliquot orationibus et declamationibus adumbrata* (Barcelona, 1756).
23 Batllori, *Cultura* (véase arriba, n. 2), 318.
24 Recientemente traducidos y estudiados por Elena Gallego Moya, *Los himnos de la "Hymnodia Hispanica"* (Alicante, 2002).

que escribió *Plura poemata latina, italica et hispana* en un manuscrito que se ha perdido;[25] sí hemos conservado, en cambio, su poema dialogado *Ignatio Boncompagno Ludovico Viro, Principi Cardenali, Amplissimo Pontificii. Legati munus Bononiae. Inevasti Studentium. Universitates D. D. D.* (1778, dedicado a Gregorio XIII, Ugo Buoncompagni). Pero en el Archivo de la Compañía de Jesús de la Provincia de Castilla (Alcalá de Henares) encontramos numerosos poemas procedentes de varios colegios jesuíticos de toda España.[26] Sobre los humanistas españoles que fueron exiliados a Italia ("más de un centenar de jesuitas españoles") afirma Batllori: "Aquella floración de literatos – en el más amplio sentido – no se formó en Italia; allí solo se abrió el germen vivísimo que traían de España: de Madrid, de Cervera, de Valencia."[27] De todos modos, desde el prisma de Italia también tenemos autores que manifiestan la supremacía cultural de los jesuitas de la provincia de Aragón – y del País Vasco – por delante de los de Castilla: "In particolare gli intellettuali e i riformatori provenienti dall'ex Corona d'Aragona e dai Paesi Baschi possiedono sensibilità e peculiarità che li distinguono dai funzionari originari delle Castiglie."[28]

Y de las colonias hemos de destacar de manera especial la provincia de México: "Solo otra provincia puede comparársele [a la de Aragón], después del exilio, en densidad de cultura, y es la de México[29] – recuérdese a Alegre, Abad, Cavo, Clavigero, Márquez ...–, que domina sobre todas las hispanoamericanas con igual superioridad. Pero adviértase que también la Nueva España [se refiere al virreinato que incluye México y toda la América Central] había comenzado su renovación humanística antes del extrañamiento".[30] De Francisco Javier Alegre hemos de señalar su epopeya *Alexandriada* (1773) sobre la conquista de Tiro por parte de Alejandro Magno;[31] en el exilio italiano publicó una traducción latina de la *Ilíada*: *Homeri Ilias latino carmine expressa* (1776), y en 1889 Joaquín García Icazbaleta editó su obra lírica bajo el título *Opúsculos inéditos latinos y castellanos del P. Francisco Xavier Alegre*. Diego José Abad, por su parte, es autor del poema heroico *De Deo Deoque Homine heroica* (1775), una compilación teológica en verso. Pero por encima de todos cabe notar la figura

---

25 Batllori, *Cultura* (véase arriba, n. 2), 148.

26 Por poner solo un ejemplo, del jesuita gaditano José de Arenas encontramos el poema *In laudem Augustissimi Dulcissimique Eucharistiæ Sacramenti* (año 1727), en 256 hexámetros (est. 3, caja 12, carp. 14, "Versos latinos de varios metros y argumentos", leg. nº 1194/16 según el *Índice-Inventario del Archivo Histórico formado por el P. Mario Laplana (1849–1921) revisado hasta el año de 1950*), entre muchos otros poemas anónimos.

27 Batllori, *Cultura* (véase arriba, n. 2), 64.

28 Guasti, *L'esilio* (véase arriba, n. 3), XI.

29 Sobre toda esta generación de jesuitas mexicanos se ocupó Gabriel Méndez Plancarte, *Humanistas del siglo XVIII* (México, 1941).

30 Batllori, *Cultura* (véase arriba, n. 2), 318.

31 Otro poemario son sus *Lyrica et Georgica in B. Mariæ Guadalupanæ elogium* (ca. 1770).

NUEVOS RETOS PARA EL ESTUDIO DE LA POESÍA JESUÍTICA LATINA   469

del guatemalteco Rafael Landívar, autor de la *Rusticatio mexicana* (1781). Sobre este tipo de literatura llega a concluir el padre Batllori: "Entre los millares de versos españoles, italianos y latinos que se escribieron en el destierro, son en verdad poéticos casi solo los inspirados por el recuerdo de aquel lejano y sugerente mundo americano, hundido para ellos en una desesperanza inevitable."[32]

Si traspasamos el ámbito hispánico para hablar de poesía jesuítica latina del XVIII, aún en el contexto del exilio hemos de citar autores portugueses que fueron desterrados en 1759. En la misma línea que Landívar, el padre Batllori hace referencia a los *De rusticis Brasiliae rebus carminum libri IV* del portugués José Rodrigues de Melo (Roma, 1781) y el poema épico didáctico *De Sacchari opificio carmen* del brasileño Prudêncio do Amaral (Pésaro, 1780).[33] En cuanto a los jesuitas del resto de Europa, su producción poética no ha dado lugar a muchos estudios; únicamente encontramos trabajos aislados como el de László Szörényi referido a la poesía de los jesuitas de Austria en los siglos XVII y XVIII.[34] Y precisamente el siglo XVIII es, en términos generales, el menos conocido y analizado en lo atingente a su producción poética, pues los estudiosos se han centrado más en su labor humanística y erudita; la poesía jesuítica, en cambio, ha recibido más atención en el siglo anterior, el Barroco.

Pero si nos limitamos al Neoclasicismo del XVIII, apenas encontramos nombres más allá de los que ya hemos visto.[35] Fuera de España tenemos algún poeta suelto como el austríaco Michael Denis (1729–1800),[36] el astrónomo croata Ruđer Josip Bošković (1711–87),[37] los franceses Jacques Vanière

---

32   Batllori, *Cultura* (véase arriba, n. 2), 46. También hay muestras de poesía latina en Sudamérica, como las *Elejías* [sic] *latinas* (1761) del chileno Juan Ignacio Molina (1740–1829), que se han conservado manuscritas y están siendo analizadas por nuestra colega María José Brañes.

33   Batllori, *Cultura* (véase arriba, n. 2), 585.

34   László Szörenyi, "De carminibus heroicis Ovidium Vergiliumque imitantibus a patribus Societatis Jesu provinciae austriacæ sæculos XVII–XVIII scriptis," en *Acta Conventus Neo-Latini Amstelodamensis*, ed. Eckhard Kessler, G. C. Kuiper y P. Tuynman (München, 1979), 964–75.

35   Gilles Banderier, en la nota preliminar que incluye en su antología, justifica el periodo estudiado (a saber: 1620–1730) en estos términos: "Tenant, avec Vissac [Jacques A. Vissac, *De la poésie latine en France au siècle de Louis XIV* (París, 1862)], que la poésie néo-latine en général, et celles des jésuites en particulier, était entrée en décadence après l'*aetas aurea* que constitua le XVIIᵉ siècle, nous n'avons pas jugé utile de nous aventurer fort loin dans le siècle suivant" (*La lyre jésuite: Anthologie de poèmes latins (1620–1730)*, Gilles Banderier, Marc Fumaroli y Andrée Thill [Ginebra, 1999], 7).

36   Autor de poesía latina como sus *Carmina quaedam* (Viena, 1794), ha sido estudiado por Schmolze, "Michael Denis, Barde und Abbé: zur 250. Wiederkehr seines Geburtstages", *Österreich in Geschichte und Literatur* 24 (1980), 160–70.

37   Con obras como sus seis cantos *De solis ac lunae defectibus* (1760), ha sido estudiado por Lancelot Law Whyte, *Roger Joseph Boscovich: S.J., F.R.S., 1711–1787. Studies of his Life and Work on the 250th Anniversary of his Birth* (Londres, 1961).

(1664–1739)[38] y Claude Griffet (1702–51)[39] o los italianos Ubertino Carrara (1654–1716; *Columbus, carmen epicum*),[40] Simone Poggi (1685–1749; *Fabularum Aesopiarum libri X*, publicados por Giuseppe Boero en 1883)[41] y Carlo Noceti (1694–1759; *Eclogae*, 1741, y *De Iride et Aurora boreali carmina*, 1747). Luego podemos encontrar estudios sobre géneros concretos, como los que han suscitado los emblemas,[42] la épica,[43] la poesía didáctica[44] o la lírica,[45] o incluso trabajos sobre tópicos literarios muy concretos.[46] En la línea de la antología de poesía lírica que cito en la penúltima nota, tenemos alguna otra antología de poesía jesuítica latina de los siglos XVII y XVIII.[47] Llama la atención comprobar

---

38   Autor de un *Praedium rusticum* (1682) en diez cantos (después aumentados hasta dieciséis en la edición de 1730) inspirados en las *Geórgicas* de Virgilio; también tiene unos *Opuscula* (colección de poemas de 1730) y un *Dictionarium poeticum* (1740) al estilo del *Gradus ad Parnassum*, que fue una compilación de citas muy utilizada por los poetas jesuitas (Banderier et al., *Lyre* [véase arriba, n. 35], XI). Se le conoce como el "Virgilio francés". Una selección de sus versos la hallamos en la citada antología (Banderier et al., *Lyre* [véase arriba, n. 35], 217–38), que incluye además un apéndice bibliográfico (219).

39   Autor del poema didáctico *Cerebrum* (Rouen, 1727), analizado por nuestra colega Johanna Luggin, forma parte de una pléyade de poetas didácticos, muchos de los cuales fueron incluidos en la antología de François Oudin *Poemata didascalica* (París, 1813; 3 vols.): François Antoine Le Febvre (*Aurum*, 1703; *Terrae motus*, 1704), Augustin Etienne Souciet (*Cometae*, 1710), Pierre Brunoy (*De arte vitraria*, 1712), Loup Thomas (*Barometrum*, 1749), Gilles Anne Xavier de La Sante (*Ferrum*, 1707), Bertrand Gabriel Fleuriau (*Aer*, 1715), el propio Oudin (*Ignis*, 1749), etc.

40   Editado por Florian Schaffenrath (Berlín, 2006).

41   Obra que ha centrado la atención de nuestro colega José Carlos Miralles.

42   Sobre emblemática jesuítica tenemos varios trabajos, especialmente centrados en el siglo XVII, pero el XVIII también se contempla en algún caso: Walther Ludwig, "Unbekannte emblematologische Jesuitendichtung: Das horazisierende Lehrgedicht *De arte symbolica ad Erastum* (1701) von Jacobus Boschius aus Sigmaringen," *Neulateinisches Jahrbuch* 10 (2008), 195–261.

43   Florian Schaffenrath, "Unedierte lateinische Jesuitenepik aus dem Fondo Gesuitico der Biblioteca Nazionale di Roma," *Neulateinisches Jahrbuch*, 9 (2007), 328–42.

44   Yasmin Annabel Haskell, *Loyola's Bees: Ideology and Industry in Jesuit Latin Didactic Poetry* (Oxford, 2003).

45   Banderier et al., *Lyre* (véase arriba, n. 35). Es una antología que incluye diez poetas jesuitas, todos del siglo XVII salvo Jacques Vanière (1664–1739, francés), y ofrece el texto en latín con su traducción al francés. En el prólogo (*Lyre*, 1) Thill aclara que ha dejado de lado los grandes géneros (la epopeya y la tragedia) y también la poesía de circunstancias, concepto este último que debemos entender en buena medida como poesía encomiástica.

46   Por ejemplo, sobre la *descriptio templi* tenemos el trabajo de Ulrich Schlegelmilch, *Descriptio templi: Architektur und Fest in der lateinischen Dichtung des konfessionellen Zeitalters* (Regensburg, 2003).

47   James J. Mertz y John P. Murphy, *Jesuit Latin Poets of the 17th and 18th Centuries: An Anthology of Neo-Latin Poets* (Wauconda [Illinois], 1989). Tan solo seis de los diecinueve poetas incluidos se pueden situar en el siglo XVIII. Esta antología quizá sea la primera

NUEVOS RETOS PARA EL ESTUDIO DE LA POESÍA JESUÍTICA LATINA 471

que estas antologías no incorporan a ningún jesuita español.[48] Seguramente hemos de relacionar esto con el llamado *Grand siècle* de la literatura francesa (1643–1715, años correspondientes al reinado de Luis XIV), que coincide en buena parte con el Barroco,[49] bastante deslucido en el caso de España en lo referente al humanismo clasicista[50] y donde sobresalió el teatro escrito en lengua vernácula. Ya hemos visto que el "gran siglo" de la literatura jesuítica en España, y sobre todo en la provincia jesuítica de Aragón, a raíz de los jesuitas de la Universidad de Cervera, fue el XVIII, especialmente a partir de la segunda mitad, y también hemos comprobado que este siglo se vio interrumpido por la expulsión de la Compañía de Jesús (1767), que continuó su labor en el exilio italiano hasta el momento de la restauración (1814), que supuso el regreso de algunos de los ya ancianos jesuitas (desde 1815). Es en este contexto que hemos de situar la poesía conservada en los archivos. En la medida que son poemas inéditos, forman parte de un gran corpus de poesía que no ha recibido ninguna atención por parte de los mismos jesuitas, que probablemente la conciben como un simple ejercicio escolar, y que solo muy recientemente está siendo estudiada por filólogos laicos porque, más allá de la intención más o menos espiritual de esta poesía, hemos encontrado composiciones poéticas dignas de interés desde el punto de vista estrictamente literario. Por eso invito a los estudiosos a sumergirse en los archivos que conservan este tipo de poesía para darla a conocer, y que sean los lectores y críticos quienes la juzguen.

Universidad de Lleida

---

    de los tiempos modernos, ya que sus precedentes se encuentran en obras como la *Imago primi saeculi Societatis Jesu* (Anveres, 1640, que también incluye textos en prosa), el *Parnassus Societatis Jesu* (Frankfurt, 1654) o, reducida a un ámbito geográfico, los *Patrum Societatis Jesus ad Rhenum inferiorem Poemata selectiora* (1758; 4 vols.).

48   En la introducción a la citada antología, el padre John P. Murphy aclara: "The Jesuit poets of England (Edmund Campion and Robert Southwell, for exemple [no son buenos ejemplos, pues estos autores son del siglo XVI, no incluido en la antología]) and the Americas (Diego Abad and Rafael Landívar, for example) are omitted in this anthology" (Mertz et al., *Jesuit* [véase arriba, n. 47], IX). No justifica esta omisión explícita, pero tampoco dice nada sobre la omisión implícita de poetas jesuíticos españoles o portugueses.

49   Hay disparidad de opiniones en lo referente al valor de esta poesía latina que los jesuitas cultivaron en época barroca. En Italia, por ejemplo, encontramos defensores como Giovanni Getto, que habla en favor de un *Seicento barocco*, quien se enfrenta a la visión de Benedetto Croce, que critica su retórica y considera a los jesuitas unos "corruptores" del Renacimiento (Banderier et al., *Lyre* [véase arriba, n. 35], IX). Se ha vindicado incluso un *furor poeticus* y un *enthusiasmus* en esta poesía (ibid., XVIII).

50   Casanovas, *Cultura* (véase arriba, n. 1), 13–36.

CHAPTER 36

Fonti scientifiche in contesti scolastici: La metafora medica nei commenti a Persio del Secondo Quattrocento

Federica Rossetti

Abstract

During the Early Modern Age, Persius was a canonic author in the scholastic curriculum: a large number of commentaries on *Satires* were created in Italy in the second half of the fifteenth century to answer pedagogical needs arising from the Renaissance teaching of the Latin language. Despite this scholastic approach, Persius is analysed not only from a grammatical and rhetorical point of view, but also for his interest on many aspects of daily life and other *Realien*. More specifically, the metaphor of the satiric poet as a surgeon of moral vices and the medical terminology used by Persius lead commentators to utilise scientific sources for interpreting *Satires*. In addition to the encyclopedic sources commonly read by Renaissance commentators, we can find citations from less common medical sources used in humanistic commentaries on the classics. The paper investigates the use of technical texts in some commentaries on Persius of the second half of fifteenth century (Cristoforo Landino, c. 1462; Bartolomeo Fonzio, 1477; Giovanni Britannico, 1481; Angelo Poliziano, 1483–84; Raffaele Regio, 1487–88) in order to analyse interactions between medical notes and the philosophical reading of the *Satires*.

Keywords

Cristoforo Landino – Bartolomeo Fonzio – Giovanni Britannico – Neo-Latin commentaries – reception of Persius

Persio fu un autore sempre privilegiato nel panorama dell'educazione scolastica, a partire dalle prime fasi della sua ricezione,[1] attraverso tutto il Medioevo

---

1 Già Girolamo, in un celebre passo dell'*Adversus Rufinum* (1,16), fa riferimento a Persio come a un autore canonico del cursus scolastico tradizionale; inoltre, pare ormai certo che il

---

© KONINKLIJKE BRILL NV, LEIDEN, 2020 | DOI:10.1163/9789004427105_037

FONTI SCIENTIFICHE IN CONTESTI SCOLASTICI 473

e fino al tardo Rinascimento.[2] Nel corso del Quattrocento, complice lo sviluppo della stampa, il dibattito critico intorno al testo delle *Satire* si amplia, sia attraverso il proliferare di commenti continui nati in ambito scolastico e poi destinati alle stampe, sia attraverso la pubblicazione di opuscoli monografici in margine a specifici *loci critici* del testo persiano o di miscellanee filologiche che toccavano, tra gli altri argomenti, questioni di critica del testo relative ai versi delle *Satire*.[3]

I commenti continui alle *Satire*, come la maggior parte dei commenti umanistici, svolgevano una funzione enciclopedica, affrontando i temi più disparati della cultura del mondo antico, dalla grammatica latina alla storia Romana, da questioni filosofiche ai *Realien*.[4]

Tra i temi cari alla poetica persiana, l'analogia tra satira e medicina (evidente anche nei satirici latini Orazio e Giovenale) si rivela di particolare interesse per gli umanisti italiani.

Il presente studio intende analizzare alcuni passaggi di commenti a Persio prodotti nella seconda metà del Quattrocento, per mostrare come l'esegesi delle *Satire* sia influenzata dal contemporaneo dibattito sul valore della medicina e dall'ampliamento delle fonti mediche a disposizione degli umanisti.

---

cosiddetto *Commentum Cornuti*, che trova il suo assetto attuale nel IX secolo nella regione di Auxerre, abbia utilizzato e rielaborato materiali esegetici più antichi. Sull'argomento vd. James E. G. Zetzel, *Marginal Scholarship and Textual Deviance. The* Commentum Cornuti *and the Early Scholia on Persius* (London 2005), 127–37.

2   Il maggiore studio sulla ricezione delle *Satire* resta la voce del *Catalogus Translationum et Commentariorum*: Dorothy M. Robathan e Edward Cranz, "A. Persius Flaccus," in CTC, vol. 3 (Washington 1976), 201–312. Sulla tradizione manoscritta delle Satire vd. Birger Munk Olsen, *L'étude des auteurs classiques latins aux XIᵉ et XIIᵉ siècles. Tome II: Catalogue des manuscrits classiques latins copiés du IXᵉ au XIIᵉ siècle* (Paris 1985), 183–225. Tra gli studi e le edizioni dedicate a singoli commenti umanistici a Persio, ricordiamo Angelo Poliziano, *Commento inedito alle* Satire *di Persio*, ed. Lucia Cesarini Martinelli e Roberto Ricciardi (Firenze 1985); Caterina Malta, *Il commento a Persio dell'umanista Raffaele Regio* (Messina 1997); Alessandra Tramontana, *In Sicilia a scuola con Persio. Le lezioni sulle Satire dell'umanista Tommaso Schifaldo* (Messina 2000); László Takács e Attila Tuhári, *Two Renaissance Commentaries on Persius. Bartholomaeus Fontius' and Ioannes Britannicus' Commentaries on Persius* (Budapest 2015); Federica Rossetti, *Il commento di Giovanni Britannico a Persio e la sua ricezione nel Cinquecento europeo. Edizione critica e studio introduttivo* (Tesi di Dottorato, Napoli – Strasbourg 2017).

3   Tra gli opuscoli monografici dedicati a Persio, bisogna ricordare il *Tadeus sive de locis Persianis* di Bartolomeo Della Fonte (1488), la *Disputatio in errores Calphurnii de locis Persii, Valerii Maximi et Ciceronis* di Raffaele Regio (1490), l'*Oratio habita in enarratione Persii poetae satyrici* (1491), la *Praelectio in Persium* e il cap. 44 dei *Miscellanea* di Poliziano (1498).

4   Sull'argomento, *Neo-Latin Commentaries and the Management of Knowledge in the Late Middle Ages and the Early Modern Period (1400–1700)*, ed. Karl Enenkel e Henk Nellen (Leuven, 2013).

Come ha dimostrato Sari Kivistö nella sua monografia,[5] la comprensione dell'analogia medica è funzionale alla comprensione della natura stessa della Satira romana. Gli autori satirici latini utilizzano immagini di debolezza fisica come metafora della malattia dell'anima e della dissolutezza morale. Nelle satire persiane, le cause della malattia (morale e fisica) vanno infatti generalmente ricercate nello stile di vita vizioso della nobiltà romana, dedita a cibo, vino e lussuria.[6]

A questo stile di vita si oppone il modello di vita stoico (o genericamente filosofico) del poeta, dedito allo studio e alla morigeratezza. La malattia morale degli uomini diventa così la giustificazione ufficiale della scrittura satirica e il poeta presenta se stesso come un medico dei vizi. L'immagine emerge ad es. in maniera lampante nella Terza Satira, che si apre con l'immagine di un giovane ozioso che cerca invano di smaltire i postumi di una sbornia bevendo della cicuta e si chiude con i celebri funerali di un crapulone che si era rifiutato di ascoltare i consigli del suo medico.

Dal canto suo, il poeta satirico, indignato di fronte allo spettacolo della depravazione del suo tempo, dichiara di avere la milza turbolenta,[7] e la *Vita Persi* attribuita allo Ps. Probo riferisce la notizia, probabilmente autoschediastica, secondo la quale Persio sarebbe morto a trent'anni per un "vitium stomachi".[8] In generale, tutte le satire di Persio sono quindi disseminate di riferimenti a malattie, reali o morali che siano.

L'analogia tra satira e medicina è direttamente correlata a quella tra filosofia e medicina. L'autore satirico è innanzitutto filosofo[9] e gli obbiettivi di satira e filosofia coincidono nella volontà di riprendere e correggere (per quanto possibile) i vizi degli uomini. Il motivo del legame tra malattia dell'animo e malattia fisica, nonché la ricerca della cura nella filosofia, è ampiamente rappresentato nella letteratura umanistica del Quattrocento, in particolare nel quadro della cosiddetta disputa delle arti, che non solo aveva riconosciuto il carattere liberale dell'arte medica, ma l'aveva integrata ed equiparata alla filosofia naturale. Sulle orme delle *Tusculanae Disputationes*, la filosofia era a sua

---

5   Sari Kivistö, *Medical Analogy in Latin Satire* (Basingstoke 2009).

6   Alla metafora medica è infatti strettamente connessa quella alimentare, su cui vd. Shadi Bartsch, *Persius. A Study in Food, Philosophy, and the Figural* (Chicago – London 2015).

7   Pers. 1,10 "quid faciam? Sed sum petulanti splene: cachinno." ("Ma che dovrei fare? Io ho la milza turbolenta, scoppio a ridere", trad. E. Barelli).

8   *Vita A. Persii Flacci de commentario Probi Valeri sublata*, 9: "decessit autem vitio stomachi anno aetatis XXX." ("morì dunque per malattia di stomaco verso i trent'anni d'età" trad. E. Barelli).

9   Persio fu poeta stoico, allievo di Lucio Anneo Cornuto, la cui profonda influenza sulla sua produzione è evidente nella satira V, esplicitamente dedicata al maestro. La *Vita Persii* riferisce ch'egli possedesse settecento libri del filosofo stoico Crisippo (cf. *Vita Persii*, 7).

FONTI SCIENTIFICHE IN CONTESTI SCOLASTICI   475

volta intesa come medicina dell'anima: per portare solo alcuni esempi, Maffeo Vegio, nel *De liberorum educatione*, sottolinea il ruolo pedagogico della filosofia, che viene paragonata a una medicina dei mali dell'animo,[10] Marsilio Ficino (medico e filosofo) mette in correlazione l'anima e le malattie fisiche,[11] Filippo Beroaldo nella sua *Declamatio, an orator sit philosopho et medico anteponendus* sostiene che un filosofo è anche un medico, dato che il primo cura le malattie dell'animo.[12]

I commentatori quattrocenteschi di Persio non rimangono indifferenti alla tematica, data l'abbondanza di tali riferimenti all'interno del testo persiano. Nella lettera di dedica del commento a Lorenzo de' Medici, Raffaele Regio gioca con l'analogia medico-satirica, trasponendo il ruolo di medico su se stesso, capace, in quanto filologo, di risanare il testo corrotto di Persio, presentato a sua volta come un concittadino[13] malato bisognoso di cure (*Ad clarissimum patriae parentem Laurentium Medicem Raphaelis Regii enarrationum in Persii Satyras praefatio* Firenze, Laur. Plut. 46.16, f. 1r):[14]

> Si quis vel exigui nominis medicus ex optimatibus tuis quempiam, cuius praeclara in rempublicam merita extarent, variis iamque deploratis

---

10   Maphei Vegii laudensis, *De educatione liberorum et eorum claris moribus, libri sex: A Critical Text of Books I–VI*, ed. Maria Walburg Fanning (Washington, 1933), 111, cap. 3,8: "Non erit vero negligendum ut, cum aetas patietur, invitentur quam maxime adulescentes ad philosophiam, quae ita ad curandos animi morbos inventa est, quemadmodum et medicina ad sanandos corporum languores."

11   Cf. ad es. l'*Oratio de laudibus medicinae*. Marsilio Ficino, *Epistolae* (Venetiis, 1495), ISTC if00154000, c. 84v: "Scribit in Carmide Plato Magos illos animae corporisque medicos Zamolsidis Zoroastrisque sectatores arbitrari omnia corporis tum bona tum mala ab anima fluere in ipsum corpus, quemadmodum oculorum qualitas fluit a cerebro, cerebri qualitas a toto corpore. Atque ut impossibile est oculos curari, nisi curetur cerebrum, et cerebrum curari nisi corpus totum, ita corpus totum, nisi anima bene valeat, non posse bene valere; valitudinem vero animae curari Apollineis incantationibus quibusdam, id est philosophicis rationibus [...]."

12   Filippo Beroaldo, *Opusculum eruditum* (Venetiis, 1495), c. A2r: "Quid quod et philosophus medicus est? Cum Philosophia (ut inquit Arpinas orator) sit animorum medicina? Quod et Galenus quoque testatur. Cum autem morbi perniciosores pluresque sint animi quam corporis, praestantior haud dubie est philosophus, qui gravioribus morbis medelas ac fomenta salutariter apponit. Qui denique tanto est quam corporis medicus nobilior utiliorque, quanto animus corpore est preciosior."

13   Che Persio, originario di Volterra, venga indicato a Lorenzo de' Medici come *civis* della Repubblica di Firenze non desta stupore, visto che la città era a quel tempo sotto il controllo dei Medici e non erano ancora troppo lontani i tempi della guerra contro Volterra del 1472.

14   Qui e nelle successive citazioni da fonti primarie la punteggiatura e l'uso delle maiuscole sono normalizzati secondo l'uso moderno.

vulneribus confectum ac imperitorum potionibus manifestam in phrenesim lapsum, pristinae restitueret sanitati, is opinor non tibi modo, Laurenti Medices, rem gratissimam faceret, verum maximo quoque gaudio universam afficeret civitatem. Quod si is esset vir qui non in patria solum sed quocunque Latinae litterae pervenissent clarissimus esset, nonne id tibi immortali gloriae futurum existimares, si opera tua potissimum ac benignitate curatus reique publicae salvus fuisse redditus ubique praedicaretur? 'Sed quisnam' inquies 'meorum civium tanta est calamitate affectus?'. Nempe A. Persius Volaterranus, poeta candidissimus [...] in huiusmodi aerumnas mihi incidisse videtur.

Angelo Poliziano, invece, nella sua *Praelectio in Persium*,[15] ribadisce il parallelo tra satira e medicina, sostenendo che la satira può essere utilizzata come rimedio per l'anima quanto la medicina per il corpo (*Commento inedito*, vd. sopra, n. 2, 4, 41–9):

> [...] ut medici saepe eiusmodi corporis partibus ferrum adhibent aut cauterium, quo scilicet vires ipsarum vel consopitae excitentur, vel fugatae revocentur, ita nos profecto his potissimum hominibus nostros curandos animos tradere debemus, qui labem pestemque illorum omnem cunctaque perturbationum semina ceu ferro et flammis radicitus extirpant, quales scilicet ei potissimum poetae censentur, qui aut Romanam hanc satyram, aut Atheniensem illam veterem comoediam scriptitarunt.

La metafora medica era quindi perfettamente compresa dai commentatori persiani, che più volte nell'interpretare i versi persiani riconoscono al poeta il ruolo di 'chirurgo' dei vizi dell'animo.[16] Bartolomeo Della Fonte, autore del

---

15   La *Praelectio in Persium* fu stampata per la prima volta postuma nel 1498 nell'edizione aldina degli *Opera omnia* di Poliziano: *Angeli Politiani Opera Omnia et alia quaedam lectu digna*, Venetiis in aedibus Aldi Romani, 1498, cc. bbii^r–bb5^r. Moderne edizioni della *Praelectio* si leggono in Poliziano, *Commento inedito* (vd. sopra, n. 2) e in Angelo Poliziano, *Praelectiones*, 2, ed. Giorgia Zollino (Firenze 2016).

16   Lo confermano ad es. alcune note dei commenti di Giovanni Britannico e Bartolomeo Fonzio. Qui e di seguito nel testo le citazioni dal commento di Giovanni Britannico sono sempre tratte dalla mia tesi di dottorato (Rossetti, *Il commento*, vd. sopra, n. 2), mentre quelle del commento di Fonzio sono tratte da Takács, *Two Renaissance* (vd. sopra, n. 2). Giovanni Britannico, *In Pers.* 5,15–6: "PALLENTES RADERE MORES / DOCTUS ET INGENUO CULPAM DEFIGERE LUDO hinc argumentum satyrae ostenditur, quae ad hominum vitia capienda emersit. [...] 15. RADERE tangere et mordere, tractum a medicis qui cultro radere et resecare vulnera solent." Bartolomeo Della Fonte, *In Pers.* 3,63: "HELLEBORUM FRUSTRA CUM IAM CUTIS AEGRA TUMEBIT Optima similitudine

FONTI SCIENTIFICHE IN CONTESTI SCOLASTICI   477

primo commento a Persio destinato alle stampe, arriva ad attribuire al poeta conoscenze in campo medico, definendolo come un "esperto dell'arte medica" ("medicinae artis peritus").[17]

Se pure l'analogia era costruita su un piano perlopiù allegorico, le satire abbondavano di termini tecnici riferiti al campo medico, che necessitavano di essere chiarite anche su un piano scientifico. In questo contesto, le fonti classiche e tardoantiche diffuse e note tra gli umanisti italiani potevano rivelarsi insufficienti all'esegesi persiana. Tra le fonti maggiormente diffuse per l'interpretazione dell'oscuro testo persiano vi erano infatti i testi normalmente utilizzati dai commentatori umanistici: la *Naturalis Historia* di Plino il Vecchio, il *De lingua latina* e il *De re rustica* di Varrone, Pomponio Mela, l'*Epitome* di Festo di Paolo Diacono, i grammatici Servio, Nonio, Prisciano, *scholia* e commenti tardo-antichi alle *Satire* latine (*Commentum Cornuti*, Ps. Acrone, Porfirione).

La necessità di ricorrere a fonti specialistiche emerge già timidamente nel commento di Cristoforo Landino, conservato nel ms. Milano, Biblioteca Ambrosiana, I 26 inf. e redatto all'inizio degli anni Sessanta del Quattrocento. Sebbene l'esegesi del Landino sia fortemente dipendente dalla *vulgata* persiana[18] e nonostante sia chiara la destinazione scolastica del commento,[19] il professore dello *Studium fiorentinum* ricorre a una citazione dalle *Epistole* di Ippocrate (ep. 21 Smith) per la definizione del termine *veratrum* (*In Pers.* 1,51):

---

    utitur. Sicut enim morbo antequam vires adaugeat, occurrendum est, quoniam illi ingravescenti frustra remedium adhibetur, sic vitiis antequam illis occupemur, repugnandum est. Nam ubi in animis nostris penitus insederint, difficillime dimoventur."

17   Cf. Bartolomeo Della Fonte, *In Pers.* 3, 90–1: "POSTQUAM TERTIA COMPOSITAS VIDIT NOX CURRERE VENAS Medicinae Persius non ignarus ea profecto ponit, quae veteres medici observaverunt." e 5,144: "CALIDO SUB PECTORE MASCULA BILIS, INTUMUIT, QUAM NON EXTINXERIT URNA CICUTAE Hoc per parenthesim legitur et poetae attribuitur. [...] Itaque cum bilis ardore intumuisse poeta dixerit, ut medicinae artis peritus, cicutam in remedio posuit."

18   Concetto Marchesi, "Gli scoliasti a Persio," in *Rivista di filologia classica* 40 (1912), 195–9 evidenziava la dipendenza del commento di Landino da un ramo della tradizione vulgata, rappresentato dai cosiddetti *scolii fiorentini* (corrispondenti alla cosiddetta *Tradition E* in Robathan-Cranz 1976, rappresentata dai manoscritti Firenze, Riccardiano 664 e Laur. 52.4 e 53.23), da cui dipenderebbe anche Fonzio.

19   Il commento risale alle lezioni tenute da Landino presso lo Studio Fiorentino probabilmente nell'anno accademico 1461–62. Cf. Roberto Cardini, *La critica del Landino* (Firenze 1973), 16 e Roberto Cardini, "Contributo ad una 'vexatissima quaestio': "maris expers" (Pers. VI 39 – nonché Hor. Sat. II 8, 15, Sen. Nat quaest. I 16, 7, Suet. Tib. 45)," in *Tradizione classica e letteratura umanistica. Per Alessandro Perosa*, ed. Roberto Cardini et al. (Roma 1985), 694, 722–3.

Haec eadem herba, ut legitur in epistula quadam Ippocratis, dicitur curando Democrito, quod legerent heleborum in altis montibus, quum omnes herbae in huiusmodi locis plus nimirum habent propter aerem puriorem et terram subtiliorem et ea herba ipsum curarent. (Milano, Biblioteca Ambrosiana, I 26 inf., f. 198r)

Il ricorso a fonti tecniche si fa poi particolarmente evidente nel commento di Bartolomeo Della Fonte a Persio, che moltiplica le notazioni riferite a termini medico-anatomici e introduce il *De medicina* di Celso tra le fonti dell'esegesi persiana. Di quest'autore, all'epoca della composizione del commento di Fonzio a Persio, non esisteva alcuna edizione a stampa, cosicché il suo utilizzo per l'esegesi ai classici era piuttosto limitato. L'anno successivo alla pubblicazione del commento a Persio, fu lo stesso Bartolomeo Della Fonte a curare l'*editio princeps* del *De medicina*,[20] stampato a Firenze per i tipi di Niccolò di Lorenzo Alemanno.[21] Nel commento a Persio Fonzio cita il *De medicina* quindici volte, per fornire dettagliate spiegazioni e definizioni di malattie e organi del corpo umano: polmoni, fegato, denti, omento, bile, muco, scabbia, e così via. Celso rappresenta quindi una fonte privilegiata per l'umanista fiorentino, che talvolta tende a sovra-interpretare il testo di Persio grazie al recupero della fonte tecnica.

Si vedano alcuni esempi: Ai vv. 58–9 della Terza Satira, Persio descrive un giovane che smaltisce la sbornia dormendo con la testa ciondoloni e la bocca aperta, immagine della dissolutezza di chi preferisce seguire i propri istinti piuttosto che i precetti della filosofia. In questo caso, Fonzio sceglie di interpretare le espressioni "conpage soluta" e "dissutis undique malis" su un piano scientifico piuttosto che metaforico e letterario, e vi coglie un riferimento alle suture craniche. Piuttosto che chiarire il valore morale della scena,[22] il commentatore cita il *De medicina* e si dilunga in una descrizione della struttura del cranio (Della Fonte, *In Pers.* 3,58–9):

---

20   Nell'epistola prefatoria a Francesco Sassetti Fonzio dichiara di aver ricevuto da questi dei manoscritti provenienti dalla Francia, che l'editore avrebbe usato per risanare il testo corrotto del *De medicina*. Tuttavia, Poliziano lo avrebbe successivamente accusato di non aver mai utilizzato i codici 'gallici' e le ricerche di Concetto Marchesi su quest'edizione hanno condotto alla conclusione che il testo sia effettivamente attinto a codici fiorentini. Cf. Concetto Marchesi, *Bartolomeo Della Fonte (Bartholomaeus Fontius). Contributo alla storia degli studi classici in Firenze nella seconda metà del Quattrocento* (Catania 1900), 142–6.

21   Cornelii Celsi *De medicina* (Florentiis, 1478, ISTC ic00364000).

22   L'immagine delle mandibole rilassate ritornerà più avanti nella descrizione della morte del crapulone, che, colto dal malore, lascia cadere pezzi di cibo dalla bocca aperta. Vd. Pers. 3,102.

FONTI SCIENTIFICHE IN CONTESTI SCOLASTICI 479

> LAXUMQUE CAPUT COMPAGE SOLUTA Apertum somno caput propter calvariae suturas dixit, quarum, ut Celsus octavo scribit, duae super aures tempora a superiore capitis parte discernunt. [Cels. 8,1,2] Tertia ad aures per verticem tendens occipitium a summo capite diducit. Quarta ab eodem vertice per medium caput ad frontem procedit. DISSUTIS UNDIQUE MALIS Hoc oscitantibus propter suturas malarum accidit. Malae enim Celso auctore in summa parte singulas transversas suturas habent. [Cels. 8,1,4] A mediisque naribus aut superiorum dentium gingivis per medium palatum una procedit alia quae transversa idem palatum secat. [Cels. 8,1,5]

Qualcosa di simile accade nel commento alla Quinta Satira, nella nota relativa al lemma "bulla": pur comprendendo che il termine vada inteso come un riferimento alla "bulla praetexta", pendente ornamentale indossato dai bambini romani fino al raggiungimento della maggiore età, Fonzio coglie l'occasione per inserire delle notazioni attinte al *De medicina* relative alla presenza di "bullulae" nelle urine (Della Fonte, *In Pers.* 5,30):

> CUSTOS PURPURA Praetextam intelligit, quae simul cum bulla in usum nobilium puerorum usurpata est. Dependebat autem bulla, hoc est monile antiquum ornamenti genus, quod collo gestabatur a pectore, ut puerilem aetatem alterius consilio regendam esse ostenderet. [...] Est vero bulla tumor quidam excrescens. Unde et diminutivum bullula derivatur. Celsus secundo de urina scribens: Aut si quasdam quasi maculas repraesentat, aut si bullulas excitat, [Cels. 2,5,3] quin et bullo verbo idem post paulo utitur. Aut si bullat, aut si male olet. [Cels. 2,7,12]

Fonzio, pur di fare sfoggio della fonte tecnica, arriva quindi a forzare l'interpretazione del passaggio del testo persiano, o quantomeno ad estendere significativamente il commento al lemma "bulla", usando questo stesso termine come pretesto per la digressione.

L'uso smodato del *De medicina* come fonte per l'esegesi persiana nel commento di Della Fonte, probabilmente grazie alla diffusione garantita dalle stampe, diventa una cifra caratteristica dei successivi commenti a Persio (a tradizione a stampa e manoscritta) prodotti negli anni Ottanta del Quattrocento, come dimostrano ad es. i commenti di Giovanni Britannico, Raffaele Regio, Angelo Poliziano.[23]

---

23 Sull'abbondante uso di Celso come fonte dell'esegesi persiana nei commenti sopraelencati, cf. Poliziano, *Commento inedito* (vedi sopra, n. 2), LVII–LVIII; Malta, *Il commento* (vedi sopra, n. 2), 54; Rossetti, *Il commento* (vedi sopra, n. 2), XCVIII–XCIX.

Un interessante caso di riutilizzo dei passaggi del *De medicina* impiegati da Fonzio si riscontra nel commento di Giovanni Britannico, laddove la notazione relativa al termine "bullulae" e alla loro presenza nelle urine come sintomo medico viene ripresa a proposito di un altro luogo del testo di Persio. Britannico, infatti, propone un emendamento al verso 10 della Seconda Satira, difendendo la variante "ebullet" in luogo della lezione tradita "ebulliat" per ragioni metriche. A sostegno della sua posizione, Britannico rileva l'occorrenza del verbo in Celso, che ne chiarirebbe anche il significato nel testo persiano (Britannico, *In Pers.* 2,10):

> EBULLET hunc ego locum emendavi. Nam cum omnes codices temporum fortasse et librariorum culpa 'ebulliat' legant, animadverti 'ebullet' legendum esse, non 'ebulliat'. [...] Hoc verbo usus est Celsus loquens de urina: "Si haec crassa carruculas quidem exiguas quasi capillos habet, aut si bullat et male olet, et interdum quasi arenam interdum quasi sanguinem trahit". [Cels. 2,7,12]

Dall'esempio traspare come l'utilizzo di fonti tecniche, inizialmente limitato alla necessità di fornire spiegazioni 'scientifiche' dei termini medici utilizzati dal poeta satirico, si estenda poi all'esegesi generale delle *Satire*.

Nel commento di Fonzio, Celso non è comunque l'unica fonte medica utilizzata per l'interpretazione delle *Satire*: in un paio di casi, l'umanista cita il *Liber Medicinalis* di Quinto Sereno, manuale di medicina in versi databile tra la fine del II e l'inizio del IV secolo d.C. La fonte, come mostrano gli studi di Anna Bellettini,[24] inizialmente diffusa per tradizione manoscritta nella cerchia pomponiana, ebbe ulteriore successo, soprattutto in ambito bresciano, a partire dalla stampa dell'*editio princeps*, avvenuta intorno al 1474.[25]

Più interessante l'uso di una fonte contemporanea a Fonzio, il *De anima* di Cristoforo Landino, trattato sulla natura dell'anima basato su fonti classiche e medievali, principalmente Aristotele, ma anche Platone, Avicenna, Averroè, Alberto Magno, Argiropulo, Bessarione. In due casi, Della Fonte illustra il significato dei termini "bilis" (bile) e "pituita" (muco) e le loro conseguenze sulla salute umana, supportando la sua spiegazione con citazioni dal secondo libro del *De anima* (Della Fonte, *In Pers.* 2,13–4; 57):

---

24   Anna Bellettini, "L'editio princeps di Quinto Sereno e la tradizione umanistica del Liber Medicinalis in Italia nord-orientale," *Italia Medioevale e Umanistica* 52 (2011), 197–226 e Anna Bellettini, "La tradizione umanistica di Quinto Sereno 'Sammonico' e l'Accademia Romana," *Italia Medioevale e Umanistica* 51 (2010), 201–33.

25   Quintus Serenus, *Carmen medicinale* (Venetiis, 1474, ISTC is00469000).

FONTI SCIENTIFICHE IN CONTESTI SCOLASTICI

ACRI BILE Bilis, quae a Graecis 'cholera' dicitur. Landino auctore secundo de anima libro, sanguinis spuma videri potest, quae ita rubet, ut etiam in candorem ignis deflectat, corpusque optime nutrit. Sed haec bona est ipsumque sanguinem acuit. Verum huic adversa et noxia, de qua Persius loquitur, duplex est. Aut enim bilis corrumpitur cum alio se admiscente humore adulteratur, aut ipsa sua sponte a se degenerat. [...] Cum vero ipsa bilis sponte sua per se corrumpitur, aut viridis herbaceaque est, et prassina a succo prassim herbae dicitur, aut aeneae aerugini similis est, et zinaria a colore denominatur. Zinam enim Arabes aeris aeruginen vocant. Ceterum noxia ipsa bilis, ut Celsus in quarto refert, commune stomachi atque intestinorum vitium videri potest. [Cels. 4,18,1] [...]

PITUITA 'Phlegma' a Graece, 'pituita' Latine, quod vitam petat Aelio auctore, ut scribit Quintilianus, dicitur. [Quint., *inst.* 1,6,36] Est autem pituita, ut Landinus secundo de anima libro refert, sanguis rudis adhuc, nec plene decoctus, sed quae quandoque sanguis absolutissime fieri possit. [...] Ceterum ut Celsus quarto volumine auctor est: Distillat humor ex capite interdum in nares, quod leve est, interdum etiam in pulmonem, quod pessimum est. [Cels. 4,5,1]

Entrambi i passaggi combinano due fonti tecniche, il *De anima* di Landino e il *De medicina* di Celso. L'utilizzo di un'opera che aveva come oggetto la natura dell'anima sembra confermare il legame tra malattia (metaforica e non) e satira, intesa come suo rimedio. Lo stesso legame sembra emergere anche dal commento di Raffaele Regio, che utilizza il *De anima* aristotelico (nella sua traduzione latina)[26] per commentare i versi 116–7 della Terza Satira, in cui viene descritto uno scoppio d'ira del giovane ozioso che rifiuta di seguire i precetti della filosofia stoica: "alludit ad irae definitionem, quae sic a physicis assignatur. Ira est accensio sanguinis circa cor ulciscendi gratia eveniens." (Raffaele Regio, *in Pers.* 3, 116, f. 45r)[27]

L'approccio etico-filosofico finora evidenziato raggiunge il suo apice nel commento di Angelo Poliziano, che, come si è detto, già nella *praelectio in*

---

26   Cf. ad es. il commento al *De anima* di Aristotele di Tommaso d'Aquino (*Sententia De anima*, lib. 1 l. 2 n. 9 "Hic enim, scilicet physicus, assignat materiam, cum dicit, quod est accensio sanguinis circa cor") o il *Commentarium Magnum* di Averroè nella traduzione di Michele Scoto (*De an.* 1,16,4–6, Crawford: "Ira est appetitus in vindictam; et sic de similibus. Naturalis autem dicit quod est ebullitio sanguinis aut caloris in corde.")

27   Arist., *De an.* 403a29–b1: διαφερόντως δ' ἄν ὁρίσαιντο ὁ φυσικός τε καὶ ὁ διαλεκτικός ἕκαστον αὐτῶν, οἷον ὀργὴ τί ἐστιν· ὁ μὲν γὰρ ὄρεξιν· ἀντιλυπήσεως τι τοιοῦτον, ὁ δὲ ζέσιν τοῦ περὶ καρδίαν αἵματος καὶ θερμοῦ.

Persium esasperava il rapporto tra filosofia, satira e medicina. Nel commento, la concezione teorica della satira come terapia per i vizi dell'anima, si traduce in uno sfoggio continuo di fonti mediche e di accurate notazioni di termini afferenti al campo medico-scientifico. Tra le fonti di Poliziano, oltre agli ormai consueti Plinio e Celso, figurano Galeno, Paolo Egineta, Aezio, Dioscoride, i *Problemata* di Aristotele e di Alessandro di Afrodisia.[28]

Nel contesto dell'esegesi persiana del secondo Quattrocento, il parallelo tra malattia morale e malattia fisica e tra medicina e satira sembra quindi svilupparsi di pari passo con l'allargamento delle fonti mediche a disposizione degli umanisti.

I commentatori italiani, e in particolare gli esponenti dell'Umanesimo fiorentino (Landino, Della Fonte, Poliziano), sensibili al tema del legame tra filosofia e medicina e influenzati dal dibattito contemporaneo sul valore dell'arte medica, trovano terreno fertile per le loro riflessioni scientifico-filosofiche nel testo persiano, in cui i riferimenti medici si intessono su un ipotesto filosofico. Lo spettro delle fonti tecniche, classiche e contemporanee, utilizzate nell'interpretazione del testo persiano si amplia considerevolmente e l'interesse per gli aspetti medico-scientifici costituirà una delle cifre caratteristiche della produzione tardoquattrocentesca intorno alle *Satire*.

---

28   Vd. Poliziano, *Commento inedito* (vedi sopra, n. 2), LVII–LIX.

CHAPTER 37

Continuidad y variación en el tratamiento de la rabia: de Gratio (s. I) a Aurifaber (s. XVI)

María de Lourdes Santiago Martínez

Abstract

Gratio (*ca.* siglo I) en su *Cynegeticon* dedicó más de 150 versos a la detección y cura de las enfermedades que atacan a los perros de caza; siglos más tarde, Demetrio Pepagomeno (*ca.* siglos XIV–XV) también escribió su opúsculo Κυνοσόφιον para brindar consejos sobre el cuidado y preservación de los perros, de manera que ambas obras persiguen un objetivo común. Por tal razón, en este trabajo se busca, en primer lugar, identificar la posible intertextualidad del Κυνοσόφιον con el *Cynegeticon* de Gratio, a partir del análisis del fragmento dedicado al diagnóstico y prescripción contra la rabia; en segundo lugar, se aborda la recepción del Κυνοσόφιον en el siglo XVI, a través de dos traducciones neolatinas: una realizada en 1535 por Rudbertus de Moshaim, la otra, en 1545, por Andreas Aurifaber, el cotejo del mismo fragmento en ambas versiones permitirá identificar si presentan diferencias sintácticas o semánticas.

Keywords

Rudbertus de Moshaim – Andreas Aurifaber – Demetrio Pepagomeno– *Cynegeticon* – Traducciones neolatinas

En este trabajo busco, en primer lugar, identificar la posible intertextualidad del tratado Κυνοσόφιον de Demetrio Pepagomeno con el poema didáctico *Cynegeticon* de Gratio, con base en el análisis del fragmento dedicado al diagnóstico y prescripción contra la rabia que se ofrece en ambas obras. En segundo lugar, me ocupo de la recepción del Κυνοσόφιον en el siglo XVI, a través de dos traducciones al latín realizadas por Rudbertus de Moshaim (1535) y Andreas Aurifaber (1545), el cotejo del fragmento en ambas versiones me permitirá identificar algunas diferencias sintácticas o semánticas.

© KONINKLIJKE BRILL NV, LEIDEN, 2020 | DOI:10.1163/9789004427105_038

1 Introducción

En la práctica de la caza que los antiguos griegos denominaron cinegética, el cazador buscaba, además de la diversión y el placer del contacto con la naturaleza, la preparación física necesaria para llevar a cabo con éxito sus futuros compromisos guerreros.

Evidentemente, un personaje protagónico en tal actividad es el perro, animal que, en opinión de Plinio el Viejo, posee características innatas para la caza (Plin., *HN* 8,61,147):

> [...] sed in venatu sollertia et sagacitas praecipua est. scrutatur vestigia atque persequitur, comitantem ad feram inquisitorem loro trahens, qua visa quam silens et occulte, set quam significans demonstratio est cauda primum, deinde rostro!

Tan importante fue el auxilio de los perros para los cazadores, que los tratados cinegéticos no solo incluían instrucciones sobre técnicas de caza o fabricación de instrumentos venatorios, sino también recetas médicas para prevenir o remediar las principales enfermedades que atacan a los perros.

2 Los autores y los textos

Entre los autores que en la Antigüedad escribieron obras cinegéticas, se encuentra Gratio, probablemente de origen siciliano, quien, a finales del siglo I a. C. o a inicios del I, escribió el poema didáctico *Cynegeticon*, que fue transmitido por cinco códices;[1] el más antiguo de ellos es el *Vindobonensis* 277, datado entre los siglos VIII y IX, y conservado en la Biblioteca Nacional de Austria, el cual sirvió en mayor medida a Crescenzo Formicola para establecer su propia edición crítica, de la que yo misma me he servido en este trabajo.

En su *Cynegeticon*, como indica su nombre, Gratio debió de transmitir la técnica de cazar con ayuda de perros;[2] sin embargo, dado que ha llegado a nosotros en forma fragmentaria y desconocemos a ciencia cierta la totalidad de su contenido, solo encontramos en él información sobre la elaboración de

---

1 Para información sobre los diversos códices, vid. Crescenzo Formicola, *Il Cynegeticon di Gratio* (Bologna, 1988), 31–42.

2 Puesto que el nombre deriva del sustantivo griego ἡ κυνηγετική, formado, a su vez, a partir del sustantivo κύων "perro" y del verbo ἄγω, "conducir", y en el que se sobreentiende el término τέχνη "técnica".

CONTINUIDAD Y VARIACIÓN EN EL TRATAMIENTO DE LA RABIA

redes, lanzas y espantajos de caza, y consejos sobre la selección, crianza y cuidado de los perros de caza.

Ahora bien, no debemos perder de vista que en el terreno de la literatura clásica difícilmente un autor desarrollaba temas nuevos e inusitados, de manera que Gratio recurrió a otros autores que le sirvieron de fuente de inspiración: utilizó como base temática de su poema el extenso tratado sobre la caza Κυνηγέτιχων, escrito en el siglo IV antes de nuestra Era por Jenofonte; además, a lo largo del poema encontramos numerosos paralelos con la obra de Lucrecio, Virgilio y Ovidio,[3] quienes constituyeron su modelo poético-métrico; a partir de tales influencias, Gratio logró dar a su poema características propias.

Asimismo, el trabajo de Gratio sirvió, sin duda, de fuente para Nemesiano, escritor del siglo III, en la elaboración de su propio poema cinegético, homónimo, y, como intento demostrar en mi exposición, para la creación del tratado en prosa Κυνοσόφιον ο Περὶ κυνῶν ἐπιμελείας, escrito por Demetrio Pepagomeno, autor bizantino cuya producción se ubica durante la dinastía de los Paleólogos. El Κυνοσόφιον fue preservado en el *Codex Monacensis Graecus* 390 del siglo XVI. Para la datación de esta obra y de su autor, contamos con la excelente investigación de Stavros Lazaris "La production nouvelle en médicine vétérinaire sous les Paléologues et l'œuvre cynégétique de Dèmètrios Pépagôménos,"[4] en la que Lazaris afirma que, en un momento preciso del Imperio Bizantino, en especial bajo el reinado de Andrónico II,[5] se vivió un renovado interés cultural, en el que los ojos se volvieron hacia la literatura antigua y que se manifestó de dos formas: en primer lugar, por el gran número de manuscritos copiados ya por monjes y otros religiosos, ya por eruditos entregados a esta actividad por interés personal o por carecer de los recursos para confiarla en manos de expertos; en segundo lugar, por la producción de obras nuevas de temática afín a la de obras clásicas, a cargo de un reducido círculo de hombres cultos.[6] Entre esas obras hubo algunos tratados de cetrería y cinegética, dedicados, en parte,

---

3   Algunos paralelos significativos son: *Cyn.* 23: Ov., *Ars am.* 1,433; *Cyn.* 45: Ov., *Ars am.* 1,13; *Cyn.* 70: Ov., *Pont.* 1,10,9; *Cyn.* 115: Verg., *Aen.* 7,353; *Cyn.* 168: Lucr. 6,1285; *Cyn.* 239: Lucr. 4,993; Verg., *Aen.* 11,669; *Cyn.* 270: Lucr. 5,30; Verg., *Georg.* 3,85; *Aen.* 7,281; *Cyn.* 290: Verg., *Aen.* 2,391; *Cyn.* 300: Ov., *Met.* 14,357; *Cyn.* 344: Ov., *Fast.* 2,9; *Cyn.* 412: Verg., *Georg.* 3,469; *Cyn.* 437: Ov., *Am.* 1,2,21; *Cyn.* 442: Verg., *Georg.* 2,81.

4   Stavros Lazaris, "La production nouvelle en médicine vétérinaire sous les Paléologues et l'œuvre cynégétique de Dèmètrios Pépagôménos," en *Philosophie et sciences à Byzance de 1204 à 1453. Les textes, les doctrines et leur transmission*, ed. Michel Cacouros y Marie-Hélène Congourdeau (Leuven, 2006), 225–67.

5   En 1282 sucedió en el trono a su padre Miguel VIII Paleólogo; su reinado se extendió hasta 1328.

6   Vid. Lazaris, "La production nouvelle" (véase arriba, n. 4), 227–8.

al tratamiento de las enfermedades de halcones y perros, que, al ser transmitidos por los manuscritos sin el nombre de su autor, salvo por la anotación posterior de otra mano, fueron atribuidos a cierto Demetrio de Constantinopla, primero en el *Codex Parisinus Graecus* 2323 (copiado hacia 1540), después, entre el 1543 y el 1544, en el *Codex Monacensis Graecus* 390 al que ya nos hemos referido. Años más tarde, Demetrio de Constantinopla fue identificado con Demetrio Pepagomeno por Angelos Vergekios,[7] editor, en 1558, de la obra *De podagra*, atribuida a Pepagomeno. La ambigüedad de la autoría de tales escritos fue también cuestionada por Nicolaus Rigaltius en la dedicatoria que hizo a Luis XIII, rey de Francia y de Navarra, en su edición bilingüe[8] de los tratados sobre el cuidado de los halcones y de los perros (20–1):

> Antiquissimus habendus is qui sub Demetrii Constantinopolitanis nomine primus apparet. nam qui secundus appingitur, longe sequioris stili et recentioris esse videtur auctoris; fortean Phenonis illius, quem aiunt in Augustana Vindelicorum bibliotheca reperiri. nisi quis malit hoc nomine citare auctorem semibarbarae ad Michaëlem Paleologum scriptiunculae, quam heic etiam edimus.

Ante tal incertidumbre, después de un exhaustivo análisis de los manuscritos en los que la obra fue transmitida, de los autores a los que el Κυνοσόφιον fue atribuido, así como de las fechas de la posible actividad literaria de su autor, Lazaris concluye que el autor del Κυνοσόφιον fue Demetrio Pepagomeno, médico, veterinario y naturalista greco-bizantino, que vivió en Constantinopla entre los siglos XIV y XV, y que estuvo ligado al círculo de intelectuales de los emperadores Manuel II y Juan VIII, Paleólogos; que fue copista además de escritor y consagró parte de su obra a la medicina veterinaria, en especial a las enfermedades de los halcones y de los perros. En efecto, al inicio del Κυνοσόφιον Pepagomeno reconoce la utilidad del perro para el hombre:

---

7 Angelos Vergekios, calígrafo cretense que realizó numerosos manuscritos griegos para el rey Francisco I de Francia. Como copista jugó un papel importante en la difusión de obras griegas entre los círculos humanistas de Francia. Su caligrafía sirvió de modelo a Claude Garamond para la creación de los caracteres llamados "Grecs du roi", utilizados por Robert Estienne. Vid. Ambroise Firmin-Didot, *Alde Manuce et l'hellénisme à Venise*, (Paris, 1875), 581.

8 Nicolaus Rigaltius, *Hierakosophion. Rei accipitrariae scriptores nunc primum editi. Accessit Cynosophion, liber de cura canum* (Lutetiae, 1612). La edición presenta, en primer lugar, los textos en griego de los diferentes tratados; en segundo, sus versiones al latín; y, en tercero, otros textos de temática afín, entre ellos, *Alcon sive de cura canum venaticorum* de Hieronymus Fracastorius.

Οὐκ ἔλαττον συντελεῖ καὶ κύων πρὸς ὑπηρεσίαν τῷ ἡμετέρῳ γένει. πῇ μὲν πρὸς φυλακήν, πῇ δὲ καὶ πρὸς θήραν, ἢ καὶ ἀμφότερα·[9]

Lazaris plantea también en su investigación las posibles fuentes del Κυνοσόφιον y señala en primer lugar el *Cynegeticon* de Arriano,[10] sin dejar de reconocer la influencia que sobre este ejerció el tratado de Jenofonte ya mencionado; sin embargo, en mi opinión no fue Arriano sino Gratio, quien proporcionó a Pepagomeno las principales recomendaciones de índole veterinaria, pues, aunque Arriano coincide con Gratio al ofrecer consejos sobre el cuidado de los perros adultos, la edad ideal para su apareamiento, el cuidado de la perra recién parida así como sobre la nutrición de los cachorros y su inicio en la caza, y, aunque da consejos generales sobre el bienestar de los perros y sobre los riesgos que conlleva, por ejemplo, que un perro duerma junto con otros que puedan contagiarlo de sarna, en ningún momento ofrece recetas para la cura de las enfermedades, como sí lo hace el poema gratiano.

3 Los fragmentos sobre la rabia

El *Cynegeticon* de Gratio ofrece más de 150 versos dedicados al diagnóstico y cura de las enfermedades que atacan a los perros; de estos, para aplicar un breve análisis comparativo y advertir la posible influencia de Gratio en la obra de Pepagomeno, he elegido el fragmento referente a la rabia (Grat., *Cyn.* 383–98):

> Pluruma per catulos / rabies / inuictaque tardis
> praecipi ⟨t⟩at / letale / malum: / sit tutius ergo
> antire auxiliis / et primas uincere causas.
> Namque subit, / nodis / qua lingua tenacibus haeret,
> —uermiculum / dixere—/ mala atque incondita pestis.
> Ille ubi salsa siti / praecepit uiscera longa,
> aestiuos / uibrans / accensi⟨s⟩ febribus ignes,
> moliturque fugas / et sedem spernit amaram.
> Scilicet hoc / motu / stimulisque potentibus acti

---

9   Ibid., 259. Nótese cómo la versión latina de Andreas Aurifaber enriquece y complementa el parco texto griego: "Non minus utilitatis adfert suo officio ac studio generi humano canis quam falco aut accipiter, partim ratione custodiae, qua securitatem praestat, partim quod feras et a fructibus et pecudibus arceat, venaturque partim utroque" (Ibid., 165).

10 Lucio Flavio Arriano fue un filósofo e historiador nacido en Nicomedia, cuya producción se ubica en el siglo II. Escribió el tratado Κυνηγέτικων, con base en la obra homónima de Jenofonte.

in furias / uertere / canes. / Ergo insita ferro
iam teneris / elementa / mali / causasque recidunt.
Nec longa in facto / medicinast ulcere: / purum
sparge salem et / tenui / permulce uolnus olivo;
ante relata suas / quam nox / bene compleat umbras,
ecce aderit / factique oblitus uolneris ultro
blanditur / mensis / Cereremque efflagitat ore.

En el fragmento encontramos, en primer lugar, la caracterización de la enfermedad como mal letal:

Pluruma per catulos / **rabies** / inuictaque **tardis**
praecipi<t>at / **letale** / **malum**: / sit tutius ergo
antire auxiliis / et **primas uincere **causas**.

Gratio manifiesta la gravedad de la enfermedad, primero, al destacar entre cesuras las palabras "rabies" y "letale malum", y luego, al utilizar varios vocablos que denotan anticipación: "**praecipitat**", "**antire**", "**primas causas**", así como el antónimo "**tardis**", con los que busca hacer énfasis en que el mal puede ser superado si se ataca desde sus primeros síntomas.

En seguida, el poeta describe los síntomas que hacen evidente la enfermedad y explica que esta provoca una alteración física que es posible detectar en la parte inferior, nudosa, de la lengua; que tal malformación ha sido llamada gusanillo ("vermiculus"), vocablo que destaca al colocarlo en la primera sede del hexámetro y que complementa, en el mismo verso, mediante una aposición que califica la enfermedad de manera general:

Namque subit, / **nodis** / **qua lingua tenacibus haeret**,
—**uermiculum** / dixere—/ mala atque **incondita pestis**.

Asimismo, Gratio explica cómo el "vermiculus" invade las entrañas del perro y cómo, ardiente, desea salir de ahí, causando fiebre y espasmos al perro y volviéndolo furioso:

Ille ubi salsa siti / praecepit uiscera longa,
aestiuos / uibrans / accensi<s> febribus ignes,
moliturque fugas / et sedem spernit amaram.
Scilicet hoc / motu / stimulisque potentibus **acti**
in furias / uertere / canes.

CONTINUIDAD Y VARIACIÓN EN EL TRATAMIENTO DE LA RABIA

En tercer lugar, propone la cura adecuada:

Ergo insita **ferro**
iam teneris / elementa / **mali / causasque recidunt.**
Nec longa in facto / medicinast ulcere: / purum
sparge salem et / **tenui** / permulce uolnus **olivo**;

La prescripción consiste en una cirugía para extirpar la malformación causante de la rabia y en la posterior curación de la herida con dos ingredientes de uso terapéutico: sal—poderoso antiséptico—y aceite de oliva—eficaz cicatrizante. Asegura que, al cabo de unas horas, el perro vuelve a su carácter y, meloso, reclama alimento:

ante relata suas / quam nox / bene compleat umbras,
ecce aderit / factique oblitus uolneris ultro
blanditur / mensis / **Cereremque efflagitat ore.**

Por otra parte, el fragmento del Κυνοσόφιον dedicado a la rabia, aunque no cuenta con el marco que ofrecen las cesuras, tiene a su favor la posibilidad de una mayor extensión, de manera que cada capítulo se identifica con un título (Rigaltius, *Hierakosophion*, véase arriba, n. 8, 264–5):

Εἰς κύνα λυττήσσοντα πρόγνωσις.
Κύνα λυττῶντα οὕτως γνώσῃ. πρῶτον μὲν ἵσταται ἀπομεμωραμένος, καὶ δοκιμάζει τοῦ δάκνειν τὸν ἄνθρωπον, καὶ δυσήκοος ἐστιν, ἑστὼς ὡς μηδὲ γνῶ κἂν τοὺς ἰδίοις δεσπότας· τοῦτο οὖν ὅταν γνῶς, δὸς αὐτῷ τοιοῦτον ποτόν· ῥόδου ἀγρίου τὰς ῥίζας, τρῖψον καὶ λείωσον δεόντως, καὶ μῖξον ὕδωρ πηγαῖον ὀλίγον, καὶ δι᾽ ὀθονίου διηθήσας, τῷ κυνὶ δὸς πίνειν, καὶ γνώσῃ τὸν λυσσῶντα.
Ἄλλο.
Ἐν τῷ κάτω μέρει τῆς γλώσσης αὐτοῦ, δεσμοῖς ποὶ κατέχεται· γίνεται δὲ εἶδος εἰς ἐκτύπωμα σκώληκος, ὅμοιον νεύρῳ λευκῷ, πρινὴ οὖν αὐξήσῃ καὶ λάβῃ πάντα τὸν λαιμὸν τοῦ κυνός, ἀπόκοψον ἐκ τῆς γλώσσης αὐτοῦ, καὶ θεραπεύσεις μόνον ἐπιτηδείως.
Προφυλακτικὸν, ἵνα μὴ λυσσήσῃ.
Λαβὼν ἀγριοσυκῆν, κόψον καὶ μετὰ ἀξουγγίου παλαιοῦ, δὸς φαγεῖν τῷ κυνί· ἢ κισσὸν ἕψησον, καὶ ὅταν εἰς τρία μέρη ἔλθῃ, δὸς αὐτῷ πρωῒ φαγεῖν, ἐν ἡμέρᾳ ἡλίου.
Ἄλλο.
Ὀρνίθων ἀφόδευμα, καὶ ὄνου αἰδοῖον, μετὰ οἴνου εὐώδους δὸς φαγεῖν.

Ἄλλο.

Βοτανήν χελιδωνίαν μετὰ ἀξουγγίου κόψας, δὸς μετὰ ἄρτου φαγεῖν.[11]

Si bien el tratado se ocupa del cuidado de los perros y del tratamiento de sus principales enfermedades, el título del apartado se centra en el reconocimiento del perro rabioso: Εἰς κύνα λυττήσσοντα πρόγνωσις, y no en la descripción abstracta de la enfermedad; de hecho, el autor nunca menciona la palabra λύττα o λύσσα "rabia", sino que se refiere a ella a través de formas verbales que denotan la afección sufrida por el perro λυττήσσοντα, λυττῶντα, λυσσῶντα, λυσσήσῃ, vocablos en los que es posible advertir, además, la alternancia entre formas áticas y jónicas.

En su primer diagnóstico, el bizantino describe los cambios en el comportamiento de un perro atacado por la rabia, a saber, se queda parado, como si estuviera fuera de sí; se torna desobediente e intenta morder a las personas, desconociendo incluso a sus propios amos; y recomienda que, tan pronto como se reconozcan tales síntomas, se dé a beber al perro, previamente filtrada, una preparación de raíz de rosa silvestre triturada y pulverizada, mezclada con agua de manantial.

En cambio, en su segundo diagnóstico, describe el cambio físico que experimenta el perro rabioso, y tal descripción nos permite aseverar que Pepagomeno no solo conoció el *Cynegeticon* de Gratio, sino que incluso lo utilizó como fuente para la redacción de su diagnóstico.

En efecto, describe el nacimiento de un tumorcillo en forma de gusano (γίνεται δὲ εἶδος εἰς ἐκτύπωμα σκώληκος), en la base de la lengua del perro atacado por la rabia, y recomienda la extirpación del mismo (ἀπόκοψον ἐκ τῆς γλώσσης αὐτοῦ) para lograr la cura. Cabe aclarar que Gratio fue el primero que relacionó el término "vermiculus" con la rabia, y que, sin duda, de su *Cynegeticon* lo tomó Plinio el Viejo, quien, en su *Naturalis historia*, lo utilizó como sinónimo de rabia: "est vermiculus in lingua canum, qui vocatur a Graecis lytta, quo exempto infantibus catulis nec rabidi fiunt nec fastidium sentient;"[12] sin embargo, no precisa en qué parte de la lengua se encuentra el "vermiculus", malformación congénita que debe ser arrancada de los cachorros (aunque no explica cómo), para que no padezcan rabia.

En cambio, como ya hemos señalado, Gratio sí precisó el lugar donde surge ("subit") tal excrecencia "en forma de gusano" y fue también quien primero recomendó que se extirpara ("recidunt") de la boca del perro "ya afectado por la rabia", pero no como el tratamiento profiláctico que se advierte en el texto de Plinio.

---

11   Transcripción a cargo de Juan Carlos Rodríguez.

12   Plin., *HN* 29,32,100.

CONTINUIDAD Y VARIACIÓN EN EL TRATAMIENTO DE LA RABIA

4   Las traducciones neolatinas

En esta sección, analizaremos la trasmisión del fragmento del Κυνοσόφιον sobre la rabia, a través de dos traducciones neolatinas del siglo XVI, porque, de acuerdo con el *Companion to Neo-Latin Studies*, las traducciones del griego antiguo o bizantino al latín están directamente conectadas con la esencia misma del Humanismo, a saber, rescatar y revivir la herencia clásica. En efecto, las traducciones al latín fueron necesarias para que el conocimiento de los clásicos tuviera un mayor alcance porque pocos humanistas tenían pleno dominio del griego, y, aunque los primeros en realizar traducciones del griego al latín fueron los humanistas italianos, como Leonardo Bruni o Marsilio Ficino, esta labor fue realizada en forma continua desde finales del siglo XV hasta el siglo XVII por eruditos de todas partes de Europa.[13]

El gusto por la actividad cinegética y por la literatura ligada a ella hizo posible que el Κυνοσόφιον se viera favorecido por esa labor traductora: fue objeto de tres traducciones, dos de ellas aparecidas durante la primera mitad del siglo XVI, la primera, realizada en 1535 por Rudbertus de Moshaim, teólogo y erudito de Patavia, hoy Passau, bajo el título: *Kynosophion ac opusculum Phemonis de cura et conservatione canum;*[14] la segunda, en 1545, por Andreas Aurifaber, médico de Vratislavia, hoy Breslavia, quien realizó su propia versión del Κυνοσόφιον, editada primero en Wittenberg, con el título: *Phaemonis veteris philosophi Cynosophion seu de cura canum liber,*[15] y después en París, en 1612, bajo el cuidado de Nicolaus Rigaltius, con el título simplificado *Cynosophium. Liber de cura canum.*[16] Cabe señalar que la misma edición de Rigaltius, pero con textos griego y latino confrontados, fue incluida en un compendio de obras cinegéticas publicado en 1699 bajo el cuidado y anotación de Thomas Johnson.[17]

Ahora bien, en la nota al lector, Rigaltius reconoce que la versión latina de Aurifaber se basa en la realizada años atrás por Moshaim; asimismo, explica que en su edición él decidió eliminar el nombre de "Phemon vetus philosophus" porque resultaba desconocido para todos y no estaba respaldado por

---

13   Vid. Jozef IJsewijn y Dirk Sacré, *Companion to Neo-Latin Studies, Part. II. Literary, Linguistic, Philological and Editorial Questions* (Leuven, 1998), 491–4.

14   Rudbertus a Moshaim, *Kynosophion ac opusculum Phemonis de cura et conservatione canum* (Viennae, 1535).

15   Andreas Aurifaber, *Phaemonis veteris philosophi Cynosophion seu de cura canum liber* (Vitenbergae, 1545).

16   Rigaltius, *Hierakosophion* (véase arriba, n. 8).

17   *Gratii Falisci Cynegeticon, cum poematio cognomine M. A. Olympii Nemesiani Carthaginensis. Accedunt Hier. Fracastorii ALCON* [...] *et Opusculum vetus* Κυνοσόφιον *dict. seu de Cura canum,* incerto auctore (Londini, 1699).

ningún códice; finalmente, señala que, aunque existió una tercera traducción al latín: "Aurifabri versionem edi curavimus, multo feliciorem accuratioremque ea quam Gillius quidam, doctissimis [sic] illius Petri Gillii nepos hieracosophiorum versioni adtexuit."[18]

Sin embargo, de la tercera traducción solo tenemos noticia a partir de tal comentario. Ya desde el título las versiones latinas presentan diferencias:

> Moshaim: "CONTRA rabiem medicina, eiusque praecognitio"[19]
> Aurifaber: "Canem rabidum cognoscendi curandi ac praeservandi ratio".[20]

Ambas versiones son interpretativas, la de Moshaim incluye "medicina", que no aparece en el original y omite "canis", protagonista del tratado; por su parte, Aurifaber, aunque es más fiel al original griego, hace más atractiva y convincente su versión mediante la *amplificatio* de "cognoscendi ratio", al añadir "curandi ac praeservandi".

En seguida, en ambas versiones se presentan los síntomas que permiten a diagnóstico de la enfermedad:

> Moshaim: Canem rabidum hoc modo cognoscere licebit: primum quidem subsistit **furore ac insania percitus** et sub inde homines rabido morsu petere conatur, et accessu et accersitu difficilis, astans itaque nec proprium quidem **agnoscit herum**.
> Aurifaber: Canem rabidum, ita certo cognosces. Primum subsistit **dementatus prorsus ac furore percitus**, ac contendit mordere hominem, neque facile audit; **adeo ut nec dominos cognoscat suos**.

Ambos trabajos respetan el original, con mínimas diferencias: en Moshaim, el "canis rabidus": "subsistit **furore ac insania percitus**", donde el complemento predicativo "percitus" es modificado por los agentes "furore" e "insania"; en cambio, en Aurifaber leemos: "subsistit **dementatus prorsus ac furore percitus**", donde el traductor prefirió coordinar dos complementos predicativos "dementatus" y "percitus", y conservar solo uno de los agentes utilizados por Moshaim. Ahí mismo, Moshaim sustituye la subordinada comparativa griega por una coordinada copulativa: "ita**que** nec proprium quidem **agnoscit** herum"; en tanto que Aurifaber conserva la subordinada, pero, para lograr mayor contundencia, la vuelve consecutiva: "**adeo ut nec** dominos **cognoscat** suos."

---

18   Rigaltius, *Hierakosophion* (véase arriba, n. 8), 258.
19   Moshaim, *Kynosophion* (véase arriba, n. 14), 5.
20   Rigaltius, *Hierakosophion* (véase arriba, n. 8), 170.

CONTINUIDAD Y VARIACIÓN EN EL TRATAMIENTO DE LA RABIA 493

Es evidente que ambas versiones transmiten la idea original de Pepagomeno, al describir los síntomas de la rabia como una "locura" que invade a los perros, como ya antes lo había expresado Gratio, mediante una metáfora (Grat., *Cyn.* 391–2):

Scilicet hoc / motu / stimulisque potentibus **acti**
in furias / uertere / canes.

Como resultado de esta locura el perro se vuelve agresivo, muerde a todos y desconoce incluso a su propio amo. Para calmarlo, Pepagomeno recomienda la poción curativa ya referida,[21] pero tal remedio no se halla en el *Cynegeticon*, sino en Plinio.[22]

Sin embargo, en seguida, en ambas versiones se hace evidente el conocimiento que el autor bizantino tuvo del poema de Gratio, porque, en un segundo diagnóstico, se describe una malformación con apariencia de gusano ("vermis"), en la parte baja de lengua y se recomienda cortarla antes de que crezca hasta tal punto que ocupe toda la garganta del perro y la obstruya. En la versión latina de Moshaim se lee:

Et rursus **in parte inferiore linguae** Canis **vinculo ac strictura quadam angustatur.** fit autem **species** quaedam **in formam vermis** neruo albo similis, quae priusquam augeatur, gutturque totum occupet **ex ipsius lingua decidito** et **hoc uno** ingeniose **curaueris.**

En cambio, en la versión de Aurifaber:

Atque canem rabie percitum cognoscere sic: **in inferiore parte, nodis qua lingua tenacibus haeret,** accrescit **lues vermiformis** neruo candido non absimilis. priusquam autem augeatur, totumque occupet gutur canis, **rescindito** et curabis sola apta diaeta.

Como ya he comentado, este segundo diagnóstico de la enfermedad y su correspondiente curación denotan la intertextualidad del Κυνοσόφιον con el *Cynegeticon*, pues en ambos textos el indicio de la rabia es una malformación en la base de la lengua, descrita como un gusano: vermiculus = εἶδος σκώληκος = in formam vermis / vermiformis.

---

21   Véase arriba pp. 489–490.
22   Vid. Plin., *HN* 8,63,152.

Hay, desde luego, diferencias en ambos traductores, Moshaim trató de mantener la enfermedad en suspenso al referirla como "**species quaedam** in forma vermis nervo albo similis"; en cambio, Aurifaber la caracterizó de inmediato como "**lues** vermiformis neruo candido non absimilis". Este último, en mi opinión, intentó ofrecer un texto retóricamente más pulido, por ejemplo, al sustituir "in formam vermis", calco del original, por el adjetivo "vermiformis", acorde con el gusto de los neolatinos por la formación de neologismos a partir de dos términos simples;[23] además, por razones de estilo y quizá para hacer énfasis en la intensidad de la blancura, prefirió el adjetivo "candido" sobre "albo" y, en lugar de "neruo albo similis", utilizó la lítote "neruo candido non absimilis", dado que, en algunos contextos, "absimilis" llegó a utilizarse como antónimo de "similis", pero, lo más importante para nuestro argumento, complementó la expresión "in inferiore parte", con una cita directa del *Cynegeticon* de Gratio: "nodis qua lingua tenacibus haeret", hecho que el propio Aurifaber explica mediante una nota, en la versión del *Cynosophium* publicada de 1545: "Versus Gratii adscribendos duxi, tum quod mali causam pluribus expliceat, tum quod rationem curandi facilem contineat."[24]

5 Conclusiones

Estoy consciente de que el alcance de esta investigación es aún muy limitado, dado que solo me he referido a una de las enfermedades abordadas en el poema de Gratio y en el tratado de Pepagomeno; de que para que tenga una mayor repercusión deberé extender mi análisis a otras secciones o incluso a todo el Κυνοσόφιον, de manera que también el análisis de las versiones neolatinas resulte más relevante, al ser más detallado; sin embargo, la muestra que he presentado me permite desde ahora concluir:

(a) Que Demetrio Pepagomeno sí conoció el *Cynegeticon* de Gratio y lo utilizó como fuente para su Κυνοσόφιον, lo que se hace patente en su prescripción contra la rabia, en la que recomienda, como antes lo hizo Gratio, la inmediata cirugía para extirpar el "vermiculus", malformación causante de la enfermedad.

(b) Que el traductor neolatino, Andreas Aurifaber, conoció tan bien el poema gratiano que incluso, en su afán por transmitir una traducción más comprensible que la de Moshaim, lo citó o parafraseó cuando consideró

---

23 Vid. IJsewijn, *Companion* (véase arriba, n. 13), 387–90.
24 Aurifaber, *Phaemonis* (véase arriba, n. 15), 62.

pertinente matizar o explicar alguna parte del Κυνοσόφιον, privilegiando la cabal comprensión de la obra frente a la literalidad.

Sin duda, queda mucho por investigar sobre el desarrollo de la literatura de tema cinegético en el mundo bizantino, así como sobre su recepción y consecuente transmisión por eruditos neolatinos, baste decir que el paralelo hallado en la versión latina de Aurifaber me invita a realizar una investigación detallada para descubrir si el uso de citas gratianas y su adecuada inserción en el Κυνοσόφιον fue una práctica recurrente del erudito breslaviense.

Universidad Nacional Autónoma de México

CHAPTER 38

Magnetism's Transformation from Natural Phenomenon to Literary Metaphor

Raija Sarasti-Wilenius

Abstract

Several scientific discoveries and concepts have inspired allusions, metaphors, analogies, and symbols that eventually entered the literature of their age. In literary metaphors, concepts are often broadened and meanings are extended beyond the limits of their rigid scientific definitions, taking on lives of their own. The aim of this paper is to examine the use of magnetism as a literary metaphor in a Latin oration, *Scientiarum magnes* (1690) by Daniel Achrelius, Professor of Eloquence at the Academy of Turku (1679–92), then the most prominent town in the eastern part of the Swedish realm. Achrelius' predilection for magnetic symbolism derived from the idea of magnetism as a force behind a variety of natural phenomena, as explained in his natural philosophical work *Contemplationes mundi* (1682). I will seek an answer to the question of whether there was some sort of a broader philosophical implication behind Achrelius' deployment of magnetic symbolism in *Scientiarum magnes*, or whether it was purely metaphorical.

Keywords

Daniel Achrelius – *Scientiarum magnes* (1690) – Neo-Latin orations – magnetism – Academy of Turku

Metaphors and analogies have been central to scientific thinking since antiquity; by connecting generally known ideas to something that is unknown, metaphors help scientists communicate and help people grasp complex ideas or concepts. Metaphors also move in the opposite direction. Several scientific discoveries and concepts have inspired allusions, metaphors, analogies, and symbols that eventually entered the literature of their age. In literary metaphors, concepts are often broadened and meanings are extended beyond the limits of

© KONINKLIJKE BRILL NV, LEIDEN, 2020 | DOI:10.1163/9789004427105_039

their rigid scientific definitions, taking on lives of their own.[1] Especially from the mid-seventeenth century on, the 'two cultures'—that is science (factual, accurate) and literature (fictive, inaccurate)—have been diverging from each other, which has brought about discussions on the proper style of scientific language and the significance and roles of truth and metaphor.[2] This paper discusses a scientific and a literary text by an author from the second half of the seventeenth century, when the 'two cultures' still overlapped in many respects and when the goal of utilizing precision and unambiguity in scientific language still needed a champion in one of the most northern universities of Europe, the Academy of Turku.[3]

My aim is to examine the use of magnetism as a literary metaphor in a Latin oration, *Scientiarum magnes* (1690) by Daniel Achrelius, Professor of Eloquence at the Academy of Turku (1679–92), then the most prominent town in the eastern part of the Swedish realm. Achrelius' predilection for magnetic symbolism derived from the idea of magnetism as a force behind a variety of natural phenomena, as explained in his natural philosophical work *Contemplationes mundi* (1682).[4] I will seek an answer to the question of whether there was a some sort of a broader philosophical implication behind Achrelius' deployment of magnetic symbolism in *Scientiarum magnes*, or whether it was purely metaphorical. Before dealing with Achrelius' *Contemplationes mundi* and *Scientiarum magnes*, I will make some general remarks on scientific research into magnetism in premodern times, and on magnetic symbolism in literature, in order to provide some background to Achrelius' writings.

Naturally occurring magnets, called lodestones, are a form of iron oxide found in certain iron mines, the knowledge of which long predates the

---

1   Pamela Gossin, "Literature and the Modern Physical Sciences," in *The Cambridge History of Science* 5, ed. Mary Jo Nye (Cambridge, 2003), 91–110, there 99–100; David R. Langslow, "The Language of Poetry and the Language of Science: The Latin Poets and 'Medical Latin'," in *Proceedings of the British Academy* 93 (1999), 183–225, there 198–202.

2   For the much-discussed topic of significance of truth and metaphor in early modern literature and science, see Wendy Beth Hyman, "Deductions from Metaphors: Figurative Truth, Poetical Language, and Early Modern Science," in *The Palgrave Handbook of Early Modern Literature and Science* (2017), 27–48, there 27–8; Mary Thomas Crane, "John Donne and the New Science," in *The Palgrave Handbook of Early Modern Literature and Science* (2017), 95–114.

3   Mary Baine Campbell, "Literature," in *The Cambridge History of Science* 3, ed. Kathrine Park and Lorraine Daston (Cambridge, 2006), 756–72, there 770.

4   Achrelius' *Contemplationes mundi* was first written as a series of dissertations, and later published as a single volume in 1682. Jorma Vallinkoski, *Die Dissertationen der alten Universität Turku (Academia Aboensis) 1642–1828* (Helsinki, 1966), Nos. 1–21.

Christian era. The name lodestone referred to the ability of this material to indicate direction; a compass needle made of lodestone could lead you to your destination in the same way that the lodestar (the North Star, Polaris), which marks north in the night sky, could guide you on your journey.[5] According to Lucretius' *De rerum natura* (first century BC), the word magnet derives from the Lydian city of Magnesia, where magnetic rock may have first been discovered or recognized.[6] Another ancient source, the *Naturalis historia* of Pliny the Elder, tells a story about a shepherd named Magnes, who discovered a magnetic field to which the iron nails of his shoes stuck fast while he pastured his flocks on Mount Ida.[7] Both Lucretius and Pliny described the basic properties of a lodestone: it draws other pieces of iron towards itself, but sometimes iron was also repelled from it.[8] Since this seemed to happen for no apparent reason, the behaviour was often considered magical, and gave rise to many superstitions: magnets were thought to be useful for thieves, and women in labour, and also effective in a love potion. It was believed that they could repel sorcery, drive demons away, and even reconcile married couples.[9] In the Middle Ages, the best-known experiments on magnetism were conducted in the thirteenth century by the French scholar Petrus Peregrinus de Maricourt (fl. 1269). During his service as an engineer in the army of the King of Sicily, Charles of Anjou, he described the properties and usage of lodestone in a letter, *Epistola de magnete*, to his soldier friend.[10] However, several misconceptions and superstitions still surrounded magnetism three centuries later, when the English physician William Gilbert's (1544–1603) serious experimental investigations took place. Gilbert's work *De magnete*, published in 1600, reported his greatest insight: that the earth itself was magnetic.[11]

Gilbert's work generated many experiments and much speculation about magnetism during the first half of the seventeenth century.[12] One of the outcomes of this exploration was a movement called magnetic philosophy,

---

5   Gerrit L. Verschuur, *Hidden Attraction: The History and Mystery of Magnetism* (Oxford, 1996), 7–8.
6   Lucretius, *De rerum natura* 6,906–9.
7   Pliny, *Naturalis historia* 36,127
8   Lucretius, *De rerum natura* 6,910–1064; Pliny, *Naturalis historia* 36,126–7.
9   Verschuur, *Hidden Attraction* (see above, n. 5), 21; Duane H. D. Roller, *The* De Magnete *of William Gilbert* (Amsterdam, 1959), 27.
10   Roller, *The* De Magnete *of William Gilbert* (see above, n. 9), 39–42.
11   Roller, *The* De Magnete *of William Gilbert* (see above, n. 9), 93–4; Verschuur, *Hidden Attraction* (see above, n. 5), 19.
12   Martha Baldwin, "Kircher's Magnetic Investigations," in *The Great Art of Knowing: The Baroque Encyclopedia of Athanasius Kircher*, ed. Daniel Stolzenberg (Stanford, 2001), 17–36, there 27.

MAGNETISM FROM NATURAL PHENOMENON TO LITERARY METAPHOR 499

whose advocates believed that magnetic forces explained a wide range of natural phenomena. For example, both the supporters of the earth-centred and sun-centred structures of the universe drew upon magnetism for inspiration.[13] The principal sources of information on magnetism in Daniel Achrelius' *Contemplationes mundi* were the Jesuit polymath Athanasius Kircher (1601–80) and his collaborator Kaspar Schott (1608–66).[14] German by birth, Kircher settled down at the Jesuit college in Rome in 1633 and concentrated on his ambition to synthesize all known fields of knowledge. The title of the recent work edited by Paula Findlen, *Athanasius Kircher. The Last Man Who Knew Everything*, illustrates his pursuits very well.[15] In addition to the magnetic studies contained in his works on astronomy, botany, geology, medicine, and theology, he also wrote two books directly addressing magnetism, his first book *Ars magnesia* (1631) and the later *Magnes sive de arte magnetica* (Rome 1641). Kircher went beyond most natural philosophers and scientists of his age, such as Francis Bacon, René Descartes, Galileo Galilei, and Isaac Newton, in seeing the magnet as the key to understanding all other fields and phenomena.[16] Kircher's theory of universal magnetism was criticized by several contemporary scientists, who did not regard Kircher's explanations as scientifically credible. Indeed, Descartes famously declared that Kircher was more of a charlatan than a scholar.[17]

Daniel Achrelius' *Contemplationes mundi* was a typical natural philosophical work of its age, studying the material world and its changes, and dealing with, amongst other things, cosmography, meteorology, the earth, minerals, plants, and animals, including human beings. In addition, it also addressed metaphysical questions, seeking the universal causes of phenomena.[18] In

---

13   Verschuur, *Hidden Attraction* (see above, n. 5), 31.

14   In addition to Kircher and Schott, *Contemplationes mundi* presented ideas compiled from various other sources, such as Daniel Sennert, Johannes Sperling, Bernhard Varenius, Isaac Vossius, Antonius Le Grand. Maija Kallinen, "Daniel Achreliuksen teos Contemplationes mundi—sen lähdepohja ja tulkintaa," *Minerva. Aate- ja oppihistorian vuosikirja* 2 (Oulu, 1991), 3–140, there 15–22.

15   *Athanasius Kircher. The Last Man Who Knew Everything*, ed. Paula Findlen (New York, 2004).

16   Baldwin, "Kircher's Magnetic Investigations" (see above, n. 12), 17.

17   Paula Findlen, "Introduction. The Last Man Who Knew everything … or Did He?," in *Athanasius Kircher* (see above, n. 15), 1–48, there 22; René Descartes, *Correspondence*, ed. Charles Adam and Gérard Milhaud (Paris, 1936–63), vol. 3, 803.

18   Brian W. Ogilvie, "Science and Medicine," in *The Oxford Handbook of Neo-Latin*, ed. Sarah Knight and Stefan Tilg (Oxford, 2015), 263–77, there 263; Kathrine Park and Lorraine Daston, "Introduction. The Age of the New," in *The Cambridge History of Science*, ed. Kathrine Park and Lorraine Daston (Cambridge, 2006), vol. 3, 1–18, there 4.

his work, Achrelius repeated the facts about magnetism that were generally known in his time, such as its power to attract iron objects, its polarity, and its utility to navigators and cartographers in the form of the compass; but he was also fascinated by the supposed mysterious powers of magnets, and went much further in his remarks.[19] He claimed that a wide variety of natural phenomena could be best explained as the result of occult magnetic powers. One of these was a botanical phenomenon known to botanists today as phototropism: Achrelius argued that a plant inclined toward its light source in the same way that a lodestone always sought to situate itself parallel to the axis of the Earth. Based on this notion, Kircher presented the design for a sunflower clock in his *Magnes.*[20] Another botanical example taken from Kircher—Achrelius himself had hardly seen a palm tree in its natural habitat—concerns the love of male and female palm trees caused by the force of sympathy.[21] This idea is also depicted in a contemporary emblem: two palm trees bending their heads towards each other (over a river), with the motto "vivite concordes".[22] The strong connection between male and female palm trees is comparable to a harmonius marriage; a solitary male tree fades away, but if it is planted next to a female tree then both flourish.

The behaviour of lodestones provided many opportunities for their use as a symbol or literary metaphor. Magnetism was used to describe both the process of attraction or repulsion and the sympathy-antipathy relationship. In the index of literary symbols provided in the Latin translation of Filippo Picinelli's *Mondo simbolico* (Venice, 1635), the symbolic meanings of magnetism associated with God, God's will, mercy, providence, Christian life, fate, contemplation, conformity, etc. are in the majority. Moreover, magnets were commonly used as symbols for many other things, such as true love, friendship, peace, unity, constancy, but also things that stand for less desired aspects or qualities, such as worldly pleasures, harmful overriding passions, and extravagance.[23] Magnetic symbolism also appeared in iconography. An emblem with the

---

19   Kallinen, "Daniel Achreliuksen teos Contemplationes mundi" (see above, note 15), 94.

20   Daniel Achrelius, *Contemplationes mundi* (Aboae, 1682), 286–8; Athanasius Kircher, *Magnes sive de arte magnetica* (Coloniae Agrippinae, 1643), 645; Baldwin, "Kircher's Magnetic Investigations" (see above, n. 12), 30.

21   Achrelius, *Contemplationes mundi* (see above, n. 20), 228: "[...] inter palmam marem & faeminam tale intercedere amoris conjugium, ut veluti veneris intellectus ijs insidere videatur. Quippe mas solus crescens contabescere dicitur, at vero si juxta illum foemina fuerit plantata, hanc amoris pignore exhilaratam, uberi foetura impraegnat, amboque jucundissime & genialiter vivunt." See Kircher, *Magnes* (see above, n. 20), 630–1.

22   Jacob Cats, *Alle de wercken* (Amsterdam, 1658), vol. 1, 108.

23   "Index rerum notabilium quae in mundo symbolico reperiuntur," in *Mundus symbolicus in emblematum universitate formatus, explicatus et tam sacris quam profanis Eruditionibus*

motto "The mind remains unmoved" ("mens immota manet") referenced the property of lodestones always pointing to the north; the connection between the image and the motto is explained as follows: "One says that the Magnet moves iron through its internal power and hence continuously shows sailors the way. For it always looks securely, without wavering, at the pole star. In this way it depicts the passage of time and warns us in various ways. If only our mind remained so directed towards heaven, unmoved, and would not suddenly waver over fickle misfortunes."[24]

Achrelius employed magnetism as a literary device in the epideictic speeches he wrote and delivered at various social functions, often in the name of the Academy of Turku. In this connection, I deal with his rhetorical masterpiece, entitled *Scientiarum magnes*, dedicated to the Swedish King and Queen, Charles XI and Ulrica Eleonora, when celebrating the King's thirty-fifth birthday and the fiftieth anniversary of the Academy of Turku in 1690.[25] Connected to a wide variety of subjects, the symbol of the magnet runs through the whole speech, tying its different parts together. The word "magnes" itself is often highlighted in the text through the use of capital letters or a larger font. The most important idea presented there, the magnetism of the sciences, was already explained in the invitation to the delivery of the speech (the academic programme): the magnetism of sciences is drawn into the human head by divine plan, and examines the poles of the Earth and the pole of Eternity by means of both human abilities and scientific methods and principles.[26]

The obvious discrepancy between the modest appearance and the inner powers of lodestones introduces the passage that exemplifies the title. Already in *Contemplationes mundi*, Achrelius had quoted verses of the late antique poet Claudius Claudianus' poem entitled *Magnes*, probably cited from Kircher's *Magnes*, pointing out that even if the unpretentious looking lodestone was not used to adorn precious and beautiful jewellery, its powers make

---

     ac Sententiis illustratus. Idiomate Italico conscriptus a D. Philippo Picinello [...] *nunc vero in latiam traductus a R. D. Augustino Erath* (Coloniae Agrippinae, 1681), s.v. *magnes*.

24   Johannes Sambucus, *Emblemata* (Antverpiae, 1564; Budapest, 1982), 84: "Dicitur interna vi Magnes ferra movere / Perpetuo nautas dirigere inque viam. / Semper enim stellam firme aspicit polarem. / Indicat hac horas, nos varieque monet. / Mens utinam in caelum nobis immota maneret, / Nec subito dubiis fluctuet illa malis."

25   In printed form, the speech comprises 70 pages in quarto size.

26   Daniel Achrelius, *Scientiarum magnes* (Aboae, 1690, henceforth *SM*), academic programme composed in lapidary style: "Vix ratio concipere/ Vix humana eloquentia/ potest exponere/ Grandia consilia coeli! qvae unice/ In exiguo humano cranio/ pinxerunt/ MAGNETEM SCIENTIARUM. / Ille / Judicio, Ingenio, Meditatione, Industria / Tangit / Norma Artium, / Scientia solida, / Prudentia cauta / Indagine sapienti / Polos mundi; polum aeternitatis."

it superior to any other stone.[27] This also applies to the so-called magnetism of the sciences; it is not valued by uncultured, uneducated, and hypocritical people, but it nevertheless embraces all the knowledge and secrets that are meaningful to humankind. The passage, structured around the repetition of the phrase "with its repulsion and attraction" ("Hujus attractu et repulsu"), specifies various sciences and disciplines as exemplifying this trait, including theology, law, medicine, moral philosophy, eloquence, and history. Through the force of the magnetism of the sciences, the prudent mind is freed from earthly affairs and approaches heaven, justice chases away fraud and injustice, medicine suppresses diseases, virtues flourish, and eloquence and history are able to promote the good in the world.[28]

After the introduction, all the disciplines taught and studied at the Academy of Turku are dealt with individually; and each of them is called a magnet, or claimed to have magnetic powers. For example, mathematics is "the true imitator ('simia') of God, solid foundation of architects and faithful magnet of clever inventions."[29] Law, as it is practiced in Finland, is "just and incorrupt, a magnet of impartiality."[30] God has given humans the art of medicine, which

---

27   Claudius Claudianus, *Carm. min.* 29,10–5: "[...] lapis est cognomine magnes / decolor obscurus vilis. non ille repexam / caesariem regum, non candida virginis ornat / colla nec insigni splendet per cingula morsu / sed nova si nigri videas miracula saxi, / tunc pulchros superat cultus [...]"; Kircher, *Magnes* (see above, n. 20), 1–5.

28   *SM* (see above, n. 26), 13–8: "Inter saxa numeratur MAGNES lapis nigricans et vilis; ille miserculus, non pendet de auribus Reginarum, non ornat eburnea Virginum colla, nullo auro unqvam incrustatur. Gaudet tamen hoc dominio, ut ambos mundi Polos liget, metallorum praestantiam superet, nitidam gemmarum puritatem longe post se relinqvat, illud orbis speculum, ille ingeniorum cor! illa Sapientium impenetrabilis profunditas. Idipsum de Scientiarum *Magnete* licebit dicere: qvamvis in nullo sit pretio apud aulas barbaricas, apud collegia ineptorum, apud Scribarum et Pharisaeorum mensas, tamen qvidqvid Sacramentorum curiosis mentibus et oculis subjicit natura, qvidqvid Virtutum catenam intrat et decet, qvidqvid in Regiminis Throno arcani latet, omnia in se conclusit SCIENTIARUM MAGNES. Hujus attractu et repulsu segregat se mens cordata a terrenis sordibus et alligatur coelo. Hujus attractu et repulsu iniqvitatis dolos in exilia pellit justitia. Hujus attractu et repulsu detruncat agmina morborum medicina. Hujus attractu et repulsu florescit Fortitudo, temperantia, bonorum copia. Hujus attractu et repulsu sonant cordata eloqvia, svavis lyra, alta Historia, qvae veritatis calamo orbi dant modulos, dant fercula, dant modulos, imo aperiunt ostia per qvae intramus in sacros Heroum consessus indeqve egredimur optimis instructi exemplis, malorum casu admoniti. Tantum valet hoc Regnum ornamentum, hic Procerum Sol, hoc doctorum lumen, hic ductor certissimus, SCIENTIARUM MAGNES!"

29   Ibid., 31: "Haec est Dei simia, architectorum basis, curiosarum inventionum fidelissimus MAGNES."

30   Ibid., 33: "Talis est Finlandiae justitia, non elegit dolosos congressus, non fictam osculatur amicitiam, non epulis flectitur; totus in se recurrit castus, purus, solidus, aeqvitatis MAGNES, MAGNES inquam & tutela bonorum, malorum pavor, curiarum ATLAS."

"heals and prevents diseases with its magnetic forces."[31] The passage closes with a rhetorical apostrophe, addressing Finland, which is encouraged to rejoice over the Academy of Turku as a manifestation of divine love: everything about the Academy is healthy ("sana"), pure ("casta"), and glorious ("gloriosa"); it is a magnet that is unrivalled.[32] The atmosphere of the Academy and relations between colleagues are described as follows: "We do not lose our temper when contradicting what our colleagues say."[33] However, the minutes of the Academic Senate tell us a different story; the professors' conflicting interests gave rise to frequent quarrels, reproaches, complaints, and accusations, in which scientific issues became entangled with private affairs. Achrelius himself became involved in such incidents several times; for instance, he was once accused of wounding the honour of the Bishop of Turku through one of his writings, and was dismissed from the Academy for some time.[34]

Since *Scientiarum magnes* also celebrated the thirty-fifth birthday (and thirty years of rule) of Charles XI, (King of Sweden 1660–97), the symbol of the magnet is also linked to the King and Queen. Charles XI and Ulrica Eleonora are praised as being "the magnets of the Swedish empire, heroes of victories and swans of peace."[35] Achrelius used the swan, a symbol of peace and tranquillity, because after the Scanian War, which ended in 1679, Charles indeed managed to maintain the peace for the remaining twenty years of his reign.

Aside from the sciences, the Academy, the King and Queen, and a few other subjects, the remainder of the references to magnets in *Scientiarum magnes* relate to Christian religion and the Christian way of life. In a navigation metaphor, Jesus is called "the bow, stern, magnet, and anchor of our faith."[36] The analogy is clearly the use of lodestones in the compass needle of ships. God is

---

31 Ibid., 32: "[...] divinam miramur bonitatem, qvae tot vexationibus, tot cruciatibus clandestinis, mortis spiculis, uncis & corvis immensam & vere Magneticam contraposuit remediorum copiam."

32 Ibid., 49–50: "Gaude ergo Finlandia, cui tantus illuxit amor! te beatam praedicabunt populi [...]. omnia sana! omnia casta! omnia gloriosa! radix sativa, stolon praegnans rami foecundi, messis uberrima, fructus aethereus, MAGNES INCOMPARABILIS."

33 Ibid., 49: "non contradicendo in collegiis exardescimus; non in petitione honorum eruditionem ac merita calcamus pedibus, jactantiis, pecunia."

34 Raija Sarasti-Wilenius, "A Finnish Master of Latin oratory: Daniel Achrelius," in *A History of Nordic Neo-Latin Literature*, ed. Minna Skafte Jensen (Odense, 1995), 321–31, there 321.

35 *SM* (see above, n. 26), 63: "Talis est CAROLUS XI cum sua ULRICA, imperii MAGNES, Victoriarum Heroes, Pacis Cygni." In Christoph Lackner's *Coronae Hungariae Emblematica descriptio* (1612), which describes royal virtues, lodestone stands for the power of virtue. Agnes Kusler, "'Maiestatis Hungariae Aquila': Christoph Lackner and the Hieroglyph of the Habsburg Eagle," in *Emblems and the Natural World*, ed. Karl A. E. Enenkel and Paul J. Smith (Leiden, 2017), 419–53, there, 427.

36 *SM* (see above, n. 26), 43: "nostrae fidei prora, puppis, MAGNES, anchora, DEI FILIUS."

referred to as the magnet of eternity.[37] The speech ends in a wish ("votum") for an eternal life in Heaven with the angels, prophets, and apostles, and before the magnet of eternity, that is God.[38]

In a time of orthodox Lutheranism and heated theological debates at Turku, was it not a form of heresy to deem God a magnet? In seventeenth-century natural philosophy, it was not unusual to use a magnet metaphor as a rhetorical device to explain religious teachings; the lodestone's attraction to iron was considered analogous to Christ's attraction to his disciples through divine love.[39] However, natural philosophers did not usually go so far as to describe God as a magnet. Kircher, however, did; he claimed that God was the central magnet of the universe, and that magnetic forces were God's means to keep the universe in order.[40] In his *Contemplationes mundi*, Achrelius tried to avoid questions related to controversial issues in theology. Kircher's wide-ranging ideas about magnetic forces influenced Achrelius' natural philosophical theories; however, in that context, describing God as a magnet would have meant crossing a distinct line. Yet, addressing God as a magnet in the rhetorical context of the *Scientiarum magnes* was an entirely different matter. It was a literary device exemplifying the inflated Baroque style prevailing at the time. It was simply a metaphor that did not provoke the academic audience, not even the most meticulous professors of theology, who readily remarked on any issue that might have been dubious from the point of view of orthodox Lutheranism.

Achrelius' oration *Scientiarum magnes* is one example of the literary works that drew their inspiration from magnetic studies in the early seventeenth century, when such references were in vogue.[41] The magnet was already an established trope in Neo-Latin literature, serving several purposes. In his oration, Achrelius fully exploited the strong impression that the phenomenon of magnetism made on the imagination, elaborating on the symbol as the cohesive thread tying together different parts of the speech. In the most important section, the praising of the sciences, the symbol is used to illustrate that just as lodestone attracts iron, so does intellectual curiosity inspire human minds to

---

37 Ibid., 16: "ad DEUM DEORUM, Maximum, ad UNICUM & SOLIDUM AETERNITATIS MAGNETEM."

38 Ibid., 70: "ultimum votorum, ut Tecum, o sanctissima TRINITAS! cum beatis angelis, cum Prophetis, cum Apostolis, cum beatorum coetu, coram Aeternitatis MAGNETE [...] concelebremus JUBILAEUM in secula seculorum."

39 Ogilvie, "Science and Medicine" (see above, n. 18), 265–6.

40 Baldwin, "Kircher's Magnetic Investigations" (see above, n. 12), 34–5.

41 Basilius Plinius' (1540–1605) poem *Carmen de magnete* (Augustae Vindelicorum, 1603), praising the city of Riga, is another example that used the magnet as a common thread of a literary work.

examine the world and the achievements of the preceding scientists, in turn encouraging the scientists of subsequent generations. This idea resembles Angelo Poliziano's use of the magnet as a metaphor for the divine inspiration of poets; he describes how poetic inspiration is transferred from one poet to another forming one long chain, similar to a chain of iron rings attracted to each other by magnetic force.[42] Although Achrelius says that it is a divine force that impels the intellectual curiosity, it is unlikely that he is suggesting that there is a some sort of general divine magnetic force similar to stoic *pneuma/spiritus*.

Achrelius was fascinated by Kircher's theory of universal magnetism as an explanation for a wide range of natural phenomena, but as a whole his natural philosophy was a compilation of ideas from various sources rather than a consistent theory about the origin and nature of the universe. His use of magnetic symbolism in *Scientiarum magnes* should be seen purely as a metaphor, which, like several other metaphors adopted from science, enjoyed a much broader freedom of expression in literary than in scientific contexts.

University of Helsinki

---

42 Angelo Poliziano, *Ambra* 14–7 and *Nutricia* 193–6. Charles Fantazzi, *Angelo Poliziano Silvae* (Cambridge, Massachusetts, 2004), 174.

CHAPTER 39

Natural and Artificial Objects in Conrad Gessner's Book on "Fossils"

Petra Schierl

Abstract

The Swiss naturalist and polymath Conrad Gessner (1516–65), best known for his *Historia animalium*, also studied *res fossiles*. In 1565 he edited the collective volume *De omni rerum fossilium genere* which includes his own treatise *De rerum fossilium, lapidum et gemmarum maxime, figuris et similitudinibus*. This work deals especially with stones and gems including fossilized remains of organisms, which were not yet recognized as such. Gessner draws extensively on the works of authors from antiquity to his own time, above all on Georgius Agricola's *De natura fossilium* (1546). He is, however, the first to illustrate *res fossiles* with numerous woodcuts and arranges them in a new way: Gessner's book falls into 15 chapters in which he groups *res fossiles* according to their similarity to or presumed relationship with the natural world. This paper examines Gessner's innovative approach and devotes special attention to two chapters which stand out as they relate *res fossiles* to artefacts, describing on the one hand natural objects which resemble artefacts and on the other hand artefacts made of metals, stones and gems.

Keywords

Conrad Gessner – *De omni rerum fossilium genere* (1565) – Neo-Latin science – fossils – nature and art

The Swiss physician and naturalist Conrad Gessner (1516–65) is known above all for his *Historia animalium*, a comprehensive study of the animal world and one of the most important zoological works of the Renaissance.[1] Four volumes— devoted to quadrupeds, amphibians, birds, and fishes—were printed between

---

1 On the *Historia animalium* cf. e.g. Urs B. Leu, *Conrad Gessner (1516–1565). Universalgelehrter der Renaissance* (Zürich, 2016), 175–231 (where further references can be found), and

---

© KONINKLIJKE BRILL NV, LEIDEN, 2020 | DOI:10.1163/9789004427105_040

NATURAL AND ARTIFICIAL OBJECTS IN GESSNER'S BOOK ON "FOSSILS"   507

1551 and 1558, whereas a fifth volume on snakes was published posthumously in 1587. The *Historia animalium* enjoyed great success not least because of its numerous illustrations.[2] However, Gessner's interests in nature went beyond zoology. When he died from the plague in 1565, he was already working on an equally ambitious project on plants and was turning to earth sciences. He had just edited a collective volume on *res fossiles*, that is on stones and other objects which can be obtained by digging or are lying on the ground.[3] This volume, printed in octavo, consists of eight studies written mostly by contemporary authors, including amongst others Gessner's correspondent Johannes Kentmann.[4] The final treatise is Gessner's own *De rerum fossilium, lapidum et gemmarum maxime, figuris et similitudinibus liber* (6 + 169 folios). This treatise focuses on forms and resemblances of objects dug up from the ground. Numerous woodcuts depict the objects from Gessner's own natural history collection or from those of his correspondents. As the illustrations show, these objects include fossils in the modern sense, i.e. petrified remains of organisms, which were not yet recognized as such by Gessner and his contemporaries.[5] The use of illustrations in a discussion of *res fossiles*, the collection of specimens as a basis for the study of these objects as well as the scholarly exchange constitute the most important innovations of Gessner's treatise.[6] In line with the general interest in forms of visual representation in the Renaissance study of nature,[7] recent research has indeed turned to the woodcuts in Gessner's

---

   Caroline A. Gmelig-Nijboer, *Conrad Gessner's Historia animalium: An Inventory of Renaissance Zoology* (Diss. Utrecht, 1977).

2 Water-colour drawings of animals that provided the models for the woodcuts were in 2010 rediscovered at the University Library of Amsterdam and ascribed to the collection of Conrad Gessner; cf. Florike Egmond, "A collection within a collection. Rediscovered animal drawings from the collections of Conrad Gessner and Felix Platter," in *Journal of the History of Collections* 25 (2013), 149–70.

3 *De omni rerum fossilium genere, gemmis, lapidibus, metallis et huiusmodi, libri aliquot, plerique nunc primum editi* (Zürich, 1565).

4 For an overview cf. Leu (see above, n. 1), 367–78.

5 To differentiate between fossils in the modern sense and *res fossiles* as understood by Gessner and his contemporaries, i.e. objects dug up from the ground, I refer to the latter either by using the Latin terms *res fossiles* and *fossilia* or by putting fossils in inverted commas.

6 Martin J. S. Rudwick, *The Meaning of Fossils* (Chicago, ²1976), there 15.

7 Pamela O. Long, "Objects of art/objects of nature. Visual representation and the investigation of nature," in *Merchants and Marvels. Commerce, Science, and Art in Early Modern Europe*, ed. Pamela H. Smith and Paula Findlen (New York, 2002), 63–82; Brian W. Ogilvie, *The Science of Describing. Natural History in Renaissance Europe* (Chicago, 2006), esp. 175–208; Florike Egmond and Sachiko Kusukawa, "Circulation of images and graphic practices in Renaissance natural history: the example of Conrad Gessner," in *Gesnerus* 73 (2016), 29–72.

treatise as well as the drawings that provide their models.[8] Besides, the palae-ontological value of the treatise has been foregrounded.[9] This paper will focus on Gessner's innovative arrangement of "fossils" according to their relation to an order perceived in nature and address the question why the treatise contains a chapter on artificial objects and artefacts made of various "fossils", including a pencil.

Research on *fossilia* in the Sixteenth Century: Georgius Agricola

Gessner's collective volume and his own treatise on "fossils" build on the work of the physician and naturalist Georgius Agricola (1494–1555). It was in fact Agricola who established *fossilia* as a collective term marking a corresponding field of research. In 1546 he published a volume which contained four studies on this topic as well as a reprint of his *Bermannus*, a very successful dialogue on mining.[10] Among these, the ten books *De natura fossilium* stand out as an exhaustive treatment of *fossilia*.[11] In his dedicatory epistle to the Duke of Saxony, Thuringia and Misena, Prince Maurice, Agricola points to Pliny the Elder as the most important ancient authority whose work on the field survived. Agricola frequently resorts to books 33–37 of Pliny's *Natural History*, devoted to things

---

8   Drawings that served as models for the woodcuts in Gessner's treatise are preserved in an album from the collection of Felix Platter at the University Library Basel (UBH K I 2; doi: 10.7891/e-manuscripta-12850). On woodcuts and drawings cf. Angela Fischel, *Natur im Bild. Zeichnung und Naturerkenntnis bei Conrad Gessner und Ulisse Aldrovandi* (Berlin, 2009); Angela Fischel, "Collections, images and form in sixteenth-century natural history: The case of Conrad Gessner," in *Intellectual History Review* 20 (2010), 147–64.

9   On Gessner's importance for palaeontology cf. Walter Etter, "Conrad Gessner als Paläontologe," in *Facetten eines Universums. Conrad Gessner 1516–2016*, ed. Urs B. Leu and Mylène Ruoss (Zürich, 2016), 175–84, and Walter Etter, "Conrad Gessner and the early history of palaeontology," in *Conrad Gessner (1516–1565). Die Renaissance der Wissenschaften / The Renaissance of Learning*, ed. Urs B. Leu and Peter Opitz (Berlin, 2019), 129–44.

10   *De ortu et causis subterraneorum lib. V, De natura eorum quae effluunt ex terra lib. IIII, De natura fossilium lib. X, De veteribus et novis metallis lib. II, Bermannus sive De re metallica dialogus, Interpretatio Germanica vocum rei metallicae, addito indice foecundissimo* (Basel, 1546).

11   Introductions are provided in modern translations: *Georgius Agricola, De natura fossilium (Textbook of Mineralogy)*, transl. from the first Latin edition of 1546 by Mark Chance Bandy and Jean A. Bandy (New York, 1955); *Georgius Agricola, Ausgewählte Werke. Gedenkausgabe des Staatlichen Museums für Mineralogie und Geologie zu Dresden*, ed. Hans Prescher, vol. 4: *Georgius Agricola, De natura fossilium libri X – Die Mineralien*, ed. Georg Fraustadt and Hans Prescher (Berlin, 1958). For a more recent reprint of the translation cf. Georgius Agricola, *De natura fossilium. Handbuch der Mineralogie* (1546), transl. Georg Fraustadt, revised Fritz Krafft (Wiesbaden, 2006).

NATURAL AND ARTIFICIAL OBJECTS IN GESSNER'S BOOK ON "FOSSILS"   509

dug up from the ground,[12] but he also complements and corrects Pliny with his own observations.[13]

Agricola takes a systematic approach to the study of *fossilia*. Book 1 provides a general introduction and lists the physical properties according to which *fossilia* can be described such as colour, taste, shape and size. The following Books treat different groups of "fossils", beginning with types of earth (*terrae*), congealed juices (*succi concreti*) as well as amber (*succinum*), stones (*lapides*),[14] gems (*gemmae*), marbles (*marmora*) and rocks (*saxa*), metals (*metalla*), products made from metal (*metalla facticia*) as well as mixtures (*mista*) and composites (*composita*). This classification of *fossilia* is primarily based on their substance.[15]

Gessner's Innovative Treatment of *fossilia*: Nature as Organizing Principle

Agricola's work provides the starting point for Gessner's *De rerum fossilium* [...] *figuris et similitudinibus*. Gessner presents his treatise as a preliminary study, which was allegedly completed in great haste and serves to prepare a comprehensive description of "fossils". In this way he also explains his exclusive focus on form and resemblance. The treatise is therefore best described as work in progress.

As stated above, it is the use of illustrations that marks its importance. Alongside the illustrations, however, the innovative arrangement of *fossilia* deserves attention. In his dedicatory epistle to the administrator of the salt-mines near Crakow, Gessner rejects both an alphabetical order and an arrangement of the *fossilia* according to their substance. He explains the organization of his book as follows (f. Aa3^{r}):

---

12   Pliny uses the term "eruta" when referring to the contents of these books in his *Natural History* (12,1).

13   Petra Schierl, "Gessners ‚Fossilienbuch': Naturforschung zwischen Autopsie und Tradition," in *Conrad Gessner (1516–1565). Die Renaissance der Wissenschaften / The Renaissance of Learning*, ed. Urs B. Leu and Peter Opitz (Berlin, 2019), 145–58.

14   Agricola, *De ortu* (see above, n. 10), 249 distinguishes four types of stones (stones, gems, marbles, rocks) and calls those of the first type, e.g. lodestone and haematite, by the generic name "lapides".

15   On Agricola's classification cf. the introduction to Bandy and Bandy, *Georgius Agricola* (see above, n. 11), vii.

Hoc vero in libro, (qui rerum fossilium, hoc est, metallorum et lapidum in primis, figuras exhibet) similitudinum et imaginum, quas ipsa genitrix natura in rebus tam variis veluti pingendo expressit, consideratione oblectatus, ipsos etiam naturae gradus ac ordines, sequi volui: hoc est, a simplicibus dimensionum ac figurarum principiis et lineamentis primis opus auspicari: inde vero ad ipsa corpora simplicia primum, ut coelum ac elementa, ab hisce rursus ad composita ex eis, meteora, plantas, animalia transire: et in singulis, quae ab eis denominantur aut aliquam eorum similitudinem habent, fossilia enumerare: atque a coelo et coelestibus paulatim ad terram et quae in ipsa aluntur vivuntque aut vigent corpora descendere [...]

In this book, however, (that presents the forms of *res fossiles*, that is above all of metals and stones) I decided—delighted by the contemplation of resemblances and images, to which Mother Nature as if by painting has given expression in such different things—to follow the very hierarchy of Nature, that is: to begin my work from the simple beginnings of dimensions and shapes and from first lines, but to proceed thence first to the simple bodies themselves, such as heaven and the elements, and thence in turn to their composites, to atmospheric phenomena, plants, and animals, and to enumerate in each case *fossilia* that are named after them or bear a resemblance to them; and from heaven and celestial phenomena to descend gradually to the earth and the bodies that grow, live and thrive on it [...]

Gessner proposes for his treatise a division into chapters that relate images on *fossilia* as well as formal features of *fossilia* to natural phenomena and are arranged according to an hierarchical order perceived in nature.[16] Contrary to the expectations raised by the opening lines of this passage as well as the title's emphasis on form and resemblance, it turns out that Gessner is not merely concerned with the visual aspects of *fossilia*. He states explicitly that both names and resemblances motivate the ascription of objects to corresponding chapters of his treatise, when he says: "et in singulis, quae ab eis denominantur aut aliquam eorum similitudinem habent, fossilia enumerare."[17]

---

16   On the concept of a *scala naturae* in Gessner's writings cf. Leu (see above, n. 1), 177 and Urs B. Leu, *Conrad Gesner als Theologe. Ein Beitrag zur Zürcher Geistesgeschichte des 16. Jahrhunderts* (Bern, 1990), 63–9.

17   Fischel, *Natur im Bild* (see above, n. 8), 28–32 and Fischel, *Collections* (see above, n. 8) points to formal properties as providing the basis for Gessner's classification of fossil objects, but does not mention the importance of the objects' names.

A survey of the fifteen chapters will indicate how this organizing principle is implemented.[18] The First Chapter treats stones and gemstones with lines or dots on their surface but also stones with a specific shape. The Second Chapter turns to stones that relate in one way or another to the sun, the moon, the stars, i.e. to "simple bodies". Chapter 3 focuses on stones named after atmospheric phenomena such as thunder and lightning. It includes, for example, the so-called *Cerauniae* which allegedly fell from the sky during thunderstorms but were in the following centuries identified as stone axes.[19] Chapter 4 discusses stones and metals named after inanimate terrestrial objects, such as gold. Chapter 5 deals with *fossilia* that bear a resemblance to artificial objects, whilst Chapter 6 is concerned with artificial objects or artefacts made of various metals, stones and gemstones. Chapters 7 to 11 treat *fossilia* which resemble plants and fossilized plants. Chapters 12 to 15 relate *fossilia* as regards their names or resemblances to body parts of humans or animals and treat stones found in their bodies. Chapter 12 focuses on the relations between *fossilia* and humans as well as quadrupeds. The following Chapters, then, do the same for birds, aquatic animals and finally snakes and insects.

As this survey shows, the chapters' sequence corresponds roughly to the sequence envisaged by Gessner in the passage cited above. At the very beginning stand basic geometric shapes and figures. In the remaining Chapters there is a general movement from the heavenly to the terrestrial spheres, and, as regards the latter, from inanimate to animate nature. Chapters 5 and 6 deal with artificial objects in different ways and appear to provide the transition between inanimate objects and living organisms. Chapter 5 includes amongst others the so-called belemnites, "fossils" resembling arrows, as the name derived from the Greek term for arrow (βέλεμνον) indicates.[20] The name codifies the resemblance to arrows and leads Gessner to attribute belemnites to the chapter on "fossils" bearing resemblance to artificial objects. This chapter may not be what one expects in a book that arranges objects primarily according to an order perceived in nature, but it is demanded by the logic of Gessner's approach.

---

18   Gessner gives a survey of the chapters in his *praefatio* and adduces even more detailed chapter titles in the treatise; a list of the latter is provided in Appendix A.

19   The *Cerauniae*, named after the Greek word for thunderbolt (κέραυνος), provide an example for objects ascribed to a chapter on the basis of their names rather than their forms, even though Gessner observes that the *Cerauniae* look like stone axes; cf. Schierl (see above, n. 13).

20   The putative stones are actually relics of an extinct order of cephalopods, cf. Etter, *Gessner als Paläontologe* (see above, n. 9), 179.

De rebus artificiosis seu arte factis: Chapter 6, the Odd One Out?

Chapters 5 and 6, as we have seen, share a focus on artefacts. In presenting a selection of manmade objects made from "fossils" such as metals, stones and gems, Chapter 6, however, stands out among the chapters of the treatise.[21] It is the only one that does not relate "fossils" to other objects or phenomena by name or appearance. Gessner rather comments on the materials used. He pictures, for example, a writing instrument that "looks like a tube of wood with a point of lead inserted in one end and a fancy knob on the other end" and can be identified as an early pencil (f. 104^v).[22] Gessner refers to the substance as some sort of lead, called by some "English antimony". In the eighteenth century the name "graphite" was coined for the material of which pencils are made.[23]

How can the inclusion of a chapter that is inconsistent with the treatise's overall organizing principle be explained? Why does Gessner even in this chapter adduce woodcuts to illustrate some of the objects under discussion? An analysis of its contents may suggest possible answers. Chapter 6 consists of altogether 29 entries arranged in alphabetical order.[24] Gessner begins with remarks on buildings, he moves to alabastra, rings (especially gemstone rings), knife handles and lancets and to spoons. In each case he names "fossils" out of which these objects can be produced. Most of these objects are everyday objects, but some like the rings are more adequately described as jewelry or adornments. However, there are also items which are neither quotidian objects nor items of jewelry such as the sixth item on the list, to which Gessner refers as "a metal body that looks like a mountain" (f. 99^v). He describes the object as a miniature mountain made up from different stones and metals. Figures of mine-workers turn this artificial mountain into a miniature mine. Gessner does not include a woodcut of this object, but miniature mountains with miners at work could be found in contemporary curiosity cabinets and extant specimens provide an idea of what he means.[25]

---

21   The title of Chapter 6 is *De rebus artificiosis seu arte factis, ex metallis, lapidibus ac gemmis* (f. 96^r–113^v).

22   Henry Petroski, *The Pencil. A History of Design and Circumstance* (London, 1990), 36–49, there 38. According to Petroski, the woodcut Gessner adduces is likely to be the first illustration of a modern pencil.

23   Petroski, *The Pencil* (see above, n. 22), 43.

24   A list of the first twelve entries is provided in Appendix B.

25   A good example is found in the Ambras collection in Innsbruck; cf. Margot Rauch, "Steinreich: Gesammeltes aus der Erde," in *Die Entdeckung der Natur. Naturalien in den Kunstkammern des 16. und 17. Jahrhunderts*, ed. Wilfried Seipel (Wien, 2006), 156–92, there 181–3 on catalogue number 3.22.

NATURAL AND ARTIFICIAL OBJECTS IN GESSNER'S BOOK ON "FOSSILS"   513

The items discussed so far suggest that the objects of Chapter 6 divide into three major groups: objects used in everyday life, jewelry and works of art or showpieces made primarily for display. Objects from all three groups are illustrated by woodcuts.[26] The woodcuts of everyday objects show a touchstone, two sharpening stones (a water stone and an oil-stone), a writing-tablet made of slate with a stylus, the pencil, mentioned above, window panes, a marble spoon, a salt bowl made from alabastrite and a vessel made from lard- or soapstone ("Lavezstein"). Most of the woodcuts in the second group show (semi-precious) stones, which are naturally conspicuous or have been worked on, such as two gemstone rings surrounded by gemstones or a chain with beads of different materials. Under the heading "Ornaments" (f. 106^v) Gessner lists, moreover, several jaspers as well as other peculiar stones, such as a green stone used for lip piercing in the New World. Works of art or showpieces illustrated by woodcuts include a relief portrait cast in clay depicting Gessner's correspondent Kentmann and his family crest as well as specimens of *terra sigillata*: Lemnian bole impressed with the figure of a goat[27] and a clay plaque stamped on one side with the scene of Christ's Resurrection and on the other side with Christ on the cross. The plaque was brought as a pilgrim's souvenir from the Holy Land by a nobleman and sent to Gessner by Kentmann.

The illustrations in this chapter have no scientific purpose, i.e. they do not serve to identify the objects under discussion. Like the woodcuts of other chapters, however, the illustrations represent specific objects: Gessner's text reveals that these are mostly objects which Gessner owned himself and had in many cases received from donors. This suggests that Chapter 6 complements the book in as much as it integrates objects which formed part of Gessner's collection. Merely six items from Gessner's collection have come down to us.[28] His book on "fossils", however, comes very close to an inventory of his collection as both the illustrations and Gessner's descriptions suggest. The aim of

---

26   Drawings that served as models for the woodcuts exist even for some of the objects discussed in Chapter 6 and are examined by Fischel, *Collections* (see above, n. 8), 150–4.

27   On the healing powers ascribed to certain earths, above all Lemnian Earth, since antiquity, cf. e.g. Pliny, *Natural History* 35,33; Dioscorides, *De materia medica* 5,97 and Effie Photos-Jones and Allan J. Hall, "Lemnian Earth, alum and astringency: A Field-Based Approach," in *Medicine and Healing in the Ancient Mediterranean World*, ed. Demetrios Michaelides (Oxford, 2014), 183–9.

28   Leu, *Conrad Gessner* (see above, n. 1), 190. After Gessner's death the collection first came into possession of the Basel physician Felix Platter and was displayed to illustrious visitors such as Jacques-Auguste de Thou, who refers explicitly to Gessner's "theca fossilium", cf. *Jacques-Auguste de Thou, La vie de Jacques-Auguste de Thou / I. Aug. Thuani vita*, ed. Anne Teissier-Ensminger (Paris, 2007), 382–3 (lib. 2,56); on the history of Gessner's collection cf. now Walter Etter and Olivier Schmidt, "Gessner's fossil crab. An icon for the early history of palaeontology," in *Journal of the History of Collections* (forthcoming 2020).

514   SCHIERL

conveying as accurately as possible Gessner's collection may therefore have motivated the inclusion of Chapter 6.

Further and partly related reasons for its inclusion suggest themselves when we take a closer look at the everyday objects on the one hand and jewelry and showpieces on the other hand. The everyday objects form the largest group in Chapter 6. Agricola provides a precedent for their treatment. In his dedicatory epistle to *De natura fossilium* Agricola announced that he would also deal with the usefulness of "fossils" ("utilitatis fructus", 167) and his descriptions do include remarks on their use in everyday life. Unsurprisingly, Gessner refers to Agricola twelve times in Chapter 6. In addition, Gessner adduces information gleaned from other writers. He refers, for example, to Erasmus Stella who reports in his book on gemstones that jasper is used for wall-panelling in public buildings in his home-town Zwickau (f. 96^v). Contemporary authors therefore provide a precedent for the description of the use made of certain *fossilia*.

As regards jewelry and display objects, Gessner often has a more pressing reason to discuss and even illustrate them. He received many of them as presents from friends and correspondents across Europe and duly mentions them by name in his treatise. Two examples may serve as illustrations. In the entry on the miniature mountain, the reader learns not only that Georgius Fabricius owned a particularly beautiful specimen, but also that Valentinus Gravius, a senator of Freiberg in Saxony, had one made for Gessner. Gravius, who had died in 1555, was a former correspondent of Gessner and had already contributed to his *Historia animalium*.[29] The reference to this object is therefore also an act of homage.

The second example is the stone used as a lip-piercing by natives of Brazil (f. 107^v–108^r). Gessner is not able to identify the stone but refers to it as "a green stone or precious stone". Besides, he proposes a name relating to its use: he suggests "oripendulus", coined in analogy to the name of the herb "filipendula". Gessner had received the stone from the humanist Johannes Ferrerius and quotes a description of the stone and its function from his accompanying letter. The quotation illustrates how Gessner brings observations from different sources together. The letter is in this case treated in the same way as a publication in print. Ferrerius had not been to Brazil himself, but had received

---

29   Leu, *Conrad Gessner* (see above, n. 1), 190–1. In a letter to Georgius Fabricius written on 22 June 1554 and published posthumously in the *Epistolarum medicinalium* [...] *libri tres* (Zürich, 1577, 131^r–132^r) Gessner, moreover, takes lifelike images or perhaps reproductions of insects and plants he had received from Valentinus Gravius as a starting point for general reflections on naturalistic representation and "the interchangeability of art and nature", cf. Katharina Pilaski Kaliardos, *The Munich Kunstkammer. Art, Nature, and the Representation of Knowledge in Courtly Contexts* (Tübingen, 2013), 159–63, there 162.

NATURAL AND ARTIFICIAL OBJECTS IN GESSNER'S BOOK ON "FOSSILS"   515

the stone as well as other objects from a friend who had undertaken an expedition to Brazil.[30] In including both this object and quoting from the letter, Gessner once more shows his gratitude. What is more, he presents Ferrerius as an example for others to follow. In putting on display Gessner's network of correspondents Chapter 6 conforms to the rest of the treatise and provides an example for the exchange of objects on which a comprehensive knowledge of nature must be based.

Conclusion

The chapters of Gessner's treatise relate *fossilia* to natural phenomena and artificial objects based on their appearance, name or provenance. Chapter 6, however, appears to stand out: it lists objects made from *fossilia*, whether everyday objects, jewelry or showpieces. While it is somewhat incongruous with the organizational principle of the book as expounded by Gessner in his programmatic statement in the dedicatory epistle (f. Aa3^r), the items listed and discussed in this chapter clearly relate to "fossils" since they share the same substance. Produced from metals, stones and gems the artificial objects and artefacts illustrate the wide range of uses to which *fossilia* may be put, if worked on and shaped to a greater or lesser extent. Gessner and his contemporaries therefore collected and exchanged them just like the "fossils" themselves as Gessner's references to donors show. Gessner, moreover, treated them in the same way as natural objects when he had watercolour drawings made of some of them and included corresponding woodcuts in his treatise. It may be deduced that the knowledge about the uses to which "fossils" are put and the ways in which they can be shaped was a vital aspect of the "fossils" themselves. The inclusion of Chapter 6 shows that it was one of the aims of the treatise to give through verbal descriptions and illustrations as complete as possible a representation of the different facets of Gessner's collection.

The discussion of artificial objects and artefacts is also in line with a prominent feature of Gessner's treatise, namely its emphasis on the proximity of nature and art. In the programmatic passage on the organization of his book Gessner draws attention to the painter-like powers of a personified Mother

---

30   Urs B. Leu, "Konrad Gessner und die neue Welt," in *Gesnerus* 49 (1992), 279–309, there
       298–9; John Durkan, "Giovanni Ferrerio, Gesner and French affairs," in *Bibliothèque d'Humanisme et Renaissance* 42 (1980), 349–60.

Nature.[31] The chapters of the treatise show Nature as an artist when she recreates—through images and forms—both natural beings and artificial objects in "fossils". In Chapter 14 on stones showing aquatic creatures Gessner discusses amongst others the image of a fish depicted on the so-called *Lapis Islebianus* (f. 162ʳ), while the belemnites looking like arrows are treated in Chapter 5 on *fossilia* that naturally resemble artificial objects (f. 89ᵛ, f. 91ʳ). As these examples show, Gessner's arrangement of *fossilia* points to striking similarities of form in objects of different substances. In this way his treatise both highlights the permeability of the boundaries between the three kingdoms of nature, especially "the ability of the mineral kingdom to serve as a repository of the images extant in the other two kingdoms,"[32] and underlines the fluidity between the natural and the artificial. It is against this background that the presence of a chapter on artificial objects and artefacts made of metals, stones and gems may be understood.[33]

University of Basel

Appendix

A. The chapter titles of Gessner's *De rerum fossilium* […] *figuris et similitudinibus*

1. De lapidibus illis in quibus lineae potissimum considerantur, aut puncta, et figura in superficie magis, quam corpus solidum aut eius forma.
2. De lapidibus illis, quibus cum stellis, sole, luna, aut elementis aliquid commune est.
3. De lapidibus qui a meteoris, id est, sublimibus in aëre corporibus nomina sua mutuantur.
4. De lapidibus et metallis, quae denominantur a rebus terrestribus inanimatis.
5. De fossilibus rebus quae natura similes sunt rei alicui artificiosae, ordine literarum.
6. De rebus artificiosis seu arte factis, ex metallis, lapidibus ac gemmis.

---

31 On the notion of *natura pictrix* cf. Paula Findlen, "Jokes of Nature and Jokes of Knowledge: The Playfulness of Scientific Discourse in Early Modern Europe," in *Renaissance Quarterly* 43 (1990), 292–331, there 297.

32 Findlen, "Jokes of Nature" (see above, n. 31), 313. Gessner's treatise is a contribution to the debate on the origins of figured stones, many of which eventually turned out to be fossils in the modern sense, but Gessner does not explicitly position himself.

33 I would like to thank the two anonymous reviewers for valuable comments that helped to further develop aspects of this paper.

7. De lithophytis, et rebus fossilibus illis, quae plantas imitantur, in genere primum, deinde privatim quae herbarum similitudinem aliquam prae se ferunt, ordine literarum.

8. De fruticibus in lapides versis, et fruticum, eorumve partium aliqua cum fossilibus similitudine.

9. De arboribus earumque partibus, et rerum fossilium cum eis affinitate.

10. De corallio.

11. De aliis quibusdam plantis marinis quae lapidescunt.

12. De lapidibus, qui ab homine aut quadrupede aliquo denominantur, aut in eis reperiuntur.

13. Lapides ab avibus denominati, aut ex avibus sumpti.

14. De lapidibus qui aquatilium animantium effigiem referunt.

15. De lapidibus qui serpentes et insecta referunt.

B. Chapter 6: *De rebus artificiosis seu arte factis, ex metallis, lapidibus ac gemmis*
The first twelve of altogether 29 lemmata in Chapter 6:

1. aedificia et structurae lautiores

2. alabastra sive pyxides unguentariae

3. annuli

4. capuli cultrorum et enchiridiorum

5. cochlearia

6. corpus metallicum montis quadam specie ex omni variorum metallorum et lapidum genere ab artifice aliquo maltha seu lithocolla tenaci summa industria coagmentato additis etiam ex argento instrumentis quibusdam fodinarum et metallicorum, hoc est in fodinis laborantium operarum, imaginibus aliquot sparsim

7. cos

8. coticula

9. facies hominum, imagines rerum, signa et literae in variis rebus fossilibus funduntur, imprimuntur, scalpuntur

10. horologium sciatericum

11. incudes

12. instrumenta varia: stylus [...] ad scribendum factus

CHAPTER 40

Educazione e politica nelle lettere di Costanza da Varano

Margherita Sciancalepore

Abstract

Nipote di Battista da Montefeltro Malatesta, dedicataria del programma pedagogico tracciato da Leonardo Bruni nel *De studiis et litteris*, e madre di Battista Sforza, insigne duchessa d'Urbino, Costanza da Varano è stata, nella sua seppur breve vita, un esempio eloquente di sintesi tra la raffinata educazione letteraria incoraggiata dalla nonna e il pragmatismo politico ereditato dalla figlia. I pochi studi ad oggi pubblicati, volti ad inserire il suo nome tra quelli delle scrittrici erudite del Quattrocento, restituiscono l'immagine di una donna tanto umile nel rispondere agli apprezzamenti espressi da umanisti coevi del calibro di Guiniforte Barzizza e di Isotta Nogarola, quanto audace nell'indirizzare richieste e suggerimenti a sovrani, signori e pontefici quali Alfonso d'Aragona, Filippo Maria Visconti ed Eugenio IV. Attraverso il recupero delle testimonianze ancora inedite, l'intervento si propone di ricostruire il travagliato clima politico e il fervido ambiente culturale nei quali Costanza crebbe e che la indussero a impegnarsi con l'unica arma a sua disposizione, quella delle lettere, nella difesa della propria casata.

Keywords

Costanza da Varano – Guiniforte Barzizza – humanism in Camerino – Neo-Latin epistolography – female humanist writers

Nell'immagine del Rinascimento italiano che le ricerche storiche hanno contribuito a delineare, al di là delle diverse sfumature conferite dalle singole interpretazioni, ciò che appare nitidamente agli occhi di chi osserva e studia il XV secolo è il netto contrasto tra luci e ombre. Ai bagliori degli esiti artistici, determinati dalla rivoluzione di un rinnovato pensiero antropocentrico, si contrappongono le tinte fosche di una realtà difficile, dominata da uno spietato individualismo politico esercitato anche attraverso il ricorso sistematico

© KONINKLIJKE BRILL NV, LEIDEN, 2020 | DOI:10.1163/9789004427105_041

EDUCAZIONE E POLITICA NELLE LETTERE DI COSTANZA DA VARANO 519

alla violenza. Gli anni che hanno visto l'affermazione degli Stati territoriali in Italia sono stati testimoni non solo di sanguinose battaglie per la conquista del potere da parte di uomini di antico lignaggio o di più recente ascesa sociale, ma anche di efferati delitti spesso consumati all'interno dei contesti dinastici e famigliari. Non stupisce, allora, che lo stesso teorico del 'mito della Rinascenza', Jacob Burckhardt,[1] designi con il termine di 'tirannidi' i governi statali sorti dopo la fine del Trecento, se di fatto tali potenze risultano accomunate dalla medesima ciceroniana manifestazione dell'*immanitas*,[2] tanto le maggiori e influenti quanto le più piccole e meno prestigiose. Anzi, proprio nelle cosiddette 'tirannidi minori', secondo Burckhardt, sono state commesse le più atroci scelleratezze e, tra le famiglie che a buon titolo possono rientrare come modello in negativo di siffatta considerazione, menziona i da Varano, signori di Camerino.[3]

La storia di questa dinastia, dalle origini ancora incerte ma presumibilmente modeste, è segnata dai privilegi ottenuti grazie allo schieramento nelle fila del partito guelfo e raggiunge il momento di massimo splendore nel Quattrocento, sia per merito sia per colpa di un innegabile pragmatismo non esente da scelte opportunistiche e da decisioni che ignorano ogni vincolo, anche quello di consaguineità.[4] Uno dei crimini certamente presenti nella memoria di Burckhardt, tale da motivare almeno in parte il giudizio prima menzionato, risale al 1433 e si consuma nel corso di un contrasto intestino e fratricida per la successione e la spartizione dei domini combattuto tra quattro figli legittimi della nutrita progenie di Rodolfo III, contrapponendo Gentilpandolfo e Berardo, nati dal primo matrimonio con Elisabetta Malatesta, a Piergentile e Giovanni, avuti in seconde nozze da Costanza Smeducci. Dopo la morte di Rodolfo III, avvenuta nel 1424, i fratelli maggiori tramarono al fine di realizzare ciò che il padre aveva sempre temuto e che inutilmente aveva cercato di evitare con un testamento che accontentasse le richieste e le aspirazioni di ciascuno dei suoi eredi. L'avidità di potere, insieme al sospetto che la maggiore popolarità dei fratellastri potesse limitare la propria autorità e forse negare ai propri figli la possibilità di ottenere in futuro i benefici derivanti dalla naturale discendenza dinastica, indussero Gentilpandolfo e Berardo a cospirare per risolvere

---

1 Jacob Burckhardt, *La civiltà del Rinascimento in Italia*, ed. Giuseppe Zippel (Firenze, 1899).

2 Cic., *de re publ.* 2,26,48.

3 Burckhardt, *La civiltà del Rinascimento* (vedi sopra, n. 1), 31.

4 Bernardino Feliciangeli, "Ricerche sull'origine dei da Varano signori di Camerino," *L'Arcadia* 3 (1918), 153–212; Maria Teresa Guerra Medici, *Famiglia e potere in una signoria dell'Italia centrale. I Varano di Camerino* (Camerino, 2002); Pier Luigi Falaschi, "Orizzonti di una dinastia," in *I Da Varano e le arti. Atti del convegno internazionale (Camerino, 4–6 ottobre 2001)*, ed. Andrea De Marchi e Pier Luigi Falaschi (Acquaviva Picena, 2003), vol. 1, 19–42.

in maniera estrema e definitiva qualsiasi motivo di tensione. Complice il legato pontificio Giovanni Vitelleschi, i quattro fratelli furono invitati a raggiungerlo nel castello di Sanseverino, a poca distanza da Camerino, ma solo Piergentile, vittima secondo le cronache della propria ingenuità, cadde nel tranello e, giunto a destinazione, fu imprigionato e successivamente decapitato a Recanati con l'accusa – non sappiamo quanto infondata – di contraffazione della moneta papale. Né la maggiore scaltrezza risparmiò Giovanni che, convocato da Gentilpandolfo, fu ucciso a tradimento dalle guardie del corpo di quest'ultimo. Nonostante il discutibile successo ottenuto dalla realizzazione dei loro intrighi, i due maggiori da Varano non mantennero a lungo il potere acquisito con il sangue perché, effettivamente invisi ai camerti, furono travolti l'anno successivo, il 1434, da un'insurrezione popolare che colpì Berardo durante i tumulti di Tolentino e Gentilpandolfo, insieme a tre dei cinque figli maschi del fratello connivente, nella strage consumata nella chiesa di San Domenico.

L'accanimento contro la linea maschile della dinastia non è casuale, in quanto i piani di Gentilpandolfo e Berardo prima e la rivolta popolare poi prevedevano una selezione tutt'altro che naturale che limitasse o impedisse del tutto la conservazione della casata. In questo contesto di brutale spietatezza, il compito di difendere la sopravvivenza e il prestigio della stirpe, con prontezza e con un coraggio di gran lunga più virile del mero ricorso alla forza esibito dagli uomini di famiglia, fu assunto dalle donne.[5] Donne come Tora da Varano, che sarebbe riuscita a mettere in salvo il nipote Giulio Cesare, figlio di Giovanni, e a sottrarlo alla furia omicida dei suoi persecutori con l'aiuto di Pascuccio Geminiano, il quale ne favorì la fuga nascondendolo in un "fascio d'herbe".[6] Donne come Elisabetta Malatesta, figlia di Galeazzo e Battista da Montefeltro, vedova di Piergentile, che con i figli riparò inizialmente nel castello di Visso e di lì si trasferì a Pesaro sotto la protezione dei genitori e che, in mancanza del marito e in attesa che il figlio e il nipote potessero assumere la guida dello Stato, seppe allacciare relazioni con Niccolò Piccinino, Francesco Sforza e Federico da Montefeltro, utili a garantirsi il ritorno a Camerino, e fu apprezzata e rispettata nel suo ruolo di reggente. Donne come Costanza da Varano che, seppur giovanissima, per difendere la propria famiglia e la legittima restaurazione del fratello Rodolfo IV al governo della signoria camerte adoperò l'unica arma in suo possesso: la cultura.[7]

---

5   Guerra Medici, "Dalla parte di lei" (vedi sopra, n. 4), 125–36; Jennifer D. Webb, "Hidden in Plain Sight: Varano and Sforza Women of the Marche," in *Wives, Widows, Mistresses, and Nuns in Early Modern Italy*, ed. Katherine A. McIver (Farnham, 2012), 13–31.

6   Camillo Lili, *Dell'historia di Camerino* (Macerata, 1652), vol. 2, 176–7.

7   Nicola Ratti, *Memorie su la vita di quattro donne illustri della casa Sforza e di Monsignor D. Virginio Cesarini* (Roma, 1785), 1–15; Domenico Michiel, *Elogio storico di Costanza da Varano degli antichi principi di Camerino* (Venezia, 1807); Girolamo Tiraboschi, *Storia della letteratura*

EDUCAZIONE E POLITICA NELLE LETTERE DI COSTANZA DA VARANO

Durante la permanenza a Pesaro, Costanza fu affidata alle cure della nonna Battista, nota per la sua erudizione e per la propensione alle *humanae litterae* che le erano valse l'ammirazione di numerosi umanisti e la dedica del libello *De studiis et litteris* da parte di Leonardo Bruni. L'educazione che pertanto la fanciulla poté ricevere fu ampia e raffinata, affatto inferiore a quella che si sarebbe potuta impartire a un rampollo della medesima estrazione sociale, e i frutti del suo apprendimento non tardarono ad arrivare. Al fianco della madre, Costanza fu impegnata a rivendicare il ruolo ingiustamente sottratto ai giovani da Varano e all'occorrenza venne esibita come motivo di vanto, adoperata come strumento per catturare l'attenzione.[8] La prima occasione in cui si espose pubblicamente fu offerta, a maggio del 1442, dalla presenza nella Marca di Francesco Sforza accompagnato dalla sua sposa, Bianca Maria Visconti, alla quale Costanza rivolse un'orazione di grande impatto ma di scarso effetto, perché il ritorno a Camerino invocato e sperato si realizzò solo sul finire del 1443 e fu coronato da una seconda orazione, scritta sicuramente dalla ragazza ma forse pronunciata o destinata a essere pronunciata dal fratello, con cui si salutavano i ritrovati concittadini.

Oltre alle due orazioni menzionate, Costanza compose cinque *carmina* e intrattenne rapporti epistolari con alcuni dei più insigni protagonisti del suo tempo, sia uomini che donne. Si tratta di lettere ad oggi variamente studiate ed edite, ma per le quali manca uno studio critico moderno che restituisca di esse testi filologicamente corretti.[9] Quanto in questa sede si propone, peraltro, sono preliminari ed embrionali esiti di un'indagine che si sta conducendo al fine di

---

italiana (Milano, 1833), vol. 3, 168–9; Pia Mestica Chiappetti, *Vita di Costanza Varano* (Jesi, 1871); Bernardino Feliciangeli, "Notizie sulla vita e sugli scritti di Costanza Varano-Sforza (1426–1447)," *Giornale storico della letteratura italiana* 23 (1894), 1–75.

8 Margaret L. King, "Book-Lined Cells: Women and Humanism in the Early Italian Renaissance," in *Beyond Their Sex: Learned Women of the European Past*, ed. Patricia H. Labalme (New York, 1980), 66–90; Holt N. Parker, "Costanza Varano (1426–1447): Latin as an Instrument of State," in *Women Writing Latin, from Roman Antiquity to Early Modern Europe*, ed. Laurie J. Churchill, Phyllis R. Brown e Jane F. Jeffrey (New York, 2002), vol. 3, 31–53; Jane Stevenson, *Women Latin Poets: Language, Gender, and Authority, from Antiquity to the Eighteenth Century* (Oxford, 2005); Virginia Cox, *Women's Writing in Italy 1400–1650* (Baltimore, 2008).

9 Per tale motivo ho deciso di non riportare citazioni tratte dalle epistole che, seppur opportune per una più compiuta fruizione dei riferimenti inseriti nel presente contributo, non sono state ancora vagliate dalla consultazione dell'intera tradizione manoscritta. Queste le edizioni nelle quali, al momento, è possibile leggere la produzione letteraria di Costanza: *Miscellanea di varie operette al Reverendiss. Padre, il P. M. Calisto M. Palombella* (Venezia, 1743), 295–330; *Catalogus codicum manuscriptorum qui in Bibliotheca Riccardiana Florentiae adservantur* [...] *exhibentur Jo. Lamio auctore* (Liburni, 1756), 145–50; Feliciangeli, "Notizie" (vedi sopra, n. 7), 50–66; *Her Immaculate Hand: Selected Works by and about the Women Humanists of Quattrocento Italy*, ed. Margaret L. King e Albert Rabil, Jr. (Binghamton, New York, 1992), 39–44, 53–6, 134–6; Parker, "Costanza Varano" (vedi sopra, n. 8), 35–53.

individuare e definire i modelli letterari e, in senso più ampio, la formazione culturale di Costanza.

Delle missive che compongono la sua esigua corrispondenza ne sopravvivono otto da lei scritte nella prima metà degli anni '40 del Quattrocento[10] e sei inviatele nello stesso arco di tempo,[11] alcune indotte da sue precedenti comunicazioni, come nel caso delle risposte di Filippo Maria Visconti, altre dettate dalla fama letteraria che la giovane stava acquisendo. Certamente di grande rilievo è la prima epistola del 2 giugno 1442 ricevuta da Guiniforte Barzizza,[12] con la quale il 'maestro' esprimeva i suoi apprezzamenti motivati dalla lettura del discorso a Bianca Maria Visconti, il cui testo gli era pervenuto dalle mani di un entusiasta mercante, Giovanni da Melzo, testimone dell'evento, che si era interessato affinché Guiniforte potesse riceverne una copia. Il messaggio è colmo di parole di encomio e di espressioni che rientrano senza dubbio in un canone diffuso e ormai quasi stereotipato all'interno del genere epistolare, ripetuto con minime variazioni in molte delle lettere scritte dagli umanisti alle donne erudite. Una prova eloquente, in tal senso, è costituita dalla missiva, non del tutto disinteressata, inviata a Costanza da Guarino Veronese che, tra complimenti ed esortazioni, ne aveva approfittato per avanzare un'esplicita richiesta, una sorta di commissione, finalizzata a ricevere un esemplare delle *Satire* di Giovenale e impostata secondo uno schema già adoperato nel 1436 con Isotta Nogarola. Ciononostante, entrambi i documenti sono degni di nota in quanto segnalano la popolarità di cui Costanza e soprattutto i suoi scritti dovettero godere tra i contemporanei.

Da parte sua, Costanza, al di là delle usuali formule di muliebre umiltà tipiche del *topos modestiae*, non perse mai occasione per inserire riferimenti ai propri studi e all'attività di scrittura o per richiamare, attraverso opportune citazioni, i libri rappresentativi della propria formazione che, a ben guardare, cambiano a seconda del sesso del destinatario e dell'obiettivo della missiva. Ad esempio, nel caso delle lettere ad Alfonso d'Aragona e a papa Eugenio IV, la prima scritta durante l'esilio pesarese per perorare la causa dei da Varano, la seconda per persuadere il pontefice a cancellare la scomunica comminata

---

10   I destinatari sono Isotta Nogarola (data non nota), Cecilia Gonzaga (1441), Guiniforte Barzizza (30 giugno 1442), Battista Malatesta (7 marzo 1443), Alfonso d'Aragona (seconda metà del 1443), Filippo Maria Visconti (28 aprile e 27 ottobre 1444) e papa Eugenio IV (inizi del 1445).

11   I mittenti sono Polissena Grimaldi (data non nota), Guarino Veronese (presumibilmente nel 1444), Guiniforte Barizza (2 giugno e 10 aprile 1444), Filippo Maria Visconti (11 settembre e 8 dicembre 1444).

12   Una seconda epistola fu inviata dal Barzizza il 10 aprile 1444.

al nonno Galeazzo Malatesta a seguito della cessione di Pesaro come clausola necessaria al matrimonio tra la stessa Costanza e Alessandro Sforza, la donna non può che corroborare i propri intenti facendo ovviamente ricorso al principe degli oratori, Cicerone, e di questi citando un'orazione specifica, ossia la *Pro Marcello*, con la quale l'Arpinate, alla ricerca di uno spazio nel nuovo assetto politico seguito alla sconfitta dei pompeiani, aveva esaltato Cesare in senato per l'indulgenza mostrata nel concedere il perdono all'esule Marco Marcello e nell'averne accettato il rientro a Roma. Sebbene non sia possibile al momento stabilire quante e quali opere ciceroniane Costanza abbia conosciuto e studiato né attraverso quali canali la ragazza fosse entrata in contatto con il testo in questione, la scelta della *suasoria* rivela comunque un uso consapevole della fonte. Nel caso della lettera al Magnanimo, infatti, la tessera è funzionale al tentativo di garantirsi il favore dell'interlocutore mediante un espediente retorico, una *climax* che, attraverso la descrizione della grande *mansuetudo*, della rara e inaudita *clementia*, dell'immenso *modus* e infine dell'incredibile e quasi divina *sapientia*, riuscisse a compiacere il sovrano e lo disponesse a impegnarsi per soddisfare la richiesta della ragazza. Lo stesso intento è perseguito nella lettera a Eugenio IV, in cui però l'esaltazione delle capacità e delle azioni del pontefice si esprime anche per mezzo del silenzio, o meglio della remissiva, benché topica, dichiarazione della propria inadeguatezza a trovare parole idonee per adempiere a un simile compito.

Quando invece scrive alle donne, i toni utilizzati da Costanza si fanno più indulgenti, arrivando a volte a sfiorare il patetico, mentre i riferimenti letterari si diversificano e si ampliano fino ad abbracciare un contesto più vasto di insegnamenti e suggestioni. Come nella lettera a Isotta Nogarola, in cui è presente una traccia che merita una riflessione. In prossimità del congedo, Costanza si complimenta con Isotta riconoscendole il ruolo acquisito grazie alla cultura e all'attività letteraria, pari a quello raggiunto dalle *dominae doctissimae* dell'antichità, tra le quali indica Aspasia, Cornelia, figlia di Scipione l'Africano, e una meno rinomata Helpe. La ricorrenza dei primi due nomi in simili contesti è abbastanza frequente e non escludo che Costanza l'abbia potuta desumere dall'*incipit* del *De studiis* bruniano, in cui vengono suggeriti appunto i modelli di Cornelia, ricordata per la fortuna delle sue epistole scritte "elegantissimo stilo", di Aspasia, "doctissima quidem mulier et eloquentia litterisque praecellens" come dimostrato dall'intimità intellettuale avuta con Socrate, e della poetessa Saffo a completare la triade. Helpe, invece, rappresenta – a quanto mi risulta dalle ricerche condotte finora – un *unicum* di fronte al quale gli editori e gli studiosi che si sono confrontati con questa lettera hanno mostrato sempre perplessità, fino a preferire piuttosto rimuoverlo, come nell'edizione

Bettinelli.[13] I dubbi sorgono fin dalla scelta dell'aspetto grafico del nome, modificato addirittura in "Nelpe" dal Lami[14] probabilmente sulla base di una scorretta interpretazione della *h* iniziale e invece, a mio avviso, correttamente rettificato da Abel.[15] Sulla base di questa lezione, è stato ipotizzato che Costanza potesse voler alludere a Elpinice, sorella di Cimone e sua sostenitrice contro le accuse di Pericle.[16] A discordare però con la veridicità di questa ipotesi, a parte un filone storiografico diffamatorio sostenuto soprattutto da Plutarco nella *Vita di Pericle*, è a mio avviso il profilo culturale del personaggio, certamente rilevante per l'attivo coinvolgimento politico, ma non altrettanto noto per *doctrina*. Ritengo invece più probabile che la familiarità con la letteratura cristiana, tanto della mittente quanto della destinataria, abbia suggerito a Costanza l'esempio di Elpide, moglie di Severino Boezio e autrice, secondo la tradizione, degli inni sacri *Felix per omnes* e *Aurea lux* in onore degli apostoli Pietro e Paolo. In questo modo, oltre che confermare la validità della formazione di Costanza, potremmo anche ammettere che la selezione dei nomi da inserire in un'epistola così importante, riservata a una rappresentante autorevole del circolo delle donne colte, sia stata meditata e costruita in base a un ben preciso criterio storico che dalla Grecia passa al mondo latino classico e giunge a quello cristiano.

Ben presto la corrispondenza di Costanza da Varano avrebbe rappresentato un modello da conoscere e imitare. Quarant'anni dopo la sua scomparsa, avvenuta il 13 luglio 1447, l'umanista dalmata Ambrogio Miches (Ambroz Mihetić) scelse proprio il magistero di Costanza per redigere un messaggio di ammirazione rivolto a Cassandra Fedele.[17] Il testo, infatti, a parte la rievocazione esplicita del nome della donna tra le erudite più stimate del XV secolo, rivela diversi indizi della conoscenza diretta dell'epistola a Isotta Nogarola prima esaminata, come la citazione pressoché identica di una frase con la quale si asserisce la maggiore 'produttività' e risonanza di una vita dedita interamente agli studi, a conferma che l'eco della fama di Costanza, conseguita nel corso della pur breve attività letteraria, aveva continuato a risuonare anche oltre la sua morte, oltre la sua terra.

Università degli Studi 'A. Moro' di Bari

---

13   *Miscellanea* (vedi sopra, n. 9), 326.

14   *Catalogus codicum manuscriptorum* (vedi sopra, n. 9), 148.

15   *Isotae Nogarolae Veronensis opera quae supersunt omnia*, ed. Eugen Abel (Vindobonae, 1886), vol. 2, 3–6, in part. 6.

16   *Her Immaculate Hand* (vedi sopra, n. 9), 136.

17   *Clarissimae feminae Cassandrae Fidelis Venetae Epistolae et Orationes [...] Iac. Philippus Tomasinus e M.SS. recensuit* (Patavii, 1636), 138–40.

CHAPTER 41

Städtelob und Zeitkritik: Die Frankfurt-Episode im *Iter Argentoratense* (1544) des Humanisten Georg Fabricius

Robert Seidel

Abstract

Das Reisegedicht (Hodoeporicon) ist eine hybride Gattung der neulateinischen Literatur, in der sich Städtelob, Zeitkritik und autobiographisches Bekenntnis mit dem narrativen Grundgerüst eines spannenden und unterhaltenden Reiseberichts verbinden können. Unter den *Hodoeporica* des sächsischen Humanisten Georg Fabricius (1516–71) sind vor allem seine Italienreisegedichte, in denen er die Spuren antiker Kultur erkundete, bereits recht gründlich erforscht. So gut wie unbeachtet blieb indessen sein *Iter Argentoratense* (1544), in dem er von einer Reise berichtet, die ihn als Begleiter zweier junger Adliger aus Thüringen über Eisenach, Fulda, Gelnhausen, Frankfurt, Mainz, Worms und Speyer bis nach Straßburg führte. Als Anhänger der Reformation nahm er zu den Zuständen der Kirche in den katholisch gebliebenen Territorien Stellung, er äußerte sich aber auch zu Themen wie dem deutsch-französischen Verhältnis oder der Haltung der Deutschen gegenüber ihrer germanischen Vor- und Frühgeschichte. Die 216 Verse umfassende Hexameterdichtung zeichnet sich durch einen eleganten Stil, kompositorisches Geschick, Reminiszenzen an klassische Autoren und nicht zuletzt eine pointierte Gedankenführung aus. Im Zentrum des Beitrages steht die Passage, die Fabricius' Besuch in Frankfurt am Main schildert. Von hier aus werden weitere Stellen insbesondere hinsichtlich der zeitdiagnostischen Tendenzen des Textes in den Blick genommen.

Keywords

Georg Fabricius – *Iter Argentoratense* (1544) – Neo-Latin travel literature – Laus urbis – Frankfurt am Main

Der Verfasser des hier vorzustellenden Textes, Georg Fabricius (1516–71), studierte in Wittenberg und Leipzig, war eine Zeitlang Lehrer in seiner

---

© KONINKLIJKE BRILL NV, LEIDEN, 2020 | DOI:10.1163/9789004427105_042

Heimatstadt Chemnitz, unternahm diverse Reisen als Begleiter junger Adliger und wurde schließlich Rektor der Fürstenschule St. Afra in Meißen.[1] Er hat sich vor allem als Verfasser eines Poetiklehrbuches (*De re poetica libri IV*, 1556) und etlicher Bände mit geistlichen Gedichten einen Namen gemacht. Die Sammlung seiner Reisegedichte (*Itinerum liber unus*, 1547) fand in Hermann Wiegands wichtiger Gattungsmonographie *Hodoeporica* Berücksichtigung, allerdings widmete sich Wiegand vorwiegend denjenigen Texten, die sich auf Fabricius' Italienreisen beziehen.[2] Das *Iter Argentoratense*, das eine Reise von Thüringen nach Straßburg literarisch verarbeitet, wurde bislang, soweit ich sehe, noch nicht näher untersucht.

Viele Hodoeporica, die ja grosso modo die Reiseroute ihres Verfassers poetisch nachzeichnen und damit mehr oder minder konsequent auch die an der Strecke liegenden Städte beschreiben, weisen Merkmale der gattungsübergreifenden Schreibart des Städtelobs, der *laus urbis*, auf. Dieses literarische Städtelob, zu dem es eine Fülle neuerer Studien gibt,[3] hat eine differenzierte Topik entwickelt, wonach Aspekte wie Gründung und Alter der Stadt, Lage, Befestigung und öffentliche Bauten, Strukturen der Regierung und Verwaltung oder bedeutende Bürger und deren Leistungen für das Gemeinwohl abzuhandeln waren.

Diese beiden im Titel des Beitrags enthaltenen Gattungszuschreibungen, also Städtelob und Reisegedicht, sind mit dessen drittem Stichwort, also 'Zeitkritik', in Verbindung zu bringen. Ziel der nachfolgenden Untersuchung ist es, die literarischen Möglichkeiten darzustellen, die sich für einen lateinischen Dichter des 16. Jahrhunderts aus der Kombination zweier Gattungsmuster mit einer zeitdiagnostischen Intention ergaben. Dafür erschien es mir sinnvoll, aus dem *Iter Argentoratense* eine Passage besonders herauszuheben, nämlich

---

1 Hermann Wiegand, "Fabricius, Georg," in *Frühe Neuzeit in Deutschland 1520–1620. Literaturwissenschaftliches Verfasserlexikon*, hg. Wilhelm Kühlmann u.a., Bd. 2 (Berlin, 2012), 272–83.

2 Hermann Wiegand, *Hodoeporica. Studien zur neulateinischen Reisedichtung des deutschen Kulturraums im 16. Jahrhundert* (Baden-Baden, 1984), 80–99.

3 Eine Zusammenfassung der durch antike Rhetoriklehrer formulierten Regeln vermittelt z.B. Wilhelm Kühlmann, "Zum Profil des postreformatorischen Humanismus in Pommern: Zacharias Orth (ca. 1535–1579) und sein Lobgedicht auf Stralsund. Mit Bemerkungen zur Gattungsfunktion der *laus urbis* [zuerst 1994]," in *Vom Humanismus zur Spätaufklärung. Ästhetische und kulturgeschichtliche Dimensionen der frühneuzeitlichen Lyrik und Verspublizistik in Deutschland*, hg. Joachim Telle u.a. (Tübingen, 2006), 287–307, hier 294–9. Einen Überblick über den Bestand einschlägiger neulateinischer Texte aus dem deutschen Sprachraum und über die zugehörige Forschung vermittelt Nikolaus Thurn, "Deutsche neulateinische Städtelobgedichte: Ein Vergleich ausgewählter Beispiele des 16. Jahrhunderts," *Neulateinisches Jahrbuch* 4 (2002), 253–69.

DIE FRANKFURT-EPISODE IM *ITER ARGENTORATENSE* DES FABRICIUS

diejenige über die Reichsstadt Frankfurt, die angemessen kontextualisiert und anschließend nach der Methode des close reading analysiert wird.[4]

Das *Iter Argentoratense* entstand 1544 als Frucht einer der erwähnten Hofmeisterreisen des Verfassers: Am 28. September jenes Jahres brach Fabricius, wie durch Briefe bezeugt ist,[5] mit zwei jungen Grafen von Werthern in dem kleinen Ort Beichlingen in Thüringen auf, um sie nach Straßburg zu begleiten, wo sie an dem berühmten, von Johannes Sturm (1507–89) geleiteten Gymnasium einen Teil ihrer Studien absolvieren sollten. Das 207 Hexameter umfassende Hodoeporicon wurde bereits am 12. Oktober unterzeichnet, womit ein *terminus ante* für die Ankunft der drei Reisenden in Straßburg gegeben ist. Die Reise, die über Eisenach, Fulda, Gelnhausen, Frankfurt, Mainz, Worms und Speyer führte, wurde demnach in etwa zwei Wochen absolviert. Außer in dem bereits genannten Erstdruck von 1547 wurde das Gedicht mehrfach publiziert und teilweise starken Veränderungen unterzogen.[6] Erhalten ist auch Fabricius' Autograph des Textes, das er am 27. November 1544 einem Brief an seinen Freund Wolfgang Meurer beifügte.[7]

Die verhältnismäßig kurzen Bemerkungen, die Fabricius zu den besuchten Städten abgibt, scheinen auf den ersten Blick nicht sehr systematisch angelegt und den unmittelbaren Reiseeindrücken geschuldet zu sein. Konfessionell sind die Nähe zur lutherischen Lehre und eine mehr oder minder prononcierte Ablehnung der Papstkirche zu erkennen. Besonders schön zeigt sich dies an der Gegenüberstellung der kurz nacheinander behandelten, nur eine Tagesreise voneinander entfernten Städte Fulda und Gelnhausen. In der Bischofsstadt wird zwar die Ausstattung des Doms bewundert, zugleich aber dessen Umgebung als "vicus Tuscus" und "Subura" bezeichnet, womit auf

---

4 Die Frankfurt-Passage, genauer ein Teil davon, wurde bereits kurz besprochen von Ursula Paintner, "Zwischen regionaler Verortung und Reichsperspektive. Frankfurt im Städtelob der Frühen Neuzeit," in *Frankfurt im Schnittpunkt der Diskurse. Strategien und Institutionen literarischer Kommunikation im späten Mittelalter und in der frühen Neuzeit,* hg. Robert Seidel und Regina Toepfer (Frankfurt am Main, 2010), 364–85; zum Lob Frankfurts vgl. jetzt, mit nur ganz sporadischem Rekurs auf Fabricius, Marina Stalljohann-Schemme, *Stadt und Stadtbild in der Frühen Neuzeit. Frankfurt am Main als kulturelles Zentrum im publizistischen Diskurs* (Berlin, 2017), 24–31 (Kapitel *Städtelob*) und passim.

5 *Georgii Fabricii Chemnicensis Epistolae ad Wolfg. Meurerum et alios aequales. Maximam partem ex autographis nunc primum edidit Detl. Carolus Guil. Baumgarten-Crusius* (Leipzig, 1845), 12: "V. Cal. Octobris, cum nos postridie iter essemus ingressuri."

6 Drucknachweise bei Wiegand, *Hodoeporica* (s.o., Anm. 2), 483–4. Statt der ursprünglich 207 umfasst das Gedicht in späteren Fassungen 216 Verse.

7 Abgedruckt in: Fabricius, *Epistolae* (s.o., Anm. 5), 13–7. Die Handschrift befindet sich in Leipzig, Universitätsbibliothek, Hs. ASL 624.

528 SEIDEL

Prostitution in unmittelbarer Umgebung der Kirche hingewiesen wird, auf 'römische Verhältnisse' sozusagen (82–3):[8]

> Nam non sacrificos hac ullos uidimus aede,
> Sed Thusci turbam uici, mediaeque Suburae.

> Wir sahen nämlich in dieser Kirche keinen einzigen Priester, doch das Gesindel aus dem vicus Tuscus und mitten aus der Suburra.

In der lutherischen Reichsstadt Gelnhausen wird hingegen das Wort Gottes hochgehalten, was Fabricius eindrucksvoll belegt durch die vier Verse umfassende Versifikation von Christusworten, die, so der Autor, auf einer Inschrift in der Stadtkirche zu lesen waren (94–7):

> Sum lux, nemo cupit talem cognoscere lucem:
> Sum uia, nostra tamen sequitur uestigia nemo.
> Sum pius et placidus, nemo audet fidere nobis:
> Sum rerum coelique potens, me nemo ueretur.[9]

> Ich bin das Licht, doch niemand verlangt ein solches Licht zu erkennen. Ich bin der Weg, doch niemand folgt unseren Spuren. Ich bin freundlich und sanft, doch niemand wagt auf uns zu bauen. Ich bin der Herr des Himmels und der Erde, doch niemand ehrt mich.

Besonders interessant ist weiterhin die Passage, die die Bischofs- und Universitätsstadt Mainz behandelt. Von kulturpatriotischer Relevanz sind die ersten Verse, die an einen Sieg der Germanen über die Römer und an die Erfindung der Buchdruckerkunst erinnern (141–6):

---

8 Zitiert wird hier und im Folgenden aus dem Erstdruck *Itinerum Georgii Fabricii Chemnicensis liber unus* (Leipzig, 1547), 39–46, in den Zitaten beschränke ich mich auf die Versziffern. Zum Vergleich werden Fabricius' Autograph von 1544 (wie Anm. 7) und der letzte zu dessen Lebzeiten erschienene Druck (Basel, 1560) herangezogen.

9 In der evangelischen Marienkirche in Gelnhausen ist heute keine entsprechende Inschrift zu finden, weder in deutschem noch in lateinischem Wortlaut. Die Worte in der bei Fabricius überlieferten Form sind auch nicht direkt an den Bibeltext angelehnt, sondern stellen eine komplexe Kompilation verschiedener christologischer Aussagen dar. Vgl. Ruben Zimmermann, *Christologie der Bilder im Johannesevangelium. Die Christopoetik des vierten Evangeliums unter besonderer Berücksichtigung von Joh 10* (Tübingen, 2004).

Vidimus hîc grandem Glandis cognomine molem,
Romani Druso quam constituisse feruntur,
Cui mortem et nomen uictrix Germania fecit.
Quid referam insignem diuini pectoris artem,
Scriptos antè manu, nunc aere excudere libros?
Qua nihil utilius dedit ingeniosa uetustas.

Wir sahen hier einen großen Felsblock, 'Eichel' [heute "Eichelstein"] genannt, den die Römer für Drusus aufgerichtet haben sollen,[10] dem das
siegreiche Germanien seinen Tod und seinen Beinamen einbrachte. Was
soll ich an die bedeutsame Kunst eines gottgleichen Geistes erinnern,
die Kunst, Bücher, die zuvor mit der Hand geschrieben wurden, jetzt
mit Blei zu drucken, eine Kunst, mit der verglichen das Altertum nichts
Nützlicheres hervorbrachte.

Hier werden also die Germanen gegenüber den Römern und die Deutschen
gegenüber den Nationen des Altertums hervorgehoben. Eine Art *revocatio*
des Städtelobs wird in den späteren Auflagen der *Itinera* vorgetragen, wenn
in einem neu hinzugefügten Abschnitt der Verfall der Mainzer Universität be-
klagt und mit der Verkommenheit des katholischen Klerus begründet wird:[11]

Hic Academiam non esse in flore, dolendum est,
Exiliumque pijs indici turpe Camoenis:
Cùm tamen interea tot corpora pigra saginet
Luxus, et haud illos congesta pecunia in usus.

Dass die Universität hier nicht in Blüte steht, ist schmerzlich, ebenso dass
den frommen Musen schändliche Verbannung angesagt ist, während un-
terdessen der Luxus und das nicht zu solchem Nutzen zusammengetra-
gene Geld so viele faule Leiber mästet.

Wohin die Musen nach Fabricius' Ansicht verbannt wurden, werden wir später noch sehen. Nun jedoch möchte ich auf den angekündigten Passus über
Frankfurt eingehen, wohin die Reisenden von Hanau, den Main entlang oder

---

10   Vgl. Michael J. Klein, "Drusus d. Ä. und seine Denkmäler in Publikationen des 16. bis 18.
Jahrhunderts," in '... *Die Augen ein wenig zu öffnen' (J. J. Winckelmann). Der Blick auf die antike Kunst von der Renaissance bis heute. Festschrift für Max Kunze* (Mainz, 2011), 289–98.

11   Wortlaut der Ausgabe 1560, S. 61. Die Verse sind zwischen V. 153 und 154 der Erstausgabe
eingeschoben zu denken.

vermutlich eher zu Schiff *auf* dem Main, gelangten. Der gesamte Absatz umfasst die Verse 104–130:

> Mox turres offert Francfordia nobilis altas,
> Vrbs decus imperij, qua primos Caesar honores   105
> Accipit, et titulum regni sceptrumque reportat.
> Lignea tota tamen, nec claris splendida tectis,
> Sed claris speciosa uiris: huc saepe Camoenas
> In sua tecta trahit facunda uoce Micyllus,
> Suspensasque tenet Phoebeo numine plenus.   110
> Hîc mihi Saxonicas aduerso in littore sedes
> Cernere non socij, sed nox spaciumque negabant.
> Quàm uellem praesens etiam Meurere fuisses,
> Cum nos ad coenam tempusque hospesque uocarent.
> Scindebantur enim studia in contraria cuncti,   115
> Vt fit, cum mentes caluissent, cumque loquentem
> Solliciti audirent, quid saeuus Turca pararet,
> Quique Dei templo, et Romanae praesidet urbi.
> Magnanimi quidam laudabant Caesaris acta:
> India cui dederit, cui tentata Africa nomen,   120
> Et sedata armis iam Gallia, sitque daturus
> Euxinus tandem Nili cum flumine pontus.
> Quae licet[12] acciperet non gratis auribus hospes,
> Poneret et uilis Lenoei munera, Gallum
> (Ignoscat Caesar) pleno laudauimus ore.   125
> Tunc facundus erat, tunc omnia dicta probabat,
> Tristia contractae deponens nubila frontis.
> Altera lux defert turritae ad moenia Hoestae,
> Ad quam Nida secans foecundos leniter agros
> Miscetur Moeno, et placido caput occulit amne.   130

Bald zeigte ihre hohen Türme die vornehme Stadt Frankfurt, die Zierde des Reiches, wo der Kaiser seine ersten Ehrungen empfängt und von wo er den Titel und die Insignien seiner Herrschaft mitnimmt. Doch die Stadt ist ganz aus Holz gebaut und erstrahlt nicht im Glanze bedeutender Häuser, sondern fällt ins Auge durch das Ansehen bedeutender Männer: Hier lockt häufig Micyllus mit beredter Stimme die Musen in sein Haus und hält sie in gespannter Aufmerksamkeit, erfüllt vom Geiste Apollons.

---

12   licet: 1547, 1560 (Drucke); quoniam: 1544 (Autograph).

Hier hielten mich nicht die Reisegefährten, sondern die Nacht und die Entfernung davon ab, Sachsenhausen auf dem gegenüber liegenden Ufer zu besichtigen.

Wie wünschte ich mir, dass auch du, mein Meurer, dabei gewesen wärest, als uns die Zeit und der Wirt zum Essen riefen. Es spalteten sich nämlich alle in gegensätzliche Leidenschaften – wie es zu geschehen pflegt –, als die Gemüter erhitzt waren und sie aufgeregt davon reden hörten, was der wütende Türke im Schilde führe und der, welcher der Kirche Gottes und der Stadt Rom vorsteht. Einige lobten die Taten des kühnen Kaisers, dem Indien, dem das angegriffene Afrika und das nun durch Waffen bezähmte Frankreich Ruhm verliehen hätten und dem endlich auch das Schwarze Meer und der Nil Ruhm verleihen würden. Mochte dies auch unser Wirt mit unwilligen Ohren vernehmen und uns Krüge mit billigem Wein vorsetzen, so lobten wir dann doch den Franzosen (der Kaiser möge es verzeihen) aus vollem Munde. Da war er redselig, da billigte er alles, was man sagte, und verbannte die trüben Wolken von seiner gerunzelten Stirn.

Der nächste Tag brachte uns flussabwärts bis zu den Mauern des turmbewehrten Höchst, wo die Nidda sanft das fruchtbare Ackerland durchziehend sich mit dem Main vereinigt und ihr Haupt in dem sanften Strome verbirgt.

Es ist unschwer zu erkennen, dass die Passage sich in einen Rahmen- und einen Binnenteil gliedert. Der Rahmenteil liefert die topographischen Angaben: Neben Frankfurt wird die auf der gegenüberliegenden Mainseite gelegene Vorstadt Sachsenhausen erwähnt, dazu das bereits auf kurmainzischem Gebiet liegende Höchst, wo die Nidda in den Main mündet. Flüsse werden in antiker Tradition oft als Götter dargestellt. Von Fabricius ist allerdings bekannt, dass er als frommer Lutheraner es ablehnte, heidnische Mythologie in seinen Texten zuzulassen, und tatsächlich deutet er hier die Personifikation von Main und Nidda nur leise an.[13] Dass die Vereinigung von Flüssen auch anders imaginiert werden konnte, zeigen etwa zeitgenössische Gedichte auf Frankfurts französisches Pendant, die Messe- und Druckerstadt Lyon, wo Rhone und Saône zusammenfließen: Die Rhone ist im Lateinischen wie im Französischen männlichen Geschlechts, ein gewaltiger Fluss, der aus den Alpen herabstürzt

---

13 Vgl. den Artikel zu Georg Fabricius in Zedler 9 (1730), 38–40, hier 39: „Er [Fabricius] war ein redlicher und gottsfürchtiger Mann, und hatte einen grossen Abscheu vor der Gewohnheit derer christlichen Poeten, welche die Namen derer heydnischen Götter unter ihre Gedichte mischten."

und mit dem sich die zierliche Saône in zärtlicher Umarmung vereinigt. Es gibt in der Tat Texte, in denen der Zusammenfluss von Rhone und Saône als veritable Liebesszene vorgestellt wird.[14] Doch zurück zu Fabricius: Frankfurt wird in seiner politischen Bedeutung vorgeführt, als Sitz der Kaiserwahlen und somit als heimliche Hauptstadt des Reiches. Interessant ist auch hier der Vergleich mit anderen Texten der Zeit: Hans Sachs, der standesbewusste Handwerksmeister aus Nürnberg, erwähnt in seinem *lobspruech der stat Franckfurt* von 1568 noch deutlicher die Reichsunmittelbarkeit der "alt herlich reichstat" und insbesondere das funktionierende bürgerschaftliche Regiment, den "ainig rat", der "Mit regiment, recht und gericht" die städtische Ordnung garantiere.[15] Bei Fabricius zeichnet sich Frankfurt allerdings auch kulturell aus: Der eher schlichten Bauweise der Häuser wird in schöner Antithese der Glanz der ansässigen Gelehrten gegenübergestellt: Kein Geringerer als Jacob Micyllus (1503–58) wirkt hier, Rektor des städtischen Gymnasiums und einer der prominentesten Philologen und Poeten im Umkreis Melanchthons – und außer Johannes Sturm die einzige Person der Zeitgeschichte, die im ganzen Gedicht namentlich erwähnt wird.[16] Er holt die Musen in sein Haus, heißt es hier in einer recht auffälligen Formulierung, eben *die* Musen, von denen es knapp 50 Verse später heißen wird, dass sie von Mainz aus ins Exil gingen (s.o.). Offenbar also nach Frankfurt, aus der kurfürstlichen Residenz Albrechts von Brandenburg, eines der bedeutendsten Gegenspieler Luthers, in die protestantische Reichsstadt, die Mitglied im Schmalkaldischen Bund war und zwar über keine Universität, wohl aber über ein aufstrebendes Gymnasium und eine Reihe mäzenatisch aktiver Patriziergeschlechter verfügte. Wer bei der Lektüre der Mainz-Passage das Lob Frankfurts noch in Erinnerung hat, dem

---

14   Vgl. Charles Fontaine, *Ode de L'Antiquité et Excellence de la ville de Lyon* (Lyon, 1557), 12–3: "Le Rône y court s'aparier / Et à la Saone s'accompagne / Pour à elle se marier, / Tesmoin le mont et la campgane. / [...] / [Le soleil] D' un aspect droit, non de trauers, / (Comme Mars et Venus) les vise: / Tous deux tous nuds, tous descouuers, / Et nullement s'en scandalize."

15   Hans Sachs, "Ain lobspruech der stat Franckfurt" [1568] in *Frankfurt am Main im Spiegel alter Reisebeschreibungen vom 15. bis zum 19. Jahrhundert. Nebst einem Anhang: Lobgedichte auf Frankfurt am Main*, hg. Robert Diehl [1939] (Würzburg, 1984), 219–22, hier 219: "Franckfurt, die alt herlich reichstat, / Alhie ir contrafactur hat / Sambt Sachsenhausen, dis stetlein klain, / Darzwischen hinlaufet der Main. / Darueber ain staine pruecken get, / Die zusam füeget die zwo stet, / Die paid der ainig rat versicht / Mit regiment, recht und gericht."

16   Micyllus war zweimal Rektor des Frankfurter Gymnasiums, sein zweites – erfolgreicheres – Rektorat währte von 1537 bis 1547. Vgl. über ihn Robert Seidel, "Micyllus, Jacobus," in *Frühe Neuzeit in Deutschland 1520–1620. Literaturwissenschaftliches Verfasserlexikon*, hg. Wilhelm Kühlmann u.a. Bd. 4 (Berlin, 2015), 410–25 (mit ausführlichen Literaturhinweisen); zum Gymnasium unter Micyllus vgl. zuletzt Carolin Ritter, "Das Gymnasium Francofurtanum – Kein Ort für Kunstbanausen. Die 'Inscriptio scholae Francofurtensis' des Jacobus Micyllus (1503–1558)," *Daphnis* 44 (2016), 501–14.

DIE FRANKFURT-EPISODE IM *ITER ARGENTORATENSE* DES FABRICIUS   533

wird suggeriert, dass die Opposition 'Germanen vs. Römer' und 'Deutsche vs. antike Nationen' im Gegensatz 'protestantisches Frankfurt' vs. 'katholisches Mainz' fortgeführt wird, dass mithin die Koalition aus lutherischen Patriziern und melanchthonianisch geprägten Humanisten das kulturelle Erfolgsmodell der Gegenwart bildet.

Wir bleiben noch bei Micyllus: Auch er hatte einst ein Hodoeporicon verfasst, in dem er seine Ankunft in Frankfurt 1527 schilderte, und Fabricius deutet möglicherweise seine Reverenz gegenüber dem Autor mit einem intertextuellen Verweis an. Micyllus hatte geschrieben: "Hinc demum egressis medias Francphurdia turres / Et domuum ostentat culmina summa procul."[17] Bei Fabricius heißt es nun: "Mox turres offert Francfordia nobilis altas." Doch es gibt im Text auch Bezüge zu Micyllus, die von dezidiert kulturpatriotischer Relevanz sind. Wenn Fabricius weiter unten im Text auf die Geschichte von Oppenheim, einer kleinen Stadt zwischen Mainz und Worms, zu sprechen kommt, äußert er sich über die Situation der historischen Studien in Deutschland (154–63):

> Inde Oppenheimum progressi naue, quod olim
> Rufiniana fuit, uel quod Bauconia dictum,   155
> Nomen enim in dubio est: nam nostri munera nunquam
> Musarum, at duri tractarunt praelia Martis,
> Nemoque res scripsit, fecerunt fortiter omnes.
> Hinc tot facta patrum, tantorum et origo locorum,
> Tot ueteres ritus, Lethea nocte sepulti.   160
> At puto tempus erit, cum nulla gloria gente
> Nostra minor, quaecunque aeuum coluere per artes,
> Seu quae pace uigent, seu quae dominantur in armis.

Von dort brachen wir zu Schiff nach Oppenheim auf, das einst ‚Rufiniana‘ oder ‚Bauconia‘ genannt wurde. Der Name ist nämlich unsicher, weil unsere Landsleute niemals das Musenhandwerk, sondern die Kämpfe des harten Krieges verrichtet haben und niemand die Ereignisse aufgeschrieben hat, wenn sie auch alle tapfer bestanden haben. Daher sind so viele Taten der Vorfahren, die Ursprünge so wichtiger Orte und so viele alte Bräuche von der Nacht des Vergessens begraben. Doch ich glaube, die Zeit wird kommen, da unser Ruhm dem keines Volkes nachstehen wird, so viele auch die Zeit durch ihre Künste bereichert haben, ob diese nun im Frieden blühen oder im Krieg ihre Stärke besitzen.

---

17   *Hodoeporicon Micylli* [Erstdruck 1527], in Jacobus Micyllus, *Sylvarum libri quinque* (Frankfurt am Main, 1564), 191–216, hier 216.

Nun muss man wissen, dass Micyllus rund zehn Jahre vorher die erste deutsche Übersetzung der *Annalen* des Tacitus verfasst und in einer programmatischen Vorrede Argumente verwendet hatte, die Fabricius offenbar in seinem Gedicht aufgriff:[18]

> Derhalben dann auch die Teutschen nit gar vnbillicher weiß gescholten werden/ als die nit alleyn jres ersten vrsprungs vnd herkommens/ sonder auch jrer thatten vnd geschichten inn gemeyn nie keyn sonderlich historien beschrieben haben. Vnd wiewol sie mit den thatten vnd mit der mannheyt allen andern völckern alwegen gleich gewesen/ doch solche jre eygene thatten vnd tugeten/ so vil an jnen selber gewesen/ vndergehn vnd inn vergeß gestalt haben lassen werden [...]

Micyllus ist also für Fabricius nicht nur in einem allgemeinen Sinne ein Musenjünger und als Rektor des Gymnasiums der führende Vertreter des Humanismus in Frankfurt, sondern auch eine kulturpatriotische Autorität in der Nachfolge eines Celtis oder Wimpfeling. Doch ist er auch der "hospes", der Gastgeber der kleinen Reisegruppe, von dem im Binnenteil des Gedichtes die Rede ist, auf den wir jetzt eingehen wollen? Die markante Wiederholung des Wortes "suspensus" (so in der Ausgabe 1560 gegenüber "Solliciti" in V. 117 der Erstausgabe und der Handschrift) am Versbeginn könnte darauf hinweisen: Wenn Micyllus die Musen, also die Musenfreunde, in sein Haus holt und in gespannter Aufmerksamkeit hält, dann können sie auch bei ihm gespannt zuhören. Die Frage ist wohl nicht abschließend zu beantworten, zumal der Text einige Schwierigkeiten bietet: Es ist nicht klar, ob das Partizip "loquentem" in V. 116 auf eine konkrete Person bezogen werden muss oder einfach mit "jemand, der redete" übersetzt werden kann, außerdem gibt es eine im Autograph bezeugte Parallelüberlieferung für "licet" in V. 123, nämlich das in seiner Bedeutung genau entgegengesetzte, dem Anschein nach besser passende, aber schon im Erstdruck nicht mehr verwendete "quoniam". Ich überspringe diese philologischen Probleme und wende mich der literarischen Struktur der Textstelle zu: Es ist ja auffällig, dass die relativ knappe, auf reichsstädtische Würde und kulturelle Kompetenz fokussierte *laus urbis* eine sehr lebendige narrative Erweiterung erfährt. Während in manchen Städtelobgedichten die lokale Geselligkeit etwa in Form einer Beschreibung von Märkten oder Lustbarkeiten thematisiert wird, berichtet der Reisende hier von einer

---

18   *Der Römischen Keyser Historienn* [...] *durch Cornelium Tacitum beschriben* [...] (Mainz, 1535), fol. aIIIᵛ; wieder abgedruckt in *Die deutschen Humanisten. Dokumente zur Überlieferung der antiken und mittelalterlichen Literatur in der Frühen Neuzeit*. Abt. 1, Bd. 3, hg. Wilhelm Kühlmann u.a. (Turnhout, 2010), 37.

DIE FRANKFURT-EPISODE IM *ITER ARGENTORATENSE* DES FABRICIUS 535

konkreten Szene, wie sie sich in seiner Herberge – einem öffentlichen Gasthaus oder eben doch dem Haus des Micyllus – abgespielt haben dürfte. Es kommt unter den Gästen, die anscheinend auch dem Alkohol zugesprochen haben, zu hitzigen politischen Debatten. Man diskutiert über die Türkengefahr und über die Pläne des Papstes, über den Nachbarn Frankreich kommt es schließlich zum Streit. Einige loben die Erfolge Kaiser Karls v. gegen den französischen König François I., vermutlich auf die Verhandlungen im Friedensschluss von Crépy im selben Jahr (18. September) anspielend.[19] Der Gastgeber scheint allerdings Sympathien für die Franzosen zu haben und rächt sich mit dem Ausschenken schlechten Weines, worauf die Gäste – „der Kaiser möge es verzeihen", heißt es da – den französischen König, "Gallum", aus vollem Munde loben. Daraufhin wird der Gastgeber seinerseits ganz liebenswürdig und die schlechte Stimmung legt sich rasch.[20] Fabricius entwirft hier ein fast burleskes Bild urbaner Geselligkeit, das insofern eng mit dem Stadtlob verbunden ist, als in der Handels- und Druckermetropole Menschen aus vielerlei Territorien zusammenkamen und die politisch wie konfessionell relativ liberale Reichsstadt offenkundig als Plattform für den Austausch divergenter Meinungen genutzt wurde. Offenbar genoss der sächsische Humanist Fabricius in Frankfurt die Offenheit einer Atmosphäre von Weltläufigkeit, in der politisches Räsonnieren relativ gefahrlos möglich war.

Eine durchgehend textnahe Untersuchung des gesamten Hodoeporicon würde dieses noch präziser im Spannungsfeld politisch-konfessioneller, kultureller und gelehrtenständischer Diskurse positionieren, aber wohl kaum gänzlich neue Aspekte zutage fördern. Die grundsätzlich reichspatriotische, auch kaisertreue Position des Verfassers wird beispielsweise auch an den Passagen über Worms und Speyer kenntlich (V. 166–79), und natürlich wird zum Abschluss das Ziel der Reise, die Bildungsmetropole Straßburg, gerühmt, unter deren Gelehrten "Sturmius excellit" (V. 204).[21] Ein abschließender, dezidiert 'neolatinistischer' Blick auf das Gedicht soll indessen noch den intertextuellen Verweisen auf antike Prätexte gelten. Dass Fabricius

---

19 Vgl. zu den einzelnen historischen Fakten Alfred Kohler, *Karl V., 1500–1558. Eine Biographie* (München, 1999).

20 François I. (1491–1547) war bei der Königswahl 1519 gegen Karl V. angetreten. In insgesamt vier Kriegen zwischen beiden Monarchen ging es um Einflusssphären in Europa, bis 1544 unterhielt der französische König ein Bündnis mit den Osmanen (vgl. "saeuus Turca" im Text). In der Reichsstadt Frankfurt war man traditionell kaisertreu, andererseits wandte man sich gegen die Rekatholisierungsversuche und gegen die feindselige Frankreichpolitik Karls V., da diese die Handelsinteressen der Stadt gefährdete. Daher konnte es in Frankfurt durchaus 'Franzosenfreunde' geben. Die Zuspitzung der Lage im Jahr 1544 ist durch Dokumente belegt. Vgl. Irene Haas, *Reformation – Konfession – Tradition. Frankfurt im Schmalkaldischen Bund 1536–1547* (Frankfurt am Main, 1991).

21 Vgl. auch das Lob Sturms im Begleitbrief an Meurer in: Fabricius, *Epistolae* (s.o., Anm. 5), 12.

solche Beziehungen herstellt, ist zu erwarten. Am auffälligsten vielleicht ist der Rekurs auf Horaz, *Satire* 1,5,51–70, das *Iter Brundisinum*, wo ebenfalls in einem Reisegedicht eine komische Wirtshausszene eingeschaltet wird. Schön ist auch die Vergilanspielung in V. 115, wo die Wirtshausstreiterei mit den Worten "Scindebantur enim studia in contraria cuncti" umschrieben wird. Dieser Hexameter ist angelehnt an *Aeneis* 2,39: "Scinditur incertum studia in contraria vulgus." Bei Vergil bezieht sich die Auseinandersetzung auf das Problem der Trojaner, wie sie mit dem hölzernen Pferd umgehen sollten. Der Wirtshausstreit wird hier also ironisch mit einer großen epischen Entscheidungsszene verglichen. Im Kontext intertextueller Bezugnahmen sei schließlich noch ein besonders kühner Gedanke vorgetragen: Es wird ja im Gedicht eine Beziehung hergestellt zwischen "Caesar", also Kaiser Karl V., und dem "Gallus", dem französischen König François I. Nun behauptet der spätantike Vergilkommentator Servius, dass Vergil ursprünglich im vierten Buch der *Georgica* einen Abschnitt "Laudes Galli" integriert habe.[22] Nachdem der Dichter Gallus bei Octavian, dem späteren Augustus, also dem "Caesar", in Ungnade gefallen und in den Selbstmord getrieben worden sei, sei diese Passage von Vergil beseitigt und durch das Aristaeus-Epyllion ersetzt worden. Und nun die Pointe: Fabricius, der wenig später, 1551, selbst eine Servius-Ausgabe veranstaltete, diese antike Hypothese also kannte,[23] könnte sich selbst als Nachfolger Vergils inszeniert und ein Lob des "Gallus", also des französischen Königs, artikuliert haben. Zugleich hätte er Karl V. als den im Vergleich mit Augustus duldsameren Kaiser charakterisiert, der ein 'Loben des Gallus' eben zulasse.[24]

Ob nun Fabricius diese abenteuerliche Lesart seines Textes vorgeschwebt hat oder nicht – in jedem Fall erweist sich das Hodoeporicon als eine raffinierte, mit ebenso viel Gelehrsamkeit wie Darstellungskompetenz und kritischem Witz konzipierte Dichtung, die den Leser ganz nah an die politische, konfessionelle und soziale Realität der Zeitgenossen heranführt.

Johann Wolfgang Goethe-Universität, Frankfurt am Main

---

22   Servius' Spekulation wird heute allgemein verworfen, vgl. *Virgil, Georgics. Vol. 1: Books I–II*, hg. Richard F. Thomas (Cambridge, 1988), 13–6.

23   *P. Vergilii Maronis Bucolica, Georgica, et Aeneis, nunc cum ueris commentariis Tib. Donati et Seruii Honorati summa cura editis* [...] (Basel, 1551), 117: "Sanè sciendum, ut supra diximus, ultimam partem huius libri esse mutatam: nam Galli laudes habuit locus ille, qui nunc Orphei contine[n]t fabulam: quae inserta est, postquam irato Augusto occisus est Gallus."

24   Diese Vermutung wurde auf einer Diskussion in Frankfurt von meinem Kollegen Hans Bernsdorff geäußert.

CHAPTER 42

Seven Types of Intertextuality, and the Emic/Etic Distinction

Minna Skafte Jensen

Abstract

In an important paper from 2007, Toon Van Hal discussed the history of Neo-Latin research and its methods, or lack of them. Among other possible tools he mentioned the emic/etic distinction, introduced by Kenneth L. Pike in 1954, and in use among linguists and anthropologists. The emic/etic approach insists on the distinction between the two and demands that researchers are conscious of their own procedures. To a modern reader Neo-Latin poetry may seem just as strange as any foreign culture. An important factor in this strangeness is the overwhelming admiration for the ancients manifesting itself in a variety of intertextual devices of which seven are discussed here with examples from Danish Latin poetry 1552–1615. Seen with an emic or an etic eye different aspects of this highly sophisticated literature are revealed, and the author reflects a little on her own approach.

Keywords

methodology of Neo-Latin studies – emic/etic – Danish Neo-Latin poetry – intertextuality – renaissance poetry

Emic/Etic

In his seminal paper, "Towards meta-Neo-Latin studies?" Toon Van Hal among other things briefly mentioned the terms *emic* and *etic* as a possible instrument in Neo-Latin studies.[1] The pair was introduced by the American linguist

---

1 Toon Van Hal, "Towards meta-Neo-Latin studies? Impetus to Debate on the Field of Neo-Latin Studies and its Methodology," *Humanistica Lovaniensia* 56 (2007), 349–65, there 363. His request was met by Heinz Hofmann, "Some Considerations on the Theoretical Status of Neo-Latin Studies," *Humanistica Lovaniensia* 61 (2017), 513–26.

© KONINKLIJKE BRILL NV, LEIDEN, 2020 | DOI:10.1163/9789004427105_043

and anthropologist Kenneth L. Pike as early as 1954. It was part of an ambitious project of developing a method to describe human behaviour in general, but it soon found a life of its own.[2] During the following decades it spread into other disciplines, and especially established itself as a basic element in anthropological methodology.[3] I first made its acquaintance in Homeric studies, as it is in use among folklorists and anthropologists doing fieldwork among singers of oral epic.[4] Let me first cite how Pike defined the pair:[5]

> It proves convenient—though partially arbitrary—to describe behavior from two different standpoints, which lead to results which shade into one another. The etic viewpoint studies behavior as from outside of a particular system, and as an essential initial approach to an alien system. The emic viewpoint results from studying behavior as from inside the system.

He also described how the anthropologist who begins to study an alien culture first has to view the foreign data from the analytical systems with which he/ she is familiar in an etic approach, gradually shifting to an emic one as the alien systems reveal themselves.[6] It seems to me that Neo-Latin literature is not quite unlike such an alien culture, and that our approach to it to some degree is similar to how a field-worker studies natives in some far away country.

In what follows I concentrate on poetry, and for a start I want to underline how strange it is. A reader who approaches it for the first time will find much to wonder at: The Christian religion fused with Greco-Roman polytheism. Odd genres such as the Latin pastoral with its use of shepherds' masks, or paraphrases of famous works, especially the Bible. The shameless eulogies of patrons. The implied learning leading to sophistication, but also to what might be felt as a lack of spontaneity. The tension between internationalism and nationalism. The uniformity of the phenomenon, with poets all over Europe composing more or less the same poems in the same way, expressing themselves in the same genres, using the same phrases. Shared internationally is also the

---

2 Kenneth L. Pike, *Language in Relation to a Unified Theory of the System of Human Behavior*, 3 parts (Glendale, 1954–60, second revised edition Berlin, 1967).

3 Thomas N. Headland, "Introduction," in *Emics and Etics: The Insider/Outsider Debate*, ed. Thomas N. Headland, Kenneth L. Pike and Marvin Harris (Newbury Park 1990), 13–27.

4 See e.g. Elizabeth C. Fine, *The Folklore Text From Performance to Print* (Bloomington 1984), 73. Lauri Honko, *Textualising the Siri Epic* (Helsinki 1998), 130–1. Isidore Okpewho, "Performance and Plot in *The Ozidi Saga*," *Oral Tradition* 19 (2004), 87. *Edige: A Karakalpak Oral Epic as Performed by Jumabay Bazarov*, ed. Karl Reichl (Helsinki 2007), 100. Minna Skafte Jensen, *Writing Homer: A Study Based on Results from Modern Fieldwork* (Copenhagen 2011), 14–5.

5 Pike, *Language* (see above, n. 2), 37.

6 Ibid., 37–9.

SEVEN TYPES OF INTERTEXTUALITY, AND THE EMIC/ETIC DISTINCTION 539

history of reception moving from contemporary admiration to later rejection. To compose Latin poetry in early modern Europe might well be called a very special kind of "human behavior".

To return to Pike, he also gives the following description of the etic approach: "Through the etic 'lens' the analyst views the data in tacit reference to a perspective oriented to all comparable events (whether sounds, ceremonies, activities), of all peoples, of all parts of the earth."[7] This is more than most of us would be able to achieve! It is normal for us, however, to have such a tacit reference to a perspective oriented to some comparable European literatures, composed in ancient Latin or the vernaculars, and to have more or less conscious ideas about what to expect from poetry.[8]

> Through the other lens, the emic one, he views the same events, at the same time, in the same context, in reference to a perspective oriented to the particular function of those particular events in that particular culture, as it and it alone is structured.

The emic/etic distinction aims at revealing overall systems consisting of units accepted as such by insiders. Since the characteristic foreignness is shared internationally the system in this case must be the Neo-Latin poetry of the international learned republic, and the units single poems. Observing through the etic lens the researcher will study the system as a synthesis of what occurred wherever it was cultivated, describing and classifying its characteristics, its place in society and its development over time. He/she will consider it as a subset of Neo-Latin literature in general, or of poetry in general, or of literature in general. Surveys as well as details will be relevant in achieving the most careful and precise mapping of the phenomenon. The etic description will aim at revealing what makes this kind of poetry special inside the broader categories it is part of: poetry, not prose; Latin, not vernacular.

Through the emic lens the researcher will look at the same system, but concentrate on how these characteristics made sense for those who were participants in it. What at a first, etic, glance seemed foreign finds its place in the emic description.

Most important of it all, so the theory goes, is that the researcher distinguishes between the two approaches and is aware of when he/she is doing what. In our wish to understand the poems we study, we instinctively aim at reaching an emic standpoint, trying to put ourselves into the poet's place or

---

7   Ibid., 41.
8   Ibid.

that of the contemporary reader. The risk is to forget the critical eye on one's own enculturated assumptions.

Unlike the anthropologist the researcher who studies Neo-Latin is unable to check his/her interpretations directly against those of poets and readers. An impression of the emic standpoints must be formed by means of paratexts in poetry volumes, commentaries, studies of what the poet in question and his contemporaries usually were engaged in, information about how the works were received, etc., thus depending on the etic approach to arrive at emic understandings.

Intertextuality

At the heart of the foreignness of Neo-Latin literature is the dialogue with antiquity, most clearly manifested in poetry. To compose in such a way that your poem alludes to one or more hypotexts is, of course, nothing special to Neo-Latin. Gérard Genette wrote his book on palimpsests studying vernacular literature.[9] However, Neo-Latin intertextuality is different in the fact that reference to ancient Latin is all-pervasive. This kind of literature always moves on at least two levels, the ancient and the modern. The poems may have other hypotexts as well, found in ancient Greek, contemporary Latin, or vernacular, but reference to classical Roman literature is the *conditio sine qua non*.

I have chosen this intertextuality as the obvious way to illustrate the emic/etic distinction in practice. It is less obvious to divide the phenomenon into seven types. There could be more or less, but seven is a beautiful number, and it allows me to have my own small play at intertextuality. My purpose is to underline the common, omnipresent intertextuality rather than the more sophisticated forms.

I have taken my examples from only five poets in order to give you an idea of their personalities. However, they were not the only ones. In Denmark as elsewhere there was a host of young men trying their hand at Neo-Latin composition. The most successful of them were richly awarded; thus Erasmus Michaëlius Laetus (1526–82) was both ennobled by King Frederick II and given a stately house in the centre of Copenhagen. In our etic approach such moral and economic recognition is a signal of the importance of Latin poetry in the eyes of the authorities.

---

9 Gérard Genette, *Palimpsestes: La littérature au second degré* (Paris 1982).

1   Use of Ancient Genres

Danish Neo-Latin poetry began c. 1550. At the time vernacular poetry in this country was mainly oral and meant for public performance; from a modern point of view the ballads were the most important genre. Compared to that, ancient Roman poetry with its richness of genres offered endless possibilities of expressing private thoughts and individual themes. Most of them were implemented, and it was part of an overall project of revitalising antiquity. Besides Laetus the most prominent of the first generation were Hans Jørgensen Sadolin (1528–1600) and Hans Frandsen (1532–84). They started out with elegies, thus choosing a Neo-Latin genre that was immensely popular, mainly in the form of letters to specific addressees. Sadolin's *Elegidia* (Small Elegies) were published in 1552 and Frandsen's *Elegiarum liber primus* (First Book of Elegies) in 1554, both in Wittenberg.[10] With his hexametric *Bucolica* (Pastorals, Wittenberg 1560) Laetus struck a more ambitious note by competing with Vergil and handling themes such as the death of King Christian III and the coronation of Frederick II,[11] and Frandsen ventured into lyrical metres in some of his *Carmina* (Songs, Lyon 1561).[12]

2   Use of Special Neo-Latin Genres Developed from Classical Models

Neo-Latin specialities such as *laudationes urbium*, anagrams, *encomiastica*, *epitaphia* or *parodiae* were all cultivated; they all respect classical metric forms. An example is Frandsen's *Iter Francicum* (The Francic Journey, in *Carminum liber*, Lyon 1561, 9–23). The poem is a *hodoeporicon*, which tells of a journey the poet undertook in the company of the German poet Petrus Lotichius Secundus, whom he had met in Heidelberg; the young Dane was immensely proud of this friendship. The genre offered him a chance of parading as a member of the *res publica literata*, travelling with eyes and ears open while discussing the experiences with a learned friend.

---

10   The mentioned or quoted Neo-Latin texts older than 1600 are accessible online: *Early European Books*, eeb.chadwyck.co.uk.

11   Cf. Peter Zeeberg, "The Bucolica (1560) of Erasmus Laetus," in *Acta Conventus Neo-Latini Budapestinensis: Proceedings of the Thirteenth International Congress of Neo-Latin Studies* (*Budapest 2006*), ed. Rhoda Schnur (Tempe, Arizona 2010), 839–45. Trine Arlund Hass, "Erasmus Laetus and Virgil's Eclogue 7: Two Cases of Intertextuality," *Neulateinisches Jahrbuch* 15 (2013), 11–26.

12   Cf. Minna Skafte Jensen, *Friendship and Poetry: Studies in Danish Neo-Latin Literature* (Copenhagen 2004).

So far I imagine that I can understand the culture from an emic standpoint. Paraphrases of psalms, another popular genre, are more foreign to me. Somehow they reveal a bewildering anxiety that for all its holiness the Bible was less elegant than classical Latin literature. Next, I find it strange that poets were composing paraphrases of the same texts again and again; for instance, versifications of the Nativity must be uncountable. Furthermore, there are cases in which poets seem to me shameless in applying the Bible to contemporary contexts. Sadolin's paraphrase of psalm 37 is a case in point (*Insignia Regum Daniae*, The Danish Kings' symbols, Copenhagen, 1569, fol. 37v–38v). It was published during the Nordic Seven Years' War 1563–70. The psalmist sings about how the Lord supports the righteous and punishes the wicked. In Sadolin's paraphrase it is all about Danes and Swedes, with the latter being those to be thrown into the oven or scattered as chaff for the wind.

3   Invention of New Genres as Implicit Intertextuality

This is rare, but with his *Colloquia Moralia* (Moral Conversations, Basel, 1573) Laetus developed a genre that I know of no precise parallel to. Like other new genres it expresses itself in a classical metre and classical language, thus by its very existence underlining the strength of the basic intertextual system. Each of the poems has two interlocutors, mostly two flowers, trees, or animals. A theme is stated at the beginning in a proverb-like form, and the two develop their points of view in hexameters. In no. 4,7 (pp. 240–53), two rivers, the Tiber and the Danish Gudius/Gudenå, discuss the theme "ingenio magnos uiuere" ("great men live by their genius"). It is stated that Europe has two famous peninsulas. Towards the south is the Italic peninsula, towards the north, Jutland; the two rivers each have their important part to play in history. Thus both rivers and peninsulas equal each other, and Laetus lets Gudius describe a row of marvellous details of nature and culture along its banks.

Here as often in Laetus' pompous works my etic reading tends to swerve towards irony. However, if the purpose is an emic understanding of the system of Latin poetry in Denmark at the time, poetry of a kind that to me seems without a sense of proportion has to be accepted as an important emic unit.

The four last types are all examples having single ancient poems as hypotexts.

4   Signalling a Hypotext in Wording

Hans Frandsen, "Ad librum, elegia II", 48 vv. (in *Elegiarum liber primus*, fol. A3v–4v)

SEVEN TYPES OF INTERTEXTUALITY, AND THE EMIC/ETIC DISTINCTION   543

PArue liber confecte mihi iuuenilibus annis
     Tun' dominum linques tam citò quaeso tuum?
Hei mihi quam uereor si scrinia nostra relinques
     Ne subeas multis multa dolenda modis [...]
Vade sed incultus, qualem te nostra Thalia
     Fecit, quae prorsus paupere fonte fluit.
Vade bonis auibus precor, et loca grata saluta
     Praemia quae lactis prima dedere mihi.
Et si quis quaerat, quid agam, me uiuere dicas
     Hîc ubi Leucoreos irrigat Albis agros [...][13]

To the book
Little book, composed by me in youthful years,
     Do you really leave your master so soon?
Alas how I fear that if you leave my book-case
     You will suffer many pains in many ways [...]
Go ahead, as unpolished as you were made
     By my Thalia who simply flows from a poor source.
Go ahead with good omens, I pray, and greet the dear localities,
     Who first nurtured me with milk.
And if somebody asks how I am, say that I live
     Here where the Elbe waters the lands of the White Mountain [...]

The poem is modelled over Ovid's *Tristia* 1,1.

Parve—nec invideo—sine me, liber, ibis in urbem:
     ei mihi, quod domino non licet ire tuo!
vade, sed incultus, qualem decet exulis esse;
     infelix habitum temporis huius habe [...]
vade, liber, verbisque meis loca grata saluta:
     contingam certe quo licet illa pede.
siquis, ut in populo, nostri non immemor illi,
     siquis, qui, quid agam, forte requirat, erit,
vivere me dices, salvum tamen esse negabis;
     id quoque, quod vivam, munus habere dei [...]

Ovid's bitterness has been replaced by the young poet's worries about the reception of his book, but soon these worries give way to a eulogy of Frandsen's native town of Ribe and the learned friends he has there. The link to Ovid is

---

13   Cf. note 9.

only the quotations and the letter-form. Etically this is just an elegiac letter like so many others, but seen from an emic standpoint it is the grand announcement of the arrival of a dominant modern European movement to Denmark.

5   Signalling a Hypotext in Scenery and Context

With the astronomer Tycho Brahe (1546–1601) we move a couple of decades onwards. Unlike the typical Latin poets he was a nobleman, but his passion for science made him unusual also for the nobility. When he made his début, publishing his sensational observation of a new star, he added to the scientific prose a long poem modelled on the first elegy in book 3 of Ovid's *Amores*, in which the Muses of Elegy and Tragedy appear to the poet. Just like Ovid, Tycho began by describing the site of the epiphany as a place you could easily imagine as a home of Muses, and Urania's errand is of the same kind as Elegia's in Ovid, to enrol the poet as her servant.

"In Uraniam", 232 vv. (in *De nova stella*, Copenhagen 1573, fol. L1r–L5r)

> ESt locus ad Rynae properantes fluminis vndas,
>   Aspicies, Musas hic habitare putes;
> Quo non fertilior, quo non iucundior extat,
>   Qua videt Arctoum SCANIA tota polum [...]
> Fortè per vmbriferae digressus limina Syluae,
>   Solus ad irriguas expatiabar aquas.
> Sol erat Hesperias se tunc missurus in vndas,
>   Lunaque nocturnos accelerauit equos.
> En DEA (nescio quae) caelo delapsa sereno,
>   Protinus hic oculos constitit ante meos [...][14]

> To Urania
> There is a locality close to the hastening waves of the river Ryna
>   If you look, you will think that the Muses might live here.
> There is no area more fertile, nor more pleasant;

---

14   Cf. note 9. Peter Zeeberg has studied the astronomer's poetry extensively for many years. Cf. e.g. "Science versus Secular Life. A Central Theme in the Latin Poems of Tycho Brahe," in *Acta Conventus Neo-Latini Torontonensis*, ed. Alexander Dalzell, Charles Fantazzi and Richard J. Schoeck (Binghamton 1991), 831–8. idem, *Tycho Brahes "Urania Titani"—et digt om Sophie Brahe* (Copenhagen, 1994). idem, "Tycho Brahe," in *Dictionary of Literary Biography* vol. 300: *Danish writers from the Reformation to Decadence, 1550–1900*, ed. Marianne Stecher-Hansen (Detroit, 2004) 105–13.

SEVEN TYPES OF INTERTEXTUALITY, AND THE EMIC/ETIC DISTINCTION

> From there Skåne views the whole of the Northern sky [...]
> (Here follows a long description of the glories of the magnificent place.)
> By chance I wandered into the area of a shadowy forest,
>   Deviating alone towards the watering stream.
> The sun was just on the point of descending into the Western waves,
>   While the moon accelerated the horses of night.
> Look! some goddess slipped down from the clear heaven,
>   Coming to stand right here before my eyes [...]

Tycho's elegy is much longer than its model, and especially its tone is much more solemn and intense. Though there are few verbal allusions, it is evident that Tycho is referring to Ovid's Muses. The divine epiphany celebrates the ambitions of the young astronomer, and implicitly he registers not only as the Muse's worshipper, but also as Ovid's heir.

On reading this poem I imagine that my immediate experience unites an emic and an etic point of view. Nevertheless, the knowledge that the young poet actually developed into a pioneer astronomer, breaking fresh ground with his precise observations and new instruments, inevitably plays a part in my reading. The level of his ambitions when composing a poem like this at the starting point of his career is shocking to a reader like me, used to more cautious behaviour. Emically, it seems that the poet felt certain of his goal in life, whereas I have no information of how contemporary readers reacted.

6   Signalling a Hypotext in Form

Hans Sadolin had a somewhat stormy life. He made a career as a clergyman and a poet and succeeded in being declared poet laureate by the king. However, in 1576 he caused a scandal, having a child with an unmarried young noblewoman. He was dismissed from his post as a dean and imprisoned for some years. The volume of *Syluae* (Sketches) was published soon after he had been released.

> "Suam in sacrarum literarum studio negligentiam deplorat", 32 vv. (in
>   *Sylvae,* Copenhagen 1581, fol. 20v–21r)
> O Deus magni fabricator Orbis,
> Dux Ducum, Rex o generose Regum,
> Dexteram cuius metuit colitque
>   Vesper et ortus:
> Te peto supplex, stabilique corde

Vota proponens cupio iuuari:
Heu mihi si non tua gratiosus
Lumina pandas [...]
Turba te transfer procul hinc maligna:
Improbo nec me studio retunde:
Audijt vocem gemitumque nostrum
   Rector Olympi.[15]

He deplores his negligence in studying the holy scripture.
O god, creator of the great universe,
Prince of princes, o generous king of kings,
Whose right hand is feared and worshipped
   By West and East,
To you I pray humbly, with steadfast heart
Reciting vows I beg for help.
Alas if you do not direct your eyes
   Generously towards me [...]
You evil crowd, get away from here
Do not repress me with wicked intentions.
My voice and lament was heard
   By the ruler of Olympus.

The poem is in Sapphic stanzas, a metre not yet in common use in Denmark, though well known especially from Horace. Furthermore, Sadolin modelled his ode specifically on Sappho's poem to Aphrodite. Like that work, Sadolin's poem consists of seven stanzas and is a prayer, opening with a solemn address to the deity. The relationship between poet and god is, however, very different; there is nothing in Sadolin to resemble the chummy atmosphere between Aphrodite and Sappho. The severe Lutheran god of sixteenth-century Denmark bore little likeness to the Greek goddess. Accordingly, Sadolin spent the first six stanzas on praying and then let the last one come as a blow directed at his enemies, much like how Sappho ended her poem. Both poems assert forcefully that the poet is under special divine protection, not to be trifled with.

Here, I should argue, Sadolin used Sappho as a shield. Sappho's poem was accessible in Denmark at the time, but hardly well known. An average reader would notice the elegant form, but he who recognised Sappho's poem would acknowledge and respect the learning and superior ease with which Sadolin celebrated his return to the courtly scene. In reading types 5 and 6 I feel emic and etic cooperating.

---

15   Cf. note 9.

7   Adhering Closely to the Hypotext

A special genre is the *parodia*, a kind of game in which a model is followed strictly so that a word is either retained or substituted with a word of the same class, preferably a synonym, resulting in a new poem with another content. It is a tour de force, presupposing great mastery of the craft. In the example quoted Aquilonius even succeeds in entering the adjective "posthumus" in v. 25, achieving a wordplay with the name of Horace's addressee.

> Bertilus Canutius Aqvilonius, "Ad Puellam suam", 28 vv. (in *Q. Horatii Manes*, Copenhagen 1615, 70–1)
> EHeu volucres Lilia Lilia
>   Labuntur anni: nec levitas moram
>   Horis senescentique vitae
>   Afferet insipidoque letho [...]
> Absumet haeres munera posthumus
>   Servata septem clavibus, et rosâ
>   Cinget sepulcretum superbâ
>   Hesperidum potiore silvis.[16]

> To his girlfriend
> Alas, the winged years, Lilia, Lilia,
>   slip away, and cheerfulness
>   will not bring delay to hours
>   or aging life or insensible death [...]
> A late-born heir will take out the gifts
>   saved under seven locks, and will wreathe
>   the tomb with proud roses
>   stronger than the forests of the Hesperids.

> Cf. Horace, *carm.* 2,14
> Eheu fugaces, Postume, Postume,
>   labuntur anni nec pietas moram
>   rugis et instanti senectae
>   adferet indomitaeque morti [...]
> absumet heres Caecuba dignior
>   servata centum clavibus et mero
>   tinguet pavimentum superbo,
>   pontificum potiore cenis.

---

16   The Royal Library, Copenhagen, Hielmst. 2179 8°.

Aquilonius composed such *parodiae* to all Horace's odes, more than one to many of them. Etically it may be difficult to see the point. Emically it might make sense as a culmination of the aspect of education and career-making common to much Neo-Latin poetry.

The terms emic/etic may also be applied to the relationship between Neo-Latin and antiquity. Some of the poets seem to have moved so close to their models as to almost identifying with them. It is striking to consider the genres Laetus chose. He started out with *Bucolica* (Pastorals), and among his overwhelming amount of further works we find a didactic poem in four books, *De Re Nautica* (On Shipping), as well as two huge epic poems on Danish history, in that way reiterating Vergil's career while at the same time surpassing his *Bucolica*, *Georgica* and *Aeneid* in quantity. Already among his contemporaries he was called a new Vergil.

Tycho Brahe announced his ambitious plans for becoming astronomer as a divine appointment by using Ovid as a model. Over the years he followed in the Roman poet's footsteps with many other poems, most remarkably in the great Heroid *Urania Titani* (From Urania to Titan). When after the death of Frederick II he lost royal support for his research and left the country, he addressed an elegiac letter to his *patria*, like Ovid lamenting his exile. Thus his life experience underlined his status as *Ovidius redivivus*. Furthermore, I suspect that Aquilonius wanted to be accepted as a new Horace.

Conclusion

Some scholarly disciplines are defined by their method. For Neo-Latin research this is not the case; we look to related fields and borrow what we find useful. When editing texts we build on classical and modern philological experience, in interpretative studies mainly on modern literary criticism, linguistics and history. Neo-Latin research is defined by its subject, texts written in Latin in the early modern period, by authors who had at least one other language at his (and rarely her) disposal.[17]

The emic/etic approach insists on the distinction between the two and demands that researchers are conscious of their own procedures. For my own part I admit that I go for poetry rather than prose simply because for no very clear reason it seems most attractive to me. Next, I tend to concentrate, more consciously, on poems that immediately appeal to me, in practice such that are

---

17 Tom Deneire, "Neo-Latin and the Vernacular: Methodological Issues," in *Encyclopedia of the Neo-Latin World*, ed. Philip Ford, Jan Bloemendal and Charles Fantazzi (Leiden 2014), 275–85.

concerned with love, friendship, or learning rather than engaged in flattery of potential patrons. This selectivity is related to the fact that I often find myself defending the strange phenomenon of Neo-Latin poetry, more or less explicitly, against the severe criticism launched at it for centuries. Accordingly, the feeling for the subject that I have built up during the years is obviously not that of an insider.

On the other hand, the timeless aesthetic and emotional aspects of reading poetry may justify an approach that emphasises the study of texts able to enter into dialogue with readers of our time. Add to this that many of these poems were actually composed with me as a part of the model readership, since they were composed not only for contemporary readers, but also for eternity. This only emphasises the strangeness of it all: these poets are my ancestors, only a few centuries removed, and yet they may seem aliens. Still I try to understand the poetry in case as part of its own emic system.

The examples given above are emic units of the Neo-Latin system, variations of a basic approach to literature uniting the first generations of Danish Neo-Latin poets with each other. They shared it with the international learned republic while at the same time displaying individual features dependent on the local vernacular culture. Like other Neo-Latin cultures it existed in a tension between ancient and contemporary, pagan and Christian, international and local, Latin and vernacular.

Since this group of poets clearly felt that they were a special subset of the learned republic with the mission of bringing Renaissance humanism to Denmark, a series of etic questions follow, such as: What was their role in the learned republic? in Denmark? in Danish literature? In what ways did they differ from the international culture, if any? How did they handle the dialogue between Latin and vernacular? Did they have special views concerning poetics or other kinds of aesthetics? Local traits are obvious when political issues are treated, but are they characteristic only in matters of content? etc.

The distinction between emic and etic approaches is no miraculous way of solving problems, but rather a useful tool in endeavouring to achieve a more precise eye for shades and refinements of meaning and form in this highly sophisticated literature. As suggested, it seems to me to lead towards an underlining of the international aspects of it, which again, perhaps paradoxically, causes a focus on the national features. At the same time, it warns the twenty-first century reader to be aware of the distance.[18]

University of Southern Denmark
University of Copenhagen

18   I am grateful to Marianne Pade for kind criticism.

CHAPTER 43

A Dowry Recovered after Three Decades: Diego Gracián's Spanish Editions of Ioannes Dantiscus' *Hymns* Revisited

Anna Skolimowska

Abstract

In 1538, the Spanish humanist Diego Gracián de Alderete married in Valladolid Juana Dantisca, the natural daughter of the secretary of Polish Kings, diplomat and Neo-Latin poet, Ioannes Dantiscus, at that time a bishop of Ermland. Among the numerous offspring of the couple there were outstanding individuals: Antonio, Jerónimo, Lucas, Tomás and Lorenzo Gracián Dantisco. Around twenty years after the death of his father-in law, Gracián published in Spain Dantiscus' late work *Hymni aliquot ecclesiastici*. This rare book is not an exact reprint of the Cracow edition, it contains a few other texts: Dantiscus' occasional poem *De nostrorum temporum calamitatibus* (1529), a *Genethliacon* for Dantiscus by Caspar Ursinus Velius (1516), and the highest praises of Dantiscus' extraordinary virtues by Gracián. Such glorification seems somewhat odd, considering their previous difficult relationships. A thorough examination of the booklet published by Gracián shows further surprises. These are some slight but significant changes and omissions, consciously and purposefully introduced by the editor in threshold poems and letters, and in *Genethliacon*.

Keywords

Ioannes Dantiscus – *Hymni aliquot ecclesiastici* (1571) – Neo-Latin hymnography – Diego Gracián de Alderete – Spanish humanism

In the year 1548 in Cracow, due to the efforts of Stanislaus Hosius (Hozjusz), a booklet consisting of religious hymns for different occasions, the Ash Wednesday, Lent Sundays, the Passion, the Resurrection, the Ascension and the Pentecost, as well as the hymns to the Blessed Virgin Mary, was published.

© KONINKLIJKE BRILL NV, LEIDEN, 2020 | DOI:10.1163/9789004427105_044

GRACIÁN'S SPANISH EDITIONS OF DANTISCUS' *HYMNS* REVISITED 551

It was an anonymous print, but it is well known that its author was Bishop of Ermland Ioannes Dantiscus, who died several months after the publication.[1]

Some twenty years later, in the prologue to the Spanish edition of Ioannes Dantiscus' *Hymni aliquot ecclesiastici*[2] Diego Gracián de Alderete speaks very highly of the author of the *Hymns* (who privately was his father-in-law). He describes him as (fol. A5r):

> vir sane pius iuxta ac doctus, qui multis legationum functus honoribus et poetica lauru coronatus, suae gentis nobilitatem ad eandem laudem accendit [...] tanto officio et pietate erga Deum praeditus fuit, ut olim iuvenis Hierosolymam reliquaque Palaestinae loca religionis ergo peragraverit [...] talis mihi olim adolescenti notus fuit pene cotidiana consuetudine.

To a researcher of Dantiscus' correspondence,[3] however, this glorification sounds a little suspicious. We know of seven letters from Gracián to Dantiscus and one letter from Dantiscus to Gracián from the years 1536–46.[4] A theme present in almost all of these letters is that of Gracián's failed attempt to obtain a dowry for his wife, Juana Dantisca. Although Gracián always addresses his father-in-law in the most respectful tone, their difficult relations are reflected, characteristically, for example, in the beginning of Gracián's last letter, sent in 1546 after a seven-year hiatus in their correspondence:

> Etsi statueram nihil umquam ad te scribere, tamen – non sum passus vacuum meis litteris abire, existimans has saltem ad manus tuas perventuras, quemadmodum mendacia et calumniae ad aures tuas pervenerunt.

---

1 [Ioannes Dantiscus], *Hymni aliquot ecclesiastici – de Quadragesimae Ieiunio, & sex eius diebus Dominicis, deque horis canonicis, Christi passionis tempore, & de resurrectione, Ascensione, Spiritus Sancti missione, matreque gloriosissima Maria virgine* (Cracow,1548) (hereafter cited as Dantiscus, *Hymni*, 1548).

2 Ioannes Dantiscus, *Hymni aliquot ecclesiastici* [...] (Salamantica, 1571, 1576) (hereafter cited as Dantiscus, *Hymni*, 1571, 1576).

3 *Corpus of Ioannes Dantiscus' Texts & Correspondence* (*dantiscus.al.uw.edu.pl*), ed. Anna Skolimowska et al.; first published online 2010-07-01 (accessed 17 April 2018, hereafter cited as CIDTC); with an extensive bibliography concerning Dantiscus, and especially complete information on the contemporary editions of his poems and correspondence.

4 Ibid., IDL 1538, IDL 1712, IDL 1656, IDL 1657, IDL 1658, IDL 1770, IDL 1862, IDL 1861, IDL 1982, IDL 2969.

The "calumniae" in question concerned Gracián's alleged self-seeking, a French disease from which he supposedly suffered, his hypothetical sexual relations with Juana's mother, and the exaggerated age difference between the spouses. These false accusations, according to Gracián, were due to the malice of the Lutherans. In his letters to his father-in-law, he also invariably stressed that he had never been motivated by self-interest and that his marriage was going very well in every way. And, he always emphasized his wife's exceptional virtues.[5]

Gracián's truthfulness about these matters finds confirmation in many subsequent sources. Among them is Juan Cristóbal Calvete de Estrella's *Ad Antonium Gratianum Dantiscum encomium*—a threshold poem included in an edition of Diego Gracián's Spanish translation of Plutarch's *Moralia* from 1571. In this poem Calvete praises the virtues of one of Diego Gracián and Juana Dantisca's sons—Antonio, anticipating his approaching career at the Spanish king's court. Among other things, he writes:[6]

> At donis aliis refers parentem
> **Ioannam** genere et pudore claram
> **Dantiscam**, et Niobe quidem superba
> Foecundam magis et beatiorem
> Tam multa roseo decore prole.

Juana Dantisca, described in the verses above, was born in Valladolid in 1527 as the daughter of Ioannes Dantiscus (1485–1548), a humanist and diplomat from the Kingdom of Poland, and his Spanish lover Isabella Delgada. The Polish envoy indeed was a member of the nobility, as the quoted poem underlines; in fact, he was both a German and a Spanish nobleman. Although he was born to a burgher family, he was ennobled by Emperor Maximilian in 1516 in recognition of his great talents and service.[7] Another emperor, Charles v who was also king of Spain, increased honours in 1528.[8] Dantiscus left Spain forever shortly afterwards, following Charles' court to Italy, Germany, and the Low Countries. It was the last time he saw his children—two-year-old Juana and her younger brother Juan who died in infancy.

---

5 Ibid., IDL 2969; cf. also Dantiscus, *Hymns*, 1571, 1576, fol. A5v.

6 *Morales de Plutarcho*, transl. by Diego Gracián (Salamanca, 1571), fol. A3v.

7 Anna Skolimowska, "Ioannes Dantiscus on the Way *ad arcem Virtutis*. Representations of the Coat of Arms as a Tool of Self-Creation of a Renaissance Humanist and Diplomat," in *Humanitas. Festskrift till Arne Jönsson*, ed. Astrid M. H. Nilsson et al. (Göteborg, 2017), 440–63, here 443–6.

8 Ibid., 451–2.

The diplomat's subsequent contacts with his family in Spain are documented by his correspondence with both Isabella Delgada and Juana, as well as the Welsers' German agents in the Iberian Peninsula—Ulrich Ehinger, Hieronymus Sailer, and Albrecht Kuon—and with his diplomat friends—Cornelis De Schepper and Johan Weze. They were all friends of the Polish rulers' envoy, and Kuon was even his daughter's godfather. At first Dantiscus supported his children and their mother financially, and later, after taking over the bishopric of Kulm in Prussia, he made plans to have his daughter join him. He promised her mother further regular support (20 ducats per annum), but she preferred a much larger one-off payment (200 ducats), which blocked Dantiscus' further efforts to bring Juana to Prussia. He accused Isabella of wanting to sell her daughter and perversely retorted that one cannot buy what is one's own, so if Isabella was proposing such a transaction, it was fair to assume that Dantiscus was not Juana's father.[9] The negotiations were made even more difficult by the enormous distance separating Prussia from Spain.

Juana was in her tenth year when Diego Gracián entered the scene. A secretary of Emperor Charles V and Empress Isabella (later serving their son, Philip II of Spain), he was a translator of Greek and Latin literature and an Erasmian whom Dantiscus knew during his time as a diplomat.[10] Gracián was engaged to Juana in June 1537[11] and married her a year later—she was just eleven-and-a-half at the time.[12] He informed his future father-in-law of his matrimonial plans, among other things arguing that the mother's poverty would soon induce her to push her daughter into prostitution.[13] Letters took so long to reach their destination that Gracián's request for Dantiscus' consent did not reach the addressee until several months after the betrothal ceremony. This caused further resentment. Despite the displeasure Dantiscus showed him, Gracián did not lose hope that the union would gain acceptance and Juana would receive a dowry, so he sent her father detailed accounts of what she was doing. After they were married he entrusted Juana into the care of his own mother, who saw to Juana's education and spiritual formation in the same way as she did to that of her own daughter, who was the same age.[14] This did little to improve family relations. Dantiscus took offence and, as mentioned above, did not pay a dowry.

---

9   CIDTC (see above, n. 3), IDL 3857.

10   Ibid., IDL 1538.

11   Ibid., IDL 1656, IDT 264.

12   Ibid., IDT 1.

13   Ibid., IDL 1862, IDL 2969.

14   Ibid., IDL 1861.

Meanwhile, Dantiscus' daughter matured into motherhood. Juana and Gracián's offspring in fact were more numerous than Niobe's children. Cristóbal Márquez, the biographer of Father Jerónimo Gracián Dantisco, OCD, probably Dantiscus' most famous grandson, who was the confessor to St Teresa of Ávila, lists twenty children of Diego and Juana, among whom as many as thirteen were known to him by name and lived to the age of maturity.[15] Besides Jeronimo, they include Antonio, Lucas, and Tomas, mentioned above, all three of them prominent men of letters and officials in the service of the Spanish royal court.

In the same year, 1571, that saw the publication in print of the aforementioned translation of Plutach's *Moralia*, also in Salamanca, the first known Spanish edition of Ioannes Dantiscus' religious hymns was published thanks to the efforts of Diego Gracián. The *Hymns* have already been the subject of many analyses and academic discussions.[16] However, some aspects of the Spanish editions have escaped the attention of researchers, who have focused mainly on the theological and literary dimensions of the hymns, merely stating the fact (noted in the print licences) that there existed another Spanish edition from before 1571 (of which no copy is known today)[17] and cursorily describing the differences in the content of the Spanish editions and of the Cracow edition. These differences do not concern the text of the *Hymns* themselves but

---

15   [*Cristóbal Márquez*], *Excelencias, vida y trabajos del padre fray Jerónimo Gracián de la madre de Dios, carmelita*, ed. Andrés del Mármol (Madrid, 1619), fol. 4v–11r (recent edition Madrid, 2012, with some textual errors, 84–96).

16   Ann Moss, "Johannes Dantiscus, Hymn-Writer," in *Munera philologica Georgio Starnawski ab amicis, collegis, discipulis oblata*, ed. Krzysztof A. Kuczyński et al. (Łódź, 1992), 155–62; Piotr Urbański, *Natura i łaska w poezji polskiego baroku : okres potrydencki : studia o tekstach* (Kielce, 1996), chapter "Hymny Jana Dantyszka – próba interpretacji", 18–41; Enrique Llamas Martínez, "Una rareza bibliográfica: Edición Española de poemas religiosos del obispo Humanista Polaco Juan Dantisco (1571, 1576)," *Monte Carmelo* 106 (1998), 275–91; Piotr Urbański, "Between Ignatianism and Stoicism (Dantiscus, Sarbievius)," *Wątki neostoickie w literaturze polskiego renesansu i baroku*, ed. Piotr Urbański (Szczecin, 1999), 173–89; idem, *Theologia fabulosa. Commentationes Sarbievianae* (Szczecin, 2000), 97–98; idem, "Joannes Dantiscus and Italian Neo-Latin Poetry," in *Acta Conventus Neo-Latini Cantabrigiensis*, ed. Jean-Louis Charlet (Tempe/AZ, 2003), 555–63; Ann Moss, "Johannes Dantiscus (1485–1548): Hymns in Context," in *Pietas Humanistica Neo-Latin Religious Poetry in Poland in European Context*, ed. Piotr Urbański (Frankfurt am Main, 2006), 71–82.

17   The relevant excerpt from the print licence reads: "un libro intitulado hymnos ecclesiasticos y Sylva de temporum calamitatibus, que otra vez con licencia nuestra avia sido impresso." Further on, the licence letter grants permission to sell the book only after comparing it with the previous edition and ascertaining it is exactly the same, cf. Dantiscus, *Hymni*, 1571, 1576 (see above, n. 2), fols. A2v–A3r.

the texts accompanying them.[18] Contrary to the Spanish editions, the Cracow edition does not include certificates of conformity with Roman Catholic doctrine, a royal licence to print, or, obviously, Diego Gracián's prologue addressed to the reader. At the Spanish editor's initiative, the opening texts also include a *Genethliacon* written for Dantiscus on his thirty-first birthday (1516) by Caspar Ursinus Velius,[19] and the publication ends with an occasional poem penned by Dantiscus, *De nostrorum temporum calamitatibus*, written for the reconciliation between Emperor Charles V and Pope Clement VII in 1529 and the imperial coronation in Bologna.[20] None of these very long works is mentioned on the volume's title page, even though this is not actually a reprint of the Cracow edition of *Hymni aliquot ecclesiastici*, but a compilation of three different prints.

The first major difference is that information on the authorship of the *Hymns* is provided.

What really takes the reader by surprise when comparing Spanish and Cracow editions of the *Hymns* is that directly after the prologue Gracián placed an epigram *AD LECTOREM* that Dantiscus wrote as an introduction to the poem *De nostrorum temporum calamitatibus silva* (published after the text of the *Hymns*). Additionally, this epigram shows some significant differences from the author's original. Gracián definitely took advantage of the fact that it was not until the eighth and sixteenth verses of the epigram that Dantiscus revealed himself to be the "Sarmata vates" found in the opening lines of the poems and thus the poem's author, by using the grammatical first person. In the Spanish editions the first person has been consistently replaced with the

---

18   The author has conducted a thorough comparative analysis of the textual variants in the hymns from all three known editions. This analysis leads to the conclusion that the 1576 edition does not copy the 1571 edition, but proves beyond any doubt the existence of a lost edition that was the basis for both the Spanish editions known to us today. The evidence includes the presence of a sizable number of both identical and completely different variants of the text (all of them copyist or typographical errors) in these two editions as compared to the Cracow edition. These variants are shown in the online edition of the corpus of Dantiscus' texts (CIDTC, see above, n. 3).

19   "C. Vrsini Velii Genethliacon Ioannis Dantisci poetae clarissimi," in *Casparis Vrsini Velii e Germanis Slesii poematum libri quinque* (Basel, 1522), fols. q–q3 (hereafter cited as Ursinus); Dantiscus, *Hymni*, 1571, 1576 (see above, n. 2), fols. A7v–A8v.

20   First edition: *Ioannis Dantisci Oratoris Serenissimi Regis, et Reginae Poloniae etc. Ad Clementem VII Pontificem Maximum et Carolum V Imperatorem Augustum De nostrorum temporum calamitatibus Sylua Bononiae aedita IX Decembris MDXXIX*, (Bologna, 1530) (hereafter cited as Dantiscus, *Sylva*); still in the same year 1530, numerous reprints—in Cracow, Ghent, Cologne, Antwerp.

third person, which makes the reader inclined to ascribe the poem's author-ship not to the book's author but to its editor.

So far no researcher studying this subject matter has taken note of these changes. They are as follows:

	author's version (1530, 1531)[21]	editor's version (1571, 1576)[22]
verse 8	Hesperiam **peragro me** didi-cisse puta!	Hesperiam **peragrat hunc** didi-cisse puta!
verse 16	**Cum** sensum teneas **nil ego** verba **moror.**	**Qui** sensum teneas **tunc quoque** verba **iuvent.**

This epigram is followed by two more, *AD EUNDEM* and *IDEM*, taken from the Cracow edition of the *Hymns*. Again, the reader gets the impression that the epigrams were written by the editor, whereas in the Cracow edition they are published under the name of Pedro Ruiz de Moros (Petrus Roisius Maureus). The texts of these epigrams are identical in the Polish edition and the Spanish editions, with the exception of the final distich of the second work. In the Cracow edition we read

> Quam doctus **sene Maeonio** potes esse **relecto**
> Tam bonus hoc lecto, tam pius esse potes

which means that reading the *Hymns* can make the reader as good and pious as reading all of Homer ("senex Maeonius") can make him learned. Meanwhile, both the Spanish editions replace the word "relecto" with "relicto", thus sug-gesting that the reader will become wise if he abandons Homer. The inspira-tion for this change was most likely provided by the beginning of the epigram, in which Dantiscus' pious work was juxtaposed with the "lies of the previous age" ("aevi ficta prioris") and the "disgusting monsters of olden days" ("foeda vetustatis monstra"). It appears that Homer's poetry has been classified as one of those ancient falsehoods (according to the topos *figmenta poetarum* vs. *vera poesis*). Of course this could be an accidental typographical error, but it is not the only change of this kind.

After the three epigrams addressed to readers, Gracián places a work he already mentioned in the prologue as proof of the piety of the writer of the *Hymns* and *Sylva*, namely the *Genethliacon* for Dantiscus written by Caspar

---

21 Dantiscus, *Sylva* (see above, n. 20), fol. A1v.

22 Dantiscus, *Hymni*, 1571, 1576 (see above, n. 2), fol. A6v.

Ursinus Velius.[23] The *Genethliacon* is in the form of a prophecy uttered by Apollo at Dantiscus' birth. It includes praise of the physical and mental qualities of the boy coming into the world, describes his future successes as a poet and diplomat as well as the journeys he is to make in the future, among them a pilgrimage to the Holy Land. Compared to Ursinus' original publication, Gracián made quite extensive changes to the *Genethliacon*. Here, I pass over unimportant typos and focus only on significant differences.

In the title of the *Genethliacon* Ursinus referred to Dantiscus as "poeta clarissimus", which Gracián changed to "vir clarissimus", perhaps in a desire to highlight the virtue of the person described in the poem.

In the distich which reads "Prima **tuos ignes** recitabunt ludicra: toto / Prospera versiculis vivet in orbe tuis",[24] Gracián has replaced "tuos ignes" with "notos lusus". Originally, the distich was definitely a reference to the amorous epigrams with which Dantiscus supposedly won world fame for his lover named Prospera (these epigrams are lost, but the existence of a lover of that name is confirmed in Dantiscus' correspondence).[25] With this change, Gracián blotted out the erotic nature of his father-in-law's youthful output. His job was made easier by the fact that the name "Prospera" comes at the beginning of the verse, so it could be treated as a common adjective despite being capitalized. This is clearly an example of moral censorship. It is also worth noting that this interference causes an error in the poem's prosody (two long syllables: "nōtos" in place of a short and a long one: "tuos").

Gracián's next change involves supplementing the description of Dantiscus' sojourn in the Holy Land, which he obviously thought to be lacking since it took up no more than three distichs:[26]

> Et Syriae populos, et inhospita vasta videbis,
>> Qua non aequoreo tutius extat iter.
> Quin et adorabis sacrum quo condita passi
>> Lurida sarcophago membra fuere dei.
> Quaeque Palaestinas loca sunt veneranda per oras
>> Bethlemiumque larem Calvariaeque solum.

---

23 Ibid., fols. A7v–A8v.
24 Ursinus (see above, n. 19), lines 21–2.
25 CIDTC (see above, n. 3), IDL 362: "Prosperam tuam, dum castra sequitur, Leopoli esse mortuam."
26 Ursinus (see above, n. 19), lines 48–52.

558 SKOLIMOWSKA

To this aim, he added three distichs taken from a completely different work, i.e. *Ad amicos Hierosolymam proficiscentes* by Giovanni Pontano:[27]

> Felicemque locum, iacuit quo rector olympi,
> Et quam divino sanguine tinxit humum,
> Hic ubi, crudeli traiectus brachia ferro est,
> Fixit et immeritos cuspis adacta pedes,
> Hausit et immeritum latus heu ferratile telum,
> Diluit et fusus crimina nostra cruor.

Of course, the editor does not indicate in any way that such an addition has been made.

The last major change from the original text involves the removal of the final six distichs from the 88 verses in this piece: in Gracián's editions the poem ends with Phoebus leaving the door of the woman in labour and the Parcae starting to spin the thread of Dantiscus' life. It is certainly a neat ending, but the original goes on to describe the birth, a blessing of the gods (including Juno as the patron of childbirth) for the new-born baby and the good wishes and cheering in his honour from friends, including the poem's author, during the birthday feast. One can only guess that, in Gracián's view, this ending may have put too much emphasis on the secular character of the birthday celebration for the author of the *Hymns*, or maybe it contained too many pagan elements. Perhaps the simplest explanation is that—since Dantiscus had been dead for a long time—Gracián removed the last scenes as concerning a real life, in order to keep the poet on a pedestal built in the Apollo's prophecies.

Evidence that Diego Gracián personally made the editing changes in Ursinus' poem includes not only his name mentioned in the licence letter from King Philip II and his authorship of the prologue, but also an existing copy of the first edition of the *Genethliacon* with notes made in Gracián's own hand reflecting the actual changes: "tuos" to "notos" and the whole added excerpt from Pontano's poem noted in the appropriate place on the margin.[28]

---

27   Giovanni Pontano, *Amorum libri duo; De amore coniugali libri tres; Tumulorum libri duo; De divinis laudibus liber unus; Hendecasyllaborum seu Baiarum libri duo; Iambici versus de obitu Lucii filii; Lyrici versus ad res varias pertinentes; In calce libri duo quibus titulus est Eridanus* (Florence, 1514), fol. 102r–v.

28   Ursinus (see above, n. 19), copy in the Complutense University Library, catalogue number a-z4, A-I4, available online: https://books.google.pl/books?id=kuE59vwQezIC&printsec=frontcover&hl=pl&source=gbs_ge_summary_r&cad=0#v=onepage&q&f=false (accessed on 11 May 2018); in this copy marginalia are present next to just this one poem dedicated to Dantiscus (disregarding vertical lines or crosses here and there next to other works

The last element in the editions of the *Hymns* discussed here that Dantiscus' son-in-law interfered with is the letter of dedication from Stanislaus Hosius (canon of Ermland at the time, later bishop and cardinal, active designer and executor of the Roman Church's post-Tridentine reform) to the bishop of Cracow and grand chancellor of the Polish Crown, Samuel Maciejowski (Cracow, 10 July 1548).[29]

In the letter, which serves as a foreword to the Cracow edition of the *Hymns*, Hosius states, among other things, that the author of the *Hymns* changed with the passing of his flighty youth and his abandoning of the immoral court:[30]

> Est autem haec admirabilis et stupenda quaedam mutatio dexterae excelsi, quod qui libelli huius auctor est, is eadem aliquando fuit infirmitate praeditus, qua sumus nos. Nam et iuvenis ab iis, quae aetas illa fert, non abhorruit, et bonam aetatis suae partem in aula consumpsit, cuiusvis rei potius, quam virtutis, magistra, ita ut longe tum ab illo distaret, quem eum nunc esse videmus.

This final fragment, in which Hosius specifies that the court "teaches people practically everything but virtue" and then underlines the change that has taken place in Dantiscus, has been left out of the Spanish editions, as has also the subsequent reference to the transformation of Saul into Paul as described in the Acts of the Apostles: "Dicas: ex Saulo Paulum, ex persecutore factum apostolum." This comparison, taken out of context, later provoked researchers into reaching the premature conclusion that when Dantiscus was already a

---

from the volume). On a blank page at the end of the print in question, the same hand that wrote the marginal notes in the *Genethliacon*, copied a poem by Pittorio, *De Christo Crucifixo*. Under Pittorio's poem is a note made in a different hand (no doubt one of Gracián and Juana Dantisca's numerous children): "de mano de mi Padre el Secr(etari)o Di(eg)o Gracian" ("in the hand of my father, secretary Diego Gracián"). (Diego Gracián's original letters to Dantiscus are also written in the same hand.) Besides the aforementioned change of "tuos" to "notos" and the excerpt from Pontano's poem, Gracián's handwritten notes explain some of the more obscure references to ancient figures in the poem and refer to Dantiscus' biography. I provided Gracián's marginalia in the edition of *Genethliacon* annexed to my article "Records of Friendship on the Threshold of a Diplomatic Career: Nardino Celinese's Propempticon & Caspar Ursinus Velius' Genethliacon, Poems Dedicated to Ioannes Dantiscus," in *De amicitia. Transdisciplinary Studies in Friendship*, ed. Katarzyna Marciniak and Elżbieta Olechowska (Warsaw, 2016), 327–47.

29 Dantiscus, *Hymni*, 1571, 1576 (see above, n. 2), fols. A9r–A10v; Dantiscus, *Hymni*, 1548 (see above, n. 1), fols. A iijr–v + two not numbered pages; CIDTC (see above, n. 3), IDT 589.

30 Dantiscus, *Hymni* 1548 (see above, n. 1), fols. Aiijr–v. Gracián's omissions here and further on in the paper are marked by wider letter-spacing.

bishop, he was suddenly converted thanks to Hosius, having previously persecuted the Roman Church and sympathized with Luther. However, Hosius' words give no grounds for this view, as he continues as follows (in a fragment censored by Gracián): "Nam ut nos vita nunc nostra persequimur Ecclesiam Dei, sic et ille persecutus est olim." There cannot be the slightest doubt that Hosius would not have accused himself, and certainly not Maciejowski, of "persecuting the Church of God", i.e. supporting the Reformation. Therefore he does not accuse Dantiscus of this, either. Dantiscus has abandoned worldly matters for matters of the spirit. It is this move away from things secular in general, and not supporting one religion or another, that Hosius means when he writes about Dantiscus:[31]

> Tandem vero, misericordia Dei non postremum honoris gradum in ea consecutus, exuit veterem hominem, novum induit, et quanto saeculi quondam, tanto nunc Christi amore exarsit, ut non alia magis in re affecta in hac et aetate, et valetudine sua, quam in iugi Christi beneficiorum meditatione versetur.

In his editions, Gracián has replaced the words "he laid aside the old self and put on the new" ("exuit [...] induit"), a direct reference to St Paul's Letter to the Colossians, with the short "est". A little further along, the Spanish editor has removed another quotation from St Paul found in Hosius' text, this time a fragment of the Letter to the Romans warning against hastily judging other people's sins:[32]

> Quis ergo est, qui iudicare deinceps audeat servum alienum, cum quem certum etiam sit multis nunc esse peccatis obnoxium, qualis ad vesperam sit futurus, certum esse queat nemini.

The texts of St Paul had an important place in the debates of Protestant theologians. Therefore things that a younger Hosius, still a long way from his later ardent Counter-Reformation self, would have seen as innocent references to the thoughts of St Augustine on abandoning vainglory in favour of humility,[33]

---

31 Dantiscus, *Hymni*, 1548 (see above, n. 1), fol. A iijv.

32 Ibid., fol. A iijv and the next, unnumbered page.

33 Augustine, *Enarrationes in Psalmos* 72,10–1; idem, *De spiritu et littera liber unus* 7,12; idem, *Confessiones* 8,4,9, cf. Anna Skolimowska, *"Ex Saulo Paulus, ex persecutore apostolus?* duchowa przemiana biskupa Dantyszka w świetle nowych źródeł," to be published within the proceedings of the conference "Reformacja w Prusach" (Olsztyn, 2017).

to Gracián twenty years later inevitably must have evoked associations with Lutheranism, which he assumedly wanted to avoid.

Thus it appears that most of the changes and cuts Gracián made to the introductory texts in his edition of the *Hymns* were of the moralizing and censorship variety. This interference may have been the effect of the editor's fear of the Spanish Inquisition or, just as likely, his fear of corrupting pious readers. Neither of these reasons rules out another, overriding motive, in my view: a desire to erect a monument to his wife's father as well as a testimony to his impeccable morals, and thus also to Juana herself and their shared offspring. The publication certainly sold well, as confirmed by further editions, supplementing the editor's household budget. At the same time, it could serve as a kind of calling card for his sons and daughters. When the first Spanish edition was released, the eldest children were on the brink of adulthood. This would make Dantiscus' *Hymni aliquot ecclesiastici* published through the efforts of Diego Gracián a dual—financial and moral—dowry for Juana Dantisca that her father "paid" from beyond the grave many years after his death.

University of Warsaw, Faculty of "Artes Liberales"

CHAPTER 44

Neo-Latin and Russian in Mikhail V. Lomonosov's *Panegyric for Elizaveta Petrovna* (1749)

Anna Smirnova

Abstract

Mikhail Lomonosov wrote his scientific and literary works both in Russian and in Latin, sometimes he translated his own works from one to another and vice versa. Furthermore, the style and syntax of Lomonosov's Russian works were considerably influenced by Latin style and syntax. His rhetorical treatises (1744–48), which had great success in Russia, were full of references to ancient authors and his own translations from Latin and Greek. In 1749, Lomonosov was told to write a panegyric for the Russian empress. Composed first in Russian and then translated into Latin, his *Panegyric for Elizaveta Petrovna* provides a particularly interesting case of Neo-Latin / vernacular bilingualism in eighteenth century Russian rhetorical prose. A close study of this bilingual text reveals a large number of syntactical and lexical correspondences in Latin and Russian. Thus, Lomonosov quoted the Church-Slavonic Bible, but he did not use the Vulgate in the respective places of the Latin text, relying on the Russian wording; sometimes he played on the similarly sounding words in Russian and Latin.

Keywords

Mikhail Lomonosov – *Panegyric for Elizaveta Petrovna* (1749) – Neo-Latin panegyrics – self-translation – Russian Neo-Latin texts

In the eighteenth century the St. Petersburg Academy of Sciences, founded by Peter the Great in 1724, was close to the tsar's court in Russia. According to its *Reglament*, it was obliged to hold assemblies, at which speeches, written by academicians, had to be delivered. In 1749 Kirill Grigorevich Razumovskiy, the President of the Academy of Sciences, ordered the organization of an assembly on the occasion of the Empress' name day. Among the academicians who were told to write speeches was a professor of chemistry Mikhail Vasilevich Lomonosov (1711–65), who was required to write a panegyric for the Empress

© KONINKLIJKE BRILL NV, LEIDEN, 2020 | DOI:10.1163/9789004427105_045

LOMONOSOV'S *PANEGYRIC FOR ELIZAVETA PETROVNA*

Elizaveta. Lomonosov was not only a scientist, he also wrote poems and by that time he had written several panegyric odes devoted to sovereigns (it is the reason why among the eighteenth-century Russian poets he received the nickname 'Russian Pindar'). Furthermore, he was known as the author of the first handbook of rhetoric composed in Russian (1748).[1]

1   Panegyric as an Example of Lomonosov's Eloquence

The *Panegyric for Elizaveta Petrovna* (*Slovo pokhval'noe Yeya Velichestvu gosudaryne imperatritse Elisavete Petrovne, samoderzhitse vserossiyskoy*) was composed by Lomonosov first in Russian (August 1749) and he then translated it into Latin (November 1749), for the benefit of foreign readers.[2] The panegyric in honor of the Empress praises her and her ancestors' statecraft, her charity and her increasing engagement with the Academy of Sciences. Two more characters in the speech—the Church and Russia—are given their own monologues addressed to God and to Elizaveta Petrovna respectively. Lomonosov presented his panegyric in the assembly that took place on November 26. It was a triumph: his speech is still considered a masterpiece of Russian and Neo-Latin oratory of the eighteenth century. The Russian version was reprinted three times during Lomonosov's lifetime, in 1751, 1755, and 1758. Later it was the first work to be included in the collection *Opera academica* (1761), which consisted of nine works chosen by Lomonosov and was circulated abroad, to foreign scientific institutions.

---

1   When Mikhail V. Lomonosov was a student he studied rhetoric (1733–34) in Latin at the Slavo-Greco-Latin Academy in Moscow. One of his teachers was Porfiriy Krayskiy, whose lectures were written down by Lomonosov (the manuscript is held in the Russian State Library: Porfiriy Krayskiy, *Artis rhetoricae praecepta*, Moscow, MS lat. Ф. 183.1. No. 279). In 1737–39 Lomonosov was taught rhetoric (in German and Latin) by a key figure of German Enlightenment Christian Wolff (see Mikhail V. Lomonosov, *Polnoe sobranie sochinenij*, vol. 10 [Moscow, 1957], 570–1) in Marburg. A reminiscence of it is still preserved in his abstract from Johann Ch. Gottsched's *Ausführliche Redekunst* (Leipzig, 1736), which he read in 1738. In general, rhetoric "played a central role in university teaching" (*A History of the University in Europe*, ed. Walter Rüegg, vol. 2 [Cambridge, 2008], 28).

2   In the complete edition of Mikhail V. Lomonosov's works, published in the middle of the twentieth century, the Latin text of the panegyric follows the Russian one: Mikhail V. Lomonosov, *Polnoe sobranie sochinenij*, vol. 8 (Moscow, 1959), 235–56; 257–72 (hereafter cited as Lomonosov 8).

The panegyric is obviously a piece of oratory, but its genre was not necessarily described in the works on rhetoric.[3] The section on the panegyric thus is lacking in Lomonosov's own rhetorical treatise *Kratkoe rukovodstvo k krasnorechiyu* (*Short Guide to Eloquence*, 1748), which was very popular in Russia. But in his earlier textbook of rhetoric, written in 1744 (*Kratkoe rukovodstvo k ritorike*, *Short Guide to Rhetoric*), the theory of the panegyric was briefly outlined. As Mikhail Ivanovich Sukhomlinov has noted, Lomonosov borrowed this section from the famous rhetorical handbook by François Pomey,[4] who devoted about a third of the whole book to panegyrics.[5] Later Lomonosov decided to divide his rhetoric course into two parts: *Short Guide to Eloquence* and *Oratory*. From his reports it is known that in 1752–53 he was working on the second book which must have included instructions for composing speeches in prose,[6] but all these materials are considered lost.[7]

2 The Latin and the Translation

In the epoch of the rise and cultivation of national languages, Latin played both the guiding and intermediary roles: it provided the model and terminology for the grammatical descriptions of vernacular languages;[8] Latin dictionaries served as basis for multilingual lexicography: terms and phraseology, used by classical authors, had to be translated in vernaculars, which learned from them and later rivaled their Latin teachers.[9]

Lomonosov learned Latin first at the Slavo-Greco-Latin Academy (1731–35)[10] in Moscow and then while studying in Marburg (1737–39), where he read and

---

3   For example, it is only briefly mentioned in the weighty *Histoire de la rhétorique dans l'Europe moderne (1450–1950)*, ed. Marc Fumaroli (Paris, 1999).

4   François Pomey, *Candidatus Rhetoricae, seu Aphthonii Progymnasmata, in optimam formam usumque redacta* (Monachii, 1664). Working on his *Short Guide to Eloquence* Lomonosov relied on several rhetoric manuals, including those by Nicolas Caussin, François Pomey, Johann Christoph Gottsched and Longin (in Nicolas Boileau's translation).

5   *Sochineniya M. V. Lomonosova s ob"yasnitel'nymi primechaniyami akademika M. I. Sukhomlinova*, vol. 3 (Saint-Petersburg, 1895), Suppl. 101–3.

6   Mikhail V. Lomonosov, *Polnoe sobranie sochinenij*, vol. 7 (Moscow, 1952), 809–10 (hereafter cited as Lomonosov 7).

7   Anton Budilovich, *M. V. Lomonosov kak naturalist i filolog* (Saint-Petersburg, 1869), 111.

8   For instance, Bartol Kašić, *Institutionum linguae illyricae libri duo* (Roma, 1604).

9   Demmy Verbeke, "Neo-Latin's Interplay with Other Languages", in *The Oxford Handbook of Neo-Latin*, ed. Sarah Knight and Stefan Tilg (Oxford, 2015), 27–40.

10   While studying in Moscow Lomonosov had to speak Latin. In the lessons the pupils taught the Latin grammar by Manuel Alvar's *De institutione grammatica libri III*, see Grigoriy

LOMONOSOV'S *PANEGYRIC FOR ELIZAVETA PETROVNA*

spoke the language. Having returned in Russia he became a member of St. Petersburg Academy of Sciences and wrote natural-science *dissertationes* both in Russian and in Latin.[11]

Though he never considered himself as a translator he was the only Russian who skillfully translated European literature (namely various excerpts, serving as examples in his *Short Guide to Eloquence*) in the 1730s and 1740s.[12]

The Latin quotations cited in Lomonosov's *Rhetoric* turn out to be, for the most part, interlinear translations, with only a little liberty allowed both in figures of speech and word order, as can be demonstrated by the example of his unique quotation from Pliny's *Panegyricus Traiani* (Plin., *Paneg.* 1,3–4):[13]

Quod enim praestabilius est, aut pulchrius munus deorum, quam castus, et sanctus, et diis simillimus, Princeps? Ac, si adhuc dubium fuisset, forte casuque rectores terris, an aliquo numine, darentur; Principem tamen nostrum liqueret diuinitus constitutum.

Кое Божие дарование краснейшее и превосходнейшее быть может, как непорочный и святый и богам подобный государь? Ежели бы еще сомнительно было, по случаю ли и ненарочно или от Бога земные обладатели даются, однако о нашем государе явно бы показалось, что он от Бога поставлен.[14]

What divine gift is more beautiful and excellent than a sovereign who is chaste, and saintly, and similar to gods? If there had been any doubt whether earthly rulers are appointed casually and not on purpose or by god, it would nevertheless have been beyond doubt that he was put there by god.

The first part of this fragment shows Lomonosov's mastery: he skillfully reproduces the thought, preserving almost every word of the original text. In the

---

      Alexandrovich Voskresenskiy, "Lomonosov i Moskovskaya Slavyano-greco-latinskaya academia," *Pribavleniya k Tvoreniyam sv. Ottsov* Chast' 47. Kn. 1 (1891), 3–94, there 16–7.

11   By 1749 he had written in two languages *De motu aeris in fodinis observato* (1747), *Dissertatio de actione menstruorum chymicorum in genere* (1749) and *Tentamen theoriae de vi aëris elastica* (1749).

12   Lomonosov's translations from his rhetoric treatise were published separately: *Pokoinago statskago sovetnika i professora Mikhayly Vasilyevicha Lomonosova sobranie raznykh sochineniy v stikhakh i v proze* (Moscow, 1778), vol. 2, 335–453.

13   C. Plinii Caecilii Secvndi *Panegyricvs Caesari Imp. Nervae Traiano Avg. dictvs*, ed. Christianus Gottlib. Schwarzius (Norimbergae, 1746), 2.

14   Lomonosov 7 (see above, n. 6), 133.

second sentence the sense is also correct, but the version of the "aliquo numine" is not exact, as Lomonosov usually omits specific details pertaining to the ancient pagan world and tries to adapt the text for Russian readers.[15]

The translation of the *Panegyric for Elizaveta Petrovna* into Latin was Lomonosov's first experience of this kind; all other works written by him in Latin were scientific, e.g. *Specimen physicum de transmutatione corporis solidi in fluidum a motu fluidi praeexistentis dependente* (1738). In this paper I shall discuss the principles of translating from the vernacular into Latin determined by the genre of the work, the sources he relied upon while composing the original text and the cultural 'code-switching'.[16]

3 Imitations in Both Versions of the *Panegyric*

It should be noted first that Lomonosov's *Panegyric* includes a number of allusions to ancient Latin literature. Some of them had been found out in the Russian version of the panegyric by M. T. Kachenovskiy, who displayed how Lomonosov presumably imitated, "appropriated thoughts [sc. of classical authors] through various changes and translated, dressing them in the gorgeous clothes of Russian words."[17] Later Sukhomlinov gathered many parallels for certain parts of Lomonosov's *Panegyric* from Cicero, Seneca, Pliny the Younger and the Bible, to which he referred in his edition of Lomonosov's works.[18]

Comparing the Russian text with the ancient prototypes M. T. Kachenovskiy quoted three places from Lomonosov's *Panegyric*, for which, according to him, the Traian's panegyrist must be regarded as a source. Here I shall compare only one of these fragments (both in Russian and in Latin) with its presumed prototype. First, Pliny's fragment, which must have been Lomonosov's model, according to Kachenovskiy (Pliny, *Paneg.* 71,4):[19]

---

15 Making the text understandable for fellow countrymen was quite widespread in the early modern vernacular translations: thus, following Ch. Wolff and J. Ch. Gottsched Lomonosov often used familiar vocabulary instead of antiquarian terms, borrowed from Latin, e.g. for "nauarchus" the Russian "мореплаватель" ("seafarer"), not "наварх" ("navarch"), or for "cohors" the Russian "баталион" ("battalion"), not "когорта" ("cohort").

16 See more about the code-switching in Verbeke, "Neo-Latin's Interplay" (see above, n. 9) and *Multilingual Practices in Language History: English and Beyond*, ed. Päivi Pahta, Janne Skaffari and Laura Wright (Boston – Berlin, 2017).

17 Mikhail Trophimovich Kachenovskiy, "Razsuzhdenie o Pokhval'nykh slovakh Lomonosova", *Trudy obshchestva lyubitelej rossijskoj slovesnosti pri imperatorskom moskovskom universitete* 3 (1812), 70–103, there 89.

18 Sukhomlinov (see above, n. 5), Suppl. 288–99.

19 Plinii *Panegyricus* (see above, n. 13), 352.

Cui nihil ad augendum fastigium superest, hic uno modo crescere potest, si se ipse submittat, securus magnitudinis suae

For when a man can improve no more on his supreme position, the only way he can rise still higher is by stepping down, confident in his greatness.[20]

Lomonosov's Russian fragment: когда, возвышенная до толикой высоты власти и величества, которой уже человеческое могущество превзотти не может, крайним к подданным Своим снисходительством превыше смертных жребия восходит.[21]

When, risen to such summit of authority and eminence, which human power cannot surpass, [Elizaveta Petrovna] outdoes all mortals by Her extreme indulgence to Her people.

Lomonosov's Latin version, which bears resemblance to Pliny's fragment by only one word ("fastigium"): cum in summo rerum humanarum fastigio constituta, inusitata erga subditos suos comitate supra mortalium sortem evecta videatur.[22]

When, risen to the summit of human affairs, by unusual behavior towards her people, she seems to have outdone all mortals [the clause, characterizing the absolute state of Elizabeth's power, is omitted from the Latin version].

Contrary to Kachenovskiy's assumption, it seems that Lomonosov's text has little in common with the supposed classical source. In the Latin version Lomonosov used some formulas and clichés which did not exist neither in the Russian original nor in Pliny's *Panegyric*. It is more likely that Lomonosov relied on Neo-Latin usage instead of the wording: "in (summo/altissimo) rerum humanarum fastigio" is quite common in early modern texts.[23]

---

20   *Pliny, Letters, books VIII–X. Panegyricus*, ed. Betty Radice (London – Cambridge, MA, 1969), 493.

21   Lomonosov 8 (see above, n. 2), 249.

22   Ibid., 267.

23   For example: *Philippi Melan[ch]thonis Opera quae supersunt omnia*, ed. Carolus Gottlieb Bretschneider, vol. 11 (Halis Saxonum, 1843), 305: "litterati in summo fastigio rerum humanarum collocati sunt;" *Dominici Bavdi Orationes quae exstant*, ed. Matthias Byvortius (Lugduni Batavorum, 1619), 199: "a principibus in altissimo rerum humanarum fastigio

Kachenovskiy and Sukhomlinov attempted to discover allusions and imitations of classical Latin prose in the Russian text of Lomonosov's *Panegyric for Elizaveta Petrovna*. We can add an example to their collection: "Прилагайте крайнее старание к естественных вещей познанию"/ "impendite indefessum laborem ad cognoscenda rerum naturalium arcana."[24]

In the phrase "старание к естественных вещей познанию" we should note the word order, which is quite unnatural in Russian, but quite natural in Latin: when dependent words come before the main one; it occurs only once in the text of *Panegyric*. It seems to be caused by borrowing from a Latin source (the sentence appears quite often both in ancient and Neo-Latin works): "Arcana rerum naturalium ne scruteris;"[25] "rerum naturalium arcana [...] ex muneris sibi impositi ratione discipulis suis traderet"[26] (due to duty he could have taught his pupils the secrets of nature); "omnia rerum omnium arcana nobis reteguntur."[27] Numerous examples of allusions to classical texts are provided by the Latin version of *Panegyric* as well. Thus, in some places Lomonosov seems to imitate *Nazarii Panegyricus Constantino Augusto dictus* from the XII Panegyrici latini, e.g.: "Non enim *se capit* exundantis *laetitiae magnitudo*, sed dedignata pectorum latebras ita *multa et candida* foris prominet ut intellegatur non ingentior esse quam verior."[28]

In Lomonosov's *Panegyric for Elizaveta Petrovna* we find the same "laetitiae magnitudo [...] multa et candida", but it is more obvious ("ex ore atque oculis [...] prorumpit"): "Non *se capit* pectoris angustiis tantae *laetitiae magnitudo*, sed ex ore atque oculis *multa et Candida* prorumpit."[29]

The search for the missing references to different Latin sources which were supposedly read or seen by Lomonosov seems still to be fruitful and promising. It is possible to assume that Lomonosov borrowed from a dictionary, anthology, or a handbook which has not yet been identified. A. Kostin recently guessed that the poetical dictionary *Gradus ad Parnassum* could have been such a source.[30] But the examination of epithets used by Lomonosov in the

---

constitutis;" *Panegyricus serenissimo Britanniae Franciae Scotiae et Hiberniae regi Vilhelmo Aravsiaco [...] dictus a Iacobo Perizonio* (Lipsiae, 1694), 21: "in summo licet rerum humanarum fastigio & sede augustissima iam positus."

24   Ibid., 255 and 271.

25   *Disticha Moralia, nomine Catonis inscripta*, ed. Maturinus Corderius (Lugduni, 1588), 46.

26   *Petri Cvnaei Ic. Orationes argumenti varii Eiusdemque alia Latina opuscula* (Lipsiae, 1693), 249–50.

27   Ibid., 287.

28   *XII Panegyrici latini*, ed. Irina Jurjevna Shabaga (Mosqvae, 2016), 286.

29   Lomonosov 8 (see above, n. 2), 259.

30   Andrei Kostin, "Slovo pochval'noye i Panegyricus Elizabetae," *Toronto Slavic Quarterly* 47 (2014), 9–23, there 21–2.

Panegyric shows that his choice of word combinations was often at variance with those listed in *Gradus* (e.g. "minax imperium"; "mitissima auctoritas"; "munificentissima manus"; "interfusum mare"; "luctuosum vestigium" etc.). Moreover, some Latin words from his panegyric are not mentioned at all there. This is true both for the vocabulary, classical in its form and meaning (e.g. indignabundus, ineffabilis, adspectabilis, depraedico, exaggeratio etc.), as well as for the Latin words used in a sense which is not attested in classical works (e.g. "generosa popularitas"—noble indulgence; *mansuetudo*—philanthropy; "devotissimus animus"—slave sincerity etc.). We must take into account that Lomonosov's panegyric contained some marks of political and scientific life of the eighteenth century. Thus, it is impossible to believe that Lomonosov, composing such a text could confine himself to quoting from a single school text.

4 Self-Translation

In order to clarify how Lomonosov recoded the Russian text of the *Panegyric* (partly based on the samples of Latin eloquence) in its Latin version, I compared both versions of the *Panegyric*, drawing attention to its syntax, style and vocabulary. Some parts of these texts, though written in different languages, correspond almost word for word. It was partly due to the fact that the Russian text of the *Panegyric to Elizaveta Petrovna* was influenced by Latin syntax and phraseology, as was noted already by Ya. M. Borovskiy.[31] For instance, the uncommon sequences for Russian nouns, in which a dependent noun in genitive is inserted between an adjective and a noun, occur in the Russian text almost as often as in its Latin translation (e.g. "разные торжеств образы"/ "perlustrata solemnium varietate"; "многословнаго мыслей распространения"/ "verbosa cogitationum exaggeratione").

Sometimes in the Russian text an auxiliary (or modal) verb is placed at the end of a long period containing a series of dependent clauses or infinitive constructions, for example:[32]

> ибо где обильнейшую материю *сыскать* красноречие, где обширнее *разпространиться* разум, где быстрее *устремиться* искренняя

---

31 Yakov Markovich Borovskiy, "Latinskiy yazyk Lomonosova [1960]," in *Opera philologica*, ed. Alexandr Konstantinovich Gavrilov, Vsevolod Vladimirovich Zelchenko and Tatyana Vladimirovna Shaburina (Saint-Petersburg, 2009), 316–26, there 321.

32 Lomonosov 8 (see above, n. 2), 238 and 259.

ревность *может*, как в преславных добродетелях толь великия Монархини?

Quod enim dicendi genus uberius *invenire* eloquentia, qua in re latius *diffundi* ingenii vires, ubi denique flagrantius *spirare* devotissimi amoris ardor *potest*, quam in laudibus tantae Principis celebrandis?

Such a sentence structure is not typical in Russian syntax and was obviously used for stylistic reasons. Thus, it is not surprising that these constructions were preserved in the Latin translation of the *Panegyric*.

A comparison of both texts of the *Panegyric* reveals that if the Russian sentence begins with a pronoun, a verb, a conjunction, or a negative particle, in the Latin translation it usually starts with the same part of speech:

Иные—Alii; Ея провидение—Illius providentia; Естьли бы— Quodsi; Коль—Quam, там—Hinc; Ни горы, ни лесы—Non sylvae, non montes; Ободрить—Exsuscitare; Отличается—Discernitur; Обращается—Versatur.

It would not be true to maintain that every part of this speech in Russian matches the Latin version in syntax. Their difference arises first of all from the use of participles. Thus, Russian active past participles (a part of speech that is lacking in Latin) are sometimes translated by adjectives (*"оставшуюся* ночь варварства"/ *"reliquam* barbariei noctem"; "дела *многотрудившагося* Российскаго Геркулеса"/ *"indefessi* Russiaci Herculis labores"), sometimes with present participles ("Россию, *начавшую* паки двигать свои мышцы"/ "Russiam, jam suos *moventem* lacertos"), or by means of dependent clauses ("ни внутрь России *вкоренившиеся* (неприятели)"/ "non illi, *qui* insederant atque *inveterarant* in visceribus Russiae"; "Восшед на высоту толикия власти, *отлучившим* Ея от законнаго наследства, *согрубившим* неистовою гордостию и бессовестным утеснением *огорчившим* кое мщение наносит?"/ "Constituta in summa rerum omnium potestate, in eos, *qui* Patria haereditate Ipsam *excludere*, *qui* nefaria insectatione *affligere*, et impudentissimo fastu *contemnere* non *dubitarunt*, quamnam vindictam exercet?").

And vice versa, the Ablativus absolutus (being a syntactic construction peculiar to the Latin language) corresponds in the Latin translation to verbal nouns ("при *окончании* благословенной *осени*"/ *"decurrente* beatissimo *autumno*", "Ея *входом*"/ "Illa *intrante*", "воссиял престол *вступлением*"/ "collustratur thronus, *ascendente*") or adverbial participles ("*обозрев разные* торжеств *образы*"/ *"perlustrata* solemnium *varietate*") in the Russian text.

LOMONOSOV'S *PANEGYRIC FOR ELIZAVETA PETROVNA*

Rhetorical repetition of words and phrases is peculiar to both versions of Lomonosov's speech; the Latin translation of such passages is particularly close to the original text. Repetition of prepositions and conjunctions indicates the progress of thought, repetition of nouns and verbs shows the importance of notions expressed by them. Anaphoras, frequently used in the long passages in both texts, make the speech more energetic and impulsive, especially when it takes the form of a prayer. This effect is notably evident in the sevenfold repetition of the thanksgiving to Elizaveta:[33]

> ибо *приносится благодарение Государыне* благочестивейшей – свидетельствуют созидаемые и украшаемые храмы Господни, пощения, молебства и трудныя путешествия благоговения ради;
>
> *приносится благодарение Государыне* мужественной – свидетельствуют над внутренними и внешними врагами Ея преславныя победы;
>
> *приносится благодарение Государыне* великодушной – свидетельствуют прощенныя преступления внутренних и продерзости внешних неприятелей и кроткое наказание Ея злодеев;
>
> *приносится благодарение Государыне* премудрой – свидетельствуют прозорливо предприемлемыя учреждения, внутреннее и внешнее спокойство утверждающия;
>
> *приносится благодарение Государыне* человеколюбивой – свидетельствует матернее к подданным Ея снисходительство и возлюбленная к ним кротость;
>
> *приносится благодарение Государыне* премилосердой – свидетельствует безчисленное множество свобожденных от смерти и данный Ей от Бога мечь на казнь повинных, кровию еще не обагренный;
>
> *приносится благодарение Государыне* прещедрой – свидетельствует преизобильное снабдение верности, избыточествующее заслуг награждение, споможение добродетельной скудости и восстановление нещастием раззоренных.

> Quandoquidem *aguntur gratiae Dominae* piissimae: testes sunt tot exornatae Divorum arae, exstructa templa, tamque crebra jejunia supplicationes et peregrinationes ad vota persolvenda institutae;
>
> *aguntur gratiae Dominae* fortissimae: testes sunt tot clarissimae victoriae a domesticis et externis hostibus reportatae;

---

33   Lomonosov 8 (see above, n. 2), 239 and 259.

aguntur gratiae Dominae magnanimae: testis concessa illis delictorum et audaciae impunitas;

aguntur gratiae Dominae sapientissimae: testis est prudentissime instituta rerum ordinatio ad pacem domi et foris firmandam;

aguntur gratiae Dominae mansuetissimae: testis est materna Illius erga subditos comitas et acceptissima lenitas;

aguntur gratiae Dominae clementissimae: testis est innumerabilis multitudo liberatorum a mortis poena, et concessus Illi a Deo gladius ad punienda crimina nondum sanguine humano tinctus;

aguntur gratiae Dominae liberalissimae: testes sunt amplissimis praemiis ornata fidelitas, honorata praeclaris muneribus merita, erecta opibus egens et fracta calamitate probitas.

Verbs of vision are particularly frequent in both texts of Lomonosov's *Panegyric*: the Empress is depicted looking at her citizens, not leaving them unnoticed: it means that they are under her protection ("радуяся взирает"/ "laetissimis oculis videt"; "ко всем человеколюбивая Государыня взор Свой обращает"/ "omnibus spectandam se praebet clementissima Princeps"). In their turn her people see that everything that is done by the Empress is good and blessed ("видим умными очами"/ "animi oculis contuemur"; "всяк видит"/ "spectant omnes"; "не озираются беспрестанно"/ "non timidos oculos circumferunt"; "пред очами имеем"/ "ante oculos habemus"; "ревностным усердия зрением [...] видит"/ "attentiore mentis oculo [...] contemplatur").

5   Differences between the Russian and Latin Version of the *Panegyric*

Lomonosov knew that Elizaveta was an orthodox devotee,[34] which is why he used the Church-Slavonic wording pleasing to her ear: the Church's monologue, addressed to God, being part of the *Panegyric*, includes quotations from Holy Writ. Quite unexpectedly Lomonosov did not quote the Vulgate in the respective places of the Latin text, preferring instead to give his own translation:

"возносит рог" / "auget dignitatem"—Cf. Ps 88,25: "exaltabitur cornu ejus"

"утверждает столпы" / "firmat columnas"—Cf. Ps 74,4: "confirmavi columnas"

---

34   Ibid., 958, n. 9.

"посещает меня посещением" / "visitat me (devotissima) visitatione"—
Cf. Gen 50, 24–5: "Deus visitabit vos"
"силою твоею свыше осени" / "virtute tua desuper tuere"—Cf. Luc 1,35:
"virtus Altissimi obumbrabit tibi"

In the Russian version of the *Panegyric* the Church-Slavonic formulas marked the solemn style of the text rather than its religious content. In the corresponding Latin text Lomonosov paraphrased the idioms, rather than searched for equivalents: "exaltare cornu alicujus" means "make famous, glorify", this sense is expressed by "augere dignitatem" in Lomonosov's Latin version; "obumbrare alicui" means "defend somebody", "tueri". Guessing Lomonosov's reasons for avoiding quotations from the Latin Bible, we can suppose that he intended to compose a secular panegyric, not a spiritual one,[35] so he did not want to preserve biblical allusions in the translation.[36]

Some phrases of the Russian version are omitted or changed in the Latin version because their meaning was strictly contextual and referred to the circumstances of the delivery of the speech by its author: "на сие здание взирали" (at this building they looked)/ "scientiarum et artium officinam [...] haberent ante oculos."

As it was said above, Lomonosov's usage of Latin vocabulary follows the classical standard, but sometimes he endowed words with a meaning, which is not attested in the Roman sources.

Thus, the Russian verbal noun "Просветитель" (Enlightener), denoting Peter the Great, occurs only once in the *Panegyric*: its correspondence in the Latin text is "sidus", which literally means "a star" (that is a source of light): "Ты Дщерь моего Просветителя"/ "et Filia mei Sideris".[37]

The verb "illustrare" (a common translation of Russian "просвещать"— "to enlighten") is also used by Lomonosov in the *Panegyric*: "*просвещенная Россия*" (enlightened Russia)—"*illustrata* Russia";[38] "представил бы я Петра именем Великаго, делами большаго, влиянною себе от Бога премудростию *просвещающаго* Россию" (I would represent Peter named the Great, the greatest by his affairs, enlightening Russia by the wisdom obtained from God)—"redigerem in memoriam vestram Petrum, nomine Magnum,

---

35 Such as works by Gedeon Krinovskiy, Amvrosiy Yushkevich, Kirill Florinskiy, see Evgeniy Mikhailovich Matveev, *Russkaya oratorskaya prosa serediny XVIII veka* (Saint-Petersburg, 2009), 37–82.

36 Lomonosov 7 (see above, n. 6), 69–72.

37 Ibid., 245 and 264.

38 Ibid., 240 and 260.

rebus gestis maximum, ut divinae sapientiae *lumine illustraret* Russiam";[39] "в *просвещенной* Петром России" (in Russia enlightened by Peter)—"in Russia, a Petro *illustrata*".[40]

Though the figurative use of the Latin noun "sidus" in the sense of "illustrator" ("enlightener") is quite understandable, it is not present in classical texts: Lomonosov could have learned it from Neo-Latin oral or written usage when he was studying in Marburg. On the other hand, it could be his own metaphor, as designating a person who is more than just an "enlightener"—he is simultaneously a "star", "glory" and "ornament" (cf. Ovid, *Pont.* 3,3,2; 6,6,9).

Sometimes Lomonosov could note the similarity of Russian and Latin words and seems to stress this similarity in the translation: есть—est, инде ("in other place")—inde ("from there", "therefore"), там ("there", "in the distance")—tum ("afterwards"),[41] видит—videt. However, such consonances of text can be appreciated only when they are read 'en regard', for instance:[42]

> *инде* при радостном звуке мирнаго оружия достигают до облаков
> торжественные плески Российскаго воинства
> *inde* insonare per aëra sociatos laetissimo pacificorum armorum fragori
> triumphales plausus Russiaci militis
> *есть* толь великое благодеяние, которое в мыслях и сердцах наших
> во веки незагладимо пребудет
> *est* amplissimum beneficium, cujus memoria nulla oblivione ex animis
> nostris delebitur

In the eighteenth century the attempts to found the assertions of national languages' richness and dignity were intensive.[43] From this point of view, the homophony of Russian and Latin forms must have corroborated Lomonosov's aspiration for the equal status of Russian and classical languages. According to Lomonosov's assumption, if the Roman Emperor Charles v, who said that it was proper to speak Spanish with God, French with a friend, German with an

---

39 Ibid.

40 Ibid., 252 and 269.

41 The repeated Russian word "там" (there) is translated by different Latin words: "hic", "tum". The same applies to the Russian word "инде": the first time conformable Latin "inde" is used, then "ibi", after that "rursus".

42 Lomonosov 8 (see above, n. 2), 236 and 257; 238 and 258.

43 Peter Burke, *Languages and Communities in Early Modern Europe* (Cambridge, 2004), 61–88.

enemy, Italian with a woman, had known Russian, he would have claimed that it is possible to speak this language with everyone.[44]

Thus, even before the text of this panegyric speech (written with constant allusions to the classical tradition) was translated into Latin it gave the reader some idea of its non-existent Latin prototype. The Latin translation, in turn, being a translation from Russian, strengthened its status as a language of oratory prose by no means inferior to its Neo-Latin counterpart.

Russian Academy of Sciences, Institute for Linguistic Studies

---

44   Lomonosov 7 (see above, n. 6), 391.

CHAPTER 45

De interpretibus Iacobi Vanierii e Societate Jesu sacerdotis inter poetas Hungaros

László Szörényi

Abstract

Fama Iacobi Vanieri Iesuitae non solum in Gallia, Britannia atque Italia longe lateque diffusa est (quod opera eius in has linguas transversa testantur), sed etiam in Hungaria auctor claruit. Gloriae ab eo captae causa est, quod cum in regno Hungariae, tum in regnis eidem annexis (Croatia, Sclavonia et Transylvania), quae sub imperio familiae Habsburg iacebant, maxima pars educationis in lyceis et universitatibus penes Societatem Iesu fuit, usque ad annum 1773, quando ordo deletus est. Iesuitae enim in saeculis decimo septimo et decimo octavo universitatem Tyrnaviensem, Zagrabiensem, Cassoviensem et Claudiopolitanam administraverunt, et iuventus studiosa praesertim carmina fratrum eiusdem ordinis in scholis poeseos legere et imitari debebat. Hac de causa opus Vanieri, quod *Praedium rusticum* inscribitur, famam magnam in Hungaria nactum est, immo poetae quidam Hungari, nomine David Baróti Szabó et Stephanus Miháltz opus illud in linguam Hungaricam tranverserunt, poesim novam creantes, quae hodie *schola Latinizans* vocatur. Cum autem lingua Hungarica hexametro apta fuerit, haec schola fundamenta poeseos modos pedesque adhibentis in lingua Hungarica (et partim Slavica) proiecit. Quae cum ita sint, receptio Vanieri in historia carminum heroicorum et didacticorum summi momenti est, saltem quod ad mediam Europe partem pertinet.

Keywords

Jacques Vanière – *Praedium Rusticum* (1682) – Neo-Latin didactic poetry – István Miháltz – Dávid Baróti Szabó

Hoc in tractatu duas versiones *Praedii rustici*, carminis a Iacobo Vanierio (Jacques Vanière, 1664–1739) conscripti, inter se comparabo, quas poetae Hungari saeculo decimo octavo fecerunt textum Latinum in Hungaricum vertentes. Alter eorum, nomine David Baróti Szabó, stilum Vergilii elegantissimum

© KONINKLIJKE BRILL NV, LEIDEN, 2020 | DOI:10.1163/9789004427105_046

DE INTERPRETIBUS IACOBI VANIERII E SOCIETATE JESU SACERDOTIS   577

imitari et in litteras Hungaricas transplantare cupiebat. Alter autem, Stephanus Miháltz, scopum alium habuit: colonos in Hungaria et Transylvania degentes opere suo docere conabatur. Quae cum ita erant, hi poetae rationes omnino diversas secuti sunt, cum terminis technicis agriculturae vel instrumentis poeticis usi essent.

Iacobus Vanierius e Societate Iesu sacerdos, auctor operis *Praedium rusticum* inscripti, qui a contemporalibus saepissime "Vergilius Gallorum" vocabatur, non solum in patria, sed etiam in Hispania, Britannia, Germania, Italia et America Meridionali fama super aethera notus est, quod clarissime patet ex eo, quod *Praedium rusticum* saepissime editum et in linguas alienas transversum est. Immo etiam in Europa Orientali auctoris ibat fama per urbes, quoniam *Praedium rusticum* lingua Hungarica et Polonica redditum erat.[1] Editionem autem huius operis in Pannonia primam, quae adhuc Latine sonabat, patres Societatis Iesu in typographia Universitatis Tyrnaviensis[2] anno 1772° confecerunt. Sed dum (vix septem annis post) editiones duae Hungaricae in lucem venerunt, nempe anno 1779°, altera ex calamo Stephani Miháltz in oppido Cibinio[3] (capite principatus Transylvaniae, quae eo tempore sub regimine domus Austriacae fuit), altera autem ex calamo Davide Baróti Szabó in duobus regni Hungariae oppidis, Posonii[4] et Cassoviae[5] est edita. Haec iterum typographice expressa est Cassoviae, anno 1794°, in forma multo meliore. Hi interpretes ambo patres Societatis Iesu fuerunt.[6]

Quamvis temporibus recentioribus philologi multi poesim Vanierii tractaverint, nondum editio critica *Praedii rustici* extat. Magni tamen aestimandum est, quod editio meliorata et appendice ornata, quam typographus nomine "Barbou" anno 1774° fecit, iam locum in interrete habet.[7] Editiones

---

1 Yasmin Annabel Haskell, *Loyola's Bees: Ideology and Industry in Jesuit Latin Didactic Poetry* (Oxford, 2003), 38. De operibus Vanierium tractantibus vide Yasmin Annabel Haskell, "Jesuit Georgic Poetry," in *Brill's Encyclopaedia of the Neo-Latin World*, ed. Philip Ford, Jan Bloemendal and Charles Fantazzi (Leiden – Boston, 2014), 1007–09.

2 Hodie Trnava, Slovacia.

3 Hodie Sibiu, Romania.

4 Hodie Bratislava, Slovacia.

5 Hodie Košice, Slovacia.

6 Notandum est, quod Kristijonas Donelaitis (1714–80), pater poesis Lithuanicae *Praedium rusticum* ut exemplum vel typum adhibuit, cum carmen suum *Metai* vocatum confecit, quamvis veri similiter non opus Latinum, sed versionem Polonicam legeret. Vide István Margócsy, "Milyenek a litván évszakok?," *2000 : irodalmi és társadalmi havi lap* 22,5 (2010), 5–7.

7 https://archive.org/details/praediumrusticum00vaniuoft (2018-11-21).

578 SZÖRÉNYI

praedicti Davidis Baróti Szabó,[8] nec non editio Stephani Miháltz[9] fatum simile sortitae sunt.

In interpretibus Hungaris – praeter statum religiosum – unum commune invenitur, nempe quod eas operis partes, quae nemini nisi Gallis utiles vel iucundae esse viderentur, non transverterunt; sed de hac re inferius. Si quis autem textu Latino neglecto editiones tantum Hungaricas inter se comparat, statim intelligit eas omnino dissimiles esse. Miháltz enim non eisdem lectoribus scribere voluit ac quibus Baróti. Hic enim munere magistri in lyceo fungebatur, praeterea fundator et scriptor actorum diurnorum Hungaricorum fuit, ergo versione *Praedii rustici* fines ad rem litterariam spectantes habuit. Ideo de rebus rusticis scripsit, ut dialecto suo Transylvanico et thesauro verborum usus, quem studio litterarum Hungaricarum antiquarum adeptus esset, demonstraret linguam Hungaricam omnino aptissimam esse ad verba Latinorum difficillima vel rarissima transvertenda.

Miháltz autem, interpres alter, finem diversum habuit, quia cum in Transylvania, tum in Hungaria Meridionali (quae regio nuperrime a Turcis bello recepta erat) non munere magistri, sed missionarii fungebatur. Ergo Miháltz opus Vanierii velut enchiridium vel librum scholasticum adhibuit et eas libri partes transvertit, quas agricolis Hungariae Transylvaniaeque ad labores quotidianos usui fore censuit.

Quae cum ita sint, versio illius Baróti stricte textum Latinum sequitur. Hic fuit ille vates, qui hexametrum et alia Graecorum Romanorumque metra magno cum successu in poesim Hungaricam transposuit, cum antea nemini idem conanti dei favissent (primus poetarum frustratorum Ioannes Sylvester fuit, professor Universitatis Viennensis, qui saeculo decimo sexto *Novum Testamentum* in linguam Hungaricam transvertens in appendice carmina metrica Hungarica posuit, neque gloriam magnam hoc conatu acquisivit).

Baróti igitur, quam sibi sortem seu ratio dediisset seu fors obiecisset, illa contentus vivebat, cum eleganter metra antiqua in carminibus Hungaricis adhibere posset. Sed brevi tempore duo ei aemuli apparuerunt, nomine Nicolaus Révai ex Scholis Piis et Iosephus Rájnis ex Societate Iesu, cum quibus Baróti Szabó vehementer de argumentis poeticis disputabat. Philologi Hungarici hos auctores "triada classicam" vel "poetas linguam clericorum imitantes" appellant (nam lingua clericorum in Hungaria linguam Latinam significavit).

Miháltz vero nihil novi in poesi cogitabat, sed metro consueto usus est, quod Alexandrinus Hungaricus vocatur, et non spondaeum vel dactylum, sed homoioteleuton requirit. Carmen eius dedicatorium, quod baroni Samueli de

---

8 http://fulltext.lib.unideb.hu/book.cgi?lf=205.lst&pn=1 (2018-11-21).
9 http://mek.oszk.hu/06900/06989/06989.pdf (2018-11-21).

DE INTERPRETIBUS IACOBI VANIERII E SOCIETATE JESU SACERDOTIS

Brukenthal, gubernatori Magni Principatus Transylvaniae scriptum est, clarissime ostendit auctorem populo misero et pauperi prodesse voluisse. Mihältz enim gubernatorem, qui imperium absolutum reginae Mariae Theresiae in Transylvania repraesentabat, duas ob causas laudavit: partim ut benefactorem viduarum orphanorumque benevolum, partim ut servitorem reginae atque ecclesiae Catholicae fidelissimum. Ergo auctor putavit opus suum et gubernatorem cum agrestibus, tum Catholicis Transylvanicis (qui undique a protestantibus circumdati fuerunt) auxilio fore. Baróti vero in operis sui praefatione de hexametro Hungarico disputavit asserens famam gloriamque Vanierii calamo nullius indigere, cum nomen eius omnibus eruditis notissimum esset. Praeterea Baróti censuit Vanierium non solum virtutes poeticas, sed etiam utilitatem in scholis habere, cum magistri contemporales in Hungaria *Praedio rustico* in doctrinis agriculturae docendis uterentur. Auctor in ultima parte praefationis iterum diserte rationes carminum Hungaricorum scribendorum tractavit, denique gratias egit Benedicto Pyber, qui olim discipulus eius fuerat, postea autem patronus editionis est factus. Praefationi autem editionis alterius argumentum unum addidit, semet excusare volens, quod verbis *Bucolicorum Georgicorumque* usus erat. Baróti ostendit Vergilium non semper classica Martia adhibuisse neque omnibus in carminibus verbis heroicis opus esse. Quod autem ad verba carminum Venereorum attinet, multi alii erant, qui poesin huius generis foedi coluere.

Praeterea Baróti Szabó pro argumentis ad Galliam pertinentibus, quae propter ignorantiam lectorum Hungaricorum omisit, argumentis ad Hungariam pertinentibus usus est; nam si talia argumenta omnino defuissent, hiatum magnum in opere transverso reliquissent. Ubicumque igitur fieri potuit, Baróti exempla Hungarica pro exemplis Vanierii attulit, poeta enim Gallus de pomis uvisque colendis vel de utilitate eorum scribens argumenta sua tantummodo ex rebus Galliae vel Europae Occidentalis sumpserat.

Iam principium partis primae methodum praedictam manifeste demonstrat, ubi Vanierius Vergilium imitatur et semet excusat, quod de re rustica nec de bellis Ludovici regis Galliae heroicis narrat:[10]

> Haud tamen arma meis male congrua moribus ausim
> Imbelli tractare manu: dat maximus amplam
> Materiem Lodoix, victo clarissimus orbe.
> Sed jam trita nimis laudum seges; atque Poetis
> (Ausint cuncta licet) vix tantum fingere, quantum
> Efficere huic promtum est: Heroum fabula veris

---

10   Jacques Vanière, *Praedium rusticum. Nova editio, caeteris emendatior* (Paris, 1774), 3–4.

580   SZÖRÉNYI

> Vincitur historiis; stupefactaque fama triumphis
> Jam silet, & longo plausus prope concidit usu.

Notandum est locis pluribus Ludovicum Galliae regem propter expulsionem protestantium a Vanierio glorificari. Interpretes tamen Hungari hos versus non transverterunt, immo Baróti pro rege Ludovico Mariam Theresiam reginam Hungariae affert, et eam ut imperatricem triumphantem repraesentat, in prima enim operis parte non solum de hac rege femineo mentionem facit, sed etiam cum duce Hungarorum fortissimo, Iano Hunyadi (qui saeculo decimo quinto floruit), nec non cum eius filio, rege Hungarorum aeque gloriosissimo Matthia Corvino reginam suam comparat. Verba interpretis, si metrum servare volumus, hoc modo se habent:[11]

> Haud tamen arma meis male congrua moribus ausim
> Imbelli tractare manu: dat maximus amplam
> Materiem Ianus Hunyadi, vel filius eius,
> Matthias, aut illi, quos in Pannonia tellus
> heroum genuit, vel Transylvanica terra.
> Maiorum possem nostrorum tempora sertis
> cingere nunc viridis, quae Martis fortiter illi
> in campis cepissent. Sed patriae mihi mater
> amplam materiem, regina altissima donat.
> Hostibus illa fuit nam fulmen, candida cuius
> arma timebant Prussi, quorum carmine dignam
> in regno laurum cepit.

In editione huius carminis altera iam deest mentio gloriae saeculis praeteritis acquisitae, quoniam interea Maria Theresia mortua erat et successores eius, nomine Iosephus, Leopoldus et Franciscus, mores consuetudinesque Hungarorum in mores Germanos transmutare, libertatem vero tollere conabantur neque veriti sunt accusationibus sycophantarum uti et iudiciis iniustis

---

11   Jacques Vanière, *Paraszti majorság, mellyet Vanierböl hat lábbal mérséklett magyar versbe foglalt Esztergam megyebéli pap, Erdélyi, Baróthi Szabó Dávid* (Bratislava – Košice, 1779), 1–2. Hi versus Hungarice sic se habent: "Hódító fegyverre de nem mérészlem erőtlen, / 'S más munkára szokott kezemet szabadítani. Vólna / Húnyadi Jánosban, és ennek vólna Fiában / Máttyásban; Magyar, és Erdély országnak ezernyi / Válogatott deli Bajnokiban tág udvar adatnék; / Zöldellö koszorut fel-füzni lehetne piartzán / Vérengző Mársnak; 's azzal diadalmas Ösinknek / Tsak nem imádandó fejiket kerekíteni. Lenne / Fö-képpen bö tárgyam, Hazánk' kegyes Anyja, Therésa, / Ellenséginknek rettentő mennyköve: gyözö / Kardja kinek Burgus vérben minap úsza: 's borostyánt / Annak dúlt mezein aratott."

DE INTERPRETIBUS IACOBI VANIERII E SOCIETATE JESU SACERDOTIS 581

omnes capite damnare, qui rem Hungaricam promovere vellent. Quae cum ita essent, Baróti Szabó versus praedictos in editione secunda sic transmutavit:[12]

> Haud tamen arma meis male congrua moribus ausim
> Imbelli tractare manu: miserabilis amplam
> Materiem daret Hungara-Transsylvanica tellus,
> quae populum heroum genuit, clarissimum in orbe.
> Mille coronas possim lauro conserere atris
> bellorum in campis vel sub tumulis dolorosis,
> maiorum ut laudes nostrorum ad sidera tollam.
> Materiem dedit amplam mi patriae pia mater,
> quae carissima erat populo, verum hostibus atrox,
> cum Prussorum sanguine terras commaculavit,
> et dignum laurato cepit Marte triumphum.
> Sed jam trita nimis laudum seges; atque Poetis
> (ausint cuncta licet) vix tantum fingere, quantum
> efficere huic promptum est, reginae namque Theresae.

Baróti, antequam poesin Hungaricam aetate provectus coluit, carmina Latina scribebat, sed haec carmina nondum edita vel saltem collecta sunt. Habemus tamen carmen quoddam Latinum, cuius auctor ignotus est, sed certo scimus id a Baróti in linguam Hungaricam transversum esse, immo fieri potest, ut carmen Latinum non solum interprete, sed auctore quoque glorietur illo. Titulus eius est *Fatum Hungariae antiquae miserabile.* Hoc opusculum anno 1786° editum est, sub regimine Iosephi huius nominis secundi, qui "rex petasatus" vocatur, quoniam noluit Sacra Hungariae Corona ornari, neque igitur rex Hungarorum legitimus dici potuit. Carmen autem Latinum hoc modo sonat:[13]

---

12 Jacques Vanière, *Paraszti majorság. Fordította Vanierből Baróti Szabó Dávid* (Košice, 1794), 15–6. Hi versus taliter Hungarice sonant: "Ám de nehéz fegyverre ki nem mérészlem erőt-len. / 'S gyenge mivekre szokott kezeim' terjeszteni: kettős / Árva Hazánk', Magyar- és Erdély-Országnak ezernyi / Válogatott deli Bajnokiban tág udvar adattván, / Füzhetnék sok ezer laurust a' vérbe-boríttott / Ütközeteknek helyinn, 's gyászos sír-halmok alatt-is / Meg-tisztelhetném azzal diadalmas Atyáink'. / Lenne kivált bő tárgyam, Hazánk' kegyes Annya Theréza, / Ellenség' félelme, saját hív népe' szerelme; / A' ki minap Mársnak meze-jét Prusz vérrel itatván, / Tartandó koszorúra jutott. De felette sokaknak / Nyomdokitól porosúlt ez az út; 's bár költsön akár-mit / Kedve szerént a' Vers-szerző; nem költhet ez annyit, / A' mennyit ki-talált örökös javainkra Theréza."

13 Dávid Baróti Szabó, "Fatum Hungariae antiquae miserabile," in *Deákos költők I.*, ed. Elemér Császár (Budapest, 1914), 104

Praecipites ubi sunt acti de nubibus imbres,
    Caeruleo surgit purior axe dies.
Aeolii postquam posuerunt proelia fratres,
    Sedibus emoti frangitur ira maris.
Hungara terra videt nunquam post nubila Phœbum:
    Semper, quod doleat, quod vereatur, habet.
Se Niobe saxum fieri post vulnera sensit,
    At fuit huic parvo tempore flere, mori.
Vivit at ista, licet vitae prope nescia, vivit
    Et stupefacta suis ingemit usque malis.

Hic necessario notandum est illum Baróti Szabó saeculo proximo a poetis Hungarorum clarissimis, nomine Francisco Kölcsey et Michaele Vörösmarty, laudibus maximis ornatum esse. Kölcsey et Vörösmarty eum imitantes talia carmina scripserunt, quae historiam Niobes memorarent, ut fatum Hungariae vel Poloniae miserabile quam manifestissime repraesentarent. Poema Francisci Kölcsey *Iustitia* inscribitur, in quo saxum speciei femineae nationem Hungaricam ingeniose repraesentat, sed hoc saxum non Niobe est, sed statua Themitis vel Iustitiae.[14] Carmen autem Michaelis Vörösmarty Poloniam ab Imperio Russico violatam et dilaceratam cum Niobe comparat, et *Statua viva* inscribitur.[15]

Nunc autem ad locos alios transeundum est, ubi non de gloria regum, sed de natura caeli et agricultura agitur: interpretes nostri vinum Gallicum, quod Vanierius fertur magis quam vina omnia unum coluisse posthabitis vinis Germanis Italicisque, omnino omiserunt, immo vinis Hungaris Transylvanicisque locum eius compleverunt. Baróti tamen Vanierium excusat, quia poeta Gallus vina Hungarica ignoravit, et misero necesse fuit vina Gallica bibere. Miháltz vero, ut missionarius, vehementius scripsit.

Baróti igitur refert Lyaeum (id est Bacchum) taedio vinorum Graecorum Gallorumque affectum in Hungariam venisse, ubi copiam immensam vinorum Hungaricorum invenit, quibus haustis nihil fuit super ei vocis in ore, lingua sed torpebat, tenuis sub artus flamma demanavit, sonitu suopte tintinnarunt aures, geminaque tecta sunt lumina nocte. Ergo Bacchus tantopere inebriatus fuit, ut necessario potionem Arabicam sive caffeam bibere deberet, ut iterum sui compos fieret. Baróti omnes regiones in carmine percurrit, quae

---

14   Ferenc Kölcsey, *Versek és versfordítások* (Budapest, 2001), 127–30.

15   Mihály Vörösmarty, *Kisebb költemények, III.* (Budapest, 1962), 22–24. Praeterea notandum est hoc carmen in linguam Germanicam, Anglicam, Gallicam et Rutenicam transversum esse.

DE INTERPRETIBUS IACOBI VANIERII E SOCIETATE JESU SACERDOTIS

uva fertiles in Hungaria sunt, eas virtuose secundum regulas metrorum enumerans. Interpretem nostrum magnopere miseret Vanierii, qui nunquam vina Hungarica temptavit, nec unum saltem dolium potionum earum vidit, quamvis ea dolia ubique Hungari venditarent.[16]

Miháltz, interpres alter, eodem modo regiones Hungariae uviferas enumerat, multo tamen plures quam Baróti, immo refert vina talia a Polonis auro emi. Praeterea Miháltz non solum vina Hungarica, verum etiam Transylvanica memorat. Huic operis parti Miháltz mythum Graecorum de Gigantibus adiungit, cum apud Ovidium, in libro quodam *Metamorphoseon* legatur uvam a transmutatione Gigantum ortam esse. Item, Miháltz non solum in praefatione fatetur partes plures operis Vanierii a se praeteritas esse, et textu diverso hiatos completos esse, sed saepe bibliographiam de quaestione affert (quoniam, ut antea iam scriptum est, Miháltz non artis, sed utilitatis causa opus suum conscripsit). Exempli gratia partem de apibus narrantem omnino eiecit, quamvis hi versus satis iucundi sint. In margine tamen opus aliud lectoribus commendat, sine nomine auctoris, sed facillime inquirere possumus, quo de libro agatur. Liber enim satis clarus fuit, quem inter quinquaginta annos sexies ediderunt, *Apis Transylvanica* (Hungarice *Erdéllyi méhecske*) inscribitur, auctor autem eius est Laurentius Pálfi, vir religiosus ex Ordine Fratrum Minorum, qui magno amore et experientia de his bestiolis dilectis pretiosisque disseruit.[17]

Ratio interpretum nostrorum, qua regiones Hungaricas pro regionibus Gallicis in textum posuerunt, carmen didacticum aliud memorat, quod *Rusticatio Mexicana* inscribitur. Auctor eius Iesuita quidam fuit, nomine Raphael Landivar, qui exul opus in Italia scripsit.[18] Notandum est hoc carmen tempore recentiore a multis philologis valde laudatum esse, cum mores rationesque Iesuitarum cum litteris classicis atque rationibus, ut ita dicam, utopisticis splendidissime coniunxerit.[19]

Postremo de cursu poetico illius Baróti loqui voluerim, qui in praefatione operis negavit se rotam Virgilianam suis poematibus secuturum esse. Utcumque tamen fuit, Baróti post *Praedium rusticum* (quod cum *Georgicis*

---

16   Jacques Vanière, *Vanier Jakabnak* [...] *paraszti majorja, mellyet Magyarra fordított* [...] *Miháltz István* (Sibiu, 1779), 38–40. Vide etiam László Szörényi, *Bacchus kocsmája* (Budapest, 2015), 97–8.

17   Elek Csetri, "Régi erdélyi méhészkönyvek," *História* 17,5–6 (1995), 53–5.

18   Vide Arnold L. Kerson, "Rafael Landívar's Rusticatio Mexicana and the Enlightenment in America," in *Acta Conventus Neo-Latini Sanctandreani*, ed. Ian D. McFarlane (Binghampton – New York, 1986), 587–96.

19   Vide Marcella Alejandra Suarez, "El didactismo landivariano: tradición clásica, identidad cultural e ideología jesuítica en la *Rusticatio Mexicana*," *Nova Tellus* 30 (2012), 187–204; Arnold L. Kerson, "El Concepto de Utopía de Rafael Landívar en la *Rusticatio Mexicana*," *Revista Iberoamericana* 42 (1976), 373–9.

comparari potest) etiam *Eclogas* Vergilii in linguam Hungaricam transtulit, aetate autem Nestoriana *Aeneidem* in duobus voluminibus lingua Hungarica donavit, praesertim ex instigatione amici, Ioannis Batsányi, qui amicus, arbiter et laudator illius Baróti fuit.[20] Multi philologi Hungariae aestimant hanc *Aeneidem* omnium versionum optimam esse. Cui sententiae mihi annuendum esse videtur, praesertim si percogitemus fere omnes poetas Hungaros saeculo undevigesimo hac *Aeneide* instimulatos esse, ut in conatibus suis epicis Vergilium imitarentur, quamvis eo tempore iam multi magistri poetaeque putarent Vergilium nimis veterem tritumque esse. Baróti enim tam eleganter et ingeniose Vergilium interpretatus est, ut fieri non posset, quin eum omnes imitari atque aemulari vellent.

Postremo, exemplo clarissimo demonstrare conabor, quomodo Miháltz et Baróti *Praedio rustico* cogitationes suas implicuerint.[21] In *Praedio rustico* enim aliquot versus de bobus emeritis narrant, nempe hoc modo:[22]

> Emeritus bos prata terit; permissaque secum
> Otia miratus, laetis pinguescit in herbis,
> Nescius heu! letho quam tristi debita cervix,
> Cui gravis impendet frangendo clava cerebro.

Miháltz hos versus taliter transvertit:[23]

> Laete bos talis in prato nunc ambulat,
> nec propter socium absentem lacrimat,
> letho assignatum esse se ignorat,
> quamquam lanionis clava iam propinquat.

Baróti autem strictissime verba Vanierii sequitur, et textus eius Hungaricus omnino idem continet ac textus Latinus, etiam regulas metricas optime servat.[24] Notandum est tamen bovem in versibus proximis a Baróti non emeritum, sed senem appellari, quo nomine etiam semet ipsum signabat. Baróti enim, licet aetate provectus, iterum atque iterum in lyceum redire debebat, ut discipulos

---

20 Vide János Batsányi, *Batsányi János Prózai művei II.* (Budapest, 1961), 307, 466, 555.

21 Vide Árpád Tőzsér, "Egy diófa és környéke, Baróti Szabó Dávid költészetének leíró elemei, egy vers és egy régi vita," in idem, *A könyv színe előtt, Irodalomtörténeti tanulmányok, kritikák, esszék, jegyzetek, interjúk* (Budapest – Pozsony, 2015), 94–135.

22 Vanière, *Praedium rusticum* 3,75.

23 Miháltz, *Vanier Jakabnak* (vide supra, n. 16) 45. Hi versus taliter in lingua Hungarica sonant: "Az ílly vágó vigan a' zöld mezöt járja, / Nem búsúl, hogy tölle el-maradott párja; / Nem érti, halálnak hogy el-lepi árja; / Mivel hogy Mészáros bárdgya ötet várja."

24 Baróti Szabó, *Paraszti majorság* (vide supra, n. 11), 74.

DE INTERPRETIBUS IACOBI VANIERII E SOCIETATE JESU SACERDOTIS

tanto magistro indignos doceret. Ergo semet cum bove, lyceum cum taberna lanionis comparavit.

Interpretes Hungari consulto cum his versibus luserunt, cum non ignorarent Vanierium adagio nisum esse. Adagium enim quoddam apud Erasmum *de bove ad praesepe* invenitur, quod etiam *bos in stabulo* dici potest. Erasmus hoc modo illud explicat:[25]

> In emeritos dici consuevit, quoque iam ob aetatem otio vitaeque molliori indulgent. Effertur et ad hunc modum: [...] *Bos in stabulo.* Congruit et in eos, qui nullis honestis negotiis exercentur, sed turpi ocio atque abdomini serviunt [...]. Congruet et in illos, qui in suum aluntur exitium, quemadmodum ii, qui se voluptatibus mundi explent, Orco quid aliud quam victimae nutriuntur, veluti *bos ad praesepe*?

Haud mirabile est igitur Hennebertum, physicum eiusdem temporis, qui de bobus disserens etiam hanc descriptionem Vanierii crudelem in linguam Gallicam transvertit, multo levius et mitius de re scripsisse:[26]

> Jouissant en paix du fruit de ses travaux, il foule d'un pas tardif, mais joyeux, l'herbe fraîche & touffue. Il ignore hélas! que ce chemin fleuri le conduit au terme fatal où l'attend la massue meurtrière. [Huic textui auctor annotavit:] J'ai cru devoir, pour ne choquer personne, rendre un peu indirectement Emeritus Bos.

Hastiquatius tamen, sive Shakespeare sine dubio immitis fuit, cum in opere dramatico, *Henricus IV.* inscripto, in actu quinto primae partis procerem quendam rebellem, nomine Worcesterum, adagio Erasmi fatum suum praedicantem afferret:[27]

> Nutriemur ut boves ad praesepe,
> quibus morte imminente optime indulgetur.

> Universitas Scientiarum Szegediensis
> (University of Szeged, Hungary)

---

25 Erasmo da Rotterdam, *Adagi, Prima traduzione italiana completa, testo latino a fronte*, a cura di Emanuele Lelli (Milano, 2013), 966–968; 2478–2479.

26 Jean-Baptiste-François Hennebert, *Cours d'histoire naturelle, ou tableau de la nature, Considérée dans l'Homme, les Quadrupédes, les Oiseux, les Poissons & les Insectes*, vol. 2 (Paris, 1770), 25.

27 *William Shakespeare, The First Part of the History of Henry IV*, ed. John Dover Wilson (Cambridge, 2009), 89.

CHAPTER 46

The Weaver of Light: Divine Origin of Nature and Natural Science in Carlo Noceti's *Iris*

Irina Tautschnig

Abstract

In eighteenth century Rome, a flourishing local tradition of Jesuit didactic poetry produced a number of scientific poems which set out to explain phenomena in physics in Latin verse. By overcoming the difficulties inherent in their subject matter and thus beautifying their topics, these didactic poets celebrated the achievements of science. Connecting science to God is a recurring literary element in their poems, but it seems to be especially prominent in the *Iris*, a poem on the rainbow by the Roman Jesuit Carlo Noceti (1694–1759). In three miniature scenes at crucial points of the text, God is depicted as designing the Newtonian laws of light, initiating the scientific endeavour and establishing the rainbow as a symbol of peace. Together with the programmatic proem, these passages closely link the search for the origin of the rainbow to God, promoting Newtonian optics, but also scientific activity as such to the audience.

Keywords

Carlo Noceti – *Iris* (1729) – Neo-Latin didactic poetry – Isaac Newton – rainbow

In eighteenth century Rome, a flourishing local tradition of Jesuit didactic poetry produced a number of scientific poems which set out to explain phenomena in physics in Latin verse.[1] As they overcame the difficulties inherent in their subject matter and beautified their topics by turning them into poetry, the Jesuit poets did not only display literary virtuosity and the virtues of their order,[2] but also tried to engage their readers by presenting scientific content in

---

1   These poems include Roger Boscovich, *De solis ac lunae defectibus* (London, 1760); Bernardo Zamagna, *Echo* (Rome, 1764); Giuseppe Mazzolari, *Electrica* (Rome, 1767); and Benedikt Stay, *Philosophia recentior*, 3 vols. (Rome, 1755–92). For an overview of the Roman 'microtradition' of scientific didactic poetry, see Yasmin Haskell, *Loyola's Bees. Ideology and Industry in Jesuit Latin Didactic Poetry* (Oxford, 2003), 178–244.
2   Cf. Haskell, *Loyola's Bees* (see above, n. 1), 11–2.

© KONINKLIJKE BRILL NV, LEIDEN, 2020 | DOI:10.1163/9789004427105_047

DIVINE ORIGIN OF NATURE AND NATURAL SCIENCE IN NOCETI'S *IRIS* 587

a simplified and delightful manner.[3] Many of these scientific poems were written by professors of the *Collegio Romano* and recited at academic occasions.[4] The authors thus addressed an audience of superiors, peers and students that would share their Jesuit ethos and appreciate the scientific poems as evidence that the study of both poetry and nature was hard work that would bear rich fruit for the dedicated 'bees of Loyola'.[5]

Early modern scientific activity and scientific writing was deeply informed by religion in general,[6] and religious sentiment had not only framed the Jesuits' scientific activity from its beginning, but also pervaded their scientific didactic poetry.[7] The *Iris*, a poem on the rainbow according to Newton's theory of light and colours written by the Roman Jesuit Carlo Noceti (1694–1759), provides an interesting example in this regard.[8] Throughout the poem, the search for the origin of the rainbow is closely connected to God, promoting Newtonian optics, but also more generally scientific activity as such to its Jesuit audience.

Noceti recited the *Iris* in the *Collegio Romano* in 1729, when he took up the post of professor of philosophy, at the festivity which marked the beginning of the academic year.[9] By integrating Newton's explanation of the colours of

---

3   Martin Korenjak, "Explaining Natural Science in Hexameter. Scientific Didactic Epic in the Early Modern Era," *Humanistica Lovaniensia* 68 (2019), 135–75 argues that scientific didactic poems ought to be seen as serious attempts to convey early modern science.

4   A recitation of a shorter version of the poem at the beginning of the academic year is recorded e.g. for Boscovich, *De solis ac lunae defectibus* (see above, n. 1), iii and Mazzolari, *Electrica* (see above, n. 1), 7. Jesuit didactic poems were of course also recited in other colleges and academies.

5   Cf. Boscovich, "Notae in Iridem," in Carlo Noceti, *De Iride et Aurora boreali carmina* (Rome, 1747), 47 on the protreptic effect of Noceti's recitation. For the recitation as a display of commitment to teaching cf. Haskell, *Loyola's Bees* (see above, n. 1), 6.

6   There is vast scholarship on the relationship between science and religion in the early modern period. For an overview cf. Rivka Feldhay, "Religion," in *The Cambridge History of Science*, vol. 3, ed. Katharine Park and Lorraine Daston (Cambridge, 2006), 727–55, and John Hendley Brooke, "Science and Religion," in *The Cambridge History of Science*, vol. 4, ed. Roy Porter (Cambridge, 2003), 741–61.

7   For the Jesuits' scientific activity cf. Steven J. Harris, "Transposing the Merton Thesis. Apostolic Spirituality and the Establishment of the Jesuit Scientific Tradition," *Science in Context* 3 (1989), 29–65; on the significance of Harris's argument for Jesuit didactic poetry cf. Haskell, *Loyola's Bees* (see above, n. 1), 1–16. Cf. also Yasmin Haskell, "Religion and Enlightenment in the Neo-Latin Reception of Lucretius," in *The Cambridge Companion to Lucretius*, ed. Stuart Gillespie and Philip Hardie (Cambridge, 2007), 185–201, there 200.

8   I am preparing an edition with translation and commentary of this text.

9   Cf. Boscovich, "Notae in Iridem" (see above, n. 5), 19. For Noceti's life and works, see Carlos Sommervogel, *Bibliothèque des écrivains de la Compagnie de Jésus*, vol. 5 (Brussels, 1894), cols. 1784–87.

the rainbow in his poem,[10] Noceti was able to highlight not only his ability as a Latin poet, but also his familiarity with the current developments in natural philosophy, which was part of the philosophy course that he would go on to teach at the Jesuit college.[11] In the *Iris*, Noceti makes a point of the close observation of nature (e.g. rainbows appearing on fountains) leading to the conclusion that the rainbow is formed by waterdrops reflecting the sunlight. He describes the angles between which the rainbow becomes visible and confirms his account with an experiment in which a glass sphere has to be raised to a certain height in order to emit the colours of the spectrum. He then explains why the rainbow has a semi-circular shape and why it seems to follow or flee from the spectator, but can in fact never be reached. Turning to Newton's theory of light and colour, Noceti lays out the principle of refraction and explains that light consists of colours which are each refracted in a slightly different angle, a fact that is illustrated by Newton's famous experiment with two prisms.[12] Between 1713 and 1813, *Iris* was printed five times in different versions, varying in length between 373 and 527 hexameter.[13] The most elaborate edition was the edition of 1747, which contained two didactic poems by Noceti—a reworked version of *Iris* and a second poem on an equally colourful phenomenon, the

---

10   Investigating the origin of the rainbow had a rich tradition from antiquity onwards. Before Newton, the rainbow had already been identified as the result of the refraction and reflection of light within the raindrops, most famously by Descartes; Newton was the first to be able to correctly explain the origin of its colours, first in a paper to the Royal Society (1672), then in his seminal *Opticks* (1704), which was published in a Latin translation two years later as *Optice sive de reflexionibus, refractionibus, inflexionibus et coloribus lucis libri tres*, transl. Samuel Clarke (London, 1706). On the history of the theory of the rainbow, see Carl B. Boyer, *The Rainbow. From Myth to Mathematics* (New York, 1959).

11   In 1729, Noceti would start the philosophy course by teaching logic, only proceeding to natural philosophy in the following year. Cf. Ignazio Iparraguirre, "Elenco dei rettori e professori del Collegio Romano (1551–1773)," in Riccardo G. Villoslada, *Storia del Collegium Romanum dal suo inizio (1551) alla soppressione della Compagnia di Gesù (1773)* (Rome, 1954), 321–36, there 331 and 333.

12   In all subsequent editions, the order is inverted, with the Newtonian colours being explained first. From the second edition onwards, Noceti also describes the formation of efficient rays by several rays that are emitted from the drop around the largest angle of deflection and merge in the spectator's eye, and adds a short account of the secondary rainbow.

13   Carlo Noceti, "De Iride carmen philosophicum," in *Novelle della Repubblica delle Lettere dell'anno MDCCXXX* (Venice, 1731), fol. e2r–f2v; Carlo Noceti, *De Iride et Aurora boreali carmina* (Rome, 1747); Carlo Noceti, "Iris. Carmen," in *Poemata didascalica*, vol. 2, ed. François Oudin (Paris, 1749), 204–23; Carlo Noceti, *L'Iride e l'Aurora boreale*, transl. Antonio Ambrogi (Florence, 1755); Carlo Noceti, "Iris. Carmen," in *Poemata didascalica*, vol. 2, ed. François Oudin (Paris, ²1813), 71–88.

DIVINE ORIGIN OF NATURE AND NATURAL SCIENCE IN NOCETI'S *IRIS* 589

Northern Lights (*Aurora borealis*)—together with extensive, mostly scientific notes by Roger Boscovich.[14]

In all these printed versions, God is depicted in three miniature scenes placed at crucial points within the poem, and the scientific topic is programmatically connected to God in the proem.[15] The paratexts to the *Iris*, including Boscovich's notes, do not comment or elaborate on those passages, which might indicate how natural they came to both the authors and their audience in the context of this literary tradition. To my knowledge, the most explicit reflection on the role of God in the Roman Jesuits' scientific didactic poetry can be found in Christoph Stay's *De poesi didascalica dialogus*. Printed in the third volume of his brother Benedikt's monumental Newtonian poem *Philosophia recentior* (1792), it forms a vindication of Neo-Latin didactic poetry which both grows out of the Roman microtradition and marks its end.[16] In the dialogue, one of the speakers argues that God is the protagonist of nature and, consequently, of scientific didactic poetry:[17]

> Cum hanc rerum molitionem ac naturae ordinem numeris et carminis vi patefactum intuebimur, non in animum irruet et sensus omnes occupabit actio varia, multiplex, infinita, una eademque simplex, integra, absoluta, rationis ac sapientiae plenissima? Quis auctorem ac moderatorem carminis non subito agnoscet, nec rerum aeque et carminis πρωταγωνίστην Deum esse perspiciet, varias corporibus vires potestatesque adiungentem atque his tamquam ministris hanc rerum summam stabilientem ac servantem?

> When we see the system of the universe and the order of nature spelt out in metre and with the power of poetry, will not this varied performance, manifold, infinite, constant, simple, perfect, flawless, full of reason and wisdom, immediately take our minds and occupy all our senses? Who

---

14   All line numbers and quotes in this paper are given according to this edition.

15   In these miniature scenes, God is portrayed as the God of *Genesis*, creating light, initiating science and letting the rainbow appear as a symbol of peace after the Flood; there is no explicit reference to Christ.

16   For the context and meaning of Stay's dialogue, see Claudia Schindler, "Didactic poetry as Elitist Poetry. Christopher Stay's De poesi didascalica dialogus in the Context of Classical and Neo-Latin Didactic Discourse," in *Neo-Latin and the Vernaculars. Bilingual Interactions in the Early Modern Period*, ed. Alexander Winkler and Florian Schaffenrath (Leiden, 2019), 232–50.

17   Christoph Stay, "De poesi didascalica dialogus," in Benedikt Stay, *Philosophia recentior*, tom. 3 (Rome, 1792), XXVIII [I corrected "servientem" to "servantem"]. All Latin texts in this paper are normalised orthographically, and all translations are my own.

will not immediately recognise the initiator and director of the poem and will not understand that the protagonist of both nature and the poem is God, who distributes different forces and powers to the bodies and uses them as his servants in order to stabilise the universe and keep it safe?

Especially in the Newtonian poems of the Roman microtradition, such a sentiment might be informed in part also by Newton and Newtonian works.[18] Newton himself had addressed the relationship between God and nature in the later editions of the *Principia* and in the *Opticks*,[19] and in another, earlier paratext by Christoph Stay to the first volume of the *Philosophia recentior* (1755), Newton was presented as a prime example of the close connection between the study of nature, knowledge about God and piety:[20]

Qua quidem in re illud nobis praecipue propositum debet esse, ut ex hac magnificentia ac pulcherrimarum rerum cognitione facile intelligamus tanti operis effectorem ac moderatorem Deum. Nam bene ac sapienter est a Bacone de Verulamio traditum eum, qui minime hunc rerum ordinem intelligeret, ignorare fortasse posse rectorem ac mundi gubernatorem Deum esse; qui vero in rerum contemplatione omnino esset versatus, qui hunc ornatum praeclare nosceret, qui tantam in rebus omnibus convenientiam consensionemque videret, eum praeesse mundo Dominum dubitare non posse. Atque hinc quidem accepimus Newtonum, qui unus omnium naturae opificium eximie ac singulariter pervidisset, tantam animo imbibisse summi artificis speciem, ut commoveri se illius praesenti numine eumque colere ac vereri palam prae se ferret: felicior quidem futurus, si, ut vim religionis, ita etiam illius castitatem intellexisset. Hoc quidem certum exploratumque est naturae contemplationem religionis, pietatisque magistram ac ducem semper fuisse habitam.

---

18 Natural theology was an integral part of the reception of Newtonian physics. For the relationship between the Italian enlightenment and Newton's natural theology, see Vincenzo Ferrone, *The Intellectual Roots of the Italian Enlightenment. Newtonian Science, Religion, and Politics in the Early Eighteenth Century*, transl. Sue Brotherton (Atlantic Highlands, New Jersey, 1995), 63–88.

19 Cf. Newton, *Optice* (see above, n. 10), 348 on science as a way to understand the human duty towards God and each other, and Isaac Newton's *Scholium generale* at the end of the *Philosophiae naturalis principia mathematica* (London, ^{2}1713), 481–4, esp. 483 for the definition of science relative to God.

20 Christoph Stay, "Ad Benedictum fratrem epistula," in Benedikt Stay, *Philosophia recentior*, tom. 1 (Rome, 1755), XIV–XXIX, there XXIX.

In this field, it must be our main purpose that, from the very grandeur and the examination of the most beautiful things, we easily recognise that God is responsible for such a great work and rules over it. For it was well and wisely said by Francis Bacon that those who do not perceive this order of things might not know that God is the ruler and governor of the world; but those who are entirely familiar with the contemplation of things, who know this beautiful cosmos intimately, who see such great harmony and coherence in all things, cannot doubt that the world is ruled by the lord. And so we know that Newton, who alone had fully grasped the work of nature in an excellent and singular way, had conceived in his heart so great an image of the highest creator, that he publicly showed himself to be excited by his presence and to revere and worship him. However, he would have been even happier, if he had recognised not only the power of religion, but also its pure form [i.e. Catholicism]. This, however, is certain and beyond doubt, that the study of nature was always seen as a teacher and guide in religion and piety.

While connecting (Newtonian) science to God is thus a typical feature of the Roman microtradition, it seems to be an especially prominent literary element in the *Iris*.[21] This might be perhaps explained by the fact that the rainbow was not only an intriguing natural phenomenon that puzzled scientists for a long time, but also, as Noceti emphasises towards the end of his poem, the biblical symbol for the covenant between God and humankind.

There are three instances where the biblical God features prominently in the poem, but the *Iris* as a whole is framed in a way that suggests that the laws of the rainbow originated with a person, not a principle. This is done in the proem, which is programmatically modelled on the proem of Vergil's *Georgics*,[22] but pointedly substitutes Vergil's impersonal "quid" and "quo sidere" with the personal "quis" and "quae dextera", thus evoking God as the creator of the rainbow who can be detected within the poem (1–5):

---

21   As there is no in-depth study of the literary phenomenon of God in (Jesuit) scientific didactic poetry so far, it is difficult to ascertain with certainty how the *Iris* relates to other scientific didactic poems within and beyond the Jesuit tradition.

22   Noceti's *Iris* was regarded as a Vergilian poem by contemporaries, cf. the *approbationes* to the 1747 edition and Giovanni Andres, *Dell'origine, progressi e stato attuale d'ogni letteratura*, vol. 2 (Parma, 1785), 198.

> Aërias quis pingat aquas, quae dextera in arcum
> flectat, et adverso cur non nisi sole coloret,
> quae demum ignotas certa experientia causas
> Iridis occultosque diu patefecerit ortus,
> hinc canere aggredior Sophiaeque recludere sedes.

> Who paints the waters in the sky, what right hand bends it into a bow, and why he colours it only when the sun is opposite, finally, which reliable experiment has revealed the unknown causes of the rainbow and its long-hidden origins: these things I will sing about and disclose the seats of Wisdom.

Therefore, when Noceti announces that he will illustrate the physics of the rainbow, he actually promises to explain *who* is responsible for the colours and the form of the rainbow. In regard to his topic, the rainbow, his decision may be inspired by the fact that in the bible, God personally lets the rainbow appear in the sky after the flood (*Gn* 9,13 "arcum meum ponam in nubibus"). The personal colouring of the opening questions connects Noceti's proem to the story of the flood told at the very end of the poem, but more importantly, it frames the didactic poem in such a way, that learning about the rainbow actually becomes a search for God by means of natural science. Through this subtle technique, Noceti generates at the very beginning of the poem the impression that there is a connection between nature and God and consequently between natural science and a better understanding of God. Moreover, this introduction lends special emphasis to passages where the biblical God is actually portrayed within the text.

The first appearance of God in the *Iris* closes the first third of the poem, in which our didactic poet had explained the fundamental principles of the rainbow, the refraction of light and, more importantly, Newton's colour spectrum. Some thirty verses before, Noceti had established the metaphor of threads for the seven colours of the rainbow, which are to become a leitmotif for the whole poem (103–6). This metaphor culminates in a grand image depicting God as the weaver of light, taking red, orange, yellow, green, blue, indigo and violet warp threads to produce a white cloth (144–54):[23]

---

23   This is the Newtonian division of the spectrum, cf. Newton, *Optice* (see above, n. 10), 127–8. Noceti had enumerated Newton's seven colours in a catalogue shortly before (111–31).

DIVINE ORIGIN OF NATURE AND NATURAL SCIENCE IN NOCETI'S *IRIS*   593

Non tamen haec rutilis non haec data foedera filis
magnorum sine mente deum, sine numine credas.
Ipse pater prima nascentis origine mundi
versicoloratam percurrens pectine telam
staminibus lucem variis ita texuit auctor,
quodlibet ut certa natum esset lege refringi,
scilicet atque oculos certa percellere forma.
Unde simul potuere seorsum inflectere cursum
et discreta aliis tela variante retexi,
continuo et leges et flexum servat eundem
quodque suum innatumque negat mutare colorem.

Do not believe that these laws are given to the bright strands without the
intention of the great gods,[24] without divine will: at the very beginning
of the world, which was just coming into existence, the father himself let
the comb run through the colourful fabric, and from warp threads of different colours, he wove together the light in such a way that each thread
was by its nature refracted by a certain law and penetrated the eyes in a
certain colour. Therefore, as soon as they were able to take different paths
and be separated from the colourful fabric, away from the others, each
thread preserves both the laws and the same angle and refuses to change
its own natural colour.

By using a vivid and intelligible metaphor taken from everyday life,[25] the poet
drives home the crucial point about Newton's theory of light: the colours do
not appear because the white light is somewhere, somehow altered during the
process of reflection and refraction: the colours are there from the very beginning. The image of a texture of light is ingeniously crafted to provide the reader
with a visualisation of how the different colours can coexist within white light.[26]
But there is more to this image than that, seeing that it is also a metaphor for
the creation of the laws of light by God, as Noceti himself emphasises in the

---

24 While it will become clear later in this passage that the Vergilian "ipse pater" refers to the
    biblical God, the introduction frames the scene with a classicising reference to the many
    ancient gods.
25 The metaphor may be inspired by the weaving competition in Ov., *met.* 6,63–7, where the
    seamlessly transitioning colours of the fabric are compared to those of the rainbow.
26 Cf. Korenjak, "Explaining Natural Science in Hexameter" (see above, n. 3), 156–7.

introduction to this passage (144–5). That the weaver (the Vergilian "ipse pater")[27] must be identified with the God of the bible becomes clear from the fact that he fabricates the light at the very beginning of the process of creation. It follows, then, that the poem confirms the Newtonian theory of light by picturing God as creating the light in a Newtonian way. God is, in a way, a Newtonian—or, to put it the other way around, what Newton found out about the colours within light, is actually a discovery about God's creation.

About one hundred and fifty verses later, the Vergilian "ipse pater" appears for a second time, when the poet, after laying out the Newtonian explanation for the colours of the rainbow, reflects on the late date of this discovery (317–9). This statement leads the poet to a reflection on natural science in general: here, he depicts science not only as a story of progress, but, crucially, as a divinely inspired endeavour. God made the laws of nature a secret not in order to hide them from humans, but in order to initiate the process of science (320–5):[28]

> Ipse pater primae permulta incognita genti
> abdidit atque aliis post invenienda reliquit,
> scilicet ut pulchri correpta cupidine veri
> altius et vitiis venientia saecla iocisque
> exsererent caput et studiorum exercita curis
> damnoso numquam torperent fracta veterno.

> The father himself hid many things unknown to the first people and left them for others to find later, so that future generations, moved by the desire for the beautiful truth, would lift their head over vices and trifles, and, through the careful exercise of study, would never stand still, broken by damaging lethargy.

In this picture, science is not only judged by its results, but at least equally by the moral effect it has on those who practise it: science is, in essence, a moral

---

27   In Verg., *Georg.* 1,353–5, which might be Noceti's model here, the "father himself" is, in a way, preoccupied with light as well, as he determines the course of moon and stars.

28   The template for this passage is, of course, the Vergilian "ipse pater" making agriculture difficult (Verg., *Georg.* 1,121–4), but the influence of Seneca's vision of progress (*nat.* 7,30,5–6) is evident, too. Scientific progress is celebrated in many Jesuit didactic poems, this passage from the *Iris* (together with a very similar account from Mazzolari's *Electrica*) is discussed by Haskell, *Loyola's Bees* (see above, n. 1), 240–4.

DIVINE ORIGIN OF NATURE AND NATURAL SCIENCE IN NOCETI'S *IRIS* 595

exercise, a continuous effort to be elevated above the world. Not only is the "labor improbus" of Vergil's *Georgics* (156–7) transformed into the good labour of science,[29] in stating that science lifts the spirits up above the vices and trifles of the world, Noceti also generalises Ovid's praise of astronomers (Ov., *fast.* 1,297–300) to encompass all of natural science. Therefore, it is not just the laws of nature that are devised by God: the process of discovering them is divinely ordained, too. To present science as godly work is a powerful preliminary to the praise of science that is about to unfold. In the light of this preface, the following catalogue of great achievements of science, alluding inter alia to the law of gravitation and the speed of light, is to be seen as a series of successful examples of fulfilling God's plan (326–44). When the catalogue culminates in an encouragement to the audience to join the scientific endeavour (345–50), this invitation becomes even more effective because it is framed by the statement that science is initiated by God himself and therefore is in itself a religious act.

Towards the end of the text, God appears for a third and last time, this time within the farewell hymn to Iris, the personified rainbow and subject of Noceti's scientific didactic poem: in a not altogether serious *correctio*, our Jesuit poet suddenly renounces mythical stories like the aetiological tale he himself invented for his poem (400–55).[30] Instead, he turns to the holy Iris of the bible. Consequently, for the standard narrative part of the hymn he chooses the biblical story of the flood, in which God installs the rainbow as a symbol of peace (512–23):

> Te rerum vera potestas
> caelicolum genitor summo ditavit honore,
> aeternumque dedit tibi ferre in saecula nomen:
> te siquidem, incestae pertaesus crimina terrae
> cum ruit immensum caelo sine nubibus imbrem
> conseruitque acrem nimbis toto aethere pugnam
> fervidus et pelago obduxit iuga summa sonante,
> paciferum iussit deferre per aëra foedus
> perpetuumque sui te fulgere pignus amoris.

---

29   Cf. ibid., 242–3.

30   On myths in Neo-Latin didactic poetry, see Heinz Hofmann, "Aristaeus und seine Nachfolger. Bemerkungen zur Rezeption des Aristaeus-Epyllions in der neulateinischen Lehrdichtung," *Humanistica Lovaniensia* 52 (2003), 343–98.

It was you, whom the true power over all things, the creator of the angels, presented with the highest honour. He gave you an ever-lasting name to bear in eternity. When he abhorred the crimes of the wicked earth and sent without any clouds boundless rain from the sky and let the rainstorms fight fiercely in the whole sky and, furious as he was, covered the highest mountains with the roaring sea, he ordered you to bring down through the air the peace-bringing covenant and to shine as an eternal token of his love.

While God can seemingly act against the laws of nature—he lets the rain pour down on the earth without there being clouds in the sky—, he is, as we have seen, also the creator of the laws of light, and, presumably, all other laws of nature. This could be intended to clarify the relationship between the omnipotent God and nature.[31] Although Noceti probably understands that the rainbow after the flood is not the first rainbow ever, but the first rainbow to signify peace,[32] this biblical myth serves to emphasise that the subject of the poem is a biblical, as well as a scientific one. Thus, one might infer that the scientific exploration of the rainbow is a worthwhile task, both from the perspective of theology and that of natural philosophy,[33] and that it is certainly worthy of a Jesuit scientific didactic poem.

To conclude, the poet of the *Iris* consciously evokes the God of *Genesis* at crucial points of the text to justify and promote a specific scientific discovery, and scientific activity (including scientific poetry) in general: in the proem, the didactic poem and the scientific question it encapsulates are framed as a search for God. By portraying God as the weaver of light, Noceti implicitly affirms and ennobles the Newtonian theory of light and colour. Not only is God the origin of nature, he is also the origin of science: scientists partake in a divinely initiated endeavour, aiming to uncover the laws of nature as God designed

---

31 Noceti might imagine here that the rain results from some sort of perforation of the boundaries between the sky and the waters above it. However, this idea is referenced, but rejected in several Jesuit commentaries, cf. Cornelius a Lapide, *Commentaria in Pentateuchum Mosis* (Antwerp, 1616), 80; Athanasius Kircher, *Arca Noe* (Amsterdam, 1675), 127–31; Alfonso Niccolai, *Dissertazioni e lezioni di sacra scrittura*, vol. 4 (Florence, 1760), 144–6.

32 Cf. a Lapide, *Commentaria* (see above, n. 31), 91; Kircher, *Arca Noe* (see above, n. 31), 177–8; Niccolai, *Dissertazioni* (see above, n. 31), 330–2.

33 A case in point are Johann Jakob Scheuchzer, *Physica sacra*, vol. 1 (Augsburg, 1731), 60–1 and Niccolai, *Dissertazioni* (see above, n. 30), 323–6, who both provide an account of the physics of the rainbow according to Newton in their commentaries on *Genesis* (in the latter case, this account is embellished with excerpts of Noceti's and Niccolai's scientific poetry).

them, thus ultimately trying to come closer to understanding the mind of God. The rainbow seems to be the perfect example for this vision of science, since it is a natural phenomenon that, after the flood, God himself made visible for humans to behold as a sign of peace, and, one might speculate, as a stimulus to wonder about its origins.[34]

University of Innsbruck

---

[34] I would like to thank Timothy King and Christopher Standley for reading and correcting my English, Martin Korenjak and my colleagues at the ERC project *NOSCEMUS—Early Modern Scientific Literature and Latin* for fruitful discussions and comments, and the anonymous reviewers for their helpful suggestions on this paper.

CHAPTER 47

Notas sobre la correspondencia manuscrita de Christoph Sand

Pablo Toribio

Abstract

This paper provides a corrected and updated inventory of Christoph Sand's (1644–80) epistolary, including letters by or to Johannes Becius, Henry Oldenburg, Constantijn Huygens Sr., Johann Georg Graevius and Pierre-Daniel Huet. It also contains the first edition of Sand's earliest preserved letter and points to previously unnoticed material related to his translation of the *Philosophical Transactions*. Sand is a relevant but neglected figure of the late seventeenth-century Republic of Letters. He was born in Königsberg, studied at the university of his native city and in Oxford, and then he established himself in Amsterdam as a proofreader and as independent writer of controversial books on theology and Church history.

Keywords

Christoph Sand – Neo-Latin epistolography – Anti-Trinitarianism – Socinianism – Radical Enlightenment

El presente[1] trabajo aporta nuevo material relativo a la correspondencia de Christoph Sand (1644–80)[2] y presenta un inventario corregido y ampliado de

---

1 El presente trabajo es parte de los realizados en el marco del proyecto *Edición y estudio de textos bíblicos y parabíblicos* (FFI2017–86726-P), financiado por AEI / FEDER (UE). Buena parte de la investigación resultante en el mismo la llevé a cabo como Scaliger Fellow en la Universidad de Leiden (verano de 2018), institución a la que agradezco su excelente acogida. Agradezco a Henk Nellen y Ad Leerintveld su amable ayuda en materia de paleografía neerlandesa, y a Stephen Snobelen su generosa colaboración para el estudio del material manuscrito de Sand en la Royal Society.

2 El trabajo más exhaustivo sobre Sand se debe a Lech Szczucki, "W kręgu spinozjańskim (Krzysztof Sandius junior)," *Przegląd filozoficzno-literacki* 3–4,18 (2007), 289–311 (actualización de Lech Szczucki, *Nonkonformiści religijni XVI i XVII wieku: Studia i szkice* [Warsaw, 1993], 105–31). Existe una traducción al húngaro: Lech Szczucki, "Ifj. Christophorus Sandius és Spinoza," in *Latinitas Polona. A latin nyelv szerepe és jelentősége a történelmi Lengyelország*

© KONINKLIJKE BRILL NV, LEIDEN, 2020 | DOI:10.1163/9789004427105_048

sus manuscritos. La mayor parte de las cartas conservadas han llegado hasta nosotros por haber acabado en los archivos de personajes ilustres a los que Sand escribió en calidad de traductor, editor o corrector de sus obras, o bien en búsqueda de mecenazgo. Casi todas ellas muestran a Sand en su papel de "corrector erudito", la categoría en que lo incluiría Zeltner,[3] y todas ellas giran en torno a libros, propios o ajenos.[4]

La primera carta: una conexión antitrinitaria (1668)

Presento a continuación el texto completo y anotado de la primera carta conservada de Sand, de acuerdo con el original en Ámsterdam, Universiteitsbibliotheek (OTM: hs. Bc 156):[5]

> A Monsieur Monsieur Jean Becius woonende in de Handbochsstraet, naest de Luytersche Kerck, bij een Boeckdrucker, tot Amsterdam.

> Doctissime Domine Beci.
> Ex apologia tua[6] [*in mg.*: (quam legi ex c<ommend>atione[7] Schwertneri)][8] satis cognovi et eruditionem tuam, et animum vere Christianum:

---

kora újkori irodalmában, ed. Enikő Békés and Rita Szilágyi Emőke (Budapest, 2014), 213–34. Véase también: Lech Szczucki, "Sandius (Sand) Jr., Christophorus," en *Biografisch Lexicon voor de geschiedenis van het nederlandse Protestantisme*, ed. J. van den Berg y otros (Kampen, 1998), vol. 4, 379–82. Se encuentran frecuentes menciones a él en la obra colectiva *Socinianism and Arminianism: Antitrinitarians, Calvinists and Cultural Exchange in Seveenteenth-Century Europe*, ed. Martin Mulsow and Jan Rohls (Leiden, 2005). Véase además mi anterior contribución: Pablo Toribio Pérez, "El *Nucleus historiae ecclesiasticae* de Christoph Sand y los escritos en latín de Isaac Newton sobre historia de la Iglesia," en *Acta Conventus Neo-Latini Monasteriensis*, ed. Astrid Steiner-Weber and Karl. A. E. Enenkel (Leiden, 2015), 553–62.

3 Johann Conrad Zeltner, *Correctorum in typographiis eruditorum centuria speciminis loco collecta* (Norimbergae, 1716), 482–6.

4 También es así en el caso de las cartas cambiadas con Samuel Gardiner (*ca.* 1619–86), conocidas solo en su versión impresa, y que por ello no incluyo aquí: véase Dmitri Levitin, *Ancient Wisdom in the Age of the New Science* (Cambridge, 2015), 504–5.

5 La única mención a ella que me ha sido posible encontrar se debe a Ruud C. Lambour, "De familie en vrienden van Daniel Zwicker (1612–1678) in Amsterdam", *Doopsgezinde Bijdragen* 25 (1999), 113–66, en 149–50.

6 Joannes Becius, *Apologia modesta et christiana I. B. M. Z. Dat is, Sedige en Christelijcke Verantwoordinge van Joannes Becius, Middelburger in Zeeland* (Eleutheropoli [=¿Ámsterdam?], 1668); cf. Philip Knijff and Sibbe Jan Visser, *Bibliographia Sociniana: A Bibliographical Reference Tool for the Study of Dutch Socinianism and Antitrinitarianism* (Hilversum, 2004), 111, no. 3001.

7 El papel está rasgado y no permite leer lo que restituyo entre corchetes triangulares.

8 Probablemente su coetáneo Georgius Schwertner (1643–1708), proveniente de Danzig y emigrado a Ámsterdam como él: Lambour, "De familie en vrienden van Zwicker" (véase arriba, n. 5), 161–2.

600   TORIBIO

praeprimis autem admiror, quod per divinam gratiam et illuminationem ad ipsam fidem pervenire merueris, ad quam multis praejudicio occupatis pervenire non licet. Sicut autem fateor apologiam illam optime elaboratam, ita quaedam etiam sunt in illa, quae ego unde probari possint, non scio. Caeterum quia humanitas tua a multis est laudata (propter quam etiam optavi saepius in numerum amicorum tuorum recipi), ista recensebo dubia, quae ut a te mihi eximantur, obnixe rogo.

Primum illorum est, quod scribis Lutherum, Bullingerum, Naogeorgum, et alios Reformatores locum 1. Joh. V. 7 pro parte scripturae non agnoscere.[9] De Luthero quidem constat illum locum dictum in versione sua non transtulisse. At quod alicubi scripserit expresse locum hunc non esse genuinum, de eo mihi non constat. Bugenhagius est ille, qui verbis dissertis *in Jonam* fuse probat locum hunc ab impiis Scripturae esse insertum.[10] Bullingerus et Naogeorgus ubi idem scribant, fateor me ignorare, imo nequidem de Naogeorgo usquam audivisse, adeoque me nescire utrum fuerit Reformatus vel Lutheranus.

Secundum est, quod scribis magnam partem Arianorum docuisse Christum non esse adorandum. Confiteor equidem Socinum in fine Anti-Wujeki sententiam illam Arianis omnibus attribuere,[11] at unde istud probari possit non video. Certe ego ex scriptis Arianorum, veluti ex Eusebio Caesar<iensi>, Origene, fonte (ut fertur) Arii, aliisque Patribus primitivae Ecclesiae, qui judice Petavio,[12] idem cum Ario docuerunt, probare ~~sust~~ possum, ipsos omnino Christum adorasse, et adorare praecepisse. Quinetiam Ariani crediderunt Christum fuisse unum ex tribus, quem Abraham adoravit.[13] At quis unquam Arianorum Abrahamum ob id reprehenderit? Nullus, quod sciam. Interea tamen laudo tuam modestiam,

---

9   Becius, *Apologia* (véase arriba, n. 6), 37: "1 Joan. 5. 7 [...] (waerom oock Lutherus, Bullingerus, Naogeorgus, en andere van d'eerste Reformateurs dat vers voor een gedeelte van Gods woort niet en erkennen)"; cf. Christoph Sand, *Interpretationes paradoxae quatuor evangeliorum, quibus affixa est Dissertatio de Verbo, una cum appendice* (Cosmopoli [= Ámsterdam], 1669), 384–5, y Grantley McDonald, *Biblical Criticism in Early Modern Europe: Erasmus, the Johannine Comma and Trinitarian Debate* (Cambridge, 2016), 111.

10   Véase McDonald, *Biblical criticism* (véase arriba, n. 9), 64–8.

11   Cf. Fausto Sozzini, "Responsio ad libellum Wuieki," en *Fausti Socini Senensis operum tomus alter, continens scripta polemica* (Irenopoli [=Ámsterdam], post annum Domini 1656), 529–624, en 619b. La *editio princeps* latina se había impreso en 1595: Kęstutis Daugirdas, *Die Anfänge des Sozinianismus* (Göttingen, 2016), 184.

12   Dionysius Petavius, *Theologicorum dogmatum tomus secundus, in quo de sanctissima Trinitate agitur* (Lutetiae Parisiorum, 1644).

13   *Genesis* 18,2.

NOTAS SOBRE LA CORRESPONDENCIA MANUSCRITA DE CHRISTOPH SAND   601

quod illud magnae parti Arianorum adscribas, quod Socinus omnibus attribuit.

Hisce dubiis si satisfacere volueris, gratissimum fuerit mihi, omnibus-~~que~~ studiis \ad/ favorem illum compensandum promptissimo,

T<ibi> observantiss<imo> Christoph<oro> Sandio.

Amsterdam, in de nieuwe sides armstege in de Harlinger kercke.[14]

El destinatario es el predicador Johannes Becius (*ca.* 1623–90), natural de Middelburg.[15] La carta no está fechada, pero puede afirmarse con seguridad que fue escrita entre 1668 y 1669 por los siguientes motivos: Sand se refiere a la *Apologia modesta et christiana* (1668) de Becius; en esta obra, Becius había escrito que Lutero, Bullinger y Naogeorgus habían negado la autenticidad del *comma Johanneum*: sobre esta información Sand expresa dudas y pide más detalles, afirmando incluso desconocer quién es Naogeorgus; en cambio, incluye sin reservas esa misma información en sus *Interpretationes paradoxae* (1669). Esto implica que la carta ha de anteceder a la publicación de las *Interpretationes*, y muy probablemente implica también que Becius respondió al prusiano y disipó sus dudas. Además, cuando Becius se unió a la comunidad remonstrante en agosto de 1669, dio una dirección amstelodamense distinta a la utilizada por Sand en su carta, y ello podría indicar una mudanza anterior a esa fecha, como sugiere Lambour.[16]

Dada la probabilidad de que el Schwertner mencionado en la carta sea el identificado por Lambour,[17] este documento muestra a Sand vinculado a la comunidad remonstrante de Ámsterdam al poco de su llegada a la ciudad, que se produjo en una fecha por determinar después de que su padre fuera destituido en Königsberg en 1668 por 'arrianismo'. Los pormenores patrísticos a los que alude Sand al respecto de las creencias de los arrianos están en sintonía con la argumentación que despliega en el *Nucleus historiae ecclesiasticae* (Ámsterdam, 1668–69), cuyo primer libro se publicó el mismo año que la

---

14   La "iglesia de Harlingen" era una pensión: véase Isabella H. van Eeghen, "De 'uitgever' Henricus Cunrath of Künraht van de polygamist Lyserus en van de philosoof Spinoza," *Amstelodamum: Maandblad voor de kennis van Amsterdam* 50 (1963), 73–80, y Lambour, "De familie en vrienden van Zwicker" (véase arriba, n. 5), 149–50. Esta carta permite situar dicha pensión en el actual Nieuwezijds Armsteeg, cerca del puerto de Ámsterdam. Llegué a esta noticia bibliográfica gracias al profesor Henk Nellen, quien además se prestó generosamente a revisar mi transcripción tanto de esta línea como de los datos del destinatario al comienzo.

15   Véase S. B. J. Zilverberg, "Becius, Joannes," en *Biografisch Lexicon voor de geschiedenis van het nederlandse Protestantisme*, vol. 4, ed. Doede Nauta (Kampen, 1998), 26–8.

16   Lambour, "De familie en vrienden van Zwicker" (véase arriba, n. 5), 149–50.

17   Véase arriba, n. 8.

602   TORIBIO

Apologia de Becius. Que Sand no haga ninguna mención a su *Nucleus* en esta carta de presentación invita a pensar que la escribió antes de publicarse este, por tanto todavía en 1668. Por lo demás, esta es la única carta privada conservada en la que nuestro autor se muestra expresamente favorable a una forma de cristianismo que rechaza el dogma de la Trinidad (las autoridades describieron la *Apologia* de Becius como "un escrito blasfemo, condenable, corruptor de almas"[18]) y considera además este cristinianismo antitrinitario como una fe a la que se llega "por medio de la gracia y la iluminación divinas", a la que "a muchos no les es posible llegar por estar cargados de prejuicios".

La correspondencia con Oldenburg (1673–74)

Las únicas cartas de Sand disponibles en una edición moderna[19] son las que intercambió con Henry Oldenburg (*ca.* 1619–77), el sajón que llegó a ser secretario de la Real Sociedad de Londres y estableció la que se considera la primera revista científica, *Philosophical Transactions* (publicada desde 1665 hasta la actualidad). Sand escribió sus cartas a Oldenburg mientras ocupaba el cargo de secretario del residente (diplomático) inglés en Hamburgo, Sir William Swan.[20]

La anotación crítica de Hall y Hall no agota las posibilidades de estudio de esta correspondencia, particularmente interesante para los neolatinistas, pues versa sobre la traducción al latín, a cargo de Sand, de los primeros números de *Philosophical Transactions*.[21] Aquí mencionaré uno solo de esos aspectos desatendidos: la identificación del prefacio escrito por Sand para el primer volumen de la traducción. Sand menciona este prefacio en su segunda carta a Oldenburg (28 de febrero de 1673); en una posterior (31 de marzo de 1673) afirma que se lo ha enviado y supone que Oldenburg ya ha debido de recibirlo, y en su última carta lamenta que dicho prefacio ha sido "castrado" por los editores (21 de septiembre de 1674).[22]

El silencio de los editores modernos al respecto se debe probablemente a que no encontraron ningún ejemplar de la primera edición (1672) del primer volumen de la traducción de Sand, que en efecto ha llegado a muchas menos

---

18   Zilverberg, "Becius" (véase arriba, n. 15), 27.
19   *The Correspondence of Henry Oldenburg, Volume IX: 1672–1673*, ed. A. Rupert Hall and Marie Boas Hall (Madison, 1973); *Volume X: June 1673 – April 1674* (London, 1975); *Volume XI: May 1674 – September 1675* (London, 1977).
20   Véase *The Correspondence of Oldenburg*, ed. Hall, (véase arriba, n. 19), vol. 9, 426.
21   Para más detalles sobre esta empresa y sobre lo que sigue remito a mi trabajo "The Latin Translation of *Philosophical Transactions* (1671–1681)," de próxima publicación.
22   *The Correspondence of Oldenburg*, ed. Hall (véase arriba, n. 19), vo. 9, 513 y 546; vol. 11, 85.

NOTAS SOBRE LA CORRESPONDENCIA MANUSCRITA DE CHRISTOPH SAND 603

bibliotecas que la edición censurada de 1674.[23] Si se comparan los prefacios de ambas es fácil detectar el "corte en el medio" del que se quejó Sand. Donde en la segunda edición se lee: "[...] autoritas hominis fallibilis. Adeo multi laudant" (Sand, *Acta philosophica anni M. DC. LXV* (1674), *5v), se leía en la original:

> [...] autoritas hominis fallibilis. Non alia certe ratione legimus olim Vigilium libris suis contra Sabellium, Arium, Photinum, praefixisse nomina Athanasii, Idacii, Ambrosii, Augustini. Quare ni uterque dolum confessus fuisset, sciri non poterat, quid Clerselirii, quid vero Cartesii? [*4r] quid Vigilii, quid Athanasii esset?[24] Nec tamen satis constat, quid Idacii, Ambrosii, Augustini, quid Vigilii sit. Adeo multi laudant [...] (Sand, *Acta philosophica anni M. DC. LXV* [1672], *3v–*4r)

Del mismo modo, donde en la segunda edición se lee: "[...] nemo non videt. Caeterum ego considerans [...]" (Sand, *Acta philosophica anni M. DC. LXV* (1674), [*6v]), la primera edición presentaba el texto siguiente :

> [...] nemo non videt. His quoque rebus tanto major est certitudo, quanto certius sensus demonstrant, quam ipsa Ratio. Absit autem ut omnem Rationis usum homini adimam: habeat sane locum in rebus divinis, et iis quas sensibus nostris subjicere non possumus. Nam sicut sensus homini dati sunt a natura ad perceptionem rerum sensibilium, ita Mens seu Lumen rationis concessum est a Deo cujus adminiculo intelligamus Entia aeterna. Initio autem facto a sensibilibus et specialibus progredien- [*5r] dum est ad divina et universalia, non praepostere incognitis illis in universalibus totum vitae curriculum inutiliter terendum. Per gradus proficit genus humanum. Quare sicut Physici sensibus posthabitis; ita Theologi ratione posthabita in absurditates infinitas prolapsi sunt: dum traditionum suarum veritatem non ratione, sed traditionibus rationem metiri

---

23   *Acta philosophica Societatis Regiae in Anglia, anni M. DC. LXV, auctore Henrico Oldenburgio, Soc. Reg. Secr. anglice conscripta, et in Latinum versa interprete C. S.* (Amstelodami, 1674). Con idéntico título existe una primera edición de 1672, debida a los mismos editores (Hendrik y Dirk Boom), de la que solo he podido localizar ejemplares en la Biblioteca Histórica de la Universidad de Valencia, en la Biblioteca Nacional de Francia y en la Biblioteca de la Royal Society en Londres.

24   Se trata, respectivamente, de Vigilio de Tapso (siglo v), que escribió un diálogo *Contra Arrianos*: ed. J.-P. Migne, *Patrologia Latina* 62 (París, 1848), 155–238; edición reciente de P.-M. Hombert, *Corpus Christianorum Series Latina* 90B (Turnhout, 2017), en el que introducía a Atanasio de Alejandría (m. 373) como defensor de la postura ortodoxa (*cf. PL* 62, 180C), y de Claude Clerselier (1614–84), editor y promotor de René Descartes (1596–1650).

604 TORIBIO

conantur, contradictoria plane scribunt, eoque devenere quidam dementiae, ut non erubuerint asserere: primum etiam Principium, *Impossibile est idem simul esse et non esse*,[25] in divinis locum non habere. Adeo illis non est Catholicus, nisi qui hominem dedicit: non Christianus, nisi qui animal rationale esse desiit: non Theologus, nisi qui mentem exuit. Ingenue itaque fatetur Jesuita Der-Kennis, *Doctores in rebus divinis plurimum adhibere arbitrariae locutionis, imo* [*5v] *saepissime ita loqui, ut se ipsos non intelligant*.[26] Utinam observantes illud, quod ipsi urgere solent, *Scrutator Majestatis, opprimitur a gloria*,[27] desinerent scrutari et definire modum generationis seu filiationis in divinis, quandoquidem facilius est dicere qualis non sit, quam qualis sit, secundum scripturam dicentem: *Generationem ejus quis enarrabit*:[28] Desinerent quoque suis loquendi modis definire Unitatem Trinitatis, et verbis scripturae insisterent, nec altius saperent, quam Spiritus S<anctus> nos sapere voluit. Quarum rerum principiis sublatis, omnes quaestiones illae spinosae frustra erunt, et cum Scholasticorum operibus vastis simul corruent, nullaeque erunt difficultates, quae tales apparebant, neque necesse erit vel in Papae, vel Lutheri, vel Calvini verba jurare. Sed diutius his immorari, mei non est insituti. / [*6r] Caeterum ego considerans [...] (Sand, *Acta philosophica anni M. DC. LXV* [1672], *4v–[*6r])

La postura antitrinitaria de Sand en este pasaje se funda en dos argumentos: que el dogma de la Trinidad contraviene los principios de la razón y que si los teólogos se atuviesen a la razón se haría posible el entendimiento entre los cristianos. Este irenicismo antitrinitario se asemeja mucho al postulado en el *Irenicum irenicorum* (Ámsterdam, 1658) por Daniel Zwicker (1612–78), otro prusiano emigrado a los Países Bajos, con quien Sand estuvo relacionado.[29]

---

25   Aristóteles, *Metafísica* 4,3,1005b19–20.

26   Sand usa la cita con idéntica formulación en la segunda edición de su *Nucleus historiae ecclesiasticae* (Coloniae [= Ámsterdam], 1676), 83. El pasaje más cercano que encuentro en la obra de Ignatius Der Kennis (1589–1656) se refiere al habla de los ángeles, en su obra *De Deo uno, trino, creatore* (Bruxellis, 1655), 459: "Hanc rem satis expeditam supposita mentalis locutionis natura difficilem et implexam faciunt sententiae variae et obscuri modi loquendi Auctorum, quos nec satis illi explicant, nec quid velint promptum est assequi."

27   *Proverbios* 25,27.

28   *Isaías*, 53,8; *Hechos*, 8,33.

29   Véase Peter G. Bietenholz, *Daniel Zwicker (1612–1678): Peace, Tolerance and God the One and Only* (Firenze, 1997), 48–9.

Un mecenas improbable: la carta a Huygens Sr. (1675)

En algún momento entre el otoño de 1674 y el del año siguiente, Sand abandonó Hamburgo y se instaló de nuevo en Ámsterdam, desde donde buscó el patronazgo del anciano Constantijn Huygens Sr. (1596–1687), secretario del Príncipe de Orange en La Haya. La carta está fechada el 31 de octubre de 1675 y escrita en neerlandés; a diferencia de todas las demás, no es de puño y letra de Sand, quien probablemente solo puso su firma.[30] A través de la web del *Instituto Huygens* es posible visualizar imágenes del original; la edición de Worp de la correspondencia de Huygens no contiene una transcripción completa, sino solo una paráfrasis.[31]

Con esta carta, de contenido breve y cortés, Sand se atrevió a enviarle al señor de Zulichem un ejemplar de la segunda edición de su *Nucleus historiae ecclesiasticae* (1676), y le pedía que, si no tenía tiempo para leerlo entero, leyese al menos el prólogo de su padre. En él Huygens habría encontrado un claro manifiesto antitrinitario, que difícilmente podría haberlo movido por sí mismo a emprender el patronazgo del joven prusiano. El libro terminó muy probablemente en la biblioteca de su hijo, Constantijn Huygens Jr. (1628–97), pues el título figura en el catálogo de la subasta de esta.[32]

La correspondencia con Huet y Graevius (1677–80)

Sand entabló contacto con Pierre-Daniel Huet (1630–1721) a través de Johann Georg Graevius (1632–1703) a propósito de la edición de Orígenes de aquel (1668). El grueso de la correspondencia se ocupa de la *Demonstratio evangelica* (1679) del francés, obra cuya edición holandesa (1680) Sand estuvo encargado de revisar. Pese a no disponerse de edición, esta correspondencia es la que ha recibido relativamente mayor atención en la literatura académica,[33] en buena

---

30 Debo esta apreciación al juicio experto del doctor Ad Leerintveld, facilitado en comunicación privada.

31 resources.huygens.knaw.nl/briefwisselingconstantijnhuygens (acceso: 21/11/18). Véase Jacob A. Worp, *De briefwisseling van Constantijn Huygens (1608–1687). Zesde deel: 1663–1687* ('s-Gravenhage, 1917), 368, número 6993. Debo la transcripción del texto completo a la generosa disponibilidad del profesor Nellen.

32 *Bibliotheca Zuylichemiana* (Leiden, 1701), 94. Véase Ad Leerintveld, "Constantijn Huygens's Library," en *Crossing Boundaries and Transforming Identities: New Perspectives in Netherlandic Studies*, ed. Margriet Bruijn Lacy and Christine P. Sellin (Münster, 2011), 11–8.

33 Elena Rapetti, *Pierre-Daniel Huet: erudizione, filosofia, apologetica* (Milano, 1999), 16 y 70; Szczucki, "Krzysztof Sandius" (véase arriba, n. 2), 300–11; April Shelford, *Transforming the Republic of Letters: Pierre-Daniel Huet and European Intellectual Life, 1650–1720* (Rochester,

medida porque contiene los juicios enfrentados de Huet y Sand sobre Baruch Spinoza (1632–77). Sin embargo, está aún pendiente de llevarse a cabo un estudio detenido, además de una edición. La consignación de los manuscritos en el anexo que se encontrará a continuación presenta una mejora notable con respecto a las descripciones previas disponibles.

Instituto de Lenguas y Culturas del Mediterráneo y Oriente Próximo (ILC, Madrid), Consejo Superior de Investigaciones Científicas (CSIC)

Anexo: inventario de la correspondencia manuscrita conservada

1668

1. Sand a Johannes Becius (Ámsterdam, sin fecha):
   Ámsterdam, Universiteitsbibliotheek (UBA), OTM: hs. Bc 156

1673

2. Sand a Henry Oldenburg (Hamburgo, 24 de enero de 1673) [CO 2135]:[34]
   Londres, Royal Society (RS), MS. S 1, no. 128
3. Sand a Oldenburg (Hamburgo, 28 de febrero de 1673) [CO 2171]:
   Londres, RS, MS. S 1, no. 122
4. Sand a Oldenburg (Hamburgo, 31 de marzo de 1673) [CO 2191]:
   Londres, RS, MS. S 1, no. 126
5. Sand a Oldenburg (Hamburgo, 10 de noviembre de 1673) [CO 2383]:
   Londres, RS, MS. S 1, no. 126
6. Sand a Oldenburg (Hamburgo, 15 de diciembre de 1673) [CO 2407]:
   Londres, RS, MS. S 1, no. 127

1674

7. Oldenburg a Sand (Londres, 11 de febrero de 1674) [CO 2429]:
   Londres, RS, MS. O 2, no. 141
8. Sand a Oldenburg (Hamburgo, 27 de febrero de 1674) [CO 2449]:
   Londres, RS, MS. S 1, no. 129

2007), 156–7; eadem, "The Quest for Certainty in Fact and Faith: Pierre-Daniel Huet and Josephus' *Testimonium Flavianum*," en *Essays in Renaissance Thought and Letters in Honor of John Monfasani*, ed. Alison Frazier and Patrick Nold (Leiden, 2015), 216–40; Ian Leask, "Speaking for Spinoza? Notes on John Toland's *Origines Judaicae*", en *Reassessing the Radical Enlightenment*, ed. Steffen Ducheyne (London, 2017), 143–59, en 151.

34 Ofrezco entre corchetes la numeración usada en *The Correspondence of Oldenburg*, ed. Hall (véase arriba, n. 19), IX, X y XI.

9. Oldenburg a Sand (Londres, 20 de marzo de 1674) [CO 2461]:
    Londres, RS, MS. S 1, no. 129a
10. Sand a Oldenburg (Hamburgo, 21 de septiembre de 1674) [CO 2543]:
    Londres, RS, MS. S 1, no. 130
11. Oldenburg a Sand (Londres, 26 de octubre de 1674) [CO 2653]:
    Leiden, Universiteitsbibliotheek (UBL), PAP 15

1675

12. Sand a Constantijn Huygens Sr. (Ámsterdam, 31 de octubre de 1675):[35]
    Ámsterdam, UBA, OTM: hs. 29 Aw

1677

13. Pierre-Daniel Huet a Sand (Versalles, 8 de junio [VI. Eid. Jun.] de 1677):[36]
    Florencia, Biblioteca Medicea Laurenziana (BML), Ashburnham (Ashb.) 1866,
    2949 (primer borrador)
    Florencia, BML, Ashb. 1866, 2640 (segundo borrador)
    París, Bibliothèque nationale de France (BnF), Latin 11432, fols. 202–8 (copia de
    Huet)
    Leiden, UBL, BUR F 8 (copia de Sand)
    Leiden, UBL, BUR Q 22: 2, fols. 216–8 (copia de Pieter Burman [1668–1741])
14. Sand a Johann Georg Graevius (Ámsterdam, 25 de agosto [VIII. Cal. Sept.] de
    1677):
    Leiden, UBL, BUR F 8.

1679

15. Huet a Sand (París, 17 de abril [XV. Cal. Maias] de 1679):[37]
    Florencia, BML, Ashb. 1866, 2957 (primer borrador)
    Florencia, BML, Ashb. 1866, 2631 (segundo borrador)
    París, BnF, Latin 11432, fols. 227–18 (*sic*; copia del autor)
    Leiden, UBL, BUR Q 22: 2, fol. 218 (copia de Burman)
16. Sand a Huet (Ámsterdam, 13 de junio [Id. Jun.] de 1679):[38]
    Florencia, BML, Ashb. 1866, 2164

---

35 Número 6993 de Worp, *De briefwisseling van Huygens* (véase arriba, n. 31).
36 Falta en Léon-Gabriel Pélissier, "Inventaire sommaire des papiers de Pierre-Daniel Huet
    à la Bibliothèque Laurentienne de Florence," *Revue des bibliothèques* 9 (1899), 1–20.
    Szczucki ("Krzysztof Sandius," 301, n. 40 (=Szczucki, "Christophorus Sandius," 224, n. 41,
    véase arriba, n. 2) la refiere como del 8 junio – 30 agosto.
37 Szczucki la refiere como del 5 de mayo.
38 Probablemente es la misma que Pélissier, "Inventaire" (véase arriba, n. 36), 18, registra
    como "id. jan".

17. Sand a Huet (Ámsterdam, 3 de agosto [III. Non. Augusti] de 1679):
Florencia, BML, Ashb. 1866, 2165

18. Huet a Sand (París, 19 de junio [XIII Cal. Sext.] de 1679):[39]
Florencia, BML, Ashb. 1866, 2869 (primer borrador)
Florencia, BML, Ashb. 1866, 2628 (segundo borrador)
París, BnF, Latin 11432, fols. 232–3 (copia del autor)
Leiden, UBL, BUR Q 22: 2, fol. 219 (copia de Burman)

19. Sand a Huet (Ámsterdam, 31 de agosto [Prid. Cal. Sept.] de 1679):
Florencia, BML, Ashb. 1866, 2166

20. Huet a Sand (París, 16 de septiembre [XVI. Cal. Oct.] de 1679):[40]
Florencia, BML, Ashb. 1866, 2875 (primer borrador)
Florencia, BML, Ashb. 1866, 2476 (segundo borrador)
París, BnF, Latin 11432, fols. 247–253 (copia del autor)
Leiden, UBL, BUR Q 22: 2, fols. 219v–222r (copia de Burman)

21. Sand a Huet (Ámsterdam, 27 de septiembre [ad v Cal. Octobr.] de 1679):[41]
Florencia, BML, Ashb. 1866, 2167

22. Huet a Sand (París, 13 de octubre [III. Eid. Oct.] de 1679):[42]
Florencia, BML, Asbh. 1866, 2876 (primer borrador)
Florencia, BML, Ashb. 1866, 2477 (segundo borrador)
Leiden, UBL, BUR Q 22: 2, fols. 229v–234r (copia de Burman)

23. Sand a Huet (Ámsterdam, 13 de noviembre [Id. Nov.] de 1679):[43]
Florencia, BML, Ashb. 1866, 2168

1680

24. Huet a Sand (Saint-Germain-en-Laye, 11 de enero [III Eid. Jan.] de 1680):[44]
Florencia, BML, Ashb. 1866, 2787 (primer borrador)
Florencia, BML, Ashb. 1866, 2614 (segundo borrador)
París, BnF, Latin 11432, fols. 260–266 (copia del autor)
Leiden, UBL, BUR Q 22: 2, fols. 222–224 (copia de Burman)

---

39 Falta en Pélissier. Szczucki la refiere como del 20 de julio. Quizás es la misma que la que Pélissier, "Inventaire" (véase arriba, n. 36), 5, refiere como del 8 de junio (*6 eid. jun.*).

40 Falta en Pélissier.

41 Szczucki la refiere como del 28 de septiembre.

42 En el segundo borrador Huet ha omitido accidentalmente el trazo I de la cifra MDCLXXIX; el año erróneo resultante (1680) se mantiene en la copia de Leiden, UBL, BUR Q 22: 2, que en consecuencia presenta esta carta como la última de la correspondencia. No se encuentra en la colección de París, BnF, Latin 11432. Falta en Pélissier; Szczucki la refiere con el año correcto.

43 Falta en Szczucki.

44 Muy probablemente es la que Pélissier, "Inventaire" (véase arriba, n. 36), 5, refiere como "4 eid. jan.".

NOTAS SOBRE LA CORRESPONDENCIA MANUSCRITA DE CHRISTOPH SAND   609

25. Sand a Huet (Ámsterdam, 24 de enero [IX. Cal. Februar.] de 1680):
     Florencia, BML, Ashb. 1866, 2169

26. Huet a Sand (Saint-Germain-en-Laye, 26 de marzo [Ad VII Cal. April.] de 1680):[45]
     Leiden, UBL, PAP 15 (original)
     Florencia, BML, Ashb. 1866, 2792 (primer borrador)
     Florencia, BML, Ashb. 1866, 2611 (segundo borrador)
     París, BnF, Latin 11432, fols. 275–277 (copia de Huet)
     Leiden, UBL, BUR Q 22: 2, fols. 224v–225r (copia de Burman)[46]

27. Sand a Huet (Ámsterdam, 9 de mayo [VII Id Maji] de 1680):
     Florencia, BML, Ashb. 1866, 2170

28. Huet a Sand (Aulnay, 24 de septiembre [VIII. Cal. Oct.] de 1680):
     Florencia, BML, Ashb. 1866, 2796 (primer borrador)
     Florencia, BML, Ashb. 1866, 2609 (segundo borrador)
     París, BnF, Latin 11432, fols. 298–307 (copia del autor)
     Leiden, UBL, BUR Q 22: 2, fols. 225v–229r (copia de Burman)

---

45 Impresa íntegramente por Johannes Brant, *Clarorum virorum epistolae centum inedi-
    tae de vario eruditionis genere, ex Museo Johannis Brant G. F. ad V. Cl. I. G. Graevium*
    (Amstelaedami, 1702), 277–9.

46 Además, Szczucki refiere otra copia en Leiden, UBL, BUR F 9, pero no se encuentra.

CHAPTER 48

Cum Apolline Christus: Personal Mottos of Humanists from the Czech Lands

Marta Vaculínová

Abstract

During the work on the *Companion to Central and East European Humanism*, attention was paid also to emblems (*insignia*) and devices (*symbola*) of humanists and their reflexion in occasional poetry. Currently, a systematic list of the initials and devices is being developed, which should be applicable also to identification of the book provenance (*supra libros* in the form of initials or handwritten *ex libris* as a *symbolum cephalonomaticum*). The objective of this paper is the analysis of the influence of profession, social status, confession, nationality, conferred honours, and values of the bearers and inventors of *symbola*. The most frequent sources of inspiration for *symbola* such as emblem books or *adagia* will also be identified. Besides preserved prints and modern inventories of book provenance, *alba amicorum* are also counted as a relevant source, in which the individual device is often associated with an emblem (similarly to printed *insignia* or printers' signets) and abbreviations in the form of initials occur in frequently used proverbs or sayings. Finally, different languages used in symbola will be discussed.

Keywords

Czech humanism – Neo-Latin emblems – adagia – symbola

Investigations into the *Companion to Central and East European Humanism*, carried out by our team over the last three years,[1] focus on the lives and works of men of letters in the Czech lands. After examining a significant amount of historical and literary sources, several questions arose in connection with this research, which are not to be included in the Lexicon, but nevertheless they

---

1 The project *Forms of Humanism in the Literature of the Bohemian Lands, 1469–1622* (GA ČR 16-09064S) is supported by the Czech Science Foundation.

PERSONAL MOTTOS OF HUMANISTS FROM THE CZECH LANDS 611

deserve to be discussed separately in the present paper. How did humanists present themselves directly? What did they use to express their personality and how did they sign their works? My answers to these questions are based on the material that were composed for the Lands of the Crown of Bohemia in the sixteenth century and the first quarter of the seventeenth century.

The most common forms of direct self-presentation comprise portraits (*effigies* or *icones*), emblems (*emblemata*), coats of arms and printer's marks (*insignia*) and personal mottos (*symbola*).[2] Each of these forms is represented by a particular type of occasional poem (*in effigiem, in emblema, in insignia* and *in symbolum*). Less well-represented in the collection are forms of self-presentation that involve the use of an image. Approximately 50 portraits,[3] some tens of *insignia* and a few personal emblems exist. By contrast, however, some 240 personal mottos have been collected. These so called *symbola* occur mainly in numerous poems which are generally entitled *in symbolum*, but they can be a part of the other forms which are mentioned above, too. Whereas *symbolum* in emblematics denotes the combination of a motto and an image,[4] these *symbola* solely consist of a personal motto, often accompanied by an explanatory poem. The prevalence of *symbola* does not necessarily signify that it was the favoured mode of self-presentation, simply that it was the cheapest one. While it was rather expensive to print a collection of emblems or portraits, the publication of collected poems on symbols was realisable even for humanists with more modest means at their disposal.

---

2 The mottos of humanists are usually mentioned in the abundant literature on printers' marks, *ex libris*, coats of arms, and *alba amicorum*. However, specialized literature about them is rare, see Walter Ludwig, "Klassische Mythologie in Druckersigneten und Dichterwappen," in *Renaissancekultur und antike Mythologie*, ed. Bodo Guthmüller and Wilhelm Kühlmann (Tübingen, 1999), 113–48; or Kristi Viiding on mottos of Livonian humanists in the seventeenth century: "Haritlaste tunnuslaused 17. sajandi Eesti- ja Liivimaal: allikad ja kasutusviis," in *Lugemise kunst* (*Acta Bibliothecae Nationalis Estoniae = Eesti Rahvusraamatukogu toimetised 13*), ed. Piret Lotman (Tallinn, 2011), 220–71. On the Czech *symbola* see the recently published work by Susann El Kholi, "Siegel und Wahlspruch des Böhmischen Dichters Leonhartus Albertus im poetischen Gewand seiner Epigrammata," *Listy filologické* 141 (2018), 221–40.

3 The oldest portrait from the Czech lands is that of Francysk Skaryna, a printer from Belarus, who incorporated the portrait into the edition of his Belarusian Bible, edited in Prague in 1517. It was somewhat of an exception, because the publication of portraits really started in Bohemia only in the second half of the sixteenth century.

4 In the Italian tradition the genre of *imprese*, cf. Ludwig, "Klassische Mythologie" (see above, n. 1), 123.

The oldest humanist personal mottos are documented in Italy in the middle of the fifteenth century[5] and they appear in Central Europe at the end of the *quattrocento*. One well known example is the motto *Concedo nulli* on the medal of Erasmus. In the Czech lands, too, one of the oldest examples of humanist mottos is on medals, as two silver portrait medals from the year 1526 show.[6] Generally, portrait medals were common in the circles of physicians, but we have no example of a medal of a poet (as, for example, Lodovico Ariosto in Italy 1555). The portraits of humanists, which often appear and are thus known from their printed works, show many similarities to those on portrait medals—besides the personal motto, they contain information about the age of the portrait's subject and the year when the image was created.

Evidence suggests that in the Czech lands, the oldest form of self-presentation to be combined with a motto is a printer's mark from 1518: this is *Spes mea ex alto* by Jan Mantuán Fencl, a printer in Pilsen in West Bohemia. This is an exceptional case for that time, because the use of a motto as a part of a printer's mark was only widely used from the second half of the sixteenth century, the most famous example that is known about being that of the humanist and printer Georgius Melantrich—*Nec igni cedit nec ferro*—from 1560, which is well known from emblem books. Since there were no printers' dynasties in Bohemia and Moravia, almost every printer's mark can be considered a personal motto.

Sometimes mottos were used as part of humanist coats of arms. From the 1540s, the number of humanists who were awarded noble titles increased in the Czech lands. Physicians, poets, teachers, printers and lawyers were decorated with their own coats of arms at the will of the emperor. Buoyed by their new status as noble burghers, they now imitated the mottos of nobility and created their own personal mottos. They often expressed their nobility with reference to the arts rather than the use of arms.[7] The motifs in the coats of arms of noble burghers were derived from the traditional symbols in the heraldry of nobility, such as a lily, star, lion, etc. Poets laureate, who had formed an exclusive group, bearing particular motifs on their coats of arms (a Pegasus, laurel wreath, swan, etc.) used to create their own unique mottos.[8]

---

5 Bernardo Bembo and his motto *Virtus et honor*, which was used on the revers of his portrait medal and as his *ex libris*, Ludwig, "Klassische Mythologie" (see above, n. 1), 122.

6 These are portraits of Wenceslaus Bayer, a personal physician of the noble family Schlick in North Bohemia. Both are held in the collection of the National Museum in Prague, Historical Museum, no. H5-150916 and 5068.

7 As, for example, *Arte, non Marte* by Henricus Clingerius, a Saxon poet living in Prague at the beginning of the sixteenth century.

8 Such as *Ingenio partum nescit obire decus* of Caspar Cropacius, or *Per levia ad gravia* of Paulus a Gisbice.

PERSONAL MOTTOS OF HUMANISTS FROM THE CZECH LANDS   613

Let us now examine the *symbola* which are not accompanied by images (later, also called *emblemata nuda*), which make up the largest part of our collected material. This genre can be traced back to the very beginning of the sixteenth century and is connected with two famous humanists—Erasmus and his collection of proverbs called *Adagia* (1500), and Lodovicus Vives and his *Satellitium animi* (1524). In the title of his *Satellitium*, Vives used the term *symbolum*,[9] which reminds us of the medieval tradition of *symbola Christiana*. The influence of these works by Erasmus and Vives in the Czech and Moravian humanist literature and culture in the period before the Battle of White Mountain was enormous.[10] There is probably also the influence of Martin Luther and his *symbola* translated by Vincentius Obsopoeus,[11] and numerous paraphrases of psalms by non-Catholic poets and theologians, such as Theodore Beza or George Buchanan.[12] This type of *symbola* is defined by Filippo Beroaldo the Elder in his commentary on the *symbola Pythagorea*:[13]

> quibus praecepta quaedam catholica, hoc est, universalia sunt involuta, ad vitam sancte beateque degendam valde congruentia.

The Christian content of the *symbola* from *Satellitium* and other mentioned moralising works might have met the needs of non-Catholic humanists more effectively than the popular genre of emblems related to alchemy and Cabala, which was made popular at the Prague court of Rudolf II by Nicolaus Reusner, Juan de Borja, or Jacobus Typotius.

---

9 Daniel Adam of Veleslavín edited the Latin text of *Satellitium* as a part of the book entitled *Ioannis Lodovici Vivis Valentini ad veram sapientiam introductio* (Pragae, 1586), cf. Knihopis českých a slovenských tisků [Czech and Slovak Early Printed Books published between years 1501–1800]: www.knihopis.cz, no. 16585, with a Czech translation by Václav Plácel. In the Latin preface, Veleslavín called *symbola* "sanctissima et utilissima praecepta ad vitam honeste, sancte, moderate et cum laude instituendam necessaria", fol. ( )(6a).

10 For some examples of re-editions and paraphrases on *Satellitium* in the Czech lands see Jan Martínek, "Drobné literární útvary za humanismu [Small Literary Genres in Humanism]," in *Martiniana. Studie o latinském humanismu v českých zemích* (Praha, 2014²), 77–90, there 80.

11 *Martini Lutheri epistolarum farrago. Epistola ad Vitebergenses […] cum Psalmorum aliquot interpretatione, in quibus multa […] praecepta ceu Symbola quaedam indicantur* (Haganoe, 1525) (VD16 L 4656).

12 For an overview of sources, see the monograph by Johann Albertus Fabricius, *Votum Davidicum, Cor novum crea in me Deus, a 150 amplius Metaphrastis* (Hamburg, 1729).

13 *Symbola Pythagorae moraliter explicata*, first edited in Bologna 1503. I used the later edition by Petrus Fabricius *Philippi Beroaldi Bononiensis Symbola Pythagorica tropologice & moraliter explicata* (Rostock, 1604), fol. A7a (VD17 23:285818V). In a similar way, Petrus Fabricius, the editor of this book, explains with pedagogical intent the utility of *symbola* as "vitae praecepta" to his pupil in the preface.

I have analysed *symbola* with regard to their date of origin, language, content, the social status of their users and their form. The first humanist personal mottos appear, as already mentioned, in the first quarter of the sixteenth century, but their more frequent use is documented from the 1570s, with the peak being at the beginning of the seventeenth century. There is a diagram, made by Josef Hejnic and Jan Martínek, which shows the frequency of humanist literature. My research has proved that the frequency of *symbola* is very similar.[14] Thus, we cannot assume that *symbola* was a fashionable genre, which began to be cultivated suddenly, for example, following an edition of a popular book of emblems or symbols. Although the interest of emperor Rudolf II in symbols and emblems is well known, it did not affect the variety of genres used in poetry in the Czech lands during that time.

Latin was the common language of symbols. Sometimes it appeared in combination with a Czech language version (mostly *symbola* of printers or humanists which were aimed predominantly at Czech speaking readers) or a Greek version (mostly in prints by way of decoration and to add cachet value). Humanists from the Unity of Brethren and some of their followers used mottos in Czech, but not as a general rule. *Symbola* written only in ancient Greek were typically those of physicians, though they occurred rather rarely. A few oriental scholars used mottos in Hebrew or Syriac.

Regarding their content, the largest number of *symbola* carried an explicitly religious meaning (35%). These mottos reflected the inner spirituality of their bearers, and expressed their profound belief in God and Christ as mediator, their hope in the power of God and in salvation and in eternal life. A quarter (25%) of the mottos pertain to human life, mainly comprising pieces of advice on a range of subjects: how to proceed and be successful in life; how to 'die well'; and how to achieve true nobility, gained not through the use of arms but through the arts. The third group of mottos (19%), that bears some resemblance to the second one, focuses on praise for ancient and Christian virtues (*virtus, pietas, fides*). The final twenty per cent, represented by widely used maxims, is known also from heraldry (for example *Festina lente*). Since a significant section of the humanists from Czech and Moravian towns were active in municipal administration, one might expect more mottos that relate to the *res publica*, but few exist. The theme of friendship, which is so frequently seen in the *alba amicorum* is conspicuous by its absence.

It might be assumed that the content of a personal motto would be influenced by the profession, confession, and social status of humanists. However,

---

14   Josef Hejnic and Jan Martínek, "O rozsahu a časovém rozložení naší humanistické literatury," *Zprávy Jednoty klasických filologů* 7 (1965), 93–7.

PERSONAL MOTTOS OF HUMANISTS FROM THE CZECH LANDS

the results of our research do not confirm this theory. With the exception of the aforementioned physicians, the content of personal mottos was similar to that of humanists from various professions, social status and confession. Why was this?

The first reason was that the majority of literate men of the time created their personal mottos during their period of study at the academy[15] or university as young students without any clear knowledge about their future career. The phenomenon is captured by Balthasar Exner in his collection of poems on his *symbolum Spero meliora* of 1619:[16]

> [...] prima sane in adolescentia mea, cum fortuna (cuius ludus perpetuo fui) me plusquam lividineis oculis nonnunquam aspiceret, Genius quidam mihi (ita credo) desubito suggessit aureum illud meum *Spero meliora.*

His words illustrate well also the way in which *symbola* originated. The second reason is that the careers of humanists in the Czech lands were sometimes complicated. The same person could be a teacher for a period of time, then a physician and, after ordination, end his life as a pastor. The typical career of a Czech humanist with a university degree was: teacher—municipal scribe—burgher.

It is impossible to discern a different content or type of *symbola* among Catholics and non-Catholics in the Czech lands. Use of mottos by Catholic humanists at the imperial court and among the higher-ranking members of the clergy, were among the minority (totalling 11 persons according to our findings), and their mottos are diverse in their content and form. Moreover, there were many convertites at the court of Rudolf II, who still used their personal motto they had prior to conversion,[17] and similar cases can be found between Czech humanist writers.[18] If there had not been such a lack of mottos among Catholics, we might have concluded that the personal mottos stood mostly

---

15 The Altdorf academy influenced the habits of Czech students in creating *symbola* and *emblemata*. Their emblems can be found, for example, in the book by the Altdorf professor Nicolaus Taurellus *Emblemata physico-ethica* (Nuremberg, 1595), second enlarged edition of 1602 (VD16 T 249 and VD17 23:626961Y).

16 *Anchora utriusque vitae Balth. Exneri de Hirschberga* (Hanau, 1619), 5 (Universal Short Title Catalogue 2156584, VD17 27:745850H).

17 For example, Johann Matthäus Wacker of Wackenfels or Ludwig Schwartzmaier of Schwarzenau.

18 One good example is Michael Pěčka Smržický z Radostic and his motto *Meum Praesidium Salus a Redemptore*, in Czech version *Můj Pomocník Spasitel z Radosti*. He used it as a signature in his work *Schola aulica* (Pragae, 1607) (Knihopis 15386).

upon confession. I should add that similar sources are documented for all groups of profession or confession, the most commonly used ones being from Vives and from the Bible (above all Psalms).

Concerning the form, the most typical for humanists from burgher circles are the so-called *symbola cephalonomatica*.[19] *Symbola cephalonomatica* are mottos in which the first letters of the sentence construct the initials of a person (for example *Jesus Anchora Nostra—Joannes Amos Nivnicensis*). They belong to the special kind of occasional poetry that played with names, such as anagrams or onomastic epigrams.[20] They were often composed on the names of patrons or friends, usually as a New Year's gift for patrons (*strena*) or on the establishing of a new city council. These *symbola* were mostly accompanied with explanatory epigrams.

The use of initials or monograms as a form of an abbreviation were very popular during the period of the late humanism in the era of Rudolf II. They can be compared to the widely used maxims, which were not only in Latin, but also in the vernacular, had their own abbreviations and were frequently used in *alba amicorum* entries.[21]

Personal mottos that incorporated musical notation seem to be quite exceptional, although they constitute a very attractive form of *symbolum*. A typical example is the personal motto of the nobleman and composer, Kryštof Harant of Polžice and Bezdružice, namely *Virtus ut sol micat*, where the notes are meant to be read as solfa syllables.[22] This principle was later imitated by other humanists who used the same motto, but even Harant had probably followed an older model.[23] However, it is very difficult to decide which mottos are genuinely original and which are only an imitation, much as it is in the case of proverbs. Several personal mottos from the Czech material were, for instance, published many years after their use in collections of emblems and other similar publications, without any reference to a person.

---

19   For the definition see Martínek, "Drobné literární útvary" (see above, n. 10), 82.

20   See Martínek, "Drobné literární útvary" (see above, n. 10), 83–4.

21   Friedrich-Carl Freiherr von Stechow, *Lexikon der Stammbuchsprüche. Stechows Stammbuchsprüche-Schlüssel* (Neustadt an der Aisch, 1996).

22   See his portrait by Aegidius Sadeler, engraved by Jacob von Sandrart in Peter Mortzfeld, *Katalog der graphischen Porträts in der Herzog August Bibliothek Wolfenbüttel 1500–1850. Reihe A: Die Porträtsammlung*, A 26357: http://portraits.hab.de/werk/26137/bild/

23   *Répertoire International des Sources Musicales*, RISM ID no.: 455036189 (canon by Michael Scheuffler). For more information on mottos using solfa syllables, see Franz Krautwurst, "Widmungskanons in einem Humanistenstammbuch der Oettingen-Wallersteinischen Bibliothek der Universitätsbibliothek Augsburg," *Jahrbuch der Universität Augsburg* (1985), 151–9.

PERSONAL MOTTOS OF HUMANISTS FROM THE CZECH LANDS 617

Personal mottos or emblems could also be used in a figurative sense. An example is the *emblema nudum* of Jan Jesenius in his edition of *Hierographia* by Jacobus Typotius in 1618.[24] Jesenius, one of his contemporaries, who was a rector and chancellor of Prague University, presents it in the introduction of his newly invented motto (*recens emblema*). Following Typotius' theory that the image precedes the text, he describes it as follows: "Struthio camelus ovo incubans pictus,[25] cum hac scriptura: Excludat oportet." The five poems by other university professors appended to the work were explained accordingly: The ostrich symbolises Prague academy under the protection of her rector Jesenius and with the favour of *facilis fautor* (the nobleman Charles of Žerotín, to whom the book is dedicated), who should after long years of sterility educate a new generation of students, to be well-educated and religious. This *emblema* was not in fact the personal motto of Jesenius, it was created for him as a rector, and it should be an address to the noble patron in the name of the university to gain his favour.

In conclusion, it may be possible to outline some of the ways in which this research into personal mottos may be used in practice. I have created a basic list of used abbreviations, taken from prints, manuscripts, book bindings and *alba amicorum*.[26] This could help to identify the authors of literary works, singular poems or *album* entries, who preferred to remain anonymous or to be known only to a small group of friends or collaborators, so they used their initials or their motto, mostly *symbolum cephalonomaticum*.[27] This list could also make it easier to identify the provenance of books. The abbreviations of names and mottos frequently appear on blind stamped Renaissance bindings, and sometimes the owner's name has not been noted in the book, or has been scratched or blackened out. In such a case, the identification of the abbreviations on the bookbinding is the only possible means to identify the owner.

Centre for Classical Studies at the Institute of Philosophy, Czech Academy of Sciences

---

24 *Jacobi Typotii Batavi* [...] *De hierographia, quae complectitur hieroglyptica atq*[*ue*] *symbola, libri duo: Opus posthumum* (Prague, 1618), see Bibliografie cizojazyčných bohemikálních tisků [Bibliography of Foreign-Language Printed Bohemica], https://clavius.lib.cas.cz/katalog/eng/baze.htm, no. 42136. Emblem with explanation poems on fols. A5a–A8a.

25 The imagine of the ostrich and its egg is probably derived from *Physiologus* or later from Albertus Magnus, *De animalibus* 23,139, known also from several works by Marsilio Ficino.

26 This list is accessible on: http://www.ics.cas.cz/upload/__files/Initials.pdf.

27 E.g. Sigismundus Podkostelsky signed his poem with his motto *Musarum Studiis Parta Brabaea Beant* (= *Magister Sigismundus Podkostelsky Bohemo-Brodenus*) in Jan Rosacius, *O hladu, pokutě Boží hrozné, kázání* (Prague 1616), fol. A8b (Knihopis 14887).

CHAPTER 49

Lettere alla corte aragonese: L'epistolario di Antonio Galateo, i re di Napoli e l'Accademia

Sebastiano Valerio

Abstract

La raccolta delle epistole latine di Antonio Galateo fu l'ultima opera a cui il letterato salentino pose mano, prima di morire nel 1517. Tràdito in primo luogo dal cod. vat. Lat. 7584, in parte autografo, l'epistolario rappresenta una vivida testimonianza degli usi della corte e dell'accademia napoletana e poi della sua crisi. In questo senso un significato particolare lo rivestono le lettere indirizzate a Ferdinando e Federico d'Aragona, a Belisario e Andrea Matteo Acquaviva, a Marino Brancaccio, a Bona Sforza e ad altri esponenti ancora dell'accademia pontaniana e della cultura umanistica napoletana. In queste lettere il Galateo fornisce uno spaccato delle discussioni accademiche, che spesso si svolgevano alla presenza dei sovrani, e rappresenta a tinte vivide le conversazioni che avevano come argomenti privilegiati i temi etici, scientifici, storici e filosofici. Proprio l'analisi di queste discussioni e dei contesti in cui avvennero sarà l'oggetto della presente comunicazione.

Keywords

Antonio Galateo – Neo-Latin epistolography – humanism in Naples – Accademia Pontaniana

L'epistolario di Antonio Galateo, medico e scrittore di cui si è recentemente celebrato il cinquecentesimo anniversario della morte (1517–2017), resta una delle più vive ed efficaci testimonianze di quel difficile e drammatico passaggio storico che fu per l'Italia il periodo a cavallo tra quindicesimo e sedicesimo secolo, da quando, nel 1494, il re di Francia Carlo VIII fece irruzione in Italia con le sue truppe per conquistare il Regno di Napoli.[1]

---

1 Cfr. Benedetto Croce, "Il Galateo (Antonio De Ferrariis)," in idem, *Poeti e scrittori del pieno e tardo rinascimento* (Bari 1945), vol. 1, 17–35, già in *Humanisme et Renaissance* 4 (1937),

L'EPISTOLARIO DI ANTONIO GALATEO, I RE DI NAPOLI E L'ACCADEMIA   619

Quell'epistolario, affidato a numerosi testimoni manoscritti, tra cui si segnala il cod. Vat. Lat. 7584, in parte autografo e in parte idiografo,[2] consta di oltre una quarantina di epistole latine, scritte lungo un arco di tempo che va dagli anni Ottanta del Quattrocento fino quasi agli ultimi giorni di vita del letterato che ebbe i propri natali nel Salento, dove ancora forte era la tradizione greca, che egli rivendicò come nutrimento primario del suo essere umanista. In quelle lettere il Galateo ripose tutto se stesso, tutto il proprio pensiero, fece convergere in esse tutto il suo mondo, in un lavoro di risistemazione della silloge che fu lungo e travagliato e che non giunse mai compiutamente a termine.[3] Il mondo aragonese viene rappresentato in primo luogo nei suoi principali interpreti. Bastino le prime lettere per comprendere questo particolare aspetto della scrittura del Galateo. La prima epistola è dedicata ad una non meglio specificata dama della corte aragonese, Maria di Portogallo; la seconda a Giovan Francesco Caracciolo;[4] la terza indirizzata a Sannazaro riporta una tipica discussione accademica; quindi si incontra il nome di Andrea Matteo Acquaviva e quello del fratello Belisario, per continuare con Marino Brancaccio, Giovanni Pontano, Cariteo, Pietro Summonte, Puderico, ecc.

Si tratta di un panorama pressoché completo dell'umanesimo napoletano, in cui un ruolo centrale l'ha proprio l'educazione, il modello culturale da proporre. In questa sede però intendo soffermarmi solo su alcune di queste epistole che ritraggono proprio la conversazione accademica o comunque erudita, quella che, per intenderci, ripropone situazioni e argomenti delle discussioni che avvenivano tra intellettuali attorno al Pontano o presso la corte, nell'intento di comprendere cosa queste riflessioni e questi ricordi potessero

---

366–80. Sull'epistolario cfr. Francesco Tateo, "Un epistolario umanistico nella Puglia del Cinquecento (il testamento intellettuale di Antonio Galateo)," *Atti e relazioni* (*1986–87*), *Accademia Pugliese delle Scienze, classe di Scienze Morali* 44,1 (s.d. [1990]), 85–109; idem, "La raccolta delle Epistolae di Antonio Galateo," in *Acta Conventus Neo-Latini Guelpherbytani*, ed. Stella P. Revard (Binghamton 1988), 551–62. L'epistolario è edito in *A. De Ferrariis Galateo. Epistole*, ed. Antonio Altamura (Lecce 1959). Alcune lettere sono in *A. De Ferrariis Galateo. Lettere*, ed. Amleto Pallara (Lecce 1996).

2   Cfr. Antonio Iurilli, *L'opera di Antonio Galateo nella tradizione manoscritta. Catalogo* (Napoli 1990), 97–8. Si veda a proposito di questo prezioso volume Carlo Vecce, "Paralipomeni al Galateo," *Studi e problemi di critica testuale* 45 (1992), 59–82; Francesco Tateo, "La storia del corpus di Antonio Galateo in una recente ricostruzione della tradizione manoscritta," in *Studi e storia di cultura meridionale* (Galatina 1992), 53–62.

3   Cfr. Sebastiano Valerio, "Nello 'scriptorium' del Galateo: per una storia dell'epistolario," in *Antonio Galateo dalla Iapigia all'Europa. Convegno internazionale di studi nel V centenario della morte di Antonio Galateo, Galatone – Nardò – Gallipoli – Lecce, 15–18 novembre 2017*, in corso di pubblicazione.

4   Cfr. Marco Santagata, "Caracciolo, Giovan Francesco," *Dizionario Biografico degli Italiani*, vol. 19 (Roma, 1976), on-line.

rappresentare quando Antonio Galateo mise mano alla revisione del suo epistolario, ad anni dalla caduta della dinastia aragonese e dalla diaspora degli intellettuali dell'Accademia.

Bisogna dire che il lavoro di revisione dell'epistolario, su cui molto è stato detto anche recentemente,[5] dovette iniziare in una fase piuttosto antica, forse subito dopo il suo rientro in Salento all'indomani della conquista spagnola del *Regnum*, se si considera che nell'epistola 7, indirizzata a Belisario Acquaviva, al f. 38v del manoscritto vaticano, in una pagina vergata dalla mano del Galateo, la dedica vede la correzione "Marchionem" ad emendare in rasura il precedente "Comitem", facendo risalire evidentemente tale intervento a dopo il 1503, quando all'Acquaviva venne concesso il titolo di Marchese dopo la battaglia del Garigliano, mentre non figura alcuna correzione, più tarda, che lo indichi come Duca, titolo che ricevette nel 1516, evidentemente troppo tardi perché un vecchio Galateo potesse tornare sul manoscritto a correggerlo ancora. È un indizio, debole ma a mio avviso significativo, di un'attività di revisione della silloge che deve datarsi ai primi anni del '500 e che, per quanto sappiamo, durò quasi fino agli ultimi giorni di vita del suo autore. La costruzione della raccolta, dunque, il suo ordinamento su cui illuminanti pagine hanno scritto Francesco Tateo, Antonio Iurilli e Isabella Nuovo,[6] deve riferirsi ad un periodo tardo, ipotesi che non esclude che fosse nelle intenzioni del Galateo procedere alla raccolta delle lettere anche in una fase precedente, cosa anzi probabilissima, ma quanto oggi abbiamo appartiene ad un momento tardo della vita del Galateo che corrisponde agli anni di crisi più profonda dell'Italia e del Regno di Napoli.

La prima lettera, indirizzata ad una non meglio nota dama aragonese, Maria di Portogallo, si apre col tema dell'ipocrisia,[7] che in qualche modo segna anche tematicamente l'inizio della raccolta e finisce, così, per diagnosticare uno dei mali delle corti italiane, segnalando in questo caso la specificità della condizione muliebre, più sana e retta di quella maschile, ma mettendo anche in luce come l'incidenza di questo male fosse tanto più perniciosa in chi era destinato a reggere le sorti di un regno, perché, se pure era vero l'antico adagio, risalente

---

5   Si veda il contributo di Antonio Manfredi nel convegno *Antonio Galateo dalla Iapigia all'Europa*, di prossima pubblicazione. Ma cfr. anche *Novità e Tradizione in Antonio Galateo. Studi e Testi*, ed. Paolo Viti (Lecce 2018).

6   Cfr. Isabella Nuovo, "Philosophia magistra vitae, la missione del sophos nelle Epistole di Antonio Galateo," *Otium e negotium. Da Petrarca a Scipione Ammirato* (Bari 2007), 179–219, edito anche in *Forme e contesti. Studi in onore di Vitilio Masiello*, ed. Francesco Tateo e Raffaele Cavalluzzi (Bari 2005), 69–102. Fondamentale per la tradizione galateana resta Iurilli, *L'opera* (vedi sopra, n. 2).

7   Cfr. Sebastiano Valerio, "Simulare e dissimulare: l'ipocrisia tra religione e corte," in *Lessico ed etica nella tradizione italiana di primo Cinquecento*, ed. Raffaele Ruggiero (Lecce 2016), 11–24.

L'EPISTOLARIO DI ANTONIO GALATEO, I RE DI NAPOLI E L'ACCADEMIA   621

a Tacito, che "qui nescit simulare nescit regnare", era altrettanto vero che questo vizio era indegno degli uomini e dei re.

Tra le lettere molte che riportano le discussioni accademiche, a cominciare dall'epistola 3, che segue la lettera a Francesco Caracciolo in cui si parla di un altro tema legato al mondo della corte, quello dei benefici ricevuti più o meno indegnamente, che così si legava al tema dell'ipocrisia che aveva aperto la raccolta. Indirizzata "Accio Sincero",[8] la cosiddetta lettera *De situ terrarum* ricorda al Sannazaro la discussione avvenuta al cospetto di Federico d'Aragona, non ancora re, attorno ad una "tabella", una carta geografica del mar Mediterraneo, forse un portolano (viene descritta come in uso da parte dei "nostri temporis navigantes"), che venne illustrato proprio da Federico il quale era divenuto, dopo la destituzione di Antonello Sanseverino, ammiraglio del regno e che qui viene definito *heros* e paragonato a quell'Ulisse che aveva visto "mores hominum multorum [...] et urbes", secondo la definizione omerica. Attorno a Federico si muovono, in una rappresentazione che ha effetti scenici, un non meglio specificato Acquaviva, che dovrebbe essere Belisario, e il conte di Potenza Antonio Guevara. Si ricordi che sempre al Sannazaro Galateo dedicò il *De situ elementorum*, operetta scientifica che ribadisce l'ordine tolemaico dell'universo.[9] La discussione accademica qui avviene secondo uno schema ben noto, con Federico che, come *magister*, imposta la questione della conformazione delle terre del Mediterraneo e i due nobili contendenti che discutono, su fronti opposti, dell'effetto delle mutazioni naturali sulla conformazione dei luoghi, adducendo fonti filosofiche e scientifiche che spaziano da Aristotele, vero fulcro della discussione, a Plinio, Seneca, Virgilio, con un richiamo problematico alla verità delle sacre scritture che andavano conciliate con questo antico sapere. L'esito del confronto tuttavia portava dalle considerazioni sulla formazione e sull'evoluzione delle terre ad una considerazione di taglio moraleggiante, alla mutevolezza del mondo umano, che dal punto di vista etico-comportamentale era stata già posta al centro dell'epistola 2, indirizzata a Francesco Caracciolo, a dimostrare la ponderata e attenta costruzione della silloge, almeno per quel che riguarda la prima parte.

---

8   La lettera è edita e tradotta da Francesco Tateo in *Puglia neo-latina. Un itinerario del Rinascimento tra autori e testi*, ed. Francesco Tateo, Mauro de Nichilo e Pietro Sisto (Bari 1994), 35–59. Le lettere qui riportate (*Ad Mariam Lusitanam de hypocrisi, Ad Accium Sincerum de situ terrarum, Ad Illustrem dominam Bonam Sforciam, Ad Chrysostomum de Prospero Columna et de Ferramusca, Ad Chrysostomum de pugna tredecim equitum*) sono state riproposte in *La prosa dell'Umanesimo*, ed. Francesco Tateo (Roma 2004), 349–92.

9   Queste e altre operette scientifiche sono edite in *La Giapigia e varii opuscoli di Antonio De Ferrariis detto il Galateo*, ed. Salvatore Grande (Lecce 1868), vol. 3, 2–114.

622 VALERIO

Ancora incentrate su discussioni accademiche sono le lettere di maggiore estensione, quasi dei trattati in forma di epistole responsive su determinate questioni, come ad esempio la dignità delle discipline, nella lettera indirizzata a Marino Brancaccio, oppure la discussione sulle lettere, posposte alla filosofia nell'epistola indirizzata a Belisario Acquaviva (36) o l'importanza della cultura greca, nella lettera in cui ringraziava Ermolao Barbaro per la dedica di una parte della traduzione di Temistio, condotta nel 1481 dal letterato veneto che aveva avuto modo di soggiornare a lungo a Napoli e lì di conoscere il Galateo. La lettera *De interpretatione Temistii* al Barbaro era ancora frutto di un incontro academico, avvenuto presso la corte, e tornava ad affermare la superiorità della sapienza greca, ribadendo anche qui la preferenza per una filosofia delle *res*, né legata alla sottigliezza dei ragionamenti, né confusa dall'uso delle parole.

La lettera a Marino Brancaccio, detta *De dignitate disciplinarum*,[10] verteva attorno tema topico della superiorità delle lettere rispetto all'arte della guerra, coinvolgendo, però, in modo più ampio, medicina e giurisprudenza, ma prendeva le mosse proprio da una precedente discussione accademica in cui proprio Brancaccio, che fu valente militare, aveva avuto occasione di parlare del modo di combattere degli italiani e dei *barbari*, un tema che, sin dai tempi della nascita del Regno aragonese di Napoli, era stato ben presente alla cultura partenopea, sin da quando nella *Vita di Braccio* Giannantonio Campano aveva introdotto la questione "de italicis bellis" e della superiorità in guerra degli italiani, questione che poi sarà ripresa dal Galateo nelle lettere sulla Disfida di Barletta.[11]

Nell'epistola detta *Vituperatio litterarum* a Belisario Acquaviva, databile ad anni tardi, veniva ancora riportata una discussione accademica ("Legi non sine maxima voluptate epistolam tuam [...]"), e si tornava sulla questione della valutazione delle lettere, che venivano giudicate negativamente se disgiunte dalla vera sapienza filosofica e dalle *res*, rimanendo solo parole vane.

Nell'epistola decima, indirizzata a Ferdinando d'Aragona, figlio di Federico, viene affrontato il tema della regalità, ripreso sul versante dell'educazione del

---

10   L'epistola *De dignitate disciplinarum*, datata agli anni Ottanta del Quattrocento, è edita nell'edizione delle *Epistole* curata da Altamura (vedi sopra, n. 1), 48–68, è stata inserita anche in Eugenio Garin, *La disputa delle arti nel Quattrocento* (Roma 1982), 103–29. L'epistola è stata edita quindi criticamente in Francesco Tateo, "La dignità delle arti in un'epistola del Galateo a Marino Brancaccio," *La parola del testo* 4 (2000), 381–414.

11   Cfr. Sebastiano Valerio, "Antonio Galateo e il 'mito' umanistico della Disfida," in *La Disfida di Barletta. Storia, fortuna, rappresentazione*, ed. Fulvio Delle Donne e Victor Rivera Magos (Roma 2017), 69–80; Tobia R. Toscano, "L'immagine letteraria della conquista: la disfida di Barletta," in *El Reino de Nápoles y la monarquía de España. Entre agregación y conquista (1485–1535)*, ed. Giuseppe Galasso e Carlos J. Hernando Sánchez (Roma 2004), 585–601.

L'EPISTOLARIO DI ANTONIO GALATEO, I RE DI NAPOLI E L'ACCADEMIA   623

principe. L'esemplarità dei modelli portati al giovane aragonese vengono anzitutto dalla sua stessa storia familiare, ma Galateo teneva, additando questi modelli, a far emergere il ruolo civile che la figura del principe, sul quale ricadevano gli occhi di tutti, veniva a ricoprire:[12] per questo motivo l'educazione del principe avrebbe dovuto elevarne i costumi ben sopra quelli dei propri sudditi, facendo fruttare i propri talenti di natura (come avrebbe scritto a Bona Sforza anni dopo) con un'educazione a modello della quale viene richiamato ancora Aristotele, citato in chiusura dell'epistola direttamente in greco, lingua materna del Galateo. I re svolgono qui la funzione esemplare di *speculum* per tutti, per il ruolo che Dio e la fortuna hanno assegnato loro in terra,[13] con una ripresa di una topica che in quegli anni (siamo prima del 1495, essendo ancora vivo Ferrandino e venendo egli stesso definito qui "adulescens") caratterizzava ampia parte della cultura aragonese: se pure era vero che le virtù regie erano ereditarie, Galateo declinava un lungo elenco di *virtutes*, attribuite ancora ai predecessori aragonesi (munificenza, umanità, clemenza, cortesia, grandezza d'animo, gloria, amore delle lettere, gravità, sapienza, gloria, prudenza, felicità, integrità di vita, giustizia, perseveranza, equilibrio dell'animo, costanza, modestia, liberalità, grandezza d'animo, sopportazione delle fatiche, arte di accamparsi, perizia di guerra, pietà, religione, strenuità, audacia, ferocia, larghezza, indulgenza, grazia e pubblica benevolenza) che erano utili a disegnare il profilo di principe in cui le virtù naturali si dovevano nutrire di pratica e studio e non a caso la lettera finisce per ricordare la funzione di guida e istitutore del conte di Potenza Antonio Guevara e quella di precettore di Crisostomo Colonna,[14] che poi troveremo nell'epistolario galateano come interlocutore quando sarà, dopo il 1506, precettore di Bona Sforza.

Nell'epistola 21, indirizzata a Ferrandino, quando questi era ancora assai giovane, spicca ancora la funzione dell'educazione del principe, perché la lettera, che sembra rispondere ad una sollecitazione del precettore del principe, il letterato pontaniano Gabriele Altilio, introduce brevemente una copia greca della lettera di Isocrate a Demonico, che il *magister* avrebbe dovuto tradurre in volgare per il futuro re, e da cui l'Altilio avrebbe dovuto apprendere "qualis esse et haberi debeat, qui principes ad bonas artes instituit"[15] e Ferrandino "qualis

---

12   De Ferrariis Galateo, *Epistole* (vedi sopra, n. 1), 119: "in vos omnium oculi intenti sunt."
13   Cfr. Guido M. Cappelli, *Maiestas. Politica e pensiero politico nella Napoli Aragonese 1443–1503* (Roma 2016), 30–2, 95–8.
14   Giuseppe Angeluzzi, *Intorno alla vita e alle opere di Grisostomo Colunna, pontaniano accademico Ragionamento* (Napoli, 1856), 13: "actendite cum omne diligentia et cum piacere al suo imparare de modo che de continuo vada avanzando et con quella sollecitudine che da voi speramo." La lettera è datata al 30 giugno 1498.
15   De Ferrariis Galateo, *Epistole* (vedi sopra, n. 1), 143.

futurus sit princeps, qui philosophorum praeceptis pareat", in ossequio a quel primato della filosofia che è centrale nella cultura del Galateo.[16] Non a caso, a questa lettera segue la lettera a Bona Sforza, probabilmente scritta nel momento in cui Crisostomo Colonna ne aveva preso la cura come precettore. Anche in questo caso il percorso che avrebbe dovuto riportare la futura regina di Polonia e figlia di Isabella d'Aragona ai fasti dei suoi antenati, dopo la caduta del regno aragonese di Napoli, avvenuta pochi anni prima, passava per la riproposizione dell'esemplarità della storia familiare ma anche e soprattutto per un piano di studi incentrato sulla lettura dei classici, a cominciare da Virgilio e Cicerone, dalle sacre scritture fino ai padri della Chiesa e al suo stesso precettore, che avrebbe dovuto distinguere la "illustris puella" dalle "mulierculae", restituendola, ancora grazie alla forza dell'educazione, alla sua dignità regale.

Sempre, insomma, rivolgendosi agli aragonesi, Galateo finiva per esaltare il ruolo dell'educazione e della cultura umanistica come fondamento e nutrimento della dignità dei re e della vera nobiltà, tutti elementi che in opere come il *De educatione*[17] e il *De nobilitate*[18] emergono in modo assolutamente evidente. Quando, nell'epistola scritta per la morte di Alfonso II (siamo dunque attorno al 1495, nel pieno della guerra contro Carlo VIII), Galateo lo paragona ad Achille, Alessandro Magno, Tito, lo ricorda vincitore non solo dei Galli, ma anche dei Turchi, con riferimento al *Bellum hydruntinum* del 1480–81, per esaltarne il profilo di uomo saggio in pace e invincibile in guerra, proprio per la capacità di saper attendere il momento in cui la fortuna si sarebbe mostrata più favorevole e domabile, dopo aver portato gli esempi classici, torna a proporre gli esempi familiari di Alfonso il Magnanimo e di Ferrante, ma mettendo ancora in evidenza come la grandezza di questo re fosse stata sì "in extruendis arcibus", ma anche "in instaurandis templis", "in ornandis domibus", e nell'aver richiamato a Napoli scultori, pittori, architetti e artisti da tutta l'Italia senza badare a spese, come con magnificenza aveva arricchito una biblioteca degna di Tolomeo.[19]

La costruzione della silloge, tuttavia, è riferibile, almeno nella forma che oggi sopravvive, ad un periodo in cui questo mondo si era dissolto, in cui il regno aragonese era diventato un ricordo, per quanto sia nelle lettere con cui riferiva i fatti della disfida di Barletta del 1503, quanto nell'epistola indirizzata

---

16   Vedi sopra, n. 6.

17   *Antonio De Ferrariis Galateo, De educatione (1505)*, ed. Carlo Vecce (Lovanio, 1993).

18   Gabriella Di Pierro (ed.), "Antonio Galateo, De nobilitate," in *Puglia Neo-Latina* (vedi sopra, n. 8), 107–75.

19   De Ferrariis Galateo, *Epistole* (vedi sopra, n. 1), 265.

L'EPISTOLARIO DI ANTONIO GALATEO, I RE DI NAPOLI E L'ACCADEMIA

a Ferdinando il Cattolico (36) *De capta Tripoli*, dunque dopo il 1511, gli spagnoli vengano in qualche modo ricondotti sotto la categoria della *latinitas*, almeno dal punto di vista culturale, contrapposti comunque ai barbari del Nord Europa, francesi (Galli) compresi.

In un'opera che ha attraversato temporalmente la storia aragonese, come l'epistolario, concepito nelle sue singole parti prima e dopo la crisi politico-bellica di fine secolo, è sempre necessario leggere i due tempi della redazione, individuare il senso microtestuale e quello macrotestuale, distinguere la singola tessera e il disegno complessivo e soprattutto il senso che la singola tessera assume quando il disegno finale prende forma, sicuramente in modo inizialmente imprevisto. Le discussioni accademiche, insomma, le *questiones* poste, che nel loro contesto originale e nel loro primo significato erano una testimonianza della vivacità e della complessità della vita culturale della corte aragonese e che avevano spesso riportato i conversari dell'accademia, finivano per assumere, alla metà degli anni '10 del sedicesimo secolo, un senso ben diverso. Nelle lettere, qui sia pur brevemente prese in esame (ed in altre ancora), veniva rappresentata la civiltà del dialogo, nelle sue articolazioni, nei suoi spesso differenti punti di vista, che però convergevano a creare un orizzonte ampio e articolato, e che originariamente trovavano una composizione nel mondo della corte aragonese e dell'accademia pontaniana; venuti meno nei fatti i luoghi propri di questa cultura, cioè accademia e corte, si scompone l'idea tutta umanistica di un sapere al servizio della comunità degli intellettuali e dei governanti, con un reciproco e mutuo scambio di funzioni, che aveva portato gli intellettuali ad educare i governanti e ad ispirare loro le pratiche del buon governo alla luce degli esempi storici antichi e moderni e della riflessione etica e filosofica, e aveva indotto per converso i governanti a farsi essi stessi intellettuali e cultori delle buone lettere e delle arti. A tenere tutto assieme, anzi a tenerlo ancora in vita, allora è la rappresentazione delle discussioni contenute nell'epistolario, ma in esse non vi è più nulla di programmatico, non c'è più la primigenia progettualità. Il quadro in movimento si è fermato, la dinamica del mondo umanistico è diventata rappresentazione statica, la speranza si tramuta in rimpianto. Sia ben inteso, questo vale se guardiamo a quella realtà dalla prospettiva del Galateo: con ciò non si può né si vuole dire che questa sia la condizione reale di quella cultura, che proprio in quegli anni produrrà opere e autori straordinari, spesso ancora da studiare e valutare pienamente. Per Galateo, la fine di quel mondo implica anche il ritorno nella periferia del regno, in quell'angolo d'Italia, come ebbe a definirlo, che è il Salento, e da ciò ne consegue una visione particolarmente negativa. Il suo ritiro in Puglia è però anche la condizione necessaria per guardare, negli ultimi malinconici anni di vita, la storia di quel primo Cinquecento da una prospettiva sghemba, che se talvolta lo marginalizza dagli sviluppi culturali che porteranno al 'gran secolo', dall'altra gli fa comprendere a tutto tondo la profondità della crisi e la sua complessità e soprattutto fa diventare un epistolario, che forse nasceva per ben altri motivi, una delle testimonianze più vive e drammatiche di quella crisi epocale.

Università di Foggia

CHAPTER 50

The Latin and the Swedish Versions of J. Widekindi's *Historia Belli Sveco-Moscovitici Decennalis*: the Nature of the Differences

Arsenii Vetushko-Kalevich

Abstract

Johannes Widekindi (c. 1620–78) was a Swedish historiographer of the Realm. His main work *Historia Belli Sveco-Moscovitici Decennalis* was published both in Latin and in Swedish (as *Thet Swenska i Ryssland Tijo åhrs Krijgz-Historie*). Although the Swedish edition appeared one year earlier than the Latin one, the latter is in no way a translation of the former. The textological relationship between the two versions is an intricate one, and they are far from identical in contents. The paper seeks to classify and to explain the differences. They turn out to be caused partly by the character of Widekindi's work with his sources in different languages (some were Latin, others Swedish and German), partly by stylistic considerations.

Keywords

Johannes Widekindi – *Historia Belli Sveco-Moscovitici Decennalis* (1672) – Neo-Latin historiography – Swedish translations of Neo-Latin texts

Introduction

The Russian 'Time of Troubles' in the beginning of the seventeenth century implicated, apart from inner turbulence in Russia, also military conflicts with Sweden and Poland. The Swedish forces came to Russia in 1609 to help the czar Vasili Shuysky against an impostor known as the Second False Dmitry and the Poles. However, after liberating Moscow from the siege in 1610 the Swedish-Russian forces suffered a bitter defeat in the battle of Klushino. Thereafter, the Swedes became discontent with the delay in payments and territorial cessions from the Russian side and began their own military actions in

---

© KONINKLIJKE BRILL NV, LEIDEN, 2020 | DOI:10.1163/9789004427105_051

628 VETUSHKO-KALEVICH

north-western Russia. This military conflict, sometimes called the Ingrian war, lasted until the Treaty of Stolbovo in 1617.[1]

The main published source for knowledge about the Ingrian war is *Historia Belli Sveco-Moscovitici Decennalis*[2] by Johannes Widekindi, Swedish Historiographer of the Realm. Widekindi was born around 1620, studied in Uppsala, received his Master's degree at Oxford in 1653 and after returning to Sweden became a teacher of Latin eloquence at Stockholm Gymnasium. His rhetorical and poetic talents soon helped him to find patrons among the aristocracy, including Count Magnus Gabriel De la Gardie, Chancellor of the Realm. Due to De la Gardie's protection Widekindi was appointed Historiographer of the Realm in 1665.[3]

The history of the war against the Muscovites, on which he worked throughout the 1660s, is his main historical work. However, *Historia Belli Sveco-Moscovitici* is important not only as a historical source, but also as an impressive piece of Swedish Neo-Latin historiography and as one of the most significant bilingual works in seventeenth century Sweden, being published both in Swedish (as *Thet Swenska i Ryssland Tijo åhrs Krijgz-Historie*) and in Latin.

The seventeenth century, especially its second half, was a heyday of Neo-Latin literature in Sweden, in science and scholarship as well as in belles-lettres.[4]

---

1 The most detailed account of the war can be found in Generalstaben, *Sveriges krig 1611–1632. Band 1: Danska och ryska krigen* (Stockholm, 1936). A good summary in English is provided by Gennadij Kovalenko, "Troubled Years. The Background to the Occupation," in *Accounts of an Occupied City. Catalogue of the Novgorod Occupation Archives 1611–1617*, ed. Elisabeth Löfstrand and Laila Nordquist (Stockholm, 2005), 27–38, complemented by Elisabeth Löfstrand, "Annals," in the same volume (39–60). For shorter overviews see e.g. Michael Roberts, *Gustavus Adolphus* (second edition, London – New York, 1992), 10–1, 36–9; Maureen Perrie, "The Time of Troubles (1603–1613)," in *The Cambridge History of Russia*, ed. Maureen Perrie (Cambridge, 2006), 409–31, there 422–9; the entries "Time of Troubles", "Polish and Swedish Intervention in Russia during the Early Seventeenth Century", "De la Gardie, Jacob Pontus" and "Stolbovo Peace Treaty of 1617" in *The Modern Encyclopedia of Russian and Soviet History*, ed. Joseph L. Wieczynski (Gulf Breeze, 1976–2000).

2 "Ten years" in the title are misleading—in fact, it took eight years from the arrival of Swedish forces under Jacob De la Gardie to Russia until the Treaty of Stolbovo. On the title-pages of both editions the year 1607 is indicated as the starting point, and some passages in the text seem to imply (although somewhat vaguely) that Widekindi has in mind the appearance of the second False Dmitry, whose campaign eventually forced tsar Vasili Shuysky to resort to the Swedish help.

3 For details on Widekindi's biography, see Johan Theodor Westrin, "Widekindi," in *Nordisk familjebok. 32:a bandet: Werth—Väderkvarn*, ed. Johan Theodor Westrin (Stockholm, 1921), 263–5 and Ingel Wadén, "Widekindi," in *Svenska män och kvinnor. Biografisk uppslagsbok. 8. Toffteen—Ö*, ed. Torsten Dahl (Stockholm, 1955), 342.

4 On the role of Latin in Sweden during its Great Power era, see Hans Helander, *Neo-Latin Literature in Sweden in the Period 1620–1720. Stylistics, Vocabulary and Characteristic Ideas* (Uppsala, 2004), 17–21 and n. 9 (for further reading).

WIDEKINDI'S *HISTORIA BELLI SVECO-MOSCOVITICI DECENNALIS* 629

Historiography was one of the areas where a certain competition between Latin and Swedish took place, but all the most important works of the period were still written in Latin. Glorifying both the remote past and the recent deeds of the Swedish rulers before the European audience was an issue of state concern in a country with flourishing imperial ambitions.

On the other hand, the Swedish language struggled against the Latin dominance and actually improved its position during the century.[5] Some works, especially those of propagandistic character and those belonging to antiquarian research,[6] were published in both Latin and Swedish.

Some of the famous bilingual writings of the period, like Olof Rudbeck's *Atlantica* (1677–1702), an enormous work arguing for the old age of Sweden as compared with Greece and Rome, or Olof Verelius' *Manuductio ad Runographiam*, one of the pioneer works on runology, combine the Swedish and the Latin text, which run as parallel columns in one edition. However, Widekindi's *Thet Swenska i Ryssland Tijo åhrs Krijgz-Historie* and *Historia Belli Sveco-Moscovitici* were published separately, the Swedish book in 1671[7] and the Latin one in 1672.[8] In this respect Widekindi's work stands closer to bilingual political writings, e.g. the official reasons for King Sigismund's dethronement, published in Swedish (four times) in 1605–09 and in Latin in 1610 or the official reasons for the so-called Torstenson war between Sweden and Denmark, published both in Swedish and in Latin in 1644.

Also the great predecessor of Widekindi in the Swedish Russian-related literature, Petrus Petrejus, published the two versions of his chronicle separately, in 1615 in Swedish (*Regni Muschovitici sciographia*) and in 1620 in German (*Historien vnd Bericht von dem Groszfürstenthumb Muschkow*). The two versions of Petrejus' work are, however, almost identical, the only significant

---

5 The breakthrough of Swedish in this and other literary genres is thoroughly treated in Stina Hansson, *Svenskans nytta, Sveriges ära. Litteratur och kulturpolitik under 1600-talet* (Göteborg, 1984), esp. 98 for illustrative statistical data regarding languages used in occasional poetry.

6 This fits well into the general European pattern: see W. Leonard Grant, "European Vernacular Works in Latin Translation," *Studies in the Renaissance* 1 (1954), 120–56, there 129 and 132–5.

7 Johannes Widekindi, *Thet Swenska i Ryssland Tijo åhrs Krijgz-Historie, Hwilket vnder twänne Sweriges Stormächtige Konungars, Konung Carls IX. Och K. Gustaf Adolphs den Andres och Stoores Baneer, Storfursten Ivan Vasilivitz Suischi och Ryssland til hielp, Först emoot the Rebeller och Lithower, sedan the Påler, på sidstone emoot sielfwe Muskowiterne, ifrån åhr 1607. in til 1617. Aff Feldtherren Gref. Iacob De La Gardie vthfördt, och medh en reputerligh Fredh bijlagdt är, i lijka många Böcker fördeelt* (Stockholm, 1671).

8 Johannes Widekindi, *Historia Belli Sveco-Moscovitici Decennalis, Quod junctis armis cum Magno Moscorum Duce Johan. Basilio Svischio, Primum adversus Rebelles et Lithuanos, mox Polonos, tandem data causa contra ipsos Moscovitas, auspiciis Regum Sveciae Caroli IX, Et Gustavi Adolphi Ductu Jacobi De La Gardie, Varia fortuna ab Anno seculi hujus Septimo, in decimum septimum gestum, et ardua pace compositum est, Totidem Libris distincta* (Holmiae, 1672).

difference being an update (a lot had happened in Russia just in the years that passed between 1615 and 1620).

That is not the case with Widekindi. The Latin version is half as extensive as the Swedish one, due to the lack of the last two of the ten books, but the eight initial books contain obvious differences as well. This fact may give rise to all kinds of speculations, and there are some in the scholarship,[9] although a systematic analysis of the differences has actually never been made. Such an analysis is the scope of this paper.

Early modern translations from and into Latin constitute a vast field of study,[10] and there are many case studies of the same kind as the present paper, i.e. concerned with specific details of translation technique. Subject to a comparative analysis have been e.g. Joachim Du Bellay's Latin and French poems[11] and the Latin text of *Diva Montis Sacri* by Bohuslav Balbín with its vernacular versions.[12] As regards material from Sweden, one can mention a dissertation dealing with a Latin translation of a Hebrew text.[13]

The Use of the Sources

Theoretically, there are three possible kinds of reasons that can explain why the Latin version is different from the Swedish one on certain points. The first one is the basic working process, primarily Widekindi's use of the sources. Another

---

9   It has been assumed that the Latin version must be influenced by the détente in the Russian-Swedish relations at the beginning of the 1670s (Геннадий Коваленко и др., "Апология Юхана Видекинда," in *Юхан Видекинд, История десятилетней шведско-московитской войны*, пер. С. А. Аннинского, А. М. Александрова, под ред. В. Л. Янина, А. Л. Хорошкевич (Москва, 2000), 521–61, there 559).

10   Peter Burke speaks about more than a thousand published translations into Latin: "Translations into Latin in early modern Europe", in *Cultural Translation in Early Modern Europe*, ed. Peter Burke and R. Po-Chia Hsia (Cambridge, 2007), 65–80, there 65, despite his strict criteria (ibid., 66–7).

11   Genevieve Demerson, "Joachim Du Bellay traducteur de lui-même," in *Neo-Latin and the Vernacular in Renaissance France*, ed. Grahame Castor and Terence Cave (Oxford, 1984), 113–28; Ellen S. Ginsberg, "Translation, Imitation, Transformation: Du Bellay as Self-Translator," in *Acta Conventus Neo-Latini Hafniensis*, ed. Rhoda Schnur (Tempe, AZ, 1997), 429–36.

12   Alena Bočková, "Balbínova Diva Montis Sancti a její dobové překlady," in *Dělám to k větší slávě Boží a chvále vlasti*, ed. Václav Chroust, Zdeňka Buršíková and Karel Viták (Klatovy, 2014), 70–91.

13   Josef Eskhult, *Andreas Norrelius' Latin Translation of Johan Kemper's Hebrew Commentary on Matthew* (Uppsala, 2007), in particular 110–23 and 247–67.

WIDEKINDI'S *HISTORIA BELLI SVECO-MOSCOVITICI DECENNALIS* 631

group is differences that have to do with a wide range of phenomena from exquisite stylistic devices to simple reader-friendliness, i.e. those dealing with the author's concern about the *form* of the Latin and the Swedish text (and not to their *contents*). Finally, the third group is eventual shifts of the author's intention and his main views on the characters, nations or specific problems.

I will begin with the general contents of the work. As already mentioned, the two last books, which mainly contain the details of the peace negotiations, are missing in the Latin version. Apart from that, there are numerous passages which are only present in either of the versions. For those present only in the Swedish text, the distribution is especially interesting. Their percentage is presented in the following table:

TABLE 1   Omissions in the Latin version

Book	% of the Swedish text without any correspondence in Latin
1	0
2	0
3	5
4	2
5	0
6	1
7	4
8	22

As may be seen, the first two books are nearly identical, whereas in the eighth the divergence reaches its peak. The difference can be explained if we turn to the sources and the process of the work:

TABLE 2   The sources and the translation order

Book	Main sources	Translation order
1	Oxenstierna (*Relatio historica*), Kobierzycki (*Historia Vladislai*) etc.	Latin → Swedish
2	Kobierzycki, Petrejus etc.	Latin → Swedish
3	Kobierzycki, archive documents	Swedish → Latin & Latin → Swedish
4	Kobierzycki, archive documents	Swedish → Latin & Latin → Swedish

632   VETUSHKO-KALEVICH

TABLE 2   The sources and the translation order (*cont.*)

Book	Main sources	Translation order
5	Kobierzycki, archive documents	Swedish → Latin & Latin → Swedish
6	Kobierzycki, archive documents	Swedish → Latin & Latin → Swedish
7	Kobierzycki, archive documents	Swedish → Latin & Latin → Swedish
8	archive documents	mostly Swedish → Latin
9	archive documents	–
10	archive documents	–

Widekindi states himself in a letter to M. G. De la Gardie that he first wrote his work in Latin and then translated it into Swedish,[14] but this is not quite true. The work is utterly compilative, and by comparing it with the sources we can easily find out which language is original for one or another passage. To put it crudely, when using literary sources, primarily *Historia Vladislai Poloniae et Sveciae principis* by the Polish historian Stanisław Kobierzycki and a sketch on the history of Swedish-Polish relations by chancellor Axel Oxenstierna, both written in Latin, Widekindi writes Latin first, whereas the Swedish version is to regard as translation. When Widekindi uses Swedish (mainly documentary) sources, in particular the reports by the leader of Swedish forces, Jacob De la Gardie, the situation is more complicated: there are some striking mistakes in Swedish that can only be explained by the existence of a Latin draft, but there are also literal correspondences with and quotations from the Swedish text of the source, suggesting that the Swedish translation from Latin was revised with the help of the sources. The final Latin text is, in its turn, sometimes translated from Swedish.

The first two books, which present a short introduction to the main narrative, were first written in Latin, even though at the end of the second book the author had to resort to the Swedish documents: he first paraphrased them in Latin, and then translated back into Swedish.[15] Books 3–7 largely consist

---

14   Stockholm, Riksarkivet, De la Gardieska samlingen, vol. E 1596, Widekindi, 15 March 1672. About Widekindi's letters to De la Gardie, in particular this one, see Arsenij Vetushko-Kalevich, "Biligual Writings on Bilingual Writings: J. Widekindi's Letters to M. G. De La Gardie," *Philologia Classica* 11 (2016), 289–300.

15   This is suggested *inter alia* by a comparison between the Swedish text of the Viborg treaty from 1609, published in *Sverges traktater med främmande magter jemte andra dit hörande handlingar. 5:e delens förra hälft: 1572–1632*, ed. Olof Simon Rydberg, Carl Hallendorff (Stockholm, 1903), 158–68, and Widekindi's paraphrase of it (Widekindi, *Krijgz-Historie*

of De la Gardie's reports, but the share of the Latin literary sources is still significant: e.g. in book 4 more than one third of the text is borrowed from Kobierzycki; some other Latin works, mainly by Polish historians, occasionally leave their traces in the text as well.

A change comes in book 8 and is marked by the following declaration—here quoted from the Latin version:[16]

> Nos illis solummodo attendimus, quae bella in Muschovia gesta concernunt, quatenus scilicet de rebus hisce, ex literis, mandatis, consilijs, decretis, relationibus, alijsque monumentis nobis constare poterit: Eaque juxta seriem annorum mensiumque memorabimus.

This remark looks somewhat awkward, as our author has by that time used all these archive materials for some hundreds of pages, and his narrative has also been more or less chronologic. What actually changes here is the situation with the literary sources: short passages from Kobierzycki appear only four times in the last three books, and geographical notes borrowed from Rossica-literature are absent altogether. So Widekindi does not begin using documents in the eighth book—he begins using *exclusively* documents. This is not surprising due to the character of the events he is dealing with. Previously it was military campaigns and the political turbulence in Russia partly described by his Polish colleague Kobierzycki and his Swedish predecessor Petrus Petrejus and often giving occasions for short or long digressions on Russian history and geography, also treated by different authors before him. Now Widekindi turns more and more to the strategic considerations and the peace negotiations, and can only find his sources in the archives. Translating into Latin all this huge Swedish and German material, which occupies about 500 pages in Widekindi's Swedish version, would be a much more demanding work than the one he had done so far; besides, he is busy enough, working on several other historiographical projects by the beginning of the 1670s. It was then that *Gustaff Adolphs Historia* was written, published posthumously in 1691. The *Additamentum* to the history

---

[see above, n. 7], 63–6 and Widekindi, *Historia Belli* [see above, n. 8], 53–4). Some details in the Latin text render the contents of the source more exactly, but even more striking is the fact that the wording of Widekindi's Swedish does not bear any resemblance to the expressions of the source.

16   "We are only occupied with the things that concern the war in Muscovy (i.e. as opposed to the war with Denmark, which is briefly mentioned before), as far as it will be possible for us to know about these from letters, mandates, counsels, decrees, relations and other documents, and we will relate about it chronologically." Widekindi, *Historia Belli* (see above, n. 8), 377. All translations are my own.

of Gustavus Vasa's reign was also ready for printing in 1672.[17] Besides that, from Widekindi's letters it is clear that he was working on the history of Kings Eric XIV and John III.[18] The historiographer of the Realm may have simply been too busy to finish the Latin version, and the dramatic shortening of book 8 is an additional reason to suspect this.

If we now turn to specific episodes, the differences can also be largely explained by the character of the sources. Left out are the passages that can easily be left out, e.g. short geographical digressions, originally written in Latin, are sometimes missing in the Swedish text,[19] and the same is true for a description of skis, borrowed from Kobierzycki's work.[20] On the other hand, when consulting De la Gardie's reports and using them in his Swedish text, Widekindi omits in his Latin text some military maneuvers of secondary importance.[21]

An interesting case is the disastrous battle of Klushino. The chapter it comprises in the fourth book is about 1,200 words long in the Latin text and about 1,100 words long in the Swedish one, whereas the Swedish text would be at least 20 per cent longer by a normal translation, be it from Latin or into Latin, due to structural differences between the languages.[22] Large passages are thus missing in the Swedish version. Did Widekindi want to make an unpleasant story shorter for the home public? This would have implied that he did it in a strange way, depriving his Swedish reader of some complimentary details, e.g.[23]

---

17   This *Additamentum* has survived only partially: two first pages of the trial print, pasted into the collection *Bibliographia Sveo-Gothica* of Elias Palmskiöld, are preserved in Uppsala (Uppsala, Uppsala Universitetsbibliotek, Palmskiöldska samlingen, vol. 348, 678–81), and an eleven pages long fragment of the draft may be found in the Royal Library in Stockholm (Stockholm, Kungliga Biblioteket, vol. D 495).

18   Vetushko-Kalevich, "Bilingual Writings" (see above, n. 14), 293.

19   As is the case with short notes about the towns of Tver, Pereslavl-Zalessky and Alexandrovskaya Sloboda in book 3.

20   Widekindi, *Historia Belli* (see above, n. 8), 119–20 after Stanislaus Kobierzycki, *Historia Vladislai Poloniae et Sueciae Principis, ejus Natales et Infantiam, Electionem in Magnum Moscoviae Ducem, Bella Moscovitica, Turcica, caeterasque res gestas continens, usque ad excessum Sigismundi III Poloniae Sueciaeque Regis* (Dantisci, 1655), 212.

21   For instance, news of the attack of a Polish squadron against the surroundings of Narva in June 1609 (Widekindi, *Krijgz-Historie* [see above, n. 7], 87) only mean that Jacob De la Gardie cannot get additional supplements for his expedition towards Moscow and are omitted in the Latin text.

22   In fact, passages accurately translated from Latin sometimes expand more than twofold in Widekindi's Swedish version—without any changes in their contents.

23   "Soon our cavalry, trying to help the troubled infantry, resumed the battle, fiercely attacked the Poles, and, although the spearmen of the enemy came to their aid instantly, bravely resisted them for four hours" Widekindi, *Historia Belli* (see above, n. 8), 165–6.

WIDEKINDI'S *HISTORIA BELLI SVECO-MOSCOVITICI DECENNALIS* 635

> Mox nostri equites laboranti pediti succurrentes, redintegrato praelio acrius Polonos invasere, ac, licet recentes subinde hostium hastatae turmae in auxilium advolarent, eos tamen quatuor integras horas fortiter sustinuere.

and a bit further:[24]

> Constat tunc universi militis ab utraque parte pugnantis egregiam virtutem enituisse, dignam certe, quae ad imitationem virtutis posteritati commendetur.

A closer look on the passages missing in the Swedish version of this chapter shows one trait that they share: all of them are borrowed from Kobierzycki's description of the battle. The Swedish historian simplified his own task here. Although Jacob De la Gardie's report about Klushino battle is not preserved nowadays (like all of his reports until the autumn 1610), there are no doubts that Widekindi used it here,[25] thus having at hand two different stories, one in Swedish and another in Latin. He had time to partly integrate the former into his Latin text, but not to translate details from the latter in his Swedish. Such tricks may also be found elsewhere in the text, in particular several chapters earlier in the same book, as military actions of the Swedish commander Evert Horn are described according to his own documentary account, but in the Latin version the translation from Swedish is partly contaminated with Kobierzycki's passage dealing with the same events.[26]

Stylistic Features

However, the situation when Latin is more or less accurately translated from Swedish or Swedish from Latin is by far the most usual one in the first seven books. So we can proceed to the details of this translation, i.e. differences in

---

24　"In fact, the soldiers on both sides displayed a conspicuous courage, worthy of a praise and imitation by posterity" Widekindi, *Historia Belli* (see above, n. 8), 166.

25　Helge Almquist, *Sverge och Ryssland 1595–1611: Tvisten om Estland, förbundet mot Polen, de ryska gränslandens eröfring och den stora dynastiska planen* (Uppsala, 1907), 190 n. 1.

26　Widekindi, *Krijgz-Historie* (see above, n. 7), 177–83; Widekindi, *Historia Belli* (see above, n. 8), 144–50; Kobierzycki, *Historia Vladislai* (see above, n. 20), 234–9; Evert Horn's report from 23 May 1610 (Stockholm, Riksarkivet, Handlingar rörande ryska kriget).

specific phrases. Widekindi's own statement about his style in Swedish is preserved in a letter to M. G. De la Gardie:[27]

> Malebam stylum populari et quo vulgus hominum loquitur modo fluere, quam aliquid verborum flosculis ambituique dare, putans omnem simplicis et ingenuae veritatis gratiam a Svecico sermone perire, si multum ornamentis litaretur.

That is not perfectly correct: for instance, the heavy syntax of lengthy periods in Latin often influences the Swedish text.[28] However, there are some traces of Widekindi's care about the reader of his Swedish text compared to the reader of the Latin one. In Swedish he often uses appositions and other ways to shortly repeat what has already been said. He also sometimes avoids circumlocutions of the Latin text: e.g. Moscow is sometimes called "domina urbs" or "sedes imperii" in Latin, whereas in Swedish it is simply "Muskou".[29]

The reader of the Swedish text is not supposed to have deep knowledge of classical literature. A comparison of the two versions in the passage dealing with the river Don is illustrative:

> Widekindi, *Historia Belli*, 346: Herodotus ejus fontes ex nescio quibus paludibus deducit. Mela eosdem Riphaeis montibus tribuit. Idem Lucanus quoque lib. 3.[30]
>
> Widekindi, *Krijgz-Historie*, 428: Den gamle Historie-skribenten Herodotus säger at denna Dona skal hafwa sitt vhrsprung vthur ett Kärr/ men förmäler intet hwar thet samma Kärret är. Den förfarne Jordennes kretz beskrifware Mela säger åter/ at hon hafwer sitt vthlopp ifrån the nampnkunnige Bergen som kallas Riphaei; medh honom instämmer och så den märckelige gamle Poeten Lucanus.[31]

---

27   "I preferred that the style would flow in a popular way, used by common people, than to care about rhetorical embellishment, as I thought that the Swedish tongue will lose all the grace of simple and ingenuous sincerity, if too much attention is given to its decoration".

28   This is especially conspicuous in the first book, where mile-long Latin sentences (which go back to Axel Oxenstierna's historical sketch) are far from always split into shorter ones in the Swedish version.

29   Cf. Widekindi, *Historia Belli* (see above, n. 8), 84, 99, 117 and Widekindi, *Krijgz-Historie* (see above, n. 7), 104, 123, 143.

30   "Herodotus traces its beginnings to some bogs. Mela attributes them to the Riphean Mountains. The same does Lucan in book 3."

31   "The ancient historiographer Herodotus says that Don has its beginning in a bog, but does not tell where this bog is. The experienced describer of the Earth Mela says, on the other hand, that it flows from the famous Riphean Mountains; the notable ancient poet Lucan agrees with him."

WIDEKINDI'S *HISTORIA BELLI SVECO-MOSCOVITICI DECENNALIS* 637

The Swedish text here has "the ancient historiographer Herodotus", "the experienced describer of the Earth Mela" and "the notable ancient poet Lucan", while in Latin we only read "Herodotus", "Mela" and "Lucanus".

In the Latin text one may find numerous references to classical mythology, whereas in the Swedish version they are usually omitted,[32] e.g.

> Widekindi, *Historia Belli*, 52: Nostrates, quorum mentes (ut dici solet) ex meliori luto finxit Iupiter [...][33]
>
> Widekindi, *Krijgz-Historie*, 62: Wåra som vprichtige woro/ och aff ett ährebarare Kynne och Sinne än the andra [...][34]
>
> Widekindi, *Historia Belli*, 199: Claudius Boye [...] multos Moschorum in Libithinae rationem misit.[35]
>
> Widekindi, *Krijgz-Historie*, 246: Clas Boye [...] lade många Ryssar neder til jorden.[36]

Somewhat more veiled allusion may be found in the description of the seizure of Novgorod.

> Widekindi, *Historia Belli*, 250–1: Moschi [...] Jacobum ut fulmen bellicum [...] prosequuntur.[37]
>
> Widekindi, *Krijgz-Historie*, 319–20: Ryssar [...] begynte på at [...] wörda och ähra Herr Iacob föga annorledes än som Gudh.[38]

Here the Russians honor Jacob De la Gardie "almost as God" in the Swedish text, whereas the Latin text has the expression "lightning of war". Perhaps it is a higher honor to be God,[39] but it is a very specific achievement to make seventeenth century citizens of Novgorod read Virgil. "Fulmina belli" is namely

---

32   Cf. Коваленко и др., "Апология Юхана Видекинда" (see above, n. 9), 559.

33   "Our people, whose minds, as the saying is, Jupiter molded out of a better clay."

34   "Our people, who were sincere and of a nobler character and mind than the others."

35   "Claes Boije sent many of the Russians into the list of Libitina."

36   "Claes Boije brought many Russians to the ground."

37   "Russians honor Jacob as a lightning of war."

38   "Russians began to revere and to honor Jacob almost as God."

39   Widekindi's references to God throughout the text are in general a good example of what is called ethnicismus styli; on this feature of Neo-Latin literature, see Hans Helander, *Neo-Latin Literature in Sweden in the Period 1620–1720. Stylistics, Vocabulary and Characteristic Ideas* (Uppsala, 2004), 75–80: the word "Deus" sometimes occurs in the Latin text, but only twice outside reported speech and direct quotations of letters or speeches. When the Swedish text has "Gud", it often corresponds to words like "caelites" and "omnipotens" or expressions with "divinus" in Latin; sometimes the mention of God is omitted altogether.

638 VETUSHKO-KALEVICH

an expression praising the Scipios in the sixth book of the *Aeneid* (6, 842–3 "geminos, duo fulmina belli, / Scipiadas, cladem Libyae"); it can also be found in Lucretius (3,1034: "Scipiadas, belli fulmen, Carthaginis horror").[40]

All that does not mean, however, that the Swedish text is totally dry. It does contain some specimens of phraseology without any correspondence in the Latin text, even when this Latin text is the original one, e. g.

> Widekindi, *Historia Belli*, 156: Moschi [...] sclopis suis Polonos petunt, pugnatur strenue, Polonis veniunt in subsidium Cosaci.[41]
>
> Widekindi, *Krijgz-Historie*, 191: Rysserna [...] anföllo Pålackerna medh sine Slungor/ så at dher höltz ett starckt qwastebad/ til dhess Cossakerna kommo Pålackerne til hielp.[42]

Here the plain "pugnatur strenue" is translated as "dher höltz ett starckt qwastebad", i.e. "there was a harsh broom bath there." Another example, again from a passage which follows Kobierzycki and is consequently first written in Latin:

> Widekindi, *Historia Belli*, 90: <Alii prolixe disserebant> ruptis imperii vinculis, munitionum ac provinciarum obtinendarum faciliorem occasionem fore.[43]
>
> Widekindi, *Krijgz-Historie*, 110: När sinnen äre skingrade/ styrelse Compassen förryckt/ och willwalla ibland Folcket/ så är lättare/ at intaga Land och Fästningar.[44]

A metaphor from the Latin text, "ruptis imperii vinculis", is substituted by another metaphor, "styrelse Compassen förryckt", i.e. "the compass of the rule is disturbed". So both texts are often quite idiomatic.

---

40 The expression was widely spread. Widekindi himself uses it ("belli illud fulmen") in his panegyric to Queen Christina (1644), this time to praise Charles IX. Lars Fornelius in his epic poem *Gustavus Sago-Togatus* (1634) calls Gustavus Vasa and Charles IX "belli duo fulmina reges", and the expression "fulmina Martis" can be found in *Carmen votivum in natalem Udalricae Eleonorae* (1682) by Johan Columbus and in *Panegyris Supra Laudibus Erici Lindschoeldi* (1690) by Gunno Eurelius Dahlstierna.

41 "The Muscovites attack the Poles with their guns, it comes to a fierce battle, the Poles are rescued by the Cossacks."

42 "The Russians attacked the Poles with their guns, so that there was a harsh broom bath there, until the Cossacks succored the Poles."

43 "Others verbosely argued that when the bonds of the state are broken it will be easier to overtake fortresses and provinces."

44 "When minds are dispersed, the compass of the rule disturbed, and there is confusion among the people, it is easier to take land and fortresses."

Conclusions

The differences between the Latin and the Swedish version of Johannes Widekindi's historiographical work are numerous, but they are caused either by stylistic considerations or by the technical side of the working process, that is, by the fact that Widekindi manages to slightly rework the text of his sources in the same language, but sometimes cuts corners on the translation into the other language, and ends up in not finishing his Latin text at all.[45] Although it has been claimed in previous research that the Latin version is more "Russian-friendly",[46] there is no evidence for this or other changes in Widekindi's attitude to what he is writing about. Jacob De la Gardie is as heroic in the Latin text, Poles are as treacherous,[47] Russians are as perfidious[48] as in the Swedish text, and so on. The only difference that is indeed "Russian-friendly" is the absence of a genealogical appendix in the Latin version. This appendix demonstrated the lack of legitimacy of the Romanov dynasty to the Russian throne and could provoke a diplomatic controversy, and from Widekindi's letter to M. G. De la Gardie we learn that the chancellor gave orders to the historiographer to erase the appendix from the Latin edition—in fact, it is not only absent there, but also shortened in some copies of the Swedish version.[49] In other respects we have to remember that Widekindi himself claims that the Swedish and the Latin version are intended to complete each other[50] and sometimes even refers to the Latin version in his Swedish text and vice versa.[51] By these conditions, any significant change of the main ideas would have been surprising.

Lund University

---

45   Differences between the Latin and the vernacular versions due to the use of different sources have also been noted in Du Bellay's case, see George H. Tucker, *The Poet's Odyssey* (Oxford, 1990), 133–6; cf. Ginsberg, "Translation, Imitation, Transformation" (see above, n. 11), 435–6.

46   Коваленко и др., "Апология Юхана Видекинда" (see above, n. 9), 559.

47   The word "callidus" often describes them and their doings; note also the recurrent expression "artes Polonicae".

48   The words "perfidus" and "perfidia" occur dozens of times.

49   That is the case with one of the copies preserved in the Royal Library in Stockholm and the copy preserved in the Russian State Library in Moscow.

50   In the dedicatory letter to De la Gardie in the Swedish version.

51   Widekindi, *Krijgz-Historie* (see above, n. 7), 157 (marginal note), Widekindi, *Historia Belli* (see above, n. 8), 127 (marginal note), 420.

CHAPTER 51

Il bestiario "non inutile e giocondo" dell'umanista Pier Candido Decembrio

Éva Vígh

Abstract

L'attività letteraria di Pier Candido Decembrio (1399–1477) rispecchia fedelmente la versatilità della civiltà dell'umanesimo italiano, siccome la sua biografia, le sue opere in diversi generi e temi culturali, le traduzioni ne sono un esempio invero singolare. Con il suo bestiario composto in latino con esigenza umanistica, scritto prima del 1460, intitolato il *De animantium naturis atque formis*, Decembrio mirava a scrivere un'opera zoologica che rispettasse l'antica tradizione oraziana dell'*utile dulci* trasmettendo conoscenze naturali e scientifiche insieme a valori letterario-estetici: le illustrazioni pure assecondano questa finalità. L'intervento traccia brevemente la storia del *De animantium naturis* accentuando il rapporto con la sua fonte primaria (il *Liber de natura rerum* di Tommaso di Cantimpré) e con altre fonti antiche e medievali. Si prende in esame anche il metodo di lavoro del Decembrio tramite la raffigurazione di alcuni mostri, cosa che dimostra come la sensibilità filologica dell'umanista e le nozioni radicate nella tradizione plurisecolare dovevano essere combaciate. Il bestiario composto alla metà del '400 e le illustrazioni eseguite cento anni dopo dimostrano chiaramente la commistione della tradizione antica e medievale, nonché la pacifica compresenza del realismo e della fantasia.

Keywords

Pier Candido Decembrio – *De animantium naturis atque formis* (before 1460) – Neo-Latin bestiaries – fantastic creatures

Studiando la complessa attività degli umanisti fra il '400 ed il '500, si avverte che il loro interesse era rivolto anche a saperi ed autori che erano rimasti fuori dal contesto degli *studia humanitatis*.[1] Il recupero dei classici e la loro

---

1 Le ricerche su questo argomento sono state realizzate nell'ambito del programma *MTA-SZTE Antiquity and Renaissance: Sources and Reception Research Group (TK2016-126)*.

© KONINKLIJKE BRILL NV, LEIDEN, 2020 | DOI:10.1163/9789004427105_052

IL BESTIARIO "NON INUTILE E GIOCONDO" 641

reintegrazione nel quadro umanistico attraverso la lettura, la traduzione, l'interpretazione e l'edizione dei testi della cultura classica, infatti, venivano accompagnati da un'attenzione particolare e da un approccio empirico alla natura a livello conoscitivo e di scoperta. In questo contesto, l'attività e l'esperienza letterario-filosofica di Pier Candido Decembrio (1399–1477), poeta e umanista di corte, testimoniano quella poliedricità intellettuale che caratterizza la civiltà dell'umanesimo latino in Italia.[2] Decembrio fu infatti attivo in tutti i campi di studi umanistici e quindi, oltre a coltivare i suoi interessi di grammatica, retorica, letteratura, storia e filosofia morale, era anche un insigne traduttore, nonché autore di un bestiario che offre tutta una serie di analisi testuale, contestuale ed iconografica. Il manoscritto miniato conservato presso la Biblioteca Vaticana, il *De animantium naturis atque formis*,[3] composto prima del 1460, costituisce un testo di transizione tra i bestiari medievali incentrati sulla natura con la spiritualità cristiana e le opere di zoologia 'scientifica' affermatasi a partire dalla fine del '500. L'idea di scrivere l'opera e dedicarla a Ludovico III Gonzaga sperando di ottenere un servizio presso la corte di Mantova gli venne durante la permanenza nella corte di Alfonso d'Aragona a Napoli. Decembrio prestava servizio a corte in qualità di segretario presso Alfonso, e poi con Ferdinando, tra il 1456 ed il 1459. Nella dedica, Decembrio riporta le circostanze e le motivazioni della composizione del *De animantium naturis*, e quindi i suoi lettori vengono informati che a Napoli, nei rari momenti di *otium,* egli aveva potuto leggere la descrizione della natura degli animali dalla penna di un autore ignoto. E sebbene il testo risultasse per l'umanista senza eleganza e stilisticamente poco convincente, la ricca materia e la sua ammirazione per la natura lo avevano stimolato ad elaborare il testo a modo suo per offrire ai lettori ("aliis prodesse possem non inutili et iucunda lectione") e per recare piacere anche a se stesso benché egli dubitasse della validità di alcune osservazioni e commenti.[4]

---

2 Fra gli studi dedicati all'attività multiforme del Decembrio rinvio al saggio di Vittorio Zaccaria, "Sulle opere di P. C. Decembrio," *Rinascimento* 7 (1956), 13–74. Per l'ambiente intellettuale si veda Massimo Zaggia, "Linee per una storia della cultura in Lombardia dall'età di Coluccio Salutati a quella del Valla," in *Le strade di Ercole. Itinerari umanistici e altri percorsi,* ed. Luca Carlo Rossi, (Firenze, 2010), 3–37.

3 Il titolo intero del codice miniato della Biblioteca Vaticana (*Urb. Lat.* 276) è *De omnium animantium naturis atque formis nec non rebus memoria et annotatione dignis ad illustrissimum principem dominum Ludovicum Gonzagam Mantuae marchionem.* Per la consultazione del manoscritto (1r–231v) e delle illustrazioni invero singolari rinvio alla versione digitalizzata (https://digi.vatlib.it/view/MSS_Urb.lat.276), nonché all'edizione facsimile: *Il Libro degli animali. Cod.Urb.Lat.276. Biblioteca Apostolica Vaticana. Codice Urbinate scritto nel 1460 ed illustrato nel secolo successivo* (Milano, 1985). Il volume di commento è a cura di Cynthia M. Pyle.

4 Cfr. Decembrio, *De omnium animantium* (vedi sopra, n. 3), fols. 1r–231v. La presente citazione: fols. 1r–1v.

Il bestiario ritenuto poco elegante, come si evince dai confronti testuali e studi filologici, era una versione del *Liber de natura rerum* di Tommaso di Cantimpré (1201–72),[5] allievo di Alberto Magno. L'enciclopedista duecentesco dedica sette libri su venti agli animali, più uno agli uomini mostruosi spesso con aspetto composito (teste di animali su corpi umani), e si riferisce anche alle sue fonti – innanzitutto ad Aristotele, Plinio, Solino, il *Fisiologo*, Sant'Isidoro, San Basilio e Sant'Ambrogio – le quali continuavano ad essere fondamentali a proposito degli animali anche ai tempi di Decembrio. Anche il nostro autore, nella dedica, fa menzione delle fonti letterarie che, del resto in gran parte presenti anche nel libro dell'enciclopedista domenicano, dimostrano chiaramente la vastità e la ricchezza del materiale in rapporto alla natura degli animali. Fra i Greci sono nominati, oltre ad Aristotele, anche Socrate, Teofrasto, Teopompo, Plutarco, Galeno, Luciano; tra i 'nostri' non mancano Virgilio, Seneca, Orazio, Giovenale, Cicerone, Varrone, Cornelio Celso, Apuleio, Pomponio Mela, Solino e naturalmente Plinio il Vecchio; gli autori cristiani sono rappresentati da Ambrogio, Girolamo, Agostino, Gregorio ed Isidoro.[6]

Il pregiatissimo codice del *De animantium naturis*, con le sue 473 illustrazioni sugli animali eseguite più di cento anni dopo la stesura del manoscritto, è stato studiato soprattutto dagli storici dell'arte per l'apparato iconografico che continua ad impostare tutta una serie di quesiti di carattere cronologico o relativi all'identità del miniatore.[7] Ludovico Gonzaga, alla fine del 1460, ringraziò

---

5   Cfr. l'edizione moderna: *Thomas Cantimpratensis, Liber de natura rerum, Editio princeps secundum codices manuscriptos*, vol. 1 (Berlin, 1973). I libri 3–9 (97–312) sono dedicati alla zoologia includendo 69 quadrupedi, 72 uccelli, 20 mostri di mare, 29 specie di pesci, 37 di serpenti, lucertole, cioè rettili, nonché 31 di lumache. È di particolare importanza per il nostro tema la sezione sulle mostruose razze umane e composite trovate in oriente (97–101: *Incipit liber III. De monstruosis hominibus orientes*).

6   Per le fonti dirette del Decembrio rinvio a Marco Petoletti, "Pier Candido Decembrio e i suoi libri: primi appunti," in *Retter der Antike*, ed. Patrizia Carmassi (Wiesbaden 2016), 147–90.

7   In base alla posizione unanime degli studiosi, sembra indiscutibile che la maggior parte delle illustrazioni rimandino alle caratteristiche di due opere di Conrad Gesner, la *Historia animalium*, edita per la prima volta nel 1551, ed il *De serpentium natura* pubblicato nel 1587. Per le storia e l'identificazione delle immagini e dell'esecutore rinvio al saggio di Giuseppe Castelli, "Codice Urbinate Latino 276. La miniatura," in *Animalia prodigiosa. Elementi di storia naturale e aspetti prodigiosi in* De omneum animantium naturis atque formis *di Pier Candido Decembrio*, ed. Marisa Laveroni (Vigevano, 2001), 64–85. A parte i dati filologicamente ricostruiti, basti dare un'occhiata all'immagine della *gallina Indiae* (ovvero il tacchino) in compagnia di altri volatili, cosa che dimostra evidentemente la datazione delle illustrazioni al '500. L'immagine del *monoceros*, a sua volta, è la copia del *rhinocerus* di Dürer (1515) o quella di Gesner, del resto identica alla raffigurazione düreriana. Gli storici dell'arte ricordano pure un particolare dell'affresco da soffitto di Bernardino Campi che rappresenta quest'animale nello studiolo del Palazzo del Giardino a Sabbioneta. Per il rapporto fra il manoscritto del Decembrio e i disegni rinascimentali della natura si veda Cynthia M. Pyle, "The Art and

IL BESTIARIO "NON INUTILE E GIOCONDO" 643

lo "spectabilis miles amice noster carissime" della copia del *De animantium naturis*, anzi, ne era rimasto entusiasta al punto che voleva che l'opera fosse illustrata "de manum de bono maestro",[8] ma la storia del manoscritto (e quella delle illustrazioni eseguite nella seconda metà del '500) rimane alquanto misteriosa poiché ci sono solo congetture più o meno plausibili relative alla nascita delle immagini invero suggestive.[9]

Considerando la vastità degli animali descritti e i tanti approcci con cui è possibile analizzare il bestiario di Decembrio, questa volta mi accingo a prendere in esame le creature fantastiche ed i mostri che in letteratura e in arte occupano un posto importante nel mostrare la visione del mondo e la mentalità dell'uomo medievale. Siccome la concezione medievale non faceva distinzione fra gli animali appartenenti alla vita quotidiana e quegli esseri la cui nozione non era minimamente sorretta dall'esperienza diretta, non era assolutamente necessario distinguere il reale dal fantastico. Esseri fantastici, mostruosi e diversi portenti popolavano i capitelli e le facciate delle chiese, le decorazioni delle miniature e degli arazzi, e le stesse creature figuravano nei fogli dei bestiari rievocati e citati dai predicatori per cui, in fin dei conti, anche queste figure animali, come esempi morali, erano familiari ai credenti. Non dobbiamo dimenticarci allo stesso tempo dell'etimologia del termine "mostro" (lat. "monstrum" "prodigio, portento") dal verbo "monere" ("avvisare, ammonire"),[10] che nell'interpretazione cristiana indica che i mostri creati da Dio vengono intesi anche come ammonimenti divini. Isidoro di Siviglia fu il primo, nell'Alto Medioevo, a classificare le diverse tipologie di mostri. Sulle orme di Varrone dichiara che essi[11]

Science of Renaissance Natural History. Thomas of Cantimpre, Pier Candido Decembrio, Conrad Gessner and Teodoro Ghisi in Vatican Library MS. Urb.Lat. 276," *Viator* 27 (1996), 265–321.

8 Per il testo integrale della lettera del marchese di Mantova cfr. Carlo Ramella, *Codice Urbinate Latino 276. Esegesi scritturale*, in Laveroni, *Animalia* (vedi sopra, n. 7), 48–86, qui 58.

9 Il codice, realizzato secondo il desiderio del Duca (ma fino alla seconda metà del '500 senza immagini), rimane conservato probabilmente nella biblioteca dei Gonzaga fino al 1630, e poi passa alla Biblioteca Ducale di Urbino. Per il trasferimento della biblioteca (e il *Codice Urbinate Latino 276*) alla Biblioteca Vaticana si veda Maria Moranti-Luigi Moranti, *Il trasferimento dei "Codices Urbinates" alla Biblioteca Vaticana. Cronistoria, documenti e inventario* (Urbino, 1981).

10 In Cicerone il "monstrum" assunse il significato di un avvertimento divino, anzi fu considerato come un presagio con connotati di un essere sovrannaturale. Egli, infatti, nel *De divinatione* (1,42,92) ricorda che "Quia enim ostendunt, portendunt, monstrant, praedicunt, ostenta, portenta, monstra, prodigia dicuntur."

11 *Isidori hispalensis episcopi Etymologiarum sive Originum Libri XX*, ed. Wallace M. Lindsay (Oxford, 1911), 11,3,1–3. Le citazioni successive da quest'opera verranno segnalate *Etym.*

contra naturam nata videntur: sed non sunt contra naturam, quia divina voluntate fiunt, cum voluntas Creatoris cuiusque conditiae rei natura sit. Unde et ipsi gentiles Deum modo Naturam modo Deum appellant. Portentum ergo fit non contra naturam, sed contra quam est nota natura. Portenta autem et ostenta, monstra atque prodigia ideo nuncupantur, quod portendere atque ostendere, monstare ac praedicare aliqua futura videntur. [...] Monstra vero a monitu dicta, quod aliquid significando demonstrent, sive quod statim monstrent quid appareat; et hoc proprietatis est, abusione tamen scriptorum plerumque corrumpitur.

Quando analizziamo le forme e le proprietà di queste creature, dobbiamo tener presenti queste considerazioni che determinano la visione cristiana degli esseri mostruosi. I termini con cui veniva designata la mostruosità, ossia "monstrum, prodigium, portentum" o "ostentum", malgrado le sottili differenze erano intercambiabili nell'Alto Medioevo. Ancora ai tempi di Decembrio i mostri indicavano qualcosa di insolito, irregolare e straordinario contro natura, ma anche un presagio o un danno nel futuro.[12] Tuttavia, il Decembrio umanista trasmetteva le informazioni, le descrizioni e gli aneddoti relativi a queste creature, provenienti dalle fonti antiche e medievali, talvolta con un distacco ossequioso nei confronti delle autorità, talaltra con una certa perplessità, oppure si lasciava persuadere cedendo alla forza delle immagini radicate nell'immaginario collettivo sin da secoli. Seguendo fedelmente la sua fonte, nei quattro libri del bestiario,[13] Decembrio descrive le creature composite distribuite in base al loro *habitat* (terra, acqua, aria), e le inserisce fra gli altri animali tenendo presente l'ordine alfabetico senza tentare di classificarle secondo uno scrupolo tassonomico. Il mondo reale e l'immaginario si mescolano così nella loro precisa classificazione alfabetica, ed è dovuto a questo metodo

---

12   Cfr. John Block Friedman, *The Monstrous Races in Medieval Art and Thought* (Cambridge, 1981), 111.

13   Il primo libro (fols. 5r–62r) descrive in ordine alfabetico, in 107 capitoli, la proprietà degli animali quadrupedi terrestri (*De animantium quadrupedum sive terrestrium natura*), partendo dal cinghiale fino allo zibellino. Il secondo libro (fols. 62v–121r) si occupa della natura e della forma di 116 uccelli (*De volucrum naturis et formis*) cominciando con l'aquila e chiudendo con il falcone. Il terzo (fols. 121v–168r), il *De beluarum maritimarum et piscium omnium naturis et formis*, contiene la descrizione dei mostri marini e di tutti gli esseri acquatici dividendo il libro in due parti: dopo i 69 mostri marini segue il catalogo di 90 pesci di fiume e di mare. Il quarto libro (168r–183v/184r–204r), con il titolo *De serpentum et vermium natura*, a sua volta viene diviso in due parti: la prima (*De serpentibus*) rappresenta 42 rettili, la seconda (*De vermibus*) si occupa di 51 specie di rane ed insetti. Il quinto libro, ormai senza immagini, parla "de rebus memoria et annotatione dignis" (fols. 204v–231v).

IL BESTIARIO "NON INUTILE E GIOCONDO" 645

tipicamente medievale che possiamo osservare nello stesso foglio per esempio il ghiro accanto alla sfinge ("fingae"), una specie di scimmia da non confondere con la mitica figura egizia (fol. 30r), o la manticora con il mosco siberiano ("musquelibet", fol. 42r), o la serra con la sirena (fol. 139r), la ficedula con il grifone (fol. 91r–91v).

Il nostro autore, nella descrizione delle creature ibride (sirena, centauro, tritone, sfinge, satiro, uomo marino, manticora) trasmette fedelmente quello che gli era imposto da una lunga tradizione plurisecolare. Nel caso dell'onocentauro ("onocentaurus"), che "habet enim caput velut asini corpus ut hominis,"[14] Isidoro di Siviglia (*Etym.* 11,3,39) viene citato per intero, e come un essere creato per innesto della parte superiore umana sulla parte inferiore dell'asino, l'onocentauro è simbolo della commistione degli istinti selvaggi e della ragione. Il miniatore cinquecentesco (ispirato probabilmente dalla descrizione di una pittura di Zeusi da parte di Luciano) accanto alla figura dell'onocentauro ne raffigurava anche la versione femminile, non riportata però nel testo di Decembrio. Da altri bestiari sappiamo che questa creatura nasce dal rapporto fra un asino dissoluto ed una donna altrettanto lussuriosa, e che vive in Africa. Conviene menzionare anche il breve riferimento all'onocentauro del *Liber monstrorum* il quale coincide con la descrizione degli enciclopedisti: l'onocentauro "quos sic diversorum generum varia naturaliter coniungit natura."[15] Decembrio segue quasi letteralmente la descrizione di Tommaso di Cantimpré (4,82) e, per rendere la voce di questo essere composito, egli completa la sua fonte medievale e ricorre al racconto di Plutarco che, a proposito della vita di Silla, fece riferimento alla cattura di un satiro uguale a quelli che scultori e pittori sono soliti raffigurare. Il catturato, infatti, emetteva una voce aspra e di un suono misto e confuso tra il nitrir del cavallo e il belare del capro.[16]

Per ciò che riguarda la sfinge (una specie di scimmia), il nostro autore fa derivare l'origine etiopica di questa creatura seguendo la descrizione di Plinio il Vecchio. Il naturalista antico racconta infatti che durante i giochi circensi offerti da Pompeo Magno si potevano vedere molte stranezze fra cui le "sfingas,

---

14   Decembrio, *De omnium animantium* (vedi sopra, n. 3), 46r.

15   *Liber monstrorum*, ed. Franco Porsia, (Napoli, 2012), 1,10, p. 148. Il libro è un enigmatico capolavoro, composto con ogni probabilità nel IX secolo e dedicato alla difformità e alla diversità. Il libro I sui tre (*Liber primus de monstris*) descrive in 56 capitoli le bestie e i popoli dalle caratteristiche straordinarie.

16   Nei pressi di Durazzo "ἐνταῦθά φασι κοιμώμενον ἁλῶναι σάτυρον, οἷον οἱ πλάσται καὶ γραφεῖς εἰκάζουσιν, ἀχθέντα δὲ ὡς Σύλλαν ἐρωτᾶσθαι δι' ἑρμηνέων πολλῶν ὅστις εἴη· φθεγξαμένου δὲ μόλις οὐδὲν συνετῶς, ἀλλὰ τραχεῖάν τινα καὶ μάλιστα μεμιγμένην ἵππου τε χρεμετισμῷ καὶ τράγου μηκασμῷ φωνὴν ἀφέντος, ἐκπλαγέντα τὸν Σύλλαν ἀποδιοπομπήσασθαι." *Plutarch's lives*, vol. 4, ed. B. Perrin (Cambridge, 1916., reprint 1968), 408–10.

fusco pilo, mammis in pectore geminis, Aethiopia generat multaque alia monstri similia."[17] È il nostro autore ad aggiungere (ricorrendo questa volta alla sua fonte medievale) che, avendo due mammelle, può partorire anche gemelli ed accentua la sua irruenza e la ferocia per cui "qui placida habere cupit contentionem a principio evitet" (fol. 30r). Anche Tritone, dio marino metà uomo e metà pesce e dal petto semiferino, viene inserito da Decembrio fra i mostri compositi (fol. 140v) con una descrizione laconica utilizzando Plinio il Vecchio e riportando gli immancabili attributi con cui il figlio di Poseidone comanda alle acque. Oltre ai tanti ricordi e riferimenti mitologici, Decembrio poteva leggere la descrizione di Tritone anche nell'*Eneide* (Virg., *Aen.* 10,209–12):

> hunc vehit immanis Triton et caerula concha
> exterrens freta, cui laterum tenus hispida nanti
> frons hominem praefert, in pristim desinit alvus,
> spumea semifero sub pectore murmurat unda.

A proposito della barca di Aulete, Virgilio, infatti, parla della figura di Tritone che dal ventre in su ha forma umana ("semifero sub pectore"), e per il resto è pesce con l'attributo della conca cerulea. Sappiamo inoltre che Tritone era considerato un mostro marino anche dal *Liber monstrorum* che ne parla assieme a sirene, satiri, arpie, ecc.:[18]

> Et Tritonem capite humano, pectore semifero et deorum ab umbelico piscibus dixerunt similem, qui in Aegyptiorum Carpathio mari et circa oras Italiae visus fuisse describitur. Et utrum a Tritone Lybiae palude an palus ab illo, hoc nomen inditum possideat ignoratur.

In tal modo, Decembrio segue fedelmente la tradizione mitologica e letteraria plurisecolare, nonché le affermazioni dei bestiari medievali senza esprimere questa volta la propria presa di posizione, che probabilmente non era troppo distante da quella delle fonti.

Era ancora più ricca ed estesa la tradizione relativa a satiri, fauni, e ad altri abitatori delle selve. Decembrio costituisce un insieme di varie creature sotto la voce "pilosus" e, riportando un passo di Girolamo dalla *Vita di San Paolo*, che ad ogni modo è stato ripreso da Isidoro sotto la voce "satiri",[19] descrive

---

17   Plinio, *Hist. nat.* 8,30.

18   *Liber monstrorum* (vedi sopra, n. 15), 1,52, p. 238.

19   *Etym.* 11,3,21 "Satyri homunciones sunt aduncis naribus; cornua in frontibus, et caprarum pedibus similes [...]"

IL BESTIARIO "NON INUTILE E GIOCONDO" 647

dettagliatamente quell'essere che si chiama ora fauno, ora satiro, ora incubo: comunque sia, hanno aspetto umano fino all'ombelico, ma portano corna ricurve, e sono provvisti di gambe e piedi caprini. Decembrio, in questo contesto, dedica maggiore spazio al cinocefalo, una creatura semiumana alquanto frequente anche nelle fonti antiche e medievali. Era stato sant'Agostino, nel *De civitate dei*, ad iniziare proprio con i cinocefali il suo discorso dedicato alle razze umane mostruose. Per i bestiari le testimonianze di Agostino ed Isidoro[20] dovevano essere fondamentali: la descrizione prevede un essere grande come un cane, con la testa di cane e con un latrato al posto della voce umana. Il *Liber monstrorum* descrive i cinocefali in modo generico, precisando anche che mangiano carne cruda.[21] Decembrio aggiunge che "cetera corporis membra homini simillima erant. Crura nuda, manus inspicere licebat. Collum est album et nudum in dorso pilos habebat. Vinum avidissime bibebat", cosa che viene evidenziata anche nell'illustrazione al margine del foglio che rappresenta il cinocefalo con un bicchiere di vino in mano. Il pudore invece impediva al miniatore cinquecentesco di mettere in evidenza il fatto che "genitale membrum ultra corporis staturam eminebat."[22] E se gli antichi attribuirono agli uomini silvestri e pelosi uno smodato appetito carnale e altri costumi negativi, nelle interpretazioni cristiane, a loro volta, essi assumevano caratteristiche diaboliche legate alla carne, ed erano simboli della lussuria e del peccato. Soprattutto ai cinocefali, veri nemici dei cristiani, venivano attribuite proprietà assolutamente negative: bestialità, crudeltà ed irrazionale ferocia.

La descrizione della sirena è altrettanto significativa perché, leggendola, possiamo renderci conto dell'atteggiamento di Decembrio nei confronti degli animali/creature ibride, la cui esistenza viene relegata dall'umanista nel campo della fantasia. A questo punto invece lo studioso cede il posto al poeta: se, infatti, nei più diversi generi letterari sin da Omero si poteva leggere di sirene, giganti, centauri, Scilla e chimere, il nostro autore poteva giustamente pensare che non fosse lecito ignorarli. Decembrio, esprimendo allo stesso tempo la propria perplessità, non riporta servilmente la descrizione molto dettagliata di Tommaso di Cantimpré, anzi è molto laconico. Egli non presta attenzione alla morfologia piuttosto varia e diversificata di questo mostro marino sebbene non gli dovesse passare inosservata la ricca e variegata tradizione testuale medievale in cui le sirene erano raffigurate in forme diverse: per metà donna, per metà pesce, con una coda biforcuta (variante con cui essa veniva raffigurata

---

20   Cfr. August., *De civ. Dei* 16,8, ed Isidoro, *Etym.* 11,3,15.
21   Cfr. *Liber monstrorum*, (vedi sopra, n. 15), 1,16, p. 165.
22   Decembrio, *De omnium animantium* (vedi sopra, n. 3), fol. 51r.

648 VÍGH

anche nel manoscritto di Decembrio), nonché con una forma a metà tra femmina ed uccello, ma si poteva leggere anche di una parte cavallina.[23]

Per ciò che riguarda la manticora,[24] Decembrio procede similmente al metodo adoperato nel caso della sirena copiando le affermazioni della fonte senza aggiungere né togliere alcun dettagio o modificarne il contenuto:[25]

> Manticora animal monstruosum ut Plinius scribit facie quasi humana oculis glaucis colore sanguineo corpore leonino cauda aculeata voce tam sibila ut fistularum concinentium modulationes imitetur. Humanas carnes avidissime affectat velocitate tam eximia ut avium volatus exequet. Id aliqui morcomoroni persimile dixerunt.

In realtà, la fonte in assoluto per i bestiari e le enciclopedie era soprattutto Plinio, che ne aveva dato una descrizione plastica:[26]

> Apud eosdem nasci Ctesias scribit quam mantichoran appellat, triplici dentium ordine pectinatim coeuntium, facie et auriculis hominis, oculis glaucis, colore sanguineo, corpore leonis, cauda scorpionis modo spicula infigentem, vocis ut si misceatur fistulae et tubae concentus, velocitas magnae, humani corporis vel praecipue adpetentem.

Anche la raffigurazione della manticora nei vari bestiari risulta ripetitiva: "carne humana desia e afecta".[27] Se diamo un'occhiata alle illustrazioni duecentesche dei bestiari inglesi e francesi[28] e a quella eseguita dell'artista cinquecentesco al margine del *De animantium naturis* decembriano, a parte il disegno invero 'rinascimentale', quindi più incline alla raffigurazione dei tratti somatici del volto, non troviamo nessuna differenza nei dettagli morfologici e

---

23 A questo proposito cfr. il testo del *Bestiario toscano* in Luigia Morini, *Bestiari medievali* (Torino, 1996), 444–5. Il *Liber Monstrorum*, a sua volta, segnala che "squamosas tamen piscium caudas habent, quibus semper in gurgite latent" (vedi sopra, n. 15), 1,6, p. 141.

24 La denominazione della creatura, riportata nella *Historia animalium* di Aristotele (2,3,501a25), venne ripresa da Plinio in forma erronea: doveva essere infatti "martichora", un animale antropofago, ma la versione pliniana passava ai testi medievali.

25 Decembrio, *De omnium animantium* (vedi sopra, n. 3), fol. 42r.

26 Plinio, *Hist. nat.* 8,30.

27 Morini, *Bestiari medievali* (vedi sopra, n. 24), 505 (*Bestiario moralizzato*, sonnet 24).

28 Per la raffigurazione alquanto ripetitiva della manticora rimando ai manoscritti seguenti: Paris, BnF, lat. 3630, f. 8or; Oxford, Bodleian Library, Ms. Bodley 533, f. 7r; Bodleian Library, Ms. Ashmole 1511, f. 22v; Bodleian Library, Ms. Bodley 764, f. 25r; Haga, Koninklijke Bibliotheek, KB, KA 16, f. 64r; New York, Morgan Library, Ms. M.81, f. 38v; Haga, Museum Meermanno, MMW, 10 B 25, f. 13r.

IL BESTIARIO "NON INUTILE E GIOCONDO" 649

cromatici. Anche in questo caso risulta evidente il fatto che le creature a proposito delle quali l'autore (e il miniatore) non potevano avere un'esperienza diretta, venivano descritte e raffigurate nella loro forma consueta in base agli schemi plurisecolari. Del resto questa rimane la pratica anche nel secolo successivo, basti sfogliare i libri di due grandi autori della zoologia rinascimentale, Conrad Gesner ed Ulisse Aldrovandi. Nelle loro opere,[29] scritte con un'esigenza ormai scientifica, continuano ad apparire animali, mostri e creature ibride accanto agli animali reali ed appartenenti alla natura e all'esperienza diretta degli autori stessi.

Studiando il testo del *De animantium naturis*, il metodo di lavoro del Decembrio umanista ci risulta evidente, e soprattutto molto istruttivo: egli si basa prevalentemente sulle descrizioni dell'enciclopedista medievale ma richiama sistematicamente alla memoria anche le sue letture della tradizione classica. Inoltre, con un atteggiamento critico, proprio dell'umanesimo, e con l'osservazione personale della natura, in alcuni casi specifici egli dimostra una nuova impostazione mentale con cui diventa il precursore dei nuovi metodi di investigazione delle scienze naturali. Nei bestiari medievali, la disposizione degli animali e la loro interpretazione venivano sistemate a due livelli di lettura: alla parte descrittiva era aggiunto il criterio teologico-moralizzante. La fonte presuntiva di Decembrio, Tommaso di Cantimpré, accentuava la descrizione zoologica, e quindi l'opera dell'umanista vigevanese a sua volta adotta questo schema enciclopedico. In tal modo, per una scelta presumibilmente consapevole dell'autore, scompare la moralizzazione in chiave teologica dimostrando anche con questo atteggiamento il richiamo dei tempi. Allo stesso tempo, l'inserimento di animali prodigiosi, creature composite o mostri mai visti da Decembrio, tramandati da tutta una serie di miti, favolose relazioni di viaggio e ricavati dalle leggende antiche e medievali, come abbiamo potuto constatare, serviva da un lato a mettere in risalto la propria cultura poliedrica. D'altro canto, il testo documenta la mentalità di un umanista quattrocentesco e soprattutto la forza dell'immaginario collettivo colto e popolare che continuava ad avvalersi di queste creature nel loro significato simbolico. La stessa posizione si rispecchia del resto anche nel lavoro del miniatore che, pur seguendo prevalentemente le descrizioni del testo, in alcuni dettagli realistici si lascia guidare dalle proprie osservazioni o da altri maestri della pittura cinquecentesca. Nel caso delle creature mitiche e leggendarie mai viste, invece, non si distacca affatto dalle immagini tramandate dai bestiari e dalla tradizione

---

29   Per la zoologia di Gesner cfr. Conrad Gesner, *Historia animalium*, 5 vols. (Zurich, 1551–58). Fra le diverse opere ed edizioni degli scritti di Aldrovandi, dal punto di vista dei mostri cfr. Ulisses Aldrovandi, *Monstrorum Historia* (Bologna, 1642).

iconografica medievale. Il Bestiario del Decembrio, composto alla metà del '400, e le decorazioni nate un secolo dopo, dimostrano la commistione e la pacifica convivenza di tradizione, realismo e fantasia poetico-artistica, elementi distintivi della civiltà rinascimentale.

Università di Szeged, Dipartimento di Italianistica
MTA-SZTE Antiquity and Renaissance: Sources and Reception Research Group

CHAPTER 52

Der Humanist in der Krise: Zur Rolle der Poesie im Leben des Rigaer Humanisten David Hilchen

Kristi Viiding

Abstract

Zu den bekanntesten und einflussreichsten Humanisten Livlands gehörte im 16./17. Jahrhundert der Rigaer Stadtsekretär und Syndikus David Hilchen (1561–1610). Sein Lebenslauf und seine Gelehrsamkeit sind dank seiner umfangsreichen Korrespondenz, Gelegenheitsdichtung, seiner Reden sowie dank von ihm verfasster Gesetzen gut dokumentiert. Seine Vermittlerrolle zwischen dem Rigaer Rat, dem livländischen Adel und der polnischen Regierung hat ihn zu Lebzeiten in große Krisen gestürzt, die er trotz vieler Gerichtsprozesse und Verleumdungen, des Raubes seines Sohnes von den Jesuiten und zehn Jahre im Exil erfolgreich überwunden hat. Der Beitrag betrachtet die Rolle der Literatur und besonders der Poesie in den Jahren seiner gesellschaftlich erfolgreichen Tätigkeit (ca. 1585–99) und in seinen Krisenjahren (1600–10). Anhand Hilchens Gedichten aus zwei Lebensperioden wird analysiert, wie sich das Verständnis der Literatur sowie die von Hilchen verwendeten antiken Vorbilder synchron mit seiner Lebenserfahrung verändert haben. Zum Schluss wird Hilchens persönliche Entwicklung mit dem Vorbild einiger zeitgenössischer Humanisten verglichen.

Keywords

David Hilchen – Neo-Latin occasional poetry – humanism in Riga – reception of Horace – crisis management with poetry

Einleitung[1]

Kristallisationspunkt der [livländischen] humanistischen Spätblüte und ihr hauptsächlicher Anreger wurde der Rigaer Syndikus David Hilchen,

---

1 Der Aufsatz entstand im Rahmen des Forschungsprojektes *Masterpieces of Humanism in Livonia: David Hilchen's epistolography as a source of language, literary, juridical and*

© KONINKLIJKE BRILL NV, LEIDEN, 2020 | DOI:10.1163/9789004427105_053

der mit der Gründung der Buchdruckerei und einer Buchhandlung, der Verbesserung der Stadtbibliothek und vor allem mit der Reform der Domschule auch die äußeren Voraussetzungen humanistischen Bildungswirkens und geistigen Lebens schuf. [...] Die [...] Bildungsreform ist in literarischen Zusammenhängen die wichtigste Leistung Hilchens, der neben lateinischen Reden und Schriften auch mit lateinischen Episteln an Freunde sowie Hochzeits- und Leichencarmina hervortrat. Sie ist aber nur ein Teilaspekt seines Wirkens als Diplomat, Jurist und ein echter *uomo universale*.[2]

Dies ist eine für das livländische Geistesleben der Frühen Neuzeit im Allgemeinen zutreffende Stellungnahme. Hilchens Gründungen und Reformen von Bildungs- und kulturellen Institutionen in Riga sowie seine gesetzgeberische Tätigkeit sind gut belegt und untersucht.[3] Seine rednerische und dichterische Tätigkeit dagegen wurde bis jetzt nur fragmentarisch betrachtet: Die deutsch(baltisch)e Forschung beschäftigte sich lediglich mit Hilchens Rigaer Arbeitsjahren (1585–1600) – zuerst war er Stadtsekretär und Syndikus, seit 1591 der Vertreter der livländischen Stände im polnischen Sejm und seit 1595 auch Sekretär des polnischen Königs.[4] Doch nachdem Hilchen im Jahre 1600 des Hochverrats angeklagt worden und aus Riga geflohen war, und besonders nachdem über ihn im Mai 1601 das Todesurteil gesprochen und er vogelfrei geworden war, blieb er als Flüchtling in Polen mit seiner literarischen Tätigkeit völlig außerhalb des Gesichtskreises der (deutsch)baltischen (Literatur-)Historiker. Von der polnischen Humanismusforschung ist Hilchen in seiner Zugehörigkeit zur dortigen Literatur während seines Exils in Zamość 1603–10 nur *en passant* als Panegyrist des Grosskanzlers Jan Zamoyski erwähnt worden.[5] Diese Fragmentierung eines Humanistenschicksals ist teilweise durch ein auf der Nation basierendes Literaturverständnis bedingt. Bei großen Humanisten ist dieser Zugang längst überwunden. Im Hilchens Fall zögern die lettischen Literaturhistoriker jedoch bis heute, die Schriften eines des Hochverrats Beschuldigten in

---

 educational history, unterstützt von Estonian Research Council (PUT-1030). Ich danke Walther Ludwig (Hamburg) und Thomas Hoffmann (Tallinn) für die Sprachkorrektur und Michał Czerenkiewicz (Krakow) für wertvolle Literaturhinweise.

2 Gero von Wilpert, *Deutschbaltische Literaturgeschichte* (München, 2005), 74–5.

3 Grundlegend Herta von Ramm-Helmsing, *David Hilchen (1561–1610): Syndikus in Riga* (Posen, 1936); Thomas Hoffmann, *Der Landrechtsentwurf David Hilchens von 1599: Ein livländisches Rechtszeugnis polnischer Herrschaft* (Frankfurt am Main, 2007).

4 Livland gehörte 1562–1625/29 zur Polnisch-Litauischen Adelsrepublik.

5 Z. B. Stanisław Łempicki, *Mecenat Wielkiego Kanclerza* (Warszawa, 1980); Jerzy Starnawski, Halina Kasprzak-Obrębska, Maria Wichowa, *Pod cieniem Hippeum: studia i materiały* (Lódz, 1995).

DER POESIE IM LEBEN DES RIGAER HUMANISTEN DAVID HILCHEN 653

die Literaturgeschichte seiner Heimat einzugliedern. Aus literaturhistorischer Perspektive können solche Schicksale jedoch für das Verständnis der Rolle der Poesie besonders in Krisenzeiten eines Humanisten äußerst wichtig sein, um die Dynamik seiner poetischen Produktion als auch metapoetische Überlegungen zu verstehen.

Die verlorenen *juvenilia*

Die erhaltenen 39 Gedichte (1096 Verse) aus Hilchens Feder sind in den zwanzig Jahren zwischen 1587 und 1608 entstanden. Die Existenz einiger weiterer Gedichte ist aus Erwähnungen in Briefen bekannt. So gibt es einen Hinweis auf ein im Jahr 1606 verfasstes *Jambicum Dunamundense*.[6] 1608 schickte Hilchen Johannes Wowerius ein Grabgedicht für Justus Lipsius zur Lektüre – jedoch mit der Bemerkung, dass es kaum die Veröffentlichung wert sei, jedoch in der Hoffnung, dass es in einer Sammlung der Grabgedichte für Lipsius veröffentlicht werden könne.[7] Wegen des Brandes der Rigaer Stadtbibliothek in 1941 ist ein viel größerer Verlust zu vermuten, nämlich der der Jugendgedichte Hilchens. Zu dieser Annahme führt nicht nur der zeittypische Poesieunterricht an der Rigaer Domschule,[8] sondern auch Bemerkungen in seinen späteren Werken. Wiederholt erwähnt er die poetischen Segel und Ruder, die ihn früher getragen haben.[9] Um 1599 nennt er am Anfang seiner Satire unter seinen Jugendwerken anspruchsvolle Gattungen wie Liebeselegien, Oden und

---

6 In seinen Briefen 1608-10-20 und 1608-10-09. Hier und im Folgenden alle Briefe von Hilchen nach dem Katalog: Kristi Viiding, Thomas Hoffmann, Hesi Siimets-Gross und Patryk Sapala, *Correspondence of David Hilchen. Early Modern Letters Online* (http://emlo-portal.bodleian .ox.ac.uk/collections/?catalogue=david-hilchen).

7 „Epitaphium quod mihi excidit non quidem lucem meretur. Mitto tamen ut tu videas" 1607-02-26. Das Epitaphium fehlt sowohl in Franciscus Sweertius, *Clariss. Viri Ivsti Lipsi Mvsae Errantes. Ex auctoris schedis partem descripsit, sparsas collegit, ac iunctim posteritati edidit Franciscvs Sweertivs f. Antverpiensis* (Antverpiae, 1610) als auch in Balthasar Moretus, *Iusti Lipsi Sapientiae et Litterarum Antistitis Fata Postuma editio secunda, varie aucta et correcta* (Antverpiae, 1613).

8 *Bernd Hollander, Geschichte der Domschule, des späteren Stadtgymnasiums zu Riga,* hg. Clara Redlich (Hannover – Döhren, 1980).

9 „si non velis omnino Poëticis, quibus olim ferri solebam, at remis tamen exprimerem" David Hilchen, *Nomina regia trajectione quadam litterarum inter litteratos hodie usitata breviter exposuit David Hilchen, Regiae Maiestatis per Livoniam Secretarius et Synd. Rigensis* (Cracoviae, 1595), AIIr–AIIv; „nec amplius remis nedum velis ferar Poëticis" 1594-07-01; in *Academiae Zamoscianae recens institutae intimatio cum Dan. Hermanni carmine in eamdem Academiam* (Riga, 1594), A2r.

654 VIIDING

heroische Epen.[10] Sei es auch nur eine Selbstinszenierung oder ein literarischer Topos, so steht doch fest, dass Hilchen sich später nie weiter um das Sammeln und die Gesamtedition weder seiner *juvenilia* noch seiner anderen Gedichte gekümmert hat, obwohl er in Riga als Druckereiherr und seit 1603 in Zamość im nächsten Kreise Zamoyskis gute Publikationsmöglichkeiten gehabt hätte. Die Widmungsgedichte an ihn sind dagegen spätestens aus seinen Studienjahren in Deutschland bekannt: Gratulationen zur Disputation und ein Reisegeleitgedicht, alle ohne jeglichen Hinweis auf Hilchens eigene Gedichte.[11]

Dichtung zu offiziellen Anlässen (1585–99)

Während seiner politischen Blütezeit in Riga (1585–99) hat Hilchen nur in Ausnahmefällen gedichtet. Er verfasste fast nichts zu üblichen Gelegenheiten wie Geburten, Trauerfeiern usw., sondern kultivierte stattdessen eine Art 'Beamtendichtung'. Sein erstes erhaltenes Gedicht in zwei Distichen ist der Königswahl in Polen gewidmet: Die Königswahl im September 1587 fand unter dem Sternzeichen der Waage statt, das auf das Abwiegen zwischen zwei Kandidaten, eines aus dem Norden, eines aus dem Süden, hindeute.[12] 1589 dankte Hilchen den polnischen Gesandten im Namen des Rigaer Rats für die Restitution einiger hoher Stadtbeamten, die als Folge der Beilegung des

---

10 „Qvi leues Elegos atque asperitate carentes / Vel consueui Odas uel amabile fundere carmen / Flare tuba heroa, didicique heroica gesta" *Catharini Santonellae Horti Musarum in Monte Helicone custodis contra Cerberum in Elysijs vallibus excubitorem Heliconi oblatrantem Satyra*, (S.l, s.a. [verm. Riga, 1599]), A2r.

11 Seiner Heidelberger Disputation sind zwei kurze lateinische Gratulationsgedichte seiner polnischen Kommilitonen Philipp von Solms (in Hexametern) und Jan Rybiński (in elegischen Distichen) beigefügt, in welchen Hilchen empfohlen wird, seine theoretische Leistung als Jurist in die Praxis umzusetzen. Vgl. *De legatis et fideicommissis disputatio in* [...] *Heidelbergensi academia sub* [...] *Domini Matthiae Entzellini u[triusque] j[uris] d[octoris] et professoris ordinarii:* [...] *publice proposita a Davide Heliconio Livono die 20. Februarii horis ante et pomeridiani discutienda* (Heydelbergae, 1585). Rybiński widmete ihm zusätzlich ein Reisegeleitgedicht in 62 Versen (*In discessum Tubinga Ingolstadium Davidis Heliconii Livoni, amici Suavissimi Elegia III*) stilisiert als Gespräch von Timelicon (Wortspiel mit dem Humanistenname von Hilchen Heliconius) und Philothemis (griech. Liebhaber des Rechtes). Neuedition der Gedichte: *Jan Rybińki, Księga Elegii Podróżnych*, hg. Elwira Buszewicz und Wojciech Ryczek (Warzawa, 2015), 122–9, 196–7.

12 *Pro* [...] *Sigismundo Tertio* [...] *electo Rege Poloniae Sueciaeque. Ad conventus in Regno et Magno Ducatu Lithuaniae indictos Elegia*, Riga, Latvijas Valsts Vēstures Arhīvs, 673-1-1242, fol. 15v.

DER POESIE IM LEBEN DES RIGAER HUMANISTEN DAVID HILCHEN 655

Kalenderstreites stattfand.[13] 1594 schickte er ein Glückwunschgedicht der Stadt Zamość zur Erweihung einer Schule,[14] 1595 zehn Anagrammgedichte an Mitglieder des polnischen Königshofs.[15] 1599 entstanden drei Lobepigramme für den litauischen Kanzler Leo Sapieha.[16] Neben diesen Gedichten, die außenpolitisch eine Demonstration der Loyalität der Stadt bezweckten, verfasste Hilchen in den nächsten Jahren auch Gedichte für innenpolitische Zwecke: 1597 entstand eine Versinschrift für das Außenportal des neuen Rigaer Kanzleigebäudes, in dem das personifizierte Gebäude dem Rat für den Bau der Kanzlei dankt, seine Funktion im Dienste des Rats thematisiert und um Gottes Segen bittet. Das Gedicht war 1598 über dem Außenportal angebracht, am 27. April 1602 jedoch im Sinne der *damnatio memoriae* des Verfassers entfernt worden.[17] 1598 verfasste Hilchen ein Dedikationsgedicht zu einem Buch des Rigaer Pastors Georg Ciegler – aber nicht als Freund des Autors, sondern als Vertreter des Rates, der die Veröffentlichung finanziert hatte.[18]

Die poetische Technik dieser offiziellen Produktion ist in fast allen 19 Gedichten anspruchslos. Sie bestehen aus vier bis zehn Versen, entweder in elegischen Distichen (14 Gedichte, 102 Verse) oder Hexametern (4 Gedichte, 74 Verse). Nur ein einziges Gedicht für Sapieha ist in zweizeiligen sapphischen Strophen verfasst.[19] Von zehn Anagrammgedichten hat Hilchen die Anagramme in sieben korrekt gebildet, während in drei jeweils einige Buchstaben fehlen

---

13   *Applausus nomine Senatus Rigensis in Restitutionem* [...] *D[omi]ni Nicolai Eckii Burgrabii,* [...] *D[omi]ni Casparis Bergii Proconsulis et* [...] *D[omi]ni Ottonis Cannii Secretarii, scriptus a D. H. S. R. carmine,* in *Oratio Davidis Hilchen Secretarii Rigensis, qua* [...] *Dominis Commissariis, nomine Senatus et Civitatis Rigensis respondet die 7. Septembris Anno 1589* (Riga, 1589), D3r–D3v.

14   *Academiae Zamoscianae* (s.o., Anm. 9), B5v.

15   Hilchen, *Nomina regia* (s.o., Anm. 9).

16   In *Epistola gratulatoria ad* [...]*Dm. Leonem Sapieha, Magni Ducatus Lithuaniae Cancellarium, Sloninensem, Mogilensem, Pernauiensemque Capitaneum: et nunc generalem in Liuoniae Commissarium: Qva felix Matrimonium illi, una cum consorte eius,* [...] *Elisabetha Radzivila* [...] *Palatini Vilnensi filia, exoptat David Hilchen, S. R. M.tis Secretarius, et Notarius in Livonia terrestris Vendensis* (Riga, 1599), sine pag., B2v–B3r, B4v.

17   Die Inschriften sind handschriftlich und ohne Titel in Riga, Latvijas Valsts Vēstures Arhīvs, 673-1-460, fol. 2v erhalten geblieben. Für die Bildungs- und Sprachgeschichte sind zwei griechische Wörter im letzten Vers des Epigramms bemerkenswert („Sic noua perpetuum durabit machina faxit, / is qui cuncta facit solus Deus αὐτὸς ἐποίη"), die die erste Verwendung des Griechischen im öffentlichen Raum Livlands bedeuten. Keine zeitgenössischen Aufzeichnungen der Inschrift sind bekannt, weshalb Fragen zur paläographischen Realisierung der Inschrift unbeantwortet bleiben.

18   Georg Ciegler, *De Incertitvdine rervm hvmanarvm: Discvrsvs, theologicus, Ethicus, Historicus* (s.l., s.n. [Riga, 1598]), Ar–A4r.

19   Hochzeitsgedicht in *Epistola gratulatoria* (s.o., Anm. 16), B4v. Auf einen kurzen Aristophaneus folgt ein großer sapphischer Vers, wie in der Horazode 1,8, vgl. Friedrich

oder übrig bleiben. Die Übernahme vereinzelter Formeln aus Gedichten römischer Dichter erlaubt es nicht, von einer bewussten Imitation zu sprechen. Seltene Bildersprache ist konventionell, der Gesamteindruck der Gedichte schlicht und übereilt.

Hilchen als Adressat poetischer Huldigungen

Hilchens Leben in Riga war jedoch nicht so arm an Poesie, wie es sein Werk glauben lassen möchte – in den 1590er Jahren war er als einflussreiche Person vor allem selbst Adressat von Dichtungen. Zu den Gelegenheiten passend dominieren Gedichte zur Begrüßung und zur glücklichen Ankunft bei Hilchens diplomatischen Reisen. Die Geburt seines Sohnes, der Tod seiner Tochter und der Jahresbeginn stehen mit Einzelbeiträgen eher im Hintergrund. Unter den Dichtern, die ihm huldigten, ist erstens die internationale humanistische Elite zu nennen – Professoren und gekrönte Poeten, die geographisch von Helmstedt (Salomon Frenzel von Friedenthal,[20] Johannes Peparinus[21]) über Liegnitz (Matthias Rudinger[22]) und Rostock (Martin Brasch[23]) bis Riga reichte (Daniel Hermann, ein Dichter preussischer Herkunft mit Erfahrung

---

Crusius und Hans Rubenbauer, *Römische Metrik. Eine Einführung* (Hildesheim, 2006), 119–20.

20 Salomon Frencelius, *ΓΛΥΚΥΠΙΚΡΟΝ ad* [...] *Davidem Hilchen,* [...] *Regiae Maiestatis per Livoniam Secretarium, et* [...] *Reipub[licae] Rigens[is] Syndicum, Leonorae Hilcheniae, puellulae* [...]*, Francisci Hilchenii Puelli* [...] (Helmaestadii, 1598); zu Frenzels Gedichten aus der Rigaer Periode vgl. Kristi Viiding, „Salomon Frenzel von Friedenthal in Riga – die Endstation eines Humanistenschicksals," in *Album alumnorum,* hg. Ludwig Braun (Würzburg, 2014), 209–27.

21 *Ad* [...] *D[omi]n[um] Davidem Hilchen I[uris]C[onsul]tum et oratorem* [...] *Reip[ublicae] Rigensis Syndicum,* [...] *Regis Poloniae per Liuoniam Secretarium, & nunc Legatum in Germaniam Ode Ioan. Peparini, qua transeunti Helmstaestadium gratulatur* (Helmaestadii, 1595).

22 Matthias Rudinger, *Lusus Anagrammatismalis novem musarum et Apollinis D[omi]n[i] Davidis Hilchenii* [...] *a Reg. Maj. in Germaniam missi* (Frankfurt, 1595); idem, *Charitum Sive Gratiarum Stichodylecta. Fautori Musarum Sideri Livonum Nestori Rigensium.* [...] *D[omi] n[o] Davidi Hilchenio* [...] *in Germaniam misso Gratitudinis loco oblata per Matthaeum Rudingerum Fraustadiensem* (Francofurti, 1595).

23 *De Felici Impetratione Ac Successu Commissionis Generalis S. R. M. & Ordinum Regni Pol. Magnique Ducatus Lithuaniae in Livoniam Ad* [...] *Dominum Davidem Hilchenium* [...] *Serenissimi Regis Liuoniam Secretarium & Notarium terrestrem Vendensem, Livoniae Commissarium Generalium Martinus Braschius Professor Academiae Rostochiensis* (Rostock, 1599).

DER POESIE IM LEBEN DES RIGAER HUMANISTEN DAVID HILCHEN 657

am Hof der Habsburger in Wien).[24] Zweitens sind Studenten livländischer Herkunft zu nennen, die mit Stipendien des Rigaer Rates in anderen Ländern studierten. Dies überrascht nicht, da Hilchen als Rigaer Scholarch über die Zuweisung von Stipendien mitentschied. Am bekanntesten ist die Huldigung des Medizinstudenten Basilius Plinius an Hilchen in einem langen Lobgedicht für Riga (*Encomium inclitae civitatis Rigae, metropolis Livoniae*) in den Versen 1519–38.[25] Auch ein anonymes Lobgedicht ist zu erwähnen, in dem besonders seine Fähigkeit, im Anagramm verborgene Wahrheiten zu äußern, gepriesen wird.[26]

Die Krisenjahre 1599–1602: Dichtung als Warnung und Waffe

Im Frühling 1599 änderten sich die Huldigungsgedichte für Hilchen wesentlich. Als er von einer Reise nach Riga rückkehrte, schrieb Daniel Hermann in einem Begrüßungsgedicht[27] über Verleumdungen, die in Riga über ihn aufgekommen waren, und bat Hilchen, standhaft zu bleiben. So verrät dieses Gedicht den Anfang eines Konfliktes in Riga. Die Dichtung fungierte seither nicht nur als Warnmedium, sondern auch als Konfliktquelle und Waffe: Hilchens Feinde attackierten nicht nur ihn, sondern auch Personen, die ihm Gedichte gewidmet hatten. So wurde der frühere Jurastudent und damalige rigische Prokurator Paul Spandko wegen der angeblich falschen Verwendung des Titels *sacrosanctus* in seinem 1596 publizierten Gedicht über Hilchen angegriffen;[28] dies sei eine widerrechtliche Anmaßung. Spandko rechtfertigte seine Wortwahl mit dem Verweis auf Hilchens Immunität als polnischer Gesandter.[29] Daraufhin griff Hilchen selbst einen seiner Feinde, den Stadtarzt Georg Herbers, mit poetischen Mitteln, nämlich mit der ersten Satire

---

24   Daniel Hermann, *Dvnae flvvii ad* [...] *Davidem Hylchen Rigen. Syndicvm, ex Aula* [...] *Poloniae Regis etc iterum redeuntem Applavsvs* (Rigae, 1599).

25   Erste Ausgabe Lipsiae 1595, weitere Editionen: Alt-Riga im Lichte eines humanistischen Lobgedichts vom Jahre 1595. Basilius Plinius, Encomium (inclitae civitatis) Rigae, hg. Arnold Spekke (Riga, 1927, zweite Ausgabe mit neier Einleitung 1997).

26   Hilchen, *Nomina regia* (s.o., wie Anm. 9) Abschrift in Krakow, Biblioteka Jagiellońska, 5575. Kod.pap.z w. XVI/XVII, fol. 92r.

27   Hermann, *Dvnae flvvii* (s.o., Anm. 25), Verse 56–70.

28   Paulus Spandko, *Abitui et reditui felicibus e Polonia in Germaniam et Livoniam, S[acro] Sancti Polonorum Legati* [...] *D[omini] Davidis Hilchen, Regiae civitatis Rigensis, Patriae suae, Syndici Paulus Spandko, AA. et SS. LL. Studio, Notarius, P. Judicijque Rigens. Procurator* (Riga, 1596).

29   *Johann Gottfried Arndt, Der Liefländischen Chronik erster und zweiter Theil*, hg. Johann Daniel Gruber (Halle, 1753), 24.

658 VIIDING

Livlands, an:[30] Herbers habe ihn wegen seiner Maßnahmen während der Kalenderunruhen verhöhnt. Die Satire (140 Verse) ist eine kräftige Allegorie über Heliconius (Hilchens Humanistenname) und Kerberus (die latinisierte Namensform von Herbers). Der Gestalt des Kerberus sind viele Details aus verabscheuenden antiken Mythen hinzugefügt, mitunter additiv und assoziativ, mitunter kontrastiv, oft sehr übertrieben. Das Ziel sei es, Herbers *hybris* zu zähmen. Am Ende der Satire nimmt Heliconius die Position Jupiters ein und droht, alle seine Feinde vom Olymp herabzuwerfen, wie er einst die Titanen unterworfen habe. Die Satire war wirksam: Herbers wurde verhaftet und wird nach 1600 in Rigaer Dokumenten nie wieder erwähnt; gleichzeitig wurde das Werk zum Anklagepunkt im Prozess gegen Hilchen.[31]

Mit dieser Satire, einem Spitzenwerk des livländischen Humanismus, verändert sich auch die Art von Hilchens metapoetischen Reflexionen. Diese sind kein nostalgischer Rückblick auf seine gelungenen Jugendwerke mehr, sondern wollen ein internationales Netzwerk von Dichtern manifestieren, die Hilchen mit Gedichten in verschiedenen Gattungen helfen werden, wenn Kerberus seine Tätigkeit nicht beende (v. 92–101):

> Nunc primam hanc Satyram ubi, mordax Cerbere, mitto.
> Si sapis, absistes lacerare Heliconis alumnum:
> Ex Helicone orti ne plures forsan alumni
> Te contra insurgant, et uersus versibus addant
> Omnes armati, cordato pectore et omnes,
> Archilochus dictis rabiosus et acer Iambus,
> Et plures alij Lyrici, regionibus orti
> Diversis, diversa canent te, Cerbere, contra.
> Ergo vide, atque in te propius descendere disce,
> Nec contra hunc latra, cui magnae patria curae est.

In den folgenden tiefsten Krisenjahren (1600–02), während Hilchens erstem Gerichtsprozess in Riga und seiner Teilnahme am Polnisch-Schwedischen Krieg, publizierte er keine Gedichte. Seine Feinde in Riga fabrizierten hingegen anonyme Spottepigramme, von welchen die Inschrift für ein fiktives goldenes

---

30 *Catharini Santonellae* (s.o., wie Anm. 10). Erhalten unter Hilchens Gerichtsdokumenten (Riga, LVVA 673-1-344b, 170r–177r) und Poznan, PAN Biblioteka Kórnicka, Cim.Qu.3073. Vgl. die kommentierte Edition mit Einleitung: Kristi Viiding, „Gefährliche Bücher, gefährliche Gattungen, gefährliche Vorlagen: Die Geburt der Satire in Livland," in *Book in context* (= Renæssanceforum 15), hg. Outi Merisalo (Kopenhagen, 2019), 73–99.

31 „Herberum vexavit satyris" Riga, Latvijas Valsts Vēstures Arhīvs, 673–1-344b, fol. 245r–253r.

DER POESIE IM LEBEN DES RIGAER HUMANISTEN DAVID HILCHEN 659

Tor in Riga erhalten ist.[32] Der Bezug zu Hilchens Inschrift auf dem Außenportal des Rigaer Kanzleigebäudes ist eindeutig. Hilchen wird als "filius infernalis" beschimpft, latinisiert aus dem Höllen- bzw. Hellenkind, einer klanglichen Assoziation mit seinem Namen. Unter den Vorwürfen (Habgier, Missbrauch der Macht als Rigaer König und andere moralische Laster) gibt es allerdings nichts, was mit seiner dichterischen Tätigkeit in Verbindung gesetzt werden kann. Wer sich hinter dem Pseudonym "Rauaelus Argentauiensis" verbirgt, ist unklar. Wichtig ist, dass der Epigrammatiker sich als kaiserlicher "poeta laureatus" präsentiert – jemanden aus der Dichterelite, die Hilchens Meinung nach allein würdig waren, über ihn zu dichten:

> Inscriptio Portae aureae filij infernalis siue Hellenkindij
> Quod volui, potui, potui quod, feci, ita factis
>   Dicere nemo mihi, quid facis? ausus erat.
> Quod potui, rapui, rapuissem, si potuissem
>   Plus, DEVS haud voluit me rapere vlterius.
> Regis ego instar eram Rigae, sed me ipsa superbo
>   Deposuit solio, nec DEVS ipse tulit.
> Nam tandem ipse DEVS fortunam euertit et ipsum
>   Me quoque nil facere et nil quoque posse, facit,
> Nunc viuo invisus terraeque, DEOque hominique,
>   Heu mea quid prosunt impia facta mihi.
> Frausque dolusque, superbia, auaritia, ambitioque
>   Hinc pia iusticiae discite castra sequi.
> Cunctorum in me vno vitiorum immensa vorago est
>   Deprecor, o ueniae, sit, precor, vsque locus.
> Areae quisquis praeis huius amplam
> Auream portam, meliora disce
> Et time Christum et cole iuste tum nec
> Quenque verere.
> Rauaelus Argentauiensis
> Poeta Caesareus D. C. Scripsit

---

32   Zwei handschriftliche Exemplare in *Hilcheniana oder Acta in Kriminalsachen des Sindikus Godemannus und Eines W. E. Rates wider den Sindikus David Hilchen, dessen wider die Stadt gehabte aufrührische, kalumiese* [*sic!*] *und höchst gefährliche Händel betreffend 1601ff* (Riga, Latvijas Valsts Vēstures Arhīvs, 673-1-344a, fol. 553r–554r).

660 VIIDING

Hilchen als ein lyrischer Hofpoet (1603–10)

In der letzten Lebensphase, d.h. nach seinem endgültigen Fortzug nach Polen (1603), setzte Hilchen zwar seinen Gerichtsprozess fort, verzichtete aber auf jegliche Verwendung der Poesie im Kampf um seine Restitution und gegen seinen Feinde – dafür benutzte er seither nur die Prosaform. Er wurde Hofpoet, der für Festtage der höchsten polnischen Elite dichtete: sechs Hochzeitsgedichte,[33] acht Trauergedichte bzw. Epitaphien[34] und drei Dedikationsgedichte zu neuen Büchern sind bekannt.[35] Livländische Adressaten verschwanden mit Ausnahme des Wendenschen Kastellans Georg Schenking, eines Vertreters der polnischen Macht in Livland.

Mit der Auswechslung des Adressatenkreises veränderte sich auch die Art seiner Poesie. Die dem Rigaer (Schul-)Humanismus eigenen elegischen Distichen sowie den Hexameter hat Hilchen nur noch in kürzeren Epitaphien und Dedikationsgedichten, vorwiegend auf seine Kinder[36] verwendet.

---

33 *Ode Nuptialis* [...] *Paullo Wolowicz Succamerario Grodnen. Sponso, et* [...] *virgini Sophiae,* [...] *Hieronymi Chodkiewicz, Castellani Vilnen. et Capitanei Brestensis filiae, Sponsae. Inscripta a Davide Hilchen Not. Ter. Vendensi, S. R. M. Secretario* (Samoscii, 1603); *Nuptiis* [...] *Iacobi Potocki Capitanei Bialocamenen. etc. Ducentis* [...] *Stanislai Comitis A Tarnov Castellani Sandomiriens. Caputanei* [sic!] *Buscen. etc, filiam Hedwigim gratulatur David Hilchen Notarius Terrestr. Venden. S. R. M. Secretar. Zamoscii Anno Domini, Millesimo Sexcentesimo tertio. Die 19. Octobris,* (s.l. [Zamoscii], 1603). *ΕΠΑΙΝΟΣ pompae Regalis in Nuptiis* [...] *Principis Sigismundi Tertij,* [...] *Poloniae et Sueciae Regis etc etc. et* [...] *Constantiae,* [...] *Caroli Archiducis Austriae, etc filiae, Auctore Dauide Hilchen Secretario Reg. Maiest. Notario Terr. Uenden.* (Zamosc, 1604); *Oda ad* [...] *D[ominum] Nicolaum Comitem ab Ostrorog, novam nuptam,* [...] *Fabiani a Czema Palatini Mariaeburgensis. etc. filiam ex Prussia in domum suam deducentem, exeunte Anno 1604. A Dauide Hilchen Notario Terr. Venden. Secret. R. M. Anno Domini M. DC. IV* (Zamoscii, 1604); *Generoso Domino Alexandro Krzywczycki, excipienti domi suae Elizabetham, Domini Joannis Gniewoszz, Capitanei Latovicien. etc* [...] *David Hilchen S. R. Maiestatis Secretarius, Notarius Terrestr. Venden.* (Zamoscii, 1607).

34 *Honori Herois Zamoscii David Hilchen Regiae Maiestati in Polonia a secretis faciebat* (Zamosci, 1605) (drei Gedichte); *Memoriae* [...] *Matronae Annae* [...] *Domini Stanislai Slupecki Castellani Lublinensis filiae* [...] *Ioannis Lipski de Gorai Succamerarii Belzensis coniugis* [...] *David Hilchen* [...] (Samoscii, 1605) (zwei Gedichte); *Epicedion Memoriae et honori* [...] *Domini Georgi Schencking Castellani in Livonia Venden. Haeredis in Antzen et Fernesse, Cracouiae die 10 Nouembr. Anno 1605 demortui et Anno ineunte 1606 Toruniae sepulti. David Hilchen Sacrae Reg. Maiest. Secretarius et Notarius Terr. Venden. faciebat* (Zamoscii, 1606) (zwei Gedichte); *Tumulus* (1606, ein Gedicht), Angaben wie Anm. 36.

35 *In Promptuarium* [...] *Pauli Szerbicii Secretarii Regii Phaleucion,* in Pawel Sczerbic, *Promptuarium Statutorum Omnium et Constitutionum Regni Poloniae* [...] *cum Indice Rerum et Verborum copiosissimo singulari eiusdem Pauli Sczerbic studio, et diligentia confecto* (Brunsbergae, 1605), sine pag. (zwei Gedichte) und Rhodomanologia (Zamoscii, 1608, ein Gedicht), Angaben wie Anm. 36.

36 1606 ein Grabepigramm für seine Tochter Beata auf dem Grabmonument in der Kollegiatskirche Zamość: *Tumulus Beatae* [...] *Davidis Hilchen, Secretarij Regii, Notarij*

DER POESIE IM LEBEN DES RIGAER HUMANISTEN DAVID HILCHEN 661

Stattdessen verfasste er zwei lange Gedichte in catullischen Elfsilblern, zwei noch längere Gratulationen in der ersten asklepiadischen Strophe (ein Anklang an das horazische *Exegi monumentum*) und fünf sehr lange Gedichte in epodischen Versmaßen – wieder in den Metren der horazischen Epoden, Hexameter mit jambischen Trimetern bzw. daktylischen Tetrametern oder jambische Trimeter mit jambischen Dimetern alternierend. Das catullische und horazische Vorbild bezog sich aber nicht nur auf die entsprechenden Versmaße, sondern erweiterte sich auch auf Motive und Strukturen. So imitiert Hilchen z.B. in seinem Hochzeitsgedicht für König Sigismund III. Wasa das Peleus-und-Thetis-Gedicht Catulls, von dem er die Motivfolge des Festzuges der Gäste und die Beschreibung des Hochzeitstages übernimmt. Hilchen wurde zu einem livländisch-polnischen Horaz: In einem seiner ersten Exilgedichte von 1603 beschrieb er sich nach horazischem Vorbild als Dichter in einer Reihe verschiedener Lebensarten. Obwohl er wisse, dass seine Gedichte die traurige Lage Livlands nicht zu bessern vermögen, gefalle es ihm nun, nach der Art des Dichters zu leben.[37]

Hilchens ästhetische Verschiebung zu den klassischen lyrischen Versmaßen und Gedichtformen in seiner Exildichtung in Zamość geschah nicht willkürlich, sondern deutet auf den Einfluss des dortigen akademischen Dichterkreises hin. Gesamteuropäischen Ruf genoss dort der 'polnische Pindar' Szymon Szymonowic, der neben Lyrik und Epik auch Tragödien verfasste. Der Rhetorikprofessor Adam Burski verfasste Handbücher über Tropen und Rhetorik, und der Medizinprofessor Jan Ursyn-Niedźwiecki wird zu den 100 besten polnischen Autoren gezählt.[38]

Genau wie in allen seinen früheren Lebensphasen hat Hilchen sich somit auch im Exil sehr schnell sowohl den äußeren Umständen als auch den poetischen Normen der Umwelt angepasst. Obwohl er in seinen Exilgedichten und -briefen über den eigenen Werdegang und über das Schicksal Livlands bis 1604 zunächst noch hoffnungslos, doch dann mit stetig wachsender Zuversicht schreibt, hat Hilchens Bindung an seine Heimat sowie seine endgültige

---

Terrae Vendensis Filiolae, in *Monumenta Sarmatarum, viam universae carnis ingressorum*, hg. Simon Starowolski (Cracoviae, 1655), 642; dazu Jerzy Kowalczyk, „Nagrobek Beaty Hilchen z 1606 roku w kolegiacie Zamojskiej," in *Studia z historii sztuki i kultury Gdańska i Europy Północnej. Prace poświęcone pamięci Doktor Katarzyny Cieślak*, hg. Jacka Friedricha und Edmunda Kizika (Gdansk, 2003), 195–203; und 1608 ein Dedikationsgedicht für jungen Thomas Zamoyski, den Sohn seines früheren Patrons, zur Neuausgabe des Epos *Rhodomanologie* zu Ehren seines Vaters: *Rhodomanologia Manibvs Magni Ioannis Zamoscii Inscripta & A duobus fratribus Dauide, & Francisco Hilchen in Academia Zamosciensi publice In anniuersario depositionis die 5 Iunij recitata, Anno Domini M. DC. VIII* (Zamoscii, 1608), A2.

37   *Ode nuptialis* (s.o., wie Anm. 33), V. 7–21.

38   Starnawski, *Pod cieniem Hippeum* (s.o. Anm. 5).

Restitution vom polnischen König im Jahre 1609 sein Poesieverständnis nicht weiter verändert bzw. auf seine Ursprünge zurückgeführt.

Fazit

Hilchens Beispiel zeigt, dass neulateinische Poesie oft eine literarisch verdichtete Dokumentation von Krisensituationen und -reaktionen der Humanisten gespeichert hat. Obwohl diese Dichtung lange vor der Entstehung der modernen Psychologie und Psychotherapie verfasst ist, kann sie trotzdem als historisches Beispiel dafür analysiert werden, wie Dichtung im Prozess individueller Krisenbewältigung funktionierte: vom Hilfsmittel zum Verständnis der ersten Krisenmerkmale (bei Hilchen etwa der Warnungen in den an ihn gerichteten Huldigungsgedichten) bis zu einer Methode der aktiven Krisenintervention (bei Hilchen die Verwendung der Gattung Satire zum Angriff auf seine Feinde und zum Aufruf seiner literarischen Unterstützer; danach kurzfristige Unterbrechung des Dichtens) und -therapie (der völlige Verzicht auf die früheren poetischen Ausdrucksmittel, das Einstellen der Kommunikation mit dem früheren Adressatenkreis). Im Hilchens Fall bestätigt eine solche Analyse die Produktivität von Krisen, d.h. dass eine politische und persönliche Krisenzeit – hier das Exil und Verleumdungen – den Humanisten zur Herausbildung eigener dichterischer Vielfalt veranlassten, für die es unter ruhigeren Umständen kaum Zeit und Motivation gegeben hätte.

Under und Tuglas Literaturzentrum der Estnischen Akademie der Wissenschaften

CHAPTER 53

Nepenthes – Trank der Helena: Die umstrittene Identität eines ‚homerischen' *pharmakon* in gelehrten Debatten des 17. Jahrhunderts

Benjamin Wallura

Abstract

An einer berühmten Stelle der Odyssee (Od. 4,219–32) bereitet Helena für Menelaos und Telemachos einen Trank zu, gemischt aus Wein und einer, wie es heißt, Kummer und Leid vertreibenden Substanz (φάρμακον νηπενθής). Die Kommentarliteratur hat über Jahrhunderte stets gerätselt, was genau diese Substanz gewesen sein mag, die Helena aus Ägypten bekommen hatte. So rätselte darüber auch das 17. Jahrhundert, das neben zahlreichen, philologischen Interessen an antiken Texten, zunehmend auch ein Interesse an der Kenntnis der genauen Wirksamkeit sämtlicher Rausch-, Genuss- und Heilsubstanzen ausbildete, um genau solche Fragen wie die nach dem *Nepenthes* Homers, wie die Substanz in der Frühen Neuzeit mehrfach verkürzt begegnet, minutiös klären zu können. Der Beitrag geht anhand neulateinischer Dissertationen und Traktate daher der Frage nach, wie die gelehrten Interpretatoren dieses ägyptische, pharmazeutische Mittel jeweils gedeutet haben und welche Argumente sie auf welche Weise für ihre Textinterpretationen vorgebracht haben. In Form einer Teilstudie sollen damit Einblicke in das Funktionieren frühneuzeitlicher, gelehrter Debattenkulturen geliefert werden. Sie soll zeigen, wie unter Anlehnung an verschiedenste medizinische, historiographische Diskurse und philologische Debatten der *Nepenthes* Homers vor allem im 17. Jahrhundert zu einem Projektionsobjekt verschiedenster gelehrter Spekulationen und Interessen werden konnte, die darin zuweilen Cannabis, Opium oder den Kaffee entdeckt zu haben glaubten.

Keywords

Giovanni Battista Persona – Pietro La Sena – Hermann Conring – Reception of Homer – Nepenthes

1

Im vierten Buch der *Odyssee* berichtet Homer von einer bemerkenswerten Substanz; genauer gesagt von einem *pharmakon*, das – wie hinreichend bekannt – bei den Griechen verschiedene Dinge bezeichnen konnte: „Gift", „Zaubertrank", aber auch schlicht das „Medikament" zur Bekämpfung von Krankheiten oder sonstigen körperlichen wie geistigen Gebrechen.[1] Dies gilt nicht zuletzt für das – so bei Homer vollständig zu lesende – φάρμακον [...] / νηπενθές τ᾽ ἄχολόν τε, κακῶν ἐπίληθον ἁπάντων (*Od.* 4,220–1), welches antike wie frühneuzeitliche Interpretatoren der *Odyssee* nicht selten – philologisch durchaus irritierend – zum Eigennamen *Nepenthes*/νηπενθές verkürzten, und das sämtlichen Kummer sowie Zorn (oder Sorgen) – überhaupt alles Schlechte – vergessen machen soll.[2] Was hatte es mit diesem in die *Odyssee* projizierten Mittel auf sich und welche unterschiedlichen Deutungen erfuhr es im Verlauf der westlich-europäischen Geistesgeschichte, insbesondere der iatrophilologischen Spekulationen des 17. Jahrhunderts?[3] Unter besonderer Fokussierung auf dieses Zentennium soll im Folgenden – *in nuce* – ein Teil der Geschichte jener Exegese, die sich mit dem *Nepenthes* beschäftigte, genauer vorgestellt werden. Anhand verschiedener Autoren des 17. Jahrhunderts, die einen Zugang zur ‚homerischen Pharmazie' gesucht haben, gilt es die diesbezüglichen Debatten exemplarisch zu skizzieren.

In der *Odyssee* sucht Telemach nach seinem Vater Odysseus. Dabei landet er in Buch vier am Hof des Menelaos in Sparta und wird dort als Gast empfangen.

---

1 Luigi Arata, „Nepenthes and Cannabis in Ancient Greece," in *Janus Head* 7.1 (2004), 34–49, 34–5; Bettina Wahrig, „Zweifelhafte Gaben: Die andere Pharmazie und das Weib," in *Pharmazie in Geschichte und Gegenwart*, hg. Christoph Friedrich und Joachim Telle (Stuttgart, 2009), 517–32, 517; Zum *medicamina*-Begriff, vor allem im lateinischen Mittelalter, vgl. jüngst Iolanda Ventura, „Wie beherrscht man die Kenntnis der *medicamina*? Fehler und Normierung in der universitären Pharmakologie," in *Irrtum – Error – Erreur*, hg. Andreas Speer und Maxime Mauriège (Berlin-Boston, 2018), 123–48.

2 Als Eigenname ist *Nepenthes* bereits antik belegt (vgl. Theophr., *h. plant.* 9,15,1: τὸ νηπενθές; Plin., *hist. nat.* 21,91: "nepenthes illud praedicatum ab Homero"; Ibid. 25,12: "nobile illud nepenthes oblivionem tristitiae veniamque adferens et ab Helena utique omnibus mortalibus propinandum"). Die Gründe, aus welchen es zu dieser Verengung des gesamten poetischen Ausdrucks kam (denn insbesondere die Bedeutung von ἄχολόν ist umstritten), können vielseitig sein; vgl. dazu Suzanne Amigues, *Théophraste. Recherches sur les Plantes*, Tome V, Livre IX (Paris, 2006), 185–6. Hier genügt der Hinweis, dass wir es bereits seit der Antike mit einer exegetischen Tradition zu tun haben, die unter dem Stichwort *Nepenthes* die Identität des Tranks der Helena diskutierte und später insbesondere für das 17. Jahrhundert einflussreich geworden ist.

3 Allgemein dazu: Herbert Jaumann, „*Iatrophilologia. Medicus philologus* und analoge Konzepte in der frühen Neuzeit," in *Philologie und Erkenntnis. Beiträge zu Begriff und Problem frühneuzeitlicher ‚Philologie'*, hg. Ralph Häfner (Tübingen, 2001), 151–76.

NEPENTHES – TRANK DER HELENA

Im Gespräch bei Tisch erinnern sich Menelaos und dessen Gattin Helena an Odysseus und versetzen damit die Anwesenden, insbesondere Telemach, in einen tiefen Kummer. Telemach wird schließlich als Sohn des Helden erkannt und Helena reicht den Trauernden ein Mittel, das dem Leid und Kummer Abhilfe schaffen soll. In *Od.* 4,219–32 lesen wir in der Übersetzung von Johann Heinrich Voß von 1781:[4]

> Aber ein Neues ersann die liebliche Tochter Kronions:
> 220 Sie warf in den Wein, wovon sie tranken, ein Mittel
> Gegen Kummer und Groll und aller Leiden Gedächtniß.
> Kostet einer des Weins, mit dieser Würze gemischet;
> Dann benetzet den Tag ihm keine Thräne die Wangen,
> Wär' ihm auch sein Vater und seine Mutter gestorben,
> 225 Würde vor ihm sein Bruder, und sein geliebtester Sohn auch
> Mit dem Schwerte getötet, daß seine Augen es sähen.
> Siehe so heilsam war die künstlichbereitete Würze,
> Welche Helenen einst die Gemahlin Thons, Polydamna,
> In Aigyptos geschenkt. Dort bringt die fruchtbare Erde
> 230 Mancherlei Säfte hervor, zu guter und schädlicher Mischung;
> Dort ist jeder ein Arzt, und übertrifft an Erfahrung
> Alle Menschen; denn wahrlich sie sind vom Geschlechte Paions.

„Ein Mittel gegen Kummer und Groll und aller Leiden Gedächtniß", wie es bei Voß heißt, ist eine mögliche und zugleich eine der gängigsten Übersetzungen der zentralen Stelle.[5] Sie stellte jedoch bereits die antike Interpretation Homers seit Theophrast vor gewisse Probleme.[6] Wie war der Text hier zu verstehen? Ging es tatsächlich um ein reales pharmazeutisches Mittel oder musste der „Sorgenbrecher" (wie er später noch auftauchen sollte) nicht doch rein allegorisch verstanden werden, etwa als das übergroße Maß an Trost, den Helena allein mit dem Reichen des Weins spenden konnte?[7] Oder hatte Homer, der Dichter, doch mit mehr medizinisch-pharmazeutischem Wissen aufwarten

---

4 Johann Heinrich Voß, *Homers Odüßee* (Hamburg, 1781), 71–2.

5 *Od.* 4,220–1: αὐτίκ’ ἄρ’ εἰς οἶνον βάλε φάρμακον, ἔνθεν ἔπινον, / νηπενθές τ’ ἄχολόν τε, κακῶν ἐπίληθον ἁπάντων.

6 Hier nur die einschlägigen Stellen, die auch explizit den *Nepenthes* erwähnen: Theophr., *h. plant.* 9,15,1; Diod. 1,97,7–9; Plin., *hist. nat.* 21,91; 23,23; 25,12; Plut., *symp.* 1,1,4.

7 Für eine Liste der hierfür grundlegenden antiken Autoritäten siehe bereits: Christian Friedrich Harless, *Die Verdienste der Frauen um Naturwissenschaft und Heilkunde sowie auch um Länder-, Völker- und Menschenkunde von der ältesten Zeit bis auf die neueste* (Göttingen, 1830), 94–9. Vgl. auch: Arata, „Nepenthes" (s.o., Anm. 1), 37–9.

können als zu erwarten gewesen war, da viele Stellen der homerischen Epen auf eine solche Expertise zumindest hinzuweisen schienen?[8]

2

Die Vorstellung vom Dichter Homer, der umfängliches Wissen besessen und dieses auch in seinen Dichtungen verarbeitet habe, ist bereits antik und wirkte weit in die frühneuzeitliche Geistesgeschichte.[9] Mit der *editio princeps* seiner Werke durch Dimetrios Chalkondyles (1423–1511) in Florenz (1488), den Aldinen-Drucken Homers in Venedig 1504, 1517 und 1524, der Edition von Adrien Turnèbe (1554) und des erst kurz zuvor (1544–50) herausgegebenen Kommentars des mittelalterlichen Kommentators Eustathius von Thessalonike († um 1195) sowie der Homer-Edition des Pariser Buchdruckers Henri Estienne (1531–98) in Genf 1566 waren wichtige Meilensteine der Beschäftigung mit dem griechischen Text im europäischen Westen erreicht, die zur einer erneuten Popularisierung des Dichters beitrugen. Durch diese Entwicklungen wurde nicht zuletzt auch die Frage nach dem medizinisch-pharmazeutischem Wissen Homers zu einer brennenden Frage, die sich vor allem im 17. Jahrhundert gelehrte Akteure immer mehr zu stellen begannen. Das *Nepenthes* Homers war somit kurz nach 1600 selbstredend längst sprichwörtlich geworden und konnte sich einer allgemein verbreiteten Kenntnis innerhalb der gelehrten Welt sicher sein. Es besaß als Projektionsobjekt ein ungeheures Potenzial, wie etwa nicht zuletzt Justus Lipsius' Beschreibung der *Constantia* in dessen gleichnamigen Traktat belegen kann.[10]

---

8   So etwa das berühmte Kraut *moly* aus *Od.* 10,302–7. Auch hier wurde in der Frühen Neuzeit vielfach ein ‚dahinterstehender‘ pharmazeutischer Effekt diskutiert, vgl.: Daniel Wilhelm Triller und Johann Jacob Wagner (resp.), *Moly Homericum detectum cum reliquis ad fabulam Circaeam pertinentibus* (Leipzig, 1716). Vgl. Jaumann, *„Iatrophilologia"* (s.o., Anm. 3).

9   Noémi Hepp, *Homère en France au xviième siècle* (Paris, 1968), 105–26 (dort auch zum *Nepenthes*); Vgl. auch Theodor und Barbara Mahlmann, *„Iliada post Homerum scribere –* Prüfstein frühneuzeitlicher Autorschaft", in *Realität als Herausforderung: Literatur in ihren konkreten historischen Kontexten*, hg. Ralf Georg Bogner, Ralf Georg Czapla, Robert Seidel und Christian von Zimmermann (Berlin – New York, 2011), 47–91.

10 Justus Lipsius, *De Constantia libri duo, qui alloquium praecipue continent in publicis malis* (Antwerpen, 1584), lib. I, c. 6: "Haec [sc. Constantia] sola illa Helena, quae verum illud legitimumque Nepenthes propinet, in quo oblivio curarum et dolorum." Zu *Nepenthes* als Trost-Allegorie in der Theologie vgl. Otto Casmann, "Nepenthes peccatorum contritorum et humilatorum," in idem, *Schola tentationum, praecipue divinarum, prima* (Frankfurt, 1604), 257–306, 259.

NEPENTHES – TRANK DER HELENA 667

1613 erschienen die *Noctes solitariae, sive De iis quae scientifice scripta sunt ab Homero in Odysseia*[11] des Giovanni Battista Persona (1575–1619), eines Philosophen und Arzt im italienischen Bergamo. Schon in der *Praefatio* breitet dieser ein unmissverständliches Lob über die homerische Weisheit aus, über die "sapientia Homerica", die besonders in ihrer „profunditas", „varietas doctrinarum" ihrem "acumen ingenii" sowie ihrer "praestantia" hervorsteche. Homer, der Dichter, sei gleichsam der Ursprung aller Wissenschaften und Disziplinen ("origo scientiarum et disciplinarum omnium") gewesen. Dies gelte, wie Persona fortführt, nicht zuletzt auch für die Arzneikunst, die "facultas medica", in der sich Homer, bereits vor Hippokrates und Galen, ausgezeichnet habe.[12] In Dialogform lässt Persona sechs Charaktere (Inclusus, Siticulosus, Providus, Anonymus, Ingeniosus, Tutus) aus den Bereichen Theologie, (aristotelischer) Philosophie, Medizin, Politik, Geschichte sowie Philologie sich miteinander über naturkundliche Phänomene in der *Odyssee* Homers unterhalten.

Die 13. Unterredung (*Colloquium*) steht dabei ganz im Zeichen des "medicamentum Nepenthes". Die Unterhaltung wird dabei dominiert durch Tutus, der den Philologen mimt, und durch Providus, der die Rolle des Arztes übernimmt. Unter minutiösen Referenzen an den berühmten italienischen Arzt Antonius Musa Brassavola (1500–55), der zu Hippokrates und Galen publiziert hatte, versucht der Philologe nachzuweisen, dass es sich beim "Nepenthes Homeri" um nichts anderes als Helenium gehandelt habe, mit dem auch Plinius der Ältere es bereits in Verbindung gebracht hatte.[13] In einer Reihe von Reden und Gegenreden führt Providus, der Arzt, schließlich das finale und schließende Argument ins Feld: Vor geraumer Zeit, wie er versichert, habe er, der Arzt, in Padua durch den Logikprofessor Bernardino Petrella (1529–95) eine Substanz erhalten, welche dieser einst vom Kurator des dortigen Botanischen Gartens, Melchior Giulandino (ca. 1520–89), bekommen habe. Dabei habe es sich um eine Art Wurzel gehandelt, vergleichbar etwa der der Crateva. Petrella hätte ihm, damals von Melancholie befallen ("me plus solito melancholicum"), diese Wurzel als Gegenmittel, gerieben in Wein (wie bei Homer), verabreicht und es hätte sich dabei folgende Wirkung eingestellt: Mehrere Stunden sei er dermaßen beschwingt und fröhlich durch Padua gelaufen als sei er über die Maßen betrunken gewesen, wie Passanten ihm später erzählt hätten. Auf die Frage, was Petrella ihm für ein Mittel verabreicht hätte, habe dieser geantwortet: eine Art des Heleniums aus Ägypten, das sich – so schließt der Arzt seine Rede –

---

11   Giovanni Battista Persona, *Noctes solitariae, sive De iis quae scientifice scripta sunt ab Homero in Odysseia* (Venedig, 1613).

12   Persona, *Noctes solitariae* (s.o., Anm. 11), *praef.* (unpaginiert).

13   Persona, *Noctes solitariae* (s.o., Anm. 11), 88.

doch hervorragend mit dem Nepenthes vergleichen ließe, das, wie bei Homer nachzulesen sei, seinen Ursprung ebenfalls in Ägypten habe.[14]

Nur wenige Jahre nach Persona sollte Pietro La Sena (1590–1636) in Laon mit seinem *Homeri Nepenthes, seu de Abolendo Luctu liber* von 1624 der Debatte neue, weitreichende Impulse verleihen.[15] La Sena fokussierte hierfür etwas eingehender die philologischen Aspekte, die die Homer-Passage betrafen. *Nepenthes*, das schien ihm zumindest notwendig festzuhalten, konnte ein Substantiv oder Epitheton sein. Er sah sich veranlasst von einem Substantiv *Nepenthes* auszugehen, das stellvertretend für eine reale Substanz stehen könne.[16] Er fügte dem allerdings wenig später gleich hinzu, dass wohl von mehreren *Nepenthea* auszugehen sei, die zwar unterschiedliche Bestandteile beinhalten konnten, in ihrer Trauer vertreibenden Wirkung jedoch vergleichbar seien.[17] La Sena nun lenkt, unter zahlreichen Reminiszenzen an die antike Kommentartradition und Medizin, die Debatte erstmals auf das Opium – bekanntlich auch ein griechischer Terminus für „Saft" (*opion*) – bzw. den allgemeinen Bereich der Opiate.[18] Über mehrere Schritte beleuchtet La Sena zunächst den allegorischen, dann den anagogischen Gehalt des Nepenthes und dessen zerstreuende Wirkung[19] und liefert schließlich für das gesamte 17. Jahrhundert eines der Referenzwerke zum Thema Nepenthes, auf das alle Folgetexte immer wieder Bezug nehmen sollten.

Dennoch: die Debatte um das Nepenthes Homers hatte sich damit keineswegs konkretisiert. Es blieb das gesamte 17. Jahrhundert über ein äußerst ambivalentes Projektionsobjekt gelehrten Wissens: Bereits 1614 hatte beim schottischen Publizisten William Barclay (ca. 1570–ca. 1630) das Nepenthes als Chiffre für den Tabak herhalten müssen.[20] Eine weitere vergleichbare Interpretation lieferte 1650 die Reisebeschreibung des Pietro della Valle (1586–1652), der in einem Eintrag vom 7. Februar 1625 über die Trinksitten der Türken Folgendes über den Kaffee vermerkte:[21]

---

14 Persona, *Noctes solitariae* (s.o., Anm. 11), 91.

15 Pietro La Sena, *Homeri Nepenthes, seu de abolendo luctu liber* (Laon, 1624).

16 La Sena, *Homeri Nepenthes* (s.o., Anm. 15), 44–109, bes. 47–8.

17 La Sena, *Homeri Nepenthes* (s.o., Anm. 15), 55–66.

18 Ibid., 85.

19 Ibid., 110–78; 179–245; 246–86.

20 William Barclay, *Nepenthes, or the Virtues of Tobacco* (Edinburgh, 1614).

21 Pietro della Valle, *Eines vornehmen Römischen Patritii Reiss-Beschreibung in unterschiedliche Theile der Welt, nemlich in Türckey, Egypten, Palestina, Persien, Ost-Indien, und andere weit entlegene Landschaften [...] Erster Theil* (Genf, 1674, zuerst auf Italienisch: Rom, 1650), 41–2.

NEPENTHES – TRANK DER HELENA 669

Wann man denselben auch mit Wein wie mit Wasser tränke, dürfte ich mir wohl einbilden, dass es vielleicht des Homeri Nepenthe sei, welches, wie er sagt, die Helena aus Ägypten bekommen: Weil es gewiss ist, dass dieses Cahve auch von daher in dieses Land gebracht worden ist; und gleich wie dieses Nepenthe Bekümmernis und Sorgen vertreibt, dient also auch der Kaffee den Türken zu ihrem gewöhnlichen Zeitvertreib und Kurzweil, indem sie damit in ihren Gesellschaften etliche Stunden zubringen und zwischen ihrem Zutrinken lustige und ergötzliche Gespräche mit untermischen, welches dann vielleicht in ihren Gemütern ein solches Vergessen der Traurigkeit bewirkt, welche der Poet der Kraft seines Nepenthes zuschreibt.

Erfolg konnte solchen Anekdoten im gelehrten Diskurs um Luxusgüter nicht beschieden sein. Schon 1685 konnte Sylvestre Dufour (1622–87) in seinem *Traitez nouveaux et curieux du café, du thé et du chocolate* feststellen, dass der homerische Text eine solche Deutung nicht zulassen konnte: Nepenthes, so Dufour, sei doch eindeutig – wie er glaubt – ein pflanzliches Narkotikum ("herba Narcotica"), das, ganz anders als der von della Valle favorisierte Kaffee, den Schlaf doch begünstige statt ihn zu bekämpfen.[22]

Über gleich mehrere Jahrzehnte zog sich die Debatte hin, die Hermann Conring (1606–81) und Ole Borch (1626–90) über das *Nepenthes Homeri* geführt hatten. Conring war Professor für Politik und Medizin an der Universität Helmstedt von 1632 bis zu seinem Tod, Borch seit 1660 Professor für Botanik und Chemie in Kopenhagen mit speziellen Interessen für Alchemik, wofür er, nicht zuletzt von Conring, gelegentlich kritisiert worden war. Das Verhältnis beider Gelehrter war ein rivalisierendes, da sowohl Conring als auch Borch enge Kontakte an den dänischen Hof pflegten, und nicht zuletzt auch in ihrer Funktion als Leibärzte diverser Herrscherpersönlichkeiten konkurrierten.

In seiner Schrift *De Hermetica Aegyptiorum vetere et Paracelsiorum Nova Medicina*, erstmals veröffentlicht 1641 in Helmstedt und dann vielfach aufgelegt,[23] äußert Conring, wie bereits der Titel nahelegt, Zweifel an der nahezu übernatürlichen Wirkung des homerischen Nepenthes. Er vermutet dahinter ein allzu topisches Lob, das Homer hier über die ägyptische Medizin und Magie ausbreite: „Es steckt keine natürliche Kraft in dem Mittel, das Homer

---

22   Sylvestre Dufour und Jacob Spon, *Tractatus novi de potu caphe, chinesium thé, et chocolata* (Paris, 1685), 85.

23   Hermann Conring, *De Hermetica Aegyptiorum vetere et Paracelsiorum Nova Medicina* (Helmstedt, 1641).

der Helena zuschreibt."[24] Die vielfach beschworene Allwissenheit des Dichters bröckelt und Conring möchte vor jeglichen Auswüchsen des Paracelsismus, ein regelrechtes Schimpfwort der Zeit, warnen. Nepenthes scheint ihm mehr eine Chiffre für den Trost zu sein und kein medizinisches Mittel, das einer solchen Wirkung gleichkäme.[25]

Anders hingegen der zwanzig Jahre jüngere Borch, der es in seiner Schrift von 1668 *Dissertatio de ortu et progressu Chemiae*[26] nicht auslässt, Conring persönlich anzugehen. Wie könne er nur auf die Idee kommen beim Nepenthes von einer übernatürlichen Kraft zu sprechen, die nur poetisch vom Dichter überhöht sei. Keinen Anlass gebe es hier, Aberglauben zu vermuten. Hinter dem poetischen Ausdruck müsse doch eine reale Substanz gestanden haben, die auch Homer möglicherweise dabei im Blick gehabt hatte.[27] Hierzu schließt Borch an La Sena und seinem einflussreichen Werk an und argumentiert erneut für die Opiate, wie etwa das sogenannte "Meslach Turcarum", das dieser bereits an entsprechender Stelle erwähnt hatte, sowie den Stechapfel ("datura"), denen allgemein, wie etwa dem "laudanum", eine sämtliche Schmerzen vertreibende Wirkung attestiert wurde.[28]

Die Kritik von Conring ließ indes nicht lange auf sich warten. Schon ein Jahr später, 1669, veröffentlichte er in einer Neuauflage seiner *Hermetica Medicina* eine Appendix, die er als direkte Apologie gegen die Vorwürfe Borchs verstanden wissen wollte.[29] Conring verteidigt sich darin, dass die Chemie bzw. Alchemie ihren Sitz zwar bereits bei den alten Ägyptern gehabt habe, besteht aber darauf, dass das Nepenthes kein derartig magisches Heilmittel gewesen sein könne, sondern von Homer nur zu einem solchen exaltiert worden sei. Wenn auch Stechapfel oder Meslach Turcarum in ihren beschriebenen Wirkungen ähnlich seien, so habe dies doch keinen magischen bzw. alchemischen Hintergrund; und schon recht sei Homer keine Kenntnis dieser altägyptischen Praktiken einzuräumen. Conring verweist Borch im Folgenden nur auf die "Problemata physica" (anspielend wohl auf Buch III), die Conring für aristotelisch hält. Dort seien solche und ähnliche Rauschzustände, vor allem die

---

24   Conring, *De Hermetica Medicina* (s.o., Anm. 23), 104.

25   Zum geistesgeschichtlichen Hintergrund hier und im Folgenden vgl. Florian Ebeling, „Ägypten als Heimat der Alchemie," in *Goldenes Wissen. Die Alchemie – Substanzen, Synthesen, Symbolik*, hg. Petra Feuerstein-Herz und Stefan Laube (Wiesbaden, 2014), 23–34, bes. 27–31.

26   Ole Borch, *De ortu et progressu Chemiae dissertatio* (Kopenhagen, 1668).

27   Borch, *De ortu et progressu* (s.o., Anm. 26), 57–8.

28   La Sena, *Homeri Nepenthes* (s.o., Anm. 15), 85; vgl. Margit Kreutel, *Die Opiumsucht* (Stuttgart, 1988), 105.

29   Hermann Conring, "Apologeticus adversus calumnias et insectationes Olaii Borrichii," in idem, *De Hermetica Medicina libri duo* (Helmstedt, 1669), 421–47.

NEPENTHES – TRANK DER HELENA

in Kombination mit Wein – ganz wie im homerischen Beispiel – diskutiert und entlässt seinen Kontrahenten damit aus der Lehrstunde. Beiden Diskutanten, so viel ist klar, schien es weniger um die Klärung des Nepenthes gegangen zu sein, als vielmehr um die Bewertung von Fragen, die in den Bereich der frühneuzeitlichen Alchemik fielen. So zeigt gerade die Debatte zwischen Conring und Borch beispielhaft, wie das Nepenthes Homers zu einem besonderen Projektionsobjekt konkurrierender Wissenskonzepte werden konnte, da es gerade in seiner extremen Wirkung sowie seiner sachlichen Ambivalenz dafür besonders geeignet schien.

Die *Hermetis, Aegyptiorum et Chemicorum Sapientia ab Hermanno Conringo animadversionibus vindicata*[30] des Kopenhagener Gelehrten von 1674 wird von Conring dann keiner antwortenden Zeile mehr gewürdigt. Borch berichtet darin von einem Stechapfeltrank (bereitet aus der "datura"), der an einem Kopenhagener Mädchen ausprobiert worden sei. Die mit dem Nepenthes vergleichbare Wirkung habe dabei einen ganzen Tag lang angehalten, genau so, wie es nicht zuletzt die Homer-Stelle selbst nahegelegt hätte (*Od.* 4,223).[31]

Hier war nun in der Nepenthes-Debatte ein Punkt erreicht, wo sich Philologie und pharmazeutisches Wissen auf eine Weise miteinander verschlungen hatten, wie es aus vielen Fällen der Iatrophilologie bekannt ist. Die Debatte hatte sich indes weiter verzweigt. Johann Heinrich Meibom (1590–1655), Professor für Medizin in Helmstedt, diskutierte in seinem postum 1668 durch seinen Sohn Heinrich Meibom d.J. (1638–1700), ebenfalls Arzt in Helmstedt, herausgegebenen und vielfach aufgelegten *De cerevisiis potibusque et ebriaminibus extra vinum aliis commentarius* noch eine ganze Reihe weiterer Substanzen, bei denen auf ähnliche Wirkung zu hoffen war.[32] So erwähnt natürlich auch er das Nepenthes und die verschiedenen Substanzen, die dafür diskutiert worden waren (Buglossum, Helenium, Datura etc.). Unter diesen finden sich bemerkenswerter Weise auch Cannabis und Coca, die Meibom entsprechend mit Argumenten zu unterfüttern suchte.[33] Auch er schloss seinen Exkurs mit dem Opium, sich der allgemeinen Tendenz der Nepenthes-Debatte anschließend. Dies verwundert nicht weiter, verbreitete sich doch das Wissen um Opium und insbesondere über den Opiumkonsum seit dem 16. Jahrhundert zunehmend

---

30   Ole Borch, *Hermetis, Aegyptiorum et Chemicorum Sapientia ab Hermanno Conringo animadversionibus vindicata* (Kopenhagen, 1674), 128–34.

31   Ibid., 130.

32   Heinrich Meibom, *De cerevisiis potibusque et ebriaminibus extra vinum aliis commentarius* (Helmstedt, 1668; 1671; 1688), c. 23.

33   Ibid.; vgl. Ole Borch, *De somno et somniferis maxime papavereis Dissertatio* (Kopenhagen – Frankfurt, 1681), 14.

schnell innerhalb gelehrter Diskurse.[34] Dies zeigen die Beispiele des James Duport (1606–79) und seiner *Homeri Gnomologia*[35] sowie des bekannten Jenaer Professor für Medizin Georg Wolfgang Wedel (1645–87), der sich gleichfalls bemühte, verschiedenste antike wie biblische Pflanzen zu identifizieren und mit den philologischen und botanischen Kenntnissen der Zeit in Einklang zu bringen.[36]

Schließlich sei noch Pierre Petit (1617–87) erwähnt, ein in Paris wirkender Philologe und Mediziner, der mit seiner Schrift *Homeri Nepenthes, sive de Helenae medicamento* (1689) 65 Jahre nach Pietro La Sena erstmals wieder eine komplette Summe zur Debatte um das fragliche Nepenthes vorlegte.[37] Darin sprach er sich zwar – schon aufgrund der Analogie zu Helena – wieder für das seit Plinius diskutierte Helenium aus, das hinter dem Nepenthes zu vermuten sein müsse,[38] schließt jedoch seine Betrachtung mit weiteren, in der Debatte bereits zuvor diskutierten Kandidaten, wie etwa dem Kaffee als geselligem, trostspendendem und Kummer vertreibendem Getränk. Diesen ergänzt er sogar noch um einen neuen, den Tee, dessen Kräfte und vielseitige Anwendungsmöglichkeiten er bereits zuvor 1685 in einem Lehr- und Lobgedicht beschworen hatte.[39] Auch hier wird deutlich, dass trotz zunehmender Konkretisierung der Nepenthes-Debatte hin zu den Opiaten, keine abschließende Festlegung erfolgte. Immer wieder konnten diverse Substanzen als Projektionsobjekte für das Nepenthes herhalten, fast, möchte man meinen, wie sie in Europa jeweils gerade im Schwange waren.

Nicht zuletzt aufgrund dieser Diskussionen erreichte Homer eine Renaissance. So finden sich nicht weit im 18. Jahrhundert nicht wenige Dissertations- und Traktatstitel, die in ihm nicht nur den Dichter, sondern auch den Arzt, den *Homerus medicus*, erkannt haben wollten.[40] Autoren, wie etwa der Apotheker, Arzt und Chemiker Johann Conrad Barchusen (1666–1723)

---

34 Andreas-Holger Maehle, "Pharmacological Experimentation with Opium in the Eighteenth Century," in *Drugs and Narcotics in History*, hg. Roy Porter und Miguláš Teich (Cambridge, 1995), 52–76, hier 52.

35 Jacob Duport, *Homeri poetarum omnium saeculorum facile principis Gnomologia* (Cambridge, 1660).

36 Georg Wolfgang Wedel, *Propempticon inaugurale de Nepenthe Homeri* (Jena, 1692).

37 Franz-Josef Kuhlen, *Zur Geschichte der Schmerz-, Schlaf-, und Betäubungsmittel in Mittelalter und Früher Neuzeit* (Stuttgart, 1983), 177.

38 Pierre Petit, *Homeri Nepenthes, sive de Helenae medicamento* (Utrecht, 1689).

39 Pierre Petit, *Thea, sive de Sinensi herba Thee Carmen ad Petrum Danielem Huetium* (Leiden, 1685).

40 So z.B. Adam Brendel und Johann Gottfried Oertel (resp.), *De Homero Medico* (Wittenberg, 1700); Johann Christian Haynisch, *Homerum artis medendi peritum fuisse* (Schleiz, 1736); Johannes Gottlieb Daehne, *Epistola de Medicina Homeri* (Leipzig, 1776).

NEPENTHES – TRANK DER HELENA

in der *Oratio de Nepenthe*, die seiner *Historia Medicinae* von 1710 beigefügt ist,[41] ließen nicht davon ab, stets das medizinisch-pharmazeutische Wissen des Dichters zu betonen und schrieben die Interpretation des Nepenthes als Opium (bzw. als Meslach Turcarum) im 18. Jahrhundert weiter fort. Doch auch die frühneuzeitliche Botanik eines Jacob Breyne (1637–93) oder des berühmten Carl von Linné (1707–78) ließ es sich nicht nehmen, Nepenthes schließlich als Bezeichnung für tropische, fleischfressende Kannenpflanzen zu usurpieren; wenn auch damit die Frage nach dem Trank der Helena mitnichten gelöst war. Linné etwa, der es von Breyne übernimmt, schreibt dazu wie folgt:[42]

> Assumsi synonymon Breynii, cum enim si haec non Helenae nepenthes, certe Botanicis omnibus erit. Quis Botanicorum longissimo itinere profectus, si mirabilem hanc plantam reperiet, non admiratione raperetur, totus attonitus, praeteritorum malorum oblitus, mirificam Creatoris manum dum obstupescens adspiceret?

Nepenthes, so Linné, wird also zu einem Symbol der – sprichwörtlich oft odysseeartigen – Reise- und Forschungstätigkeit des Botanikers an sich. Endlich am Ziel dieser einzigartigen, göttlichen Pflanzengeschöpfe angekommen, wirken sie so sehr auf den Betrachter, dass alle vorherigen Mühen und Entbehrungen vergessen sind.

3

Wenn auch eine Einordnung der hier präsentierten Aspekte in den viel größeren Kontext der (oftmals vor allem spekulativen) Homer-Exegese des 17., 18. und natürlich auch 19. Jahrhunderts im hier gesetzten Rahmen unterbleiben musste, zeigt der Beitrag in aller Kürze und trotz Verzicht auf eine eingehendere Betrachtung der oft vielfach verzweigten frühneuzeitlichen Argumentationsgänge, wie heterogen die Debatte um das *Nepenthes* im 17. Jahrhundert ausfallen konnte und wie diskontinuierlich ihr Verlauf gewesen war. In der Debatte um die reale Substanz hinter dem homerischen Stoff blieb das Nepenthes nicht zuletzt durch die im Text des Dichters beschriebenen

---

41 Johann Conrad Barchusen, "Oratio de Nepenthe," in idem, *Historia Medicinae* (Amsterdam, 1705), 610–32.

42 Carl von Linné, *Hortus Cliffortianus* (Amsterdam, 1737), 431; Breynes Beschreibung findet sich in Jacob Breyne, *Prodomi fasciculi rariorum planatarum primus et secundus* (Gdańsk, 1739), vol. 2, 85, die erst postum herausgegeben worden sind.

Eigenschaften ein vielseitig brauchbares Projektionsobjekt frühneuzeitlichen, gelehrten Wissens. Es blieb damit äußerst anschlussfähig an eine ganze Reihe von Diskursen um bekannte Luxusgüter und/oder Heilmittel im 17. Jahrhundert und konnte seine Präsenz in stets ambivalenter Erscheinung unter diesen behaupten. Mit Bezug auf die (Iatro-)Philologie des 17. Jahrhunderts und die Exegese der homerischen Realien lässt sich hier zweifellos von einem ‚Rausch des Homer' sprechen, der sich im 18. und 19. Jahrhundert noch um ein Weiteres intensivieren und dynamisieren sollte.

Danksagung

Ich danke allen aufmerksamen Leser/innen für die hilfreichen Anmerkungen zu meinem Text. Der Artikel entstand im Rahmen des DFG-Projekts „Der Aristotelismus in Helmstedt – Die Karriere eines europäischen Paradigmas" an der Freien Universität Berlin und der Herzog August Bibliothek Wolfenbüttel (Leitung: Prof. Dr. Bernd Roling/Dr. Hartmut Beyer/Ulrike Gleixner) sowie des Projekts „Late Medieval and Early Modern Libraries as Knowledge Repositories, Guardians of Tradition and Catalysts of Change, Lamemoli, Academy of Finland and University of Jyväskylä no. 307635" (Leitung: Outi Merisalo).

Herzog August Bibliothek Wolfenbüttel

CHAPTER 54

Martinus Szent-Ivany's Notion of *scientia*: Some Preliminary Notes on the Semantics of Neo-Latin Science

Svorad Zavarský

Abstract

The voluminous intellectual output of the Tyrnavian Jesuit Martinus Szent-Ivany (1633–1705), comprised in his *Curiosiora et selectiora variarum scientiarum miscellanea* (1689–1709) and *Opuscula polemica* (1699–1709), provides a unique opportunity to explore how science was conceived of by a Central European scholar and university teacher towards the end of the seventeenth century. Focusing on his dissertation *De scientiis in genere*, which occupies a prominent position within his *Miscellanea*, I wish to highlight some basic aspects of the terms *scientia* and *scientiae* as applied in the texts of his miscellaneous corpus. By doing so, I hope to be able to make a propaedeutic contribution to the semantics of the Neo-Latin notion of *scientia*. Was science thought of as an abstract system, or rather as a collection of concrete pieces of information? What types of knowledge did it comprise? How did it relate to reason and faith? Szent-Ivany's works can give us a relatively complete picture of *scientiae* (plural), that synthesis of knowledge which was only possible thanks to the medium of Neo-Latin.

Keywords

Martinus Szent-Ivany – *Curiosiora et selectiora variarum scientiarum miscellanea* (1689–1709) – Neo-Latin science – *scientia* – Jesuit literature

© KONINKLIJKE BRILL NV, LEIDEN, 2020 | DOI:10.1163/9789004427105_055

Introduction

A brief note on the man in the title of this paper is needed at the beginning. Martinus Szent-Ivany (1633–1705)[1] was a Jesuit scholar based predominantly at the University of Tyrnavia (nowadays Trnava, Slovakia) which once was the most important center of scholarship in the Hungarian Kingdom. His rather extensive literary output includes a nine-part collection of dissertations, observations, *ephemerides* and chronological synopses entitled *Curiosiora et selectiora variarum scientiarum miscellanea* (further referred to as *Miscellanea*) and a corpus of more than twenty works of polemical theology.[2] His polymathy, as well as his engagement in both theological and non-theological disciplines, makes his texts an ideal basis for an inquiry into the Neo-Latin notion of *scientia*.

Let it be noted beforehand that, in the interest of shortness, I shall only concentrate on a few selected aspects of Szent-Ivany's notion of *scientia*—which, however, I consider the most crucial ones—and I shall combine things which at first sight may seem to have little in common. Yet, I believe this approach, highlighting a few extra-scientific aspects of early modern science, can bring us closer to a better understanding of how the term *scientia* was used three or four hundred years ago.[3] It is generally known that the Neo-Latin word *scientia* encompasses a reality incomparably greater than that designated by the modern English term *science*. Nevertheless, the understanding of what connotations this word precisely evoked in early modern minds remains rather vague.

Although the discovery and exploration of the New World and the invention of the telescope brought it about that the universe grew considerably bigger in

---

1   I intentionally use the Latin forms of personal and geographical names when speaking about people and places of the early modern Kingdom of Hungary, a multi-national state where Latin not only had the status of the official language but was also widely spoken until the mid-nineteenth century. In this case, the use of vernacular names often does not correspond to historical reality, but it rather tends to reflect the modern historians' ethnic affiliation.

2   The volumes of his *Curiosiora et selectiora variarum scientiarum miscellanea* (further abbreviated as csvsm) were published by the university press of Trnava in the period 1689–1709. His polemical works started to appear in 1699 with the same publisher. At that time, Szent-Ivany was director of the university printing office at Trnava and censor of books for the Hungarian Kingdom. For a general discussion of csvsm, see Svorad Zavarský, "Between the Universe and Universal Knowledge: Martinus Szent-Ivany's Curiosiora et selectiora variarum scientiarum miscellanea," in *Acta Conventus Neo-Latini Vindobonensis. Proceedings of the Sixteenth International Congress of Neo-Latin Studies (Vienna 2015)*, ed. Astrid Steiner-Weber and Franz Römer (Leiden 2018), 788–801.

3   Extra-scientific aspects are so named here with respect to the modern notion of science commonly accepted today. They are meant to refer mainly to the religious, moral, and artistic dimensions of knowledge.

MARTINUS SZENT-IVANY'S NOTION OF *SCIENTIA*

the minds of men, nevertheless the world in the days of Martinus Szent-Ivany, i.e. toward the end of the seventeenth century, was, if viewed from the perspective of our contemporary understanding, a very small one, both in terms of space and in terms of time. The duration of its temporal existence was commonly thought not to exceed five to seven thousand years, and the distance between the Earth and the end of the universe, surrounded by the empyreum, was imagined not to be much greater than the distance which we now know separates the Sun from Neptune.[4] Indeed, it was a tiny universe compared with ours, of which we know that its time can be measured in billions of years and its space only described with the help of the speed of light. The way men imagine their world doubtlessly determines the ways in which they approach that world by reason.[5] Hence, the simple fact of today's conception of the universe being so very different from the conception held three hundred years ago makes it obvious to us how much the early modern notion of *scientia* must have differed from what we understand by the word *science* today.[6] Therefore, aiming to prevent misunderstanding, I shall use the Latin term *scientia* throughout this paper whenever referring to the texts of Martinus Szent-Ivany.

In those texts, the word "scientia" often appears together with nouns such as "cognitio, notitia, doctrina, disciplina, sapientia, philosophia, prudentia", all of which are either used as synonyms or they express different shades of meaning.

---

4 This estimate is based on Martinus Szent-Ivany's cosmological dissertation *De systemate mundi* in which the size of the universe is discussed. See the critical edition of the relevant passage in Svorad Zavarský, *Martin Sentiváni: Dissertatio cosmographica seu De systemate mundi / Sústava sveta—kozmologická štúdia* (Bratislava, 2011), 28–31. For more information on Szent-Ivany's cosmology, see Svorad Zavarský, "The Cosmology of Martinus Szent-Ivany SJ (1633–1705): Some Philological Notes on his Dissertatio cosmographica seu De mundi systemate," in *Knowing Nature in Early Modern Europe*, ed. David Beck (London, 2015), 101–17 and 208–12.

5 Cf. Edward Harrison, *Masks of the Universe: Changing Ideas on the Nature of the Cosmos* (Cambridge, 2003), introduction. However, we must admit that early modern scholars also stood before the vastness of the universe in mute awe, declaring that the Earth in it was only "instar puncti" (as tiny as a point), which, taken geometrically (an approach typical of seventeenth-century Jesuit thought), accentuates the vastness of the universe all the more. Nevertheless, later development in science and technology dramatically shifted the boundaries of "vastness" beyond all early modern imagination.

6 This position may be perhaps better explained by the fact that early modern science, continuing the traditions of antiquity and the Middle Ages, aspired, until well into the eighteenth century, to preserve the unity, or the common fundament, of all intelligible reality, and that with traditional, relatively simple methods and gnoseological tools. These aspirations, however, gradually grew untenable proportionately with the fast growth of scientific data and, perhaps due to lack of adequate tools and methods, the wished-for unity of knowledge got disintegrated. Nowadays, cutting-edge technologies once more seem to be able to revive the Baroque aspirations of a great synthesis.

Particularly interesting would be to examine the relationship of "scientia" to the nouns "opinio" and "fides" (see below). In addition, there are specific verbs frequently occurring in connection with "scientia", such as "discere", "investigare", and others. An exploration of the relationships among these and other related terms would no doubt yield a treasury of relevant results. However, the present paper can only offer a preliminary to such a detailed semantic study. Therefore, much is only sketched and simply stated as a matter of fact.[7]

The key text of Szent-Ivany's *Miscellanea*, with respect to the notion of *scientia*, is his dissertation entitled *De scientiis in genere* which appeared only posthumously in 1709.[8] This dissertation is basically built up of two parts: first comes a theoretical discussion of the basic aspects of science (or knowledge) and the ways of its acquisition, which is then practically backed up by a proposal of a compendious knowledge-generating method applicable to all sciences. Therefore, in order to grasp both, the following remarks are also split in two parts.

1   General Discussion of Science

1.1   *Concrete vs. Abstract*

In Szent-Ivany's *De scientiis in genere*, the term *scientia* is basically used in two meanings: It either denotes human cognition and knowledge, in which case it functions as an abstract noun and always appears in singular ("scientia"), or else the term is employed to designate specific disciplines, or specific fields of study, in which case, interesting to note, it regularly comes up in plural ("scientiae"). The regular use of the plural form in the latter meaning indicates eloquently that Szent-Ivany did not operate with any general, abstract notion of science (Wissenschaft) as a separate sphere of human activity. No 'virtual reality' of science, as it were, seems to have played a role in his thought, there were only scientific disciplines ("scientiae") and the learned men ("eruditi") possessing their knowledge ("scientia"). This, I would say, brings early modern science ("scientiae") and art ("artes") very close together, and that in two ways. Firstly, they were both conceived as concrete objects,[9] and secondly, they

---

7   My research on the Neo-Latin works of M. Szent-Ivany has been previously presented at the Congresses of the IANLS in Uppsala (2009), Münster (2012) and Vienna (2015) as well as at the *Scientiae* conferences in Warwick (2013), Vienna (2014), Oxford (2016), Padua (2017) and Minneapolis (2018). Some of it has already been published, as indicated in footnotes.

8   Martinus Szent-Ivany, "De scientiis in genere," in CSVSM 3:2 (1702), 1–47.

9   Just as craft or art was associated with making concrete objects or artifacts from concrete material, so was science concerned with collecting and organizing data, endeavouring to shape them into meaningful structures.

MARTINUS SZENT-IVANY'S NOTION OF *SCIENTIA* 679

were mutually interdependent.[10] Today, in contrast, both these notions have acquired much more abstract meanings and, interestingly, they have also become rather estranged from each other.

The term "scientia", as used by Szent-Ivany, obviously denotes the result rather than the process of acquiring knowledge. It regularly seems to refer almost exclusively to the sum of information gained, not the way that leads that information. What we today comprise in the general concept of science, including scientific methods, would have probably best corresponded to the notion of *philosophia* in the days of Szent-Ivany. The problem, however, is not that simple, for Szent-Ivany himself divided the whole of *scientiae* into five classes identical with the five faculties of the university ("theologia, philosophia, juris-prudentia, medicina, artistica") since according to him all *scientiae* could most conveniently be reduced to these.[11] Philosophy, comprising what we now denote as natural sciences, was obviously not considered by him as the only legitimate framework of knowledge. On the other hand, his reduction of *scientiae* proper to no more than five general classes makes us alert to another important aspect of Szent-Ivany's attitude toward science: He clearly disapproved of the ever-growing specialization of scientific disciplines which he considered a disadvantage for the scholarly community.[12]

1.2   Science, Faith, and Truth

The dissertation *De scientiis in genere* first offers a general idea of *scientiae* by discussing their utility, necessity, and delightfulness. The last aspect, the delightfulness of knowledge, is of special interest to us as it is related to curiosity ("curiositas"), a concept of utmost importance for the Neo-Latin *scientiae*, which, however, provoked ambivalent reactions among early modern

---

10   In early modern times, this fact is also manifest in the interchangeability of the notions of "ars" and "scientia". So, e.g., poetics could be referred to as "scientia poetica/poetices" while astronomy was often spoken of as "ars astronomiae".

11   Note that "artistica" is included as one of the five classes. This faculty of arts (identical with the Jesuit *classes inferiores*, i.e. *gymnasium*) covered Latin grammar, stylistics, poetics, and rhetoric. This is of considerable significance to us since it shows that seventeenth-century *scientia* was also bound with the poetic and rhetoric *inventio* and imagination (see part 2 of this paper). At the same time, though, the inclusion of both "juris-prudentia" and "medicina" in the list clearly points to the emphasis Szent-Ivany placed on the axiomatic, aphoristic, and normative elements of science.

12   In his *De scientiis in genere*, he particularly refers to the "unnecessary" subdivision of geometry into trigonometry, planimetry, etc., affirming that such compartmentation of scientific disciplines is an obstacle to the dissemination of scientific knowledge since it slows down the process of learning.

scholars.[13] At one point in his discourse, Szent-Ivany deals with the problem of the compatibility of sanctity and erudition, i.e. spiritual life and scholarship, quoting his contemporary Hieronymus Hirnhaim (1637–79) who in his work *De typho generis humani* contended that there was hardly a man to whom the Apostle's words "scientia inflat" (1Cor 1,8) could not be applied, and consequently, that *scientiae* were harmful to man's salvation.[14] Szent-Ivany explicitly polemicizes against this, demonstrating that, on the contrary, *scientiae* beckon us to humility. He writes:[15]

> What do we know for certain in individual disciplines? And yet, certainty belongs to the innermost essence of *scientia*. Is it not true that many things are exposed to disputation? And is it not true that there is often discordance about the very principles of sciences? Indeed, almost all our statements about things are mere opinions. Consequently, there is no reason for us to boast about our knowledge as though we were in possession of some great *scientia*.

The requirement of certainty constitutes a link between science and faith since for theologian Szent-Ivany it is faith that imparts the highest degree of certainty. I can illustrate this relationship between *scientia* and *fides* very poignantly.

In one of his polemical works, Szent-Ivany writes that those who wish to find the true faith must first of all pray and ask God for grace and for the light of faith. Second, they must strive to abstain from sin, above all from carnal desires, and keep their hearts clean "because," as the Book of Wisdom (1,4) says, "into a soul that plots evil, wisdom enters not, nor dwells she in a body under debt of sin." These moral requirements are then followed by a set of theological

---

13   There has been a large discussion of this subject going on in contemporary scholarship. For a fundamental semantic study of the word *curiositas*, see Neil Kenny, *Curiosity in Early Modern Europe: Word Histories* (Wiesbaden, 1998).

14   Hieronymus Hirnhaim, *De typho generis humani sive scientiarum humanarum inani et ventoso tumore* (Prague, 1676), 234–247. With respect to Szent-Ivany's refutation of Hirnhaim, the thought of St Augustine should indispensably be taken into account.

15   Szent-Ivany, *De scientiis* 20: "Quid enim in singulis facultatibus à nobis procerto scitur? & tamen certitudo est, de ratione intrinseca scientiæ. Nonnè pleraque disputationibus, & ventilationibus subjecta sunt? Et de ipsius quandoque principijs litigatur, & controvertitur? Adeoque omnes ferè nostræ de rebus sententiæ sunt opiniones meræ [...] Non erit igitur fundamentum, ut ex rerum notitia, quam habemus superbiamus & gloriemur, tanquam de magna scientia [...]." This slant of Szent-Ivany's thinking deserves increased attention as it brings him close to skepticism, though being in substantial tension with his otherwise very optimistic view of scientific progress.

MARTINUS SZENT-IVANY'S NOTION OF *SCIENTIA* 681

axioms and principles of sound reasoning.[16] Now, in his *De scientiis in genere* Szent-Ivany discusses the means that should be applied by a student wishing to acquire knowledge. He writes that the student must first of all pray and ask God for grace. Second, he must lead a virtuous life and preserve the purity of his heart "because into a soul that plots evil, wisdom enters not, nor dwells she in a body under debt of sin." These moral prerequisites are then followed by the description of a universal method of teaching and learning the *scientiae*.[17] Thus, the acquisition of a (true) *scientia* is conditioned on the same requirements as the acquisition of a (true) *fides*.[18] It is good to remember that in the times of confessionalization the attributes 'true' and 'false' were heavily stamped by their religious meaning, and as such they were not seldom also applied in other spheres of thought. The fact that the matters of *fides* and *scientia* were approached by the same method is accounted for by both of them being based on truth, which was considered to be only one, regardless of whether it outwardly manifested itself in science or religion. The requirement of certitude with respect to *scientia* is, in addition, very well reflected in the fact that, when wishing to express the idea of what we today would refer to as 'findings' or 'pieces of knowledge,' Szent-Ivany uses the word "veritates".

1.3 *Scientia and the Kingdom of Heaven*

For Szent-Ivany, *scientiae* are inexhaustible and no man on earth is capable of acquiring an encyclopaedic knowledge of all of them.[19] He asserts that no matter how much knowledge one acquires there still will be a greater amount of data left to be learned.[20] This infiniteness of science, which cannot be exhausted in time, implies, in the thought of theologian Szent-Ivany, eschatological connotations. In his dissertation *Ratio status futurae vitae* (1699), Szent-Ivany discusses the nature of the beatific vision in heaven. For him, the vision of God coincides with knowledge—*scientia* (it must be emphasized

---

16 Martinus Szent-Ivany, *Quinquaginta rationes* (Trnava, 1702), 5–13. For a more detailed discussion, see Svorad Zavarský, "Quinquaginta Rationes—Fifty Reasons: From an Opusculum Polemicum Tyrnaviense to a Standard Catholic Book in America," in *Acta Conventus Neo-Latini Monasteriensis. Proceedings of the Fifteenth International Congress of Neo-Latin Studies (Münster 2012)*, ed. Astrid Steiner-Weber and Karl A. E. Enenkel (Leiden, 2015), 614–25.

17 Szent-Ivany, *De scientiis* 16 and 22.

18 The problem is much more complex, and we cannot address it here in detail. The major difficulty consists in the fact that the notion of *fides* was frequently synonymous to and alternated with the notions of *religio* and *ecclesia*.

19 The specification "on earth" is made with respect to the distinction among human, angelic, and divine knowledge ("scientia humana, angelica, divina").

20 Szent-Ivany, *De scientiis* 6 and 8.

in this connection that for him, like for many of his contemporaries, ocular testimony represented the highest level of evidence attainable in the natural world)—and accordingly, he enquires what exactly it is which a blessed soul sees *in* and *with* God: It is not only God's essence and the divine perfections, all the mysteries of faith and Scripture, celestial glory and infernal doom, but also the universe and all its parts, the qualities, size, and proportions of all the things a soul can see and know in God.[21] In short, there is no spiritual or corporeal thing of which a soul in heaven would be ignorant. Furthermore, this vision and knowledge comprises the entire history from the beginning of the world, all things past, present, and future. Consequently, the least saint in heaven who lived as an absolute simpleton while on earth, has a much greater knowledge than any of the greatest philosophers and scientists of human history. It is clear to anyone familiar with the works of Martinus Szent-Ivany that this series of things which he explicitly made part of the beatific vision is actually identical with the contents of his *Miscellanea*. What, then, is the purpose of science if any 'uneducated' soul in heaven is given greater knowledge than the wisest sage on earth? Is science, with respect to eternity, just a waste of time? Szent-Ivany gives us a clue when he writes that no creature in this world is so mean as to be incapable of bringing man to the knowledge of some of God's perfections and hence of prompting him to praise, love, and serve God more.[22] I would like to argue that this is one of the motives which lay at the root of early modern scientific enquiry: Every creature, no matter how small, can bring man closer to knowing and loving God. What, therefore, is essential here is the connection of knowledge and love ("amor", not "caritas").[23] If there is the link of love, there is a meaningful continuity between science on earth and the beatific vision in heaven. Thus, the eschatological aspect of *scientia* has far-reaching implications for the ethics of human knowledge and its application.[24] This also may be one of the reasons why Szent-Ivany considered ascetic theology ("theologia ascetica") to be the highest science of all, referring to it as "scientia scientiarum".[25]

---

21 Martinus Szent-Ivany, *Ratio status futurae vitae* (Trnava, 1699), 65–6.

22 Ibid., 25.

23 For a more detailed discussion of this, see Svorad Zavarský, "The Idea of Encyclopaedia at the University of Trnava around 1700," in *Early Modern Universities and the Scientiae*, ed. Vittoria Feola and Giovanni Silvano (in press).

24 For Szent-Ivany and his contemporaries, there obviously was good (genuine) and bad (distorted) science, of which the first provided its followers with a foretaste of heaven and assisted the implementation of God's kingdom in human society.

25 Basically, ascetic theology, in Szent-Ivany's perspective, can be defined as a discipline directing all human actions so as to make him capable of attaining his final goal, i.e. the highest good.

MARTINUS SZENT-IVANY'S NOTION OF *SCIENTIA*

2 The Practical Tool of *scientia*

To make the access to knowledge easier, Szent-Ivany offers in his *De scientiis in genere* a compact solution: *Brevissima methodus tradendi et assequendi quascunque humanas scientias*. His method, being an original combination of then existing approaches based on Sebastián Izquierdo (1601–81), Caspar Knittel (1644–1702), and Athanasius Kircher (1602–80), is distinguished by being extraordinarily short and plain. It consists of six parts, or founts ("fontes"), as they are referred to by the author: observation, axiomatics, analogy, analysis and sythesis (taken together), the great art of Kircher and Lullus (*Ars Magna Kirchero-Lulliana*), and combinatorics. A very brief consideration of each of these reveals interesting information on the meaning of the term *scientia* as used by Szent-Ivany. At the same time, it provides a useful supplement to what has been said in the first part of this paper, demonstrating the tight interrelations of reason, faith, and art in early modern *scientia*.

2.1 *Observation*

As the historians of science Lorraine Daston and Elizabeth Lunbeck have pointed out, the notion of *observatio* was so widely used in early modern times that it almost seems to have coincided with science in general.[26] This is also true of the texts of Szent-Ivany. Following Sebastián Izquierdo, he distinguished three kinds of observation: "experimentalis", "idealis", and "doctrinalis".[27] The last mentioned kind ("observatio doctrinalis") is definitely the one most frequently employed by Szent-Ivany, who I believe did not differ much in this respect from the majority of Neo-Latin authors. It may be surprising to learn that this kind of observation is basically identical with taking notes and excerpts from books. This is a simple but very significant fact: reading and excerpting was an important, if not the foremost, tool of early modern *scientia*.[28] This means that a great deal of research into Neo-Latin science must indispensably consist in intertextual investigation.

2.2 *Axiomatics*

Szent-Ivany belongs to those scholars who emphasized the necessity of basing every discourse on a set of clearly defined and unquestionable principles, a

---

26 Lorraine Daston and Elizabeth Lunbeck (eds.), *Histories of Scientific Observation* (Chicago, 2011), 1.

27 Sebastián Izquierdo, *Pharus scientiarum* (Lyon, 1659), vol. 2, 291–7.

28 For further reading, let it suffice here to refer the reader to the publications by Helmut Zedelmaier (LMU Munich) recently written on the early modern practice of excerption.

method he called geometrical. This tool of *scientia* was to be applied not only to what we would call exact sciences but to all *scientiae* in general. Szent-Ivany, for example, made ample use of axioms in his polemical theological writings, as also did some other great Jesuit theologians of the seventeenth century. The purpose of axiomatics, besides guaranteeing brevity, was to attain the highest possible degree of certainty (see above).

2.3 *Analogy*

Particularly interesting is the third tool of *scientia*, the third fount of Szent-Ivany's *Brevissima methodus*—namely, analogy. When reading Szent-Ivany's texts, one finds it very instructive to notice that it is often simply a metaphor or a simile that the author adopts when proceeding by way of analogy, especially in his polemical theological treatises. Analogy is thus a tool of knowing which not only brings early modern *scientia* close to *poesis* but, vice versa, it also makes us alert to the fact that the function of rhetorical devices in Neo-Latin literature may exceed the limits of purely artistic expression. The importance of analogy for early modern *scientia* clearly shows that reason, i.e. the substance of *scientia*, once followed a path quite different from the one it takes today. *Artes* and *scientiae* were siblings, a fact of which didactic poetry is only one example.

2.4 *Analysis and Synthesis*

The fourth fount or tool of *scientia* is analysis and synthesis, a method highly praised by Szent-Ivany and referred to by him as mathematical. Like the other parts of his *Brevissima methodus*, analysis, too, is a concept not wholly corresponding with what we might expect it to be. At one time it takes on the form of a simple division or classification of the subject under discussion, at another time, though, it is represented by deducing logical consequences in a series of propositions. It is again striking that it is in his polemical theology, a genre we would expect to be very rhetorical, that Szent-Ivany applied the analytical method, in its strictly logical form, most consistently. He even authored a separate treatise devoted to the deductive analysis of the main articles of faith.[29] Having in mind what has been said of analogy, we can see that there is in Szent-Ivany's approach to *scientia* an intriguing tension between a close relation to rhetoric on the one hand and a strong tendency toward a certain de-rhetorization on the other (see below).

---

29 Martinus Szent-Ivany, *Analysis seu resolutio duodecim praecipuorum erroneorum dogmatum in fide modernorum acatholicorum* (Trnava, 1703; Cologne, 1704).

2.5 Ars Magna Kirchero-Lulliana

Szent-Ivany's *Ars Magna Kirchero-Lulliana* is an extremely simplified version of Athanasius Kircher's modification of the Lullian art. It is obviously meant to fulfil the function of generating new questions and propositions, and thus it may be regarded as a powerful tool of one of the three kinds of observation—namely, "observatio idealis", i.e. mental observation based on the operations of the intellect.

2.6 *Combinatorics*

The last fount, combinatorics, is in this case not strictly conceived as a discipline of mathematics but is simply fashioned as making combinations of things. In his *De scientiis in genere*, Szent-Ivany draws an analogy between anagrams and knowledge, saying that not all anagrams can produce meaningful messages just like not all questions and propositions are capable of yielding useful results.[30] I find his spontaneous mentioning of anagrams in connection with *scientia* particularly interesting as it shows how much the acquisition of knowledge was considered to be a product of mechanical practices. On the other hand, however, Szent-Ivany made it clear that the right selection was always to be done by an intelligent mind. It should be noted here that the last two founts of Szent-Ivany's *Brevissima methodus*, i.e. the Kirchero-Lullian art and combinatorics, can certainly be regarded as a scientific counterpart of the rhetorical concept of *inventio*.

2.7 *Considering Observation in Particular (a Micro Case Study)*

A detailed examination of how and to what extent Szent-Ivany's concept of *scientia*, as outlined in his *Brevissima methodus*, was really put into practice in his works must be left for further investigation. For the time being, it is possible to insert here a brief note on how Szent-Ivany utilized the tool of *observatio* (i.e., the first fount of his concise method) throughout his works, both those contained in his *Miscellanea* and those belonging to his polemical theological corpus.[31] After a thorough examination, it has turned out that the term "observatio" can denote different types of texts, ranging from a mere recording of data to a whole treatise on a specific subject, regardless of the discipline concerned. Yet, there are certain characteristics that can be associated with this notion. The most obvious ones that immediately come to mind, based on my reading of Szent-Ivany's texts, are shortness, plainness, and factualness;

---

30 Szent-Ivany, *De scientiis* 8.

31 I discussed Szent-Ivany's use of the tool of *observatio* at the Seventh *Scientiae* Conference held at the University of Minnesota in May 2018.

but also incompleteness, open-endedness, tentativeness—and even subjectiveness, not in the sense of being biased, but in the sense of being the expression of a personal opinion or preference. The kind of discourse distinguished by these characteristics can be denoted as *observatio*. I propose to call it the observational mode of discourse. This kind of discourse is, in a way, unrhetorical, or even anti-rhetorical as regards its structure and outward appearance. It tends to be fragmented. In it, bits of information are juxtaposed alongside one another, often with no linguistic connectors being employed (see above on the concreteness of *scientia*). Its function is not at all aesthetic, it is purely informational. Nor is it meant to persuade the reader, its sole task being to inform. And yet it remains rhetorical in the way it comes into being, for each of the six sources or founts of Szent-Ivany's concise method has, to a greater or lesser degree, to do with rhetorical invention. This formal de-rhetorization of scientific discourse is, I believe, closely related to the unprecedented growth of information and the ever-increasing specialization of scientific disciplines in the course of the seventeenth century.

3   Conclusion

In the end, let me highlight a few points which may have an impact on the semantics of the word *scientia* in early modern times.

1. Around 1700, the Neo-Latin notion of *scientia* seems to have been a very concrete one and rather remote from the abstractness with which we tend to conceive of science today. With Szent-Ivany, the focus of this term was unambiguously on data, the sum of concrete pieces of information, rather than on an abstract system.
2. This very concreteness of *scientia* makes it akin to the arts.
3. The strong association of *scientia* with truth accounts for its close relationship with faith and religion, which, in turn, gives it a strong ethical dimension.

Martinus Szent-Ivany's works are representative of only one strand of early modern scientific thinking—namely, the Catholic, or more specifically, the Jesuit scholarship. Yet, this particular tradition within the early modern *scientiae* certainly deserves increased attention—especially in comparison with and in contrast to the concept of 'universal reform' which is nowadays intensely investigated—if we wish to obtain a balanced idea of the early modern notion of *scientia*. Another particular characteristic of Szent-Ivany's works lies in the fact that they came into existence on a scientific periphery, as it were, away from the big centers of European learning. This, however, makes them perhaps, paradoxically, more representative of the mainstream scholarly practice of the period.

The aim of this paper has been to emphasize that every discourse on early modern science should be preceded by a proper and authentic understanding of the very notion of *scientia* as conceived in the early modern period, taking into account those aspects and connotations of the term which may seem to be of little relevance when judged by present-day criteria, but may turn out to be decisive for a successful interpretation of early modern scientific works. I believe a deeper semantic and contextual study of the Neo-Latin notion *scientia* would often help us avoid errors and anachronistic misinterpretation. The better we know the content of this word, the less likely we are to expect from the works of Neo-Latin scholarship that which they cannot give and the more sensitive we will be to that which we actually can learn from them.

Societas studiis Slavo-Latinis provehendis, Bratislava

Index

This index has been compiled with the help of Delila Jordan.

Abad, Diego José   468, 471
Accolti, Benedetto   298, 303
Achrelius, Daniel   496–497, 499–505
Acidalius, Valens   202–203, 211–212
Acquaviva, Andrea Matteo   618–619
Acquaviva, Belisario   227, 618–622
Acron (Ps.-)   477
Aegina   see Paul of Aegina
Aelianus, Claudius   157, 378, 384
Aesop   469–470
Aëtius of Amida   440, 458, 482
Agricola, Georg   506, 508–509, 514
Agricola, Rodolph   378
Agrippa, Marcus Vipsanius   216, 398–399
Ahaz (king of Judah)   402–404
Al-Battānī (Albategno)   430–431
Al-Farghānī (Alfragano)   430–431, 436
Al-Razi   440
Alberti, Leon Battista   81
Albertus Magnus   480, 617, 642
Aldrovandi, Ulisse   227–228, 508, 649
Alegre, Francisco Javier   468
Alexander (the Great)   208–209, 211, 468, 624
Alexander of Aphrodisias   275, 277–278, 482
Alexander of Tralles   440, 458
Alexander VI (pope)   393–394
Alexander VII (pope)   352
Alexandria   see Arius; Athanasius; Philo
Alexandrou, Jorge   282
Alfonso d'Avalos   230–231
Alfonso de Cartagena   121–122, 125–126, 128–129
Alfonso II (king of Naples)   624
Alfonso V (king of Aragon)   93, 518, 522–523, 624, 641
Alfonso X (king of Castile)   125
Alighieri   see Dante
Altilio, Gabriele   623–624
Álvarez, Manuel   564–565
Amaral, Prudentius de   469
Amboise, Michel d'   350
Ambrogi, Antonio   588

Ambrose, St.   603, 642
Amerbach, Basilius   147–148
Amerbach, Johann   147–148
Amerinus, Hans Lauridsen   330
Ammianus Marcellinus   394
Ancona   see Cyriacus
Andreae, Johann Valentin   89
Andrés, Juan (Andres, Giovanni)   591, 466–467
Andronikos II Palaiologos)   485
Angeli, Pietro da Barga   223–235
Anjou   see Charles; Robert
Antonius   see Mark Antony
Aphrodisias   see Alexander
Aphthonius   378
Apollonios Rhodios   350
Aponte, Pedro Jerónimo de   266
Apostolis, Michael   59–60
Appian   166, 389–392, 397–398
Apuleius   81, 296, 378–379, 642
Aquilonius, Bertilus Canutius   547–548
Aquinas, Thomas, St.   109, 133, 415, 421, 481
Aranda, Conde de   275
Archimedes   432
Aretaios   440
Arévalo, Faustino   467
Argyropoulos, Ioannes   275, 480
Arian, Antuono   194
Arian, Marco   194
Ariosto, Ludovico   297, 303, 348, 612
Ariovist   394
Aristarchus of Samos   432
Aristarchus of Samothrace   219–220
Aristides   59
Aristippus   386
Aristotle   11, 14, 16, 50, 56–58, 62, 64–65, 92–114, 164, 254, 273–282, 314–315, 317, 378–379, 390, 431–432, 436, 440, 480–482, 621, 623, 642, 648, 667
Arius of Alexandria   600–601, 603
Armagnac, George d'   389–390, 397
Arredondo, Gonzalo de   117–118, 125–129
Arrianus, Lucius Flavius   208, 211, 487

690 INDEX

Arsilli, Francesco 299
Arteaga, Esteban de 467
Aspasia of Miletus 523
Athanasius of Alexandria 603
Athenaeus, Harmonius 282
Atticus, Titus Pomponius 204, 425
Atumanus, Simon 51
Aubéry, Antoine 397
Augustine, St. 40–41, 332, 403, 560–561, 603,
 642, 647
Augustus (Roman emperor) 393, 396, 398,
 466–467, 536, 680
Aulus Gellius 157–158, 160, 378
Aurelianus, Lucius Domitius 87
Aurifaber see Goldschmidt
Aurillac, Gerbert de 148
Aurispa, Giorgio 392–393
Ausonius, Decimus Magnus 220–221, 447
Averara see Giovanni
Averroes 440, 480–481
Avicenna 440, 458, 480
Avila see Teresa
Aymerich, Mateo 467

Baarland, Adriaan van 378–380
Bachelier, Nicolas 397
Bacon, Francis 499, 590–591
Balbín, Bohuslav 630
Balde, Jakob 347, 351–353
Barbara, St. 180
Barbaro, Ermolao 622
Barbaro, Francesco 58–59
Barbato da Sulmona 29
Barbo, Pietro 391
Barbosa, Arias 420
Barchusen, Johann Conrad 673
Barclay, John 68, 71, 73–80, 83–85, 87, 89,
 330
Barclay, William 668
Barga see Angeli
Barker, William 303
Baróti Szabó, Dávid 576–584
Bartelón, Pantaleón 447
Barzizza, Guiniforte 518, 522
Basil, St. 642
Bassi Veratti, Laura María Caterina 465
Batsányi, Ioannes 584
Bayer, Wenceslaus 612
Bayle, Pierre 401–402, 409–410

Beccadeli, Antonio 379
Becchi, Gentile de 216
Becius, Johannes 598–602, 606
Bellay, Joachim du 630, 639
Belon, Pierre 227
Bembo, Bernardo 612
Bembo, Bonifacio 393
Bembo, Pietro 350
Benagli, Bernardino 241
Bentley, Richard 144
Benucci, Alessandra 297
Benucci, Lattanzio 297
Benucci, Lelio 297
Benvenuto da Imola 288
Bergantini, Giovanni Pietro 224, 227, 233
Bernardus Silvestris 287, 289
Beroaldo, Filippo 156–159, 161, 296, 378,
 474–475, 613
Bersuire, Pierre 287–288
Bessarion, Basilios 66–67, 282, 480
Bettinelli, Saverio 466
Bettinelli, Tommaso 523–524
Bettini, Mario 361–366
Beza, Theodore 301, 399, 613
Biancuzzi, Benedetto 158–159
Birago, Lampugnino 391–392
Birken, Sigmund von 79
Bissel, Johannes 80, 85, 89–90
Bisticci, Vespasiano da 92
Bituriensis see Guido
Blanc, Guillaume du 389–390, 397
Boccaccio, Giovanni 25, 32–36, 48–50,
 285–286, 348
Bodianus, Franciscus Vitalis 143, 145, 149,
 151, 155
Boethius 524
Boije, Claes 637
Bonardo, Diomedes 240
Bonardus, Johannes 393
Bonifacio, Giovanni Bernardino 302
Boom, Dirk 603
Boom, Hendrik 603
Borch, Ole 669–672
Borja, Juan de 613
Boschius, Jacobus 470
Boscovich, Roger Joseph 469–470, 586–587,
 589
Bourbon, Nicolas 335–346
Boxhorn, Marcus Zuerius 3–4, 6, 9

INDEX

Boyd, Marc Alexander 347, 350–352
Bracciolini, Poggio 60–61, 390
Brahe, Tycho 544–545, 548
Brancaccio, Marino 618–619, 622
Brandenburg, Albrecht von 532
Brasch, Martin 656
Brassavola, Antonius Musa 667
Braunschweig, Anton Ulrich von 79
Brendel, Adam 673
Bretschneider, Carolus Gottlieb 567
Breyne, Jacob 673
Britannicus, Ioannes 472–473, 476–477, 479–480
Brossano, Francescuolo da 36
Brukenthal, Samuel of 578–579
Bruni, Antonio 348–349
Bruni, Leonardo 46, 48, 55, 57–58, 61–65, 67, 91–114, 289, 415–416, 491, 521
Brunoy, Pierre 470
Brutus, Marcus Iunius 330
Buchanan, George 613
Budé, Guillaume 140
Bullinger, Heinrich 600–601
Buondelmonti, Cristoforo 248–258
Burckhardt, Jacob 519
Buridan, John 433
Burman, Pieter 607–609
Burski, Adam 661
Bussi, Giovanni Andrea 216

Caelius, Marcus Rufus 166
Caesar, Gaius Iulius 41, 137, 330–333, 393–394, 396–399, 523
Calderini, Domizio 156–157, 161
Calenus, Quintus Fufius 398–399
Calepino, Ambrogio 297
Caligula (Roman emperor) 209, 395
Callistus, Nicephorus 378
Calvete de Estrella, Juan Cristóbal 552
Calvin, Johannes 8, 372–373, 409, 599, 604
Campano, Giannantonio 622
Campi, Bernardino 642
Campion, Edmund 471
Canter, Dirk 164
Cantimpré, Tommaso di 640–641, 645, 647–649
Capdevila, Francesc 465
Capitolinus, Julius Julio 378, 394
Capote, Truman 83

Caracciolo, Giovan Francesco 619, 621
Caracciolo, Tristano 215
Cardano, Gerolamo 8, 13
Carducci, Giosue 38
Cariteo, Benedetto 619
Carnicer, Joaquín 466
Carolus a Wehingen 135
Carondelet, Jean de 368
Carranza de Miranda, Sancho 274
Carrara, Ubertino 469–470
Cartagena see Alfonso
Carvajal, Juan de 118, 414, 418
Carvejal, Lorenzo Galíndez de 118–120, 128
Casimir III (the Great) 178–179
Casmann, Otto 667
Cassiodorus 378
Cassius Dio 166, 356, 389–390, 392–394, 397–400
Castellio, Sebastian 372
Castiglionchio, Lapo da 27–28
Castiglione, Baldassare 47
Castilla, Diego 266
Castner, Jodocus 139
Castro, León de 271
Catherine of Alexandria, St. 180, 185
Cato, Marcus Porcius 132, 140
Cats, Jacob 500
Catullus 160, 336, 661
Caussin, Nicolas 564
Cavalicensis, Philippus 25
Cavo, Andrés 468
Celsus, Aulus Cornelius 478–482, 642
Celsus, Iulius 127
Celtis, Conrad 445, 534
Cerda, Ana de la 419
Cervantes, Miguel de 267
Chalkokondyles, Demetrios 216, 666
Charles V (Emperor) 118, 175, 251, 342, 395, 535–536, 552–553, 555, 574, 575
Charles VIII (king of France) 216, 618, 624
Charles IX (king of France) 330
Charles III (king of Spain) 275
Charles IX (king of Sweden) 638
Charles XI (king of Sweden) 501, 503
Charles I (Duke of Savoy) 217
Charles of Anjou 498
Charles of Žerotín 617
Charondas 99, 103, 109
Chimienti, Giuseppe 224

Chouet, Jean-Robert   411
Christian III (king of Denmark)   168–177,
   330, 541
Christina (queen of Sweden)   638
Christus   see Jesus Christ
Chrysippus   474
Chrysoloras, Manuel   52–59, 62–64, 67
Chytraeus, Nathan   303
Cicero   18–19, 27–28, 43, 46–47, 49, 53, 55,
   77, 132, 137, 162, 165–166, 204–205, 208,
   220, 289–290, 340, 378–379, 393,
   397–399, 413–416, 418, 420–427, 464,
   473, 519, 523, 566, 624, 642–643
Ciegler, Georg   655
Cimon   524
Cinozzi, Girolamo   218
Cipelli   see Veneto
Cisneros, Francisco Jiménez de   274
Claerhout, Jacques de   7–9
Clarke, Samuel   588
Claudian   179, 501–502
Clavigero, Francisco Javier   468
Clement VII (pope)   369, 555
Clerselier, Claude   603
Clingerius, Henricus   612
Cocceius, Lucius Auctus   215–216
Coleridge, Samuel Taylor   72
Colet, John   419
Colines, Simon de   210, 241
Colomes, Juan Bautista   467
Colonna, Crisostomo   623–624
Colonna, Giovanni   26, 43
Colonna, Mario   223
Colucci, Giovanbattista   299
Columbus, Christopher   469–470
Columbus, Johann   638
Commodus, Lucius Aurelius   395
Conca, Antonio   467
Conches, Guillaume de   289
Conradinus, Henning   326
Conring, Hermann   669–671
Conti, Natale   226
Conti, Pietro Ginori   213, 219
Contursino, Brusonio   378–379
Contzen, Adam   80, 85
Copernicus, Nicolaus   428–430, 432,
   435–436
Cornarius, Janus   245

Cornelius a Lapide   596
Cornutus, Lucius Annaeus   473–474, 477
Corvinus, Matthias   580
Corycius, Johannes   299
Costeo, Giovanni   246
Cremona   see Gerard
Crescenzi, Pietro de   227
Cropacius, Caspar   612
Ctesias   648
Curione, Celio Secondo   389–390, 398–400
Curtius Rufus   202–212, 390
Cusanus, Nicholas   418
Cuspian, Johannes   378–380
Cyriacus of Ancona   250–254, 257–258
Cyril, St.   260, 263–264, 271

Dahlstierna, Gunno Eurelius   638
Damascus   see John
Dante Alighieri   39, 193, 285–286, 289, 324,
   348
Dantisca, Juana   550–554, 559, 561
Dantisco, Juan (son of Ioannes)   552
Dantiscus, Ioannes   179, 550–561
Decembrio, Pier Candido   64, 67, 168,
   390–391, 640–650
Delgada, Isabella   552–553
Demetrios Palaiologos   486
Demosthenes   49, 61, 64
Denis, Michael   469–470
Der-Kennis, Ignatius   604
Deroziers, Claude   393–394
Desbordes, Henri   409
Descartes, René   499, 588, 603
Diaconus   see Paulus
Díaz, Hernando   440
Diodorus Siculus   60, 208, 211, 390, 665
Diogenes Laertius   378–379, 384–385
Dionigi di Borgo San Sepolcro   29, 33
Dionís, Dinis   266
Dionysius of Halicarnassus   141, 389–392,
   400
Dioscorides   458, 482, 513
Dolet, Etienne   47–48, 335–337, 339–340,
   346
Donatus, Aelius   134
Donelaitis, Kristijonas   577
Donne, John   497
Dorán, Gregorius   467

INDEX

Dorca, Francisco Javier   466
Doria, Miguel   465–466
Dousa, Janus   445
Drusus, Decimus Claudius   529
Dubravius, Johannes   145
Ducher, Gilbert   335–337, 339, 342, 346
Dufour, Sylvestre   669
Duport, James   672
Dürer, Albrecht   380, 642

Edward VI (king of England)   372, 398–399
Ehinger, Ulrich   553
Elagabalus   395
Elias   39
Elizabeth I (queen of England)   75
Elizaveta Petrovna (Russian empress)
    562–563, 566–572
Ennius   29, 423
Epimenides   103
Episcopius, Nikolaus   244–245
Erasmus, Desiderius   18, 131, 135, 140, 182,
    203–206, 210–212, 301, 312–322, 367–375,
    377–379, 394–397, 399, 408, 410, 413,
    419–420, 423, 426–427, 553, 585, 612–613
Erath, Augustinus   500
Eric XIV (king of Sweden)   634
Ertl, Anton Wilhelm   79, 85
Este, Borso d' (duke of Ferrara)   466
Estienne   see Stephanus
Étaples, Jacques Lefèvre d'   91, 108, 110, 113,
    421
Euclid   432
Eugenius IV (pope)   93, 522–523
Euripides   18
Euryphontis   111, 113
Eusebius of Caesarea   53, 378, 600
Eustathius   666
Eutecnius, Sophistes   228
Eutropius   378, 394
Eximeno, Antonio   467
Exner, Balthasar   615

Fabre, Jean-Henri   38
Fabricius, Georgius   514, 525–536
Fabricius, Johann Albertus   613
Fabricius, Petrus   613
Farri, Dominico   242
Favolio, Hugo   250–255, 257–258

Favorinus   378
Febvre, François Antoine le   470
Fedele, Cassandra   524
Fendt, Tobias   303
Ferdinand II (Emperor)   624–625
Ferdinand III (Emperor)   125
Ferdinand of Aragona (king of Naples)   103,
    618, 622–623, 641
Ferdinand VI (king of Spain)   466
Fernando de Aragón   103
Fernel, Jean François   440
Ferrari, Scipione   241
Ferrerius, Johannes   514–515
Ficino, Marsilio   219, 440, 474–475, 491, 617
Filelfo, Francesco   55–56, 63, 391
Finestres, José   462–464
Firmin-Didot, Ambroise   486
Fleuriau, Bertrand Gabriel   470
Florus   135, 397–398
Foix, Henri de   339
Fontaine, Charles   532
Fontius, Bartholomaeus   472–473, 476–482
Fornelius, Lars   638
Fortunatus   see Venantius
Fracastoro, Girolamo   350, 440, 486, 491
France, François de (duc d'Alençon)   9–10
Francis I (king of France)   338–341, 486,
    535, 536
Frandsen, Hans   541–544
Frederick I (king of Denmark and
    Norway)   168
Frederick II (king of Denmark and
    Norway)   176–177, 330, 540–541, 548
Frederick III (Friedrich III; Holy Roman
    Emperor)   414
Frederick III of Saxony (Friedrich III von
    Sachsen)   395–396, 399
Frederick of Naples (king of Naples)   618,
    621–623
Freinsheim, Johannes   202–203
Frellon, Jean   245
Freud, Sigmund   4
Fridolin of Säckingen   133
Friedenthal, Salomon Frenzel von   656
Frisch, Max   82
Froben, Hieronymus   244–245
Fuente, Rodrigo of   266–267, 271
Fulgosio, Baptista   378–379

694 INDEX

Gadaldini, Agostino 243–245
Galateo, Antonio 618–626
Galen 8–9, 11, 15, 22, 237–247, 439–440, 444, 448, 455, 458, 460, 475, 482, 642, 667
Galilei, Galileo 430, 432, 499
Galiot de Genouillac, Jacques 337–339
Gallicanus see Vulcacius
Gallus, Gaius Cornelius 300, 536
Gamaliel 372–373
Garcés, Gregorio 467
García, Alonso 439, 441–443, 445–449
Gardie, Jacob de la 628, 632–635, 637, 639
Gardie, Magnus Gabriel de la 628, 632, 636, 639
Gardiner, Samuel 599
Gaudanus, Theodoricus Gerardus 236–247
Gaza, Theodore 64
Geisshüsler see Myconius
Gelenius, Sigismund 398
Gellius see Aulus
Geminiano, Pascuccio 520
Gemusaeus, Hieronymus 245
Genazzano, Mariano da 218
Genette, Gérard 89, 540
Gentil, René 301, 303, 308–309
George of Trapezunt 64–65, 390
George the Bearded (George of Saxony) 395–396
Gerald of Wales 35
Gerard of Cremona 239–240
Gessner, Conrad 158, 227–228, 245–246, 506–517, 642–643, 649
Ghisi, Teodoro 643
Gibbon, Edward 395
Gilbert, William 498
Gilles, Pierre 492
Giovanni di Averara 196, 198
Giovio, Paolo 230–231
Giraldi, Lilio Gregorio 233
Gisbice, Paulus a 612
Giulandino, Melchior 667–668
Giunta, Giovanni Maria 244
Giunta, Lucantonio 241, 244–247
Giunta, Tommaso 244
Glareanus Heinrich 130–142, 203, 207–212
Glimes, Jean IV de 9
Goldschmidt, Andreas 483, 487, 491–495
Gómez de Castro, Álvar 262–263

Gonzaga, Aloisius of 465–466
Gonzaga, Cecilia 522
Gonzaga, Ludovico III 641–643
Gothein, Eberhard 214–215
Gott, Samuel 80, 85–86
Gottius, Johannes 222
Gottsched, Johann Christoph 563–564, 566
Gracián Dantisco, Antonio 550, 552, 554
Gracián Dantisco, Jerónimo 550, 554
Gracián Dantisco, Lorenzo 550
Gracián Dantisco, Lucas 550, 554
Gracián Dantisco, Tomas 550, 554
Gracián de Alderete, Diego 550–561
Graevius, Johann Georg 598, 605, 607
Grand, Antonius Le 499
Grattius Faliscus 483–485, 487–494
Gravius, Valentius 514
Gregory I (pope) 196–201, 416, 642
Gregory XIII (pope) 468
Gremesius, Vitantonius 282
Gribaldi, Matteo 372–373
Griffet, Claude 469–470
Grimaldi, Polissena 522
Groesbeek, Gerard van 147
Groot, Willem de 401
Grotius, Hugo 143–146, 151–155, 260, 401–402, 404–412
Grotius, Janus 152
Gruterus, Janus 158–159, 163
Gryphius, Sebastian 335
Guarino, Battista 393–394
Guevara, Antonio 621, 623
Guicciardini, Francesco 399
Guido Bituriensis 379
Gustà, Francisco 467
Gustav I (king of Sweden) 633–634, 638
Gustav II Adolf (king of Sweden) 633–634
Gymnich, Johann 210

Hadrianus (Emperor) 393–394
Hadrianus, Junius 157–158, 162–164
Hal, Toon van 537
Han, Ulrich 122
Hangest, Jean de 241–242
Hangest, Jérôme de 302
Harant of Polžice and Bezdružice, Kryštof 616
Harvey, Gabriel 399–400

INDEX 695

Hegelund, Peder 168–177
Heinsius, Daniel 260
Hejnic, Josef 614
Hennebert, Jean-Baptiste-François 585
Henry (king of Portugal) 377
Henry IV (king of France) 75, 152, 330
Henry IV (king of Spain) 120, 122, 125, 127
Henry IV (king of England) 585
Henry VI (king of England) 91–92
Henry VIII (king of England) 313
Herbers, Georg 657–658
Hermann, Daniel 656–657
Herodianus 378, 392
Herodotus 78, 378, 390, 636, 637
Hervás y Panduro, Lorenzo 467
Herwart, Johann Heinrich 397–398
Hesiod 96, 98, 388
Hessus, Helius Eobanus 182
Hilary of Poitiers, St. 368
Hilchen, Beata 660–661
Hilchen, David 651–662
Hilchen, Franciscus 661
Hippocrates 246, 439–440, 443–444, 448, 458, 460, 477–478, 667
Hirnhaim, Hieronymus 680
Hobbes, Thomas 411
Holanda, Francisco de 296
Holberg, Ludvig 81, 85–87
Hollywood, John 432, 436
Homer 29, 48–52, 79, 317, 321, 338, 341, 468, 538, 556, 647, 663–674
Horace 16, 31, 35, 43, 47, 53, 62, 137, 161, 165, 183–188, 227, 288–289, 293, 299–300, 354–359, 365–366, 445, 473, 477, 536, 546–548, 642, 661
Horn, Evert 635
Hosius, Stanislaus 550, 559–561
Huarte de San Juan, Juan 439–441
Huet, Pierre-Daniel 406, 598, 605–609
Hume, David 330
Hunyadi, Janus 580
Hutten, Ulrich von 203, 205–207, 210, 212, 445
Huttich, Johannes 304
Huygens, Constantijn (the Elder) 598, 605, 607
Huygens, Constantijn (the Younger) 605
Hyginus 287

Ifflinger, Daniel 132
Ignatius of Loyola, St. 353, 363
Immanuel 402, 404
Imola see Benvenuto
Isabella (queen of Spain) 553
Isabella I (queen of Castile) 120–121, 127–128
Isabella of Aragón 624
Isaiah 402–406
Isidore of Seville 150, 154, 287, 289, 642–647
Isla, José Francisco de 467
Isocrates 62–63, 395, 623
Iustinus 135, 211
Iuvenalis 473, 522, 642
Izquierdo, Sebastián 683

Jacopo da Volterra 393
Jagiello, Ladislaus 178–179
James I (king of England) 84–85, 330, 350
James VI Stuart 350
Jerome, St. 46, 49–50, 53, 63, 66, 219–220, 403–404, 416, 421, 472, 642, 646–647
Jesenius, Jan 617
Jesus Christ 32, 132–133, 196–200, 288, 290–291, 372, 403–406, 410, 419, 421, 502, 513, 528, 589, 600
Joachim I (Elector) 169, 171–172, 174–175
Joana of Castile 120–121
Joana of Portugal 127–128
Joanna of Austria 234
Johannes VIII Palaiologos 486
John II (king of Aragón) 104
John III (king of Sweden) 634
John of Damascus 421
John the Baptist 290–291
Johnson, Thomas 491
Joseph II (Emperor) 580–581
Joyce, James 72, 82
Juan de Aragón (archbishop of Zaragoza) 104
Judas 199

Kachenovskiy, Mikhail Trophimovich 566–568
Kallierges, Zacharias 282
Kašic, Bartol 564
Kemper, Johan 630
Kentmann, Johannes 507, 513

696 INDEX

Kidder, Richard   411
Kircher, Athanasius   499–502, 504–505, 596, 683, 685
Knittel, Caspar   683
Kobierzycki, Stanisław   631–635, 638
Krayskiy, Porfiriy   563
Krosno   see Paul
Kühn, Karl Gottlob   239
Kuon, Albrecht   553

La Sena, Pietro   668, 670, 672
Lackner, Christoph   503
Laetus, Erasmus   330, 540–542, 548
Laetus, Julius Pomponius   394
Lami, Giovanni   524
Lampillas, Francisco Javier   467
Lampridius, Aelius   378, 394
Landiano, Gerardo   93
Landino, Cristoforo   472, 477–478, 480–482
Landívar, Rafael   468–469, 471, 583
Larraz, Blas   463–464
Lascaris, Ioannes   281
Łaski, Jan   134
Lassala, Manuel   466–467
Lautrec, Henri de   339–341
Lautrec, Odet de   340–341
Laval, Claude-Guy de   339
Leclerc, Jean   401–402, 406–412
Leiva, Antonio de   342
Lenfant, Jacques   408–409
Leo x (pope)   368, 393, 399
León, Luis of   271
Leoniceno, Niccolò   237, 393–394
Leontorius, Conradus   148
Leopold II (Emperor)   580, 581
Lepidus, Marcus Aemilius   396
Lili, Camillo   520
Limborch, Philippus van   407
Lindenbrog Erpold   152
Lindenbrog Friedrich   152
Linné, Carl of   673
Lipsius, Justus   157, 162–166, 653, 666–667
Livy   39–41, 125, 135, 137, 208, 390, 398, 400
Lloses, Francisco   466
Llull, Ramon   683, 685
Locke, John   407
Logau, Georg von   188
Lombardus, Petrus   421

Lomonosov, Mikhail Vasilyevich   562–575
Longinus, Gaius Cassius   330, 564
Lorenzo, Niccolò di   478
Loriti   see Glareanus
Loschi, Antonio   50–51
Lotichius Secundus, Petrus   541
Louis xi (king of France)   338
Louis xiii (king of France)   75, 83, 486
Louis xiv (king of France)   471
Louis xv (king of France)   465
Louis of Granada   376–388
Lucan   179, 227, 344, 636–637
Lucian   88, 642, 645
Lucretius   227, 344–345, 445–446, 485, 498, 637–638
Lucullus   215
Luis Fernando of Spain   465
Luna, Álvaro de   126–127
Lusitanus, Amatus   450–461
Luther, Martin   169, 171, 367–374, 527, 531–533, 546, 552, 560–561, 599–601, 604, 613
Lycosthenes, Conrad   379
Lycurgus   98, 110, 384

Machays, Abraham le   301, 308–309
Machiavelli, Niccolò   47, 399–400
Maciejowski, Samuel   559–560
Macrobius   378
Maecenas   398–399
Magyi, Sebastién   179–180
Maillard, Nicolas   301–302, 308–309
Malatesta, Battista   522
Malatesta, Elisabetta   519–520
Malatesta, Galeazzo   520, 522–523
Maludan, Jean   296
Manardo, Giovanni   440
Manetti, Gianozzo   65, 67
Manrique, Jorge   259
Mantuán Fencl, Jan   612
Manuel II Palaiologos   486
Manuzio, Aldo   237–239, 278–281, 283
Marcellus   523
Margarit, Joan   129
María Teresa Rafaela of Spain   465
Maria Theresa (queen of Hungary)   579–581
Marineo Sículo, Lucio   129
Marino, Giovan Battista   348, 350–351

INDEX

Mark Antony 393–394, 396, 398
Marnix, Jean de 8
Marnix, Philippe de 8, 260
Márquez, Cristóbal 554
Márquez, Pedro José 468
Martial 32, 296, 300, 336, 357, 446–447, 466
Martianus Capella 143–155, 287
Martínek, Jan 614, 616
Martini, Simone 29–30
Mary I of England 399
Mary, Virgin 132, 185, 403, 406, 550
Masdeu, Baltasar 467
Masdeu, José Antonio 467
Masdeu, Juan Francisco 467
Mata, Alonso de 440–441
Matthew 195, 371, 402–405, 407–408, 414–415
Maximilian I (Emperor) 80, 380, 399, 552
Mazzocchi, Giacomo 294–295, 303
Mazzolari, Giuseppe 586–587, 594
Medici, Cosimo de' 223–224
Medici, Francesco de 223–225, 234–235
Medici, Julio de 275
Medici, Lorenzo de 475–476
Medina, María de 441
Medinaceli, Duque de 260
Meibom, Heinrich (the Younger) 671–672
Meibom, Johann Heinrich 671–672
Melanchthon, Philipp 113, 532–533, 567
Melantrich, Georgius 612
Melissa, Antonius 378
Mella, Carvajal de 118
Mella, Juan de 118
Melzo, Giovanni da 522
Mendoza y Bobadilla, Francisco de 260, 262–268
Mendoza, Diego de 419
Mendoza, Fernando de 260, 266, 268
Menéndez Pelayo, Marcelino 467
Mennio, Giovanni Rinaldo 104
Mentelin, Johann 94, 105
Mercuriale, Girolamo 246
Merula, Giorgio 393–394
Mesmes, Henri de 296–297
Messala 425
Mesue, Johannes (Masawaih, Yuhanna ibn) 458

Meurer, Wolfgang 527, 535
Meursius, Johannes 152
Michael VII Ducas 392
Michael VIII Palaiologos 485–486
Michelozzi, Bernardo 213–222
Michelozzi, Niccolò 213, 215
Micyllus, Jacob 530–535
Miháltz, Stephanus 576–579, 582–584
Mihetić, Ambroz 524
Miletus see Aspasia
Milio, Giuseppe 226
Millás, Joaquín 467
Mithridates, Flavius 219
Modius, François 203, 210–212
Moerbeke, William of 109, 274
Molina, Juan Ignacio 469
Mollet, Antonio 465
Molza, Francesco Maria 298, 303
Mondor, Claude 342
Montaigne, Michel de 367–368, 370–372, 374–375
Montano, Giovanni Battista 243–244
Montefeltro, Battista da 520
Montefeltro, Federico da 520
Montengón, Pedro de 467
Morales, Ambrosio de 119, 262–263, 266, 269
More, Thomas 80
Moretus, Balthasar 653
Moschos, Demetrios 282
Moses 39, 411, 425
Mosham, Ruprecht von 483, 491–492, 494
Mountjoy, William 313
Müller, Johannes 428–438
Münster, Johann von 3
Muret, Marc-Antoine 158–159, 161, 163–165
Murmellius, Johannes 132
Mutius, Macarius 182
Myconius, Oswald 138–139

Nannius, Petrus 161–162
Naogeorgus, Thomas 600–601
Nassau, Guillaume de 9
Nebrija, Antonio de 118, 121–124, 128, 419–420
Nemesianus 228, 485
Nemorarius, Jordanus 432

Nero (Emperor)   209, 395
Nerva (Emperor)   393–394
Newton, Isaac   465, 499, 586–594, 596
Niccolai, Alfonso   596
Niccoli, Niccolò   57–58
Niccolò de Reggio   239–240, 246
Nicholas V (pope)   59–60, 390–391
Nicolau, Sebastián   463, 467
Noceti, Carlo   469–470, 586–589, 591–596
Noeux, Rasse des   301
Nogarola, Isotta   518, 522–524
Nonius, Marcellus   477
Norrelius, Andreas   630

Obsopoeus, Vincentius   613
Oertel, Johann Gottfried   673
Oldenburg, Henry   598, 602–604, 606–607
Oporinus, Ioannes   9, 94, 112–113
Oppian   228
Oresme, Nicola   433
Origenes   403, 600, 605
Orsini, Giordano   249
Orth, Zacharias   526
Osius, Hieronymus   169, 176
Osório, Jerónimo   379
Oudin, François   470, 588
Ovid   18, 179, 227, 233, 254–256, 286–288,
   297, 300, 337, 343, 349–353, 423,
   444–445, 447, 469, 485, 543–545, 548,
   574, 583, 593, 595
Oxenstierna, Axel   631–632, 636

Páez de Castro, Juan   262, 266, 271–272
Palencia, Alfonso de   129
Pálfi, Laurentius   583
Palmart, Lambert   94, 106
Palmerius Janus   163, 211
Palmskiöld, Elias   634
Pannagl, Bernardo   353
Pannonius, Janus   187
Panormita   see Beccadelli
Panzano, Girolamo da   219–220
Paolini, Fabio   246
Papeus, Petrus   419–420, 422–423
Pascasius, Justus   3–22
Pascoli, Giovanni   223
Patetta, Federico   214–217, 221
Paul, St.   373, 524, 559–560

Paul of Aegina   242, 440, 458, 482
Paul of Krosno   178–188
Paulus Diaconus   394, 477
Paungartner, Johann Georg   136
Pausanias   287
Pedro Alfonso of Portugal   266
Peisistratos   314
Pekah (king of Israel)   402–403
Pepagomeno, Demetrio   483, 485–487,
   489–494
Peparinus, Johannes   656
Peramato, Pedro de   440
Peregrinus de Maricourt, Petrus   498
Perényi, Gábor   179–180, 187
Pérez de Guzmán, Alonso   441
Pérez de Guzmán, Fernán   118
Pericles   524
Perizonius, Jacobus   568
Perotti, Niccolò   59–60
Persius   166, 179, 289, 472–481
Persona, Giovanni Battista   667–668
Pétau, Denis   600
Peter I (the Great)   562, 573–574
Peter of Ravenna   179
Peter, St.   524
Petit, Pierre   672
Petrarca, Francesco   24–44, 48–52, 55–57,
   66–67, 214, 284–293, 430
Petrarca, Gherardo   290
Petreio, Giovanni   429–430, 432
Petreius, Petrus   629–631, 633
Petrella, Bernardino   667–668
Petremot, François   330
Petronius   88
Petrus, Henricus   145–151, 153, 204
Peuerbach, Georg   432, 434–435
Peutinger, Conrad   303–304
Philipp II (king of Spain)   7, 75, 261–262,
   268–271, 553, 558
Philipp le Bon (duc de Bourgogne)   338
Philipp V (king of Macedonia)   39–40
Philipp V (king of Spain)   462, 465
Philo of Alexandria   378
Philostratus   378
Photinus   603
Piccinino, Niccolò   520
Piccolomini, Enea Silvio   119, 379, 413–418,
   420, 422

INDEX 699

Picinelli, Filippo 500
Pico della Mirandola, Giovanni 217–219, 222
Piendibeni, Francesco 288
Pike, Kenneth 537–539
Pilato, Leonzio 49–52
Pinazo, Antonio 466–467
Pindar 661
Pinzi, Aurelio 241
Pinzi, Filippo 240
Pio, Alberto 277
Pio, Giovanni Battista 161–162, 393
Pires, Henrique 451
Pithou, Pierre 160
Pittacus 314
Pittorio, Ludovico 559
Pla, Joaquín 467
Planoudes, Maximos 282
Plato Tiburtinus 430–431
Plato 57–58, 64, 287, 315–316, 379–381, 385, 390, 432, 440, 480
Platter, Felix 507–508, 513
Plautus 343, 419–420
Plessis, Armand-Jean du (cardinal Richelieu) 84
Plinius, Basilius 504, 657
Pliny the Elder 32, 164, 166, 219, 252–253, 287, 378, 477, 482, 484, 490, 493, 498, 508–509, 513, 621, 642, 645–646, 648, 664–665, 667, 672
Pliny the Younger 565–567
Plutarch 51, 59, 211, 231, 376, 378–379, 381, 390, 397–398, 524, 552, 554, 642, 645, 665
Pocatela, Giacomo 241
Podkostelsky, Sigismundus 617
Poggi, Simone 469–470
Poggio, Giovanni 6–8
Poliziano, Angelo 157–164, 213–214, 219–220, 222, 392–393, 472–473, 476, 478–479, 481–482, 505
Pollio, Trebellius 394
Polybius 59–60, 400
Pomey, François-Antoine 564
Pompeius Magnus 397, 645–646
Pompeius Trogus 135, 390
Pomponazzi, Pietro 274
Pomponius Mela 39–41, 477, 636–637, 642
Ponce de León, Pedro 119

Ponce de León, Rodrigo (Duke of Arcos) 441
Poncher, Étienne 140
Pongelli, Girolamo 224
Pons i Massana, José 465
Pontano, Giovanni 182, 188, 300, 352, 379, 558–559, 619
Popoleschi, Giovanni Antonio 231
Porcia, Jacopo di 227, 232
Porphyrion, Pomponius 477
Posthumus, Herman 297
Pou, Bartolomé 462–465, 467
Prasch, Ludwig 81
Prasch, Susanne 81
Pratdesaba, Onofre 466
Pratensis, Jason 440
Prats, Buenaventura 467
Priscianus 378–379, 477
Probus 393, 474
Procler, John 179
Propertius 161, 227
Prospera 557
Prudentius 182–183
Ptolemaios 390, 431–432, 434, 436
Pucci, Francesco 213–222
Puderico, Errico 619
Pyber, Benedictus 579
Pythagoras 613

Quintilian 35, 52, 62–63, 205–206, 208, 289, 378, 481

Radbert, Paschasius 6
Rájnis, Iosephus 578
Rantzau, Heinrich 324–333
Rantzau, Johann 324–325, 327–330
Rantzau, Katharina 325
Rasario, Giovanni Battista 245–246
Ravenna see Peter
Ravisius, Johannes 445
Razumovskiy, Kirill Grigorevich 562
Recanati, Menachem 219
Reggio see Niccolò
Regio, Raffaele 472–473, 475, 479, 481
Regiomontanus see Müller
Reigersberch, Nicolaes van 401
Reinhold, Erasmus 431
Remigius of Auxerre 148–149, 289

Requeno, Vicente 467
Resende, André de 296
Reusner, Nicolaus 613
Révai, Nicolaus 578
Rezin (king of Aram-Damascus) 402–403
Rhegius, Urbanus 367
Rhenanus, Beatus 207
Rheticus, Joachim 429
Rho, Antonio da 64
Ricchi, Agostino 242–243, 247
Richelieu   see Plessis
Ridolfi, Niccolò 281
Rieger, Urban 140
Rigault, Nicolas 486, 489–492
Rincio, Bernardino 302
Rivet, André 401–402, 406
Rivirius, Joannes Nebriensis 240–241
Robert of Anjou 292
Robortello, Francesco 159, 161–165, 336–337
Rodrigues de Melo, José 469
Rodríguez de Almela, Diego 121, 125, 128
Roisius   see Ruiz
Roncaglia, Francesco 195
Ronchadele, Bortolameus da 194
Ronsard, Pierre de 290, 350
Rosacius, Jan 617
Rossi, Giovanni Vittorio 86–87
Rota, Marziano 241
Rubiales, Ana de Vargas 441
Rudbeck, Olof 629
Rudinger, Matthias 656
Rudolf II (Emperor) 613–616
Ruiz de Moros, Pedro 556
Rustici, Cencio de 52–54
Rustico, Pietro Antonio 241
Rybinski, Jan 654

Sabellius 603
Sacchi, Cesare 299–300, 303–305
Sachs, Hans 532
Sacrobosco   see Hollywood
Sadolin, Hans Jørgensen 541–542, 545–546
Sailer, Hieronymus 553
Sallust 61, 166, 203, 206, 212, 397–399
Salmasius, Claudius 144
Salutati, Coluccio 50–52, 55, 285, 390, 641
Salvini, Salvino 225–226
Sambucus, Johannes 501

Sánchez de Arévalo, Rodrigo 117–129
Sand, Christoph 598–609
Sannazaro, Jacopo 619, 621
Sanseverino, Antonello 621
Sante, Gilles Anne Xavier de La 470
Sapieha, Leo 655
Sappho 523, 546
Sarbiewski, Maciej Kazimierz 354–366
Sascerides, Johannes 169, 176
Sassetti, Francesco 478
Savonarola, Girolamo 217–218
Saxo Grammaticus 182
Scaliger, Joseph Justus 145–146, 152,
    154
Scève, Maurice 335–336
Schenking, Georg 660
Schepper, Cornelius de 553
Scheuchzer, Johann 596
Schifaldo, Tommaso 473
Schöner, Johannes 428–431, 435
Schoppe, Caspar 159
Schott, Andreas 122, 159
Schott, Kaspar 499
Schrader, Laurentius 303
Schwartzmaier, Ludwig 615
Schwertner, Georgius 599, 601
Scipio, Cornelia 523
Scipio, Publius Cornelius Aemilianus
    Africanus (the Younger) 637–638
Scipio, Publius Cornelius Africanus
    (the Elder) 291, 523, 637–638
Scotus, Michael 481
Sebastian, St. 185
Seneca 11, 127, 160, 163, 179, 186, 356–357,
    376, 378–380, 477, 566, 621
Senensis, Francisco 378–379
Sennert, Daniel 499
Sepúlveda, Juan Ginés de 273–283
Serenus, Quintus 480
Serra y Ferragut, Buenaventura 463
Serrano, Tomás 466–467
Servet, Michel 372
Servius 30, 287, 289, 329–332, 477, 536, 594,
    642
Sette, Guido 28, 31, 37
Sforza, Alessandro 522–523
Sforza, Bona (queen of Poland) 618, 621,
    623–624

INDEX

Sforza, Francesco   520–521
Shakespeare, William   585
Sidney, Philip   78
Sigismund III (king of Poland)   629, 661
Silber, Eucharius   94, 109
Silius Italicus   254, 344, 445
Simon, Richard   401–402, 407, 409–410
Siviglia, Giovanni da   430–431
Skaryna, Francysk   611
Smeducci, Costanza   519
Smržicky, Michael Pěčka   615
Socrates   383, 523, 642
Soderini, Fiammetta   234
Solinus   642
Solms, Philipp von   654
Souastre, Charles de   9
Souciet, Augustin Etienne   470
Southwell, Robert   471
Sozzini, Fausto   405–406, 409, 600
Spandko, Paul   657
Spartianus, Aelius   394
Sperling, Johannes   499
Speyer, Wendelin von   202–203
Spiegel, Jakob   379–380
Spindeler, Nicolaus   94, 108
Spineda, Paolo   295–296
Spinoza, Baruch   409–410, 606
Spon, Jacob   669
Stabluco, Piligrini de   194
Statius   157, 343
Stay, Benedikt   586, 589–591
Stay, Christoph   589–591
Stella, Erasmus   514
Stephanus, Henricus   94, 666
Stephanus, Robertus   394, 486
Stobaeus, Johannes   378
Stobnicensis, Ioannes   180
Stoppani, Giovanni Niccolò   399
Strabo   208, 215–216, 390
Strada, Zanobi da   27
Strozzi, Palla   92
Stuart, John   339
Sturm, Johannes   239, 241, 527, 532, 535
Suetonius   41, 137, 166, 168, 204, 378,
    394–395, 397–398, 477
Suidas   397
Sukhomlinov, Mikhail Ivanovich   564, 566,
    568

Suleiman I   251
Sulmona   see Barbato
Summonte, Pietro   619
Suriano, Girolamo   240–241
Swan, William   602
Sweertius, Franciscus   653
Sylvester, Ioannes   578
Szent-Ivany, Martinus   675–687
Szymonowic, Szymon   661

Tacitus   207, 212, 390, 397–398, 534, 620–621
Tasso, Torquato   348
Taurellus, Nicolaus   615
Tegli, Silvestro   399
Tell, Wilhelm   133
Tempesta, Antonio   227
Terence   185, 419
Teresa of Ávila, St.   554
Textor   see Ravisius
Thapsus   see Vigilius
Themistius   278, 622
Theodosius (of Bithynia)   432
Theophrastus   390, 642, 665
Theopompus   642
Theotokópoulos, Doménikos   267
Thomas, Loup   470
Thomesen, Hans   169, 174, 176
Thou, François de   341
Thou, Jacques-Auguste de   513
Thucydides   46, 59, 61, 390
Thurzo, Sigismund   188
Thurzo, Stanislaus   182, 186, 188
Tiberius (Emperor)   86, 209
Tifernas, Gregorius   216
Tiglath-Pileser III (king of Assyria)   403
Todeschini, Francesco   393
Torquemada, Juan de   118
Tortario, Rodolfo   445
Tortelli, Giovanni   297
Toscano, Giovan Matteo   298
Traianus (Emperor)   393–394, 396, 565–566
Tralles   see Alexander
Trapezunt   see George
Triller, Daniel Wilhelm   666
Trincavelli, Vittore   242–243, 247
Trivulzio, Gian Giacomo   299
Trivulzio, Scaramuccia   299
Turnèbe, Adrien   165, 666

702 INDEX

Turner, William 227
Tuy, Lucas de 119
Typotius, Jacobus 613, 617

Ulrica, Eleonora 501, 503
Ursyn-Niedzwiecki, Jan 661
Utenhof, Wolfgang von 170–172

Vadian, Joachim 336
Váez, Pero 440
Valera, Diego de 125
Valeriano, Pierio 299
Valerius Flaccus 344
Valerius Maximus 125, 185, 207, 378, 473
Valgrisi, Vincenzo 245
Valla, Lorenzo 46, 59, 61, 67, 137
Vallambert, Simon de 336
Valle, Pietro della 668–669
Valleriola, Francisco 440
Vallés, Francisco 440
Valli da Todi, Antonio 227
Valois, Elizabeth of 263, 269–270, 272
Vanegas (or Venegas), Alexius 413, 418–427
Vanière, Jacques 469–470, 576–585
Varano, Berardo da 519–520, 522–523
Varano, Costanza da 518–524
Varano, Gentilpandolfo da 519–520, 522–523
Varano, Giovanni da 519–520, 522–523
Varano, Giulio Cesare da 519–520, 522–523
Varano, Piergentile da 519–520, 522–523
Varano, Rodolfo III da 519, 522–523
Varano, Rodolfo IV da 519–520, 522–523
Varano, Tora da 519–520, 522–523
Varenius, Bernhard 499
Varro 164, 289, 477, 642–644
Vasili IV (tsar of Russia) 627–628
Vauzelles, Georges de 337
Vecellio, Tiziano 22
Vegio, Maffeo 474–475
Velásquez, Andrés 439–444, 448–449
Veleslavín, Daniel Adam 613
Velius, Kaspar Ursinus 188, 550, 555–559
Velleius Paterculus 397–398
Venantius Fortunatus 183
Veneto, Egnazio 394
Verelius, Olof 629
Vergekios, Angelos 486

Vergil, Polydor 231
Vergil 30, 34, 49, 175, 179, 205, 226–227, 232, 253–254, 285–287, 291, 299–300, 328–333, 338–340, 342–345, 350, 414, 444, 446, 469–470, 485, 536, 541, 548, 576–577, 579, 583–584, 591–595, 621, 624, 637–638, 642, 646
Veronese, Guarino 55, 58, 62–63, 67, 216, 522
Veronese, Battista 55
Vésale, André 9
Vettori, Piero 158, 162–163
Vibius Sequester 39
Victor, Sextus Aurelius 394
Vida, Girolamo 226
Vienne, Paschase de 6
Vigilius of Thapsus 603
Vilafranca, Luis de 463
Vilar i Costa, Joan 465
Villanova, Arnaldus de 460
Vinci, Leonardo da 433
Visagier, Jean 335–337, 342, 346
Visconti, Bianca Maria 521–522
Visconti, Filippo Maria 522
Visconti, Luchino 37
Vitali, Pietro 282
Vitalis, Janus 445
Vittelischi, Giovanni 519–520
Vives, Juan Luis 113, 419, 613, 616
Volterra see Jacopo
von Höfen see Dantiscus
Voorbroek see Perizonius
Vopiscus, Flavius 87, 378, 394
Vossius, Isaac 144, 499
Voß, Johann Heinrich 665
Vulcacius Gallicanus 394
Vulcanius Bonaventura 145–148, 150–154, 259–272

Wacker, Johann Matthäus 615
Wagner, Johann Jacob 666
Walstorp, Anna 324–329, 331–333
Walstorp, Gert 325
Walther, Bernard 431
Wechsel, Andreas 122
Wedel, Georg Wolfgang 672
Wehingen see Carolus
Weze, Johan 553

INDEX

Widekindi, Johannes 627–639
Wimpfeling, Jacob 534
Witelo, Erazmus Ciolek 432
Wolff, Christian 563, 566
Wonnegger, Johann 134
Worp, Jacob 605
Wowerius, Johanens 653

Xenophon 60, 390, 485, 487
Xiphilinus, Joannes 389–390, 392–393, 397
Xylander, Wilhelm 391, 397–398

Yourcenar, Marguerite 83

Zamagna, Bernardo 586
Zamoyski, Jan 652, 654, 661
Zamoyski, Thomas 661
Zeltner, Johann Conrad 599
Žerotín see Charles
Zipfel, Frank 68, 71–72, 78, 81–83, 88–89, 325, 333
Žižka, Jan 414
Zurita, Jerónimo de 267
Zwicker, Daniel 599, 601, 604

Printed in the United States
By Bookmasters